Men's & Boys' Wear Buyers™

2005-06 Edition

Published by The Salesman's Guide™, an imprint of Douglas Publications, Inc.

International Standard Book Number (ISBN): 0-87228-236-8
International Standard Serial Number (ISSN): 0077-5983
Federal I.D. Number: 56-1492630

Douglas Publications, Inc. makes its products available at special discounts for bulk purchases in the U.S. by corporations, institutions and other organizations. For more information, please contact the Group Sales Department at 2807 N. Parham Rd., #200, Richmond, VA 23294 or call (800) 223-1797, ext. 236.

Men's & Boys' Wear Buyers™

2005-06 Edition

The Salesman's Guide™
An Imprint of Douglas Publications, Inc.
Richmond, VA

The 2005-06 edition of *Men's & Boys' Wear Buyers*™ was prepared by The Salesman's Guide™, an imprint of Douglas Publications, Inc.

Frank Finn, V.P., Editor-in-Chief
Tammy Hudson, Production Manager
Megan Southwick, Assistant Editor
Kimberly Sprankle, Editorial & Production Assistant
Marie Adkins, Editorial Research Assistant
Naimah Black, Editorial Research Assistant
Arnold Molish, Editorial Research Assistant
Scott Sota, Customer Service & Fulfillment Manager
Chris Bonner, Database Administrator
Patrick Snyder, Database Sales Director

Cover design by Karyn Heebner

HEADQUARTERS

Douglas Publications, Inc.
2807 N. Parham Rd., Suite 200
Richmond, VA 23294
804-762-9600/Fax: 804-935-0271
Sales: 800-223-1797
www.douglaspublications.com
E-mail: info@douglaspublications.com

LOS ANGELES OFFICE

The Salesman's Guide
Linda Brand
110 E. Ninth St., Suite B-286
Los Angeles, CA 90079
Fax: 213-623-1809

Contents

Preface

The 2005-06 edition of *Men's & Boys' Wear Buyers*™ lists more than 14,000 buyers and executives for over 6,700 retail firms in the United States and Canada that sell men's & boys' apparel, furnishings, accessories and footwear.

Companies listed in the previous edition of the directory were sent questionnaires to update their listings. Those that did not respond were contacted by telephone for listing verification. Companies that could not be located were dropped from this edition. Firms listed for the first time in this edition were obtained using publicly available sources, and information was collected and verified through telephone surveys conducted directly with the companies.

ARRANGEMENT OF THE DIRECTORY

Company profiles are arranged geographically, beginning on page 1. In addition to the mailing address, telephone numbers, fax numbers and Web site addresses, company profiles include: the president or owner; merchandise manager(s) and buyer(s) of the items carried; merchandise price points; and the buying office associated with the firm.

A sample entry describing the entry format and codes used in each listing can be found on pages xi and xiii.

INDICES

Mail Order & Catalog House Index: Beginning on page 481, this index alphabetically lists companies that operate a mail order or catalog business in the men's & boys' wear field. Reference is made to the location of each company in the main section.

Online Retailers Index: Starting on page 485 this index alphabetically lists men's & boys' wear retailers who sell their products directly to customers via the internet. This includes retailers who operate exclusively online as well as those companies who operate traditional retail store locations or mail order catalog divisions. Reference is made to their location in the main section.

Alphabetical Index to Companies: To assist the user in finding a company when its location is not known, an alphabetical index by company name is included in the back of the directory, starting on page 495. This index references the location of each company's full listing in the main section.

ADDITIONAL SERVICES

The Salesman's Guide™ publishes a wide range of directories serving a variety of markets. Other retail directories include *Women's & Children's Wear Buyers™; Mass Merchandisers & Off-Price Apparel Buyers™; Sporting Goods & Activewear Buyers™; Gift, Housewares & Home Textiles Buyers™; Corporate Gift Buyers™;* and the *RN & WPL Encyclopedia™*. Hospitality titles include *Association Meeting & Event Planners™; Safety Award & Incentive Buyers™; Exhibit & Trade Show Display Buyers™, Premium, Incentive & Travel Buyers™*; *Medical Meeting & Event Planners* and *Corporate Meeting & Event Planners™*. Healthcare industry specific titles include the *The Hospital Phone Book™* and *The Insurance Phone Book™*. You may obtain information on purchasing any of these titles by calling (800) 223-1797 and asking for THE SALESMAN'S GUIDE SALES DEPARTMENT.

Our MAILING LIST DEPARTMENT will assist you in segmenting our directories toward specific buyers for any of your direct mail programs. If you prefer, you may purchase directories on diskette in either a label program or database format on CD-ROM or magnetic tape. Information on purchasing these products may be obtained by calling (800) 793-4568.

Our research staff is available to answer any questions or to supply you with additional information about the content of our directories. Our research department may be reached at (804) 762-9600, Monday through Friday, from 9:00 A.M. to 5:30 P.M. Eastern Standard Time. Ask for the Directories Editorial Department.

We take pride in bringing you this latest edition of the *Men's & Boys' Wear Buyers*™. We are grateful to everyone whose efforts made possible the publishing of this year's volume. Particular gratitude is owed to the many firms that have assisted in updating their listings.

Comments and suggestions are encouraged and should be directed to the editors, *Men's & Boys' Wear Buyers*, The Salesman's Guide, 2807 N. Parham Rd., Suite 200, Richmond, VA 23294.

Megan Southwick
Assistant Editor

KEY TO CODES

EXPLANATION OF TYPES OF BUSINESS CODES INCLUDED IN THIS DIRECTORY

AN .... Army Navy Store

CBO.. Corporate Buying Offices

CLO .... Family Clothing Store

DEPT .... Department Store

DG.. Dry Goods

FW.. Footwear Specialty Store

GM..General Merchandise

GS.. Gift Shop

KS .... Children's Specialty Store

MO.. Mail Order

MW .... Men's Wear Store

OL .... Online Retailer

OT..Manufacturer's Outlet

PX .... Military Post Exchange

RB .... Resident Buying Office

SG ....Sporting Goods

SP .... Specialty Store

WW.. Western Wear

PRICE CODES USED TO INDICATE RANGE OF MERCHANDISE CARRIED

des..Designer

b..Better

m..Moderate

p..Popular

bud..Budget

SAMPLE ENTRY

OREGON – Astoria

[1]DOUBLE O NEGATIVE CLOTHING, INC.
[5](MW – 2)
(ROCKY ROAD STREET WEAR)
[2]138 Goondocks Ln. (p-m)[7]
Astoria, OR 78532
[8](Henry Doneger)
[3]448-562-7895/ FAX: 448-562-7789[4]
[6]Sales: Over $10 Million
[10]Website: www.00neg.com
[11]Email: slickshoes@00neg.com
[12]Retail Locations: OR, WA, CA
[9]LAWRENCE COHEN (President & C.E.O.)
ANDREA CARMICHAEL (V.P. & G.M.M.)
LOTNEY FRATELLI – Men's Overcoats, Suits, Tailored Jackets, Tailored Slacks, Raincoats, Sweaters, Sport Shirts, Leather Apparel, Dress Shoes, Boots, Dress Shirts, Ties, Underwear, Robes, Hosiery, Big & Tall Men's Wear
ELGIN PERKINS – 4 to 20 Boys' Wear, Boys' Accessories, Underwear, Hosiery
RICHARD WANG – Store Displays, Fixtures, Supplies

KEY TO ENTRIES

1. Company Name
2. Address
3. Telephone Number
4. Fax Number
5. Type of Business - Numbers following type of business abbreviations indicate number of units operated by multiple-unit retail operations
6. Sales Volume - Annual sales as reported by the firms that are listed
7. Price Range of Merchandise Carried
8. Buying Offices Used
9. Executives/Buyers - Individuals at the firms who are responsible for purchasing men's and boys' wear and accessory items
10. Website
11. E-mail Address
12. Geographic Retail Analysis - Indicates in which states the company has a retail operation

Men's & Boys' Wear Buyers in the United States

ALABAMA - Albertville

GUNTERSVILLE OUTLET (CLO-135)
(FACTORY CONNECTION)
701 Railroad Ave. (bud-p)
Albertville, AL 35951
256-878-2866 / Fax: 256-878-0629
TERRY SCOTT (President & Real Estate Contact) & Buys Men's Apparel, Men's Denim Apparel, Men's Accessories, Men's Outerwear, Men's Sportswear
KENNY LITTLETON (V.P. - Opers.) & Buys Men's Apparel, Men's Denim Apparel, Men's Accessories, Men's Outerwear, Men's Sportswear
DEBBIE STEPPE-Men's Sportswear

HAMMER'S (CLO-10)
P.O. Box 686 (p)
102 E. Main St.
Albertville, AL 35950
256-878-2961 / Fax: 256-878-6857
Sales: $1 Million-$10 Million
FRED HAMMER (Co-Owner) & Buys Men's Suits, Tailored Jackets, Raincoats, Urban Contemporary, Dress Shirts, Ties, Robes, Underwear, Hosiery, Belts, Small Leather Goods, Footwear
ROBERT HAMMER, SR. (Co-Owner) & Buys Men's Suits, Tailored Jackets, Raincoats, Urban Contemporary, Dress Shirts, Ties, Robes, Underwear, Hosiery, Belts, Small Leather Goods, Footwear
EARL HAMMER (Co-Owner) & Buys Men's Suits, Tailored Jackets, Raincoats, Urban Contemporary, Dress Shirts, Ties, Robes, Underwear, Hosiery, Belts, Small Leather Goods, Footwear

WHITTEN'S TOWN & COUNTRY CLOTHES, INC. (CLO)
113 Sand Mountain Dr. (b-des)
P.O. Box 1005
Albertville, AL 35950
256-878-3901 / Fax: 256-582-1741
Sales: $1 Million-$10 Million
THOMAS T. WHITTEN, Sr. (Owner & Real Estate Contact) & Buys Men's Footwear, Leather Goods, Men's Casualwear, Men's Denim Apparel, Men's Formalwear, Men's Accessories, Men's Hosiery, Men's Outerwear, Men's Sportswear, Men's Suits, Men's Swimwear
THOMAS T. WHITTEN, Jr. (Sls. Mgr.) & Buys Men's Footwear, Leather Goods, Men's Casualwear, Men's Denim Apparel, Men's Formalwear, Men's Accessories, Men's Hosiery, Men's Outerwear, Men's Sportswear, Men's Suits, Men's Swimwear

CARLISLE CLOTHING (MW)
53 Main St. (p)
Alexander City, AL 35010
256-234-5321 / Fax: 218-326-8604
Sales: $500,001-$1 Million
JAMES C. CARLISLE (Owner) & Buys Men's Sportswear, Furnishings, Headwear, Accessories, Footwear, Store Displays, Fixtures, Supplies

ANSLEY PLACE (CLO)
1214 E. Three Notch St. (m-b)
Andalusia, AL 36420
334-222-0450 / Fax: 334-427-0450
Sales: $100,001-$500,000
LOUISA MANN (Owner) & Buys Men's & Boys' Apparel, Small Leather Goods

RONNIE'S MEN'S & BOYS' WEAR (MW-2)
425 Broadway Ave. (m-b)
Ashford, AL 36312
334-899-3148
Sales: $500,001-$1 Million
RONNIE BROWN (Owner) & Buys Men's Suits, Tailored Jackets, Tailored Slacks, Sportswear, Furnishings, Accessories, Footwear, Big & Tall Men's Wear, Young Men's Wear, 8 to 20 Boys' Wear, Store Displays, Fixtures, Supplies

BENNETT'S DEPARTMENT STORE (DEPT-2)
215 W. Washington St. (m-b)
Athens, AL 35611
256-232-8431 / Fax: 256-232-8443
Sales: $1 Million-$10 Million
MIKE BENNETT (President) & Buys Men's Suits, Tailored Jackets, Tailored Slacks, Coats, Sweaters, Sport Shirts, Outer Jackets, Casual Slacks, Furnishings, Headwear, Accessories, Footwear, Boys' Wear, Leather Apparel, Young Men's Wear, Store Displays, Fixtures, Supplies

SMITH'S MEN'S & BOYS' WEAR, INC. (MW)
207 W. Washington St. (b)
Athens, AL 35611
256-232-1640 / Fax: 256-233-3593
ANDY SMITH (Partner) & Buys Men's Overcoats, Suits, Tailored Jackets, Tailored Slacks, Raincoats, Sweaters, Sport Shirts, Outer Jackets, Casual Slacks, Leather Apparel, Active Apparel, Dress Shirts, Ties, Robes, Underwear, Hosiery, Gloves, Headwear, Belts, Small Leather Goods, Men's Footwear, Store Displays, Fixtures, Supplies
RAY SMITH (Partner) & Buys Men's Overcoats, Suits, Tailored Jackets, Tailored Slacks, Raincoats, Sweaters, Sport Shirts, Outer Jackets, Casual Slacks, Leather Apparel, Active Apparel, Dress Shirts, Ties, Robes, Underwear, Hosiery, Gloves, Headwear, Belts, Small Leather Goods, Men's Footwear, Store Displays, Fixtures, Supplies

ANDERSON'S SHOES & BOOTS, LLC (FW)
115 Gilbertsferry Rd. (m-b)
Attalla, AL 35954
256-538-5582 / Fax: 256-538-5580
Sales: $100,001-$500,000
TAMMY ANDERSON (Owner & G.M.M.) & Buys Boys' Footwear, Men's Footwear

AUBURN UNIVERSITY BOOK STORE (SP)
Auburn University
1360 Haley Ctr.
Auburn, AL 36849
334-844-4241 / Fax: 334-844-1697
Sales: $10 Million-$50 Million
AMY COAN (Apparel Mgr.) & Buys Men's & Boys' Fleece, Jackets, Hosiery, Licensed Apparel

THOMPSON'S FINE FASHIONS (CLO)
112 Courthouse Sq. (m)
Bay Minette, AL 36507
251-937-2941 / Fax: 251-937-2951
Sales: $500,001-$1 Million
ALBERT M. THOMPSON, III (President & G.M.M.) & Buys Men's Wear, Young Men's & Boys' Wear, Men's Footwear, Furnishings, Accessories, Store Displays, Fixtures, Supplies

BARON'S MEN STORE (MW)
1910 2nd Ave. North (m)
Bessemer, AL 35020
205-425-2131
Sales: $500,001-$1 Million
ROLAND ARMSTRONG (Owner) & Buys Men's Footwear, Leather Goods, Men's Apparel, Men's Big & Tall Apparel, Men's Casualwear, Men's Denim Apparel, Men's Outerwear, Men's Suits

ECONOMY CLOTHING & FURNITURE (DEPT)
112 N. 20th St. (p-m-b)
Bessemer, AL 35020
205-425-3578
Sales: $500,001-$1 Million
JOHN E. BOYD, JR. (Owner)
RENEE SNIDERMAN-Men's Overcoats, Suits, Tailored Jackets, Tailored Slacks, Big & Tall Men's Wear, Sweaters, Sport Shirts, Outer Jackets, Casual Slacks, Active Apparel, Dress Shirts, Ties, Robes, Underwear, Hosiery, Belts, Jewelry, Small Leather Goods, Young Men's Wear, B

THE CAMBRIDGE SHOP (MW)
(ROUTMAN'S, INC.)
624 Montgomery Hwy. (m-b)
Birmingham, AL 35216
205-823-1123 / Fax: 205-822-1916
Sales: $500,001-$1 Million
STANLEY ROUTMAN (Owner)
ROBERT RIOSA (G.M.M.) & Buys Men's Sportswear, Furnishings, Headwear, Accessories, Footwear, Young Men's Wear, Leather Apparel, Store Displays, Fixtures, Supplies

ALABAMA - Birmingham

COTTON'S (CLO)

400 19th St. (m-b)
Birmingham, AL 35218
205-787-1212 / Fax: 205-787-4905
Sales: $1 Million-$10 Million

HARRY WEINBERG (Owner) & Buys Men's Sportswear, Furnishings, Accessories, Men's Footwear, Store Displays, Fixtures, Supplies

DAVID BARRY'S TALL & BIG (MW-2)

(UNITED MEN'S STORE)
P.O. Box 531221
Birmingham, AL 35253
205-870-4436 / Fax: 205-870-3844
Sales: $1 Million-$10 Million

BARRY LEVIN (President) & Buys Men's Sportswear, Furnishings, Headwear, Accessories, Big & Tall Men's Wear, Leather Apparel, Store Displays, Fixtures, Supplies

FINE TRADITIONS (MW)

1917 3rd Ave. North
Birmingham, AL 35203
205-251-9519

J.D. MARTIN (Owner) & Buys Men's Furnishings, Accessories, Footwear, Young Men's Wear, Boys' Wear

GUS MAYER (CLO-2)

604 Brookwood Village (b)
Birmingham, AL 35209
205-870-3300 / Fax: 205-877-8553
Sales: $1 Million-$10 Million
Website: www.gusmayer.com

MICHAEL PIZITZ (Co-Owner)

JEFF PIZITZ (Co-Owner & President) & Buys Men's Overcoats, Tailored Jackets, Tailored Slacks, Suits, Raincoats, Sportswear, Furnishings, Headwear, Accessories, Footwear

CATHY PEREZ-Store Displays, Fixtures, Supplies

INDIA SHOPPE (CLO-2)

118 Century Plaza Mall (p)
Birmingham, AL 35210
205-591-8933 / Fax: 205-591-6275
Sales: $500,001-$1 Million

MARK CHANDIRAMANI (Owner) & Buys Men's T-shirts, Leather Apparel, Men's Wear, Sports Wear, Furnishings, Accessories, Men's Footwear, Store Displays, Fixtures, Supplies

MAGIC CITY SPORTSWEAR (CLO)

3131 4th Ave. South
Birmingham, AL 35207
205-871-9100 / Fax: 205-871-8736

JOHN JARMON (Owner) & Buys Men's Sportswear, T-shirts

MASSEY'S CORRAL (WW)

2421 2nd Ave. North (m)
Birmingham, AL 35203
205-323-6969 / Fax: 205-328-4320

HUGH MASSEY, JR. (Owner)

RON MASSEY (Mgr.) & Buys Men's, Young Men's & Boys' Western Wear, Related Accessories, Furnishings, Boots, Store Displays, Fixtures, Supplies

McMILLAN'S BIG & TALL, INC. (MW-2)

7893 Creswood Blvd. (m-b)
Birmingham, AL 35210
205-956-8086 / Fax: 205-956-3356

AUTREY McMILLAN, SR. (President & Owner) & Buys Big & Tall Men's Wear, Sportswear, Furnishings, Accessories, Store Displays, Fixtures, Store Supplies

MOBLEY & SONS (MW)

(VARSITY SHOP, INC.)
112 Euclid Ave. (m)
Birmingham, AL 35213
205-870-7929

MR. MOBLEY (Owner) & Buys Men's Sportswear, Furnishings, Footwear, Store Displays, Fixtures, Supplies

MR. BURCH FORMAL WEAR (MW-6)

2420 1st Ave. North (m-b)
Birmingham, AL 35203
205-252-3600 / Fax: 205-252-3737
Website: www.mrburchformalwear.com

DWAYNE BURCH (Owner) & Buys Men's, Young Men's & 8 to 18 Boys' Formal Wear, Footwear, Store Displays, Fixtures and Supplies

LONNIE MIMS (Gen. Mgr.) & Buys Men's, Young Men's & 8 to 18 Boys' Formal Wear, Footwear, Store Displays, Fixtures and Supplies

PARISIAN, INC. (DEPT-43)

(Div. of SAKS, INC.)
750 Lakeshore Pkwy. (m-b)
Birmingham, AL 35211
205-940-4000 / Fax: 978-256-4723
Sales: $500 Million-$1 Billion
Website: www.saksincorporated.com
Retail Locations: AL, AZ, CA, CO, CT, FL, GA, HI, IA, IL, IN, KS, KY, LA, MA, MD, MI, MN, MO, MS, MT, NC, ND, NE, NJ, NV, NY, OH, OK, OR, PA, SC, SD, TN, TX, VA, WI, WV, WY

MARK SATRIANS (D.M.M.-Children's)

TRAVIS SAUCER (President & C.E.O.)

NICK STRANGE (Sr. V.P.-Stores)

JIM MITCHELL (Store Planning) & Buys Store Fixtures

JENNIFER DAY (Real Estate Contact)

ERNEST BROWN (G.M.M.-Men's & Children's) (@ 205-940-4540)

STEVE EVANS (D.M.M.-Men's)

ROBIN GRAHAM-Men's Suits, Tailored Jackets, Tailored Slacks, Overcoats, Raincoats

BART TINGLE-Men's Woven Tops, Knit Tops, Sweaters

BILL COWAN-Men's Furnishings

JIM CLARK-Men's Active Apparel, Outer Jackets, Casual Slacks, Shorts, Outerwear

LIZ LANG-Men's Updated Collections, Polo

LYN FRANKS-8 to 20 Boys' Sportswear, Clothing, Young Men's Denim, Basics, Jeans

DAVE NERI (D.M.M.-Footwear)

JOE MOYNIHAN-Men's Footwear

BARBARA QUINN-Children's Footwear

PLAIN CLOTHES (CLO)

2820 Linden Ave. (b)
Birmingham, AL 35209
205-871-3391 / Fax: 205-871-9098

MARTHA FAZIO (President) & Buys Supplies

STEVE FAZIO (Secy.) & Buys Men's Overcoats, Suits, Tailored Jackets, Tailored Slacks, Raincoats, Sportswear, Furnishings, Headwear, Accessories, Footwear, Store Displays, Fixtures

ROGERS TRADING CO. (CLO)

4639 Hwy. 280 East (p-m)
Birmingham, AL 35242
205-408-9378 / Fax: 205-408-8126

LEE ROGOFF (Owner)

JOHN SEGAL-Men's Overcoats, Belts, Small Leather Goods, Sportswear, Knitwear, Hosiery, Headwear, Footwear, Furnishings, Boys' Clothing, Store Displays, Fixtures and Supplies

ALABAMA - Birmingham

SHAIA'S OF HOMEWOOD, INC. (GM)

2818 18th St. South (des)
Birmingham, AL 35209
205-871-1312 / Fax: 205-871-3055
Sales: $1 Million-$10 Million
Website: www.shaias.com

J.L. SHAIA (President) & Buys Men's Footwear, Fragrances, Leather Goods, Men's Apparel, Men's Casualwear, Men's Denim Apparel, Men's Designer Apparel, Men's Formalwear, Men's Hosiery, Men's Outerwear, Men's Sleepwear, Men's Sportswear, Men's Activewear, Men's Suits, Men's Swimwear, Men's Underwear, Watches

KEN SHAIA (V.P.) & Buys Men's Footwear, Fragrances, Leather Goods, Men's Apparel, Men's Casualwear, Men's Denim Apparel, Men's Designer Apparel, Men's Formalwear, Men's Hosiery, Men's Outerwear, Men's Sleepwear, Men's Sportswear, Men's Activewear, Men's Suits, Men's Swimwear, Men's Underwear, Watches

LEO SHAIA (V.P.) & Buys Men's Footwear, Fragrances, Leather Goods, Men's Apparel, Men's Casualwear, Men's Denim Apparel, Men's Designer Apparel, Men's Formalwear, Men's Hosiery, Men's Outerwear, Men's Sleepwear, Men's Sportswear, Men's Activewear, Men's Suits, Men's Swimwear, Men's Underwear, Watches

SHOE CORPORATION OF BIRMINGHAM, INC. (FW & MO)

(SHOE CORPORATION FOOTWEAR)
1415 1st Ave. South (m-b)
Birmingham, AL 35223
205-326-2800 / Fax: 205-326-2808
Sales: $1 Million-$10 Million

JAMES F. CALHOUN (President) & Buys Boys' Footwear, Men's Footwear, Men's Apparel, Men's Hosiery

BRENDA CALHOUN (V.P.) & Buys Boys' Footwear, Men's Footwear, Men's Apparel, Men's Hosiery

CHRIS ADAMS (Mgr.-Sales) & Buys Boys' Footwear, Men's Footwear, Men's Apparel, Men's Hosiery

THE SHOE INN (FW)

3728 Lorna Rd. (m-b-des)
Birmingham, AL 35216
205-987-9728
Sales: $100,001-$500,000

ROSLYNN BUDOFF (Partner)

STUART BUDOFF (Partner) & Buys Men's, Young Men's & Boys' Footwear

SLATER SALES, INC. (CLO)

2209 1st Ave. North (bud-p-m-b-h)
Birmingham, AL 35203
205-328-8003 / Fax: 205-328-6347
Sales: $1 Million-$10 Million

BARRY M. SLATER (President & G.M.M.) & Buys Men's & Young Men's Overcoats, Suits, Tailored Jackets, Tailored Slacks, Raincoats, Leather Apparel, Furnishings, Sportswear, Accessories, Men's Footwear, Big & Tall Men's Wear, Store Displays, Fixtures, Supplies

SNOOZY'S COLLEGE BOOKSTORE (SP-4 & OL)

(UNIV. OF ALABAMA)
1321 10th Ave. South
Birmingham, AL 35205
205-328-2665 / Fax: 205-933-2229
Sales: $501,000-$1 Million
Website: www.follett.com

GEORGE JONES, SR. (Owner) (@ 205-995-5580) & Buys Outerwear, Sportswear, Accessories, Activewear

THE TRAK SHAK (FW)

2839 18th St. South (b)
Birmingham, AL 35209
205-870-5644 / Fax: 205-870-5645
Sales: $500,001-$1 Million
Website: www.trakshak.com

VALERIE MCLEAN (Owner)

SCOTT STRAND (G.M.M.) & Buys Boys' Footwear, Men's Footwear, Men's Accessories, Men's Apparel, Hosiery

UNITED MENS, INC. (MW-2)

(DAVID BARRY'S TALL & BIG STORE)
P.O. Box 531221 (m-b-des)
733 Brookwood Village, #B
Birmingham, AL 35209
205-870-4436 / Fax: 205-870-3844
Sales: $1 Million-$10 Million

BARRY LEVIN (President) & Buys Leather Goods, Men's Apparel, Men's Big & Tall Apparel, Men's Casualwear, Men's Denim Apparel, Men's Accessories, Men's Hosiery, Men's Outerwear, Men's Sleepwear, Men's Sportswear, Men's Suits, Men's Underwear, Young Men's Apparel

P. BAER DEPARTMENT STORE (DEPT)

P.O. Box 169 (p)
Main St.
Calera, AL 35040
205-668-2733
Sales: $1 Million-$10 Million

PHILLIP A. BAER (President & Co-Owner) & Buys Men's Suits, Tailored Jackets, Tailored Slacks, Sport Shirts, Outer Jackets, Leather Apparel, Casual Slacks, Dress Shirts, Ties, Robes, Underwear, Hosiery, Gloves, Belts, Jewelry, Small Leather Goods, Fragrances, Footwear, Big & Tall Men's Wear, Store Displays, Fixtures, Supplies

ELIZABETH BAER (Co-Owner) & Buys Men's Suits, Tailored Jackets, Tailored Slacks, Sport Shirts, Outer Jackets, Leather Apparel, Casual Slacks, Dress Shirts, Ties, Robes, Underwear, Hosiery, Gloves, Belts, Jewelry, Small Leather Goods, Fragrances, Footwear, Big & Tall Men's Wear, Store Displays, Fixtures, Supplies

WETHERBEE'S DEPARTMENT STORE (DEPT)

103 Claiborne St. (p-m-b)
Camden, AL 36726
334-682-9118
Sales: $500,001-$1 Million

CHARLIE WETHERBEE (Owner) & Buys Men's Sportswear, Headwear, Accessories, Footwear, Boys' Wear, Store Displays, Fixtures, Supplies

SOMETHING SPECIAL (CLO)

96 Court Sq. (m)
Carrollton, AL 35447
205-367-8071

MICHELLE SHIELD (President) & Buys Men's Denim, Sport Shirts, Sweaters, Casual Slacks, Active Apparel, Ties, Underwear, Hosiery, Gloves, Belts, Small Leather Goods, Store Displays, Fixtures and Supplies

MADDOX FAMILY FASHIONS (CLO)

1110 W. Main St. (m-b)
Centre, AL 35960
256-927-5112 / Fax: 256-927-4717

LARRY P. MADDOX (Owner) & Buys Men's Sportswear, Furnishings, Headwear, Accessories, Boys' Wear, Leather Apparel, Store Displays, Fixtures, Supplies

PATRICK'S (CLO)
1117 Walnut St. (m)
Centreville, AL 35042
205-926-4793 / Fax: 205-926-4793
Sales: $500,001-$1 Million
TIM PATRICK (Co-Owner) & Buys Boys' Apparel, Leather Goods, Men's Apparel, Men's Big & Tall, Men's Casualwear, Men's Formalwear, Men's Accessories, Men's Hosiery, Men's Sportswear, Men's Suits
LUCY PATRICK (Co-Owner) & Buys Boys' Apparel, Leather Goods, Men's Apparel, Men's Big & Tall, Men's Casualwear, Men's Formalwear, Men's Accessories, Men's Hosiery, Men's Sportswear, Men's Suits
BETTY JO FRANKLIN (Store Mgr.)

DUVY'S MEN'S STORE (MW)
33320 US Hwy. 280 (p)
Childersburg, AL 35044
256-378-7841 / Fax: 256-378-3391
Sales: $500,001-$1 Million
TOM DUVALL (President) & Buys Men's Overcoats, Suits, Tailored Jackets, Tailored Slacks, Big & Tall Sportswear, Furnishings, Headwear, Belts, Fragrances, Footwear, Young Men's Wear, Store Displays, Fixtures & Supplies
JOYCE DUVALL (V.P.) & Buys Men's Overcoats, Suits, Tailored Jackets, Tailored Slacks, Big & Tall Sportswear, Furnishings, Headwear, Belts, Fragrances, Footwear, Young Men's Wear, Store Displays, Fixtures & Supplies

TRAFFANSTEDT'S TOWN COUNTRY (CLO)
P.O. Box 676 (bud-p-m)
90 Main St.
Collinsville, AL 35961
256-524-2183
JANE SIMPSON (Owner) & Buys Men's Sportswear, Furnishings, Accessories, Leather Apparel, 8 to 20 Boys' Sportswear, Furnishings, Accessories, Leather Apparel, Footwear, Store Displays, Fixtures, Supplies

JACK'S WESTERN WEAR (WW)
1591 County Rd. 437
Cullman, AL 35055
256-739-3612 / Fax: 256-739-3643
Sales: $1 Million-$10 Million
LARRY ALLRED (Owner) & Buys Men's, Young Men's & Boys' Western Style Jeans, Shirts, Hats, Jackets, Footwear, Store Displays, Fixtures, Supplies

WERNER SHOES (FW)
317 2nd Ave. SW (bdes)
Cullman, AL 35055
256-734-7494
Sales: $1 Million-$10 Million
JOHN WERNER (Owner & G.M.M.) & Buys Boys' Footwear, Men's Footwear, Licensed Apparel, Men's Apparel, Hosiery, Watches

BURNHAM SHOES (FW-2)
P.O. Box 700 (p)
3811 Ross Clark Cir.
Dothan, AL 36303
334-794-5682 / Fax: 334-794-1940
WILLIAM BURHNAM (Owner)
JOE WESTON-Men's & Boys' Dress Shoes, Casual Shoes, Athletic Footwear, Hiking Boots, Western Boots, Hosiery, Store Displays, Fixtures, Supplies

D. ETHRIDGE, INC. (CLO)
1728 W. Main St. (b)
Dothan, AL 36301
334-792-0747 / Fax: 334-792-6728
Sales: $1 Million-$10 Million
DAVID ETHRIDGE (Owner & Real Estate Contact) & Buys Men's Footwear, Leather Goods, Men's Apparel, Men's Casualwear, Men's Sportswear
SHEILA HEASLETT-Men's Footwear, Leather Goods

MARK TWAIN SHOPPE (KS)
2954 Ross Clark Cir. (m-b)
Dothan, AL 36301
334-794-7021
JULIA HUNTER (Owner) & Buys Store Displays, Fixtures, Supplies

S. BRANNON CLOTHING (MW)
3074 Ross Clark Cir., #12 (b)
Dothan, AL 36301
334-712-1367 / Fax: 334-712-0185
STEVE BRANNON (President) & Buys Men's Suits, Tailored Jackets, Tailored Slacks, Sportswear, Furnishings, Accessories, Footwear, Young Men's Wear, Store Displays, Fixtures, Supplies

SANDRA JEAN UNIFORM SHOP (SP)
2493 Montgomery Hwy. (p-m)
Dothan, AL 36303
334-792-4553 / Fax: 334-792-3636
JAY SOLOMON (Owner) & Buys Men's & Big & Tall Men's Medical Uniforms, Industrial Uniforms, Municipal Uniforms, Related Footwear, Store Displays, Fixtures, Supplies

SOUTHEASTERN APPAREL (MO)
142 S. Woodburn Dr. (m)
Dothan, AL 36305
334-793-1576 / Fax: 334-793-7381
Website: www.southeastern-performance-apparel.com
JIM PAXTON (V.P.) & Buys Men's Apparel, Accessories

YANCEY PARKER'S (MW)
Westgate Shopping Ctr. (p)
Enterprise, AL 36330
334-347-8134 / Fax: 334-347-8134
Sales: $500,001-$1 Million
MELISSA PARKER-PAUL (Owner) & Buys Men's & Boys' Wear, Accessories, Headwear, Knitwear, Hosiery, Sportswear, Swimwear, Outerwear, Underwear, Hosiery, Furnishings, Leather Apparel
ADDISON PAUL-Footwear, Store Displays, Fixtures

NEAL LOGUE CO. (MW)
129 E. Broad St. (m)
Eufaula, AL 36027
334-687-2001
Sales: $1 Million-$10 Million
BEN MITCHELL (Co-Owner) & Buys Men's Formalwear, Suits, Tailored Jackets, Tailored Slacks, Sportswear, Furnishings, Accessories, Big & Tall Men's Wear, Young Men's Wear, Boys' Wear, Store Displays, Fixtures, Supplies
ANN MITCHELL (Co-Owner) & Buys Men's Footwear

THE COLONY SHOP, INC. (CLO)
27 S. Section St. (b-des)
Fairhope, AL 36532
251-928-8172
VERONA BEISER (President) & Buys Boys' Apparel
DEBBIE MOFFETT (V.P.) & Buys Boys' Apparel
KIM McLEMORE (Treas.) & Buys Boys' Apparel

EAST BAY CLOTHIERS (MW)
225 Fairhope Ave.
Fairhope, AL 36532
251-928-6848 / Fax: 251-928-6918
Website: www.eastbayclothiers.com
JEANIE McCOWN (Owner) & Buys Men's Wear, Men's Accessories, Furnishings, Footwear

FISHER'S MEN'S SHOP (MW-2)
118 Temple Ave. North (m-b)
Fayette, AL 35555
205-932-3259
Sales: $1 Million-$10 Million
DENNIS FISHER (President) & Buys Store Displays, Fixtures, Supplies, Men's Sportswear, Furnishings, Headwear, Accessories, Footwear, 14 to 20 Boys' Wear
ROBERT FISHER (G.M.M.) & Buys Store Displays, Fixtures, Supplies, Men's Sportswear, Furnishings, Headwear, Accessories, Footwear, 14 to 20 Boys' Wear

ROBBIE'S OF FAYETTE, INC. (CLO)
132 Temple Ave. North (m-b)
Fayette, AL 35555
205-932-4451 / Fax: 205-932-7356
Sales: $1 Million-$10 Million
DONNA KERR (President) & Buys Boys' Apparel, Leather Goods

ALABAMA - Florence

ALL AMERICAN SWIM SUPPLY (CLO)

614 Thompson St.
Florence, AL 35630
256-767-5762 / Fax: 256-718-2095
Website: www.americanswim.com

LOU ANN CHANDLER (Co-Owner) & Buys Men's & Boys' Surf & Swimwear, Fashion Accessories, T-shirts, Imprinted Sportswear, Sandals

JEFF CHANDLER-Men's & Boys' Surf & Swimwear, Fashion Accessories, T-shirts, Imprinted Sportswear, Sandals

GEM-TEX, INC. (CLO)

509 Wilhite St.
Florence, AL 35630
256-764-8447 / Fax: 256-764-8407

JIM MORRIS-Men's T-shirts, Imprinted Sportswear

GOLDEN SPUR WESTERN WEAR (WW)

3519 Florence Blvd. (m)
Florence, AL 35634
256-767-7440 / Fax: 256-767-0011

RONNIE GISH (Owner) & Buys Men's Suits, Sport Coats, Sport Shirts, Outer Jackets, Casual Slacks, Dress Shirts, Hosiery, Headwear, Jewelry, Small Leather Goods, Boys' Shirts, Boots, Hats, Footwear, Store Displays, Fixtures, Supplies

THE LONDON SHOPS (MW)

English Village Shopping Ctr. (m)
Florence, AL 35630
256-767-1880 / Fax: 256-767-1894
Sales: $500,001-$1 Million

JOHNNY McCLANAHAN (Owner) & Buys Men's Overcoats, Suits, Tailored Slacks, Raincoats, Sportswear, Dress Shirts, Ties, Underwear, Hosiery, Gloves, Accessories, Boys' Wear, Footwear, Store Displays, Fixtures, Supplies

STUDENT BOOKSTORE OFF CAMPUS (CLO)

(UNIVERSITY OF NORTH ALABAMA)
P.O. Box 423 (m)
Florence, AL 35630
256-764-7507 / Fax: 256-764-0454

MARTHA TRUITT (Owner)

BRAD NICHOLS (Mgr.) & Buys Men's T-shirts, Fleecewear, Shorts, Headwear, Gloves, Belts, Small Leather Goods, Store Displays, Fixtures, Supplies

THORNTON LAKES CLOTH BARN (DG)

576 Thornton Lake Rd. (m)
Gadsden, AL 35903
256-492-2773 / Fax: 256-492-9660
Website: www.thorntonlakes.com

A. R. THORNTON, JR. (Owner)

VICKI CHRISTOPHER-Men's Fleece, T-shirts

LOUIS CREW & CO. (DEPT)

P.O. Box 14 (p)
Goodwater, AL 35072
256-839-5321
Sales: $100,001-$500,000

JOHNNY WATSON (Owner) & Buys Men's Overcoats, Suits, Tailored Jackets, Tailored Slacks, Raincoats, Sweaters, Sport Shirts, Outer Jackets, Leather Apparel, Casual Slacks, Active Apparel, Dress Shirts, Ties, Robes, Underwear, Hosiery, Gloves, Belts, Boys' Wear, Sportswear, Furnishings, Footwear, Store Displays, Fixtures, Supplies

GREENVILLE SHOE SHOP (FW)

P.O. Box 26 (m-b)
128 W. Commerce St.
Greenville, AL 36037
334-382-8802
Sales: $500,001-$1 Million

ERNIE SMITH (Owner & G.M.M.) & Buys Men's Footwear, Boys' Footwear, Accessories, Hosiery, Leather Goods, Watches

BEACH BAZAAR (CLO-3)

(SOUVENIR OUTLET)
(T SHIRT OUTLET)
616 Hwy. 59 South (p-m-b)
Gulf Shores, AL 36542
251-967-2255 / Fax: 251-948-8766
Sales: $1 Million-$10 Million

KARRIE RONA (Owner) & Buys Men's Swimwear, Shorts, T-shirts, Young Men's, Size 8-20 Boys' Wear, Sandals, Store Displays, Fixtures, Supplies

OCEAN EDDIE'S T-SHIRT CO. (CLO-5)

P.O. Box 3647
1140 Gulf Shores Parkway
Gulf Shores, AL 36542
251-948-6111 / Fax: 251-948-8505

STEVE HORVAT (Co-Owner) & Buys T-shirts, Resortwear, Footwear, Accessories

GAYE HORVAT (Co-Owner) & Buys T-shirts, Resortwear, Footwear, Accessories

NORTH ALABAMA NAUTIQUES, INC. (CLO)

8858 US Hwy. 31
Hanceville, AL 35077
256-739-9940 / Fax: 256-739-9972

KEVIN MARSH-Men's Surfwear, Swimwear & Wetsuits, Boats, Sunglasses, Fashion Accessories

JAMES WHITAKER-Men's Surfwear, Swimwear & Wetsuits, Boats, Sunglasses, Fashion Accessories

CRAIG ARCHOR-Men's Surfwear, Swimwear & Wetsuits, Boats, Sunglasses, Fashion Accessories

TINA BLACKMON-Men's Surfwear, Swimwear & Wetsuits, Boats, Sunglasses, Fashion Accessories

KENNETH BLACKMON-Men's Surfwear, Swimwear & Wetsuits, Boats, Sunglasses, Fashion Accessories

ROMINE'S (CLO)

108 Commercial St. (p-m-b)
Hanceville, AL 35077
256-352-4343
Sales: $100,001-$500,000

SUE ROMINE (Owner) & Buys Men's Sportswear, Headwear, Accessories, Boys' Wear, Footwear, Store Displays, Fixtures, Supplies

MAISON MORGAN, INC. (CLO)

240 Hwy. 31 SW (p-m)
Hartselle, AL 35640
256-773-5456 / Fax: 256-773-5457
Sales: $1 Million-$10 Million

MACK R. TAYLOR (C.E.O. & G.M.M.)

JOE LYNN TAYLOR (President) & Buys Men's Overcoats, Suits, Tailored Jackets, Tailored Slacks, Raincoats, Big & Tall Men's Wear, Sweaters, Sport Shirts, Outer Jackets, Casual Slacks, Active Apparel, Furnishings, Headwear, Accessories, Footwear, Young Men's Wear, Store Displays, Fixtures, Supplies

SIKES' SHOE CO. (FW-2)

(SIKES CHILDREN'S SHOES)
2920 18th St. South (b)
Homewood, AL 35209
205-879-3433 / Fax: 205-879-7453
Sales: $1 Million-$10 Million

FRANK YOUNGS (Owner)

STEVEN YOUNGS (G.M.M.) & Buys Accessories, Boys' Footwear

ESCAPADE (CLO)

1935 Hoover Ct., #C
Hoover, AL 35226
205-822-0048

ROD GAINES-Swimwear, Men's Apparel, Urban Streetwear, Footwear

KATRINA HALE-Swimwear, Men's Apparel, Urban Streetwear, Footwear

GARYWOOD CLOTHING (CLO)
3062 Allison Bonnett Dr., #A (m-b)
Hueytown, AL 35023
205-491-6734 / Fax: 205-491-6121
Sales: $1 Million-$10 Million
BOB NEFF (Owner) & Buys Men's Sportswear, Furnishings, Accessories, Leather Apparel, Big & Tall Men's Wear, 8 to 20 Boys' Wear, Young Men's Wear, Leather Apparel, Store Displays, Fixtures, Supplies

U.S. SPACE-ROCKET (CLO)
1 Tranquility Base SW
Huntsville, AL 35805
256-837-3400 / Fax: 256-890-3367
KIM WINGARD-Shorts, Sweat Pants, T-shirts, Denim Shirts, Headwear, Sunglasses
JIM JOHNSON-Shorts, Sweat Pants, T-shirts, Denim Shirts, Headwear, Sunglasses

BERNARD'S STORE FOR MEN (MW)
217 19th St. West (b)
Jasper, AL 35501
205-384-6421 / Fax: 205-384-0509
Sales: $500,001-$1 Million
GEORGE A. RICHARDSON (Owner) & Buys Men's Footwear, Fragrances, Leather Goods, Men's Apparel, Men's Big & Tall Apparel, Men's Casualwear, Men's Denim Apparel, Men's Formalwear, Men's Accessories, Men's Outerwear, Men's Sleepwear, Men's Sportswear, Men's Suits, Men's Swimwear, Men's Underwea

JENNY 'N' ME (KS)
Jasper Mall (m-b)
300 Hwy. 78 East, #430
Jasper, AL 35501
205-387-7268
Sales: $500,001-$1 Million
LARRY D. AKINS (Co-Owner) & Buys Boys' Wear, Store Displays, Fixtures, Supplies

THE PANTS STORE (MW-2)
(THE TAYLOR CO.)
P.O. Box 127 (p)
717 Parkway Dr. SE
Leeds, AL 35094
205-699-6166 / Fax: 205-699-4790
Sales: $1 Million-$10 Million
Website: www.pantsstore.com
MICHAEL GEE (President) (@ 205-699-0166) & Buys Men's Sportswear, Furnishings, Headwear, Accessories, Boys' Wear, Leather Apparel, Men's Footwear, Store Displays, Fixtures & Supplies
SHAWN WILLIAMSON (Mgr.) & Buys Men's Sportswear, Furnishings, Headwear, Accessories, Boys' Wear, Leather Apparel, Men's Footwear, Store Displays, Fixtures & Supplies

THE PANTS BARN, INC. (CLO-2)
P.O. Box 467 (bud-p)
11770 Hwy. 231 North
Meridianville, AL 35759
256-828-0381 / Fax: 256-828-0381
Sales: $1 Million-$10 Million
LARRY BRYANT (President) & Buys Men's Sportswear, Furnishings, Headwear, Accessories, Footwear, Athletic Footwear, Young Men's Wear, Boys' Wear, Store Displays, Fixtures, Supplies

AL'S 5 AND 10 (GM-6)
(L & M ENTERPRISES, INC.)
4358 Old Shell Rd. (bud)
Mobile, AL 36608
251-343-6703 / Fax: 251-344-8600
AL LOEB (Co-Owner) (@ 251-343-4554) & Buys Men's & Boys' Underwear, Hosiery, Swimwear, Beach Shoes
MARK LOEB (Co-Owner) & Buys Men's & Boys' Underwear, Hosiery, Swimwear, Beach Shoes, Store Displays, Fixtures and Supplies

BARNETT-SIMMONS (MW)
4413 Old Shell Rd. (b)
Mobile, AL 36608
251-342-8780 / Fax: 251-342-9438
Sales: $500,001-$1 Million
PHILLIP BARNETT (Owner) & Buys Men's Suits, Tailored Jackets, Tailored Slacks, Raincoats, Sweaters, Sport Shirts, Outer Jackets, Leather Apparel, Casual Slacks, Dress Shirts, Ties, Robes, Underwear, Hosiery, Headwear, Belts, Jewelry, Fragrances, Footwear, Store Displays, Fixtures, Supp

HANNON & WILLIAMS (MW)
3700 Dauphin St. (b)
Mobile, AL 36608
251-343-5740 / Fax: 251-343-5752
Website: www.hannon-williams.com
JOHN WILLIAMSON (Mgr.) & Buys Men's Sportswear, Furnishings, Accessories, Footwear, Store Displays, Fixtures, Supplies

HOLIDAY, INC. (GS)
4513 Old Shell Rd. (m-b)
Mobile, AL 36608
251-342-4911
Sales: $1 Million-$10 Million
NANCY BROCK (Co-Owner) & Buys Boys' Apparel, Boys' Footwear, Leather Goods
MICHAEL P. FEORE (Co-Owner) & Buys Boys' Apparel, Boys' Footwear, Leather Goods
PERRY STEWART (Co-Owner) & Buys Boys' Apparel, Boys' Footwear, Leather Goods

J-RAY SHOES (FW & OL)
121 University Blvd. South (m-b-des)
Mobile, AL 36608
251-342-6322 / Fax: 251-342-9270
Sales: $500,001-$1 Million
Website: www.jrayshoes.com
MARIAN DOMINICK (Partner) & Buys Boys' Footwear
JOHN DOMINICK (Partner) & Buys Boys' Footwear, Apparel, Accessories
LEIGH KERCHER-Boys' Footwear

JUST IN FASHIONS (MW)
2994 Spring Hill Ave. (m)
Mobile, AL 36607
251-471-4261 / Fax: 251-471-3865
SAMIR SAYYAD (President) & Buys Men's Overcoats, Suits, Tailored Jackets, Tailored Slacks, Raincoats, Sportswear, Furnishings, Accessories, Footwear, Big & Tall Men's Wear, Young Men's Wear, Boys' Wear, Store Displays, Fixtures, Supplies
HADAYA SAYYAD (V.P.) & Buys Men's Overcoats, Suits, Tailored Jackets, Tailored Slacks, Raincoats, Sportswear, Furnishings, Accessories, Footwear, Big & Tall Men's Wear, Young Men's Wear, Boys' Wear, Store Displays, Fixtures, Supplies

LEO'S WESTERN WEAR & UNIFORM SUPPLY (WW)
3756 Government Blvd. (p-m-b)
Mobile, AL 36693
251-666-7723 / Fax: 251-666-7724
JEFF REDISCH (Owner) & Buys Store Displays, Fixtures, Supplies, Men's, Young Men's & Boys' Sportswear, Riding Wear, Western Style Clothing, Furnishings, Accessories, Men's Footwear, Boots

METZGER'S, INC. (CLO)
3704 Dauphin St. (m-b)
Mobile, AL 36608
251-342-6336 / Fax: 251-342-4223
Sales: $1 Million-$10 Million
KEN METZGER (Chmn.) & Buys Store Displays, Fixtures
ALAN DAY (Gen. Mgr.) & Buys Overcoats, Suits, Tailored Jackets, Tailored Slacks, Sweaters, Sport Shirts, Outer Jackets, Casual Slacks, Active Apparel, Furnishings, Headwear, Accessories, Footwear, Big & Tall Men's Wear

ALABAMA - Mobile

NAMAN'S DEPARTMENT STORE (MW-2)
(RITZ FOR MEN)
204 Dauphin St. (m)
Mobile, AL 36602
251-433-3893 / Fax: 251-433-2410
Sales: $500,001-$1 Million
EMILE NAMAN (Co-Owner) & Buys Men's Overcoats, Suits, Tailored Jackets, Tailored Slacks, Raincoats, Sportswear, Big & Tall Men's Wear, Young Men's & Boys' Wear, Footwear, Store Displays, Fixtures, Supplies
VIRGINIA NAMAN (Co-Owner) & Buys Men's Overcoats, Suits, Tailored Jackets, Tailored Slacks, Raincoats, Sportswear, Big & Tall Men's Wear, Young Men's & Boys' Wear, Footwear, Store Displays, Fixtures, Supplies
DAVID NAMAN (Mgr.) & Buys Men's Overcoats, Suits, Tailored Jackets, Tailored Slacks, Raincoats, Sportswear, Big & Tall Men's Wear, Young Men's & Boys' Wear, Footwear, Store Displays, Fixtures, Supplies

SHOE STATION, INC. (FW-9)
(SHOE STATION)
450 Bel Air Blvd. (m-b)
Mobile, AL 36606
251-476-7472 / Fax: 251-476-1902
Sales: $10 Million-$50 Million
TERRY BARKIN (President) & Buys Men's Footwear, Accessories, Hosiery
TOM HALE-Men's Footwear, Boys' Footwear

SMART SHOE STORES, INC. (FW)
(PICK-N-SAVE SHOES)
P.O. Box 1078 (bud-p-m)
5451 Halls Mill Rd., #15
Mobile, AL 36619
251-661-2741 / Fax: 251-661-1078
Sales: $100,001-$500,000
ALMA HAVEEB (President) & Buys Boys' Footwear, Men's Footwear, Men's Accessories, Hosiery

WHITE'S BIG & TALL (CLO)
3980 Airport Blvd., #H (m)
Mobile, AL 36608
251-380-0064 / Fax: 251-380-0067
Sales: $500,001-$1 Million
JOHN WHITE (Co-Owner) & Buys Big & Tall Men's Wear, Furnishings, Accessories, Men's Footwear, Store Displays, Fixtures, Supplies
MARVINE WHITE (Co-Owner) & Buys Big & Tall Men's Wear, Furnishings, Accessories, Men's Footwear, Store Displays, Fixtures, Supplies
STEVE WHITE (Mgr.) & Buys Big & Tall Men's Wear, Furnishings, Accessories, Men's Footwear, Store Displays, Fixtures, Supplies

AZAR'S BIG & TALL MEN'S STORE (MW-2)
3659 Debby Dr. (m-b)
Montgomery, AL 36111
334-288-1660 / Fax: 334-288-1642
Sales: $1 Million-$10 Million
ZACK N. AZAR, JR. (Co-Owner) & Buys Big & Tall Men's Sportswear, Furnishings, Accessories, Footwear, Store Displays, Fixtures, Supplies
ZACK N. AZAR, III (Co-Owner) & Buys Big & Tall Men's Sportswear, Furnishings, Accessories, Footwear, Store Displays, Fixtures, Supplies

BUCKELEW'S, INC. (CLO-2)
7012 Vaughn Rd. (b)
Montgomery, AL 36116
334-279-5147 / Fax: 334-279-5179
Sales: $1 Million-$10 Million
TOM BUCKELEW (President) & Buys Men's Footwear, Leather Goods, Men's Apparel, Men's Casualwear, Men's Denim Apparel, Men's Formalwear, Men's Accessories, Men's Hosiery, Men's Outerwear, Men's Sportswear, Men's Suits

JIM MASSEY (MW-12)
531 South St.
Montgomery, AL 36104
334-262-8852 / Fax: 334-265-5461
JIM MASSEY, JR. (Owner)
TIM HAIGLER (Gen. Mgr.-Stores) & Buys Men's, Young Men's & Boys' Suits, Formal Wear, Footwear, Store Displays, Fixtures, Supplies

THE LOCKER ROOM OF MONTGOMERY, INC. (MW)
1717 Carter Hill Rd. (b)
Montgomery, AL 36106
334-262-1788 / Fax: 334-262-7750
Sales: $500,001-$1 Million
GEORGE WILDER (Owner) & Buys Men's Wear, Accessories, Furnishings, Men's Footwear, Store Displays, Fixtures, Supplies

LOOKIN' GOOD (CLO-2)
71 Dexter Ave. (h)
Montgomery, AL 36104
334-263-7372 / Fax: 334-263-7405
Sales: $500,001-$1 Million
ARCHIE DARYNANI (Owner) & Buys Men's Sportswear, Big & Tall Men's Wear, Young Men's Wear, Boys' Wear, Furnishings, Accessories, Men's Footwear, Store Displays, Fixtures, Supplies

THE NAME DROPPER (KS)
1721 Eastern Blvd. (b)
Montgomery, AL 36117
334-277-7118 / Fax: 334-244-0001
Sales: $1 Million-$10 Million
SID SCHROLL (Co-Owner) & Buys Boys' Wear, Accessories, Furnishings, Boys' Footwear, Store Displays, Fixtures, Supplies
SHEA SCHROLL (Co-Owner) & Buys Boys' Wear, Accessories, Furnishings, Boys' Footwear, Store Displays, Fixtures, Supplies

NEW FASHION LINE (CLO)
2264 E. South Blvd.
Montgomery, AL 36116
334-280-3334 / Fax: 334-280-3325
Website: www.newfashionline.com
JOE KENNEDY (Owner) & Buys Men's Urban Contemporary, Accessories

THE NEW HOBNOB (CLO)
1603 S. Decatur St. (m-des)
Montgomery, AL 36104
334-263-2254 / Fax: 334-262-6013
Sales: $1 Million-$10 Million
EVELYN JETER (Co-Owner) & Buys Men's Footwear, Leather Goods, Men's Apparel, Men's Casualwear, Men's Denim Apparel, Men's Accessories, Men's Hosiery, Men's Outerwear, Men's Sportswear, Men's Suits
JANET JETER (Co-Owner) & Buys Men's Footwear, Leather Goods, Men's Apparel, Men's Casualwear, Men's Denim Apparel, Men's Accessories, Men's Hosiery, Men's Outerwear, Men's Sportswear, Men's Suits
PAULINE WATLEY (Co-Owner) & Buys Men's Footwear, Leather Goods, Men's Apparel, Men's Casualwear, Men's Denim Apparel, Men's Accessories, Men's Hosiery, Men's Outerwear, Men's Sportswear, Men's Suits
BELINDA JETER (Co-Owner) & Buys Men's Footwear, Leather Goods, Men's Apparel, Men's Casualwear, Men's Denim Apparel, Men's Accessories, Men's Hosiery, Men's Outerwear, Men's Sportswear, Men's Suits
BETTY JETER (Co-Owner) & Buys Men's Footwear, Leather Goods, Men's Apparel, Men's Casualwear, Men's Denim Apparel, Men's Accessories, Men's Hosiery, Men's Outerwear, Men's Sportswear, Men's Suits

WEBBER'S DEPARTMENT STORE (DEPT)
(THE JAMES STORES)
39 N. Perry St. (bud-p)
Montgomery, AL 36104
334-264-7376
Sales: $1 Million-$10 Million

WALTER JAMES (Co-Owner) & Buys Men's Sportswear, Furnishings, Big & Tall Men's Wear, Accessories, Young Men's Wear, Boys' Wear, Men's Footwear, Boys' Footwear

ALLEN JAMES (Co-Owner) & Buys Men's Sportswear, Furnishings, Big & Tall Men's Wear, Accessories, Young Men's Wear, Boys' Wear, Men's Footwear, Boys' Footwear, Store Displays, Fixtures and Supplies

WEIL'S, INC. (CLO-14)
64 Monroe St. (bud-p)
Montgomery, AL 36104
334-262-0093 / Fax: 334-263-3004

ALAN WEIL, JR. (President) & Buys Men's & Boys' Wear, Footwear, Accessories, Furnishings, Store Displays, Fixtures, Supplies

KING'S DEPARTMENT STORE (CLO)
P.O. Box 516 (m)
Moulton, AL 35650
256-974-0444
Sales: $1 Million-$10 Million

ED KING (Owner) & Buys Men's Suits, Sport Shirts, Outer Jackets, Casual Slacks, Furnishings, Accessories, Leather Apparel, Men's Footwear, Store Displays, Fixtures, Supplies

VICKIE HALE (Mgr.) & Buys Men's Suits, Sport Shirts, Outer Jackets, Casual Slacks, Furnishings, Accessories, Leather Apparel, Men's Footwear, Store Displays, Fixtures, Supplies

SHELTON CLOTHING, INC. (CLO)
2524 County Rd. 87 (m)
Moulton, AL 35650
256-974-9079 / Fax: 256-974-9095

BOBBY LEE SHELTON (Owner) & Buys Men's Sportswear, Western Headwear, Footwear, Big & Tall Men's Wear, Young Men's Wear, 8 to 14 Boys' Wear, Store Displays, Fixtures, Supplies

ROGERS, INC. (DEPT-2)
(THE DUNLAP COMPANY)
519 W. Avalon Ave. (m-b)
Muscle Shoals, AL 35661
256-383-1828 / Fax: 256-389-8299
Sales: $10 Million-$50 Million

EDWARD MARTIN (President & G.M.M.)

COURTNEY TURNER-Men's Overcoats, Suits, Tailored Jackets, Tailored Slacks, Raincoats, Big & Tall Men's, Sweaters, Sport Shirts, Outer Jackets, Casual Slacks, Leather Apparel, Active Apparel, Dress Shirts

LYNN ALMOND-Furnishings, Accessories, Men's & Boys' Wear

KIM LUCE-Boys' Wear, Footwear

SHANKY'S MENSWEAR OF ALABAMA, INC. (MW)
711 Woodward Ave. (m-b)
Muscle Shoals, AL 35661
256-383-1551 / Fax: 256-383-9837
Sales: $500,001-$1 Million
Website: www.shankys.com

GREG SHARP (Owner) & Buys Men's Wear, Leather Apparel, Furnishings, Accessories, Young Men's Wear, Footwear, Store Displays, Fixtures, Supplies

THE WHARF (CLO)
220 McFarland Blvd. (m)
Northport, AL 35476
205-752-2075
Sales: $1 Million-$10 Million

LEE LOVOY (Co-Owner)

MARK LOVOY (Co-Owner) & Buys Men's & Boys' Casual Sportswear,Young Men's Wear, Furnishings, Accessories, Leather Apparel, Footwear, Store Displays, Fixtures

JULIE LOVOY-Store Supplies

BENNETT'S DEPARTMENT STORE (DEPT)
222 1st Ave. East (m-b)
Oneonta, AL 35121
205-274-2288
Sales: $1 Million-$10 Million

GORDON BENNETT (Owner) & Buys Men's & Boys' Wear, Footwear, Accessories, Furnishings, Store Displays, Fixtures & Supplies

PRICKETT'S MEN'S STORE (MW)
206 1st Ave. (b)
Oneonta, AL 35121
205-274-2267 / Fax: 205-625-0148
Sales: $500,001-$1 Million

DAVID NATION (Co-Owner) & Buys Men's Overcoats, Suits, Tailored Slacks, Tailored Jackets, Raincoats, Sportswear, Furnishings, Headwear, Belts, Small Leather Goods, Fragrances, Footwear, Young Men's Wear, Big & Tall Men's Wear, Store Displays, Fixtures, Supplies

MARTHA NATION (Co-Owner) & Buys Men's Overcoats, Suits, Tailored Slacks, Tailored Jackets, Raincoats, Sportswear, Furnishings, Headwear, Belts, Small Leather Goods, Fragrances, Footwear, Young Men's Wear, Big & Tall Men's Wear, Store Displays, Fixtures, Supplies

SOUVENIR CITY (CLO)
24644 Perdido Beach Blvd.
Orange Beach, AL 36561
251-974-1658 / Fax: 251-974-1659

GEORGE FRANKLIN-Boys' Apparel, Boys' Swimwear, Dive Apparel, Sunglasses, Accessories, Footwear, Hats, Men's Apparel, Men's Surf & Swimwear, Outdoor Gear, Outdoor Apparel, Resortwear

ANDY'S SUIT STORE & BIG & TALL (MW)
527 Quintard Dr. (m)
Oxford, AL 36203
256-835-0054 / Fax: 256-831-0752
Sales: $500,001-$1 Million
Website: www.andysstoreformen.com

ANDY WEEMS (Owner) & Buys Leather Goods, Men's Apparel, Big & Tall Men's Wear, Men's Casualwear, Men's Denim Apparel, Men's Formalwear, Men's Hosiery, Men's Outerwear, Men's Sportswear, Men's Suits, Men's Underwear

PHIL MATTHEWS (Mgr.) & Buys Leather Goods, Men's Apparel, Big & Tall Men's Wear, Men's Casualwear, Men's Denim Apparel, Men's Formalwear, Men's Hosiery, Men's Outerwear, Men's Sportswear, Men's Suits, Men's Underwear

SLACKS SHACK (MW)
6 N. Court Sq. (m)
Ozark, AL 36360
334-774-7211

DAN SPANO (Owner) & Buys Men's Wear, Casual Slacks, Tailored Slacks, Store Displays, Fixtures & Supplies

MP SURPLUS, INC. (DEPT)
1229 E. Hwy. 134 (p-m)
Pinckard, AL 36371
334-983-3164 / Fax: 334-983-1242
Sales: $1 Million-$10 Million
Website: www.mpsurplus.com

BOB G. PAGE (Owner) & Buys Store Displays, Fixtures, Supplies, Overcoats, Raincoats, Big & Tall Men's, Sweaters, Sport Shirts, Outer Jackets, Leather Apparel, Active Apparel, Dress Shirts, Underwear, Hosiery, Gloves, Headwear, Belts, Jewelry, Small Leather Goods, Footwear

SHARON SEWELL (Mgr.) & Buys Store Displays, Fixtures, Supplies, Overcoats, Raincoats, Big & Tall Men's, Sweaters, Sport Shirts, Outer Jackets, Leather Apparel, Active Apparel, Dress Shirts, Underwear, Hosiery, Gloves, Headwear, Belts, Jewelry, Small Leather Goods, Footwear

SIKES' AND KOHN'S COUNTRY MALL (DEPT)
P.O. Box 60 (m-b)
22150 Troy Hwy.
Pine Level, AL 36065
334-584-7402 / Fax: 334-584-7700
Sales: $1 Million-$10 Million

JAMES SIKES (Owner) & Buys Men's Overcoats, Suits, Tailored Jackets, Tailored Slacks, Raincoats, Big & Tall Men's Wear, Sweaters, Sport Shirts, Outer Jackets, Leather Apparel, Dress Shirts, Ties, Robes, Underwear, Hosiery, Gloves, Headwear, Belts, Jewelry, Small Leather Goods, Young Men's Wear, Boys' Wear, Sportswear, Furnishings, Accessories, Footwear, Store Displays, Fixtures

DANNY SIKES (Gen. Mgr.) & Buys Store Supplies

ALABAMA - Roanoke

CHRIS GAY SPORTSWEAR (CLO)
2064 US Hwy. 431 (m-b)
P.O. Box 336
Roanoke, AL 36274
334-863-8993 / Fax: 334-863-8941
Sales: $100,001-$500,000
BILL HARVEL (Co-Owner) & Buys Leather Goods, Men's Apparel, Men's Big & Tall Apparel, Men's Casualwear, Men's Denim Apparel, Men's Suits
JUDY HARVEL (Co-Owner) & Buys Leather Goods, Men's Apparel, Men's Big & Tall Apparel, Men's Casualwear, Men's Denim Apparel, Men's Suits

BAR D OUTFIT (CLO)
2400 US Hwy. 80 West (m-b)
Selma, AL 36701
334-872-7333 / Fax: 334-874-9200
D. C. BEVILLE (Co-Owner) & Buys Store Displays, Fixtures, Supplies
DELORES BEVILLE (Co-Owner) & Buys Men's Western Sport Coats, Sport Shirts, Casual Slacks, Dress Shirts, Small Leather Goods, Big & Tall Men's Shirts, Jeans, Footwear
DONNA BEVILLE-Men's Western Sport Coats, Sport Shirts, Casual Slacks, Dress Shirts, Small Leather Goods, Big & Tall Men's Shirts, Jeans, Footwear

ON TIME FASHIONS (MW-2)
1120 Alabama Ave. (m)
Selma, AL 36701
334-874-9997
Sales: $1 Million-$10 Million
SAM DABIT (Co-Owner) & Buys Store Displays, Fixtures, Supplies
ZUHER DABIT (Co-Owner) & Buys Men's Sportswear, Boys' Wear, Leather Apparel, Big & Tall Men's Wear, Men's Footwear, Boys' Footwear, Furnishings, Accessories

A & M CLOTHING (CLO)
115 N. Norton Ave. (m-b)
Sylacauga, AL 35150
256-249-9620 / Fax: 256-249-9620
Sales: $100,001-$500,000
BETTY BLADES (Co-Owner) & Buys Men's Footwear, Men's Apparel, Men's Casualwear, Men's Denim Apparel
RICHARD BLADES (Co-Owner) & Buys Men's Footwear, Men's Apparel, Men's Casualwear, Men's Denim Apparel

GRIFFIN JEWELERS, INC. (JWLY-6)
704 Battle St. East
Talladega, AL 35160
256-362-5282 / Fax: 256-362-5858
Sales: $1 Million-$10 Million
Website: www.griffinsjewelers.com
MILLARD GRIFFIN (President) & Buys Jewelry, Watches
TIM GRIFFIN (V.P.) & Buys Jewelry, Watches

MICHAEL'S MENSWEAR (CLO)
127 W. Court Sq. (m)
Talladega, AL 35160
256-362-2631
Sales: $1 Million-$10 Million
JOHN GEE (Owner) & Buys Men's Wear, Leather Apparel, Furnishings, Accessories, Men's Footwear, Store Displays, Fixtures, Supplies
MIKE GEE-Men's Wear, Leather Apparel, Furnishings, Accessories, Men's Footwear, Store Displays, Fixtures, Supplies

DON WALKER SHOES (FW)
814 Hwy. 231 South, #B (bud-p-m-b-des)
Troy, AL 36081
334-566-0044
Sales: $500,001-$1 Million
FRANCIS WALKER (Owner) & Buys Boys' Apparel, Uniforms, Footwear, Watches, Men's Accessories, Men's Apparel, Hosiery

OLIVER SHOES, INC. (FW)
60 S. Court Sq. (b)
Troy, AL 36081
334-566-5516 / Fax: 334-566-4439
Sales: $1 Million-$10 Million
TIM OLIVER (President & G.M.M.) & Buys Men's Accessories, Hosiery, Footwear, Boys' Footwear

STANTON'S (CLO-2)
(OLIVER ENTERPRISES)
P.O. Box 1107 (p)
52 E. Court Sq.
Troy, AL 36081
334-566-4504
Sales: $1 Million-$10 Million
DORIS OLIVER (President)
DAVIS DOGGETT (Mgr.) & Buys Men's, Young Men's & Boys' Wear, Store Displays, Fixtures, Supplies
RICHMOND WATKINS (Mgr.) (@ 256-245-6381) & Buys Men's, Young Men's & Boys' Wear, Store Displays, Fixtures, Supplies

BRITTAN'S MEN'S & BOYS' WEAR (MW)
2312 6th St. (m)
Tuscaloosa, AL 35401
205-758-3544
Sales: $500,001-$1 Million
DONALD LAFOY (President) & Buys Men's Furnishings, Accessories, Footwear, Store Displays, Fixtures, Supplies
GEORGE JONES (G.M.M.) & Buys Men's Furnishings, Accessories, Footwear, Store Displays, Fixtures, Supplies

BURCH & HATFIELD FORMAL SHOPS (MW-12)
1810 University Blvd. (bud-p-m-b-h)
Tuscaloosa, AL 35401
205-345-2938 / Fax: 205-345-2966
Website: www.tuxedo4u.com
DAVID BURCH (Owner) & Buys Men's & Boys' Formal Wear, Footwear, Store Displays, Fixtures, Supplies

GINGER'S TRUNK (GS)
(CORNER INVESTMENTS, INC.)
1012 8th Ave.
Tuscaloosa, AL 35401
205-345-0407 / Fax: 205-752-4101
JENNY SWAIN (Co-Owner) & Buys Men's, Young Men's & Boys' T-shirts, Headwear, Store Displays, Fixtures, Supplies
GINGER UNDERWOOD (Co-Owner) & Buys Men's, Young Men's & Boys' T-shirts, Headwear, Store Displays, Fixtures, Supplies

THE LOCKER ROOM (MW)
1218 University Ave.
Tuscaloosa, AL 35401
205-752-2990 / Fax: 205-758-4329
ALEX GATEWOOD (Owner) & Buys Men's Sportswear, Furnishings, Accessories

SHIRT SHOP (MW)
525 Greensboro Ave. (p)
Tuscaloosa, AL 35401
205-752-6931 / Fax: 205-752-6939
Sales: $500,001-$1 Million
CHARLES SPURLIN (Owner) & Buys Men's Suits, Sport Coats, Dress Shirts, Sport Shirts, Casual Slacks, Tailored Slacks, Ties, Accessories, Big & Tall Men's Wear, Men's Footwear

UNIVERSITY SUPPLY STORE (SP-2)
(UNIVERSITY OF ALABAMA)
Box 870291 Ferguson Ctr.
McCorvey Dr.
Tuscaloosa, AL 35487
205-348-6168 / Fax: 205-348-9239
Sales: $2 Million-$5 Million
Website: www.supestore.ua.edu
ROBERT PALMER (Dir.)
NOELE BUTLER-Activewear

ARDEAN'S FASHIONS (CLO)
101 Westside St. (m)
Tuskegee, AL 36083
334-727-7690
Sales: $100,001-$500,000
ARDEAN LEWIS (Owner) & Buys Leather Goods, Men's Casualwear, Men's Formalwear, Men's Accessories, Men's Suits

TOWN & COUNTRY CLOTHING (CLO)

P.O. Box 367 (p)
105 Columbus Ave.
Vernon, AL 35592
205-695-7024
Sales: $100,001-$500,000

EDDIE McNEES (Owner) & Buys Men's Suits, Tailored Slacks, Sweaters, Sport Shirts, Casual Slacks, Furnishings, Accessories, Big & Tall Men's Wear, Men's Footwear, Store Displays, Fixtures, Supplies

MARIE McNEES-Store Displays, Fixtures and Supplies

W.B. CLEARMAN STORE (CLO)

P.O. Box 424 (p)
1st Ave. NW
Vernon, AL 35592
205-695-9558
Sales: $100,001-$500,000

W. B. CLEARMAN (Owner) & Buys Men's Casual & Work Clothes, Western Wear, Western Footwear, Dress & Casual Footwear, Store Displays, Fixtures, Supplies

WARRIOR MERCANTILE CO. (CLO)

305 Main St. (p-m)
Warrior, AL 35180
205-585-3743 / Fax: 205-647-0534
Sales: $100,001-$500,000

MERVYN EPSMAN (Owner) & Buys Men's Suits, Tailored Jackets, Tailored Slacks, Raincoats, Sweaters, Sport Shirts, Outer Jackets, Casual Slacks, Active Apparel, Dress Shirts, Ties, Robes, Underwear, Hosiery, Gloves, Belts, Jewelry, Small Leather Goods, Fragrances, Footwear, Big & Tall Men's Wear, Young Men's Wear, 8 to 20 Boys' Wear, Store Displays, Fixtures, Supplies

ALASKA - Anchorage

ALASKA COMMERCIAL CO. (GM-24)

550 W. 64th Ave., #200 (m)
Anchorage, AK 99518
907-273-4600 / Fax: 907-273-4800
Sales: $100 Million-$500 Million
Website: www.alaskacommercial.com
Retail Locations: AK, CA

JERRY BITTNER (President)
EDWARD KENNEDY (C.E.O.)
JOHN TOONE (Real Estate Contact) (@ 800-782-0391)
BONNIE OSGOOD-Men's & Boys' Sportswear, Footwear, Store Displays, Fixtures, Supplies

ANDRE'S CUSTOM TAILORS, INC. (MW-2)

4007 Old Seward Hwy. (h)
Anchorage, AK 99503
907-562-3714 / Fax: 907-563-2905
Sales: $1 Million-$10 Million

ANDRES CASTRO (Partner) & Buys Men's Sportswear, Furnishings, Accessories, Footwear, Small Leather Goods, Belts, Gloves, Store Displays, Fixtures, Supplies

ARMY NAVY STORE (AN)

(EAGLE RIVER, INC.)
320 W. 4th Ave.
Anchorage, AK 99501
(World Wide Distributors)
907-279-2401 / Fax: 907-278-7174
Sales: $2 Million-$5 Million
Website: www.army-navy-store.com

MARK CRUVER (Owner) & Buys Men's & Boys' Outerwear, Denim, Tops, Bottoms, Underwear, Hosiery, Belts, Gloves, Small Leather Goods, Store Displays, Fixtures & Supplies
JEFF STULTZ-Boots

BOOT COUNTRY (FW)

7901 Old Seward Hwy. (b)
Anchorage, AK 99518
907-349-8413
Sales: $500,001-$1 Million
Website: www.bootcountryalaska.com

COLLIN LEARY (Owner) & Buys Men's Footwear

BREWSTER'S CLOTHING & FOOTWEAR, INC. (MW-2)

3825 Mt. View Dr. (p)
Anchorage, AK 99508
907-279-0533 / Fax: 907-276-0180
Sales: $1 Million-$10 Million
Website: www.brewstersak.com

CHARLES BREWSTER (Owner)
KAREN MEYER (President)
MATT MARTH (Mgr.) & Buys Men's Work Clothing, Footwear, Western Wear, Accessories, Furnishings, Store Displays, Fixtures, Supplies

BRUCE'S T-SHIRTS (SP)

800 E. Diamond Blvd., #146
Anchorage, AK 99515
907-522-3526 / Fax: 907-522-3526
Website: www.brucestshirts.com

MICHAEL FORMAN (Owner) & Buys Activewear, T-shirts

JUNIOR TOWNE (KS)

1017 W. Fireweed Ln. (b)
Anchorage, AK 99503
907-279-2824 / Fax: 907-276-6375
Sales: $1 Million-$10 Million

LYNN BOOTS (Owner) & Buys Boys' Clothing, Sweaters, Sport Shirts, Outer Jackets, Leather Apparel, Casual Slacks, Tailored Slacks, Tailored Jackets, Active Apparel, Furnishings, Accessories to Size 20, Footwear, Store Displays, Fixtures, Supplies

PIA'S SCANDANAVIAN WOOLENS (SP & MO)

445 W. 4th Ave.
Anchorage, AK 99501
907-277-7964 / Fax: 907-279-4912
Sales: $100,001-$500,000

KARIN WANAMAKER-Men's Woolen Apparel

THE SILVA SADDLE, INC. (WW)

2808 E. Tudor Rd., #7 (b)
Anchorage, AK 99507
907-561-8780 / Fax: 907-561-8832

DEA SILVA (Owner) & Buys Men's Western Wear, Boys' Western Wear, Related Accessories, Furnishings, Footwear, Store Displays, Fixtures, Supplies

SIXTH AVENUE OUTFITTERS (CLO)

520 W. 6th Ave.
Anchorage, AK 99501
907-276-0233 / Fax: 907-276-0360

RAY WILLIAMS (Owner) & Buys Sweaters, Outer Jackets, Parkas, T-shirts, Jeans, Fleece, Active Apparel, Outer Clothing, Hosiery, Underwear, Gloves, Headwear, Footwear, Boots, Hiking Boots, Store Displays, Fixtures and Supplies
BRIAN WILLIAM (Mgr.) & Buys Sweaters, Outer Jackets, Parkas, T-shirts, Jeans, Fleece, Active Apparel, Outer Clothing, Hosiery, Underwear, Gloves, Headwear, Footwear, Boots, Hiking Boots, Store Displays, Fixtures and Supplies

THE CLOTHES COMPANY (MW-2)

P.O. Box 218 (m)
Craig, AK 99921
907-826-3939 / Fax: 907-826-3940
Sales: $500,001-$1 Million

MARSHA HOWARD (Owner) & Buys Men's & Young Men's Wear, Sportswear, Belts, Small Leather Goods, Work Clothes, Men's Footwear, Boys' Wear, Boys' Footwear, Store Displays, Fixtures and Supplies
NANCY LUCAS (Mgr.) & Buys Men's & Young Men's Wear, Sportswear, Belts, Small Leather Goods, Work Clothes, Men's Footwear, Boys' Wear, Boys' Footwear, Store Displays, Fixtures and Supplies

SAVVY WEAR (CLO)

Westwind Plaza Mall (m-b)
Cold Storage Rd.
Craig, AK 99921
907-826-3945 / Fax: 907-826-3946

VICTORIA MARVIN (Owner) & Buys Men's, Young Men's & Boys' Wear, Footwear, Accessories, Furnishings, Store Displays, Fixtures, Supplies

BIG RAY'S STORE (MW-2)

(ARMY/NAVY STORE)
507 2nd Ave. (p)
Fairbanks, AK 99701
907-452-3458 / Fax: 907-456-2413
Sales: $1 Million-$10 Million

MONTY ROSTAD (Owner) & Buys Men's Sportswear, Work Clothes, Arctic Gear, Footwear, Boys' Clothes, Store Displays, Fixtures, Supplies
STEVE JOHNSON (Floor Mgr.) & Buys Men's & Boys' Footwear

CARR'S CLOTHING STORE (MW)

404 Cushman (b)
Fairbanks, AK 99701
907-452-2370 / Fax: 907-452-5896
Sales: $100,001-$500,000

DANIEL F. BLOOD (President) & Buys Men's Sportswear, Furnishings, Accessories, Store Displays, Fixtures, Supplies

FAMILY SHOE STORE, INC. (FW)

1235 Airport Way, #4 (m-b)
Fairbanks, AK 99701
907-452-2353 / Fax: 907-452-2365
Sales: $500,001-$1 Million

GARY CONTENTO (President)
JUDY COOPER (G.M.M.) & Buys Men's Apparel, Boys' Apparel, Men's Footwear, Boys' Footwear, Accessories

HOMER'S JEANS (CLO)

564 E. Pioneer, #1 (m-b)
Homer, AK 99603
907-235-6234 / Fax: 907-235-4972
Sales: $500,001-$1 Million

LESLIE MASTICK (Owner) & Buys Men's Sport Shirts, Casual Slacks, Active Apparel, Underwear, Hosiery, Big & Tall Men's Sport Shirts, Casual Slacks, Active Apparel, Underwear, Hosiery, Footwear, Young Men's Wear, Store Displays, Fixtures, Supplies

GALLIGASKINS (CLO-2 & MO)

219 S. Franklin St. (b)
Juneau, AK 99801
907-586-8953 / Fax: 907-586-8154
Sales: $1 Million-$10 Million
Website: www.galligaskins.com

GAILE SWOPE (Owner) & Buys Men's Resortwear, T-shirts, Casualwear, Headwear, Footwear, Boys' Wear

NUGGET ALASKAN OUTFITTER (MW)

8745 Glacier Hwy., #145 (m-b)
Juneau, AK 99801
907-789-0956 / Fax: 907-789-3635
Sales: $1 Million-$10 Million

RON FLINT (President & G.M.M.) & Buys Men's Work & Outdoor Apparel, Related Footwear

NANCY POTTS (Asst. Mgr.) & Buys Men's Athletic Apparel, Outdoor Apparel, Related Footwear & Accessories

SOS VALUE MART, INC. (CLO)

P.O. Box 177 (bud)
Mile 2.5 Keku Rd.
Kake, AK 99830
907-785-6444 / Fax: 907-785-3201
Sales: $1 Million-$10 Million

DAVE OHMER (Co-Owner)

JOE SHORT (Co-Owner)

AUDREY McNELLY-Jeans, Underwear, Hosiery, Boots, Store Displays, Fixtures, Supplies

LARRY ELLSWORTH-Jeans, Underwear, Hosiery, Boots, Logging Wear, Store Displays, Fixtures, Supplies

KASIGLUK, INC. (DEPT-2)

P.O. Box 39 (m)
Kasigluk, AK 99609
907-477-6113 / Fax: 907-477-6026
Sales: $1 Million-$10 Million

HOWARD TINKER (President)

MIKE MARTIN (Mgr.) & Buys Men's Sweaters, Sport Shirts, Outer Jackets, Casual Slacks, Active Apparel, Furnishings, Footwear, Boys' Wear, Store Displays, Fixtures, Supplies

MALSTON'S MEN'S (MO)

405 Overland Ave., #105 (p-m)
Kenai, AK 99611
907-283-4966 / Fax: 907-283-5685
Sales: $500,001-$1 Million

RON MALSTON (Owner) & Buys Suits, Tailored Slacks, Tailored Jackets, Big & Tall Men's Wear, Tuxedos, Dress Shirts, Ties, Hosiery, Store Displays, Fixtures and Supplies

TONGASS TRADING (DEPT-3)

201 Dock St. (m)
Ketchikan, AK 99901
907-225-5101 / Fax: 907-225-0481
Sales: $1 Million-$10 Million
Website: www.tongasstrading.com

CHRIS PARKS (G.M.M.) & Buys Store Displays, Fixtures, Supplies

WAYNE McMURCHIE-Men's Overcoats, Suits, Tailored Jackets, Tailored Slacks, Raincoats, Big & Tall Men's Wear, Sweaters, Sport Shirts, Outer Jackets, Casual Slacks, Furnishings, Headwear, Accessories, Footwear, Young Men's Wear

COAST GUARD EXCHANGE SYSTEMS (PX)

P.O. Box 195024 (m)
U.S. Coast Guard Support Ctr.
Kodiak, AK 99619
907-487-5113 / Fax: 907-487-5051

ANNA BISHOP-Men's Sweaters, Sport Shirts, Outer Jackets, Casual Slacks, Active Apparel, Furnishings, Headwear, Accessories, Boys' Wear, Men's & Boys' Footwear, Store Displays, Fixtures, Supplies

CY'S SPORTING GOODS (SG)

117 Lower Mill Bay Rd. (m-b-h)
Kodiak, AK 99615
907-486-3900 / Fax: 907-486-5620
Website: www.kodiak-outfitters.com

CY HOEN (President) & Buys T-shirts, Fleece, Active Apparel, Athletic Hosiery, Hats, Athletic Footwear, Hunting Clothes & Footwear

SHARON MOORE-T-shirts, Fleece, Active Apparel, Athletic Hosiery, Hats, Athletic Footwear, Hunting Clothes & Footwear

SUTLIFF'S TRUE VALUE HARDWARE, INC. (GM)

P.O. Box 1157
210 Shelikof Ave.
Kodiak, AK 99615
907-486-5797 / Fax: 907-486-4977

DON ZIMMERMAN (G.M.M.) & Buys Store Displays, Fixtures and Supplies

L. J. EURBANO (Mgr.-Housewares, Clothing) & Buys Men's Sportswear, Underwear, Hosiery, Gloves, Headwear, Belts, Footwear, Young Men's & Boys' Wear

MICHELLE CAGUIOA-Men's Sportswear, Underwear, Hosiery, Gloves, Headwear, Belts, Footwear, Young Men's & Boys' Wear

DELAR'S CLOTHING & BRIDAL BOUTIQUE (CLO)

P.O. Box 8209 (m-b)
Nikishka, AK 99635
907-776-8347 / Fax: 907-776-5491
Sales: $500,001-$1 Million

DELORES M. RAPPE (Owner) & Buys Sweaters, Outer Jackets, Underwear, Hosiery, Gloves, Belts, Store Displays, Fixtures, Supplies

NOTE-Specializing in Men's Work Clothing Only.

LEE'S CLOTHING, INC. (CLO)

P.O. Box 747 (m)
Petersburg, AK 99833
907-772-4229 / Fax: 907-772-3542
Sales: $1 Million-$10 Million

CYNTHIA LEE-MATHISED-Men's Clothing, Accessories & Footwear

THE TRADING UNION, INC. (DEPT)

P.O. Box 489 (m-b)
Petersburg, AK 99833
907-772-3881 / Fax: 907-772-9309
Sales: $50 Million-$100 Million

A. K. SLAVIN (President & G.M.M.) & Buys Store Displays, Fixtures, Supplies

ELAINE HAYWOOD-Men's Raincoats, Big & Tall Men's, Sweaters, Sport Shirts, Outer Jackets, Leather Apparel, Casual Slacks, Active Apparel, Dress Shirts, Ties, Robes, Underwear, Hosiery, Gloves, Headwear, Belts, Jewelry, Small Leather Goods, Fragrances, Footwear, Young Men's Wear, 8 to 20 Boys' Clothing, Sportswear, Furnishings, Accessories, Men's Footwear

BROWN & HAWKINS DEPARTMENT STORE (DEPT. & MO)

P.O. Box 149
209 4th Ave.
Seward, AK 99664
907-224-3011 / Fax: 907-224-2343
Sales: $100,001-$500,000

IRIS DARLING (Co-Owner) & Buys Apparel, Skiwear, Athletic Footwear, Outdoor Footwear

HUGH DARLING (Co-Owner) & Buys Apparel, Skiwear, Athletic Footwear, Outdoor Footwear

URBACH'S (MW)

P.O. Box 249 (p-m)
218 4th St.
Seward, AK 99664
907-224-3088 / Fax: 907-224-2484
Sales: $500,001-$1 Million

DOROTHY URBACH (Owner) & Buys Men's Sportswear, Furnishings, Headwear, Belts, Footwear, Boys' Furnishings, Accessories, Store Displays, Fixtures, Supplies

ALASKA - Sitka

R & D CLOTHING, INC. (KS)
(THE CELLAR)
203 Harbor Dr. (m)
Sitka, AK 99835
907-747-8020 / Fax: 907-747-3777
Sales: $1 Million-$10 Million
VICKY DENKINGER (Owner) & Buys Boys' Wear, Accessories, Furnishings, Boys' Footwear, Store Displays, Fixtures, Supplies

RUSSEL'S STORE FOR MEN (MW-4)
(WILMAC CORP.)
(RAIN COUNTRY)
(HALIBUT HOLE)
213 Harbor Dr. (p)
Sitka, AK 99835
907-747-3395 / Fax: 907-747-5885
Sales: $1 Million-$10 Million
RON McCLAIN (Co-Owner) & Buys Store Displays, Fixtures & Supplies
CATHY HANSON-Men's Sweaters, Sport Shirts, Outer Jackets, Leather Apparel, Casual Slacks, Active Apparel, Furnishings, Headwear, Accessories, Men's Athletic Footwear
SHIRLEY BAYNE-Men's Sweaters, Sport Shirts, Outer Jackets, Leather Apparel, Casual Slacks, Active Apparel, Furnishings, Headwear, Accessories, Men's Athletic Footwear

NUNAKAUIAK YUPIK CORP. (DEPT)
P.O. Box 37068
Toksook Bay, AK 99637
907-427-7929 / Fax: 907-427-7326
ALAN ALIRKAN-Men's & Boys' Wear, Accessories, Furnishings, Store Displays, Fixtures, Supplies

SUGAR & SPICE & EVERYTHING NICE (CLO)
P.O. Box 186 (m-b)
200 Egan Dr.
Valdez, AK 99686
907-835-4336 / Fax: 907-835-5342
Sales: $500,001-$1 Million
ANN DERIFIELD (Owner) & Buys Boys' Apparel, Boys' Footwear, Men's Apparel, Leather Goods

ANGERMAN'S, INC. (MW)
P.O. Box 928 (m-b)
Wrangell, AK 99929
907-874-3640 / Fax: 907-874-2447
Sales: $500,001-$1 Million
DAWN ANGERMAN (Co-Owner) & Buys Young Men's Apparel & Accessories
JEFFREY ANGERMAN (Co-Owner) & Buys Men's Overcoats, Raincoats, Tailored Slacks, Sweaters, Sport Shirts, Outer Jackets, Casual Slacks, Active Apparel, Furnishings, Small Leather Goods, Footwear, Young Men's Wear, Store Displays, Fixtures, Supplies

MILLIE'S (CLO)
P.O. Box 291 (m-b)
22 Front St.
Wrangell, AK 99929
907-874-3831 / Fax: 907-874-3831
Sales: $500,001-$1 Million
MILDRED GRANT (Owner)
NOEL SMITH (Gen. Mgr.) & Buys Boys' Apparel, Leather Goods

MALLOTT'S GENERAL STORE, INC. (DEPT)
P.O. Box 159 (p)
Yakutat, AK 99689
907-784-3355 / Fax: 907-784-3258
Sales: $1 Million-$10 Million
LARRY POWELL (Co-Owner)
CAROLINE POWELL (Co-Owner) & Buys Men's Sweaters, Sport Shirts, Outer Jackets, Leather Apparel, Casual Slacks, Active Apparel, Footwear, Boys' Clothing, Sportswear, Furnishings, Accessories, Store Displays, Fixtures, Supplies

4 FUN ORIGINALS, INC. (CLO)
6552 E. Creek Rd., #5 (m)
Cave Creek, AZ 85020
480-575-1199
Sales: $500,001-$1 Million
Website: www.4funoriginals.com
LAURY KLASKY (President) & Buys Men's Apparel, Men's Sportswear
JOEL KLASKY (V.P.) & Buys Men's Apparel, Men's Sportswear

BOWLING DYNAMICS (SG)
6225 W. Chandler Blvd. (m)
Chandler, AZ 85226
480-940-0940
Sales: $500,001-$1 Million
DAVID CIRIGLIANO (Owner) & Buys Men's Footwear, Men's Apparel

SABA'S WESTERN STORES, INC. (WW-8)
3270 N. Colorado St., #101 (m)
Chandler, AZ 85225
480-969-7122 / Fax: 480-833-6494
Sales: $1 Million-$10 Million
Website: www.sabaswesternwear.com
ROGER SABA, SR. (President & Co-Owner)
RICHARD SABA (V.P., Gen. Mgr. & Co-Owner)
NORMAN SABA (Secy., Treas. & Co-Owner) & Buys Store Displays, Fixtures, Supplies
MARK SABA (Co-Owner)
ROGER SABA, JR.-Men's Western Sweaters, Sport Shirts, Outer Jackets, Leather Apparel, Casual Slacks, Boots, Related Accessories, Boys Wear & Footwear

COLEMAN CLOTHIERS, INC. (MW)
919 G Ave. (m-b)
Douglas, AZ 85607
520-364-3373 / Fax: 520-364-3373
Sales: $500,001-$1 Million
LESLEY DAVIDSON (Owner) & Buys Men's & Students' Clothing, Sweaters, Sport Shirts, Outer Jackets, Leather Apparel, Casual Slacks, Active Apparel, Dress Shirts, Men's Western Wear, Young Men's, Store Displays, Fixtures, Supplies
ROLANDO DAVIDSON (Mgr.) & Buys Men's & Students' Clothing, Sweaters, Sport Shirts, Outer Jackets, Leather Apparel, Casual Slacks, Active Apparel, Dress Shirts, Men's Western Wear, Young Men's, Store Displays, Fixtures, Supplies

MARLIN'S SADDLE SHOP (WW)
930 G Ave. (m-b)
Douglas, AZ 85607
520-364-2541 / Fax: 520-364-2723
JERRY BOHMFALK (Owner) & Buys Men's & Boys' Western Wear, Footwear, Related Accessories, Furnishings, Store Displays, Fixtures, Supplies

LEHMAN'S, INC. (CLO)
201 Railroad Blvd. (m)
Duncan, AZ 85534
928-359-2571
STEVE LEHMAN (Owner) & Buys Western Apparel, Sportswear, Dress Shirts, Underwear, Hosiery, Gloves, Headwear, Belts, Jewelry, Young Men's Wear, Store Displays, Fixtures and Supplies

BABBITT'S SPORTS CENTER (SG)
109 N. Leroux St. (m)
Flagstaff, AZ 86001
928-774-2960 / Fax: 928-774-6448
Sales: $1 Million-$10 Million
JIM BABBITT (Owner)
ADAM TURNER (Store Mgr.) & Buys Boys' Apparel, Boys' Footwear, Men's Footwear, Men's Sportswear
BRYAN THOMPSON-Boys' Apparel, Boys' Footwear, Men's Footwear, Men's Sportswear

CIRCLE Q WESTERN WEAR (WW)
1716 Rt. 66 East (h)
Flagstaff, AZ 86004
928-774-4672 / Fax: 928-774-3817
MARGO CHILDERS (Co-Owner) & Buys Men's Western Wear, Young Men's & Boys' Western Wear, Men's, Young Men's & Boys' Cowboy Boots, Footwear, Related Accessories, Furnishings, Store Displays, Fixtures, Supplies
ROBERT CHILDERS (Co-Owner) & Buys Men's Western Wear, Young Men's & Boys' Western Wear, Men's, Young Men's & Boys' Cowboy Boots, Footwear, Related Accessories, Furnishings, Store Displays, Fixtures, Supplies

MOUNTAIN SPORTS (SG-2)
24 N. San Francisco (m-b-h)
Flagstaff, AZ 86001
800-286-5156 / Fax: 928-774-5509
Website: www.mountainsport.com
MARK LAMBERSON (Owner)
MAT CLARKE-Outdoor Clothing, Outer Jackets, Raincoats, Gloves, Headwear

COWPOKE WESTERN STORE (WW)
5754 W. Glendale Ave. (p)
Glendale, AZ 85301
623-937-5929
Sales: $500,001-$1 Million
KATHY MUNNINGER (Co-Owner) & Buys Men's Sweaters, Tailored Slacks, Big & Tall Men's Wear, Young Men's Wear, Active Apparel, Store Displays, Fixtures and Supplies
JIM EGGLESTON (Co-Owner) & Buys Men's Sport Shirts, Outer Jackets, Casual Slacks, Furnishings, Belts, Hats,, Active Apparel, Store Displays, Fixtures, Supplies

MILLER SHOES, INC. (FW)
5801 W. Glendale Ave. (m-b)
Glendale, AZ 85301
623-937-5511
Sales: $500,001-$1 Million
SAM MILLER (Owner & G.M.) & Buys Men's Footwear & Hosiery

CANYON VILLAGE MARKETPLACE (DEPT-3)
P.O. Box 159
Grand Canyon, AZ 86023
928-638-2262 / Fax: 928-638-9204
JAMIE HODGSON (Gen. Mgr.)
JEN KATES-Skiwear, Outdoor Apparel & Footwear

LEISURE CONCEPTS INTERNATIONAL (CLO)
1990 McCulloh Blvd., #D278
Lake Hauasa City, AZ 86403
928-453-3250 / Fax: 928-453-1151
MARLENE MARTINEZ-Boys' Apparel, Boys' Swimwear, Dive Apparel & Accessories, Sunglasses, Accessories, Footwear, Hats, Men's Apparel, Men's Surf & Swimwear, Outdoor Gear & Apparel
ALEX MARTINEZ-Boys' Apparel, Boys' Swimwear, Dive Apparel & Accessories, Sunglasses, Accessories, Footwear, Hats, Men's Apparel, Men's Surf & Swimwear, Outdoor Gear & Apparel

ANDREA'S DRESS SHOPPE (CLO)
3045 W. Hwy. 260
Lakeside, AZ 85929
928-368-8322
ANDREA PEASLEY-Men's & Boys' Sportswear, Women's Dresses, Novelty T-shirts, Hats

CLOTHING CITY, INC. (MW-3)
2910 S. Alma School Rd. (m)
Mesa, AZ 85210
480-345-0684 / Fax: 480-345-0686
Sales: $1 Million-$10 Million
JIM ROBERTS (G.M.M.) & Buys Men's Suits, Tailored Jackets, Tailored Slacks, Raincoats, Big & Tall Men's Wear, Sportswear, Sweaters, Sport Shirts, Outer Jackets, Casual Slacks, Active Apparel, Furnishings, Dress Shirts, Ties, Robes, Underwear, Hosiery, Gloves, Young Men's Wear, Boys' Wear, Men's & Boys' Footwear, Store Displays, Fixtures, Supplies

JUST SPORTS (CLO-12)
(SPORTS VENTURE, INC.)
1445 W. Southern Ave., #2286
Mesa, AZ 85202
480-615-8183 / Fax: 480-615-8165
Website: www.ijustsports.com
KELLY ROBERTS (President) & Buys Men's Licensed Active Apparel, Headwear, Small Leather Goods, Store Displays, Fixtures, Supplies

ARIZONA - Mesa

LARADA'S ARMY SURPLUS STORE (AN)

764 W. Main St. (p-m)
Mesa, AZ 85201
480-834-7047 / Fax: 480-834-1388
Sales: $1 Million-$10 Million
Website: www.laradas.com

BRENT PENDLETON (Mgr.) & Buys Men's, Young Men's & Boys' Camouflage Wear, Furnishings, Accessories, Footwear, Military Clothing, Outdoor Wear, Store Displays, Fixtures, Supplies

O'NEAL'S SHOE CO. (FW)

6712 E. Broadway Rd., #4 (m)
Mesa, AZ 85206
480-985-6448 / Fax: 480-985-1178
Sales: $100,001-$500,000
Website: www.onealshoe.com

ELAINE O'NEAL (Partner) & Buys Men's Footwear, Men's Accessories, Leather Goods

PAUL O'NEAL (Partner & G.M.M.) & Buys Men's Footwear, Men's Accessories, Leather Goods

BRIAN O'NEAL (Mgr.)

POMEROY'S MEN'S STORES, INC. (MW & OL)

136 W. Main St. (m)
Mesa, AZ 85201
480-833-0733 / Fax: 480-834-4322
Sales: $1 Million-$10 Million
Website: www.pomeroysmissionary.com

WAYNE C. POMEROY (President) & Buys Store Displays, Fixtures, Supplies

DOUG WIMMER (Mgr.) & Buys Men's & Young Men's Wear, Suits, Overcoats, Accessories, Furnishings, Footwear

PHELPS - DODGE MERCANTILE CO. (DEPT)

172 Plaza Dr. (p-m)
P.O. Drawer 9
Morenci, AZ 85540
928-865-4121 / Fax: 928-865-2935
Sales: $1 Million-$10 Million

RAUL QUASALIA (Store Mgr.) & Buys Store Displays, Fixtures, Supplies

CARLA HICKS (Mgr.) & Buys Men's, Boys' & Students Wear, Footwear, Tailored Suits, Sports Shirts, Casual Slacks, Active Apparel, Dress Shirts, Ties, Underwear, Hosiery, Gloves, Belts, Jewelry, Small Leathers, Young Men's Shop, Boys' Wear 7+, Sportswear, Furnishings, Accessories

CARMEN CABBEJO-Men's, Boys' & Students Wear, Footwear, Tailored Suits, Sports Shirts, Casual Slacks, Active Apparel, Dress Shirts, Ties, Underwear, Hosiery, Gloves, Belts, Jewelry, Small Leathers, Young Men's Shop, Boys' Wear 7+, Sportswear, Furnishings, Accessories

ALEXANDER'S, INC. (MW)

144 N. Morley Ave. (p-m-b)
Nogales, AZ 85621
520-287-5103 / Fax: 520-287-3411
Sales: $1 Million-$10 Million

ALEX KORY (Owner) & Buys Men's Sportswear, Dress Shirts, Underwear, Hosiery, Accessories, Footwear

TERRY CRESPO-Young Men's Wear, Footwear

ANA KORY-Young Men's, Store Displays, Fixtures, Supplies

BRACKER'S DEPARTMENT STORE (DEPT-2)

P.O. Box 1489 (m-b)
68 N. Morley Ave.
Nogales, AZ 85628
520-287-3631 / Fax: 520-287-7137
Sales: $1 Million-$10 Million

PAUL BRACKER (Sr. Partner & Owner)

BRUCE BRACKER (Partner) & Buys Men's Sportswear, Furnishings, Headwear, Accessories, Footwear, Young Men's Wear, Store Displays, Fixtures, Supplies

ALMA AVILES-Boys' Wear, Footwear

CAPIN & CO. (DEPT)

P.O. Box 1117 (m-b)
32 N. Morley Ave.
Nogales, AZ 85628
520-397-6100 / Fax: 520-287-4110
Sales: $1 Million-$10 Million

NILS URMAN (Partner & Owner) & Buys Men's Footwear, Sport Shirts, Casual Slacks, Active Apparel, Sportswear, Furnishings, Accessories, Store Displays, Fixtures & Supplies

DANDY'S JEAN STORE (CLO)

(DANDY'S JEAN STORE)
367 W. Mariposa Rd. (m)
Nogales, AZ 85621
520-281-0259 / Fax: 520-281-0219
Sales: $500,001-$1 Million

EDWARD JEONG, JR. (President & Owner) & Buys Men's Footwear, Leather Goods, Licensed Apparel, Casualwear, Denim Apparel, Designer Apparel, Outerwear, Sportswear, Activewear, Watches, Young Men's Apparel, Boys' Footwear

LUPITA NEGATE (Mgr.) & Buys Men's Footwear, Leather Goods, Licensed Apparel, Casualwear, Denim Apparel, Designer Apparel, Outerwear, Sportswear, Activewear, Watches, Young Men's Apparel, Boys' Footwear

JACOBO DABDOUB (MW)

66 N. Terrace Ave.
Nogales, AZ 85621
520-287-2611 / Fax: 520-287-9687
Website: www.viaveneto.mx

JACOBO DABDOUB-Apparel

NORRIS DEPARTMENT WESTERN WEAR (WW)

1212 California Ave. (m)
Parker, AZ 85344
928-669-2718

TONY LOPEZ (Co-Owner) & Buys Men's Western Wear, Leather Apparel, Footwear, Young Men's Shop, Accessories, Furnishings, Store Displays, Fixtures & Supplies

DORA NORRIS (Co-Owner) & Buys Men's Western Wear, Leather Apparel, Footwear, Young Men's Shop, Accessories, Furnishings

PEGGY'S PAYSON PLACE (CLO-2)

109 W. Main St. (m-b)
Payson, AZ 85541
928-474-5500
Sales: $500,001-$1 Million

PEGGY WYATT (Owner) & Buys Men's Wear, Footwear, Accessories, Furnishings, Store Displays, Fixtures, Supplies

THE MAD CATFISH (CLO)

8248 W. Deer Valley Rd.
Peorie, AZ 85382
623-572-9974 / Fax: 623-572-0714

TROY ABRAHAMS-Boys' Apparel, Sunglasses, Accessories, Footwear, Hats, Men's Apparel, Men's Surf & Swimwear, Skate Apparel, T-shirts

SHANE TERRELL-Boys' Apparel, Sunglasses, Accessories, Footwear, Hats, Men's Apparel, Men's Surf & Swimwear, Skate Apparel, T-shirts

ARIZONA TACTICAL, INC. (SG)

3828 N. 28th Ave. (m-b)
Phoenix, AZ 85017
602-266-2600 / Fax: 602-230-0930
Sales: $10 Million-$50 Million
Website: www.azshootersworld.com

PHILIP ROUX (President)

JEFF GREGORY (Gen. Mgr.) & Buys Men's Footwear, Men's Apparel

AZ-TEX HAT CO. (CLO)

15044 N. Cave Creek Rd. (m-b-des)
Phoenix, AZ 85032
602-971-9090 / Fax: 602-971-9199
Sales: $500,001-$1 Million
Website: www.aztexhats.com

HEATHER HARDING (Owner) & Buys Leather Goods, Men's Apparel, Men's Accessories

BIG DEAL CO. (CLO)

3616 W. Thomas Rd., #9
Phoenix, AZ 85019
602-212-9731 / Fax: 602-269-3549

RICH PHILLIPS-Men's Apparel, Men's Surf & Swimwear, Skate Apparel, Skateboards & Accessories, Snowboards, Wakeboards & Accessories, Wetsuits

BILL'S SHOE HUT (FW)

P.O. Box 4807 (m)
7611 W. Thomas Rd., #426
Phoenix, AZ 85033
623-873-2991

CHARLIE KIM (Owner) & Buys Boys' Footwear, Men's Footwear, Men's Accessories, Hosiery

CALIFORNIA DAZE (CLO-2)

302 E. Flower St. (m-b)
Phoenix, AZ 85012
602-279-1747 / Fax: 602-279-4360
Sales: $1 Million-$10 Million
Website: www.californiadaze.com

LOUIS BOCCHINI (Owner) & Buys Men's T-shirts, Casual Slacks, Active Apparel, Hosiery, Headwear, Young Men's & 8 to 14 Boys' Wear, Men's & Boys' Footwear, Store Displays, Fixtures, Supplies

VINCENT BOCCHINI (@ 480-946-1882)-Men's & Boys' Sportswear, Athletic Footwear

CALL JEWELERS, INC. (JWLY-12)

8335 N. 7th St.
Phoenix, AZ 85020
602-996-4064 / Fax: 602-861-4712
Sales: $10 Million-$50 Million
Website: www.calljewelers.com

TERRY CALL (President & C.E.O.) & Buys Jewelry, Watches

DAVID JOHNSON (V.P.-Mdse.) & Buys Jewelry, Watches

CARTER'S (MW)

5045 N. 44th St. (b)
Phoenix, AZ 85018
602-952-8646 / Fax: 602-840-6590

MIKE CARTER (Owner) & Buys Men's Suits, Tailored Jackets, Tailored Slacks, Sportswear, Furnishings, Dress Shirts, Ties, Robes, Underwear, Hosiery, Headwear, Accessories, Belts, Small Leather Goods, Fragrances, Footwear, Store Displays, Fixtures, Supplies

CASTLE SUPERSTORE CORP. (CLO-13 & OL)

7102 W. Roosevelt St.
Phoenix, AZ 85043
623-478-1477 / Fax: 623-478-1489

TAYLOR COLEMAN (Owner)

LAURY BURNS-Swimwear

THE CLOTHERIE LTD. (GM)

2552 E. Camelback Rd. (b-des)
Phoenix, AZ 85016
602-956-8600
Website: www.theclotherie.com

JACKSON LaBAER (President) & Buys Men's Footwear, Fragrances, Leather Goods, Big & Tall Apparel, Casualwear, Denim Apparel, Designer Apparel, Formalwear, Accessories, Outerwear, Sportswear, Suits, Underwear, Young Men's Apparel

GREG EVELOFF (V.P.) & Buys Men's Footwear, Fragrances, Leather Goods, Big & Tall Apparel, Casualwear, Denim Apparel, Designer Apparel, Formalwear, Accessories, Outerwear, Sportswear, Suits, Underwear, Young Men's Apparel

DEL RE WESTERN OUTDOOR SPORT STORES (WW)

5437 S. Central Ave. (p-m)
Phoenix, AZ 85040
602-276-1409 / Fax: 602-276-6397

AL DEL RE (Co-Owner) & Buys Men's Western Wear, Boys' Denims, Related Accessories, Furnishings, Boots, Store Displays, Fixtures, Supplies

JOE DEL RE (Co-Owner) & Buys Men's Western Wear, Boys' Denims, Related Accessories, Furnishings, Boots, Store Displays, Fixtures, Supplies

HERITAGE HAT CO. (MW)

13602 N. Cave Creek Rd. (m)
Phoenix, AZ 85022
602-867-3323
Sales: $500,001-$1 Million

RICHARD GLISSON (Owner) & Buys Men's Headwear, Accessories

JOHN'S UNIFORMS, INC. (CLO)

1749 E. McDowell Rd. (m-b)
Phoenix, AZ 85006
602-254-9217 / Fax: 602-271-0435

JOHN TINCOMBE (Owner) & Buys Men's Police Uniforms, Footwear, Store Displays, Fixtures, Supplies

K-MOMO, INC. (CLO-17)

6070 S. Central Ave. (m-b-des)
Phoenix, AZ 85040
602-484-9722 / Fax: 602-484-9792
Sales: $1 Million-$10 Million
Website: www.k-momo.com

JOHN SO (President & C.E.O.) & Buys Boys' Footwear, Men's Footwear, Leather Goods, Men's Apparel, Men's Big & Tall Apparel, Men's Casualwear, Men's Denim Apparel, Men's Accessories, Men's Outerwear, Men's Sportswear

CHARLES KWEON (Gen. Mgr.) & Buys Boys' Footwear, Men's Footwear, Leather Goods, Men's Apparel, Men's Big & Tall Apparel, Men's Casualwear, Men's Denim Apparel, Men's Accessories, Men's Outerwear, Men's Sportswear

MILLS TOUCHE, INC. (MW-2)

2466 E. Camelback Rd. (b)
Phoenix, AZ 85016
602-955-8160 / Fax: 602-955-4594
Sales: $1 Million-$10 Million

ALBERT TOUCHE (President)

TOM ALLEN (G.M.M.) & Buys Men's Sportswear, Sweaters, Sport Shirts, Outer Jackets, Leather Apparel, Casual Slacks, Active Apparel, Furnishings, Headwear, Accessories, Footwear, Store Displays, Fixtures, Supplies

MODA GEORGIO (MW)

2414 E. Camelback Rd. (b-des)
Phoenix, AZ 85016
480-955-2003 / Fax: 480-391-1905
Sales: $500,001-$1 Million
Website: www.modageorgio.com

NICK ESPOSITO, SR. (President) & Buys Men's Footwear, Fragrances, Leather Goods, Men's Apparel, Men's Casualwear, Men's Formalwear, Men's Accessories, Men's Hosiery, Men's Outerwear, Men's Sportswear, Men's Suits, Men's Underwear

NICK ESPOSITO, JR. (G.M.)

JEFF ESPOSITO (Sales Mgr.)

PANTS SHACK (WW)

3654 W. Van Buren St. (m)
Phoenix, AZ 85009
602-272-6245 / Fax: 602-272-8771

ERNIE SILVA (President & Owner) & Buys Jeans, Western Wear, Accessories, Footwear, Furnishings, Store Displays, Fixtures, Supplies

PARR OF ARIZONA (CLO)

1318 E. Indian School Rd. (bud-p-m-b)
Phoenix, AZ 85014
602-264-3270 / Fax: 302-212-2636
Sales: $500,001-$1 Million
Website: www.parr-intl.com

KIM DYE (Owner) & Buys Men's Apparel

ARIZONA - Phoenix

PEGASUS DIAMONDS (JWLY-4)
(PEGASUS DIAMOND OUTLET)
1801 E. Camelback Rd. (b)
Phoenix, AZ 85016
602-230-2236 / Fax: 602-230-8332
Sales: $1 Million-$10 Million

ANCA PERON (President & G.M.) & Buys Jewelry, Watches

GARY PAPAA (Mgr.) & Buys Jewelry & Watches

PERRYMAN WESTERN WEAR (WW)
4648 N. 16th St. (m-b)
Phoenix, AZ 85016
602-279-5814 / Fax: 602-279-1106
Sales: $500,001-$1 Million

RON PERRYMAN (Owner) & Buys Boys' Footwear, Men's Footwear, Men's Apparel, Men's Casualwear, Men's Denim Apparel, Men's Accessories, Men's Outerwear, Men's Suits

JENNIFER HOLLAND (Asst. Store Mgr.) & Buys Boys' Footwear, Men's Footwear, Men's Apparel, Men 's Casualwear, Men's Denim Apparel, Men's Accessories, Men's Outerwear, Men's Suits

POPULAR OUTDOOR OUTFITTERS (DG-21)
4331 N. 44th Ave.
Phoenix, AZ 85031
(Nation's Best Sports)
623-848-6600 / Fax: 623-848-9640
Sales: $1 Million-$10 Million
Website: www.popularoutdooroutfitters.com
Retail Locations: AZ, NM

KIRK LIPSON (President)

JIM SCOTT (V.P.-Mdse.) & Buys Men's & Boys' Footwear

MITCH MEAD (V.P.-Opers.) & Buys Store Displays, Fixtures, Supplies

MATT LAGERGREN-Men's Sportswear, Outerwear, Sweaters, Outer Jackets, Leather Apparel, Casual Slacks, Apparel, Headwear, Belts, Small Leather Goods, Men's Footwear, Boys' Footwear

CURTIS LIPSON (Real Estate Contact)

RUNNER'S DEN, INC. (CLO)
6505 N. 16th St. (m-b)
Phoenix, AZ 85016
602-277-4333 / Fax: 602-277-4372
Sales: $500,001-$1 Million

ROB WALLACK (Owner) & Buys Men's Footwear, Boys' Footwear, Watches, Men's Accessories, Men's Apparel, Hosiery

RON FRENCH-Men's Footwear, Watches, Men's Accessories, Men's Apparel, Hosiery, Boys' Footwear

STONECREEK - THE GOLF CLUB (SG)
4435 E. Paradise Ln. (m-b)
Phoenix, AZ 85032
602-935-9110 / Fax: 602-953-3297
Sales: $1 Million-$10 Million

JOHN LIENEMANN (Chmn. & C.E.O. & President) & Buys Men's Footwear, Men's Accessories

THAKU'S MENSWEAR, INC. (MW-2)
9201 N. 29th Ave. (b)
Phoenix, AZ 85051
602-943-8800 / Fax: 602-943-8844
Sales: $1 Million-$10 Million
Website: www.bigtallshort.com

GEORGE VASWANI (President) & Buys Men's Apparel, Big & Tall Apparel, Casualwear, Denim Apparel, Designer Apparel, Formalwear, Accessories, Hosiery, Outerwear, Sleepwear, Sportswear, Suits, Swimwear, Underwear, Young Men's Apparel

KASH VASWANI (Exec. V.P.) & Buys Men's Apparel, Big & Tall Apparel, Casualwear, Denim Apparel, Designer Apparel, Formalwear, Accessories, Hosiery, Outerwear, Sleepwear, Sportswear, Suits, Swimwear, Underwear, Young Men's Apparel

NEIL VASWANI (V.P.) & Buys Men's Apparel, Big & Tall Apparel, Casualwear, Denim Apparel, Designer Apparel, Formalwear, Accessories, Hosiery, Outerwear, Sleepwear, Sportswear, Suits, Swimwear, Underwear, Young Men's Apparel

BOB VASWANI (Treas.) & Buys Men's Apparel, Big & Tall Apparel, Casualwear, Denim Apparel, Designer Apparel, Formalwear, Accessories, Hosiery, Outerwear, Sleepwear, Sportswear, Suits, Swimwear, Underwear, Young Men's Apparel

TOTAL FASHIONS (CLO)
3341 N. 19th Ave. (m)
Phoenix, AZ 85015
602-265-7040
Sales: $100,001-$500,000

MI KIM (Owner) & Buys Men's Apparel

TRAILS DEPARTMENT STORES (DEPT-8)
4111 N. 32nd Ave. (m-b)
Phoenix, AZ 85017
602-336-8537 / Fax: 602-336-1002
Sales: $500,001-$1 Million

ARTHUR KRUGLICK (President) & Buys Boys' Apparel, Leather Goods, Men's Apparel, Men's Casualwear, Men's Denim Apparel, Men's Accessories, Men's Hosiery, Men's Outerwear, Men's Sleepwear

UPTOWN FASHION EXCHANGE (MW)
751 W. Camelback Rd. (m-b-des)
Phoenix, AZ 85013
602-265-1992
Sales: $500,001-$1 Million

DAVID HILTON (President) & Buys Men's Footwear, Fragrances, Leather Goods, Men's Big & Tall Apparel, Casualwear, Denim Apparel, Designer Apparel, Formalwear, Accessories, Sportswear, Uniforms, Workclothes, Watches

ACTION SKI RENTAL (SG)
713 E. White Mountain Blvd. (b)
Pinetop, AZ 85935
928-367-3373 / Fax: 928-367-2099
Sales: $500,001-$1 Million

NADIA ROSE (Co-Owner) & Buys Men's Footwear, Men's Sportswear, Men's Swimwear

CHARLES ROSE-Men's Footwear, Men's Sportswear, Men's Swimwear

GARY ROSE (Co-Owner) & Buys Men's Footwear, Men's Sportswear, Men's Swimwear

CROSBY'S MEN'S SHOP (CLO)
P.O. Box 9 (m)
Pinetop, AZ 85935
928-367-2311

BUDDY WISE (Owner) & Buys Men's Suits, Sport Shirts, Outer Jackets, Casual Slacks, Active Apparel, Dress Shirts, Ties, Robes, Underwear, Hosiery, Belts, Small Leathers, Store Displays, Fixtures and Supplies

SAVOINI'S, INC. (WW)
1117 Iron Spring Rd.
Prescott, AZ 86301
928-445-5713 / Fax: 928-445-8168
Sales: $1 Million-$10 Million

ART SAVOINS (Co-Owner) & Buys Store Displays, Fixtures, Supplies

SUE SAVOINS-Men's Western Wear, Big & Tall Men's Western Wear, Young Men's Western Wear, Related Accessories, Furnishings, Boys' Western Wear, Men's & Boys' Boots, Footwear, Hats, Store Displays, Fixtures and Supplies

JIM SAVOINS-Men's Western Wear, Big & Tall Men's Western Wear, Young Men's Western Wear, Related Accessories, Furnishings, Boys' Western Wear, Men's & Boys' Boots, Footwear, Hats, Store Displays, Fixtures and Supplies

SOLTS, INC. (CLO)
120 W. Gurley St. (m-b)
Prescott, AZ 86301
928-445-6000 / Fax: 928-445-6038

RON SOLT (Owner) & Buys Men's Sweaters, Sport Shirts, Outer Jackets, Casual Slacks, Furnishings, Suits, Dress Slacks, Dress Shirts, Ties

STEWARD'S FAMILY SHOE STORE (FW)

1641 Meadowridge Rd. (m-b)
Prescott, AZ 86305
928-445-2421 / Fax: 928-541-0163
Sales: $100,001-$500,000
Website: www.stewards.com

WILLIS STEWARD (President)
JOHN STEWARD (V.P.) & Buys Men's Footwear

ELLSWORTH TEXTILE & APPAREL (SP)

6479 Cooper Hill Dr.
Prescott Valley, AZ 86314
928-772-5010 / Fax: 928-772-5062
Sales: $501,000-$1 Million
Website: www.clothplus.com

BILL ELLSWORTH (Owner & Mgr.) & Buys Skiwear, Outdoor Footwear, Outdoor Apparel, Skate Apparel, Sportswear & Accessories

POLLOCK'S WESTERN OUTFITTERS (WW)

610 5th St. (b-h)
Safford, AZ 85546
928-428-0093 / Fax: 928-348-9102
Sales: $1 Million-$10 Million

NORMA POLLOCK BROWN (President) & Buys Men's Suits, Outer Jackets, Men's & Boys' Western & Casual Wear, Footwear, Fragrances, Leather Apparel, Dress Shirts, Belts, Jewelry, Small Leathers, Boys' Clothing, Store Displays, Fixtures, Supplies
COLLEEN POLLOCK (Secy. & Treas.)
JEAN CARPENTER (Mgr.)

ARTIGIANOS, INC. (CLO)

(DE ANDREA, INC.)
6166 N. Scottsdale Rd. (b)
Scottsdale, AZ 85253
480-585-0161
Sales: $500,001-$1 Million

DIANE ANDREASEN (Owner) & Buys Men's Wear, Suits, Dress Shirts, Outer Jackets, Jewelry, Small Leather Goods, Belts, Store Displays, Fixtures & Supplies

AT EASE OF SCOTTSDALE (CLO-2)

7014 E. Camelback Rd., #1260 (b)
Scottsdale, AZ 85251
480-947-3800 / Fax: 480-947-3852

RON BEALE (Chmn.)
LINDA BEALE (C.E.O.) & Buys Men's Dress Furnishings, Better Men's Sportswear, Footwear, Belts, Hosiery, Store Fixtures, Displays, Supplies

EQUATOR'S MEN'S SHOP (MW)

(THE PHOENICIAN)
6000 E. Camelback Rd.
Scottsdale, AZ 85251
480-941-8200 / Fax: 480-947-4311

SHERYL McCORMICK-Apparel

EXCLUSIVELY BIG & TALL MEN'S STORE (MW)

6107 N. Scottsdale Rd. (b)
Scottsdale, AZ 85250
480-998-9069 / Fax: 480-998-0727
Sales: $1 Million-$10 Million
Website: www.exclusivelybigandtall.com

LYNN LUTZKER (Owner) & Buys Big & Tall Men's Sportswear, Sweaters, Outer Jackets, Leather Apparel, Casual Slacks, Active Apparel, Furnishings, Robes, Ties, Accessories, Footwear, Store Displays, Fixtures, Supplies

FITIGUES, INC. (CLO-24)

9364 E. Raintree Dr. (b)
Scottsdale, AZ 85260
480-391-9800
Sales: $10 Million-$50 Million
Website: www.fitigues.com

STEVE ROSENSTEIN (President)
ANDREA ROSENSTEIN (V.P.)
PATRICE METZLER (Mdsg. Mgr.)
ELLEN FOLEY-Boys' Apparel, Leather Goods, Men's Apparel, Sportswear

PORTERS OF SCOTTSDALE (WW)

3944 N. Brown Ave. (b-h)
Scottsdale, AZ 85252
480-945-0868 / Fax: 480-945-1416
Sales: $1 Million-$10 Million

MARGIE MEADOWS (Owner) & Buys Men's Western Overcoats, Western Wear, Big & Tall Western Wear, Young Men's Western Wear, Leather Apparel, Active Apparel, Ties, Gloves, Belts, Jewelry, Small Leathers, Fragrances, Boys' Accessories, Men's & Boys' Boots

THE TENNIS SHOPPE LTD. (CLO)

7023 5th Ave. (m-b)
Scottsdale, AZ 85251
480-947-9111 / Fax: 480-947-8804
Sales: $100,001-$500,000

KATARINA IVARSSON (Owner) & Buys Men's & Boys' Tennis Apparel, Men's Shoes, Store Displays, Fixtures, Supplies

VAN'S CALIFORNIA DAZE (SP-4 & OL)

7607 E. McDowell Rd.
Scottsdale, AZ 85257
480-946-1882 / Fax: 480-946-2007

VINCE BOCCHINI-Skiwear
ANGIE BOCCHINI-Skiwear

JOE WILCOX WESTERN WEAR (WW)

(WILCOX INDIAN ARTS, INC.)
320 Hwy. 89A North, #F (m-b)
Sedona, AZ 86336
928-282-1348 / Fax: 928-282-4205
Sales: $1 Million-$10 Million

WILMA WILCOXSON (Co-Owner) (@ 928-282-1701) & Buys Men's & Boys' Western Wear, Related Accessories, Furnishings, Men's & Boys' Boots, Store Displays, Fixtures, Supplies
SHIRLEY TOLLEY (Co-Owner) & Buys Men's & Boys' Western Wear, Related Accessories, Furnishings, Men's & Boys' Boots, Store Displays, Fixtures, Supplies

RICHARD DAVID FOR MEN (MW-2 & OL & MO)

320 N. Hwy. 89A, #12 (b)
Sedona, AZ 86336
928-282-6938
Sales: $500,001-$1 Million
Website: www.richarddavid.com

STACIE BYRNES (Partner) & Buys Fragrances, Leather Goods, Men's Apparel, Men's Big & Tall Apparel, Men's Casualwear, Men's Denim Apparel, Men's Accessories, Men's Hosiery, Men's Outerwear, Men's Sleepwear, Men's Sportswear, Men's Swimwear, Men's Underwear
JEFF BYRNES (Partner) & Buys Fragrances, Leather Goods, Men's Apparel, Men's Big & Tall Apparel, Men's Casualwear, Men's Denim Apparel, Men's Accessories, Men's Hosiery, Men's Outerwear, Men's Sleepwear, Men's Sportswear, Men's Swimwear, Men's Underwear

ABBOTT'S MEN'S SHOP (MW)

10726 W. Bell Rd. (p)
Sun City, AZ 85351
623-972-1441 / Fax: 623-972-6594
Sales: $500,001-$1 Million

GENE TAPFER (Owner) & Buys Men's Suits, Tailored Slacks, Tailored Jackets, Raincoats, Big & Tall Men's Wear, Sportswear, Furnishings, Accessories, Slippers, Store Displays, Fixtures, Supplies

ALL ABOUT TENNIS (SG)

3114 S. McClintock Dr., #4 (m-b)
Tempe, AZ 85282
480-820-7805 / Fax: 480-820-8814
Sales: $500,001-$1 Million
Website: www.allabouttennis.com

PAM PONWITH (Owner) & Buys Boys' Apparel, Boys' Footwear, Men's Apparel, Men's Accessories, Men's Sportswear
JESSE PONWITH (Store Mgr.)

ARIZONA SHORTS & SPORTS, INC. (SP)

425 S. Mill Ave., #101
Tempe, AZ 85281
480-966-9199 / Fax: 480-921-7363

GIL SCHMITT (Mgr.) & Buys Women's Activewear, Sunglasses, Footwear

ARIZONA - Tempe

AS IS (CLO-2)
1290 N. Scottsdale Rd. (m-b)
Tempe, AZ 85281
480-829-7171 / Fax: 480-967-3995
Sales: $1 Million-$10 Million
BRADLEY GREENHALPH (Co-Owner) & Buys Boys' Apparel, Boys' Footwear, Leather Goods, Men's Apparel, Men's Casualwear, Men's Denim Apparel, Men's Accessories, Men's Outerwear, Men's Sportswear, Men's Suits
MATHEW LOPATA (Co-Owner) & Buys Boys' Apparel, Boys' Footwear, Leather Goods, Men's Apparel, Men's Casualwear, Men's Denim Apparel, Men's Accessories, Men's Outerwear, Men's Sportswear, Men's Suits
JERRY WILKOFF-Boys' Apparel, Boys' Footwear, Leather Goods, Men's Apparel, Men's Casualwear, Men's Denim Apparel, Men's Accessories, Men's Outerwear, Men's Sportswear, Men's Suits

ASU BOOK STORE (SP-4)
Arizona State University
Tempe, AZ 85287
480-965-7928 / Fax: 480-965-9108
Website: www.bookstore.asu.edu
VAL ROSS (Dir.)
KELLY DIETRICH-Fleece, Jackets, Hosiery, Apparel, Licensed Apparel
LELA CAPE-Licensed Apparel

DILLARD'S DEPARTMENT STORES, INC. - PHOENIX DIV. (DEPT-48 & MO & OL)
1616 S. Priest Dr. (m-b)
Tempe, AZ 85281
480-736-2000 / Fax: 480-736-2201
Sales: $100 Million-$500 Million
Website: www.dillards.com
Retail Locations: AR, AZ, FL, MO, TX, GA, KS, KY, NC, VA
G. KENT BURNETT (Chmn.)
DAN JENSEN (V.P. & District Mgr.)
TOM SULLIVAN (V.P. & G.M.M.-Men's)
GEORGE PHILLIPS (D.M.M.-Men's Clothing, Furnishings & Sportswear)
MICHELLE KING-Men's Dress Shirts, Neckwear, Underwear, Hosiery
JAMIE SCHERER-Men's Gloves, Belts, Jewelry, Small Leather Goods, Accessories, Robes, Pajamas
SAM BARG-Men's Active Sportswear, Outerwear, Leather Apparel, Swimwear, Licensed Apparel, Sweaters, Casualwear
RUSTY HAYES-Men's Sport Shirts, Knit Shirts, Shorts, Sweaters, Casual Slacks, Men's Contemporary Sportswear, Perry Ellis, Claiborne, Golf Apparel
JULIE BUCKLEY-Polo Sportswear, Nautica, Daniel Cremieux
NANCY GERNAND-Traditional Sportswear, Tommy Hilfiger, Mossimo, Big & Tall Men's Wear, Seasonal Apparel, Coordinates
ROSE BEER-Men's Fragrances

JIM NORTHUP (D.M.M.-Shoes)
BEN CALDERON-Men's Dress & Moderate Casual Shoes
JESSICA BASSETT-Men's & Boys' Athletic Shoes

JIM CHRISTIE (D.M.M.-Children's)
PENNIE McGOWAN-Men's Denim, Young Men's Outerwear
HUU DONG-Boys' Wear 4 to 7 & Toddlers
LOUANNE ROHE-Size 8 to 20 Boys' Wear, Better Boys' Wear

DON SAINT (Dir.-Visual) & Buys Store Displays, Fixtures, Store Supplies
JOE STORY (Real Estate Contact) (@ 501-376-5200)
NOTE:-Men's Suits & Tailored Wear Buying Performed @ DILLARD'S, Little Rock, Ar. - See Listing.

FORMAL FASHIONS, INC. (MO)
1500 W. Drake (h)
Tempe, AZ 85283
480-897-0766 / Fax: 480-491-2228
KEITH HOFFMAN (President)
SHERYL CARITY-Men's Formal Wear, Tailored Jackets, Tailored Slacks, Formal Dress Shirts, Ties, Jewelry, Store Displays, Fixtures, Supplies

SHOE MILL (FW)
398 S. Mill Ave., #100 (m-b)
Tempe, AZ 85281
480-966-3139 / Fax: 480-350-9741
Sales: $1 Million-$10 Million
BEVERLY NELSON (Partner) & Buys Boys' Footwear, Men's Footwear, Leather Goods, Bags, Wallets, Accessories, Shoe Care
MELINDA HENDERSON (Mgr.) & Buys Boys' Footwear, Men's Footwear, Leather Goods

ALAN'S SHOES, INC. (FW-2 & OL)
6030 N. Oracle Rd. (m-b)
Tucson, AZ 85704
520-297-1319 / Fax: 520-544-7824
Sales: $1 Million-$10 Million
Website: www.walkingco.com
STEVEN ADLER (President)
JASON GAVE (Mgr.-Sales)
BARBARA CARO-Men's Footwear
DARA OLSON-Leather Goods, Men's Accessories, Hosiery

BUFFALO EXCHANGE LTD., INC. (CLO-30)
P.O. Box 40488
209 E. Helen St.
Tucson, AZ 85705
520-622-2711 / Fax: 520-622-7015
Sales: $10 Million-$50 Million
Website: www.buffaloexchange.com
KERSTIN BLOCK (President)
DANA WHITNEY (Real Estate Contact)
KRISTIN HODGSON-Men's Footwear, Men's Apparel, Men's Casualwear, Men's Denim Apparel, Men's Accessories, Men's Hosiery, Men's Outerwear, Men's Sportswear, Men's Swimwear

CAMPUS ATHLETIC (CLO)
936 E. University Blvd. (m-b)
Tucson, AZ 85719
520-628-7622
Sales: $100,001-$500,000
Website: www.campusathletic.com
DAVID BRESSLER (Owner) & Buys Boys' Apparel, Men's Apparel, Men's Casualwear, Men's Denim Apparel, Men's Sportswear

COFFEE ETC., INC. (CLO)
2830 N. Campbell Ave.
Tucson, AZ 85719
520-881-8070 / Fax: 520-881-0029
STEVEN MEINHAUSEN (Owner)
MIKE HAYDEN (Dir.-Purch.) & Buys Men's Sportswear, Sweaters, Active Apparel, T-shirts, Shorts, Store Displays, Fixtures, Supplies

ARIZONA - Tucson

CORRAL WEST RANCHWEAR (WW-96)
4525 E. Broadway (m-b)
Tucson, AZ 85711
520-322-6001 / Fax: 520-322-9540
Sales: $1 Million-$10 Million
Website: www.corralwest.com
Retail Locations: Mid-West States
LESLIE A. BALL (C.E.O.)
DARWIN STOVER (Real Estate Contact)
RON THRING (@ 307-632-0951)-Men's Apparel
CATHY HABERCORN (@ 307-632-0951)-Boys' Wear

FIRENZE BOUTIQUE (CLO)
2951 N. Swan Rd. (b-des)
Tucson, AZ 85718
520-299-2992 / Fax: 520-299-1197
Sales: $500,001-$1 Million
CEROOS PARSA (Owner) & Buys Boys' Apparel, Leather Goods, Men's Apparel, Men's Big & Tall Apparel, Men's Casualwear, Men's Denim Apparel, Men's Hosiery

L.J.M., INC. (CLO-3)
(THE PANT WAREHOUSE)
6383 E. 22nd St. (p-m-b)
Tucson, AZ 85710
/ Fax: 520-747-8761
JEFF BERNSTEIN (Owner) & Buys Men's Sportswear, Sweaters, Sport Shirts, Outer Jackets, Leather Apparel, Casual Slacks, Active Apparel, Casual Sportswear, Furnishings, Boys' Casual Sportswear, Footwear, Store Displays, Fixtures, Supplies

MAYA PALACE (CLO-2)
6332 E. Broadway Blvd. (m)
Tucson, AZ 85710
520-748-0817 / Fax: 520-748-0745
Sales: $1 Million-$10 Million
JOHN KOPPLIN (Co-Owner) & Buys Men's Apparel
SUSANA KOPPLIN (Co-Owner) & Buys Men's Apparel

RUNNING SHOP (SP)
3055 N. Campbell Ave., #153
Tucson, AZ 85719
520-325-5097 / Fax: 520-325-5056
SHARON BART (Owner) & Buys Women's Activewear, Athletic Footwear

TUCKER ENTERPRISES (SP)
930 N. Stone Ave.
Tucson, AZ 85705
520-325-7782 / Fax: 520-670-1149
TOM TUCKER (Owner) & Buys Activewear, T-shirts, Fleecewear

UNIVERSITY OF ARIZONA BOOKSTORE (SP-5 & OL)
University of Arizona
P.O. Box 210019
Tucson, AZ 85721
520-621-2426 / Fax: 520-621-8098
Sales: $1 Million-$10 Million
Website: www.uofabookstores.com
FRANK FARIAS (Dir.-Store) (@ 520-621-8857)
DEBBY SHIVELY (Assoc. Dir.-Non-Book Mdse.) (@ 520-621-7151) & Buys Fleece, Activewear, Athletic Footwear, Licensed Apparel
YADHIRA AVECEDO-Golf Apparel

QUINN & LOE CLOTHIERS (MW)
13576 Camino Del Sol, #18 (m-b)
West Sun City, AZ 85375
623-584-0949 / Fax: 623-546-1472
Sales: $1 Million-$10 Million
JAY QUINN (Co-Owner) & Buys Men's Suits, Tailored Jackets, Tailored Slacks, Sweaters, Sport Shirts, Casual Slacks, Active Apparel, Dress Shirts, Ties, Robes, Underwear, Hosiery, Headwear, Accessories, Store Displays, Fixtures, Supplies
BARBARA QUINN (Co-Owner) & Buys Men's Suits, Tailored Jackets, Tailored Slacks, Sweaters, Sport Shirts, Casual Slacks, Active Apparel, Dress Shirts, Ties, Robes, Underwear, Hosiery, Headwear, Accessories, Store Displays, Fixtures, Supplies

JOHNSON DRY GOODS CO. (DG)
P.O. Box 931 (p)
72 N. Tegner St.
Wickenberg, AZ 85358
520-684-2212
Sales: $500,001-$1 Million
MRS. L. L. CHRISTIAN (Co-Owner) & Buys Men's Sweaters, Sport Shirts, Outer Jackets, Leather Apparel, Casual Slacks, Active Apparel, Jeans, Dress Shirts, Ties, Underwear, Hosiery, Gloves, Headwear, Accessories, Belts, Jewelry, Small Leather Goods, Boys' Clothing, Men's & Boys' Boots, Store Disp
MR. L. CHRISTIAN (Co-Owner) & Buys Men's Sportswear, Sweaters, Sport Shirts, Outer Jackets, Leather Apparel, Casual Slacks, Active Apparel, Jeans, Furnishings, Dress Shirts, Ties, Underwear, Hosiery, Gloves, Headwear, Accessories, Belts, Jewelry, Small Leather Goods, Boys' Clothing, Men's

APPAREL BY JOHNNY (MW)
1338 S. 4th Ave. (p-m)
Yuma, AZ 85364
928-783-4774 / Fax: 928-376-7438
Sales: $500,001-$1 Million
JOHNY RODRIGUEZ (Owner) & Buys Formal Wear, Sport Shirts, Casual Slacks, Dress Shirts, Ties, Belts, Jewelry, Small Leathers, Hosiery, Gloves, Store Displays, Fixtures & Supplies

YUMA OUTLET BLUES (MW)
1404 S. 4th Ave.
Yuma, AZ 85364
928-783-8583 / Fax: 928-783-8583
ROBERTO RAMIREZ (Owner) & Buys Men's Sportswear, Furnishings, Underwear, Hosiery, Men's Westernwear & Boots, Store Displays, Fixtures, Supplies

ARKANSAS - Arkadelphia

SOUTHWEST SPORTING GOODS CO., INC. (SG)
115 S. 6th St. (b)
P.O. Box 471
Arkadelphia, AR 71923
870-246-2311 / Fax: 870-246-3932
REGGIE SPEIGHTS (President) & Buys Men's Footwear, Men's Apparel, Men's Accessories, Men's Hosiery, Men's Sportswear, Men's Swimwear

CHARLIE'S MENSWEAR (MW)
250 E. Main St. (m-b)
Batesville, AR 72501
870-698-1505 / Fax: 870-698-2260
Sales: $1 Million-$10 Million
Website: www.charliesmenswear.com
CHARLES INSELL (Co-Owner) & Buys Men's Sportswear, Sweaters, Sport Shirts, Outer Jackets, Leather Apparel, Casual Slacks, Active Apparel, Furnishings, Accessories, Boys' Wear, Store Displays, Fixtures, Supplies
DAVY INSELL (Co-Owner) & Buys Men's Clothing,Sportswear, Sweaters, Sport Shirts, Outer Jackets, Leather Apparel, Casual Slacks, Active Apparel, Furnishings, Accessories, Boys' Wear, Store Displays, Fixtures, Supplies

HEUER'S FAMILY SHOES (FW)
226 E. Main St. (m-b)
Batesville, AR 72501
870-793-7311
Sales: $500,001-$1 Million
BARBARA FITZPATRICK (President & G.M.M.) & Buys Boys' Footwear, Men's Footwear, Hosiery

VAN ATKINS STORE (DEPT-4)
Town Plaza Shopping Center (p)
1295 E. Main St.
Batesville, AR 72501
870-793-7673 / Fax: 870-793-4349
Sales: $1 Million-$10 Million
ROBERT VAN HOOK (President)
BROOK MAYS (G.M.M.) & Buys Men's Sportswear, Sweaters, Sport Shirts, Outer Jackets, Leather Apparel, Casual Slacks, Active Apparel, Furnishings, Headwear, Accessories, Footwear, Store Displays, Fixtures, Supplies

GINGLES DEPARTMENT STORE (DEPT)
145 W. South St. (m-b)
Benton, AR 72015
501-778-2516 / Fax: 501-778-4605
Sales: $1 Million-$10 Million
Website: www.gingles.com
JOHN YOUNG (President & G.M.M.) & Buys Store Displays, Fixtures, Supplies
FRANK BAPTIST-Men's Sweaters, Sport Shirts, Outer Jackets, Leather Apparel, Casual Slacks, Active Apparel, Furnishings, Headwear, Accessories, Boys' Wear

RHEA'S MEN'S STORE (MW)
128 N. Market St. (m-b)
Benton, AR 72015
501-778-3307 / Fax: 501-778-5271
Sales: $100,001-$500,000
MACK McMANUS (G.M.M.) & Buys Men's Sweaters, Sport Shirts, Outer Jackets, Leather Apparel, Casual Slacks, Active Apparel, Furnishings, Headwear, Accessories, Footwear, Young Men's & Boys' Wear, Store Displays, Fixtures, and Supplies

DAY'S MEN'S STORE, INC. (MW)
P.O. Box 65 (m-b)
322 W. Main St.
Blytheville, AR 72315
870-762-2721 / Fax: 870-762-2722
Sales: $1 Million-$10 Million
NEIL BURGE (President) & Buys Men's Sportswear, Leather Apparel, Furnishings, Accessories, Headwear, Young Men's Wear, Urban Contemporary, Store Displays, Fixtures, Supplies
LEON JONES-Men's Sportswear, Leather Apparel, Furnishings, Accessories, Headwear, Young Men's Wear, Urban Contemporary, Men's Footwear, Store Displays, Fixtures, Supplies

HAWKS, INC. (SG)
P.O. Box 207 (p)
322 E. Main St.
Blytheville, AR 72315
870-763-8288 / Fax: 870-763-0473
Sales: $100,001-$500,000
Website: www.hawksinc.com
BRAD HAWKS (President) & Buys Men's & Boys' Trousers, Hunting Apparel, Shorts, Leather Apparel, Footwear, Store Displays, Fixtures, Supplies

BRUCE'S, INC. (MW)
114 Adams St. SW (m-b)
Camden, AR 71701
870-836-3590 / Fax: 870-836-3448
Sales: $500,000-$1 Million
BRUCE MURRY (Owner) & Buys Men's Footwear, Store Displays, Fixtures, Supplies
JERRY ROWLAND (Mgr.) & Buys Men's Wear, Big & Tall Men's, Swimwear, Outerwear, Footwear, Headwear, Knitwear, Underwear, Accessories, Hosiery, Furnishings, Formalwear

THE CREDIT SHOP (CLO)
145 Adams St. (p)
Camden, AR 71701
870-836-3630
Sales: $100,001-$500,000
JAMES BRANYAN (Owner) & Buys Men's Wear, Accessories, Furnishings, Young Men's Wear, Footwear, Store Displays, Fixtures, Supplies

LOLLIPOP SHOP, INC. (KS-2)
1137 W. Washington St., #132 (p-m-b)
Camden, AR 71701
870-836-2611 / Fax: 870-836-2610
Sales: $500,001-$1 Million
PEGGY FENWICK (President) & Buys Boys' Sportswear, Clothing Accessories, Furnishings to Size 20, Store Displays, Fixtures, Supplies

RAINBOW CONNECTION (KS)
106 W. Washington St. (m-b)
Camden, AR 71701
870-836-5287
Sales: $100,001-$500,000
DEBRA LANEY (Owner) & Buys Infant to 20 Boys' Wear, Urban Contemporary, Store Displays, Fixtures, Supplies

MORGAN'S FASHIONS (CLO-4)
(YOUNG WORLD)
116 E. Main St. (p-m-b)
Clarksville, AR 72830
479-754-8130 / Fax: 479-754-4417
Sales: $1 Million-$10 Million
Website: www.morganfashions.com
DAVID MORGAN (Owner) & Buys Men's Sweaters, Sport Shirts, Outer Jackets, Leather Apparel, Casual Slacks, Active Apparel, Furnishings, Footwear, Accessories, Young Men's Wear, Boys' Wear, Store Displays, Fixtures, Supplies

LEFLER'S FASHIONS (CLO-4)
105 Griggs St. (m-b)
P.O. Box 370
Clinton, AR 72031
501-329-3424 / Fax: 501-336-9801
Sales: $1 Million-$10 Million
MARTIN LEFLER (Owner) & Buys Men's Footwear, Leather Goods, Men's Apparel, Men's Casualwear, Men's Denim Apparel, Men's Accessories, Men's Outerwear, Men's Sportswear, Men's Suits, Men's Swimwear

ED CAMP'S MEN'S STORE (MW)
1116 Oak St. (b)
Conway, AR 72032
501-329-5816 / Fax: 501-329-8667
Sales: $1 Million-$10 Million
LORI RYAN (Owner) & Buys Men's Wear, Sportswear, Footwear, Accessories, Furnishings, Store Displays

ARKANSAS - Conway

OK CORRAL WESTERN STORES, llc (WW-2)
1627 E. Oak St (p-b)
Conway, AR 73032
501-329-6860 / Fax: 501-329-5731
NICK KEATHLEY-Men's Outer Jackets, Western Wear, Leather Apparel, Dress Shirts, Headwear, Belts, Jewelry, Young Men's & Boys' Western Wear, Boys' Accessories, Store Displays, Fixtures, Supplies
DEBIE KEATHLEY-Men's Outer Jackets, Western Wear, Leather Apparel, Dress Shirts, Headwear, Belts, Jewelry, Young Men's & Boys' Western Wear, Boys' Accessories, Store Displays, Fixtures, Supplies

WILKINSON'S MALL (DEPT)
P.O. Box 217 (p)
Harrison & Mill
Conway, AR 72032
501-329-6819 / Fax: 501-329-7102
Website: www.wilkmall.com
JENNY WOODARD (V.P.) & Buys Men's T-shirts, Shorts, Accessories, Furnishings, Store Displays, Fixtures, Supplies
MIKE WILKINSON-Footwear

REESE GENERAL MERCANTILE (DEPT)
(EMPORIUM)
P.O. Box 7 (m)
212 Main St.
Dierks, AR 71833
870-286-2554 / Fax: 870-286-2335
Sales: $500,001-$1 Million
ROSE REESE (Co-Owner) & Buys Men's Sweaters, Sport Shirts, Casual Slacks, Active Apparel, Furnishings, Belts, Small Leather Goods, Fragrances, Boys' Clothing, Sportswear, Store Displays, Fixtures, Supplies
ROSE DEERE (Co-Owner) & Buys Men's Sweaters, Sport Shirts, Casual Slacks, Active Apparel, Furnishings, Belts, Small Leather Goods, Fragrances, Boys' Clothing, Sportswear, Store Displays, Fixtures, Supplies

WOLFF BROTHERS DEPARTMENT STORE (DEPT)
168 S. Main St. (p)
Dumas, AR 71639
870-382-6600
H. WOLFF (Owner) & Buys Men's & Boys' Wear, Sportswear, Accessories, Furnishings, Footwear, Store Displays, Fixtures, Supplies

EMERALD FOREST TRAVEL & ADVENTURE CLOTHING (CLO-2)
31 Spring St. (p-m-b)
Eureka Springs, AR 72632
479-253-6959
Website: www.emeraldforestclothing.com
DARLENE SCHRUM (Owner) & Buys Men's Raincoats, Sweaters, Sport Shirts, Outer Jackets, Casual Slacks, Active Apparel, Store Displays, Fixtures, Supplies

UNIVERSITY OF ARKANSAS BOOKSTORE (SP)
(THE RAZORBACK SHOP)
Arkansas Union Bldg., #202E
Fayetteville, AR 72701
479-575-2617 / Fax: 479-575-5761
Website: www.uark.edu/bookstore
ALI SADEGHI (G.M.M.) (@ 479-575-2979)
LANCE CHERAMIE (G.M.M.) (@ 479-575-5154) & Buys Men's Fleecewear, Jackets, Licensed Apparel, Young Men's Wear, Boys' Wear

WALKER BROTHERS DRY GOODS (MW)
(COLE & CO.)
577 E. Millsap Rd., #3
Fayetteville, AR 72703
479-521-0077 / Fax: 479-521-8963
JOHN W. COLE (Owner) & Buys Men's Furnishings, Accessories, Footwear

WOODEN NICKEL SPORTSWEAR (SP & MO)
845 N. Gregg St.
Fayetteville, AR 72701
479-443-3023 / Fax: 479-443-9207
Sales: $501,000-$1 Million
KAREN WIST-Apparel, Skiwear, Custom Apparel

THE FASHION CENTER (CLO-2)
(WORDS)
P.O. Box 653 (p)
Fordyce, AR 71742
870-352-3733
Sales: $500,000-$1 Million
BETTY WORD (Owner) & Buys Men's Sportswear, Accessories, Store Displays, Fixtures, Supplies
PHIL WORD-Men's Sportswear, Accessories, Store Displays, Fixtures, Supplies

HICKEY'S, INC. (DEPT)
P.O. Box 728 (p)
209 Main St.
Fordyce, AR 71742
870-352-2945 / Fax: 870-352-5748
Sales: $500,001-$1 Million
MR. LYNN HORTON (Partner) & Buys Men's Sportswear, Sweaters, Tailored Slacks, Sport Shirts, Casual Slacks, Active Apparel, Dress Shirts, Raincoats, Ties, Robes, Underwear, Hosiery, Gloves, Belts, Sportswear, Store Displays, Fixtures, Supplies

EDWIN HOUSTON, INC. (SP)
P.O. Box 1014 (m-b)
Forrest City, AR 72336
870-633-5100 / Fax: 870-633-5112
Sales: $500,001-$1 Million
SCOTT CARROLL (Owner) & Buys Store Displays, Fixtures, Supplies
LARRY HUETT (G.M.M.) & Buys Men's & Boys' Clothing, Sportswear, Furnishings, Accessories, Young Men's Wear

TAYLOR CASBEER, INC. (CLO)
401 Cleveland St. (b)
Forrest City, AR 72335
870-633-4011 / Fax: 870-633-3937
Sales: $500,001-$1 Million
JOHN CASBEER (Owner & G.M.M.) & Buys Men's Sweaters, Sport Shirts, Outer Jackets, Leather Apparel, Casual Slacks, Active Apparel, Furnishings, Footwear, Headwear, Accessories, Young Men's Wear, Store Displays, Fixtures, Supplies

D. S. CLOTHIERS (MW)
709 Garrison Ave. (b)
Fort Smith, AR 72901
479-783-2400
Sales: $100,001-$500,000
DANIEL SMITH-Men's Wear, Suits, Sportswear, Tuxedos, Formalwear, Accessories, Furnishings, Store Displays, Fixtures, Supplies

RAINWATER'S (CLO-2)
9700 Rogers Ave.
Fort Smith, AR 72903
479-452-5836 / Fax: 479-484-1937
Sales: $1 Million-$10 Million
DOYLE RAINWATER (Owner) & Buys Footwear
GAIL DEAN RAINWATER-Boys' Clothing, Sportswear, Dress Shirts, Hosiery, Big & Tall Men's Wear, Urban Contemporary, Store Displays, Fixtures, Supplies
PAUL RAINWATER-Boys' Clothing, Sportswear, Dress Shirts, Hosiery, Big & Tall Men's Wear, Urban Contemporary, Formalwear

RIK'S SHOES, INC. (FW-2)
704 Garrison Ave. (m-b)
Fort Smith, AR 72901
479-782-3474 / Fax: 479-782-9323
Sales: $500,001-$1 Million
DAVID BUSHKUHL (President & Mgr.) & Buys Men's Footwear
SUSAN BUSHKUHL-Leather Goods, Men's Accessories

ARKANSAS - Fort Smith

TIP TOP WESTERN WEAR, INC. (WW)

512 Garrison Ave.
Fort Smith, AR 72901
479-783-0840 / Fax: 479-783-0575

DAN WALD (Partner) & Buys Men's, Young Men's & Boys' Western Wear & Sportswear, Jeans, Accessories, Store Displays, Fixtures, Supplies

SAM WALD (Partner) & Buys Footwear, Furnishing

HARRISON'S DEPARTMENT STORE (DEPT)

103 E. Adams St. (m-b)
Hamburg, AR 71646
870-853-5294 / Fax: 870-853-8531
Sales: $1 Million-$10 Million

DEBBIE LADD-Men's Footwear, Boys' Footwear

NELL MILLER FASHIONS (SP)

603 Oakland Ave., #607 (b)
Helena, AR 72342
870-338-8122 / Fax: 870-338-6086
Sales: $500,001-$1 Million

NELL MILLER (Owner) & Buys Men Accessories, Stores Displays, Fixtures, Supplies

KT'S (CLO)

225 Malvern Ave. (m-b-des)
Hot Springs National Park, AR 71901
501-321-9602 / Fax: 501-321-1555
Sales: $500,001-$1 Million

KATI FISH (President) & Buys Men's Apparel, Men's Formalwear

NANCY FISH (V.P.) & Buys Men's Apparel, Men's Formalwear

OAKLAWN SPORTSWEAR, INC. (CLO)

120 Central Ave. (m)
Hot Springs National Park, AR 71901
501-624-2181
Sales: $100,001-$500,000

STUART PENNINGTON (President) & Buys Men's Sportswear, Sweaters, Outer Jackets, Leather Apparel, Casual Slacks, Furnishings, Headwear, Accessories, Store Displays, Fixtures, Supplies

ARKY HOUSE, INC. (MW)

218 E. Grand Ave. (m)
Hot Springs Nationall, AR 71901
501-624-0605 / Fax: 501-624-0835
Sales: $1 Million-$10 Million

EARL WELLS (President & Owner) & Buys Men's Wear, Men's Accessories, Furnishings, Footwear, Stores Displays

MIKE WELLS-Men's Sportswear, Footwear

ANDERSON WESTERN STORE (WW)

241 S. Main St. (m)
Jonesboro, AR 72401
870-932-7600 / Fax: 870-931-6700

WAYNE ANDERSON-Men's Western Wear, Women's Jeans

ARKANSAS SPORTS FAN (GS)

2810 E. Highland Dr., #O
Jonesboro, AR 72401
870-931-6949
Sales: $100,001-$500,000
Website: www.arksportsfan.com

LINDA ROBINSON (Owner) & Buys Women's & Children's Licensed Apparel

BROADWAY MEN'S STORE (CLO)

(THE BROADWAY MENS STORE)
Caraway Plaza (m)
2235 S. Caraway Rd.
Jonesboro, AR 72401
870-932-7302 / Fax: 870-935-7302
Sales: $100,001-$500,000

DALE McKINNEY (Owner) & Buys Men's Sportswear, Furnishings, Accessories Men's Footwear, Boys' Wear, Urban Contemporary, Store Displays, Fixtures, Supplies

GRISHAM'S CLOTHING (CLO)

2209 E. Highland Dr. (b-des)
Jonesboro, AR 72401
870-932-4562 / Fax: 870-935-0631
Sales: $1 Million-$10 Million

LARRY GRISHAM (President)

FRANK HURST (G.M.M.) & Buys Men's Sportswear, Furnishings, Accessories, Footwear, Young Wear, Leather Apparel, Stores Displays

JEAN JOINT (CLO)

2612 E. Nettelton Ave. (p-m)
Jonesboro, AR 72401
870-935-1870 / Fax: 870-910-3833

DICK DEMAINE (Owner) & Buys Men's Sportswear, Shorts, Belts, Hosiery, Leather Apparel, Footwear, Store Displays, Fixtures, Supplies

GAILON DEMAINE-Women's Sportswear, Shorts, Belts, Hoisery, Leather Apparel, Footwear, Accessories

ISTHMUS (MW)

55 S. Lake Havasue, #L
Lake Havasu, AR 86403
928-855-8800

BUCK REYNOLDS-Men's Apparel, Accessories, Furnishings

BAUMAN'S, INC. (MW)

8201 Cantrell Rd., #150 (m)
Little Rock, AR 72227
501-227-8797 / Fax: 501-227-0326
Sales: $1 Million-$10 Million
Website: www.baumans.com

WAYNE RATCLIFF (Owner) & Buys Men's & Boys' Sportswear, Dress Shirts, Underwear, Hosiery, Accessories, Footwear, Store Displays, Fixtures, Supplies

BENNETT'S MILITARY SUPPLIES (AN)

302 Main St. (bud)
Little Rock, AR 72201
501-372-2944 / Fax: 501-372-6399
Website: www.bennettsmilitary.com

JOE KAUFMAN (Owner) & Buys Men's Sportswear, Underwear, Hosiery, Gloves, Headwear, Belts, Footwear, Boys' Sportswear, Store Displays, Fixtures, Supplies

CRK ENTERPRISE, INC. (CLO-2)

(FASHION USA)
(MR COOL)
301 Main St. (bud-p-m)
Little Rock, AR 72201
501-378-0107 / Fax: 775-305-6601
Sales: $500,001-$1 Million

TOM CHOI (President) & Buys Boys' Apparel, Boys' Footwear, Men's Apparel, Men's Big & Tall, Men's Casualwear, Men's Denim Apparel, Men's Formalwear, Men's Accessories, Men's Hosiery, Men's Outerwear, Men's Sportswear, Men's Suits

SUSIE CHOI (V.P.) & Buys Boys' Apparel, Boys' Footwear, Men's Apparel, Men's Big & Tall, Men's Casualwear, Men's Denim Apparel, Men's Formalwear, Men's Accessories, Men's Hosiery, Men's Outerwear, Men's Sportswear, Men's Suits

ARKANSAS - Little Rock

DILLARD'S DEPARTMENT STORES, INC. - LITTLE ROCK DIV. (DEPT-83 & MO & OL)

1600 Cantrell Rd. (m-b)
Little Rock, AR 72201
501-376-5200 / Fax: 501-376-5182
Sales: Over $1 Billion
Website: www.dillards.com
Retail Locations: MT, ID, UT, CO, OK, NE, IA, IL, IN, KS, TX, CA, NV, AZ, NM, AR, WY, MO, FL, AL, MS, LA, TN, SC, NC, VA, OH, KY

MIKE DILLARD (Chmn. & G.M.M.)
JAMES FREEMAN (Sr. V.P. & C.F.O.)
RICH WILLEY (V.P.-Construction; Mgr.-Store Fixtures)
TIM HOLMES (Visual Presentation Mgr.) & Buys Store Displays, Fixtures and Supplies
WEST CHERRY (Real Estate Contact) (@ 501-376-5200)

ROGER WILLIAMS (D.M.M.) & Buys Men's Sportswear & Accessories
CHRIS PLANK (D.M.M.) & Buys Footwear, Men's Dress Shoes, Men's Moderate Casual Footwear, Men's Contemporary Footwear, Men's Better Casual Footwear
MISSY KING-Men's Dress Shirts, Men's R&Y Dress Shirts
DOUG SALMI-Men's Suits, Tailored Slacks, Tailored Jackets, Tailored Sportswear, Sport Coats
MIKE FITNEY-Men's Large Sizes, Tommy Hilfiger, Polo, Nautica, Golf Apparel
LLOYD KASSLER-Active Sportswear, Swimwear, Outdoor Wear, Outerwear, Leather Apparel
DAVID ZACHARY-Men's Perry Ellis, Claiborne for Men, Advanced Sportswear, Tommy Hilfirger, Traditional Collections, Golf Big & Tall
CLINT CARMEAUX-Polo, Nautica
LINDA WRIGHT (@ 817-831-5171)-Polo, Daniel Cremieux, Nautica
TIM MARTIN-DKNY Jeans
LYNN BATTON-Knit Shirts, Sport Shirts, Men's Shorts, Casual Slacks, Sweaters
ROBERT BAUHOFFER (@ 817-831-5487)-Ties
MELINDA BARRETT-Young Men's Denim Bottoms & Tops
CINDY HINRICHS (D.M.M.) (@ 817-505-4842) & Buys Cosmetics, Men's Fragrances
VAL OFFILL (@ 817-505-4817)-Men's Fragrances
ROSE MARIE BAER (@ 817-505-4816)-Men's Fragrances
MICHELLE KING-Dress Shirts
STEVE DILLARD (D.M.M-Children)
CHERYL CALVA-Infants, Layette, Newborn, Infants and Toddlers Polo, Infant's and Toddlers Tommy
JOYCE DAILY-Polo, Tommy 8-20, Toys, Boys' Swimwear, Sweaters, Outerwear
JEFF BROWN-Boys' Footwear

DUNDEE SMART CLOTHES (MW)

306 Main St. (bud)
Little Rock, AR 72201
501-372-0610

WILLIAM KEY (Owner) & Buys Men's Sportswear, Furnishings, Accessories, Headwear, Men's Footwear, Store Displays, Fixtures, Supplies
SAMMIE STEWART (Mgr.) & Buys Men's Sportswear, Furnishings, Accessories, Headwear, Men's Footwear

GREENHAW'S, INC. (CLO)

10301 Rodney Parham Rd. (b)
Little Rock, AR 72227
501-227-8703 / Fax: 501-227-7918
Sales: $1 Million-$10 Million
Website: www.greenhaws.com

STEVE GREENHAW (Owner) & Buys Men's Sportswear, Sweaters, Sport Shirts, Outer Jackets, Leather Apparel, Casual Slacks, Active Apparel, Young Men's Wear, Furnishings, Headwear, Accessories, Men's Footwear, Store Displays, Fixtures, Supplies
GREG HERR (Mgr.) & Buys Men's Sportswear, Sweaters, Sport Shirts, Outer Jackets, Leather Apparel, Casual Slacks, Active Apparel, Young Men's Wear, Furnishings, Headwear, Accessories, Men's Footwear, Store Displays, Fixtures, Supplies

HORN'S, INC. (MW & DISC)

624 Center St. (bud-b)
Little Rock, AR 72201
501-376-3866 / Fax: 501-376-3867
Sales: Under $100,000

NANCY HORN ROY (Owner) & Buys Men's Suits, Tailored Jackets, Tailored Slacks, Casual Slacks, Dress Shirts, Ties
LINDA DAVIS (G.M.M.) & Buys Men's Suits, Tailored Jackets, Tailored Slacks, Casual Slacks, Dress Shirts, Ties, Overcoats
LINDA STOGNER-Dress Shirts, Ties, Belts, Jewelry
BETTY BAILEY (Office Mgr.) & Buys Store Displays, Fixtures, Supplies

J.E. PHILLIPS MEN'S STORE (MW)

608 Main St. (p)
Little Rock, AR 72201
501-376-3146

CHARLES PHILLIPS-Big & Tall Men's Wear, Suits, Men's Wear, Accessories, Furnishings, Store Displays

M.M. COHN CO. (DEPT-2)

(LITTLE ROCK DIV.)
(DUNLOP CO.)
300 S. University Ave. (m-b)
Little Rock, AR 72205
501-664-5501 / Fax: 501-664-2582
Sales: $10 Million-$50 Million

RUSSELL WOMACK (President)
TOM BALDWIN (Display Coord.) & Buys Store Displays, Fixtures, Supplies
BOB JACKSON-Men's Sportswear, Furnishings, Headwear, Jewelry, Small Leather Goods, Footwear, Young Men's, Boys' Wear, Women's Sportwear

MR. WICKS, INC. (MW)

5924 R St. (b)
Little Rock, AR 72207
501-664-3062 / Fax: 501-664-3648
Sales: $1 Million-$10 Million

CHARLES F. CARROLL, JR. (President) & Buys Men's Clothing
MARK C. CARROLL (V.P. & G.M.M.) & Buys Men's Sportswear, Furnishings, Accessories, Headwear, Men's Footwear, Store Displays, Fixtures, Supplies

PARTNERS MEN'S STORE (MW)

5700 B St., #B (m)
Little Rock, AR 72205
501-224-4466
Sales: $500,001-$1 Million

W. B. LOYD (Owner) & Buys Men's Suits, Sportswear, Furnishings, Accessories, Footwear, Urban Contemporary, Store Displays, Fixtures, Supplies

PAUL BUNYAN'S (MW)

8511 W. Markham St. (b)
Little Rock, AR 72205
501-227-5440 / Fax: 501-227-9468
Sales: $1 Million-$10 Million

JERRY BOOE (Owner) & Buys Men's Big & Tall Sportswear, Furnishings, Accessories, Store Displays
DANNY BRADBERRY-Footwear

SPORTSTOP, INC. (CLO)

10720 N. Rodney Parham Rd. (m)
Little Rock, AR 72212
501-224-4033 / Fax: 501-224-4210

JAY ROGERS-Men's Sportswear, Outer Jackets, Footwear, Accessories, Furnishings, Store Displays

ARKANSAS - Little Rock

THE TOGGERY, INC. (KS-2)

5919 R St. (b)
Little Rock, AR 72207
501-663-8662 / Fax: 501-663-9152
Sales: $1 Million-$10 Million

PENNY OLINGHOUSE (Co-Owner) (@ 501-227-8492) & Buys Newborn to 20 Boys' Wear, Store Displays, Fixtures, Supplies

PHIL OLINGHOUSE (Co-Owner) & Buys 8 to 20 Boys' Wear, Store Displays, Fixtures, Supplies

UNIVERSITY OF ARKANSAS LITTLE ROCK BOOKSTORE (SP)

2801 S. University Ave.
Little Rock, AR 72204
501-569-3245 / Fax: 501-569-8987

RICK BURTON (Mgr.) & Buys Fleece, Jackets

McCRARY & CO., INC. (CLO)

115 W. Front St. (p-m)
Lonoke, AR 72086
501-676-2317 / Fax: 501-676-3170
Sales: $1 Million-$10 Million

WALLS McCRARY (Owner) & Buys Men's Sportswear, Furnishings, Accessories, Footwear, Young Men's Shop, Store Displays, Fixtures, Supplies

BUFFALOES II (WW)

109 N. Jefferson St. (m)
Magnolia, AR 71753
870-234-2932 / Fax: 870-234-7742

ARLINDA YATES (Co-Owner) & Buys Men's Sportswear, Wester Wear, Furnishings, Accessories, Young Men's Wear, Boots, Boys' Wear, Store Displays, Fixtures, Supplies

MIKE MOONEY (Co-Owner) & Buys Men's Sportswear, Western Wear, Furnishings, Accessories, Young Men's Wear, Boots, Boys' Wear, Store Displays, Fixtures, Supplies

TALBOT'S DEPARTMENT STORE, INC. (DEPT)

100 Northside Sq. (m)
Magnolia, AR 71753
870-234-1050 / Fax: 870-234-1053
Sales: $1 Million-$10 Million

DUDLEY A. TALBOT (President) & Buys Store Displays, Fixtures, Supplies

KEN BOSWORTH (Exec. V.P. & Chief Mdsg. Ofcr.)

STEVE THOMPSON-Men's Overcoats, Suits, Tailored Jackets, Sportswear, Sweaters, Outer Jackets, Casual Slacks, Active Apparel, Furnishings, Headwear, Accessories, Leather Apparel, Young Men's Wear, Boys' Wear, Men's Footwear, Boys' Footwear

RONNY'S (CLO-2)

P.O. Box 568 (bud-p)
101 Mann St.
Marianna, AR 72360
870-295-6130 / Fax: 870-295-6100
Sales: $1 Million-$10 Million

STEVE O'MELL (Owner) & Buys Men's Sportswear, Young Men's Wear, Boys' Suits, Pants, Tops, Accessories, Furnishings, Men's Footwear, Store Displays

HEROD'S DEPARTMENT STORE (DEPT)

821 S. Mena St. (p)
Mena, AR 71953
479-394-4864 / Fax: 479-394-7528
Sales: $500,001-$1 Million

STOKES HEROD (Owner) & Buys Men's Overcoats, Suits, Tailored Jackets, Tailored Slacks, Sportswear, Sweaters, Sport Shirts, Outer Jackets, Casual Slacks, Active Apparel, Furnishings, Dress Shirts, Ties, Robes, Underwear, Hosiery, Gloves, Accessories, Belts, Jewelry, Small Leather Goods

RUBY'S FOR KINGLY MEN (MW)

Hwy. 71 North (m)
Mena, AR 71953
501-394-6616
Sales: $100,001-$500,000

RUBY GIBBENS (President) & Buys Men's Overcoats, Suits, Tailored Jackets, Tailored Slacks, Sportswear, Leather Apparel, Furnishings, Accessories, Headwear, Store Displays, Fixtures, Supplies

GREER'S, INC. (CLO)

115 E. Broadway (m)
Morrilton, AR 72110
501-354-3186 / Fax: 501-354-4214
Sales: $1 Million-$10 Million

RAY MOLL (Owner) & Buys Men's Sportswear, Leather Apparel, Furnishings, Accessories, Young Men's & Boys' Wear, Urban Contemporary, Store Displays, Fixtures, Supplies

C & K CLOTHING (CLO-3)

1014 Highland Cir. (p-m-b)
Mountain Home, AR 72653
870-425-9455 / Fax: 870-424-5082
Sales: $1 Million-$10 Million

CHARLES MONTGOMERY (President)

SHANNA HEAD (Mgr.) & Buys Men's Sportswear, Sweaters, Sport Shirts, Casual Slacks, Active Apparel, Dress Shirts, Hosiery, Young Men's & Boys' Wear

JOBETH MONTGOMERY-Men's Sportswear, Sweaters, Sport Shirts, Casual Slacks, Active Apparel, Dress Shirts, Hosiery, Young Men's & Boys' Wear

DOX SPORTING GOODS SHOP (SG)

113 N. Main St. (m)
Nashville, AR 71852
870-845-2213 / Fax: 870-845-4390
Sales: $1 Million-$10 Million
Website: www.doxsportshop.com

JEFF McBRIDE (Owner) & Buys Active Wear, T-shirts, Shorts, Headwear, Athletic Footwear, Store Displays, Fixtures, Supplies

VAN ATKINS OF MONTICELLO, INC. (DEPT-4)

Village Mall Shopping Center (m-b)
Newport, AR 72112
870-523-2330 / Fax: 870-523-4103

ROBERT VAN HOOK (President)

BROOK MAYS-Men's Overcoats, Suits, Tailored Jackets, Tailored Slacks, Raincoats, Big & Tall Wear, Sweaters, Sport Shirts, Outer Jackets, Casual Slacks, Active Apparel, Furnishings, Dress Shirts, Ties, Robes, Underwear, Hosiery, Gloves, Accessories, Belts, Footwear, Young Men's & Boys' Wear, Store Displays, Fixtures, Supplies

CAMP ROBINSON CANTEEN (PX & OL)

Bldg. 5400, Camp Robinson
North Little Rock, AR 72119
501-753-9017 / Fax: 501-753-9430
Website: www.mwr-arng.com

JACK SCARBROUGH-Military Insignia, Apparel & Accessories, Men's Uniforms, Casual Slacks, Dress Shoes, Ties, Underwear, Hoisery, Gloves, Headwear, Belts, Footwear, Store Displays

LITTLE ROCK APPAREL, INC. (CLO-13)

(PUFF'S WAREHOUSE)
(THE WEARHOUSE)
4653 John F Kennedy Blvd. (m)
North Little Rock, AR 72116
501-753-1086 / Fax: 501-758-6071
Sales: $10 Million-$50 Million

DON FELGATE (Owner) & Buys Boys' Apparel, Leather Goods, Men's Apparel, Men's Casualwear, Men's Denim Apparel, Men's Hosiery, Men's Outerwear, Men's Sportswear, Men's Swimwear

GERRI MUCH (G.M.M.) & Buys Boys' Apparel, Leather Goods, Men's Apparel, Men's Casualwear, Men's Denim Apparel, Men's Hosiery, Men's Outerwear, Men's Sportswear, Men's Swimwear

SHARPS (SP)

14 N. Elm St. (m-b)
Paris, AR 72855
479-963-3636

JACKIE FLEETWOOD (Mgr.) & Buys Men's Apparel

ARKANSAS - Pine Bluff

BURT'S STORE FOR MEN (MW)

(BURT'S, INC.)
205 S. Main St. (m-b)
Pine Bluff, AR 71601
870-534-0372 / Fax: 870-534-8072
Sales: $500,001-$1 Million

THOMAS CURRY (President) & Buys Men's Sportswear, Furnishings, Accessories, Footwear, Young Men's Wear, Big & Tall Men's, Store Displays, Fixtures, Supplies

JERRY'S DEPARTMENT STORE (MW)

313 S. Main St. (m)
Pine Bluff, AR 71601
870-534-4430 / Fax: 870-536-0283
Sales: $500,001-$1 Million

LINDA RICE-Men's Wear, Urban Contemporary, Uniforms, Footwear, Accessories, Sportswear, Furnishings

LOOKING GOOD (CLO)

300 Main St.
Pine Bluff, AR 71601
870-535-6143 / Fax: 870-535-1794
Sales: $500,001-$1 Million

KAREN TOLANI (Co-Owner) & Buys Men's, Young Men's & Boys' Clothing, Sportswear, Furnishings, Accessories, Footwear, Urban Contemporary, Store Displays, Fixtures, Supplies

BOBBY DADLANI (Co-Owner) & Buys Men's Overcoats, Suits, Tailored Jackets, Tailored Slacks, Sportswear, Dress Shirts, Underwear, Headwear, Jewelry, Small Leather Goods, Footwear, Young Men's Wear, Boys' Wear, Store Displays, Fixtures, Supplies

DANNY MELVANI (Co-Owner) & Buys Men's & Boys' Wear, Urban Contemporary, Footwear, Store Displays, Fixtures, Supplies

MARK MAHTNI (Co-Owner) & Buys Men's Sportswear, Urban Contemporary, Furnishings, Accessories, 8 to 20 Boys' Suits, Suits, Dress Pants, Dress Shirts, Big & Tall Men's Wear, Hosiery, Footwear, Store Displays, Fixtures, Supplies

SPIKES' CLOTHING, INC. (CLO)

107 N. Marr St. (m-b)
Pocahontas, AR 72455
870-892-3736

CHARLOTTE SPIKES (President & Co-Owner) & Buys Men's Sportswear, Headwear, Young Men's & Boys' Wear, Store Displays, Accessories, Furnishings, Fixtures, Supplies

STEVE SPIKES (Co-Owner) & Buys Men's Sportswear, Headwear, Young Men's & Boys' Wear, Store Displays, Accessories, Furnishings, Fixtures, Supplies

NORMAN'S, INC. (MW)

Heritage Square (b)
900 W. Main
Russellville, AR 72801
479-968-1457 / Fax: 479-858-6367
Sales: $500,001-$1 Million

NORMAN WATSON (Co-Owner) & Buys Men's Footwear, Men's Sportswear, Leather Apparel, Furnishings, Accessories, Headwear, Store Displays, Fixtures, Supplies

COTHERN'S MEN'S STORE (MW)

1547 E. Race Ave. (m-b)
Searcy, AR 72143
501-268-2858
Sales: $500,001-$1 Million

LOGAN COTHERN (Owner) & Buys Men's Overcoats, Suits, Tailored Jackets, Tailored Slacks, Raincoats, Sportswear, Sweaters, Sport Shirts, Outer Jackets, Casual Slacks, Active Apparel, Furnishings, Headwear, Footwear, Store Displays, Fixtures, Supplies

AFTER GLOWS TANNING (CLO)

511 W. Tulsa St., #102
Siloam Springs, AR 72761
479-524-6319 / Fax: 479-736-8261

TERESA LOWERY-Sunglasses, Accessories, Footwear, Hats, Apparel, Men's Surf & Swimwear

FELTS' FAMILY STORES (CLO-2)

(FELTS' FAMILY SHOES)
P.O. Box 96 (m)
215 N. Wright St.
Siloam Springs, AR 72761
479-524-5671 / Fax: 479-524-9047
Sales: $1 Million-$10 Million

ROBERT FELTS (President & G.M.M.) & Buys Boys' Footwear, Men's Footwear, Leather Goods, Hosiery

IMOGENE FELTS (Treas. & Secy.) & Buys Boys' Footwear, Men's Footwear, Leather Goods, Hosiery

RYAN'S CLOTHING, INC. (DG)

200 E. Emma Ave., #202 (p-m-b)
Springdale, AR 72764
479-751-2177 / Fax: 479-751-2177
Sales: $1 Million-$10 Million

TROY RYAN (Co-Owner)

MAX RYAN (G.M.M.) & Buys Men's Sportswear, Leather Apparel, Furnishings, Accessories, Young Men's & Boys' Wear, Urban Contemporary, Store Displays, Fixtures & Supplies

WESTERN SPORTING STORE (SP & MO)

606 N. Lincoln Ave.
Star City, AR 71667
870-628-3832
Sales: $100,001-$500,000

PAMELA FISH (Mgr.) & Buys Outdoor Footwear, Hunting Apparel, Work & Hunting Boots, Accessories

C.V.'S DEPARTMENT STORE (DEPT)

106 E. Ruby St. (p-m-b)
Stephens, AR 71764
870-786-5395
Sales: $1 Million-$10 Million

C. V. ARRINGTON (Owner) & Buys Men's Sportswear, Furnishings, Accessories, Big & Tall Men's Wear, Young Men's Wear, Footwear, Store Displays, Fixtures, Supplies

MACK'S SPORT SHOP (MW)

(MACK'S PRAIRIE WING)
2335 Hwy. 63 North (m-b)
Stuttgart, AR 72160
870-673-6960 / Fax: 870-673-3687
Website: www.mackspw.com

MARION McCULLUM (President & Owner)

CHUCK LOCK (Mgr.) & Buys Sportswear, Outer Jackets, Men's Footwear, Boots, Furnishings, Accessories, Store Displays, Fixtures, Supplies

COLLINS & WILLIAMS (MW)

104 E. Broad St. (m)
Texarkana, AR 71854
870-772-2765 / Fax: 870-773-3324
Sales: $500,001-$1 Million

DON WILLIAMS (Co-Owner) & Buys Men's Sportswear, Sweaters, Furnishings, Accessories, Dress Shirts, Footwear, Urban Contemporary

RAYMOND TOLLETT (Co-Owner) & Buys Men's Overcoats, Leather Apparel, Headwear, Young Men's & Boys' Wear, Footwear, Store Displays, Fixtures, Supplies

CUFF & COLLAR (MW)

301 E. Broad St. (bud-p)
Texarkana, AR 71854
870-774-9200 / Fax: 870-772-5068

BETTY BOREN (Owner) & Buys Big & Tall Men's Wear, Young Men's Big & Tall Wear, Urban Contemporary, Suits

TAMMY THOMPSON-Big & Tall Men's Wear, Young Men's Big & Tall Wear, Urban Contemporary, Suits

GQ LOOK (MW)

209 E. Broad St. (b)
Texarkana, AR 71854
870-772-3316 / Fax: 870-773-0533
Sales: $1 Million-$10 Million

GEORGE GAWIREH-Young Men's Wear, Urban Contemporary, Footwear, Accessories, Furnishings, Suits, Boys' Wear, Men's Big and Tall, Sportswear, Store Displays

MARTIN'S DEPARTMENT STORE (DEPT)
200 S. Main St. (p)
Warren, AR 71671
870-226-3531 / Fax: 870-226-2990
Sales: $100,001-$500,000

BRYAN MARTIN (Owner) & Buys Men's Overcoats, Suits, Tailored Jackets, Tailored Slacks, Raincoats, Sportswear, Sweaters, Sport Shirts, Outer Jackets, Casual Slacks, Boys' Jeans, Furnishings, Dress Shirts, Ties, Robes, Underwear, Hosiery, Gloves, Hats, Accessories, Belts, Jewelry, Small Leather Goods, Fragrances, Store Displays, Fixtures, Supplies

COUNTRY SQUIRE, INC. (MW)
1399 Missouri (m)
West Memphis, AR 72301
870-735-8801 / Fax: 870-735-8807
Sales: $1 Million-$10 Million
Website: www.hogsport.com

JAY EARNEY, JR. (President) & Buys Men's Sportswear, Sweaters, Sport Shirts, Outer Jackets, Casual Slacks, Active Apparel, Underwear, Hosiery, Accessories, Young Men's Wear, Urban Contemporary, Boys' Sportswear, Accessories, Leather Apparel, Footwear, Store Displays, Fixtures, Supplies

SAIG CLOTHES FOR MEN (MW)
(SAM SAIG & SONS, INC.)
710 E. Broadway (m-b)
West Memphis, AR 72301
870-735-5236
Sales: $500,001-$1 Million

ALFRED SAIG (Secy.) & Buys Men's Sportswear, Furnishings, Accessories, Headwear, Footwear, Store Displays, Fixtures, Supplies

REGINALD LEE'S DEPARTMENT STORE, INC. (DEPT)
1816 Oakwood Falls Shopping Center
Wynne, AR 72396
870-238-2494 / Fax: 870-238-7417
Sales: $1 Million-$10 Million

REGINALD LEE (Owner)

TERRIE LEE (Mgr.) & Buys Men's Overcoats, Suits, Sportswear, Dress Shirts, Underwear, Hosiery, Accessories, Big & Tall Men's Wear, Young Men's Wear, Urban Contemporary, Store Displays, Fixtures, Supplies

PRO LOOK SPORTSWEAR (SP-1)

5731 Kanan Rd.
Agoura Hills, CA 91301
818-735-0456 / Fax: 818-735-0634

RICHARD SCLAR (Owner) & Buys Activewear, Athletic Footwear, Licensed Apparel

DEE BEE'S UNIFORM SHOP, INC. (MW-3)

(DEE BEE'S ELEGANT CLEANERS)
P.O. Box 5041
U.S. Coast Guard Island #22
Alameda, CA 94501
510-536-4252 / Fax: 510-536-4252

FRANK DE BIASI (President) & Buys Men's Overcoats, Raincoats, Formal Wear, Casual Slacks, Dress Shirts, Hosiery, Military Headwear, Military Jewelry, Small Leather Goods, Military Uniforms, Accessories, Footwear, Surplus Products, Store Displays, Fixtures, Supplies

ADORABLE SHOP (KS)

50 S. Garfield Ave. (b)
Alhambra, CA 91801
626-282-6181 / Fax: 626-282-1349
Sales: $1 Million-$10 Million

LISA KORNBLAU (President) & Buys Young Men's Overcoats, Suits, Tailored Jackets, Tailored Slacks, Sportswear, Dress Shirts, Ties, Belts, Jewelry, 8 to 20 Boys' Wear

JOSE RODRIGUEZ-Young Men's Overcoats, Suits, Tailored Jackets, Tailored Slacks, Sportswear, Dress Shirts, Ties, Belts, Jewelry, 8 to 20 Boys' Wear, Footwear, Store Displays, Fixtures & Supplies

TOM'S MENSWEAR & UNIFORMS, INC. (MW)

301 E. Main St. (p)
Alhambra, CA 91801
626-281-5341 / Fax: 626-281-3380
Sales: $500,000-$1 Million
Website: www.tomsuniforms.com

JEFF SHULMAN (Owner)

JOE CARR-Men's Work Uniforms, Men's Sportswear, Leather Apparel, Furnishings, Accessories, Work Shoes & Boots, Urban Contemporary, Store Displays, Fixtures, Supplies

ROBERT GILLIAM-Men's Work Uniforms, Shoes, Boots, Career Apparel, Police Uniforms, Fire Uniforms, Security Uniforms, Medical Uniforms

BEACH FUN USA (CLO)

10211 Corkwood Ct.
Alta Loma, CA 31737
909-941-9676 / Fax: 909-483-2578

SERGIO CASTILLO (Partner)

FERNANDO LARA-Boys' Swimwear, Sportswear, Sunglasses, Footwear, Hats, Men's Surf & Swimwear

CALIFORNIA KIDS & TEENS (KS)

6787 Carnelian St., #A (m-b)
Alta Loma, CA 91701
909-941-1004

SANDY DAVIS (Owner) & Buys Infants, Young Men's, 8 to 20 Boys' Wear, Store Displays, Fixtures, Supplies

ERLANDER'S NATURAL PRODUCTS (CLO)

2279 N. Lake St. (m)
Altadena, CA 91001
626-797-7004 / Fax: 626-798-2663

LEATRICE ERLANDER (Co-Owner) & Buys Men's & Young Men's Cotton Shirts, Pants, Underwear, Hosiery, Footwear, Store Displays, Fixtures, Supplies

ARDIE'S CLASSIE LASSIE (CLO)

(CALICO COW)
301 S. Main St.
Alturas, CA 96101
530-233-5599 / Fax: 530-233-2296

ARDITH FERRY (Owner) & Buys Men's Sportswear, Swimwear, Accessories

JAY'S MENSWEAR (CLO)

108 S. Main (p-m)
Alturas, CA 96101
530-233-2903 / Fax: 530-233-4583

STELLA HIGHT (Co-Owner) & Buys Men's Apparel, Accessories, Footwear

BREWER HAWAII (CLO)

(BREWER SNOWBOARDS, INC.)
3620 E. Miraloma Ave.
Anaheim, CA 92806
714-630-4311

KELLY NOVAC-Beachwear, Swimwear, Activewear

MATHEW NOVAC-Beachwear, Swimwear, Activewear

FRIAR TUX (MW-28)

1711 S. Claudina Way (m-b)
Anaheim, CA 92805
714-635-1262 / Fax: 714-635-2701
Website: www.friartux.com

MIKE MESKELL (Owner/Real Estate Contact)

GREG GOODWIN (President) & Buys Men's & Boys' Formal Wear, Men's & Boys' Formal Footwear, Related Accessories, Store Displays, Fixtures, Supplies

PACIFIC SUNWEAR, INC. (CLO-612 & OL)

(d.e.m.o.)
(PAC SUN OUTLET)
3450 E. Miraloma Ave. (p)
Anaheim, CA 92806
714-414-4000 / Fax: 714-414-4251
Sales: $500 Million-$1 Billion
Website: www.pacsun.com
Retail Locations: AL, AK, AZ, CA, CO, CT, DC, DE, FL, GA, HI, ID, IL, IN, IA, KS, KY, LA, ME, MD, MA, MI, MN, MS, MO, MT, NE, NV, NH, NJ, NM, NY, NC, ND, OH, OK, OR, PA, PR, RI, SC, SD, TN, TX, UT, VT, VA, WA, WV, WI

TIMOTHY HARMON (President & Chief Mdsg. Officer)

LARRY FESLER (V.P.-Stores)

GREG WEAVER (C.F.O.)

MARK KIBLER (V.P.-Dist.)

FRANK SCHOLLS (V.P. - Finance)

ABBY ARNOFF (V.P. - H.R.)

MARK KIBLER (V.P. - Dist.)

DIANE NANCE (V.P. - Sourcing)

WILLIAM ROSENBAUM (V.P. - Young Men's)

SHELLEY SMITH (Sr. V.P. - Real Estate)

BOB ENTERSZ (V.P. - Mdse. & e-Commerce)

DEBBIE SHINN (V.P & G.M.M. - Juniors) & Buys Young Men's Bottoms & Denims, T-Shirts, Fleece Outerwear

JEFF BUSCHE-Young Men's Bottoms & Denims

JAIMIE GARVIN-Young Men's Bottoms & Denims

CURTIS HILDAGO-Young Men's Knits & Wovens

JAMES SHIRAI-Young Men's Knits & Wovens

ROBERT THOMSEN-Young Men's T-Shirts & Fleece Outerwear

JON BOLINGER (D.M.M - Accessories & Footwear)

PAMELA MILCETICH-Young Men's Accessories

VERONICA MRACEK-Young Men's Footwear & Accessories

HEIDI MUHLER (D.M.M. - d.e.m.o.) & Buys Young Men's & Juniors' Accessories

PRISCILLA FUHREE-Young Men's d.e.m.o.

KANNA PLACE-Young Men's d.e.m.o. & Accessories

KIM BENNETT-Store Displays, Fixtures & Supplies

STEVENS' FORMAL WEAR (MW)

5642 E. La Palma Ave.
Anaheim, CA 92807
714-970-1717

GARY STEVENS (Owner) & Buys Men's, Young Men's & Boys' Formal Wear, Store Displays, Fixtures, Supplies

WIN, LOSE OR DRAW SPORTSWEAR (CLO)
510 S. State College
Anaheim, CA 92806
714-776-5077
BRUCE GERSHENOFF (President) & Buys Licensed Sports Apparel

WINNER'S CIRCLE WESTERN WEAR (WW)
1623 A St. (m)
Antioch, CA 94509
925-757-0202 / Fax: 925-757-8502
SUSAN PEDERSEN (Owner) & Buys Men's Western Wear & Accessories, Big & Tall Men's Western Wear, Young Men's & Boys' Western Wear, Footwear, Store Displays, Fixtures, Supplies

ADVANTIS RIDE (SP)
1041 S. Baldwin Ave.
Arcadia, CA 91007
626-445-6680 / Fax: 626-447-7104
STAN O'HARA (Owner) & Buys Snowboards, Surfboards, Skateboards, Related Activewear, Athletic Footwear

TEAM WEAR ATHLETIC (SP)
1350 Broadway
Atwater, CA 95301
209-358-5063 / Fax: 209-358-5216
MARK RIEDEMAN (Owner) & Buys Athletic Apparel, Athletic Footwear, Sports Apparel
FLOYD STUBBS-Athletic Apparel, Athletic Footwear, Sports Apparel

FOOTPATH (FW)
825 Lincoln Way
Auburn, CA 95603
530-885-2091 / Fax: 530-885-3074
Sales: $100,001-$500,000
JERRY LAWTON (President) & Buys Men's Footwear

NAT'S MENSWEAR (MW)
155 Belmont Dr. (m)
Auburn, CA 95603
530-885-9329
NAT GIULIANI (Owner) & Buys Men's Furnishings, Footwear, Store Displays, Fixtures, Supplies

SWEAT SHOP (SP)
13416 Lincoln Way
Auburn, CA 95603
530-823-5353 / Fax: 530-823-3740
TOM HENDERSON (Owner) & Buys Activewear

BUOYS & GULLS MENSWEAR (CLO)
417 Crescent Ave.
Avalon, CA 90704
310-510-0416 / Fax: 310-510-1840
JERRY DUNN (Owner) & Buys Sport Shirts, Outerwear, Active Apparel, T-shirts, Sportswear,. Footwear

THE SAND BOX (KS)
P.O. Box 8 (bud-p-m-b)
519 Crescent Ave.
Avalon, CA 90704
310-510-2130 / Fax: 310-510-0854
BARBARA COTTER (Owner) & Buys 8 to 18 Boys' Wear, Footwear, Store Displays, Fixtures, Supplies

VERONICA RAYES (SP)
105 Pebble Beach Rd.
Avalon, CA 90704
310-510-9525 / Fax: 310-510-9526
NORBERT REYES-Boys' Apparel, Boys' Swimwear, Sunglasses, Fashion Accessories, Footwear, Hats, Men's Surf & Swimwear, Men's Swimwear, Resortwear, T-shirts, Imprinted Sportswear

YOSHI'S FASHIONS (CLO-2)
(YOSHI'S ISLAND GIRL)
106 Catalina St.
Avalon, CA 90704
310-510-2538 / Fax: 310-510-9443
YOSHI WEEKS (Owner) & Buys Sportswear, Swimwear

CASA NOVA L'UOMO (WW-6)
241 E. Gladstone St.
Azusa, CA 91702
626-633-1077
ALFREDO CASANOVA (Mgr.) & Buys Western Wear, Casual Slacks, Headwear, Footwear, Suits, Related Accessories

PASEO FASHIONS (MW)
840 Alosta Ave.
Azusa, CA 91702
626-633-0022 / Fax: 626-969-4022
HUSSEIN ELKANTAR (Owner) & Buys Men's Sportswear, Accessories, Boys' Sportswear

BOOTS 'N' BRITCHES (CLO)
1340 Roberts Ln., #S1 (m)
Bakersfield, CA 93308
661-399-1151
Sales: $100,001-$500,000
PAULA MAYNARD (Owner) & Buys Men's, Big & Tall Men's, Young Men's & Boys' Western Clothing, Sportswear, Hosiery, Gloves, Accessories, Store Displays, Fixtures, Supplies

EMPORIUM WESTERN STORE (WW)
1031 19th St. (p)
Bakersfield, CA 93301
661-325-8476 / Fax: 661-325-2924
Sales: $1 Million-$10 Million
CAROL DURST (Co-Owner)
STEPHEN GOLDWATER (Co-Owner & G.M.M.) & Buys Men's & Boys' Footwear, Men's Western Clothing, Sportswear, Furnishings
DEBORAH BAKER (Gen. Mgr.) & Buys Men's Western Clothing, Sportswear, Furnishings
AL GONZALES-Men's Western Belts, Headwear

FLOYD STORES, INC. (DEPT-5)
P.O. Box 2940 (p-m)
Bakersfield, CA 93301
661-410-4602 / Fax: 661-410-4613
Website: www.floyds.com
RUSSELL SEARCY (Mdse. Mgr.) & Buys Men's Western Wear, Sportswear, Boys' Jeans, Footwear, Urban Contemporary, Store Displays, Fixtures, Supplies

H. WALKER'S CLOTHING STORE (CLO)
(HERB WALKER'S)
1700 K St. (m-b-h)
Bakersfield, CA 93301
661-283-4500 / Fax: 661-283-4505
Sales: $500,000-$1 Million
TRACY WALKER (Owner) & Buys Men's Suits, Tailored Jackets, Tailored Slacks, Sportswear, Dress Shirts, Underwear, Hosiery, Footwear, Store Displays, Fixtures, Supplies

J.M. BABY NEWS (KS)
930 Wible Rd. (b)
Bakersfield, CA 93304
661-834-7277 / Fax: 661-834-0502
Sales: $1 Million-$10 Million
MOLLY CLIFTON (Co-Owner) & Buys 4 to 7 Boys' Wear, Footwear, Store Displays, Fixtures, Supplies
CRAIG CLIFTON (Co-Owner) & Buys 4 to 7 Boys' Wear, Footwear, Store Displays, Fixtures, Supplies

MICHAEL'S (MW-4)
3616 Ming Ave. (m)
Bakersfield, CA 93309
661-832-7124 / Fax: 661-832-6653
MICHAEL GONZALES (Owner) & Buys Men's &Young Men's Big & Tall Wear, Sportswear, Leather Apparel, Store Displays, Fixtures, Supplies

SABA'S (MW)
915 Baker St. (b)
Bakersfield, CA 93305
661-323-7834 / Fax: 661-323-0507
Sales: $100,001-$500,000
JAMES SABA (Co-Owner) & Buys Men's Sportswear, Leather Apparel, Footwear
JACK SABA (Co-Owner) & Buys Men's Sportswear, Leather Apparel, Footwear, Store Displays, Fixtures, Supplies

SNEAD'S FOR MEN (MW)
5127 Ming Ave. (m-b)
Bakersfield, CA 93309
661-832-4270
SNEAD PRICE (Owner) & Buys Men's Wear, Sportswear, Furnishings, Accessories, Leather Goods, Jewelry, Fragrances, Big & Tall Men's Wear, Footwear, Store Displays, Fixtures and Supplies

THE UNIFORM SHOP (MW)
4450 California Ave.
Bakersfield, CA 93309
661-322-1587
LAUREL COLEMAN (Owner) & Buys Men's Medical Uniforms, Footwear

WALL STREET ALLEY T-SHIRT CO. (CLO)
3700 Easton Dr., #17
Bakersfield, CA 93309
661-324-6207 / Fax: 661-324-5604
DOMINIC WEBBY (Owner) & Buys Men's, Young Men's & Boys' T-shirts, Pants, Jackets, Headwear, Store Displays, Fixtures, Supplies

SUN & FUN OF NEWPORT BEACH (SP-2)
307 Main St.
Balboa, CA 92661
949-675-4353 / Fax: 949-673-3376
RICHARD TULSIANI (Owner) & Buys Surfwear, Activewear, Leisurewear, Headwear, Swimwear

ALEX'S FASHION CENTER (CLO)
214 Marine Ave.
Balboa Island, CA 92662
949-723-1267
ALEX KOYOUMJIAN (Owner)
NAZAARET KOYOUMJIAN (G.M.M.) & Buys Men's, Young Men's & Boys' Sportswear, Swimwear, Sunglasses Sandals, Athletic Footwear
RACHEL KOYOUMJAIN-Men's, Young Men's & Boys' Sportswear, Swimwear, Sunglasses Sandals, Athletic Footwear

J.P. MAXWELL (CLO)
(MARINE ISLAND, INC.)
204 Marine Ave.
Balboa Island, CA 92662
949-673-7211 / Fax: 949-673-1637
MAXWELL PHILLIPS (Owner) & Buys Men's Sportswear, Sport Shirts, Outwear, Active Apparel, Headwear, Store Displays, Fixtures, Supplies

MATHERSON'S DEPARTMENT STORE (DEPT)
260 W. Ramsey St. (p-m)
Banning, CA 92220
909-849-4347 / Fax: 909-849-5967
BUD MATHERSON (Owner) & Buys Men's Suits, Tailored Jackets, Tailored Slacks, Raincoats, Sportswear, Furnishings, Accessories, Young Men's Wear, Urban Contemporary, Boys' Wear, Store Displays, Fixtures and Supplies

MARINE CORPS EXCHANGE (PX)
Marine Corps Logistics Base
Bldg. 319
Barstow, CA 92311
760-256-0212 / Fax: 760-256-7027
ANTHONY CISNEROS (Staff Sgt. & Retail Mgr.)
ANTHONY E. SPRAGUE-Men's Sportswear, Accessories, Footwear, Boys' Sportswear, Boys' Accessories, Boys' Footwear

1ST UNITED SHOE (FW)
9818 Artesia Blvd. (bud-p-m-b-des)
Bellflower, CA 90706
562-867-3502 / Fax: 562-866-7733
Sales: $500,001-$1 Million
EASTON CRAWFORD (Partner) & Buys Boys' Apparel, Boys' Footwear, Men's Footwear, Leather Goods, Men's Accessories, Men's Apparel, Hosiery
ARTHUR CASTANEDA (Partner) & Buys Boys' Apparel, Boys' Footwear, Men's Footwear, Leather Goods, Men's Accessories, Men's Apparel, Hosiery

DOUGHBOY'S SURPLUS BAZAAR (CLO)
9826 E. Artesia Blvd. (p)
Bellflower, CA 90706
562-867-2063 / Fax: 562-867-2763
Sales: $1 Million-$10 Million
MARK FRANKEL (Owner) & Buys Men's Sport Shirts, Outer Jackets, Casual Slacks, Active Apparel, Leather Apparel, Work Clothes, Dress Shirts, Underwear, Hosiery, Gloves, Belts, Big & Tall Men's Wear, Urban Contemporary, Boys' Clothing, Sportswear, Headwear, Store Displays, Fixtures, Supplies, Footwear
CHRISTINE AVALOS-Footwear

BILL'S MEN'S SHOP (MW)
2386 Telegraph Ave. (m)
Berkeley, CA 94704
510-848-5436
MARTY BERG (Owner) & Buys Men's Sports Jackets, Sportswear, Furnishings, Footwear, Accessories, Store Displays, Fixtures and Supplies

DISCOVERY CHANNEL STORES (GS-120 & OL)
(THE NATURE CO.)
(Div. of DISCOVERY COMMUNICATIONS, INC.)
1608 4th St. (b)
Berkeley, CA 94710
510-528-9924 / Fax: 510-558-6312
Sales: $100 Million-$500 Million
Website: www.discovery.com
Retail Locations: WA, OR, NV, UT, CO, AZ, CA, KS, MI, KY, NY, VT, MN, NH, MT, RI, CT, NJ, PA, MD, DC, VA, NC, SC, GA, FL, AL, TN, MA, WI, MI, TX, LA, OK, OH, IL
GREGORY DURIG (Exec. V.P. & C.F.O.) & Buys Belts, Jewelry, Sweaters, Sport Shirts, Outer Jackets, Active Apparel, Ties, Hosiery, Gloves, Headwear, T-shirts

SUNSHINE FASHIONS (CLO)
2529 Telegraph Ave.
Berkeley, CA 94704
510-843-9062
PAUL PHILOGENE (Owner) & Buys Young Men's & Boys' Wear, Sportswear, Activewear, Footwear, Store Displays, Fixtures & Supplies

BATTAGLIA SHOP (MW)
306 N. Rodeo Dr. (b-h)
Beverly Hills, CA 90210
310-276-7184 / Fax: 310-276-8853
DOW THANOMBHAND (Mgr.) & Buys Men's Overcoats, Suits, Tailored Jackets, Tailored Slacks, Raincoats, Sportswear, Dress Shirts, Ties, Underwear, Hosiery, Belts, Jewelry, Small Leather Goods, Footwear, Store Displays, Fixtures, Supplies

BIJAN (CLO)
(BIJAN FRAGRANCES)
(FASHION WORLD, INC.)
420 N. Rodeo Dr.
Beverly Hills, CA 90210
310-273-6544 / Fax: 310-273-6535
Website: www.bijan.com
BIJAN PAKZAD (Owner & Chmn.) & Buys Men's Overcoats, Suits, Tailored Jackets, Tailored Slacks, Raincoats, Sportswear, Sweaters, Sport Shirts, Outer Jackets, Casual Slacks, Active Apparel, Leather Apparel, Furnishings, Dress Shirts, Ties, Robes, Headwear, Belts, Jewelry, Small Leather Goods, Fragrances, Footwear, Store Displays, Fixtures, Supplies
DARYOUSH MAHBOUBI-FARDI (C.E.O.)
MANIJEH MESSA (G.M.) & Buys Men's Fragrances

CARROLL & CO. (MW)
425 N. Canyon Dr. (b)
Beverly Hills, CA 90210
310-273-9060 / Fax: 310-273-7974
Sales: $1 Million-$10 Million
RICHARD CARROLL (Owner)
STUART NEWMARK (G.M.M.) & Buys Men's Dress Shirts, Ties, Robes, Underwear, Hosiery, Gloves, Headwear, Belts, Jewelry, Small Leathers, Fragrances, Footwear
JOHN CARROLL-Men's Dress Shirts, Ties, Robes, Underwear, Hosiery, Gloves, Headwear, Men's Dresswear, Belts, Jewelry, Small Leathers, Fragrances, Footwear, Men's Overcoats, Suits, Tailored Jackets, Tailored Slacks, Raincoats, Sweaters, Sportshirts, Outerjackets, Leather Apparel, Casual Slacks

CALIFORNIA - Beverly Hills

G. B. HARB & SON LTD. (MW-2)
336 N. Camden Dr.
Beverly Hills, CA 90210
310-274-8466 / Fax: 310-274-7916
Sales: $100,001-$500,000
Website: www.gbharbclothier.com
GEORGE B. HARB (Owner) & Buys Men's Sportswear, Furnishings, Leather Apparel, Accessories, Ties, Footwear, Store Displays, Fixtures, Supplies

GIANFRANCO FERRE BOUTIQUE (CLO)
270 N. Rodeo Dr. (des)
Beverly Hills, CA 90210
310-273-6311 / Fax: 310-273-5230
Sales: $10 Million-$50 Million
HARRY MOSS (Owner)
KARINA GOLUMBIC (Gen. Mgr.) & Buys Men's Footwear, Leather Goods, Men's Casualwear, Denim Apparel, Formalwear, Accessories, Outerwear, Sleepwear, Sportswear, Suits, Swimwear

JACK TAYLOR (MW)
341 N. Camden Dr. (b-h)
Beverly Hills, CA 90210
310-274-7276 / Fax: 323-272-9900
JACK TAYLOR (Owner) & Buys Men's Overcoats, Suits, Tailored Jackets, Tailored Slacks, Raincoats, Sportswear, Furnishings, Accessories, Store Displays, Fixtures, Supplies

MADISON INTERNATIONAL, INC. (FW-3 & OL)
9630 Brighton Way (m-b)
Beverly Hills, CA 90210
310-273-4787 / Fax: 310-273-4785
Sales: $1 Million-$10 Million
Website: www.madisonstyle.com
DAVID ASSIL (President & Owner)
BRIGETTE ASSIL (V.P.) & Buys Men's Footwear, Leather Goods, Men's Accessories, Hosiery, Apparel, Jewelry

PIXIE TOWN (KS)
(M & E, INC.)
400 N. Beverly Dr. (b-h)
Beverly Hills, CA 90210
323-272-6415 / Fax: 310-278-2829
BRAD LEVY-Footwear

VELAZCO'S TAILORING (MW)
317 1/2 S. Robertson Blvd. (b)
Beverly Hills, CA 90211
310-659-5606
FRED VELAZCO (Owner) & Buys Men's Ties, Belts, Store Displays, Fixtures, Supplies

ALPINE SPORTS CENTER (SG)
41530 Big Bear Blvd. (m)
Big Bear Lake, CA 92315
909-866-7541 / Fax: 909-866-8666
Website: www.alpinesportscenter.com
JIM BOLLINGMO (Owner) & Buys Active Apparel, Shorts, T-shirts, Headwear, Hosiery, Fleece

LEROY'S (CLO-3)
P.O. Box 801 (m)
598 Paine Rd.
Big Bear Lake, CA 92315
909-866-4887 / Fax: 909-866-1084
DAVID LEROY (Owner) & Buys Men's Slacks, Tops, Sweaters, Shorts, Jackets, Hosiery, Belts, Small Leather Goods, Footwear, Young Men's Urban Contemporary, Store Displays, Fixtures, Supplies

TOGGERY (WW)
115 N. Main St. (m)
Bishop, CA 93514
760-872-3211
HERB SESSUMS (President & Owner)
GARY WILLIAMSON-Western Clothing, Sportswear, Accessories, Young Men's Wear, Boys' Wear, Work Clothes

HALBY'S STORE FOR MEN & JEWELRY (MW)
217 W. Hobsonway (m)
Blythe, CA 92225
760-922-4514 / Fax: 760-922-4590
GEORGE HALBY (Owner) & Buys Men's Sportswear, Leather Apparel, Furnishings, Corrections Uniforms & Accessories, Store Displays, Fixtures, Supplies

INDIA MERCANTILE, INC. (CLO)
(YELLOW MART)
228 W. Hobson Way (m-b)
Blythe, CA 92225
760-922-4215 / Fax: 760-922-1008
Sales: $1 Million-$10 Million
JOHN FRIESTAD (President) & Buys Boys' Apparel, Boys' Footwear, Men's Footwear, Leather Goods, Men's Denim Apparel, Accessories, Hosiery, Outerwear, Sportswear, Underwear

COLLAGE (CLO)
13089 Central Ave. (m)
Boulder Creek, CA 95006
831-338-4044
LAUREL FARMER (Owner) & Buys Men's Sportswear, Sweaters, Sport Shirts, Outer Jackets, Casual Slacks, Active Apparel, Leather Apparel, Outerwear, Big & Tall Men's Wear, Footwear, Store Displays, Fixtures, Supplies

ELLIS' (CLO)
632 Main St. (m)
Brawley, CA 92227
760-344-1475
MITCHELL ELLIS (Owner) & Buys Men's Sportswear, Leather Apparel, Boys' Sportswear, Footwear, Store Displays, Fixtures, Supplies

ART'S TAILORING & FASHIONS (MW)
1010 E. Imperial Hwy. (p-m-b)
Brea, CA 92821
714-529-4888 / Fax: 714-529-9305
ART HAROUTOUNIAN (Owner)
ROBERT HAROUTOUNIAN (Mgr.) & Buys Men's Wear, Footwear, Store Displays, Fixtures, Supplies

BOARDWALK SURF-SKATE-SNOW (SP-3)
1036 Brea Mall
Brea, CA 92821
714-529-2053 / Fax: 714-529-2844
Sales: $1 Million-$10 Million
Website: www.boardwalk-skate.com
JIM BOETEL (President) & Buys Men's Apparel, Men's Accessories
Faye FREDERICKS (Gen. Mgr.) & Buys Men's Footwear, Big & Tall Men's Wear, Men's Casualwear, Denim Apparel, Accessories, Outerwear, Sportswear, Sleepwear, Swimwear

GUCCINI (MW)
2010 Brea Mall (b-h)
Brea, CA 92621
714-671-2072 / Fax: 714-671-6885
ASADULLAH ABEULLAH (Owner) & Buys Men's Overcoats, Suits, Tailored Jackets, Tailored Slacks, Raincoats, Sportswear, Sweaters, Sport Shirts, Outer Jackets, Casual Slacks, Leather Apparel, Footwear, Store Displays, Fixtures, Supplies
NOTE:-Italian Imports Only

Z CLOTHING (MW)
11677 San Vincente Blvd., #215
Brentwood, CA 90049
310-826-4500 / Fax: 310-207-6603
BARRY ZELDES-Men's Apparel

BOB'S MEN'S SHOP (MW-2)
Knott's Berry Farm (p-m-b)
Buena Park, CA 90620
714-995-1706 / Fax: 714-995-7438
Sales: $1 Million-$10 Million
DAVE ANDERSON (Owner) & Buys Men's Overcoats, Suits, Tailored Jackets, Tailored Slacks, Casual Slacks, Raincoats, Dress Shirts, Ties, Gloves, Belts, Jewelery, Young Men's Wear, Boys' Shorts, T-shirts, Surfwear, Store Displays, Fixtures and Supplies

INTERMOUNTAIN CLOTHING (CLO)
37017 Main St. (m)
Burney, CA 96013
530-335-4893
Sales: $100,001-$500,000
LORI MARTIN (Co-Owner) & Buys Men's Sportswear, Sweaters, Sport Shirts, Outer Jackets, Casual Slacks, Dress Shirts, Accessories, Belts, Robes, Underwear, Hosiery, Gloves, Big & Tall Men's Wear, 8 to 20 Boys' Wear, Store Displays, Fixtures, Supplies
DARRELL MARTIN (Co-Owner) & Buys Men's Sportswear, Sweaters, Sport Shirts, Outer Jackets, Casual Slacks, Dress Shirts, Accessories, Belts, Robes, Underwear, Hosiery, Gloves, Big & Tall Men's Wear, 8 to 20 Boys' Wear, Store Displays, Fixtures, Supplies

DURAZO'S (MW)
218 Heffernan Ave. (m)
Calexico, CA 92231
760-357-4071 / Fax: 760-357-0616
ALFONSO DURAZO (Owner) & Buys Men's Wear, Sportswear, Furnishings, Accessories, Young Men's Wear, Urban Contemporary, Store Displays, Fixtures and Supplies

ECONCENTRO (CLO-2)
201 E. 2nd St. (p-m)
Calexico, CA 92231
760-357-2437 / Fax: 760-357-6881
CLEMENTE WONG (Owner) (@ 619-357-6666)
EDI CUETO (Mgr.) & Buys Men's Sportswear, Leather Apparel, Accessories, Young Men's Wear, Boys' Wear, Store Displays, Fixtures, Supplies

GARLAN'S (CLO)
130 2nd St. (m-b)
Calexico, CA 92231
760-357-6846 / Fax: 760-357-3464
Website: www.garlans.com
CLARA GRONICH (Owner)
ROBERT GRONICH (President) & Buys Store Displays, Fixtures, Supplies
LUIS MACIAS (G.M.M.) & Buys Men's Sportswear, Furnishings, Accessories, Young Men's Wear
GRISELDA SANTIBANEZ-4 to 18 Boys' Wear

SAM ELLIS STORE, INC. (DEPT)
1st & Heffernan Ave. (m-b)
Calexico, CA 92231
760-357-3211 / Fax: 760-357-5836
Sales: $1 Million-$10 Million
MRS. ALMA ELLIS HEMS (President)
RICHARD ELLIS (Store Mgr.)
MIMI ELLIS HOLLOWAY (V.P.)
BENNY MENDEZ-Men's & Young Men's Wear, Store Displays, Fixtures, Supplies
MARK HOLLOWAY-Sport Shirts, Childrens, Young Men's
ELSA CABALLERO-Footwear

TIENDA DEL ARMY, INC. (AN)
115 E. 2nd St. (p-m)
Calexico, CA 92231
760-357-6661
Sales: $1 Million-$10 Million
JOEL REISIN (Owner)
ABRAHAM REISIN (Mgr.) & Buys Men's Sportswear, Leather Apparel, Belts, Small Leathers, Young Men's & Boys' Jeans, Footwear
WILLIAM REISIN (Mgr.) & Buys Store Displays, Fixtures, Supplies

THE FAIR STORE (DEPT)
P.O. Box 329 (p)
112 E. Main St.
Calipatria, CA 92233
760-348-5439 / Fax: 760-348-7571
Sales: $100,001-$500,000
ARTHUR VALDEZ (Co-Owner) & Buys Men's Sportswear, Headwear, Accessories, Boys' Wear, Footwear, Raincoats, Furnishings, Small Leather Goods, Belts, Store Displays, Fixtures, Supplies
LYDIA VALDEZ (Co-Owner) & Buys Footwear, Store Displays, Fixtures, Supplies

FUNKE'S (CLO)
(L. FUNKE & SON)
1417 Lincoln Ave. (p-m)
Calistoga, CA 94515
707-942-6235
Sales: $500,000-$1 Million
BRUCE DILL (Co-Owner) & Buys Men's & Young Men's Wear, Footwear, Leather Apparel, Store Displays, Fixtures, Supplies
DONNA DILL (Co-Owner) & Buys Store Displays, Fixtures, Supplies

MARINE CORPS EXCHANGE (PX)
Marine Corps Base
Camp Pendleton, CA 92055
760-725-6233 / Fax: 760-385-0446
JOE ALLISON (Retail Mgr.)
ANDREE BERGMAN (G.M.M.-Hardlines)
ROBERT COLLETTA (G.M.M.-Softlines) & Buys Men's Sportswear, Emblematic Apparel
MEG HARKINS-Boys' Sportswear
KERRI ROBLES-Sunglasses, Men's and Boys' Footwear
TERRY VANDEVER-Military Clothing

MOUNTAIN VIEW (AN)
2045 S. Bascom Ave.
Campbell, CA 95008
408-377-1362 / Fax: 408-377-1322
Sales: $500,001-$1 Million
ROGER BONNER (Owner) & Buys Apparel, Footwear

SILVER BUCKLE WESTERN WEAR (WW)
275 E. Campbell Ave.
Campbell, CA 95008
408-378-1111 / Fax: 408-374-2366
ALEX PRANDI (Owner) & Buys Men's Western Overcoats, Suits, Tailored Jackets, Tailored Slacks, Sport Coats, Sweaters, Sport Shirts, Outer Jackets, Casual Slacks, Dress Shirts, Headwear, Jewelry, Small Leather Goods, Footwear, Store Displays, Fixtures, Supplies

BIG KAHUNA (MW)
217 Capitola Ave. (m-b)
Capitola, CA 95010
831-462-5320 / Fax: 831-888-5720
Sales: $100,001-$500,000
Website: www.aloha-bigkahuna.com
AMY TOGEAZZINI (Owner) & Buys Men's Casualwear, Men's Accessories
RACHEL MAXWELL (Mgr.-Opers.)

HOT FEET (FW)
(THE BIG KAHUNA)
219 Capitola Ave. (bud-p-m-b-des)
Capitola, CA 95010
831-476-3960
Sales: $100,001-$500,000
AMY TOGEAZZINI (Owner) & Buys Men's Footwear, Men's Accessories, Hosiery

ATHLEISURE, INC. (CLO-6)
(SUN DIEGO)
5925 Priestly Dr., #120 (p)
Carlsbad, CA 92008
760-476-9201 / Fax: 760-476-9202
Sales: $1 Million-$10 Million
Website: www.sundiego.com
DAVID NASH (President) & Buys Men's Sportswear, Swimwear, Headwear, Footwear
SHARON NASH (Exec. V.P.) & Buys Store Displays, Fixtures, Supplies

H. GLADSTONE FOR MEN & WOMEN (CLO)
2945 State St. (m-b)
Carlsbad, CA 92008
760-434-4332
HOWARD GLADSTONE (Co-Owner) & Buys Men's Sportswear, Young Men's Wear, Urban Contemporary, Footwear, Store Displays, Fixtures, Supplies
CAROLE GLADSTONE (Co-Owner) & Buys Men's Sportswear, Young Men's Wear, Urban Contemporary, Footwear, Store Displays, Fixtures, Supplies

JAZZERTOGS (SP & MO)
(JAZZERCISE)
2460 Impala Dr.
Carlsbad, CA 92008
760-476-1750 / Fax: 760-602-7180
Sales: $1 Million-$10 Million
Website: www.jazzercise.com
JUDI SHEPPARD-MISSETT (President)
JOAN MARIE WALLACE-Sportswear, Activewear, Sandals, Athletic Footwear
FRANCES CORNING-Sportswear, Activewear, Sandals, Athletic Footwear

KHAKI'S MEN'S CLOTHIER (MW)
3744 The Barnyard
Carmel, CA 93923
831-625-8106 / Fax: 831-625-6515
Website: www.khakisofcarmel.com
JIM OCKERT (Owner) & Buys Men's Wear, Clothing, Furnishings, Accessories

RITTMASTER LTD. (CLO-2)
Ocean Ave. & Lincoln St. (b-des)
P.O. Box 516
Carmel, CA 93921
831-624-4088
Sales: $1 Million-$10 Million
RICHARD RITTMASTER (President)
PHILIP GEIGER (Gen. Mgr.) & Buys Men's Footwear, Leather Goods, Casualwear, Formalwear, Accessories, Outerwear, Suits
JENNIFER GEIGER-Men's Footwear, Leather Goods, Casualwear, Formalwear, Accessories, Outerwear, Suits

THE TREADMILL (SP)
111 Crossroads Blvd.
Carmel, CA 93923
831-624-4112 / Fax: 831-624-4131
Sales: $1 Million-$10 Million
SIMON ROTHHOUSE (Co-Owner)
DEBORAH ROTHHOUSE (Co-Owner) & Buys Activewear, Athletic Footwear & Accessories
KIM WILKINSON-Athletic Footwear
JUDY O'NEILL-Activewear, Accessories

MR. BIG & TALL (MW)
(HUNT-PACKWOOD, INC.)
3364 El Camino Ave. (m)
Carmichael, CA 95821
916-482-8150 / Fax: 916-482-5912
Sales: $1 Million-$10 Million
RAY PACKWOOD (President & G.M.M.) & Buys Big & Tall Men's Sportswear, Furnishings, Headwear, Belts, Footwear, Store Displays, Fixtures, Supplies

FREEWAY CLOTHING (MW)
(FREEWAY ARMY & NAVY)
21809 S. Avalon Blvd. (m)
Carson, CA 90745
310-549-8700 / Fax: 310-834-2534
Sales: $500,000-$1 Million
DON DeMARINI (Co-Owner) & Buys Men's Wear, Big & Tall Men's, Store Displays, Fixtures, Supplies
JIM BARKER (Co-Owner) & Buys Men's Wear, Big & Tall Men's, Store Displays, Fixtures, Supplies

MEN'S LAND, INC. (CLO)
20700 S. Avalon Blvd., #665
Carson, CA 90746
310-527-7901 / Fax: 310-527-7903
CARLOS-Men's Pants, Shirts, Accessories, Hosiery, Shoes

GUYS & GALS UNIFORMS (CLO)
68100 Ramon Rd.
Cathedral City, CA 92234
760-324-9170 / Fax: 760-324-2164
CHUCK McGEE (Owner) & Buys Men's Municipal, Industrial & Medical Uniforms, Footwear, Store Displays, Fixtures, Supplies

WILD OCEAN (SP)
9310 Mason Ave.
Chatsworth, CA 91311
818-341-5766 / Fax: 818-341-4234
SENDER HART (Owner)
GUY HART (V.P.) & Buys Activewear

AYOOB DEPARTMENT STORE (DEPT)
201 Main St. (m)
P.O. Box 645
Chester, CA 96020
530-258-2628
KAREN KEMP (President & Owner)
WILLIAM KEMP-Sportswear, Furnishings, Accessories, Young Men's Wear, Urban Contemporary, Boys' Wear, Store Displays, Fixtures and Supplies

CORWIN & SON CLOTHIERS (CLO)
130 W. 3rd St. (m)
Chico, CA 95928
530-342-6521 / Fax: 530-898-1111
Sales: $1 Million-$10 Million
Website: ww.corwinandson.com
DAVID CORWIN (Co-Owner) & Buys Men's Suits, Sportswear, Furnishings, Accessories, Store Displays, Fixtures, Supplies, Young Men's Wear, Urban Contemporary, Formal Wear, Footwear

WEEKEND WEARHOUSE (CLO)
1950 E. 20th St., #905
Chico, CA 95928
530-893-1567
DAN TORRES (Owner) & Buys Sportswear, Resortwear, Swimwear, Accessories

MANSOUR CLOTHING (MW)
5405 Riverside Dr. (bud)
Chino, CA 91710
909-627-1990
ANTON MANSOUR (Owner) & Buys Men's Casual Wear, Boys' Wear, Footwear, Store Displays, Fixtures, Supplies

THE HIGHLANDER (MW)
5500 Grossmont Dr., #127 (m-b)
Chula Vista, CA 91942
619-465-2300 / Fax: 619-465-4290
Sales: $1 Million-$10 Million
DAVID PHAIR (President)
PETER DANIELSON (V.P.-Display & G.M.M.) & Buys Men's Suits, Tailored Jackets, Tailored Slacks, Raincoats, Sportswear, Sweaters, Sport Shirts, Outer Jackets, Leather Apparel, Casual Slacks, Active Apparel, Furnishings, Headwear, Belts, Jewelry, Small Leather Goods, Fragrances, Store Displays, Fixtures, Supplies

WARNACO (OL)
(SPEEDO AUTHENTIC FITNESS)
6040 Bandini Blvd. (m-b)
City of Commerce, CA 90040
323-726-1262 / Fax: 323-726-5086
Sales: $100 Million-$500 Million
Website: www.speedo.com
ROGER WILLIAMS (President & C.E.O.)
PATRICIA RAMIREZ-Men's Sportswear, Accessories, Swimwear

BENISON APPAREL (CLO)
(STYLES USA, INC.)
15328 E. Valley Blvd.
City of Industry, CA 91746
626-336-8223 / Fax: 626-336-7373
Website: www.benisonapparel.com
JAY ZHANG-Activewear, Resortwear, Sportswear

CALIFORNIA - City of Industry

HOT TOPIC, INC. (CLO-420 & OL)
(HOTTOPIC.COM)
(TORRID)
18305 E. San Jose Ave. (bud-p-m)
City of Industry, CA 91748
626-839-4681 / Fax: 626-839-4686
Sales: $100 Million-$500 Million
Website: www.hottopic.com
Retail Locations: CA, AZ, NV, OR, WA, MN, NY, IL, NJ, MA, PA, DE, MD, CT, VA, OH, NM, WI, NH, MT, IN, CO, NE, GA, WV, UT, MO, TN, SC, NC, KS, TX, LA, OK, IA, LA, FL, KY, ID, SD, NY, RI, HI, VT, WV

ELIZABETH M. MCLAUGHLIN (C.E.O.)
JERRY COOK (President)
TRICIA HIGGINS (Dir.- e-Commerce)
DARRELL KINSLEY (V.P.-Store Opers.)
JASON SHELBY (V.P. & G.M.M.) & Buys Men's Tops, Bottoms, T-shirts
SCOTT MORGAN-Men's Accessories, Small Leather Goods
CARA SCHREINER-Men's Shoes
DAN HEITKEMPER-Rock T-Shirts
NOTE:-Items are music oriented.

SASSANO'S MENSWEAR (MW)
448 Pollasky Ave. (p)
Clovis, CA 93612
559-299-4430

LES SASSANO (Owner & Mgr.) & Buys Men's Sportswear, Western Wear, Leather Apparel, Work Clothes, Big & Tall Sport Shirts, Store Displays, Fixtures, Supplies

GENTLEMAN'S EXCLUSIVE (MW)
345 N. La Cadena Dr. (m)
Colton, CA 92324
909-825-0868

ABE SIMON (Owner) & Buys Men's Wear, Sportswear, Furnishings, Accessories, Store Displays, Fixtures and Supplies

AQ MENSWEAR (MW)
222 E. Compton Blvd. (m-b)
Compton, CA 90220
310-604-9954 / Fax: 310-604-3309

MISS KIM (Owner) & Buys Men's Wear, Urban Contemporary, Footwear, Store Displays, Fixtures, Supplies

HILDA'S CHILDREN'S SHOP, INC. (KS)
1001 E. Compton Blvd. (m-b)
Compton, CA 90221
310-631-7474 / Fax: 310-631-9679

VIVIAN CHANG (Owner) & Buys 8 to 20 Boys' Wear, Store Displays, Fixtures, Supplies

HOBIE SPORTS LTD. (CLO)
2831 East Coast Hwy. (p-m-b)
Corona Del Mar, CA 92625
949-675-9700 / Fax: 949-675-1427
Website: www.hobiecm.com

R. B. ALEXANDER (Owner) & Buys Men's & Boys' Swimwear, Surf Wear, Sandals
K.C. BULAR-Store Displays, Fixtures, Supplies

THE ARTS MARKET (CLO)
4000 Coronado Bay Rd.
Coronado, CA 92118
619-424-4000 / Fax: 619-424-4464

DENISE NELSON (Owner) & Buys Sportswear, Swimwear, Leisurewear

BRADYS (MW-4)
1500 Orange Ave. (b)
Coronado, CA 92118
619-437-1144 / Fax: 619-437-1497
Sales: $100,001-$500,000

RICHARD BRADY (President) & Buys Men's Sportswear, Furnishings, Headwear, Accessories, Store Displays, Fixtures, Supplies

KIPPY'S (CLO-6)
1114 Orange Ave.
Coronado, CA 92118
619-435-6218 / Fax: 619-435-6358
Website: www.kippys.com

ROBERT KIPPERMAN (Owner) & Buys Men's Wear Clothing, Overcoats, Suits, Tailored Jackets & Slacks, Raincoats, Sportswear, Sweaters, Sport Shirts, Outer Jackets, Leather Apparel, Casual Slacks, Active Apparel, Furnishings, Dress Shirts, Ties, Accessories, Belts, Jewelry, Small Leather Goods, Young Men's Shop

LA CAMISA (GS & CLO)
1201 1st St., #109 (m)
Coronado Island, CA 92118
619-435-8009

JOHN ROMERO (Owner) & Buys Men's & Boys' T-shirts, Store Supplies

BARCELINO CONTINENTAL CORP. (MW-9)
111 Lucky Dr. (b)
Corte Madera, CA 94925
415-927-7779 / Fax: 415-927-1081
Website: www.barcelino.com

SHARAM SHAREI (President) & Buys Men's Sportswear, Leather Apparel, Footwear
NOTE-Store Carries Primarily Imported European Merchandise.

LOUIS THOMAS MEN'S APPAREL (MW-2)
211 Corte Madera Town Ctr. (m-b)
Corte Madera, CA 94925
415-924-1715 / Fax: 415-924-1759

TOM MALVINO (Owner) & Buys Men's Wear, Sportswear, Furnishings, Accessories, Store Displays, Fixtures and Supplies

ALEX SEBASTIAN (MW)
Southcoast Plz. (b)
3333 S. Bristol St.
Costa Mesa, CA 92626
714-545-3821 / Fax: 714-549-1703

LANA OBER (Partner)
LARRY DOUGLAS (Partner) & Buys Men's Sportswear, Furnishings, Accessories, Store Displays, Fixtures, Supplies

ALEXANDER'S SHOE STORE (FW)
751 Baker St. (b)
Costa Mesa, CA 92626
714-751-9220 / Fax: 714-751-6214
Sales: $100,001-$500,000

BORIS ALEXANDER (President) & Buys Men's Footwear

THE GRANT BOYS, INC. (MW & SG & OL)
1750 Newport Blvd. (p-m-b)
Costa Mesa, CA 92627
949-645-3400 / Fax: 949-645-2603
Sales: $1 Million-$10 Million
Website: www.grantboys.com

RANDY J. GARELL (President)
ALEXA GARELL (V.P.) & Buys Men's Sweaters, Sport Shirts, Outer Jackets Casual Slacks, Jeans, Underwear, Hosiery, Gloves, Headwear, Belts, Young Men's Wear, Footwear, Store Displays, Fixtures, Supplies

LUBIANI II (MW-3)
1794 Newport Blvd. (h)
Costa Mesa, CA 92627
949-515-7813 / Fax: 949-515-4195
Website: www.lubiani.qpg.com

TONY LUBIANI (Owner) & Buys Men's Suits, Ties, Tailored Jackets, Accessories, Furnishings, Footwear

NORDSTROM - SOUTHERN DIV. (DEPT-6)
3333 Bristol St. (m-b)
Costa Mesa, CA 92626
714-549-8300 / Fax: 714-850-3795
Website: www.nordstrom.com

JULIE KUNS (V.P. & Gen. Mgr.)
TOM NEVELL (D.M.M.-Men's Div.-SCA, NV, & AZ) (@ 714-648-3780)
DAVID STEWART-Men's Facconible
TINA ANIVERSARO (@ 714-648-2580)-Men's Rail
JOHN SARNI (@ 714-648-2579)-Men's Sportswear Bottoms & Tops, Young Men's Brass Rail
JIM ADDIS (@ 714-648-2576)-Men's Clothing, Suits, Sportscoats
KATHLEEN CHEELY (@ 714-648-2578)-Men's Furnishings, Accessories, Headwear
STEVE DUNN-Men's Footwear
VERNON BOYD-8 to 20 Boys' Wear

CALIFORNIA - Covina

CREATE A TEE (SP)
1208 E. Cypress St.
Covina, CA 91724
626-966-8250 / Fax: 626-966-6495
Website: www.catspecialties.com
MARK BREVES (Owner) & Buys Activewear, Outerwear, Imprintable Sportswear, Knitwear, Accessories

MILLIE'S DANCEWEAR (SP-2)
129 W. Badillo St.
Covina, CA 91724
626-915-8949 / Fax: 626-915-8940
KATRINA MORAMARCO (Owner) & Buys Active Apparel, Dancewear, Related Footwear & Accessories

ALANDALES, INC. (MW)
9715 Washington Blvd. (b)
Culver City, CA 90232
310-838-5100 / Fax: 310-838-5141
Sales: $1 Million-$10 Million
GLENN LAIKEN (Owner) & Buys Men's Sportswear, Furnishings, Accessories, High End Men's Wear, Store Displays, Fixtures, Supplies
BOBBY YOSTEN-Men's Sportswear, Furnishings, Accessories, High End Men's Wear, Store Displays, Fixtures, Supplies

BERTONI'S MEN'S FASHIONS (MW-7)
131 Foxhill Mall
Culver City, CA 90230
310-391-6784 / Fax: 310-391-6785
FAROUK TAR (President) & Buys Men's Overcoats, Suits, Tailored Jackets, Tailored Slacks, Raincoats, Sportswear, Furnishings, Headwear, Accessories, Big & Tall Men's Wear, Footwear, Store Displays, Fixtures, Supplies

ICE & HUGO BOSS LAS VEGAS (CLO-5)
(HUGO BOSS)
(ICE ACCESSORY)
3615 Hayden Ave. (b-des)
Culver City, CA 90232
310-202-0900 / Fax: 310-202-6565
Sales: $1 Million-$10 Million
HARVEY KALE (President & C.E.O.)
DOTTIE CHANIN (Co-Owner) & Buys Leather Goods, Men's Casualwear, Denim Apparel, Formalwear, Accessories, Hosiery, Outerwear, Sportswear, Suits, Underwear
MARVIN CHANIN (Co-Owner) & Buys Leather Goods, Men's Casualwear, Denim Apparel, Formalwear, Accessories, Hosiery, Outerwear, Sportswear, Suits, Underwear
TRACEY FRIEDMAN (V.P.-Opers.)

SACKS, INC. (CLO-5)
(SACKS SFO)
9608 Venice Blvd. (m-b)
Culver City, CA 90232
310-559-5448 / Fax: 310-288-6013
Sales: $1 Million-$10 Million
DAVID SACKS-Men's Sportswear, Furnishings, Store Displays, Fixtures, Supplies
RANDI LEVIN-Accessories

SHERWOOD MANAGEMENT CO. (JWLY-45)
(DANIEL'S JEWELERS)
P.O. Box 3750
Culver City, CA 90231
310-665-2100 / Fax: 310-665-2101
Sales: $10 Million-$50 Million
Website: www.danielsjewelers.com
Retail Locations: CA
JOSEPH SHERWOOD (Chmn. & Dir.-Opers.)
HOWARD SHERWOOD (Co-President)
LARRY SHERWOOD (Co-President)
JOAN REESE (V.P.-Mdse.)
ROBERT OGHOUBIAN-Jewelry, Watches

DICK'S APPAREL (CLO)
39581 Rd. 128 (b)
Cutler, CA 93615
559-528-3206
Sales: $500,001-$1 Million
DEAN PARENTO (Owner) & Buys Boys' Apparel, Men's Footwear, Leather Goods, Casualwear, Denim Apparel, Accessories, Hosiery, Outerwear, Sportswear, Swimwear, Underwear, Uniforms/Workclothes

DUKE & DUCHESS, INC. (MW)
9091 Walker St. (p)
Cypress, CA 90630
714-826-5540 / Fax: 714-826-2914
Sales: $1 Million-$10 Million
ALAN DeKOVNER (Co-Owner) & Buys Men's, Young Men's & Boys' Jeans, Active Apparel, Underwear, Hosiery, Big & Tall Men's Outer Jackets, Active Apparel, Underwear, Hosiery, Footwear
FRAN DeKOVNER (Co-Owner) & Buys Men's, Young Men's & Boys' Jeans, Active Apparel, Underwear, Hosiery, Big & Tall Men's Outer Jackets, Active Apparel, Underwear, Hosiery, Footwear, Store Displays, Fixtures & Supplies

GOLDEN GALLEON BOUTIQUE (CLO-2)
34677 Golden Lantern St.
Dana Point, CA 92629
949-493-8521 / Fax: 949-498-3470
MARLA SHERMAN (Owner) & Buys Sportswear, Sandals

TOP BRASS (CLO)
34679 Golden Lantern St.
Dana Point, CA 92629
949-496-4140
JENNIFER RENTZIPERIS (Owner) & Buys Active Apparel, Swimwear, Leisurewear, Resortwear, Outerwear

DAVID LOUIS LTD., INC. (MW)
200 Hartz Ave. (m-b)
Danville, CA 94526
925-837-3300 / Fax: 925-837-3547
LOUIS PAGNINI (Owner) & Buys Men's Sportswear, Footwear, Store Displays, Fixtures, Supplies

CC DUDE'S FAMILY FOOTWEAR (FW)
605 2nd St. (p)
Davis, CA 95616
530-756-0388 / Fax: 530-756-0539
DOUG DULUDE (President & Owner) & Buys Belts, Hosiery, Footwear

JAMES ANTHONY MENSWEAR (MW)
207 F St. (m)
Davis, CA 95616
530-753-2465
NICK GOJKOVICH (Owner) & Buys Men's Wear, Sportswear, Furnishings, Accessories, Young Men's Wear, Store Displays, Fixtures and Supplies

TOPPER'S MENSWEAR (MW)
(VEEMA CORP.)
1107 Main St. (m-b)
Delano, CA 93215
661-725-9338 / Fax: 661-725-7128
Sales: $500,000-$1 Million
CHRIS GONZALES (Owner) & Buys Men's Sportswear, Leather Apparel, Dress Shirts, Ties, Men's Robes, Underwear, Headwear, Hosiery, Belts, Gloves, Footwear, Store Displays, Fixtures, Supplies

CONKLIN CLOTHING & FORMAL WEAR (MW)
100 N. L St. (m)
Dinuba, CA 93618
559-591-2422 / Fax: 559-591-2423
Sales: $100,001-$500,000
TIM CONKLIN (Owner) & Buys Men's Formal Wear, Sportswear, Leather Apparel, Furnishings, Accessories, Boys' Wear, Young Men's Wear, Urban Contemporary, Footwear, Store Displays, Fixtures, Supplies

ROBBEN'S DEPARTMENT STORE (DEPT)
111 N. 1st St. (p)
Dixon, CA 95620
707-678-5763
Sales: $100,001-$500,000
ROBERT ROBBENS (Owner) & Buys Men's Overcoats, Suits, Raincoats, Sportswear, Furnishings, Headwear, Accessories, Big & Tall Men's Wear, 8 to 20 Boys' Wear, Western Wear, Footwear, Store Displays, Fixtures, Supplies

FOLEY & BONNY, INC. (MW)
400 El Cerrito Plz. (b)
El Cerrito, CA 94530
510-524-5215
Sales: $500,000-$1 Million
Website: www.foleyandbonny.com
HERBERT FOLEY (President) & Buys Men's Overcoats, Suits, Tailored Jackets, Tailored Slacks, Raincoats, Sportswear, Furnishings, Headwear, Accessories, Footwear, Store Displays, Fixtures, Supplies

EL PASO SHOES, INC. (FW-9)
10820 Valley Mall (m-b)
El Monte, CA 91731
626-575-3455 / Fax: 626-582-7034
Sales: $1 Million-$10 Million
PAUL ALVAREZ, SR. (President) (@ 626-582-7030) & Buys Boys' Footwear, Men's Footwear, Leather Goods, Men's Accessories, Hosiery
ELIZABETH ALVAREZ (V.P.) (@ 626-582-7030)

PETE'S SPORTSWEAR, INC. (CLO)
(SPORTING THREADS)
2250 Park Pl. (m-b)
El Segundo, CA 90245
310-643-0117 / Fax: 310-643-7425
Sales: $100,001-$500,000
PETER ABRAHAM (Owner) & Buys Men's Active Apparel, Sportswear, T-shirts, Shorts, Beachwear, Swimwear, Hosiery, Headwear, Footwear, Store Displays, Fixtures, Supplies

JOE HASSAN'S (DG-3)
9117 Stockton Blvd. (p)
Elk Grove, CA 95624
916-686-1949 / Fax: 916-685-7292
Sales: $500,001-$1 Million
JOE HASSAN (Owner)
MIKE MIKBEL (Gen. Mgr.) & Buys Men's & Boys' Western Wear, Big & Tall Men's Western Wear, Young Men's Western Wear, Footwear, Work Clothes, Store Displays, Fixtures, Supplies

ALL PRO SPORTS (SP)
16919 Ventura Blvd.
Encino, CA 91316
818-981-5264 / Fax: 818-981-5265
Sales: $100,001-$500,000
Website: www.allprosportshoes.com
WIN SEVERN (Owner) & Buys Activewear, Athletic Footwear, Licensed Apparel

MEL FOX CO. (MW)
17255 Ventura Blvd.
Encino, CA 91316
818-995-1264 / Fax: 818-784-7243
ANDY FOX-Men's Pants, Shirts, Accessories

RUDNICK'S (KS)
17047 Ventura Blvd. (b)
Encino, CA 91316
818-788-9170 / Fax: 818-788-4525
Sales: $1 Million-$10 Million
MARTY RUDNICK (President) & Buys Young Men's & 8 to 20 Boys' Clothing, Sportswear, Leather Apparel, Store Displays, Fixtures, Supplies

ULTIMA MODA BY HAL (MW)
16101 Ventura Blvd. (m-b)
Encino, CA 91436
818-990-5676 / Fax: 818-981-4176
Sales: $1 Million-$10 Million
HAL STEARNS (Owner) & Buys Men's Sportswear, Furnishings, Footwear, Store Displays, Fixtures, Supplies
GARY STEARNS-Men's Sportswear, Furnishings, Footwear, Store Displays, Fixtures, Supplies
STEVE STEARNS-Men's Sportswear, Furnishings, Footwear, Store Displays, Fixtures, Supplies

KOKOPILAU (CLO)
515 2nd St.
Eureka, CA 95502
707-442-5893 / Fax: 707-442-5705
TED ANDERSON (Owner) & Buys Ladies' Sportswear, Sandals, Athletics

PHIL'S MEN'S SHOP, INC. (MW)
832 Texas St. (p-m)
Fairfield, CA 94533
707-425-4622 / Fax: 707-425-4453
Sales: $100,001-$500,000
PHIL ZUMPANO (Co-Owner) & Buys Men's Casual Slacks, Sweaters, Leather Apparel, Sport Shirts, Furnishings, Headwear, Footwear, Uniforms, Store Displays, Fixtures, Supplies
GRACE MESCHENDORF (Co-Owner) & Buys Men's Casual Slacks, Sweaters, Leather Apparel, Sport Shirts, Furnishings, Headwear, Footwear, Uniforms, Store Displays, Fixtures, Supplies
MARK MARINO (Mgr.) & Buys Men's Casual Slacks, Sweaters, Leather Apparel, Sport Shirts, Furnishings, Headwear, Footwear, Uniforms, Store Displays, Fixtures, Supplies

BASES LOADED (SP & SP)
337 E. Bidwell
Folsom, CA 95630
916-983-0633 / Fax: 916-983-0682
CHERYL CHRISTIAN-Apparel, Athletic Footwear, Outdoor Footwear, Sports Apparel, Custom Apparel

DELA ROSA'S BRIDAL & TUXEDO (SP)
319 E. Bidwell St. (m-b)
Folsom, CA 95630
916-983-3400 / Fax: 916-983-3475
Sales: $500,001-$1 Million
RICHARD DE LA ROSA (Owner) & Buys Boys' Footwear, Men's Footwear, Big & Tall Men's Wear, Formalwear, Accessories, Suits
FLORENCE DE LA ROSA (V.P.) & Buys Boys' Footwear, Men's Footwear, Big & Tall Men's Wear, Formalwear, Accessories, Suits
LIZ EISEN (Store Mgr.) & Buys Boys' Footwear, Men's Footwear, Big & Tall Men's Wear, Formalwear, Accessories, Suits

HANDLEY'S (MW)
314 E. Bidwell (m)
Folsom, CA 95630
916-983-2668
Sales: $500,000-$1 Million
DONELLA HANDLEY (Owner) & Buys Men's Tailored Slacks, Big & Tall Men's Wear, Sportswear, Dress Shirts, Ties, Underwear, Hosiery, Gloves, Western Style Headwear, Jewelry, Small Leather Goods, Young Men's Wear, 8 to 20 Boys' Wear, Footwear, Store Displays, Fixtures, Supplies

BALD MOUNTAIN MOCCASINS (FW)
P.O. Box 1363
6450 1st St., #J
Forestville, CA 95436
435-645-9037
Sales: $100,001-$500,000
DORA BALLARD (Owner) & Buys Men's Footwear

CALIFORNIA - Fort Bragg

REYNOLDS MENSWEAR (MW)
349 N. Franklin St. (bud-p-m)
Fort Bragg, CA 95437
707-964-5294
Sales: $100,001-$500,000
JAMES REYNOLDS (Owner) & Buys Men's Suits, Tailored Jackets, Sweaters, Sport Shirts, Outer Jackets, Casual Slacks, Active Apparel, Dress Shirts, Ties, Robes, Underwear, Hosiery, Headwear, Belts, Small Leather Goods, Store Displays, Fixtures, Supplies

A SNAIL'S PACE (SP-4)
8780 Warner Ave.
Fountain Valley, CA 92708
714-842-2337 / Fax: 714-842-6347
Website: www.runasnailspace.com
EDDIE JOHNSON (Co-Owner) & Buys Activewear, Athletic Footwear
DAVE REYNOLDS (Co-Owner) & Buys Activewear, Athletic Footwear

THE MEN'S WEARHOUSE (MW-482)
40650 Encyclopedia Cir.
Fremont, CA 94538
510-657-9821 / Fax: 510-623-8491
Sales: Over $1 Billion
Website: www.menswearhouse.com
Retail Locations: AL, AK, AZ, AR, CA, CO, CT, DE, FL, GA, HI, ID, IL, IN, IA, KS, KY, LA, MD, MA, MI, MN, MS, MO, NE, NV, NH, NM, NY, NC, OH, OK, OR, PA, RI, SC, SD, TN, TX, UT, VA, WA, WI
GEORGE ZIMMER (Chmn. & C.E.O.) (@ 510-777-8580, Ext.: 8591)
ERIC LANE (C.O.O. & President)
DOUG EWERT (Sr. V.P.)
NEILL DAVIS (V.P. & Treas.)
ROBERT E. ZIMMER (Sr. V.P. & Real Estate Contact)
TOM JENNINGS (V.P. & Real Estate Contact)
STEVE ROTHCHILD (Real Estate Contact)
SCOTT NORRIS (Dir.-Visual Mdsg.) (@ 510-723-8353) & Buys Store Displays, Fixtures and Supplies
TONY FINOCCHIARO-Men's Sportswear
ED STEINER (@ 713-664-3692)-Men's Dress Shirts
STEVE DONALDSON-Men's Slacks, Outerwear
JIM ZIMMER (@ 713-664-3692)-Men's Suits, Sportcoats
MIKE BATLIN-Men's Belts, Suspenders, Small Leather Goods, Footwear
SCOTT NORTH-Men's Underwear, Neckwear, Outerwear, Formal Accessories, Hosiery

ALL AMERICAN SPORTS FAN (SP-13)
3480 W. Holland St.
Fresno, CA 93722
559-221-8822 / Fax: 559-221-8830
TONY ADAMO (Owner) & Buys Licensed Apparel

DICK'S MENSWEAR & SHOES (MW & FW)
1526 Kern (b)
Fresno, CA 93706
559-233-5351
Sales: $100,001-$500,000
DICK AVAKIAN (Owner) & Buys Men's Furnishings, Headwear, Belts, Small Leather Goods, Footwear, Store Displays, Fixtures, Supplies

GOTTSCHALK'S, INC. (DEPT-63 & SP-10)
7 River Park Place E. (p-m-b)
Fresno, CA 93720
559-434-8000 / Fax: 559-434-4801
Sales: $100 Million-$500 Million
Website: www.gottschalks.com
Retail Locations: AK, CA, ID, NV, OR, WA
JOE LEVY (Chairman)
JAMES R. FAMALETTE (C.E.O.)
GARY GLADDING (Exec. V.P.-Mdsg.)
ROBERT CRIVELLO (Corp. Dir.-Visual Presentation) & Buys Store Displays, Fixtures, Supplies
FLYNN CHERNOS (D.M.M.-Men's)
DAVID MATSUDAIRA-Men's Knits, Wovens, Sweaters
MIRTA NAJIMIAN-Men's Collections, Casual Bottoms
TIM DAVIS-Men's Furnishings, Accessories, Dress Shirts, Ties
LUIS RAMIREZ-Young Men's Wear, Men's Activewear
RICHARD WRIGHT-8 to 20 Boys' Wear
ADI ALMANI-Footwear
SUSAN RUTH LEOWE-Footwear
CATHIE HIGISHIDA-Footwear
LISA COULSON-Men's Clothing, Outerwear, Big & Tall

HERB BRAUER SPORTING GOODS (SG)
6264 N. Blackstone Ave. (m)
Fresno, CA 93710
559-435-8600 / Fax: 559-435-8605
Sales: $1 Million-$10 Million
BARRY BAUER (Owner & Gen. Mgr.)
JIM CORBET-Men's Casualwear, Men's Sportswear

PATRICK JAMES, INC. (MW-15 & OL)
3457 W. Shaw Ave. (b)
Fresno, CA 93711
(Kreiss & Gordon)
559-275-4300 / Fax: 559-275-0137
Sales: $10 Million-$50 Million
Website: www.patrickjames.com
PATRICK J. MONPERE, SR. (President & C.E.O.) & Buys Men's Suits, Tailored Jackets, Tailored Slacks, Raincoats, Sportswear, Sweaters, Sport Shirts, Outer Jackets, Leather Apparel, Casual Slacks, Active Apparel, Furnishings, Ties, Robes, Underwear, Hosiery, Gloves, Headwear, Accessories, Belts, Jewelry, Small Leather Goods, Fragrances, Footwear
WILLIAM E. SOMMERS (V.P. & C.F.O.)
PAUL MONPERE (G.M.M.) & Buys Accessories
PATRICK M. MONPERE, JR. (Mgr.) & Buys Men's Suits, Tailored Jackets, Tailored Slacks, Raincoats, Sportswear, Sweaters, Sport Shirts, Outer Jackets, Leather Apparel, Casual Slacks, Active Apparel, Furnishings, Ties, Robes, Underwear, Hosiery, Gloves, Headwear, Accessories, Belts, Jewelry, Small Leather Goods, Fragrances, Footwear
TERRIE BACHMAN-Store Fixtures, Store Displays, Supplies

SUNNYSIDE DEPARTMENT STORE (WW)
3554 E. Butler Ave. (p-m)
Fresno, CA 93702
559-237-1505 / Fax: 559-237-1506
ERNA BONETTO (Owner) & Buys Western Shirts, Furnishings, Dance Wear, Footwear, Accessories

TRI-SPORT (SP)
132 W. Nees St., #111
Fresno, CA 93711
559-432-0800 / Fax: 559-432-0876
Sales: $500,001-$1 Million
Website: www.tri-sport.com
BEN MEDRANO (Owner) & Buys Activewear, Athletic Footwear

THE WILLIAMS CO. (MW)
112 E. Commonwealth (p)
Fullerton, CA 92632
714-525-7560 / Fax: 714-525-5528
Sales: $100,001-$500,000
BRIAN WILLIAMS (Owner) & Buys Men's Raincoats, Sportswear, Dress Shirts, Ties, Underwear, Hosiery, Gloves, Headwear, Belts, Small Leather Goods, Boys' Levis, Footwear, Urban Contemporary, Store Displays, Fixtures, Supplies

GARDENA DEPARTMENT STORE (DEPT)

1106 W. Gardena Blvd. (m)
Gardena, CA 90247
310-323-6242 / Fax: 310-327-5020

PHILIP SHAR (Owner) & Buys Men's Sportswear, Furnishings, Accessories, Young Men's Wear, Urban Contemporary, Footwear, Store Displays, Fixtures, Supplies

J.M. FALLAS-PAREDIS (CLO-75)

(NATIONAL STORES, INC.)
15001 S. Fidueroa St. (b)
Gardena, CA 90248
310-324-9962 / Fax: 310-324-9129
Sales: $1 Million-$10 Million

JOE FALLAS (Co-Owner)
MICHAEL FALLAS (Co-Owner)
JACK KATRI-Men's & Boys' Wear, Footwear, Store Displays, Fixtures, Supplies

ARTISTIC WEAR (SP-2)

(NOK JOZ, INC.)
1313 Glendale Galleria
Glendale, CA 91210
818-240-9640
Sales: $100,001-$500,000

NEHAMA MEGED (Owner) & Buys Activewear, Licensed Apparel, Golf Apparel

THE DISNEY STORE, INC. (CLO-623)

101 N. Brand Blvd., #1000 (m-b)
Glendale, CA 91203
818-265-3435 / Fax: 818-547-3485
Sales: $50 Million-$100 Million
Retail Locations: CA, IN, KY, MO, ME, TX, UT, VA, LA, VT, MA, IL, OH, MN, KS

PETER WHITFORD (President)
JODI ROSEBLACK (D.M.M.-Men's & Boy's Wear) & Buys Men's Accessories & Sleepwear
TANDY AVERY-Boys' Wear
MELISSA ROZANSKY-Children's Softlines

JIMMY AU'S (MW)

2168 Glendale Galleria (m)
Glendale, CA 91210
818-243-9898 / Fax: 818-243-0117
Sales: $500,000-$1 Million

JIMMY AU (Owner) & Buys Extra Short & Short Men's Overcoats, Suits, Tailored Jackets, Tailored Slacks, Sweaters, Outer Jackets, Dress Shirts, Hosiery, Belts, Jewelry, Store Displays, Fixtures, Supplies

POST & M CO. (CLO)

6218 San Fernando Rd.
Glendale, CA 91201
818-637-7810 / Fax: 818-637-7811

MASARU YAMASE (Owner)
KAY KANESHIRO-Men's & Boys' Contemporary Sportswear, Beachwear, Active Apparel, Swimwear, Store Displays, Fixtures & Supplies

ROBBINS BROTHERS (JWLY-7)

P.O. Box 4097
Glendale, CA 91222
800-610-7464 / Fax: 818-265-5498
Sales: $10 Million-$50 Million
Website: www.robbinsbros.com

STEVE ROBBINS (President & C.E.O.) & Buys Jewelry
SALLY FURRER (V.P.-Mdse.) & Buys Jewelry

THREE DAY SUITS BROKER (MW-10)

1222 E. Colorado Ave. (m)
Glendale, CA 91205
818-703-7848
Sales: $1 Million-$10 Million

SAM SHAHINIAN-Men's Sportswear, Furnishings, Headwear, Accessories, Young Men's Wear, Store Displays, Fixtures, Supplies
LEO SHAHINIAN-Men's Sportswear, Furnishings, Headwear, Accessories, Young Men's Wear, Store Displays, Fixtures, Supplies

BILLY'S COMFORT SHOES (FW)

1185614 Balboa Blvd. (bud-p-b)
Granada Hills, CA 91344
818-242-8832 / Fax: 818-363-6124
Sales: $100,001-$500,000

BILL STANLEY (Owner) & Buys Boys' Footwear, Men's Footwear, Leather Goods, Watches, Men's Accessories, Men's Apparel, Hosiery

BRITTON & BRITTON, INC. (MW-4)

(BASELINE)
P.O. Box 2170 (bud)
6857 Itchy Acres Rd.
Granite, CA 95740
916-791-4139
Sales: $500,000-$1 Million

ALFRED BRITTON (President) & Buys Men's Sport Shirts, Outer Jackets, Active Apparel, T-shirts
PAT BRITTON (V.P.) & Buys Store Displays, Fixtures, Supplies

ARCH RIVAL, INC. (SP-2)

150 Bon Air Ctr.
Greenbree, CA 94904
415-461-6588 / Fax: 415-461-6417

JOEL FRUCHTMAN (Owner) (@ 415-456-4469)
DEBBIE MAXINE (Mgr.) & Buys Activewear, Athletic Footwear

CONTINENTAL WESTERN WEAR (WW)

8972 E. Lacey Blvd. (p)
Hanford, CA 93230
559-584-6638 / Fax: 559-584-5202

GUY BADASCI, SR. (President)
JOE BADASCI-Men's Western Suits, Tailored Jackets, Tailored Slacks, Sweaters, Active Apparel, Dress Shirts, Ties, Hosiery, Gloves, Belts, Jewelry, Small Leather Goods, Fragrances, Leather Apparel, Big & Tall Men's Western Wear, Boys' Western Clothing, Footwear, Store Displays, Fixtures, Supplies

VAN ANDEL'S, INC. (MW)

210 W. 7th St. (m)
Hanford, CA 93230
559-584-8319 / Fax: 559-584-9673
Sales: $100,001-$500,000
Website: www.vanandels.com

JOHN VAN ANDEL (Owner) & Buys Men's Wear, Sportswear, Footwear, Furnishings, Accessories, Young Men's Wear, Store Displays, Fixtures and Supplies
VICTOR CAMPOS (Mgr.) & Buys Men's Wear, Sportswear, Footwear, Furnishings, Accessories, Young Men's Wear, Store Displays, Fixtures and Supplies

WORKINGMAN'S STORE FOR GUYS & GALS (CLO)

P.O. Box 144 (m)
216 N. Irwin
Hanford, CA 93232
559-584-3914 / Fax: 559-584-1598
Sales: $500,000-$1 Million

ROBERT L. TOS (President)
TIM KOELEWYN (Asst. Mgr.) & Buys Men's Sportswear, Sweaters, Outer Jackets, Casual Slacks, Underwear, Hosiery, Gloves, Headwear, Sport Shirts, Western Wear, Footwear, Store Displays, Fixtures, Supplies

SAV-ON SURPLUS (MW)

12711 Hawthorne Blvd. (p)
Hawthorne, CA 90250
310-675-8782 / Fax: 310-675-8468
Sales: $500,000-$1 Million

FARLEY MANILL (President) & Buys Men's Work Clothes
SCOTT WHITMAN-Young Men's Wear, Urban Contemporary, Boys' Wear, Footwear

WESTERN SURPLUS (WW)

12251 Hawthorne Blvd.
Hawthorne, CA 90250
310-675-3349 / Fax: 310-675-2476

NORMAN ZALBEN (Owner)
FELIX HOFFMAN-Men's Western Wear, Clothing, Accessories, Furnishings, Footwear

CALIFORNIA - Hayward

MERVYN'S CALIFORNIA (DEPT-267)
(TARGET CORP.)
22301 Foothill Blvd. (p)
Hayward, CA 94541
(Associated Mdsg. Corp.)
510-727-3000 / Fax: 510-727-3003
Sales: $4 Billion
Website: www.mervyns.com
Retail Locations: AZ, CA, CO, MI, MN, NV, OK, OR, TX, UT, WA
DIANA NEAL (President)
GEORGE SHERMAN (Sr. V.P.-Stores)
PETE DALEIDEN (V.P. Merch. Mgr.-Men's)
GEOFF SORRICK-Men's Pants & Shorts
RICHARD RIGOWSKI-Men's Activewear, Young Men's, Outerwear
SIMON BLACK-Men's Knits, Wovens, Sweaters
JESSE ROMERO-Men's Dress Furnishings, Basics
KEISH CARNAHAN-Sleepwear, Hosiery
JUDY HOWARD (V.P. Merch. Mgr.-Children's)
OPEN-Infant Boys
STACEY RINEY-Infant, Toddler Sleepwear, Basics, Accessories
KRISTIN LIGHTTISER-Toddler Boys
ILIANA WISE-Boys'/Students' 4-20
ALINE TEWES (V.P.-Merch. Mgr.-Shoes)
SARAH BARROW-Adult Athletic & Men's Fashion Footwear
LAURA NAWROCKI-Children's Footwear

SELIX FORMAL WEAR (MW-19)
(DICK BRUHN, INC.)
P.O. Box 29 (b)
22423 Foothill Blvd.
Hayward, CA 94543
510-881-0333 / Fax: 510-881-8387
Sales: $100,001-$500,000
Website: www.selix.com
Retail Locations: CA, NV
RICHARD BRUHN (Owner)
JOHN HORNEY (Real Esate Contact) & Buys Men's & Boys' Formal Wear, Men's Furnishings, Accessories, Footwear, Store Displays, Fixtures, Supplies

SHIEKH, LLC (FW-63)
(SHIEKH SHOES)
2247 Commerce Pl. (bud-p-b-des)
Hayward, CA 94545
510-732-8900 / Fax: 510-732-2955
Sales: $10 Million-$50 Million
Website: www.shiekhshoes.com
Retail Locations: CA
SHIEKH ELLAHI (President & Real Estate Contact)
Alex KIM-Footwear
NELSON CHOY-Apparel, Footwear

BEACH CITIES CYCLE (SP-2)
219 Pacific Coast Hwy.
Hermosa Beach, CA 90254
310-318-6030
Sales: $100,001-$500,000
BRIAND LINDQUIST (Owner)
CARL PEDERSEN (G.M.M.)
RUSSEL DOCKERY-Biking Apparel & Accessories

BEACHY KEEN BAY (SP)
1038 Hermosa Ave.
Hermosa Beach, CA 90254
310-376-4416 / Fax: 310-376-0511
GREG STAGER (Owner)
DONNA MITCHELL (Mgr.) & Buys Leisurewear, Resortwear, Swimwear, Beachwear

GLOBAL SOUL (CLO)
424 Pacific Coast Hwy.
Hermosa Beach, CA 90254
310-374-0299
GREG ELLINGSON-Accessories, Footwear, Hats, Apparel, Men's Surf & Swimwear, Men's Apparel, Private Label, Skate Apparel, T-shirts, Imprinted Sportswear, Urban Streetwear

GREEKO'S SANDALS (MW)
1120 Hermosa Ave. (p)
Hermosa Beach, CA 90254
310-374-9040 / Fax: 310-376-3110
Sales: $100,001-$500,000
STEVE YERKES (Owner) & Buys Men's Sportswear, Belts, Jewelry, Headwear, Footwear

BOOT HILL BOOTERY (FW)
14377 Main St. (m-b)
Hesperia, CA 92345
760-949-0288
Sales: $500,001-$1 Million
MARK CULLENS (Owner) & Buys Men's & Boys' Footwear, Leather Goods, Men's Accessories, Hosiery

ANTENNA (CLO)
6363 Hollywood Blvd.
Hollywood, CA 90028
323-463-5363 / Fax: 323-463-3863
KEN BATEMAN-Men's Clothing & Furnishings

TUXEDO CENTER, INC. (MW-2)
7401 Sunset Blvd. (m-b)
Hollywood, CA 90046
323-874-4200 / Fax: 323-874-2495
GARY MARTIN (Owner) & Buys Men's, Young Men's & Boys' Tuxedos, Men's Furnishings, Accessories, Footwear, Store Displays, Fixtures, Supplies

BEACH STORE (SP)
200 Main St., #114
Huntington Beach, CA 92648
714-969-6653
Website: www.beachstorehb.com
LEIA CHA (Owner) & Buys Sportswear, Beachwear, Swimwear, Dancewear, Clubwear, Footwear, Accessories

DANCEWORKS DANCEWEAR (SP)
7174 Edinger Ave.
Huntington Beach, CA 92647
714-847-8820 / Fax: 714-847-7815
SANDY BLAIN (Owner) & Buys Dancewear, Activewear, Related Footwear

DEWEY RUDOLPH & SONS (MW)
16531 Bolsa Chica St., #310 (m-b)
Huntington Beach, CA 92649
714-377-0212 / Fax: 714-377-9233
DEWEY RUDOLPH (Owner) & Buys Men's Sportswear, Furnishings, Accessories, Footwear, Store Displays, Fixtures, Supplies

ELECTRIC CHAIR (CLO-3)
(SUNLINE ELECTRIC CHAIR)
410 Main St.
Huntington Beach, CA 92648
714-536-0784 / Fax: 714-960-0272
Website: www.electricchair.com
ABDUL MEMON (President)
SHANNON COFFIELD-Tailored Jackets, Tailored Slacks, Sportswear, Dress Shirts, Ties, Belts, Young Men's Wear, Urban Contemporary
RACHEL PULIKOLSKY-Men's Shoes

JACK'S SURF BOARDS (SG)
101 Main St.
Huntington Beach, CA 92648
714-536-4516 / Fax: 715-536-7861
Sales: $1 Million-$10 Million
Website: www.jackssurf.com
KIRA FUKUDA (President & Gen. Mgr.)
BOBBY ABEDELFATTAH-Men's Apparel, Swimwear

KOOKIES (CLO)
17214 Pacific Coast Hwy. (m)
Huntington Beach, CA 92649
562-592-2388
STEVE M. PAVLICK (Owner) & Buys Men's & Boys' Activewear, Swimwear, Accessories, Footwear

BUY RITE (MW)
(CHARLES REIFF CORP.)
6434 Pacific Blvd. (p-m)
Huntington Park, CA 90255
323-587-4108 / Fax: 323-587-1261
Sales: $500,000-$1 Million
JACOB GIVERTZ (V.P.) & Buys Men's & Boys' Sportswear, Activewear, Furnishings, Store Displays, Fixtures, Supplies

MODERN CASUALS (CLO)
6433 Pacific Blvd. (p)
Huntington Park, CA 90255
213-622-3236 / Fax: 323-583-0200
Sales: $100,001-$500,000
STEVE KIM (Owner) & Buys Men's & Boys' Dress Pants, Men's Suits, Casual Slacks, Gloves, Jeans, Dress Shirts, Sport Shirts, Underwear, Hosiery, Urban Contemporary, Store Displays, Fixtures, Supplies

TRES HERMANOS CLOTHING STORE (MW-16)
6801 Pacific Blvd.
Huntington Park, CA 90255
323-585-1618 / Fax: 323-585-1674
Sales: $1 Million-$10 Million
MONIR AWADA (Owner & Real Estate Contact) & Buys Men's Suits, Tailored Jackets, Tailored Slacks, Sportswear, Furnishings, Headwear, Belts, Young Men's & Boys' Wear, Men's & Boys' Leather Apparel, Store Displays, Fixtures, Supplies

BONNIE'S HAPPY LOOK (CLO)
P.O. Box 1555 (p-m)
54320 N. Circle Dr.
Idyllwild, CA 92549
909-659-3313
BONNIE WOLF (Owner) & Buys Men's & Young Men's Wear, Footwear

YELLOW MART STORE (MW-2)
82850 Miles Aves (m)
Indio, CA 92201
760-347-1107 / Fax: 760-347-6838
BRUCE JERNISAN (Owner) & Buys Jeans, Sweaters, Sport Shirts, Casual Slacks, Active Apparel, Headwear, Hosiery, Underwear, Belts, T-shirts, Shorts

BLACK KNIGHTS SHOE (FW)
139 S. Market St. (m-des)
Inglewood, CA 90301
310-671-0786
Sales: $100,001-$500,000
KIM SANG (Owner) & Buys Boys' Footwear, Men's Footwear
CLAUDIA BARAJAS (Mgr.) & Buys Boys' Footwear, Men's Footwear

JEAN JUNGLE (CLO-4)
(CASUAL TEXTILE)
713 S. Hindry Ave. (m-b)
Inglewood, CA 90301
310-670-4685 / Fax: 310-670-4687
OLIVER HAUG (Owner) & Buys Men's & Young Men's Sportswear, Active Apparel, Casual Wear, Footwear, Wear

COUNTRY FEED BARN (CLO)
1345 3rd St. (m)
Inyokern, CA 93527
760-377-4532
NORMA MARQUARDT (Owner) & Buys Western Apparel & Related Accessories For Men's, Men's & Young Men's Wear, Store Displays, Fixtures and Supplies

BEACH ACCESS, INC. (SP-4)
17801 Sky Park Circle
Irvine, CA 92614
949-224-0765 / Fax: 949-224-0767
Sales: $100,001-$500,000
TOM MOORE (Owner)
DAVE MORELAND-Apparel, Licensed Apparel, Athletic Footwear, Custom Apparel

PRODUCT RESOURCES, INC. (MW)
2712 McGaw Ave.
Irvine, CA 92614
949-622-5122 / Fax: 949-622-9082
MARTY HAMBURGER (Owner) & Buys Store Displays, Fixtures, Supplies
MIKE DeBONO (President) & Buys Men's & Boys' Sportswear

TILLY'S SPORTSWEAR (CLO-36 & OL)
10 Whateny (p)
Irvine, CA 92618
949-609-5599 / Fax: 949-609-5500
Website: www.tillys.com
HEZY SHAKED (Owner) & Buys Men's & Boys' Sportswear, Activewear, Accessories, Footwear

ASCOT SHOP (MW)
7750 Girard Ave. (b-h)
La Jolla, CA 92037
858-454-4222 / Fax: 858-454-4331
Sales: $1 Million-$10 Million
WILLIAM WHITE (President) & Buys Footwear, Men's Suits, Tailored Jackets, Tailored Slacks, Raincoats
BART O'ROURKE-Men's Suits, Tailored Jackets, Tailored Slacks, Raincoats
DAVID SEARLE-Men's Suits, Tailored Jackets, Tailored Slacks, Raincoats, Furnishings, Accessories, Headwear, Belts, Store Displays, Fixtures
JACK BENNETT-Store Supplies

CUSTOM SHIRTS OF LA JOLLA, INC. (CLO)
7872 Girard Ave. (b-des)
La Jolla, CA 92037
858-459-6147 / Fax: 858-459-4703
Sales: $500,001-$1 Million
GERHARD BENDL (President) & Buys Men's Footwear, Leather Goods, Casualwear, Denim Apparel, Formalwear, Accessories, Hosiery, Sportswear, Sportswear, Suits
ELIZABETH BENDL (V.P.) & Buys Men's Footwear, Leather Goods, Casualwear, Denim Apparel, Formalwear, Accessories, Hosiery, Sportswear, Sportswear, Suits

GENTLEMAN'S QUARTER, INC. (CLO)
1200 Prospect St. (b-des)
La Jolla, CA 92037
858-459-4253 / Fax: 858-459-8581
Sales: $1 Million-$10 Million
RUBY EICHLER (President) & Buys Men's Footwear, Leather Goods, Casualwear, Denim Apparel, Formalwear, Accessories, Hosiery, Outerwear, Sleepwear, Sportswear, Suits, Swimwear, Underwear
ROMY EICHLER (Gen. Mgr.) & Buys Men's Footwear, Leather Goods, Casualwear, Denim Apparel, Formalwear, Accessories, Hosiery, Outerwear, Sleepwear, Sportswear, Suits, Swimwear, Underwear

SHOE WAREHOUSE (FW-2)
(BLACK KNIGHT SPORT)
17307 Valley Blvd. (m-b-des)
La Puente, CA 91744
626-913-7773
Sales: $1 Million-$10 Million
BRUCE LEE (Partner) & Buys Boys' Footwear, Men's Footwear, Hosiery
KAREN LEE (Partner) & Buys Boys' Footwear, Men's Footwear, Hosiery

McCAULOU'S, INC. (DEPT-14)
(DAVID M. BRIAN)
3512 Mt. Diablo Blvd. (bud-p)
Lafayette, CA 94549
925-283-3380 / Fax: 925-932-3158
Sales: $10 Million-$50 Million
DAVE McCAULOU (President) & Buys Store Displays, Fixtures, Supplies
LYNN ZIMMER (Mdse. Mgr.) & Buys Men's Sportswear, Furnishings, Accessories, 8 to 20 Young Men's & Boys' Wear
DENISE WONG (@ 510-947-1991)-Men's Sportswear, Furnishings, Accessories, 8 to 20 Young Men's & Boys' Wear

INDIAN SUMMER STORE (CLO)
686 S. Coast Hwy. (m)
Laguna Beach, CA 92651
949-494-2595 / Fax: 949-494-2282
DENNIS McBRIDE (Owner) & Buys Sportswear, Dress Shirts, Ties, Underwear, Hosiery, Belts, Small Leather Goods, Store Displays, Fixtures and Supplies

MERRILEE'S (CLO-2)
790 S. Coast Hwy.
Laguna Beach, CA 92651
949-497-6743 / Fax: 949-497-8701
MERRILEE MADRIGAL (Owner) & Buys Beachwear, Swimwear, Sandals, Beach Footwear

DUKES MEN'S STORE (MW)
2 Lakewood Center Mall (m)
Lakewood, CA 90712
562-633-0046 / Fax: 562-633-9576
Sales: $500,001-$1 Million
ABDEL KARIM MILBES (President) & Buys Men's Footwear, Fragrances, Leather Goods, Men's Apparel, Men's Big & Tall Apparel, Men's Casualwear, Men's Designer Apparel, Men's Formalwear, Men's Accessories, Men's Hosiery, Men's Outerwear, Men's Sportswear, Men's Suits, Young Men's Apparel

WHITES SURPLUS STORES (DEPT-2)
564 West Ave., #I (p)
Lancaster, CA 93534
661-942-2091
Sales: $100,001-$500,000
SERGIO BLANCO (Owner) & Buys Men's Work Clothes, Overcoats, Raincoats, Sweaters, Sport Shirts, Leather Apparel, Underwear, Hosiery, Gloves, Belts, Boys' Shirts, Sportswear, Accessories, Footwear

BAILEY'S (MW-2 & OL & MO)
P.O. Box 550 (m)
44650 Hwy. 101
Laytonville, CA 95454
707-984-6133
Sales: $10 Million-$50 Million
Website: www.baileys-online.com
WILLIAM G. BAILEY (President)
MIKE WILWAND (V.P.-Purch.) & Buys Men's Apparel, Men's Accessories, Footwear

GEIGER'S (DEPT)
(LAYTONVILLE MERCANTILE CO.)
P.O. Box 3 (p)
Laytonville, CA 95454
707-984-6913 / Fax: 707-984-6914
MICHAEL BRAUGHT (Owner) & Buys Men's & Boys' Underwear, Hosiery, Store Displays, Fixtures, Supplies

DIAMOND D BAR WESTERN STORE (WW)
615 5th St.
Lincoln, CA 95648
916-645-8710 / Fax: 916-645-7029
Website: www.diamondbar.qpg.com
GAYLE LANG (Owner) & Buys Western Wear, Work Boots, Leather Jackets, Boots, Outerwear, Hats, Cowboy Shirts
DAVID BORLONGAN-Western Wear, Work Boots, Leather Jackets, Boots, Outerwear, Hats, Cowboy Shirts

BAUGHMAN'S (WW-2)
(CHRISTESEN'S)
2029 1st St. (m-b)
Livermore, CA 94550
925-447-5767 / Fax: 925-447-0578
Website: www.baughmans.com
RORY JANES (Owner) & Buys Men's Leather Apparel, Western Wear, Boys' Western Wear, Footwear, Urban Contemporary,Store Displays, Fixtures, Supplies

DOM'S OUTDOOR OUTFITTERS (DEPT & OL)
1870 First St. (p)
Livermore, CA 94550
925-447-9629 / Fax: 925-447-0195
Website: www.domsoutdoor.com
JEFF SACCULLO (G.M.M.) & Buys Men's Overcoats, Sweaters, Sport Shirts, Outer Jackets, Gloves, Belts, Levis, Work Clothes, Big & Tall Men's Wear, Boys' Clothing, Accessories, Camouflage Military Clothing, Footwear, Store Displays, Fixtures, Supplies

JOE HASSAN'S CLOTHING & WESTERN WEAR (DG-3)
100 N. Sacramento St. (p)
Lodi, CA 95240
209-369-6500 / Fax: 209-369-6328
Sales: $1 Million-$10 Million
JOE HASSAN (Owner) & Buys Men's Footwear
JIM HASSAN (G.M.M.) & Buys Men's Tailored Jackets, Tailored Slacks, Raincoats, Sweaters, Sport Shirts, Dress Shirts, Underwear, Gloves, Headwear, Belts, Small Leather Goods, Big & Tall Men's Wear, Young Men's Wear, Boys' Clothing, Leather Apparel, Footwear, Store Displays, Fixtures, Supplies

LLOYD'S OF LONE PINE, INC. (WW)
P.O. Box 763 (p-m-b)
141 N. Main St.
Lone Pine, CA 93545
760-876-4371 / Fax: 760-876-4212
Sales: $100,001-$500,000
ROD AYERS (Owner) & Buys Men's & Boys' Western Wear, Store Displays, Fixtures, Supplies, Footwear
ARLENE MAYFIELD (Mgr.) & Buys Footwear

BODELL'S SHOES, INC. (FW)
490 Viking Way (b)
Long Beach, CA 90808
562-425-1426
Sales: $500,001-$1 Million
Website: www.bodellshoes.com
LEWIS BODELL (President)
RICHARD BODELL (V.P.) & Buys Boys' Footwear, Men's Footwear, Hosiery, Boys' Footwear

DE SANTIS STYLES FOR MEN (MW)
3840 Atlantic Ave. (b)
Long Beach, CA 90807
562-428-3927 / Fax: 562-424-9429
Sales: $100,001-$500,000
EDWARD DE SANTIS (Owner) & Buys Men's Suits, Tailored Jackets, Tailored Slacks, Raincoats, Sweaters, Sport Shirts, Dress Shirts, Ties, Robes, Hosiery, Belts, Jewelry, Fragrances

LITTLE BARNEY'S, INC. (MW)
5527 Stearns St. (m-b)
Long Beach, CA 90815
562-594-4797
Sales: $500,000-$1 Million
GEORGE AMARANTOS (President) & Buys Men's Suits, Overcoats, Tailored Jackets, Tailored Slacks, Raincoats, Big & Tall Men's Wear, Men's Sweaters, Sport Shirts, Outer Jackets, Leather Apparel, Casual Slacks, Active Apparel, Men's Furnishings, Accessories

UMBERTO INTERNATIONAL CLOTHIER (MW)
2141 N. Bellflower Blvd. (b)
Long Beach, CA 90815
562-597-0391 / Fax: 562-597-0276
Sales: $1 Million-$10 Million
Website: www.umbertoclothing.net
UMBERTO AUTORE (Owner) & Buys Leather Goods, Men's Casualwear, Denim Apparel, Formalwear, Accessories, Hosiery, Outerwear, Sportswear, Suits, Swimwear, Underwear
TOM JOHNSON-Leather Goods, Men's Casualwear, Denim Apparel, Formalwear, Accessories, Hosiery, Outerwear, Sportswear, Suits, Swimwear, Underwear

CASSARA BROTHERS CLOTHIERS (MW-2)
981 N. San Antonio Rd. (m-b)
Los Altos, CA 94022
650-948-4335 / Fax: 650-948-1142
Website: www.cassarabrothers.com
MARIO CASSARA (President) & Buys Men's Suits, Sportswear, Ties, Hosiery, Big & Tall Men's Sizes, Footwear, Store Displays, Fixtures, Supplies

DENNIS RICH (MW)
334 Main St.
Los Altos, CA 94022
650-941-3350
DENNIS RICH (Owner) & Buys Men's Apparel

THAI SILKS (CLO)
252 State St. (m-b)
Los Altos, CA 94022
650-948-8611 / Fax: 650-948-3426
Sales: $10 Million-$50 Million
Website: www.thaisilks.com
DEANNE M. SHUTE (Owner) & Buys Men's Sleepwear, Men's Underwear
ROSI VALQUI (Mgr.-Retail Opers.)
MARY CARTER (Sls. Mgr.) & Buys Men's Apparel, Hosiery, Sleepwear, Underwear

AARDVARK'S ODD ARK, INC. (CLO-5)
7579 Melrose Ave. (bud)
Los Angeles, CA 90046
323-655-6769 / Fax: 323-655-1162
Sales: $1 Million-$10 Million
JOSEPH STROMEI (Owner) & Buys Men's & Young Men's Overcoats, Suits, Tailored Jackets, Tailored Slacks, Raincoats, Sweaters, Sport Shirts, Outer Jackets, Leather Apparel, Casual Slacks, Active Apparel, Furnishings, Headwear, Accessories, Store Displays, Fixtures, Supplies

ACADEMY AWARD CLOTHES (MW)
821 S. Los Angeles St. (b)
Los Angeles, CA 90014
213-622-9125 / Fax: 213-622-8719
PETER D. KAPLAN (President) & Buys Men's Overcoats, Suits, Tailored Jackets, Raincoats, Formal Wear, Tailored Slacks, Dress Shirts, Ties, Hosiery, Belts, Store Displays, Fixtures, Supplies

ADRIAN IN CALIFORNIA (CLO)
P.O. Box 15517
425 W. 11th St.
Los Angeles, CA 90015
213-746-5230
ADRIAN DAMENSTEIN (President) & Buys Men's Apparel, Boys' Apparel, Men's Footwear, Boys' Footwear, Accessories

AGAPE UNIFORM CO. (SP)
3606 W. Washington Blvd. (m-b)
Los Angeles, CA 90018
323-731-0621 / Fax: 323-731-0690
Sales: $500,001-$1 Million
MOZELL ENGLISH (President) & Buys Boys' Apparel, Men's Footwear, Leather Goods, Accessories, Hosiery, Uniforms/Workclothes

AL WEISS MEN'S CLOTHING (MW)
942 S. Maple Ave. (m)
Los Angeles, CA 90015
213-622-0986 / Fax: 213-622-3356
MARIO WEISS (President) & Buys Men's Sportswear, Accessories, Footwear, Store Displays, Fixtures, Supplies

AMERICAN RAG CIE (CLO-4)
150 S. La Brea Ave. (b)
Los Angeles, CA 90036
323-935-3154 / Fax: 323-935-2238
MARK WERTS (Owner)
STEPHAINE SEELEY (Head Buyer) & Buys Men's Overcoats, Suits, Tailored Jackets, Tailored Slacks, Sweaters, Activewear, Leather Jackets, Furnishings, Accessories, 8 to 20 Boys' Wear, Footwear, Store Displays, Fixtures, Supplies

ANGEL SHOE (FW)
2206 Cesare Chavez Ave. (m-b-des)
Los Angeles, CA 90033
323-264-8629
Sales: $100,001-$500,000
SONYA GONZALEZ (Owner) & Buys Boys' Footwear, Men's Footwear

AVEDON, INC. (MW)
8620 Melrose (b)
Los Angeles, CA 90069
310-659-9606 / Fax: 310-659-5447
RENEE AVEDON (Owner) & Buys Men's Overcoats, Suits, Tailored Jackets, Tailored Slacks, Raincoats, Sweaters, Sport Shirts, Outer Jackets, Casual Slacks, Active Apparel, Dress Shirts, Ties, Hosiery, Belts, Jewelry, Store Displays, Fixtures, Supplies

BALI COLLECTION (CLO)
953 Santee St.
Los Angeles, CA 90015
213-624-1280 / Fax: 213-624-6816
HARRY JETHANI-Sportswear, Active Apparel, Swimwear

BELL SALES CO., INC. (DEPT)
910 W. Martin Luther King Jr. Blvd. (p-m-b)
Los Angeles, CA 90037
323-234-7883 / Fax: 323-234-8911
Sales: $1 Million-$10 Million
STEPHEN R. BELL (President) & Buys Men's Ties, Underwear, Hosiery, Gloves, Headwear, Belts
NEIL M. KULUVA (V.P.) & Buys Men's Overcoats, Suits, Tailored Jackets, Tailored Slacks, Raincoats, Big & Tall Men's Wear, Sweaters, Sport Shirts, Outer Jackets, Leather Apparel, Casual Slacks, Active Apparel, Dress Shirts, Robes, Footwear

BENO'S (CLO-2)
1512 Santee St. (m)
Los Angeles, CA 90015
213-748-2222 / Fax: 213-741-2329
Sales: $1 Million-$10 Million
Website: www.benos501.com
MAX SALTER (Chmn.)
LARRY JOHNSON (President) & Buys Boys' Apparel, Leather Goods, Big & Tall Men's Wear, Casualwear, Denim Apparel

BERNARDI OF CALIFORNIA (MW-2)
(BERNARD CLOTHES)
(DARMANI BY BERNARD)
3137 S. Alameda St. (m-b)
Los Angeles, CA 90058
323-232-0537 / Fax: 323-232-4001
Sales: $1 Million-$10 Million
BERNARD REIN (President) & Buys Men's Casualwear, Formalwear, Accessories, Outerwear, Sportswear, Suits

BERNINI, INC. (MW-35)
10401 Venice Blvd. (m-b)
Los Angeles, CA 90034
310-815-1786 / Fax: 310-842-7860
Website: www.bernini.com
Retail Locations: CA, CO, DC, FL, GA, HI, IL, MI, NV, NJ, NY, PA
JOSEPH TAR (Owner) & Buys Store Displays, Fixtures, Supplies
STEVEN HILL-Men's Sportswear, Denim Sportswear, Leather Apparel, Furnishings, Accessories, Young Men's Wear, Footwear
YOUSUF TAR (Real Estate Contact)

THE BIG MAN'S SHOP (MW)
1069 N. Fairfax Ave. (m)
Los Angeles, CA 90046
323-656-4460 / Fax: 323-656-7134
Sales: $500,001-$1 Million
Website: www.bigmansshop.com
TONY INCORVAIA (Partner) & Buys Big & Tall Men's Wear, Store Displays, Fixtures, Supplies
IRVING KERZNER (Partner) & Buys Big & Tall Men's Wear, Store Displays, Fixtures, Supplies

THE BROADWAY WEARHOUSE (CLO-2)
(SY ZAGHA, INC.)
(HOMBRE L.A.)
333 S. Broadway (p)
Los Angeles, CA 90013
213-625-0153 / Fax: 213-617-0911
SY ZAGHA (Owner) & Buys Men's Sportswear, 8 to 20 Young Men's & Boys' Wear, Urban Contemporary, Store Displays, Fixtures, Supplies

BROOKLYN PANTS (MW)
2226 Ceasar Chavez (m-b)
Los Angeles, CA 90033
323-780-1909 / Fax: 323-780-2831
HUDA CHAHINE (President) & Buys Store Displays, Fixtures, Supplies
HUSSCINE CHAHINE-Men's & Boys' Jeans, Belts

CALIFORNIA - Los Angeles

BUSONI MEN'S CLOTHING (MW)
8275 Los Angeles Ave. (m)
Los Angeles, CA 90014
213-623-6404 / Fax: 213-627-0027
Website: www.lamenswear.com
MICHAEL DAMAVANDI-Men's Sportswear, Furnishings, Accessories, Formal Wear, Store Displays, Fixtures, Supplies

CABARET (MW)
1331 Maple Ave. (p-m)
Los Angeles, CA 90015
213-749-8535 / Fax: 213-749-2770
MOREL NAIM (Partner) & Buys Men's Casual Wear, Store Displays, Fixtures, Supplies

CALIFORNIA SURPLUS MART (AN)
6263 Santa Monica Blvd. (p)
Los Angeles, CA 90038
323-465-5525 / Fax: 323-465-2418
OVI LALO (Mgr.) & Buys Casual Clothes, Levis For Men, Military Surplus Clothing For Men, Sportswear, Leather Apparel, Furnishings, Accessories, Headwear, Footwear, Store Displays, Fixtures, Supplies

CANDY CANE'S CHILDREN'S SHOP (KS)
2310 E. Cesar Chavez Ave. (m-b)
Los Angeles, CA 90033
323-268-7097 / Fax: 323-268-7099
STEPHANIE HOU (Owner) & Buys Boys' Wear, Store Displays, Fixtures, Supplies

CINDERELLA CLOTHING STORE (CLO)
4111 South Centinela (m)
Los Angeles, CA 90066
310-391-5562 / Fax: 310-448-1801
HILARIO ARTOLA (Owner) & Buys Men's & Boys' Levis, Shirts, Hosiery, Urban Contemporary, Store Displays, Fixtures, Supplies

COOPER & KRAMER (MW)
1401 Santee St. (bud-p)
Los Angeles, CA 90015
213-747-5221
RICHARD TIKKER (Co-Owner) & Buys Men's Furnishings, Accessories, Footwear, Store Displays, Fixtures, Supplies
ROBERT TIKKER (Co-Owner) & Buys Men's Furnishings, Accessories, Footwear, Store Displays, Fixtures, Supplies

DIPLOMAT CLOTHING CO. (CLO-3)
4789 E. Whittier Blvd. (p-m-b-h)
Los Angeles, CA 90022
323-780-9610 / Fax: 323-780-1128
MOUNIR NASSER (Owner) & Buys Men's Overcoats, Suits, Sportswear, Dress Shirts, Underwear, Hosiery, Boots, Fragrances, Young Men's Wear, Boys' Levis & Jeans, Men's Shoes, Store Displays, Fixtures, Supplies

DIRECTIVES WEST - L.A. (RB)
110 E. 9th St., #A1126 (p-m-b)
Los Angeles, CA 90079
213-627-5921 / Fax: 213-614-0176
Website: www.directiveswest.com
SANDY RICHMAN (Co-Owner)
SANDY POTTER (Co-Owner & D.M.M.-Young Men's, Boys')
CARRIE HARRIS (Mdse. Mgr.) & Buys All Young Men's Wear, 8 to 20 Boys' Sportswear

DNLA (CLO)
1334 S. Main St., #C
Los Angeles, CA 90015
213-745-4575 / Fax: 213-745-4599
DOUG NILI-Sportswear, Swimwear, Surfwear

DOPO DOMANI (MW)
928 S. Western Ave., #243 (b)
Los Angeles, CA 90006
213-480-0802 / Fax: 213-480-0890
JOANN LIM (Owner) & Buys Men's Sportswear, Furnishings, Accessories (Imports Only), Store Displays, Fixtures, Supplies

ENTERPRISE 99 (CLO & OL)
1423 58th Pl.
Los Angeles, CA 90001
323-585-0099 / Fax: 323-585-1711
Sales: $500,000-$1 Million
Website: www.sockman.com
WON IM (Owner) & Buys Men's & Boys' Hosiery, Underwear, Briefs, Store Displays, Fixtures, Supplies

EUROSTAR, INC. (FW-36)
(WAREHOUSE SHOE SALES)
13425 S. Figueroa St. (bud-p-m-b)
Los Angeles, CA 90061
310-715-9300 / Fax: 310-767-2169
Sales: $50 Million-$100 Million
Website: www.wss-footwear.com
Retail Locations: CA
ERIC ALON (President)
PETER TRUONG (Mdse. Mgr.) & Buys Men's Footwear, Licensed Apparel, Men's Accessories, Men's Apparel, Hosiery
AISHA McKINNEY-Boys' Footwear
MICHAEL CONNOR-Boys' Apparel
JOSE GONZALES-Men's Footwear

FAMILY PANTS (MW-6)
731 S. Broadway
Los Angeles, CA 90014
213-622-6433 / Fax: 213-622-6430
ADEL KASPY (Owner) & Buys Men's Furnishings, Belts, Footwear

FASHION FIVE II (CLO)
1714 W. Sunset Blvd.
Los Angeles, CA 90026
213-483-6789
MR. TAEKIM (Owner) & Buys Sportswear, Activewear, Leisurewear

FASHION GUIDE (CLO)
1129 Wall St.
Los Angeles, CA 90015
213-748-6788 / Fax: 213-748-7014
JOE CHO (Owner) & Buys Sportswear, Activewear, Leisurewear

THE FIRST STREET STORE, LTD. (DEPT-2)
3640 E. 1st St. (p)
Los Angeles, CA 90063
323-269-7471 / Fax: 323-269-6423
Sales: $1 Million-$10 Million
OLIVE M. KEMP (President)
MARTA DELAHOYA (Exec. V.P. & G.M.M.) & Buys Store Fixtures, Supplies, Displays
THERESA AMAYA-Men's Overcoats, Suits, Tailored Jackets, Tailored Slacks, Raincoats, Sweaters, Sport Shirts, Outer Jackets, Casual Slacks, Apparel, Furnishings, Headwear, Accessories, Young Men's & Boys' Wear, Footwear

FOR KIDS ONLY (KS-2)
746 N. Fairfax Ave. (b-h)
Los Angeles, CA 90046
323-650-4885 / Fax: 323-651-4754
Sales: $1 Million-$10 Million
STEVEN MILLER (Owner) & Buys Infant to 22 Boys' Overcoats, Suits, Sweaters, Sport Shirts, Outer Jackets, Leather Apparel, Dress Shirts, Ties, Robes, Underwear, Hosiery, Headwear, Belts, Accessories, Footwear, Store Displays, Fixtures, Supplies

FRIAR TUX SHOP (MW)
(A TUXEDO SHOP, INC.)
10546 W. Pico Blvd. (p)
Los Angeles, CA 90064
310-559-4889 / Fax: 310-559-2934
MIKE MESCAL (Owner) (@ 714-685-1262) & Buys Men's & Boys' Formal Wear, Accessories, Footwear, Store Displays, Fixtures, Supplies

FRIEDEN'S DEPARTMENT STORE, INC. (DEPT)
2619 N. Broadway (p)
Los Angeles, CA 90031
323-225-0713 / Fax: 323-225-4127
Sales: $1 Million-$10 Million
LEON FRIEDEN (Owner) & Buys Men's & Boys' Sweaters, Sport Shirts, Outer Jackets, Casual Slacks, Active Apparel, Belts, Dress Shirts, Underwear, Hosiery, Furnishings, Footwear

CALIFORNIA - Los Angeles

FRONTRUNNER'S (CLO)
11620 San Vicente Blvd. (m)
Los Angeles, CA 90049
310-820-7585 / Fax: 310-826-4840
Sales: $1 Million-$10 Million
PAUL TORDELLA (Owner) & Buys Boys' Apparel, Boys' Footwear, Men's Footwear, Casualwear, Accessories, Outerwear, Sportswear, Swimwear, Furnishings

GIORGIO ROSSI (MW)
830 S. Los Angeles St. (m-b-des)
Los Angeles, CA 90014
213-623-9909 / Fax: 213-892-8475
Sales: $500,001-$1 Million
NASSIR KOHANZADEH (Partner) & Buys Leather Goods, Men's Apparel, Men's Big & Tall Apparel, Men's Designer Apparel, Men's Formalwear, Men's Accessories, Men's Sportswear, Men's Suits, Young Men's Apparel
MINNO KOHANZADEH (Partner) & Buys Leather Goods, Men's Apparel, Men's Big & Tall Apparel, Men's Designer Apparel, Men's Formalwear, Men's Accessories, Men's Sportswear, Men's Suits, Young Men's Apparel

GOOD OLD TIMES, INC. (CLO)
7739 Santa Monica Blvd.
Los Angeles, CA 90046
323-654-7103 / Fax: 323-654-7416
Sales: $100,001-$500,000
LISA KARAKO (Owner) & Buys Men's & Boys' Sportswear, Dress Shirts, Ties, Robes, Headwear, Accessories, Footwear

GUESS?, INC. (CLO-217)
(GUESS)
(GUESS FACTORY OUTLETS)
(GUESS KIDS)
1444 S. Alameda St. (b)
Los Angeles, CA 90021
213-765-3100 / Fax: 213-744-7838
Sales: $500 Million-$1 Billion
Website: www.guess.com
MAURICE MARCIANO (Co-Chmn.)
PAUL MARCIANO (Co-Chmn.)
CARLOS ALBERINI (President & C.E.O.)
NANCY SHACHMAN (President-Whsl. Opers.)
BRYAN TIMM (C.I.O.)
VINCENT DELL'OSA (V.P.-Store Opers.)
ROBERT HIGGINS (V.P.-Retail Opers & Bus. Dev. & Mdsg.)
LLONA CYRUS (V.P.-Sls.)
BRIAN DWAN (V.P.-Real Estate)
LINDA WHITEHEAD (V.P.-Mdsg.)
STEPHANIE ZOCCOTI (Sr. Buyer) & Buys Men's Accessories, Apparel, Footwear

HIGH SOCIETY (CLO)
2974 Wilshire Blvd. (des)
Los Angeles, CA 90010
213-382-0148 / Fax: 213-382-7476
Sales: $500,001-$1 Million
RICHARD LIM (Owner) & Buys Men's Apparel, Outerwear, Suits, Accessories

HOLLYWOOD HATTERS (CLO)
6915 Melrose Ave. (b)
Los Angeles, CA 90038
323-525-1912
Sales: Under $100,000
SALVADOR ROVERO-Headwear

HURRICANE MEN'S SHOP (MW-2)
6666 Hollywood Blvd.
Los Angeles, CA 90028
323-465-1696 / Fax: 323-465-0125
OLIVIA LEE (Owner) (@ 323-465-1236) & Buys Men's Suits, Tailored Slacks, Sweaters, Sport Shirts, Casual Slacks, Jeans, Athletic Apparel, Leather Jackets, Dress Shirts, Ties, Hosiery, Belts, Footwear, Store Displays, Fixtures, Supplies

JAMES & WILLIAMS SHOE CO. (FW)
5552 Wilshire Blvd. (bdes)
Los Angeles, CA 90036
323-938-3505 / Fax: 323-938-3500
Sales: $100,001-$500,000
HARLEY STEGNER (President) & Buys Boys' Footwear, Men's Footwear
RIGO HERNANDEZ (Mgr.) & Buys Boys' Footwear, Men's Footwear

JOHNNY'S CLOTHING CO. (MW)
8840 S. Western (m)
Los Angeles, CA 90047
323-778-0745
JOHNNY CHU (Owner) & Buys Men's Sportswear, Furnishings, Accessories, Boys' Wear, Footwear, Store Displays, Fixtures, Supplies

JOSEPH'S MENSWEAR (MW)
(MATTHEW JAMES, INC.)
238 E. 1st St. (m-b)
Los Angeles, CA 90012
213-626-1830
Sales: $500,000-$1 Million
KEN OKUBO (President & Owner) & Buys 'Short Men's' Overcoats, Suits, Tailored Jackets, Tailored Slacks, Raincoats, Sweaters, Sport Shirts, Outer Jackets, Casual Slacks, Active Apparel, Furnishings, Accessories

K-BOND (MW)
7257 Beverly Blvd.
Los Angeles, CA 90036
323-939-8866 / Fax: 323-939-0406
JAMES BOND-Men's Apparel

KIK-WEAR, INC. (CLO & OL)
1813 E. Washington Blvd.
Los Angeles, CA 90021
213-746-5317 / Fax: 213-746-5312
Website: www.kikwear.com
GREG OSTROW-Sportswear, Beachwear, Athletic Apparel

KIM'S CLOTHING STORE (MW)
1600 W. Slauson Ave. (p-m)
Los Angeles, CA 90047
323-565-3413 / Fax: 323-565-3414
JIM KIM (President) & Buys Men's Jeans, Casual Shirts, Belts, Dress Shirts, Sportswear, Ties, Store Displays, Fixtures, Supplies

LA COMERCIAL (MW-2)
4713 Whittier Blvd. (p-m)
Los Angeles, CA 90022
323-265-1020 / Fax: 323-265-0156
JOE SAAB (Owner) & Buys Men's Sportswear, Furnishings, Accessories, Boys' Wear, Boots, Urban Contemporary, Store Displays, Fixtures, Supplies

LEFT COAST STYLE (CLO)
110 E. 9th St., #529
Los Angeles, CA 90079
213-628-0882 / Fax: 213-688-0121
SUZANNE R. KARGER-Swimwear
ELLEN BRADLEY-Swimwear

LISA KLINE (CLO)
136 S. Robertson Blvd.
Los Angeles, CA 90048
310-248-2423 / Fax: 310-248-2849
LISA KLINE (Owner) & Buys Sportswear, Active Apparel, Swimwear

LITTLE PARIS (MW & GS)
5334 Hollywood Blvd. (m)
Los Angeles, CA 90027
323-462-0094 / Fax: 323-953-8090
ARMEN MKHSIAN (Owner) & Buys Men's & Boys' Wear, Footwear, Store Supplies

MARCEL COLLECTIONS (MW)
205 E. 12th St.
Los Angeles, CA 90015
213-749-1795 / Fax: 213-749-3008
KEVIN NAIM (Owner) & Buys Men's Sportswear, Furnishings, Accessories, Store Displays, Fixtures, Supplies

CALIFORNIA - Los Angeles

MARSHALL KLINE BUYING SERVICE (RB)
112 W. 9th St., #825 (bud-p-m-b-h)
Los Angeles, CA 90015
213-689-1269 / Fax: 213-689-9671
Sales: $1 Million-$10 Million
- MARSHALL KLINE (Owner) & Buys Men's Sportswear, Furnishings, Budget Men's Wear, Leather Apparel, All Footwear
- SAMMY KLINE-8 to 20 Boys' Wear
- MRS. GARY RUSSELL-Young Men's & Boys' Wear, Accessories
- FRED AMINI-Men's & Boys' Promotional Items
- GERT GERBER-Store Displays, Fixtures, Supplies

MAXFIELD (CLO-2)
(MAX BLUE)
8825 Melrose Ave. (b)
Los Angeles, CA 90069
310-274-8800 / Fax: 310-657-8880
Sales: $1 Million-$10 Million
- THOMAS PERSE (President)
- DEIRDRE WHEATON (G.M.M.)
- VINCENT EHLY-Men's Sweaters, Sport Shirts, Outer Jackets, Casual Slacks, Furnishings, Headwear, Accessories, Leather Apparel, Young Men's & Boys' Wear, Footwear, Store Displays, Fixtures, Supplies

MEN'S WORLD (MW)
1404 Los Angeles St. (b)
Los Angeles, CA 90015
213-746-2081 / Fax: 213-748-5741
Sales: $100,001-$500,000
- YUN B. KIM (Owner) & Buys Men's Sport Shirts, Outer Jackets, Casual Slacks, Active Apparel, Dress Shirts, Ties, Belts, Store Displays, Fixtures, Supplies

MODA GENTLEMAN (MW)
1426 Paloma St. (m-b)
Los Angeles, CA 90021
213-745-6040 / Fax: 213-746-9922
Sales: $1 Million-$10 Million
- BEN BAHARI (Owner) & Buys Men's Wear, Footwear, Sports Shirts, Big & Tall Wear, Sweaters, Leather Apparel, Store Displays, Fixtures, Supplies

NEW YORK TOWN CLOTHING (MW)
701 S. Los Angeles St. (p-m-b)
Los Angeles, CA 90014
213-627-9379 / Fax: 213-627-4412
- HELEN CHU (Owner) & Buys Men's Sportswear, Furnishings, Accessories, Footwear, Store Displays, Fixtures, Supplies

NO PROBLEM, INC. (CLO-5)
920 N. Formosa Ave. (m-b)
Los Angeles, CA 90046
323-969-1962 / Fax: 323-969-9485
- MICHAEL DOVAN (Owner) & Buys Men's Sportswear, Accessories, Footwear, Store Displays, Fixtures, Supplies

ORLY FASHIONS (MW-2)
325 E. 12th St. (m-b)
Los Angeles, CA 90015
213-749-0034 / Fax: 213-749-0059
- JOSEPH YAMINI (Owner) & Buys Men's Sportswear, Furnishings, Accessories, Store Displays, Fixtures, Supplies

PALAIS DES MODES (MW)
7660 Melrose Ave. (m-b)
Los Angeles, CA 90046
323-651-0384 / Fax: 323-653-9418
Sales: $500,000-$1 Million
- SYRUS RASMI (Owner) & Buys Men's Leather Apparel, Leather Jackets, Leather Pants, Gloves, Belts, Small Leather Goods, Footwear

PAOLO CELLINI (MW)
(SAFIR INTERNATIONAL, INC.)
751 S. Los Angeles (b)
Los Angeles, CA 90014
213-892-0026 / Fax: 213-892-8475
- MR. NASIR (Owner) & Buys Men's Suits, Shirts, Ties, Store Displays, Fixtures, Supplies

PARKWAY MENSWEAR (MW)
715 S. Los Angeles St. (m-b)
Los Angeles, CA 90014
213-689-1468 / Fax: 213-689-0032
- HYUK PARK (President)
- MONTE PARRISH (G.M.M.) & Buys Men's Furnishings, Accessories, Store Displays, Fixtures, Supplies

ROGER STUART CLOTHES, INC. (MW)
729 S. Los Angeles St. (m-b)
Los Angeles, CA 90014
213-627-9661 / Fax: 213-627-7748
- ROGER KELLER (President) & Buys Men's Overcoats, Suits, Tailored Slacks, Sport Coats, Raincoats, Dress Shirts, Ties, Belts, Hosiery

RON HERMAN (CLO)
(FRED SEGAL)
8100 Melrose Ave. (p-m-b)
Los Angeles, CA 90046
323-651-4129 / Fax: 323-651-3897
Sales: $10 Million-$50 Million
Website: www.ronherman.com
- RON HERMAN (President)
- BRET WAGNER (V.P. & G.M.M.) & Buys Men's Denim, Store Displays, Fixtures, Supplies
- NINA GARDUNO-Men's Denim, Ties, Hosiery, Headwear, Jewelry, Men's Suits, Dress Shirts

RON ROBINSON, INC. (MW-2)
2500 La Cienega Blvd.
Los Angeles, CA 90034
310-815-0606 / Fax: 310-815-0707
Website: www.apothia.com
- RON ROBINSON (Owner)
- KAREN MEENO-Men's Sportswear, Sleepwear, Underwear, Urban Contemporary, Store Displays, Fixtures, Supplies

ROYAL MODE, INC. (MW)
807 S. Los Angeles St. (m-b-des)
Los Angeles, CA 90014
213-622-2123
Sales: $500,001-$1 Million
- JACOB RASH (Partner) & Buys Leather Goods, Men's Apparel, Men's Big & Tall Apparel, Men's Designer Apparel, Men's Formalwear, Men's Accessories, Men's Sportswear, Men's Suits, Young Men's Apparel, Men's Footwear, Men's Casualwear
- MOUSSA AGHAI (Partner) & Buys Leather Goods, Men's Apparel, Men's Big & Tall Apparel, Men's Designer Apparel, Men's Formalwear, Men's Accessories, Men's Sportswear, Men's Suits, Young Men's Apparel, Men's Footwear, Men's Casualwear

SALEH SPORTSWEAR (CLO-2)
2227 Cesar E. Chavez Ave.
Los Angeles, CA 90033
323-264-0428 / Fax: 323-264-2665
- HOSNI SALEH, SR. (Owner)
- MOHAMMED SALEH-Men's Sportswear, Leisurwear, Accessories, Footwear

SAVY STORES (WW-2)
2036 E. Cesar Chavez Ave. (m)
Los Angeles, CA 90033
323-264-1589 / Fax: 323-264-4511
Sales: $1 Million-$10 Million
- JACK ROVERO (President) & Buys Men's & Boys' Western Wear, Footwear, Store Displays, Fixtures, Supplies

SCOTT HILL, INC. (MW)
100 S. Robertson Blvd. (m-b-des)
Los Angeles, CA 90048
310-777-1190
Sales: $1 Million-$10 Million
- JEFF FOX (Exec. V.P.) & Buys Men's Footwear, Leather Goods, Fragrances, Men's Apparl, Men's Denim Apparel, Men's Formalwear, Men's Accessories, Men's Outerwear, Men's Sleepwear, Men's Suits

STIEGLER, INC. (MW)
(HUGO BOSS)
10250 Santa Monica Blvd., #7 (m-b-des)
Los Angeles, CA 90067
310-553-7171 / Fax: 310-553-7242
Sales: $1 Million-$10 Million
JOHN STIEGLER, SR. (Owner)
PATRICK NAIMI (Gen. Mgr.) & Buys Mens Footware, Leather Goods, Casualwear, Denim Apparel, Designer Apparel, Formalwear, Accessories, Hosiery, Outerwear, Sportswear, Suits, Swimwear, Underwear, Sleepwear

THEODORE (MW-2)
6083 W. Pico Blvd. (b)
Los Angeles, CA 90035
323-965-2707 / Fax: 323-965-9406
HERBERT FINK (Owner) & Buys Men's Suits, Sportswear, Footwear, Store Displays, Fixtures, Supplies
TRACY FINK-Men's Suits, Sportswear, Footwear, Store Displays, Fixtures, Supplies

UCLA STUDENTS' STORE (SP-2)
(UNIVERSITY OF CALIFORNIA-LA)
308 Westwood Plz.
Los Angeles, CA 90024
310-206-0814 / Fax: 310-825-2794
Sales: $1 Million-$10 Million
Website: www.uclastore.com
PATRICK HEALEY (Dir.) & Buys Fleece, Jackets, Hosiery, Athletic Footwear, Men's Apparel, Licensed Apparel
MONICA LEAHEY-Men's Sportswear
LEE GLADDEN-Licensed Apparel

UNIFORMS, INC. (SP-3)
(CALIFORNIA UNIFORM)
1630 W. Olympic Blvd. (m-b)
Los Angeles, CA 90015
213-383-1395 / Fax: 213-383-6774
Sales: $1 Million-$10 Million
GEORGE ADRIAN (President & Mgr.-Real Estate)
MIKE HEGAZY (V.P.) & Buys Men's Footwear
WAYNE ADRIAN (Gen. Mgr.) & Buys Men's Footwear, Leather Goods, Apparel, Accessories, Outerwear, Uniforms/Workclothes

UNITED COLORS OF BENETTON (CLO-24)
7771 Melrose Ave. (m)
Los Angeles, CA 90046
323-658-8645 / Fax: 323-658-8764
Sales: $10 Million-$50 Million
ANDREA ROSSETTO (President) & Buys Boys' Apparel, Boys' Footwear, Men's Footwear, Leather Goods, Casualwear, Denim Apparel, Accessories, Outerwear, Sportswear, Suits, Underwear
AJIT DODANI (C.F.O.)
PAOLO SCOLERI (Dir.-Opers.)
BRUCE HUNERBERG (Mgr.-Real Estate)

UNIVERSITY SPORTING GOODS PLACE (SP-2)
3625 S. Vermont St.
Los Angeles, CA 90007
323-734-4707 / Fax: 323-734-4847
HYOK CHIN (Owner) & Buys Activewear, Athletic Footwear, Licensed Apparel

URGENT GEAR (MW)
1016 E. 14th Pl. (m)
Los Angeles, CA 90021
213-741-9926 / Fax: 213-741-9928
Website: www.urgentgear.com
RAMIN ROOFIAN (Co-Owner) & Buys Store Displays, Fixtures, Supplies, Men's & Boys' Jeans, Tops, Shirts, Shorts, Slacks
BOB ROOFIAN (Co-Owner) & Buys Men's & Boys' Jeans, Tops, Shirts, Shorts, Slacks

USC BOOKSTORES (SP-3)
(USC GIFT STORE)
(USC DENTAL BOOKSTORE)
(USC HEALTH & SCIENCES BOOKSTORE)
(UNIVERSITY SOUTHERN CALIFORNIA)
840 Childs Way, # 400
Los Angeles, CA 90089
213-740-5200 / Fax: 213-740-5203
Sales: $20 Million-$50 Million
Website: www.uscbookstore.com
DAN ARCHER (Director)
DAN STIMMLER (G.M.M.)
TRACY ENOS-Men's & Boys' Activewear, Athletic Footwear, Golf Apparel, Licensed Apparel

VENCCI (MW)
10800 W. Pico Blvd., #170 (b)
Los Angeles, CA 90064
818-991-5076 / Fax: 323-851-6936
AMI PERETZ (Owner) & Buys Men's Suits, Sportswear, Big & Tall Suits, Sportswear, Men's Furnishings, Accessories, Footwear

ZACHARY ALL, INC. (MW)
5467 Wilshire Blvd. (p)
Los Angeles, CA 90036
323-931-1484
ED NALBANDIAN, SR. (Owner) & Buys Men's Suits, Sport Coats, Sweaters, Formal Wear, Raincoats, Dress Shirts, Ties, Sportswear, Belts, Outer Jackets, Big & Tall Men's Wear, Shorts (Up to Size 60), Tailored Jackets, Tailored Slacks, Store Displays, Fixtures, Supplies
ED NALBANDIAN, JR. (Secy.) & Buys Men's Suits, Sport Coats, Sweaters, Formal Wear, Raincoats, Dress Shirts, Ties, Sportswear, Belts, Outer Jackets, Big & Tall Men's Wear, Shorts (Up to Size 60), Tailored Jackets, Tailored Slacks, Store Displays, Fixtures, Supplies

RUNNER'S FACTORY (SP)
51 University Ave.
Los Gatos, CA 95030
408-395-4311 / Fax: 831-479-0669
Sales: $100,001-$500,000
JEFF NEWKIRK (Owner) & Buys Activewear, Athletic Footwear, Triathalon Apparel, Licensed Apparel

MILBE'S MENSWEAR (MW)
3100 E. Imperial Hwy. (m-b)
Lynwood, CA 90262
310-635-1762
MUSTAS A. HASAN (Owner) & Buys Men's & Boys' Wear, Footwear, Store Displays, Fixtures, Supplies

WILLIAM & CAROL FASHIONS (MW)
135 E. Yosemite Ave. (p)
Madera, CA 93638
559-674-4633 / Fax: 559-674-4244
BILL ALESSINI (Owner) & Buys Men's Sportswear, Leather Apparel, Furnishings, Accessories, Young Men's Wear, Footwear, Store Displays, Fixtures, Supplies

MALIBU BEACH CLUB (SP)
(MALIBU LAUNDRY)
3898 S. Cross Creek Rd.
Malibu, CA 90265
310-456-2706 / Fax: 310-589-3939
Sales: $500 Million-$1 Billion
NATASHA PEDERSON (Co-Owner)
JESTA PEDERSON (Co-Owner) & Buys Beachwear, Sportswear, Leisurewear, Sandals, Beach Footwear

MALIBU LIFE STYLES MEN'S SPORTSWEAR (MW & CLO)
(MALIBU LIFE STYLES SOFT CASUAL)
3835 Cross Creek Rd., #10 (m-b)
Malibu, CA 90265
805-985-8366
Sales: $1 Million-$10 Million
GENE FORD (C.E.O.)
JOE RENNA (President) & Buys Men's Overcoats, Suits, Tailored Jackets, Tailored Slacks, Sweaters, Sport Shirts, Outer Jackets, Leather Apparels, Casual Slacks, Active Apparel, Dress Shirts, Ties, Robes, Underwear, Hosiery, Belts

ANOTHER T-SHIRT SHOP (DEPT)
P.O. Box 8887
Mammoth Lakes, CA 93546
760-934-8652 / Fax: 818-760-2299
Sales: $100,001-$500,000
MARTY SHAPIRO (Owner) & Buys Apparel, Licensed Apparel, Custom Apparel

CALIFORNIA - Mammoth Lakes

KITTREDGE SPORTS (SG-4)
P.O. Box 598 (m-b)
3218 Main St.
Mammoth Lakes, CA 93546
760-934-7566 / Fax: 760-934-6391
Website: www.kittredge.net
TOM CAGE (President & Owner)
JOE JOERGER (Partner) & Buys Active Apparel, Outdoor Clothing, Ski Wear, Beach Wear, Fleece, Long Underwear, Athletic Hosiery, Store Displays, Fixtures and Supplies, Footwear

VILLAGE CLOTHIER LTD. (CLO-2)
P.O. Box 3939
Mammoth Lakes, CA 93546
760-934-8220 / Fax: 760-934-6391
Sales: $2 Million-$5 Million
JOE JOERGER (V.P.) & Buys Athletics, Men's Activewear, Golf Apparel
DARLENE JOERGER-Activewear

SKECHERS U.S.A., INC. (FW-43 & MO & OL)
(SKECHERS MAGALOG)
228 Manhattan Beach Blvd. (m-b)
Manhattan Beach, CA 90266
310-318-3100 / Fax: 310-318-3019
Sales: $100 Million-$500 Million
Website: www.skechers.com
Retail Locations: AZ, CA, FL, HI, MA, NV, NJ, NY, NC, TN, TX
MICHAEL GREENBERG (President)
ROBERT GREENBERG (C.E.O.)
MARK NASON (V.P.-Opers. & Mdse.) & Buys Boys' Footwear, Men's Footwear

FREMONT HOUSE (MW)
P.O. Box 726 (m)
5030 State Hwy. 140
Mariposa, CA 95338
209-966-3657 / Fax: 209-966-2723
MIKE RADONOVICH-Men's Wear, Sportswear, Dress Shirts, Ties, Belts, Store Displays, Fixtures and Supplies

COTTON'S COWBOY CORRAL (WW)
320 5th St. (m-b)
Marysville, CA 95901
530-742-2401 / Fax: 530-742-7375
Sales: $500,001-$1 Million
COTTON ROSSER (C.E.O., President & Real Estate Contact)
MELINDE RODDA (C.F.O.) & Buys Boys' Apparel, Boys' Footwear, Men's Footwear, Leather Goods, Casualwear, Denim Apparel, Accessories, Hosiery, Outerwear, Sportswear
KARIN ROSSER (Gen. Mgr.) & Buys Boys' Apparel, Boys' Footwear, Men's Footwear, Leather Goods, Casualwear, Denim Apparel, Accessories, Hosiery, Outerwear, Sportswear

CIRCA (CLO)
P.O. Box 128 (p-m-b-h)
530 Main St.
Mendocino, CA 95460
707-937-4110
GLEN RICARD (Co-Owner) & Buys Men's Wear, Furnishings, Accessories, Store Displays, Fixtures and Supplies
MARY RICARD (Co-Owner) & Buys Men's Wear, Furnishings, Accessories, Store Displays, Fixtures and Supplies

MENDOSA BROS. (DEPT)
10501 Lansing St. (m)
Mendocino, CA 95460
707-937-5879 / Fax: 707-937-0563
BOB BRADLEY (Head Mgr.)
KATIE WHITNEY-Men's Jeans, Shirts, Underwear, Hosiery, Footwear (Rubber Boots Only), Store Displays, Fixtures, Supplies

JUST ADD WATER (CLO)
989 El Camino Real
Menlo Park, CA 94025
650-327-1834 / Fax: 650-327-1789
MAURICE THORESON (Owner)
HEIDI BORTOLIN-Beachwear, Resortwear, Sunglasses, Goggles, Swimwear

RILEY'S (KS)
310 Strawberry Vlg. (m-b)
Mill Valley, CA 94941
415-388-2446 / Fax: 415-388-2122
WILLIAM RILEY (President) & Buys Men's Apparel, Footwear & Accessories

AIDA'S APPAREL (SP)
401 Broadway
Millbrae, CA 94030
650-692-0123 / Fax: 650-692-5123
Sales: $100,001-$500,000
AIDA MALENJAKE (Owner) & Buys Swimwear

GONE BANANAS (CLO)
3785 Mission Blvd.
Mission Beach, CA 92109
858-488-4900 / Fax: 858-488-7129
TOM O'HARA (Owner) & Buys Swimwear, Beach Footwear

CELINI FOR MEN (MW-2)
184 The Shops at Mission Viejo (m-b)
Mission Viejo, CA 92691
949-347-9092 / Fax: 949-347-9712
MICHAEL T. QUISSINY (President) & Buys Men's Sportswear, Accessories, Furnishings, Footwear, Store Displays, Fixtures, Supplies

MISS MUFFET SHOPPE (KS)
25316 Staysail (m)
Mission Viejo, CA 92691
949-348-2260 / Fax: 949-493-7188
LYNDA J. CREEL (G.M.M.) & Buys Infant to Size 14 Boys' Wear, Accessories, Footwear

HUFFMAN'S BIG & TALL (MW & OL)
1203 14th St. (m-b)
Modesto, CA 95354
209-527-0420
Sales: $1 Million-$10 Million
Website: www.huffmansbigandtall.com
ED HUFFMAN (Owner) & Buys Men's Big & Tall Clothing, Sportswear, Accessories, Sandals, Flip Flops, Store Displays, Fixtures, Supplies

KENNETH'S FINE MENSWEAR (MW)
3500 Sisk Rd. (m)
Modesto, CA 95356
209-545-2601 / Fax: 209-545-2605
KEN TOMATIS (Owner) & Buys Men's Sportswear, Furnishings, Accessories, Footwear, Store Displays, Fixtures, Supplies

PRO SPORTSWORLD, INC. (SP-3 & OL)
Vintage Fair Mall
3401 Dale Rd., #528
Modesto, CA 95356
209-523-1621 / Fax: 209-545-5853
Website: www.prosportsworld.com
DARRYL CABRAL (Owner) & Buys Licensed Apparel, Athletic Apparel, Golf Apparel

ROGERS JEWELRY CO. (JWLY-11)
P.O. Box 3151
1408 10th St.
Modesto, CA 95354
209-578-1873 / Fax: 209-578-6523
Sales: $10 Million-$50 Million
Website: www.rogersjewelryonline.com
ROGER MARKS (President)
JAMES CARROLL-Jewelry, Watches

ROSSINI'S FORMAL WEAR & GENTLEMAN'S APPAREL (MW)
(RRT, INC.)
(ROSSINI'S GENTLEMEN'S APPAREL)
3224 McHenry Ave. (b)
Modesto, CA 95350
209-529-6860 / Fax: 209-529-1908
Sales: $100,001-$500,000
Website: www.rossinitux.com
JOE ROSSINI (President) & Buys Men's Suits, Sport Coats, Tailored Slacks, Dress & Sport Shirts, Underwear, Hosiery, Belts, Sportswear, Headwear, Formal Wear, Footwear, Store Displays, Fixtures, Supplies

SPECIAL DAYS (CLO)
3330 Oakdale Rd. (m)
P.O. Box 577318
Modesto, CA 95355
209-551-3297 / Fax: 209-551-0905
Sales: $1 Million-$10 Million
Website: www.specialdaysbridal.com
GEORGIA CHAPMAN (Owner) & Buys Men's Formalwear, Accessories
KEN CHAPMAN (Gen. Mgr.)

VITOS (MW)
2625 Coffee Rd., #U (h)
Modesto, CA 95355
209-521-6181
MIKE VITO (President & Owner) & Buys Men's Wear, Sportswear, Furnishings, Accessories

THE NEW BONDS (MW)
5404 Moreno St. (m-b)
Montclair, CA 91763
909-931-2500 / Fax: 909-931-2502
EZRA LEE (Owner) & Buys Men's Sportswear, Furnishings, Accessories, Headwear, Footwear, Store Displays, Fixtures, Supplies

TALLY FOR MEN (MW)
2116 Montclair Plaza Ln. (b)
Montclair, CA 91763
909-621-7990
Sales: $100,001-$500,000
MICHAEL TALAEE (Owner) & Buys Men's Sportswear, Furnishings, Accessories, Footwear, Store Displays, Fixtures, Supplies

HOWARDS (MW)
(HIRSHAP, INC.)
(FASHIONS FOR MEN)
1816 Montebello Town Center Dr. (p-m)
Montebello, CA 90640
323-722-4413 / Fax: 323-722-4417
Sales: $500,000-$1 Million
ROBERT D. BAKER (President) & Buys Men's Overcoats, Suits, Tailored Jackets, Tailored Slacks, Sweaters, Sport Shirts, Outer Jackets, Casual Slacks, Raincoats, Sportswear, Dress Shirts, Ties, Hosiery, Gloves, Accessories, Young Men's Wear, Footwear

BILLY'S SKI & SPORT (CLO)
2031 Verdugo Blvd.
Montrose, CA 91020
818-249-3600 / Fax: 818-249-0434
ALAN AMITIN (Owner) & Buys Men's & Boys' Sportswear, Jeans, Underwear, Shirts, Hosiery, Outer Jackets, Ski Wear, Leather Apparel, Headwear, Young Men's Wear, Urban Contemporary, Men's, Young Men's & Boys' Shoes & Sandals, Store Displays, Fixtures, Supplies

CUDDLE ME (KS)
2256 Honolulu Ave. (b)
Montrose, CA 91020
818-249-3941 / Fax: 818-249-9101
Sales: $1 Million-$10 Million
LIVCY KUMJIAN (Owner) & Buys Infant to 14 Boys' Clothing, Sportswear, Ties, Footwear, Store Displays, Fixtures, Supplies

KIMMEL & MEEHAN CLOTHIERS (MW)
2227 Honolulu Ave. (b)
Montrose, CA 91020
818-249-5085 / Fax: 818-249-6165
Sales: $500,000-$1 Million
BRYAN WALKER (Owner) & Buys Men's Overcoats, Suits, Tailored Jackets, Tailored Slacks, Raincoats, Sweaters, Sport Shirts, Outer Jackets, Casual Slacks, Furnishings, Headwear, Ties, Accessories, Leather Apparel, Store Displays, Fixtures, Supplies

FOX RACING, INC. (SG & MO)
18400 Sutter Blvd.
Morgan Hill, CA 95037
408-776-8633 / Fax: 408-776-8610
Sales: $10 Million-$50 Million
Website: www.foxracing.com
GREG FOX (President) & Buys Men's Apparel, Sportswear
GEOFF FOX (C.E.O.)
PETE FOX (V.P.-Displays) & Buys Store Displays, Fixtures & Supplies

BOARDGARDEN (FW)
2740 Jefferson St. (m-b)
Napa, CA 94558
707-253-7949 / Fax: 707-253-0808
Sales: $100,001-$500,000
WES DEBOW (Owner) & Buys Boys' Apparel, Boys' Footwear, Men's Footwear, Leather Goods, Licensed Apparel, Watches, Men's Accessories, Men's Apparel, Hosiery
KEVIN O'BRIEN (Mgr.)

CRAIG WILLIAMSON'S MENSWEAR (MW)
3204 Jefferson St. (b)
Napa, CA 94558
707-224-5284 / Fax: 707-224-8964
JAY WILLIAMSON (President) & Buys Store Displays, Fixtures, Supplies, Men's Sportswear, Furnishings, Accessories, Young Men's Wear, Urban Contemporary, Men's & Boys' Tuxedos, Headwear, Hawaiian Shirts
ALAN CLARK (Mgr.) & Buys Men's Sportswear, Furnishings, Accessories, Young Men's Wear, Urban Contemporary, Men's & Boys' Tuxedos, Headwear, Hawaiian Shirts

NORCAL SWIM SHOP (SP)
2449 2nd St.
Napa, CA 94559
707-252-3574 / Fax: 707-252-7244
Sales: $500,001-$1 Million
CRAIG DILLINGHAM (Mgr.) & Buys Activewear, Swimwear

WORKING MAN BIG & TALL (MW)
1315 1st St. (m)
Napa, CA 94559
707-255-4994
JERRY DAVIS (Owner) & Buys Men's Wear, Sportswear, Furnishings, Belts, Young Men's Wear, Urban Contemporary, Store Displays, Fixtures and Supplies

LEE'S MENSWEAR (MW)
1420 E. Plaza Blvd. (p-m)
National City, CA 91960
619-477-1037 / Fax: 619-477-2218
WON PARK (Owner) & Buys Men's Overcoats, Tailored Jackets, Tailored Slacks, Suits, Sweaters, Outer Jackets, Sport Shirts, Casual Slacks, Leather Apparel, Furnishings, Belts, Jewelry, Fragrances, Big & Tall Men's Wear, Young Men's Wear, 8 to 20 Boys' Clothing, Store Displays, Fixtures and Supplies

HAT STORE (CLO)
314 Broad St. (m-b)
Nevada City, CA 95959
530-265-4070
GREG SPORTS (Owner) & Buys Headwear

NOVAK'S (MW)
305 Broad St. (p-m)
Nevada City, CA 95959
530-265-4684
Sales: $500,000-$1 Million
MATHEW BOWDEN (Owner & President) & Buys Men's Sportswear, Furnishings, Accessories, Leather Apparel, Men's Docksider Shoes, Store Displays, Fixtures, Supplies

J.P. MAXWELL (MW)
204 Marine Ave.
New Port Beach, CA 92662
714-673-7211
MR. MAXWELL (Owner) & Buys Men's Wear, Footwear, Furnishings, Accessories

J Q, INC. (MW)
1121 New Park Mall (m)
Newark, CA 94560
510-792-0486 / Fax: 510-792-0488
ADEL BADAWY (Owner) & Buys Men's Sportswear, Furnishings, Accessories, Urban Contemporary, Young Men's Wear, Store Displays, Fixtures, Supplies

AT EASE OF NEWPORT BEACH (CLO)
579 Newport Center Dr. (b)
Newport Beach, CA 92660
949-759-7979 / Fax: 949-759-7902
Sales: $1 Million-$10 Million
RON BEALE (Chairman)
LINDA BEALE (C.E.O.) & Buys Men's Belts, Hosiery, Dress Furnishings, Better Men's Sportswear, Footwear, Store Displays, Fixtures, Supplies

CALIFORNIA - Newport Beach

ATKINSON'S MEN'S CLOTHING (MW)

3430 Via Lido (b)

Newport Beach, CA 92663

949-673-0653 / Fax: 949-642-6117

GORDON C. ATKINSON, JR. (President) & Buys Men's Suits, Tailored Jackets, Tailored Slacks, Raincoats, Dress Shirts, Furnishings, Headwear, Sportswear, Ties, Accessories, Fragrances, Footwear, Store Displays, Fixtures, Supplies

GARY'S (CLO-14)

(GARY'S ISLAND STORES)

1065 Newport Center Dr. (b)

Newport Beach, CA 92660

949-759-1622 / Fax: 949-759-1843

RICHARD BRAEGER (Co-Owner) & Buys Men's Sportswear, Active Apparel, Casual Wear, Leather Apparel, Furnishings, Accessories, Footwear

JOHN BRAEGER (Co-Owner) & Buys Men's Sportswear, Active Apparel, Casual Wear, Leather Apparel, Furnishings, Accessories, Footwear

CLAUDIO ROBLES-Store Displays, Fixtures, Supplies

L. GAYLORD SPORTSWEAR (CLO)

894 Production Pl. (m-b)

Newport Beach, CA 92663

949-548-5427 / Fax: 949-548-2756

Website: www.gaylordsportswear.com

LAURIE GAYLORD (Owner) & Buys Men's Sportswear, Men's & Boys' T-shirts, Custom Screen Printing & Embroidery, Store Displays, Fixtures, Supplies

PERSIMMON TREE (CLO)

229 Marine Ave.

Newport Beach, CA 92662

949-673-4280 / Fax: 945-675-3458

PAMELA HUBBARD (Owner) & Buys Sportswear, Accessories, Swimwear

POSH GENTLEMEN'S CLOTHING (MW)

(P.O.S.H. CLOTHING, INC.)

561 Newport Center Dr. (b)

Newport Beach, CA 92660

949-640-8310 / Fax: 949-640-8322

Sales: $1 Million-$10 Million

RICHARD BRAEGER (Owner) & Buys Men's Wear, Sportswear, Dress Shirts, Ties, Hosiery, Headwear, Belts, Jewelry, Small Leather Goods

BJORN SEDLENICK (Dir.-Opers.) & Buys Men's Sportswear, Furnishings, Accessories, Footwear, Store Displays, Fixtures, Supplies

JOHN BRAEGER-Men's Sportswear, Furnishings, Accessories, Footwear, Store Displays, Fixtures, Supplies

ALL-PRO ATHLETIC SHOE, INC. (FW-2)

12650 Sherman Way, #12 (m)

North Hollywood, CA 91605

818-764-1908 / Fax: 818-764-2198

Sales: $500,001-$1 Million

JIM K. YU (Owner) & Buys Boys' Footwear, Men's Footwear, Hosiery

SHIRLEY YU-Boys' Footwear, Men's Footwear, Hosiery

ROBINSONS-MAY (DEPT-71)

(MAY DEPARTMENT STORES)

6160 Laurel Canyon Blvd. (m-b-h)

North Hollywood, CA 91606

818-508-5226 / Fax: 818-509-5483

Sales: $1.9 Billion

Website: www.robinsonsmay.com

Retail Locations: AZ, CA, NV

ROBERT M. SOROKA (Chmn.)

CRAIG ISRAEL (President & C.E.O.)

JOSEPH CUNTI (V.P.-Visual Mdsg.) & Buys Store Displays, Fixtures, Supplies

KEVIN SHOENER (D.M.M. - Young Men's, Boys' 8-20, Men's Pants, Denim Collections)

CHARLIE CONOVER-Young Men's Levis Jeans, Seasonal Pants, Casual Pants, Levi Knits & Wovens, Shorts, Levi Shorts, Boys' Separates, Furnishings, Casual Pants, Levi Bottoms & Shorts

MAVET PEARSON-Young Men's Levis Jeans, Seasonal Pants, Casual Pants, Levi Knits & Wovens, Shorts, Levi Shorts, Boys' Separates, Furnishings, Casual Pants, Levi Bottoms & Shorts

KEVIN LUENEBRINK-Young Men's Urban Collections, South Pole, Rocawear, Ecko, Sean John, Ocean Pacific, Beachwear, Puma, Quiksilver, Young Men's Swimwear, Wovens, Knits, Sweaters, Novelty Tees, Outerwear

JONATHAN RODGERS-Young Men's Urban Collections, South Pole, Rocawear, Ecko, Sean John, Ocean Pacific, Beachwear, Puma, Quiksilver, Young Men's Swimwear, Wovens, Knits, Sweaters, Novelty Tees, Outerwear

LIZ FISKE AMELUXEN-Boys' 8-20 Woven Tops, Russell, Knit Tops, Activewear, Sweaters, Outerwear, Ocean Pacific, Guess, Polo, Quiksilver, Calvin Klein, Nautica, Tommy Hilfiger

TROY MILEHAN-Boys' Woven Tops, Russell, Knit Tops, Activewear, Sweaters, Outerwear, Ocean Pacific, Guess, Polo, Quiksilver, Calvin Klein, Nautica, Tommy Hilfiger

BETH WHITE-Men's Dress Slacks, Slates Pants, SKNY Pants, Perry Ellis Pants, Dockers Pants, Casual Slacks, Lauren Pants, Claiborne Pants

OKENA HODGES-Men's Dress Slacks, Slates Pants, SKNY Pants, Perry Ellis Pants, Dockers Pants, Casual Slacks, Lauren Pants, Claiborne Pants

CHRIS GRATTAN-Men's Tommy Jeans, Polo Jeans, Nautica Jeans, Guess Jeans, Calvin Klein Jeans, DKNY Jeans, Lucky Brand Jeans

FRANK COCONATO (D.M.M. - Men's Sportswear & Collections)

ART PANOSSIAN-Men's Sportshirts, Izod, Caribbean Joe, Chaps R.I.

KIRK LOHMOLDER-Men's Better Sportscoats, Blazers, Better Dress Slacks

JANNA LEIGHTY-Men's Knit Shirts, Lauren, Golf Knits, Sweaters

(ROBINSONS-MAY Cont. on next

(ROBINSONS-MAY Cont.)

JENNIFER DUNAJSKI-Men's Knit Shirts, Lauren, Golf Knits, Sweaters

STEVE CORVI-Men's Sportshirts, Izod, Caribbean Joe, Izod Jeans, Ralph Lauren Chaps

JEFF STEINBERG-Men's Active Separates, Swimwear, Russell Athletic, Nike, Licensed Apparel, Outerwear, Walkshorts, Designer Shorts, Dockers Shorts, Izod

CHRIS JAMIESON-Men's Active Separates, Swimwear, Russell Athletic, Nike, Licensed Apparel, Outerwear, Walkshorts, Designer Shorts, Dockers Shorts, Izod

JAY MORRISON-Men' Quicksilver, Polo Belts, Nautica, TommyHilfiger, Polo, LaCoste

MIKE BRAVO-Men' Polo, Nautica, TommyHIlfiger, LaCoste

LYNN SARVER-Men's Claiborne, Perry Ellis, Jones NY, DKNY, Kenneth Cole

HENRY MONTALVO-Men's Suits, Suit Separates, Pant Suits, Rainwear/Topcoats

STEVE HAAS (D.M.M. - Men's Furnishings)

RICK HLAD-Men's Izod Shirts, Private Label Shirts, Van Heusen Shirts, Designer Shirts, G. Beene Shirts, Ralph Lauren Dress Shirts

JONATHAN URATA-Men's Izod Shirts, Private Label Shirts, Van Heusen Shirts, Designer Shirts, G. Beene Shirts, Ralph Lauren Dress Shirts

SHAWN SALAS-Neckwear

JUSTIN DAE-Neckwear

KARA AYERS-Underwear, Hosiery, Jockey, Sleepwear, Robes

SAIGE HASELKORN-Underwear, Hosiery, Jockey, Sleepwear, Robes

SUE KIEFFER-Belts, Sunglasses, Small Leather Goods, Gifts, Seasonal Accessories, Personal Electronics

LEAH KLINGER-Belts, Sunglasses, Small Leather Goods, Gifts, Seasonal Accessories

THE SPORTS SECTION, INC. (CLO)

8300 Corbin Ave. (m)
Northridge, CA 91324
818-998-6200 / Fax: 818-998-7100
Sales: $1 Million-$10 Million
Website: www.sportssection.com

ARRI GUBNER (President) & Buys Boys' Apparel, Men's Apparel, Accessories

MIKE GUBNER (C.F.O.)

JESSICA TAYLOR (Mgr.-Mktg.)

SMITH & HAWKEN (MO & OL & GS)

Hanger No. 4, Hamilton Landing
Novato, CA 94949
415-506-3700 / Fax: 415-506-3909
Website: www.smith-hawken.com

KARYN BARSA (C.E.O.) & Buys Outdoor Men's Headwear, Casual Shoes, Sandals

OAKDALE FEED & SEED (CLO-3)

(SHELDON FEED & SUPPLY)
141 N. Yosemite Ave.
Oakdale, CA 95361
209-847-0307 / Fax: 209-847-6460

DAN DONNELLY (President)

PAT GULLEY (G.M.M.) & Buys Men's & Boys' Western Wear, Boots, Related Accessories, Store Displays, Fixtures, Supplies

PANTS 'N' THINGS (CLO)

40135 Hwy. 41 (m-b)
Oakhurst, CA 93644
559-683-7220 / Fax: 559-683-7979
Sales: $100,001-$500,000
Website: www.pantsandthings.com

CHESTER SANTOS (Co-Owner) & Buys Men's Sportswear, Furnishings, Store Displays, Fixtures, Supplies

RUTH SANTOS (Co-Owner) & Buys Men's Sportswear, Furnishings, Store Displays, Fixtures, Supplies

ARYA FOOTWEAR (FW)

2648 E. 14th St., #11 (m-b)
Oakland, CA 94601
510-535-2229
Sales: $100,001-$500,000

DON DEVEE (Owner)

MOE DEVEE (Mgr.) & Buys Men's Footwear

CRESCENT JEWELERS, INC. (JWLY-148)

315 11th St.
Oakland, CA 94607
510-874-7600 / Fax: 510-835-0906
Sales: $100 Million-$500 Million
Website: www.crescentonline.com
Retail Locations: AZ, CA, NV, NM, OR, TX, WA

RANDY POE (President)

BRAD STINN (C.E.O.)

TERI FRANK (V.P.-Mdse.) & Buys Jewelry, Watches

DAN GOULD & SON (CLO)

1611 17th St.
Oakland, CA 94607
510-832-0676 / Fax: 510-839-2635

ROBERT RICH (Owner) & Buys Men's Ties, Underwear, Hosiery, Gloves, Belts, Hats, Boys' Underwear, Thermal Underwear, Hosiery, Gloves

H. JOHNS MEN'S CLOTHIERS (MW)

(GOLDEEN & SONS, INC.)
1929 Broadway (m)
Oakland, CA 94612
510-465-2220 / Fax: 510-465-3258

JOHN S. GOLDEEN (President) & Buys Men's Sportswear, Furnishings, Headwear, Accessories, Formal Wear, Young Men's & Boys' Special Order Clothing, Store Displays, Fixtures, Supplies

JOHN L. GOLDEEN (V.P.) & Buys Men's Sportswear, Furnishings, Headwear, Accessories, Formal Wear, Store Displays, Fixtures, Supplies

HAT GUYS (CLO)

1764 Broadway (m)
Oakland, CA 94612
510-834-6868 / Fax: 510-444-3104
Website: www.hatguys.com

CORRIE ORANJE (Owner) & Buys Men's Hats, Gloves, Fragrances, Store Displays, Fixtures, Supplies

MONTCLAIR SPORTING GOODS (SG)

1970 Mountain Blvd. (b)
Oakland, CA 94611
510-339-9313 / Fax: 510-339-6092

TOM REVELLI (Owner) & Buys Store Displays, Fixtures and Supplies

PEGGY TORBELL-Men's, Young Men's & Boys' Sportswear, Athletic Footwear

SAN FRANCISCO DANCE WEAR (SP-2)

5900 College Ave.
Oakland, CA 94618
510-655-3608 / Fax: 415-882-1693

SUSAN SPINNER (Owner) & Buys Dancewear, Bodywear, Dance Footwear

SPACCIO (MW)

(SPACCIO, INC.)
140 Frank H. Ogawa Plz. (m-b)
Oakland, CA 94612
510-251-8600 / Fax: 510-251-8606

MAURICE HIMY (Owner) & Buys Men's Sportswear, Furnishings, Accessories, Leather Apparel, Footwear, Store Displays, Fixtures, Supplies

A STEP FORWARD SHOES (FW)

4018 Piedmont Ave. (m-b)
Oakland, CA 94611
510-339-0500 / Fax: 510-339-3111
Sales: $500,001-$1 Million

ULLA LUNDGREN (Owner) & Buys Men's Footwear, Leather Goods, Men's Accessories, Men's Apparel, Hosiery

CALIFORNIA - Ocean Beach

SOUTH COAST SURF SHOP (CLO-5)

5023 Newport Ave. (p)
Ocean Beach, CA 92107
619-223-7017 / Fax: 619-223-9215
Website: www.southcoast.com

ROB ARD (Owner) & Buys Men's Beach Wear, Sweatsuits, T-shirts, Shorts, Oxford Shirts, Footwear
BRIAN BOSSEN (Office Mgr.) & Buys Store Displays, Fixtures, Supplies

COTTON PATCH (SP)

307 N. Coast Hwy.
Oceanside, CA 92054
760-722-3191 / Fax: 760-722-1547
Sales: $100,001-$500,000

HARRY CATHEY (Owner) & Buys Shirts, Headwear, Jackets, Uniforms, Licensed Apparel

HAWAIIAN HUT (CLO)

270 Harbor Dr. South, #A
Oceanside, CA 92054
760-722-6000

ROSA AVILA (Owner) & Buys Sportswear, Swimwear

SURF RIDE BOARD SHOP (SG)

1909 S. Coast Hwy. (b)
Oceanside, CA 92054
760-433-4020 / Fax: 760-439-0574
Website: www.surfride.com

RICHARD BERNARD (Co-Owner)
BILL BERNARD (Co-Owner)
SUE BERNARD (Co-Owner)
KATIE BERNARD (Co-Owner) & Buys Store Displays, Fixtures, Supplies
NADINE EISENKERCH (Mgr.) & Buys Men's & Boys' Jeans, Sport Shirts, Active Apparel, Swimwear, Shirts, T-shirts, Pants, Shorts, Men's & Boys' Sandals & Beach Shoes, Urban Contemporary

BARBARA BOWMAN, INC. (CLO-3)

125 E. Ojai Ave. (m-b)
Ojai, CA 93023
805-646-2970 / Fax: 805-646-3955
Sales: $1 Million-$10 Million

BARBARA BOWMAN (President) & Buys Leather Goods, Men's Accessories, Men's Apparel

RAINS DEPARTMENT STORE (DEPT & OL)

(A. RAINS, INC.)
218 E. Ojai Ave. (m)
Ojai, CA 93023
805-646-1441 / Fax: 805-646-1442
Sales: $1 Million-$10 Million
Website: www.rainsofojai.com

ALAN RAINS (Owner)
JEFF RAINS (President) & Buys Men's Sportswear, Active Apparel, Furnishings, Accessories, Young Men's Sportswear, Men's Footwear, Store Displays, Fixtures, Supplies
LIDA DELATORRE-Men's Accessories, Casualwear, Hosiery, Outerwear, Activewear, Swimwear
MELYNDA HOLDREN-Men's Accessories, Activewear

ANCHOR BLUE (CLO-170)

(HUB DISTRIBUTING, INC.)
(AMERICAN RETAIL GROUP)
P.O. Box 5996 (p-m)
2501 E. Guasti Rd.
Ontario, CA 91761
909-605-5000 / Fax: 909-988-5664
Sales: $100 Million-$500 Million
Website: www.millersoutpost.com
Retail Locations: WA, OR, NV, NM, TX, OK, AZ, CA, UT, ID, MT, WI, MI, IL, IN

HOWARD GROSS (President)
JOHN BURGESS (Sr. V.P. & Real Estate Contact)
DON HAYES (D.M.M.-Young Men's Wear)
LISA WASSEN-Young Men's Hosiery, Headwear, Belts, Jewelry, Leather Goods
VITO SPANO-Young Men's Knit Shirts, Sweaters
OPEN-Young Men's Woven Tops
JEFF DAVIS-Shorts, Outerwear, Juniors Bottoms, Long Bottoms
JACKIE DEACKOFF-Young Men's Denim, Shorts, Outerwear
LISA HOLSTEIN (Purch. Agent) & Buys Store Displays, Fixtures, Supplies

ARMY-NAVY STORE (AN)

(ALVAREZ BROS. CO., INC.)
131 S. Glassell St. (p-m)
Orange, CA 92666
714-639-7910 / Fax: 714-639-5587
Sales: $1 Million-$10 Million
Website: www.orangearmynavy.com

CONNIE ALVAREZ (Owner)
STEVE ALVAREZ (Gen. Mgr.)
DAVE O'BRIEN-Men's Sweaters, Sport Shirts, Outer Jackets, Casual Slacks, Active Apparel, Young Men's Wear, Boys' Wear, Men's Underwear, Hosiery, Gloves, Headwear, Belts, Small Leather Goods, Footwear, Urban Contemporary, Store Displays, Fixtures, Supplies

BOOT BARN (WW-21 & OL)

1636 W. Collins Ave. (m-b)
Orange, CA 92867
714-288-8181 / Fax: 714-288-8182
Sales: $1 Million-$10 Million
Website: www.bootbarn.com
Retail Locations: CA, NV

KEN MEANY (Owner)
LAURIE G. GIRIJALUA-Men's Sportcoats, Sportswear, Western Wear, Young Men's Wear, Boys' Western Wear, Store Displays, Fixtures, Supplies
MIKE CISOWSKI-Men's & Boys' Boots, Related Western Accessories

SUNNY SMITH (MW)

1814 N. Tustin Ave. (m)
Orange, CA 92665
714-998-5522 / Fax: 714-998-5566

JASON NUNUZ (Owner) & Buys Men's Sportswear, Furnishings, Accessories, Young Men's & Boys' Wear, Footwear, Store Displays, Fixtures, Supplies

WICKET SHO-BIZ (SP-2)

100 S. Glassell St. (bud-p)
Orange, CA 92866
714-639-6431 / Fax: 714-998-3308

CARROLL JOHNSON (Owner) & Buys Suits, Tailored Slacks, Tailored Jackets, Dress Shirts, Ties, Belts, Young Men's & Boys' Wear, Zoot Suits, Formal Wear

BROWN & CO. (CLO)

2005 Bird St. (p-m)
Oroville, CA 95965
530-533-2626 / Fax: 530-533-4051
Sales: $100,001-$500,000

MILTON BROWN (Owner) & Buys Men's Sweaters, Sport Shirts, Jackets, Casual Slacks, Active Apparel, Hosiery, Belts, Small Leather Goods, Store Displays, Fixtures, Supplies

GORDON'S WESTERN & SPORTS WEAR (WW)

446 S. Oxnard Blvd. (p-m-b)
Oxnard, CA 93030
805-483-4933 / Fax: 805-483-1255

ROBERT LUNA (Owner) & Buys Men's & Boys' Western Wear, Sportswear, Boots, Store Displays, Fixtures, Supplies

LA TIENDA NUEVA (MW & WW)

114 E. 5th St.
Oxnard, CA 93030
805-483-0411 / Fax: 805-483-3112

JOSE MORALES (Owner) & Buys Men's Clothing

MIKE'S GENERAL MERCHANDISE (DEPT)

P.O. Box 387 (m-b)
480 Meta St.
Oxnard, CA 93030
805-483-5919 / Fax: 805-483-6369
Sales: $100,001-$500,000

MELBA B. NASSER (Owner) & Buys Men's & Boys' Pants, Shirts, Outer Jackets, Sweaters, Underwear, Hosiery, Jewelry, Raincoats, Footwear

PARTS UNKNOWN (SP-5)

(LEATHER BOUND)
1701 Pacific Ave.
Oxnard, CA 93033
805-483-1615 / Fax: 805-483-6439

DAN SCULLY (Owner)
ROBERT SWINK (V.P. & Gen. Mgr.)
LYNN SWINK-Adventure Wear, Active Apparel, Men's Leather Wear, Casual Shirts, Pants, Hats, Hiking Footwear

SINGERS BIG & TALL MEN'S STORE (MW-3)

360 Esplanade Dr. (b)
Oxnard, CA 93036
805-983-2311 / Fax: 805-988-1004
Sales: $1 Million-$10 Million

BRUCE SINGER (Co-Owner) & Buys Big & Tall Men's Suits, Tailored Jackets, Tailored Slacks, Raincoats, Sweaters, Sport Shirts, Outer Jackets, Leather Apparel, Casual Slacks, Active Apparel, Furnishings, Footwear, Accessories
BOB SINGER (Co-Owner) & Buys Big & Tall Men's Suits, Tailored Jackets, Tailored Slacks, Raincoats, Sweaters, Sport Shirts, Outer Jackets, Leather Apparel, Casual Slacks, Active Apparel, Furnishings, Accessories

BENTON'S SPORTS SHOP (CLO)

1038 Swarthmore Ave. (m-b)
Pacific Palisades, CA 90272
310-459-8451 / Fax: 310-459-0186

BOB BENTON (Owner) & Buys Men's Shorts, T-shirts, Shirts, Pants, Boys' Wear, Footwear, Store Displays, Fixtures, Supplies

CHAPMAN ENTERPRISES, INC. (MW-2)

73375 El Pasco (m)
Palm Desert, CA 92260
760-340-2642 / Fax: 760-779-1810

SCOTT CHAPMAN (Owner) & Buys Men's Sportswear, Furnishings, Accessories, Store Displays, Fixtures, Supplies

RICHARD BARRY SHOE COLLECTION, INC. (FW)

73750 El Paseo (bdes)
Palm Desert, CA 92260
760-346-2316 / Fax: 760-340-5565
Sales: $1 Million-$10 Million

RICHARD B. MALVIN (President) & Buys Men's Footwear, Leather Goods
RICHARD CONRAD (Mgr.) & Buys Men's Footwear, Leather Goods

DILLONS (CLO)

320 N. Palm Canyon Dr. (m-b)
Palm Springs, CA 92262
760-327-6449
Sales: $500,000-$1 Million

KEN BALZHISER (Owner) & Buys Men's Sweaters, Sport Shirts, Denim Jackets, Leather Jackets, Casual Slacks, Active Apparel, Headwear, Beachwear, Young Men's & Boys' Sportswear, Headwear, Beachwear, Beach Shoes, Store Displays, Fixtures, Supplies

DON VINCENT MENSWEAR (MW-2)

123 N. Palm Canyon Dr. (b-h)
Palm Springs, CA 92262
760-323-3232 / Fax: 760-323-3310
Sales: $1 Million-$10 Million

VINCENT J. PUCCIO (President) & Buys Men's Suits, Tailored Jackets, Tailored Slacks, Raincoats, Sweaters, Sport Shirts, Outer Jackets, Leather Apparel, Casual Slacks, Furnishings, Hats, Accessories, Footwear
DON PUCCIO (V.P.) & Buys Men's Suits, Tailored Jackets, Tailored Slacks, Raincoats, Sweaters, Sport Shirts, Outer Jackets, Leather Apparel, Casual Slacks, Furnishings, Hats, Accessories, Footwear

GERRY MALOOF'S MEN'S SHOP (MW-3)

186 S. Palm Canyon Dr. (m-b)
Palm Springs, CA 92262
760-325-2586 / Fax: 760-325-1170
Sales: $500,000-$1 Million

FRANK GROSSO (Owner) & Buys Men's Suits, Tailored Jackets, Tailored Slacks, Sweaters, Sport Shirts, Casual Slacks, Active Apparel, Dress Shirts, Ties, Underwear, Hosiery, Belts, Big & Tall Men's, Footwear, Store Displays, Fixtures, Supplies

PLAZA CUSTOM TAILORS (MW)

(PLAZA TAILORS MEN'S SHOP)
134 La Plaza (m)
Palm Springs, CA 92262
760-325-5817

JAN ZYGMUNT (Owner) & Buys Men's Tuxedos, Suits, Tailored Jackets, Tailored Slacks, Ties, Sweaters, Sport Shirts, Casual Slacks, Hosiery, Jewelry, Formal Footwear, Young Men's & Boys' Tuxedos, Store Displays, Fixtures, Supplies

R & R MENSWEAR (MW & OL)

333 N. Palm Canyon Dr., #101B (b)
Palm Springs, CA 92262
760-320-3007 / Fax: 760-320-2990
Sales: $500,001-$1 Million

RICHARD ERWIN (Owner) & Buys Men's Wear, Sportswear, Dress Shirts, Ties, Robes, Underwear, Hosiery, Belts, Small Leathers, Store Displays, Fixtures and Supplies

L'UOMO INTERNATIONAL (MW-2)

(CIELO BOUTIQUE, INC.)
122 Stanford Shopping Ctr. (m)
Palo Alto, CA 94304
650-321-2593 / Fax: 650-321-5566

BALGODIRO JAISWAL (Owner) (@ 650-329-8833) & Buys Men's Sportswear, Furnishings, Accessories, Footwear, Hosiery, Belts, Store Displays, Fixtures, Supplies

ROBERT KROHN SHOES (FW-7)

(BIRKENSTOCK PLUS)
(SHUZ OF DANVILLE)
(SHUZ OF LOS GATOS)
825 El Camino Real (m)
Palo Alto, CA 94301
650-326-0525 / Fax: 650-326-7842
Sales: $1 Million-$10 Million

JOHN RIKER (President & G.M.M.) & Buys Men's Footwear, Leather Goods, Men's Accessories, Men's Apparel, Hosiery

BUTTONS & BOWS, INC. (CLO)

6200 Clark Rd. (m-b)
Paradise, CA 95969
530-877-8151 / Fax: 530-877-0191

RALPH HEIN (Owner) & Buys Men's Sportswear, Furnishings, Accessories, Tuxedos, Young Men's Wear, Footwear, Store Displays, Fixtures, Supplies

HIP HOP CONNECTIONS (CLO)

8530 1/2 E. Rosencrans Ave.
Paramount, CA 10062
562-630-6303 / Fax: 562-630-9051

ALI ERADO-Men's Pants, Shirts, Accessories

NEW FAMILY SHOES (SP)

14488 S. Garfield Ave.
Paramount, CA 90723
562-529-8988 / Fax: 562-529-7642
Sales: $20 Million-$50 Million
Website: www.shoes4all.com

WON YOO (Owner) & Buys Men's & Boys' Athletic Footwear

FINE KICKS (FW & OL)

88 E. Colorado Blvd.
Pasadena, CA 91105
626-744-0656 / Fax: 626-744-0657

HELENA JOSEPH (Owner) & Buys Footwear, Leather Apparel, Accessories, and Belts

CALIFORNIA - Pebble Beach

PEBBLE BEACH GOLF SHOP (GOLF)
P.O. Box 658
Pebble Beach, CA 93953
831-624-3811 / Fax: 831-622-8795
Website: www.pebble-beach.com
ARCHIE HARPER (Exec. Dir.)
R. J. HARPER (Dir. - Golf)
DALE KINKADE (1st Asst. Golf Pro) (@ Ext. 7560) & Buys Golf Apparel, Licensed Apparel
MARK THUSH-Activewear

PEBBLE BEACH TENNIS SHOP (SP-2)
P.O. Box 1128
1576 Cypress Dr.
Pebble Beach, CA 93953
831-625-8509 / Fax: 831-625-8580
Sales: $100,001-$500,000
Website: www.pebblebeach.com
KIE FOREMAN (Dir.-Tennis)
KELLY WALTHOUR-Men's Licensed Apparel

SHOE PAVILION, INC. (FW-112 & OL)
1380 Fitzgerald Dr. (p-m-b)
Pinole, CA 94564
510-222-4405 / Fax: 510-222-4506
Sales: $1 Million-$10 Million
Website: www.shoepavilion.com
Retail Locations: CA, CO, IL, IA, KS, MO, NE, OK, OR
JIM ANDERSON (C.E.O.) & Buys Boys' Footwear, Men's Footwear
DAN LANNING (C.O.O.) & Buys Boys' Footwear, Men's Footwear
STEVE GREENBERG-Accessories

BEACH WEST (SP)
175 Pomeroy, #E
Pismo Beach, CA 93449
805-773-3225 / Fax: 805-773-6805
KORI GOMEZ (Owner) & Buys T-shirts, Swimwear, Sportswear, Beachwear, Sandals, Underwear, Beach Shoes

COMBELLACK'S (CLO)
339 Main St.
Placerville, CA 95667
530-622-2582 / Fax: 530-295-8035
GAIL ROHL-COMBELLACK (Owner) & Buys Men's Wear, Sportswear, Furnishings, Accessories, Store Displays, Fixtures and Supplies

ALDER'S WIDE SHOES, INC. (FW)
1745 Contra Costa Blvd. (m-b)
Pleasant Hill, CA 94523
925-687-1745 / Fax: 925-687-8122
Sales: $1 Million-$10 Million
RICHARD S. ALDER (President) & Buys Men's Footwear, Leather Goods, Men's Accessories, Hosiery
WENDY ALDER (Exec. V.P.) & Buys Men's Footwear, Leather Goods, Men's Accessories, Hosiery
NANCY CORREIA (Mgr.)

RHINESTONE COWBOY (CLO)
963 Contra Costa Blvd. (p-m-b-h)
Pleasant Hill, CA 94523
925-676-2075 / Fax: 925-676-6861
DEBBIE CACCAUO (Mgr.) & Buys Men's Western Overcoats, Suits, Raincoats, Sport Coats, Sport Shirts, Outer Jackets, Casual Slacks, Dress Shirts, Headwear, Young Men's & Boys' Wear, Boots, Store Displays, Fixtures, Supplies

SCHEER'S MEN'S & BOYS' WEAR (MW)
73 N. Main St. (m)
Porterville, CA 93257
559-784-9202 / Fax: 559-784-9162
Sales: $100,001-$500,000
SCOTT SCHEER (Owner) & Buys Men's & Boys' Wear, Men's & Boys' Boots, Store Displays, Fixtures, Supplies

AYOOB'S (DEPT)
P.O. Box A (p-m)
515 E. Main St.
Quincy, CA 95971
530-283-0940 / Fax: 530-283-1747
JOHN CULLEN (Owner) & Buys Men's Overcoats, Suits, Tailored Jackets, Tailored Slacks, Raincoats, Sweaters, Sport Shirts, Outer Jackets, Leather Apparel, Active Apparel, Big & Tall Men's, Furnishings, Belts, Fragrances, Young Men's & Boys' Wear, Footwear, Store Displays, Fixtures, Supplies

SPORTS LTD. (SG)
950 Hilltop Dr. (m)
Redding, CA 96003
530-221-7333 / Fax: 530-221-6432
DAVID KEPON (Owner) & Buys Active Apparel, T-shirts, Hosiery

THOMPSON'S MEN'S STORE, INC. (MW)
1448 Pine St. (b)
Redding, CA 96001
530-243-1351
Sales: $500,000-$1 Million
SCOTT THOMPSON (Co-Owner) & Buys Men's Sportswear, Furnishings, Accessories, Store Displays, Fixtures, Supplies
JAY THOMPSON (Co-Owner) & Buys Store Displays, Fixtures & Supplies

TUXEDO DEN, INC. (MW)
(Mr. Formal)
1580 Charles Dr. (m-b)
Redding, CA 96003
530-245-1905 / Fax: 530-245-1911
Website: www.tuxedoden.com
ED HONEYCUTT (President) & Buys Men's & Boys' Formal Wear
RON BENBROOK (V.P.) & Buys Men's & Boys' Formal Wear, Furnishings, Footwear, Related Accessories
NANCY FOX (V.P.-Opers.) & Buys Store Displays, Fixtures, Supplies

WILD IRIS ACTIVEWEAR (SP)
1738 Churn Creek Rd.
Redding, CA 96002
530-221-3045 / Fax: 530-221-3042
CATHY CUNDY (Owner) & Buys Activewear, Sportswear, Swimwear

JONATHAN (CLO)
1707 S. Catalina Ave. (m-b)
Redondo Beach, CA 90277
310-373-8708 / Fax: 310-375-7888
Sales: $1 Million-$10 Million
SUSAN GILBERT (Owner) & Buys Men's Footwear, Leather Goods, Casualwear, Formalwear, Accessories, Hosiery, Outerwear, Sportswear, Suits
TAMIRA HALE (Store Mgr.) & Buys Men's Apparel

NORDSTROM - LOS ANGELES DIV. (DEPT-9 & OL)
1835 Hawthorne Blvd. (m-b-h)
Redondo Beach, CA 90278
310-542-9440 / Fax: 310-214-7679
Website: www.nordstrom.com
JULIE KUNS (V.P. - Orange County Div.) (@ 714-850-2500)
JOHN SULLIVAN (D.M.M.-Men's Wear) (@ 415-977-5004) & Buys Men's Suits, Overcoats, Tailored Jackets, Raincoats, Sportswear
WENDY THOMPSON-Men's Accessories
SHERRE HADDIX (D.M.M.-Boys' Wear)
VERNON BOYD-Boys' 8 to 20
BRUCE ANDERSON (D.M.M.-Men's Shoes)
GEORGE STAIKUS-Men's Footwear
GAIL LALUMIERE (D.M.M.- Children's) & Buys Boys' Shoes
ANISSA WILLIAMS (Display Mgr.) & Buys Store Displays, Fixtures, Supplies

REDONDO SPORTSWEAR (MW)
100 Fishersmens Wharf (m)
Redondo Beach, CA 90277
310-379-3499
SOON OH (Owner) & Buys Men's Sportswear, Casual Shoes, Store Displays, Fixtures and Supplies

THREADS FOR MEN (MW)

1907 S. Catalina Ave. (m)
Redondo Beach, CA 90277
310-375-7575 / Fax: 310-375-9703

GENE MUNTEAN (Owner) & Buys Men's Sportswear, Furnishings, Accessories, Store Displays, Fixtures and Supplies

MICHAEL SORIANO (Mgr.)

REDWOOD TRADING POST (SG)

1305 El Camino Real (b)
Redwood City, CA 94063
650-363-2033 / Fax: 650-363-2056
Sales: $1 Million-$10 Million
Website: www.redwoodtradingpost.com

RANDOLPH WEBER (Co-Owner) & Buys Men's & Boys' Military Clothes, Store Displays, Fixtures and Supplies

LARRY WEBER (Co-Owner) & Buys Sportswear, Store Displays, Fixtures and Supplies

RONALD WEBER (Co-Owner) & Buys Men's & Boys' Raincoats, Boots, Store Displays, Fixtures and Supplies

THE CLOTHING BROKER (MW-5)

5327 Jacuzzi St., #3C (bud-p)
Richmond, CA 94804
510-528-2196 / Fax: 510-528-8196
Website: www.clothingbroker.com

CHUCK KROGH (Owner) & Buys Men's Sportswear, Furnishings, Accessories, Footwear, Store Displays, Fixtures and Supplies

GOLDEN GATE (WW-2)

12153 San Pablo Ave. (m-b)
Richmond, CA 94805
510-232-3644
Sales: $500,000-$1 Million
Website: www.goldengatewesternwear.com

BILL KNUDSEN (Owner) (@ 510-232-0379) & Buys Men's Leather Vests, Western Wear, Boys' Western Wear, Belts, Hats, Boots, Store Displays, Fixtures and Supplies

LANDON'S MEN'S, WOMEN'S & BOYS' WEAR (CLO)

3327 Santa Fe St.
Riverbank, CA 95367
209-869-2010 / Fax: 209-869-2453

STUART LANDON (Owner) & Buys Men's Suits, Sportswear, Activewear, Big & Tall Men's Wear, Furnishings, Accessories, Young Men's Wear, Urban Contemporary, Boys' Wear, Footwear, Store Displays, Fixtures and Supplies

BOARD SHOPS OF AMERICA (MW)

3971 Tyler St. (p)
Riverside, CA 92503
909-351-1015 / Fax: 909-351-2300

RUTH GERBER (Co-Owner)

DAVE GERBER (Co-Owner) & Buys Men's Sportswear, Surf Wear, Headwear, Young Men's & Boys' Wear, Urban Contemporary, Store Displays, Fixtures and Supplies

HAWAII SWIMWEAR (SP)

3652 Van Buren Blvd.
Riverside, CA 92503
909-688-1141

MARY DeMONT-Swimwear, Beachwear, Related Accessories

SAM'S WESTERN WEAR (WW & OL)

(HAMDY SALEM, INC.)
8930 Limonite Ave. (p)
Riverside, CA 92509
909-685-2206 / Fax: 909-681-9316
Website: www.samswest.com

SAM SALEM (Owner) & Buys Men's & Boys' Western Clothing, Boots

MIKE STANOFF (Mgr.) & Buys Men's & Young Men's Western Clothing, Western Furnishings, Western Accessories

WINSTON INTERNATIONAL (MW)

550 Deep Valley Dr., #223 (m-b)
Rolling Hill Estates, CA 90274
310-541-2446 / Fax: 310-541-8638

GENE MUNTEAN (Owner) & Buys Men's Overcoats, Suits, Tailored Jackets, Tailored Slacks, Raincoats, Furnishings, Accessories, Polo Sportswear

JOSEPH CIPOLLA (G.M.M.) & Buys Men's Overcoats, Suits, Tailored Jackets, Tailored Slacks, Raincoats, Furnishings, Accessories, Polo Sportswear

RICHARDSON'S MEN STORE (MW)

1129 Roseville Sq. (m)
Roseville, CA 95678
916-782-1215 / Fax: 916-782-2881
Sales: $1 Million-$10 Million
Website: www.wagner-bigandtall.com

JIM WAGNER (V.P.)

JOHN WAGNER (V.P.) & Buys Men's Suits, Tailored Jackets, Raincoats, Big & Tall Men's Wear, Casual Slacks, Overcoats, Tailored Slacks, Sweaters, Sport Shirts, Outer Jackets, Active Apparel, Underwear, Small Leather Goods, Dress Shirts, Ties, Robes, Hosiery, Belts, Footwear, Tuxedos, Big & Tall Men's Tuxedos, Store Displays, Fixtures, Supplies

TOM WAGNER (V.P.) & Buys Men's Suits, Tailored Jackets, Raincoats, Big & Tall Men's Wear, Casual Slacks, Overcoats, Tailored Slacks, Sweaters, Sport Shirts, Outer Jackets, Active Apparel, Underwear, Small Leather Goods, Dress Shirts, Ties, Robes, Hosiery, Belts, Footwear, Tuxedos, Big & Tall Men's Tuxedos, Store Displays, Fixtures, Supplies

BONNEY & GORDON STORE FOR MEN (MW & OL)

2651 Town & Country Pl. (b)
Sacramento, CA 95821
916-485-9999 / Fax: 916-481-2662
Sales: $1 Million-$10 Million
Website: www.bonneygordon.com

FRED KNOWLES (President & G.M.M.) & Buys Men's Overcoats, Suits, Tailored Jackets, Tailored Slacks, Sportswear, Footwear, Raincoats, Store Displays, Fixtures, Supplies

LEE WHITAKER (V.P.) & Buys Men's Sweaters, Sport Shirts, Outer Jackets, Leather Apparel, Casual Slacks, Active Apparel, Dress Shirts, Furnishings, Accessories

DE ROW & SHARMA TAILORS & CLOTHIERS (MW)

1009 10th St. (m)
Sacramento, CA 95814
916-447-7312

VENILAL NAGIN (Owner) & Buys Men's Wear, Dress Shirts, Ties, Store Displays, Fixtures and Supplies

DEVON'S JEWELERS (JWLY-14)

P.O. Box 162285
1910 29th St.
Sacramento, CA 95816
916-451-6583 / Fax: 916-456-2514
Sales: $10 Million-$50 Million
Website: www.devonsjewelers.com

GERALD MERKSAMER (President) & Buys Jewelry, Watches

LARRY MILLER (C.F.O.)

CALIFORNIA - Sacramento

JOE SUN & CO. (CLO)
704 K St. (p)
Sacramento, CA 95814
916-442-3754 / Fax: 916-442-4216
Sales: $1 Million-$10 Million
Website: www.joesunco.com
DENNIS SHUN (G.M.M.) & Buys Men's & Young Men's Wear, Casual Shoes
EUGSON WONG-Store Displays, Fixtures and Supplies

JULIUS (CLO)
580 Pavilions Ln. (b)
Sacramento, CA 95825
916-929-0500 / Fax: 916-929-6436
Sales: $1 Million-$10 Million
SAM ANAPOLSKY (Owner) & Buys Men's Overcoats, Suits, Tailored Jackets, Tailored Slacks, Raincoats, Sweaters, Sport Shirts, Outer Jackets, Leather Apparel, Casual Slacks, Active Apparel, Dress Shirts, Ties, Hosiery, Belts, Jewelry, Small Leather Goods, Store Displays, Fixtures and Supplies
PAT BROUSSEAU (Mgr.) & Buys Men's Overcoats, Suits, Tailored Jackets, Tailored Slacks, Raincoats, Sweaters, Sport Shirts, Outer Jackets, Leather Apparel, Casual Slacks, Active Apparel, Dress Shirts, Ties, Hosiery, Belts, Jewelry, Small Leather Goods

KID-E-KORRAL (KS)
3194 Arden Way (p-m-b)
Sacramento, CA 95825
916-483-7331 / Fax: 916-483-4274
Sales: $500,000-$1 Million
JAMES K. BONNEY (President) & Buys Store Displays, Fixtures and Supplies
NANCY BONNEY-8 to 20 Boys' Wear

MENS LTD. (MW)
(HUNT-PACKWOOD, INC.)
3364 El Camino Ave. (m-b)
Sacramento, CA 95821
916-489-9505 / Fax: 916-482-5912
RAY PACKWOOD (Owner) & Buys Men's Wear, Footwear, Store Displays, Fixtures, Supplies

NAVIN'S CUSTOM CLOTHIERS (CLO)
324 K St. (b-h)
Sacramento, CA 95814
916-448-6295 / Fax: 916-554-7507
NAVIN PETER (Owner) & Buys Custom Made Clothing, Ties

OXFORD (MW-2)
5907 Florin Rd. (m)
Sacramento, CA 95814
916-391-3337 / Fax: 916-391-1903
DAVID HASHUA (Owner & Buyer) & Buys Men's Wear, Sportswear, Furnishings, Accessories, Young Men's Wear, Urban Contemporary, Boys' Wear, Store Displays, Fixtures and Supplies

TOPS YOUNG MEN'S FASHION (MW-3)
5967 Florin Rd. (p)
Sacramento, CA 95823
916-427-8444 / Fax: 916-427-1126
HASSAN OSMAN (Owner) & Buys Men's Sportswear, Furnishings, Accessories, Young Men's Wear, Footwear, Store Displays, Fixtures and Supplies

MARIO'S MEN'S CLOTHING (MW)
1223 Main St. (h)
Saint Helena, CA 94574
707-963-1603 / Fax: 707-963-1633
Website: www.mariosnapavalley.com
DOUG CHAMPAIGN (Owner) & Buys Men's Tailored Jackets, Tailored Slacks, Raincoats, Sportswear, Furnishings, Accessories, Footwear, Store Displays, Fixtures and Supplies

DICK BRUHN FAMILY OF STORES (MW-6)
P.O. Box 81600 (b)
300 Main St.
Salinas, CA 93912
831-758-4684 / Fax: 831-422-2620
Sales: $10 Million-$50 Million
JOHN D. MANESS (President)
RUDY SANCHEZ (D.M.M.) & Buys Men's Sweaters, Sport Shirts, Outer Jackets, Leather Apparel, Active Apparel, Young Men's Wear, Men's Tailored Slacks, Sport Shirts, Casual Slacks, Men's Dress Shirts, Ties

JOCK SHOP (SP)
536 Abbott St.
Salinas, CA 93901
831-757-2447 / Fax: 831-757-2441
Sales: $100,001-$500,000
Website: www.myjockshop.com
RAMON VALENZUELA (Owner & G.M.M.) & Buys Activewear, Athletics, Football

GIANNI (MW-2)
221 Carousel Mall (b-h)
San Bernardino, CA 92401
909-888-4179 / Fax: 909-888-2088
Sales: $1 Million-$10 Million
Website: www.gianni.com
OMAR GANI (Owner) & Buys Men's Overcoats, Suits, Tailored Jackets, Tailored Slacks, Leather Apparel, Raincoats, Sweaters, Sport Shirts, Outer Jackets, Casual Slacks, Active Apparel, Furnishings, Accessories, Young Men's Wear, Footwear, Store Displays, Fixtures, Supplies

M & R CLOTHIERS (MW)
254 Carousel Mall (b)
San Bernardino, CA 92401
909-885-1144
Sales: $100,001-$500,000
OMAR MELBES (Owner) & Buys Men's Sportswear, Furnishings, Accessories, Footwear, Store Displays, Fixtures, Supplies

WESTWAY WESTERN WEAR (WW)
1650 SE St. (m-b)
San Bernardino, CA 92408
909-885-7559
CANDICE COHEN (Owner) & Buys Men's Western Wear, Leather Apparel, Boys' Western Wear, Footwear, Store Displays, Fixtures, Supplies

TURTURICI NEW GENERATIONS (MW)
(BEN TURTURICI, INC.)
740 Laurel St. (b)
San Carlos, CA 94070
650-592-9190 / Fax: 650-592-9192
Sales: $100,001-$500,000
FREDDIE MICHELES (Owner) & Buys Men's Overcoats, Suits, Tailored Jackets, Tailored Slacks, Raincoats, Sweaters, Outer Jackets, Leather Apparel, Casual Slacks, Active Apparel, Dress Shirts, Ties, Robes, Belts, Jewelry, Fragrances, Store Displays, Fixtures, Supplies

AUSSIE DOGS (FW & MO)
P.O. Box 2933 (m-b)
315 N. El Camino Real
San Clemente, CA 92672
949-366-6727 / Fax: 949-366-0899
Sales: $500,001-$1 Million
Website: www.aussie-dogs.com
CHRIS WATT (Owner)
JAN FOLEY (G.M.M.) & Buys Boys' Footwear, Men's Footwear

BEACH CLUB (SP)
128 Avenida Del Mar
San Clemente, CA 92672
949-492-2305 / Fax: 949-369-1432
Sales: $1 Million-$10 Million
MARIA MORALES (Owner) & Buys Activewear, Swimwear, Footwear

DON ROBERTO JEWELERS, INC. (JWLY-55)
1020 Calle Recodo, # 100
San Clemente, CA 92673
949-361-6700 / Fax: 949-498-8917
Sales: $10 Million-$50 Million
Retail Locations: CA, TX
ROBERT TRETTE (President)
SHANNON TRETTE-Jewelry, Watches

BIG DEAL BIG & TALL (MW-2)
8199 Clairmont Mesa Blvd. (m-b)
San Diego, CA 92111
858-576-1194 / Fax: 858-576-1195
GEORGE WILSON (Co-Owner) & Buys Big & Tall Men's Sportswear, Furnishings, Accessories, Store Displays, Fixtures, Supplies
MICHAEL HAYDEN (Co-Owner) & Buys Big & Tall Men's Sportswear, Furnishings, Accessories, Store Displays, Fixtures, Supplies

CALIFORNIA SPORTS (SG-2)
(CAL'S STORES)
4030 Sports Arena Blvd. (p-m-b)
San Diego, CA 92110
619-223-2325 / Fax: 619-223-0758
Sales: $10 Million-$50 Million
OSCAR DAVILA (President) & Buys Men's Sportswear, Sport Shirts, Active Apparel, Urban Contemporary, Athletic Footwear, Young Men's & Boys' Wear
JEAN CURTIS (V.P.) & Buys Men's Sportswear, Sport Shirts, Active Apparel, Urban Contemporary, Athletic Footwear

FACTORY 2-U STORES, INC. (CLO-248)
4000 Ruffin Rd. (bud-p-m)
San Diego, CA 92123
858-627-1800 / Fax: 858-637-4199
Sales: $500 Million-$1 Billion
Website: www.factory2-u.com
NORMAN PLOTKIN (C.E.O.)
NORM DOWLING (C.F.O. & Exec. V.P.-Finance)
TRACY PARKS (C.I.O.)
A.J. NEPA (Exec. V.P.-Mdsg.)
SHARON LITTLE (Sr. V.P.-Mktg.)
PEGGY CORNETT (V.P. & M.M.)
JIM CRUMP (V.P.-Men's & Footwear Div.)
ANGELA DAWSON-Men's Hosiery, Furnishings, Fleece & T-Shirts
MIKE WELCH-Men's Footwear
STEVEN RAFSTEDT-Men's Traditional Tops, Bottoms, Shorts & Outwear
ASANTE TRUONG-Young Men's Traditional Tops, Bottoms & Activewear
PEGGY SAMSON (Merch. Mgr.-Children's)
GAEANNE SOVIERO-Newborns, Infants Apparel, Accessories
CYNDEE BERG-Sizes 2-14: All Sets, Seasonal
RHONDA BROWN-Boys' Sizes 2-16: Separates
JANELLE JOHNSON-Boys' Apparel
DAVID EVANS (V.P.- Store Planning)

INTERNATIONAL MALE (MO & OL)
(BRAWN OF CALIFORNIA, INC.)
741 F St. (m-b)
San Diego, CA 92101
619-544-9900 / Fax: 619-881-3942
Sales: $10 Million-$50 Million
Website: www.internationalmale.com
NICKKI PEAVEY (Asst. Buyer) & Buys Wovens, Vests, Pants
CONNIE WILSON-Knits, Sweaters, Outerwear, Denim, Shorts, Surplus, Sport Suits
MARINA PARSONS-Underwear, Swimwear, Loungewear, Athletic Apparel, Maximum Exposure
CHERYL BERGLUND (Asst. Buyer) & Buys Off-Price, Footwear, Leather Apparel, Jewelry
LINDA ELDRIDGE-Shoes & Accessories

JIGSAW HILLCREST (CLO)
412 University Ave. (m-b)
San Diego, CA 92103
619-297-7920
MR. SAEED SAEED KATAME (Owner) & Buys Men's Sport Shirts, Outer Jackets, Leather Apparel, Casual Slacks, Dress Shirts, Hosiery, Belts, Small Leather Goods, Footwear, Urban Contemporary, Store Displays, Fixtures, Supplies

MARINE CORPS EXCHANGE (PX)
MWR 0171-MCRD (m)
3800 Chosin Ave.
San Diego, CA 92140
619-297-2500 / Fax: 619-296-8400
Sales: $50 Million-$100 Million
ROLAND GRIFFIN (Dir.-Retail)
ZELLA PRICE-Men's Clothing, Footwear, Accessories,Sportswear, Furnishings, Belts, Small Leather Goods, Young Men's Shop, Boys' Sportswear
ROBB BOWER-Store Displays, Fixtures and Supplies

MEN'S FASHION DEPOT (MW)
3730 Sports Arena Blvd. (bud-p-m-b-des)
San Diego, CA 92110
619-222-9570
Sales: $1 Million-$10 Million
DENNIS BASSON (President) & Buys Leather Goods, Men's Apparel, Men's Big & Tall Apparel, Men's Casualwear, Men's Designer Apparel, Men's Formalwear, Men's Accessories, Men's Outerwear, Men's Sportswear, Men's Suits, Young Men's Apparel

RANGONI U.S. CORP. (FW-15)
(RANGONI OF FLORENCE SHOES)
6191 Cornerstone Ct. East, Suite 114 (m-b-des)
San Diego, CA 92121
858-404-0014 / Fax: 858-404-0013
Sales: $1 Million-$10 Million
Website: www.rangonishoes.com
NICCOLO RANGONI (President)
BART CRAWFORD (V.P.) & Buys Men's Footwear, Men's Accessories, Hosiery

RICCARDO (MW)
111 Horton Plz. (b)
San Diego, CA 92101
619-232-6211 / Fax: 619-236-9520
JOHN NOURI (Mgr.) & Buys Men's Sportswear, Designer Italian Apparel, Furnishings, Accessories, Store Displays, Fixtures, Supplies

ROAD RUNNER SPORTS, INC. (CLO & OL & MO)
5549 Copley Dr. (m-b)
San Diego, CA 92111
858-974-4200 / Fax: 858-636-7689
Sales: $1 Million-$10 Million
Website: www.roadrunnersports.com
MICHAEL GOTFREDSON (Owner & C.E.O.)
DAWN MOORE (V.P.-Mdse.)
TINA CONRAD-Men's Accessories, Watches
DAVID JEWELL-Boys' Footwear, Men's Footwear, Accessories
CLARK MASON-Men's Apparel

RON-STUART & ASSOCIATES (MW)
1110 5th Ave. (m)
San Diego, CA 92101
619-232-8850 / Fax: 619-232-8868
RON FORD (Owner) & Buys Men's Sportswear, Furnishings, Accessories, Store Displays, Fixtures, Supplies

UNIVERSAL BOOT SHOPS (FW-2)
939 5th Ave. (m-b)
San Diego, CA 92101
619-233-6566 / Fax: 619-235-9487
Sales: $1 Million-$10 Million
ERIK HEIMBURGE (Partner) & Buys Men's Footwear
KATHERINE HERON (Partner) & Buys Men's Footwear
HELEN JACKMAN (Partner) & Buys Men's Footwear

JEANS PLUS (MW)
1109 San Fernando Rd. (m)
San Fernando, CA 91340
818-361-3955
AHMED SALEH (Owner) & Buys Men's Sportswear, Furnishings, Boys' Wear, Store Displays, Fixtures, Supplies

K-PANTS (MW)
1016 S. San Fernando Rd. (m)
San Fernando, CA 91340
818-361-4687
Sales: $100,001-$500,000
AHMED KASIM (Owner) & Buys Men's Sportswear, Furnishings, Accessories, Store Displays, Fixtures, Supplies

ACME SURPLUS STORE (CLO)
5159 Mission St. (bud-p-m)
San Francisco, CA 94112
415-586-4343 / Fax: 415-586-5615
Sales: $500,001-$1 Million
BILL LUTCHFIELD (Owner) & Buys Boys' Apparel, Men's Footwear, Casualwear, Uniforms/Workclothes

CALIFORNIA - San Francisco

ALL AMERICAN BOY (MW)

463 Castro (m-b)
San Francisco, CA 94114
415-861-0444 / Fax: 415-861-3749
Sales: $1 Million-$10 Million
Website: www.citysearch7.com

TIM OVIATT (Owner) & Buys Men's Sweaters, Sport Shirts, Outer Jackets, Leather Apparel, Casual Slacks, Active Apparel, Ties, Underwear, Hosiery, Belts, Urban Contemporary, Swimwear, Store Displays, Fixtures, Supplies

SCOTT SHARP (G.M.M.) & Buys Men's Sweaters, Sport Shirts, Outer Jackets, Leather Apparel, Casual Slacks, Active Apparel, Ties, Underwear, Hosiery, Belts, Urban Contemporary, Swimwear, Store Displays, Fixtures, Supplies

ALL AMERICAN TEAM SHOP (SP)

2800 Leavenworth St., #62
San Francisco, CA 94133
415-885-0704 / Fax: 415-885-4798
Sales: $100,001-$500,000

KAREN LUI (Owner) & Buys Activewear, Athletics, Licensed Apparel

THE ART CLOTHING CO. (MW)

914 Grant Ave. (p)
San Francisco, CA 94108
415-982-3247
Sales: $100,001-$500,000

E. W. FAY (President)

HANK LOUIE (Mgr.) & Buys Men's & Boys' Overcoats, Suits, Tailored Jackets, Tailored Slacks, Raincoats, Accessories, Headwear, Footwear

JOHNNY LAU-Men's & Boys' Sportswear

L. K. WONG-Men's & Boys' Furnishings, Store, Displays, Fixtures, Supplies

ARTHUR BEREN SHOES, INC. (FW-2 & MO)

474 Bryant St. (des)
San Francisco, CA 94107
415-365-9300 / Fax: 415-371-0163
Sales: $10 Million-$50 Million
Website: www.berenshoes.com

DAVID BEREN (President)

ARTHUR BEREN (C.E.O.)

KEN PETERSON (Mgr.)

SID BURGER-Men's Footwear, Leather Goods, Men's Accessories

AUSTRALIA FAIR (CLO)

700 Sutter St. (b)
San Francisco, CA 94109
415-441-5319 / Fax: 415-441-4078
Sales: $1 Million-$10 Million
Website: www.australiafair.net

JOHN RAWSON (Owner) & Buys Men's Footwear, Leather Goods, Big & Tall Men's Wear, Casualwear, Hosiery, Outerwear, Sportswear

ANNETTE WARNER (Store Mgr.)

BANANA REPUBLIC (CLO-297 & MO & OL)

(Div. of THE GAP, INC.)
345 Spear St. (b)
San Francisco, CA 94105
415-777-0250 / Fax: 415-427-7030
Website: www.bananarepublic.com
Retail Locations: AL, AK, AZ, AR, CA, CO, CT, DE, DC, FL, GA, HI, ID, IL, IN, IA, KS, KY, LA, ME, MD, MA, MN, MI, MS, MO, NE, NH, NJ, NM, NY, NC, SC, SD, TN, RI, PR, PA, UT, VT, VA, WA, WV, WI, WY

MARKA HANSEN (President)

MICHAEL J. DADARIO (Exec. V.P.-Stores & Opers.)

DEBRA LLOYD (Exec. V.P.-Product Design & Dev.)

KATHY BOYER (V.P. & G.M.M.-Men's)

MATTHEW CORIN (Mdse. Mgr.-Men's Outerwear) & Buys Outerwear, Sweaters, Activewear, Knits, Pants

LISA ROSTOKER (Visual Design) & Buys Store Displays, Fixtures and Supplies

BILLYBLUE (MW)

54 Geary St. (h)
San Francisco, CA 94108
415-781-2111 / Fax: 415-781-4042
Sales: $1 Million-$10 Million
Website: www.billyblue.com

BILLY BRAGMAN (Partner) & Buys Men's Furnishings, Belts, Tailored Jackets, Tailored Slacks, Raincoats, Dress Shirts, Store Displays, Fixtures, Supplies

J. B. BICKERS (Partner) & Buys Men's Furnishings, Belts, Tailored Jackets, Tailored Slacks, Raincoats, Dress Shirts, Store Displays, Fixtures, Supplies

BODY OPTIONS (SP-9)

2108 Chestnut St., 2nd Fl.
San Francisco, CA 94123
415-921-7857 / Fax: 415-567-7036

NISSIM LANYADOO (Owner & President)

CHRYSSA GIANNARES-Activewear, Leisurewear, Sandals, Swimwear

NOTE:-Only 1 store carries Men's Clothing

BUTTON DOWN (MW)

3415 Sacramento St.
San Francisco, CA 94118
415-563-1311
Sales: $1 Million-$10 Million

MICHAEL SABINO (Owner) & Buys Men's Apparel, Men's Sports/Activewear

JOHN DIQUATTRO (Mgr.)

CABLE CAR CLOTHIERS (MO & MW & OL)

115 Sansome St. (b)
San Francisco, CA 94104
415-397-4740 / Fax: 415-616-8998
Sales: $1 Million-$10 Million
Website: www.cablecareclothiers.com

CHARLES PIVNICK (President) & Buys Men's Robes, Underwear, Pajamas, Sportswear, Ties, Dress Shirts, Hosiery, Gloves, Accessories

HARRY SIEWERT-Accessories

TIM SIEWERT-Store Displays, Fixtures, Supplies

CITIZENS (MW-2)

536 Castro (m-b)
San Francisco, CA 94114
415-558-9429 / Fax: 415-575-3564

PETER KANE (Owner) & Buys Store Displays, Fixtures, Supplies, Men's Sportswear, Furnishings, Accessories, Footwear

PAUL NISBIT (Mgr.) & Buys Men's Sportswear, Furnishings, Accessories

CITY FITNESS (SP)

3251 Pierce St.
San Francisco, CA 94123
415-345-9326

MI MI TOWBIS (Owner) & Buys Activewear, Athletic Footwear

DAVID STEPHEN CO. (MW & OL)

(JAY BRIGGS, INC.)
50 Maiden Ln. (h)
San Francisco, CA 94108
415-982-1612 / Fax: 415-553-0123
Sales: $1 Million-$10 Million
Website: www.davidstephen.com

KURT GRONOWSKI (President)

HANS GRONOWSKI (V.P.)

DAVID GRONOWSKI (Gen. Mgr.) & Buys Men's Overcoats, Suits, Tailored Jackets, Tailored Slacks, Raincoats, Sweaters, Sport Shirts, Outer Jackets, Leather Apparel, Dress Shirts, Ties, Hosiery, Belts, Jewelry, Store Displays, Fixtures and Supplies

CALIFORNIA - San Francisco

DFS MERCHANDISING LTD. (GS-150)

525 Market St., 31st Fl. (p-m-b)
San Francisco, CA 94105
415-977-2700 / Fax: 415-977-2956
Sales: Over $1 Billion
Website: www.dfs.com
Retail Locations: AZ, AK, AZ, AR, CA, CO, CT, DE, DC, FL, GA, HI, ID, IL, IN, IA, KS, KY, LA, ME, MD, MA, MI, MN, MS, MO, MT, NE, NV, NH, NJ, NM, NY, NC, ND, OH, OK, OR, PA, RI, SC, SD, TN, TX, UT, VT, VA, WA, WV, WI, WY, Canada, Mexico

- EDWARD J. BRENNAN (President & C.E.O.)
- MICHAEL SHRIVER (Exec. V.P.-H.R. & Mdse. Planning)
- BRAD LATSUM (Mdse. Mgr.-Men's Ready to Wear) & Buys Men's Domestic & Imported Workwear, Footwear, Accessories, Leather Apparel
- OPEN (Sr. V.P.-Adv. & Sls. Prom.) & Buys Store Displays, Fixtures, Supplies

FIRST STEP (SP-3)

939 Market St.
San Francisco, CA 94103
415-989-9989 / Fax: 415-397-7811
Website: www.firststepsf.com

- SCOTT KIM (Owner) & Buys Athletic Footwear, Activewear
- JOE KIM (Mgr.) & Buys Athletic Footwear, Activewear

FLEET FEET (FW)

2086 Chestnut St. (m-b)
San Francisco, CA 94123
415-921-7188 / Fax: 415-921-3898
Sales: $500,001-$1 Million
Website: www.fleetfeet.com

- MITCHELL MASIA (Owner) & Buys Men's Footwear, Watches, Men's Accessories, Men's Apparel, Hosiery
- KIMBERLY SPARR-Men's Footwear, Watches, Men's Accessories, Men's Apparel, Hosiery

FRANCISCAN SHOPS (SP)

(SAN FRANCISCO STATE UNIVERSITY)
1650 Holloway Ave.
San Francisco, CA 94132
415-338-2665 / Fax: 415-338-1450
Sales: $10 Million-$20 Million
Website: www.bookstore.sfsu.edu

- ROBERT STRONG (Mgr.)
- KRISTIN SYMES-Fleece, Jackets, Hosiery, Licensed Apparel

FTC SKI & SPORTS (SG-2)

1360 Bush St. (p-b)
San Francisco, CA 94109
415-673-8363 / Fax: 415-771-9210

- LLOYD UYEHARD-Active Apparel, T-shirts, Sweat Outfits, Athletic Hosiery, Long Underwear, Headwear, Ski Clothing, Golf Apparel, Skate Clothing

G & M SALES, INC. (SG)

1667 Market St. (p-m)
San Francisco, CA 94103
415-863-2855 / Fax: 415-863-2154
Website: www.gmsales.com

- PERRY KERSON (President & Owner)
- KAREN GIKAS-Outdoor Clothing, Long Underwear, Work Clothing, Hosiery, Store Displays, Fixtures and Supplies

THE GAP, INC. (CLO-3100 & OL)

(GAP KIDS)
(BABY GAP)
1 Harrison St. (p-m-b)
San Francisco, CA 94105
650-952-4400 / Fax: 415-427-7046
Sales: $11 Billion
Website: www.gap.com

- PAUL PRESSLER (President & C.E.O.)
- GARY MUTO (President- Gap U.S.)
- JEROME JESSUP (Exec. V.P.-Product Design & Dev.)
- KYLE ANDREW (V.P.- Mktg.)
- MARK DVORAK (V.P.)
- KIM ZACHARY (Dir.- Fixtures) & Buys Store Displays, Fixtures, Supplies
- CHRIS CHOY (Assoc. Mdse. Mgr.) & Buys Men's Jeans, Men's Outerwear
- JIMMY OLSSON (Mdse. Mgr.) & Buys Knits

GUMP'S, INC. (GS & MO & OL)

135 Post St.
San Francisco, CA 94108
415-982-1616 / Fax: 415-984-9415
Website: www.gumps.com

- MARILU KLAR (V.P.) & Buys Men's Jewelry

THE HOUND SHOP, INC. (MW)

140 Sutter St. (b-des)
San Francisco, CA 94104
415-989-0429 / Fax: 415-788-6178
Sales: $1 Million-$10 Million
Website: www.thehound.com

- WALT SCHORNO (President & Partner) & Buys Leather Goods, Fragrances, Men's Designer Apparel, Men's Formalwear, Men's Accessories, Men's Activewear, Men's Suits, Young Men's Apparel, Men's Footwear, Men's Casualwear, Men's Swimwear, Underwear
- MIKE BLUNDEN (Partner & Mgr.) & Buys Leather Goods, Fragrances, Men's Designer Apparel, Men's Formalwear, Men's Accessories, Men's Activewear, Men's Suits, Young Men's Apparel, Men's Footwear, Men's Casualwear, Men's Swimwear, Underwear

THE IDEAL (CLO)

2370 Mission St. (bud-p)
San Francisco, CA 94110
415-826-6020 / Fax: 415-852-6022
Sales: $500,001-$1 Million

- MARIA RUBIO-Boys' Apparel, Men's Casualwear, Denim Apparel, Hosiery, Outerwear, Sleepwear, Sportswear, Underwear
- ROBERT MILLS (Owner) & Buys Boys' Apparel, Men's Casualwear, Denim Apparel, Hosiery, Outerwear, Sleepwear, Sportswear, Underwear

IMPERIAL FASHION (CLO-3)

(FAR EAST FASHION)
(IMPERIAL FASHION)
(RELIN)
564 Grant Ave. (m)
San Francisco, CA 94108
415-362-8112 / Fax: 415-362-6115
Sales: $1 Million-$10 Million

- RAYMOND LAM (President) & Buys Boys' Apparel, Men's Apparel, Outerwear, Sportswear
- CELIN LAM (V.P.) & Buys Boys' Apparel, Men's Apparel, Outerwear, Sportswear
- MAXINE WONG (Gen. Mgr.) & Buys Boys' Apparel, Men's Apparel, Outerwear, Sportswear
- JEANNIE LEE (Store Mgr.)

IN-JEAN-IOUS (MW)

432 Castro St. (m-b)
San Francisco, CA 94114
415-864-1707 / Fax: 415-864-3651
Sales: $1 Million-$10 Million

- BILL TULL (Owner) & Buys Leather Goods, Fragrances, Men's Apparel, Men's Designer Apparel, Men's Formalwear, Men's Accessories, Men's Activewear, Men's Suits, Young Men's Apparel, Men's Footwear, Men's Casualwear, Men's Sleepwear, Men's Swimwear, Underwear, Watches
- WOODY EVANS (Mgr.) & Buys Leather Goods, Fragrances, Men's Apparel, Men's Designer Apparel, Men's Formalwear, Men's Accessories, Men's Activewear, Men's Suits, Young Men's Apparel, Men's Footwear, Men's Casualwear, Men's Sleepwear, Men's Swimwear, Underwear, Watches

JEFF'S JEANS (CLO)

5201 Geary Blvd. (p-m-b)
San Francisco, CA 94118
415-221-1802 / Fax: 415-221-2045

- MRS. HANNA (Owner) & Buys Men's Jeans, Slacks, Tops, Sweaters, Dress Shirts, Levi Jackets, Hosiery, Belts, Store Displays, Fixtures, Supplies
- RICHARD HANNA (Mgr.) & Buys Jeans, Active Apparel, T-shirts, Fleece, Shorts, Underwear, Hosiery, Belts, Store Displays, Fixtures and Supplies

CALIFORNIA - San Francisco

LOMBARDI SPORTS, INC. (SG)

1600 Jackson St.
San Francisco, CA 94109
415-771-0600 / Fax: 415-771-1891
Website: www.lombardisports.com

STEVE LOMBARDI (President)
KEVIN DePALMER-Outdoor Clothing
CHRIS PEAKE-Hosiery, Footwear
MAZ HATTORI-Active Apparel, T-shirts, Fleece & Shorts
DIANA DeFARIO-Exercise Apparel, Underwear

MACY'S WEST (DEPT-99 & OL)

(FEDERATED DEPT. STORES, INC.)
P.O. Box 7888 (p-m-b)
170 O'Farrell Street
San Francisco, CA 94102
(Federated Merchandising Group)
415-954-6000 / Fax: 415-984-7807
Sales: $4 Billion
Website: www.federated-fds.com
Retail Locations: AZ, CA, MN, NV, NM, TX

ROBERT L. METTLER (Chmn. & C.E.O.)
MIKE OSBORN (President & C.O.O.)
RUDOLPH J. BORNEO (Vice-Chmn.)
ROBERT GILMARTIN (V.P. & Real Estate Contact)

PAUL FITZPATRICK (Sr. V.P./G.M.M.-Men's/Children's)
RICK SMITH (D.M.M.-Men's Casual Pants, Shoes & Tailored Clothing)
CHERYL PATTISON-Men's Joseph Abboud, La Coste, Tommy Bahama, Polo Ralph Lauren
ED LARA-American Designers, European Designers, Armani AX, Traditional Collection, DKNY Men's, Kenneth Cole
CRAIG ROBERTSON-Men's Walkshorts, Outerwear, Dress/Casual Pants, Slacks, Dress Slacks
CHENOAH BELCHER (Asst. Buyer) & Buys Dress Slacks, Casual Slacks, Jeans, Better Casual Slacks
KATHLEEN HOLLIWELL-Men's Casual Slacks
CHRISTINE O'NEILL-Men's Denim
STEPHEN ETLING-Better Suits, Designer Suits, Topcoats, Rainwear, Sportscoats, Tailored Clothing, Suit Separates
MARK RESNIK-Men's Dress Shoes, Designer Shoes
DAWN ECKERLE-Men's Athletic Shoes, Moderate Shoes
TONY BROWN (D.M.M.-Men's Casual Tops, Activewear & Outerwear) (@ 415-984-7335) & Buys 4 to 7 Boys' Wear
PHYLLIS KIVETT-Golf Wear, Knits, Sweaters
JULIE BARBIERI (Asst. Buyer) & Buys Golf Wear, Knits, Sweaters
KRISTEN KOH (Asst. Buyer) & Buys Golf Wear, Knits, Sweaters
BECKY KIM-Men's Tasso Elba, Wovens, Related Separates
CATHY STRACQUADANIO-Young Men's Eminem, Ecko, Sean John, Streetwear, Rocawear
DENNI LOCKE-Activewear, Swimwear, Walkshorts, Outerwear, Nike, Licensed Team

MICHELLE MONIGAL (D.M.M.- Young Mens)
JOHN HUNT-Boys' 8-20 Surf & Skate wear, Oakley, Levi, Quicksilver
MICHELLE HOUGHTON (Asst. Buyer) & Buys Boys' 8-20 Polo, Boys' 8-20 Calvin Klein, Boys' 8-20 Nautica, Boys' 8-20 Clothing, Boys' 8-20 Hilfiger, Boys' 8-20 Collections, Boys' 8-20 Furnishings, Boys' 8-20 Outerwear
RUQAYYUH ROLLINS (Asst. Buyer) & Buys Boys' 8-20 Active, Surf
CHRIS O'NEIL-DKNY Young Men's Jeans, Young Men's Guess, Tommy Denim, Young Men's Polo Denim, Young Men's CK Jeans, Nautica Denim, Kenneth Cole Denim
JESSICA MORTON (Asst. Buyer) & Buys DKNY Young Men's Jeans, Young Men's Guess, Tommy Denim, Young Men's Polo Denim, Young Men's CK Jeans, Nautica Denim, Kenneth Cole Denim
ANDY NGUYEN-Young Men's Collections, Boys' 8-20 Collectios, Union Bay, Trend Tops, Trend Bottoms, Denim, Levi's Bottoms
BETSY VALDES (Asst. Buyer) & Buys Boys' 8-20 Trend Tops, Boys' 8-20 Bottoms
SARAH HERNANDEZ (Asst. Buyer) & Buys Modern Dressing, Streetwear
SCOTT KEMNITZ-Boys' 8-20 Polo, Streetwear, Nautica, Tops, Bottoms, Active, Hilfiger, Collections, Furnishings
JULIE CASHION (D.M.M.-Infants, Toddlers & Boys 4-7)
THAI PHAM-Infant Layette, Newborn-9 mos.
DELORA LEE (Asst. Buyer) & Buys Infant Layette, Newborn-9 mos.
OPEN-Infants 12-24 mos. & Infant Collections
JAMIE WHITMORE (Asst. Buyer) & Buys Infants 12-24 mos. & Infant Collections
PHYLISS KIVETT-Men's Golfwear, Knit Shorts, Sweaters
BUFF MORGAN-Toddler Boys', Toddler Boys' Collection, License, Boys' 4-7 Sportswear, Boys' 4-7 Tommy, Boys' Collection 4-7, Boys' 4-7 Polo
CYNTHIA COOPER

MIKE HASKELL (D.M.M.-Men's Dress & Basic Furnishings)
JACKIE HOWARD-Men's Basic Dress Shirts, Status Dress Shirts, Designer Dress Shirts, Neckwear
LAUREN ALTBAIER-Men's Seasonal Accessories, Small Leather Goods
BUFF MORGAN-Leather Goods, Men's Belts, Men's Jewelry
MICHELLE LEE (Asst. Buyer) & Buys Leather Goods, Men's Belts, Men's Jewelry
JOE ROSSI-Men's Underwear, Men's Sleepwear & Robes, Men's Hosiery
JOLIE LEONG (Asst. Buyer) & Buys Men's Underwear, Men's Sleepwear & Robes, Men's Hosiery
HELEN D'OLIVERA (D.M.M.-Sportswear Collections)
CHERI EHRLICH-Men's INC, Claiborne, Reunion, Perry Ellis, Kenneth Cole, Emanuel
PATTY STARK-Men's Timberland, Update Traditional, Hilfiger, Nautica, Swim

(MACY'S WEST Cont. on next page)

(MACY'S WEST Cont.)

ED LARA-Men's American Designer, European Designer, DKNY

DINA KHALID-Men's Diesel, Impulse, Impulse Collections

MARIAN'S MERCHANDISING CO., INC. (CLO)

2040 Mission St. (b-des)
San Francisco, CA 94110
415-863-5897 / Fax: 415-863-0297
Sales: $500,001-$1 Million

JOE ANKER (President)

DAVID ANKER (C.E.O.) & Buys Leather Goods, Men's Casualwear, Denim Apparel, Sportswear

ANDREW THOMPSON (Treas.) & Buys Leather Goods, Men's Casualwear, Denim Apparel, Sportswear

THELMA ZAMORA-Leather Goods, Men's Casualwear, Denim Apparel, Sportswear

MILLS, INC. (CLO-15 & OL)

1834 Market St. (m)
San Francisco, CA 94102
415-864-1899 / Fax: 415-864-1110
Sales: $1 Million-$10 Million
Website: www.millswear.com

SUZETTE MILLS FOLEY (President)

LINDA VOGEL (Dir.) & Buys Men's Tailored Slacks, Tailored Jackets, Sweaters, Sport Shirts, Casual Slacks, Outer Jackets, Active Apparel, Dress Shirts, Ties, Hosiery, Belts, Young Men's Wear, 8 to 20 Boys' Wear, School Uniforms, Footwear

MODERN APPEALING CLOTHING (CLO-2)

5 Claude Ln. (m-b)
San Francisco, CA 94108
415-837-0615 / Fax: 415-296-7455

BEN OSPITAL (Co-Owner) & Buys Men's Apparel, Accessories, Outerwear, Sportswear, Suits

CHRIS OSPITAL (Co-Owner) & Buys Men's Apparel, Accessories, Outerwear, Sportswear, Suits

JERI OSPITAL (Co-Owner) & Buys Men's Apparel, Accessories, Outerwear, Sportswear, Suits

NFL SHOP (MW & OL)

(Div. of COURTNEY ENTERPRISES)
Pier 39 (p-m-b)
Bldg. Q, #Q215
San Francisco, CA 94133
415-397-2027 / Fax: 415-397-4374
Website: www.nflshop39.com

RON COURTNEY (Owner)

EDWARD LAO (Mgr.) & Buys Store Displays, Fixtures, Supplies

RICH BLEVENS-Men's Licensed T-shirts, Clothing, Young Men's & Boys' Licensed Clothing

NORDSTROM NORTHERN DIV. - CITY REGION (DEPT-9 & OL)

865 Market St. (m-b)
San Francisco, CA 94103
415-243-8500 / Fax: 415-977-5297
Website: www.nordstrom.com

DAVID WITMAN (Corp. Mdsg. Mgr. & V.P. - Men's Wear)

MATT ALBRIGHT (D.M.M. - Men's Wear) (@ 925-975-5600)

SHERI DERSHIMAN-PHILLIPS (R.M.M. - Suits)

BRUCE EMBREE-Men's Suits

JIM ADDIS-Men's Suits

JULINE FUJII-Men's Sportswear

JODI WILSON-Men's Sportswear

GREG SCOTT-Men's Wear

CHARLES SPISAK-Men's Rail Apparel

GERIL OLSEN (D.M.M. - Accessories) (@ 415-977-5078)

DIANE KANTOR (D.M.M. - Jewelry) (@ 310-750-2513)

LARA GRACE (@ 925-975-5542)-Men's Furnishings

RAMINA OUSHANA (@ 311-075-0251)-Men's Gloves

TINA FOWLER-Men's Belts, Sunglasses

CAROLYN MEISTER (@ 415-977-5093)-Small Leather Goods

KATIE DONLAN-Men's Watches

ANDREA NAKAGAKI (D.M.M - Fragrances)

PENNY APPLEFORD-Men's Fragrances

CHRISTIE COTTLER (D.M.M - Children's Wear)

VERNON BOYD-Boys' Wear

TAMMY LEONG-Boys' Wear

BRUCE ANDERSON (D.M.M. - Men's Footwear)

GAIL LALUMIERE (D.M.M. - Children's Footwear)

STEVE HILL-Men's Athletic Footwear

DAVE BEAUDIN-Men's Footwear

GORDON STILL-Men's Better & Moderate Footwear

JOE MARCH-Men's & Young Men's Athletic Footwear

ALYSHA LUJAN-Boys' Footwear

SHANNON BRAEGELMANN-Boys' Hosiery

NORTH BEACH LEATHER (SG-5)

224 Grant Ave. (b-h)
San Francisco, CA 94108
415-362-8300 / Fax: 415-362-0585

SKIP PAS (Dir.-Purch.) & Buys Men's Leather Apparel, Furnishings, Accessories

OLD NAVY CLOTHING CO. (CLO-706 & OL)

(Div. of THE GAP, INC.)
345 Spear St. (p)
San Francisco, CA 94105
650-952-4400 / Fax: 415-427-4875
Website: www.oldnavy.com
Retail Locations: AL, AK, AR, AZ, CA, CO, CT, DE, DC, FL, GA, HI, ID, IL, IN, IA, KS, KY, LA, ME, MD, MT, MN, MA, MI, MS, NE, NV, NH, NJ, NM, NY, NC, ND, OH, OK, OR, PA, PR, RI, SC, SD, TN, TX, UT, VT, VA, WA, WV, WI

JENNY MING (President)

KEVIN LONERGAN (Exec. V.P. & C.O.O.-Old Navy Clothing Co.)

ALAN BEVROCAS (Sr. V.P. & Real Estate Contact)

RICHARD GOLDEN (V.P.-South & Midwest Regions)

HENRY STAFFORD (Mdse. Mgr.) & Buys Men's Wear, Knits, Sweaters, Accessories

REBECCA SALMONSON-Men's Accessories, Underwear, Hosiery

TOBY JACKSON-Boys' 4-18 Wovens, Accessories

ON THE ROAD AGAIN (CLO)

Pier 39, #D2
San Francisco, CA 94133
415-434-1482 / Fax: 415-434-1482

BRUCE DOBEKIN-Travelwear

ON THE RUN SHOE STORE (FW)

1310 9th Ave. (m-b)
San Francisco, CA 94122
415-665-8384 / Fax: 415-665-3740
Sales: $1 Million-$10 Million
Website: www.shoesontherun.com

LIDIA WACHTER (President)

LUBA REEVES (V.P.) & Buys Men's Footwear

MARK WACHTER (V.P.) & Buys Men's Footwear

PARK GENERAL, INC. (MW)

349 Sutter St. (m-b)
San Francisco, CA 94108
415-781-2666 / Fax: 415-781-6740
Sales: $500,001-$1 Million

NASSER ZAGHI (President) & Buys Men's Footwear, Leather Goods, Big & Tall Men's Wear, Casualwear, Denim Apparel, Formalwear, Accessories, Hosiery, Outerwear, Sportswear, Suits, Swimwear, Underwear

NINA YAHID (Store Mgr.) & Buys Men's Footwear, Leather Goods, Big & Tall Men's Wear, Casualwear, Denim Apparel, Formalwear, Accessories, Hosiery, Outerwear, Sportswear, Suits, Swimwear, Underwear

CALIFORNIA - San Francisco

PIONEER ARMY & NAVY STORE (AN)
1133 Market St.
San Francisco, CA 94103
415-621-8909 / Fax: 415-566-4121
JULES HOLTZ (Owner) & Buys Hunting Apparel, Boots, Sneakers, Licensed Apparel

ROCHESTER BIG & TALL CLOTHING, INC. (MW-21)
(CALIFORNIA BIG & TALL)
P.O. Box 882406 (m-b)
San Francisco, CA 94188
415-536-4181 / Fax: 415-896-2668
Sales: $50 Million-$100 Million
Website: www.rochesterclothing.com
ROBERT SOCKOLOV (President) & Buys Men's Footwear
STEVE SOCKOLOV (V.P. & G.M.M.) & Buys Big & Tall Men's Overcoats, Suits, Tailored Jackets, Tailored Slacks, Big & Tall Men's Raincoats, Sweaters, Sport Shirts Outer Jackets, Casual Slacks, Active Apparel, Furnishings, Accessories, Footwear
BILL SOCKOLOV (Dir.) & Buys Store Displays, Fixtures, Supplies

ROLO SAN FRANCISCO, INC. (CLO-3 & OL)
(ROLO GARAGE)
(ROLO SOMA)
2351 Market St. (p-m-b)
San Francisco, CA 94114
415-431-4545 / Fax: 415-431-0139
Sales: $1 Million-$10 Million
Website: www.rolo.com
MARK SCHULTZ (President)
ROLAND PETERS (Co-Owner) & Buys Men's Sportswear, Furnishings, Headwear, Accessories

SEYMOUR'S FASHIONS (MW)
211 Sutter, 7th Fl. (b)
San Francisco, CA 94108
415-421-6103 / Fax: 415-421-0641
GEORGE BULCHANDANI (Owner) & Buys Men's Dress Shirts, Ties, Belts, Jewelry, Store Displays, Fixtures, Supplies

SFO FORECAST (CLO)
211 Jefferson St.
San Francisco, CA 94133
415-931-3624 / Fax: 415-931-1976
RODRICK JONES-Men's Apparel

SIEGEL'S CLOTHING SUPERSTORE (CLO-2)
(SIEGEL'S TUXEDO SHOP)
2366 Mission St. (bud-p-m-b-des)
San Francisco, CA 94110
415-824-7729 / Fax: 415-824-7256
Sales: $1 Million-$10 Million
Website: www.zootsuitstore.com
MICHAEL GARDNER (President & Gen. Mgr.) & Buys Boys' Apparel, Men's Footwear, Big & Tall Apparel, Casualwear, Denim Apparel, Formalwear, Accessories, Hosiery, Outerwear, Sleepwear, Sportswear, Suits, Swimwear, Underwear
JOSE GONZALEZ (Sls. Mgr.)

THE TAILORED MAN, INC. (MW)
360 Sutter St. (b-h)
San Francisco, CA 94108
415-397-6906 / Fax: 415-362-4792
PETER DOMENICI, SR. (Owner) & Buys Store Displays, Fixtures, Supplies, Men's Overcoats, Suits, Tailored Jackets, Tailored Slacks, Sportswear, Leather Apparel, Furnishings, Accessories
PETER DOMENICI, JR.-Men's Overcoats, Suits, Tailored Jackets, Tailored Slacks, Sportswear, Leather Apparel, Furnishings, Accessories

VILLAIN'S (CLO-3)
(VILLAIN'S VAULT)
1672 Haight St. (m-b-des)
San Francisco, CA 00000
415-626-5939 / Fax: 415-621-0766
Website: www.villainssf.com
DAVID ENGEL (Owner) & Buys Men's Sportswear, Dress Shirts, Leather Jackets, Casual Headwear, Jeans, Footwear, Store Displays, Fixtures, Supplies
RANDY BREWER (Gen. Mgr.) & Buys Men's Sportswear, Dress Shirts, Leather Jackets, Casual Headwear, Jeans, Footwear, Store Displays, Fixtures, Supplies

WALTER FONG & SONS (MW)
459 Geary St. (h)
San Francisco, CA 94102
415-775-2900 / Fax: 415-775-8800
Sales: $1 Million-$10 Million
WALTER FONG (President) & Buys Men's Overcoats, Men's Suits, Tailored Jackets, Tailored Slacks, Raincoats, Sweaters, Sport Shirts, Outer Jackets, Leather Apparel, Casual Slacks, Furnishings, Accessories, Footwear, Store Displays, Fixtures, Supplies
WILLIAM FONG (G.M.M.) & Buys Men's Overcoats, Men's Suits, Tailored Jackets, Tailored Slack, Raincoats, Sweaters, Sport Shirts, Outer Jackets, Leather Apparel, Casual Slacks, Furnishings, Accessories, Footwear, Store Displays, Fixtures, Supplies

WILKES BASHFORD (CLO)
375 Sutter St. (h)
San Francisco, CA 94108
415-986-4380 / Fax: 415-956-3772
WILKES BASHFORD (Owner) & Buys Men's Wear, Store Displays, Fixtures and Supplies
ROSS HUNTER-Sportswear, Furnishings, Accessories

BECK'S SHOES, INC. (FW-8)
3687 Union Ave. (bud-p-m-b-des)
San Jose, CA 95124
408-559-1601 / Fax: 408-559-1643
Sales: $1 Million-$10 Million
Website: www.beckshoes.com
BLAINE BECK (President)
BILL BECK (C.E.O.)
DAN L. BECK (V.P.-Opers.) & Buys Men's Footwear, Leather Goods, Hosiery

DALE'S SHIRT WHEEL (MW & OL)
1375 Blossom Hill Rd. (p)
San Jose, CA 95118
408-266-4122 / Fax: 408-266-4124
Website: www.shirtwheel.com
DALE LASSNER (Owner) & Buys Men's Sportswear, Furnishings, Headwear, Accessories, Young Men's Wear, Boys' Wear, Store Displays, Fixtures, Supplies

DIAZ MENSWEAR (MW)
70 E. Santa Carla St. (m)
San Jose, CA 95113
408-297-8443
ALFRED DIAZ (Owner) & Buys Young Men's Wear, Sportswear, Store Displays, Fixtures and Supplies

ELI THOMAS THE COMPLETE MEN'S (MW)
400 S. Winchester Blvd., #120 (b)
San Jose, CA 95128
408-247-1024 / Fax: 408-244-3820
ELI THOMAS (President & Owner)
JIM THOMAS-Men's Wear, Sportswear, Furnishings, Accessories, Store Displays, Fixtures and Supplies

HAMMER & LEWIS FASHIONS (MW-2)
19 S. 1st St. (p-m)
San Jose, CA 95113
408-295-5808
Sales: $1 Million-$10 Million
SELA VELEZ (Co-Owner) & Buys Men's & Boys' Clothing, Urban Contemporary, Sportswear, Leather Apparel, Accessories, Store Displays, Fixtures, Supplies
IRVING VELEZ (Co-Owner) & Buys Men's & Boys' Clothing, Sportswear, Leather Apparel, Accessories, Men's Footwear, Urban Contemporary, Store Displays, Fixtures, Supplies

CALIFORNIA - San Jose

KETTMANN'S (MW-2)

1560 Alum Rock Ave. (m)
San Jose, CA 95116
408-251-0346 / Fax: 408-251-6761
Sales: $100,001-$500,000
Website: www.school-clothes.com

JOHN KETTMANN (President) & Buys Men's Sportswear, Headwear, Accessories, Furnishings, Boys' Public & Private School Uniforms, Store Displays, Fixtures, Supplies

DEBRA KETTMANN (V.P.) & Buys Men's Sportswear, Headwear, Accessories, Furnishings, Boys' Public & Private School Uniforms, Store Displays, Fixtures, Supplies

NOTE:

MEL COTTON'S, INC. (CLO-2)

1266 W. San Carlos St. (b)
San Jose, CA 95126
408-287-5994 / Fax: 408-298-3536
Sales: $10 Million-$50 Million
Website: www.melcottons.com

STEVE ZERHING (President, Gen. Mgr. & Real Estate Contact)

NEAL COLLIN (Gen. Mgr.) & Buys Boys' Footwear, Men's Footwear, Big & Tall Apparel, Casualwear, Accessories, Outerwear, Sportswear, Swimwear, Underwear

JAY LAURSSA-Boys' Footwear, Men's Footwear, Big & Tall Apparel, Casualwear, Accessories, Outerwear, Sportswear, Swimwear, Underwear

ONE EYED JACK'S WESTERN WEAR (WW)

2845 Moorepark Ave.
San Jose, CA 95128
408-244-1346 / Fax: 408-244-0566
Website: www.oneeyedjackswesternwear.com

JACK KOZLOWSKI (Owner) & Buys Men's Western Wear, Jewelry, Boots, Vests, Headwear, Wedding Apparel

SAN JOSE BLUE JEANS (CLO-2)

3062 Story Rd. (m-b)
San Jose, CA 95127
408-926-9606 / Fax: 408-929-3333
Sales: $1 Million-$10 Million

OSMAN PATEL (Owner) & Buys Boys' Apparel, Boys' Footwear, Men's Footwear, Leather Goods, Big & Tall Apparel, Casualwear, Denim Apparel, Accessories, Hosiery, Outerwear, Sportswear, Swimwear, Underwear

SAN JOSE MENSWEAR, INC. (MW)

1175 S. King Rd. (m)
San Jose, CA 95122
408-251-3326 / Fax: 408-251-3387
Sales: $500,001-$1 Million

JOSE MENDOZA (President) & Buys Boys' Apparel, Boys' Footwear, Men's Footwear, Fragrances, Leather Goods, Men's Apparel, Men's Casualwear, Men's Denim Apparel, Men's Accessories, Men's Hosiery, Men's Outerwear, Men's Sportswear, Men's Suits, Men's Underwear, Men's Western Wear, Young Me

CONSUELO MENDOZA (V.P.) & Buys Boys' Apparel, Boys' Footwear, Men's Footwear, Fragrances, Leather Goods, Men's Apparel, Men's Casualwear, Men's Denim Apparel, Men's Accessories, Men's Hosiery, Men's Outerwear, Men's Sportswear, Men's Suits, Men's Underwear, Men's Western Wear, Young Me

SANTA TERESA GOLF CLUB (SG)

260 Bernal Rd. (m)
San Jose, CA 95119
408-225-2650 / Fax: 408-226-9598

MIKE RAWITSER (President)

ROBI KRAMER-Men's Sportswear, Belts, Store Displays, Fixtures and Supplies

SPARTAN BOOKSTORE (SP)

(SAN JOSE STATE UNIVERSITY)
1125 N. 7th St.
San Jose, CA 95112
408-947-6920 / Fax: 408-924-1818
Sales: $500,001-$1 Million
Website: www.spartanshops.sjsu.edu

JEN SKEBBA (Mgr.) & Buys Fleece, Jackets, Hosiery

WARREN COURT (Dir. & Mgr.) (@ 408-924-1831)

STEVENS CREEK SURPLUS (MW)

3449 Stevens Creek Blvd. (p)
San Jose, CA 95117
408-244-0773 / Fax: 408-244-1839
Website: www.scssurplus.com

HOWARD SUSMAN (Owner)

SIVA RAO-Men's & Young Men's Wear, Levis, Working Clothes, Footwear, Raincoats, Sport Shirts, Underwear, Gloves, Headwear, Belts, Store Displays, Fixtures, Supplies

FRECKLES & FRILLS (MW-2)

(BANCROFT MEN'S WEAR)
590 Dutton Ave. (m)
San Leandro, CA 94577
510-638-1622 / Fax: 510-638-3302
Sales: $500,000-$1 Million

BRUCE BARNES (Owner) & Buys Men's Overcoats, Suits, Tailored Jackets, Tailored Slacks, Sweaters, Sport Shirts, Outer Jackets, Casual Slacks, Active Apparel, Furnishings, Accessories, 8 to 20 Boys' Better Suits, School Uniforms, Store Displays, Fixtures, Supplies

JOSEF DURAN MENSWEAR (MW-2)

177 Pelton Center Way (m-b-h)
San Leandro, CA 94577
510-483-7266

JOSEF DURAN (Owner) & Buys Suits, Tailored Jackets, Tailored Slacks, Sportswear, Furnishings, Accessories, Store Displays, Fixtures and Supplies

THE NORTH FACE (SG-11)

2013 Farlallon Dr. (m-b)
San Leandro, CA 94577
510-618-3500 / Fax: 510-618-3532
Website: www.thenorthface.com

BERNEY BISHOP-Men's Accessories, Furnishings, Outerwear, Sweaters, Hosiery, Headwear, Footwear

PACIFIC APPAREL (MW)

16276 E. 14th St. (m)
San Leandro, CA 94578
510-351-5237 / Fax: 510-278-7158
Sales: $500,000-$1 Million

ALLAN BARNES (Owner) & Buys Men's Raincoats, Work & Western Shirts, Outer Jackets, Casual Slacks, Work Pants, Underwear, Work Hosiery, Work Gloves, Headwear, Hats, Belts, Footwear, Store Displays, Fixtures, Supplies

CHARLES SHOES (FW-2)

867 Higuera St. (m-b)
San Luis Obispo, CA 93401
805-543-4054 / Fax: 805-543-4833
Sales: $1 Million-$10 Million

KEN PORCHE (Partner) & Buys Men's Footwear, Leather Goods, Men's Accessories, Hosiery

RUBY PORCHE (Partner) & Buys Men's Footwear, Leather Goods, Men's Accessories, Hosiery

BALLARD'S UNIFORM CENTER (SP)

715 S. B St. (m-b)
San Mateo, CA 94401
650-347-3240 / Fax: 650-347-9491
Sales: $500,001-$1 Million

MONICA GRIFFIN (Store Mgr.)

OTIS GRIFFIN (Owner) & Buys Men's Footwear, Apparel, Accessories, Uniforms, Workclothes

CALIFORNIA - San Mateo

DAN NEWELL, INC. (MW)
35 E. 4th Ave. (b)
San Mateo, CA 94401
650-348-4042 / Fax: 650-348-4153
ROBERT NUTINI (Owner) & Buys Men's Wear, Sportswear, Furnishings, Accessories, Store Displays, Fixtures and Supplies

SCHNEIDER'S APPAREL (MW-2)
208 E. 3rd Ave. (p-m)
San Mateo, CA 94401
650-342-3216 / Fax: 650-342-3367
JANET ROBB (President)
BILL NAUGHTON-Men's Wear, Sportswear, Furnishings

WINNERS (SP-2)
1730 S. Amphlett Blvd., #112
San Mateo, CA 94402
650-570-7937 / Fax: 650-570-4391
Sales: $2 Million-$5 Million
VINCE WARNER (President)
JOHN MURPHY (Gen. Mgr.) & Buys Athletic Footwear, Activewear

MANNINO'S TUX & TAILS (MW)
683 W. 9th St. (m-b)
San Pedro, CA 90731
310-832-4098 / Fax: 310-832-5052
BILL MANNINO (Store Mgr.) & Buys Men's & Boys' Formal Wear, Store Displays, Fixtures, Supplies

NORMAN'S MEN'S & BOYS', INC. (MW)
(NORMAN'S)
371 W. 6th St. (m)
San Pedro, CA 90731
310-832-8342
Sales: $1 Million-$10 Million
NICK D'AMBROSI (Owner) & Buys Boys' Apparel, Men's Footwear, Leather Goods, Men's Apparel, Men's Casualwear, Men's Denim Apparel, Men's Formalwear, Men's Accessories, Men's Hosiery, Men's Outerwear, Men's Sportswear, Men's Swimwear, Men's Underwear, Watches

UNION WAR SURPLUS STORE, INC. (DEPT)
355 W. 6th St. (p-m)
San Pedro, CA 90731
310-833-2949 / Fax: 310-833-3549
Website: www.unionwar.com
AL KAYE (Owner) & Buys Men's Jeans, Sport Shirts, Western Shirts, Jackets, Underwear, Hosiery, Belts, Footwear, Store Displays, Fixtures, Supplies

FRENCH'S HITCHING POST, INC. (WW)
1323 2nd St. (p)
San Rafael, CA 94901
415-453-6000 / Fax: 415-453-9114
Sales: $500,000-$1 Million
JEANIE O'NEILL (V.P.) & Buys Men's & Boys' Western Wear, Footwear

JEANS TO A T (MW)
1314 2nd St. (p)
San Rafael, CA 94901
415-456-6841 / Fax: 415-456-6842
TOM DIETTRICH (Owner) & Buys Sportswear, Jeans, T-shirts, Activewear, Hosiery, Belts, Young Men's Wear, Urban Contemporary, Boys' Wear, Store Displays, Fixtures and Supplies

EL PROGRESO (DEPT)
157 Virginia Ave. (p-m-b)
San Ysidro, CA 92073
619-428-2888 / Fax: 619-428-2888
Sales: $1 Million-$10 Million
JACK YUFE (Owner) & Buys Men's Tailored Slacks, Raincoats, Sweaters, Sport Shirts, Casual Slacks, Jeans, Leather Jackets, Dress Shirts, Hosiery, Gloves, Underwear, Headwear, Belts, Active Apparel, Jewelry, Young Men's Wear, 7 to 20 Boys' Wear, Store Displays, Fixtures, Supplies
MARIA VEGA-Men's Tailored Slacks, Raincoats, Sweaters, Sport Shirts, Casual Slacks, Jeans, Leather Jackets, Dress Shirts, Hosiery, Gloves, Underwear, Headwear, Belts, Active Apparel, Jewelry, Young Men's Wear, 7 to 20 Boys' Wear, Store Displays, Fixtures, Supplies
JOE MEZA-Men's Tailored Slacks, Raincoats, Sweaters, Sport Shirts, Casual Slacks, Jeans, Leather Jackets, Dress Shirts, Hosiery, Gloves, Underwear, Headwear, Belts, Active Apparel, Jewelry, Young Men's Wear, Footwear, 7 to 20 Boys' Wear, Store Displays, Fixtures, Supplies

AL'S SHOP (MW)
216 E. 4th St. (p-m)
Santa Ana, CA 92701
714-542-6639 / Fax: 714-542-4820
PHOUN CHAN (Owner) & Buys Men's Wear, Sportswear, Furnishings, Accessories, Young Men's Wear, Boys' Wear, Store Displays, Fixtures and Supplies

GINGISS FORMAL WEAR (MW)
3713 S. Bristol St. (m-b)
Santa Ana, CA 92704
714-751-4160 / Fax: 949-495-9417
Website: www.gingiss.com
JUAN HONG (Owner) & Buys Men's Formal Wear, Young Men's Formal Wear, Boys' Formal Wear, Footwear, Store Displays, Fixtures, Supplies

GUADALAJARA JEWELRY, INC. (JWLY-2)
P.O. Box 924
200 E. 4th St.
Santa Ana, CA 92701
714-547-5622 / Fax: 714-547-5385
Sales: $1 Million-$10 Million
LOUIS R. PESCARMONA (President) & Buys Jewlery, Watches

INDUSTRIAL SHOE CO. (FW-7 & MO)
1421 E. 1st St. (m)
Santa Ana, CA 92701
714-796-1976 / Fax: 714-796-1975
Sales: $1 Million-$10 Million
Website: www.industrialshoeco.com
CHARLES CUMMINGS (President & C.E.O.)
RICHARD FLOOD (G.M.) & Buys Men's Accessories, Hosiery
RICK SALEH (Mgr. Purch.) & Buys Men's Footwear

LA MODA MEN'S SPORTSWEAR (MW-2)
120 E. 4th St. (b)
Santa Ana, CA 92701
714-541-2727 / Fax: 714-547-9157
NASSER KASSIRA (@ 714-547-9173)-Men's Sportswear, Leather Apparel, Tops, Bottoms, Store Displays, Fixtures, Supplies

PANTS PLUS (MW-2)
3740 W. McFadden Ave. (p-m)
Santa Ana, CA 92704
714-775-8300
Sales: $1 Million-$10 Million
DEBRA SALERNO (President & Coord.) & Buys Men's Sweaters, Sport Shirts, Outer Jackets, Casual Slacks, Dress Shirts, Underwear, Hosiery, Belts, Boys' Clothing, Sportswear, Footwear
JEFF SALERNO-Footwear, Store Displays, Fixtures and Supplies

PERFECT SHOES (FW-3)
116 W. 4th St. (p-m)
Santa Ana, CA 92701
714-547-6724 / Fax: 714-542-4820
PHOUN CHAN (Owner) & Buys T-shirts, Fleece, Active Apparel, Western Hats, Belts, Jeans, Footwear, Store Displays, Fixtures and Supplies

R & R SPORTSWEAR (MW)
308 E. 4th St. (m)
Santa Ana, CA 92701
714-543-3648
RAYMOND RANGEL (Owner) & Buys Men's Sportswear, Furnishings, Accessories, Boys' Wear, Leather Apparel, Store Displays, Fixtures, Supplies

RANDY'S MENSWEAR LTD., INC. (MW)
2800 N. Main St., #1034 (m)
Main Place Mall
Santa Ana, CA 92701
714-479-0855 / Fax: 714-479-0656
ABRAHAM HAMIDEH (Owner) & Buys Men's Sportswear, Furnishings, Accessories, Footwear, Store Displays, Fixtures, Supplies

CALIFORNIA - Santa Ana

SPORTS PLUS (SP)
307 E. 1st St.
Santa Ana, CA 92701
714-547-4994 / Fax: 714-667-0612
IMAD DAKELBAB (Owner) & Buys Athletic Footwear

BIG DOG SPORTSWEAR (CLO-198)
121 Gray Ave. (m-b)
Santa Barbara, CA 93101
805-963-8727 / Fax: 805-963-8048
Sales: $100 Million-$500 Million
Website: www.bigdogs.com
ANDREW FESHBACH (C.E.O. & President)
ANTHONY WALL (Exec. V.P.-Purch.)
DOUG NILSON (Exec. V.P.-Mdsg.)
ANDREW WADHAMS (Sr. V.P.-Retail Opers.)
DAVID WOLF (Sr. V.P.-Mktg. & Sls.)
SUSIE MINIER (V.P.-Mdsg.)
KAREN CAHILL (Dir.-Sls.) & Buys Boys' Apparel, Men's Casualwear, Accessories, Hosiery, Outerwear, Sportswear, Swimwear, Underwear, Sleepwear

CENTRO MUSICAL OF SANTA BARBARA (MW)
514 N. Milpas St. (p)
Santa Barbara, CA 93103
805-962-2785
MARIA PEREZ (Owner) & Buys Men's Sportswear, Furnishings, Footwear, Store Displays, Fixtures, Supplies

THE CHANDLERY ON THE BREAKWATER (CLO)
132 B Harbor Way, #B (m)
Santa Barbara, CA 93109
805-965-4538 / Fax: 805-966-5237
Sales: $1 Million-$10 Million
TIFFANY REYES (Mgr.) & Buys Men's Sweaters, Sport Shirts, Active Apparel, Shorts, Belts, Footwear, Store Displays, Fixtures, Supplies

JEDLICKA'S SADDLERY (WW-2 & OL)
2605 De La Vina St. (m-b)
Santa Barbara, CA 93105
805-687-0747 / Fax: 805-687-7376
Sales: $1 Million-$10 Million
Website: www.jedlickas.com
J. C. JENKINS, SR. (President) & Buys Store Displays, Fixtures, Supplies
KAREN JENKINS (Secy.)
J. F. JENKINS, JR. (G.M.M.) & Buys English Riding Apparel, Men's Western Wear, Overcoats, Suits, Tailored Jackets, Tailored Slacks, Sport Shirts, Outer Jackets, Leather Apparel, Casual Slacks, Dress Shirts, Robes, Sweaters, Active Apparel, Fragrances, Boys' Clothing, Belts, Jewelry, Small Leather Goods, Footwear, Headwear & Belts
SHARON FROWISS-Clothing, Jewelry
GEORGE AIGNER-Footwear
APRIL STEWART-Saddlery

OUTFOOTERS, INC. (FW)
136 S. Hope Ave. (m-b)
Santa Barbara, CA 93105
805-687-4533 / Fax: 805-687-1034
Sales: $500,001-$1 Million
FRANK DEJOHN (Owner) & Buys Men's Footwear, Licensed Apparel, Men's Accessories, Men's Apparel, Hosiery
JENNIFER CANNON (Mgr.)

PANOYAN CUSTOM TAILORING & MENSWEAR (MW)
2964 State St. (h)
Santa Barbara, CA 93105
805-687-8521
GARY PANOYAN (Owner) & Buys Suits, Tailored Jackets, Tailored Slacks, Dress Shirts, Ties, Belts

SUNDANCE BEACH SPORTS (SG)
(BENBAR, INC.)
809 State St.
Santa Barbara, CA 93109
805-966-2474 / Fax: 805-968-0031
RICHARD BENNETT (Owner) & Buys Activewear, Athletic Footwear, Swimwear

SURF 'N' WEAR'S BEACH HOUSE (CLO)
(SURF 'N' WEAR INTERNATIONAL, INC.)
10 State St. (p)
Santa Barbara, CA 93101
805-963-1281 / Fax: 805-965-7485
Website: www.surfnwear.com
ROGER NANCE (President) & Buys Men's & Boys' Activewear, Sport Shirts, Shorts, Tops, Sweaters, Swimwear, Licensed Apparel
KIM LIPP (Mgr.) & Buys Men's & Boys' Activewear, Sport Shirts, Shorts, Tops, Sweaters, Swimwear, Store Displays, Fixtures and Supplies

THE TERRITORY AHEAD, INC. (CLO-4 & MO)
419 State St.
Santa Barbara, CA 93101
805-962-5558 / Fax: 805-509-2648
Sales: $10 Million-$50 Million
Website: www.territoryahead.com
GEORGE ITTNER (C.E.O. & President)
MARK CARMODY (C.F.O.)
STEVE TRAER (V.P.-Men's Apparel)
BEAU LAWRENCE-Men's Outerwear, Leather Goods
DAVID BROWN-Men's Woven Shirts, Apparel, Accessories, Footwear

W.A. KING CO. (MW)
9 E. Figueroa St. (m-b)
Santa Barbara, CA 93101
805-966-3333 / Fax: 805-966-4038
W. ALEX KING (Owner) & Buys Men's Sportswear, Furnishings, Leather Apparel, Footwear, Store Displays, Fixtures, Supplies

RYAN'S SPORTS SHOP (SP)
1171 Homestead Rd.
Santa Clara, CA 95050
408-985-6886 / Fax: 408-985-0278
Sales: $500,001-$1 Million
STEVEN GOETTLEMAN (Co-Owner) & Buys Activewear, Athletic Footwear
GARY GOETTELMANN (Co-Owner) & Buys Activewear, Athletic Footwear

TEAM CONCEPT (SP)
(ENTERPRISE, INC.)
3064 Lawrence Expwy.
Santa Clara, CA 95051
408-739-1671 / Fax: 408-739-2654
Website: www.teamconcept.com
GLORIA FLESNER (Owner) & Buys Activewear, Athletic Footwear
MICHELLE PUCCINELLI (Partner) & Buys Activewear, Athletic Footwear

BILLS WHEELS, INC. (FW-2 & MO)
(PHANTOM)
1240 Soquel Ave. (m-b)
Santa Cruz, CA 95062
831-469-0904 / Fax: 831-469-0214
Sales: $500,001-$1 Million
Website: www.billswheels.com
BILL ACKERMAN (Owner & G.M.) & Buys Boys' Apparel, Boys' Footwear, Leather Goods, Licensed Apparel, Men's Apparel, Men's Footwear

O'NEILL SURF SHOP (SP-5)
1071 41st Ave.
Santa Cruz, CA 95062
831-475-7500 / Fax: 831-475-0544
Sales: $1 Million-$10 Million
JOSEPH ROSE (Retail Mgr.) & Buys Activewear, Athletic Footwear, T-shirts, Shorts, Boardshorts

O'NEILL, INC. (CLO-3)
(O'NEILL BOARDWALK SHOP)
(O'NEILL BEACH SHOP)
(O'NEILL SURF SHOP)
1115 41st Ave. (p)
Santa Cruz, CA 95010
831-475-7500 / Fax: 831-479-5677
Sales: $10 Million-$50 Million
Website: www.oneill.com
PAT O'NEILL (President)
ELFIN SAFER (District Mgr.)
JOSH SHERROCK-Men's Sportswear, Footwear, Urban Contemporary, Store Displays, Fixtures, Supplies

CALIFORNIA - Santa Cruz

PORTS OF CALL (CLO-4)
(SHORELAND)
(NOLAND'S)
(FLOTSAM OF CALIFORNIA, INC.)
415 Spring St.
Santa Cruz, CA 95060
831-426-9699 / Fax: 831-426-0408
GINGER NOLAND (Owner)
TODD NOLAND (C.E.O.) & Buys Active Apparel, Swimwear, Resortwear, Beach Footwear
BRUCE NOLAND (V.P.) & Buys Active Apparel, Swimwear, Resortwear, Beach Footwear

SANTA CRUZ T & C CORP. (CLO)
1306 Pacific Ave. (m-b)
Santa Cruz, CA 95060
831-427-1040 / Fax: 831-427-1042
Sales: $500,001-$1 Million
TOM JACKSON (Co-Owner) & Buys Boys' Apparel, Men's Apparel, Hosiery
CAROL JACKSON (Co-Owner) & Buys Boys' Apparel, Men's Apparel, Hosiery

OXMAN SURPLUS, INC. (AN & OL)
14128 E. Rosecrans Ave. (p-m)
Santa Fe Springs, CA 90670
562-921-1106 / Fax: 562-921-1106
JEROME OXMAN (Chmn.)
MURRAY OXMAN (President) & Buys Men's Footwear, Men's & Boys' Military Clothing, Store Displays, Fixtures, Supplies

VANS, INC. (FW-160 & OL)
15700 Shoemaker Ave. (m-b)
Santa Fe Springs, CA 90670
562-565-8267 / Fax: 562-565-8406
Sales: $100 Million-$500 Million
Website: www.vans.com
STEVE MURRAY (President & C.E.O.)
KEVIN BAILEY (President-Retail Stores)
ALEX GONZALEZ (V.P.-Apparel)
STEVE MILLS (V.P.-Mdse.)
SYLVIN NYLES-Boys' Apparel, Boys' Footwear, Men's Apparel, Men's Footwear, Men's Accessories, Leather Goods

LA BONITA (CLO)
501 W. Main St. (bud-p)
Santa Maria, CA 93458
805-922-3721
P. CORTEZ (Owner) & Buys Sportswear, Young Men's Wear, Furnishings, Accessories, Work Clothes

B. NY (CLO)
2449 Main St. (b-h)
Santa Monica, CA 90405
310-396-1616 / Fax: 310-399-0466
Sales: $500,000-$1 Million
GREGORY NIEBEL (Owner) & Buys Men's Overcoats, Suits, Tailored Jackets, Tailored Slacks, Sweaters, Sport Shirts, Active Apparel, Footwear, Store Displays, Fixtures, Supplies

BEL MONDO (CLO)
1413 Montana Ave.
Santa Monica, CA 90403
310-394-7272 / Fax: 310-394-0271
GEORGE DOW-Men's Apparel

CANYON BEACHWEAR (SP-16)
106 Entrada Dr.
Santa Monica, CA 90402
310-459-5070 / Fax: 310-573-1228
Website: www.canyonbeachwear.com
KATHLEEN MUDD (Owner) & Buys Men's Swimwear

FLAP HAPPY, INC. (CLO & MO)
2330 Michigan Ave.
Santa Monica, CA 90404
310-453-3527 / Fax: 310-829-1485
Sales: $1 Million-$10 Million
LAURIE SNYDER (President) & Buys Boys' Apparel, Men's Apparel

FRED SEGAL (SP)
500 Broadway, #H (b)
Santa Monica, CA 90401
310-394-9652 / Fax: 310-394-2782
BETTY GOLDIE (Owner) & Buys Men's Sportswear, Leather Apparel, Denim, Swimwear, Accessories, Clothing, Furnishings, Store Displays, Fixtures and Supplies

HANSEL & GRETEL (KS)
225 26th St. (m-b)
Santa Monica, CA 90402
310-394-2619 / Fax: 310-394-2619
Sales: $500,001-$1 Million
WILLIAM COULTER (Co-Owner) & Buys Store Displays, Fixtures, Supplies
LOUISE COULTER (Co-Owner) & Buys Boys' Wear 0 to 20

MIKE CARUSO CLOTHIERS (MW)
631 Wilshire Blvd. (b)
Santa Monica, CA 90401
310-393-9996 / Fax: 310-395-8338
Sales: $1 Million-$10 Million
Website: www.mikecaruso.com
JACK CARUSO (Owner) & Buys Men's Suits, Tailored Jackets, Tailored Slacks, Men's Dress Shirts, Hosiery, Fragrances, Raincoats, Sportswear, Ties, Robes, Underwear, Footwear, Store Displays, Fixtures, Supplies

TOP TO TOP (CLO-2)
2621 Wilshire Blvd.
Santa Monica, CA 90403
310-829-7030 / Fax: 310-315-0412
AMIR GHADOUSHI (Owner) & Buys Athletic Apparel, Athletic Footwear

BARBARA FRIDAY WEEKEND WEAR (CLO)
2413 Magowan Dr.
Santa Rosa, CA 95405
707-575-7119
BARBARA HOPP (Owner) & Buys Sportswear, Resortwear, Leisurewear, Swimwear, Related Accessories

THE COMPETITOR (SP)
713 Village Court Mall
Santa Rosa, CA 95405
707-578-5689 / Fax: 707-578-2014
Sales: $500,001-$1 Million
KATHY SCHAACK (Owner) & Buys Activewear, Athletic Footwear, Golf Apparel, Fitness Apparel

KING'S CLOSET, INC. (MW)
3581 Cleveland Ave. (p)
Santa Rosa, CA 95404
707-528-8906
RAY STATZER (Owner) & Buys Big & Tall Size Men's, Sportswear, Furnishings, Accessories, Store Displays, Fixtures, Supplies

PAOLINI'S MENSWEAR (MW)
512 Wilson St. (p)
Santa Rosa, CA 95401
707-545-1260 / Fax: 707-545-1263
Sales: $100,001-$500,000
LYNN SCURI (Owner)
PERRY SMITH (Store Mgr.) & Buys Men's Work Clothes, Western Wear, Belts, Footwear, Store Displays, Fixtures, Supplies

GENE HILLER EXCLUSIVE MENSWEAR (MW)
729 Bridgeway (b)
Sausalito, CA 94965
415-332-3636 / Fax: 415-332-6899
Sales: $1 Million-$10 Million
Website: www.genehiller.com
EUGENE HILLER (President) & Buys Men's Overcoats, Suits, Tailored Jackets, Tailored Slacks, Raincoats, Sweaters, Sport Shirts, Outer Jackets, Coats, Furnishings, Belts, Leather Apparel, Footwear, Store Displays, Fixtures, Supplies
TOM GANGITANO-Men's Overcoats, Suits, Tailored Jackets, Tailored Slacks, Raincoats, Sweaters, Sport Shirts, Outer Jackets, Coats, Furnishings, Belts, Leather Apparel, Footwear, Store Displays, Fixtures, Supplies

MACKE'S SWEATERS (CLO)

26 El Portal (m-b)
Sausalito, CA 94965
415-332-4357

MIMI KAHN (Owner) & Buys Men's Sweaters, Jackets, Store Displays, Fixtures, Supplies

PEGASUS LEATHER CO. (CLO)

28 Princess St. (b)
Sausalito, CA 94965
415-332-5624 / Fax: 415-332-4327
Sales: $500,001-$1 Million
Website: www.pegasus.com

CHARLES HONTALAS (Owner) & Buys Leather Goods, Men's Casualwear, Accessories, Outerwear

KOALA MEN'S SWIMWEAR (OL & MO)

(KOALA SWIMWEAR)
P.O. Box 5519 (m)
Sherman Oaks, CA 91413
818-904-3301 / Fax: 818-780-5170
Sales: $1 Million-$10 Million
Website: www.koalaswim.com

MICHAEL D. YOUNG (President) & Buys Men's Swimwear

RICK PALLACK (MW)

4554 Sherman Oaks Ave. (m-b)
Sherman Oaks, CA 91403
818-789-7000 / Fax: 818-789-1825
Sales: $1 Million-$10 Million

RICK PALLACK (President & G.M.M.) & Buys Men's Wear, Store Displays, Fixtures, Supplies

BASSETT'S STATION (DEPT)

Hwy. 49 & Gold Lake Rd.
Sierra City, CA 96125
916-862-1297 / Fax: 916-862-1520
Sales: $100,001-$500,000

JOYCE DOUGHERTY (Mgr.) & Buys Apparel, Skiwear, Sports Apparel

LEE DOUGHERTY-Apparel, Skiwear, Sports Apparel

HIS PLACE (MW)

2824 Cochran St. (p-m)
Simi Valley, CA 93065
805-522-5029 / Fax: 805-577-7654

SANG HAN (Owner) & Buys Formal Wear, Related Furnishings & Accessories

ERALDI'S MENSWEAR (MW)

475 1st St. West (m-b)
Sonoma, CA 95476
707-996-2013 / Fax: 707-996-0508
Sales: $500,000-$1 Million

DANIEL J. ERALDI (Partner) & Buys Men's Overcoats, Tailored Jackets, Tailored Slacks, Raincoats, Sweaters, Sport Shirts, Outer Jackets, Casual Slacks, Dress Shirts, Ties, Robes, Underwear, Hosiery, Headwear, Belts, Small Leather Goods, Footwear

DONALD A. ERALDI (Partner) & Buys Men's Overcoats, Tailored Jackets, Tailored Slacks, Raincoats, Sweaters, Sport Shirts, Outer Jackets, Casual Slacks, Dress Shirts, Ties, Robes, Underwear, Hosiery, Headwear, Belts, Small Leather Goods, Footwear

KYRIAKOS OF HYDRA (MW-2)

240 2nd St. East (p-m)
Sonoma, CA 95476
707-939-8249

CHARLES DAPANTELES (Owner) & Buys Men's Wear, Sportswear, Accessories, Hand-Woven Items, Store Displays, Fixtures and Supplies, Furnishings

GREENSPAN'S DEPARTMENT STORE (MW)

3405 Tweedy Blvd. (m)
South Gate, CA 90280
323-566-5124
Website: www.greenspans.com

EDWARD GREENSPAN (Co-Owner) & Buys Men's & Young Men's Wear, Store Displays, Fixtures, Supplies

EVAN GREENSPAN (Co-Owner) & Buys Men's & Young Men's Wear, Urban Contemporary, Footwear, Headwear, Furnishings, Store Displays, Fixtures, Supplies

ONE THOUSAND BATHING SUITS (SP-2)

3986 Lake Tahoe Blvd.
South Lake Tahoe, CA 96150
530-544-0359 / Fax: 530-542-8789

RUSSELL PENN (Owner) & Buys Sportswear, Beachwear, Swimwear, Sandals, Sunglasses

SHIRT STOP (CLO-5)

(TAHOE SUMMERS)
P.O. Box 16282 (p-m)
4083 Hwy. 50
South Lake Tahoe, CA 96151
530-542-2707 / Fax: 530-542-0574

STEVE MYERS (Co-Owner)

MARGIE KOVARIK (Co-Owner & Mgr.) & Buys Men's & Boys' T-shirts, Fleece, Sweatshorts, Store Displays, Fixtures, Supplies

SPORTAGO (CLO)

1224 Adams St.
St. Helena, CA 94574
707-963-9042
Website: www.sportago.com

COREY WING-Men's Sportswear, Outer Wear

STANFORD BOOK STORE (SP-3)

White Plz.
Stanford, CA 94305
650-329-1217 / Fax: 650-322-1936
Website: www.stanfordbookstore.com

JANE LAPORTA-Activewear, Fleecewear, Jackets, Hosiery, Shorts, Athletic Footwear

BOGGIANO'S (MW)

363 Lincoln Ctr. (b)
Stockton, CA 95207
209-951-5581
Sales: $100,001-$500,000

REID BOGGIANO (Owner) & Buys Men's Sportswear, Headwear, Belts, Young Men's & Boys' Wear, Footwear, Store Displays, Fixtures, Supplies

CAMPBELL'S IN THE VILLAGE (CLO)

P.O. Box 7975 (p-m)
345 Lincoln Ctr.
Stockton, CA 95267
209-477-5568 / Fax: 209-477-6765
Sales: $1 Million-$10 Million

MR. TERRY J. COSSETTE (President)

MR. A. A. CARROLL CAMINATA (G.M.M.) & Buys Men's, Young Men's & Boys' Wear, Store Displays, Fixtures, Supplies

THE MAD HATTER (MW)

2007 Pacific Ave. (m-b)
Stockton, CA 95204
209-942-4287

ERNEST PROVOST (Owner) & Buys Men's & Boys' Headwear, Store Displays, Fixtures, Supplies

MARIANI'S MEN'S & BOYS' CLOTHING (MW)

345 S. El Dorado St. (p)
Stockton, CA 95203
209-466-3092 / Fax: 209-466-0539
Sales: $1 Million-$10 Million

PAUL L. MARIANI (President & G.M.M.) & Buys Men's Tailored Slacks, Sweaters, Sport Shirts, Outer Jackets, Leather Apparel, Active Apparel, Furnishings, Belts, Small Leather Goods, Boys' Clothing, Sportswear, Furnishings, Accessories, Footwear, Store Displays, Fixtures, Supplies

MAXINE'S BRIDAL (SP)

5 E. Harding Way (m-b)
Stockton, CA 95204
209-463-4041 / Fax: 209-464-5336
Sales: $500,001-$1 Million
Website: www.maxinesbridal.com

ANGELA DIAS-REYES (Owner) & Buys Men's Formalwear

CALIFORNIA - Stockton

STAN'S IMAGE UNIFORMS (CLO-2)
1351 W. Oak St. (m-b)
Stockton, CA 95203
209-462-2622 / Fax: 209-462-2652
STAN KANEKO (Owner) & Buys Men's Police, Fire Department & Security Uniforms, Store Displays, Fixtures, Supplies
KOKO PARKER (Mgr.) & Buys Men's Police, Fire Department & Security Uniforms, Store Displays, Fixtures, Supplies

DANIELLI (MW)
12208 Ventura Blvd. (b)
Studio City, CA 91604
818-760-8919 / Fax: 818-761-7881
DANNY HAMPARIAN (Owner) & Buys Men's Sportswear, Furnishings, Accessories, Store Displays, Fixtures, Supplies

KING'S WESTERN WEAR, INC. (WW & OL)
11450 Ventura Blvd.
Studio City, CA 91604
818-761-1162 / Fax: 818-761-3639
Sales: $500,001-$1 Million
Website: www.westernwear.com
ROSEMARY VALASCK-Men's Jewelry
GREG PARSONS-Men's Western Shirts, Outerwear, Clothing
RANDY KING (V.P.) & Buys Men's Suits, Tailored Jackets, Tailored Slacks, Footwear
GEORGETTE KING-Young Men's & Boys' Sportswear, Clothing, Furnishings, Accessories

SY DEVORE VALLEY SHOP (MW)
12930 Ventura Blvd. (b)
Studio City, CA 91604
818-783-2700 / Fax: 818-501-4302
Sales: $1 Million-$10 Million
MARTY DEVORE (Owner)
LEONARD FREEDMAN (President)
DANIEL MARSH (V.P.) & Buys Men's Overcoats, Suits, Tailored Jackets, Tailored Slacks, Raincoats, Sportswear, Furnishings, Headwear, Accessories, Store Displays, Fixtures, Supplies

LAS PALMAS TENNIS SHOP (SG)
800 Russet Dr. (m)
Sunnyvale, CA 94087
408-732-2130
Sales: $100,001-$500,000
JAN YOUNG (President & Owner)
HENNY DALHUISEN-Apparel, Active Apparel

RICARDO'S TAILORING (MW)
765 E. El Camino Real
Sunnyvale, CA 94087
408-736-4194 / Fax: 408-736-1984
RICARDO TORRES (Owner) & Buys Men's Wear, Sportswear, Dress Shirts, Ties, Hosiery, Belts, Young Men's Wear, Urban Contemporary, Store Displays, Fixtures and Supplies

SPORTSMAN SPORT SHOP (SP)
242 Commercial St.
Sunnyvale, CA 94085
408-736-6148 / Fax: 408-736-6170
Sales: $100,001-$500,000
ALAN LEE (Owner) & Buys Activewear, Athletics

PARDNER, INC. (WW)
702-100 Johnstonville (m)
Susanville, CA 96130
530-257-5176 / Fax: 530-257-6060
KURT MORAN (President & Owner)
JO ELLEN WOOD (Partner) & Buys Western Wear, Related Furnishings, Accessories

THE CLOTHES MINE (CLO-2)
P.O. Box 926 (p-m)
Sutter Creek, CA 95685
209-267-0417 / Fax: 209-267-0417
Sales: $100,001-$500,000
LOUISE NUNN (Owner) & Buys Formal Wear, Related, Furnishings, Accessories, Work Clothes, Underwear, Headwear, Belts, Hosiery, Store Displays, Fixtures and Supplies, Tuxedo Rental

MAJOR MOTION SPORTSWEAR (CLO)
12424 Gladstone Ave. (m)
Sylmar, CA 91342
818-837-7200 / Fax: 818-837-0880
JOHN LEVINE (President) & Buys Men's Fleecewear, T-shirts, 8 to 20 Boys' Fleecewear, T-shirts, Store Displays, Fixtures, Supplies

PORTER'S SKI & SPORT (SG-4)
P.O. Box 6983 (p-m)
Tahoe City, CA 96145
530-583-8501 / Fax: 530-583-0914
Website: www.poerterstahoe.com
JOHN CHAPMAN (President & Owner) & Buys Men's Footwear
LONNIE MAURICE-Ski Clothing, Active Apparel, T-shirts, Sweaters, Outer Jackets, Athletic Hosiery, Belts, Fleece, Shorts

SPORTS TAHOE (CLO-2)
P.O. Box 166
Tahoe City, CA 96145
530-583-1990 / Fax: 530-583-1996
JAMES A. GREGORY (Owner) & Buys Athletic Footwear
MICKEY GREGORY-Activewear, Leisurewear, Athletic Apparel, Beachwear

APPAREL WAREHOUSE (CLO-2)
6010 Yolanda Ave. (m-b)
Tarzana, CA 91356
818-344-3224 / Fax: 818-708-7221
Sales: $1 Million-$10 Million
TERRY SEEMAN (Co-Owner) & Buys Boys' Apparel, Boys' Footwear, Men's Apparel, Hosiery, Sportswear

RECON-1, INC. (AN)
19423 Ventura Blvd.
Tarzana, CA 91356
818-342-2666 / Fax: 818-345-6020
Sales: $500,001-$1 Million
Website: www.recon-1.com
GARY KALAYDJIAN (President)
SAKO RAFAELIAN (G.M.M.) & Buys Hunting Apparel, Hiking Boots

RANCHO ARMY-NAVY STORE (AN)
27999 Jefferson (p-m)
Temecula, CA 92590
909-676-0057 / Fax: 909-676-0536
CARLOS ALVAREZ (Owner)
PATTY MILLER (Head Mgr.) & Buys Men's & Boys' Casual Wear, Work Clothes, Jeans, Levis, Tops, Furnishings, Accessories, Store Displays, Fixtures, Supplies
RICK WINTERS (Mgr.) & Buys Men's & Boys' Casual Wear, Work Clothes, Jeans, Levis, Tops, Furnishings, Accessories, Store Displays, Fixtures, Supplies

GABRIEL'S MENSWEAR (MW)
9578 Las Tunas Dr. (m-b)
Temple City, CA 91780
626-285-0562 / Fax: 626-285-9315
DOMINIC ZOCCOLI (Co-Owner)
TONY ZOCCOLI (Co-Owner)
FRED WRIGHT (D.M.M.) & Buys Big & Tall Men's Wear, Store Displays, Fixtures, Supplies

SHOE RACKS, INC. (FW)
(999 SHOE OUTLET)
4417 Broadway (bud-p-m)
Thorn, CA 90250
310-331-1666 / Fax: 310-331-1616
Sales: $500,001-$1 Million
LARRY SCHWARTZ (President) & Buys Men's Footwear, Leather Goods, Men's Accessories

CONEJO SWIMWORKS (CLO)
688 N. Moore Park Rd.
Thousand Oaks, CA 91360
805-379-4734 / Fax: 805-496-7382
BARBARA MANDICH-Swimwear, Beachwear, Related Accessories & Footwear

HILLTOP FEED & RANCH STORE (WW)
2727 E. Hillcrest Dr. (m)
Thousand Oaks, CA 91362
805-495-3516
BILL ADKINS (Owner)
SYDNEY KANE (Mgr.) & Buys Men's & Boys' Western Wear, Footwear, Store Displays, Fixtures, Supplies

CALIFORNIA - Torrance

DANIEL JAMES CUSTOM SHIRT & CLOTHING (MW)
24203 Hawthorn Blvd. (b-h)
Torrance, CA 90505
310-791-2188 / Fax: 310-791-2189
Sales: $100,001-$500,000
DANNY BABB (Owner) & Buys Men's Sportswear, Furnishings, Accessories, Store Displays, Fixtures, Supplies

DOMANI (MW)
(STUDIO DOMANI)
83 Del Amo Fashion Ctr. (m)
Torrance, CA 90503
310-370-4479
Sales: $100,001-$500,000
CHUCK JAY (Owner) & Buys Men's Suits, Tailored Jackets, Tailored Slacks, Sweaters, Sport Shirts, Dress Shirts, Footwear, Store Displays, Fixtures, Supplies

SHOE LORD, INC. (CLO)
227 Del Amo Fashion Ctr.
Torrance, CA 90503
310-371-1620 / Fax: 310-542-1690
MUHAMMED ALI-Men's & Boys' Shoes, Hosiery, Accessories

THE SURPRISE STORES (SP)
23118 Hawthorne Blvd.
Torrance, CA 90505
310-378-0338
Sales: $500,001-$1 Million
JEROME HESS (Owner)
GARY BRANDFELLNER (Mgr.) & Buys Activewear, Athletic Footwear

RICHARD'S MENSWEAR (MW)
70 W. 10th St. (p-m-b)
Tracy, CA 95376
209-835-4684 / Fax: 209-835-1232
RICHARD HUGHES (Owner) & Buys Men's Wear, Sportswear, Furnishings, Accessories, Formal Wear, Store Displays, Fixtures and Supplies

CAMARA'S CLOTHIER (MW)
107 W. Main (m)
Turlock, CA 95380
209-667-9022 / Fax: 209-634-9950
JOSEPH CAMARA (Owner) & Buys Men's Wear, Big & Tall Men's Wear, Store Displays, Fixtures, Supplies

FRANK'S ITALIAN MENSWEAR (MW-2)
(SIR WICKET)
13011 Newport Ave. (m-des)
Tustin, CA 92780
714-730-5945
Sales: $1 Million-$10 Million
FRANK JOHNSON (Co-Owner) & Buys Store Displays, Fixtures, Supplies
CARROLL JOHNSON (Co-Owner) & Buys Men's Suits, Tailored Jackets, Tailored Slacks, Raincoats, Sweaters, Sport Shirts, Outer Jackets, Leather Apparel, Casual Slacks, Dress Shirts, Ties, Robes, Headwear, Belts, Jewelry, Men's Shoes

MacNAB'S MENSWEAR (MW)
111 N. State St. (bud-p-m-b)
Ukiah, CA 95482
707-462-2767 / Fax: 707-462-6964
Sales: $100,001-$500,000
SANDY MacNAB (Partner)
BILL MacNAB (Partner) & Buys Men's Suits, Tailored Jackets, Tailored Slacks, Raincoats, Sweaters, Sport Shirts, Outer Jackets, Leather Apparel, Casual Slacks, Dress Shirts, Ties, Robes, Underwear, Hosiery, Gloves, Headwear, Belts, Small Leather Goods, Big & Tall Men's Wear, Young Men's Wear, Footwear, Store Displays, Fixtures, Supplies

THE TACK ROOM (CLO)
1296 N. State St. (m)
Ukiah, CA 95482
707-462-3477 / Fax: 707-462-2278
DORETHA RUNNINGS (Owner) & Buys Men's Footwear, Western Wear, Leather Apparel, Tack, Store Displays, Fixtures, Supplies

CHORUS LINE DANCEWEAR (SP)
23300 Cinema Dr.
Valencia, CA 91355
661-253-0300
MEREDITH WEST-Dancewear, Dance Footwear, Related Accessories

MR. RIC (MW)
629 Marin St. (b-h)
Vallejo, CA 94590
707-643-8786
RICK LEMKE (Owner) & Buys Men's Sportswear, Furnishings, Accessories, Store Displays, Fixtures, Supplies

VICTORY ARMY-NAVY STORES, INC. (AN)
P.O. Box 7007 (m)
435 Virginia St.
Vallejo, CA 94590
707-642-0467 / Fax: 707-642-0467
TERRY ROSS PRATHER (President) & Buys Store Displays, Fixtures, Supplies
RAYMOND PRATHER (Mgr.) & Buys Men's Sportswear, Furnishings, Accessories, Footwear, Store Displays, Fixtures and Supplies

COUNTRY GENERAL STORE (CLO & OL)
(SURPLUS DISTRIBUTORS)
6279 Van Nuys Blvd. (p-m-b)
Van Nuys, CA 91401
818-782-8327 / Fax: 818-782-2182
Website: www.countrygeneralstore.com
RICK STANOFF (Owner) & Buys Men's Sportswear, Underwear, Hosiery, Headwear, Belts, Footwear, Store Displays, Fixtures, Supplies

EL PANTALON (MW-2)
(GLOBE TRADING CORP.)
6645 Van Nuys Blvd. (p-m)
Van Nuys, CA 91405
818-908-1912
JOSEPH MICHAEL (Owner) & Buys Men's Sportswear, Belts, Footwear, Store Displays, Fixtures, Supplies

PHIL'S WEAR-HOUSE (KS)
13819 Saticon (m)
Van Nuys, CA 91402
818-908-8808
GERDA JOSOVICZ (Owner & Mgr.) & Buys 8 to 16 Boys' Wear, Footwear, Store Displays, Fixtures, Supplies

POLITIX (MW-2)
(MOBA, INC.)
14141 Covelo St., #2A (m)
Van Nuys, CA 91405
818-780-2410 / Fax: 818-780-3875
VIKEN MOMBJIAN (President)
ELIE KEVORKIAN-Men's Overcoats, Suits, Raincoats, Tailored Jackets, Sportswear, Dress Shirts, Underwear, Hosiery, Accessories, Footwear, Store Displays, Fixtures, Supplies

VAN NUYS ARMY & NAVY STORE, INC. (AN)
6179 Van Nuys Blvd. (bud-p)
Van Nuys, CA 91401
818-781-3500 / Fax: 818-781-5162
Sales: $500,000-$1 Million
BENJAMIN M. SUSMAN (President & C.E.O.) & Buys Store Displays, Fixtures, Supplies, Men's Sport Shirts, Outer Jackets, Leather Apparel, Men's & Boys' Military Suits, Raincoats, Sweaters, Jeans, Work Clothes, Underwear, Hosiery, Gloves, Headwear, Belts, Headwear, Footwear

INSIDE TRACK (SG)
1410 E. Main St. (p-m)
Ventura, CA 93001
805-643-1104
GARY TUTTLE (Owner) & Buys Active Apparel, Running Clothes, Hosiery, Headwear

LUCKY BRAND DUNGAREES, INC. (CLO-75)
5233 Alcoa Ave. (b)
Vernon, CA 90058
323-282-4100 / Fax: 323-585-7771
Sales: $50 Million-$100 Million
Website: www.luckybrandjeans.com
BARRY PERLMAN (President)
GENE MONTESANO (C.E.O.) & Buys Men's Denim Apparel, Outerwear, Sportswear, Swimwear, Underwear
TRENT MERRILL (C.F.O.)
JASON JOHNSON (V.P.-Mktg.)

WINDSOR FASHIONS (CLO-30)
4533 Pacific Blvd.
Vernon, CA 90058
(Directives West-L.A.)
323-282-9000 / Fax: 323-973-4309
Sales: $10 Million-$50 Million
Website: www.windsorfashions.com
Retail Locations: AZ, CA, CT, NV, NJ, TX
LEON ZEKARIA (Owner)
CYNTHIA LOPEZ-Outerwear, Sportswear
TRACY KING-Watches, Sunglasses

BIG GUYS TUXEDO (MW & CLO)
(TUXEDO/THE BRIDAL CONNECTION)
16970 Bear Valley Rd., # B (bud-p-m-b)
Victorville, CA 92392
760-241-5099 / Fax: 760-951-5809
Sales: $500,000-$1 Million
CAROL THARP (Co-Owner) & Buys Big & Tall Men's Wear, Tuxedos, Accessories, Men's Footwear

JERSCHEID'S MEN'S APPAREL (MW)
14400 Bear Valley Rd., #107 (b)
Victorville, CA 92392
760-241-1194 / Fax: 760-241-0307
PHYLLIS JERSCHEID (Owner) & Buys Men's Wear, Sportswear, Dress Shirts, Ties, Hosiery, Headwear, Belts, Small Leathers, Store Displays, Fixtures and Supplies

LINKS MEN'S & WOMENSWEAR (CLO)
115 E. Main St. (b)
Visalia, CA 93291
559-732-4858 / Fax: 559-732-2837
TOM LINKS (Owner) & Buys Men's Wear, Sportswear, Furnishings, Accessories, Store Displays, Fixtures and Supplies

McWILLIAMS AND MOSLEY (MW)
215 E. Main St. (m)
Visalia, CA 93291
559-732-5617 / Fax: 559-732-5617
LLOYD MOSLEY (Owner) & Buys Men's Wear, Western Wear, Big & Tall Men's Wear, Footwear, Store Displays, Fixtures, Supplies

ROBERTSON'S BIG 'N' TALL (MW)
3288 S. Mooney Blvd. (m-b)
Visalia, CA 93277
559-732-2354
MIKE ROBERTSON (Owner) & Buys Big & Tall Men's Sportswear, Furnishings, Leather Apparel, Footwear, Store Displays, Fixtures, Supplies

SPORTS NUT, INC. (SP)
1935 E. Main St.
Visalia, CA 93229
559-625-1540 / Fax: 559-625-9008
MARK WALKER (Owner) & Buys Activewear, Sports Apparel

PACIFIC EYES & T'S (CLO-39 & OL)
1221 Liberty Way
Vista, CA 92083
760-597-9600 / Fax: 760-597-1300
Website: www.pacificeyes.com
Retail Locations: AZ, CA, HI, NV, TX
DANIEL GOODMAN (C.O.O. & Real Estate Contact)
JILL PICKERING (Opers. Mgr.)
JIM JOHNSON-Men's Activewear
ANDY TOWNS-Sunglasses
LORI HUMPHRIES-Licensed Apparel, Boys' Activewear
SHARON GLEASON-Men's Activewear

DASKALO'S EUROPEAN MEN'S FASHIONS (MW)
1216 Broadway Plz. (h)
Walnut Creek, CA 94596
925-937-1808 / Fax: 925-937-1723
TOM DASKALO (Owner) & Buys Men's Sportswear, Furnishings, Belts, Footwear, Store Displays, Fixtures, Supplies

NORDSTROM NORTHERN DIV. - EAST BAY REGION (DEPT-11)
1200 Broadway Plz. (m-b)
Walnut Creek, CA 94596
925-930-7959 / Fax: 925-975-5589
Website: www.nordstrom.com
MATT ALBRIGHT (D.M.M.-SW Men's Div.-NCA & LA) (@ 925-975-5680)
JOHN SULLIVAN (Prdt. Mgr.-Men's) (@ 415-243-8500)
JULINE FUJII (@ 925-975-5579)-Men's Better Sportswear, Moderate Sportswear, Activewear
TRENT KAMMAN (@ 415-243-8500)-Men's Suits, Tailored Jackets, Tailored Slacks
DAVE STEWART (@ 925-975-5516)-Men's Faconnable
BRUCE EMBREE (@ 925-975-5576)-Men's Suits, Sportscoats
CHARLES SPISAK (@ 925-975-5545)-Young Men's Rail
LARA GRACE (@ 925-975-5542)-Men's Furnishings
GAIL LALUMIERE-Men's Footwear
DON MARTIN-Men's Footwear
MEYLENE GARCIA (@ 925-227-4157)-Infants/Layette
LORRAINE BELTRAN (@ 925-227-4057)-Infants/Layette
NOTE:-Store Supplies, Fixtures Buying Performed By NORDSTROM in Seattle, WA-See Listing.

WATSONVILLE JEANS (MW)
311 Main St.
Watsonville, CA 95076
831-728-1171 / Fax: 831-728-2750
RAMIRO ROMO (Owner) & Buys Men's Wear, Boys' Jeans, Leather Apparel, Footwear, Store Displays, Fixtures, Supplies

GROUP NINE ASSOCIATES, INC. (FW-14)
(J. STEPHENS)
(ROCKPORT)
6700 Fallbrook Ave., #152 (m-b-des)
West Hills, CA 91307
818-884-2260 / Fax: 818-884-7967
Sales: $1 Million-$10 Million
DALTON HAUSS (President & C.E.O.)
GARY HAUSS (Exec. V.P.) & Buys Men's Footwear, Accessories, Hosiery, Apparel

JOHN VARVATOS (CLO-2)
8800 Melrose Ave.
West Hollywood, CA 90069
310-859-2970
Website: www.johnvarvatos.com
Retail Locations: NY, CA
JOHN VARVATOS (Owner) (@ 212-812-8000) & Buys Men's Apparel

PLEASURE CHEST LTD. (CLO & OL)

7733 Santa Monica Blvd. (b)
West Hollywood, CA 90046
323-650-1022 / Fax: 323-650-1176
Website: www.thepleasurechest.com

DAVID BALLOW (Gen. Store Mgr.) & Buys Men's Leather Jackets, Pants, Vests, Underwear

JEAN DEPOT (CLO)

3065 W. Capitol Ave. (m-b)
West Sacramento, CA 95691
916-371-5326 / Fax: 916-371-2473

AL ZANUSSI (Owner) & Buys Store Displays, Fixtures, Supplies

LINDA SHAVER-Men's & Boys' Wear, Leather Apparel

CARRIERE FINE MENSWEAR (MW)

982 S. Westlake Blvd., #6 (m-b)
Westlake, CA 91361
805-497-6601 / Fax: 805-497-3032

ROBERT CARRIERE (President) & Buys Men's Sportswear, Leather Apparel, Footwear, Store Displays, Fixtures, Supplies

PAUL JARDIN OF USA (MW-11)

(3 DAY SUIT BROKER)
6415 De Soto Ave. (m-b)
Woodland Hills, CA 91367
818-703-7848 / Fax: 818-703-6600
Sales: $10 Million-$50 Million
Website: www.3daysuitbroker.com

SAM SHAHINIAN (President & C.E.O.)

LEO SHAHINIAN (V.P.) & Buys Men's Footwear, Leather Goods, Men's Apparel, Men's Big & Tall Apparel, Men's Casualwear, Men's Accessories, Men's Hosiery, Men's Outerwear, Men's Sportswear, Men's Suits, Young Men's Apparel, Formal Wear

SHAWN SHAHINIAN (V.P.) & Buys Men's Footwear, Leather Goods, Men's Apparel, Men's Big & Tall Apparel, Men's Casualwear, Men's Accessories, Men's Hosiery, Men's Outerwear, Men's Sportswear, Men's Suits, Young Men's Apparel, Formal Wear

BULLSEYE ENTERPRISES, INC. (FW-4)

(DAVE'S SHOES)
(RYDEL SHOES)
441 Bridge St. (bud-p-m-b-des)
Yuba City, CA 95991
530-674-7780 / Fax: 530-674-0934
Sales: $1 Million-$10 Million

KENT SLANGSTROM (President) & Buys Boys' Footwear, Men's Footwear, Leather Goods, Men's Accessories, Hosiery

DONNA POLNMANTEER (G.M.M.) & Buys Boys' Footwear, Men's Footwear, Leather Goods, Men's Accessories, Hosiery

COLORADO - Alamosa

CARLUCCI'S, INC. (DEPT)
630 Main St. (m)
Alamosa, CO 81101
719-589-6449 / Fax: 719-589-6418
Sales: $1 Million-$10 Million

BOB CARLUCCI (President) & Buys Men's & Boys' Wear, Sportswear, Accessories, Furnsihings, Footwear, Urban Contemporary, Store Displays, Fixtures, Supplies

H & R SUPPLY CO., INC. (GM-2)
P.O. Box 2001 (m)
Alamosa, CO 81101
719-589-4581 / Fax: 719-589-5692
Sales: $1 Million-$10 Million

HERB MOSHER (Co-Owner) & Buys Men's & Boys' Shirts, Jeans, Western Apparel, Outdoor Boots, Footwear, Store Displays, Fixtures, Supplies

TED CURTIS (Co-Owner) & Buys Men's & Boys' Shirts, Jeans, Western Apparel, Outdoor Boots, Store Displays, Fixtures, Supplies

MOUNTAIN MUNCHKIN (KS)
505 State Ave.
Alamosa, CO 81101
719-587-2229 / Fax: 719-587-9819

AMANDA GARCIA (Owner) & Buys Boys' Clothing, Sportswear, Furnishings, Accessories

SPENCER SPORTING GOODS (SG)
616 Main St. (p-m)
Alamosa, CO 81101
719-589-4361 / Fax: 719-589-4681

ERIC GULE (Owner) & Buys Men's T-shirts, Fleece, Swimwear, Store Displays, Fixtures, Supplies

HIGH COUNTRY WESTERN WEAR (WW-2 & CBO)
4900 Allison St. (m)
Arvado, CO 80002
303-425-0055 / Fax: 303-940-8917

JOHN NOWLEN (Owner) & Buys Men's & Boys' Western Wear, Leather Apparel, Related Accessories, Furnishings, Footwear, Store Displays, Fixtures, Supplies

ART TEE GALLERY (SP)
401 E. Hyman Ave.
Aspen, CO 81611
970-920-2648 / Fax: 970-920-3665
Sales: $501,000-$1 Million
Website: www.artteegallery.com

MICHAEL SHADLING (Owner & Mgr.) & Buys Men's Apparel

ASPEN SPORTS (CLO-15)
709 E. DurantAve.
Aspen, CO 81611
970-925-6333 / Fax: 970-925-2755
Sales: $1 Million-$10 Million
Website: www.friendskis.com

JEFF TURNER-Men's Sportswear, Dress Shirts, Headwear, Swimwear, Footwear, Store Displays, Fixtures, Supplies

LAURA PESSEL-Men's Sportswear, Dress Shirts, Headwear, Swimwear, Footwear, Store Displays, Fixtures, Supplies

BARBARA BLECKER-Accessories

NOTE-Contact Via Mail Only.

BOOGIE'S DINER (CLO)
(PEPS OF ASPEN, INC.)
534 E. Cooper St. (b)
Aspen, CO 81611
970-925-6111 / Fax: 970-920-1560
Sales: $1 Million-$10 Million
Website: www.boogiesaspen.com

LEONARD WEINGLASS (President)

PENNIE LEIGHTON (Bookkeeper)

MATTI BOURGAN-Men's Wear, Sportswear, Accessories, Furnishings, Men's Footwear, Store Displays, Fixtures & Supplies

GORSUCH LTD. (CLO)
419 E. Cooper Ave.
Aspen, CO 81611
970-925-7576 / Fax: 970-925-7577
Website: www.gorsuchltd.com

RENEE GORSUCH (Co-Owner) & Buys Skiwear

JEFF GORSUCH (Co-Owner) & Buys Skiwear

PITKIN COUNTY DRY GOODS (DG)
(PITKIN COUNTY DRY GOODS & LEATHERS)
520 E. Cooper Ave. (m-b)
Aspen, CO 81611
970-925-1681 / Fax: 970-925-1683
Sales: $1 Million-$10 Million

DAVID FLEISHER (Owner) & Buys Men's Sportswear, Furnishings, Hats, Accessories, Leather Coats, Hats, Jackets, Footwear, Urban Contemporary, Store Displays, Fixtures, Supplies

STEIN ERIKSEN, INC. (CLO-2)
Upper Village Mall
P.O. Box 5096
Aspen, CO 81615
970-923-3665 / Fax: 970-925-1265
Sales: $1 Million-$10 Million

STEIN ERIKSEN (Owner)

INGER GERNON (Mgr.) & Buys Activewear, Fitness & Exercise Apparel, Skiing Apparel

MAN'S WORLD (MW)
2495 S. Havana St. (m-b)
Aurora, CO 80014
303-745-7100
Sales: $500,001-$1 Million

JOE BUTLER (Owner) & Buys Men's Sportswear, Furnishings, Accessories, Casual Shoes, Athletic Footwear, Store Displays, Fixtures, Supplies

GENE EISEN (President) & Buys Leather Goods, Men's Apparel, Men's Designer Apparel, Men's Formalwear, Men's Accessories, Men's Hosiery, Men's Outerwear, Men's Sportswear, Men's Suits, Young Men's Apparel, Men's Uniforms

R & N SPORTS (SP)
10700 E. Bethany Dr., #100
Aurora, CO 80014
303-695-1985 / Fax: 303-695-1940
Sales: $100,001-$500,000

RICHARD PEROVICH (Owner) & Buys Apparel, Sports Collectibles

BOULDER T-SHIRT CO. (SP)
2602 Baseline Rd.
Boulder, CO 80301
303-440-7050 / Fax: 303-494-4610
Sales: $100,001-$500,000

KIRO KANCHAR (Mgr.) & Buys Custom & Readymade T-shirts

CU BOOKSTORE (SP)
(UNIVERSITY OF COLORADO)
Campus Box 36
Boulder, CO 80309
303-492-6411 / Fax: 303-492-8329
Sales: $1 Million-$10 Million
Website: www.cubooks.colorado.edu

PAM MILLS (Mgr.) & Buys Activewear, Sweats, Jackets, Hosiery, Shorts

HI POINT SWIM & SPORT (SP-2)
1738 Pearl St.
Boulder, CO 80302
303-545-2090 / Fax: 303-544-9091

PAUL GAYER (Owner)

BARBARA GAYER-Surf & Swimwear, Wetsuits, Beach Shoes

JIM MORRIS ENVIRONMENTAL T-SHIRT (CLO)
5660 Valmont Rd. (m-b)
P.O. Box 18270
Boulder, CO 80301
303-444-6430 / Fax: 303-786-9095
Sales: $1 Million-$10 Million

JIM MORRIS (President) & Buys Boys' Apparel, Men's Apparel

COLORADO - Boulder

KINSLEY & CO. (MW)
1155 13th St. (m-b-des)
Boulder, CO 80302
303-442-7260 / Fax: 303-442-7286
Sales: $1 Million-$10 Million
Website: www.kinsleyco.com
COURT DIXON (Co-Owner)
EDWARD KAPSON (Co-Owner) & Buys Men's Sportswear, Furnishings, Accessories, Footwear, Store Displays, Fixtures, Supplies
DO PHAN (Co-Owner) & Buys Men's Sportswear, Furnishings, Accessories, Footwear, Store Displays, Fixtures, Supplies

RUNNER'S CHOICE (SP)
2460 Canyon Blvd.
Boulder, CO 80302
303-449-8551
Sales: $501,000-$1 Million
JACK SMITH (Co-Owner)
PAUL ROBERTS (Co-Owner) & Buys Activewear, Athletic Footwear
CAROL SMITH (Co-Owner) & Buys Apparel, Athletic Footwear, Outdoor Footwear

STARR'S CLOTHING & SHOES (CLO & FW)
1630 Pearl St. (m)
Boulder, CO 80302
303-442-3056 / Fax: 303-245-9099
Sales: $1 Million-$10 Million
Website: www.starrsclothing.com
STEVE WIGOTOW (Owner) & Buys Men's Urban Contemporary, Sportswear, Furnishings, Accessories, Store Displays, Fixtures, Supplies

WEEKENDS (DEPT)
1101 Pearl St.
Boulder, CO 80302
303-444-4231 / Fax: 303-444-4380
JOHN SCHOPBACH (Owner) & Buys Men's Wear, Men's Accessories, Furnishings, Footwear

GOODS (CLO-2)
105 S. Main St. (p-m-b)
Breckenbridge, CO 80424
970-453-2880 / Fax: 970-453-7850
Website: www.goodsbreckenbridge.com
JOHN BALMA (President & Owner) & Buys Sportswear, Furnishings, Accessories, Young Men's Wear, Urban Contemporary, Boys' Wear, Men's Footwear, Boys' Footwear, Store Displays, Fixtures and Supplies

JOY OF SOX & EXCESSORIES (SP)
P.O. Box 3909
Breckenridge, CO 80424
970-453-4534 / Fax: 970-453-1030
Sales: $100,001-$500,000
ANN EVANS-Men's Outdoor Apparel, Sportswear

MOUNTAIN TEES (SP-6)
P.O. Box 1189
120 S. Main St.
Breckenridge, CO 80424
970-453-9515 / Fax: 970-453-7636
Sales: $10 Million-$50 Million
Website: www.mountaintees.com
CHUCK STRUVE (Owner) & Buys Apparel, Skiwear, Custom Apparel

THE SHIRT OFF MY BACK (CLO-8)
P.O. Box 309 (p-m)
124 S. Main St.
Breckenridge, CO 80424
970-453-1717 / Fax: 970-453-7033
Website: www.shirtoffmyback.com
JEAN TAYLOR (Co-Owner)
RICK TAYLOR (Co-Owner)
PATRICK SUMMERS (Co-Owner)
SHERRY FLACK (Co-Owner) & Buys Apparel
MICHAEL FLACK (Co-Owner) & Buys Apparel
HEIDI ROY-Men's & Boys' T-shirts, Fleece Jackets, Shorts, Store Displays, Fixtures, Supplies

TWISTED PINE FUR & LEATHER (CLO-2)
P.O. Box 2825 (m-b)
411 S. Main St.
Breckenridge, CO 80424
970-453-6615 / Fax: 970-453-8092
JIM B. BESTERFELDT (Owner) & Buys Men's Leather Overcoats, Sport Coats, Outer Jackets, Jewelry, Small Leather Goods, Footwear, Slippers, Cowboy Boots

ORTH'S DEPARTMENT STORE (CLO)
431 14th St. (p)
Burlington, CO 80807
719-346-8314 / Fax: 719-346-6049
Sales: $100,001-$500,000
HELMUTH ORTH (Co-Owner) & Buys Footwear
DENNIS ORTH (Co-Owner) & Buys Men's Sportswear, Furnishings, Headwear, Accessories, Footwear, Store Displays, Fixtures, Supplies
JEAN ORTH-Boys' Wear, Footwear

CANON WESTERN WEAR (WW)
502 Main St. (m)
Canon City, CO 81212
719-275-9512 / Fax: 719-275-9519
MICHAEL HADLEY (President & Owner) & Buys Western Clothing, Sportswear, Furnishings, Accessories, Young Men's Wear, Boys' Wear, Boots, Store Displays, Fixtures and Supplies

DONNA'S BROKEN SPOKE WESTERN SHOP (CLO)
2345 E. Boulder St. (m)
Colorado Springs, CO 80909
719-632-3131
Sales: $500,001-$1 Million
DONNA BROCK (Owner & Gen. Mgr.) & Buys Boys' Apparel, Boys' Footwear, Men's Footwear, Men's Apparel, Leather Goods, Men's Denim Apparel

*DYER & CO. (KS)
520 Ridgewood Ave.
Colorado Springs, CO 80906
804-762-4455 / Fax: 804-217-8999
A. DYER (Owner) & Buys Men's Apparel, Accessories, Footwear

LORIG'S, INC. (WW)
112 E. Colorado Ave. (m-b)
Colorado Springs, CO 80903
719-633-4695
HAROLD EICHENBAUM (Owner) & Buys Men's Western Wear, Leather Apparel, Related Accessories, Furnishings, Footwear, Store Displays, Fixtures, Supplies

RUTLEDGE'S (CLO)
1 S. Tejon St. (b)
Colorado Springs, CO 80903
719-632-7654 / Fax: 719-632-7694
Sales: $1 Million-$10 Million
JERRY RUTLEDGE (Owner) & Buys Men's Overcoats, Suits, Tailored Jackets, Tailored Slacks, Raincoats, Sportswear, Sweaters, Sport Shirts, Casual Slacks, Active Apparel, Furnishings, Headwear, Accessories, Footwear, Store Displays, Fixtures, Supplies

TEE SHIRT GALLERY (SP-2)
750 Citadel Dr. East, #1068
Colorado Springs, CO 80909
719-591-8721
Sales: $501,000-$1 Million
SANJAY KANCHANLAL (Owner) & Buys Skiwear, Sports Apparel

COMMERCE CITY ACE HARDWARE (DEPT)
6900 Eudora Dr. (p-m)
Commerce City, CO 80022
303-288-6641 / Fax: 303-288-6080
CAROL WOODBUM (Co-Owner)
KENNY JAY-Men's Work Clothes, Jeans, Shirts, Underwear, Hosiery, Headwear, Footwear, Store Displays, Fixtures, Supplies

COLORADO - Cortez

THE TOGGERY (CLO)
1 E. Main St. (p)
Cortez, CO 81321
970-565-3167 / Fax: 970-565-3167
Sales: $1 Million-$10 Million
ROBERT HELMS (President) & Buys Men's & Boys' Wear, Sportswear, Accessories, Furnishings, Store Displays, Fixtures, Supplies
PATTI MOSS-Men's Footwear, Boys' Footwear

CRITTER MOUNTAIN WEAR (CLO)
P.O. Box 975 (m-b)
Crested Butte, CO 81224
970-349-9326 / Fax: 970-389-3900
Sales: $500,001-$1 Million
Website: www.crittermountainwear.com
RICHARD KOCUREK, Jr. (President) & Buys Men's Outdoor Apparel

THE DAVIS CLOTHING CO. (MW)
P.O. Box 246 (m-b)
401 Main St.
Delta, CO 81416
970-874-4370 / Fax: 970-874-9978
Sales: $1 Million-$10 Million
BRADFORD G. DAVIS (President) & Buys Men's Overcoats, Suits, Raincoats, Big & Tall Men's Wear, Sportswear, Furnishings, Headwear, Accessories, Boys' Clothing, Furnishings, Footwear, Store Displays, Fixtures, Supplies

ANDRISEN MORTON CO. (MW)
270 Saint Paul (m-b)
Denver, CO 80206
303-377-8488 / Fax: 303-377-8858
CRAIG ANDRISEN (Co-Owner) & Buys Men's Sportswear, Leather Apparel, Furnishings, Headwear, Accessories, Footwear
DAVID MORTON (Co-Owner) & Buys Store Displays, Fixtures, Supplies

DUMAN'S CUSTOM TAILORS (MW)
438 E. Colfax Ave. (m)
Denver, CO 80203
303-832-1701 / Fax: 303-832-3535
STEVE DUMAN (President & Owner) & Buys Men's Overcoats, Suits, Tailored Jackets, Tailored Slacks, Big & Tall Men's Wear, Sportswear, Furnishings, Dress Shirts, Ties, Men's Footwear, Underwear, Hosiery, Gloves, Headwear, Accessories, Belts, Small Leathers, Uniforms, Store Displays, Fixtures and Supplies

DUNCAN MEN'S STORE (MW & OL)
1001 E. 26th Ave. (m-b)
Denver, CO 80205
303-295-2010 / Fax: 303-295-3109
Sales: $1 Million-$10 Million
CURTIS WASHINGTON-Men's Sportswear, Furnishings, Accessories, Footwear, Store Displays, Fixtures, Supplies

EBONY/ROCHE FASHIONS, INC. (MW)
1305 Krameria (m)
Denver, CO 80220
303-320-1977 / Fax: 303-680-9750
BRIAN ROCHE (President) & Buys Men's Sportswear, Furnishings, Accessories, Headwear, Young Men's Wear, Boys' Suits, Footwear, Urban Contemporary, Store Displays, Fixtures, Supplies

GARMENT DISTRICT, INC. (MW-2)
2595 S. Colorado Blvd. (m-b)
Denver, CO 80222
303-757-3371 / Fax: 303-757-3375
Sales: $1 Million-$10 Million
JIM STEVENS (Owner) & Buys Men's Suits, Tailored Jackets, Tailored Slacks, Sportswear, Dress Shirts, Furnishings, Ties, Underwear, Hosiery, Accessories, Belts, Footwear, Urban Contemporary, Store Displays, Fixtures, Supplies

HILLS BROTHERS BOOTS, INC. (FW)
1901 S. Broadway (m)
Denver, CO 80210
303-722-4995
Sales: $100,001-$500,000
DOYLE ROTH (Owner) & Buys Men's Footwear

HOMER REED LTD. (MW-3)
1717 Tremont Pl. (b)
Denver, CO 80202
303-298-1301 / Fax: 303-298-8195
Sales: $1 Million-$10 Million
MARK REED (President) & Buys Men's Wear, Leather Apparel, Footwear
BROOKS WHITWORTH-Men's Wear, Leather Apparel, Footwear

LAWRENCE COVELL (CLO)
225 Steele St. (b-h)
Denver, CO 80206
303-320-1027 / Fax: 303-320-6476
LAWRENCE COVELL (Co-Owner) & Buys Men's Sportswear, Furnishings, Headwear, Accessories, Urban Contemporary, Store Displays, Fixtures, Supplies
KATHY COVELL (Co-Owner) & Buys Men's Sportswear, Furnishings, Headwear, Accessories, Urban Contemporary, Store Displays, Fixtures, Supplies

LEO'S BODYWEAR (SP)
201 Fillmore St.
Denver, CO 80206
303-399-1627
Sales: $100,001-$500,000
BRENDA MOORE (Owner) & Buys Apparel, Skiwear

MARIO DiLEONE (CLO)
2820 E. 3rd Ave. (h)
Denver, CO 80206
303-333-1414 / Fax: 303-333-5151
MARIO GHAZANFARI (President & Owner) & Buys Men's Wear, Sportswear, Furnishings, Accessories, Men's Footwear, Store Displays, Fixtures and Supplies

THE RIGHT STUFF (SP & MO)
150 W. Louisiana
Denver, CO 80223
303-744-8700 / Fax: 303-744-7878
Sales: $100,001-$500,000
JEANE MANCHESTER-Apparel, Custom Apparel

RUNNER'S ROOST LTD. (FW-5)
1685 S. Colorado Blvd., Unit J (b)
Denver, CO 80222
303-759-8455 / Fax: 303-691-9164
Sales: $1 Million-$10 Million
Website: www.runnersroost.com
DENNIS GIANNANGELI (Owner) & Buys Men's Footwear, Licensed Apparel, Watches, Men's Accessories, Men's Apparel, Hosiery
GREG SUTTON (Mgr.)

SHIRT BROKER (MW)
1201 16th St. (b)
Denver, CO 80202
303-892-1482
Sales: $500,001-$1 Million
RON NEEL (President & Owner) & Buys Men's Wear, Sportswear, Dress Shirts, Ties, Robes, Gloves, Belts, Jewelry, Store Displays, Fixtures and Supplies

SKAGGS TUXALL UNIFORM & EQUIPMENT, INC. (CLO-8)
(C.E. SMITH & ASSOCIATES)
1705 E. 66th Ave. (m)
Denver, CO 80216
303-227-1529 / Fax: 303-297-1439
Sales: $10 Million-$50 Million
CLAYTON C. SMITH (President) & Buys Men's Uniforms, Footwear, Store Displays, Fixtures, Supplies

SPORTS FAN (SP-15 & MO & OL)
1720 Federal Blvd.
Denver, CO 80204
303-455-6303 / Fax: 303-295-3429
Sales: $1 Million-$10 Million
Website: www.sportsteams.com
JOHN BRENNAN (Owner) & Buys Licensed Team Products

COLORADO - Denver

SWIM 'N' THINGS, INC. (CLO & SG)

5494 E. Evans Ave. (m)
Denver, CO 80222
303-757-8866 / Fax: 303-756-9188
Sales: $500,001-$1 Million
Website: www.swimnthings.com

LOIS FAHEY (President & Co-Owner) & Buys Men's Swimwear, T-shirts, Store Displays, Fixtures, Supplies
DENISE GLASS (Co-Owner) & Buys Sandals, Beach Footwear

TREVA'S, INC. (CLO)

6460 E. Yale Ave. (m)
Denver, CO 80222
303-691-9991
Website: www.trevas.com

TREVA STETZMAN (President & Owner) & Buys Men's Robes & Underwear, T-shirts, Thongs, Store Displays, Fixtures & Supplies
CATHY JONES (Mgr.) & Buys Men's Robes & Underwear, T-shirts, Thongs, Store Displays, Fixtures & Supplies

VARSITY FORMAL WEAR (MW)

70 Broadway (p-m)
Denver, CO 80203
303-778-8073 / Fax: 303-722-2629
Website: www.varsityformalwear.com

MIKE LUCHETTA (President & Owner) & Buys Store Displays, Fixtures, Supplies
SANDY LEWIS-Men's & Boys' Formal Wear, Footwear, Related Accessories, Furnishings
DIANE ROY-Men's & Boys' Formal Wear, Footwear, Related Accessories, Furnishings

HOGAN'S STORE (MW)

P.O. Box 598 (p-m)
828 Main Ave.
Durango, CO 81302
970-247-0446 / Fax: 970-247-0446
Sales: $1 Million-$10 Million

G. MICHAEL HOGAN (Owner) & Buys Men's Suits, Tailored Jackets, Tailored Slacks, Raincoats, Sportswear, Sweaters, Sport Shirts, Outer Jackets, Casual Slacks, Active Apparel, Furnishings, Belts, Big & Tall Men's Wear, Footwear, Store Displays, Fixtures, Supplies
JERRY POER (G.M.M.) & Buys Men's Suits, Tailored Jackets, Tailored Slacks, Raincoats, Sportswear, Sweaters, Sport Shirts, Outer Jackets, Casual Slacks, Active Apparel, Furnishings, Robes, Belts, Big & Tall Men's Wear, Footwear, Store Displays, Fixtures, Supplies

STUART'S OF DURANGO, INC. (CLO)

713 Main Ave. (b)
Durango, CO 81301
970-247-0136
Sales: $500,001-$1 Million

ANNA PRICE (Co-Owner) & Buys Men's Footwear, Leather Goods, Men's Apparel, Men's Casualwear, Men's Denim Apparel, Men's Accessories, Men's Formalwear, Men's Hosiery, Men's Outerwear, Men's Sleepwear, Men's Sportswear, Men's Suits, Men's Swimwear, Men's Underwear
DENNIS JOHNSON (Co-Owner) & Buys Men's Footwear, Leather Goods, Men's Apparel, Men's Casualwear, Men's Denim Apparel, Men's Accessories, Men's Formalwear, Men's Hosiery, Men's Outerwear, Men's Sleepwear, Men's Sportswear, Men's Suits, Men's Swimwear, Men's Underwear

O'BOS ENTERPRISES, LLC (GS-8)

(COVERED BRIDGE STORE)
(BEAVER CREEK GEAR)
P.O. Box 2000 (m-b)
Edwards, CO 81632
970-926-9300 / Fax: 970-926-9305
Sales: $1 Million-$10 Million

ROBERT BOSELLI (President & Owner)
ERIN BOSELLI-T-shirts, Headwear, Belts, Small Leathers, Active Apparel, Jewelry

KAUFMAN'S TALL & BIG MEN'S SHOP (MW & OL)

3395 S. Broadway (p-m-b)
Englewood, CO 80110
303-761-6000 / Fax: 303-761-3395
Sales: $1 Million-$10 Million
Website: www.kaufmans.com

FRED KAUFMAN (President)
SAM KAUFMAN (V.P.) & Buys Big & Tall Men's Wear, Related Sportswear, Accessories, Furnishings, Store Displays, Fixtures, Supplies
MAX KERN (G.M.M.) & Buys Big & Tall Men's Wear, Related Sportswear, Accessories, Furnishings, Store Displays, Fixtures, Supplies
MARK BOAGLIO-Footwear

TED'S CLOTHIERS (MW)

3476 S. Broadway (m-b-h)
Englewood, CO 80113
303-781-1382 / Fax: 303-781-1407
Website: www.tedsclothiers.com

TED VASILAS (President & Owner) & Buys Men's Sportswear, Business Wear, Accessories

WESTERN TRADING CO. (CLO-2)

3524 S. Broadway (m-b-des)
Englewood, CO 80110
303-789-1827 / Fax: 303-761-0644
Sales: $1 Million-$10 Million
Website: www.armysurplusforless.com

ALBERT J. FINER (President)
STEVEN A. FINER (V.P.)
MARK LANDERS-Boys' Apparel, Boys' Footwear, Men's Footwear, Men's Apparel, Leather Goods, Men's Big & Tall Apparel, Men's Casualwear, Men's Denim Apparel, Men's Accessories, Men's Hosiery, Men's Outerwear, Men's Underwear

FUN WEAR BRANDS, INC. (MO & CLO-2)

(OUTDOOR WORLD)
(ROCKY MOUNTAIN CONNECTION)
P.O. Box 2800 (m)
141 E. Elkhorn Ave.
Estes Park, CO 80517
970-586-3361 / Fax: 970-586-3302
Sales: $1 Million-$10 Million
Website: www.rmconnection.com

E. J. PETROCINE (C.E.O.)
BILL SCOTT-Men's Western Sportswear, Outdoor Apparel, Leather Apparel, Furnishings, Headwear, Boys' Clothing, Sportswear, Urban Contemporary, Footwear

VILLAGE STORE (CLO)

900 Moraine Ave. (p-m)
Estes Park, CO 80517
970-586-2776 / Fax: 970-586-8547

SCOTT WEBERMEIER (President & Owner) & Buys Store Displays, Fixtures & Supplies
KATIE WEBERMEIER-Men's Outdoor Clothing, Sweaters, Sport Shirts, Outer Jackets, Dress Shirts, Active Apparel, Gloves, Headwear, Moccasins

AUSTRALIAN OUTBACK COLLECTION (CLO)

Showbarn Plaza Bldg. (b-h)
Evergreen, CO 80439
303-670-3933 / Fax: 303-670-3839

CHRIS BLONDEL (President & Owner) & Buys Outerwear, Store Displays, Fixtures & Supplies

BLEACHERS (MW)

1153 Bergen Pkwy. (m)
Evergreen, CO 80439
303-674-6515 / Fax: 303-674-0125

TERRE GLEASON (Co-Owner) & Buys Men's Sportswear, Furnishings, T-shirts, Fleece, Jeans, Shorts, Store Displays, Fixtures, Supplies
DAVID GLEASON (Co-Owner) & Buys Men's Sportswear, Furnishings, T-shirts, Fleece, Jeans, Shorts, Store Displays, Fixtures, Supplies

COLORADO - Florence

JIM'S CLOTHING (CLO)
114 W. Main St. (m-b)
Florence, CO 81226
719-784-3558 / Fax: 719-784-4420
Sales: $500,001-$1 Million
JAMES PROVENZANO (President & Owner) & Buys Men's Jeans, Suits, Sport Shirts, Casual Slacks, Hosiery, Underwear, Belts, Young Men's Shop, Boys' Wear 7+, Men's Footwear, Boots, Store Displays, Fixtures & Supplies

J. PITNER CLOTHING CO. (MW)
125 S. College Ave.
Fort Collins, CO 80524
970-221-2131 / Fax: 970-221-2145
CHRIS HUTCHINSON (Owner) & Buys Men's Sportswear, Furnishings, Jewelry, Small Leather Goods, Urban Contemporary, Footwear, Store Displays, Fixtures, Supplies

JAX (SG & CLO & OL)
(JAX MERCANTILE, INC.)
1200 N. College Ave, (p-m-b)
Fort Collins, CO 80524
970-221-0544 / Fax: 970-493-1013
Sales: $1 Million-$10 Million
Website: www.jaxoutdoor.com
JIM QUINLAN (Co-Owner)
NAN QUINLAN (Co-Owner)
NANCY RAINEY-Men's Outerwear, Activewear, Sport Shirts, Outer Jackets, Leather Apparel, Casual Slacks, Hosiery, Headwear, Store Displays, Fixtures, Supplies
KATE REYNOLDS-Men's Outerwear, Activewear, Sport Shirts, Outer Jackets, Leather Apparel, Casual Slacks, Hosiery, Headwear, Store Displays, Fixtures, Supplies
DAVE CHADSTAY-Footwear

SOPHIE GALLY (CLO)
606 6th St. (m-b-h)
Georgetown, CO 80444
303-569-2434 / Fax: 303-569-2434
PATTIE FRALEY (President & Owner) & Buys Men's Raincoats, Outer Jackets, Sport Shirts, Gloves, Headwear, Store Displays, Fixtures & Supplies

ANDERSON'S CLOTHING (MW)
826 Grand Ave. (p-m)
Glenwood Springs, CO 81601
970-945-6671 / Fax: 970-945-8460
GARY MILLER (President & Owner) & Buys Formal Wear, Sportswear, Sweaters, Sport Shirts, Outer Jackets, Casual Slacks, Furnishings, Dress Shirts, Ties, Belts, Jeans, Young Men's Wear, Store Displays, Fixtures and Supplies

BILL BULLOCK'S, INC. (DEPT)
P.O. Box 609 (m-b)
1526 Grand Ave.
Glenwood Springs, CO 81602
970-945-5066 / Fax: 970-947-0676
Sales: $100,001-$500,000
BILL BULLOCK, SR. (Owner) & Buys Men's Sportswear, Furnishings, Belts, Jewelry, Small Leather Goods, Store Displays, Fixtures, Supplies

HJ FOSS (CLO & OL)
1224 Washington Ave. (bud)
Golden, CO 80401
303-279-7555 / Fax: 303-278-9556
Website: www.fossco.com
BOB LOWRY (President)
SANDRA BANTELE-Sportswear, Underwear, Hosiery, Belts, Urban Contemporary, Store Displays, Fixtures and Supplies

INTERMOUNTAIN SAFETY SHOES (FW-2 & MO)
P.O. Box 878 (m)
15400 W. 44th Ave.
Golden, CO 80403
303-278-2871 / Fax: 303-278-2041
Sales: $1 Million-$10 Million
TONY PENNA (President) & Buys Leather Goods, Watches, Men's Accessories, Hosiery

TRAZ BODY GEAR (SP)
504 28 1/4 Rd.
Grand Junction, CO 81501
970-241-4433 / Fax: 970-255-1527
Sales: $100,001-$500,000
HAROLD MARTINEZ (Co-Owner) & Buys Skiwear, Athletic Footwear, Outdoor Footwear, Skate Apparel, Snowboard Apparel
TOM LEVALLEY (Co-Owner) & Buys Skiwear, Athletic Footwear, Outdoor Footwear, Skate Apparel, Snowboard Apparel

BIG R OF GREELEY, INC. (DEPT)
310 8th St. (m)
Greeley, CO 80631
970-352-0544 / Fax: 970-356-2054
Website: www.bigrgreeley.com
DUANE FRANCIS (Owner)
KRISTINA BABCOCK-Men's Sportswear, Furnishings, Work Clothes, Big & Tall Men's Wear, Footwear, Boys' Wear, Store Displays, Fixtures, Supplies

SCHEUNEMANN'S DEPARTMENT STORE (DEPT)
105 S. Interocean Dr. (m-b)
Holyoke, CO 80734
970-854-3434 / Fax: 970-854-3434
Sales: $1 Million-$10 Million
FREEMAN SCHEUNEMANN (Owner) & Buys Men's & Boys' Wear, Footwear, Urban Contemporary, Young Men's Wear, Store Displays, Fixtures, Supplies

JOHNSTOWN CLOTHING (CLO)
P.O. Box 57 (m)
18 S. Parish St.
Johnstown, CO 80534
970-587-4502 / Fax: 970-587-4509
Sales: $100,001-$500,000
ED REICHERT (Owner) & Buys Men's Sportswear, Clothing, Accessories, Furnishings, Boys' Wear, Store Displays, Fixtures, Supplies
SUSAN WADAS-Men's Sportswear, Clothing, Accessories, Furnishings, Boys' Wear, Store Displays, Fixtures, Supplies
MARGIE COUFAL-Men's Sportswear, Clothing, Accessories, Furnishings, Boys' Wear, Store Displays, Fixtures, Supplies

AMAZONIA'S SWEATERS (CLO)
195 River Run Rd. (b)
P.O. Box 767
Keystone, CO 80435
970-262-6655 / Fax: 970-453-6956
Sales: $100,001-$500,000
WALTER CAAMANO (Owner) & Buys Men's Apparel, Men's Casualwear
MARY CAAMANO (Gen. Mgr.) & Buys Men's Apparel, Men's Casualwear

ESMIOL'S DEPARTMENT STORE (DEPT)
104 S. 2nd St. (m)
Kremmling, CO 80459
970-724-3355
ELDO GALLAGHER (Co-Owner) & Buys Footwear
MARCELLINE GALLAGHER (Co-Owner) & Buys Men's Raincoats, Sportswear, Furnishings, Jewelry, Small Leather Goods, Swimwear, Boys' 8 to 14 Sportswear, Store Displays, Fixtures, Supplies

HIGH POINT SWIM, INC. (SP-4)
1535 S. Kipling Pkwy., #1
Lakewood, CO 80232
303-989-2724 / Fax: 303-989-2746
Sales: $100,001-$500,000
BARBARA GAYER (Owner) & Buys Apparel, Athletic Footwear, Custom Apparel

BIG R, INC. (CLO-7 & OL)

P.O. Box 1049 (p-m-b)
310 W. Washington St.
Lamar, CO 81052
719-336-7864 / Fax: 719-336-3136
Website: www.bigronline.com

DAVE BLAIN (President) & Buys Store Displays, Fixtures, Supplies
LEE ANN BROOKS-Men's & Boys' Wear, Footwear
SHAWN HANSON-Men's & Boys' Wear, Footwear
ADAM CAROL-Men's & Boys' Wear, Footwear

TIME OUT SPORTS LETTERING, INC. (SP)

6905 S. Broadway
Littleton, CO 80122
303-794-8169 / Fax: 303-794-7540
Sales: $500,001-$1 Million
Website: www.timeoutsportsinc.com

BRENT BAILEY (Owner) & Buys Activewear
DARREN BARROWS (Mgr.) & Buys Activewear

MR. NEAT'S FORMAL WEAR, INC. (MW-18)

5677 Boeing Dr. (b)
Loveland, CO 80538
970-667-4444 / Fax: 970-669-9226
Website: www.misterneats.com

MARK BURKE (Owner & C.E.O.) & Buys Men's & Boys' Formal Wear, Related Accessories, Furnishings, Men's & Boys' Footwear, Store Displays, Fixtures, Supplies
NANCY HABOUSH (President)
KEITH LONGWELL (Senior V.P.) & Buys Men's & Boys' Formal Wear, Related Accessories, Furnishings, Men's & Boys' Footwear, Store Displays, Fixtures, Supplies

QUALITY SHOES CO., INC. (FW)

224 E. 4th St. (m-b-des)
Loveland, CO 80537
970-667-6735 / Fax: 970-667-6763
Sales: $500,001-$1 Million

FRANK MUSSO (President) & Buys Men's Footwear, Leather Goods, Hosiery
SALLY MUSSO-Men's Footwear, Leather Goods, Hosiery

SNEAKERS (SP)

257 E. 29th St., #A
Loveland, CO 80538
970-663-4880 / Fax: 970-622-2058

ROB RAMSAY (Owner) & Buys Athletic Footwear, Licensed Apparel

WHITESIDE'S (WW)

(VANDERBILT #7, INC.)
202 SE 19th St. (m-b)
Loveland, CO 80537
970-669-7808 / Fax: 970-669-7824

JOHN WHITESIDE (Owner) & Buys Men's & Boys' Western Wear, Footwear, Related Accessories, Furnishings, Store Displays, Fixtures, Supplies

MANITOU SPRINGS T-SHIRT CO. (SP-3 & MO)

(MOUNTAIN WEST T & TRADING CO.)
744 Manitou Ave.
Manitou Springs, CO 80829
719-685-4005 / Fax: 413-828-2569
Sales: $501,000-$1 Million
Website: www.mountain-west.com

PAIGE BARTON (Co-Owner) & Buys Apparel, Custom Apparel
TODD BARTON (Co-Owner) & Buys Apparel, Custom Apparel

DOWN HOME MEN'S STORE, INC. (MW)

316 Main St.
Montrose, CO 81401
970-240-4323 / Fax: 970-240-4323

JEFF BUTTERBAUGH (Owner) & Buys Men's Sportswear, Furnishings, Accessories, Headwear, Young Men's Wear, Store Displays, Fixtures, Supplies

JEANS WESTERNER, INC. (CLO-2 & OL)

120 N. Townsend Ave.
Montrose, CO 81401
970-249-8757 / Fax: 970-249-5205
Sales: $1 Million-$10 Million
Website: www.jeanswesterner.com

MARY K. MATHIS (President) & Buys Athletic Apparel
STEVE OMERNIK (G.M.M.) & Buys Athletic Footwear, Athletic Apparel
TOM OMERNIK-Athletic Apparel

GOODMAN'S (DEPT)

P.O. Box 68 (m-b)
Pagosa Springs, CO 81147
970-264-5460 / Fax: 970-264-2223

ROBERT GOODMAN (Owner) & Buys Men's Sportswear, Leather Apparel, Boys' Jeans, Tops, Underwear, Footwear, Urban Contemporary, Store Displays, Fixtures, Supplies

CLARK'S WESTERN STORES (WW-2)

300 N. Main St. (m-b)
Pueblo, CO 81003
719-544-3780 / Fax: 719-546-1590
Sales: $1 Million-$10 Million

ALEX CLARK, III (President) & Buys Men's & Boys' Western Wear, Suits, Sweaters, Furnishings, Small Leather Goods, Belts, Jewelry, Leather Apparel
BARCLAY CLARK (V.P.) & Buys Men's & Boys' Western Wear, Suits, Sweaters, Furnishings, Small Leather Goods, Belts, Jewelry, Leather Apparel, Store Displays, Fixtures and Supplies
PATRICK FIRESTONE-Footwear, Boots

MILLER'S DRY GOODS (DG)

118 E. 3rd St. (m)
Rifle, CO 81650
970-625-1737 / Fax: 970-625-1737

GARY MILLER (Owner) & Buys Men's Tailored Jackets, Tailored Slacks, Sportswear, Furnishings, Jewelry, Small Leather Goods, Swimwear, Western Boots, Work Boots, Store Displays, Fixtures, Supplies

J. HENRY OUTFITTERS (CLO-2)

P.O. Box 948 (m)
Silverthorne, CO 80498
970-468-2920 / Fax: 970-468-5568

ANN MARIE OHLY (Owner) & Buys Outer Jackets, Ski Clothing, Sportswear, Sport Shirts, Casual Slacks, Active Apparel, Store Displays, Fixtures & Supplies
DAVID SHAPIRIO (Mgr.) & Buys Outer Jackets, Ski Clothing, Sportswear, Sport Shirts, Casual Slacks, Active Apparel, Store Displays, Fixtures & Supplies

F.M. LIGHT & SONS (SP-3)

(BUSHWACKERS)
830 Lincoln Ave.
Steamboat Springs, CO 80487
(Sports, Inc.)
970-879-1822 / Fax: 970-879-0089

TY LOCKHART (Owner) & Buys Athletic Footwear, Athletic Apparel
MICHELLE BAUKNECHT-Athletic Footwear, Athletic Apparel

OLD TOWN SHIRT CO. (SP)

833 Lincoln Ave.
Steamboat Springs, CO 80487
970-879-5099 / Fax: 970-879-1107

LEON RINCK (Owner) & Buys Apparel

THE SHIRT STOP (SP & MO)

P.O. Box 880760
Steamboat Springs, CO 80488
970-879-5440 / Fax: 970-879-5440

LIL GONZALEZ (Co-Owner) & Buys Apparel, Licensed Apparel
BEN GONZALEZ (Co-Owner) & Buys Apparel, Licensed Apparel

COLORADO - Sterling

CLOTHES LION (CLO)
119 Main St. (m-b)
Sterling, CO 80751
970-521-0828
THEODORA YOST (Owner) & Buys Boys' Apparel, Boys' Footwear, Men's Footwear, Men's Apparel, Men's Big & Tall Apparel, Men's Casualwear, Men's Denim Apparel, Men's Outerwear, Men's Suits
YOLANDA GUERRA (Gen. Mgr.)

HERALD'S MEN'S STORE (MW)
206 Main St.
Sterling, CO 80751
970-522-3708
Website: www.heraldsmenswear.com
HAL SPERBER (Owner) & Buys Men's Sportswear, Furnishings, Accessories, Headwear, Young Men's Wear, Store Displays, Fixtures, Supplies

TELLURIDE TRAPPINGS & TOGGERY (CLO)
109 E. Colorado Ave. (b)
P.O. Box 1138
Telluride, CO 81435
970-728-3338 / Fax: 970-728-3367
Sales: $1 Million-$10 Million
TERRY TICE (Owner) & Buys Boys' Apparel, Boys' Footwear, Men's Footwear, Men's Apparel, Men's Casualwear, Men's Denim Apparel, Men's Accessories, Men's Hosiery, Men's Sleepwear, Men's Sportswear, Men's Swimwear, Men's Underwear

TOPS OF THE ROCKIES (SP)
305 N. Commercial St.
Trinidad, CO 81082
719-846-7555
Sales: $100,001-$500,000
MARTIN SOLANO (Owner) & Buys Apparel, Custom Apparel

CHARLIE'S SHIRTS, INC. (CLO-9)
641 Lionshead Cir. West (b)
Vail, CO 81657
970-476-9737 / Fax: 970-476-4930
Website: www.vail.net/shops/charlies
STEVE MELZER (Co-Owner) & Buys Men's & Boys' Shirts, Urban Contemporary, Active Apparel, Hats, Hosiery, Store Displays, Fixtures, Supplies
STEVE MELZER (Co-Owner) & Buys Men's & Boys' Shirts, Urban Contemporary, Active Apparel, Leisure Suits, Hats, Underwear, Hosiery, Store Displays, Fixtures, Supplies

GORSUCH LTD. (CLO-7 & MO & SG)
263 E. Gore Creek Dr. (m-b)
Vail, CO 81657
970-476-2294 / Fax: 970-476-4323
Sales: $10 Million-$50 Million
Website: www.gorsuchltd.com
JEFF GORSUCH (Co-Owner)
RENEE GORSUCH (Co-Owner & G.M.M.) & Buys Men's Ski Wear, Store Displays, Fixtures, Supplies, Footwear
JUDY CONN-Men's Outerwear, Leather Apparel, Footwear
JOHN GORSUCH-Sportswear, Outer Jackets, Leather Apparel, Footwear

WILD BILL'S EMPORIUM (SP)
225 Wall St.
Vail, CO 81657
970-476-5738
BILL HANLON (Owner) & Buys Apparel

THE VILLAGE SHOP (CLO)
205 Main St. (m)
Westcliffe, CO 81252
719-783-2541 / Fax: 719-783-2541
GARY KING (Co-Owner) & Buys Fleece, T-shirts, Sweaters, Outer Jackets, Active Apparel, Jeans, Dress Shirts, Bolo Ties, Underwear, Belts, Small Leathers, Jewelry, Hosiery, Gloves, Headwear, Young Men's Wear, Boys' Wear, Store Displays, Fixtures and Supplies
JANICE KING (Co-Owner) & Buys Fleece, T-shirts, Sweaters, Outer Jackets, Active Apparel, Jeans, Dress Shirts, Bolo Ties, Underwear, Belts, Small Leathers, Jewelry, Hosiery, Gloves, Headwear, Young Men's Wear, Boys' Wear, Store Displays, Fixtures and Supplies

SHOE EXTREME (SP-3)
5481 W. 88th Ave., #124
Westminster, CO 80030
303-426-0138
Sales: $501,000-$1 Million
JUDY LUNN (Owner) & Buys Apparel, Athletic Footwear, Outdoor Footwear
JASON LUNN-Apparel, Athletic Footwear, Outdoor Footwear

THE SHIRT OFF MY BACK (SP)
P.O. Box 266
Woody Creek, CO 81656
970-923-3917 / Fax: 970-923-5967
Sales: $100,001-$500,000
SHERRY FLACK (Co-Owner) & Buys Apparel
MICHAEL FLACK (Co-Owner) & Buys Apparel

B & L MEN'S & BOYS' (MW)

350 W. Main St. (p)
Ansonia, CT 06401
203-734-2607 / Fax: 203-735-0332
Sales: $1 Million-$10 Million

CARMEN DICENSO (Owner) & Buys Men's Overcoats, Suits, Tailored Jackets, Tailored Slacks, Raincoats, Sweaters, Sport Shirts, Outer Jackets, Leather Apparel, Casual Slacks, Active Apparel, Dress Shirts, Ties, Robes, Underwear, Hosiery, Gloves, Headwear, Belts, Jewelry, Small Leather Goods, Fragrances, Big & Tall Men's Wear, Young Men's Wear, Size 8 to 20 Boys' Wear, Urban Contemporary, Store Displays, Fixtures, Supplies

JEFF CAVANAUGH (G.M.M.) & Buys Men's Overcoats, Suits, Tailored Jackets, Tailored Slacks, Raincoats, Sweaters, Sport Shirts, Outer Jackets, Leather Apparel, Casual Slacks, Active Apparel, Dress Shirts, Ties, Robes, Underwear, Hosiery, Gloves, Headwear, Belts, Jewelry, Small Leather Goods, Fragrances, Big & Tall Men's Wear, Young Men's Wear, Size 8 to 20 Boys' Wear, Urban Contemporary, Store Displays, Fixtures, Supplies

SECCOMBE'S MEN'S SHOP, INC. (MW)

171 Main St. (m-b)
Ansonia, CT 06401
203-734-1536
Sales: $100,001-$500,000

CHARLES T. SECCOMBE (Co-Owner) & Buys Men's Sportswear, Furnishings, Accessories, Tuxedos, Store Displays, Fixtures, Supplies

GREGG SECCOMBE (Co-Owner) & Buys Men's Sportswear, Furnishings, Accessories, Tuxedos, Store Displays, Fixtures, Supplies

MADISON SHOP OF AVON, INC. (MW)

395 W. Main St. (m)
Avon, CT 06001
860-676-9449 / Fax: 860-677-5453

MARTIN BRODER (Owner) & Buys Men's Sportswear, Furnishings, Accessories, Young Men's Wear, Urban Contemporary, Men's Footwear, Store Displays, Fixtures, Supplies

MICKEY FINN STORES (CLO-3)

P.O. Box 8315 (m-b)
874 Wilbur Cross Tnpk.
Berlin, CT 06037
860-828-6547 / Fax: 860-829-1863
Sales: $10 Million-$50 Million

JEROME SKOLNICK (Co-Owner)

DANIEL SKOLNICK (Co-Owner)

DAVID SKOLNICK-Sweaters, Sport Shirts, Ties, Underwear, Young Men's Wear, Boys' Wear, Leather Apparel, Dress Shirts

SCOTT COHEN-Outer Jackets

DOUG COHEN-Casual Slacks

JAY SKOLNICK-Active Apparel, Athletic Footwear

CHRIS FAGIAN-Hosiery, Men's Footwear

LAURA WILSON-Gloves, Belts, Small Leather Goods

ARCTIC SPORTS, LLC (CLO)

353 Huntington Tnpk. (m)
Bridgeport, CT 06610
203-371-8326 / Fax: 203-373-9655
Sales: $1 Million-$10 Million

RICK PICCIRILLO (President) & Buys Boys' Apparel, Men's Footwear, Men's Apparel, Men's Casualwear, Men's Denim Apparel, Men's Accessories, Men's Hosiery, Men's Outerwear, Men's Sportswear, Men's Swimwear, Men's Underwear

WALTER DUNN (V.P. & G.M.M.) & Buys Boys' Apparel, Men's Footwear, Men's Apparel, Men's Casualwear, Men's Denim Apparel, Men's Accessories, Men's Hosiery, Men's Outerwear, Men's Sportswear, Men's Swimwear, Men's Underwear

JIMMY'S ARMY & NAVY (AN-5)

(M. SCHNEIDER, INC.)
1000 Main St. (p)
Bridgeport, CT 06604
203-333-3939 / Fax: 203-334-6150

BOB SCHNEIDER (Owner) & Buys Men's Raincoats, Overcoats, Casual Slacks, Active Apparel, Underwear, Headwear, Small Leather Goods, Urban Contemporary, Footwear, Store Displays, Fixtures, Supplies

DAVE SCHNEIDER-Men's Raincoats, Overcoats, Casual Slacks, Active Apparel, Underwear, Headwear, Small Leather Goods, Urban Contemporary, Footwear, Store Displays, Fixtures, Supplies

MISTER JERRY (MW)

1191 Main St. (m-b)
Bridgeport, CT 06604
203-335-0474
Sales: $500,001-$1 Million

JERRY ARDUS (Owner) & Buys Men's Sportswear, Furnishings, Accessories

BOB HARRIS-Men's Footwear, Store Displays, Fixtures, Supplies

INSANE IRVING'S, INC. (CLO)

900 Farmington Ave. (bud-p-m)
Bristol, CT 06010
860-582-0691 / Fax: 860-589-6604
Sales: $1 Million-$10 Million
Website: www.insaneirvings.com

NORM GINSBURG (President) & Buys Boys' Apparel, Boys' Footwear, Men's Footwear, Leather Goods, Men's Apparel, Men's Casualwear, Men's Denim Apparel, Men's Formalwear, Men's Accessories, Men's Hosiery, Men's Outerwear, Men's Sportswear, Men's Swimwear

IRVING GINSBURG (V.P.) & Buys Boys' Apparel, Boys' Footwear, Men's Footwear, Leather Goods, Men's Apparel, Men's Casualwear, Men's Denim Apparel, Men's Formalwear, Men's Accessories, Men's Hosiery, Men's Outerwear, Men's Sportswear, Men's Swimwear

BIANCHI'S (CLO)

89 Main St. (b)
Canaan, CT 06018
860-824-7608
Sales: $500,001-$1 Million

FRAN ENGLISH (Owner) & Buys Men's Sportswear, Furnishings, Accessories, Store Displays, Fixtures, Supplies

PAUL'S FINE CLOTHING, INC. (MW)

112 Elm St. (m-b)
Cheshire, CT 06410
203-272-9212

PAUL CAMARATO (Owner) & Buys Men's Sportswear, Furnishings, Accessories, Headwear, Footwear, Store Displays, Fixtures, Supplies

DANIELSON'S SURPLUS SALES (CLO)

151 Main St. (p-m)
Danielson, CT 06239
860-774-6287 / Fax: 860-779-3572

WARREN ROSENBERG (Owner) & Buys Men's Sportswear, Furnishings, Headwear, Accessories, Young Men's & Boys' Wear, Men's Footwear, Boys' Footwear

MARK GOLDBERG-Store Displays, Fixtures, Supplies

CONNECTICUT - Darien

DARIEN SPORT SHOP, INC. (SG)

1127 Post Rd. (h)
Darien, CT 06820
203-655-2575 / Fax: 203-655-2751
Sales: $1 Million-$10 Million
Website: www.dariensport.com

STEVE ZANGRILLO, SR. (President)
STEVE ZANGRILLO, JR. (Store Mgr.) & Buys Athletic Footwear
GINA REILLY (Bus. Mgr.) & Buys Store Displays, Fixtures, Supplies
MATT KAPTEINA-Men's Sportswear, Headwear, 8 to 20 Boys' Wear, Furnishings, Accessories, Men's Footwear
LOU ARGYROPOULIS-Size 4 to 7 Boys' Wear

EDWARD TUNICK (MW)

(M.L.T., INC.)
340 Heights Rd. (m)
Darien, CT 06820
203-655-1688 / Fax: 203-655-1492
Sales: $500,001-$1 Million

EDWARD TUNICK (Owner) & Buys Men's Sportswear, Furnishings, Accessories, Store Displays, Fixtures, Supplies

JOHNNY'S (SP)

45 Tokeneke Rd. (m)
Darien, CT 06820
203-655-0157

JOHN KONRAD (Owner) & Buys Men's & Boys' Novelty, Music & Movie T-shirts, Store Displays, Fixtures, Supplies
NOTE-This Store Sells Movie & Music Related Goods Only.

CARLINO TAILOR & MENS (MW)

63 Elizabeth St. (m)
Derby, CT 06418
203-735-5751
Sales: $100,001-$500,000

NICK CARLINO (Owner) & Buys Men's Sportswear, Furnishings, Accessories, Store Displays, Fixtures, Supplies

SHERMAN'S MENSWEAR (MW)

1003 Main St. (m-b)
East Hartford, CT 06108
860-528-2934
Sales: $100,001-$500,000

LEON DARESSKY (Owner) & Buys Neck Ties, Men's Wear, Accessories, Furnishings, Store Displays, Fixtures, Supplies

ATTILLIO'S MEN'S CLOTHING (MW)

827 Foxon Rd. (b)
East Haven, CT 06513
203-469-1275
Sales: $500,001-$1 Million

ATTILLIO DELVECCHIO (Owner) & Buys Men's Sportswear, Leather Apparel, Ties, Accessories, Footwear, Store Displays, Fixtures, Supplies
GIULIO DELVECCHIO (Mgr.) & Buys Men's Sportswear, Leather Apparel, Ties, Accessories, Footwear, Store Displays, Fixtures, Supplies

YOUNG FOLK'S STORE (KS)

(Y.F.S., INC.)
309 Main St. (m-b)
Ensonia, CT 06401
203-734-7394 / Fax: 203-732-4730
Sales: $100,001-$500,000

BERNIE BENEDETTO-Size 8 to 20 Boys' Wear, Accessories, Sportswear, Furnishings, Store Displays, Fixtures, Supplies

J. ALDEN (MW)

17 Main St.
Essex, CT 06426
860-767-7633 / Fax: 860-767-3120

JIM DALESSIO (Owner) & Buys Men's Wear, Accessories, Furnishings, Footwear

GROSSMAN SHOES, INC. (FW)

88 Greenwich Ave. (des)
Greenwich, CT 06830
203-869-2123 / Fax: 203-869-5104
Sales: $1 Million-$10 Million

LEE GROSSMAN (President & G.M.) & Buys Men's Footwear

HENRY LEHR CO., INC. (CLO-5)

116 Greenwich Ave. (m-b)
Greenwich, CT 06830
203-255-9008 / Fax: 203-255-9059
Sales: $1 Million-$10 Million

TONI LEHR (President & Real Estate Contact) & Buys Leather Goods, Men's Apparel, Men's Denim Apparel, Men's Accessories, Men's Outerwear, Men's Sportswear, Men's Swimwear

RICHARD'S OF GREENWICH (MW-2)

359 Greenwich Ave. (m-b)
Greenwich, CT 06830
203-622-0551 / Fax: 203-622-7352
Sales: $1 Million-$10 Million

JACK MITCHELL (Owner)
ROBERT MITCHELL-Men's Sportswear, Furnishings, Accessories, Footwear, Store Displays, Fixtures, Supplies
BILL MITCHELL-Men's Sportswear, Furnishings, Accessories, Footwear, Store Displays, Fixtures, Supplies

VAN DRIVER, INC. (MW)

24 E. Elm St. (b-des)
Greenwich, CT 06830
203-869-5358 / Fax: 203-869-2250

MICHAEL OSSORIO (President)
TOM MOLNAR (Partner) & Buys Men's Sportswear, Furnishings, Accessories, Store Displays, Fixtures, Supplies

FLEISCHMAN'S DEPARTMENT STORE (DEPT)

1067 Boston Post Rd. (m)
Guilford, CT 06437
203-453-3355 / Fax: 203-458-7684
Website: www.fleischmans.com

JOSEPH FLEISCHMAN (Co-Owner) & Buys Men's & Boys' Footwear

TRAILBLAZER (CLO-4)

102 Broad St. (m-b)
Guilford, CT 06437
203-458-2267 / Fax: 203-458-1813
Sales: $1 Million-$10 Million
Website: www.trailblazerdirect.com

DAVID VENABLES (Co-Owner)
CHRIS HOWE (Co-Owner) & Buys Men's Raincoats, Sweaters, Sport Shirts, Outer Jackets, Casual Slacks, Active Apparel, Furnishings, Swimwear, Young Men's Wear, Urban Contemporary, Hiking Boots, Athletic Footwear, Children's Outdoorwear, Store Displays, Fixtures, Supplies

FRANKLIN FORMALS (MW)

399 Franklin Ave. (b)
Hartford, CT 06114
860-296-2889 / Fax: 860-296-8067
Sales: $100,001-$500,000

JERRY MESSINA (Owner) & Buys Men's & Boys' Formalwear

NEW YORK FASHIONS (MW)

633 Park St. (m)
Hartford, CT 06106
860-249-4006

BILL DAMGANBARA (Owner) & Buys Men's Sportswear, Furnishings, Accessories, Urban Contemporary, 7 to 20 Boys' Wear, Men's Footwear, Boys' Footwear, Store Displays, Fixtures, Supplies
GERARDO MALAVE (Mgr.) & Buys Men's Sportswear, Furnishings, Accessories, Urban Contemporary, 7 to 20 Boys' Wear, Men's Footwear, Boys' Footwear, Store Displays, Fixtures, Supplies

CONNECTICUT - Hartford

STACKPOLE MOORE TRYON CO. (MW)
242 Trumbull St. (b-des)
Hartford, CT 06103
860-522-0181 / Fax: 860-706-0460
Sales: $1 Million-$10 Million
CYNTHIA L. GARDNER (President) & Buys Men's Sportswear, Accessories, Furnishings, Store Displays, Fixtures, Supplies
DENNIS QUIGLEY-Men's Overcoats, Suits, Tailored Jackets, Tailored Slacks, Raincoats, Furnishings

COUNTRY CLOTHES (CLO)
11 N. Main St. (m)
Kent, CT 06757
860-927-4064
CAROL JALBERT (Owner) & Buys Men's Casual Wear, Store Displays, Fixtures, Supplies

ASHFIELD CLOTHIER (CLO)
44 Stock Pl. (m-b)
Manchester, CT 06040
860-646-9502 / Fax: 860-646-4988
Sales: $100,001-$500,000
GARETH WITKEWICZ (Owner) & Buys Men's Sportswear, Furnishings, Accessories, Headwear, Store Displays, Fixtures, Supplies
NOTE:-Primarily Supply Clothing For Nursing Home Residents.

LUCA'S TAILOR SHOP (CLO)
180 Spruce St. (m-b)
Manchester, CT 06040
860-643-7757 / Fax: 860-646-5000
Sales: $500,001-$1 Million
MR. LUCA (Owner) & Buys Men's Sportswear, Furnishings, Accessories, Store Displays, Fixtures, Supplies

MARLOW'S, INC. (DEPT)
867 Main St. (p)
Manchester, CT 06040
860-649-5221
GEORGE MARLOW (President) & Buys Men's Headwear, Accessories, Boys' Wear, Store Displays, Fixtures, Supplies
LESTER MINER (G.M.M.) & Buys Men's Sportswear, Furnishings

BOB'S STORES (CLO-36)
160 Corporate Ct. (m)
Meriden, CT 06450
203-235-5775 / Fax: 203-634-0433
Sales: $50 Million-$100 Million
Website: www.bobstores.com
Retail Locations: CT, MA, NH, NJ, NY, RI
DAVID FARRELL (President, C.E.O. & Real Estate Contact)
MIKE ZIBEL (V.P. & G.M.M.)
AVA HILL-GAUNT (D.M.M. - Men's) & Buys Men's Apparel, Footwear, Activewear, Accessories
LISA RAMOS-Men's Sweaters, Sport Shirts, Dress Shirts, Young Men's Wear, Urban Contemporary, Young Men's Bottoms
PAUL BETTAN-Men's Tops
JIM TOKARZ-Men's Traditional, Outerwear, Leather Apparel, Workwear
PAUL DeTAN-Young Men's Bottoms
STEVE TURCO-Men's Big & Tall
TORI PACE-Men's Denim

JIM BECHARD (D.M.M.-Accessories)
CHRISTINE VALE de SERRA-Men's Accessories
KATHY RACZKA-Men's Underwear, Hosiery, Gloves, Ties, Robes, Accessories

ANDY ANNUNZIALLA (D.M.M.-Activewear)
BERRY GARVIN-Men's Active Apparel
JAMIE HOLLIS-Young Men's Action Sports, Outerwear
BARRY GARVIN-Men's Active Tops & Bottoms

AVA HILL-GAUNT (D.M.M.-Children's)
KIM LIBERTORE-Boys' Activewear, Accessories
CATHY RACZKA-Boys' Accessories, Boys' Wear
NANCY SANELLO-Boys' 8-20

ANDY ANNUNZIATA (D.M.M.-Footwear) & Buys Athletic Footwear
CAROLYN SWENSON-Men's & Boys' Athletic Footwear, Cleats
KATHY ECKE-Workboots, Hunting Shoes
GAYLE PEACOCK-Men's Shoes
RITA BERTONE (Visual Display Mgr.) & Buys Store Displays, Fixtures & Supplies

REGAL MEN'S SHOP (MW)
308 Main St. (m)
Middletown, CT 06457
860-347-2889 / Fax: 860-343-7702
Sales: $100,001-$500,000
JAMES SALONIA (President) & Buys Men's & Young Men's Wear, Sportswear, Furnishings, Accessories, Footwear, Store Displays, Fixtures, Supplies

CAPRICORN UNIFORM SHOP (SP)
764 Boston Post Rd. (m-b)
Milford, CT 06460
203-878-9070
Sales: $500,001-$1 Million
PEGGY DE CAPUA (Owner) & Buys Men's Footwear, Men's Apparel, Men's Accessories, Men's Hosiery, Men's Uniforms/Workclothes

ROSENBLATT'S, INC. (MW)
85 Maple St. (p-m-b)
Naugatuck, CT 06770
203-729-3742
HOWARD ROSENBLATT (Owner) & Buys Men's Sportswear, Urban Contemporary, 8 to 20 Boys' Wear, Furnishings, Accessories, Store Displays, Fixtures, Supplies

FANTASTIC FASHIONS (MW)
148 E. Main St. (p)
New Britain, CT 06051
860-224-2297 / Fax: 860-223-2299
Sales: $500,001-$1 Million
MIKE MIN (Owner)
SUE MIN-Men's Casual Wear, Sportswear, Accessories, Furnishings, Store Displays, Fixtures, Supplies

THE BEACH CORNER (CLO)
102 Main St.
New Canaan, CT 06840
203-966-4644 / Fax: 203-972-6663
KIM RIBEIRO-Boys' Apparel, Boys' Swimwear, Sunglasses, Fashion Accessories, Footwear, Hats, Men's Surf & Swimwear, Resortwear
MARCIA CHLUDZINSKI-Boys' Apparel, Boys' Swimwear, Sunglasses, Fashion Accessories, Footwear, Hats, Men's Surf & Swimwear, Resortwear

ENSON'S, INC. (MW)
1050 Chapel St. (b)
New Haven, CT 06510
203-562-4136 / Fax: 203-789-1834
Sales: $1 Million-$10 Million
JAMES CIVITELLO (President) & Buys Men's Leather Apparel, Sportswear, Furnishings, Accessories, Store Displays, Fixtures, Supplies

FERRUCCI LTD., INC. (MW)
53 Elm St. (m-b-des)
New Haven, CT 06510
203-787-2928
Sales: $500,001-$1 Million
VINCENT FERRUCCI (Owner) & Buys Men's Wear, Sportswear, Accessories, Furnishings, Footwear, Store Displays, Fixtures, Supplies
VINCENT FERRUCCI, JR.-Men's Wear, Sportswear, Accessories, Furnishings, Footwear, Store Displays, Fixtures, Supplies

CONNECTICUT - New Haven

HAROLD'S FORMALWEAR (MW-2)

19 Elm St. (p)
New Haven, CT 06511
203-562-7433 / Fax: 203-239-6404
Website: www.haroldsformalwear.com

HAROLD PELLEGRINO (Owner) & Buys Men's, Young Men's & Boys' Formal Wear, Accessories, Furnishings, Footwear, Store Displays, Fixtures, Supplies

HE & SHE CLOTHING CO., INC. (CLO)

105 Church St. (m)
New Haven, CT 06510
203-624-3512 / Fax: 203-287-8100

CARMELLO TORRES (Owner) & Buys Men's Wear, Sportswear, Accessories, Furnishings, Men's Footwear, Young Men's Wear, Store Displays, Fixtures, Supplies

HOROWITZ BROTHERS, INC. (MW)

760 Chapel St. (m-b)
New Haven, CT 06510
203-787-4183 / Fax: 203-787-4186
Sales: $1 Million-$10 Million

ARTHUR HOROWITZ (Owner) & Buys Men's Wear, Store Displays, Fixtures, Supplies

LEONARD HOROWITZ-Men's Wear, Sportswear, Accessories, Furnishings

J. CANDIDO DEPARTMENT STORE (DEPT)

335 Grand Ave. (p-m-b)
New Haven, CT 06513
203-562-2929
Sales: $100,001-$500,000

JULIE CANDIDO (Owner) & Buys Men's Sportswear, 4 to 20 Boys' Wear, Urban Contemporary, Accessories, Store Displays, Fixtures, Supplies

RAGGS (MW)

1020 Chapel St. (m-b)
New Haven, CT 06510
203-865-3824 / Fax: 203-624-5728
Sales: $500,001-$1 Million

TOM MALONEY (Owner) & Buys Men's Sportswear, Furnishings, Accessories, Headwear, Footwear, Store Displays, Fixtures, Supplies

SWIMWEAR OUTLET (CLO)

1175 State St., 2nd Fl.
New Haven, CT 06511
203-777-6630 / Fax: 203-777-6648
Website: www.swimwearoutlet.com

JOE LABANARO-Boys' Swimwear, Men's Surf & Swimwear, Resortwear, Footwear, Accessories

DONNA LABANARO-Boys' Swimwear, Men's Surf & Swimwear, Resortwear, Footwear, Accessories

WHALLEY SAMPLE SHOP (MW)

61 Whalley Ave. (bud-p)
New Haven, CT 06511
203-562-2621 / Fax: 203-562-8100
Sales: $1 Million-$10 Million

GEORGE LEHRER (Partner) & Buys Men's Overcoats, Suits, Tailored Jackets, Tailored Slacks, Raincoats, Sweaters, Sport Shirts, Outer Jackets, Casual Slacks, Active Apparel, Belts, Furnishings, Leather Apparel, Young Men's Wear, Boys' Wear, Urban Contemporary, Big & Tall Men's Wear, Men's Footwear, Boys' Footwear, Store Displays, Fixtures, Supplies

ALEX LEHRER (Partner) & Buys Men's Overcoats, Suits, Tailored Jackets, Tailored Slacks, Raincoats, Sweaters, Sport Shirts, Outer Jackets, Casual Slacks, Active Apparel, Belts, Furnishings, Leather Apparel, Young Men's Wear, Boys' Wear, Urban Contemporary, Big & Tall Men's Wear, Men's Footwear, Boys' Footwear, Store Displays, Fixtures, Supplies

H. MARCUS & CO., INC. (CLO)

21 Bank St. (m-b)
New London, CT 06320
860-443-0471 / Fax: 860-443-0908
Sales: $1 Million-$10 Million

SAM RUBENSTEIN (President)

RICHARD RUBENSTEIN (G.M.M.) & Buys Men's Outer Jackets, Embroidery, Store Displays, Fixtures, Supplies

US COAST GUARD EXCHANGE SYSTEM (PX)

US Coast Guard Academy (p-m)
15 Mohegan Ave., Johnson Hall
New London, CT 06320
860-444-8487 / Fax: 860-444-8492
Sales: $1 Million-$10 Million

TOM BIRCH (CGES Mgr.)

NANCIE BENNETT (Retail Mgr.) & Buys Jewelry, Fragrances

MARY ISHERWOOD-Men's Overcoats, Tailored Jackets, Tailored Slacks, Raincoats, Sportswear, Furnishings, Belts

FOOTPRINTS FASHION FOOTWEAR, INC. (FW)

(FOOTPRINTS)
79 Costello Rd. (m-b-des)
Newington, CT 06111
860-666-3100 / Fax: 860-666-4192
Sales: $1 Million-$10 Million
Website: www.footprintsshoes.com

JERILYN D. COHEN (President) & Buys Boys' Apparel, Boys' Footwear, Men's Footwear, Leather Goods, Hosiery, Watches

SCOTT COHEN (V.P.) & Buys Boys' Apparel, Boys' Footwear, Men's Footwear, Leather Goods, Hosiery, Watches

DAVID COHEN (Treas.) & Buys Boys' Apparel, Boys' Footwear, Men's Footwear, Leather Goods, Hosiery, Watches

JULIE ALLEN BRIDAL (SP)

154 S. Main St. (b-des)
Newtown, CT 06470
203-426-6830 / Fax: 203-270-1839
Sales: $500,001-$1 Million

JAY MATTEGAT (Co-Owner) & Buys Men's Apparel, Men's Big & Tall Apparel, Men's Accessories, Men's Hosiery, Men's Suits, Men's Formalwear

MELANIE ALLEN-MATTEGAT (Co-Owner & Store Mgr.) & Buys Men's Apparel, Men's Big & Tall Apparel, Men's Accessories, Men's Hosiery, Men's Suits, Men's Formalwear

P. HUTTON & SON, INC. (MW)

117 Washington Ave. (b)
North Haven, CT 06473
203-239-3702 / Fax: 203-234-0475
Sales: $500,001-$1 Million

RICHARD HUTTON (President)

DOUG HUTTON-Men's Wear, Sportswear, Accessories, Furnishings, Leather Apparel, Footwear, Store Displays, Fixtures, Supplies

PAUL GRENIER-Men's Wear, Sportswear, Accessories, Furnishings, Leather Apparel, Footwear, Store Displays, Fixtures, Supplies

CAMILLO, INC. (MW-2)

(CAMILLO TUXEDOS)
155 Main St.
Norwalk, CT 06851
203-849-1466 / Fax: 203-846-1894
Sales: $1 Million-$10 Million
Website: www.camillos.com

CAMILLO TRAMONTANA (Owner) & Buys Store Displays, Fixtures, Supplies, Men's & Boys' Tuxedos, Related Accessories, Furnishings, Footwear

COUSIN'S OF NORWALK, INC. (MW)

32 Main St. (m)
Norwalk, CT 06851
203-853-2737
Sales: $100,001-$500,000

LEE CHAVKIN (Owner) & Buys Men's Sportswear, Furnishings, Accessories, Headwear, Young Men's Wear, 7 to 20 Boys' Wear, Men's Footwear, Store Displays, Fixtures, Supplies

BACKER'S CLOTHES (MW)

236 Boston Post Rd. (m-b-des)
Orange, CT 06477
203-795-3399 / Fax: 203-795-3910
Sales: $1 Million-$10 Million

FRANK BACKER (Owner) & Buys Men's Sportswear, Suits, Sportcoats, Furnishings, Accessories, Footwear, Store Displays, Fixtures, Supplies

DIMENSION POLYANT (CLO)

78 Highland Dr.
Putnam, CT 06260
800-441-2424 / Fax: 860-928-0161

TETSUYA O'HARA-Windsurf Apparel & Accessories

DAVID McGILL-Windsurf Apparel & Accessories

CHAMBERS ARMY/NAVY STORE (AN)

38 Danbury Rd. (p)
Ridgefield, CT 06877
203-438-5797 / Fax: 203-438-3794

STEVE CHAMBERS (Owner) & Buys Men's & Boys' Denim, Shirts, Outer Jackets, Underwear, Hosiery, Active Apparel, Men's Footwear, Store Displays, Fixtures, Supplies

THE RUN IN (SP)

2172 Silas Deane Hwy.
Rocky Hill, CT 06067
860-563-6136 / Fax: 860-871-1300
Sales: $100,001-$500,000

JOHN VITALE (Co-Owner) & Buys Men's Activewear, Athletic Footwear

RAY CROTHERS (Co-Owner) & Buys Men's Activewear, Athletic Footwear

MELLUZZO'S, INC. (MW)

842 Queen St. (m-b)
Southington, CT 06489
860-276-8106 / Fax: 860-621-6784
Sales: $500,001-$1 Million

PAUL MELLUZZO (Owner) & Buys Men's Sportswear, Furnishings, Accessories, Headwear, Footwear, Store Displays, Fixtures, Supplies

EBLEN'S CASUAL CLOTHING & FOOTWEAR, INC. (CLO-21 & FW)

299 Industrial Ln. (p-b)
Torrington, CT 06790
860-489-3073 / Fax: 860-496-7446
Sales: $10 Million-$50 Million
Website: www.eblens.com
Retail Locations: CT, MA, RI

RICHARD SEAMAN (President, Real Estate Contact)

ROBERT SEAMAN-Men's Footwear, Boys' Footwear, Athletic Footwear

TONI DeGRANDI-Men's Wear, Sportswear, Sport Shirts, Outer Jackets, Casual Slacks, Active Apparel, Young Men's Wear, Leather Apparel, Accessories, Furnishings

AMBER VAN-Boys' Wear, Accessories, Furnishings, Sportswear

MICHAEL SARTINSKI-Store Displays, Fixtures, Supplies

SPINO'S MENSWEAR (MW)

84 Main St. (b)
Torrington, CT 06790
860-482-9930
Sales: $500,001-$1 Million

DAVID SPINO (Owner) & Buys Men's Sportswear, Furnishings, Accessories, Tuxedos, Dress Shirts, Ties, Store Displays, Fixtures, Supplies

ZAHNER'S CLOTHIERS (MW)

(D.L.S. OUTFITTERS)
520 Hartford Tnpk. (m-b)
Vernon, CT 06066
860-872-7349 / Fax: 860-872-2105
Sales: $500,001-$1 Million

SCOTT ZAHNER (President & G.M.M.) & Buys Men's Overcoats, Suits, Tailored Jackets, Tailored Slacks, Raincoats, Big & Tall Men's Wear, Sweaters, Sport Shirts, Outer Jackets, Leather Apparel, Casual Slacks, Active Apparel, Dress Shirts, Ties, Robes, Hosiery, Gloves, Belts, Boys' Suits

SPORTSTUFF (GS)

23 S. Main St.
Waterbury, CT 06704
203-757-9126

RICK GILEAU (Mgr.) & Buys Licensed Apparel

ALLEN COLLINS, INC. (CLO)

8 Ellsworth Rd. (m-b-des)
West Hartford, CT 06107
860-236-2541 / Fax: 860-232-0590
Sales: $1 Million-$10 Million

ALLEN COLLINS (Owner) & Buys Men's Sportswear, Dress Shirts, Underwear, Hosiery, Accessories, Furnishings, Store Displays, Fixtures, Supplies

ART CLOTHES - THE TUXEDO SHOP (MW-2)

Bishops Corner (m)
2529 Albany Ave.
West Hartford, CT 06117
860-233-4666
Sales: $100,001-$500,000

ERIC SCHULMAN (Owner) & Buys Men's, Young Men's & Boys' Formalwear, Store Displays, Fixtures, Supplies

RAJENDRA RAMNARACE (Mgr.) & Buys Men's, Young Men's & Boys' Formalwear, Store Displays, Fixtures, Supplies

BAZILIAN'S & CO. (CLO)

229 Park Rd. (m)
West Hartford, CT 06119
860-236-6877

MARK BAZILIAN (President) & Buys Men's Sportswear, Furnishings, Headwear, Accessories, Footwear, Store Displays, Fixtures, Supplies

BIG & TALL MEN'S APPAREL OF WEST HARTFORD (MW)

Corbins Corner (p-m-b)
1457 New Britain Ave.
West Hartford, CT 06110
860-521-8800 / Fax: 860-521-8972

BARRY PORTOFF (Owner) & Buys Big & Tall Men's Wear, Store Displays, Fixtures, Supplies

DASWANI & SONS, INC. (CLO)

131 S. Main St. (m-b)
West Hartford, CT 06107
860-561-4435 / Fax: 860-561-4636
Website: www.daswaniclothiers.com

JACK DASWANI (Co-Owner) & Buys Men's Overcoats, Tailored Jackets & Slacks, Raincoats, Sportswear, Sweaters, Outer Jackets, Leather Apparel, Casual Slacks, Dress Shirts, Ties, Hosiery, Gloves, Accessories, Belts, Jewelry, Store Displays, Fixtures, Supplies

DEEPA DASWANI (Co-Owner) & Buys Men's Sportswear, Furnishings, Accessories, Store Displays, Fixtures, Supplies

DENNIS REISS-Overcoats, Tailored Jackets & Slacks, Raincoats, Sportswear, Sweaters, Outer Jackets, Leather Apparel, Casual Slacks, Dress Shirts, Ties, Hosiery, Gloves, Accessories, Belts, Jewelry, Store Displays, Fixtures, Supplies

QUEST ATHLETIC FACILITY (SP)

544 Campbell Ave.
West Haven, CT 06516
203-933-0052 / Fax: 203-937-8517
Sales: Under $100,000

CAROLYN SIRES (Owner) & Buys Men's Athletic Footwear, Licensed Apparel

ALLEN COLLINS (CLO)

8 Ellsworth Rd. (m-b)
West Waterford, CT 06107
860-236-2541 / Fax: 860-232-0590

BRIAN ROSSO (President & Gen. Mgr.) & Buys Leather Goods, Men's Apparel, Men's Casualwear, Men's Formalwear, Men's Accessories, Men's Hosiery, Men's Outerwear, Men's Sleepwear, Men's Sportswear, Men's Suits

TINA ROSSO-Leather Goods, Men's Apparel, Men's Casualwear, Men's Formalwear, Men's Accessories, Men's Hosiery, Men's Outerwear, Men's Sleepwear, Men's Sportswear, Men's Suits

ED DUNN-Leather Goods, Men's Apparel, Men's Casualwear, Men's Formalwear, Men's Accessories, Men's Hosiery, Men's Outerwear, Men's Sleepwear, Men's Sportswear, Men's Suits

BEACH NUT SPORTS CENTER (SP)

(DICK'S MARINA)
314 Boston Post Rd.
Westbrook, CT 06498
860-399-6534
Sales: $100,001-$500,000

TIM SWAIN (Mgr.) & Buys Men's Apparel

OLD GLORY DISTRIBUTING (CLO-2)

90 Knothe Rd. (bud-p)
Westbrook, CT 06490
860-399-0064 / Fax: 860-399-7786
Sales: $1 Million-$10 Million
Website: www.oldglory.com

GLENN MORELLI (President) & Buys Men's Apparel

STEVE SCHOFIELD (Dir.-Opers.)

LIBERTY ARMY & NAVY STORES, INC. (AN-2)

1439 Post Rd. East (bud-p)
Westport, CT 06880
203-255-6066 / Fax: 203-255-6066
Sales: $1 Million-$10 Million

IRIS ROSE (Co-Owner) & Buys Men's Sportswear, Hosiery, Gloves, Leather Apparel, Young Men's Wear, Boys' Wear, Urban Contemporary, Store Displays, Fixtures, Supplies

EVE ROTHBARD (Co-Owner) & Buys Men's Sportswear, Hosiery, Gloves, Leather Apparel, Young Men's Wear, Boys' Wear, Urban Contemporary, Store Displays, Fixtures, Supplies

MITCHELL'S OF WESTPORT (CLO-2)

670 Post Rd. East (m-b)
Westport, CT 06880
203-227-5165 / Fax: 203-454-2617
Sales: $1 Million-$10 Million

JACK MITCHELL (Co-Owner)

BILL MITCHELL (Co-Owner)

BOB MITCHELL-Men's Sportswear, Leather Apparel, Furnishings, Headwear, Accessories, Big & Tall Men's Wear, Men's Footwear, Store Displays, Fixtures, Supplies

DAN FARRINGTON-Men's Sportswear, Leather Apparel, Furnishings, Headwear, Accessories, Big & Tall Men's Wear, Men's Footwear, Store Displays, Fixtures, Supplies

LAGANA CLOTHIERS (MW)

967 Silas Deane Hwy. (b)
Wethersfield, CT 06109
860-529-7975

JOE LAGANA (Owner) & Buys Men's Clothing, Sportswear, Furnishing, Accessories

HENRY MILLER, INC. (MW)

35 Lasalle Rd. (m-b-des)
Whartford, CT 06107
860-920-0157 / Fax: 860-920-0160
Sales: $1 Million-$10 Million

JOHN P. HAROVAS (President) & Buys Men's Footwear, Leather Goods, Big & Tall Men's Wear, Casualwear, Accessories, Hosiery, Outerwear, Sportswear, Suits

DOROTHY HAROVAS (V.P.) & Buys Men's Footwear, Leather Goods, Big & Tall Men's Wear, Casualwear, Accessories, Hosiery, Outerwear, Sportswear, Suits

HURLEY'S, INC. (MW)

699 Main St. (m)
Willimantic, CT 06226
860-423-0208
Sales: $500,001-$1 Million

RICHARD ANTHONY (President) & Buys Men's Footwear, Leather Goods, Big & Tall Men's Wear, Casualwear, Accessories, Hosiery, Outerwear, Sportswear, Suits, Young Men's Wear, Denim Apparel

NANCY ANTHONY (V.P.) & Buys Men's Footwear, Leather Goods, Big & Tall Men's Wear, Casualwear, Accessories, Hosiery, Outerwear, Sportswear, Suits, Young Men's Wear, Denim Apparel

OUTDOOR SPORTS CENTER (SG)

80 Danbury Rd. (m)
Wilton, CT 06897
203-762-8797 / Fax: 203-761-0812

JACK MAXWELL (Owner) & Buys Store Displays, Fixtures, Supplies

PAT DACON-Active Apparel, T-shirts, Shorts, Headwear

MARTY HEIR-Hiking & Outdoor Clothing

TALLMADGE'S WILTON STORE (CLO)

89 Old Ridgefield Rd. (m-b)
Wilton, CT 06897
203-762-3341 / Fax: 203-762-9455

LYLE TALLMADGE (Owner) & Buys Men's Sportswear, Furnishings, Leather Apparel, Accessories, Headwear, Store Displays, Fixtures, Supplies

WILTON SPORT SHOP, INC. (SG)

426 Danbury Rd. (m-b)
Wilton, CT 06897
203-762-8631 / Fax: 203-762-8632
Sales: $500,001-$1 Million

KEN CYR (Owner) & Buys Boys' Apparel, Boys' Footwear, Men's Footwear, Men's Apparel, Men's Big & Tall Apparel, Men's Hosiery, Men's Outerwear, Men's Sportswear, Men's Swimwear

DELAWARE - Bethany Beach

FISHTALES (CLO-3)
(BREAKER'S SURF & SPORT)
(RHODES 5 & 10)
107 Garfield Pkwy. (m)
Bethany Beach, DE 19930
302-539-7676 / Fax: 302-539-9636
Sales: $500,001-$1 Million
BOB TERNAHAN (Co-Owner) & Buys Men's & Boys' Apparel, Swimwear & Footwear
DIANE TERNAHAN (Co-Owner) & Buys Men's & Boys' Apparel, Swimwear & Footwear

BRIDAL & TUXEDO OUTLET, INC. (CLO-2)
Tri State Mall
Claymont, DE 19703
302-798-4000 / Fax: 302-798-3306
CATHY SAWDON (Owner) & Buys Men's Tuxedos, Formal Accessories, Store Displays, Fixtures, Supplies

SIMON'S BRIDAL SHOPS (SP)
215 W. Loockerman St. (b)
Dover, DE 19904
302-678-8160 / Fax: 302-678-4401
Sales: $1 Million-$10 Million
Website: www.simonsbridal.com
JANET LAWRENCE (President & Gen. Mgr.) & Buys Men's Formalwear

SOUTHERN EXPOSURE (CLO-2)
(SOUTHERN EXPOSURE BEACH LIFE)
(OCEAN AVE.)
(RIGHT ANGLE)
1200 Coastal Hwy. (bud-p-m-b)
Box 442
Fenwick Island, DE 19944
302-539-8606 / Fax: 302-539-4665
TIM COLLINS (Owner) & Buys Men's Sweaters, Sport Shirts, Outer Jackets, Casual Slacks, Activewear, Men's Footwear, Store Displays, Fixtures, Supplies

MARJORIE SPEAKMAN, INC. (KS)
P.O. Box 3781 (b)
4017 Kennett Pike
Greenville, DE 19807
302-658-3521
GAIL WATSON (Owner) & Buys Size 8 to 20 Boys' Wear, Store Displays, Fixtures, Supplies

WILMINGTON COUNTRY STORE (CLO-3)
(Lily Pulitzer)
4013 Kennett Pike (b)
Greenville, DE 19807
302-656-4409 / Fax: 302-652-3242
Website: www.wilmingtoncountrystore.com
G. STEVENSON SMITH (Owner) & Buys Men's Sweaters, Sport Shirts, Outer Jackets, Casual Slacks, Leather Apparel, Ties, Hosiery, Belts, Young Men's Wear, Urban Contemporary, Store Displays, Fixtures, Supplies

PHILLIPS' MEN'S SHOP, INC. (CLO)
115 W. Market St. (b)
Laurel, DE 19956
302-875-7554 / Fax: 302-846-9686
Sales: $1 Million-$10 Million
DON PHILLIPS (President & G.M.M.) & Buys Men's Overcoats, Suits, Tailored Jackets, Tailored Slacks, Raincoats, Sweaters, Sport Shirts, Casual Slacks, Outer Jackets, Active Apparel, Leather Apparel, Dress Shirts, Ties, Belts, Robes, Underwear, Hosiery, Gloves, Headwear, Jewelry, Small Leather Goods, Fragrances, Big & Tall Men's Wear, Store Displays, Fixtures, Supplies

GRAVES UNIFORMS (SP)
102 Savannah Rd. (m-b)
Lewes, DE 19958
302-645-7771 / Fax: 302-645-5894
Sales: $1 Million-$10 Million
Website: www.gravesuniforms.com
WILLIAM D. GRAVES (President) & Buys Men's Footwear, Men's Apparel, Men's Uniforms, Workclothes
TERRY HAVENS (Gen. Mgr.) & Buys Men's Footwear, Men's Apparel, Men's Uniforms, Workclothes

STYLE GUIDE, INC. (CLO)
Mid Sussex Shopping Center (m)
Millsboro, DE 19966
302-934-8144
Sales: $100,001-$500,000
JACK BURBAGE (President) & Buys Leather Goods, Men's Apparel, Men's Big & Tall Apparel, Men's Casualwear, Men's Denim Apparel, Men's Accessories, Men's Hosiery, Men's Outerwear, Men's Sleepwear, Men's Sportswear, Men's Suits, Men's Swimwear, Men's Underwear
JOHN H. BURBAGE, Sr. (V.P.)
BUZZ TAYLOR (Store Mgr.)

FORMAL AFFAIRS (CLO-3)
129 E. Main St.
Newark, DE 19711
302-737-1519 / Fax: 302-738-4425
CHRIS LOCKE (Owner) & Buys Men's Formal Wear, Footwear, Accessories, Store Displays, Fixtures, Supplies

TREASURE ISLAND FASHIONS, INC. (CLO)
P.O. Box 939 (p)
Cedar Neck Rd.
Ocean View, DE 19970
302-539-6597 / Fax: 302-539-5847
Sales: $500,001-$1 Million
KEN CROOKS (Owner) & Buys Men's Sportswear, Furnishings, Accessories, Footwear, Store Displays, Fixtures, Supplies

CARLTON'S MENSWEAR, INC. (MW)
31 Rehoboth Ave. (m-b)
Rehoboth Beach, DE 19971
302-227-7990 / Fax: 302-227-2873
ROBERT W. DERRICKSON (Owner) & Buys Men's Wear, Footwear, Young Men's Wear, Urban Contemporary, Store Displays, Fixtures, Supplies

NORM GERSHMAN'S THINGS TO WEAR (CLO)
43 Rehoboth Ave. (p-m-b)
Rehoboth Beach, DE 19971
302-366-8135 / Fax: 302-226-5007
DAVID GERSHMAN (President) & Buys Men's Overcoats, Sweaters, Sport Shirts, Outer Jackets, Casual Slacks, Active Apparel, Ties, Underwear, Hosiery, Young Men's Wear, Urban Contemporary, Big & Tall Men's Wear, Boys' Sport Shirts, Licensed Jackets, Store Displays, Fixtures, Supplies
NORMAN GERSHMAN-Men's Overcoats, Sweaters, Sport Shirts, Outer Jackets, Casual Slacks, Active Apparel, Ties, Underwear, Hosiery, Young Men's Wear, Urban Contemporary, Big & Tall Men's Wear, Boys' Sport Shirts, Licensed Jackets, Store Displays, Fixtures, Supplies

SUMMER WINDS (CLO)
77 Rehoboth Ave.
Rehoboth Beach, DE 19971
302-227-1434 / Fax: 302-227-6050
DEEPAK CHATANI (Co-Owner) & Buys Accessories, Men's Apparel, Men's Surf & Swimwear, Resortwear, T-shirts, Imprinted Sportswear
PREM N. CHATANI (Co-Owner) & Buys Accessories, Men's Apparel, Men's Surf & Swimwear, Resortwear, T-shirts, Imprinted Sportswear

SCOTTY'S CLOTHING (MW)
Church & Main Sts. (p)
Selbyville, DE 19975
302-436-8424
BRUCE SCOTT (V.P.) & Buys Men's Overcoats, Suits, Tailored Jackets, Raincoats, Sportswear, Furnishings, Headwear, Accessories, Footwear, Store Displays, Fixtures, Supplies

DECOURCELLE'S, INC. (FW)
(B&B SHOES)
3919 Kirkwood Hwy. (bud-p-m)
Wilmington, DE 19808
302-994-3870
Sales: $100,001-$500,000
HARRY BRATTON (President & Mgr.) & Buys Boys' Footwear
ROBERT MOSCATO (V.P.) & Buys Boys' Footwear

DELAWARE - Wilmington

FASHION PLACE, INC. (MW)
717 Market St. (m-b)
Wilmington, DE 19801
302-654-4350 / Fax: 302-654-4365

CHAE PARK (Co-Owner) & Buys Men's Sportswear, Furnishings, Accessories, Young Men's Wear, Urban Contemporary, Store Displays, Fixtures, Supplies

CLINT PARK (Co-Owner) & Buys Men's Sportswear, Furnishings, Accessories, Young Men's Wear, Urban Contemporary, Store Displays, Fixtures, Supplies

KID'S KLOSET (KS)
2309 Concord Pike (b-h)
Fairfax Shopping Ctr.
Wilmington, DE 19803
302-658-3299

LIN Y. CHENG-Size 8 to 22 Boys' Wear, Boys' Suits, Boys' Formal Wear, Boys' Designer Sportswear, Store Displays, Fixtures, Supplies

THE SWIM SHOP (CLO)
2115 Concord Pike
Wilmington, DE 19803
302-575-1224 / Fax: 302-575-0364

JUDY WARD-Swimwear, Pool Accessories

MICHAEL ROCCIA-Swimwear, Pool Accessories

WRIGHT & SIMON, INC. (MW)
911 Market St. (b-h)
Wilmington, DE 19801
302-658-7345
Sales: $1 Million-$10 Million

LEONARD SIMON (C.E.O.) & Buys Men's Wear, Furnishings, Accessories, Store Displays, Fixtures and Supplies

DISTRICT OF COLUMBIA - Washington

A & A ATHLETIC & RECREATION (SG)

212 7th St. SE (m-b)
Washington, DC 20003
205-543-0556 / Fax: 202-543-0556
Sales: $1 Million-$10 Million

HAROLD GOFFNEY (Owner) & Buys Boys' Apparel, Men's Footwear, Men's Apparel, Men's Casualwear, Men's Denim Apparel, Men's Sportswear

OSCAR FUNDURBERK (Gen. Mgr.) & Buys Boys' Apparel, Men's Footwear, Men's Apparel, Men's Casualwear, Men's Denim Apparel, Men's Sportswear

BEAU MONDE (MW)

(TONY J. LTD.)
1814 K St. NW (b)
Washington, DC 20006
202-466-7070 / Fax: 202-429-3147
Sales: $100,001-$500,000

TONY JAHANSOOZI (Owner) & Buys Better Priced Men's Suits, Tailored Jackets, Tailored Slacks, Raincoats, Sweaters, Outer Jackets, Sport Shirts, Casual Slacks, Leather Apparel, Dress Shirts, Ties, Underwear, Hosiery, Belts, Urban Contemporary

FRANKLIN'S (CLO)

3234 11th St. NW (m-b)
Washington, DC 20010
202-328-3499 / Fax: 202-328-3499
Sales: $500,001-$1 Million

FRANKLIN HALL (Owner) & Buys Boys' Apparel, Boys' Footwear, Men's Footwear, Men's Apparel

GEORGE'S PLACE LTD. (MW)

101 H St. NE (m)
Washington, DC 20002
202-397-4113 / Fax: 202-396-1299

GEORGE BUTLER (Owner) & Buys Men's Sportswear, Furnishings, Accessories, Young Men's Wear, Footwear, Store Displays, Fixtures, Supplies

HIGHCLIFFE CLOTHIERS LTD. (CLO)

1120 20th St. NW (h)
Lafayette Ctr.
Washington, DC 20036
202-872-8640 / Fax: 202-872-8641
Website: www.customshirtmakers.com

MARK METZGER (Owner) & Buys Men's Tailored Jackets, Tailored Slacks, Suits, Accessories, Footwear

LA MONDE (MW)

960 14th St. (b)
Washington, DC 20005
202-371-9230 / Fax: 202-371-1135
Sales: $500,001-$1 Million

CAMERON FOROUGHI (Owner) & Buys Men's Overcoats, Men's Suits, Tailored Jackets, Sweaters, Sport Shirts, Outer Jackets, Leather Apparel, Casual Slacks, Active Apparel, Fragrances, Furnishings, Accessories, Young Men's Wear, Footwear, Store Displays, Fixtures, Supplies

LONG RAP, INC. (CLO)

1420 Wisconsin Ave. NW
Washington, DC 20007
202-337-6610

IZZY SMITH-Sportswear, Accessories

M. STEIN & CO. (MW)

1900 M St. NW (m-b)
Washington, DC 20036
202-659-1434 / Fax: 202-452-9362
Website: www.mstein.com

DARRLY RUSSO (Owner) & Buys Men's & Boys' Formal Wear, Footwear, Accessories, Hosiery, Furnishings

MARRIOTT INTERNATIONAL (GS-387)

1 Marriott Dr. (m-b)
Washington, DC 20058
301-380-3000 / Fax: 301-380-8228
Sales: $10 Million-$50 Million
Website: www.marriott.com
Retail Locations: AL, AK, AZ, CA, CO, CT, DC, FL, GA, HI, IL, IN, IA, KS, KY, LA, MA, MD, MT, MN, MI, MO, NE, NH, NJ, NM, NY, NC, OH, OK, OR, PA, RI, SC, TN, TX, UT, VA, WA, WV, WI

ANNA MANCEBO (Dir.-Retail Svcs.)

MICHAEL FISCHETTI (National Mdse. Mgr.) & Buys Men's Furnishings, Headwear, Accessories, Store Displays, Fixtures, Supplies

MEN'S FASHION CENTER (MW)

918 H St. NE (m)
Washington, DC 20002
202-543-4464 / Fax: 202-543-4465

JERRY GOLDKIND (Owner) & Buys Men's Sportswear, Accessories, Footwear

MILANO COLLECTION (MW)

1408 Wisconsin Ave. NW (b-des)
Washington, DC 20007
202-342-1616
Sales: $1 Million-$10 Million

KAMI RABARAN (Owner) & Buys Men's Footwear, Men's Apparel, Men's Accessories, Men's Outerwear, Men's Sportswear, Men's Suits

MODA (MW)

1510 Wisconsin Ave. (b)
Washington, DC 20007
202-298-8598 / Fax: 202-337-0347

ASMA ETEMADI (Owner) & Buys Men's Overcoats, Suits, Tailored Slacks, Tailored Jackets, Raincoats, Sweaters, Sport Shirts, Outer Jackets, Leather Apparel, Casual Slacks, Dress Shirts, Hosiery, Accessories, Footwear, Store Displays, Fixtures, Supplies

PRINCE & PRINCESS (FW-4)

1400 Wisconsin Ave. NW (bdes)
Washington, DC 20007
202-337-4211 / Fax: 202-337-4212
Sales: $1 Million-$10 Million

PERVIS MIZRAHI (Owner) & Buys Boys' Footwear, Men's Footwear, Leather Goods, Watches, Men's Accessories, Men's Apparel, Hosiery

LIDA MIZRAHI (Mgr.) & Buys Boys' Footwear, Men's Footwear, Leather Goods, Watches, Men's Accessories, Men's Apparel, Hosiery

KEVIN MIZRAH-Boys' Footwear, Men's Footwear, Leather Goods, Watches, Men's Accessories, Men's Apparel, Hosiery

ROCK CREEK (MW-2)

2029 P St. NW
Washington, DC 20036
202-429-6940 / Fax: 202-296-0975

RANDY MASON (Co-Owner)

JOE MORIARTY (Co-Owner) & Buys Men's Wear, Men's Casual Wear, Accessories, Furnishings, Footwear

SCOGNA FORMAL WEAR (MW)

1908 L St. NW
Washington, DC 20036
202-296-4555 / Fax: 703-525-4235

ISRAEL SHEINBEIN (Owner) & Buys Men's & Boys' Formal Wear, Footwear, Accessories, Hosiery

SOLBIATO (MW)

(MOTTAGHI & SON, INC.)
1511 Wisconsin Ave. (b-h)
Washington, DC 20007
202-338-4005 / Fax: 202-338-4008

MR. SOLBIATO (Owner) & Buys Sportswear, Sweaters, Sport Shirts, Outer Jackets, Leather Apparel, Casual Slacks, Active Apparel

DISTRICT OF COLUMBIA - Washington

STARTING LINE, INC. (FW)

(FLEET FEET)
1841 Columbia Rd. NW
Washington, DC 20009
202-387-3888 / Fax: 202-387-3175
Sales: $100,001-$500,000
Website: www.dcnet.com/fleetfeet

JAN FENTY (Partner) & Buys Men's Footwear, Licensed Apparel, Watches, Men's Accessories, Men's Apparel, Hosiery

PHIL FENTY (Partner) & Buys Men's Footwear, Licensed Apparel, Watches, Men's Accessories, Men's Apparel, Hosiery

SHAWN FENTY (Mgr.) & Buys Men's Footwear, Licensed Apparel, Watches, Men's Accessories, Men's Apparel, Hosiery

UNIVERSAL GEAR, INC. (MW-2 & OL)

(UNIVERSALGEAR.COM)
1621 U St. NW (m-b)
Washington, DC 20009
202-319-1157 / Fax: 202-319-1158
Sales: $1 Million-$10 Million
Website: www.universalgear.com

KEITH CLARK (Co-Owner) & Buys Men's Sportswear, Furnishings, Accessories, Footwear, Store Displays, Fixtures, Supplies

DAVID FRANCO (Co-Owner) & Buys Men's Sportswear, Furnishings, Accessories, Footwear, Store Displays, Fixtures, Supplies

UP AGAINST THE WALL (CLO-21)

(COMMANDER SALAMANDER)
(LONG RAP, INC.)
1420 Wisconsin Ave. (m-b)
Washington, DC 20007
202-337-6610 / Fax: 202-333-1246
Sales: $10 Million-$50 Million
Website: www.upagainstthewall.com

STUART EZRAILSON (President) & Buys Men's Sweaters, Sport Shirts, Outer Jackets, Leather Apparel, Casual Slacks, Urban Contemporary, Store Displays, Fixtures, Supplies

WENDY EZRAILSON (V.P.)

ANHTU LU-Men's Accessories, Footwear

WASHINGTON UNIFORM, INC. (CLO)

900 11th St. NW (m)
Washington, DC 20001
202-393-8200 / Fax: 202-393-8201
Website: www.washingtonuniform.com

JANE FRENKIL (President) & Buys Career Apparel, Ties, Belts, Footwear, Men's Suits, Tailored Jackets, Tailored Slacks

WM. FOX & CO. (MW)

1427 G St. NW (m-b)
Washington, DC 20005
202-783-2530 / Fax: 202-347-8513
Website: www.wmfox.com

CRAIG FOX (Owner) & Buys Clothing, Sportswear, Furnishings, Accessories, Headwear, Store Displays, Fixtures, Supplies

WESTERN TEPEE, INC. (WW)

15981 NW Hwy. 441 (m)
Alachua, FL 32615
386-462-4626 / Fax: 386-462-4816

MICHAEL JARVIS (Owner) & Buys Men's & Boys' Western Apparel, Related Furnishings, Headwear, Accessories, Boots, Moccasins, Store Displays, Fixtures, Supplies

ROXBARRY, INC. (CLO-5)

(INLAND OCEAN)
(THE BOARDWALK SURF & SPORT)
(Accelerate)
1000 Pine Hollow Point (m-b-des)
Altamonte Springs, FL 32714
407-682-2693 / Fax: 407-682-1941
Sales: $1 Million-$10 Million
Website: www.surfinlandocean.com

JERALD SCHIEDEL (President & Real Estate Contact)

BARRY SCHIEDEL (Exec. V.P.) & Buys Boys' Apparel, Men's Footwear, Leather Goods, Men's Apparel, Men's Casualwear, Men's Denim Apparel, Men's Hosiery, Men's Outerwear, Men's Sportswear, Men's Swimwear

ROXANE SCHIEDEL-MANN (V.P.)

JESSIE MILLER (Mgr.-Opers.)

AMELIA INN GIFT SHOP (CLO)

4924 1st Coast Hwy., #4
Amelia Island, FL 32034
904-491-4218 / Fax: 904-277-2093

DAVE CASTO-Sunglasses, Fashion Accessories, Footwear, Hats, Outdoor Gear & Apparel, Resortwear,T-shirts, Imprinted Sportswear, Urban Streetwear, Men's Apparel, Men's Swimwear

CAROL GREY-Sunglasses, Fashion Accessories, Footwear, Hats, Outdoor Gear & Apparel, Resortwear, T-shirts, Imprinted Sportswear, Urban Streetwear, Men's Apparel, Men's Swimwear

AMELIA ISLAND CLOTHING CO. (CLO)

308 Center St.
Amelia Island, FL 32034
904-491-7716

ERIK PRICE-Fashion Accessories, T-shirts, Imprinted Sportswear, Men's Apparel

EVE PRICE-Fashion Accessories, T-shirts, Imprinted Sportswear, Men's Apparel

TIDEWATER OUTFITTERS, INC. (CLO)

P.O. Box 8001
Amelia Village Villa 40
Amelia Island, FL 32034
904-261-2202 / Fax: 904-321-2205

ALLYSON SIMMONS-Fashion Accessories, Footwear, Hats, Men's Apparel, Men's Surf & Swimwear, Outdoor Gear & Apparel, Men's Apparel

LOU SIMMONS-Fashion Accessories, Footwear, Hats, Men's Apparel, Men's Surf & Swimwear, Outdoor Gear & Apparel, Men's Apparel

BEACH STYLE SPORTSWEAR (SP)

(BEACH STYLE SILK SCREEN, INC.)
P.O. Box 1156
10010 Gulf Dr.
Anna Maria, FL 34216
941-778-4323 / Fax: 941-778-4323
Sales: $100,001-$500,000

JOSEPH HUTCHINSON (President) & Buys Apparel, Skiwear, Licensed Apparel, Licensed Apparel, Athletic Footwear, Custom Apparel

STEWART NORMAN (CLO-2)

(ARDEN ROSE CORP.)
19575 Biscayne Blvd. (m-b-h)
Aventura, FL 33180
305-936-8006 / Fax: 305-936-8029

STEWART NORMAN (Co-Owner) & Buys Suits, Tailored Jackets, Tailored Slacks, Sportswear, Sport Shirts, Casual Slacks, Active Apparel

WALESKA NORMAN (Co-Owner) & Buys Suits, Tailored Jackets, Tailored Slacks, Sportswear, Sport Shirts, Casual Slacks, Active Apparel

TOTAL SWIMWEAR (CLO)

3205 NE 184th St., #9204
Aventura, FL 33160
800-940-7946 / Fax: 561-637-5828
Website: www.totalswimwear.com

JAY LEVY-Men's Surf & Swimwear, Private Label

ENRICO (FW)

9700 Collins Ave., #236 (h)
Bal Harbour, FL 33154
305-866-4117 / Fax: 305-866-4019
Website: www.enrico.qpg.com

SCOTT CHANDLER (Owner) & Buys Men's Italian Shoes, Belts, Leather Jackets, and Accessories

OXGENE (CLO)

9700 Collins Ave.
Bal Harbour, FL 33154
305-864-0202 / Fax: 305-861-4977

FELIX COHEN (Owner)

ROCIO CAMPODONIC-Surf & Swimwear, Wet Suits

BARTOW MALL MENSWEAR (MW)

234 E. Vanfleet Dr. (p-m)
Bartow, FL 33830
863-533-5056 / Fax: 863-534-3401

WALLACE SEMANDEL (Owner) & Buys Men's Wear, Young Men's Wear, Urban Contemporary, Work Clothing, Headwear, Shorts, Work Boots

DIANA'S, INC. (CLO)

1033 Kane Concourse (b)
Bay Harbor Islands, FL 33154
305-866-1700 / Fax: 305-866-1785
Sales: $500,001-$1 Million

ABRAHAM SRETER (Owner) & Buys Boys' Apparel, Leather Goods, Men's Apparel, Men's Sportswear, Men's Suits

SARA STEINBERG (Store Mgr.)

CASHMERES ETC., INC. (CLO-3 & OL)

1160 Kane Concourse
Bay Harbour Islands, FL 33154
305-865-5351 / Fax: 305-865-2065

JENNIFER TYLER (Owner) & Buys Men's Cashmere Sweaters, Better Sweaters, Store Displays, Fixtures, Supplies

BELLE GLADE CLOTHING (CLO)

361 W. Ave. A (m)
Belle Glade, FL 33430
561-996-9919
Sales: $100,001-$500,000

DAMEN HALUM (Owner) & Buys Men's & Boys' Wear, Urban Contemporary, Footwear, Store Displays, Fixtures, Supplies

MISSOURI DEPARTMENT STORE (DEPT-2)

317 W. Avenue A (m)
Belle Glade, FL 33430
561-996-4465 / Fax: 561-996-4465
Sales: $100,001-$500,000

MOHAMAD MUSLET (Owner) & Buys Men's Sweaters, Sport Shirts, Outer Jackets, Leather Apparel, Casual Slacks, Urban Contemporary, Active Apparel, Furnishings, Headwear, Accessories, Footwear, Boys' Wear, Store Displays, Fixtures, Supplies

FAISAI MUSLET-Men's Sweaters, Sport Shirts, Outer Jackets, Leather Apparel, Casual Slacks, Urban Contemporary, Active Apparel, Furnishings, Headwear, Accessories, Footwear, Boys' Wear, Store Displays, Fixtures, Supplies

MODA (CLO-2)
(OMAR FASHION)
256 SW Ave. A (p-m-b)
Belle Glade, FL 33430
561-996-4548 / Fax: 561-996-0049
Sales: $100,001-$500,000
ABBY MATARI (Co-Owner) & Buys Men's, Young Men's & Boys' Clothing, Sportswear, Leather Apparel, Furnishings, Accessories, Footwear, Headwear, Store Displays, Fixtures, Supplies
OMAR MATARI (Co-Owner) & Buys Men's, Young Men's & Boys' Clothing, Sportswear, Leather Apparel, Furnishings, Accessories, Footwear, Headwear, Store Displays, Fixtures, Supplies

SUPER MERCHANDISE (DEPT)
265 W. Ave. A (b)
Belle Glade, FL 33430
561-996-2158
Sales: $100,001-$500,000
AHMAD ZAYYAD (Owner) & Buys Men's Suits, Tailored Jackets, Raincoats, Sport Shirts, Outer Jackets, Leather Apparel, Urban Contemporary, Furnishings, Belts, Jewelry, Footwear, Young Men's Shop, Boys' Wear, Sportswear, Accessories, Headwear, Store Displays, Fixtures, Supplies
SHAKE ZAYYAD (President)

T.U.R.F. URBAN GEAR (CLO)
8 Magnolia Ave.
Belle Glade, FL 33430
561-996-2234
Website: www.turfurbangear.qpg.com
MARVIN DIXON (Owner) & Buys Men's Urban Contemporary, Jeans, Baggy Jeans, T-shirts, Outer Jackets, Performance Fleece

YAQUB BROTHERS STORE (GM)
257 W. Ave. A (m)
Belle Glade, FL 33430
561-996-5833 / Fax: 561-992-2370
MAHMUD YAQUB (Owner) & Buys Men's Sportswear, Furnishings, Accessories, Boots, Young Men's & Boys' Wear, Store Displays, Fixtures, Supplies

CAPTAINS & KINGS WEAR (MW)
100 Indian Rocks Rd., #2
Belleair Bluffs, FL 33770
727-586-3482
NANCY TRAGER (Owner) & Buys Men's Sportswear, Active Wear, Beach Wear, Men's Accessories, Footwear, Store Displays, Fixtures, Supplies

FUGATES (DEPT-2)
P.O. Box 721 (b)
4th St. & Park Ave.
Boca Grande, FL 33921
941-964-2323 / Fax: 941-964-1200
TOBY WIENER (Owner) & Buys Men's Resort Wear, Belts, Sportswear, Leather Apparel, Furnishings, Accessories, Headwear, Footwear, Store Displays, Fixtures, Supplies

THE ISLAND BUMMER (CLO)
P.O. Box 1502
Railroad Plz.
Boca Grande, FL 33921
941-964-2636
SANDRA JAMES-Men's High-End Resortwear, Urban Streetwear, Men's Apparel

ANDOVER REED (MW)
2100 N. Federal Hwy.
Boca Raton, FL 33432
561-392-0878 / Fax: 561-392-1339
MICHAEL RUDIKOFF (President) & Buys Men's Suits, Tailored Jackets, Tailored Slacks, Sportswear, Furnishings, Headwear, Store Displays, Fixtures, Supplies

THE DESANTIS COLLECTION (MW & MO & OL)
(HASSLER CONSORTIUM)
4500 Oak Circle, # B9 (p-m-b-des)
Boca Raton, FL 33431
561-391-9939 / Fax: 561-391-0343
Website: www.desantiscollection.com
JUDY FOX (President & C.E.O.)
LAURA FISH-Casual Wear, Custom Dress Shirts, Custom Trousers, Ties, Belts, Accessories

DOREEN'S SWIMWEAR (CLO)
293 E. Palmetto Park Rd.
Boca Raton, FL 33432
561-750-6755
DOREEN GARGANO (Owner) & Buys Swimwear

EXPORTRADE (CLO)
1499 W. Palmetto Park Rd., #161
Boca Raton, FL 33486
561-447-8520 / Fax: 561-447-8521
JEFFREY FIRESTONE-Men's Apparel, T-shirts, Imprinted Sportswear

FRANK MICHAEL TAILORS (MW)
241 E. Palmetto Park Rd.
Boca Raton, FL 33432
561-392-3113
PAUL PINSKY (Owner) & Buys Men's Clothing, Furnishings, Accessories

KELLY GREENE, INC. FOR MEN (MW)
7050 W. Palmetto Park Rd. (m-b)
Boca Raton, FL 33433
561-338-3838 / Fax: 561-367-0278
ALAN GREENE (Co-Owner) & Buys Men's Sportswear, Furnishings, Accessories, Footwear, Store Displays, Fixtures, Supplies
JAY GREENE (Co-Owner) & Buys Men's Sportswear, Furnishings, Accessories, Footwear, Store Displays, Fixtures, Supplies

KIDDIE WEAR (CLO & OL)
8183 Springlake Dr.
Boca Raton, FL 33496
561-218-1021 / Fax: 561-218-2706
Website: www.kiddiewear.com
ABE RENKO (Owner) & Buys Boys' Hats, Fleecewear, T-shirts, Accessories, Store Displays, Fixtures, Supplies

KING JAMES CORNER BIG & TALL (MW)
(THE SCOT SHOP, INC.)
2200 W. Glades, #903 (b)
Boca Raton, FL 33431
561-368-4227 / Fax: 561-368-4270
JAMES MAYER (Owner) & Buys Men's Big & Tall Clothing, Sportswear, Furnishings, Accessories, Footwear, Store Displays, Fixtures, Supplies

KIWI'S OF BOCA, INC. (CLO)
335 Plaza Real
Boca Raton, FL 33432
561-392-8880 / Fax: 561-362-7126
CATHIE McVAY-Boys' Apparel, Men's Apparel, Dive Apparel, Resortwear
RICK McVAY-Boys' Apparel, Men's Apparel, Dive Apparel, Resortwear

LINBAR GROUP (CLO)
19489 Sedgefield Ter.
Boca Raton, FL 33498
561-483-7780 / Fax: 561-483-8288
Website: www.linbarapparel.com
BARRY HOROWITZ-Boys' Apparel, Men's Apparel, Men's Swimwear, Private Label, Resortwear, T-shirts, Imprinted Sportswear

MARK, FORE & STRIKE (CLO-11 & OL & MO)
6500 Park of Commerce Blvd. NW (b)
Boca Raton, FL 33487
561-742-4234
Sales: $10 Million-$50 Million
Website: www.markforeandstrike.com
LARRY AUTREY (President)
JIM MORTON (Reg. Opers. Mgr. & Real Estate Contact) & Buys Store Displays, Fixtures, Supplies
PATTY BORNSTEIN-Men's Sportswear, Accessories, Leather Apparel, Clothing, Furnishings, Headwear

SHAPE SHOP (SP)
9882 Glades Rd.
Boca Raton, FL 33434
561-482-7009 / Fax: 561-852-1652
FLORENCE APPEL (Owner) & Buys Activewear, Dancewear, Related Hosiery

SUZI SAINT TROPEZ (CLO)
430 Plaza Real
Boca Raton, FL 33432
561-391-0913 / Fax: 561-272-3096
Website: www.fashionangel.com
SUZI DUNETZ (Co-Owner) & Buys Swimwear, Resortwear
RODNEY DUNETZ (Co-Owner) & Buys Swimwear, Resortwear

TATTOO ALTERNATIVES (CLO)
22275 Rushmore Pl.
Boca Raton, FL 33428
561-852-1060 / Fax: 561-479-2092
HULYA ATIS-Boys' Apparel, Fashion Accessories,T-shirts, Imprinted Sportswear
BRETT BERNSTEIN-Boys' Apparel, Fashion Accessories,T-shirts, Imprinted Sportswear

USEPP ISLAND CLUB (CLO)
P.O. Box 640
Bokeelia, FL 33922
941-283-1061 / Fax: 941-283-0290
NEIL BRERETON-Boys' Apparel, Footwear, Hats, Apparel, Men's Apparel, Men's Apparel, Men's Surf & Swimwear, Outdoor Gear & Apparel, Private Label, Resortwear,T-shirts, Imprinted Sportswear, Urban Streetwear
ANGELA LIKEWISE-Boys' Apparel, Footwear, Hats, Apparel, Men's Apparel, Men's Apparel, Men's Surf & Swimwear, Outdoor Gear & Apparel, Private Label, Resortwear,T-shirts, Imprinted Sportswear, Urban Streetwear

CREATIONS BY CONNIE (SP)
11902 Bonita Beach Rd.
Bonita Springs, FL 34135
941-498-7520
CONSTANCE D'ATTILIO (Owner) & Buys Beachwear, Activewear, Resortwear

TROPICAL TREASURES (CLO-5)
24509 Claire St.
Bonita Springs, FL 34135
239-495-9291 / Fax: 239-495-9295
KIMBERLY STAIGER-Men's Apparel, Boys' Apparel, Men's Surf & Swimwear, Resortwear, T-shirts, Imprinted Sportswear
CONNIE MINOR-Men's Apparel, Boys' Apparel, Men's Surf & Swimwear, Resortwear, T-shirts, Imprinted Sportswear
CAROL GRIFFITH-Men's Apparel, Boys' Apparel, Men's Surf & Swimwear, Resortwear, T-shirts, Imprinted Sportswear
MARILYN FRANCE-Men's Apparel, Boys' Apparel, Men's Surf & Swimwear, Resortwear, T-shirts, Imprinted Sportswear
SEEMON COHEN-Men's Apparel, Boys' Apparel, Men's Surf & Swimwear, Resortwear, T-shirts, Imprinted Sportswear

DOLPHIN BEACH (CLO)
531 E. Ocean Ave.
Boynton Beach, FL 33435
561-732-3838
JOAN BONE-Boys' Apparel, Men's Apparel, Men's Swimwear
GLORIA AKERS-Boys' Apparel, Men's Apparel, Men's Swimwear
COLLEEN STOCKER-Boys' Apparel, Men's Apparel, Men's Swimwear
LAURA ECKERT-Boys' Apparel, Men's Apparel, Men's Swimwear

KNOLLWOOD GROVES, INC. (CLO)
8053 Lawrence Rd.
Boynton Beach, FL 33436
561-734-4800 / Fax: 561-737-6700
Website: www.knollwoodgroves.com
BARBARA DWYER-Fashion Accessories, Hats, Men's Apparel, Resortwear,T-shirts, Imprinted Sportswear, Men's Apparel
TOM DWYER-Fashion Accessories, Hats, Men's Apparel, Resortwear,T-shirts, Imprinted Sportswear, Men's Apparel

NEW YORK MEN'S CLOTHING, INC. (MW-5)
(Ascot Enterprises)
438 N. Federal Hwy. (p)
Boynton Beach, FL 33435
561-732-5566
KHAIR ASKAR (Owner) & Buys Men's Overcoats, Suits, Tailored Jackets, Tailored Slacks, Sweaters, Sport Shirts, Outer Jackets, Leather Apparel, Casual Slacks, Active Apparel, Furnishings, Headwear, Accessories, Men's & Boys' Big & Tall Wear, Footwear, Store Displays, Fixtures, Supplies

NOMAD SURF & SPORTS WEAR (SG)
4655 N. Ocean Blvd. (m-b)
Boynton Beach, FL 33435
561-272-2882 / Fax: 561-272-4212
Sales: $500,001-$1 Million
RON HEAVYSIDE, Sr. (Owner) & Buys Boys' Apparel, Boys' Footwear, Men's Footwear, Men's Apparel, Men's Hosiery, Men's Outerwear, Men' Sportswear, Men's Swimwear
RON HEAVYSIDE, Jr. (Gen. Mgr.) & Buys Boys' Apparel, Boys' Footwear, Men's Footwear, Men's Apparel, Men's Hosiery, Men's Outerwear, Men' Sportswear, Men's Swimwear
JEN CALLAWAY (Store Mgr.) & Buys Boys' Apparel, Boys' Footwear, Men's Footwear, Men's Apparel, Men's Hosiery, Men's Outerwear, Men' Sportswear, Men's Swimwear

IN STYLE ACCESSORIES, INC. (CLO)
801 N. Congress Ave.
Boyton Beach, FL 33426
561-733-1535 / Fax: 561-733-6838
KEYLA MOON (Owner) & Buys Men's Beachwear, Accessories, Hawaiian Shirts, Belts

THE TAN FACTORY (CLO)
1899 N. Congress Ave.
Boyton Beach, FL 33426
561-736-2636 / Fax: 561-272-1951
TIFFANY LABAR-Men's Swimwear
ROB LABAR-Men's Swimwear

FLORIDA - Bradenton

BEALL'S DEPARTMENT STORE, INC. (DEPT-69)
(BEALL'S, INC.)
P.O. Box 25207 (p-m)
1806 38th Ave. East
Bradenton, FL 34208
(Henry Doneger)
941-747-2355 / Fax: 941-745-2813
Sales: $100 Million-$500 Million
Website: www.beallsflorida.com
Retail Locations: AL, AZ, FL, GA
- BOB BEALL (Chmn.)
- CONRAD SZYMANSKI (President)
- RICK EDGAR (G.M.M.-Men's)
- KIM OLSEN-All Men's Pants & Shorts
- SEAN PILON-Active Apparel, Collections, Outer Jackets
- MANDI BUTURBAUGH-Men's Main Floor, Sport Shirts, Active Apparel, Walk Shorts, Sweaters, Outerwear
- BRIAN RESTID-Robes, Underwear, Hosiery, Gloves, Headwear, Belts, Jewelry, Small Leathers, Licensed Apparel
- TODD THOMA-Young Men's Shop, Urban Contemporary
- MAURICE COOPER-Men's & Boys' Footwear
- JIM KNAPP (D.M.M.- Young Men's)
- LINDA KELLER-8 to 20 Boys' Clothing, Sportswear, Furnishings, Accessories
- GARY ZIMMERMAN-8 to 20 Boys' Accessories, Infants, Toddlers
- TIFFANY COBLE (Dir.-Visual) & Buys Store Displays
- FRANK DePALMA (Proj. Mgr.) & Buys Store Fixtures
- KARL BERVEN (Corp. Svces. Supv.) & Buys Store Supplies
- CHARLIE BUSCARINO (Div. V.P.-Real Estate)

JOHNSON - SMITH CO. (CLO)
(BETTY'S ATTIC)
(LIGHTER SIDE)
(THINGS YOU NEVER KNEW EXISTED)
4514 19th St., #E (bud-p)
P.O. Box 25600
Bradenton, FL 34206
941-747-5566 / Fax: 800-551-4406
Sales: $1 Million-$10 Million
Website: www.johnsonsmith.com
- GRAIG TARBECK (Dir.-Purch.) & Buys Men's Apparel, Men's Footwear

M. KESTEN (MW)
6773 Manatee Ave. West
Bradenton, FL 34209
941-792-5334 / Fax: 941-794-3767
- CAROL KESTEN (Co-Owner) & Buys Men's Sportswear, Sports Shirts, Casual Slacks, Active Apparel, Furnishings, Accessories, Footwear
- MURRAY KESTEN (Co-Owner) & Buys Men's Sportswear, Sports Shirts, Casual Slacks, Active Apparel, Furnishings, Accessories, Footwear

SK & COMPANY (CLO)
424 Old Main St.
Bradenton, FL 34205
941-749-7487 / Fax: 941-748-2838
- TERI KIRKPATRICK-Men's Surf & Swimwear, Boys' Apparel, Sunglasses, Fashion Accessories, Footwear, Hats, Apparel, Swimwear, Men's Apparel
- SHERMAN KIRKPATRICK-Men's Surf & Swimwear, Boys' Apparel, Sunglasses, Fashion Accessories, Footwear, Hats, Apparel, Swimwear, Men's Apparel

TEAM EDITION APPAREL (CLO)
4208 19th St. Court East
Bradenton, FL 34208
941-747-5300 / Fax: 941-747-9575
Website: www.footlocker.com
- CHRIS BULZIS-Men's Apparel
- KIM CARTANO-Men's Apparel
- SAM JENKINS-Men's Apparel
- KEVIN BOYD-Men's Apparel

CHAPAE (CLO)
119 Bridge St., #C
Bradenton Beach, FL 34217
941-778-1451 / Fax: 941-778-7614
- RON COFFEY-Men's Sportswear

MONOPOLI CLOTHING (CLO)
4601 E. Hwy. 100
Bunnell, FL 32100
386-439-5665
- TONY MONOPOLI-Accessories, Men's Apparel, Men's Swimwear, Private Label, Resorts Wear
- NICK CRISTELLO-Accessories, Men's Apparel, Men's Swimwear, Private Label, Resorts Wear

TROPICAL WORLD GIFTS (CLO)
125 SW 13th Terr.
Cape Coral, FL 33991
941-332-7774 / Fax: 941-458-7174
- CHERYL STEURY-Sunglasses, Fashion Accessories
- CRAIG ZENTZ-Sunglasses, Fashion Accessories

PALM ISLAND RESORT (CLO)
7092 Placida Rd.
Cape Haze, FL 33946
941-697-7309 / Fax: 941-697-0696
Website: www.palmisland.com
- KIMMER MANERA (Owner) & Buys Resortwear, T-shirts & Imprinted Sportswear
- JOHN MANERA-Resortwear, T-shirts & Imprinted Sportswear

BEACH STUFF, INC. (SP-2)
P.O. Box 992
14900 Captiva Dr.
Captiva, FL 33924
941-472-3544 / Fax: 941-472-9466
- GARY BAUGHER (Co-Owner) & Buys Beachwear, Swimwear, Headwear, Beach Shoes
- JOAN BAUGHER (Co-Owner) & Buys Beachwear, Swimwear, Headwear, Beach Shoes
- SUSAN BECKER-Boys' Apparel, Boys' Swimwear, Apparel, Swimwear, Sunglasses

ISLAND BEACH CO., INC. (CLO-3)
14820 Captiva Dr. (m-b)
Captiva, FL 33924
239-472-3272 / Fax: 239-395-1818
Sales: $1 Million-$10 Million
- MOREY HARTLEY (Owner) & Buys Men's & Boys' Casual Wear, Beach Wear, Footwear, Store Displays, Fixtures, Supplies

PELICAN ROOST (CLO-2 & GS)
(T.H. OSPREY)
P.O. Box 249
Captiva, FL 33924
941-472-5161 / Fax: 941-472-0249
- CINDY SCRAGG-Resortwear

HAMMOCK HOUSE (CLO)
P.O. Box 120
Dock St.
Cedar Key, FL 32625
352-543-5322
- CONNIE BROWN-Sportswear, Headwear, Leisurewear, Resortwear, T-shirts, Imprinted Sportswear

WESTERNER, INC. (DEPT & OL)
1095 Hwy. 90 (m)
Chipley, FL 32428
850-638-1124 / Fax: 850-638-8595
Website: www.westernerinc.com
- RODNEY SEWELL (Co-Owner) & Buys Men's Suits, Sportswear, Dress Shirts, Underwear, Headwear, Accessories, Swimwear, Young Men's & Boys' Wear, Swimwear, Footwear, Store Displays, Fixtures, Supplies

FLORIDA - Clearwater

FLIPPERZ BEACH SHOP (SP)
437 S. Gulfview Blvd.
Clearwater, FL 33767
727-446-0687 / Fax: 727-446-0687
DEBRA PURCELL-Swimwear, Beach Shoes, Headwear, Beachwear, Surfwear
NINA KIRIAKIDIS-Swimwear, Beach Shoes, Headwear, Beachwear, Surfwear
JOAN FRANGEDIS-Swimwear, Beach Shoes, Headwear, Beachwear, Surfwear
JAMES BOUTZOUKAS-Swimwear, Beach Shoes, Headwear, Beachwear, Surfwear
MIA BOUTZOUKAS-Swimwear, Beach Shoes, Headwear, Beachwear, Surfwear

FONTAINE APPAREL, INC. (KS)
1603 Sunshine Dr.
Clearwater, FL 34625
727-441-3702 / Fax: 727-443-1770
TYLER FONTAINE (Owner) & Buys 8 to 20 Boys' Uniforms, Store Displays, Fixtures, Supplies

FRENCHY'S OFF THE HOOK (CLO)
49 Baymont St.
Clearwater, FL 34630
727-446-1522 / Fax: 727-446-0588
Website: www.frenchysonline.com
CHRIS UCKER-T-shirts, Imprinted Sportswear, Headwear, Sunglasses, Beach Shoes

LEVINE'S FAMILY SHOES (FW & OL)
25897 US Hwy. 19 North (m-b-des)
Clearwater, FL 33763
727-796-2100 / Fax: 508-302-0357
Sales: $500,001-$1 Million
Website: www.webbedfoot.com
KEN LEVINE (Owner)
REGGIE LEVINE-Boys' Footwear, Men's Footwear

MANDALAY SURF & SPORT (CLO-2)
499 Mandalay Ave. (b)
Clearwater, FL 33767
727-443-3884 / Fax: 727-442-3227
Sales: $1 Million-$10 Million
BILL McKENNA-Sportswear, Young Men's Wear, Urban Contemporary

UNCLE MILTY'S (CLO)
1867 Gulf to Bay Blvd.
Clearwater, FL 33765
727-443-2027 / Fax: 727-443-2027
MILTON JAMES-Sportswear, Beachwear, Surfwear, Swimwear, Resortwear, Sunglasses, Footwear, Headwear, Skate Apparel, T-shirts, Imprinted Sportswear
ROSE JAMES-Sportswear, Beachwear, Surfwear, Swimwear, Resortwear, Sunglasses, Footwear, Headwear, Skate Apparel, T-shirts, Imprinted Sportswear

WEBB'S GENTLEMEN'S APPAREL, INC. (MW)
(WEBB'S OF CLEARWATER)
501 S. Fort Harrison Ave.
Clearwater, FL 33756
727-443-1578 / Fax: 727-461-0551
Sales: $1 Million-$10 Million
KERNAN WEBB (Owner) & Buys Leather Goods, Men's Big & Tall Apparel, Men's Apparel, Men's Casualwear, Men's Denim Apparel, Men's Formalwear, Men's Accessories, Men's Hosiery, Men's Outerwear, Men's Sportswear, Men's Suits, Men's Swimwear, Men's Underwear, Men's Sleepwear

WILDCHILD (CLO)
205 Bayshore Blvd.
Clearwater, FL 33759
727-712-8191
KENNY YOUNG-Resortwear, Swimwear, Surfwear, Sunglasses, Headwear, T-shirts, Imprinted Sportswear

WILLIAM SHORT CLOTHIERS (MW-2)
2454 N. McMullen Booth Rd., #301
Clearwater, FL 33759
727-796-1067 / Fax: 727-726-7058
Sales: $1 Million-$10 Million
WILLIAM W. SHORT, JR. (President)
BRUCE D. RABON (G.M.M.) & Buys Men's Suits, Tailored Jackets, Tailored Slacks, Raincoats, Sportswear, Leather Apparel, Accessories, Furnishings, Footwear, Store Displays, Fixtures, Supplies

DANA'S TOUCH (CLO-2)
790 S. Gulfview Blvd.
Clearwater Beach, FL 34630
727-443-7004 / Fax: 727-443-7004
DANA KOTYLAK-Resortwear, Sportswear, Accessories
CONRAD KOTYLAK-Resortwear, Sportswear, Accessories

SOUTH BEACH PAVILION (GS-2)
(FOUR SUNS, INC.)
332 S. Gulf View Blvd.
Clearwater Beach, FL 34630
727-447-5356 / Fax: 727-446-4255
HOWARD HAMILTON (President)
ALISA ACOSTA-Beachwear, Resortwear, Beach Footwear, Swimwear

MAR CHIQUITA (CLO)
1 N. Atlantic Ave.
Cocoa Beach, FL 32932
321-868-0868 / Fax: 321-784-2626
Website: www.marchiquita.net
REBECCA DUHIGG (Owner) & Buys Beachwear, Resortwear, Swimwear

RON JON SURF SHOP OF FLORIDA, INC. (SG-5)
3850 S. Banana River Blvd. (p-m-b-h)
Cocoa Beach, FL 32931
321-799-8888 / Fax: 321-868-7555
Website: www.ronjons.com
AL GUSE-Men's Sportswear, Accessories, Resortwear
EMMA WHITE-Young Men's & Boys' Footwear, Clothing, Swimwear

SELECT SCREEN PRINTING (CLO)
10050 Griffin Rd.
Cooper City, FL 33328
954-680-8496 / Fax: 954-680-9376
Website: www.flselect.com
MICKIE MOEN (Co-Owner) & Buys Men's, Young Men's & 8 to 20 Boys' T-shirts, Fleecewear, Shorts, Headwear, Store Displays, Fixtures, Supplies
VICKI MOEN (Co-Owner) & Buys Men's, Young Men's & 8 to 20 Boys' T-shirts, Fleecewear, Shorts, Headwear, Store Displays, Fixtures, Supplies

FRANCO B (MW)
350 Miracle Mile (b)
Coral Gables, FL 33134
305-444-7318 / Fax: 305-444-0443
JORGE MIRANDA (Co-Owner) & Buys Men's Overcoats, Suits, Tailored Jackets, Tailored Slacks, Sweaters, Outer Jackets, Leather Apparel, Casual Slacks, Urban Contemporary, Active Apparel, Dress Shirts, Ties, Robes, Underwear, Hosiery, Gloves, Headwear, Belts, Store Displays, Fixtures, Supplies
RICARDO LAZOFF (Co-Owner) & Buys Men's Overcoats, Suits, Tailored Jackets, Tailored Slacks, Sweaters, Outer Jackets, Leather Apparel, Casual Slacks, Urban Contemporary, Active Apparel, Dress Shirts, Ties, Robes, Underwear, Hosiery, Gloves, Headwear, Belts, Store Displays, Fixtures, Supplies

GALLERIA BORGHESE (MW-2)
2030 Ponce De Leon Blvd. (b)
Coral Gables, FL 33134
305-529-0300 / Fax: 305-529-1060
Sales: $1 Million-$10 Million
ALBERTO STIMAMIGLIO (Owner) & Buys Men's Overcoats, Suits, Tailored Jackets, Tailored Slacks, Sport Shirts, Leather Apparel, Casual Slacks, Store Displays, Fixtures, Supplies
MATILDE STIMAMIGLIO-Men's Dress Shirts, Ties, Underwear, Belts

FLORIDA - Coral Gables

J. BOLADO CLOTHIER, INC. (MW)
336 Miracle Mile (b)
Coral Gables, FL 33134
305-448-2507 / Fax: 305-448-8998
Sales: $500,000-$1 Million
JOSE BOLADO, SR. (Co-Owner)
JOSE BOLADO, JR. (Co-Owner)
CARLOS BOLADO (G.M.M.) & Buys Men's Sportswear, Furnishings, Accessories, Footwear, Store Displays, Fixtures, Supplies

MODIGLIANI, INC. (MW)
(BERTINI)
315 Miracle Mile (h)
Coral Gables, FL 33145
305-461-3374 / Fax: 305-461-3884
Sales: $1 Million-$10 Million
Website: www.pepibertini.com
JOSE GONZALES (Owner) & Buys Men's Sportswear, Headwear, Furnishings, Accessories, Store Displays, Fixtures, Supplies

UNIVERSITY OF MIAMI BOOKSTORE (SP)
(UNIVERSITY OF MIAMI)
Student Union Bldg.
Coral Gables, FL 33124
305-284-4101 / Fax: 305-284-4462
Sales: $500,001-$1 Million
Website: www.miami.bksc.com
ED MOEHLE (Mdse. Coord.) & Buys Active Apparel, Licensed Apparel
KATHERINE LOVE (Store Mgr.)

C.R. JEWELERS DIAMOND OUTLET (JWLY-15)
(CHAIN REACTION)
3111 N. University Dr., # 604
Coral Springs, FL 33065
954-796-2060 / Fax: 954-796-2066
Sales: $10 Million-$50 Million
Website: www.crjewelers.com
LAWRENCE WEINBERG (President)
DONALD WEINBERG (V.P.-E-Commerce)
RICK FITZGERALD-Jewelry

JONATHAN REED (MW-2)
4649 University Dr.
Coral Springs, FL 33067
954-346-2533 / Fax: 954-346-3370
JONATHAN REED (Owner) & Buys Men's Furnishings, Accessories, Boys' Wear, Boys' Accessories, Boys' Furnishings

WELFIT KIDS SHOES (FW)
9112 Wiles Rd. (m-b)
Coral Springs, FL 33067
954-345-9677
Sales: $100,001-$500,000
JANET JOHNSON (Owner) & Buys Boys' Footwear

CLASSIC MENSWEAR (MW)
290 N. Main St. (m-b)
Crestview, FL 32536
850-682-6315 / Fax: 850-689-1656
Sales: $100,001-$500,000
HILDA BLUE (Owner) & Buys Men's Wear, Urban Contemporary, Store Displays, Fixtures, Supplies

GRIF'S WESTERN, INC. (WW-2)
6211 SW 45th St. (m-b)
Davie, FL 33314
954-587-9000 / Fax: 954-587-9734
ALFRED GRIFFIN, JR. (President) & Buys Men's Western Suits, Sportswear, Furnishings, Accessories, Young Men's & Boys' Western Sportswear, Footwear, Store Displays, Fixtures & Supplies

RITCHIE SWIMWEAR (CLO-5 & OL)
(DOUBLE J. OF BROWARD, INC.)
15712 SW 41st St., #6
Davie, FL 33331
954-659-8880 / Fax: 954-659-8954
Website: www.ritchieswimwear.com
MICHAEL BERGER (President) & Buys Store Displays, Fixtures, Supplies
RICHARD BERGER (C.E.O.)
RAY BIRD (Sls. Mgr.) & Buys Men's Swimwear

ANYTHING GOES (CLO)
22 S. Ocean Ave. (b)
Daytona Beach, FL 32118
386-255-5280
Sales: $100,001-$500,000
JUDA MORALI (Owner) & Buys Boys' Apparel, Boys' Footwear, Men's Footwear, Men's Apparel, Men's Casualwear, Men's Sportswear, Men's Swimwear

BEACH TOWNE USA, INC. (CLO-2)
(MAUI-NIX SURF SHOP)
611 N. Atlantic Ave. (m-b)
Daytona Beach, FL 32118
386-238-1000 / Fax: 386-238-3099
Sales: $1 Million-$10 Million
GEORGE KARAMITOS (Co-Owner) & Buys Boys' Footwear, Men's Footwear, Men's Apparel, Men's Accessories, Men's Swimwear
NICK KARAMITOS (Co-Owner)
PETER KARAMITOS (Co-Owner)

CHRISTINA'S BEACHWEAR & GIFTS (CLO)
1019 Main St. (p-m)
Daytona Beach, FL 32118
386-255-9132 / Fax: 386-673-6585
STAVROULA PETROPOULES (Owner)
STEVE PETROPOULES-Men's Beachwear, Store Displays, Fixtures, Supplies

DAYTONA BEACH 'N' SPORT, INC. (SP)
411 N. Atlantic Ave., #2
Daytona Beach, FL 32118
386-257-7621
ERIC LALGHAND-Swimwear, Surfwear, T-shirts, Beachwear, Resortwear, Related Accessories

DAYTONA SHIRT SHOP (CLO)
825 E. International Speedway, #B (m)
Daytona Beach, FL 32118
386-252-5699
Sales: $100,001-$500,000
ZOLTAM KEREKES (Owner) & Buys Boys' Apparel, Boys' Footwear, Men's Footwear, Men's Apparel, Men's Casualwear, Men's Denim Apparel, Men's Sportswear, Men's Swimwear

JUST OFF CAMPUS (CLO)
725 Dr. Mary McLeod Bethune Blvd. (des)
Daytona Beach, FL 32114
386-257-9944 / Fax: 386-257-0698
Sales: $500,001-$1 Million
Website: www.justoffcampusdaytona.com
CLIFF WRIGHT (Owner) & Buys Boys' Apparel, Leather Goods, Men's Apparel, Men's Casualwear, Men's Sportswear

MAUL NIX (CLO-2)
635 N. Atlantic Ave.
Daytona Beach, FL 32118
386-253-1234 / Fax: 386-254-0516
MELISSA SMITH-Beachwear, Swimwear, Athletic Apparel
BRIAN WHITE-Athletic Shoes, Sandals, Flip Flops

MISTI-LEIGH, INC. (CLO-13)
555 8th St., #1 (m-b)
Daytona Beach, FL 32118
386-255-8898 / Fax: 386-323-1917
Sales: $1 Million-$10 Million
GARY HUNTER (Owner) & Buys Boys' Apparel, Leather Goods, Men's Apparel, Men's Casualwear, Men's Accessories, Men's Sportswear, Men's Swimwear

THE SALTY DOG (CLO-4)
100 S. Atlantic Ave. (m)
Daytona Beach, FL 32128
386-253-2755 / Fax: 386-252-2083
Website: www.saltydogsurfshop.com
BRUCE MILLER (Owner) & Buys Men's & Boys' Sport Shirts, Outer Jackets, Shorts, Headwear, Footwear, Store Displays, Fixtures, Supplies

THE SAND BOX, INC. (CLO-3)

1310 S. Atlantic Ave. (m-b)
Daytona Beach, FL 32118
386-252-0676 / Fax: 386-252-9061

TRUDY TABASKY (President) & Buys Men's & Boys' Swimwear, Footwear, Store Displays, Fixtures, Supplies

ROB TABASKY (V.P.) & Buys Men's & Boys' Swimwear, Footwear, Store Displays, Fixtures, Supplies

TOTAL FASHION (CLO-2)

411 N. Atlantic (p)
Daytona Beach, FL 32118
386-238-1903 / Fax: 386-257-7719

CHARLES FEDIDA (Owner) & Buys Men's Sport Shirts, Outer Jackets, Casual Slacks, Jeans, T-shirts, Urban Contemporary, Hosiery, Hats, Sandals, Belts, Store Displays, Fixtures, Supplies

PURE ATLANTIC SURF & SKI (SP-2)

2540 S. Atlantic Ave.
Daytona Beach Shores, FL 32118
386-322-1143 / Fax: 904-322-9478

JOHN ANDRIOROPOULOS (President & Owner)

TIFFANY GANGI (Gen. Mgr.) & Buys Activewear, Athletic Footwear, Athletic Apparel, Swimwear, Headwear, Sandals, Beachwear, Accessories

JACK'S FOR SLACKS (CLO)

(ANDOVER REED)
1560 SE 3rd St. (b)
Deerfield Beach, FL 33441
954-428-8188 / Fax: 954-428-1678

STANLEY GRAFF (Co-Owner) & Buys Men's Wear, Furnishings, Sportswear

MICHAEL RUBIKOFF (Co-Owner) & Buys Men's Wear, Furnishings, Sportswear

EPIC SURF & SWIM (SP)

1122 E. Atlantic Ave.
Delray Beach, FL 33483
561-272-2052

AMANDA CODNER (Owner) & Buys Beachwear, Surf & Swimwear, Wet Suits, Athletic Shoes, Sandals, Flip Flops, Water Sport Accessories

FRANCES BREWSTER, INC. (CLO-4)

1100 E. Atlantic Ave.
P.O. Box 2136
Delray Beach, FL 33486
561-276-4148 / Fax: 561-266-0847
Sales: $1 Million-$10 Million

WILLIAM G. BREWSTER (President & Real Estate Contact) & Buys Leather Goods, Men's Apparel, Men's Casualwear, Men's Formalwear, Men's Accessories, Men's Outerwear, Men's Sportswear, Men's Suits, Men's Swimwear

JANET CREESE-Leather Goods, Men's Apparel, Men's Casualwear, Men's Formalwear, Men's Accessories, Men's Outerwear, Men's Sportswear, Men's Suits, Men's Swimwear

MERCER WENZEL, INC. (DEPT)

P.O. Box 2170 (b)
401 E. Atlantic Ave.
Delray Beach, FL 33483
561-278-2885 / Fax: 561-276-3483
Sales: $500,000-$1 Million

BRUCE B. WENZEL (President & G.M.M.)

MARK WENZEL-Men's & Young Men's Wear, 14 to 20 Boys' Wear

CHRIS WENZEL-8 to 14 Boys' Wear, Store Displays, Fixtures, Supplies

SIMPLY SWIMWEAR (CLO)

Carnival Flea Market Magic Way, #135
Delray Beach, FL 33484
561-637-2727

BERT APPLEBAUM (Co-Owner) & Buys Beachwear, Swimwear, Headwear, Beach Shoes, Beach & Swim Accessories

GAIL APPLEBAUM (Co-Owner) & Buys Beachwear, Swimwear, Headwear, Beach Shoes, Beach & Swim Accessories

SOUTH OCEAN BEACH SHOP (CLO)

28 S. Ocean Blvd.
Delray Beach, FL 33483
561-278-3336 / Fax: 561-278-3350

DIANA PANK-Beachwear, Swimwear, Headwear, Athletic Shoes, Beach Footwear

THE TROUSER SHOP (CLO & OL)

(OCEAN 12, INC.)
439 E. Atlantic Ave. (m-b)
Delray Beach, FL 33483
561-278-5626 / Fax: 561-740-1018
Sales: $100,001-$500,000
Website: www.trousershop.com

BRUCE GIMMY (President) & Buys Men's Tailored Slacks, Tailored Jackets, Tuxedos, Belts, Suspenders, Big & Tall Men's Wear, Sport Shirts, Casual Slacks, Store Displays, Fixtures, Supplies

BEACH BUMS (CLO)

9539 Hwy. 98 West
Destin, FL 32550
850-837-7111 / Fax: 850-837-6530

CHARLES JARVIS (Owner) & Buys Beachwear, Swimwear, Beach Footwear, Beach & Swim Accessories

SHERRI JARVIS-Beachwear, Swimwear, Beach Footwear, Beach & Swim Accessories, Headwear

PETE SMITH, INC. (CLO)

(JAMAICA JOE'S)
106 Benning Dr., #8
Destin, FL 32541
850-837-1149 / Fax: 850-650-8148

DEBRA SMITH (Owner) & Buys Beachwear, Swimwear, Headwear, Beach Footwear

SOCKEYE'S BEACH & SPORT (SG)

20011 Emerald Coast Pkwy.
Destin, FL 32541
850-654-8954 / Fax: 850-654-8963
Website: www.sockeyesonline.com

MATT CASSIDY (Store Mgr.) & Buys Athletic Footwear, Active Apparel, Outerwear

DAVE SETTON (Mgr.-Men's) & Buys Athletic Footwear, Active Apparel, Outerwear

SPUNKY MONKEY (CLO)

(LONG VARIETIES, INC.)
500 E. Hwy. 98 (b)
Destin, FL 32541
850-837-6171 / Fax: 850-837-6172

JOY WAMBLE (Owner) & Buys Men's Swimwear, Sweaters, Sport Shirts, Outer Jackets, Casual Slacks, Active Apparel, Headwear, Jewelry, Small Leather Goods, Footwear, Store Displays, Fixtures, Supplies

ADAMO CLOTHIER, INC. (CLO-2)

5975 N. Federal Hwy. (b)
Fort Lauderdale, FL 33308
954-491-4719 / Fax: 954-491-2523

JIM CROWE (Owner) & Buys Men's Sportswear, Contemporary, Sportswear, Furnishings

AUDACE (SP & OL)

813 E. Las Olas Blvd. (p-m-b-h)
Fort Lauderdale, FL 33301
954-522-7503 / Fax: 954-522-7504
Website: www.audace.com

PIERRE JUBINVILLE (Owner) & Buys Men's & Young Men's Shorts, Sportswear, T-shirts, Underwear, Store Displays, Fixtures, Supplies

FLORIDA - Fort Lauderdale

BARBARA'S BOATIQUE, INC. (CLO-2 & OL)
(CHARLIE'S LOCKER)
1465 SE 17th St.
Fort Lauderdale, FL 33316
954-523-3350 / Fax: 954-523-5846
Website: www.charlieslocker.com
BARBARA BIRER (Co-Owner) & Buys Yachtwear, Resortwear, Related Footwear
ROBERT BIRER (Co-Owner) & Buys Yachtwear, Resortwear, Related Footwear

BERMUDA BAY CLOTHING (CLO-6)
349 Idlewyld Dr. (m-b)
Fort Lauderdale, FL 33301
954-463-5546 / Fax: 954-832-0843
Sales: $1 Million-$10 Million
MICHAEL EVANGELISTI (Owner) & Buys Men's Apparel, Men's Casualwear, Men's Accessories, Men's Outerwear, Men's Sportswear, Men's Swimwear, Men's Footwear

CARRIAGE CLOTHIERS (MW-3)
(TAFFY'S)
(PHILIPS)
1461 SE 17th St. Causeway
Fort Lauderdale, FL 33316
954-523-3545 / Fax: 954-583-2832
Sales: $1 Million-$10 Million
STEVE BEAN (President) & Buys Men's Suits, Tailored Jackets, Tailored Slacks, Sport Shirts, Outer Jackets, Casual Slacks, Active Apparel, Furnishings, Headwear, Accessories, Store Displays, Fixtures, Supplies

CASUAL AIRE CLOTHING (MW)
3005 E. Las Olas Blvd. (m-b)
Fort Lauderdale, FL 33316
954-523-7403
ISAAC WAGCER (Owner) & Buys Men's Wear

CLIMAX FASHIONS (CLO)
2941 E. Las Olas Blvd.
Fort Lauderdale, FL 33316
954-761-8354 / Fax: 954-525-0581
ISSAC ASULIN (Owner) & Buys T-shirts, Shorts, Beachwear, Swimwear, Beach Footwear

CLOUD 9 CLOTHING (MW)
1350 SE 17th St. (p-m)
Fort Lauderdale, FL 33316
954-463-1961 / Fax: 954-463-1961
PHYLLIS (Owner) & Buys Young Men's Wear, Accessories, Footwear

COOL VIBRATIONS (CLO-2)
12801 W. Sunrise Blvd. (bud-p)
Fort Lauderdale, FL 33323
954-846-0409 / Fax: 954-437-2370
Sales: $500,001-$1 Million
Website: www.rootz.com
RAY EPKU (Sls. Mgr.)
ANDREW BAINES (Owner) & Buys Men's Apparel

GOLD COAST T-SHIRT, INC. (CLO)
3200 NE 5th Ave. (p-m-b)
Fort Lauderdale, FL 33334
954-565-6554 / Fax: 954-565-7655
Website: www.goshirts.com
JEAN CHENAULT, JR. (Owner) & Buys Men's & Boys' T-shirts, Polo Shirts, Dress Shirts, Store Displays, Fixtures, Supplies

HIP POCKETS (CLO)
(STERLING CO., INC.)
1344 SE 17th St. (m)
Fort Lauderdale, FL 33316
954-761-7677 / Fax: 954-760-9190
STAN STERLING (Owner) & Buys Men's Sportswear, Store Displays, Fixtures, Supplies

LACE TO LUST, INC. (CLO-2)
139 E. Oakland Park Blvd. (p-m)
Fort Lauderdale, FL 33334
954-566-1880 / Fax: 954-566-2443
CHERYL PARRY (Owner) & Buys Men's Underwear, Swimwear, Small Leather Goods, Store Displays, Fixtures, Supplies

MAUS & HOFFMAN, INC. (CLO-5 & MO & OL)
P.O. Box 2000 (h)
800 E. Las Olas Blvd.
Fort Lauderdale, FL 33301
954-463-1472 / Fax: 954-463-1587
Sales: $1 Million-$10 Million
Website: www.mausandhoffman.com
WILLIAM H. MAUS, JR. (Co-Owner) & Buys Men's Overcoats, Suits, Tailored Jackets, Tailored Slacks, Raincoats, Sweaters, Sport Shirts, Outer Jackets, Furnishings, Accessories, Footwear, Store Displays, Fixtures, Supplies
THOMAS B. MAUS (Co-Owner) & Buys Men's Overcoats, Suits, Tailored Jackets, Tailored Slacks, Raincoats, Sweaters, Sport Shirts, Outer Jackets, Furnishings, Accessories, Footwear, Store Displays, Fixtures, Supplies
JOHN MAUS (Co-Owner) & Buys Men's Overcoats, Suits, Tailored Jackets, Tailored Slacks, Raincoats, Sweaters, Sport Shirts, Outer Jackets, Furnishings, Accessories, Footwear, Store Displays, Fixtures, Supplies

MODA MARIO, INC. (MW)
820 E. Las Olas Blvd. (b-des)
Fort Lauderdale, FL 33301
954-467-3258 / Fax: 954-467-3277
Sales: $1 Million-$10 Million
Website: www.modamario.com
MARIO ARGIRO (Owner) & Buys Men's Sportswear, Leather Apparel, Accessories, Footwear, Store Displays, Fixtures, Supplies

THE PRO IMAGE, INC. (CLO)
(UTAR, INC.)
12801 W. Sunrise Blvd.
Fort Lauderdale, FL 33323
954-846-2548 / Fax: 954-432-9801
VIMAL PATEL (Mgr.) & Buys Licensed Apparel

RS LORDS, INC. (MW)
5251 N. Powerline Rd. (p-m)
Fort Lauderdale, FL 33309
954-772-6285 / Fax: 954-491-3630
RAY SAMUEL (Owner) & Buys Men's Suits, Slacks, Jackets, Shirts, Ties, Belts, Store Displays, Fixtures, Supplies

RUNNING WILD, INC. (SP)
5437 N. Federal Hwy.
Fort Lauderdale, FL 33308
954-492-0077 / Fax: 954-492-8202
Sales: $500,001-$1 Million
Website: www.runningwild.com
PATRICIA UFHEIL (Mgr.)
MEG BRUCH (Owner) & Buys Activewear, Athletic Footwear

SMALLWOOD'S, INC. (CLO & MO & OL)
1001 SE 17th St.
Fort Lauderdale, FL 33316
954-523-2282 / Fax: 954-523-4312
Website: www.smallwoods.com
HELEN SMALLWOOD (Owner)
BARBARA BJORK-Men's Suits, Raincoats, Tailored Slacks, Sportswear, Dress Shirts, Footwear, Store Displays, Fixtures, Supplies

SUNUP SUNDOWN, INC. (CLO & OL)
P.O. Box 11899
Fort Lauderdale, FL 33339
954-238-3289 / Fax: 954-564-1515
Sales: $500,001-$1 Million
Website: www.sunupsundown.com
THOMAS FARLEY (President) & Buys Men's Apparel

SUPREME MENSWEAR (MW)
3211 N. Ocean Blvd. (m-b)
Fort Lauderdale, FL 33308
954-563-3100
Sales: $100,001-$500,000
MAC WEISS (President) & Buys Men's Wear, Store Displays, Fixtures, Supplies

TIME FASHION (MW-2)
3161 W. Oakland Park Blvd. (p)
Fort Lauderdale, FL 33111
954-777-4849
HYO YOUNG (Owner) & Buys Men's Sportswear, Furnishings, Headwear, Accessories, Young Men's Wear, Store Displays, Fixtures, Supplies

WIPE OUT OF FT. LAUDERDALE, INC. (CLO-2)
203 S. Atlantic Blvd. (bud-p)
Fort Lauderdale, FL 33316
954-832-0745 / Fax: 954-463-9455
SHLOMO D. JAMAL (Owner)
DAVID-Men's Raincoats, Sweaters, Sport Shirts, Outer Jackets, Active Apparel, Dress Shirts, Urban Contemporary, Underwear, Hosiery, Belts, Jewelry, Fragrances, Boys' Clothing, Sportswear, Furnishings, Accessories, Footwear, Store Displays, Fixtures, Supplies

THE GOLF & CASUAL SHOP (CLO)
11900 S. Cleveland Ave. (m-b)
Fort Myers, FL 33907
941-936-8753 / Fax: 239-936-5646
BOB ISENHOWER (President)
FERN ISENHOWER (V.P.) & Buys Men's Sweaters, Sport Shirts, Casual Slacks, Active Apparel, Hats, Golf Appare, Footwear, Store Displays, Fixtures, Supplies

HAY LOFT, INC. (WW-2)
4300 Lexington Ave. (m-b)
Fort Myers, FL 33905
941-694-4916 / Fax: 941-694-7707
Website: www.hayloftwestern.com
KELLY PALMER (Partner) & Buys Men's Footwear, Store Displays, Fixtures, Supplies
MICHELE MUSCO-Men's & Boys' Western Wear, Denim, Headwear, Accessories, Big & Tall Wear

HIGH FASHIONS MENSWEAR (CLO)
4901 Palm Beach Blvd., #3
Fort Myers, FL 33905
941-694-2622 / Fax: 863-422-7295
OMAR HAMDAN (Owner) & Buys T-shirts, Fleece, Shorts, Activewear, Swimwear, Shoes
ZEIAD HAMDAN-T-shirts, Fleece, Shorts, Activewear, Swimwear, Shoes

MANGO BAY BEACH COMPANY (CLO)
151 Old San Carlos Blvd.
Fort Myers, FL 33931
941-463-4114 / Fax: 941-463-4357
BRIAN SCANLAN (Owner)
JEFFREY LUSK-Activewear, Resortwear, Beachwear, Swimwear, Headwear, Beach Shoes, Sandals, Beach & Swim Accessories

SHARKY'S BEACH MART (SP)
(BLOCKHEAD ENTERPRISES)
11563 Marshwood Ln.
Fort Myers, FL 33908
941-433-2723 / Fax: 239-454-6039
MARK COLBERT-Beachwear, T-shirts, Fleece, Shorts, Headwear, Sandals, Swimwear

STANLEY'S ARMY & NAVY STORE (AN)
3280 Palm Beach Blvd.
Fort Myers, FL 33916
941-334-4085 / Fax: 941-332-2261
Sales: $100,001-$500,000
JIM CHESTER (Owner) & Buys Men's Apparel, Footwear & Accessories

SWIMWEAR (CLO)
13300 S. Cleveland Ave., #53
Cypress Trace
Fort Myers, FL 33907
941-481-1350 / Fax: 941-481-6610
Website: www.swimworldftmyers.com
WILLIAM MENKE (Co-Owner) & Buys Swimwear, Beach Footwear, Sandals
JODI MENKE (Co-Owner) & Buys Resortwear, Beachwear, Headwear

BEACH CONNECTION (CLO-2)
2401 Estero Blvd. (m-b)
Fort Myers Beach, FL 33931
941-765-1345
Sales: $500,001-$1 Million
NIRI COHEN (Owner) & Buys Boys' Apparel, Boys' Footwear, Men's Footwear, Men's Apparel, Men's Swimwear

WEST COAST SURF SHOP (CLO-2)
1035 Estero Blvd. (p-m)
Fort Myers Beach, FL 33931
941-463-1989 / Fax: 941-463-1990
BRIAN ANDERSON (Owner) & Buys Men's Sport Shirts, Active Apparel, Swimwear, Cruise Wear, Boys' Swimwear, Accessories, Young Men's Wear, Footwear, Store Displays, Fixtures and Supplies

BIG JOHN'S FEED & WESTERN SUPPLIES (WW)
6100 Orange Ave.
Fort Pierce, FL 34947
561-461-7712 / Fax: 561-461-7736
CLYDE CROUCH (Co-Owner)
SANDRA CROUCH (Co-Owner) & Buys Men's & Boys' Western Wear, Boots, Store Displays, Fixtures, Supplies

MEN'S RAGS (MW)
2053 US Hwy. 1 South (p-m)
Fort Pierce, FL 34950
561-461-3553 / Fax: 561-461-3655
MIKE ABRAHAM (Owner) & Buys Men's & Boys' Clothing, Sportswear, Urban Contemporary, Furnishings, Accessories, Footwear, Headwear, Store Displays, Fixtures, Supplies

ISLANDERS SURF & SPORT SHOPS (CLO-5)
(SURF & SPORT, INC.)
191 Miracle Strip Pkwy. (p-m)
Fort Walton Beach, FL 32548
850-244-0451 / Fax: 850-243-7607
Website: www.islandsurf.com
JOHN HAMILTON (Owner) & Buys Men's & Young Men's Apparel, Casual Slacks, Urban Contemporary, Swimwear, Store Displays, Fixtures, Supplies

JIMMY'S MEN'S STORE & PAWN SHOP, INC. (MW)
P.O. Box 547 (m)
22 Eglin Pkwy. SE
Fort Walton Beach, FL 32548
850-244-5184 / Fax: 850-244-5120
Sales: $100,001-$500,000
ROY MAJORS (President) & Buys Men's Sport Shirts, Active Apparel, Furnishings, Headwear, Accessories, Men's Big & Tall Wear, Boots, Store Displays, Fixtures, Supplies

ETTK (CLO)
1307 E. Commercial Blvd.
Ft. Lauderdale, FL 33334
954-689-3511 / Fax: 954-689-3655
ANDREW KRANCE-Swimwear, Men's Apparel
ETI KRANCE-Swimwear, Men's Apparel

BEACH HOUSE SWIMWEAR (SP-9 & MO)
(AQUA BEACHWEAR)
15870 Pine Ridge Rd., #2
Ft. Myers, FL 33908
239-466-3414 / Fax: 239-466-5973
Sales: $501,000-$1 Million
Website: www.thebeachhouseswimwear.com
DON BAUER (Owner) & Buys Outdoor Footwear, Swimwear
MARY BAUER-Outdoor Footwear, Swimwear
FRANNIE SAMPSON-Outdoor Footwear, Swimwear

BENCHMARK (MW)
3301 W. University Ave.
Gainesville, FL 32606
352-377-4468
EVANS SMITH (Owner) (@ 904-332-0807) & Buys Men's Suits, Tailored Jackets, Tailored Slacks, Sportswear, Dress Shirts, Underwear, Small Leather Goods, Store Displays, Fixtures, Supplies

FLORIDA - Gainesville

BILL PINNER FOOTWEAR, INC. (FW)

3411 W. University Ave. (des)

Gainesville, FL 32607

352-376-7001 / Fax: 352-336-4560

Sales: $500,001-$1 Million

DUKE PINNER (Owner) & Buys Men's Footwear, Leather Goods, Men's Hosiery

GATOR PLUS, INC. (CLO)

1620 W. University Ave.

Gainesville, FL 32604

352-375-8115 / Fax: 352-375-5950

Website: www.gatorsplus.com

BILL OLANDER (Owner) & Buys Activewear, Licensed Apparel

GATOR SHOP (CLO & OL)

1702 W. University Ave. (p-m-b-h)

Gainesville, FL 32603

352-376-5191 / Fax: 352-376-2334

Website: www.gatorshop.com

JOE FINCHER (Owner)

AMY FINCHER (Mgr.) & Buys Men's T-shirts, Shorts, Urban Contemporary, Footwear, Store Displays, Fixtures, Supplies

JUDI HAYES-Men's T-shirts, Shorts, Urban Contemporary, Footwear, Store Displays, Fixtures, Supplies

THE RANCHER, INC. (CLO)

4821 NW 6th St.

Gainesville, FL 32609

352-376-4595 / Fax: 352-374-8149

Sales: $100,001-$500,000

Website: www.therancher.com

LUTHER WHITE (Co-Owner)

JUANITA WHITE (Co-Owner) & Buys Men's Western Wear, Boots, Pants, Shirts, Headwear

SOUL TRAIN STOP (MW)

2 E. University Ave. (p)

Gainesville, FL 32601

352-372-7922 / Fax: 352-372-7599

JAMES OUM (Owner) & Buys Young Men's Wear, Urban Contemporary, Sportswear, Dress Shirts, Accessories, Men's Wear, Footwear

SWIM & SKI COUNTRY (SG)

(Div. of RUDDY'S, INC.)

Creekside Mall

3501 SW 2nd Ave.

Gainesville, FL 32607

352-378-8751 / Fax: 352-371-4364

JERRY RUDDERMAN (Owner) & Buys Ski Apparel, Related Apparel, Swimwear

UNIVERSITY OF FLORIDA BOOK STORES (SP-5)

(UNIVERSITY OF FLORIDA)

P.O. Box 118450

Gainesville, FL 32611

352-392-0194 / Fax: 352-392-3660

Sales: $5 Million-$10 Million

Website: www.ufl.bkstr.com

LYNN VAUGHAN (Dir.)

PAMELA HOUGHTON (Asst. Dir.) & Buys Activewear, Fleece, Jackets, Hosiery, Shorts, Golf Apparel, Headwear

GOLDEN LARIAT WESTERN SHOP (WW)

1353 Hwy. 69 (m-b)

Grand Ridge, FL 32442

850-592-6058 / Fax: 850-592-4180

MICHAEL ADKINS (Owner) & Buys Men's Western Wear, Accessories, Boots, Store Supplies

EMILIO HOWARD CO. (KS)

1899 Reserve Blvd., #98

Gulf Breeze, FL 32563

804-762-4455 / Fax: 804-217-8999

EMILIO HOWARD (Owner) & Buys Men's Apparel, Footwear, Accessories & Furnishings

HIGH FASHIONS MENSWEAR (MW-3)

35910 US Hwy. 27 North (m-b)

Haines City, FL 33844

863-422-7295

Website: www.menswearonline.com

YOUSIF HAMDAM (Owner)

RAY HAMDAM (Mgr.) & Buys Men's Sportswear, Urban Contemporary, Accessories, Furnishings, Footwear, Store Displays, Fixtures, Supplies

ZAYAS MEN'S SHOP, INC. (MW-2)

990 W. 49th St. (m-b)

Hialeah, FL 33012

305-557-5371 / Fax: 305-885-8005

Sales: $500,000-$1 Million

JOSE ZAYAS, JR. (President) & Buys Men's Tailored Jackets, Tailored Slacks, Sweaters, Sport Shirts, Outer Jackets, Casual Slacks, Active Apparel, Dress Shirts, Ties, Underwear, Hosiery, Belts, Jewelry, Small Leather Goods, Young Men's Wear, Leather Apparel, Footwear, Store Displays, Fixtur

IGGY DIAZ (Asst. Comptroller) (@ 305-885-1122) & Buys Men's Tailored Jackets, Tailored Slacks, Sweaters, Sport Shirts, Outer Jackets, Casual Slacks, Active Apparel, Dress Shirts, Ties, Underwear, Hosiery, Belts, Jewelry, Small Leather Goods, Young Men's Wear, Leather Apparel, Footwear, Store Displays, Fixtur

JIM'S TRADING (MW)

689 W. 26th St.

Hialeh, FL 33010

305-883-1856 / Fax: 305-883-5664

SOLOMON SUSI (Owner) & Buys Men's Big & Tall, Men's Wear, Accessories, Furnishings, Footwear

ATLANTIC EYE'S & TEE'S (CLO)

320 N. Broadwalk

Hollywood, FL 33019

954-921-5818 / Fax: 954-894-1568

RAN AYALON (Owner) & Buys Beachwear, T-shirts, Fleece, Shorts, Swimwear, Beach Shoes, Sandals, Sunglasses, Goggles

DISTINCTIVE USA (CLO)

1000 N. Broadwalk, #A

Hollywood, FL 33019

954-925-1404

LUZ EVGI (Co-Owner)

ELI EVGI (Co-Owner) & Buys Resortwear, Beachwear, Swimwear, Beach Footwear, Sandals, Sunglasses

IRVING BERLIN CASUALS, INC. (MW)

1919 Hollywood Blvd. (b)

Hollywood, FL 33020

954-921-2561 / Fax: 954-921-2563

Sales: $500,000-$1 Million

LEWIS COHEN (President) & Buys Men's Sportswear, Furnishings, Footwear, Store Displays, Fixtures, Supplies

RONNI COHEN (V.P.) & Buys Men's Sportswear, Furnishings, Footwear, Store Displays, Fixtures, Supplies

OCEAN WAVE BEACHWEAR (CLO)

600 N. Surf Rd.

Hollywood, FL 33019

954-922-2427 / Fax: 954-925-8757

JIMMY MORAD (Owner) & Buys Men's & Boys' Sportswear, Footwear, Store Displays, Fixtures, Supplies

TEEPEE WESTERN WEAR, INC. (WW)

3560 N. State Rd. 7 (m)

Hollywood, FL 33021

954-983-4352 / Fax: 954-962-2932

Sales: $1 Million-$10 Million

CHUCK FULLERTON (Owner)

CINDY POOL (Gen. Mgr.) & Buys Men's Sportswear, Headwear, Boys' Jeans, Boots, Store Displays, Fixtures, Supplies

SHIRTERY (CLO-2)

1416 N. Boardwalk (p-m-b)

Hollywood Beach, FL 33019

954-922-3635

MR. MENASSE SATTON (Co-Owner)

DANIEL SATTON (Co-Owner) (@ 954-927-9236) & Buys Men's Sportswear, Furnishings, Accessories, etc.

SUN & SURF BEACH SHOP (SP)
5418 Marina Dr.
Holme Beach, FL 34217
941-778-2169 / Fax: 941-778-6497
AMY JULINE STICKLER (Owner) & Buys Resortwear, Beachwear, Swimwear, Headwear, Beach Footwear, Sandals

SUNSET ENGLISH & WESTERN WEAR (WW-2)
16300 SW 296th St. (p-m-b)
Homestead, FL 33033
305-245-2935 / Fax: 305-246-1721
JESS BUTT (Co-Owner)
ANNA BUTT (Co-Owner) & Buys Men's & Boys' Western Wear, Boots, Store Displays, Fixtures, Supplies

DOUB'S WESTERN WEAR (WW)
307 New Market Rd..
Immokalee, FL 34142
239-657-2707 / Fax: 239-657-2707
WILLIAM DOUB (Owner) & Buys Men's & Boys' Western Wear, Related Furnishings, Accessories, Men's & Boys' Boots, Store Displays, Fixtures, Supplies

SHUTTLE PRODUCTS INTERNATIONAL INC. (CLO & MO & OL)
1101 S. Miramar Ave., #203
P.O. Box 34117
Indialantic, FL 32903
321-773-4020 / Fax: 321-779-5090
Sales: $500,001-$1 Million
Website: www.shuttleproducts.com
CHIP ROHLKE (President) & Buys Boys' Apparel, Men's Apparel

THE SWIM SHOP (CLO)
401 2nd St.
Indian Rocks Beach, FL 33785
727-593-7946 / Fax: 727-596-7946
KIM CONNER-Boys' Apparel, Boys' Swimwear, Accessories, Footwear, Hats, Men's Apparel, Men's Surf & Swimwear, Resortwear,T-shirts, Imprinted Sportswear
JOYCE CONNER-Accessories, Footwear, Hats, Men's Apparel, Men's Surf & Swimwear, Resortwear,T-shirts, Imprinted Sportswear

MICHAEL'S MEN'S STORE, INC. (CLO)
(MICHAEL'S STORE FOR MEN & WOMEN)
201 5th Ave. (m-b)
Indiatlantic, FL 32903
321-723-8400 / Fax: 321-723-1991
MICHAEL JABLAOUI (Owner) & Buys Men's Sportswear, Furnishings, Accessories, Store Displays, Fixtures, Supplies

EYE CANDY BOUTIQUE (CLO)
80925 Overseas Hwy.
Islamorada, FL 33036
305-664-3100 / Fax: 305-664-2339
Website: www.eyecandyboutique.com
JOANNE McCORKLE-Men's, Young Men's & Boys' Apparel

LATITUDE 25 (CLO-2)
82748 Overseas Hwy. (b)
Islamorada, FL 33036
305-664-4421 / Fax: 305-664-2544
GAIL SCHNEIDER (Co-Owner) & Buys Men's Sweaters, Sport Shirts, Outer Jackets, Casual Slacks, Active Apparel, Headwear, Small Leather Goods, Footwear, Store Displays, Fixtures, Supplies

PARADISE COVE SWIM & SURF (SP)
P.O. Box 1904
Islamorada, FL 33036
305-664-4726 / Fax: 305-664-2703
Website: www.bikinisinparadise.com
STEVEN GIULIANO-Swimwear, Surfwear, Beachwear

ALOHA PARADISE (CLO)
1009 Park St.
Jacksonville, FL 92204
904-350-0355 / Fax: 904-350-0365
Website: www.alohaparadise.net
ROBIN HOLTON-Boys' Apparel, Sunglasses, Accessories, Footwear, Hats, Men's Apparel
DEBBIE GOLPE-Boys' Apparel, Sunglasses, Accessories, Footwear, Hats, Men's Apparel
HARRY HOFFMAN-Boys' Apparel, Sunglasses, Accessories, Footwear, Hats, Men's Apparel

BELK, INC. - SOUTHERN DIV. (DEPT-46)
5210 Belfort Rd., # 400 (bud-p-m-b-h)
Jacksonville, FL 32256
(Belk Stores Services)
904-296-2014 / Fax: 904-296-7590
Website: www.belk.com
Retail Locations: AL, AZ, TX, MS, GA, FL, SC, NC, VA, MD, WV, KY, TN
THOMAS M. BELK, JR. (President-Store Divisions & Real Estate Contact)
JIM MADDEN (President-Southern Div.)
JOAN FLUKE (D.M.M.-Men's Better, Moderate, Young Men's)
DONNA LOMBARDO-Men's Better, Moderate, Young Men's
PHILIP MABE (D.M.M. -Men's Furnishings & Accessories)
ANDY ANDERSON-Men's Accessories, Furnishings
GARY FULKERSON-Men's Ties, Dress Shirts
GEORGE METTRICK (D.M.M.-Children's)
JIM GAMEZ-Boys' 4 to 20
DILL GRABART (D.M.M.-Footwear)
JANET WALSH-Men's Footwear

BROTHERS (MW-2)
5238 Norwood Ave., #1 (bud-p)
Jacksonville, FL 32208
904-768-6004 / Fax: 904-766-9111
Sales: $500,000-$1 Million
VICTOR AMKI (Owner) & Buys Men's Sportswear, Urban Contemporary, Furnishings, Accessories, 8 to 20 Boys' Suits, Slacks, Men's & Boys' Footwear, Store Displays, Fixtures, Supplies

IMAGE FASHIONS, INC. (CLO)
9501 Arlington Expwy., #505
Jacksonville, FL 32225
904-855-0581 / Fax: 904-885-0582
JAY OLIN-Men's & Boys' Pants, Shirts, Accessories

JIM TATUM'S FASHION SHOWROOM (MW)
P.O. Box 37559 (bud)
5318 Normandy Blvd.
Jacksonville, FL 32236
904-786-8770 / Fax: 904-783-9491
Sales: $1 Million-$10 Million
Website: www.jimtatums.com
TIM TATUM (President & G.M.M.) & Buys Men's Wear

FLORIDA - Jacksonville

KARL'S (MW-2)
3579 St. Johns Ave. (b-h)
Jacksonville, FL 32205
904-389-1900 / Fax: 904-387-3614
Sales: $1 Million-$10 Million
JAY JABOUR (Owner) & Buys Upscale Men's Sportswear, Furnishings, Accessories

ON STAGE (CLO)
(FASHION KING, INC.)
5156 Norwood Ave., #1 (bud)
Jacksonville, FL 32208
904-768-4435 / Fax: 904-768-4436
JOE MENAGED (Owner) & Buys Men's Overcoats, Suits, Tailored Jackets, Tailored Slacks, Sweaters, Sport Shirts, Outer Jackets Leather Apparel, Casual Slacks, Active Apparel, Furnishings, Accessories, Headwear, Young Men's & Boys' Wear, Men's, Young Men's & Boys' Footwear, Store Displays, Fixtures, Supplies
DAVID MEYER-Men's Overcoats, Suits, Tailored Jackets, Tailored Slacks, Sweaters, Sport Shirts, Outer Jackets, Leather Apparel, Casual Slacks, Active Apparel, Furnishings, Accessories, Headwear, Young Men's & Boys' Wear, Men's, Young Men's & Boys' Footwear, Store Displays, Fixtures, Supplies

PIER 17 MARINA, INC. (MW)
4619 Roosevelt Blvd. (m-b)
Jacksonville, FL 32210
904-387-4669 / Fax: 904-389-1161
GRACE ROGERS (Co-Owner)
CYNTHIA SEGRAVES (Co-Owner) & Buys Men's Sportswear, Shorts, Shirts, Casual Shoes, Store Displays, Fixtures, Supplies

ROSENBLUM'S (CLO)
5500 San Jose Blvd. (m-b)
Jacksonville, FL 32207
904-733-8633 / Fax: 904-739-2437
Sales: $1 Million-$10 Million
ROBERT ROSENBLUM (President & G.M.M.)
RICHARD M. ROSENBLUM (V.P.) & Buys Men's Sportswear, Formalwear, Furnishings, Accessories, Leather Apparel, Men's Footwear, Store Displays, Fixtures, Supplies

SHEL-MAR, INC. (FW-4)
(ICEMAN BIG)
(ICE MAN, INC.)
(ICEMAN KICKS)
(MR. KICKS)
5100 Norwood Ave. (m-b)
Jacksonville, FL 32208
904-765-3814 / Fax: 904-765-6567
Sales: $1 Million-$10 Million
SHELDON TEITELBAUM (President) & Buys Boys' Apparel, Men's & Boys' Footwear, Leather Goods, Licensed Apparel, Men's Apparel, Men's Accessories, Men's Hosiery
ANITA TEITELBAUM (V.P.) & Buys Boys' Apparel, Men's & Boys' Footwear, Leather Goods, Licensed Apparel, Men's Apparel, Men's Accessories, Men's Hosiery

SOUL TRAIN STOP FASHIONS (MW-2)
5000 Norwood Ave., #4 (m)
Jacksonville, FL 32208
904-768-9446 / Fax: 904-768-2002
CHARLES OUM (Owner)
JAY OUM-Men's Sportswear, 8 to 20 Boys' Men's & Boys' Footwear

SPORTS MANIA (SP-2 & OL)
11112 San Jose Blvd., #21
Jacksonville, FL 32257
904-886-2442 / Fax: 904-886-4710
Sales: $500,001-$1 Million
Website: www.sports-mania.com
JOHN SMITH (President)
TERRY TRINIDAD (Mgr.) & Buys Men's, Young Men's & Boys' Activewear, Athletic Footwear, Licensed Apparel

STEIN MART (DEPT)
3560 University Blvd. West
Jacksonville, FL 32217
904-731-8544
JAY STEIN (Owner) & Buys Men's & Boys' Apparel, Accessories, Furnishings, Footwear

SUIT TOWN (MW)
769 University Blvd. North (p)
Jacksonville, FL 32211
904-743-6767 / Fax: 904-743-2070
WILLIAM T. McQUAIG (President) & Buys Men's Accessories, Casual Slacks, Dress Shirts, Sport Shirts, Sweaters, Suits, Sportswear

VENUS SWIMWEAR, INC. (MO)
11711 Marco Beach Dr.
Jacksonville, FL 32224
904-647-4377 / Fax: 904-641-0977
Sales: $501,000-$1 Million
GERALD FOSTER (Owner) & Buys Swimwear, Sportswear
JODI RANDOLPH (V.P.-Design)

CD CONNECTION (CLO)
1908 3rd St. South
Jacksonville Beach, FL 92250
904-246-0550 / Fax: 904-246-0538
TERRY DIXON (Owner) & Buys Hats, T-shirts, Imprinted Sportswear

CUSTOM CLOTHIERS, INC. (CLO)
2425 S. 3rd St. (b)
Jacksonville Beach, FL 32250
904-241-8141 / Fax: 904-241-8142
Sales: $1 Million-$10 Million
L. DALE SPRADLIN (President) & Buys Men's Suits, Tailored Jackets, Raincoats, Sportswear, Dress Shirts, Underwear, Hosiery, Accessories, Resort Wear, Small Leather Goods, High End Custom Made Clothing

AMERICA'S 1 BIG & TALL (MW)
3249 NW Federal Hwy. (m)
Jensen Beach, FL 34957
772-692-4542 / Fax: 772-692-4542
RANDY SEGAL (Owner & President) & Buys Men's Big & Tall Clothing, Sportswear, Furnishings

GRAND SLAM (CLO)
261 N. A1A
Jupiter, FL 33477
561-746-0526 / Fax: 561-746-0969
RICHARD BLACK (Owner) & Buys Outdoor Gear & Apparel

JUPITER OUTDOOR CENTER, INC. (CLO)
18095 A1A
Jupiter, FL 33477
561-747-9666 / Fax: 561-747-3469
Website: www.jupiteroutdoorcenter.com
RICHARD CLEGG-Dive Apparel & Accessories, Headwear, Men's Apparel, Outdoor Gear & Accessories, Resortwear

MOONDOG CREATIONS (CLO)
815 W. Indiantown Rd.
Jupiter, FL 33458
561-744-4848 / Fax: 561-745-8860
Sales: $100,001-$500,000
MIKE GROSS (President & Owner)
ARLEEN TAITZ-Activewear, T-shirts, Golf Apparel

BURNS LTD. (MW)
(KEN-BERN, INC.)
624 Crandon Blvd. (b)
Key Biscayne, FL 33149
305-361-2568 / Fax: 305-361-9996
MICHAEL RUBIN (Owner) & Buys Men's Wear

FLORIDA - Key Biscayne

SCOTTS (CLO)
650 Crandon Blvd.
Key Biscayne, FL 33149
305-361-2300 / Fax: 305-361-5411
Sales: $100,001-$500,000
OLIVIA FLOWERS (Co-Owner) & Buys Swimwear, Sandals, Sunglasses
LINDA WHITE (Co-Owner) & Buys Swimwear, Sandals, Sunglasses

SONESTA SWIM & SPORTSWEAR (CLO)
Sonesta Beach Resort
350 Ocean Dr.
Key Biscayne, FL 33149
305-361-2021 / Fax: 305-361-3096
Website: www.sonesta.com
BEVY YUZ (President)
FELIX MADERA-Activewear, Swimwear

RANDY'S (CLO)
99609 Overseas Hwy.
Key Largo, FL 33037
305-459-9229 / Fax: 305-453-9229
RANDY ALTHOUSE (Owner) & Buys Resortwear, Beachwear, Activewear, T-Shirts, Shorts, Headwear, Sandals, Beach Footwear

SUNSATIONAL, INC. (SP)
103400 Overseas Hwy.
Key Largo, FL 33037
305-451-2002 / Fax: 305-451-2002
Sales: $100,001-$500,000
MARTHA WINFIELD (President) & Buys Men's Apparel, Skiwear, Outdoor Apparel, Skatewear

ASSORTMENT (MW)
P.O. Box 6404 (b)
514 Fleming St.
Key West, FL 33041
305-294-4066 / Fax: 305-294-4068
CLAUDE REANS (Co-Owner) & Buys Sportswear, Casual Slacks, Sport Shirts, Elegant Casual, Sport Coats
JOE CARR (Co-Owner) & Buys Sportswear, Casual Slacks, Sport Shirts, Elegant Casual, Sport Coats

BEACH CLUB USA (SP)
210 Duval St.
Key West, FL 33040
305-292-7975 / Fax: 305-292-7975
ANGELA SAIDA (Owner) & Buys Beachwear, Resortwear, Swimwear, Headwear, Sandals, Beach Footwear

FAST BUCK FREDDIE'S, INC. (DEPT)
500 Duval St. (p-m-b-h)
Key West, FL 33040
305-294-2007 / Fax: 305-295-2684
Website: www.fastbuckfreddies.com
TONY FALCONE (Owner) & Buys Men's Suits, Furnishings, Sweaters, Sport Shirts, Outer Jackets, Leather Apparel, Casual Slacks, Active Apparel, Accessories, Footwear, Swimwear
BARRY SIEGEL-Men's Suits, Furnishings, Sweaters, Sport Shirts, Outer Jackets, Leather Apparel, Casual Slacks, Active Apparel, Accessories, Footwear, Swimwear

ISLAND ANGLER (CLO)
5110 US Hwy. 1
Key West, FL 33040
800-295-2866 / Fax: 305-295-2866
Website: www.almostthere.net
MARIANNE McGUFFEY-Boys' Apparel, Sunglasses, Accessories, Footwear, Hats, Outdoor Gear & Apparel, Resortwear, T-shirts, Imprinted Sportswear, Men's Apparel, Tropical Clothing, Sportswear, Footwear
ROC McGUFFEY-Boys' Apparel, Sunglasses, Accessories, Footwear, Hats, Outdoor Gear & Apparel, Resortwear, T-shirts, Imprinted Sportswear, Men's Apparel, Tropical Clothing, Sportswear, Footwear

KEY WEST HAND PRINT FABRICS (CLO)
201 Simonton St.
Key West, FL 33040
305-292-8951 / Fax: 305-292-8965
Website: www.keywestfashion.com
DEBBIE LEE (Mgr.) & Buys Accessories, Men's Apparel

MACHOTI RESORT WEAR (CLO)
721 Duval St.
Key West, FL 33040
305-294-9950
ALEXANDRA ROBINSON (Owner) & Buys Men's, Young Men's & Boys' T-shirts, Tank Tops, Shorts, Swimwear

SOUTH BEACH SOUTHERN SWIMWEAR (CLO-3)
507 South St., #B
Key West, FL 33040
305-295-0015 / Fax: 305-294-4801
Adriana (Owner) & Buys Beachwear, Resortwear, Activewear, Surf & Swimwear, Headwear, Athletic Shoes, Sandals, Beach Footwear

SOUTHERN MOST SPORTSWEAR (CLO)
208 Duval St.
Key West, FL 33040
305-294-9222 / Fax: 305-294-7861
Sales: $500 Million-$1 Billion
JOSEPH COHEN (Owner & G.M.M.) & Buys Swimwear, Sandals

A & K INVESTMENTS (CLO-2)
4137 W. Vine St.
Kissimmee, FL 34741
407-238-1890 / Fax: 407-846-1355
SALLISHA EBRAHIM-Men's Apparel, Men's Swimwear, Surfwear, Resortwear, T-shirts, Imprinted Sportswear, Boys' Apparel, Boys' Swimwear, Footwear, Hats

ALI'S MARKETING MANAGEMENT (CLO)
4301 W. Vine St., #A113
Kissimmee, FL 34746
407-396-0076
QUDRAT ULLAH ALI-Men's Beach Apparel, T-shirts, Fashion Accessories

GOOLD'S DEPARTMENT STORE, INC. (DEPT)
26 Broadway (p-m-b)
Kissimmee, FL 34741
407-847-4791 / Fax: 407-847-4350
Sales: $500,000-$1 Million
HARRY LOWENSTEIN (President) & Buys Men's Suits, Tailored Jackets, Tailored Slacks, Urban Contemporary, Store Displays, Fixtures, Supplies
DAVID H. LOWENSTEIN (G.M.M.) & Buys Men's Western Sport Shirts, Outer Jackets, Leather Apparel, Casual Slacks, Dress Shirts, Ties, Hosiery, Headwear, Belts, Small Leather Goods, Fragrances, 8 to 20 Boys' Sportswear, Men's & Boys' Boots

MOD COWBOY (CLO)
2530 E. Irlow Bronson Hwy. (m)
Kissimmee, FL 34744
407-847-5937 / Fax: 407-933-4725
VERNON HENDERSON (Owner) & Buys Men's Western Sportcoats, Sport Shirts, Outer Jackets, Casual Slacks, Dress Shirts, Men's Jeans, Headwear, Small Leather Goods, Young Men's Jeans, Shirts, Belts, Boys' Jeans, Shirts, Belts, Store Displays, Fixtures, Supplies

RADISSON RESORT PARKWAY (CLO)
2900 Parkway Blvd.
Kissimmee, FL 34747
407-396-7000 / Fax: 407-396-6792
Website: www.radissonresortparkway.com
BOB CARDONA-Boys' Apparel, Boys' Swimwear, Accessories, Hats, Men's Apparel, Men's Surf & Swimwear, Resortwear, T-shirts, Imprinted Sportswear

FLORIDA - Kissimmee

SHORE'S MENSWEAR (MW)

201 Broadway (m)
Kissimmee, FL 34741
407-847-4727 / Fax: 467-847-3037
Sales: $100,001-$500,000

HELEN SHORE (Owner) (@ 407-846-6922) & Buys Men's Suits, Tailored Jackets, Tailored Slacks, Raincoats, Sweaters, Sport Shirts, Outer Jackets, Leather Apparel, Casual Slacks, Active Apparel, Dress Shirts, Ties, Robes, Underwear, Hosiery, Gloves, Headwear, Belts, Jewelry, Small Leather Goods, Fragrances, Men's Footwear, Young Men's Wear, Store Displays, Fixtures, Supplies

GEORGE CROSS (Mgr.) & Buys Men's Suits, Tailored Jackets, Tailored Slacks, Raincoats, Sweaters, Sport Shirts, Outer Jackets, Leather Apparel, Casual Slacks, Active Apparel, Dress Shirts, Ties, Robes, Underwear, Hosiery, Gloves, Headwear, Belts, Jewelry, Small Leather Goods, Fragrances, Men's Footwear, Young Men's Wear, Store Displays, Fixtures, Supplies

TUNA ENTERPRISES (CLO)

4301 W. Vine St.
Kissimmee, FL 34746
407-397-0607 / Fax: 407-935-1414

SHAHJAHAN ALI-Men's Apparel, Fashion Accessories, Men's Swimwear

SALAUDDIN CHAWDHURY-Men's Apparel, Fashion Accessories, Men's Swimwear

WALT DISNEY WORLD CO., INC. (CLO-346 & OL & MO)

P.O. Box 10000
Lake Buena Vista, FL 32830
407-397-6000 / Fax: 407-397-6050
Website: www.store.disney.go.com
Retail Locations: CA, FL, IL, IN, KS, KY, LA, MA, ME, MI, MN, MO, OH, TX, UT, VT, VA

JOAN RYAN (Sr. V.P.) & Buys Men's Sportswear, Leather Apparel, Furnishings, Accessories, Headwear, Young Men's Wear (Non-Character Mdse.)

FRANK HUFF-Men's ESPN Active Apparel

SILVIE CRUMBAUGH-Men's Character Sportswear & Headwear

JENNIFER MOCIERNO-Men's Character Furnishings & Accessories

DONALD FERRO-Men's Imprintable T-shirts

MARLOU SY HOLLINS-8 to 20 Boys' Wear, Character Boys' Accessories

NATURE QUEST (CLO)

P.O. Box 2999
Lake City, FL 32056
904-755-5252 / Fax: 904-758-5821
Website: www.naturequestusa.com

JIM FREE-Dive Apparel & Accessories, Sunglasses, Hats, Men's Apparel, Resortwear, T-shirts, Imprinted Sportswear, Men's Swimwear

B-C CORRAL, INC. (WW)

4509 Hwy. 92 East (p-m)
Lakeland, FL 33801
863-666-2200 / Fax: 863-666-9573

DAVID HUDDLESTON (Owner) & Buys Men's & Boys' Western Wear, Men's & Boys' Boots

CLEGHORN'S, INC. (MW)

2125 S. Florida Ave. (m-b)
Lakeland, FL 33803
863-687-3656 / Fax: 863-680-2666

TOM LANCI (Owner) & Buys Men's Suits, Sweaters, Sport Shirts, Outer Jackets, Leather Apparel, Casual Slacks, Urban Contemporary, Active Apparel, Furnishings, Accessories, Men's Footwear, Young Men's Wear, Store Displays, Fixtures, Supplies

NATHAN'S MEN'S STORE (MW & OL)

(NEW FASHION SHOP, INC.)
221 E. Main St. (m-b)
Lakeland, FL 33801
863-682-2811 / Fax: 863-683-7013
Sales: $1 Million-$10 Million

HARRIS ESTROFF (President) & Buys Headwear, Accessories, Formalwear, Scout Uniforms

DEWEY SLACK (Mgr.) & Buys Regular Men's Wear, Big & Tall Men's Wear, Suits, Shoes, Casual Wear, Sportswear

WILLIAMS & WILLIAMS, INC. (CLO)

1145 E. Main St. (bud-p-m-b)
Lakeland, FL 33801
863-683-5487 / Fax: 863-683-6420

TOM WILLIAMS (President) & Buys Sportswear

ATTITUDES FASHION FOR ACTION, INC. (CLO)

13002 Seminole Blvd.
Largo, FL 33778
727-526-0447 / Fax: 727-587-9906

DONNA HAMBOETON (Owner) & Buys Activewear, Resortwear

LARRY'S BIG & TALL MENSWEAR, INC. (MW-2)

3200 E. Bay Dr. (m-b)
Largo, FL 33771
727-531-8449 / Fax: 727-538-0573
Sales: $1 Million-$10 Million

BILL GOODALL (Owner) & Buys Big & Tall Men's Suits, Sportcoats, Sweaters, Sport Shirts, Outer Jackets, Leather Apparel, Casual Slacks, Active Apparel, Furnishings, Store Displays, Fixtures, Supplies

SOUTHERN APPAREL CORP. (CLO)

(SAC DISTRIBUTORS)
12420 73rd Ct.
Largo, FL 33773
727-536-8672 / Fax: 727-539-0752
Website: www.sacplus.com

ROBERT PALMIERO (Owner) & Buys Men's Wear, Sportswear, Golf Apparel, T-shirts

CABANA SHOP (SP)

4733 N. Ocean Dr.
Lauderdale Sea, FL 33308
954-941-7235

WILLIAM MICHAELSON (Owner) & Buys Beachwear, Resortwear, Activewear, Surf & Swimwear, Wet Suits, Athletic Shoes, Sandals

TEMPO, INC. (MW)

(HIGH SCORE, INC.)
1323 State Rd. 7 (p-m)
Lauderhill, FL 33313
954-587-8525 / Fax: 954-864-0652
Sales: $500,000-$1 Million

ALBERT LUSKY (Co-Owner) & Buys Men's Sweaters, Sport Shirts, Casual Slacks, Active Apparel, Dress Suits, Shirts, Shoes, Furnishings

GISELA LUSKY (Co-Owner) & Buys Men's Sweaters, Sport Shirts, Casual Slacks, Active Apparel, Dress Suits, Shirts, Shoes, Furnishings

THE MAIN EVENT (SP-2)

700 W. Main St. (b)
Leesburg, FL 34748
352-787-3242 / Fax: 352-728-2500

JoANN BOSWELL (Owner) & Buys Men's Formal Wear, Accessories, Store Displays, Fixtures, Supplies

LE TENNIQUE, INC. (CLO)

1620 Gulf of Mexico Dr.
Longboat Key, FL 34228
941-383-7576 / Fax: 941-387-0250
Sales: $501,000-$1 Million
Website: www.colonybeach.com

MURG KLAUBER (Owner) & Buys Men's Apparel

KATIE MOULTON (President) & Buys Activewear, Swimwear, Sunglasses, Athletic Footwear

DEBBIE DENSMORE (Gen. Mgr.) & Buys Activewear, Swimwear, Sunglasses, Athletic Footwear

SEA STABLE (CLO-6)

3170 Gulf Of Mexico Dr. (m-b)
Longboat Key, FL 34228
941-383-2288 / Fax: 941-383-4396

JOE FALLS (Owner) & Buys Men's Sportswear, Swimwear, Footwear

MADCAT GRAPHICS (CLO)
701 Industrial Rd., #4
Longwood, FL 32750
407-695-4600 / Fax: 407-695-1743
Website: www.mad-cat.com
ROBERT PETERSON-T-shirts, Imprinted Sportswear

FLAMINGOS (CLO)
174 Johns Pass Boardwalk
Madeira, FL 33708
727-392-7423
PAT CONGINO (Co-Owner) & Buys Beachwear, Resortwear, Beach Shoes, Headwear
CRICKET FINGER (Co-Owner) & Buys Beachwear, Resortwear, Beach Shoes, Headwear

CASUAL MENSWEAR, INC. (MW)
15130 Municipal Dr. (m)
Madeira Beach, FL 33708
727-392-0196
JAMES QUAGLIANA (Owner) & Buys Men's Sportswear, Men's Sandals, Store Displays, Fixtures, Supplies

COOL STYLE, INC. (CLO)
12921 Village Blvd.
Madeira Beach, FL 33708
727-397-2525 / Fax: 727-319-6203
MALLI EINY-Boys' Apparel, Sunglasses, Accessories, Hats, Men's Apparel, Men's Surf & Swimwear, Resortwear, T-shirts, Imprinted Sportswear
MOTI EINY-Boys' Apparel, Sunglasses, Accessories, Hats, Men's Apparel, Men's Surf & Swimwear, Resortwear, T-shirts, Imprinted Sportswear
SHOSHI EINY-Boys' Apparel, Sunglasses, Accessories, Hats, Men's Apparel, Men's Surf & Swimwear, Resortwear, T-shirts, Imprinted Sportswear

SEACRETS (SP)
15235 Gulf Blvd.
Madeira Beach, FL 33708
727-399-1976
SHELLEY McDUFFIE-Boys' Apparel & Swimwear, Sunglasses, Accessories, Hats, Footwear, Men's Apparel, Men's Surf & Swimwear

KRAMER'S (CLO)
204 S. Range St. (m)
Madison, FL 32340
850-973-2580
MILDRED HAUSMAN (Partner) & Buys Young Men's Wear, Footwear, Men's Wear
NORMAN GOLIBESKY (G.M.M.) & Buys Young Men's Wear, Footwear, Men's Wear

T.J. BEGGS & CO. (MW)
106 S. Range Rd. (m-b)
Madison, FL 32340
850-973-6163
JIM STANLEY-Men's Overcoats, Suits, Raincoats, Sweaters, Sport Shirts, Outer Jackets, Casual Slacks, Active Apparel, Dress Shirts, Ties, Robes, Footwear, Underwear, Hosiery, Gloves, Headwear, Belts, Jewelry, Small Leather Goods, Fragrances, Big & Tall Men's Wear, Store Displays, Fixtures, Supplies

BE-XTREME, INC. (CLO)
900 S. Orlando Ave.
Maitland, FL 32751
407-628-2453 / Fax: 407-975-9176
GINA GARCIA-Activewear, Athletic Footwear

BAYSHORE CLOTHING (CLO)
Quay Village (m)
MM #54
Marathon, FL 33050
305-743-8430 / Fax: 305-743-0619
Sales: $100,001-$500,000
JOAN ANDERSON (Owner) & Buys Boys' Apparel, Boys' Footwear, Men's Apparel

KEY BANA RESORT APPAREL (CLO)
Key Colony Beach Causeway
P.O. Box 123
Marathon, FL 33051
305-289-1161 / Fax: 305-289-0151
EVELYN LAY (President & Owner) & Buys Men's Resort Wear

KAY'S ON THE BEACH (SP-4)
1089 Bald Eagle Dr.
Marco Island, FL 34145
239-394-1033
JEANE HILT (Owner) & Buys Men's Activewear, Resortwear, Sunglasses, Swimwear

McFARLANDS' OF MARCO, INC. (MW)
111 S. Barfield Dr. (b)
Marco Island, FL 34145
941-394-6464 / Fax: 941-642-7117
CHARLES McFARLAND (Co-Owner) & Buys Men's Sweaters, Sport Shirts, Outer Jackets, Casual Slacks, Active Apparel, Furnishings, Store Displays, Fixtures, Supplies
SHELLY McFARLAND (Co-Owner) & Buys Men's Sweaters, Sport Shirts, Outer Jackets, Casual Slacks, Active Apparel, Furnishings, Store Displays, Fixtures, Supplies

CIRCLE D WESTERN SHOP (WW)
3121 Drive Dr. (m)
Marianna, FL 32446
850-352-3300 / Fax: 850-352-4761
Sales: $500,001-$1 Million
MATT DRYDEN (Mgr.) & Buys Western Clothing, Boots, Hats, Jeans, Shirts, Leather Goods

DON ALANS' (MW-2)
300 Mary Esther Blvd., #53 (b)
Mary Esther, FL 32569
850-243-3686 / Fax: 850-664-5180
Website: www.donalans.com
DON ALANS (Owner) & Buys Men's Wear, Young Men's Wear, Accessories, Footwear

TWO BLONDES (CLO)
300 Mary Esther Blvd.
Mary Esther, FL 32569
850-301-9229 / Fax: 850-654-1432
Website: www.twoblondesonline.com
YVETTE MANCINI-Fashion Accessories, Footwear, Hats, Apparel, Private Label, T-shirts, Imprinted Sportswear, Urban Sportswear
MICHELE KULICH-Fashion Accessories, Footwear, Hats, Apparel, Private Label, T-shirts, Imprinted Sportswear, Urban Sportswear

BARONI'S TALL & BIG (MW-2)
1755 W. New Haven Ave. (m)
Melbourne, FL 32904
321-724-8160
NANCY SHARP (Owner) & Buys Big & Tall Men's Sportswear, Furnishings, Accessories, Store Displays, Fixtures, Supplies

PAUL MANN SALES (CLO)
P.O. Box 1257
Melbourne, FL 32902
321-727-0099
PAUL MANN-Apparel & Swimwear

ADVENTURE CYCLES, INC. (CLO-2)
625 N. Courtenay Pkwy. (m-b)
Merritt Island, FL 32953
321-452-3550 / Fax: 321-453-2253
Sales: $500,001-$1 Million
DAVID HORNER (President) & Buys Men's Footwear, Men's Apparel, Men's Casualwear, Men's Outerwear, Men's Sportswear, Men's Swimwear
PETE JONES (Store Mgr.) & Buys Men's Footwear, Men's Apparel, Men's Casualwear, Men's Outerwear, Men's Sportswear, Men's Swimwear
CAROL HORNER (Store Mgr.) & Buys Men's Footwear, Men's Apparel, Men's Casualwear, Men's Outerwear, Men's Sportswear, Men's Swimwear

GOLD-ING (CLO)
(ELECTRIC BEACH)
262 E. Merritt Island Causeway, #4
Merritt Island, FL 32952
321-459-1230
CARRIE ZAVODNY-Men's Surf & Swimwear
CYNTHIA ORTON-Men's Surf & Swimwear

FLORIDA - Merritt Island

SID'S MEN'S FASHIONS (MW-2)
(MALE ATTRACTION)
Merritt Square Mall (m-b)
777 E. Merritt Island Causeway
Merritt Island, FL 32952
321-453-6731 / Fax: 321-453-6731
Sales: $1 Million-$10 Million
SIDNEY ABRAHAM (Owner & President) & Buys Men's Overcoats, Suits, Tailored Jackets, Tailored Slacks, Raincoats, Sweaters, Sport Shirts, Outer Jackets, Leather Apparel, Casual Slacks, Active Apparel, Dress Shirts, Ties, Robes, Underwear, Hosiery, Belts, Footwear, Jewelry, Small Leather Goods, Leather Jackets, Fragrances, Young Men's & Boys' Accessories, Store Displays, Fixtures, Supplies

AA UNIFORM CO., INC. (CLO-2)
8820 SW 131st St. (m)
Miami, FL 33176
305-254-0000 / Fax: 305-254-0303
BARBARA BLANCK (President)
CYNTHIA BLANCK (V.P.) & Buys Men's Uniforms, Work Clothes, Casual Slacks, Knit Sport Shirts, Boys' School Uniforms, Boys' School Shoes, Store Displays, Fixtures, Supplies

ACTON UNIFORM CO. - FLORIDA (CLO)
1607 NE 2nd Ave.
Miami, FL 33132
305-358-8730 / Fax: 305-358-4484
HUGH MOSS (President) & Buys Men's Cruise Wear, Footwear, Work Uniforms

ARTHUR SNYDER (SP)
16851 W. Dixie Hwy.
Miami, FL 33160
305-948-2947 / Fax: 305-919-8007
Sales: $100,001-$500,000
ALBERT MORA-Racquetball Apparel

ASIS MENSWEAR (MW)
7795 W. Flagler St. (m)
Miami, FL 33010
305-264-2224 / Fax: 305-262-6781
FIDEL LOPEZ (Owner) & Buys Men's Sportswear, Furnishings, Accessories, Footwear

ATHLETIC X PRESS (SP)
(FOOTLOCKER)
1455 NW 107th Ave.
Miami, FL 33172
305-594-4616 / Fax: 305-594-4616
Sales: $100,001-$500,000
Website: www.footlocker.com
MIKE CALVO-Licensed Apparel, Athletic Footwear, Outdoor Footwear, Apparel

AUSTIN BURKE OF FLORIDA (MW)
2601 NW 6th Ave. (m-b)
Miami, FL 33127
305-576-2714 / Fax: 305-576-0878
Sales: $1 Million-$10 Million
BARRY BURKE (President) & Buys Men's Sweaters, Sport Shirts, Outer Jackets, Suits, Leather Apparel, Casual Slacks, Active Apparel, Furnishings, Headwear, Accessories, Store Displays, Fixtures, Supplies
KEN SAGER (V.P.) & Buys Men's Sweaters, Sport Shirts, Outer Jackets, Suits, Leather Apparel, Casual Slacks, Active Apparel, Furnishings, Headwear, Accessories, Store Displays, Fixtures, Supplies

B-SCREENED, INC. (CLO)
10834 NW 27th St. (bud)
Miami, FL 33172
305-592-7505 / Fax: 305-471-0462
Website: www.b-screened.com
LENNY BOOTH (Owner) & Buys Young Men's Wear, Men's Wear, Athletic Apparel, T-shirts

BEACH MOB (FW)
1127 Washington Ave. (bud-p)
Miami, FL 33139
305-532-5494 / Fax: 305-532-5495
Sales: $100,001-$500,000
MOISES COHEN (Owner) & Buys Men's & Young Men's Apparel, Footwear
PABLO HERMAN (Mgr.)

BEST BRANDS (CLO-10)
(SHOE EXPERT)
269 Geraida Ave., #302
Miami, FL 33134
305-567-2031 / Fax: 305-567-2033
ANDRE BURGUERA (Owner) & Buys Beachwear, Sportswear, Headwear, Sandals
MARIEZ MUNIZ-Swimwear

BOJANGLES MEN'S SHOP (MW)
Northside Shopping Center (m)
Miami, FL 33147
305-836-3606
Sales: $100,001-$500,000
BERTHA SPITZ (President & Owner) & Buys Men's Apparel, Young Men's Apparel, Urban Contemporary, Accessories

BURDINES (DEPT-55 & OL)
(FEDERATED DEPT. STORES, INC.)
22 E. Flagler St. (p-m-b)
Miami, FL 33131
(Federated Merchandising Group)
305-577-2000 / Fax: 305-577-2598
Sales: $1.4 Billion
Website: www.burdines.com
Retail Locations: FL
TIM ADAMS (Chmn. & C.E.O.)
NIRMAL "TRIP" TRIPATHY (President & C.O.O.)
DAVID KINTZ (V.P.-Store Dev. & Property Mgmt.)
DON BRENNAN (Sr. V.P.-Men's, Boys' & Children's Wear)
DARIN FINKELSTEIN (Mdse. V.P.-Men's Sportswear & Collections)
KELLIE HENLEY (G.M.M.)
CLAUDIA ZOROVICH (Mdse. V.P. - Men's & Boys' Wear) & Buys Contemporary, Young Men's 8-20
CAROLINA SALCEDO-Boys' Tommy Hilfiger, Polo, Nautica, Contemporary Collections, Streetwear, Dress Up, Furnishings
YASMIN LEON-Boys' Tommy Hilfiger, Polo, Nautica, Contemporary Collections, Streetwear, Dress Up, Furnishings
SARAH DAVIS-Boys' 8 to 20 Tops, 8 to 20 Bottoms, Activewear, Outerwear, Trend Bottoms, Trend Tops, Club, American Rag
REBECCA EVANS-Boys' 8 to 20 Tops, 8 to 20 Bottoms, Activewear, Outerwear, Trend Bottoms, Trend Tops, Club, American Rag
JAVIER SANCHEZ-Young Men's Streetwear, Ecko, Sean Jean, Quiksilver, Rocawear, Shady, Activewear
RAQUEL NOSWORTHY-Young Men's Streetwear, Ecko, Sean Jean, Quiksilver, Rocawear, Shady, Activewear
DEANNA TAYLOR-Men's Contemporary Collections, DKNY, Guess, Tommy Denim, Polo Jeans, Nautica Jeans, Diesel, Levi Bottoms, Calvin Klein Jeans, Premium Denim
PATTY RODRIGUEZ-Men's Contemporary Collections, DKNY, Guess, Tommy Denim, Polo Jeans, Nautica Jeans, Diesel, Levi Bottoms, Calvin Klein Jeans, Premium Denim
CYL BUSKO-Men's Knitwear, Wovens, Tasso Elba, Chaps, Golf, Nautica
CHRISTINA CIANI-Men's Knitwear, Wovens, Tasso Elba, Chaps, Golf, Nautica
DONNA LOMBARDO-Men's Activewear, Walkshorts, Swimwear, Nike, Outerwear, Sweaters
DION CAVATAIO-Men's Activewear, Walkshorts, Swimwear, Nike, Outerwear, Sweaters
JOHN KALTYNSKI-Men's Collections, Hugo Boss, INC, Perry Ellis, DKNY, Kenneth Cole
JESSICA ST. FRANCIS-Men's Collections, Hugo Boss, INC, Perry Ellis, DKNY, Kenneth Cole

(BURDINES Cont. on next page)

FLORIDA - Miami

(BURDINES Cont.)

SORAYA CARRASCO-Men's Collections, Polo, Claiborne, LaCoste, Tommy Hilfiger, Tommy Bahama, Quiksilver Edition

NICKIE JONES-Men's Collections, Polo, Claiborne, LaCoste, Tommy Hilfiger, Tommy Bahama, Quiksilver Edition

VERONICA ROBERSON-Men's Moderate Dress Shirts, Status Dress Shirts, Designer Dress Shirts

JULIE ROISMAN-Men's Small Leather Goods, Belts, Underwear, Loungewear, Hoisery

JENNIFER BARNES-Men's Suits, Sportcoats, Blazers, Rainwear, Suit Separates, Neckwear

LONNIE POLSYN-Men's Casual Pants, Dress Casual Pants, Better Casual Pants, Dress Slacks

PHILLIP HADJIYEROU-Men's Casual Pants, Dress Casual Pants, Better Casual Pants, Dress Slacks

MARY ALICE HUGHES (Creative Dir.) & Buys Store Displays, Fixtures & Supplies

CAVALIER MENSWEAR, INC. (MW-2)

2 W. Flagler St. (p-m-b)
Miami, FL 33130
305-379-8784
Sales: $1 Million-$10 Million

ISAAC RAIJMAN (President) & Buys Men's Sportswear, Furnishings, Accessories, Store Displays, Fixtures, Supplies

COMGLEN FASHION & ALTERATIONS (MW)

11750 NW 7th Ave. (bud-p)
Miami, FL 33168
305-688-8300 / Fax: 305-688-8320

COMPTON CANTERBURY (Owner) & Buys Men's Big & Tall, Men's Wear, Suits, Tailored Jackets, Tailored Slacks, Sportswear, Dress Shirts, Accessories, Furnishings, and Ties

COTTON IMAGES (CLO)

12930 SW 132nd Ct.
Miami, FL 33186
305-251-2560 / Fax: 305-969-9966
Website: www.cottonimages.com

SCOTT HERTZBACH-T-shirts, Imprinted Sportswear

SANDI HERTZBACH-T-shirts, Imprinted Sportswear

COWBOY CENTER (CLO & OL & MO)

3221 NW 79th St.
Miami, FL 33147
305-691-6605 / Fax: 305-691-4122
Website: www.cowboycenter.com

KILOS CAMPOS (Owner & G.M.M.) & Buys Men's Western & English Riding Wear, Boots, Store Displays, Fixtures, Supplies

DANCE DUDS, INC. (SP)

8670 SW 137th Ave.
Miami, FL 33183
305-382-2600

TERRI ZUCKER (Owner) & Buys Dancewear, Dancing Shoes

DE HOMBRE, INC. (MW)

26 SE 1st Ave. (m)
Miami, FL 33010
305-358-0392

DORA MYLINSKI (Owner) & Buys Young Men's Wear, Men's Wear

DINORA'S SPORTSWEAR SCREENPRINTING (CLO)

1780 NW 20th St. (bud)
Miami, FL 33142
305-633-1488 / Fax: 305-560-2240
Sales: $1 Million-$10 Million

RUBEN VARELA (President) & Buys Men's T-shirts, Tank Tops, Men's Shorts, Store Displays, Fixtures, Supplies

ENEIDA FASHIONS CORP. (CLO)

11241 SW 40th St.
Miami, FL 33165
305-220-4700

JOSE PENA (Owner) & Buys Men's Suits, Tailored Jackets, Sportswear, Dress Shirts, Underwear, Hosiery, Store Displays, Fixtures, Supplies

ESQUIRE BARBER & CLOTHING SHOP (MW)

1487 NW 54th St. (bud)
Miami, FL 33142
305-693-1363 / Fax: 305-693-1363

RALPH PRESSLEY (Owner) & Buys Young Men's Wear, Men's Wear, Boys' Wear, Accessories

FASHION CLOTHIERS, INC. (MW)

2650 NW 5th Ave. (p-m-b-h)
Miami, FL 33127
305-573-5890 / Fax: 305-573-8667

SHELDON BLOOM (Owner) & Buys Men's Suits, Tailored Jackets, Tailored Slacks, Sport Coats, Sweaters, Sport Shirts, Active Apparel, Men's Footwear, Dress Shirts, Hosiery, Small Leather Goods, Store Displays, Fixtures, Supplies

FLAGLER SURPLUS, INC. (DEPT)

1798 W. Flagler St. (bud-p-m-b)
Miami, FL 33135
305-642-3436 / Fax: 419-735-1223

MARC SCHULBERG (Owner) & Buys Men's Work Clothes, Jeans, Leather Apparel, Urban Contemporary, Shirts, Underwear, Hosiery, Belts, Headwear, Young Men's & Boys' Wear, Men's Work Shoes, Men's Military Dress Shoes, Store Displays, Fixtures, Supplies

GALTRUCCO SHOP (MW)

Bal Harbour Village (b)
9700 Collins Ave.
Miami, FL 33154
305-866-0477 / Fax: 305-866-6544
Sales: $1 Million-$10 Million

JULIE RODRIGUEZ (Owner) & Buys Men's Overcoats, Suits, Tailored Jackets, Tailored Slacks, Sweaters, Sport Shirts, Leather Apparel, Urban Contemporary, Dress Shirts, Ties, Underwear, Hosiery, Belts

ALFREDO BASHARA (Gen. Mgr.) & Buys Men's Overcoats, Suits, Tailored Jackets, Tailored Slacks, Sweaters, Sport Shirts, Leather Apparel, Urban Contemporary, Dress Shirts, Ties, Underwear, Hosiery, Belts

GAMBINO OF NEW YORK (MW)

20505 S. Dixie Hwy.
Store #1735, Cutler Ridge Mall
Miami, FL 33189
305-234-0142 / Fax: 305-235-0038

SALVADOR GAMBINO (Owner) & Buys Men's Wear, Suits, Ties, Tailored Jackets, Tailored Slacks, Dress Shirts, Accessories, Furnishings

GRAND PRIX SHOPS (MW)

49 E. Flagler St. (p-m-b)
Miami, FL 33131
305-371-8220
Sales: $1 Million-$10 Million

ISAAC TUCHMAN (Owner) & Buys Men's Tailored Slacks, Leather Apparel, Sport Shirts, Casual Slacks, Dress Shirts, Underwear, Hosiery, Headwear, Belts, Small Leather Goods, Young Men's Wear, Jeans, Boys' Wear

HERITAGE HOUSE (CLO)

11355 S. Dixie Hwy. (m-b)
Miami, FL 33156
305-232-1776
Website: www.boyssuits.com

HOWARD TENDRICH (Owner) & Buys Men's Sportswear, Furnishings, Accessories, Young Men's Wear, Boys' Wear, Urban Contemporary, Men's & Boys' Footwear, Store Displays, Fixtures, Supplies

CHARLES MERRILL (Mgr.) & Buys Men's Sportswear, Furnishings, Accessories, Young Men's Wear, Boys' Wear, Urban Contemporary, Men's & Boys' Footwear, Store Displays, Fixtures, Supplies

KIDDING AROUND (KS-2)

(BRANDALS, INC.)
8888 Howard Dr. (b)
Miami, FL 33176
305-255-7879 / Fax: 305-254-3256

LESLIE SAIONTZ (President) & Buys Boys' Clothing, Sportswear, Leather Apparel, Urban Contemporary, Furnishings, Accessories, Headwear, Footwear, Store Displays, Fixtures, Supplies

FLORIDA - Miami

KIDZ (KS-4)
(MIGENE CORP.)
10201 SW 69th Ave. (h)
Miami, FL 33156
305-666-5900 / Fax: 305-666-3339
MICHAEL KRAMER (Owner) & Buys 8 to 12 Boys' Clothing, Sportswear, Leather Apparel, Furnishings, Accessories

LA EPOCA DEPARTMENT STORE, INC. (DEPT-2)
96 NE 2nd Ave. (bud-p-m-b)
Miami, FL 33132
305-374-7731 / Fax: 305-374-1689
Sales: $1 Million-$10 Million
PEPE ALONSO (Co-Owner & Mgr.) & Buys Men's, Young Men's & Boys' Wear, Store Displays, Fixtures, Supplies
ANTONIO ALONSO (Co-Owner) & Buys Men's, Young Men's & Boys' Wear, Store Displays, Fixtures, Supplies

LA IDEAL (DEPT-2)
(IDEAL CORP.)
1119 W. Flagler St. (m-b)
Miami, FL 33130
305-548-3296 / Fax: 305-545-0866
Website: www.laideal.com
BERNARDINO RODRIGUEZ (Owner) & Buys Men's Wear, 8 to 18 Boys' Wear, Men's & Boys' Footwear, Store Displays, Fixtures, Supplies

LA REVOLTOSA (CLO-2)
10771 W. Flagler St. (p-m-b)
Miami, FL 33125
305-225-7977 / Fax: 305-225-7086
FERMIN HERNANDEZ (Owner) & Buys Men's Raincoats, Sweaters, Sport Shirts, Outer Jackets, Casual Slacks, Dress Shirts, Ties, Robes, Underwear, Hosiery, Gloves, Headwear, Belts, Small Leather Goods, Fragrances, Boys' Wear, Store Displays, Fixtures, Supplies
MILAGROS PARDO-Men's Raincoats, Sweaters, Sport Shirts, Outer Jackets, Casual Slacks, Dress Shirts, Ties, Robes, Underwear, Hosiery, Gloves, Headwear, Belts, Small Leather Goods, Fragrances, Boys' Wear, Store Displays, Fixtures, Supplies

LINDA FABRICS (KS)
100 N. Miami Ave. (b)
Miami, FL 33010
305-371-6907 / Fax: 305-371-5001
CLARA SAPOZNIK (Co-Owner)
ROSA PAPIR (Mgr.) & Buys Uniforms

LOS HISPANOS OF MIAMI (CLO-2)
1068 W. Flagler
Miami, FL 33010
305-324-8177 / Fax: 305-324-5717
RALPH MAYA (Co-Owner) & Buys Men's Wear, Footwear, Store Displays, Fixtures, Supplies
SAL TACHER (Co-Owner) & Buys Men's Wear, Urban Contemporary

LOS NUEVOS LATINOS (CLO)
(MIANASA, INC.)
3721 NW 7th St. (p-m)
Miami, FL 33010
305-649-4440 / Fax: 305-643-3491
CLARA CHOEFF (Owner)
JOSE CHOEFF-Men's Suits, Tailored Slacks, Sport Coats, Sport Shirts, Casual Slacks, Dress Shirts, Men's Footwear, Underwear, Hosiery, Small Leather Goods, Men's Big & Tall Shop, Young Men's Wear, Store Displays, Fixtures, Supplies

LUCKY'S MEN'S CLOTHING (MW)
7537 Dadeland Blvd. (b)
Miami, FL 33186
305-669-0124 / Fax: 305-665-5717
Sales: $1 Million-$10 Million
JEFF COHEN (Owner) & Buys Men's Suits, Tailored Jackets, Tailored Slacks, Sport Shirts, Outer Jackets, Leather Apparel, Urban Contemporary, Belts, Footwear, Store Displays, Fixtures, Supplies

MARK'S ATHLETIC SHOES (MO)
4235 SW 71st Ave.
Miami, FL 33155
305-260-4205 / Fax: 305-665-8989
Sales: $501,000-$1 Million
PAT McCABE (Dir.-Finance)
REYNOL DIAZ-Apparel, Athletic Footwear

MIAMI BIG & TALL (MW)
7294 SW 117th Ave.
Miami, FL 33183
305-271-2611 / Fax: 305-279-6043
MANNY FENRA (Owner) & Buys Men's Wear, Men's Big & Tall, Accessories, Furnishings

MIRAGE TWO (CLO)
(HOUSE OF DENIM)
1931 Collins Ave.
Miami, FL 33139
305-532-5534
BEN SHOAFF-Active Apparel, Athletic Apparel
MARCELLE SHOAFF-Active Apparel, Athletic Apparel

MR. TONY MEN'S SHOP (MW)
146 E. Flagler St. (m)
Miami, FL 33131
305-373-1493 / Fax: 305-373-1490
BENNY KOZOLCHYK (Owner) & Buys Men's Jeans, Sport Shirts, Outer Jackets, Casual Slacks, Accessories, Furnishings, Store Displays, Fixtures, Supplies

NAUTICAL BOATIQUE, INC. (MO & OL)
P.O. Box 593516 (bud-p-b)
Miami, FL 33159
305-633-6660 / Fax: 305-633-6586
Sales: $500,001-$1 Million
Website: www.nauticalboatique.com
MARTHA BOLANOS (President)
MIKE BOLANOS (V.P.-Opers.) & Buys Men's Boat Shoes, T-shirts, Shorts, Sportswear

NICK'S (MW)
12 NE 3rd. St. (m-b)
Miami, FL 33132
305-379-9417 / Fax: 305-379-9417
JOSE KERBEL (President) & Buys Men's Sweaters, Sport Shirts, Casual Slacks, Dress Shirts, Young Men's & Boys' Wear, Store Displays, Fixtures, Supplies

PENROD INTERNATIONAL (MW)
140 SE 1st Ave.
Miami, FL 33010
305-379-4135 / Fax: 305-373-8899
JAIME MATLA (Owner) & Buys Men's Sport Shirts, Casual Slacks, Jeans, T-shirts, Hosiery, Underwear, Hats, Belts, Store Displays, Fixtures, Supplies

PERRY ELLIS INTERNATIONAL (CLO-37)
(PERRY ELLIS)
3000 NW 107th Ave. (m)
Miami, FL 33172
305-592-2730 / Fax: 305-594-2307
Sales: $100 Million-$500 Million
Website: www.perryellis.com
OSCAR FELDENKRIES (President)
GEORGE FELDENKRIES (C.E.O.)
TIMOTHY PAGE (V.P. & C.F.O.)
DAVE STEWART (Real Estate Contact)
OPEN (Sr. V.P.-Opers. & G.M.M.) & Buys Fragrances, Leather Goods, Men's Apparel, Men's Casualwear, Men's Denim Apparel, Men's Accessories, Men's Hosiery, Men's Outerwear, Men's Sportswear

RANI'S BOUTIQUE, INC. (CLO)
3432 Main Hwy. (m)
Miami, FL 33133
305-448-0567 / Fax: 305-442-0056
Sales: $500,001-$1 Million
ZAHIR MERALI (Owner) & Buys Men's Footwear, Men's Casualwear, Men's Denim Apparel
PATRICIA E. NASSI (G.M.M.)

RICHARD'S GEMS & JEWELRY (JWLY & OL)
33 E. Flagler St.
Miami, FL 33131
305-379-3800 / Fax: 305-577-4522
Sales: $1 Million-$10 Million
Website: www.richards-diamonds.com
AIRL PAZ (President)
FERNANDO SCHLAEN-Jewelry, Watches

FLORIDA - Miami

RICK'S MENSWEAR, INC. (MW)

226 E. Flagler St. (b)
Miami, FL 33010
305-374-3728 / Fax: 305-373-8509

SARAH KUPER (Owner) & Buys Men's Suits, Tailored Jackets, Tailored Slacks, Sweaters, Sport Shirts, Casual Slacks, Accessories, Furnishings, Boys' Wear, Store Displays, Fixtures, Supplies

SORREN OF FLORIDA, INC. (CLO)

134 NE 1st St. (m-b)
Miami, FL 33132
305-379-4521 / Fax: 305-371-7527

WILLIAM SORREN (Owner) & Buys Men's & Boys' Sportswear, Shoes, Store Displays, Fixtures, Supplies

SUAYAS' (CLO-2 & OL)

272 E. Flagler St. (m)
Miami, FL 33131
305-374-0484 / Fax: 305-579-2183
Website: www.suayas.com

EMILIO SUAYAS (Owner) (@ 305-579-8679) & Buys Young Men's Wear, Urban Contemporary, Men's Wear, Footwear, Accessories

SURREY'S (MW-23)

5125 NW 77th Ave. (m-b)
Miami, FL 33010
305-592-8300 / Fax: 305-592-6850
Sales: $10 Million-$50 Million
Website: www.surreys.com
Retail Locations: CA, FL, TX

STEVEN SHIEKMAN (President) & Buys Men's Sportswear, Dress Shirts, Ties, Robes, Underwear, Hosiery, Accessories

MICHAEL BLOCK (Exec. V.P. & Real Estate Contact) & Buys Men's Suits, Tailored Jackets, Tailored Slacks, Leather Apparel, Headwear, Shoes

FRANK KIICK (V.P. & G.M.M.) & Buys Men's Suits, Tailored Jackets, Tailored Slacks, Leather Apparel, Headwear, Shoes

SWIM 'N' SPORT SHOP, INC. (SP-30)

2396 NW 96th Ave.
Miami, FL 33172
305-593-5071 / Fax: 305-593-2669
Sales: $1 Million-$10 Million
Website: www.swimsport.com

MARK SIDLE (President & G.M.M.)

ALBERT ABRAMS-Activewear, Swimwear, Sandals, Beach Footwear

TEXAS SUPPLY WHOLESALE (DEPT)

950 NE 2nd Ave. (p-m-b)
Miami, FL 33132
305-371-6723 / Fax: 305-381-9989

BUDD WEISS (Co-Owner)

JUDD ZISQUIT (President) & Buys Men's Sportswear, Boys' Wear, Urban Contemporary, Store Displays, Fixtures, Supplies

TUPELO HONEY (CLO-2)

3585 NE 207th St. (m)
Miami, FL 33180
305-936-9300 / Fax: 305-936-0086
Sales: $1 Million-$10 Million

IRA BLUM (President) & Buys Men's Apparel, Men's Casualwear, Men's Denim Apparel, Men's Outerwear, Men's Sportswear

UNDERWEAR HOUSE (CLO-2)

10755 SW 72nd St.
Miami, FL 33173
305-598-7800 / Fax: 305-598-9224

DAVID SCHARLIN (Owner) & Buys Swimwear

VIALEX EXPORT, INC. (MW)

3942 NW 27th St.
Miami, FL 33010
305-871-1912 / Fax: 305-871-1417

MANUEL RODRIGUEZ (Owner) & Buys Men's Sportswear, Furnishings, Accessories, Fragrances, Footwear, Store Displays, Fixtures, Supplies

VILLA CLARA STORE, INC. (CLO)

1951 W. Flagler St. (m)
Miami, FL 33135
305-642-2162 / Fax: 305-541-3730
Sales: $1 Million-$10 Million

GILBERT NIEMAN (Co-Owner & President) & Buys Boys' Apparel, Boys' Footwear, Leather Goods

BERNARDO NIEMAN (Co-Owner & Gen. Mgr.) & Buys Boys' Apparel, Boys' Footwear, Leather Goods

NURY NIEMAN-Boys' Apparel, Boys' Footwear, Leather Goods

WINDJAMMER SEACHEST (CLO-6)

1759 Bay Rd. (m)
Miami, FL 33139
305-672-6453 / Fax: 305-538-3784
Sales: $1 Million-$10 Million
Website: www.windjammerseachest.com

POLLY BURTON (President) & Buys Boys' Apparel, Men's Apparel, Men's Casualwear

MARK BURTON (C.F.O.) & Buys Boys' Apparel, Men's Apparel, Men's Casualwear

BARUCCI HIGH FASHION (CLO)

750 Ocean Dr.
Miami Beach, FL 33139
305-534-1303

BENARD HALLAR (Owner)

ALAIN COHEN (Mgr.) & Buys Swimwear

DAN & STEVE, INC. (MW)

(DB DUNGAREE)
840 Ocean Dr.
Miami Beach, FL 33139
305-538-2884 / Fax: 305-673-9909

MR. DROR (Owner) & Buys Men's Sportswear, Furnishings, Headwear, Accessories, Footwear, Store Displays, Fixtures, Supplies

THE ETE STORES, INC. (CLO)

530 Lincoln Rd. (m-b)
Miami Beach, FL 33139
305-672-4742 / Fax: 305-672-6826
Sales: $500,001-$1 Million

KURT SCHROEDER (President) & Buys Men's Footwear, Men's Apparel, Leather Goods, Men's Casualwear, Men's Denim Apparel, Men's Accessories, Men's Sleepwear, Men's Sportswear, Men's Suits, Men's Swimwear, Men's Underwear

IDIOM EYEWEAR (SP)

16200 NW 59th Ave., #106
Miami Beach, FL 30014
305-556-3434 / Fax: 305-531-8187
Website: www.idiomeyewear.com

LES KOCSIS-Sunglasses

ILLUSIONS BY RAQUEL (CLO-2)

1231 Washington Ave.
Miami Beach, FL 33139
305-935-3504 / Fax: 305-372-1225

RAQUEL GREEN (Owner) & Buys Beach Cover Ups, Swimwear

MIAMI CLOTHING 2, INC. (CLO)

(MIAMI CLOTHING)
229 N. Miami Ave. (p)
Miami Beach, FL 33139
305-377-1339

JOSE BLACHER (Owner) & Buys Men's Sweaters, Sport Shirts, Outer Jackets, Casual Slacks, Accessories, Dress Shirts, Ties, Underwear, Hosiery, Belts, Big & Tall Men's Wear, Young Men's Wear, Men's & Young Men's Jeans, Store Displays, Fixtures, Supplies

PALM PRODUCE RESORTWEAR (CLO-9)

657 Lincoln Rd.
Miami Beach, FL 33139
305-534-3335 / Fax: 305-534-3233
Website: www.palmproduceresortwear.com

STEPHEN LICATA (Owner) & Buys Beachwear, Resortwear, Swimwear, Headwear, Sandals, Beach Footwear

POST BLUE JEAN CO. (CLO)

836 Lincoln Rd.
Miami Beach, FL 33139
305-673-2124 / Fax: 305-673-2824
Sales: $500,001-$1 Million

JUAN PLASENCIA (Owner) & Buys Leather Goods, Men's Apparel, Men's Denim Apparel, Men's Sportswear

FLORIDA - Miami Beach

REGGAE WEAR SOUTH BEACH (CLO-3)
1143 Washington Ave. (m-des)
Miami Beach, FL 33139
305-538-2888
Sales: $500,001-$1 Million
TROVEL WILLIAMS (Co-Owner) & Buys Men's Apparel, Men's Casualwear, Men's Accessories
MICHELE WILLIAMS (Co-Owner)
OMAR SHOUCAR (Co-Owner) & Buys Men's Apparel, Men's Casualwear, Men's Accessories
DONNA SHOUCAIR (Co-Owner)

WATERLOO CLOTHING CORP. (CLO)
1672 Collins Ave., #A
Miami Beach, FL 33139
305-538-8932
INEZ MATO-Men's & Boys' Wear, Store Displays, Fixtures, Supplies

WILD THING (CLO)
900 Ocean Dr.
Miami Beach, FL 33139
305-532-8815 / Fax: 305-532-7014
DAVID HARAR (Owner) & Buys Activewear, Licensed Apparel

MERC TRADING, INC. (CLO)
6043 NW 167th St., # A20
Miami Lakes, FL 33015
305-556-3655 / Fax: 305-556-1077
Website: www.merctrading.com
SIGGY ALMEIDA-Boys' Apparel, Sunglasses, Fashion Accessories, Footwear, Hats, Apparel, Men's Apparel, Outdoor Apparel

BEACH HOUSE OF NAPLES (SP-2)
1300 3rd St. South
Naples, FL 34102
239-261-1366 / Fax: 239-261-1482
Sales: $1 Million-$10 Million
CONI SUTTER (Owner) & Buys Resortwear
TARA BEE (Mgr.) & Buys Beachwear, Activewear, Footwear

BETH MONE CHILDREN'S SHOPPES OF NAPLES (KS)
381 12th Ave. South (b-h)
Naples, FL 34102
941-261-3447 / Fax: 941-262-2577
Sales: $500,000-$1 Million
SUSAN TIGWELL (Owner) & Buys 8 to 20 Boys' Wear, Store Displays, Fixtures, Supplies

CAPTAIN'S CLOSET (CLO)
1200 5th Ave. South
Naples, FL 34102
941-261-5125 / Fax: 941-262-5487
Website: www.captainscloset.com
JAMES KENT (Owner) & Buys Men's Sportswear, Footwear, Store Displays, Fixtures, Supplies

CHIMERE INTERNATIONAL (SG & OL)
5534 Yahl St.
Naples, FL 34109
562-824-7682 / Fax: 562-598-2662
Website: www.chimere.com
MIKE BOYER (Owner) & Buys Men's Outdoor Clothing, Store Displays, Fixtures, Supplies

CRICKET SHOP, INC. (CLO-9)
(JOHNSON'S CRICKET SHOPS, INC.)
1161 Sun Century Rd., #2
Naples, FL 34110
239-566-3232 / Fax: 239-566-3824
DAVID COX (Owner) & Buys Activewear, Swimwear, Athletic Footwear, Beachwear, Sandals

EVERGLADES ANGLER, INC. (CLO)
810 12th Ave. South
Naples, FL 34102
941-262-8228 / Fax: 941-262-0572
Sales: $100,001-$500,000
Website: www.evergladesangler.com
MARK WARD (Owner) & Buys Fly Fishing Boots, Apparel
DOROTHY WARD-Men's Apparel, Resortwear

HUBBARD'S LTD. OF NAPLES, INC. (CLO)
5400 Taylor Rd., #109 (p-m-b)
Naples, FL 34109
239-566-3242 / Fax: 239-556-3626
Website: www.affordabletuxedos.com
ROBERT HUBBARD (Co-Owner) & Buys Men's Sportswear, Furnishings
KAREN HUBBARD (Co-Owner) & Buys Men's Sportswear, Furnishings, Store Displays, Fixtures, Supplies

KEPP'S MEN'S SHOPS OF FLORIDA, INC. (MW & OL)
3541 Mercantile Ave. (b)
Naples, FL 34104
941-643-1234 / Fax: 941-643-5347
Sales: $1 Million-$10 Million
Website: www.kepps.com
JONATHAN C. RUSSELL (G.M.M. & V.P.) & Buys Men's Overcoats, Suits, Tailored Jackets, Tailored Slacks, Raincoats, Sweaters, Sport Shirts, Casual Slacks, Active Apparel, Dress Shirts, Ties, Robes, Underwear, Hosiery, Headwear, Belts, Small Leather Goods, Store Displays, Fixtures, Supplies

MONDO UOMO, INC. (MW-2)
4232 Gulf Shore Blvd. North (b)
Naples, FL 34103
941-434-9484 / Fax: 941-434-8246
LYNN MANAGANIAN (Owner) & Buys Men's Sportswear, Furnishings, Accessories, Footwear, Store Displays, Fixtures, Supplies

NAPLES BEACH HOTEL & GOLF CLUB (GOLF)
851 Gulf Shore Blvd. North
Naples, FL 34102
941-261-2222 / Fax: 941-261-8019
Sales: $100,001-$500,000
KATE KEATING (Dir.-Retail) & Buys Golf Apparel, Footwear
MICHAEL WATKINS (Mgr.)

QUIET STORM SURF & SPORT, INC. (CLO-10)
4360 Gulf Shore Blvd. North, #608 (p)
Naples, FL 33103
239-434-6488 / Fax: 239-434-2434
BILLY DREIBELBIS (Owner) & Buys Men's Sportswear & Footwear, Store Displays, Fixtures, Supplies

WILL O THE WISP (CLO-5)
(D. W. ENTERPRISES OF NAPLES)
1455 Real Head Blvd., #25 (m-b)
Naples, FL 34110
239-514-0425 / Fax: 239-514-0825
DON MULLARKY (Co-Owner) & Buys Men's & Boys' T-shirts, Shorts, Swimwear, Store Displays, Fixtures, Supplies
WILLA MULLARKY (Co-Owner) & Buys Men's & Boys' T-shirts, Shorts, Swimwear, Store Displays, Fixtures, Supplies
ELAINE SWEET-Men's & Boys' Footwear

INLET CHARLEY'S SURF SHOP (CLO)
510 Flagler Ave. (p-m-b)
New Smyrna Beach, FL 32169
386-423-2317 / Fax: 386-426-0955
JOE ARMSTRONG (Owner) & Buys Men's & Boys' Sportswear, Accessories, Headwear, Young Men's Wear, Store Displays, Fixtures, Supplies
DUSTIN MARKLAND-Men's & Boys' Sportswear, Accessories, Headwear, Young Men's Wear, Footwear, Store Displays, Fixtures, Supplies

SUN MAGIC BEACHWEAR (SP)
504 Flagler Ave.
New Smyrna Beach, FL 32169
386-424-8420
LINDA THURMAN-Men's T-shirts, Imprinted Sportswear, Headwear, Footwear, Accessories, Jewelry

ARMY & NAVY OUTDOORS (AN-4)
(CRIS MERCANTILE COMPANY, INC.)
1701 S. State Rd. 7
North Fort Lauderdale, FL 33068
954-973-6289 / Fax: 954-979-4571
SAMUEL ZACKOWITZ (Owner) & Buys Activewear, Athletic Footwear, Military Apparel, Footwear
COOKIE GOODMAN (G.M.M.) & Buys Activewear, Athletic Footwear, Military Apparel, Footwear

ABC DISTRIBUTING CO. (MO & OL)
2000 NE 146th St. (p-m-b)
North Miami, FL 33181
305-944-6900 / Fax: 305-944-4931
Website: www.abcdistributing.com
KAREN WALLACE (V.P.-Sls. & Mktg.)
CAROLINE ARMSTRONG-Men's Sportswear, Leather Apparel, Furnishings, Accessories, Young Men's & Boys' Shirts
VALERIE SCHWARTZ-Footwear

BENGE, INC. (CLO-3)
(DECO DENIM)
17700 Collins Ave. (p-m)
North Miami Beach, FL 33160
305-932-3389 / Fax: 305-932-3271
Website: www.decodenim.com
BARRY SHELOMOVITZ (Owner) & Buys Men's & Boys' Sportswear, Jeans, Footwear, Store Displays, Fixtures, Supplies

IZZY'S BIG & TALL (MW)
3061 NE 163rd St. (m-b)
North Miami Beach, FL 33160
305-956-3956 / Fax: 305-956-3939
ISRAEL FRANCO (Owner) & Buys Big & Tall Men's Suits, Sportswear, Furnishings, Accessories, Footwear, Store Displays, Fixtures, Supplies

HAROLD GRANT FOR MEN (MW-2)
11616 US Hwy. 1 (b)
Oakbrook Sq.
North Palm Beach, FL 33408
561-626-0002 / Fax: 561-622-3375
ROBERT GRANT (President) & Buys Men's Sweaters, Sport Shirts, Outer Jackets, Leather Apparel, Casual Slacks, Active Apparel, Dress Shirts, Ties, Robes, Hosiery, Headwear, Accessories, Store Displays, Fixtures, Supplies
HAROLD GRANT (C.E.O.)

DUNNIGAN'S MENSWEAR (MW)
3161 W. Oakland Park Blvd. (p)
Oakland Park, FL 33311
954-486-7628
SUKJA DUNNIGAN (Owner) & Buys Men's Sportswear, Urban Contemporary, Furnishings, Accessories, Store Displays, Fixtures, Supplies

DUKE'S MEN'S SHOP (MW)
18 SE Broadway St. (p-m)
Ocala, FL 34471
352-629-0781
Sales: $100,001-$500,000
ROBERT DECONNA (Owner) & Buys Men's Sportswear, Furnishings, Accessories, Headwear, Footwear, Store Displays, Fixtures, Supplies

FALVEY'S STORE FOR MEN (MW-2)
3100 W. College Rd., #352 (m-b)
Ocala, FL 34474
352-237-3060
Sales: $500,000-$1 Million
JIM FALVEY (President & G.M.M.) & Buys Men's Suits, Tailored Jackets, Tailored Slacks, Raincoats, Men's Big & Tall Wear, Sweaters, Sport Shirts, Outer Jackets, Leather Apparel, Casual Slacks, Active Apparel, Furnishings, Accessories, Store Displays, Fixtures, Supplies

WISHFUL THINKING WESTERN WORLD, INC. (WW)
2230 NW 10th St. (p)
Ocala, FL 34475
352-629-7676 / Fax: 352-622-9474
Sales: $100,001-$500,000
CARMEN G. MURVIN (Owner) & Buys Men's & Boys' Western Clothing, Sportswear, Leather Apparel, Furnishings, Accessories, Boots, Store Displays, Fixtures, Supplies

DONATO CLOTHING GROUP (CLO)
9401 W. Colonial Dr., #334
Ocoee, FL 34761
407-293-7626 / Fax: 407-293-2306
JOSE RODRIGUEZ-Boys' Apparel, Boys' Swimwear, Sunglasses, Accessories, Hats, Men's Apparel, Resortwear, T-shirts, Imprinted Sportswear
CHAD YOAS-Boys' Apparel, Boys' Swimwear, Sunglasses, Accessories, Hats, Men's Apparel, Resortwear, T-shirts, Imprinted Sportswear

HMS CORP. (CLO)
P.O. Box 310
Ocoee, FL 34761
407-532-3622 / Fax: 407-532-9949
Website: www.hmshost.com
LYNN FLEMING-Sunglasses, Hats, Resortwear, T-shirts, Imprinted Sportswear

ATLANTIC HOSIERY OUTLET (CLO-3)
4700 NW 132nd St. (m)
Opa Locka, FL 33054
305-685-7617 / Fax: 305-685-3872
Sales: $1 Million-$10 Million
NEIL GOTTLIEB (Co-Owner) & Buys Boys' Apparel, Men's Apparel, Men's Casualwear, Men's Hosiery, Men's Underwear
RUBEN KLODA (Co-Owner)
DON WHITEBOOK (Co-Owner)

COAST GUARD EXCHANGE SYSTEM (PX-4)
US Coast Guard Air Station Miami
Opa Locka, FL 33054
305-688-6851 / Fax: 305-769-5872
Sales: $1 Million-$10 Million
Website: www.coastguardexchange.com
BRIAN O'CONNOR (District Mgr.)
EVELYN RAWLS (Retail Mgr.) & Buys Men's Wear, Young Men's & Boys' Wear, Footwear, Store Displays, Fixtures, Supplies

D & N SPORTS (CLO)
17201 NW 27th Ave. (m)
Opa Locka, FL 33056
305-628-4408
Sales: $1 Million-$10 Million
DOUGLAS ROSS (Owner) & Buys Men's Apparel, Men's Casualwear, Men's Sportswear

ABED BROTHERS (MW-4)
(MEN'S CLOSET)
(METROPOLITAN MEN'S WEAR)
(SUIT CITY)
7840 W. Colonial Dr. (m)
Orlando, FL 32808
407-578-4878 / Fax: 407-292-0577
SAMMY ABED (Co-Owner) & Buys Young Men's Wear, Urban Contemporary, Suits, Men's Wear, Footwear, Accessories
ABED ABED (Co-Owner) (@ 407-292-1998) & Buys Suits, Tailored Jackets, Tailored Slacks, Big & Tall Men's Wear, Sportswear, Sport Shirts, Dress Shirts, Ties, Hosiery, Headwear, Footwear, Belts

AL'S ARMY STORE (AN)
23 N. Orange Blossom Trl. (p)
Orlando, FL 32801
407-425-4932 / Fax: 407-423-7644
NEIL CRASNOW (Co-Owner) & Buys Camouflage Young Men's Wear
FRANK CRASNOW (Co-Owner) & Buys Camouflage Young Men's Wear
FAYE COHON (Co-Owner) & Buys Camouflage Young Men's Wear

BAKER LEISURE GROUP (CLO)
5401 Kirkman Rd., #610
Orlando, FL 32819
407-351-0425 / Fax: 407-363-0716
KAREN TRYMAN-T-shirts, Imprinted Sportswear

BIMINI SHOES (SP)
9101 International Dr., #1184
Orlando, FL 32819
407-354-9898
JOE PINDER (Owner) & Buys Men's Shoes, Hosiery, Accessories

FLORIDA - Orlando

BOMB'S THREADZ (CLO)
318 W. Colonial Dr.
Orlando, FL 32801
407-650-9232 / Fax: 407-447-3751
KHA LY-Men's Sportswear
HEATHER CUTBILL-Men's Sportswear

BROADWAY MEN'S FASHIONS (MW)
4510 S. Orange Blossom Trl. (m)
Orlando, FL 32839
407-855-6868 / Fax: 407-855-6104
JIM SHATARA (Owner) & Buys Men's Sportswear, Urban Contemporary, Furnishings, Accessories, Footwear, 8 to 20 Boys' Suits, Store Displays, Fixtures, Supplies

DELTA ORLANDO RESORT (CLO)
5715 Major Blvd.
Orlando, FL 32819
407-351-3340 / Fax: 407-351-5117
Website: www.deltaorlandoresort.com
DAVID GILMORE-Boys' Apparel, Sunglasses, Accessories, Men's Apparel, T-shirts, Imprinted Sportswear
AIMEE KOLLER-Boys' Apparel, Sunglasses, Accessories, Men's Apparel, T-shirts, Imprinted Sportswear

EVERYTHING BUT WATER, INC. (CLO-37)
5615 Windhover Dr. (m-b)
Orlando, FL 32819
407-351-4069 / Fax: 407-363-0967
Sales: $10 Million-$50 Million
Website: www.everythingbutwater.com
STACEY SIEGEL (President) & Buys Boys' Apparel, Men's Apparel, Men's Furnishings, Men's Swimwear, Footwear
ANN TUCKER (C.F.O.) & Buys Boys' Apparel, Men's Apparel, Men's Furnishings, Men's Swimwear, Footwear
LEANNA STOKER (Dir.-Opers.) & Buys Boys' Apparel, Men's Apparel, Men's Furnishings, Men's Swimwear, Footwear

FAIRVILLA ADULT MEGA STORE (CLO)
1740 N. Orange Blossom Trl.
Orlando, FL 32804
407-425-6005 / Fax: 407-644-0467
Website: www.fairvillaonline.com
WILLIAM MURPHY (Owner)
DEBI LLOYD-Swimwear

THE G SPOT (CLO)
5617 E. Colonial Dr.
Orlando, FL 32807
407-306-8777 / Fax: 407-306-0125
Website: www.wheresyourgspot.com
TROY FISH (Co-Owner) & Buys Sunglasses, Men's Apparel, Men's Surf & Swimwear, T-shirts, Imprinted Sportswear
JAY HENING (Co-Owner) & Buys Sunglasses, Men's Apparel, Men's Surf & Swimwear, T-shirts, Imprinted Sportswear

HE (CLO)
P.O. Box 550936
Orlando, FL 32821
407-816-9311
Website: www.heswimwear.com
RON SERASS-Sunglasses, Footwear, Hats, Men's Apparel, Men's Surf & Swimwear, T-shirts, Imprinted Sportswear

LOOKING GOOD (MW-2)
5333 W. Colonial Dr. (m-b)
Orlando, FL 32808
407-291-4212 / Fax: 407-291-4416
MARK MAHTNI (Owner) & Buys Men's Sportswear, Urban Contemporary, Furnishings, Accessories, 8 to 20 Boys' Suits, Suits, Dress Pants, Dress Shirts, Big & Tall Men's Wear, Hosiery, Footwear, Store Displays, Fixtures, Supplies

ROBINSON ENTERPRISES (CLO)
2730 N. Orange Blossom Trl.
Orlando, FL 32804
407-467-7092 / Fax: 407-246-1797
DARLENE ROBINSON-Boys' Apparel, Accessories, Hats, Men's Apparel, Outdoor Gear & Apparel, Resortwear, T-shirts, Imprinted Sportswear
TERRY ROBINSON-Boys' Apparel, Accessories, Hats, Men's Apparel, Outdoor Gear & Apparel, Resortwear, T-shirts, Imprinted Sportswear
JOHN WOOD-Boys' Apparel, Accessories, Hats, Men's Apparel, Outdoor Gear & Apparel, Resortwear, T-shirts, Imprinted Sportswear

THE SPORTS DOMINATOR (CLO & SG)
(BIG BARGAIN WORLD)
5858 Lakehurst Dr.
Orlando, FL 32819
407-370-9600 / Fax: 407-270-4555
Website: www.sportsdominator.com
JESSIE MAALL (President & Owner) & Buys Athletic Apparel, Sporting Goods, Golf Apparel, Leisure Wear, Headwear, Athletic Footwear

SUPER VISION (CLO)
8210 Presidents Dr.
Orlando, FL 32809
407-857-9900 / Fax: 407-857-0050
BRET KINGSTONE (Owner) & Buys Outdoor Gear & Apparel

THE SWIMWEAR COMPANY (CLO)
8422 International Dr.
Orlando, FL 32819
407-352-9955 / Fax: 407-352-9055
Website: www.swimwearcompany.com
KATHY McCOY (Mgr.) & Buys Boys' Swimwear, Men's Surf & Swimwear,T-shirts, Imprinted Sportswear

TEMPUS RESORTS (CLO)
7547 Commerce Center Dr.
Orlando, FL 32819
407-226-0497 / Fax: 407-352-7225
Website: www.tempusresorts.com
ROGER FARWELL (President) & Buys Resortwear, Golf Apparel
JIM TINNEY-Resortwear, Golf Apparel

THREE MASK (CLO)
417 W. Church St.
Orlando, FL 32801
407-426-7355 / Fax: 407-426-7355
TIMOTHY ADEBULE (Owner) & Buys Beachwear, T-shirts, African Clothing

TITANIC SHIP OF DREAMS (CLO)
8445 International Dr., #202
Orlando, FL 32819
407-248-1166 / Fax: 407-248-1925
Website: www.titanicshipofdreams.com
PAUL BURNS (Gen. Mgr.) & Buys Sportswear, Beachwear
PAM SHEETS-Sportswear, Beachwear
ANN LeBLANC-Sportswear, Beachwear

TRACK SHACK (SP)
1104 N. Mills Ave.
Orlando, FL 32803
407-898-1313 / Fax: 407-898-2196
Sales: $500,001-$1 Million
Website: www.trackshack.com
JON HUGHES (Co-Owner)
BETSY HUGHES (Co-Owner)
JERRY PEGRAM (G.M.M.) & Buys Activewear, Running Footwear, Running Accessories
ANTHONY O'NEIL (Store Mgr.) & Buys Activewear, Running Footwear, Running Accessories

TYRONE'S TAILORING & FORMAL WEAR (MW)
9480 S. Orange Blossom Trl. (m)
Orlando, FL 32837
407-251-6900 / Fax: 407-251-4883
Website: www.tailoringandtuxedos.com
TYRONE PERSAUD (Owner) & Buys Men's Suits, Dress Shirts, Tuxedos, Formal Wear, Tailored Jackets, Tailored Slacks, Accessories, Furnishings, Footwear

ULTIMATE SPORTSFAN, INC. (GS)
8001 S. Orange Blossom Trl.
Orlando, FL 32809
407-851-1017 / Fax: 407-851-9454
Sales: $1 Million-$10 Million
YOUNG HWANG (President) & Buys Skiwear, Licensed Apparel
ELLEN JONES (Mgr.) & Buys Apparel, Footwear

UNIVERSITY OF CENTRAL FLORDIA KNIGHTWEAR (SP)
UCF St. Union Bldg. 52, #102H
Orlando, FL 32816
407-823-3201
Website: www.knightwear.com
PHILIP SHEARER-T-shirts, Imprinted Sportswear, Urban Streetwear, Men's Apparel, Boys' Apparel

VISTA ENTERPRISES, INC. (CLO)
8725 Wittenwood Cove
Orlando, FL 32836
407-239-1414 / Fax: 407-239-1117
TARIQ JAVAID (Owner) & Buys Boys' Swimwear, Sunglasses, Fashion Accessories, Hats, Men's Swimwear

WALT DISNEY COSTUMING (CLO)
590 N. Stage Ln.
Orlando, FL 32830
407-560-3847 / Fax: 407-560-3646
MATT DAVIDSON (Owner) & Buys Fashion Accessories, Footwear, Hats, Men's Apparel, Men's Surf & Swimwear, T-shirts, Imprinted Sportswear

WOD MANAGEMENT CO., LLC (CLO-7)
(World of Denim, Inc.)
(Designer Outlet)
(DENIM PLACE)
(DENIM OUTLET)
7509 Exchange Dr. (p)
Orlando, FL 32809
407-859-6634 / Fax: 407-826-0401
Sales: $1 Million-$10 Million
Website: www.worldofdenim.com
VERA STEINFELD (Owner)
DAMIEN CROSKEY-Men's Jeans, Shorts, Footwear, Boys' Wear, Store Displays, Fixtures, Supplies

BIKINI COMPANY (CLO-2)
235 Granada Blvd.
Ormond Beach, FL 32176
904-676-2525 / Fax: 904-676-7702
Sales: $100 Million-$500 Million
LOUISE ROUTZAHN (Owner)
JOY MYERS-Beachwear, Swimwear, Sandals, Beach Footwear

C.J. MINERAL AND BEAD (CLO)
37 Corbin Ave.
Ormond Beach, FL 32174
386-677-3242 / Fax: 386-615-8957
JOHN GEORGOUDIOU (Owner) & Buys Jewelry, Accessories
CINDY VORHEES-Jewelry, Accessories

JAMES HAGEN DISTRIBUTORS (CLO)
44 Bay Point Dr.
Ormond Beach, FL 32174
386-672-2259 / Fax: 386-672-0893
JAMES HAGEN (Owner) & Buys T-shirts, Imprinted Sportswear

SKIP'S WESTERN OUTFITTERS (WW-5)
300 N. State Rd., #415 (p-m-b)
Osteen, FL 32764
407-321-1000 / Fax: 407-324-9940
Website: www.skipsboots.com
SKIP PATSOS (Owner) & Buys Men's & Boys' Western Wear, Footwear, Store Displays, Fixtures, Supplies

ARISTOKIDS, INC. (FW-2 & OL)
309 S. County Rd., #A (b)
Palm Beach, FL 33480
561-832-3596 / Fax: 561-832-8869
Sales: $1 Million-$10 Million
Website: www.aristokids.com
JODI WENTLEY (President) & Buys Boys' Apparel, Boys' Footwear, Watches
JAMIE APPLEFIELD (V.P.)
RICHARD WENTLEY (Secy.) & Buys Boys' Apparel, Boys' Footwear, Watches, Accessories

C. ORRICO, INC. (CLO & OL)
336 S. County Rd. (m)
Palm Beach, FL 33480
561-659-7820 / Fax: 561-832-2410
Website: www.corrico.com
CASEY ORRICO (Co-Owner) & Buys Boys' Apparel, Boys' Swimwear, Sunglasses, Fashion Accessories, Footwear, Hats, Men's Apparel, Men's Surf & Swimwear, Resortwear, T-shirts, Imprinted Sportswear
KATHY ORRICO (Co-Owner) & Buys Boys' Apparel, Boys' Swimwear, Sunglasses, Fashion Accessories, Footwear, Hats, Men's Apparel, Men's Surf & Swimwear, Resortwear, T-shirts, Imprinted Sportswear
COLLEEN ORRICO (Co-Owner) & Buys Boys' Apparel, Boys' Swimwear, Sunglasses, Fashion Accessories, Footwear, Hats, Men's Apparel, Men's Surf & Swimwear, Resortwear, T-shirts, Imprinted Sportswear

GIORGIO'S (CLO)
230 Worth Ave.
Palm Beach, FL 33480
561-655-2446 / Fax: 561-655-3751
BECKY BELL-Handmade Italian Men's Apparel

KASSATLY'S, INC. (CLO)
250 Worth Ave. (b)
Palm Beach, FL 33480
561-655-5655 / Fax: 561-835-9808
Sales: $500,001-$1 Million
ROBERT KASSATLY (Co-Owner) & Buys Men's Apparel, Men's Hosiery, Men's Outerwear, Men's Sleepwear, Men's Sportswear, Men's Underwear
EDWARD KASSATLY (Co-Owner) & Buys Men's Apparel, Men's Hosiery, Men's Outerwear, Men's Sleepwear, Men's Sportswear, Men's Underwear
MONICA MACLOUD (Store Mgr.)
LINDA HAYES (Mgr.-Opers.)

PALM BEACH BOYS' CLUB (SP)
305 S. County Rd.
Palm Beach, FL 33480
561-832-9335 / Fax: 561-832-8869
Website: www.pbboysclub.com
JODI WENTLEY (Co-Owner) & Buys Boys' Apparel, Boys' Swimwear, Accessories, Hats, Men's Apparel, Men's Surf & Swimwear, Resortwear, T-shirts, Imprinted Sportswear
RICK WENTLEY (Co-Owner) & Buys Boys' Apparel, Boys' Swimwear, Accessories, Hats, Men's Apparel, Men's Surf & Swimwear, Resortwear, T-shirts, Imprinted Sportswear
JAMIE APPLEFIELD (Co-Owner) & Buys Boys' Apparel, Boys' Swimwear, Accessories, Hats, Men's Apparel, Men's Surf & Swimwear, Resortwear, T-shirts, Imprinted Sportswear

PASTEL (CLO)
139 N. Country Rd.
Palm Beach, FL 33480
561-655-7995 / Fax: 561-655-5583
SONIA PERALTA (Owner) & Buys Swimwear, Headwear

TRILLION SARTORIA (CLO)
315 Worth Ave. (b)
Palm Beach, FL 33480
561-832-3525 / Fax: 561-832-3888
Sales: $1 Million-$10 Million
DAVID NEFF (Owner) & Buys Men's Overcoats, Suits, Tailored Jackets, Tailored Slacks, Raincoats, Sweaters, Sport Shirts, Outer Jackets, Casual Slacks, Active Apparel, Dress Shirts, Ties, Hosiery, Belts, Store Displays, Fixtures, Supplies

OUTHOUSE, INC. (CLO)

2494 Habor Ln.
Palm Beach Gardens, FL 33140
561-775-6648 / Fax: 561-775-6648

MATT EAKES (Co-Owner) & Buys Hats, Apparel, Swimwear, Men's Apparel, Men's Surf & Swimwear, Private Label, Skate Apparel, Skateboarding Accessories, Surfboarding Accessories, T-shirts, Imprinted Sportswear, Wetsuits

LISA EAKES (Co-Owner) & Buys Hats, Apparel, Swimwear, Men's Apparel, Men's Surf & Swimwear, Private Label, Skate Apparel, Skateboarding Accessories, Surfboarding Accessories, T-shirts, Imprinted Sportswear, Wetsuits

PALM BEACH GOLF CENTER, INC. (GOLF-2)

7700 N. Military Trl.
Palm Beach Gardens, FL 33410
561-842-7100 / Fax: 561-842-7288
Website: www.golfshoes4u.com

LAWRENCE SUGARMAN (Owner)

TERRY HALL-Golf Accessories

MARLENE CHRISTOPHER-Golf Apparel

MARCUS COOPER-Golf Footwear

BENTFRAME (CLO)

37160 US Hwy.19 North
Palm Harbor, FL 34684
727-942-9930 / Fax: 727-942-9707
Website: www.bentframeclothing.com

BRANDI TICHENOR (Co-Owner) & Buys Swimwear, Men's Apparel, Men's Surf & Swimwear

RONNIE TICHENOR (Co-Owner) & Buys Swimwear, Men's Apparel, Men's Surf & Swimwear

JOHN GOTTSCHALK-Swimwear, Men's Apparel, Men's Surf & Swimwear

LORIE MAHONY-Swimwear, Men's Apparel, Men's Surf & Swimwear

CMA (CLO)

1538 Largo Vista Blvd.
Palm Harbor, FL 34685
727-772-7447 / Fax: 727-772-7557

JAMES FOGGETT (Owner) & Buys Footwear

RENA'S WILD WEAR (CLO)

36649 US Hwy. 19 North
Palm Harbor, FL 34684
727-939-0397 / Fax: 727-939-8430
Website: www.renas.com

ERIN ROGER (Co-Owner) & Buys Fashion Accessories, Footwear, Hats, Resortwear, Men's Apparel, Dancewear, Swimwear

TIM HENNEBERRY (Co-Owner) & Buys Fashion Accessories, Footwear, Hats, Resortwear, Men's Apparel, Dancewear, Swimwear

NICK HENNEBERRY-Fashion Accessories, Footwear, Hats, Resortwear, Men's Apparel, Dancewear, Swimwear

CAROLYN HENNEBERRY-Fashion Accessories, Footwear, Hats, Resortwear, Men's Apparel, Dancewear, Swimwear

CRUMS MINI MALL (DEPT)

1321 Coastal Hwy. (p)
Panacea, FL 32346
850-984-5501

ELOISE CRUM (Owner) & Buys Men's Footwear, Men's T-shirts, Shorts, Swimwear, Hosiery, Store Displays, Fixtures, Supplies

RHONDA CRUM PLOUSSE-Men's T-shirts, Shorts, Swimwear, Hosiery, Store Displays, Fixtures, Supplies

BAY POINT RETAILERS, INC. (CLO)

204 Ellen Ln., #A
Panama City, FL 32408
850-234-6112 / Fax: 850-233-6837

EDWINA McLANE (Retail Mgr.) & Buys Resortwear, Swimwear, Sunglasses, Leisure Wear

KAREN WAKSTEIN-Resortwear, Swimwear, Sunglasses, Leisure Wear

BLUE ISLAND BEACH CO. (CLO)

15628 Front Beach Rd.
Panama City, FL 32413
850-234-6278 / Fax: 850-234-5924

MARK HESS (Owner) & Buys Beachwear, Swimwear, Surfwear, Sunglasses, Headwear, Beach Shoes

THERESA ROBYCK-Beachwear, Swimwear, Surfwear, Sunglasses, Headwear, Beach Shoes

C & G SPORTING GOODS (SG-2)

137 Harrison Ave.
Panama City, FL 32401
850-769-2317 / Fax: 850-785-4305

RONALD GROOM (Owner) & Buys Big & Tall Men's Wear, Sportswear, Raincoats, Outer Jackets

NOTE:-This Store Sells Camouflage Clothing Only.

CO-CO'S (CLO-2)

12620 Front Beach Rd. (m)
Panama City, FL 32407
850-233-1269
Sales: $1 Million-$10 Million

JACOB MAMAN (Owner) & Buys Leather Goods, Men's Casualwear, Men's Denim Apparel, Men's Sportswear, Men's Swimwear

IMAGE NATION (CLO)

302 S. Glades Trl.
Panama City, FL 32407
850-234-3446 / Fax: 850-233-6335

DIANA HOLMES (Owner) & Buys Beachwear, Resortwear, Swimwear, Headwear

THE JOINT (CLO)

14600 Front Beach Rd., #B (m-b)
P.O. Box 14061
Panama City, FL 32413
850-230-3007 / Fax: 850-230-9948
Sales: $500,001-$1 Million
Website: www.joint.com

CHRIS McLAUGHLINE (Owner) & Buys Men's Footwear, Leather Goods, Men's Sportswear

MOLLY ALLEN (Store Mgr.) & Buys Men's Footwear, Leather Goods, Men's Sportswear

CARL ALLEN-Men's Footwear, Leather Goods, Men's Sportswear

JOYCE'S TOUCH OF CLASS, INC. (CLO)

632 W. 23rd St. (m-b)
Panama City, FL 32405
850-769-6336 / Fax: 850-769-3234
Sales: $500,001-$1 Million

JOYCE WILLIAMSON (President)

BEVERLY HUMPHERYS-Men's Apparel, Men's Sleepwear, Men's Swimwear, Men's Underwear

PRO-MARK, INC. (CLO)

P.O. Box 15932
Panama City, FL 32406
850-763-8618 / Fax: 850-763-2973

NORM GULKIS-Swimwear, Resortwear, T-shirts, Imprinted Sportswear, Sunglasses, Beach Shoes, Headwear

ALVIN'S STORES (CLO-14)

(Division of Marco Destin, Inc.)
14520 Front Beach Rd. (m)
Panama City Beach, FL 32413
850-234-8897
Sales: $10 Million-$50 Million
Website: www.alvinsisland.com

JAY ARDEN (@ 305-471-9394)-Men's Sweaters, Sport Shirts, Casual Slacks, Swimwear, Active Apparel, Belts, Underwear, Hosiery, Boys' Accessories, Jewelry, Fragrances, Footwear, Men's & Boys' T-shirts

FLORIDA - Panama City Beach

BEACH SCENE (SP)
10059 Hutchinson Blvd.
Panama City Beach, FL 32407
850-233-1662 / Fax: 850-233-1663
Sales: $1 Million-$10 Million
BOB ECKER (Co-Owner) & Buys Resortwear, Swimwear, Beach Footwear
MYNETTE ECKER (Co-Owner) & Buys Resortwear, Swimwear, Beach Footwear

HARBOR WEAR (CLO-2)
537 Beckrich Rd.
Panama City Beach, FL 32407
850-230-8111 / Fax: 850-230-3436
EDDIE GREEN (Co-Owner) & Buys Beachwear, Resortwear, T-shirts, Imprinted Apparel
LAURA GREEN (Co-Owner) & Buys Beachwear, Resortwear, T-shirts, Imprinted Apparel

HY'S TOGGERY, INC. (MW)
495 Beckrich (m-b)
Panama City Beach, FL 32407
850-235-1177
Sales: $500,000-$1 Million
GARY WAKSTEIN (President)
RONNIE MARTIN (G.M.M.) & Buys Men's Sweaters, Sport Shirts, Outer Jackets, Leather Apparel, Casual Slacks, Active Apparel, Hosiery, Headwear, Belts, Small Leather Goods, Footwear, Fragrances, Store Displays, Fixtures, Supplies

SHIPWRECK MERCANTILE CO. (CLO-2)
P.O. Box 18229
Panama City Beach, FL 32417
850-235-7800 / Fax: 850-234-6233
Sales: $1 Million-$10 Million
Website: www.shipwreckltd.com
JIM BRADLEY (Owner)
NIKI BALL-Swimwear, Leisure Wear, T-shirts

SURF & TURF (CLO)
10414 Front Beach Rd. (m)
Panama City Beach, FL 32407
850-234-8579
RON HAIBACH-Men's Wear, Sportswear, Young Men's Wear

SURFWEAR (SP)
8730 Thomas Dr., #1109
Panama City Beach, FL 32407
850-233-1079
RANDY CLEMENT-Surfwear, Dive Apparel & Accessories, Sunglasses, Related Footwear, Headwear, Kayaking Accessories, Surfboarding Accessories, Jewelry

T-SHIRT EXPRESS (CLO)
11832 Front Beach Rd.
Panama City Beach, FL 32407
850-235-8960 / Fax: 850-235-0118
Website: www.tshirtexpress.org
GEORGE OUTMEZGUINE-T-shirts, Imprinted Sportswear, Sunglasses

U2 JOSEF'S FUNWEAR (CLO)
P.O. Box 9377
Panama City Beach, FL 32417
850-234-0082
DANNY SADEH (Owner) & Buys Sportswear, Leisurewear, Sunglasses
NISIM SADEH-Sportswear, Leisurewear, Sunglasses
YAIER SADEH-Sportswear, Leisurewear, Sunglasses

SWIMLAND (CLO-9)
3149 W. Hallandale Beach Blvd.
Pembroke Park, FL 33309
954-966-5055 / Fax: 954-966-5074
Sales: $2 Million-$5 Million
SANDY LABATON (Owner) & Buys Activewear, Swimwear, Sandals, Sunglasses
EVERATE ORTEGA (Asst. V.P.) & Buys Activewear, Swimwear, Sandals, Sunglasses

SPARLON HOSIERY (MW)
1600 SW 66th Ave. (m)
Pembroke Pines, FL 33023
954-966-2050 / Fax: 954-966-6428
ISAAC COCHRAN-Men's & Boys' Hosiery, Underwear, Store Displays, Fixtures, Supplies
JEFFREY KERNUTS-Footwear

ABBOTT MILITARY TAILORS (MW-2)
200 S. Palafox St. (p)
Pensacola, FL 32501
850-438-9868 / Fax: 850-436-2063
Website: www.abbottuniforms.com
WILLIAM H. WARREN, JR. (G.M.M.) & Buys Uniforms

BLUE DOLPHIN (CLO)
8826 Grow Dr.
Pensacola, FL 23514
850-478-6500 / Fax: 850-428-4343
Website: www.bluedolphindesigns.com
DARLENE ARENZ-Beachwear, Swimwear, Surfwear

BROADWAY MENSWEAR (MW)
6249 N. Davis Hwy., #A (m)
Pensacola, FL 32504
850-475-0700
Sales: $100,001-$500,000
TEO ADVANI (Owner) & Buys Men's Sportswear, Furnishings, Accessories, 8 to 20 Boys' Suits, Dress Pants, Casual Pants, Shirts, Footwear, Store Displays, Fixtures, Supplies

DINAH'S SHORE SHOP (CLO-3)
14110 Perdido Key Dr. (m)
Pensacola, FL 32507
850-492-9411 / Fax: 850-497-1112
Sales: $500,001-$1 Million
DINAH WELLS (Owner) & Buys Men's Wear & Accessories

DIXON BROTHERS SPORTING GOODS (SG)
312 W. Detroit Blvd. (m)
Pensacola, FL 32534
850-476-3924 / Fax: 850-474-4791
JACK DIXON (Owner) & Buys Boys' Apparel, Men's Apparel, Men's Big & Tall Apparel, Men's Casualwear, Men's Denim Apparel, Men's Accessories, Men's Hosiery, Men's Outerwear, Men's Sportswear
PETE FOREHAND (Store Mgr.)

WEATHERFORD'S FOUR SEASON APPAREL (CLO)
3009 E. Cervantes St. (m-b)
Pensacola, FL 32503
850-469-9922 / Fax: 850-434-5605
Sales: $100,001-$500,000
Website: www.weatherfordsoutback.com
DAVID DODSON (Owner) & Buys Men's Sportswear, Belts, Headwear, Footwear, Store Displays, Fixtures, Supplies

HERBIE T'S (CLO)
45 Via De Luna Dr., #B (m-b)
Pensacola Beach, FL 32561
850-932-0721 / Fax: 850-931-0721
Sales: $500,001-$1 Million
HERB TURNER (Owner) & Buys Boys' Apparel, Men's Apparel, Men's Hosiery, Men's Outerwear, Men's Sleepwear, Men's Sportswear, Men's Suits, Men's Swimwear
PAUL EMANUEL (Store Mgr.)

THE FAIR STORE, INC. (DEPT)
123 N. Jefferson St. (p-m-b)
Perry, FL 32347
850-584-2247 / Fax: 850-838-1900
Sales: $500,000-$1 Million
HERBERT S. GLICKMAN (Owner) & Buys Men's Sportswear, Leather Apparel, Urban Contemporary, Furnishings, Accessories, Headwear, Footwear, Young Men's & Boys' Wear, Store Displays, Fixtures, Supplies

WAHINE BLUE (CLO)

11645 S. Dixie Hwy.
Pinecrest, FL 33156
786-242-6585 / Fax: 786-242-6575

STEPHANIE WILLIAMS (Owner) & Buys Sportswear, Swimwear, Beachwear, Headwear, Related Footwear, Leisurewear

NICOLE WILLIAMS-Sportswear, Swimwear, Beachwear, Headwear, Related Footwear, Leisurewear

BLACKIE CABRAL-Sportswear, Swimwear, Beachwear, Headwear, Related Footwear, Leisurewear

SPENCER'S WESTERN WORLD, INC. (WW-2 & OL)

7108 66th St. North (m-b)
Pinella, FL 33781
727-544-2606 / Fax: 727-544-2668
Website: www.westernstore.net

MARK SPENCER (Co-Owner) & Buys Men's & Young Men's Western Clothing, Sport Coats, Sport Shirts, Outer Jackets, Casual Slacks, Furnishings, Jewelry, Small Leather Goods, Boots, Store Displays, Fixtures, Supplies

GULFSHORE SPORT STORE, INC. (SG)

7686 49th St. (bud-p-m-b)
Pinellas Park, FL 33781
727-541-6488 / Fax: 721-544-3958

MIKE McKENNA (Owner) & Buys Sportswear, Footwear

NATIVE SUN SPORTSWEAR (CLO)

(ROCK 'N' ROLL CUSTOM SCREEN SHIRTS)
4590 62nd Ave. North (m)
Pinellas Park, FL 33781
727-528-2111 / Fax: 727-528-8441
Website: www.nativesunmarketing.com

GEORGE MITCHESON (Owner) & Buys Men's T-shirts, Fleecewear, Jackets, Hats, Store Displays, Fixtures, Supplies

SAM'S MEN'S FASHIONS (MW)

225 W. Alexander St. (m)
Plant City, FL 33566
813-752-8499 / Fax: 813-752-8499
Sales: $100,001-$500,000

SAM HIGEZ (Owner) & Buys Men's Wear, Young Men's Wear, Urban Contemporary, Sportswear, Tailored Jackets, Footwear, Accessories

BELL'S BEACH STORE (SP)

1201 S. Ocean Blvd.
Pompano Beach, FL 33062
954-782-6966 / Fax: 954-630-1743

RANDY BELL (Co-Owner) & Buys Beachwear, Swimwear, Headwear, Sandals

PATRICIA TUCKER (Co-Owner) & Buys Beachwear, Swimwear, Headwear, Sandals

FLORIDA NOVEL-TEES (CLO)

(SIAMESE TRADER O.G., INC.)
1404 SW 13th Ct.
Pompano Beach, FL 33069
954-946-7800 / Fax: 954-781-4652

GAIL SCHNEIDER (President) & Buys Men's & Boys' Casual Sportswear, Swimwear, Store Displays, Fixtures, Supplies

MARTONE'S MENSWEAR (MW)

2635 E. Atlantic Blvd. (b)
Pompano Beach, FL 33062
954-941-6493

GARY MARTONE (Owner) & Buys Men's Wear

MIAMI BLUES, INC. (CLO)

3400 E. Atlantic Blvd.
Pompano Beach, FL 33062
954-781-3501 / Fax: 954-782-0803

DANNY ROSS (Co-Owner) & Buys Surf & Beachwear, Swimwear, Sandals, Athletic Footwear

ISAAC ROSS (Co-Owner) & Buys Sandals, Athletic Footwear

POMPANO BEACH GOLF SHOP (GOLF)

1101 N. Federal Hwy.
Pompano Beach, FL 33062
954-781-0426 / Fax: 954-781-4653

BOB LORING (Owner) & Buys Golf Apparel, Footwear, Activewear, Licensed Apparel

POMPANO BEACH TENNIS CENTER (SP)

920 NE 18th Ave.
Pompano Beach, FL 33060
954-786-4115 / Fax: 954-786-4113
Website: www.mypompanobeach.org

BARBARA HERRMANN (Mgr.) & Buys Tennis Apparel & Footwear

VICTOR VICTORIA (MW-2)

2621 W. Atlantic Beach Blvd. (p)
Pompano Beach, FL 33069
954-968-7044

TERENCE YANG (Owner) & Buys Men's & Boys' Clothing, Sportswear, Urban Contemporary, Furnishings, Accessories, Store Displays, Fixtures, Supplies

WICKETS OF SAWGRASS (CLO)

P.O. Box 1586 (b)
200 Sawgrass Village Dr.
Ponte Verde Beach, FL 32082
904-285-7200 / Fax: 904-285-5034

CLIFF BROWN (Owner) & Buys Men's & Boys' Accessories

TYSON'S MENSWEAR, INC. (MW)

Town Center Mall (m)
1441 Tamiami Trl.
Port Charlotte, FL 33948
941-629-6411 / Fax: 941-629-6715

BOB YOUNG (President) & Buys Men's Sportswear, Suits, Slacks, Sportcoats, Caps, Furnishings, Belts

DAY DREAMS UNIFORMS, INC. (SP-2)

9304 US Hwy. 1 South (m)
Port Saint Lucie, FL 34952
561-335-7424 / Fax: 561-335-8707
Sales: $500,001-$1 Million

NELL ROGERS (President)

BOB ROGERS (Sls. Mgr.) & Buys Boys' Apparel, Men's Footwear, Leather Goods, Men's Uniforms

CAPTAIN'S LANDING (MW)

(TYSONS MENS WEAR, INC.)
1200 W. Retta Esplanade (m-b)
Punta Gorda, FL 33950
941-637-6000 / Fax: 941-637-6213

TRENT YOUNG (Mgr.) & Buys Men's Resort Wear, Footwear, Headwear, Store Displays, Fixtures, Supplies

LARAINE'S SWIMWEAR & RESORTWEAR (SP)

1200 W. Retta Esplanade
Fishermans Village, #M19
Punta Gorda, FL 33950
941-639-4233 / Fax: 941-627-4568
Website: www.laraines.com

LARAINE PROVENCE (Owner) & Buys Beachwear, Resortwear, Swimwear, Headwear, Sandals, Beach Footwear

GQ FASHION (MW)

22 E. Washington St. (m)
Quincy, FL 32351
850-627-6699

TALAL ABDEL (Owner) & Buys Men's & Boys' Clothing, Sportswear, Urban Contemporary, Furnishings, Accessories, Footwear, Store Displays, Fixtures, Supplies

MEDALLION SPORTS OF RIVIERA BEACH, INC. (SG-3)

2311 Broadway
Riviera Beach, FL 33404
561-848-7977 / Fax: 561-848-7988
Sales: $500,001-$1 Million

VINCE LICATA (President) & Buys Activewear, Athletic Footwear, Licensed Apparel

SURF RIVIERA (SG-3)
2601 N. Ocean Dr. (m-b)
Riviera Beach, FL 33404
561-881-4401 / Fax: 561-881-4401
Sales: $500,001-$1 Million
DAVID ZISLIN (Co-Owner) & Buys Boys' Apparel, Boys' Footwear, Men's Footwear, Men's Casualwear, Men's Swimwear
MOSES BRACHA (Co-Owner) & Buys Boys' Apparel, Boys' Footwear, Men's Footwear, Men's Casualwear, Men's Swimwear

THE 187 (CLO)
970 Francis St.
Saint Augustine, FL 32084
904-825-0448 / Fax: 904-829-8413
Website: www.the187.com
SARAH PACETTI-Beachwear, Swimwear
VINTON PACETTI-Beachwear, Swimwear

BONGO BAY (CLO)
1021 King St.
Saint Augustine, FL 32084
904-810-2233 / Fax: 904-810-5060
JIM ELLIS-Men's Sportswear
DONNA ELLIS-Men's Sportswear

FRESH LAUNDRY (CLO)
122 Saint George St.
Saint Augustine, FL 32084
904-824-6809
JOE McCLURE (Owner) & Buys Men's Resortwear, Sportswear, Western Wear

H.W. DAVIS, INC. (MW)
152 St. George
Saint Augustine, FL 32084
904-829-3742 / Fax: 904-829-1150
ROBERT LICHTER (Owner) & Buys Men's Sportswear

NAUTILUS AT THE BEACH (MW)
Hwy. A1A South at Rio Del Mar Rd.
Saint Augustine Beach, FL 32080
904-471-6280
SYLVIA SAMS (Owner) & Buys Men's Sportswear, Swimwear, Belts, Headwear, Footwear, Young Men's & Boys' Wear, Store Displays, Fixtures, Supplies

THE SUNSHINE SHOP (CLO)
645 A1A Beach Blvd.
Saint Augustine Beach, FL 32080
904-471-6899 / Fax: 904-471-7692
Website: www.sunshineshop.com
ALAN GREENE (Co-Owner) & Buys Resortwear, Swimwear, Sunglasses, Sandals
LYN GREENE (Co-Owner) & Buys Resortwear, Swimwear, Sunglasses, Sandals

FOREVER FLORIDA (CLO)
4755 N. Kenansville Rd.
Saint Cloud, FL 34773
407-957-9794 / Fax: 407-957-9157
MELLA JACOBS-Fashion Accessories, Hats, Men's Apparel, Outdoor Apparel
KIM DEL CAMPO-Fashion Accessories, Hats, Men's Apparel, Outdoor Apparel
CINDY LEIBRING-Fashion Accessories, Hats, Men's Apparel, Outdoor Apparel
KEITH LEIBRING-Fashion Accessories, Hats, Men's Apparel, Outdoor Apparel

AIRBRUSH MAGIC (CLO)
12979 Village Blvd.
Saint Petersburg, FL 33708
727-397-1638
MIKE GORDON (Owner) & Buys Imprintable T-shirts, Headwear, Sportswear

BOND JEWELERS, INC. (JWLY-8)
33 3rd Ave. North, #500
Saint Petersburg, FL 33701
727-821-2581 / Fax: 727-821-6733
Sales: $10 Million-$50 Million
Website: www.bonddiamonds.com
MARVIN SHAVLAN (President)
MICHAEL SHAVLAN (V.P.-Opers.) & Buys Jewelry
PATRICIA SHAVLAN-Jewelry

DOLPHIN BAY (CLO)
6255 Gulf Blvd.
Saint Petersburg, FL 33706
727-363-4449 / Fax: 727-363-4449
EYAL KADURY (Co-Owner) & Buys Swimwear, Surfwear, Beachwear, Surfboarding Accessories, T-shirts, Imprinted Sportswear
GALIT KADURY (Co-Owner) & Buys Swimwear, Surfwear, Beachwear, Surfboarding Accessories, T-shirts, Imprinted Sportswear

HELIOS (CLO)
909 Central Ave.
Saint Petersburg, FL 33705
727-822-8016 / Fax: 727-897-4079
LORI JOHNS (Owner) & Buys Sportswear, Leisurewear, Resortwear, Related Footwear

PANTS TOWNE (CLO)
6901 22nd Ave. North (p)
Saint Petersburg, FL 33710
727-341-0099 / Fax: 727-341-0008
RICK ALVAREZ (Co-Owner) & Buys Men's Sportswear, Jeans, Tops, Shorts, Store Displays, Fixtures, Supplies
SANDI BECKER (Co-Owner) & Buys Men's Sportswear, Jeans, Tops, Shorts, Store Displays, Fixtures, Supplies
MIKE ALVAREZ-Footwear

PARADISO, INC. (CLO)
104 8th Ave. (b)
Saint Petersburg, FL 33706
727-363-8831
Website: www.paradisoinc.qpg.com
SUSAN WESSON (Co-Owner) & Buys Men's & Boys' Clothing, Accessories, Active Apparel, Headwear, Hosiery, Casual Slacks, Boys' Accessories
MARTINA THORNE (Co-Owner) & Buys Men's & Boys' Clothing, Accessories, Active Apparel, Headwear, Hosiery, Casual Slacks, Boys' Accessories

RED BEAR CLOTHING (CLO)
4773 58th Ave. North
Saint Petersburg, FL 33714
727-522-6619 / Fax: 727-522-5109
JIM HUBRET (Owner) & Buys T-shirts, Imprinted Sportswear

SACINO'S FORMAL WEAR (MW-25)
3430 Fairfield Ave. South (m-b)
Saint Petersburg, FL 33711
727-323-1940 / Fax: 727-328-2814
Website: www.sacinos.com
RON SACINO (President & C.E.O.) & Buys Men's Tuxedoes & Formal Accessories, Footwear, Store Displays, Fixtures, Supplies

US COAST GUARD EXCHANGE (PX-4)
1301 Beach Dr. SE (p)
Saint Petersburg, FL 33701
727-896-2816 / Fax: 727-821-5033
Sales: $1 Million-$10 Million
TONI CARTISANO (Retail Mgr.) & Buys Men's Sportswear, Furnishings, Headwear, Belts, Jewelry, Small Leather Goods, Young Men's Wear, Men's Fragrances, Footwear

ATR ENTERPRISES, INC. (CLO)
431 Corey Ave. (m-b)
Saint Petersburg Beach, FL 33706
727-360-5142 / Fax: 727-360-5700
ALAIN RIMAR (Owner) & Buys Men's Active Apparel, Headwear, Footwear

FOOTLOOSE OUTFITTERS (CLO-4)
1700 Perwinkle Way
Sanabell, FL 33957
239-472-4717 / Fax: 239-472-3614
BRIAN BAUGHER (Owner) & Buys Knives, Watches, Headwear, Outdoor Apparel & Footwear, Beachwear, Beach Shoes, Sunglasses

FLORIDA SPORT WEAR (CLO)
1910 Park Ave.
Sanford, FL 32771
407-321-5354
DONNIE GREEN (Owner) & Buys Sportswear, Athletic Apparel, Resortwear

FLORIDA - Sanford

MEN'S DEN (MW)
3609 Orlando Dr. (m)
Sanford, FL 32773
407-323-7301 / Fax: 561-461-3655
MIKE KORODOR (Owner) & Buys Men's Sportswear, Furnishings, Accessories, 8 to 20 Boys' Suits, Sportswear, Store Displays, Fixtures, Supplies

SAI RAM FASHIONS (CLO)
4289 S. Orlando Dr.
Sanford, FL 32773
407-330-7792
PETER RAITWAINO (Owner) & Buys T-shirts, Beachwear, Imprinted Sportswear

BILLY'S CONCESSION CONSULTING (CLO)
1024 S. Yachtman Dr.
Sanibel, FL 33957
941-472-4919 / Fax: 914-472-0348
Website: www.bikesanibel.com
ALLI KIRKLAND (Owner) & Buys Men's Hats, Men's Apparel, Men's Surf & Swimwear, Outdoor Apparel, T-shirts, Imprinted Sportswear, Urban Contemporary

CARIBBEAN COAST (CLO-4)
(T-SHIRT PLACE)
(TAHITIAN SURF SHOP)
(WESTWIND SURF SHOP)
2075 Periwinkle Way
Sanibel, FL 33957
239-472-2993 / Fax: 239-432-0467
RALPH CANNATI (Owner)
MARY KAISER-Surfwear, Beachwear, Resortwear, Swimwear

MANGO BAY BEACH CO. (SP)
(CC-O WETZEL, INC.)
1700 Periwinkle Way, #2-3
Sanibel, FL 33957
239-472-6678 / Fax: 239-472-8473
DERRECK RYAN (Co-Owner) & Buys Beachwear, Swimwear, Resortwear, Headwear, T-shirts, Imprinted Sportswear
SUSAN LABOUNTY (Co-Owner) & Buys Beachwear, Swimwear, Resortwear, Headwear, T-shirts, Imprinted Sportswear

SHALIMAR INTERNATIONAL, INC. (CLO)
1997 Periwinkle Way
Sanibel, FL 33957
941-472-3310
ANGI UTTAMCHANDANI (Co-Owner) & Buys Beachwear, Sunglasses, Beach Shoes
JACK UTTAMCHANDANI (Co-Owner) & Buys Beachwear, Sunglasses, Beach Shoes

SPORTY SEAHORSE SHOP (DEPT)
362 Periwinkle Way (m-b)
Sanibel, FL 33957
941-472-1858 / Fax: 941-395-1858
JOHN NAPPI (Co-Owner)
JOANNE NAPPI (Co-Owner)
JUDY HOLTZLEITER (G.M.M.) & Buys Men's Sweaters, Sport Shirts, Outer Jackets, Casual Slacks, Active Apparel, Swimwear, Hosiery, Headwear, Footwear, Jewelry, Fragrances, Store Displays, Fixtures, Supplies

T-SHIRT HUT (CLO)
1504 Periwinkle Way
Sanibel, FL 33957
941-472-1415 / Fax: 941-395-0457
STAN FAGAN-Boys' Apparel, Fashion Accessories, Hats, Men's Surf & Swimwear, Resortwear
NICH TICHICH-Boys' Apparel, Fashion Accessories, Hats, Men's Surf & Swimwear, Resortwear

MEMORIES OF SANIBEL (CLO)
630 Tarpan Bay Rd.
Sanibel Island, FL 33957
941-395-1410
KAUSHILIA SAMTANI (Owner) & Buys Boys' Apparel, Sunglasses, Accessories, Footwear, Hats, Resortwear, T-shirts, Imprinted Sportswear, Men's Apparel

NANNY'S (CLO)
2340 Periwinkle Way, #D
Sanibel Island, FL 33957
941-472-0304
JAN GABRIELSON (Owner) & Buys Boys' Apparel, Boys' Swimwear, Footwear, Hats

COMPLEMENTS (CLO-2)
26 E. Logan Ln.
Santa Rosa Beach, FL 32459
850-231-0515 / Fax: 850-231-0258
SUSAN THORNTON (Owner) & Buys Men's Apparel

ONO SURF SHOP (SP)
2236 E. Country Rd., #30A
Santa Rosa Beach, FL 32459
850-231-1573 / Fax: 850-231-1593
JIM CALDWELL (Owner) & Buys Boys' Apparel, Boys' Swimwear, Accessories, Hats, Men's Apparel, Men's Surf & Swimwear, Resortwear, T-shirts, Imprinted Sportswear

ALPHABET SHOP (CLO)
386 Saint Armand's Cir.
Sarasota, FL 34236
941-388-1505 / Fax: 941-377-1765
JENNY LENZ-Boys' Apparel, Boys' Swimwear, Sunglasses, Footwear, Hats, Apparel, Swimwear, Resortwear

ANIMALE (CLO)
354 Saint Armand's Cir.
Sarasota, FL 34236
941-388-1476
ASIA TAYLOR-Sunglasses, Fashion Accessories, Resortwear, Men's Apparel
BLAIR TAYLOR-Sunglasses, Fashion Accessories, Resortwear, Men's Apparel

BEACH BAZAAR (SP)
5211 Ocean Blvd.
Sarasota, FL 34242
941-346-2995 / Fax: 941-346-3300
SUSAN BALES (Owner) & Buys Beachwear, Surf & Swimwear, Wet Suits, Headwear, Sandals, Beach Footwear

C.B.'S SALTWATER OUTFITTERS (CLO)
(SIESTA MR. C.B.'S RENTALS, INC.)
1249 Stickney Pt. Rd.
Sarasota, FL 34242
941-349-4400 / Fax: 941-346-1148
Sales: $500,001-$1 Million
Website: www.cbsoutfitters.com
ALEDIA TUSH (Co-Owner) & Buys Men's Apparel, Water Ski Apparel, Beach & Boating Apparel
CHERYL TOWNE (Co-Owner) & Buys Men's Apparel, Dive Apparel & Accessories, Sunglasses, Fashion Accessories, Footwear, Hats, Men's Surf & Swimwear, Outdoor Gear & Apparel, Resortwear

CRAVATS' CUSTOM SHIRTS & CLOTHIERS (MW)
222 Sarasota Quay (b)
Sarasota, FL 34236
941-366-7780 / Fax: 941-366-2874
Sales: $100,001-$500,000
Website: www.cravatscustomclothier.com
HENRY "HANK" BATTIE (Owner) & Buys Men's Custom Sportswear, Accessories, Footwear, Store Displays, Fixtures, Supplies

DELMAR SPORTSWEAR (SP)
6227 N. Washington Blvd.
Sarasota, FL 34243
941-360-8777 / Fax: 941-355-7260
Website: www.delmarsportswear.com
TOM CORELLO (Owner) & Buys Boys' Apparel, Boys' Swimwear, Sunglasses, Accessories, Hats, Men's Apparel, Private Label, Resortwear, T-shirts & Imprinted Sportswear

FRESH PRODUCE (CLO)
1 N. Blvd. of Presidents
Sarasota, FL 34236
941-388-1883 / Fax: 941-388-1886
SCOTT BROGAN (Owner) & Buys Boys' Apparel, Boys' Swimwear, Hats, Men's Apparel, Men's Surf & Swimwear, Resortwear
CHRISSY BASTURK-Boys' Apparel, Boys' Swimwear, Hats, Men's Apparel, Men's Surf & Swimwear, Resortwear
CEM BASTURK-Boys' Apparel, Boys' Swimwear, Hats, Men's Apparel, Men's Surf & Swimwear, Resortwear

GIANNINI DESIGNER FASHIONS (MW)
2144 Gulf Gate Dr. (b)
Sarasota, FL 34231
941-923-1752
FRANK GIANNINI (Co-Owner) & Buys Men's Sportswear, Leather Apparel, Furnishings, Accessories, Store Displays, Fixtures, Supplies
ANNA GIANNINI (Co-Owner) & Buys Men's Sportswear, Leather Apparel, Furnishings, Accessories, Store Displays, Fixtures, Supplies

GLENWITS MENSWEAR (MW)
1476 Main St. (m)
Sarasota, FL 34236
941-955-5022
JOE BOROME (Owner) & Buys Men's Outerwear, Sportswear, Furnishings, Accessories, Store Displays, Fixtures, Supplies

HOT FLASH (CLO)
4858 S. Tamiami Trl.
Sarasota, FL 34231
941-921-7027 / Fax: 941-921-7278
FRANKIE RUSHMORE (Owner) & Buys Men's Apparel, Men's Swimwear, Resortwear, Urban Contemporary, T-shirts, Imprinted Sportswear, Fashion Accessories, Hats, Footwear

ISLAND COTTON COMPANY (CLO-1)
5221 Ocean Blvd., #4
Sarasota, FL 34242
941-349-1170
GEORGE ANDRASI (Co-Owner) & Buys Men's Apparel, Fashion Accessories, Hats, Resortwear
ED ADRASI (Co-Owner)

JOLIES (CLO)
17 N. Blvd. Of Presidents
Sarasota, FL 34236
941-388-3040 / Fax: 941-388-4467
DARRELL ROBERTSON (Co-Owner) & Buys Men's Apparel, Resortwear, Hats
VALERIE ROBERTSON (Co-Owner) & Buys Men's Apparel, Resortwear, Hats

KATIE-DID'S ORIGINALS, INC. (CLO)
6851 Whitefield Industrial Ave.
Sarasota, FL 34243
941-756-8338 / Fax: 941-753-9387
Website: www.katie-dids.com
TRAVIS CUNDIFF (Owner) & Buys Men's Apparel, Boys' Apparel, T-shirts, Imprinted Sportswear, Outddoor Apparel, Hats

KING JAMES BIG & TALL MEN'S STORE (MW-3)
(KING JAMES, INC.)
4333 S. Tamiami Trl. (b)
Sarasota, FL 34231
941-922-3790 / Fax: 941-922-2430
Sales: $1 Million-$10 Million
JAMES MONTONEY (Owner) & Buys Store Displays, Fixtures, Supplies
MATT MONTONEY-Big & Tall Men's Wear

LUBA'S FASHION (CLO)
8918 Huntington Pointe Dr.
Sarasota, FL 34238
941-366-1079 / Fax: 941-955-7472
MARTIN CHYORY-Men's Apparel, Boys' Apparel, Men's Surfwear, T-shirts, Imprinted Sportswear, Resortwear, Fashion Accessories
VLADIMIR SHAPIRO-Men's Apparel, Boys' Apparel, Men's Surfwear, T-shirts, Imprinted Sportswear, Resortwear, Fashion Accessories
LUBA SHAPIRO-Men's Apparel, Boys' Apparel, Men's Surfwear, T-shirts, Imprinted Sportswear, Resortwear, Fashion Accessories

MY GENERATION GRAPHICS (CLO)
1090 Commerce Blvd. North
Sarasota, FL 34243
941-358-1373 / Fax: 941-358-1430
JON SCHUM (Co-Owner) & Buys Boys' Apparel, Hats, Men's Apparel, Resortwear, Private Label, T-shirts, Imprinted Sportswear
CONNIE SCHUM (Co-Owner) & Buys Boys' Apparel, Hats, Men's Apparel, Resortwear, Private Label, T-shirts, Imprinted Sportswear
HEATHER PAGES-Boys' Apparel, Hats, Men's Apparel, Resortwear, Private Label, T-shirts, Imprinted Sportswear

SIESTA TEES (CLO)
5239 Ocean Blvd.
Sarasota, FL 34242
941-349-4540 / Fax: 941-346-7514
MARILYN ADAMS (Owner) & Buys Boys' Apparel, Boys' Swimwear, Sunglasses, Hats, Men's Apparel, Men's Surf & Swimwear, T-shirts, Imprinted Sportswear
PAT DODGE (Mgr.) & Buys Boys' Apparel, Boys' Swimwear, Sunglasses, Hats, Men's Apparel, Men's Surf & Swimwear, T-shirts, Imprinted Sportswear

SISCO (CLO)
7707 33rd Ln. East
Sarasota, FL 34243
941-351-9877 / Fax: 941-358-1196
HARRY CLOUGH (Owner) & Buys Sheepskin Slippers & Boots

STOCKYARD (CLO)
1010 Cattleman Rd. (m)
Sarasota, FL 34232
941-371-6591 / Fax: 941-378-9754
Sales: $1 Million-$10 Million
CY BISPHAM (Owner) & Buys Boys' Apparel, Boys' Footwear, Men's Footwear, Leather Goods, Men's Apparel, Men's Big & Tall, Men's Casualwear, Men's Denim Apparel, Men's Accessories
TIM DROWN (Store Mgr.)

SWIM CITY (CLO)
1960 Stickney Point Rd.
Sarasota, FL 34231
941-922-4545 / Fax: 941-923-0640
MARY GRONINGER (President) & Buys Swimwear, Sandals, Beachwear

SWIM MART (SP-7)
(SWIM WORLD, INC.)
5250 S. McIntosh Rd.
Sarasota, FL 34233
941-927-8445 / Fax: 941-927-8645
Sales: $1 Million-$10 Million
Website: www.swimmart.com
JUDY JOHNSON (Owner) & Buys Swimwear, Beachwear, Loungewear, Sunglasses, Sandals

TAFFY'S (MW-3)
14 S. Blvd. of Presidents (b-h)
Sarasota, FL 34236
941-388-1155 / Fax: 941-388-2701
Sales: $1 Million-$10 Million
STEVE BEAN (Co-Owner & President) (@ 954-523-3545) & Buys Men's Overcoats, Suits, Tailored Jackets, Tailored Slacks, Sweaters, Sport Shirts, Outer Jackets, Casual Slacks, Active Apparel, Leather Apparel, Furnishings, Accessories
FOREST HESTER (Co-Owner) & Buys Men's Overcoats, Suits, Tailored Jackets, Tailored Slacks, Sweaters, Sport Shirts, Outer Jackets, Casual Slacks, Active Apparel, Leather Apparel, Furnishings, Accessories
JACK PEFFLEY (G.M.M.) & Buys Men's Overcoats, Suits, Tailored Jackets, Tailored Slacks, Sweaters, Sport Shirts, Outer Jackets, Casual Slacks, Active Apparel, Leather Apparel, Furnishings, Accessories

FLORIDA - Sarasota

WALL STREET FOR MEN (MW-3)
3501 S. Tamiami Trl. (m)
Sarasota, FL 34239
941-365-2881
GHAZI ABRAHAM (Owner)
JEAN ABRAHAM (Mgr.) & Buys Men's Sportswear, Urban Contemporary, Furnishings, Accessories, Footwear, Store Displays, Supplies

MACHO PRODUCTIONS (CLO)
10045 102nd Ter.
Sebastian, FL 32958
561-388-9892 / Fax: 561-388-9859
CHARLES FERRER-Boys' Apparel, Boys' Swimwear, Dive Apparel & Accessories, Sunglasses, Accessories, Footwear, Hats, Men's Apparel, Men's Surf & Swimwear, Skate Apparel, T-shirts, Imprinted Sportswear, Windsurf Apparel & Accessories
ALI FERRER-Boys' Apparel, Boys' Swimwear, Dive Apparel & Accessories, Sunglasses, Accessories, Footwear, Hats, Men's Apparel, Men's Surf & Swimwear, Skate Apparel, T-shirts, Imprinted Sportswear, Windsurf Apparel & Accessories

BOB'S MENSWEAR (MW)
906 SE Lakeview Dr. (m)
Sebring, FL 33870
863-385-8546 / Fax: 863-314-9665
Sales: $100,001-$500,000
JIM GOSE (Co-Owner)
PAT GOSE (Co-Owner & G.M.M.) & Buys Men's Suits, Tailored Jackets, Tailored Slacks, Sweaters, Sport Shirts, Outer Jackets, Leather Apparel, Urban Contemporary, Casual Slacks, Dress Shirts, Ties, Robes, Underwear, Hosiery, Belts, Jewelry, Small Leather Goods, Fragrances, Footwear, Store Displays, Fixtures, Supplies

CONRAD EGAN (CLO)
5116 Ocean Blvd. (m-b)
Siesta Key, FL 34242
941-349-8777 / Fax: 941-349-9716
SONNY SEARS (Owner) & Buys Men's Sportswear, Furnishings, Accessories, Young Men's Wear, Store Displays, Fixtures, Supplies

LANE'S EXCELLENCE IN MEN'S CLOTHING (MW)
5700 Sunset Dr. (b)
South Miami, FL 33143
305-667-7560 / Fax: 305-669-4790
Sales: $1 Million-$10 Million
EDWARD BOAS (President) & Buys Men's Overcoats, Suits, Tailored Jackets, Tailored Slacks, Sportswear, Furnishings, Accessories, Store Displays, Fixtures, Supplies

THE AMERICAN BAG (CLO)
5568 Commercial Way (p)
Spring Hill, FL 34606
352-666-7227
Sales: $100,001-$500,000
PHIL SCHICK (Owner) & Buys Men's & Boys' Jeans, T-shirts, Sportswear, Leather Apparel, Urban Contemporary, Headwear, Young Men's Wear, Western Wear, Store Displays, Fixtures, Supplies

GATOR & NOLE COUNTRY (GS)
2121 US Hwy. 1 South
St. Augustine, FL 32086
904-794-4897 / Fax: 904-797-2549
GINGER LUCAS (Owner) & Buys Men's Sportswear, Headwear, Golf Apparel, Accessories, 8 to 20 Boys' T-shirts, Jackets, Store Displays, Fixtures, Supplies

BEACH MART, INC. (SP-4)
5297 Gulf Blvd.
St. Pete Beach, FL 33706
727-360-0776 / Fax: 727-363-4155
STEVE LUPER (President) & Buys Activewear, Beachwear, Footwear
AMANDA SHENISE (Mgr.)

MAD MUSIC (SP)
(MADEIRA BEACH SURF SHOP)
6630 Central Ave.
St. Petersburg, FL 33707
727-381-0100
Website: www.madmusiconline.com
ROB PORTER (Co-Owner) & Buys Music Oriented Sportswear, Accessories
GINA PORTER (Co-Owner) & Buys Music Oriented Sportswear, Accessories

GORE CREEK OUTFITTERS (CLO)
41 W. Osceoloa St., #B
Stuart, FL 34994
561-221-8554 / Fax: 561-283-6903
Website: www.gorecreekflyfisherman.com
CHRIS KOKEY-Fashion Accessories, Footwear, Men's Apparel, Resortwear, T-shirts, Imprinted Sportswear

HUTCHISON ISLAND MARRIOT BEACH RESORT (CLO)
555 NE Ocean Blvd. (m-b)
Stuart, FL 34996
772-225-3700 / Fax: 772-225-0003
JIM WENTLEY (Supv.) & Buys Men's Wear & Footwear, Store Displays, Fixtures, Supplies

MALE TRENDS OF FLORIDA, INC. (MW-2)
3744 SE Ocean Blvd. (m)
Stuart, FL 34996
561-220-1454 / Fax: 561-220-2910
HARVEY TOBACK (Owner) & Buys Men's Sportswear, Custom Suits, Furnishings, Accessories, Urban Contemporary, Store Displays, Fixtures, Supplies

TAYLOR'S CLOTHING SALES (CLO)
610 SE 10th St. (m)
Stuart, FL 34994
561-287-4696
CLAUDIUS TAYLOR (President) & Buys Men's Suits, Sportswear, Urban Contemporary, Big & Tall Men's Wear, Store Displays, Fixtures, Supplies
RUBY TAYLOR (V.P.)

SUMMERLAND STYLES (CLO)
24748 Overseas Hwy.
Summerland Key, FL 33042
305-744-4405
JANET FUNK (Co-Owner) & Buys Beachwear, T-shirts, Shorts
CHERYL SMITH (Co-Owner) & Buys Beachwear, T-shirts, Shorts

ANANIAS, INC. (CLO)
10287 NW 46th St.
Sunrise, FL 33351
954-747-7810 / Fax: 954-747-7811
Website: www.ananias.com
SUZANNE PARTENZA-Fashion Accessories, Footwear, Private Label
LOU PARTENZA-Fashion Accessories, Footwear, Private label

MAYOR'S JEWELERS, INC. (JWLY-28)
14051 NW 14th St., #200
Sunrise, FL 33323
954-835-3400 / Fax: 954-835-3361
Sales: $100 Million-$500 Million
Website: www.mayors.com
Retail Locations: FL, GA
TOM ANDRUSKOVICH (President, C.E.O. & Dir.-Real Estate)
IDA ALVAREZ (Mdse. Mgr.)
ALISON ROBERTS-Jewelry

BROADWAY MENSWEAR (CLO)
2547 S. Adams St. (m-b)
Tallahassee, FL 32301
850-942-7200
MUSONG YI (Owner) & Buys Men's Wear, Boys' Suits, Leather Apparel, Footwear, Store Displays, Fixtures, Supplies

FLORIDA STATE BOOK STORE (SP)
(FLORIDA STATE UNIVERSITY)
Follett 208
Tallahassee, FL 32306
850-644-2072 / Fax: 850-644-9953
Sales: $100,001-$500,000
Website: www.fsu.bkstr.com
MIKE DUFFY (Gen. Mgr.)
TROY CORBIN-Activewear, Fleece, Pants, Jackets, Hosiery, Shorts, Sport Headwear, Licensed Apparel

NIC'S TOGGERY, INC. (MW-3)

212 S. Monroe St. (b)
Tallahassee, FL 32301
850-222-0687 / Fax: 850-224-5579
Sales: $10 Million-$50 Million
Website: www.nicstoggery.com

VICTOR GAVALAS (President) & Buys Men's Overcoats, Suits, Tailored Jackets, Tailored Slacks, Raincoats, Sweaters, Sport Shirts, Outer Jackets, Casual Slacks, Leather Apparel, Belts, Footwear

SPORTS BEAT, INC. (CLO)

2020 W. Pensacola St., #20 (m-b)
Tallahassee, FL 32304
850-576-3338 / Fax: 850-575-6956
Sales: $500,001-$1 Million
Website: www.sportsbeatinc.com

SHANNON SULLIVAN (Owner) & Buys Boys' Apparel, Boys' Footwear, Men's Footwear, Men's Apparel, Men's Casualwear, Men's Denim Apparel, Men's Accessories, Men's Hosiery, Men's Outerwear, Men's Sportswear, Men's Swimwear

GEORGE WEST (Dir.-Opers.) & Buys Boys' Apparel, Boys' Footwear, Men's Footwear, Men's Apparel, Men's Casualwear, Men's Denim Apparel, Men's Accessories, Men's Hosiery, Men's Outerwear, Men's Sportswear, Men's Swimwear

TAILS 'N' TWEEDS (MW)

1410 Market St., #C5 (b)
Tallahassee, FL 32301
850-893-8446 / Fax: 850-893-5654
Website: www.tailsntweeds.com

BILL THOMAS (Owner) & Buys Men's & Boys' Formal Wear

GOLD COAST FORMAL WEAR, INC. (MW)

5308 NW 22nd Ave. (m-b)
Tamarac, FL 33309
954-735-4440 / Fax: 954-484-6154

CHARLIE WALTERS (Owner) & Buys Men's & Boys' Formal Wear, Footwear, Store Displays, Fixtures, Supplies

DENIM CITY OF TAMPA (CLO)

8857 N. Florida Ave. (m)
Tampa, FL 33604
813-935-4809 / Fax: 813-933-7609

DOROTHY STEINFELD (President & Owner)
ANN SHAPIRO-Sportswear, Accessories
TISHA BLAIR-Sportswear, Accessories

GEORGE LTD. (MW)

4315 W. Kennedy Blvd. (b)
Tampa, FL 33609
813-877-1223 / Fax: 813-282-8447
Sales: $1 Million-$10 Million

ROBERT ESPINOLA (Owner) & Buys Men's Overcoats, Suits, Tailored Jackets, Sweaters, Sport Shirts, Outer Jackets, Leather Apparel, Casual Slacks, Active Apparel, Dress Shirts, Ties, Underwear, Hosiery, Gloves, Store Displays, Fixtures, Supplies

JOHN HRIFKO (G.M.M.) & Buys Men's Overcoats, Suits, Tailored Jackets, Sweater, Sport Shirts, Outer Jackets, Leather Apparel, Casual Slacks, Active Apparel, Dress Shirts, Ties, Underwear, Hosiery, Gloves, Men's Wear, Store Displays, Fixtures, Supplies

GREINER'S OF TAMPA, INC. (MW)

117 Whiting St. (b)
Tampa, FL 33602
813-226-3207 / Fax: 813-229-3548

DOUG TOZIER (Co-Owner) & Buys Men's Sportswear, Furnishings, Accessories

CHRIS BLOWERS (Co-Owner) & Buys Men's Sportswear, Furnishings, Accessories

HOMBRE CLOTHIER, INC. (MW)

Tampa Bay Center (b)
3302 W. Martin Luther King Blvd.
Tampa, FL 33607
813-875-3009 / Fax: 813-875-0644
Sales: $100,001-$500,000

FRED SALEM (Owner) & Buys Men's Sportswear, Furnishings, Accessories, Store Displays, Fixtures & Supplies

SAM BAL (Mgr.) & Buys Men's Sportswear, Footwear, Furnishings, Accessories

NEW YORK FASHIONS (MW)

2323 Hillsborough Ave. (m)
Tampa, FL 33610
813-237-2545

SONNY SAJNANI (Owner) & Buys Men's Sportswear, Furnishings, Footwear, Accessories, Young Men's Wear, 8 to 20 Boys' Wear, Store Displays, Fixtures, Supplies

THE SWIMWEAR COMPANY (CLO)

(UJENA SWIMWEAR)
2790 E. Fowler Ave.
Tampa, FL 33612
813-978-8057 / Fax: 813-558-8487
Website: www.swimwearcompany.com

RICHARD HUG (President & Owner) & Buys Activewear, Swimwear, Accessories

FAKLIS DEPARTMENT STORE (DEPT)

139 E. Tarpon Ave. (m)
Tarpon Springs, FL 34689
727-937-3602 / Fax: 727-938-1669
Sales: $100,001-$500,000

MICHAEL V. FAKLIS (Co-Owner) & Buys Men's Sportswear, Urban Contemporary, Furnishings, Young Men's & Boys' Wear, Store Displays, Fixtures, Supplies

GEORGE V. FAKLIS (President) & Buys Men's Footwear, Men's Sportswear, Furnishings, Young Men's & Boys' Wear, Store Displays, Fixtures, Supplies

PARK SHOES, INC. (FW-3)

(VILLAGE BOOTERY)
245 S. US Hwy. 1 (m-b)
Tequesta, FL 33469
561-746-3536 / Fax: 561-744-7851
Sales: $1 Million-$10 Million

THOMAS SCHUEMANN (President & Treas.) & Buys Men's Footwear, Leather Goods, Men's Accessories, Men's Hosiery

DEBORAH SCHUEMANN (V.P.) & Buys Men's Footwear, Leather Goods, Men's Accessories, Men's Hosiery

TIM O'BRIEN (Gen. Mgr.) & Buys Men's Footwear, Leather Goods, Men's Accessories, Men's Hosiery

GAIL'S BRIDAL BOX (SP)

2400 S. Hopkins Ave. (bud-p-m-b)
Titusville, FL 32780
321-268-1311
Sales: $500,001-$1 Million

GAIL WARD (President) & Buys Men's Apparel, Men's Big & Tall, Men's Formalwear, Men's Accessories

MALE IMAGE (MW)

2500 S. Washington Ave. (m)
Titusville, FL 32780
321-269-4589
Sales: $100,001-$500,000

FAREE KADUR (Owner) & Buys Men's Sport Coats, Sweaters, Sport Shirts, Outer Jackets, Casual Slacks, Furnishings, Accessories

SAAD CHEHAB-Men's Footwear, Urban Contemporary

BEACH HOUSE OF TREASURE ISLAND (SP)

10621 Gulf Blvd.
Treasure Island, FL 33706
727-367-5172

JOE GIROLANO (Co-Owner) & Buys Beachwear, Surf & Swimwear, Wet Suits, Headwear, Sandals, Beach Footwear

LYNN GIROLANO (Co-Owner) & Buys Beachwear, Surf & Swimwear, Wet Suits, Headwear, Sandals, Beach Footwear

FLORIDA - Vero Beach

THE BEACHED WHALE (SP)
3143 Ocean Dr.
Vero Beach, FL 32963
561-231-0244 / Fax: 561-231-8883
MARY WALKER (Owner) & Buys Boys' Apparel, Boys' Swimwear, Sunglasses, Accessories, Footwear, Hats, Men's Apparel, Men's Surf & Swimwear, Resortwear, T-shirts, Imprinted Sportswear

DISNEY'S VERO BEACH RESORT (GS)
9250 Island Rd. Ter.
Vero Beach, FL 32963
561-234-2023 / Fax: 561-234-2030
TERESA MAGES-Beachwear, Surf & Swimwear, Wet Suits, Headwear, Sandals

G.T. RHODES MEN'S CLOTHING (MW)
Sexton Plaza (b-h)
1008 Beachland Blvd.
Vero Beach, FL 32963
561-231-6424 / Fax: 561-231-7917
MS. GERRE RHODES (Owner) & Buys Men's Wear, Suits

HANLON'S MEN'S SHOES (FW)
3343 Cardinal Dr. (h)
Vero Beach, FL 32963
561-231-2334
TOM HANLON (President & Owner) & Buys Men's Wear, Footwear

J. RANS (CLO)
818 Beachland Blvd. (b)
Vero Beach, FL 32963
561-234-1401 / Fax: 561-234-1403
RANDY HINDERT (Owner) & Buys Men's Wear, Tailored Jackets, Tailored Slacks, Furnishings, Sportswear

VERNON SCOTT MENSWEAR (MW)
3240 Cardinal Dr. (b)
Vero Beach, FL 32963
561-234-3066
VERNON ROSCHACH (Owner) & Buys Men's Sportswear, Furnishings, Accessories, Footwear, Store Displays, Fixtures, Supplies

VERO BEACH CYCLING & FITNESS (SP)
1865 14th Ave.
Vero Beach, FL 32960
561-562-2781 / Fax: 561-562-5552
Sales: $501,000-$1 Million
JAMES DeBULA (Co-Owner)
JOANN FOLLETTE (Co-Owner) & Buys Apparel, Footwear, Skiing Apparel
EVERETT L. FOLLETTE (Co-Owner) & Buys Apparel, Footwear, Skiing Apparel
BRIAN DeBULA-Apparel, Athletic Footwear

POLO GEAR (MW & OL)
3500 Fairlane Farms Rd., #15
Wellington, FL 33414
561-795-1719 / Fax: 561-795-1731
Website: www.pologearusa.com
GARY FELLERS (Owner) & Buys Men's Sportswear, Furnishings, Accessories

ARMY NAVY OUTDOORS (AN)
1649 N. Military Trl.
West Palm Beach, FL 33409
561-684-5533 / Fax: 561-684-6363
ADELE ABBOTT (Owner) & Buys Athletic Footwear, Activewear

EPIC SURF & SWIM (SP-2)
13873 Wellington Terr.
West Palm Beach, FL 33414
561-795-5470
DAVID FITCH (Owner) & Buys Beachwear, Surf & Swimwear, Wetsuits, Headwear, Athletic Shoes, Sandals, Skateboards

FIELD'S ARMY & NAVY STORE (AN)
811 Belvedere Rd., #A (m)
West Palm Beach, FL 33405
561-832-1242
Sales: Under $100,000
JACK KIRSCHNER (Owner) & Buys Men's Pants, Tops, Underwear, Hosiery, Gloves, Headwear, Belts, Boys' Bottoms, Tops, Leather Apparel, Outerwear, Footwear, Store Displays, Fixtures, Supplies

J.C. HARRIS & CO. (MW)
335 Clematis St. (p-m-b)
West Palm Beach, FL 33401
561-832-7747 / Fax: 561-832-7747
JIM HARRIS (Owner) & Buys Men's Wear, Sportswear, Furnishings, Accessories, Young Men's Wear, Footwear, Tailored Jackets, Tailored Slacks

J.C. WESTERN SUPPLY (WW-2)
1200 S. Congress Ave. (m-b)
West Palm Beach, FL 33406
561-967-0100 / Fax: 561-967-0127
BRIGITTE HALSEY (Owner) & Buys Men's & Boys' Western Wear, Men's Sportswear, Furnishings, Accessories, Boots, Headwear, Store Displays, Fixtures, Supplies
MAXENE SCHMIDT-Men's & Boys' Western Wear, Men's Sportswear, Furnishings, Accessories, Boots, Headwear, Store Displays, Fixtures, Supplies

SELBY SHOES (FW-2 & OL)
3161 Forest Hill Blvd. (bud-p-m-b-des)
West Palm Beach, FL 33406
561-969-9369 / Fax: 561-439-2977
Sales: $1 Million-$10 Million
Website: www.selbyshoeswpb.com
RIAD BATRUNY (Owner) & Buys Men's Footwear, Leather Goods, Men's Hosiery
ANDREW HICKS (Mgr.)

ZEIDEL'S ANCHORS AWEIGH (CLO)
203 6th St. (m)
West Palm Beach, FL 33401
561-655-2311 / Fax: 561-655-9642
Website: www.zeidel.com
BRUCE ZEIDEL-Sportswear, Men's Wear, Footwear

ATHLETIC ATTIC (SP)
Indian Trace Shopping Center
1382 SW 160th Ave.
Weston, FL 33326
817-284-3479 / Fax: 954-349-8440
Sales: $100,001-$500,000
SALLY WILHELM (Owner) & Buys Active Apparel, Athletic Footwear, Licensed Apparel, Athletics

ANDY THORNAL EXPEDITION OUTFITTERS (CLO)
336 Magnolia Ave. SW (m-b)
Winter Haven, FL 33880
863-299-9999 / Fax: 863-297-8025
Website: www.andythornal.com
ANDY THORNAL (Owner)
SCOTT HART (V.P.) & Buys Men's Sportswear, Leather Apparel, Furnishings, Headwear, Accessories, Store Displays, Fixtures, Supplies
KEN HART-Men's Footwear

DOWNEAST SPORTING CLASSICS (SG-2)
(OLDE PARKE TRADING CO.)
538 Park Ave. South (m-b)
Winter Park, FL 32789
407-645-5100 / Fax: 407-628-9544
Sales: $1 Million-$10 Million
DON SEXTON (Co-Owner)
CARINA SEXTON (Co-Owner) & Buys Men's Sportswear, Furnishings, Accessories, Footwear, Outerwear, Store Displays, Fixtures, Supplies

JOHN CRAIG LTD. (MW)
132 S. Park Ave.
Winter Park, FL 32789
407-629-7944 / Fax: 407-629-1096
CRAIG DeLONGY (Owner) & Buys Men's Wear, Men's Accessories, Footwear

GEORGIA - Albany

2BIGFEET.COM (OL & FW)
717 N. Slappey Blvd., #B
Albany, GA 31701
229-434-0000 / Fax: 706-882-8103
Website: www.2bigfeet.com
BRANDON ELEE-Men's Athletic, Dress and Casual Footwear, Oversize Footwear

CONNIE'S CORNER (MW)
301 S. Jackson St. (bud-m-b)
Albany, GA 31701
229-432-6911
Sales: $100,001-$500,000
MR. CONNIE V. FORD (Owner) & Buys Men's Suits, Tailored Jackets, Pants, Sportswear, Urban Contemporary, Young Men's Wear, Furnishings

FRIEDMAN'S CLOTHING, INC. (MW)
719 N. Westover Rd. (p-m-b)
Albany, GA 31707
229-431-0304 / Fax: 229-431-1164
Sales: $100,001-$500,000
Website: www.friedmansclothing.com
BRUCE BITTERMAN (President) & Buys Men's Sportswear, Furnishings, Hosiery, Accessories, Footwear, Store Displays, Fixtures, Supplies

MARINE CORPS EXCHANGE (PX)
MCCS (bud)
814 Radford Blvd., #20322, Bldg. 7500
Albany, GA 31704
229-888-6801 / Fax: 229-439-0324
WARD OFFICER WHITAKER (Exchange Ofcr.-Retail)
DIANE SUTKO-Men's & Boys' Sportswear, Leather Apparel, Store Displays, Fixtures, Supplies

SOUL FASHIONS OF NEW YORK (MW)
240 W. Broad Ave. (m)
Albany, GA 31701
912-436-3241
Sales: $100,001-$500,000
PETER MELWANI (Owner) & Buys Men's Sportswear, Furnishings & Accessories, Store Displays, Fixtures, Supplies

COHEN'S OF ALMA, INC. (CLO)
420 W. 12th St. (p-m-b)
Alma, GA 31510
912-632-5273 / Fax: 912-632-5765
Sales: $500,000-$1 Million
MARK COHEN (Co-Owner) & Buys Men's Sportswear, Furnishings, Headwear, Men's Dress Shoes, Sneakers, Accessories, Young Men's & Boys' Wear, Store Displays, Fixtures, Supplies
JERALD COHEN (Co-Owner) & Buys Men's Men's Furnishings, Headwear, Men's Dress Shoes, Sneakers, Accessories, Young Men's & Boys' Wear
WAYNE GOLDEN (G.M.M.) & Buys Store Displays, Fixtures, Supplies

TNT FASHIONS (MW)
417 W. 12th St. (m)
Alma, GA 31510
912-632-6900 / Fax: 912-632-4586
Sales: $100,001-$500,000
TERRELL SALLET (Owner) & Buys Men's Sportswear, Furnishings & Accessories, Young Men's Wear, Urban Contemporary, Store Displays, Fixtures, Supplies

THE FAIR STORE (CLO)
127 W. Forsyth St. (m-b)
Americus, GA 31709
229-924-2796 / Fax: 229-931-0444
Sales: $100,001-$500,000
JOHNNY MEMHOOD (Owner) & Buys Men's Suits, Tailored Jackets, Tailored Slacks, Sportswear, Furnishings, Footwear, Accessories, Young Men's Shop, Boys' Wear, Store Displays, Fixtures, Supplies

KINNEBREW CO., INC. (CLO)
208 W. Lamar St. (m-b)
Americus, GA 31709
229-924-8888 / Fax: 229-924-9858
Sales: $1 Million-$10 Million
HULME KINNEBREW, III (President) & Buys Men's Furnishings, Sportswear, Clothing, Underwear, Hosiery, Accessories, Dress & Casual Footwear
LINDA ROBERSON (Office Mgr.) & Buys Store Displays, Fixtures, Supplies

DICK FERGUSON CLOTHING STORES, INC. (CLO)
196 Alps Rd. (m-b)
Athens, GA 30606
706-548-7246 / Fax: 706-548-3061
DICK FERGUSON (President) & Buys Men's Sportswear, Furnishings, Headwear, Accessories, Dress Shoes, Store Displays, Fixtures, Supplies

GEORGE DEAN'S MEN'S STORE (MW)
P.O. Box 1427 (m-b)
227 E. Clayton St.
Athens, GA 30603
706-548-4406 / Fax: 706-548-4469
Sales: $500,000-$1 Million
GEORGE DEAN (Owner)
WAYNE DEAN-Men's Overcoats, Suits, Tailored Jackets, Tailored Slacks, Raincoats, Sweaters, Sport Shirts, Outer Jackets, Casual Slacks, Leather Apparel, Furnishings, Headwear, Dress Footwear, Accessories, Young Men's Wear, Store Displays, Fixtures, Supplies

GEORGE GIBSON'S MENSWEAR (MW)
196 Alps Rd. (p-m-b)
Beechwood Shopping Center
Athens, GA 30606
706-548-4663 / Fax: 706-353-8350
Sales: $100,001-$500,000
ANDY GIBSON (Owner) & Buys Men's Overcoats, Suits, Tailored Jackets, Tailored Slacks, Raincoats, Big & Tall Men's Wear, Sportswear, Sweaters, Sport Shirts, Outer Jackets, Leather Apparel, Casual Slacks, Active Apparel, Furnishings, Dress Shirts, Ties, Robes, Underwear, Hosiery, Gloves, Headwear, Accessories, Belts, Small Leather Goods

JUNKMAN'S DAUGHTER'S BROTHER (CLO)
458 E. Clayton St. (p-m)
Athens, GA 30601
706-543-4454 / Fax: 706-369-1600
Sales: $100,001-$500,000
MARK GAVRON (President) & Buys Men's Overcoats, Raincoats, Sportcoats, Sweaters, Sport Shirts, Outer Jackets, Casual Slacks, Hosiery, Headwear, Jewelry, Small Leather Goods, Footwear, Urban Contemporary, Store Displays, Fixtures, Supplies
BRIAN KING (Asst. Mgr.) & Buys Men's Overcoats, Raincoats, Sportcoats, Sweaters, Sport Shirts, Outer Jackets, Casual Slacks, Hosiery, Headwear, Jewelry, Small Leather Goods, Footwear, Store Displays, Fixtures, Supplies

KUM'S FASHIONS (CLO-2)
115 E. Clayton St. (p-m-b)
Athens, GA 30601
706-546-6945
Sales: $100,001-$500,000
PETER AH (Owner) & Buys Tailored Jackets & Slacks, Raincoats, Big & Tall Wear, Sportswear, Sweaters, Sport Shirts, Outer Jackets, Leather Apparel, Casual Slacks, Active Apparel, Furnishings, Dress Shirts, Ties, Robes, Underwear, Hosiery, Gloves, Headwear, Accessories, Belts, Jewelry, Small Leather Goods, Young Men's Shop, Boys' Sportswear, Furnishings, Accessories, Footwear, Store Displays, Fixtures & Supplies

GEORGIA - Athens

UNIVERSITY OF GEORGIA BOOK STORE (SP)
P.O. Box 2217
Athens, GA 30612
706-542-3171 / Fax: 706-542-7243
Website: www.bookstore.uga.edu
HENRY BRYAN (Mgr.)
BETH BAKER-Activewear, Pants, Jackets, Hosiery

BALBOA, INC. (CLO)
70 Alabama St. SW
Atlanta, GA 30303
404-525-1445
STEVE SULT-Men's Pants, Shirts, Accessories

BENNIE'S SHOES (FW-3)
2625 Piedmont Rd. NE (m-b)
Atlanta, GA 30324
404-262-1966 / Fax: 404-262-7528
Sales: $100,001-$500,000
Website: www.benniesshoes.com
LOUIS SHEMARIA (President) & Buys Men's Dress Footwear, Hosiery, Belts, Accessories

BOY NEXT DOOR (MW)
1447 Piedmont Ave. (m)
Atlanta, GA 30309
404-873-2664 / Fax: 404-873-1486
Sales: $100,001-$500,000
DAVID BOSWELL (Mgr.) & Buys Men's Sportswear, Urban Contemporary, Dress Shirts, Underwear, Hosiery, T-shirts, Jeans, Shorts, Belts, Small Leather Goods, Sandals, Store Displays, Fixtures, Supplies

BRITE CREATIONS, INC. (MW-6)
(WHAT'S HAPPENING)
(CITY WIDE FASHIONS)
60-62 Decatur St. SE (m)
Atlanta, GA 30303
404-588-1164 / Fax: 770-695-9595
Sales: $100,001-$500,000
MICHAEL RAMA (President)
NEIL RAMA-Men's Suits, Sportswear, Dress Shirts, Headwear, Young Men's Wear, Urban Contemporary, Boys' Wear, Store Displays, Fixtures, Supplies
DAN RAMA-Men's Dress & Casual Apparel, Furs, Leather Apparel, Footwear
RAJ GIDWANI-Big & Tall Men's Wear, Plus Sizes

COLONIAL UNIFORMS (MW)
3102 Oakcliff Industrial St. (m-b)
Atlanta, GA 30340
770-457-0447 / Fax: 770-457-4157
Sales: $100,001-$500,000
JACK WILLIS (Co-Owner)
TERRIE WILLIS (Co-Owner)
JOE HERZOG-Men's Hotel Office & Industrial Uniforms

EDGAR POMEROY LTD. (CLO)
2985 Piedmont Rd. NE
Atlanta, GA 30305
404-365-0405 / Fax: 404-262-1144
Sales: $1 Million-$10 Million
EDGAR POMEROY (Owner) & Buys Men's Footwear, Men's Apparel, Men's Accessories, Men's Suits

EXECUTIVE SHOP (MW)
56 Walton St. NW (m-b)
Atlanta, GA 30303
404-577-2898
Sales: $100,001-$500,000
RICK LINKWALD (Owner) & Buys Men's Sportswear, Furnishings, Accessories, Shoes

FRIEDMAN'S SHOES (FW-2 & OL & MO)
209 Mitchell St. SW (b)
Atlanta, GA 30303
404-524-1311 / Fax: 404-524-3831
Sales: $1 Million-$10 Million
Website: www.largefeet.com
BRUCE FRIEDMAN (President)
BRETT FRIEDMAN (V.P. - e-Commerce) & Buys Men's Footwear, Hosiery, Accessories
RANDY FRIEDMAN-Men's Apparel
MURRAY TEILHABER-Men's Hosiery

GEORGIO'S BIG & TALL (MW)
Greenbriar Mall (m)
Atlanta, GA 30331
404-344-8411 / Fax: 404-349-4353
Sales: $100,001-$500,000
JEAN CLAUDE TORIZ (Owner) & Buys Men's Wear

GOLDEN TREASURES, INC. (CLO-5)
21 Peachtree St. SW (m-b)
Atlanta, GA 30303
404-658-9933 / Fax: 404-880-4123
Sales: $500,001-$1 Million
BENNY GABBI (Owner) & Buys Men's Sportswear, Furnishings & Accessories, Young Men's Wear, Store Displays, Fixtures & Supplies
SAM EITAN (Mgr.) & Buys Men's Sportswear, Furnishings & Accessories, Young Men's Wear
BOB YAIR-Footwear

GUFFEY'S OF ATLANTA, INC. (MW)
3340 Peachtree Rd. (b)
Atlanta, GA 30326
404-231-0044 / Fax: 404-237-4091
Sales: $1 Million-$10 Million
Website: www.guffeys.com
DON W. GUFFEY (President) & Buys Men's Clothing and Overcoats, Suits, Tailored Jackets, Tailored Slacks, Raincoats, Sweaters, Sportswear, Sport Shirts, Ties, Furnishings, Accessories, Footwear, Store Displays, Fixtures, Supplies

H. STOCKTON - ATLANTA, INC. (MW-5)
4505 Ashford Dunwoody Rd. (b)
Atlanta, GA 30346
770-396-1300 / Fax: 770-396-2416
Sales: $1 Million-$10 Million
CHIP STOCKTON (President) & Buys Men's Tailored Slacks, Sportswear, Urban Contemporary, Men's Overcoats, Suits, Tailored Jackets, Furnishings, Accessories, Store Displays, Fixtures and Supplies

HATSHACK.COM (SP & MO & OL)
3731 Northcrest Rd., #13
Atlanta, GA 30340
770-454-8301 / Fax: 770-454-8303
Website: www.hatshack.com
MARK MONROE (President)
MICHAEL COOK (D.M.M.)
MARK DEAL (V.P.) & Buys Men's & Boys' Headwear
CRAIG WILLIS (Asst.) & Buys Men's & Boys' Headwear

HATVANTAGE (OL)
(ROBLEY HATS, INC.)
44 Peachtree Cir. (m-b)
Atlanta, GA 30309
404-876-4287 / Fax: 404-607-7131
Sales: Under $100,000
Website: www.hatvantage.com
ROBERT GERSON (Owner) & Buys Men's & Boys' Headwear

HONG KONG TAILORS (MW)
(ELEGANT FASHIONS)
5378 Buford Hwy. (b)
Atlanta, GA 30340
770-458-8682 / Fax: 770-457-8482
Sales: $100,001-$500,000
L.G. VASWANI (Owner) & Buys Men's Furnishings & Accessories

INTERNATIONAL MAN (MW)
Phipps Plz. (m-b)
3500 Peachtree Rd. NE
Atlanta, GA 30326
404-841-0770
Sales: $100,001-$500,000
LEE GAJESKI (Owner) & Buys Men's Sportswear, Urban Contemporary, Dress Shirts, Ties, Robes, Hosiery, Gloves, Accessories, Store Displays, Fixtures, Supplies

GEORGIA - Atlanta

JUNKMAN'S DAUGHTER (CLO)

464 Moreland Ave. NE (m-b)
Atlanta, GA 30307
404-577-3188 / Fax: 404-223-0880
Sales: $1 Million-$10 Million

PAM MAJORS (President) & Buys Men's Footwear, Leather Goods, Men's Apparel, Men's Casualwear, Men's Denim Apparel, Men's Accessories, Men's Hosiery, Men's Outerwear, Men's Sportswear, Men's Suits

SUSANNE GIBBONEY (Gen. Mgr.) & Buys Men's Footwear, Leather Goods, Men's Apparel, Men's Casualwear, Men's Denim Apparel, Men's Accessories, Men's Hosiery, Men's Outerwear, Men's Sportswear, Men's Suits

MEN'S FASHION CORNER (MW)

1366 Morland Ave. (m)
Atlanta, GA 30316
404-622-5504 / Fax: 404-622-5504
Sales: $100,001-$500,000

JIN CHOY (Owner) & Buys Men's Sportswear, Furnishings & Accessories, Young Men's Wear, Store Displays, Fixtures, Supplies

NEW YORK FASHIONS (MW)

69 Peachtree St. SW, #C (m)
Atlanta, GA 30303
404-522-6738 / Fax: 404-522-6766
Sales: $100,001-$500,000

TONY MULCHANDANI (Owner) & Buys Men's Sportswear, Furnishings & Accessories, Young Men's Wear, Urban Contemporary, Store Displays, Fixtures, Supplies

NEIL MULCHANDANI-Men's Sportswear, Furnishings & Accessories, Young Men's Wear, Urban Contemporary, Store Displays, Fixtures, Supplies

NORTH FULTON (CLO)

500 Abernathy Rd. NE (b)
Atlanta, GA 30328
404-256-3591 / Fax: 404-256-3591
Sales: $500,001-$1 Million

SCOTT JONES (Owner) & Buys Boys' Apparel, Boys' Footwear, Men's Footwear, Men's Apparel, Mens's Big & Tall, Men's Casualwear, Men's Denim Apparel, Men's Accessories, Men's Sportswear

MARK FAIRCHILD (Gen. Mgr.)

OXFORD STREET (MW-3 & CLO)

Greenbriar Mall (m-b)
2841 Greenbriar Pkwy.
Atlanta, GA 30331
404-508-1445 / Fax: 404-349-4353
Sales: $500,001-$1 Million

ELIE KARAM (Owner) & Buys Men's & Boys' Wear, Dress Shoes, Casual Shoes, Footwear, Store Displays, Fixtures & Supplies

THE PARADIES SHOPS (GS-300)

P.O. Box 43485 (m)
5950 Fulton Industrial Blvd. SW
Atlanta, GA 30336
404-344-7905 / Fax: 404-349-7539
Sales: $500,001-$1 Million
Website: www.theparadiesshops.com

GREG PARADIES (President)

RICHARD DICKSON (Chmm)

LYNN BENNETT (V.P. - Mktg)

TIM KINDER (V.P. - Mdsg.)

JEFF MASON (Dir. - Visual)

MICHELLE SENIGO-Men's & Boys' Souvenir & Fashion Clothing, T-Shirts, Shorts

RICH'S, INC. (DEPT-74)

(Div. of FEDERATED DEPARTMENT STORES)
(GOLDSMITH'S)
(LAZARUS)
(MACY'S)
223 Perimeter Center Pkwy. (p-m-b)
Atlanta, GA 30346
(Federated Merchandising Group)
770-913-4000 / Fax: 770-913-5809
Sales: Over $3 Billion
Website: www.federated-fds.com
Retail Locations: AL, GA, SC

DAVID NICHOLS (President)

RON KLEIN (C.E.O.)

RONALD W. TYSOE (Vice Chmn.-Finance)

GARY J. NAY (Real Estate Contact)

BECKY DEMHOUSER (V.P. & G.M.M.-Men's & Boys' Wear) (@ 770-913-5555)

SCOTT WILTSEY (D.M.M.-Men's Sportswear) (@ 770-913-4128)

RICK PAYNE (D.M.M.-Men's Clothing, Pants, & Shoes) (@ 770-913-4098)

BRYAN NOSAL (@ 770-913-4506)-Men's Knits, Sweaters, Golf Apparel, Men's Activewear, Swimwear, Shorts, Tommy Active

MATTHEW BRAWNING (@ 770-913-5494)-Men's Casual Slacks, Levi Basic Jeans, Dress Casual Slacks, Better Casual Slacks

HOWARD SALLERSON (@ 770-913-4257)-Men's Suits, Tailored Jackets, Tailored Slacks, Sport Coats, Top Coats, Raincoats

MICHELLE MANN (@ 770-913-4015)-Men's Wovens, Outerwear, CHAPS

OPEN-Men's Dress Shirts, Neckwear, Ties, Polo Dress Shirts, Fashion Dress Shirts

STEPHEN RECTOR (@ 770-913-4588)-Men's Tommy Hilfiger, Fila, Perry Ellis, Inc.

DAVID RAYMOND (@ 770-913-4121)-Men's Polo, Nautica, Claiborne

CHRIS MANNING (D.M.M.-Men's Furnishings) (@ 770-913-5522)

RESA HALLER (@ 770-913-4258)-Men's Accessories, Small Leathers, Belts, Seasonal

JOHN WALSH (@ 770-913-4166)-Men's Underwear, Sleepwear, Pajamas, Robes, Hosiery

NATASHA LEBOWITZ-8 to 20 Boys' Bottoms, Tommy Hilfiger, Polo, Guess, Calvin Klein, Collections

KAREN NETTLES-Young Men's Jeans, Tommy Hilfiger, Calvin Klein, Guess, Nautica, DKNY

MARY VORUS-8 to 20 Boys' Tops, Clothing, Outerwear, Furnishings, Accessories, Moderate Coordinates

RICH FLEMMING (@ 770-913-4883)-Men's Footwear

GEORGIA - Atlanta

ROGUE, INC. (MW)
284 Buckhead Ave. (p)
Atlanta, GA 30305
404-233-2245
Sales: $500,001-$1 Million
BRUCE NELSON (Owner) & Buys Men's Sportswear, Furnishings & Accessories, Footwear, Store Displays, Fixtures, Supplies

SAVVI FORMAL WEAR (MW-14)
(HEIGHTS, INC.)
140 James Ulridge Blvd. (m-b)
Atlanta, GA 30336
404-691-7610 / Fax: 404-691-2026
Sales: $500,001-$1 Million
TOM PACER, SR. (Owner) & Buys Men's Tuxedos, Dress Shirts, Hosiery, Boys' Formalwear, Store Displays, Fixtures & Supplies

SEBASTIAN'S CLOSET, INC. (MW)
3222 Peachtree Rd. NE (p)
Atlanta, GA 30305
404-365-9033 / Fax: 404-365-9726
ROBERT KUCHENBECKER (Owner) & Buys Men's Sportswear, Furnishings & Accessories, Young Men's Wear, Footwear, Store Displays, Fixtures, Supplie

SHOEMAKERS' WAREHOUSE (FW)
500 Amsterdam Ave. NE, #A (m-b-des)
Atlanta, GA 30306
404-881-1896 / Fax: 404-881-9227
Sales: $500,001-$1 Million
Website: www.shoemakerswarehouse.com
BETSY ROBBINS (Owner) & Buys Men's Footwear, Leather Goods, Men's Accessories
TRACEY THOMAS (Mgr.) & Buys Men's Footwear, Leather Goods, Men's Accessories

SHOES ITALIANO (FW)
63 Forsyth St. NW
Atlanta, GA 30303
404-589-8134
DAN RAMA (V.P.) & Buys Men's Shoes, Hosiery, Accessories

STYLE CRAFT OF ATLANTA (MW)
11 Decatur St. (m)
Atlanta, GA 30303
404-524-5177
Sales: $500,001-$1 Million
JOHN LEE (Owner) & Buys Men's Sportswear, Urban Contemporary, Furnishings & Accessories, Store Displays, Fixtures, Supplies

TERRY SALES CO. (CLO)
4360 Commerce Cir., #B (p-m)
Atlanta, GA 30336
404-691-3403 / Fax: 404-691-3404
TERRY ARONOFF (Owner) & Buys Men's Sportswear, Headwear, Accessories, Big & Tall Men's Wear, Young Men's & Boys' Wear, Store Displays, Fixtures, Supplies

THONY'S CLOTHING (MW)
(HOLLYWOOD FASHIONS, INC.)
111 Peachtree St. SW (p)
Atlanta, GA 30303
404-525-0711 / Fax: 404-525-0734
Sales: $500,000-$1 Million
RITA TURETSKY (President) & Buys Men's Overcoats, Suits, Tailored Jackets, Tailored Slacks, Raincoats, Sportswear, Dress Shirts, Ties, Underwear, Hosiery, Gloves, Belts, Dress Shoes, Big & Tall Men's Wear, Size 8 to 20 Boys' Wear, Urban Contemporary, Store Displays, Fixtures, Supplies

UNDERNEATH.COM (CLO & OL)
2109 Faulkner Rd. NE
Atlanta, GA 30324
404-329-0096 / Fax: 404-329-0097
Sales: $500,001-$1 Million
Website: www.underneath.com
MIKE WATERS (V.P.)
JEFF JOHNSON (C.E.O.) & Buys Boys' Apparel, Men's Accessories, Men's Hosiery, Men's Underwear

WEST END MENSWEAR (MW)
826 Ralph Davis Abernathy (m)
Atlanta, GA 30310
404-756-0566
Sales: Under $100,000
HAE KIM (Owner) & Buys Men's Sportswear, Dress Shoes, Furnishings & Accessories, Young Men's Wear, Boys' Suits, Urban Contemporary, Store Displays, Fixtures, Supplies

BOARDROOM, INC. (CLO)
3604 Verandah Dr. (b)
Augusta, GA 30909
706-733-6203 / Fax: 706-733-4660
Sales: $500,001-$1 Million
HAMILTON KUHLKE (Chmn.)
STAN REYNOLDS (President) & Buys Men's Overcoats, Suits, Sport Coats, Slacks, Sportswear, Footwear, Store Displays, Fixtures, Supplies
DAVID HALLDEN (G.M.M.) & Buys Men's Overcoats, Suits, Sport Coats, Slacks, Sportswear, Footwear, Store Displays, Fixtures, Supplies

DAVID'S MENSWEAR (MW)
948 Broad St.
Augusta, GA 30901
706-724-1440
Sales: $100,001-$500,000
DAVID ALANDAITCH-Men's Wear

GENTRY MEN'S SHOP (MW)
Surrey Ctr. (b)
Augusta, GA 30909
706-733-2256 / Fax: 706-733-2261
Sales: $100,001-$500,000
BRUCE JACKSON (Owner) & Buys Men's Casual and Dress Clothes

HARRINGTON'S SPORTSWEAR (MW)
2827 Washington Rd. (m)
Augusta, GA 30909
706-738-4810 / Fax: 706-737-4045
Sales: $100,001-$500,000
REGIS A. HARRINGTON (President) & Buys Men's & Boys' Sportswear, Sweaters, Sportshirts, Outer Jackets, Casual Slacks, Active Apparel, Dress Shirts, Headwear

MANHATTAN (MW)
3450 Wrightsboro Rd. (m)
Augusta, GA 30909
706-736-6595 / Fax: 706-736-6595
Sales: $100,001-$500,000
DON LEE (Owner) & Buys Men's Sportswear, Urban Contemporary, Furnishings & Accessories, Footwear, Store Displays, Fixtures, Supplies

OUR SHOP MEN'S FURNISHINGS (MW)
1014 Broad St. (p)
Augusta, GA 30902
706-724-0402
Sales: $1 Million-$10 Million
DAVID DAITCH (Owner & G.M.M.) & Buys Men's Overcoats, Suits, Tailored Jackets, Leather Apparel, Raincoats, Big & Tall Men's Wear, Sportswear, Dress Shirts, Footwear, Ties, Underwear, Hosiery, Headwear, Accessories, Young Men's Wear, Urban Contemporary, Store Displays, Fixtures, Supplies

RUBEN'S DEPARTMENT STORES OF AUGUSTA, INC. (DEPT)
914 Broad St. (m-b)
Augusta, GA 30901
706-722-6671 / Fax: 706-724-6671
Sales: $1 Million-$10 Million
BONNIE RUBEN (President) & Buys Boys' Wear
JEFF GORELICK-Men's Sportswear, Leather Apparel, Furnishings, Headwear, Accessories, Footwear, Young Men's Wear, Boys' Wear, Store Displays, Fixtures, Supplies

SIDNEY'S DEPARTMENT STORE & UNIFORMS, INC. (DEPT)
550 Broad St. (m)
Augusta, GA 30901
706-722-3112 / Fax: 706-722-2262
Sales: $100,001-$500,000
M. STEVEN FISHMAN (President) & Buys Men's Sportswear, Furnishings, Accessories, Uniforms, Work Clothing, Footwear, Store Displays, Fixtures, Supplies

RAY'S JEANS & TOPS (CLO)
30168 Veterans Memorial Hwy. (m)
Austell, GA 30168
770-944-8242
Sales: $500,001-$1 Million
RAY NEWMAN (Owner) & Buys Men's & Boys' Jeans, Shirts, T-shirts, Jackets, Belts

T-SHIRT DESIGNS, INC. (CLO)
2869 Washington St. (bud-p)
Avondale Estates, GA 30002
404-296-4555 / Fax: 404-296-0319
Sales: $1 Million-$10 Million
Website: www.catalogsportswear.com
JEFF DRAKER (Owner) & Buys Boys' Apparel, Men's Apparel, Men's Casualwear, Men's Accessories, Men's Outerwear, Men's Sportswear

TONY BATTEN'S MEN'S SHOP, INC. (MW)
256 E. Main St. (b)
Blackshear, GA 31516
912-449-5565 / Fax: 912-449-5566
Sales: $100,001-$500,000
TONY BATTEN (Owner) & Buys Men's Sportswear, Furnishings & Accessories, Dress Shoes, Store Displays, Fixtures, Supplies

ALEXANDER'S STORE (DEPT)
4966 Town Creek School Rd. (p-m-b)
Blairsville, GA 30512
706-745-6450 / Fax: 706-745-2381
Sales: $500,001-$1 Million
EDDIE ALEXANDER (Owner)
SANDY ALEXANDER-Men's Wear, Urban Contemporary, Casual Boots, Work Boots, Store Displays, Fixtures, Supplies

HAYES MENSWEAR (MW)
210 Columbia St., #6 (m)
Blakely, GA 31723
229-723-8825 / Fax: 229-723-8825
Sales: $500,001-$1 Million
BILLY W. HAYES (Owner) & Buys Sportswear, Suits, Furnishings, Casual Slacks, Shorts, Denim, Urban Contemporary, Young Men's Wear, Accessories

MULTI-LINE INDUSTRIES, INC. (MW)
124 Commerce St. (m-b)
Bowdon, GA 30108
770-258-5500 / Fax: 770-258-3007
Sales: $500,001-$1 Million
JAMES JONES (President) & Buys Men's Suits, Raincoats, Tailored Slacks, Sportcoats, Sweaters, Sport Shirts, Outer Jackets, Casual Slacks, Dress Shirts, Headwear, Big & Tall Men's, Store Displays, Fixtures, Supplies
BECKY JONES-Men's Suits, Raincoats, Tailored Slacks, Sportcoats, Sweaters, Sport Shirts, Outer Jackets, Casual Slacks, Dress Shirts, Headwear, Big & Tall Men's, Store Displays, Fixtures, Supplies

ATHLETIC ATTIC (SP-2)
Colonial Mall
100 Mall Blvd., #C1
Brunswick, GA 31525
912-264-6568 / Fax: 912-264-8633
Sales: $1 Million-$10 Million
FRANK STILL, JR. (President) & Buys Athletic Footwear, Activewear, Licensed Apparel, acc

GENTLEMAN'S OUTFITTERS, INC. (MW-2)
100 Mall, #C1 (m)
Brunswick, GA 31526
912-264-1023 / Fax: 912-264-8633
Sales: $500,001-$1 Million
FRANK STILL (Owner)
ELIZABETH ALYWARD (V.P.) & Buys buy Men's Jackets, Slacks, Sportswear, Furnishings & Accessories, Casual Shoes, Young Men's Wear, Boys' Wear, Store Displays, Fixtures, Supplies

P S MENSWEAR, INC. (MW)
4420 Altama Ave. (p)
Brunswick, GA 31520
912-265-1069 / Fax: 912-265-1069
Sales: $100,001-$500,000
ARTHUR COOK (Owner) & Buys & Buy Men's Sportswear, Furnishings & Accessories, Big & Tall Men's Wear, Store Displays, Fixtures, Supplies

PETER'S MALE APPAREL, INC. (MW)
1521 Newcastle St. (m-b)
Brunswick, GA 31520
912-265-7446 / Fax: 912-264-8551
Sales: $100,001-$500,000
PETER VIVENZIO (Co-Owner) & Buys Men's Sportswear, Urban Contemporary, Furnishings, Accessories, Store Displays, Fixtures, Supplies

KEENE'S FASHIONS (CLO)
P.O. Box 54 (m)
109 Court St.
Calhoun, GA 30701
706-629-3703
Sales: $100,001-$500,000
NETTIE HOLLINGSWORTH (President) & Buys Men's Tailored Slacks, Sportswear, Dress Shirts, Ties, Robes, Underwear, Hosiery, Belts, Small Leather Goods, Men's Big & Tall, Young Men's & Boys' Clothing, Sportswear, Store Displays, Fixtures, Supplies

MEN'S DEN, INC. (MW)
306 Hwy. 53 (p)
Calhoun, GA 30701
706-629-8369
Sales: $100,001-$500,000
EMMETT DUPREE (Owner) & Buys Men's Sportswear, Leather Apparel, Furnishings, Boys' Wear

MOORE MEN'S & BOY'S SHOP, INC. (MW)
514 S. Wall St. (p)
Calhoun, GA 30701
706-629-3633
Sales: $100,001-$500,000
DeETTE MOORE (Owner) & Buys Men's Suits, Tailored Jackets, Sweaters, Outer Jackets, Casual Slacks, Active Apparel, Leather Apparel, Furnishings, Belts, Footwear, Jewelry, Boys' Wear, Urban Contemporary, Store Displays, Fixtures, Supplies

SPECIAL OCCASIONS BRIDAL & FORMAL SHOP (CLO)
309 Bellwood Rd. (m-b)
Calhoun, GA 30701
706-625-2865
Sales: $100,001-$500,000
TERESA FARRIS (Owner) & Buys Men's Formalwear

E-BOOT.COM (CLO & OL)
(BOOTS PLUS)
Carnesville Sq. (p)
181 Athens St.
Carnesville, GA 30521
706-384-4243
Website: www.e-boot.com
BILL LITTLE (Owner) & Buys Men's Work Boots, Furnishings, Accessories, Store Displays, Fixtures, Supplies
SHIRLEY LITTLE-Men's Work Boots, Furnishings, Accessories, Store Displays, Fixtures, Supplies

PHOENIX FASHIONS FOR BUSINESS (CLO)
39 S. Public Sq. (bud-p-m)
Cartersville, GA 30120
770-386-5770 / Fax: 770-382-4122
Sales: $1 Million-$10 Million
Website: www.phoenixfb.com
BOB POSTON (Owner)
PETE POSTON (G.M.M.)
DALE KEITH-Men's Footwear, Men's Apparel, Men's Casualwear, Men's Denim Apparel, Men's Sportswear, Men's Uniforms

BARRY MANUFACTURING CO. (MW-19 & OL)
(BARRY BETTER MEN'S WEAR)
2303 John Glenn Dr. (bud)
Chamblee, GA 30341
770-451-5476 / Fax: 770-451-8095
Website: www.bettermenswear.com
BARRY ZEEMAN (President & C.E.O.) & Buys Men's Wear, Clothing, Furnishings, Accessories
KEITH McSurley (Dir. - Store Opers.) & Buys Men's Wear, Clothing, Furnishings, Accessories, Footwear

HOUSE OF TYROL, INC. (GM & MO)
P.O. Box 909
66 E. Kytle St.
Cleveland, GA 30528
706-865-5115 / Fax: 706-865-7794
Sales: $500,001-$1 Million
LINDA NAGY (Co-Owner)
BERNARD NAGY (Co-Owner) & Buys Men's Sportcoats, Sweaters, Sport Shirts, Headwear, Accessories, Store Displays, Fixtures, Supplies
BERNIE PURK-Men's Sportcoats, Sweaters, Sport Shirts, Headwear, Accessories, Store Displays, Fixtures, Supplies
LISA PURK-Men's Sportcoats, Sweaters, Sport Shirts, Headwear, Accessories, Store Displays, Fixtures, Supplies

LYLES' (CLO)
208 2nd St. (m)
Cochran, GA 31014
478-934-6911 / Fax: 478-934-1171
Sales: $100,001-$500,000
MR. JODY LYLES (Owner) & Buys Men's Wear, Casual Shoes

IN FASHION MENSWEAR OUTLET (MW)
4853 Old National Rd., #B (p)
College Park, GA 30337
404-766-1035 / Fax: 404-763-8337
Sales: $500,001-$1 Million
MIKE PARMANAND (Co-Owner) & Buys Men's Sportswear, Furnishings & Accessories, Footwear, Store Displays, Fixtures, Supplies

BOB DOW'S RACQUETS SPORTSWEAR (SP)
3551 Macon Rd.
Columbus, GA 31907
706-561-9292 / Fax: 706-563-7077
BOB DOW (Mgr.) & Buys Apparel, Footwear, Racquetball Apparel

CHANCELLOR'S (MW)
1108 Broadway (b)
Columbus, GA 31901
706-322-8819 / Fax: 706-323-9178
Sales: $500,000-$1 Million
J. EDGAR CHANCELLOR, III (President) & Buys Men's Overcoats, Suits, Tailored Jackets, Tailored Slacks, Raincoats, Sweaters, Sport Shirts, Outer Jackets, Casual Slacks, Furnishings, Headwear, Accessories, Dress Shoes, Store Displays, Fixtures, Supplies

HENRI'S FORMAL WEAR (MW-3)
2312 Francis St.
Columbus, GA 31906
706-322-4466 / Fax: 706-596-8191
Sales: $500,001-$1 Million
Website: www.sunraycleaners.com
JACK WILENSKY (Owner) & Buys Store Displays, Fixtures, Supplies
CONNIE COXS-Men's, Young Men's & Boys' Formal Wear, Dress Shoes, Related Accessories & Furnishings, Store Displays, Fixtures and Supplies

JOE'S DEPARTMENT STORE (CLO)
310 6th St. (bud)
Columbus, GA 31901
706-571-0996
Sales: $100,001-$500,000
JOE LAUDEDALE (Owner) & Buys Men's Wear, Furnishings, Accessories

KRAVTIN'S NOVELTY SHOP (CLO)
(KRAVTIN'S, INC.)
1027 Broadway (m)
Columbus, GA 31901
706-323-1651 / Fax: 706-324-0170
Sales: $500,000-$1 Million
BYRNA MYERS (Co-Owner)
BILLY KRAVTIN (C.E.O.) & Buys Men's, Young Men's & Boys' Wear, Urban Contemporary, Footwear, Store Displays, Fixtures, Supplies

THE MOVIN MAN (MW)
(HEWELL INTERNATIONAL, INC.)
1021 Broadway
Columbus, GA 31901
706-327-1836
WALTER HEWELL (Owner) & Buys Suits, Sportswear, Urban Contemporary, Underwear, Hosiery, Headwear, Belts, Footwear, Store Displays, Fixtures, Supplies

ON TIME FASHION, INC. (MW)
1010 Broadway (m)
Columbus, GA 31901
706-324-3212
Sales: $100,001-$500,000
GEORGE SAAD (Owner) & Buys Men's Suits, Tailored Jackets, Tailored Slacks, Casual Slacks, Sportswear, Shoes, Urban Contemporary

RANGER JOE'S INTERNATIONAL (SP-3 & MO)
325 Farr Rd.
Columbus, GA 31907
706-689-0082 / Fax: 706-689-0954
Website: www.rangerjoes.com
PAUL VOORHEES (Co-Owner)
JANICE VOORHEES (Co-Owner)
VANESSA WHATLEY-Apparel, Footwear, Outdoor Apparel, Hunting and Shooting Apparel, Military Clothing, Police Unifrom, Camouflage
TRACY ROLON-Apparel, Footwear, Outdoor Apparel, Hunting and Shooting Apparel, Military Clothing, Police Unifrom, Camouflage

JAY'S DEPARTMENT STORE (DEPT)
P.O. Box 875 (p-m-b)
1710 S. Broad St.
Commerce, GA 30529
706-335-4300 / Fax: 706-335-4300
Sales: $100,001-$500,000
NATHAN JAY (President) & Buys Store Displays, Fixtures, Supplies, Men's & Boys' Wear, Footwear
TERRY MINISH (Mgr.) & Buys Men's & Boys' Wear, Urban Contemporary, Footwear

WALL'S FACTORY OUTLET STORE, INC. (CLO)
3730 US Hwy. 280 East (m)
Cordele, GA 31015
229-273-5299 / Fax: 229-273-5962
Sales: $100,001-$500,000
AUDREY HOBBS (Owner)
BILLY HOBBS (G.M.M.) & Buys Men's Raincoats, Big & Tall Men's Wear, Sport Shirts, Outer Jackets, Casual Slacks, Active Apparel, Furnishings, Headwear, Accessories, Boots, Young Men's Wear, Size 8 to 20 Camouflage Boys' Wear, Store Displays, Fixtures, Supplies

GOLD'S DEPARTMENT STORE, INC. (DEPT)
643 Irvin St. (p)
Cornelia, GA 30531
706-778-2921
Sales: $100,001-$500,000
NATHAN BURGEN (Owner) & Buys Men's Wear, Casual Shoes, Dress Shoes, Boys' Sportswear, Furnishings, Store Displays, Fixtures, Supplies

COHEN'S MEN'S SHOP (MW)

P.O. Box 30015 (m-b)
1132 Monticello St.
Covington, GA 30014
770-786-9033 / Fax: 770-786-8268
Sales: $500,000-$1 Million

BRITT SMITH (Owner) & Buys Men's Sportswear, Leather Apparel, Accessories, Furnishings, Dress Shoes, Casual Shoes, Big & Tall Men's, Young Men's Wear, Boys' Wear, Store Displays, Fixtures, Supplies

BOBBY SMITH (Gen. Mgr.) & Buys Men's Sportswear, Leather Apparel, Accessories, Furnishings, Dress Shoes, Casual Shoes, Big & Tall Men's, Young Men's Wear, Boys' Wear, Store Displays, Fixtures, Supplies

RAMEY'S DEPARTMENT STORE (CLO)

212 Canton Hwy. (m)
Cumming, GA 30130
770-887-5033 / Fax: 770-889-8770
Sales: $500,001-$1 Million

DOUGLAS RAMEY (Owner) & Buys Men's & Boys' Clothing, Sportswear, Boots, Store Displays, Fixtures, Supplies

F & R SALES CO., INC. (SP)

2101 S. Dixie Hwy. (m)
Dalton, GA 30720
706-226-8564 / Fax: 706-226-7582
Sales: $1 Million-$10 Million

EDDIE HALL (Co-Owner) & Buys Men's T-shirts, Golf Apparel Shirts, Headwear, Store Displays, Fixtures, Supplies

FRED HALL (Co-Owner) & Buys Men's T-shirts, Golf Apparel Shirts, Headwear, Urban Contemporary, Store Displays, Fixtures, Supplies

GARMANY'S LTD. (MW)

601 S. Thornton Ave.
Dalton, GA 30720
706-278-1350 / Fax: 706-272-3247
Sales: $100,001-$500,000
Website: www.garmanysltd.com

JAY GARMANY (President)

DOUG GARMANY (V.P.) & Buys Men's Sportswear, Dress Shoes, Store Displays, Fixtures, Supplies

BERNARD'S (MW)

60 S. Dekalb Mall (p)
Decatur, GA 30034
404-241-7208
Sales: $100,001-$500,000

BERNARD DASHER (Owner) & Buys Men's Sportswear, Furnishings & Accessories, Store Displays, Fixtures, Supplies

GQ FASHIONS, INC. (MW)

2800 Candler Rd. (p)
Decatur, GA 30034
404-244-7162 / Fax: 404-241-5787
Sales: $100,001-$500,000

MAHMOOD MASHAEYKH (Owner) & Buys Men's Sportswear, Furnishings & Accessories, Big & Tall Men's Wear, Young Men's Wear, Boys' Wear, Store Displays, Fixtures, Supplies

JACK SMRR (G.M.M.) & Buys Men's Sportswear, Furnishings & Accessories, Big & Tall Men's Wear, Young Men's Wear, Boys' Wear, Store Displays, Fixtures, Supplies

HAT MANIA (MW)

60 S. DelCab Mall (p)
Decatur, GA 30034
404-244-8614

GARY DUGAN (Owner) & Buys Men's Headwear, Store Displays, Fixtures, Supplies

HEBRON SPORTS & FASHION, INC. (SP & MO & OL)

5265 Buford Hwy. NE
Doraville, GA 30340
770-986-8257 / Fax: 770-458-5221

HUNG LEE (President) & Buys Apparel, Racquet Apparel, Licensed Apparel

LOUIS JUNG (Mgr.)

BUY FOR LESS (DEPT)

942 S. West Bowens Mill Rd. (m)
Douglas, GA 31533
912-384-6147
Sales: $500,001-$1 Million

BILLY MANCIL (Owner) & Buys Men's Suits, Raincoats, Tailored Slacks, Sportswear, Dress Shirts, Underwear, Hosiery, Accessories, Swimwear, Dress Shoes, Casual Shoes, Big & Tall Sportswear, Young Men's Shop, Boys' Wear, Store Displays, Fixtures, Supplies

EARL WATKINS, INC. (MW)

P.O. Box 810 (b)
110 N. Peterson Ave.
Douglas, GA 31534
912-384-2656 / Fax: 912-384-9133
Website: www.earlwatkins.com

EARL WATKINS, JR. (Owner) & Buys Men's & Boys' Wear, Dress Shoes, Casual Shoes, Store Displays, Fixtures, Supplies

TOMMY WATKINS-Boys' Wear, Dress Shoes, Casual Shoes, Store Displays, Fixtures, Supplies

GREG BARBAREE-Men's & Boys' Wear, Urban Contemporary, Dress Shoes, Casual Shoes, Store Displays, Fixtures, Supplies

PEACOCK'S MENSWEAR, INC. (MW)

2001 Veteran's Blvd. (b)
Dublin, GA 31021
478-272-0233 / Fax: 478-275-1247
Sales: $500,001-$1 Million

L.C. PEACOCK (Owner) & Buys Men's Sportswear, Furnishings & Accessories, Store Displays, Fixtures, Supplies

MIKE PEACOCK-Men's Sportswear, Furnishings & Accessories, Dress Shoes, Casual Shoes

PETER ISLAND RESORT (CLO)

6470 E. John's Crossing, #490
Duluth, GA 30097
770-476-3723 / Fax: 770-476-3824
Website: www.peterisland.com

JUDY HOPE-Dive Apparel & Accessories, Sunglasses, Accessories, Footwear, Hats, Men's Apparel, Men's Surf & Swimwear, Resortwear, T-shirts, Imprinted Sportswear

J. MAXWELL'S BOUTIQUES (MW)

1820 Washington Rd. (m)
East Point, GA 30344
404-762-7668
Sales: $500,001-$1 Million

GEORGETTE HAMILTON (Co-Owner) & Buys Men's Coats, Suits, Tailored Jackets, Tailored Slacks, Sportswear, Furnishings, Accessories, Footwear, Store Displays, Fixtures, Supplies

HAROLD HAMILTON (Co-Owner) & Buys Men's Coats, Suits, Tailored Jackets, Tailored Slacks, Sportswear, Furnishings, Accessories, Footwear, Store Displays, Fixtures, Supplies

J & R CLOTHING (CLO-2)

P.O. Box 142490 (m-b)
Fayetteville, GA 30214
770-461-3440 / Fax: 770-461-4876
Sales: $500,001-$1 Million
Website: www.jandrclothing.com

RICHARD DUMAS (Owner) & Buys Store Displays, Fixtures, Supplies

DAVID DUMAS (@ 404-719-9961)-Men's Wear, Furnishings, Accessories, Big & Tall Men's, Young Men's Wear, Footwear

SMITH & DAVIS (CLO)

1552 Hwy. 54 (m-b)
Fayetteville, GA 30215
770-487-4183 / Fax: 770-487-3934
Sales: $100,001-$500,000

RONALD DAVIS (Owner)

TONY DAVIS (V.P.) & Buys Boys' Tops, Bottoms, Underwear, Men's Tops, Bottoms, Underwear, Leather Apparel, Footwear, Young Men's Wear, Store Displays, Fixtures, Supplies

GEORGIA - Fort Valley

KHOURY'S MEN'S (MW)
120 E. Main St. (m)
Fort Valley, GA 31030
478-825-0065
Sales: $100,001-$500,000
WILLIAM KHOURY (Owner) & Buys Men's Casual and Dress Wear

NEW YORK HIGH FASHION (MW)
119 Main St. (m)
Fort Valley, GA 31030
478-825-1400
Sales: $100,001-$500,000
KENNY BUXANI (Owner) & Buys Formal, Casual and Urban Contemporary

A.D. MATHIS (MW)
623 Green St. NE, #G
Gainesville, GA 30501
770-532-9001
AMY JOHNSON (Owner)
DALE JOHNSON-Men's Wear, Men's Accessories, Furnishings, Footwear

BURTON'S (CLO)
118 Washington St.
Gainesville, GA 30501
770-532-3660
Sales: $100,001-$500,000
NATHAN BURGEN (Owner) (@ 770-536-1033) & Buys Footwear, Men's Sportswear, Furnishings, Headwear, Belts, Small Leather Goods, Big & Tall Men's, Young Men's Wear, Store Displays, Fixtures, Supplies
VIRGINIA BLACKLEY (Mgr.) & Buys Men's Sportswear, Furnishings, Headwear, Belts, Small Leather Goods, Big & Tall Men's, Young Men's Wear, Store Displays, Fixtures, Supplies

LIPSITZ DEPARTMENT STORE (DEPT)
104 W. Bernard St. (p-m-b)
Glennville, GA 30427
912-654-2340
Sales: $100,001-$500,000
DORSEY THOMPSON (Owner) & Buys Men's & Boys' Wear, Urban Contemporary, Footwear, Store Displays, Fixtures, Supplies

BEAR PAW SALES, INC. (AN)
1424 Hwy. 16 West
Griffin, GA 30223
770-228-6334 / Fax: 770-228-6334
Sales: $100,001-$500,000
JOHNNIE ADAMS (Owner) & Buys Activewear, Athletic Footwear

GODARD'S CLOTHING, INC. (CLO)
129 N. Hill St. (m-b)
Griffin, GA 30223
770-227-2356
Sales: $500,001-$1 Million
MARION C. GODARD (President & Real Estate Contact)
KERRY GODARD-Boys' Apparel, Men's Footwear, Leather Goods, Men's Apparel, Men's Big & Tall, Men's Casualwear, Men's Denim Apparel, Men's Accessories, Men's Hosiery, Men's Outerwear, Men's Sportswear, Men's Suits, Men's Swimwear, Men's Underwear, Men's Uniforms
FRANCES GODARD-Boys' Apparel, Men's Footwear, Leather Goods, Men's Apparel, Men's Big & Tall, Men's Casualwear, Men's Denim Apparel, Men's Accessories, Men's Hosiery, Men's Outerwear, Men's Sportswear, Men's Suits, Men's Swimwear, Men's Underwear, Men's Uniforms

HIKS FASHIONS OF NEW YORK (MW)
1593 North Expy.
Griffin, GA 30223
770-227-9094 / Fax: 770-227-9094
Sales: $100,001-$500,000
ROGER VASNANI (Owner) & Buys Men's Suits, Sportswear, Footwear, Young Men's Wear, Urban Contemporary, Boys' Wear, Furnishings, Accessories, Store Displays, Fixtures, Supplies

SPALDING HOSIERY SHOPPE, INC. (CLO-3)
(SOCK SHOP)
(KID'S SHOP)
432 E. Broad St. (m-b)
P.O. Box 593
Griffin, GA 30223
770-227-4362 / Fax: 770-228-7865
Sales: $1 Million-$10 Million
Website: www.sockshoppe.com
WILLIAM F. TURNER (President & G.M.M.) & Buys Boys' Apparel, Boys' Footwear, Men's Footwear, Leather Goods, Men's Apparel, Men's Big & Tall, Men's Casualwear, Men's Denim Apparel, Men's Accessories, Men's Hosiery, Men's Outerwear, Men's Sleepwear, Men's Sportswear, Men's Underwear, Men's Uniforms
BARBARA TURNER (C.E.O.)
MEREDITH DEPALMA (V.P.) & Buys Boys' Apparel, Boys' Footwear, Men's Footwear, Leather Goods, Men's Apparel, Men's Big & Tall, Men's Casualwear, Men's Denim Apparel, Men's Accessories, Men's Hosiery, Men's Outerwear, Men's Sleepwear, Men's Sportswear, Men's Underwear, Men's Uniforms
MIKE BROWN (Store Mgr.)

YOUNG FASHION (MW)
119 S. Hill St. (m)
Griffin, GA 30223
770-227-2040
Sales: $100,001-$500,000
SEUNG LEE (Owner) & Buys Men's Sportswear, Furnishings, Accessories, Boys' 8 to 20

BAILES-COBB CO. (CLO)
P.O. Box 517 (p-m-b)
358 Howell St.
Hartwell, GA 30643
706-376-7156 / Fax: 706-376-7157
LOUISE JOHNSON (Co-Owner)
EARL JOHNSON (Co-Owner) & Buys Men's & Boys' Wear, Footwear, Store Displays, Fixtures, Supplies

SUPER STYLE (CLO)
9 Carolina St. (p-m-b)
Hartwell, GA 30643
706-376-4366
BOBBY KARAM (Co-Owner) & Buys Men's & Boys' Wear, Footwear, Store Displays, Fixtures, Supplies
VICTOR KARAM (Co-Owner) & Buys Men's & Boys' Wear, Footwear, Store Displays, Fixtures, Supplies

ROPER CLOTHING (CLO)
8016 S. Main St., #C2 (m-b-h)
Helen, GA 30545
706-878-2734
Sales: $100,001-$500,000
BARBARA ROPER (Owner) & Buys Men's & Boys' Casual Dress, Western Wear

DAVID DERANEY DEPARTMENT STORE (DEPT)
36 2nd St. (m-b)
Jackson, GA 30233
770-775-2518
Sales: $1 Million-$10 Million
LARRY DERANEY (President) & Buys Men's Wear, Big & Tall Men's, Footwear, Young Men's Wear, Boys' Wear, Store Displays, Fixtures, Supplies

JEANS STOP, INC. (CLO)
2700 Hwy. 16 (m)
Jackson, GA 30233
770-228-6696
Sales: $100,001-$500,000
GARY T. ST. CLAIR (Owner) & Buys Men's Wear, Big & Tall Men's, Young Men's & Boys' Jeans, Sportswear, Store Displays, Fixtures, Supplies

BENNETT'S ATHLETIC WEAR (SG)
44 E. Public Sq.
Jefferson, GA 30549
706-367-1139 / Fax: 706-367-1254
CHRIS BENNETT (Mgr.) & Buys Men's Footwear, Outdoor Apparel, Hunting and Shooting Apparel
MARK BENNETT-Men's Footwear, Outdoor Apparel, Hunting and Shooting Apparel

JEKYLL ISLAND BEACHWEAR, INC. (SP-2)
20 N. Beachview Dr.
Jekyll Island, GA 31527
912-635-2727 / Fax: 912-634-8720
MOCHE WAANAOUNOU (Owner) & Buys Boys' Apparel, Boys' Swimwear, Accessories, Footwear, Hats, Men's Apparel, Men's Surf & Swimwear, Resortwear

DAVID'S CLOTHING FOR MEN (MW-2)
162 W. Cherry St. (m)
Jesup, GA 31545
912-427-3133 / Fax: 912-427-9215
Sales: $1 Million-$10 Million
LAROD BOWEN (President) & Buys Men's Wear, Footwear, Big & Tall Men's
DAVID BOWEN (V.P.) & Buys Urban Contemporary

S & R MEN'S SHOP, INC. (MW)
191 W. Cherry St. (m)
Jesup, GA 31545
912-427-2775 / Fax: 912-427-9985
Sales: $500,000-$1 Million
DON MILLER (Owner) & Buys Men's & Boys' Wear, Footwear, Store Displays, Fixtures, Supplies

THE ATHLETE'S FOOT (FW-435 & OL)
(THE ATHLETE'S FOOT FOR HER)
(RALLYE)
1950 Vaughn Rd. NW (m-b)
Kennesaw, GA 30144
770-514-4500 / Fax: 770-514-4903
Sales: $100 Million-$500 Million
Website: www.theathletesfoot.com
Retail Locations: MN, IA, MO, AR, LA, MS, AL, WA, ID, MT, ND, SD, NE, OK, TX, NM, CO, WY, UT, AZ, CA, NV, GA, FL, NC, SC, VA, KY, IL, IN, OH, PA, NY, VT, NH, MA
ROBERT J. CORLISS (President & C.E.O.)
DON CUMACHI (C.F.O. & Exec. V.P.)
CHRIS EGGERS (Exec. V.P. & G.M.M.)
TONY QUAS-Athletic Footwear
SCOTT BALOT-Athletic Footwear
DENNIS KIJOWSKI-Men's Accessories, Men's Hosiery, Watches, LP, Men's Apparel

BRIGADE QUARTERMASTERS LTD. (SP & MO & OL)
1025 Cobb International Dr. (b)
Kennesaw, GA 30152
770-428-1248 / Fax: 770-421-8504
Website: www.actiongear.com
MITCHEL WERBELL (President)
GEOFFREY WERBELL (Secy. & Treas.)
MIKE McCOURT (Dir.-Mdsg.)
WENDY ABNEY (Showroom Mgr.) & Buys Men's Outdoor & Hunting Clothes, Footwear, Store Displays, Fixtures, Supplies

MANSOUR'S, INC. (MW-2)
26 W. Lafayette Sq. (b)
La Grange, GA 30240
706-884-7305 / Fax: 706-883-7302
Sales: $1 Million-$10 Million
Website: www.mansours.com
NASAR MANSOUR, III (C.E.O.) & Buys Men's Sportswear, Footwear
TONY PALMER (V.P.) & Buys Big & Tall Men's Wear, Men's Furnishings, Accessories
CHAD HERRINGTON (Adv. Dir.) & Buys Store Displays, Fixtures, Supplies
SCOTT DAVIS-Footwear

SOLOMON'S DEPARTMENT STORE (DEPT)
108 Bull St. (p-m-b)
La Grange, GA 30241
706-884-5951
Sales: $1 Million-$10 Million
CHARLES E. SOLOMON, SR. (President) & Buys Store Displays, Fixtures, Supplies
ELLIS A. SOLOMON-Men's Sportswear, Robes, Furnishings, Hats, Accessories, Dress Shirts, Ties, Footwear, Urban Contemporary, Store Displays, Fixtures and Supplies
FRANCES SOLOMON-Boys' Clothing, Sportswear, Furnishings, Store Displays, Fixtures and Supplies

THE ARMY STORE (AN)
(EDELSON BROTHERS)
111 Lafayette Park West
LaGrange, GA 30241
706-884-8043 / Fax: 706-845-1008
Sales: $100,001-$500,000
STEPHEN EDELSON (Owner) & Buys Activewear, Athletics

CLAYTON BIG & TALL (MW)
5400 Jonesboro Rd. (m)
Lake City, GA 30260
404-363-3618
Sales: $100,001-$500,000
DAVE SHILLER (Owner) & Buys Men's Big & Tall Clothing, Sportswear, Furnishings & Accessories, Store Displays, Fixtures, Supplies

SPRADLEY'S (DEPT-2)
(W.T. SPRADLEY, INC.)
114 Main St. (p)
Lakeland, GA 31635
229-482-3514 / Fax: 229-482-2445
Sales: $500,001-$1 Million
JERRI SPRADLEY (Co-Owner) & Buys Men's, Young Men's & Boys' Jeans, Urban Contemporary, Shirts, Sportswear, Store Displays, Fixtures, Supplies
W. T. SPRADLEY (Co-Owner) & Buys Men's, Young Men's & Boys' Jeans, Shirts, Sportswear, Store Displays, Fixtures, Supplies

GOLDMAN & WENGROW (CLO)
142 N. Peachtree St. (bud-p-m-b)
Lincoln, GA 30817
706-359-3612
MICHAEL WENGROW (Owner) & Buys Casual Jeans

BOWEN BROTHERS CLOTHIERS (MW)
484 Mulberry St. (m-b)
Macon, GA 31201
478-745-4543 / Fax: 478-745-1233
Sales: $500,001-$1 Million
HARRY BOWEN (Co-Owner) & Buys Men's Suits, Sportswear, Formal Wear, Big & Tall, Furnishings, Accessories, Store Displays, Fixtures, Supplies
GEORGE BOWEN (Co-Owner) & Buys Men's Footwear, Men's Suits, Sportswear, Formal Wear, Big & Tall, Store Displays, Fixtures, Supplies

HOUSE OF HINES, INC. (CLO)
2028 Vineville Ave (b-h)
Macon, GA 31204
912-746-8582 / Fax: 912-746-1778
Sales: $100,001-$500,000
HINES CAUSEY-Tuxedos and Formal Wear

KAYBEE OF MACON, INC. (MW)
446 3rd St. (p)
Macon, GA 31201
478-743-5833 / Fax: 478-738-0094
Sales: $500,000-$1 Million
BESS BAYME COTTON (President) & Buys Men's Overcoats, Suits, Tailored Jackets, Tailored Slacks, Sweaters, Sport Shirts, Outer Jackets, Leather Apparel, Active Apparel, Dress Shirts, Ties, Belts, 8 to 20 Boys' Clothing, Sportswear, Furnishings
SCOTT BAYME (V.P.) & Buys Men's Overcoats, Suits, Tailored Jackets, Tailored Slacks, Sweaters, Sport Shirts, Outer Jackets, Leather Apparel, Active Apparel, Dress Shirts, Ties, Belts, 8 to 20 Boys' Clothing, Sportswear, Men's Footwear, Furnishings

GEORGIA - Macon

MAN'S WORLD, INC. (MW)
3640 Eisenhower Pkwy. (p)
Macon, GA 31206
478-781-1909 / Fax: 478-781-1904
Sales: $100,001-$500,000
EUGENE KINARD (Owner) & Buys Big and Tall Men's Sportswear, Furnishings & Accessories, Store Displays, Fixtures, Supplies

GOLDSTEIN'S, INC. (MW)
58 S. Park Sq. (p)
Marietta, GA 30060
770-428-5313 / Fax: 770-428-5322
Sales: $100,001-$500,000
HERBERT GOLDSTEIN (Owner)
PAULA GOLDSTEIN-SHEA (Opers. Mgr.) & Buys Men's Furnishings & Accessories, Boys' Wear, Footwear, Store Displays, Fixtures, Supplies

HODGE ARMY & NAVY STORE (AN)
507 Cobb Pkwy. SE
Marietta, GA 30062
770-427-9331 / Fax: 770-514-9628
Sales: $1 Million-$10 Million
LATRELLE HODGE (President)
PAUL EARLS (Mgr.) & Buys Activewear, Outdoor Apparel, Camouflage, Footwear

LAMB CUSTOM APPAREL (CLO)
3410 Canton Hwy.
Marietta, GA 30066
770-424-6298 / Fax: 770-919-0060
Website: www.lambcustomapparel.com
LINDA BINIASZ (Mgr.) & Buys Imprintable Apparel
MARK BINIASZ-Imprintable Apparel

LEITER'S BIG & TALL (CLO)
1355 Church St. Ext.
Marietta, GA 30060
770-428-6136
Sales: $100,001-$500,000
FRANKLIN D. LEITER (Co-Owner) & Buys Men's Sportswear, Leather Apparel, Furnishings, Headwear, Belts, Big & Tall Men's Wear, Urban Contemporary, Store Displays, Fixtures, Supplies

PORTO BANUS (CLO)
1395 Marietta Pkwy. SE
Marietta, GA 30067
678-581-1001
GARGES PURTER (Owner) & Buys Beachwear, Surf & Swimwear, Wet Suits, Headwear, Sandals

BAYNE'S ARMY STORE (AN)
118 S. Wayne St. (m)
Milledgeville, GA 31061
478-452-2384 / Fax: 478-457-0014
Sales: $100,001-$500,000
VICTOR BAYNE (Co-Owner) & Buys Men's Footwear, Men's & Young Men's Work Clothes, Store Displays, Fixtures, Supplies
RANDY NEW (Co-Owner) & Buys Men's & Young Men's Work Clothes, Store Displays, Fixtures, Supplies

BRIDALS BY HARROLDS (SP)
146 W. Hancock St. (b)
P.O. Box 721
Milledgeville, GA 31061
478-453-7519 / Fax: 478-452-3168
Sales: $100,001-$500,000
Website: www.bridalsbyharolds.com
AMANDA MERCER (Owner) & Buys Men's Formalwear

C. GOLDSTEIN'S & SON INC. (DEPT)
P.O. Box 1847 (bud)
131 S. Wayne St.
Milledgeville, GA 31061
478-452-0571
Sales: $100,001-$500,000
J. L. GOLDSTEIN (Owner) & Buys Men's, Boys' & Students Wear, Men's Accessories, Fragrances, University Shop, Store Displays, Fixtures, Supplies
I.M. GOLDSTEIN-Men's Footwear, Urban Contemporary

MAFFETT'S CASUAL SHOP (MW)
206 S. Dooley St. (m-b)
Montezuma, GA 31063
478-472-7664 / Fax: 478-472-1280
Sales: $100,001-$500,000
JACK H. MAFFETT, JR. (Owner) & Buys Men's Sportswear, Leather Apparel, Accessories, Footwear, Big & Tall Men's, Young Men's Wear, Urban Contemporary, Boys' Wear, Store Displays, Fixtures, Supplies

LAZARUS, INC. (CLO)
103 1st St. SE (m-b)
Moultrie, GA 31768
229-985-1006 / Fax: 229-980-8142
Sales: $1 Million-$10 Million
STEVE LAZARUS (President) & Buys Boys' Apparel, Boys' Footwear, Men's Footwear, Leather Goods, Men's Apparel, Men's Big & Tall, Men's Casualwear, Men's Denim Apparel, Men's Formalwear, Men's Outerwear, Men's Sleepwear, Men's Sportswear, Men's Suits, Men's Swimwear, Men's Underwear, Men's Uniforms
JILL LAZARUS-Boys' Apparel, Boys' Footwear, Men's Footwear, Leather Goods, Men's Apparel, Men's Big & Tall, Men's Casualwear, Men's Denim Apparel, Men's Formalwear, Men's Outerwear, Men's Sleepwear, Men's Sportswear, Men's Suits, Men's Swimwear, Men's Underwear, Men's Uniforms

BROTHERS LTD. (CLO)
6 E. Court Sq. (m-b)
Newnan, GA 30263
770-253-5792 / Fax: 770-253-5733
Sales: $100,001-$500,000
CHARLIE MANSOUR (Co-Owner) & Buys Store Displays, Fixtures, Supplies
ELLIS MANSOUR-Men's Sportswear, Leather Apparel, Accessories, Footwear, Store Displays, Fixtures and Supplies

AFTER HOURS FORMAL WEAR (MW-241)
4444 Shackleford Rd. (bud-p-m-b-h)
Norcross, GA 30093
770-448-8381 / Fax: 770-449-6707
Sales: $25 Million-$50 Million
Website: www.afterhours.com
CINDY ONGERTH-Formal Accessories, Fashion Jewelry, Furnishings
ROD MOLITERNO-Men's & Boys' Tuxedos, Tailored Slacks, Jackets, Dress Footwear
JAMIE SINGLETON (V.P. - Merch.) & Buys Store Displays, Fixtures, Supplies

DIVOT'S SPORTSWEAR CO., INC. (MW)
6900 Peachtree Industrial Blvd.
Norcross, GA 30071
770-447-4800 / Fax: 770-448-3244
Sales: $100,001-$500,000
Website: www.divot.com
BOB FRIEDMAN (Owner) & Buys Men's Sportswear, Headwear, Young Men's Wear, 8 to 20 Boys' Wear

GEORGIA - Norcross

IT'S ABOUT TIME, INC. (JWLY-11)
3250 Peachtree Corners Cir., #F
Norcross, GA 30092
770-441-9088 / Fax: 770-447-8079
Sales: $10 Million-$50 Million
CHARLES BLANCHET (President & Partner) & Buys Watches
RON ALBRITTON (Partner) & Buys Watches
STEVE MILLER (G.M.) & Buys Watches

CASUAL SHOP (CLO)
618 E. Elm St. (m)
Rockmart, GA 30153
770-684-6639
Sales: $100,001-$500,000
BOBBY G. SMITH (Owner) & Buys Men's Tailored Jackets, Sportswear, Leather Apparel, Furnishings, Accessories, Hats, Young Men's Wear, Urban Contemporary, Boys' Wear, Store Displays, Fixtures, Supplies

H. RICHARDS CLOTHING CO. (CLO)
13 E. 3rd Ave. (b)
Rome, GA 30161
706-291-9634 / Fax: 706-290-9897
Sales: $500,000-$1 Million
HAL RICHARD (Owner) & Buys Men's Sportswear, Furnishings, Accessories

FRIEND'S UNLIMITED ATHLETICS (SP-2)
795 Old Roswell Rd.
Roswell, GA 30076
770-594-1778 / Fax: 770-594-0970
TERRY HAMMOND (Owner) & Buys Apparel, Athletic Apparel and Footwear

GO WITH THE FLOW SPORTS (SP)
4 Elizabeth Way
Roswell, GA 30075
770-992-3200 / Fax: 770-992-3200
Website: www.gowiththeflowsports.com
KYLE HAGADORN-Men's Sandals, Sunglasses

RACER WHOLESALE (CLO & MO)
1020 Sun Valley Dr.
Roswell, GA 30076
770-998-7777 / Fax: 770-993-4417
Sales: $500,001-$1 Million
Website: www.racerwholesale.com
BOB POSTELL (President)
BOB MANELL (Gen. Mgr.)
MIKE LORENSON (Mgr.-Purch.) & Buys Men's Apparel

PHILLIPS VARIETY STORE (CLO)
P.O. Box 466 (m)
168 Church St.
Royston, GA 30662
706-245-8259
Sales: Under $100,000
J. W. SHIPP (Co-Owner)
AGNES P. SHIPP (Co-Owner) & Buys Men's Casual Wear, Work Clothes, Underwear, Hosiery, Store Displays, Fixtures, Supplies

ST. SIMONS BEACHWEAR (SP-4)
(BEACHWEAR EXPRESS, INC.)
401 Mallory St.
Saint Simons Island, GA 31522
912-638-5029 / Fax: 912-638-2289
MOSHE WAANOUNOU (Co-Owner) & Buys Activewear, Beachwear, Resort Wear, Swimwear
MIKE WAANOUNOU (Co-Owner) & Buys Activewear, Beachwear, Resort Wear

THOMAS P. DENT CLOTHIER, INC. (MW)
206 Redfurn Village (b)
Saint Simons Island, GA 31522
912-638-3118 / Fax: 912-638-8021
THOMAS DENT (Owner) & Buys Men's Footwear, Store Displays, Fixtures, Supplies, Men's Sportswear, Furnishings & Accessories

VOGUES MEN'S STORE (MW)
P.O. Box 111 (m)
114 N. Harris St.
Sandersville, GA 31082
478-552-2448 / Fax: 478-552-6639
Sales: $100,001-$500,000
SAM GOODRICH (Owner) & Buys Suits, Tailored Jackets, Tailored Slacks, Casual Slacks, Dress Shirts, Sport Shirts, Furnishings, Traditional Sportswear

CITI TRENDS (CLO-182)
102 Fahm St. (m-b)
P.O. Box 2407
Savannah, GA 31401
912-236-1561 / Fax: 912-443-3674
Sales: $50 Million-$100 Million
Website: www.cititrends.com
GEORGE BELLINO (President)
ED ANDERSON (Exec. V.P.-Opers.)
TOM STOLTZ (V.P.-Fin.)
ALLISON SMITH (Mgr.-Mdsg.)
JOHN DEBORKIN (G.M.M.) & Buys Boys' Apparel, Boys' Footwear, Men's Footwear, Leather Goods, Men's Apparel, Men's Casualwear, Men's Denim Apparel, Men's Accessories, Men's Hosiery, Men's Outerwear, Men's Sportswear, Men's Suits, Men's Underwear
TOM GLISSON-Men's Apparel, Casualwear, Denim Apparel, Men's Accessories, Outerwear, Sportswear, Men's Suits, Men's Furnishings
LINDA FRANCISCO-Leather Goods
JENNIFER CAMPBELL-Boys' Apparel, Accessories, Furnishings
REX BOLTIN-Men's & Boys' Footwear

DUCK HEAD (CLO-29)
11 Gateway St, #47 (m-b)
Savannah, GA 31401
912-925-9132
Sales: $50 Million-$100 Million
Website: www.duckhead.com
WILLIAM ROBERTI (Chmn. & C.E.O.)
SCOTT GRASSMYER (C.F.O. & Sr. V.P. & Real Estate Contact)
MIKE PRENDERGAST (Sr. V.P.-Sls. & Mktg.)
WILLIAM B. MATTISON, Jr. (V.P.-Mdsg.) & Buys Boys' Apparel, Men's Apparel, Men's Casualwear, Men's Outerwear, Men's Sportswear
GWEN VENABLE (Dir.-Mktg.) & Buys Store Displays, Fixtures, Supplies

HEYMAN & SONS, INC. (MW)
28 W. Broughton St. (m-b)
Savannah, GA 31401
912-232-5503 / Fax: 912-233-0665
Sales: $100,001-$500,000
JOE DABIT (Owner) & Buys Men's Formal Wear, Footwear, Big & Tall, Young Men's Wear, Urban Contemporary, Boys' Wear, Store Displays, Fixtures, Supplies

J. PARKER LTD. (MW)
4813 Waters Ave. (m-b)
Savannah, GA 31404
912-352-9995 / Fax: 912-352-2766
Sales: $100,001-$500,000
JAMES PARKER (President) & Buys Men's Sportswear, Big & Tall Men's Wear

GEORGIA - Savannah

JOHN B. ROURKE (MW)
7135 Hodgson Memorial Dr. (b)
Savannah, GA 31406
912-355-1211 / Fax: 912-355-4411
Sales: $500,000-$1 Million
DON McELVEEN (Co-Owner & President) & Buys Men's Furnishings & Accessories, Footwear, Urban Contemporary, Store Displays, Fixtures, Supplies
ALAN TANENBAUM (Co-Owner) & Buys Men's Furnishings & Accessories, Footwear, Urban Contemporary, Store Displays, Fixtures, Supplies

ON TIME FASHIONS (MW)
26 W. Broughton St. (m)
Savannah, GA 31401
912-233-2320 / Fax: 912-233-0665
Sales: $500,000-$1 Million
SAM FASHHO (Co-Owner) & Buys Men's Wear, Young Men's Wear, Tailored Jackets, Tailored Slacks, Footwear, Accessories, 8 to 20 Boys' Wear
JOE DABIT (Co-Owner) & Buys Men's Sportswear, Leather Apparel, Footwear, 8 to 20 Boys' Wear, Urban Contemporary, Store Displays, Fixtures, Supplies

PUNCH & JUDY, INC. (KS)
4511 Habersham St. (m-b)
Savannah, GA 31405
912-352-0906 / Fax: 912-352-0945
Sales: $100,001-$500,000
SALLY KRISSMAN (President) & Buys Urban Contemporary
ERIC KARP (V.P.) & Buys 8 to 20 Boys' Wear, Store Displays, Fixtures, Supplies

RICK'S BIG & TALL MEN'S SHOP (MW)
7805 Abercorn St. (m-b)
Savannah, GA 31406
912-356-5425 / Fax: 912-352-4080
Sales: $100,001-$500,000
RICK JOSEY (Owner) & Buys Big & Tall Men's Sportswear, Footwear, Urban Contemporary, Store Displays, Fixtures, Supplies

SIMON'S FORMAL WEAR (MW-4)
7804 Abercorn St. (b-h)
Savannah, GA 31406
912-352-1251 / Fax: 912-354-5712
Sales: $100,001-$500,000
Website: www.simonsformal.com
WARREN LOKEY (Owner) & Buys Tuxedos & Formal Wear, Accessories, Footwear

STAGG SHOPPE LTD. (MW)
184 Oglethorpe Mall (b)
Savannah, GA 31406
912-352-2361 / Fax: 912-352-2361
Sales: $100,001-$500,000
BUTCH MILTIADES (Owner) & Buys Men's Sportswear, Furnishings, Accessories

THOMPSON SPORT SHOP (CLO)
8110 White Bluff Rd. (m)
P.O. Box 13683
Savannah, GA 31406
912-920-0977 / Fax: 912-920-1351
Sales: $1 Million-$10 Million
LARRY A. THOMPSON, Sr. (President) & Buys Boys' Apparel, Boys' Footwear, Men's Footwear, Men's Apparel, Men's Casualwear, Men's Accessories, Men's Hosiery, Men's Outerwear, Men's Sportswear
LARRY THOMPSON, Jr. (Store Mgr.) & Buys Boys' Apparel, Boys' Footwear, Men's Footwear, Men's Apparel, Men's Casualwear, Men's Accessories, Men's Hosiery, Men's Outerwear, Men's Sportswear

CLOISTER COLLECTION LTD. (CLO)
P.O. Box 30257 (m-b)
1 1st St.
Sea Island, GA 31561
912-638-5106 / Fax: 912-638-5117
Sales: $100,001-$500,000
IRA MOORE (Owner) & Buys Store Displays, Fixtures, Supplies
MARIANNE SANBORN-Men's Resort Wear, Outer Jackets, Sport Coats, Tailored Slacks, Casual Slacks, Active Apparel, Accessories, Underwear, Hosiery

LEON'S SPORTSWEAR, INC. (MW)
Statesboro Mall (bud)
Statesboro, GA 30458
912-764-5176 / Fax: 912-764-5650
Sales: $100,001-$500,000
LEON SHELKOFF (Owner) & Buys Men's Overcoats, Suits, Tailored Jackets, Tailored Slacks, Sportswear

R. J. POPE MENSWEAR (MW-2)
5 S. Main St. (m-b-h)
Statesboro, GA 30458
912-764-4306 / Fax: 912-764-7663
RONNIE POPE (Owner) & Buys Men's Casual, Men's Suits

SOUTH GEORGIA APPAREL, INC. (CLO)
P.O. Box 557
Statesboro, GA 30459
912-764-5501 / Fax: 912-764-4111
FRED GRIST (Owner) & Buys Men's Wear

RICHIE'S (CLO)
P.O. Box 122
10098 N. Commerce St.
Summerville, GA 30747
706-857-4512 / Fax: 706-857-4507
JAMES RICHIE (President) & Buys Men's Formal Wear, Suits, Sportswear, Footwear, Big & Tall, Young Men's Wear, Boys' Wear, Store Displays, Fixtures, Supplies
ALTHEA RICHIE (V.P.)

LORD & MASTER (MW)
P.O. Box 242 (m)
108 N. Main St.
Sylvania, GA 30467
912-564-2943
Sales: $100,001-$500,000
THOMAS E. ROBERTS (Owner) & Buys Men's Tailored Suits, Sportswear, Furnishings

JERE GREER STORE FOR MEN, INC. (MW)
P.O. Box 1164 (m-b)
114 E. Main St.
Thomaston, GA 30286
706-647-3687 / Fax: 706-646-9629
Sales: $100,001-$500,000
JERE GREER (Owner) & Buys Men's Sportswear, Furnishings & Accessories, Footwear, Young Men's Wear

YOUNG'S FASHIONS (CLO)
110 W. Main St. (p-m-b)
Thomaston, GA 30286
706-647-1700
Sales: $100,001-$500,000
MAEI NAPIER (Owner) & Buys Men's Sportswear, Furnishings, Accessories, Boys' 4 to 7 & 8 to 20

G.Q. FASHION (MW & OL)
15107 U.S. Hwy. 19 S. (b)
Thomasville, GA 31792
912-227-0980 / Fax: 334-333-0131
Sales: $100,001-$500,000
Website: www.gqfashion.com
VAK ASALI (Owner) & Buys Men's Sportswear, Furnishings & Accessories, Footwear, Young Men's Wear, Urban Contemporary, Boys' Wear, Store Displays, Fixtures, Supplies

HICKS CLOTHING CO. (CLO)
115 N. Broad St. (p-m-b)
Thomasville, GA 31792
229-226-4363 / Fax: 229-226-1802
Sales: $500,000-$1 Million
JOHN HICKS (Co-Owner) & Buys Men's Suits, Formal Wear, Sportswear, Outerwear, Men's Footwear, Big & Tall, Furnishings, Accessories, Store Displays, Fixtures, Supplies
CHARLOTTE KANNING (Co-Owner) & Buys Men's Suits, Formal Wear, Sportswear, Outerwear, Big & Tall, Furnishings, Accessories, Store Displays, Fixtures, Supplies

STAFFORD'S (DG & OL)
P.O. Box 2055 (b)
808 Smith Ave.
Thomasville, GA 31799
229-226-4306 / Fax: 229-226-4320
Sales: $100,001-$500,000
Website: www.stafford-catalog.com
WARREN STAFFORD (Co-Owner) & Buys Men's Hunting Apparel, Outdoor Apparel, Sportswear, Big & Tall Men's
BETH STAFFORD (Co-Owner) & Buys Store Displays, Fixtures, Supplies
TODD WHIDDON-Men's Footwear

YOUR DREAM BRIDAL & FORMAL SHOP, INC. (SP)
3430 Lawrenceville Hwy. (m-b)
Tucker, GA 30084
770-938-0833 / Fax: 770-938-7583
Sales: $500,001-$1 Million
BARBARA HELMS (President & Gen. Mgr.) & Buys Men's Formalwear

T.S. CHU AND CO. (DEPT)
P.O. Box 700 (b)
6 16th St.
Tybee Island, GA 31328
912-786-4561 / Fax: 912-786-4562
Sales: $1 Million-$10 Million
MOLA JUNG (Owner) & Buys Men's & Boys' Beachwear, Store Displays, Fixtures, Supplies

CLOTHING CARNIVAL, INC. (CLO)
P.O. Box 346 (m)
I-75 Hwy. 230
Unadilla, GA 31091
478-627-3466 / Fax: 478-627-3466
Sales: $1 Million-$10 Million
Website: www.clothingcarnival.com
DON CAMERON (Store Mgr.) & Buys Men's Sportswear, Work Wear, Casual Wear, Boys' Sportswear, Urban Contemporary, Furnishings, FootwearStore Displays, Fixtures, Supplies
JERRY McFARLIN-Men's Sportswear, Work Wear, Casual Wear, Boys' Sportswear, Urban Contemporary, Furnishings, FootwearStore Displays, Fixtures, Supplies
ROSS TURRENTINE-Men's Sportswear, Work Wear, Casual Wear, Boys' Sportswear, Urban Contemporary, Furnishings, FootwearStore Displays, Fixtures, Supplies

FASHION KING (MW)
117 N. Ashley St. (m)
Valdosta, GA 31601
229-244-2229 / Fax: 229-247-9448
Sales: $100,001-$500,000
CLYDE ARMSTRONG (Owner) & Buys Men's Sportswear, Furnishings & Accessories, Young Men's Wear, Urban Contemporary, Boys' Wear, Store Displays, Fixtures, Supplies

IVEY'S THE MAN'S SHOP, INC. (MW)
1723 Norman Dr. (m-b)
Valdosta, GA 31601
229-247-7729 / Fax: 229-247-7039
Sales: $100,001-$500,000
IVEY PLAIR, SR. (Owner) & Buys Men's Footwear, Store Displays, Fixtures, Supplies, Men's Sportswear, Furnishings & Accessories, Young Men's Wear
IVEY PLAIR, JR.-Men's Sportswear, Furnishings & Accessories, Young Men's Wear

FASHION VILLA (CLO)
13 N. Main St. (bud-p-m)
Wadley, GA 30477
478-252-5654 / Fax: 478-252-5654
Sales: $100,001-$500,000
JAMES M. BLOCKER (Co-Owner) & Buys Men's, Young Men's & Boys' Wear, Footwear, Store Displays, Fixtures, Supplies

SCARBOROUGH'S (MW-2)
12 Robert Toombs Ave. (m)
Washington, GA 30673
706-678-3495 / Fax: 706-678-3462
Sales: $500,000-$1 Million
DEAN SCARBOROUGH (Co-Owner)
MIKE SCARBOROUGH (Co-Owner) & Buys Men's Overcoats, Tailored Jackets, Tailored Slacks, Big & Tall, Sport Shirts, Workwear, Outer Jackets, Casual Slacks, Footwear, Accessories, Furnishings, Store Displays, Fixtures & Supplies

JAKE & ED'S, INC. (MW)
P.O. Box 743 (m-b)
314 Mary St.
Waycross, GA 31501
912-283-2545 / Fax: 912-283-2545
Sales: $100,001-$500,000
STEVE FLEMING (Owner) & Buys Men's Sportswear, Furnishings, Footwear, Big & Tall Men's, Store Displays, Fixtures, Supplies

PRIM'S MEN'S SHOP, INC. (MW)
508 Elizabeth St. (p-m-b)
Waycross, GA 31501
912-283-4411
Sales: $100,001-$500,000
MALCOLM LEO BRADDY, JR. (Owner) & Buys Men's Accessories
MIKE BRADDY-Men's Sportswear, Furnishings, Big & Tall Men's, Young Men's Wear, Size 8 to 20 Boys' Wear, Store Displays, Fixtures, Supplies

SPORT SHOP (CLO-3)
P.O. Box 715 (bud)
801 Frances St.
Waycross, GA 31502
912-283-3406 / Fax: 912-283-3347
BENJAMIN JAMES (Owner) & Buys Men's & Boys' Active Apparel

HAWAII - Aiea

CATHAY KAI, INC. (JWLY-3 & OL)

(AGUA GEM)
(CATHAY KAI JEWELRY)
98-1005 Moanalua Rd. #209
Aiea, HI 96701
808-486-7908 / Fax: 808-486-7907
Sales: $1 Million-$10 Million
Website: www.cathaykai.com

KATHLEEN HSIUNG (Owner) & Buys Jewelry, Watches

CRAZY SHIRTS, INC. (CLO-43 & OL)

99-969 Iwaena St. (m)
Aiea, HI 96701
808-487-9919 / Fax: 808-486-1276
Sales: $10 Million-$50 Million
Website: www.crazyshirts.com

MARK HOLLANDER (President)
TODD TANIGUCHI (C.F.O. & Real Estate Contact)
LANA KAEO-Men's Imprintable Sweaters, Sport Shirts, Outer Jackets, Active Apparel, Boys' T-shirts
TOM OZON (Retail Opers. Mgr.) & Buys Store Fixtures, Displays
LOUANN McNULTY (Mdse. Mgr.)

UNIFORMS BY MALIA (SP-2)

98-019 Kamehameha Hwy. (m)
Aiea, HI 96701
808-487-5399 / Fax: 808-486-0942
Sales: $1 Million-$10 Million

ROBERT PROCTOR (Owner)
JEANEEN PROCTOR (Sls. Mgr.)
NANCY DEARDEN (Store Mgr.) & Buys Leather Goods, Men's Apparel, Mens's Big & Tall, Men's Casualwear, Men's Denim Apparel, Men's Formalwear, Men's Accessories, Men's Outerwear, Men's Sportswear, Men's Suits, Men's Uniforms

SILVER MOON (CLO)

Kamehameha Hwy. (m)
Haleiwa, HI 96712
808-637-7710 / Fax: 808-637-7710
Sales: $100,001-$500,000

LUCY HOLU (Owner) & Buys Leather Goods, Men's Sportswear

HASEGAWA GENERAL STORE, INC. (GM)

P.O. Box 68 (p-m)
Hana Maui, HI 96713
808-248-8231 / Fax: 808-248-7344
Sales: $100,001-$500,000

HARRY HASEGAWA (Owner) & Buys Store Displays, Store Fixtures
NEIL HASEGAWA (Mgr.) & Buys Store Supplies
NITA HASEGAWA-Men's Sportswear, Furnishings, Footwear, Boys' Wear, Store Displays, Fixtures and Supplies

ROBERT'S OF KAUAI, INC. (CLO-2)

P.O. Box C (p)
Hanapepe Kauai, HI 96716
808-335-5332 / Fax: 808-335-5493
Sales: $1 Million-$10 Million

ROBERT T. OZAKI (President) & Buys Men's Overcoats, Suits, Tailored Jackets, Tailored Slacks, Hosiery, Boys' Clothing, Store Displays, Fixtures, Supplies
MILTON R. OZAKI-Men's Sportswear, Sweaters, Sport Shirts, Outer Jackets, Leather Apparel, Casual Slacks, Active Apparel, Furnishings, Dress Shirts, Accessories, Ties Robes, Underwear, Headwear Belts, Boys' Furnishings, Accessories, Store Displays, Fixtures and Supplies

MEN'S SHOP, INC. (MW-5)

Prince Kuhio Plaza, 111 E. Puainako St. (m-b)
Hilo, HI 96720
808-959-5866 / Fax: 808-961-0121
Sales: $1 Million-$10 Million

TSUNEO AKIYAMA (President & G.M.M.) & Buys Men's Wear, Store Displays, Fixtures, Supplies
KEVIN AKIYAMA (V.P.) & Buys Young Men's Wear, Urban Contemporary, Store Displays, Fixtures and Supplies

UNCLE BILLY'S GENERAL STORE (GM)

(UNCLE BILLY'S HILO BAY HOTEL)
87 Banyan Dr. (p)
Hilo, HI 96720
808-935-0658 / Fax: 808-935-7903
Sales: $100,001-$500,000
Website: www.unclebilly.com

SANDRA YOKOMIZO (Gen. Mgr.-Hotel)
DOREEN JOHNSON-Men's & Boys' Tops, Shorts, Store Displays, Fixtures, Supplies

S. HASEGAWA LTD. (DEPT)

P.O. Box 187 (p)
Honokaa, HI 96727
808-775-0668
Sales: $100,001-$500,000

KENNETH HASEGAWA (President)
MYRA ITO (Mgr.) & Buys Men's & Boys' Pants, Shorts, Dress Shirts, Robes, Underwear, Hosiery, Hats, Belts, Small Leather Goods, Fragrances, Store Displays, Fixtures, Supplies

Ala Moana Center-Hilo Hattie (CLO-14 & OL)

(POMARE LTD.)
700 Nimitz Hwy. (p)
Honolulu, HI 96817
808-973-3266 / Fax: 808-533-6809
Sales: $10 Million-$50 Million
Website: www.hilohattie.com

PAUL DeVILLE (President & C.E.O.)
JOHN SCOTT (V.P.-G.M.M.)
BILL WARING (Visual Mdsg. Mgr.) & Buys Store Displays, Fixtures, Supplies
TERRI FUNAKOSHI-Men's Resort Wear, T-shirts, Active Apparel, Young Men's Wear, Urban Contemporary, Surfwear
YUNAH LEE-Boys' Wear, T-shirts, Active Apparel, Surfwear

COAST GUARD EXCHANGE (PX)

U.S. Coast Guard Base (p-m)
400 Sand Island Pkwy.
Honolulu, HI 96819-4326
808-832-2564 / Fax: 808-832-2566
Sales: $1 Million-$10 Million

LLOYD NYAGUJU (CGES Mgr.)
BETH OKAZAKI-Men's Sport Shirts, Dress Shirts, Robes, Underwear, Footwear

HALE-NIU WEDDING COURT (CLO)

1014 Kapahulu Ave. (p)
Honolulu, HI 96816
808-734-2125 / Fax: 808-735-6002
Sales: $100,001-$500,000

BERTON KATO (President) & Buys Men's & Boys' Formalwear, Store Displays, Fixtures, Supplies

HAWAII RYOWA CORP. (CLO-2)

2250 Kalakaua Ave., Suite 108 (m-b-des)
Honolulu, HI 96815
808-922-2302 / Fax: 808-926-0592
Sales: $1 Million-$10 Million

KATSUHISA SASAKI (President)
JUNICHI NAKAMURA (V.P. & Gen. Mgr.) & Buys Men's Footwear, Leather Goods, Men's Apparel, Men's Casualwear, Men's Outerwear, Men's Sportswear

ISLAND WEAR LTD. (CLO)

2005 Kalia Rd. (m)
Honolulu, HI 96815
808-947-5669
Sales: $100,001-$500,000

HELEN LEE (Owner) & Buys Men's Hawaiian Wear, Furnishings, Store Displays, Fixtures, Supples

KING'S SPORTS (SP)

131 Kaiulani Ave., #27
Honolulu, HI 96815
808-926-8216 / Fax: 808-923-2706

DEAN KANG (Mgr.) & Buys Licensed Apparel, Activewear

HAWAII - Honolulu

KRAMER'S MENSWEAR (MW-2 & OL)
1450 Ala Moana Shopping Ctr. (m)
Honolulu, HI 96814
808-951-0567 / Fax: 808-845-3812
Sales: $100,001-$500,000
Website: www.bigandtallbykramers.com
SAM KRAMER (Owner)
JEFF KRAMER (G.M.M.) & Buys Big & Tall Men's Wear
DEIDRE BISHAW-Young Men's Wear, Urban Contemporary

LANAI SPORTSWEAR LTD. (MW-4)
P.O. Box 88003 (m)
866 Iwilei Rd.
Honolulu, HI 96830
808-592-7722 / Fax: 808-522-1900
Sales: $1 Million-$10 Million
BERNARD WALTHALL (President) & Buys Men's Sport Shirts, Outer Jackets, Leather Apparel, Casual Slacks, Active Apparel, Furnishings, Headwear, Accessories, Boys' Wear, Store Displays, Fixtures and Supplies

LIBERTY HOUSE - HAWAII (DEPT-52)
(Div. Of MACY'S WEST)
P.O. Box 2690 (m-b)
1450 Ala Moana Blvd.
Honolulu, HI 96845
808-941-2345 / Fax: 808-945-5571
Sales: $100 Million-$500 Million
Website: www.raynor.com
Retail Locations: GU, HI
JOHN MONAHAN (President & C.E.O.)
MARK STORFER (V.P.)
RIT PIERCE (V.P.-Visual Mdsg.) & Buys Store Displays
JIM TUCKER (Dir.-Store Planning) & Buys Store Fixtures
DEAN VITTETOE (V.P. & G.M.M.)
DINA HERSH-Men's Furnishings, Men's Dress Furnishings, Men's Accessories, Tommy, Nautica, Better Sportswear
KENT REISDORF-Young Men Classification, Surf, Levis, Guess, Active Sportswear
ALDEN YAMANE-Men's Sport Coats
SHERI SATO-Sweaters, Sports Shirts, Outer Jackets, Leather Apparel

LOCAL MOTION (CLO-10 & OL)
424 Sumner St.
Honolulu, HI 96817
808-523-7873 / Fax: 808-521-6413
Sales: $100,001-$500,000
Website: www.localmotioninc.com
TIM MOCK-Hawaiian Style Sportswear, Surfwear, Swimwear

PANIOLO TRADING CO. (CLO)
Shop 1204 Ala Moana (p-m-b-h)
Honolulu, HI 96814
808-973-1333 / Fax: 808-951-6046
Sales: $100,001-$500,000
HARUMI VALENZUELA (Owner) & Buys Western & Indian Clothing, Related Furnishings, Accessories, Store Displays, Fixtures and Supplies

PIVOT SPORTS (SP)
2233 Kalakaua Ave., #305
Honolulu, HI 96815
808-923-1073 / Fax: 808-922-0177
ROY DIAS (Co-Owner) & Buys Activewear
ERWIN DIAS (Co-Owner) & Buys Activewear

THE POSSIBILITES CO. (JWLY-60)
(H.F. WICHMAN & CO.)
(HAWAIIAN ISLAND GEM)
(PEARL FACTORY)
3049 Ualena St.
Honolulu, HI 96819
615-487-1847 / Fax: 651-697-1077
Sales: $50 Million-$100 Million
Website: www.theposs.com
ED SULTAN, III (President)
STEVE BOOKATZ-Jewelry, Watches, Pearl Jewelry
VICKI PINNICCHIA-Pearl Jewelry

RUNNERS ROUTE LTD. (SP)
1050 Ala Moana Blvd.
Honolulu, HI 96814
808-591-9155
Website: www.runnersroute.com
TOMIO KUBO (Owner) & Buys Activewear, Athletic Footwear

SAMPLE SHOP, INC. (CLO)
2335 Kalakaua Ave. (m)
P.O. Box 119
Honolulu, HI 96815
808-923-1366
Sales: $500,001-$1 Million
MAUREEN KILCOYNE (President) & Buys Men's Footwear, Men's Apparel, Men's Swimwear
MARK BUCK (V.P.)

SEA WIND CHALLENGE (SP)
353 Royal Hawaiian Ave., #A
Honolulu, HI 96813
808-922-0036 / Fax: 808-683-0114
BOBBY SAKATA (Co-Owner)
MICHIKO SAKATA (Co-Owner) & Buys Surfwear, Accessories

SERA'S SURF & SHORE (MW)
(SERA'S, INC.)
1450 Ala Moana Blvd., #1074 (bud-p-m-b)
Honolulu, HI 96814
808-949-7828 / Fax: 808-941-1120
Sales: $1 Million-$10 Million
PEGGY F. SERA (President) & Buys Men's Sportswear, Belts, Jewelry, Small Leather Goods, Boys' Clothing, Store Displays, Fixtures, Supplies
CAROL SERA (Mgr.) & Buys Men's Sportswear, Belts, Jewelry, Small Leather Goods, Boys' Clothing, Store Displays, Fixtures, Supplies
CHRIS HAGA-Men's Footwear, Sportswear, Belts, Jewelry, Small Leather Goods, Boys' Clothing, Store Displays, Fixtures, Supplies

SEVERSON SURFING ENTERPRISES (CLO)
(TAHITI IMPORTS)
1174 Waimanu St. (m)
P.O. Box 8571
Honolulu, HI 96814
808-591-2929 / Fax: 808-591-2926
Sales: $500,001-$1 Million
Website: www.tahitiimports.com
BETTY SEVERSON (President) & Buys Men's Apparel, Men's Casualwear, Men's Swimwear

SLIPPER HOUSE (FW)
1450 Ala Moana Blvd. (m)
Honolulu, HI 96814
808-949-0155
Sales: $100,001-$500,000
KAREN FRIX (Owner) & Buys Men's Footwear

SPLASH HAWAII (SP-2 & MO)
(BLUE JEANS 'N' BIKINIS, INC.)
641 Keeaumoku St., #6
Honolulu, HI 96814
808-946-8896 / Fax: 808-946-0983
Website: www.splashhawaii.com
GARY McCARTY (Co-Owner) & Buys Swimwear, Surfwear, Resort Wear, Related Footwear
DENNIS FALLAS (Co-Owner) & Buys Swimwear, Surfwear, Resort Wear, Related Footwear
LAURINDA BUTLER-Swimwear, Surfwear, Resort Wear, Related Footwear

SPORTIQUE (SP)
(M.B.K. CO., INC.)
2552 Kalakaua Ave.
Honolulu, HI 96815
808-922-2253
Sales: $500,001-$1 Million
MICHAEL KIM (Owner) & Buys Activewear

HAWAII - Honolulu

TUXEDO JUNCTION (CLO-2)
1218 Waimanu St. (bud-m-h)
Honolulu, HI 96814
808-591-1889 / Fax: 808-593-8889
Sales: $1 Million-$10 Million
Website: www.matzki.com
JACK TAKEDA (Owner)
KRISTIE LAU (Gen. Mgr.) & Buys Men's & Boys' Formal Wear, Suits, Tuxedos, Outer Jackets, Dress Shirts, Ties, Hosiery, Gloves, Footwear, Store Displays, Fixtures, Supplies

UYEDA SHOE STORE (FW)
2615 S. King St. (m-b)
Honolulu, HI 96826
808-941-1331
CLAIRE TAKASHIMA (Owner) & Buys Men's Footwear, Leather Goods, Men's Hosiery

WAIKIKI TRADER CORP. (CLO-39)
(KUPONO INVESTMENTS)
2330 Kalakaua Ave., #704 (p)
Honolulu, HI 96815
808-971-2999 / Fax: 808-971-1034
Website: www.digitalcity.com
Retail Locations: HI
RON ROBERTSON (Owner)
JAMES R. GEIGER (President & Co-Owner)
AL COTTRAL (C.E.O. & Real Estate Contact) (@ 808-483-7600)
ALEX AH TOU, JR.-Men's, Young Men's & Boys' Hawaiian Wear, Men's Sweaters, Sport Shirts, Outer Jackets, Casual Slacks, Furnishings, Young Men's & Boys' Wear, Active Apparel, Men's, Young Men's & Boys' T-shirts, Men's Headwear, Accessories, Men's T-shirts, Store Displays, Fixtures and Supplies
KIM BORGES-Golf Apparel, Shirts, Shorts
ORLANDO GONZAGA (Visual Mdse. Mgr.) & Buys Store Displays, Fixtures, Supplies

WATUMULL BROTHERS (CLO-6)
307 Lewers St., 6th Fl. (m)
Honolulu, HI 96815
808-971-8800 / Fax: 808-971-8824
Sales: $1 Million-$10 Million
GULAB WATUMULL (President)
J.D. WATUMULL (V.P.)
ELAINE BEASLEY-Men's & Boys' Hawaiian Wear

YOKOHAMA OKADAYA - USA CORP. (CLO-13)
(HUNTING WORLD)
2005 Kalia Rd. (bud-p-m-b-des)
P.O. Box 88124
Honolulu, HI 96815
808-941-8804 / Fax: 808-923-8141
Sales: $10 Million-$50 Million
KEIJIRO HARADA (President) & Buys Men's Footwear, Leather Goods, Men's Apparel, Men's Casualwear, Men's Denim Apparel, Men's Hosiery, Men's Outerwear, Men's Sportswear
MITSUJI MIYAO (Mgr.-Store Opers.)
HARUO OTA (Dir.-Opers.)

JEANS FACTORY (CLO)
Maui Mall Shopping Ctr.
Kahului, HI 96732
808-877-3625
Sales: $100,001-$500,000
CHRISTIAN LAUX (President & Owner) & Buys Jeans, T-shirts, Active Apparel

NAISH HAWAII LTD. (SP)
155A Hamakua Dr.
Kailua, HI 96734
808-262-6068 / Fax: 808-263-9723
Website: www.naish.com
CAROL NAISH (Owner) & Buys Activewear

MARINE CORPS EXCHANGE (PX)
Marine Corps Base - Hawaii
Kaneohe Bay, HI 96863
808-254-7522 / Fax: 808-254-6627
LINDA GULOSH (Retail Dir.)
IRIS TOKITA-YOUNG-Logo Apparel, Men's Wear, Men's & Boys' Footwear
PATRICIA SASAKI-Boys' Apparel

MIURA STORES (CLO-4)
(ISLAND SURF SHOP)
(DEJA VU)
4-1419 Kuhio Hwy. (m)
Kapaa, HI 96746
808-822-4401 / Fax: 808-822-5603
Sales: $100,001-$500,000
TAD MIURA (Co-Owner)
ANN LOW (Co-Owner)
ERIC MIURA (Co-Owner) & Buys Men's & Boys' Sportswear, Swimwear, Licensed T-shirts, Urban Contemporary, Store Displays, Fixtures, Supplies, Men's Footwear

MANDALAY (CLO-2)
3900 Wailea Alanui Dr.
Kihei, HI 96753
808-874-5111 / Fax: 808-879-5773
Sales: $500,001-$1 Million
PUNDY YOKOUCHI (President)
PHYLLIS BOWEN (V.P.)
PAULA WRIGHT (Gen. Mgr.) & Buys Men's Accessories, Men's Sportswear

TREASURY (CLO)
875-5744 Alii Dr.
Kona, HI 96740
808-329-9121 / Fax: 808-326-6057
PETER DUNGATE (Co-Owner) & Buys T-shirts, Fleece, Shorts, Resortwear, Beachwear
ANGELICA DUNGATE (Co-Owner) & Buys T-shirts, Fleece, Shorts, Resortwear, Beachwear

ISLAND SWIMWEAR (CLO-2)
(RAINBOW BEACH SWIMWEAR)
900 Front St., #J8
Lahaina, HI 96761
808-661-4573 / Fax: 808-667-0427
Sales: $1 Million-$10 Million
Website: www.islanddesignerswimwear.com
CYNTHIA STESSEL (Partner & G.M.M.)
MORRIS STESSEL (Partner)
JEANNE STESSEL (Partner) & Buys Boys' Apparel, Men's Swimwear

LEOLA OF HAWAII, INC. (CLO-4)
872 Front St.
Lahaina, HI 96761
808-661-3279 / Fax: 808-661-3279
Sales: $100,001-$500,000
LEOLA VIERRA (Owner) & Buys Men's Sportswear, Footwear, Store Displays, Fixtures, Supplies

MAUI CLOTHING CO., INC. (CLO-22)
1000 Limahana Pl., #N (bud-p-m-b)
Lahaina, HI 96761
(Directives West-L.A.)
808-667-2647 / Fax: 808-661-7610
Sales: $100,001-$500,000
Website: www.mauiclothing.com
EDWARD D. WAYNE (Owner)
PATTY NIEMEYER (Store Mgr.) & Buys Store Fixtures, Supplies
REA DeMAR-Men's Sport Shirts, Casual Slacks, Active Apparel, Shorts
BETSY McCLINTOCK-Belts, Furnishings, Accessories

MAUI FOUR WINDS FASHIONS (CLO-3)
820 Front St.
Lahaina, HI 96761
808-661-7177 / Fax: 808-661-4263
DON DUDA (President & Owner) & Buys Resort Wear, Swimwear, T-shirts, Fleece, Store Displays, Fixtures and Supplies

WEST MAUI SPORTS & FISHING (SP)
1287 Front St.
Lahaina, HI 96761
808-661-6252 / Fax: 808-661-8700
DOUG STACY (Owner) & Buys Golf Apparel, Accessories and Footwear

HAWAII - Lanai City

THE LOCAL GENTRY (CLO)

P.O. Box 630718
Lanai City, HI 96763
808-565-9130 / Fax: 808-565-6771

JENNA GENTRY (Owner) & Buys Men's Sportswear, Swimwear, Casual Wear, Active Apparel, Beach Footwear and Related Accessories

RICHARD'S SHOPPING CENTER, INC. (DEPT)

P.O. Box 489 (bud-p)
434 8th St.
Lanai City, HI 96763
808-565-6047 / Fax: 808-533-7694
Sales: $1 Million-$10 Million

WALLACE TAMASHIRO (President) & Buys Men's Sportswear, Furnishings, Accessories, Boys' Wear, Urban Contemporary, Store Displays, Fixtures, Supplies

M.K.B. SPORTS (SP)

94-515 Ukee St., # 210
Pearl City, HI 96797
808-676-3990 / Fax: 808-696-3992

GERALD TAOKA (President) & Buys Athletic Apparel, Licensed Apparel, Activewear

DUKE'S CLOTHING (CLO)

723 California Ave. (p-m)
Wahiawa, HI 96786
808-621-5331 / Fax: 808-683-3322
Sales: $100,001-$500,000

GAIL NAKASONE (Owner) & Buys Men's Sportswear, Underwear, Hosiery, Belts, Young Men's Wear

KUNAH'S (CLO)

(MALIA CORP.)
250 Waikoloa Beach Dr., #E4 (p-m-b)
Waikoloa, HI 96738
808-886-6422- / Fax: 808-886-0066
Sales: $100,001-$500,000

MARY FOOT (Owner) & Buys Men's & Young Men's Surfwear, Swimwear, Beachwear, T-shirts, Shorts

IDAHO - Aberdeen

VILLAGER (CLO)
24 S. Main St. (m)
Aberdeen, ID 83210
208-397-4434
MAUREEN DRISCOLL (President & Owner) & Buys Men's Sportswear, Furnishings, Accessories, Young Men's Wear, Urban Contemporary, Store Displays, Fixtures and Supplies

DRAGONFLY (CLO)
414 W. Main St. (m)
Boise, ID 83702
208-338-9234 / Fax: 208-342-6861
Sales: $500,001-$1 Million
CINDY BEAUCLAIR (President) & Buys Boys' Apparel, Leather Goods, Men's Apparel, Men's Casualwear, Men's Accessories, Men's Hosiery, Men's Sportswear
SANDY ERICKSON (V.P.) & Buys Boys' Apparel, Leather Goods, Men's Apparel, Men's Casualwear, Men's Accessories, Men's Hosiery, Men's Sportswear, Store Displays, Fixtures, Supplies
SIERRA HEAVEIN-Boys' Apparel, Leather Goods, Men's Apparel, Men's Casualwear, Men's Accessories, Men's Hosiery, Men's Sportswear

EYES OF THE WORLD IMPORTS (CLO)
804 W. Fort St. (m-b)
Boise, ID 83702
208-331-1212 / Fax: 208-331-3388
Sales: $500,001-$1 Million
MISHEL VANDENBUSCH (Owner) & Buys Boys' Apparel, Leather Goods, Men's Apparel, Men's Accessories

FORM (CLO)
113 N. 11th St. (p-m)
Boise, ID 83702
208-336-5034
Sales: $100,001-$500,000
Website: www.neurolux.com/form.html
ALAN IRELAND (Owner) & Buys Men's T-shirts, Young Men's Wear, Urban Contemporary, Clubwear, Active Apparel, Shorts, Headwear, Gloves, Small Leather Goods, Jewelry, Footwear, Store Displays, Fixtures, Supplies

L & L SHIRT SHOP (CLO)
5620 Fairview Ave. (m)
Boise, ID 83706
208-376-8881 / Fax: 208-376-0229
LYLE SHOCKEY (Owner) & Buys Men's T-shirts, Fleece, Suits, Overcoats, Tailored Slacks, Dress Shirts, Store Displays, Fixtures, Supplies

M. ALEXANDER, INC. (MW)
(ALEXANDER DAVIS MENS CLOTHING)
P.O. Box 697 (b)
812 W. Bannock St.
Boise, ID 83702
208-343-4824 / Fax: 208-345-3115
Sales: $1 Million-$10 Million
WILLIAM F. SIMONS (President) & Buys Men's Furnishings, Hats, Accessories, Sportswear, Footwear, Store Displays, Fixtures, Supplies
DAVID GRAVES (V.P.) & Buys Men's Furnishings, Hats, Accessories, Sportswear, Store Displays, Fixtures, Supplies

MADE IN IDAHO, INC. (GS-2)
350 N. Milwaukee Ave.
Boise Town Square Mall
Boise, ID 83788
208-378-1188 / Fax: 208-322-7309
Website: www.madeinidaho.com
MIKE STEINMETZ (Owner) & Buys Men's T-shirts, Young Men's Shop, Boys' T-shirts
PEGGY-Men's T-shirts, Young Men's Shop, Boys' T-shirts
NOTE:-Buying of Men's Wear & Store Displays, Fixtures, Supplies Performed Individually Per Store.

PETERSEN'S ENTERPRISES (MW)
(PETERSEN'S CLOTHING & ACCESSORIES)
6630 Overland Rd. (m)
Boise, ID 83709
208-375-3905 / Fax: 208-376-3822
Sales: $100,001-$500,000
WAYNE PETERSEN (Owner) & Buys Men's Furnishings, Sportswear, Accessories, Footwear, Suits, Tailored Jackets & Slacks, Raincoats, Big & Tall Wear, Sweaters, Outer Jackets, Ties, Robes, Hosiery, Gloves, Store Displays, Fixtures, Supplies

SWIM AND RUN SHOP, INC. (CLO-2 & OL)
514 N. 16th St. (m)
Boise, ID 83702
208-385-0105
Website: www.swimrun.com
NINA SHELTON (Owner) & Buys Men's & Boys' Active Apparel, T-shirts, Shorts, Running Clothes, Swimwear, Sandals, Store Displays, Fixtures, Supplies

UNIFORMITY (CLO)
3427 N. Cole Rd. (m)
Boise, ID 83704
208-672-8821 / Fax: 208-672-8831
Sales: $500,001-$1 Million
CAROL HOKE (President) & Buys Men's & Boys' Uniforms & Footwear
STEVE HOKE (V.P.) & Buys Men's & Boys' Uniforms & Footwear

D & B SUPPLY (WW-10)
3303 E. Linden St.
Caldwell, ID 83605
208-459-7446 / Fax: 208-459-7447
Website: www.dbsupply.com
Retail Locations: ID, OR
DICK SCHRANDT (President)
KEITH ALLCOTT (Purch. Mgr.) & Buys Men's & Boys' Western Wear, Hats, Boots, Jewelry, Underwear, Boots, Store Displays, Fixtures, Supplies
LARRY CIGLER-Men's & Boys' Western Wear, Hats, Boots, Jewelry, Underwear, Boots, Store Displays, Fixtures, Supplies

IDAHO'S COWBOY SUPPLY, INC. (CLO)
415 N. 21st Ave. (b)
Caldwell, ID 83605
208-459-1571 / Fax: 208-459-1572
MOLLY MENCHOCA (Owner) & Buys Men's & Boys' Western Jackets, Shirts, Slacks, Jeans, Ties, Hosiery, Accessories, Boots, Store Displays, Fixtures, Supplies

T-SHIRTS PLUS (CLO-3)
(IDAHO UNLIMITED)
4155 Yellowstone Ave. (m)
Pine Ridge Mall
Chubbuck, ID 83202
208-237-8484 / Fax: 208-237-1201
STAN THYBERG (Owner) & Buys Men's & Boys' T-shirts, Sweat Suits, Fleece, Shorts, Polo Shirts, Golf Apparel Shirts, Store Displays, Fixtures, Supplies
SONJA NORRIS (Mgr.) & Buys Store Displays, Fixtures, Supplies

CHADWICK'S (DEPT)
P.O. Box 346 (bud)
20 S. Main St.
Grace, ID 83241
208-425-3903
Sales: $100,001-$500,000
FRANK CHADWICK (Owner) & Buys Men's & Boys' Wear, Footwear, Men's Work Wear, Store Displays, Fixtures, Supplies

NORTH & CO., INC. (SP-2)
P.O. Box 550
101 S. Main St.
Hailey, ID 83333
208-788-2783 / Fax: 208-788-4943
Sales: $500,001-$1 Million
ROGER FLEENOR (President)
JENNIFER HAZARD (Mgr.)
AMY ANDERSON-Men's Activewear

DE MARCO'S (CLO-7)
Grand Teton Mall (b)
2300 E. 17th St.
Idaho Falls, ID 83404
208-524-3611 / Fax: 208-524-3611
LEN MARCOVITZ (Owner) & Buys Men's Suits, Sportswear, Furnishings, Accessories, Headwear, Young Men's Wear, Urban Contemporary, Footwear, Store Displays, Fixtures, Supplies

FERRELL'S CLOTHING (CLO)
(APPAREL, INC.)
P.O. Box 2094 (p-m)
417 Broadway
Idaho Falls, ID 83403
208-522-8293 / Fax: 208-522-8297
Sales: $1 Million-$10 Million
BRENT TUELLER (Owner) & Buys Young Men's Wear, Urban Contemporary, Raincoats, Big & Tall Men's Wear, Sweaters, Sport Shirts, Outer Jackets, Casual Slacks, Active Apparel, Furnishings, Headwear, Belts, Jewelry, Small Leather Goods, Footwear, Store Displays, Fixtures, Supplies

VICKERS WESTERN STORES (WW-2)
3855 5th St. East (b)
Lewisville Hwy.
Idaho Falls, ID 83401
208-522-5030 / Fax: 208-524-8048
Website: www.vickerswesternstores.com
BILL VICKERS (Owner) & Buys Western Clothing, Sportswear, Furnishings, Headwear, Boots, Accessories, Store Displays, Fixtures, Supplies

HOFFMAN SHOES (FW)
(HOFFMAN BOOTS)
100 E. Riverside Ave. (m-b)
Kellogg, ID 83837
208-786-4851 / Fax: 208-786-4301
Sales: $1 Million-$10 Million
Website: www.hoffmanboots.com
JIM HOFFMAN (Partner) & Buys Men's Footwear, Leather Goods, Men's Apparel, Hosiery
TOM HOFFMAN (Partner) & Buys Men's Footwear, Leather Goods, Men's Apparel, Hosiery
BETH HOFFMAN (Real Estate Contact)

KETCHUM DRY GOODS CO. (MW)
511 Sun Valley Rd. East
Ketchum, ID 83340
208-726-9624 / Fax: 208-726-9625
JAY EMMER (Owner) & Buys Men's Wear, Men's Accessories, Furnishings, Footwear

SHEEPSKIN COAT FACTORY & FUR SALON (CLO)
P.O. Box 838 (b)
511 Sun Valley Rd.
Ketchum, ID 83340
208-726-3588 / Fax: 208-726-4063
Website: www.sheepskincoat.com
DAVID NORTON (Owner & President) & Buys Men's Sheepskin Coats, Fur Coats, Jackets, Leather Coats, Accessories, Store Displays, Fixtures, Supplies
BRENDA NORTON-Slippers

ARMY NAVY ECONOMY STORE, INC. (AN)
827 D St.
Lewiston, ID 83501
208-746-6430 / Fax: 208-746-2104
Sales: $500,001-$1 Million
JIM McCULLOUGH (President) & Buys Hunting & Apparel, Apparel, Hiking Boots

MYKLEBUST'S (CLO)
609 Main (m-b)
Lewiston, ID 83501
208-746-0429 / Fax: 208-746-0420
ROD MYKLEBUST (President) & Buys Men's Sportswear, Big & Tall Men's Wear, Leather Apparel, Footwear, Store Displays, Fixtures, Supplies

PAULUCCI'S TAILOR & MENSWEAR (MW)
520 Main St. (m-b)
Lewiston, ID 83501
208-743-5701 / Fax: 208-746-8242
Sales: $100,001-$500,000
JOHN PAULUCCI (Co-Owner) & Buys Men's Overcoats, Suits, Men's Formal Wear, Tailored Jackets, Tailored Slacks, Raincoats, Headwear, Belts, Jewelry, Small Leather Goods, Young Men's Dress Shirts, Big & Tall Men's Wear, Store Displays, Fixtures, Supplies

SHAVER'S, INC. (DEPT-3)
411 Deinhard Ln. (m)
McCall, ID 83638
208-634-7023 / Fax: 208-634-7025
Sales: $1 Million-$10 Million
DENNIS SHAVER (President)
LARRY BOUCK (Mgr.) & Buys Clothing, Sportswear, Furnishings, Boys' Wear, Store Displays, Fixtures, Supplies

CREIGHTON'S, INC. (CLO)
P.O. Box 9125 (m)
401 S. Jackson St.
Moscow, ID 83843
208-882-2423 / Fax: 208-882-2484
STEVE NELSON (Owner) & Buys Men's Sportswear, Furnishings, Accessories, Headwear, Footwear, Store Displays, Fixtures, Supplies

TRI-STATE DISTRIBUTORS, INC. (CLO-4)
1104 Pullman Rd.
Moscow, ID 83843
208-882-4555 / Fax: 208-882-8427
Sales: $10 Million-$50 Million
Website: www.t-state.com
Retail Locations: ID, WA
GERARD CONNELLY (President & Gen. Mgr.)
EDDIE TOUT (G.M.M.)
PAUL LAFERRIERE-Apparel
ROBERT SCHMIDT-Footwear

MYATT'S SHOES & SPORTS (SP)
604 12th Ave. South
Nampa, ID 83647
208-467-2526 / Fax: 208-467-2579
MIKE MYATT (Owner) & Buys Men's Apparel, Footwear, Hosiery, Accessories

NAFZIGER'S (MW)
1309 1st St. South (m-b)
Nampa, ID 83651
208-466-5511 / Fax: 208-466-6711
Sales: $500,001-$1 Million
DAVE LANCASTER (Owner) & Buys Men's Sportswear, Big & Tall Men's Wear, Furnishings, Accessories, Headwear, Footwear, Urban Contemporary, Store Displays, Fixtures, Supplies

FASHION CENTER (DEPT)
53 S. State St. (p)
Preston, ID 83263
208-852-1208
KEITH BOSWORTH (Co-Owner) & Buys Men's Sportswear, Furnishings, Accessories, Young Men's Shop, Boys' Wear, Store Displays, Fixtures, Supplies
NORMA BOSWORTH (Co-Owner) & Buys Men's Sportswear, Furnishings, Accessories, Young Men's Shop, Boys' Wear, Store Displays, Fixtures, Supplies
TINA HINCKLEY-Footwear

COUNTRY FAIR (CLO)
824 Main St. (bud-p-m)
Saint Maries, ID 83861
208-245-2312 / Fax: 208-245-7196
Sales: $100,001-$500,000
MICHELLE SLACK (Owner) & Buys Men's Sportswear, Urban Contemporary, Furnishings, Accessories, Headwear, Footwear, Boys' Sportswear, Store Displays, Fixtures, Supplies

ARFMANN'S FOUR SEASONS (CLO)
(ARFMANN'S DEPARTMENT STORE, INC.)
522 Main St. (p-m)
Salmon, ID 83467
208-756-2422 / Fax: 208-756-4369
LOREN ARFMANN (Owner) & Buys Men's, Young Men's & Boys' Sportswear, Headwear, Accessories, Footwear, Store Displays, Fixtures, Supplies

IDAHO - Salmon

McPHERSON'S DRY GOODS CO. (DEPT & OL)

301 Main St. (p)
Salmon, ID 83467
208-756-3232 / Fax: 208-756-4279
Sales: $500,000-$1 Million
Website: www.mcphersonsdrygoods.com

FLORIN BELLER (President)
STEVE BELLER (Asst. Mgr.) & Buys Men's, Young Men's & Boys' Wear, Outerwear, Leather Apparel, Footwear, Store Displays, Fixtures, Supplies
KEN BELLER (Asst. Mgr.) & Buys Footwear, Store Displays, Fixtures, Supplies
SHAWNDA ADAMS-Western Jewelry

ATHLETE'S CHOICE (SP)

313 N. 1st St.
Sandpoint, ID 83864
208-263-8158

DAN VAN POLEN (Owner) & Buys Activewear, Athletic Footwear

FINAN McDONALD CLOTHING CO. (CLO)

305 N. 1st St. (p)
Sandpoint, ID 83864
208-263-3622 / Fax: 208-263-9518

BEN TATE (Co-Owner) & Buys Men's Sportswear, Footwear, Furnishings, Accessories, Store Displays, Fixtures, Supplies
RHONDA TATE (Co-Owner) & Buys Men's Sportswear, Footwear, Furnishings, Accessories, Store Displays, Fixtures, Supplies

LARSON'S, INC. (CLO-2)

327 N. 1st St. (p-m)
Sandpoint, ID 83864
208-263-2414 / Fax: 208-263-3069
Sales: $500,000-$1 Million

RICHARD LARSON (President) & Buys Men's Sportswear, Ties, Robes, Underwear, Hosiery, Headwear, Accessories, Footwear, Store Displays, Fixtures, Supplies
BONNIE McEWAN (Asst. Mgr.) & Buys Men's Workwear, Denim Apparel, Western Wear
LINDA LARSON-Boys' Wear

JENSEN JEWELERS OF IDAHO, INC. (JWLY-10)

P.O. Box 1295
130 2nd Ave. North
Twin Falls, ID 83301
208-734-7920 / Fax: 208-734-9574
Sales: $10 Million-$50 Million
Website: www.jensen-jewelers.com
Retail Locations: ID, MT, NV

JOHN S. JENSEN (President) & Buys Jewelry, Watches
SHAUNA REEVES-Jewelry, Watches

RULLMAN'S (MW)

(CAM'S)
418 6th St. (m-b)
Wallace, ID 83873
208-752-3111

MICHAEL ALLDREDGE (Owner)
JOANNE WALLACE (Mgr.) & Buys Men's Overcoats, Tailored Jackets, Tailored Slacks, Raincoats, Sweaters, Sport Shirts, Outer Jackets, Casual Slacks, Active Apparel, Furnishings, Headwear, Belts, Jewelry, Small Leather Goods, Big & Tall Men's Wear, Young Men's Wear, Footwear, Western Wear, Store Displays, Fixtures, Supplies

FASHION CREATORS (CLO)
70 W. Lake St.
Addison, IL 60101
630-543-8181 / Fax: 630-543-8181
MOHAMMED JALIAWALA (Owner) & Buys Men's Suits, Sportswear, Fragrances, Young Men's Wear, Shoes, Boys' Wear

GINGISS FORMAL WEAR (MW-271)
(GINGISS INTERNATIONAL)
2101 Executive Dr. (m-b)
Addison, IL 60101
630-620-9050 / Fax: 630-620-8840
Website: www.gingiss.com
Retail Locations: AL, AZ, AR, CA, CO, CT, DC, FL, GA, IL, IN, KS, KY, LA, MD, MA, MN, MS, MO, NV, NJ, NM, NC, OH, OK, OR, SC, TN, TX, UT, VA, WA, WI
MICHELLE OLDANI (V.P.-Mdse.) & Buys Displays
ARNOLD CAPITANELLY (V.P.)
CATHY DIETRICH-Men's Formal Wear & Accessories, Men's & Boys' Footwear
LARRY O'DONNELL-Fixtures, Supplies
TOM RYAN (Real Estate Contact)
NOTE-41 Company Owned Stores, 230 Franchised Stores

HANLON & HAEGELE, INC. (MW)
223 E. Cente Dr. (b)
Alton, IL 62002
618-462-7327 / Fax: 618-462-7327
Sales: $100,001-$500,000
DON LANDUYT (Owner) & Buys Men's Sportswear, Furnishings & Accessories, Footwear, Store Displays, Fixtures, Supplies

KALEEL'S CLOTHING & SHOES (MW & FW)
226 Main St. (p-m)
Amboy, IL 61310
815-857-2512
Sales: $100,001-$500,000
MONA KALEEL (Co-Owner)
GEORGE KALEEL (Co-Owner) & Buys Men's Overcoats, Suits, Tailored Jackets, Tailored Slacks, Big & Tall Men's Wear, Sweaters, Sport Shirts, Outer Jackets, Casual Slacks, Active Apparel, Men's Furnishings, Headwear, Leather Apparel, Footwear, Store Displays, Fixtures, Supplies

JIM & DOT'S SHOE STORE & WESTERN WEAR (WW)
113 W. Davie St. (p-m)
Anna, IL 62906
618-833-5245 / Fax: 618-833-3722
DOT FULLER (Co-Owner) & Buys Men's & Young Men's Western Wear, Related Furnishings, Headwear, Accessories, Western Boots, Moccasins, Work Clothes, Work Boots, Store Displays, Fixtures, Supplies
JIM FULLER (Co-Owner) & Buys Men's & Young Men's Western Wear, Related Furnishings, Headwear, Accessories, Western Boots, Moccasins, Work Clothes, Work Boots, Store Displays, Fixtures, Supplies

ELITE EMBROIDERY (CLO)
893 Main St.
Antioch, IL 60002
847-395-5584 / Fax: 847-395-9365
Sales: $100,001-$500,000
DIANE GALL (Owner) & Buys Activewear

JACK'S FOUR SQUIRES (CLO)
(MARTIN BAYER)
414 Lake St. (m-b)
Antioch, IL 60002
847-395-6880 / Fax: 847-395-1568
Sales: $1 Million-$10 Million
JACK SIEGMEIER (President) & Buys Men's Sportswear, Furnishings, Accessories, Footwear, Young Men's Shop
SCOTT BURRELL (Mgr.) & Buys Men's Sportswear, Furnishings, Accessories, Footwear, Young Men's Shop, Store Displays, Fixtures, Supplies

B. J. HINCH & ASSOCIATES (KS)
350 S. Newbury Pl.
Arlington Heights, IL 60005
804-762-4455 / Fax: 804-217-8999
B. J. HINCH (President) & Buys Men's Suits, Tailored Jackets, Tailored Slacks, Sport Shirts

DELBERT'S CLOTHING, INC. (MW & OL)
123 S. Vine St. (m-b)
Arthur, IL 61911
217-543-2322 / Fax: 217-543-3520
Sales: $1 Million-$10 Million
Website: www.delberts.com
ROBERT J. WATKINS (Owner) & Buys Men's Wear, Footwear, Big & Tall Men's Wear, Store Displays, Fixtures, Supplies
TERRY CLARK (V.P. & Mgr.) & Buys Men's Wear, Footwear, Big & Tall Men's Wear, Store Displays, Fixtures, Supplies

THE BIG CHOICE BIG & TALL (MW-2)
4342 New York St. (m-b)
Aurora, IL 60504
630-851-6105 / Fax: 630-851-6167
LEN SCHINKOETH (Owner) & Buys Men's Big & Tall Clothing, Sportswear, Dress Shirts, Underwear, Hosiery, Accessories, Footwear, Urban Contemporary, Store Displays, Fixtures, Supplies

MEPHISTO GREAT LAKES SHOE COMPANY (FW)
2515 Waukegan Rd. (des)
Bannockburn, IL 60015
847-948-7463 / Fax: 847-948-7457
Sales: $500,001-$1 Million
Website: www.mephistogreatlakes.com
RAY SAND (Owner) & Buys Men's Footwear, Hosiery

CHUCK HINES IN BARRINGTON (MW)
141 W. Main St. (b)
Barrington, IL 60010
(DLS Outfitters)
847-381-6616 / Fax: 847-381-6620
Sales: $1 Million-$10 Million
GARY HINES (Owner) & Buys Men's Sportswear, Footwear, Big & Tall Men's, Young Men's Wear, Boys' Wear, Store Displays, Fixtures, Supplies
SCOTT MORTON-Men's Furnishings, Accessories, Footwear, Dress Shirts
JIM GILBERT-Boys' Wear, Sportswear, Footwear, Accessories

FLORSHEIM GROUP, INC. (FW-250)
(FLORSHEIM FACTORY OUTLET)
(FLORSHEIM SHOE SHOP)
1250 S. Gruvest, Suite 200
Barrington, IL 60010
312-458-2500 / Fax: 312-458-7470
Sales: $100 Million-$500 Million
Website: www.florsheim.com
Retail Locations: AZ, AK, AZ, AR, CA, CO, CT, DE, DC, FL, GA, HI, ID, IL, IN, IA, KS, KY, LA, ME, MD, MA, MI, MN, MS, MO, MT, NE, NV, NH, NJ, NM, NY, NC, ND, OH, OK, OR, PA, RI, SC, SD, TN, TX, UT, VT, VA, WA, WV, WI, WY
PETER CORRITORI (President & C.E.O.)
DAVID SANGUINETTI (President-Retail Div.)
THOMAS JOSEPH (President-Intl. Div. & Real Estate Contact)
KAREN MCKENZIE (Sr. V.P.-Mktg. & Prod. Dev.) & Buys Men's Footwear, Leather Goods, Men's Accessories, Men's Hosiery

PETER DANIEL, INC. (CLO)
200 Applebee St. (m-b)
Barrington, IL 60010
847-382-6676 / Fax: 847-382-3220
Sales: $1 Million-$10 Million
Website: www.peter-daniel.com
PETER HAMMOND (Owner)
DENNIS HAMPTON (Mgr.) & Buys Men's Suits, Raincoats, Tailored Jackets, Tailored Slacks, Sweaters, Sport Shirts, Outer Jackets, Casual Slacks, Active Apparel, Big & Tall Men's, Furnishings, Small Leather Goods, Fragrances, Accessories, Store Displays, Fixtures, Supplies

SPECIAL OCCASIONS (CLO)
2 N. Batavia Ave. (m)
Batavia, IL 60510
630-406-1515 / Fax: 630-406-1545
Sales: $500,001-$1 Million
TERESA STEUER (Owner) & Buys Men's Footwear, Formalwear

ALAMO SHOES (FW)
6548 W. Cermak Rd. (m-b)
Berwyn, IL 60402
708-795-8181 / Fax: 708-484-0078
SOL PRICE (Owner) & Buys Men's Dress Shoes, Casual Shoes, Athletic Footwear, Slippers, Sandals, Hosiery, Belts, Store Displays, Fixtures, Supplies
DENNIS HODES (Mgr.) & Buys Men's Dress Shoes, Casual Shoes, Athletic Footwear, Slippers, Sandals, Hosiery, Belts, Store Displays, Fixtures, Supplies
MONYCA FLACK (Mgr.) & Buys Men's Dress Shoes, Casual Shoes, Athletic Footwear, Slippers, Sandals, Hosiery, Belts, Store Displays, Fixtures, Supplies

MOBERLY & KLENNER (MW)
(ULBRICH & KRAFT)
318 N. Main St. (b)
Bloomington, IL 61701
309-829-4444 / Fax: 309-452-3275
Sales: $500,001-$1 Million
KENNETH WOODS (President) & Buys Men's Sportswear, Footwear, Men's Big & Tall Wear
ROCKY WOODS (V.P.) & Buys Men's Sportswear, Footwear, Men's Big & Tall Wear

MURRAY'S SHOES, INC. (FW)
1701 E. Empire St. (m-b-des)
Bloomington, IL 61704
309-663-1441 / Fax: 309-663-0351
Sales: $500,001-$1 Million
JOSEPH MURRAY (Owner) & Buys Men's Footwear
ROY RAMBO (Mgr.)

WEST SIDE CLOTHING STORE (MW)
1014 W. Washington St. (m)
Bloomington, IL 61701
309-828-4823 / Fax: 309-820-9900
Sales: $100,001-$500,000
CLARK TAMINGER (Owner) & Buys Men's Tailored Jackets, Tailored Slacks, Sportswear, Big & Tall Men's Wear, Furnishings, Hats, Headwear, Belts, Small Leather Goods, Boots, Store Displays, Fixtures, Supplies

DAUBE CO. (RB)
P.O. Box 5649
Buffalo Grove, IL 60089
847-520-9090 / Fax: 847-520-9133
PAUL H. DAUBE, JR. (President & Owner)
SHIRLEE DAUBE (V.P.) & Buys Men's Big & Tall Apparel, Furnishings, Accessories

SOUTHERN SISTERS ROOTS TOO (CLO)
400 S. Illinois Ave. (bud-p-m-b-h)
Carbondale, IL 62901
618-549-5560
ANITA HAYDEN (Owner) & Buys Men's Accessories, Footwear, Furnishings, Jewelry

GRANT'S CLOTHING (CLO)
P.O. Box 1001 (p)
8 Main St.
Carrier Mills, IL 62917
618-994-2052 / Fax: 618-994-2052
Sales: $100,001-$500,000
VINCENT BESHERES (Co-Owner) & Buys Men's Raincoats, Outer Jackets, Jeans, Furnishings, Belts, Small Leather Goods, Young Men's Jeans, Boys' Western Shirts, Jeans, Work Boots, Rubber Boots, Store Displays, Fixtures, Supplies
CAROLYN BESHERES (Co-Owner) & Buys Men's Raincoats, Outer Jackets, Jeans, Furnishings, Belts, Small Leather Goods, Young Men's Jeans, Boys' Western Shirts, Jeans, Work Boots, Rubber Boots, Store Displays, Fixtures, Supplies

ROYALTY'S, INC. (CLO-2)
10 S. Madison St. (p)
Carthage, IL 62321
217-357-2323 / Fax: 217-357-2323
Sales: $500,001-$1 Million
CHARLES ROYALTY (President)
DENNIS ROYALTY (V.P.) & Buys Men's Young Men's & Boys' Slacks, Jeans, Tops, Underwear, Belts, Hosiery, Leather Apparel, Headwear, Footwear, Suits, Sportswear, Urban Contemporary, Store Displays, Fixtures, Supplies
BRIAN ROYALTY (V.P.) & Buys Boys' Sportswear, Outerwear

JIM FORD MENSWEAR, INC. (MW)
119 S. Locust St. (p-m)
Centralia, IL 62801
618-532-1113 / Fax: 618-532-1113
Sales: $500,001-$1 Million
J. MICHAEL FORD (President & G.M.M.) & Buys Men's Overcoats, Suits, Tailored Jackets, Tailored Slacks, Raincoats, Big & Tall Wear, Sweaters, Sport Shirts, Outer Jackets, Leather Apparel, Casual Slacks, Active Apparel, Dress Shirts, Ties, Robes, Underwear, Hosiery, Gloves, Headwear, Belts

BODY 'N' SOLE SPORTS (SP-2)
701 S. 6th St.
Champaign, IL 61820
217-367-2891 / Fax: 217-383-1006
Sales: $500,001-$1 Million
Website: www.bodynsolesports.com
MIKE LINDEMANN (Co-Owner) & Buys Running Apparel, Athletic Footwear
JED BUNYAN (Co-Owner)

CHAMPAIGN SURPLUS STORE (AN)
303 S. Neil St. (p)
Champaign, IL 61820
217-356-4703 / Fax: 217-356-5530
Website: www.champaignsurplus.com
IRA WACHTEL (Owner) & Buys Men's Sportswear, Belts, Hosiery, Leather Apparel, Footwear, Urban Contemporary, Store Displays, Fixtures, Supplies

JOSEPH KUHN (MW)
33 Main St. (p-m-b)
Champaign, IL 61820
217-352-7666 / Fax: 217-352-7669
Website: www.joskuhn.com
DR. WILLIAM YOUNGERMAN (Owner)
BILL BLANKENBEKER (Mgr.) & Buys Men's Big & Tall Wear, Men's Wear, Store Displays, Fixtures, Supplies

ADAMS JOSEPH'S (MW)
544 W. Roosevelt Rd. (des)
Chicago, IL 60607
312-913-1855
Sales: $500,001-$1 Million
ALAN FEDERMAN (President) & Buys Leather Goods, Men's Casualwear, Denim Apparel, Formalwear, Accessories, Hosiery, Outerwear, Sportswear, Suits, Uniforms/Workclothes

ALCALA WESTERN WEAR (WW & OL)
1733 W. Chicago Ave.
Chicago, IL 60622
312-226-0152 / Fax: 312-226-4387
Website: www.alcalas.com
RICHARD ALCALA (President) & Buys Men's Sportswear, Western Wear, Leather Apparel, Furnishings, Accessories, Boys' Western Wear, Men's & Boys' Boots, Store Displays, Fixtures, Supplies

ILLINOIS - Chicago

ALTERNATIVE SHOES, INC. (FW-2 & OL)
1969 N. Halsted St.
Chicago, IL 60614
312-943-1591
Sales: $1 Million-$10 Million
Website: www.alternativeshoes.com
SANDRO VADAR (Owner) & Buys Men's Footwear, Men's Jackets

ANDY'S FASHIONS (CLO)
1242 N. Milwaukee Ave. (p-m-b)
Chicago, IL 60622
773-862-5678
Sales: $100,001-$500,000
YOUNG PARK (Owner) & Buys Men's Sportswear, Underwear, Headwear, Store Displays, Fixtures, Supplies

APARTMENT NUMBER 9 (MW)
1804 N. Damen Ave.
Chicago, IL 60647
773-395-2999
AMY BLESSING (Co-Owner) & Buys Men's Apparel, Accessories
SARAH BLESSING (Co-Owner) & Buys Men's Apparel, Accessories

ARM-SHEFF GASLIGHT MEN'S SHOP (MW)
1654 W. Chicago Ave. (m)
Chicago, IL 60622
312-733-3553 / Fax: 312-733-6824
Sales: $100,001-$500,000
WILFREDO AVILES (President) & Buys Men's Sportswear, Furnishings, Accessories, Men's & Young Men's Shoes, Young Men's Shop, Urban Contemporary, Store Displays, Fixtures, Supplies
ERIC AVILES (Gen. Mgr.) & Buys Men's Sportswear, Furnishings, Accessories, Men's & Young Men's Shoes, Young Men's Shop, Urban Contemporary, Store Displays, Fixtures, Supplies

B & B SALES (AN)
(HERMAN'S ARMY)
11212 S. Michigan Ave.
Chicago, IL 60628
773-785-7885
Sales: $100,001-$500,000
DON COHEN (Owner & Gen. Mgr.) & Buys Big & Tall Activewear, Athletic Footwear, Athletics, Licensed Apparel

BELMONT ARMY SURPLUS (AN)
945 W. Belmont Ave. (p-m-b)
Chicago, IL 60657
773-549-1038 / Fax: 773-549-1075
Sales: $1 Million-$10 Million
CHANG YOO (Owner)
CRAIG SCHOLLA-Men's Sportswear, Ties, Underwear, Hosiery, Headwear, Accessories, Footwear, Urban Contemporary, Store Displays, Fixtures, Supplies

BENVIDES' SHOES (FW)
5220 S. Pulaski Rd. (m-b-des)
Chicago, IL 60632
773-585-2021
Sales: $100,001-$500,000
PEDRO BENVIDES (Owner) & Buys Men's Footwear, Hosiery, Boys' Footwear

BIG 'N' LITTLE SHOES, INC. (FW)
3142 W. 111th St. (b)
Chicago, IL 60655
773-239-6066
Sales: $100,001-$500,000
BRUCE KAMINSKI (Owner) & Buys Boys' Footwear, Men's Footwear, Men's Accessories, Boys' Accessories

BUY-A-TUX (MW)
615 W. Roosevelt Ave. (m-b)
Chicago, IL 60607
312-243-5465 / Fax: 312-243-5067
Sales: $1 Million-$10 Million
MICHAEL A. SHEA (President) & Buys Men's & Boys' Apparel, Men's Formalwear, Accessories, Hosiery, Outerwear, Suits, Uniforms/Workclothes
RENEE SHEA-Men's & Boys' Apparel, Men's Formalwear, Accessories, Hosiery, Outerwear, Suits, Uniforms/Workclothes

C & K FASHIONS (CLO)
4012 W. North Ave. (m)
Chicago, IL 60639
773-486-6035 / Fax: 773-486-6035
Sales: $100,001-$500,000
CHANG KIM (Owner)
JEAN KIM-Men's Casual Wear, Furnishings, Accessories, Leather Apparel, Footwear, Urban Contemporary

CAPRIO'S SHOES, INC. (FW)
3958 W. 63rd St. (bdes)
Chicago, IL 60629
773-767-6060
Sales: $500,001-$1 Million
VITO CAPRIO (Owner) & Buys Boys' Footwear, Men's Footwear

CHICAGO SHOE MART (FW-2)
(STAR SHOES)
(CHICAGO SHOES)
11232 S. Michigan Ave.
Chicago, IL 60628
773-928-6417 / Fax: 773-928-6420
MIKE YANG (Owner) & Buys Men's & Boys' Dress Shoes, Casual Shoes, Slippers, Athletic Footwear, Related Accessories, Store Displays, Fixtures, Supplies

COHN & STERN (MW)
1500 E. 55th St. (m-b)
Chicago, IL 60615
773-752-8100 / Fax: 773-752-8102
Sales: $500,001-$1 Million
Website: www.cohnandstern.com
HOWARD COHN (Owner) & Buys Store Displays, Fixtures, Supplies, Men's Sportswear, Leather Apparel, Accessories, Furnishings
MIKE AARON-Men's Sportswear, Leather Apparel, Accessories, Furnishings

CONCOURSE MEN'S FASHIONS (MW)
6300 S. Halstead St.
Chicago, IL 60621
773-483-3121 / Fax: 773-483-4123
MR. LEE (Owner) & Buys Men's Furnishings, Accessories

D & L APPAREL (SP)
4639 N. Milwaukee Ave.
Chicago, IL 60630
773-736-0855 / Fax: 773-736-0367
LEE COOPERMAN (Owner) & Buys Activewear, Licensed Apparel, Sportswear, Specialty, Closeouts

DAVIS FOR MEN (MW-2)
824 W. North Ave. (b)
Chicago, IL 60622
312-266-9599 / Fax: 312-751-0571
Sales: $1 Million-$10 Million
STEPHEN DAVIS (Owner) & Buys Men's Sportswear, Leather Apparel, Accessories, Footwear, Store Displays, Fixtures, Supplies

DELAWARE CLOTHING, INC. (MW)
1 E. Delaware Pl. (b-des)
Chicago, IL 60611
312-664-8902 / Fax: 312-664-3169
Sales: $1 Million-$10 Million
RACHEL BOE (President)
MEL CAMM-Leather Goods, Men's Big & Tall Apparel, Casualwear, Denim Apparel, Formalwear, Accessories, Hosiery, Outerwear, Sportswear, Suits, Swimwear

EAST BANK CLUB (CLO)
500 N. Kingsbury St. (b)
Chicago, IL 60610
312-527-5800 / Fax: 312-527-5481
Sales: $500,001-$1 Million
Website: www.eastbankclub.com
JAMES P. McHUGH (Co-Owner)
DANIEL LEVIN (Co-Owner)
HOLLY HARRIS-Men's Footwear, Casualwear, Hosiery, Outerwear, Sportswear, Swimwear, Underwear
TARA EVANS-Men's Footwear, Casualwear, Hosiery, Outerwear, Sportswear, Swimwear, Underwear

ILLINOIS - Chicago

G.K. TOPS & BOTTOMS (MW)
3940 W. Madison St. (m-b)
Chicago, IL 60624
773-722-5500 / Fax: 773-722-6855
DAVID KASSIM (Co-Owner) & Buys Men's Sportswear, Furnishings, Accessories, Leather Apparel, Young Men's Shop, Men's & Young Men's Footwear, Urban Contemporary, Store Displays, Fixtures, Supplies

HANIG'S FOOTWEAR CO. (FW-5)
(HANIG'S BIRKENSTOCK)
(HANIG'S SLIPPER BOX)
2754 N. Clark St. (bud-p-m-b-des)
Chicago, IL 60614
773-248-1977 / Fax: 773-248-0793
Sales: $1 Million-$10 Million
Website: www.hanigs.com
PETER HANIG (President) & Buys Men's Footwear, Watches, Men's Accessories, Hosiery
RICH HOGAN (Mgr.) & Buys Men's Footwear, Watches, Men's Accessories, Hosiery

HAWK QUARTERS (CLO)
333 N. Michigan Ave. (m-b)
Chicago, IL 60601
312-464-2957 / Fax: 312-759-0083
Sales: $500,001-$1 Million
PETER WIRTZ (President)
HARRY LACAVAR (Dir.-Mdsg.) & Buys Boys' Apparel, Leather Goods, Men's Big & Tall Wear, Casualwear, Denim Apparel, Accessories, Hosiery, Sportswear
JOHN HORMEOGEM (Store Mgr.) & Buys Boys' Apparel, Leather Goods, Men's Big & Tall Wear, Casualwear, Denim Apparel, Accessories, Hosiery, Sportswear

IN CHICAGO FOR MEN (MW)
61 E. Oak St. (m-b)
Chicago, IL 60611
312-787-9557 / Fax: 312-787-6327
Sales: $1 Million-$10 Million
DAVID PERLOW (Owner) & Buys Men's Sportswear, Leather Apparel, Belts, Hosiery, Footwear, Store Displays, Fixtures, Supplies
WILLY DAVIS-Men's Sportswear, Leather Apparel, Belts, Hosiery, Footwear, Store Displays, Fixtures, Supplies

JACK ROBBINS' CLOTHES, INC. (MW)
5613 W. Belmont Ave. (m)
Chicago, IL 60634
773-637-9000 / Fax: 773-637-8351
Sales: $500,000-$1 Million
LAWRENCE ROBBINS (President) & Buys Men's Sportswear, Leather Apparel, Accessories, Footwear, Store Displays, Fixtures, Supplies

KALE UNIFORM, INC. (CLO-5 & MO)
555 W. Roosevelt Rd. (m)
Chicago, IL 60607
312-563-0022 / Fax: 312-563-0080
Sales: $10 Million-$50 Million
TOM VAZZANO (Sls. Mgr.) & Buys Men's Footwear, Apparel, Accessories, Uniforms

KINDERLAND MODA (KS)
4753 N. Lincoln Ave. (m)
Chicago, IL 60625
773-784-0506 / Fax: 773-784-4244
Sales: Under $100,000
MARTHA P. TAPIA (Owner) & Buys 8 to 16 Boys' Wear, Store Displays, Fixtures, Supplies

KOHN'S (CLO-2)
6004 W. North Ave. (m-b)
Chicago, IL 60639
773-637-5175
Sales: $500,000-$1 Million
GEORGE KOHN (Owner) & Buys Men's & Young Men's Sportswear, Leather Apparel, Furnishings, Store Displays, Fixtures, Supplies

LAKESHORE ATHLETIC CLUB (SP)
1320 W. Fullerton Ave.
Chicago, IL 60614
773-477-9888 / Fax: 773-477-9714
Sales: $100,001-$500,000
Website: www.lsac.com
CHRIS WILSON (Mgr.) & Buys Activewear, Athletic Footwear, Running & Aerobic Apparel

M. STUART'S LTD. (MW)
568 W. Roosevelt Rd.
Chicago, IL 60607
312-663-3125
MARK FRANK (Owner) & Buys Men's Casual Slacks, Furnishings, Accessories, Footwear

MARSHALL FIELD'S (DEPT-62)
(Div. of TARGET CORP.)
111 N. State St. (m-b-h)
Chicago, IL 60602
(Associated Mdsg. Corp.)
312-781-1000 / Fax: 312-781-4326
Sales: Over $1 Billion
Website: www.marshallfields.com
Retail Locations: IL, IN, MN, MI, ND, OH, SD, WI
JOANN SITT (Real Estate Contact) (@ 612-761-3724)
NOTE-All Buying Performed By TARGET CORPORATION in Minneapolis, MN-See Listing.

MARTIN'S BIG & TALL (MW-2)
(DAUBE CO.)
4745 N. Lincoln Ave. (p-m)
Chicago, IL 60625
773-784-5853 / Fax: 773-784-2758
Sales: $1 Million-$10 Million
Website: www.martinsbigtall.com
GARY KRAUS (President) & Buys Big & Tall Men's Sweaters, Sport Shirts, Outer Jackets, Leather Apparel, Casual Slacks, Active Apparel, Dress Shirts, Ties, Robes, Underwear, Hosiery, Gloves, Headwear, Urban Contemporary
BRUCE KRAUS (V.P.) & Buys Big & Tall Men's Tailored Slacks, Store Displays, Fixtures, Supplies
JEFF ALBAUM-Men's Big & Tall Overcoats, Suits, Raincoats
MURRAY ZISKING-Men's Accessories

MAXI'S STORE FOR MEN (MW)
9737 S. Western Ave. (b)
Chicago, IL 60643
773-238-9200 / Fax: 773-238-6927
Sales: $1 Million-$10 Million
ROBERT RAFFELD (President) & Buys Men's Sportswear, Leather Apparel, Furnishings, Hats, Footwear

MEYERS ON CHICAGO AVE., INC. (DEPT)
1535 W. Chicago Ave. (p)
Chicago, IL 60622
312-421-3774 / Fax: 312-421-3481
DONALD ESRIG (President) & Buys Store Displays, Fixtures, Supplies
NORMAN MOTIN-Men's & Boys' Clothing, Sportswear, Leather Apparel, Accessories, Footwear, Urban Contemporary

MEYERSON & ASSOCIATES CLOTHING CO., INC. (MW)
555 W. Roosevelt Rd., #4 (b)
Chicago, IL 60607
312-421-5580 / Fax: 312-421-5685
Sales: $1 Million-$10 Million
RUBEN MEYERSON (Co-Owner) & Buys Men's Sportswear, Furnishings, Headwear, Accessories, Tuxedos, Young Men's Wear, Store Displays, Fixtures, Supplies
MAX ISRAEL (Co-Owner) & Buys Men's Sportswear, Furnishings, Headwear, Accessories, Tuxedos, Young Men's Wear, Store Displays, Fixtures, Supplies

ILLINOIS - Chicago

MEYSTEL, INC. (DEPT)
4666 S. Halsted St. (m)
Chicago, IL 60609
773-843-7200 / Fax: 773-843-7210
Sales: $1 Million-$10 Million
JERRY ALLEN (President)
RANDALL BURNEY (G.M.M.) & Buys Suits, Sweaters, Store Displays Fixtures, Supplies
STU ROSENTHAL-Leather Apparel, Casual Slacks, Active Apparel, Furnishings, Dress Shirts
OPEN-Men's Wear, Boys' Wear, Men's & Boys' Footwear, Urban Contemporary
IRA MOLTZMAN-Overcoats, Tailored Jackets, Tailored Slacks, Raincoats, Ties, Robes, Underwear, Hosiery, Gloves

MORRIS & SONS (CLO)
555 W. Roosevelt Rd. (b)
Chicago, IL 60607
312-243-5635 / Fax: 312-243-9085
Sales: $1 Million-$10 Million
Website: www.morrisandsons.com
GARY MORRIS (Owner) & Buys Men's Suits, Sportswear, Leather Apparel, Furnishings, Belts, Footwear

MR. KAY'S, INC. (MW-2)
(HELEN KAY)
1719 E. 87th St. (m-b-des)
Chicago, IL 60617
773-221-5297 / Fax: 773-375-8686
Sales: $1 Million-$10 Million
MAZEN KAY (President) & Buys Leather Goods, Men's Big & Tall Apparel, Casualwear, Denim Apparel, Formalwear, Accessories, Hosiery, Outerwear, Sportswear, Suits

PANTS BOX (CLO-2)
4216 S. Archer Ave. (m-b)
Chicago, IL 60632
773-847-3360 / Fax: 773-847-8360
Sales: $1 Million-$10 Million
ROGER ZAK (Owner) & Buys Store Displays, Fixtures, Supplies, Men's Sportswear, Denim
CHRISTINE WILZZECK (@ 312-847-3636)-Men's Sportswear, Denim
RODGER TOVALIN-Men's Furnishings, Accessories

PLAZA MENSWEAR (MW)
6405 S. Halsted St. (m)
Chicago, IL 60621
773-846-2712
BEN HA (Owner) & Buys Men's Sportswear, Furnishings & Accessories, Footwear, Urban Contemporary, Store Displays, Fixtures, Supplies

RASENICK'S MENSWEAR (MW)
3940 N. Cicero Ave. (bud-p)
Chicago, IL 60641
773-736-7705 / Fax: 773-736-7706
Sales: $500,000-$1 Million
ROBERT SHUMAN (President) & Buys Big & Tall Men's Suits, Casual Slacks, Tailored Jackets, Tailored Slacks, Sportswear, Sweaters, Sport Shirts, Outer Jackets, Leather Apparel, Active Apparel, Dress Shirts, Ties, Robes, Underwear, Hosiery, Gloves, Headwear, Belts, Small Leather Goods, Foot

SALAMANDER SHOES, INC. (FW & MO)
(SALAMANDER OF CHICAGO)
4762 N. Lincoln Ave. (b)
Chicago, IL 60625
773-784-7463 / Fax: 773-784-0022
Sales: $500,001-$1 Million
Website: www.salamandershoes.com
CHRISTINE LUSCHER (Owner) & Buys Boys' Footwear, Men's Footwear, Leather Goods, Men's Accessories, Hosiery, Boys' Footwear

SHIRTS OUR BUSINESS LTD. (CLO)
4949 Northwestern Ave. (p)
Chicago, IL 60625
773-271-0600 / Fax: 773-271-1274
RON WEISS (Owner) & Buys Men's Imprintable T-shirts, Fleece, Jackets & Headwear, Store Displays, Fixtures, Supplies

STANDARD HOSIERY (CLO)
2816 W. Cermak Rd. (m-b)
Chicago, IL 60623
773-927-1602 / Fax: 773-927-4851
Sales: $500,001-$1 Million
SOL KAPLAN (President) & Buys Boys' Apparel, Boys' Footwear, Men's Footwear, Casualwear, Hosiery, Sportswear

SYD JEROME (MW)
2 N. LaSalle St. (b)
Chicago, IL 60602
312-346-0333 / Fax: 312-346-9222
SYDNEY SHAPIRO (Owner) & Buys Men's Sportswear, Leather Apparel, Furnishings, Headwear, Accessories, Footwear, Store Displays, Fixtures, Supplies

TONY'S SPORTS, INC. (SG-4)
(Div. of HERMESCO, INC.)
3941 N. Sheridan Rd. (bud-p-m-b)
Chicago, IL 60613
773-477-4944 / Fax: 773-477-1721
Sales: $1 Million-$10 Million
JUAN TONY FERNANDEZ, SR. (President) & Buys Boys' Apparel, Boys' Footwear, Men's Footwear, Leather Goods, Watches, Men's Accessories, Men's Apparel, Boys' Apparel, Boys' Footwear
SANDRA FERNANDEZ (V.P.) & Buys Boys' Apparel, Boys' Footwear, Men's Footwear, Leather Goods, Watches, Men's Accessories, Men's Apparel, Boys' Apparel, Boys' Footwear
LAVAL SYKES (G.M.M.) & Buys Boys' Apparel, Boys' Footwear, Men's Footwear, Leather Goods, Watches, Men's Accessories, Men's Apparel, Boys' Apparel, Boys' Footwear

TWO BROTHERS MENSWEAR (MW)
4631 N. Broadway (m-b)
Chicago, IL 60640
773-878-5969
Sales: $500,001-$1 Million
JOHN KIM (President) & Buys Men's Overcoats, Suits, Tailored Jackets, Tailored Slacks, Raincoats, Sweaters, Sport Shirts, Outer Jackets, Leather Apparel, Casual Slacks, Active Apparel, Furnishings, Accessories, Men's Footwear, Big & Tall Men's, Boys' Wear, Store Displays, Fixtures

U.S. MEN'S FASHIONS (MW)
6331 S. Halsted St. (b)
Chicago, IL 60621
773-873-1622 / Fax: 773-873-1629
Sales: $1 Million-$10 Million
KWANG LEE (Owner) & Buys Men's Sportswear, Leather Apparel, Headwear, Accessories, Footwear, Store Displays, Fixtures, Supplies

ILLINOIS - Chicago

ULTRA STORES, INC. (JWLY-110 & OL)
(FINE JEWELRY AT DAFFY'S)
(FINE JEWELRY AT BURLINGTON COAT FACTORY)
(NEW YORK JEWELRY OUTLET)
(PREMIER FINE JEWELRY DIRECT)
(ULTRA DIAMOND OUTLETS)
(ULTRA DIAMOND FLAGSHIP STORE)
122 S. Michigan Ave., #800
Chicago, IL 60603
312-922-3800 / Fax: 312-922-3933
Sales: $50 Million-$100 Million
Website: www.ultrastores.com
Retail Locations: AZ, CA, CO, CT, FL, GA, IA, IL, IN, MA, MD, MI, MN, MO, MS, NV, NJ, NY, NC, OH, OR, PA, RI, SC, TN, TX, UT, VA, WI
DANIEL MARKS (President)
JOE DONAGHY (C.F.O.)
KIMBERLY MEYER (V.P.-Opers.)
MEGAN KANNER (V.P.-Mdse.)
DAVID SCHOEPHOESTER (V.P.-Mdse.) & Buys Jewelry
MEGAN KANNER (G.M.) & Buys Precious Colored Stones, Gold
DAVID PETRARCA-Watches
FRANK SCHMIDT (Real Estate Contact)

V.C.G. LTD. (MW)
5050 W. Irving Park Rd. (p-m)
Chicago, IL 60641
773-545-3676 / Fax: 773-545-0876
Sales: $1 Million-$10 Million
FRANK GERAGE (President)
PAULETTE GERAGE (V.P.) & Buys Men's Sweaters, Sport Shirts, Outer Jackets, Leather Apparel, Casual Slacks, Dress Shirts, Ties, Gloves, Headwear, Big & Tall Men's Wear, Belts, Footwear, Store Displays, Fixtures, Supplies

VIVA MENSWEAR (MW)
1620 W. Chicago Ave. (p)
Chicago, IL 60622
312-733-8266 / Fax: 312-733-0968
MR. CHUNG (Owner) & Buys Men's Sportswear, Furnishings, Headwear, Accessories, Footwear, Young Men's Wear, Urban Contemporary, Store Displays, Fixtures, Supplies

WESLEY SHOES (KS)
2120 Halsted St. (bud-p-m)
Chicago, IL 60614
773-755-0904 / Fax: 773-755-0904
Sales: $100,001-$500,000
BRUCE WESLEY (Owner) & Buys Boys' Footwear, Hosiery

WHITEHALL JEWELLERS, INC. (JWLY-367 & OL)
(LUNDSTROM JEWELERS)
(MARKS BROTHERS JEWELERS)
(WHITEHALL CO. JEWELERS)
155 N. Wacker Dr.
Chicago, IL 60606
312-782-6800 / Fax: 312-782-8299
Sales: $100 Million-$500 Million
Website: www.whitehalljewellers.com
Retail Locations: AL, AZ, CA, CO, CT, FL, GA, IL, IN, KY, LA, MA, MD, MN, MO, NC, NH, NM, NJ, NY, NV, OK, OR, TN, VA, WA, WV
HUGH M. PATINKIN (President & C.E.O.)
TRISH HERBERT-Colored Stones
JUDY FISHER-Diamonds
MARCIA WILBURN-Gold
DEBBIE VOLKER-Watches
JAY LEPSELPER (Real Estate Contact) (@ 312-782-8299, Ext.: 720)

ZEMSKY'S FAMILY FASHION STORES (CLO-3)
(THE ZEMSKY CORP)
4181 S. Archer Ave. (m)
Chicago, IL 60632
(Henry Doneger)
773-247-4600 / Fax: 773-523-3514
Sales: $1 Million-$10 Million
Website: www.zemskys.com
EUGENE ZEMSKY (Owner, President & Chmn.) & Buys Store Displays, Fixtures, Supplies
OPEN (G.M.M.) & Buys Men's Sportswear, Work Wear, Big & Tall Men's Wear, Furnishings, Accessories, Boys' Wear 8-18
ROSE DE LaTORRE-Boys' Wear 2-7

ZOOTS (MW)
3908 N. Cicero Ave., #10 (p-m)
Chicago, IL 60641-2709
773-545-2296
Sales: $100,001-$500,000
MICHAEL TATZ (Owner) & Buys Men's Sportswear, Furnishings, Work Clothes, Outerwear, Big & Tall Wear, Men's Work Shoes, Boots, Store Displays, Fixtures, Supplies

HAYMAN - HAWKINS, INC. (CLO)
1542 S. Halsted St. (m)
Chicago Heights, IL 60411
708-754-0440 / Fax: 708-754-3050
Sales: $100,001-$500,000
JOSEPH HAWKINS (President & G.M.M.) & Buys Men's Sweaters, Sport Shirts, Outer Jackets, Furnishings (No Robes), Headwear, Footwear, Store Displays, Fixtures, Supplies

STEVEN EDWARDS' MENSWEAR (MW & KS)
(CHILDREN'S CLOSET)
41 N. Williams St. (m-b)
Crystal Lake, IL 60014
815-459-7666
STEVE YOPP (Co-Owner) & Buys Men's Sportswear, Suits, Outer Jackets, Overcoats, Tailored Jackets, Raincoats, Sweaters, Leather Apparel, Furnishings, Accessories, Footwear, Big & Tall Men's Wear
MICHELE YOPP (Co-Owner) (@ 815-459-8883) & Buys Young Men's Wear, Boys' Wear

JOHNNY'S BIG & TALL MEN'S (MW)
51 N. Vermilion St. (m)
Danville, IL 61832
217-431-1680 / Fax: 217-431-1675
JOHN TURNER (President) & Buys Men's Big & Tall Wear, Sweaters, Furnishings, Headwear, Accessories, Urban Contemporary, Store Displays, Fixtures, Supplies, Sportswear, Footwear

MAGS MENSWEAR (MW)
55 N. Vermilion St. (m)
Danville, IL 61832
217-431-0385
GENE SCHOEDER (Owner) & Buys Men's Sportswear, Furnishings, Headwear, Accessories, Store Displays, Fixtures, Supplies

LAN SIRS, LTD. (MW)
112 E. Lincoln Hwy. (m-b)
De Kalb, IL 60115
(DLS Outfitters)
815-758-0671 / Fax: 815-758-6158
LANCE HANSEN (Owner) & Buys Men's Wear, Furnishings, Accessories, Footwear

BACHRACH CLOTHING (MW-53 & MO & OL)
1 Bachrach Ct. (m-b)
Decatur, IL 62526
217-875-1020 / Fax: 217-875-0030
Website: www.bachrach.com
Retail Locations: CA, CT, GA, IL, IN, IA, KS, KY, MD, MN, MA, MI, NJ, OH, OK, OR, PA, TN, TX, VA, WV
EDGAR BACHRACH (President)
JIM JACOBSON (Dir.-Catalog & On-line)
MARIA MARUSICH-Sportswear, Men's Active Apparel
LISA MacGREGOR-Knitwear
WAYNE KLEBE-Dress Shirts, Neckwear
EDITH STANLEY-Pants, Wovens
BRIAN CARL-Suits, Sportscoats
LANTVA YOUNG-Shoes, Belts, Sweaters, Outerwear

BRASS HORN LTD. (MW)
108 E. Prairie Ave. (b)
Decatur, IL 62523
217-422-9112
GEORGE STRECKFUSS (Owner) & Buys Men's Sportswear, Furnishings, Headwear, Accessories, Footwear, Store Displays, Fixtures, Supplies

IMAGES ALIVE LTD. (CLO & MO)
444 Lake Cook Rd.
Deerfield, IL 60015
847-947-5550 / Fax: 847-948-5551
Sales: $1 Million-$10 Million
ELLEN ROBINSON (President)
AARON KRIMBEIN (C.E.O.) & Buys Men's Apparel, Accessories

COMPETITIVE EDGE (SP)
700 E. Peace Rd.
DeKalb, IL 60115
815-758-0056 / Fax: 815-758-0057
Sales: $100,001-$500,000
JEFF RICHARDSON (Owner) & Buys Activewear

LANSIRS ON LINCOLN (MW)
112 E. Lincoln Hwy. (m-b)
DeKalb, IL 60115
815-758-0671 / Fax: 815-758-6158
LANCE HANSEN (Owner) & Buys Men's Sportswear, Accessories, Furnishings, Store Displays, Fixtures, Supplies

CHICAGO SPORTS LTD. (SP)
1655 Oakton St.
Des Plaines, IL 60018
847-296-9655
Sales: $100,001-$500,000
Website: www.chicagoscreenprinting.com
TRENT WILKERSON (Owner) & Buys Activewear

RICHARD'S MENSWEAR (MW)
1524 S. Lee St. (m)
Des Plaines, IL 60018
847-298-5575
RICHARD WHALEN (Owner) & Buys Men's Sportswear, Furnishings, Headwear, Accessories, Young Men's Wear, Urban Contemporary, Store Displays, Fixtures, Supplies

BOOT OUTLET (FW)
I-55 & Rte. 104, Exit 82 (bdes)
Divernon, IL 62530
217-628-3048 / Fax: 217-628-9059
Sales: $100,001-$500,000
JACK WELSH (President) & Buys Men's Apparel, Boys' Apparel, Men's Footwear, Boys' Footwear, Accessories, Hosiery, Leather Goods, Watches, Western Apparel
SANDRA WELSH (V.P.) & Buys Men's Apparel, Boys' Apparel, Men's Footwear, Boys' Footwear, Accessories, Hosiery, Leather Goods, Watches, Western Apparel

HERBERTS MEN'S SHOP OF DOWNERS GROVE, INC. (MW)
5123 Main St. (m-b)
Downers Grove, IL 60515
630-968-0404 / Fax: 630-968-0437
Sales: $500,001-$1 Million
Website: www.herbertsofdg.com
DUANE BAKER (President & G.M.M.) & Buys Sweaters, Outer Jackets, Leather Apparel, Active Apparel, Ties, Raincoats, Accessories, Men's Overcoats, Suits, Tailored Jackets, Gloves, Men's Tailored Slacks, Casual Slacks, Hosiery, Robes, Footwear, Store Displays, Fixtures, Supplies, Men's Dress Shirt
PAUL BAKER-Sportswear, Casual Wear, Dress Slacks, Jeans, Young Men's Apparel

SPIEGEL OUTLET STORES (CLO-18 & OL)
(Div. Of THE SPIEGEL GROUP)
3500 Lacey Road (p-m-b)
Downers Grove, IL 60515
(Directives West, L.A.)
630-986-8800 / Fax: 630-769-2067
Website: www.ultimate-outlet.com
Retail Locations: VA, GA, FL, TX, CO, NV, MO, IN, OH, MI, PA, MN, IL
BILL KOSTUROS (C.E.O.)
BRIAN LIES (Div. V.P.)
TERRY PIENIACEK (Real Estate Contact) (@ 630-769-2329)
CINDY JARTZ (G.M.M.) & Buys Men's Overcoats, Suits, Tailored Jackets, Tailored Slacks, Raincoats, Sweaters, Sport Shirts, Casual Slacks, Active Apparel, Leather Apparel, Outer Jackets, Furnishings

SPIEGEL, INC. (MO & OL)
(THE SPIEGEL GROUP)
3500 Lacey Rd. (p-m-b)
Downers Grove, IL 60515
630-986-8800 / Fax: 630-769-3102
Sales: Over $1 Billion
Website: www.spiegel.com
GERALYNN MADONNA (President)
SHARON SMITH (Mdse. Div. V.P.) & Buys Jeans, T-shirts, Accessories

EAST ST. LOUIS CLOTHING CO. (MW)
218 Collinsville Ave. (m)
East Saint Louis, IL 62201
618-271-0222
DAVID YANG (Owner) & Buys Men's Sportswear, Furnishings, Headwear, Accessories, Footwear, Young Men's Wear, Urban Contemporary, 8 to 20 Boys' Wear, Store Displays, Fixtures, Supplies

IMBER'S MENSWEAR (MW)
P.O. Box 263 (m)
144 N. Main St.
Edwardsville, IL 62025
618-656-6112
ALAN LEGOW (President) & Buys Men's Overcoats, Suits, Tailored Jackets, Tailored Slacks, Raincoats, Sweaters, Sport Shirts, Outer Jackets, Casual Slacks, Leather Apparel, Active Apparel, Furnishings, Headwear, Accessories, Big & Tall Men's Wear, Footwear, Store Displays, Fixtures, Supplies
JERRY LEGOW (V.P.) & Buys Men's Overcoats, Suits, Tailored Jackets, Tailored Slacks, Raincoats, Sweaters, Sport Shirts, Outer Jackets, Casual Slacks, Leather Apparel, Active Apparel, Furnishings, Headwear, Accessories, Big & Tall Men's Wear, Footwear, Store Displays, Fixtures, Supplies

ROSE LYNN FASHIONS (CLO)
900 Elizabeth St. (m)
Elgin, IL 60120
847-741-8337 / Fax: 847-741-6000
ROSE SPAK (Co-Owner) & Buys Men's Overcoats, Sweaters, Sport Shirts, Work Shirts, Outer Jackets, Casual Slacks, Work Pants, Active Apparel, Underwear, Headwear, Small Leather Goods, Store Displays, Fixtures, Supplies

RUGBY CUSTOM SPORTSWEAR CO. (SP & MO)
(AMERICAN RUGBY SUPPLY, INC.)
1510 Midway Ct.
Elk Grove Village, IL 60007
847-981-1242 / Fax: 847-981-1244
Website: www.americanrugby.com
CURTIS HACKER (President) & Buys Apparel, Footwear

LEONARD'S THE STORE FOR MEN (MW)

129 N. York St. (b)
Elmhurst, IL 60126
630-833-8900 / Fax: 630-833-8909
Sales: $1 Million-$10 Million

WILLIAM PATTERSON (President) & Buys Men's Overcoats, Suits, Tailored Jackets, Tailored Slacks, Raincoats, Sweaters, Sport Shirts, Leather Apparel, Outer Jackets, Casual Slacks, Headwear, Dress Shirts, Ties, Robes, Young Men's Wear, Men's Furnishings, Men's Underwear, Hosiery, Footwear, Store Displays, Fixtures, Supplies

JIM BECKER (G.M.M.) & Buys Men's Overcoats, Suits, Tailored Jackets, Tailored Slacks, Raincoats, Sweaters, Sport Shirts, Leather Apparel, Outer Jackets, Casual Slacks, Headwear, Dress Shirts, Ties, Robes, Young Men's Wear, Men's Furnishings, Men's Underwear, Hosiery, Belts, Jewelry, Small Leather Goods, Footwear, Store Displays, Fixtures, Supplies

DEI GIOVANI (MW-2)

2434 N. Harlem Ave. (m-b)
Elmwood Park, IL 60707
708-452-1800 / Fax: 708-452-1865
Sales: $1 Million-$10 Million

LARRY FURIO (President)

NICHOLAS FURIO (G.M.M. & V.P.) & Buys Men's Sportswear, Leather Apparel, Furnishings, Accessories, Footwear, Urban Contemporary, Store Displays, Fixtures, Supplies

JACK ROBBINS CLOTHING CO., INC. (MW)

7219 W. Grand Ave. (m-b)
Elmwood Park, IL 60707
708-453-2112
Sales: $1 Million-$10 Million

GEORGE FRIEDMAN (President)

DON LEALI (Mgr.) & Buys Men's Sportswear, Furnishings, Footwear, Urban Contemporary, Store Displays, Fixtures, Supplies

NORRIS CENTER BOOK STORE (SP)

1999 S. Campus Dr.
Evanston, IL 60208
847-491-3990 / Fax: 847-491-7088
Website: www.bkstore.com/northwestern

DARWIN BARNES-Fleece, Jackets, Hosiery, Hats

LEADING MAN (MW-2)

9506 S. Western Ave.
Evergreen Park, IL 60805
708-499-0406 / Fax: 708-499-6897

STEVE SCHNEIDER (President) & Buys Men's Suits, Furnishings, Accessories, Footwear

FARMERS' STORE (CLO)

706 W. Main St. (bud-p-m-b)
Fairfield, IL 62837
618-842-6581 / Fax: 618-842-2244

MARY JON LEHR (Co-Owner) & Buys Men's Suits, Sportswear, Leather Apparel, Dress Shirts, Ties, Underwear, Hosiery, Belts, Gloves, Robes, Accessories, Overcoats, Tailored Jackets, Tailored Slacks, Raincoats, Big & Tall Men's Wear, Boys' Wear, Men's & Boys' Footwear, Urban Contemporary, Store Displays, Fixtures, Supplies

ONZALEE JONES (Co-Owner) & Buys Men's Suits, Sportswear, Leather Apparel, Dress Shirts, Ties, Underwear, Hosiery, Belts, Gloves, Robes, Accessories, Overcoats, Tailored Jackets, Tailored Slacks, Raincoats, Big & Tall Men's Wear, Boys' Wear, Men's & Boys' Footwear, Urban Contemporary, Store Displays, Fixtures, Supplies

GENTLEMEN'S SHOPPE (MW)

113 E. North Ave. (m)
Flora, IL 62839
618-662-2815

DONNA WHITT (Owner) & Buys Men's Sportswear, Furnishings, Accessories, Store Displays, Fixtures, Supplies

VALENTINO'S, INC. (MW)

2626 Flossmoor Rd. (h)
Flossmoor, IL 60422
708-206-2300 / Fax: 708-206-1191

TONY DISTASIO (Co-Owner) & Buys Men's Sportswear, Small Leather Goods, Store Displays, Fixtures, Supplies, Dress Shirts, Ties, Hosiery, Gloves, Belts, Fragrances, Footwear, Leather Apparel, Suits, Tailored Jackets, Tailored Slacks, Casual Slacks, Outer Jackets

JOE DISTASIO (Co-Owner) & Buys Men's Sportswear, Small Leather Goods, Store Displays, Fixtures, Supplies, Dress Shirts, Ties, Hosiery, Gloves, Belts, Fragrances, Footwear, Leather Apparel, Suits, Tailored Jackets, Tailored Slacks, Casual Slacks, Outer Jackets

RAYMOND LEVINE, INC. (MW)

19919 S. Lagrange Rd. (b)
Frankfort, IL 60423
815-464-5766 / Fax: 815-464-2610

JEFF GLICK (Owner) & Buys Men's Sportswear, Furnishings, Footwear, Accessories, Store Displays, Fixtures, Supplies

ALLEN'S MENSWEAR (MW)

26 W. Stephenson St. (b)
Freeport, IL 61032
815-233-9689
Sales: $500,001-$1 Million

ALLEN KRAUS (Owner) & Buys Men's Footwear, Leather Goods, Casualwear, Denim Apparel, Outerwear, Sportswear, Suits, Hosiery

MARY PETERS-Men's Footwear, Leather Goods, Casualwear, Denim Apparel, Outerwear, Sportswear, Suits, Hosiery

TREND ROOM MENSWEAR (MW)

21 S. Chicago Ave.
Freeport, IL 61032
815-232-6373 / Fax: 815-232-6373
Sales: $500,001-$1 Million

AL LUTZ (Owner) & Buys Leather Goods, Men's Big & Tall Apparel, Boys' Apparel, Men's Casualwear, Denim Apparel, Formalwear, Accessories, Hosiery, Outerwear, Sportswear, Suits, Swimwear, Uniforms/Workclothes, Sleepwear

CONTINENTAL CLOTHING HOUSE (MW)

370 E. Simmons St. (m)
Galesburg, IL 61401
309-342-0016 / Fax: 309-342-0416
Sales: $100,001-$500,000

PATRICK J. BURNS (President) & Buys Men's Sportswear, Leather Apparel, Headwear, Big & Tall Men's Wear, Store Displays, Fixtures, Supplies

DOUGLAS LARSON-Men's Furnishings, Robes, Accessories

JOSEPHSON'S MEN'S STORE (MW)

352 Front St. (m)
Galva, IL 61434
309-932-3086

RUSSELL JOSEPHSON (Owner) & Buys Men's Work Clothes, Sweaters, Sport Shirts, Casual Slacks, Dress Slacks, Ties, Underwear, Hosiery, Gloves, Belts, Footwear, Store Displays, Fixtures, Supplies

ERDAY'S (MW)

P.O. Box 308 (m-b)
10 N. 3rd St.
Geneva, IL 60134
630-232-0151 / Fax: 630-232-8220
Sales: $500,001-$1 Million

VICTOR ERDAY, III (President)

BOB ERDAY-Men's Sportswear, Belts

JIM ERDAY-Big & Tall Men's Wear, Underwear, Hosiery, Small Leather Goods, Robes, Gloves, Headwear, Dress Shirts, Ties

TIM WHITE-Men's Overcoats, Suits, Dress Slacks, Raincoats, Tailored Jackets, Dress Shirts, Ties

DEAN OLSON MENSWEAR (MW)

524 Crescent Blvd. (b)
Glen Ellyn, IL 60137
630-469-1219 / Fax: 630-858-2002
Sales: $500,001-$1 Million

WESS KUNKEL (Co-Owner) & Buys Men's Sportswear, Leather Apparel, Furnishings, Headwear, Accessories, Big & Tall Men's Wear, Store Displays, Fixtures, Supplies

D. RANDALL OLSON (Co-Owner) & Buys Men's Sportswear, Leather Apparel, Furnishings, Headwear, Accessories, Big & Tall Men's Wear, Store Displays, Fixtures, Supplies

COUNTRY GOBBLER, INC. (FW-3)
1708 Glenview Rd. (m-b)
Glenview, IL 60025
847-724-3131 / Fax: 847-724-3181
Sales: $1 Million-$10 Million
Website: www.thecountrygobbler.com
JAMES ADAMS (President & G.M.M.) & Buys Boys' Footwear, Men's Footwear, Leather Goods, Accessories, Hosiery
CHRIS LOWKIS-Boys' Footwear, Men's Footwear, Leather Goods, Accessories, Hosiery

BARLEFF'S, INC. (MW)
5727 Godfrey Rd. (b)
Godfrey, IL 62035
618-466-6720
HENRY SAENZ (Owner) & Buys Men's Sportswear, Furnishings, Accessories, Headwear, Footwear, Store Displays, Fixtures, Supplies

CAROLE FREW'S BRIDAL & TUXEDO SHOPPE (SP)
200 W. Homer M. Adams Pkwy. (b)
Godfrey, IL 62035
618-466-8820 / Fax: 618-466-7802
Sales: $1 Million-$10 Million
CAROLE L. FREW (President) & Buys Men's Apparel, Formalwear
JOHN S. FREW (V.P.) & Buys Men's Apparel, Formalwear

GLIK'S STORES (DEPT-57)
3248 Nameoki Rd. (p)
Granite City, IL 62040
618-876-6717 / Fax: 618-876-7819
Sales: $50 Million-$100 Million
Website: www.gliks.com
JEFF GLIK (President & G.M.M.) & Buys Store Displays, Fixtures, Supplies
JOE GLIK (C.E.O.)
JIM GLIK (V.P.) & Buys Men's Sweaters, Sport Shirts, Casual Slacks, Active Apparel, Urban Contemporary
CARMEN WILKE-Men's Sportswear, Athletic Footwear, Young Men's Sportswear

CAMPUS COLORS, INC. (CLO-3)
1860 1st St. (m-b)
Highland Park, IL 60035
847-433-2300 / Fax: 847-433-2626
Website: www.ecampuscolors.com
NEIL RUBENSTEIN (Owner) & Buys Men's Sportswear, T-shirts, Shorts, Hats, Belts, Young Men's Sportswear, Store Displays, Fixtures, Supplies
NOTE:-Store Sells Only College Merchandise.

THE FELL CO. (CLO & OL)
595 Central Ave. (b)
Highland Park, IL 60035
847-432-5300 / Fax: 847-446-4651
JOHN FELL (Co-Owner) & Buys Men's Sportswear, Leather Apparel, Furnishings, Accessories, Headwear
HAROLD FELL (Co-Owner) & Buys Men's Sportswear, Leather Apparel, Furnishings, Accessories, Headwear
DAVID FELL (Co-Owner) (@ 847-446-8983) & Buys Men's Sportswear, Leather Apparel, Furnishings, Accessories, Headwear
NEIL FELL (Co-Owner) (@ 847-446-8983) & Buys Men's Sportswear, Leather Apparel, Furnishings, Accessories, Headwear
DEBORAH FELL (Co-Owner)

FOREST BOOTERY II (FW-2)
(FOREST BOOTERY LTD.)
342 Central Ave. (m-b)
Highland Park, IL 60035
847-433-1911 / Fax: 847-433-2007
Sales: $1 Million-$10 Million
ROGER WOLFF (Partner) & Buys Boys' Footwear, Men's Footwear, Leather Goods, Men's Accessories, Hosiery, Athletic Footwear, Casual Dress Footwear
PAUL GARRISON (Partner) & Buys Boys' Footwear, Men's Footwear, Leather Goods, Men's Accessories, Hosiery, Athletic Footwear, Casual Dress Footwear
DOUG SWANSON (Mgr.) & Buys Boys' Footwear, Men's Footwear, Leather Goods, Men's Accessories, Hosiery, Athletic Footwear, Casual Dress Footwear

RUNNING RIGHT, INC. (SP)
1770 1st St.
Highland Park, IL 60035
847-432-2884 / Fax: 847-432-9497
Website: www.runningright.com
BILL MOSS (President) & Buys Activewear, Athletic Footwear

THE STYLE SHOP (KS)
794 Central Ave. (m-b)
Highland Park, IL 60035
847-432-6944 / Fax: 847-432-7056
MICHAEL POWELL (Owner) & Buys Young Men's & Boys' Wear, Sportswear, Furnishings, Headwear, Accessories, Store Displays, Fixtures, Supplies

HINDSDALE CLOTHIERS (MW)
777 N. York Rd.
Hinsdale, IL 60521
630-323-1858 / Fax: 630-323-2732
STEVE POTTER (President) & Buys Men's Wear, Accessories

VILLAGE BOOTERY (FW-2)
(CAROUSEL SHOE LIMITED)
52 S. Washington St. (m-b-des)
Hinsdale, IL 60521
630-323-0234 / Fax: 630-323-0257
Sales: $500,001-$1 Million
CHERYL FREY (Mgr.) & Buys Boys' Footwear, Men's Footwear, Leather Goods, Accessories, Hosiery

SEARS, ROEBUCK & CO. (DEPT-850 & OL)
3333 Beverly Rd. (p-m)
Hoffman Estates, IL 60179
847-286-2500 / Fax: 847-286-1616
Sales: $41 Billion
Website: www.sears.com
Retail Locations: AZ, AK, AZ, AR, CA, CO, CT, DE, DC, FL, GA, HI, ID, IL, IN, IA, KS, KY, LA, ME, MD, MA, MI, MN, MS, MO, MT, NE, NV, NH, NJ, NM, NY, NC, ND, OH, OK, OR, PA, PR, RI, SC, SD, TN, TX, UT, VT, VA, WA, WV, WI, WY
ALAN C. LACY (Chmn. & C.E.O.)
MARY CONWAY (President)
MARK COSBY (President - Full Line Stores)
GLENN RICHTER (C.F.O.)
PAUL LISKA (V.P. & Real Estate Contact)
WAYNE SPEARS (G.M.M.-Men's)
MIKE HASKELL (D.M.M.-Men's)
JEFF BUDD-Men's Knit Shirts, Sweaters, Flannel Shirts, Dockers
DEREK KALLETA-Men's Woven Shirts
ANDY PIKEL-Men's Jeans, Western Wear, Work Outerwear, Work Pants & Shorts, Levi's Shirts
PATRICK GROSS-Men's Licensed Apparel, Activewear, Outerwear, Swimwear
RAY STEWART-Young Men's Wear
MICHAEL ALLEN-Men's Shorts
SARAH BELINSKI-Men's Shorts, Casual Bottoms

OPEN (D.M.M.)
JANET ARCHIBALD-Men's Headwear, Mufflers, Accessories, Hosiery, Underwear, Nightwear
MIKE COOK-Dress Shirts, Ties, Men's Suits Separates, Tailored Jackets, Raincoats, Overcoats, Blazers
MIKE ALLEN-Pants & All Bottoms
MEG OSTROM (Div. V.P. & G.M.M.-Children's)
LES TOWNSEN (D.M.M.-Infants)
NANCE CZAPLISKIE-Boys' Nightwear, Underwear, Hosiery, Underwear, 8 to 20 Boys' Outerwear, Headwear, Gloves
PAULA OBERTANCE-8 to 20 Boys' Activewear, Coordinates, Fleecewear, Licensed Apparel, Dress Clothes
KAREN MILLER-8 to 20 Boys' Tops, Coordinates, Casual Bottoms, Shorts, Jeans, Denim Shorts

LITTLE COLONY, INC. (KS-2)
18360 Governors Hwy. (m-b)
Homewood, IL 60430
708-799-4100 / Fax: 708-799-6042
GENE KUIPER (Owner)
AGNES KUIPER (President) & Buys 7 to 20 Boys' Wear, Store Displays, Fixtures, Supplies
SUE (Mgr.) (@ 708-246-4770) & Buys 7 to 20 Boys' Wear, Store Displays, Fixtures, Supplies

LUKEMAN'S CLOTHING CO. (MW)
901 W. Morton, Bldg. 1A (b)
Jacksonville, IL 62650
217-243-1612
Sales: $500,000-$1 Million
JACK LUKEMAN (Owner) & Buys Men's Sportswear, Leather Apparel, Furnishings, Headwear, Accessories, Footwear, Young Men's Wear, Store Displays, Fixtures, Supplies

RUDOLPH'S, INC. (CLO)
P.O. Box 280 (p-m)
116 N. State St.
Jerseyville, IL 62052
618-498-3812 / Fax: 618-498-3114
Sales: $1 Million-$10 Million
HARVEY RUDOLPH (Chmn.)
DAVID RUDOLPH (V.P.) & Buys Men's & Boys' Sportswear, Active Wear, Denim, Underwear, Hosiery, Young Men's Wear, Store Displays, Fixtures, Supplies

DON EDWARDS, INC. (CLO)
201 N. Ottawa St. (p-m)
Joliet, IL 60432
815-726-8200 / Fax: 815-726-8066
Sales: $500,000-$1 Million
DON EDWARD KOZLOWSKI (President) & Buys Men's Sportswear, Furnishings, Headwear, Accessories, Footwear, Store Displays, Fixtures, Supplies

FITWELL MEN'S STORE, INC. (MW)
(DAVID YOUNG CORP.)
160 N. Chicago St. (m)
Joliet, IL 60431
815-722-7113 / Fax: 815-722-1009
Sales: $100,001-$500,000
PAUL LEE (President & Mgr.) & Buys Men's Suits, Raincoats, Sportswear, Furnishings, Headwear, Belts, Footwear, Urban Contemporary, Formalwear, Store Displays, Fixtures, Supplies

J.J. SPORT (CLO)
1932 Essington Rd. (m-b)
Joliet, IL 60435
815-436-4300 / Fax: 815-436-3330
JAN SKELDON (Owner) & Buys Men's, Young Men's & Boys' Sportswear, Swimwear, Hosiery, Headwear, Store Displays, Fixtures, Supplies

JIMMY HOLMES - A MAN'S STORE (MW)
185 S. Schuyler Ave. (m-b)
Kankakee, IL 60901
815-933-8200
Sales: $100,001-$500,000
JIMMY HOLMES (Owner) & Buys Men's Sportswear, Furnishings, Headwear, Accessories, Footwear, Young Men's Wear, Urban Contemporary, 8 to 20 Boys' Wear, Men's & Boys' Formal Wear, Store Displays, Fixtures, Supplies

ARGYLE'S (MW)
950 N. Western Ave. (b)
Lake Forest, IL 60045
847-295-0200 / Fax: 847-295-0203
JOE COSTANZA (Owner) & Buys Men's Sportswear, Furnishings, Belts, Jewelry, Young Men's Wear, Store Displays, Fixtures, Supplies

LILLY ALEXANDER BOUTIQUE (KS)
197 E. Westminster Rd. (b)
Lake Forest, IL 60045
847-234-5858 / Fax: 847-234-9345
Sales: $500,000-$1 Million
LILLY ALEXANDER (Owner) & Buys 4 to 18 Boys' Clothing, Sportswear, Furnishings, Headwear, Accessories, Young Men's Wear, Store Displays, Fixtures, Supplies

TADEL & YORE, INC. (MW)
(SMITH'S MEN'S STORE)
770 Western Ave. (m-b)
Lake Forest, IL 60045
847-234-5866 / Fax: 847-234-6483
JOHN TADEL (Owner) & Buys Men's Sportswear, Furnishings, Headwear, Accessories, Store Displays, Fixtures, Supplies

VOLLE'S BRIDAL BOUTIQUE, INC. (SP)
53 S. Old Rand Rd. (des)
Lake Zurich, IL 60047
847-438-7603 / Fax: 847-438-7686
Sales: $1 Million-$10 Million
VOLLE HALTHEN (Co-Owner & C.E.O.) & Buys Men's Footwear, Formalwear, Hosiery
KERRY DEAN (Co-Owner) & Buys Men's Footwear, Formalwear, Hosiery

TROPICS TANNING SALON (CLO)
3234 Ridge Rd.
Lansing, IL 33024
708-895-6883 / Fax: 708-885-7850
MOE PIZANA (Co-Owner) & Buys Footwear, Swimwear, Men's Apparel, Men's Surf & Swimwear, Resortwear
CATHY PIZANA (Co-Owner) & Buys Footwear, Swimwear, Men's Apparel, Men's Surf & Swimwear, Resortwear

LIBERTYVILLE SADDLE SHOP (SG & MO & OL)
P.O. Box M (m-b)
306 Peterson Rd.
Libertyville, IL 60048
847-362-0570 / Fax: 847-680-3200
Website: www.saddleshop.com
J. L. MARTIN (President)
BEVERLY MARTIN (Mdse. Mgr.) & Buys Men's & Boys' Western Wear, Overcoats, Suits, Sweaters, Sport Shirts, Leather Apparel, Headwear, Dress Shirts, Ties, Hosiery, Gloves, Headwear, Footwear, Western Boots, Riding Boots, Store Displays, Fixtures, Supplies

ROBERT VANCE (CLO)
185 Milwaukee Ave. (b)
Lincolnshire, IL 60069
847-478-0988 / Fax: 847-478-0989
JACK SHNIDERMAN (President) & Buys Men's Sportswear, Furnishings, Accessories, Leather Apparel, Headwear

YOUTHFUL SHOES, INC. (FW-18)
(YOUTHFUL STRIDE RITE)
15 E. Madison St. (bud-p-m-b)
Lombard, IL 60148
630-953-0700 / Fax: 630-953-0767
Sales: $10 Million-$50 Million
MARK S. SPYRISON (President & G.M.M.) & Buys Boys' Apparel, Boys' Footwear, Men's Accessories, Hosiery
BILL KEYLIE-Boys' Apparel, Boys' Footwear, Men's Accessories, Hosiery

HI-FIVE SPORTSWEAR (MW)
7836 N. 2nd St. (m)
Machesney Park, IL 61115
815-637-6044 / Fax: 815-637-4912
Sales: $100,001-$500,000
PHIL SLATEY (Owner) (@ 815-961-0440) & Buys Men's Sportswear, Store Displays, Fixtures, Supplies

GUMBART'S (SP)
33 Eastside Sq.
Macomb, IL 61455
309-833-2491
Sales: $500,001-$1 Million
Website: www.gumbarts.com
HUGH ANDERSON (Co-Owner) & Buys Activewear, Jackets, Headwear, T-shirts, Sweatshirts, Sweatpants, Golf Apparel
DOUG ANDERSON (Co-Owner) & Buys Activewear, Jackets, Headwear, T-shirts, Sweatshirts, Sweatpants, Golf Apparel

NELSON'S CLOTHING (MW)

P.O. Box 303 (p-m-b)
104 N. Side Sq.
Macomb, IL 61455
309-833-2493 / Fax: 309-833-3710
Sales: $500,000-$1 Million

JOHN NELSON (President) & Buys Overcoats, Suits, Tailored Jackets, Tailored Slacks, Raincoats, Sweaters, Sport Shirts, Outer Jackets, Leather Apparel, Casual Slacks, Active Apparel, Dress Shirts, Ties, Robes, Underwear, Hosiery, Gloves, Headwear, Belts, Jewelry, Small Leathers, Fragran

WELLS' BIG & TALL (MW)

1010 E. Dickinson Dr. (p-m)
Marion, IL 62959
618-998-8651 / Fax: 618-993-1466
Sales: $100,001-$500,000

SABRINA YEARACK (Owner) & Buys Big & Tall Men's Wear, Sportswear, Furnishings, Headwear, Accessories, Young Men's Wear, Urban Contemporary, Footwear, Store Displays, Fixtures, Supplies

D TO Z SPORTS (SG)

P.O. Box 123 (m)
1611 Broadway Ave.
Mattoon, IL 61938
217-234-3691 / Fax: 217-234-2120
Sales: $500,001-$1 Million

BOB REID (Owner) & Buys Boys' Apparel, Men's Apparel, Accessories, Outerwear, Sportswear

RURAL KING SUPPLY CO., INC. (GM-25 & OL)

4216 Dewitt Ave. (bud-p)
Mattoon, IL 61938
217-235-7102 / Fax: 217-234-7115
Website: www.ruralking.com
Retail Locations: IL, IN, KY, TN

GARY MELVIN (Owner)

DON DAVIS (Controller & Real Estate Contact)

TAMMY HUDSON-Men's Sportswear, Leather Apparel, Furnishings, Headwear, Accessories, Young Men's & Boys' Wear, Footwear, Store Displays, Fixtures, Supplies

BERRY - CUTLER DISTRIBUTORS (CLO)

2036 George St. (bud)
Melrose Park, IL 60160
708-410-2500 / Fax: 708-410-1181
Sales: $100,001-$500,000

IRA BERRY (Co-Owner) & Buys Men's Underwear, Hosiery, Fleece, Big & Tall Men's, Active Apparel, Boys' Apparel

LARRY CUTLER (Co-Owner) & Buys Men's Underwear, Hosiery, Fleece, Big & Tall Men's, Boys' Apparel

SCHWENKER & MOUGIN, INC. (FW-6)

(HOLMES FLORSHEIM)
(HOLMES SHOE SUPERSTORE)
(HOLMES SHOES)
1614 5th Ave. (m-b)
Moline, IL 61265
309-764-5431 / Fax: 309-764-9550
Sales: $1 Million-$10 Million

ARTHUR HOLMES (President) & Buys Men's Footwear, Leather Goods, Men's Accessories, Hosiery

JESSIE JOHNSON (V.P.) & Buys Men's Footwear, Leather Goods, Men's Accessories, Hosiery

DAVE HOLMES (V.P.) & Buys Men's Footwear, Leather Goods, Men's Accessories, Hosiery

B & A SCREEN PRINTING (CLO)

350 W. Burnside Rd. (p-m)
Monticello, IL 61856
217-762-2632 / Fax: 217-762-2012
Sales: $500,000-$1 Million

AL ARNEY (Owner) & Buys Men's Imprintable T-shirts, Fleece, Jackets & Hats, Store Displays, Fixtures, Supplies

SKLUT'S MEN'S SHOP (MW)

307 Liberty St. (m-b)
Morris, IL 60450
815-942-1000 / Fax: 815-942-2157
Sales: $500,001-$1 Million

JIM RIEBE (Owner) & Buys Leather Goods, Men's Big & Tall Apparel, Boys' Apparel, Men's Casualwear, Denim Apparel, Formalwear, Accessories, Hosiery, Outerwear, Sportswear, Suits, Swimwear, Underwear

ARROWSMITH SHOES, INC. (FW-6)

(WILD WILD WEST)
6352 Oakton St. (m-b)
Morton Grove, IL 60053
847-965-2400 / Fax: 847-965-2549
Sales: $1 Million-$10 Million
Website: www.arrowsmithshoes.com

TED ISHAQ (President)

SAL ISHAQ (V.P.) & Buys Boys' Outerwear, Boys' Footwear, Leather Goods, Men's Outerwear, Accessories, Western Casual Boots

FRANK JONES (G.M.M.) & Buys Boys' Outerwear, Boys' Footwear, Leather Goods, Men's Outerwear, Accessories, Western Casual Boots

ABERNATHY'S (CLO-2)

506 N. Seymor (m-b)
Mundelein, IL 60060
847-566-6832 / Fax: 847-949-6385

MARK ABERNATHY (Owner) & Buys Men's Underwear, Hosiery, Headwear, Furnishings & Accessories, Sportswear, Casual Wear, Work Clothes, Boys' Sportswear, Casual Wear, Underwear, Hosiery, Headwear, Furnishing, Accessories, Men's & Boys' Footwear, Store Displays, Fixtures, Supplies

SQUARE DEAL CLOTHING HOUSE (MW)

801 Walnut St. (p-m)
Murphysboro, IL 62966
618-684-3011

PHYLLIS GROB (Co-Owner) & Buys Men's Sportswear, Work Clothes, Headwear, Young Men's Wear, Store Displays, Fixtures, Supplies

CAROLYN GALLEGLY (Mgr.) & Buys Men's Sportswear, Work Clothes, Headwear, Young Men's Wear, Store Displays, Fixtures, Supplies

BRIAN CAMDEN-Men's Sportswear, Work Clothes, Headwear, Young Men's Wear, Store Displays, Fixtures, Supplies

DEAN'S MEN'S AND LADIES' CLOTHING (CLO)

226 S. Main St. (b)
Naperville, IL 60540
630-355-3007 / Fax: 630-355-3089
Sales: $1 Million-$10 Million

GREG DEGEETER (Owner) & Buys Men's Sportswear, Leather Apparel, Headwear, Young Men's Wear, Big & Tall Men's, Store Displays, Fixtures, Supplies

AL DEGEETER-Men's Accessories, Furnishings

THE ALAMO II (SP)

319 North St.
Normal, IL 61761
309-452-7400 / Fax: 309-888-1101
Website: www.thealamoii.com

ORVAL YARGER (Partner)

CHRIS JENSEN-Activewear, Athletics, Licensed Apparel

MISTER SHOPS (MW-2)

4200 N. Harlem Ave., #E (b)
Norridge, IL 60706
708-456-9848
Sales: $1 Million-$10 Million
Website: www.themistershop.com

RANDY KURTZ (Owner) & Buys Men's Sportswear, Leather Apparel, Accessories, Footwear, Big & Tall Men's, Urban Contemporary, Store Displays, Fixtures, Supplies

KEN KURTZ (President) & Buys Men's Sportswear, Leather Apparel, Accessories, Footwear, Big & Tall Men's, Urban Contemporary, Store Displays, Fixtures, Supplies

LEONARD'S MEN'S & BOYS' LTD. (MW)

1929 Cherry Ln., #B (b)
Northbrook, IL 60062
847-272-5670 / Fax: 847-272-3167

LEONARD HOCHMUTH (Co-Owner) & Buys Men's & Boys' Clothing, Sportswear, Furnishings, Accessories, Footwear, Urban Contemporary, Footwear, Store Displays, Fixtures, Supplies

EDWARD C. HOCHMUTH (Co-Owner) & Buys Footwear, Store Displays, Fixtures, Supplies

M. HYMAN & SON, INC. (MW)

425 Huehl Rd., #11A (b)
Northbrook, IL 60062
847-205-5556 / Fax: 847-205-1011
Sales: $1 Million-$10 Million

CLARENCE PERMUT (Exec. V.P.) & Buys Big & Tall Men's Sportswear, Leather Apparel, Accessories

NORDSTROM, INC. - CENTRAL STATES DIV. (DEPT-14)

701 Harger Rd. (m-b)
Oak Brook, IL 60523
630-571-2121 / Fax: 630-218-2295
Website: www.nordstrom.com

ROBERT J. MIDDLEMAS (Exec. V.P. & Gen. Mgr.-Central States Div.)
JOHN HUNT (D.M.M.-Men's Div.) (@ 630-218-2280)
DAVID BIRD (@ 630-218-2276)-Men's Clothing, Suits, Sportscoats
DENNIS GAFFNEY (@ 630-218-2278)-Men's Furnishings & Accessories
VALERIE TIDQUIST-TAYLOR (@ 630-218-2277)-Men's Sportswear
BRIDGETT LIEDKE (@ 630-218-2275)-Young Men's Shop, The Rail & Faconnable
KRIS MAYER-Men's Footwear
EMILY GREENFIELD (D.M.M.- Kidswear) (@ 630-218-2258)
LAURA WEINBERG (@ 630-218-2460)-Infants/Layette
CHRISTINE ALAIMO (@ 630-218-2361)-Infants/Layette
NANCY BRINKMAN (@ 630-218-2359)-Boys' Wear
PAULA LUWANJA (@ 630-218-2259)-Boys' Wear
CHRIS LOOMIS (Midwest Display Designer) & Buys Store Displays
JOANNE HOLDER (Reg. Display Mgr.) & Buys Store Displays
NOTE:-Buying of Store Fixtures & Supplies is Performed in Seattle, WA - See Listing.

BLACK TIE FORMAL WEAR (MW-5)

11016 S. Cicero Ave. (m-b)
Oak Lawn, IL 60453
708-423-3530 / Fax: 708-423-3533
Sales: $1 Million-$10 Million
Website: www.blacktietuxes.com

SAM CARLSON (Owner) & Buys Men's Formal Wear, Boys' Formal Wear, Footwear, Related Furnishings, Accessories, Store Displays, Fixtures, Supplies

MAL'S MEN'S SHOP, INC. (MW)

5201 W. 95th St. (m-b)
Oak Lawn, IL 60453
708-424-3210 / Fax: 708-424-5883
Sales: $100,001-$500,000

JOSEPH M. DINOVO (President) & Buys Men's Sportswear, Furnishings, Leather Apparel, Accessories, Footwear, Store Displays, Fixtures, Supplies

PORTO CHICO STORE, INC. (CLO-2)

6603 North Ave. (m-b)
Oak Park, IL 60302
708-383-4073 / Fax: 708-383-4166
Sales: $500,001-$1 Million

CAMELIA SAUCEDO-Men's Sportswear, Suits
JOSE JORGE (President)

SPAULDING STORE FOR MEN (MW)

110 N. Marion St. (b)
Oak Park, IL 60301
708-386-1802 / Fax: 708-386-1616

DONALD MICHELI (Owner) & Buys Men's Sportswear, Furnishings, Leather Apparel, Headwear, Accessories, Footwear, Store Displays, Fixtures, Supplies
DAN DEMARTE-Men's Sportswear, Furnishings, Leather Apparel, Headwear, Accessories, Footwear, Urban Contemporary, Store Displays, Fixtures, Supplies

FOLLETT HIGHER EDUCATION GROUP (SP-700)

1818 Swift Dr.
Oakbrook, IL 60523
630-279-2330 / Fax: 630-279-2569
Sales: $50 Million-$100 Million
Website: www.fheq.follett.com
Retail Locations: AL, AZ, AR, CA, CO, CT, DE, DC, FL, GA, ID, IL, IN, IA, KS, KY, LA, ME, MD, MA, MI, MN, MS, MO, MT, NE, NV, NH, NJ, NM, NY, NC, OH, OK, OR, PA, RI, SC, TN, TX, UT, VT, VA, WA, WV, WI, WY, Canada

JAMES BAUMANN (President)
CHAD PHILLIPS-Fleece, Jackets, Shorts, Hats, Licensed Apparel
MELISSA MILES-Men's Apparel

DICK FESSEL LTD. (CLO)

112 Whittle Ave. (m-b)
Olney, IL 62450
618-395-4389 / Fax: 618-395-4380
Sales: $500,000-$1 Million

JOHN L. FYE (Owner) & Buys Men's Sportswear, Furnishings, Accessories, Young Men's Wear, Footwear, Urban Contemporary, Store Displays, Fixtures, Supplies

THREADS BIG & TALL, INC. (MW-2)

14846 S. LaGrange Rd. (bud-p-m-b-h)
Orland Park, IL 60462
708-403-1199 / Fax: 708-403-1276

GARY ABRAHAM (Owner) & Buys Big & Tall Men's Wear

AMERICAN MALE & CO. (MW)

27 Main St.
Oswego, IL 60543
630-554-8661 / Fax: 630-554-8702

GREG KALEEL (Owner) & Buys Men's Suits, Sportswear, Furnishings, Accessories, Footwear

PINES STORE FOR MEN AND BOYS (MW)

(PINES MENSWEAR, INC.)
43 S. Prospect Ave. (m-b)
Park Ridge, IL 60068
847-823-1320 / Fax: 847-823-1323
Sales: $500,000-$1 Million
Website: www.pinesofparkridge.com

DAVID IGLOW (Owner) & Buys Men's Sportswear, Furnishings, Accessories, Boys' Wear, Men's & Boys' Tuxedos, Store Displays, Fixtures, Supplies
ROBIN IGLOW (Mgr.) & Buys Men's Sportswear, Furnishings, Accessories, Boys' Wear, Men's & Boys' Tuxedos, Store Displays, Fixtures, Supplies

THE BELL CLOTHING & SHOE HOUSE, INC. (MW & FW)

4314 N. Sheridan Rd. (m-b)
Peoria, IL 61614
309-688-8767 / Fax: 309-688-8790
Sales: $1 Million-$10 Million

BRUCE FRANKEL (Chmn.)
DAVID FRANKEL (President & C.O.O.) & Buys Men's Overcoats, Tailored Jackets, Tailored Slacks, Suits, Leather Apparel, Big & Tall Men's, Men's Sportswear, Accessories, Footwear, Furnishings

BRITCHES 'N' BLOOMERS LTD. (KS)

5901 N. Prospect Rd. (b)
Peoria, IL 61614
309-692-2266 / Fax: 309-692-9531
Sales: $100,001-$500,000

NAN REID (Owner) & Buys 8 to 20 Boys' Wear, Store Displays, Fixtures, Supplies

RUNNING CENTRAL SHOES & GEAR (SP)

700 W. Main St.
Peoria, IL 61606
309-676-6378 / Fax: 309-676-7866
Sales: $100,001-$500,000

JOY KESSLER (Co-Owner) & Buys Activewear, Athletic Footwear
STEVE SHOSTROM (Co-Owner) & Buys Activewear, Athletic Footwear
GREG WHITE (Co-Owner) & Buys Activewear, Athletic Footwear

WESTERN CATTLE COMPANY FACTORY OUTLET (WW)

1320 38th St. (m)
Peru, IL 61354
815-224-2668 / Fax: 815-224-2686
Website: www.westernbootoutlet.com

KAREN STARKS (Owner) & Buys Men's & Boys' Western Wear, Related Accessories, Boots, Headwear, Store Displays, Fixtures, Supplies

CLOTHING CENTER (MW)

115 N. Madison St. (b)
Pittsfield, IL 62363
217-285-6623
Sales: $100,001-$500,000

DON LESTER (Owner) & Buys Men's Sportswear, Furnishings, Headwear, Accessories, Young Men's Wear, Store Displays, Fixtures, Supplies

JIM HERMETE-Men's Sportswear, Furnishings, Headwear, Accessories, Young Men's Wear, Store Displays, Fixtures, Supplies

SQUARE WEST (MW)

(MILL TEAM, INC.)
205 N. Mill St. (m)
Pontiac, IL 61764
815-844-3337 / Fax: 815-844-6316
Sales: $100,001-$500,000

COLLINS MILLER (President) & Buys Men's Sportswear, Furnishings, Belts, Leather Goods, Store Displays, Fixtures, Supplies

JACK VIETTI (Mgr.) & Buys Men's Sportswear, Furnishings, Belts, Leather Goods, Store Displays, Fixtures, Supplies

ECKDAHL'S CLOTHING (MW)

519 S. Main St. (m-b)
Princeton, IL 61356
815-875-1873

FRED ECKDAHL (President) & Buys Men's Sweaters, Overcoats, Suits, Tailored Jackets, Tailored Slacks, Raincoats, Sport Shirts, Outer Jackets, Leather Apparel, Casual Slacks, Active Apparel, Furnishings, Accessories, Big & Tall Men's Wear, Footwear, Store Displays, Fixtures, Supplies

RAGAMUFFINS (KS)

444 S. Main St. (b)
Princeton, IL 61356
815-875-2686 / Fax: 815-872-8006

WILLIAM JOINER (Co-Owner)

CAROL JOINER (Co-Owner)

PATRICIA CARLSON-8 to 16 Boys' Sportswear, Outerwear, Footwear, Headwear, Accessories, Hosiery

V.A. ANDERSON CLOTHING & SHOES (DEPT)

930 N. Main St. (b)
Princeton, IL 61356
815-875-1754

MARY LOU ANDERSON (Owner) & Buys Men's Sportswear, Leather, Furnishings, Headwear, Accessories, Young Men's Wear, Footwear, Store Displays, Fixtures, Supplies

RACK CLOTHING, INC. (MW-2)

(IRV'S)
610 Milwaukee Ave. (m-b)
Prospect Heights, IL 60070
847-459-8060 / Fax: 847-459-8131
Sales: $10 Million-$50 Million
Website: www.irvsmensstores.com

TODD WEINSTEIN (President) & Buys Men's Leather Apparel, Dress Shirts, Ties, Underwear, Gloves, Sportswear

DIDIER CHEVALIER-Sportswear

BEN SCADUTO-Men's Hosiery, Belts, Footwear

JEFF ADDELSON-Boys' Wear & Accessories

BUSY BEE MERCANTILE CO. (CLO)

617 Hampshire St. (p)
Quincy, IL 62301
217-222-3472

BOB NACHENBERG (Owner) & Buys Men's Sportswear, Furnishings, Headwear, Accessories, Big & Tall Men's, Young Men's Wear, Boys' Wear, Store Displays, Fixtures, Supplies

INTERSTATE BUYING GROUP (RB)

(MENSWEAR SOLUTIONS)
529 Hampshire St., #400 (p-m-b)
Quincy, IL 62301
217-224-2480 / Fax: 217-224-2495
Sales: $100 Million-$500 Million

GORDON B. FORBES (President) & Buys Men's & Young Men's Leather Apparel, Casualwear, Accessories, Headwear, Furnishings

MERKEL'S, INC. (SG)

1724 Spring St. (b)
Quincy, IL 62306
217-223-2400 / Fax: 217-222-3375
Sales: $1 Million-$10 Million
Website: www.merkelsinc.com

RUSSELL J. MERKEL (President) & Buys Men's Hunting Apparel

JANE BURTON-Men's Active Apparel, Footwear

BARKAN'S, INC. (CLO)

P.O. Box 4145 (b-h)
1709 2nd Ave.
Rock Island, IL 61201
309-786-5409 / Fax: 309-786-5400
Sales: $500,001-$1 Million

STEVE BARKAN (Owner) & Buys Men's Sportswear, Dress Shirts, Ties, Hosiery, Belts, Small Leather Goods, Footwear, Young Men's Wear, Urban Contemporary, 8 to 20 Boys' Wear, Store Displays, Fixtures, Supplies

PARKSIDE BIG & TALL (MW)

293 Executive Pkwy. (p-m-b)
Rockford, IL 61107
815-397-0110 / Fax: 815-397-8922
Sales: $1 Million-$10 Million

JAY W. SKLAR (President) & Buys Big & Tall Men's Sportswear, Leather Apparel, Furnishings, Headwear, Accessories, Footwear, Urban Contemporary, Store Displays, Fixtures, Supplies

DAVID SKLAR (V.P.) & Buys Big & Tall Men's Sportswear, Leather Apparel, Furnishings, Headwear, Accessories, Footwear, Urban Contemporary, Store Displays, Fixtures, Supplies

THE SYMBOL CLOTHING (MW)

316 W. State St. (m)
Rockford, IL 61101
815-965-2450

DAL LEE (Owner) & Buys Men's Sportswear, Furnishings, Accessories, Footwear, Store Displays, Fixtures, Supplies

RICH'S BRITCHES (CLO)

5017 Oakton St. (p-m)
Skokie, IL 60077
847-676-0085

JUDY WEIL (Co-Owner) & Buys Men's & Young Men's Dress Shirts, Belts, Sportswear, Store Displays, Fixtures, Supplies

FOUR SQUIRES (MW-2)

735 Scheider Dr.
South Elgin, IL 17711
(DLS Outfitters)
847-697-7750 / Fax: 847-697-7850

GARY HINES (President) & Buys Men's Wear, Furnishings, Accessories

HOOKER'S MEN'S STORE (MW)

Broadway Plz., #2 (p)
Sparta, IL 62286
618-443-5013

ROBERT GRAHAM (Owner) & Buys Men's Sportswear, Furnishings, Headwear, Accessories, Store Displays, Fixtures, Supplies

ILLINOIS - Springfield

JIM HERRON LTD. (MW & OL)
700 E. Adams St. (b)
Springfield, IL 62701
217-753-8036 / Fax: 217-753-8074
Sales: $500,000-$1 Million
Website: www.jimherronltd.com

JIM HERRON (Owner) & Buys Men's Sportswear, Accessories, Footwear, Store Displays, Fixtures, Supplies

MARC MASLANSKI (Mgr.) & Buys Men's Sportswear, Accessories, Footwear, Store Displays, Fixtures, Supplies

WEBER CLOTHING, INC. (MW)
P.O. Box 610 (m-b)
114 E. Main St.
Teutopolis, IL 62467
217-857-6351 / Fax: 217-857-1705
Sales: $100,001-$500,000

HENRY WEBER (Owner)

TONY WEBER (V.P.) & Buys Men's Sportswear, Furnishings, Accessories, Footwear, Store Displays, Fixtures, Supplies

THE SPORTS STATION, INC. (SP)
7060 W. 171st St.
Tinley Park, IL 60477
708-429-0500 / Fax: 708-429-0572
Sales: $2 Million-$5 Million

JOHN SLOVEY (President) & Buys Men's, Young Men's & Boys' Activewear, Athletics, Athletic Footwear, Licensed Apparel

DAVE GLENN-Men's, Young Men's & Boys' Activewear, Athletics, Athletic Footwear, Licensed Apparel

JIM'S FORMAL WEAR (RB & OL & SP-8)
1 Tuxedo Park
Trenton, IL 62293
618-224-9211 / Fax: 618-224-7924
Website: www.jimsformalwear.com

GARY DAVIS (President)

DAVID VASAOLLER (V.P.-Corporate Development) & Buys Men's, Young Men's & Boys' Formal Wear, Ties, Footwear

STEVE DAVIS (V.P.-Marketing)

CLIP CRANDALL (National Dir.-Dealer Relations) & Buys Store Displays, Fixtures, Supplies

JIM'S MEN'S & LADIES' SHOP (CLO)
13 W. Broadway (m-b)
Trenton, IL 62293
618-224-9322

MARK LOCKOWITZ (Co-Owner) & Buys Men's Sportswear, Furnishings, Headwear, Accessories, Young Men's Wear, Dress Shoes, Casual Shoes, Work Boots, Store Displays, Fixtures, Supplies

BARBARA LOCKOWITZ (Co-Owner) & Buys Men's Sportswear, Furnishings, Headwear, Accessories, Young Men's Wear, Dress Shoes, Casual Shoes, Work Boots, Store Displays, Fixtures, Supplies

MANNY'S (MW)
133 W. Roosevelt Rd. (p-m)
Villa Park, IL 60181
630-268-0500 / Fax: 630-268-1156

MANNY BEGUM (Owner) & Buys Men's Sportswear, Furnishings, Headwear, Accessories, Footwear, Big & Tall Men's Wear, Store Displays, Fixtures, Supplies

MARTIN'S BIG & TALL, INC. (MW-2)
15 W. North Ave. (m)
Villa Park, IL 60181
630-279-0024 / Fax: 630-279-0073
Website: www.martinsbigtall.com

GARY KRAUSE (President) & Buys Tops, Outerwear

BRUCE KRAUSE (V.P.) & Buys Bottoms, T-shirts

JEFF ALBAUM (Mgr.) & Buys Suits, Sportswear, Dress Outerwear, Accessories, Footwear, Urban Contemporary

AMERICAN OUTFITTERS (SP)
3700 Sunset Ave.
Waukegan, IL 60087
847-623-3959 / Fax: 847-623-0053
Sales: $2 Million-$5 Million
Website: www.americanoutfitters.com

GARY RETTIG (Owner)

BELINDA DYAO-Activewear, Bowling Apparel, Licensed Apparel

STERN'S STORE FOR MEN (MW)
37 S. Genesee St. (m)
Waukegan, IL 60085
847-336-2597 / Fax: 847-336-0254

WILLIAM DEVORE (Co-Owner) & Buys Men's & Young Men's Sportswear, Furnishings, Accessories, Men's Big & Tall Wear, Footwear, Store Displays, Fixtures, Supplies

NANCY DEVORE (Co-Owner) & Buys Men's & Young Men's Sportswear, Furnishings, Accessories, Men's Big & Tall Wear, Footwear, Store Displays, Fixtures, Supplies

GAEDE'S, INC. (CLO)
P.O. Box 714 (b)
124 N. Hale St.
Wheaton, IL 60189
630-653-6770 / Fax: 630-653-7275
Sales: $1 Million-$10 Million

HAROLD GAEDE (Chmn.)

WILLIAM GAEDE (President) & Buys Men's Sportswear, Outer Jackets, Footwear, Overcoats, Tailored Jackets, Tailored Slacks, Suits, Raincoats, Furnishings, Headwear, Accessories

BARRY KATZ-Men's Sportswear, Outer Jackets, Footwear, Overcoats, Tailored Jackets, Tailored Slacks, Suits, Raincoats, Furnishings, Headwear, Accessories

JOAN GAEDE-Store Displays, Fixtures, Supplies

HUNTLEY'S (MW)
(IRWIN LIPS LTD.)
1515 Sheridan Rd. (b)
Wilmette, IL 60091
847-853-0666 / Fax: 847-853-0719

IRWIN LIPS (President) & Buys Men's Sportswear, Accessories

RICHARD FOLTOS (Mgr.) & Buys Store Displays, Fixtures & Supplies

JOSEPH MARTIN (Asst. Mgr.)

MR. EDDIE, INC. (MW)
114 Skokie Blvd. (m-b-des)
Wilmette, IL 60091
847-251-0500 / Fax: 847-251-0514

EDWARD PALAY (Co-Owner) & Buys Men's Sportswear, Dress Shirts, Hosiery, Headwear, Men's Big & Tall Wear, Young Men's Wear, Boys' Wear, Footwear, Store Displays, Fixtures, Supplies

GARY PALAY (Co-Owner) & Buys Men's Sportswear, Dress Shirts, Hosiery, Headwear, Men's Big & Tall Wear, Young Men's Wear, Boys' Wear, Footwear, Store Displays, Fixtures, Supplies

THE RUNNING SHOP (SP)
(HUBBARD WOODS SKI CHALET)
911 Green Bay Rd., #A
Winnetka, IL 60093
847-446-6467 / Fax: 847-446-5430
Sales: $100,001-$500,000

TOM SWARSEN (Owner) & Buys Running Apparel & Footwear, Activewear, Aerobic Footwear, Walking Footwear

MARK SHALE (MW-8 & OL)
(AL BASKIN CO.)
10441 Beaudin Blvd., #100 (b)
Woodridge, IL 60517
(Martin Bayer)
630-427-1100 / Fax: 630-427-1200
Sales: $10 Million-$50 Million
Website: www.markshale.com

SCOTT BASKIN (Co-Owner)
STEVE BASKIN (Co-Owner)
MIKE BASKIN (Co-Owner)
DAN ROBBINS (D.M.M.)
PHIL BORNTRAGER-Footwear, Men's Suits, Formal Wear, Tailored Slacks, Men's Dress Shirts, Hats, Belts, Hosiery, Underwear, Footwear, Casual Slacks, Robes, Sleepwear
PAT ROBBINS-Men's Sweaters, Active Apparel, Sport Shirts
DAN PAULEY-Outerwear
JILL KURTH-Store Displays, Fixtures, Supplies

FRAME'S, INC. (MW)
120 N. Benton St. (m-b)
Woodstock, IL 60098
815-338-2757

BARRY FRAME (Owner) & Buys Men's Sportswear, Furnishings, Headwear, Accessories, Store Displays, Fixtures, Supplies

KOHLSDORF'S QUALITY CORNER, INC. (CLO)
13 Circle St. (m)
Zeigler, IL 62999
618-596-6666
Sales: $500,001-$1 Million

MICHAEL RESTIVO (Owner) & Buys Men's Suits, Tailored Jackets, Tailored Slacks, Raincoats, Sweaters, Sport Shirts, Outer Jackets, Leather Apparel, Casual Slacks, Active Apparel, Dress Shirts, Ties, Robes, Underwear, Hosiery, Belts, Footwear, Store Displays, Fixtures, Supplies

INDIANA - Anderson

THE SHED, INC. (CLO)
509 S. Scatterfield Rd. (p)
Anderson, IN 46012
765-643-2605 / Fax: 765-643-5165
WAYNE MASTERSON (Owner) & Buys Men's Suits, Sportswear, Dress Shirts, Belts, Leather Apparel, Footwear, Young Men's Wear, Urban Contemporary, Store Displays, Fixtures, Supplies

BOB'S SPORT SHOP (SP)
30 N. Public Sq.
Angola, IN 46703
260-665-3614
Sales: $100,001-$500,000
RICHARD PLAXTON (Mgr.) & Buys Men's Athletic Footwear & Apparel

J & J MENSWEAR (MW)
40 Public Sq. (m)
Angola, IN 46703
260-665-5640
JIM BURNAHM (Owner) & Buys Men's Sportswear, Furnishings, Accessories, Store Displays, Fixtures, Supplies

SAM NEWMARK STORE, INC. (MW)
107 S. Perry St. (p-m)
Attica, IN 47918
765-764-4228 / Fax: 765-764-4373
ISADORE FOGEL (Co-Owner) & Buys Men's Overcoats, Suits, Tailored Jackets & Slacks, Raincoats, Big & Tall Men's Wear, Sportswear, Sweaters, Sport Shirts, Outer Jackets, Leather Apparel, Casual Slacks, Active Apparel, Furnishings, Dress Shirts, Ties, Robes, Underwear Hosiery, Gloves, Headwear, Accessories, Belts, Jewelry, Small Leather Goods, Young Men's Wear
MIRRIAM NEWMARK FOGEL (Co-Owner) & Buys Men's Overcoats, Suits, Tailored Jackets & Slacks, Raincoats, Big & Tall Men's Wear, Sportswear, Sweaters, Sport Shirts, Outer Jackets, Leather Apparel, Casual Slacks, Active Apparel, Furnishings, Dress Shirts, Ties, Robes, Underwear Hosiery, Gloves, Headwear, Accessories, Belts, Jewelry, Small Leather Goods, Young Men's Wear

TANDY'S MEN'S WAREHOUSE (MW)
312 2nd St. (bud-p-m-b-h)
Aurora, IN 47001
812-926-2325
DELORES D. TANDY (Owner) & Buys Men's & Young Men's Wear, Leather Apparel, Big & Tall Men's Wear, Store Displays, Fixtures, Supplies

AVON SPORTS APPAREL (CLO-3)
7127 E. Hwy. 36
Avon, IN 46123
317-272-3831 / Fax: 317-272-3926
Website: www.avonsportsapparel.com
PHIL ORLANDO (President) & Buys Men's Active Apparel & Footwear

STAN'S MENSWEAR (CLO)
168 W. Main St. (p-m)
Berne, IN 46711
260-589-2907 / Fax: 928-962-0765
CRAIG SPRUNGER (Owner) & Buys Men's Wear, Sportswear, Furnishings, Accessories, Store Displays, Fixtures and Supplies

CHANEY'S FASHIONS (CLO)
48 E. Main St. (m)
Bloomfield, IN 47424
812-384-8045 / Fax: 812-384-8045
Sales: $500,001-$1 Million
WILLIAM CHANEY (Owner & Gen. Mgr.) & Buys Men's Footwear, Big & Tall Men's Wear, Men's Casualwear, Denim Apparel, Formalwear, Accessories, Hosiery, Outerwear, Sleepwear, Sportswear, Suits, Swimwear, Underwear, Uniforms

THE ARMY NAVY STORE (AN)
(HOOSIER WORKWEAR OUTLET, INC.)
207 S. Rogers St.
Bloomington, IN 47404
812-336-4130 / Fax: 812-332-4685
Sales: $100,001-$500,000
Website: www.hoosierworkwear.net
JOHN RATLIFF (Owner) & Buys Men's Athletic Footwear, Activewear

FORMAL WEAR UNLIMITED (MW)
1000 N. Walnut St. (bud)
Bloomington, IN 47401
812-336-9007 / Fax: 812-961-1011
Sales: $100,001-$500,000
Website: www.formalwear.com
LISA SAMARO (Co-Owner) & Buys Men's, Young Men's & Boys' Tuxedos & Formal Accessories, Store Displays, Fixtures, Supplies
LARRY HOLTZ (Co-Owner) & Buys Men's, Young Men's & Boys' Tuxedos & Formal Accessories, Store Displays, Fixtures, Supplies

INDIANA UNIVERSITY BOOK STORE (SP-2)
Indiana Memorial Union
900 E. 7th St.
Bloomington, IN 47405
812-855-4352 / Fax: 812-855-4984
Sales: $5 Million-$10 Million
Website: www.iubookstore.com
PAUL HAZEL (Dir.)
DEANNA HALL (G.M.M.) & Buys Men's Activewear, Golf Apparel, Athletics

J.R. STALLSMITH & CO. (MW)
120 Fountain Sq. (b)
Bloomington, IN 47404
812-332-1953 / Fax: 812-332-2451
Website: www.jrstallsmith.com
J. R. STALLSMITH (Owner) & Buys Men's Wear, Sportswear, Furnishings, Accessories, Footwear

MASTERPIECE TUX (MW)
221 N. Walnut St. (b-h)
Bloomington, IN 47404
812-333-2200 / Fax: 812-333-2210
JACK LOGAN (Owner & Mgr.) & Buys Men's Formalwear & Accessories, Store Displays, Fixtures, Supplies

SULLIVAN'S, INC. (MW)
115 N. Washington St. (m)
Bloomington, IN 47408
812-339-3444 / Fax: 812-339-8330
EUGENIE SULLIVAN (Co-Owner)
ROBERT SULLIVAN (Co-Owner) & Buys Men's Sportswear, Furnishings, Accessories, Footwear, Store Displays, Fixtures, Supplies

MASTERSON'S, INC. (MW)
127 W. Market St. (m-b)
Bluffton, IN 46714
260-824-0712
DICK MAYER (Owner) & Buys Men's Sportswear, Furnishings, Accessories

R.J.'S FASHIONS (SP)
5 W. National Ave. (m)
Brazil, IN 47834
812-446-1441
RICK JEFFRIES (Owner) & Buys Men's Formal Wear, Related Furnishings, Accessories, Store Displays, Fixtures and Supplies

LAUGHLIN'S, INC. (MW)
1032 E. Main St. (m-b)
Brownsburg, IN 46112
317-852-5101
STEVEN LAUGHLIN (Owner) & Buys Men's Sportswear, Furnishings, Accessories, Store Displays, Fixtures, Supplies

ADAMS SUNSATIONAL (CLO)
124 Hwy. 131 West
Clarksville, IN 47129
812-949-9770 / Fax: 812-944-1549
BECKY ADAMS (Co-Owner) & Buys Men's Apparel, Swimwear, Surfwear, Resortwear, T-shirts, Imprinted Sportswear, Urban Contemporary
ERNIE ADAMS (Co-Owner) & Buys Men's Apparel, Swimwear, Surfwear, Resortwear, T-shirts, Imprinted Sportswear, Urban Contemporary

ROSENBLATT'S (CLO)
335 S. Main St. (m)
Clinton, IN 47842
765-832-6572 / Fax: 765-832-3147
Sales: $100,001-$500,000
MIKE SMITH (Owner) & Buys Men's Overcoats, Suits, Tailored Jackets, Tailored Slacks, Sweaters, Sport Shirts, Outer Jackets, Casual Slacks, Active Apparel, Furnishings, Headwear, Belts, Jewelry, Store Displays, Fixtures, Supplies

DELL BROTHERS (MW-2)
P.O. Box 209
416 Washington St.
Columbus, IN 47202
812-372-4486 / Fax: 812-376-9247
Website: www.dellbrothers.com
TOM CHARLES DELL (Owner) & Buys Men's Sportswear, Furnishings, Urban Contemporary, Store Displays, Fixtures, Supplies
MICHAEL DELL (@ 765-447-6356)-Men's Sportswear, Furnishings, Young Men's Wear, Urban Contemporary, Store Displays, Fixtures, Supplies

MAC'S, INC. (MW)
103 E. Main St. (m-b)
Crawfordsville, IN 47933
765-364-0820 / Fax: 765-364-6900
WILLIAM McCORMICK (Owner) & Buys Store Displays, Fixtures, Supplies, Men's Sportswear, Furnishings, Accessories
MARSHA SMITH (Mgr.) & Buys Men's Sportswear, Furnishings, Accessories

HOT SPOT (SP-2)
3979 Kingsway Dr.
Crownpoint, IN 46307
219-756-8337
Sales: $501,000-$1 Million
TERRY MACHOWICZ (Owner) & Buys Men's Custom T-shirts

LOCKER ROOM (SP)
58 W. Main St.
Danville, IN 46122
317-745-6393 / Fax: 317-745-6590
Sales: $100,001-$500,000
JOAN MILLER (Owner) & Buys Men's Activewear, Athletic Apparel

THREADS APPAREL, INC. (CLO-3)
401 N. Halleck St. (m-b)
DeMotte, IN 46310
219-987-2416 / Fax: 219-987-6469
VERL VAN RIESSEN (Owner) & Buys Men's & Boys' Wear, Urban Contemporary, Store Displays, Fixtures, Supplies

C-MART (MW)
807 W. Chicago Ave. (m)
East Chicago, IN 46312
219-398-7729
IN CHUNG (Co-Owner) & Buys Men's Sportswear, Furnishings, Accessories, Urban Contemporary, Store Displays, Fixtures, Supplies

MAIN SPORTING GOODS (SG)
P.O. Box 3280 (m)
3822 Main St.
East Chicago, IN 46312
219-397-5870 / Fax: 219-397-5991
Sales: $1 Million-$10 Million
MICHAEL RADBEL (President) & Buys Boys' Apparel, Boys' Footwear, Men's Footwear, Denim Apparel, Accessories, Hosiery, Outerwear, Sportswear, Swimwear, Uniforms
DIANE HUDACIN (V.P.) & Buys Boys' Apparel, Boys' Footwear, Men's Footwear, Denim Apparel, Accessories, Hosiery, Outerwear, Sportswear, Swimwear, Uniforms

GENTLEMEN'S DEN (MW)
1808 E. Bristol St., #B
Elkhart, IN 46514
574-264-7086 / Fax: 574-264-7086
KIM CALLESSA (Owner) & Buys Men's Formalwear, Furnishings, Accessories, Store Displays, Fixtures, Supplies

LEATHER BANANA (MW)
154-21 W. Hively Ave.
Elkhart, IN 46517
800-915-9015 / Fax: 574-296-7495
Website: www.leatherbanana.biz
MICHAEL LEIPPERT (Owner) & Buys Men's Wear, Leather Apparel, Outer Jackets, Small Leather Goods, Furnishings, Accessories

SKINNER THE PRINTER (CLO)
226 S. Main St.
Elkhart, IN 46516
574-295-8900
MIKE COOPER (Owner) & Buys Men's Activewear

VALVE CENTER BIG & TALL (MW)
1333 S. Nappanee St.
Elkhart, IN 46516
574-293-0111 / Fax: 574-293-2333
GREG HEETER (Owner) & Buys Big & Tall Men's Wear, Footwear, Accessories, Furnishings

C & C SPORTS (CLO-2)
130 N. Rosenberger Ave. (p)
Evansville, IN 47712
812-429-0220 / Fax: 812-429-0209
ANITA CAMPBELL (Owner) & Buys Men's T-shirts, Shorts, Active Apparel, Store Displays, Fixtures, Supplies

De JONG'S (CLO)
800 N. Green River Rd. (b)
Evansville, IN 47715
812-473-3000 / Fax: 812-475-2190
Sales: $1 Million-$10 Million
HOWARD ABRAMS (President & C.E.O.) (@ 812-423-1161) & Buys Store Displays, Fixtures, Supplies
STEVE SANDERS (Mdsg. Mgr.-Men's) & Buys Men's Overcoats, Suits, Tailored Jackets, Tailored Slacks, Raincoats, Sportswear, Sweaters, Sport Shirts, Outer Jackets, Casual Slacks, Furnishings, Headwear, Accessories, Leather Apparel, Men's Footwear

FORMALWEAR (MW)
1910 W. Franklin St. (m)
Evansville, IN 47712
812-424-3809
MARION HUTCHINSON (Owner) & Buys Men's Formal Wear, Furnishings, Accessories, Store Displays, Fixtures, Supplies

PAUL'S MENSWEAR, INC. (MW)
2225 W. Franklin St. (p-m)
Evansville, IN 47712
812-423-2624 / Fax: 812-423-4821
Sales: $1 Million-$10 Million
STEVE EICKHOFF (President) & Buys Men's Overcoats, Suits, Tailored Jackets, Tailored Slacks, Sportswear, Sweaters, Sport Shirts, Outer Jackets, Leather Apparel, Casual Slacks, Active Apparel, Furnishings, Headwear, Accessories, Big & Tall Men's Wear, Store Displays, Fixtures, Supplies

ROGERS JEWELERS (JWLY-13)
(ELLENSTEIN STORES, INC.)
(STARS JEWELER)
3800 N. 1st Ave.
Evansville, IN 47710
812-464-3900 / Fax: 812-465-6640
Sales: $10 Million-$50 Million
LARRY McCOY (President)
MICHAEL S. ELLENSTEIN, JR. (C.E.O.)
TANI WHEAT (D.M.M.) & Buys Jewelry, Watches
DARLA MINNIN-Jewelry, Watches

INDIANA - Evansville

SHOE CARNIVAL, INC. (FW-180)
(CLOSET FLOOR)
8233 Baumgart Rd. (bud-p-m-b)
Evansville, IN 47725
812-867-6471 / Fax: 812-867-3625
Sales: $100 Million-$500 Million
Website: www.shoecarnival.com
Retail Locations: AL, AK, FL, GA, IL, IN, IA, KS, KY, LA, MD, MI, MS, MO, NC, OH, OK, SC, TN, TX, VA, WV, WI
MARK L. LEMOND (President)
PAUL KINNEY (Real Estate Contact) (@ 812-867-4105)
CLIFF SIFFORD (Senior V.P. & G.M.M.)
ANDY CHANDLER (D.M.M.-Footwear & Athletics) & Buys Licensed Apparel
WILLIAM D. LACKEY (D.M.M.-Footwear) & Buys Hosiery
RON DERRICK (D.M.M.-Footwear) & Buys Men's Footwear, Leather Goods, Men's Accessories
ANGIE PEMBERTON-Boys' Footwear
TUCKER ROBINSON-Men's Footwear

SIEGEL'S BIG & TALL (MW)
503 N. Green River Rd. (p-m)
Evansville, IN 47715
812-473-2900 / Fax: 812-858-2846
Sales: $1 Million-$10 Million
RON COLLINS (Co-Owner) & Buys Big & Tall Men's Wear, Sportswear, Furnishings, Accessories, Leather Apparel, Store Displays, Fixtures, Supplies
BILLIE COLLINS (Co-Owner) & Buys Big & Tall Men's Wear, Sportswear, Furnishings, Accessories, Leather Apparel, Store Displays, Fixtures, Supplies

STROUSE & BROTHERS, INC. (CLO)
4601 Lincoln Ave. (m-b)
Evansville, IN 47714
812-471-7153 / Fax: 812-428-7673
Sales: $1 Million-$10 Million
SCOTT STROUSE (President) & Buys Men's Wear, Leather Apparel, Store Displays, Fixtures, Supplies

DADDY-O'S THREADS & NOSTALGIA (CLO)
120 S. Main St.
Fairmount, IN 46928
765-948-3357
Sales: $500,001-$1 Million
Website: www.daddyos.com
CHRISTY BERRY (Co-Owner) & Buys Men's Footwear, Apparel, Casualwear
BOB BERRY (Co-Owner) & Buys Men's Footwear, Apparel, Casualwear

BRATEMAN'S, INC. (CLO)
5326 Coldwater Rd. (b)
Fort Wayne, IN 46825
219-484-8665 / Fax: 219-484-8713
Sales: $500,001-$1 Million
Website: www.bratemans.com
ADOLPH BRATEMAN (President & Dir.-Fin.)
ADRIENNE BRATEMAN (V.P.)
MIKE BRATEMAN (Store Mgr.)
PAUL BRATEMAN (Treas.) & Buys Men's Footwear, Leather Goods, Apparel, Denim Apparel, Sportswear, Uniforms

ROGER'S FORMAL WEAR (MW)
3518 Broadway (p)
Fort Wayne, IN 46807
260-744-5100
Sales: $100,001-$500,000
RICHARD PAPE (Owner) & Buys Men's & Boys' Formal Wear, Furnishings, Store Displays, Fixtures, Supplies

PANACHE (MW)
French Lick Springs Hotel (m)
8670 W. State Rd. 56
French Lick, IN 47432
812-936-9300 / Fax: 812-936-2100
Website: www.frenchlick.com
AMANDA ELLIS (Mgr.) & Buys Men's Sportswear, Furnishings, Accessories, Store Displays, Fixtures, Supplies

BRADY'S, INC. (CLO)
P.O. Box 6098 (p)
5306 W. 25th Ave.
Gary, IN 46406
219-844-1130 / Fax: 219-845-6667
RON COHEN (Owner) & Buys Store Displays, Fixtures, Supplies, Men's Work Clothes, Denim, Athletic Apparel, Accessories, Headwear, Boys' Wear
DON GALE (Retail Coord.) & Buys Store Displays, Fixtures, Supplies, Men's Work Clothes, Denim, Athletic Apparel, Accessories, Headwear, Boys' Wear

ESQUIRE MEN'S STORE (MW)
1536 Broadway (m-b)
Gary, IN 46407
219-882-0904 / Fax: 218-882-0772
Sales: $100,001-$500,000
ROZELLE HAMMOND (Owner) & Buys Men's Sweaters, Sport Shirts, Outer Jackets, Casual Slacks, Furnishings, Headwear, Accessories, Leather Apparel, Big & Tall Men's Wear, Store Displays, Fixtures, Supplies

MAX CLOTHING (MW)
4689 Broadway (m)
Gary, IN 46409
219-985-1145 / Fax: 219-985-1145
MR. CHONG (Owner) & Buys Men's Sportswear, Furnishings, Accessories, Urban Contemporary, Store Displays, Fixtures, Supplies

NEW MIMI FASHIONS (CLO-2)
3503 Grant St., #3506 (m-b)
Gary, IN 46408
219-981-1744 / Fax: 219-884-7090
Sales: $1 Million-$10 Million
DOOIL BAUM (Owner) & Buys Boys' Apparel, Boys' Footwear, Men's Footwear, Leather Goods, Apparel, Casualwear, Sportswear

B & K GRAPHICS & SPORTING GOODS (SG)
P.O. Box 734 (m-b)
115 N. Main St.
Geneva, IN 46740
219-368-9500 / Fax: 219-368-9500
Sales: $100,001-$500,000
THOMAS DULL (President) & Buys Boys' Apparel, Men's Big & Tall Apparel, Denim Apparel, Outerwear, Sportswear, Swimwear
THOMAS A. DULL (Sls. Mgr.)

SNYDER'S MEN'S SHOP, INC. (MW)
126 S. Main St. (m-b-des)
Goshen, IN 46526
219-533-5630 / Fax: 219-533-3447
Sales: $500,001-$1 Million
VIRGIL L. SNYDER (President) & Buys Leather Goods, Big & Tall Men's Wear, Boys' Wear, Men's Casualwear, Denim Apparel, Formalwear, Accessories, Hosiery, Outerwear, Sportswear, Suits, Swimwear, Underwear
JEFF SNYDER (V.P.) & Buys Leather Goods, Big & Tall Men's Wear, Boys' Wear, Men's Casualwear, Denim Apparel, Formalwear, Accessories, Hosiery, Outerwear, Sportswear, Suits, Swimwear, Underwear

BRACKNEY'S WESTERN STORE (WW)
(BRACKNEY'S MENS STORE)
1260 N. Jackson St. (m-b)
Greencastle, IN 46135
765-653-9464 / Fax: 765-653-8554
Sales: $1 Million-$10 Million
Website: www.brackneyswesternstore.com
KEITH BRACKNEY (Co-Owner) & Buys Men's Casual Wear, Suits, Big & Tall Men's Wear, Footwear, Young Men's Wear, Boys' Denim, Belts, T-shirts, Men's & Boys' Western Wear, Store Displays, Fixtures, Supplies
DARRELL BRACKNEY (Co-Owner) & Buys Men's Casual Wear, Suits, Big & Tall Men's Wear, Footwear, Young Men's Wear, Boys' Denim, Belts, T-shirts, Men's & Boys' Western Wear, Store Displays, Fixtures, Supplies

MORRIS, INC. (SG)
20 E. Main St. (m)
Greenfield, IN 46140
317-462-9613 / Fax: 317-462-9698
PHILIP MORRIS (Owner) & Buys Store Displays, Fixtures, Supplies
KELLY GUZMAN-Men's T-shirts, Sweatsuits, Fleece, Headwear, Jackets, Shorts, Men's Footwear

MINEAR'S, INC. (DG-2)
107 N. Broadway (m-b)
Greensburg, IN 47240
812-663-4601
Sales: $500,000-$1 Million
GLENN D. MOORE (President)
JEFF W. MOORE (G.M.M.) & Buys Men's Overcoats, Suits, Tailored Jackets, Tailored Slacks, Raincoats, Big & Tall Men's Wear, Sportswear, Sweaters, Sport Shirts, Outer Jackets, Casual Slacks, Furnishings, Robes, Hats, Accessories, Young Men's & Boys' Wear, Leather Apparel, Men's Dress Sh

SPORTS FANATICS, INC. (SP)
1251 US Hwy. 31
Greenwood, IN 46142
317-887-6776 / Fax: 317-887-1391
CORINNE SNYDER (Mgr.) & Buys Men's Licensed Apparel, Activewear

SKLAREWITZ UNIFORM CO. (SP)
7242 Kennedy Ave. (m-b)
Hammond, IN 46323
219-844-2870 / Fax: 219-844-3511
Sales: $500,001-$1 Million
JIM CROWELL (Owner) & Buys Men's Footwear, Apparel, Uniforms

ZANDSTRA'S STORE FOR MEN, INC. (MW)
2629 Highway Ave. (b)
Highland, IN 46322
219-923-3545 / Fax: 219-923-1807
Sales: $1 Million-$10 Million
DALE TANIS (Owner) & Buys Men's Suits, Sportswear, Furnishings, Accessories, Leather Apparel, Footwear, Store Displays, Fixtures, Supplies

GREENER'S STORE FOR MEN (MW)
201 Main St. (m-b)
Hobart, IN 46342
219-942-5544 / Fax: 219-942-2554
Sales: $100,001-$500,000
ELINOR GREENER (Owner)
LISA FIELD (G.M.M.) & Buys Men's Overcoats, Suits, Tailored Jackets, Tailored Slacks, Raincoats, Big & Tall Men's Wear, Sportswear, Sweaters, Sport Shirts, Outer Jackets, Leather Apparel, Casual Slacks, Footwear, Young Men's Wear, Store Displays, Fixtures, Supplies

AMERICA'S SHIRT (MW-1 & OL)
427 S. Illinois St (p-m-b)
Indianapolis, IN 46225
317-321-9999 / Fax: 317-321-9988
Website: www.hugestore.com
CARL LEVINSON (President & Owner) & Buys Men's Suits, Tailored Jackets, Tailored Slacks, Big & Tall Men's Wear, Leather Apparel, Sport Shirts, Casual Slacks, Furnishings, Dress Shirts, Ties, Underwear, Jeans

ARNOLD'S MEN'S STORE, INC. (OL)
1 Virginia Ave., #50 (m-b)
Indianapolis, IN 46204
317-875-8887 / Fax: 317-875-0826
Sales: $1 Million-$10 Million
Website: www.arnoldsmensstore.com
ARNOLD SIEGEL (President) & Buys Men's Sportswear, Furnishings, Store Displays, Fixtures, Supplies

ATHLETIC ANNEX (SG)
1411 W. 86th St. (m)
Indianapolis, IN 46260
317-872-0000 / Fax: 317-871-0025
Sales: $1 Million-$10 Million
Website: www.athleticannex.com
BOB WEDDEL (President)
TOM BURLESON (Gen. Mgr.) & Buys Men's Footwear, Apparel, Sportswear
ROBBIN SCHNEIDER (Mgr.-Acct. & Info Sys.)
MATT EBERSOLE (Store Mgr.) & Buys Men's Footwear, Apparel, Sportswear
MIKE ORBAN (Store Mgr.) & Buys Men's Footwear, Apparel, Sportswear

BEACH BABY SURF & SWIM (SP-2)
8687 River Crossing Blvd.
Indianapolis, IN 46240
317-574-4948 / Fax: 317-837-1780
Website: www.beach-baby.com
DEBBIE ROBERTS (Co-Owner) & Buys Men's Swimwear, Men's Surfwear, Resortwear, T-shirts, Imprinted Sportswear
RANDY ROBERTS (Co-Owner) & Buys Men's Swimwear, Men's Surfwear, Resortwear, T-shirts, Imprinted Sportswear
KELLY DeWITT-Men's Swimwear, Men's Surfwear, Resortwear, T-shirts, Imprinted Sportswear
LISA ROBERTS-Men's Swimwear, Men's Surfwear, Resortwear, T-shirts, Imprinted Sportswear

CASH BARGAIN CENTER, INC. (GM)
P.O. Box 18448 (p-m-b)
3712 E. 25th St.
Indianapolis, IN 46218
317-546-4606 / Fax: 317-542-7578
ELLIOT SCHANKERMAN (Gen. Mgr.) & Buys Men's & Boys' Wear, Big & Tall Men's Wear, Footwear, Store Displays, Fixtures, Supplies

CLASSIC FASHIONS (CLO-3)
3825 N. Illinois St. (b)
Indianapolis, IN 46208
317-924-9451 / Fax: 317-283-6038
PATRICK SUBER (Owner) & Buys Men's Sportswear, Furnishings, Accessories, Footwear, Young Men's Wear, Urban Contemporary, Denim, Store Displays, Fixtures, Supplies

THE FINISH LINE (SP-445)
3308 N. Mitthoeffer Rd.
Indianapolis, IN 46235
317-899-1022 / Fax: 317-899-0237
Sales: $50 Million-$100 Million
Website: www.finishline.com
Retail Locations: MA, NH, CT, NJ, NY, PA, DE, VA, MD, WV, NC, SC, GA, FL, AL, TN, MS, KY, ID, AZ, NM, NV, OH, IN, MI, IA, WI, MN, SD, ND, IL, MO, KS, NE, LA, AR, OK, TX, CO, CA, OR, WA
ALAN COHEN (President)
DAVID KLAPPER (Exec. V.P.)
GEORGE SANDERS (@ 317-899-3370)
JOE WOOD (Sr. V.P.-Mdsg.)
TOM SICARI (G.M.M.)
AMY PRODOUZ-Branded Apparel
DOUG CONROY-Accessories
TIM GEIS (D.M.M.)
JASON SHORT-Men's Athletic Footwear
JOHN NICHWITZ-Athletic Footwear, Hiking Boots
JEFF MORRELL-Boys' Athletic Footwear, Hiking Boots
ROBERT MARQUARDT-All Cleated Footwear, Shoes

HAT WORLD, INC. (SP-450)
(LIDS)
8142 Woodland Dr. (m-b)
Indianapolis, IN 46278
317-334-9428 / Fax: 317-337-1428
Sales: $10 Million-$50 Million
Website: www.hatworld.com
BOB DENNIS (Chmn. & C.E.O.)
JIM HARRIS (President & C.O.O.)
KEN KOCHER (C.F.O.)
TODD CAMPBELL (Sr. V.P.-Opers.)
SCOTT MOLANDER (Exec. V.P.-Real Estate)
LARRY HAVLIK (V.P.-Info. Sys.)
JON GLESING (Dir.-Mktg.)
TONY CARLISSE (Dir.-H.R.)
RICH VOELLNER (Mgr.-Store Fixtures)
CHARLES BRODT-Boys' Apparel, Men's Apparel, Men's Accessories

INDIANA - Indianapolis

J. SHEPARD, INC. (CLO)
8702 Keystone Crossing (b)
Indianapolis, IN 46240
317-575-9665
Sales: $1 Million-$10 Million
JOHN SHEPARD (President) & Buys Men's Casualwear, Denim Apparel, Accessories, Outerwear, Sleepwear, Sportswear, Suits
LINDA SHEPARD (V.P.)
KIM SHEPARD (Store Mgr.)

L.S. AYRES & CO. (DEPT-15)
(FAMOUS BARR)
(MAY DEPT. STORE CO.)
6101 N. Keystone Ave. (m-b)
Indianapolis, IN 46220
317-255-6611 / Fax: 317-255-2932
Sales: $100 Million-$500 Million
Website: www.maycompany.com
JENNIFER KING (Mgr.) & Buys Men's & Boys' Wear
NOTE:-All Buying Performed By FAMOUS BARR, St. Louis, Mo-See Listing

MAN ALIVE (CLO-35)
(THE HANG UP SHOPPES, INC.)
3919 Lafayette Rd. (m)
Indianapolis, IN 46254
(Henry Doneger)
317-291-3900 / Fax: 317-337-2127
Website: www.manalive.com
Retail Locations: MO, IL, IN, MI, OH, KY, MD, GA
JEFFREY BUBLICK (President & Real Estate Contact) & Buys Store Displays, Fixtures, Supplies
BENJAMIN BUBLICK (D.M.M.) & Buys Young Men's Wear, Urban Contemporary, Active Apparel, Outerwear, Clubwear, Streetwear, Surfwear, Skatewear, Related Accessories, Men's & Young Men's Footwear

ONE STEP, INC. (MW-2)
2802 Lafayette Rd. (p)
Indianapolis, IN 46222
317-923-1605 / Fax: 317-923-1605
IN SONG IN (Owner) & Buys Men's Sportswear, Furnishings, Accessories, Young Men's Wear, Store Displays, Fixtures, Supplies

RALEIGH LTD., INC. (MW)
8702 Keystone Crossing (b)
Indianapolis, IN 46240
317-844-1148 / Fax: 317-571-1144
Sales: $1 Million-$10 Million
MARK KOPLOW (Owner) & Buys Men's Suits, Sportswear, Footwear, Store Displays, Fixtures, Supplies

RAPP'S MENSWEAR (MW)
3816 N. Illinois St. (m)
Indianapolis, IN 46208
317-926-5500
HAROLD RAPP (Owner) & Buys Men's Tailored Jackets, Tailored Slacks, Sportswear, Furnishings, Accessories, Store Displays, Fixtures, Supplies

STYLE STORE FOR BIG & TALL (MW)
2432 E. 62nd St. (m-b)
Indianapolis, IN 46220
317-253-7656 / Fax: 317-253-9212
Sales: $1 Million-$10 Million
JOE ZUCKERBERG (President) & Buys Big & Tall Men's Overcoats, Suits, Tailored Jackets, Tailored Slacks, Raincoats, Leather Apparel, Outer Jackets, Casual Slacks, Shorts, Active Sportswear, Dress Shirts, Robes, Hosiery, Underwear, Gloves, Belts, Fragrances, Store Displays, Fixtures
CHERYL GOLDBERG (Office Mgr.) & Buys Store Supplies

SURPLUS BARGAIN CENTER (MW)
2611 W. Michigan St. (bud)
Indianapolis, IN 46222
317-637-8513
DOUG COMBS (Owner) & Buys Men's Sportswear, Dress Shirts, Hosiery, Gloves, Headwear, Belts, Young Men's Wear, Boys' Wear, Store Displays, Fixtures and Supplies

TARKINGTON TWEED, INC. (CLO)
5631 N. Illinois St. (b)
Indianapolis, IN 46208
317-257-6917 / Fax: 317-251-2325
Sales: $500,001-$1 Million
KELLI NORWALK (President)
ALYSSA SWEENEY (Store Mgr.) & Buys Leather Goods, Men's Casualwear, Denim Apparel, Accessories, Hosiery, Outerwear, Sportswear

TUXES & TAILS (MW)
4925 W. 38th St.
Indianapolis, IN 46254
317-297-3556
DAVID HAGER (Owner) & Buys Men's Formal Wear, Furnishings, Accessories, Store Displays, Fixtures and Supplies

SIEBERT'S, INC. (MW)
P.O. Box 417 (m-b)
6th & Main St.
Jasper, IN 47546
812-482-5514 / Fax: 812-482-9324
Sales: $1 Million-$10 Million
Website: www.siebertsclothing.com
JIM SIEBERT (President)
JANE SIEBERT (V.P. & G.M.M.)
BRIAN WRIGHT (Dept. Mgr.) & Buys Men's Overcoats, Suits, Tailored Jackets, Tailored Slacks, Raincoats, Outer Jackets, Leather Apparel, Big & Tall Men's Wear, Sportswear, Sweaters, Sport Shirts, Casual Slacks, Active Apparel, Furnishings, Dress Shirts, Ties, Robes, Underwear, Gloves, Headwear, Accessories, Belts, Jewelry, Small Leather Goods, Fragrances

SHOE SENSATIONS (FW-60)
(Div. of ACTON ENTERPRISES)
(KICKS)
253 America Pl. (m)
Greentree Mall
Jeffersonville, IN 47130
812-283-0755 / Fax: 812-288-7747
Website: www.shoesensation.com
Retail Locations: SC, TN, KY, WV, PA, IN, OH, MI, IA, IL
MIKE BERNARD (Owner)
MARK ROCHE-Men's Dress Shoes, Casual Shoes, Athletic Footwear, Slippers
DAVE SCHONGANT (V.P.-Opers.) & Buys Store Displays, Fixtures, Supplies

FINE LINE FASHIONS (MW)
419 E. Monroe St.
Kokomo, IN 46901
765-236-1078 / Fax: 765-236-1683
Website: www.finelinefashion.qpg.com
VERONICA CANNON (Owner) & Buys Men's Wear, Clothing, Sportswear, Furnishings, Accessories, Urban Contemporary

FLEET SUPPLY, INC. (DEPT-7)
(BIG R STORES, INC.)
1900 E. North St. (p-b)
Kokomo, IN 46901
765-452-4038 / Fax: 765-456-1257
Sales: $10 Million-$50 Million
Website: www.bigr.com
LES JOHANNING (President)
JIM MILNER (G.M.M. & Treas.)
WAYNE MORRIS-Men's Fleecewear, Outer Jackets, Hosiery, Big & Tall Men's Wear, Footwear, Denim, Boys' Wear
BRUCE KUHN (District Mgr.) & Buys Store Displays, Fixtures, Supplies

BEACHWOOD PRO SHOP (GOLF)
2222 Woodlawn Dr.
La Porte, IN 46350
219-362-2651
Sales: $501,000-$1 Million
NANCY BISHOP (Golf Pro) & Buys Men's Golf Apparel, Footwear
WILLIAM MURRAY (Mgr.) & Buys Men's Golf Apparel, Footwear

DROEGE'S, INC. (MW)
822 Lincolnway (m-b)
La Porte, IN 46350
219-362-3615 / Fax: 219-325-8262
Sales: $100,001-$500,000
Website: www.droeges.com
PHIL DROEGE (President)
KELLY BRAINERD (G.M.M.) & Buys Men's Leather Apparel, Raincoats, Headwear, Men's Sweaters, Sportswear, Sport Shirts, Outer Jackets, Casual Slacks, Active Apparel, Men's Overcoats, Suits, Tailored Jackets, Tailored Slacks, Footwear, Furnishings, Accessories

E. J.'S SPORTS & SPORTSWEAR (SP)
602 I St.
La Porte, IN 46350
219-362-2565 / Fax: 219-362-2565
Sales: $100,001-$500,000
CARLENE OTT (Owner) & Buys Men's Athletic Apparel, Activewear, Imprintable Apparel

LA PORTE SPORTING GOODS (SG)
816 Lincolnway (p-m)
La Porte, IN 46350
219-362-3447 / Fax: 219-324-7773
JOHN YATES (Owner)
KATHY KRENTZ-Men's Active Apparel, T-shirts, Sweatsuits, Headwear, Athletic Hosiery

BRIDAL BOUTIQUE & MR. PENGUIN TUXEDO (CLO)
200 Farabee Dr. North, #A (p-m-b)
Lafayette, IN 47905
765-449-1474 / Fax: 765-449-1475
Sales: $500,001-$1 Million
Website: www.misterpenguin.com
FRED SCHMUCK (Owner) & Buys Men's & Boys' Formalwear, Store Displays, Fixtures, Supplies

GOLDDEN CORP. (SP-3)
115 S. 4th St.
Lafayette, IN 47901
765-423-4366 / Fax: 765-423-2936
GARY EDMONDSON (Owner) & Buys Men's Activewear, Licensed Apparel

OXFORD SHOP (MW)
911 N. 18th St. (m-b)
Lafayette, IN 47904
765-447-9169
RICHARD MICHAEL (Owner) & Buys Men's Wear, Sportswear, Furnishings, Accessories, Store Displays, Fixtures, Supplies

VIERK'S FINE JEWELRY & EXCHANGE (AN)
1650 Main St.
Lafayette, IN 47904
765-447-1367 / Fax: 765-447-0200
Sales: $1 Million-$10 Million
DAN A. VIERK (Owner)
ELIZABETH FUNDERBURG (G.M.M.) & Buys Men's Outdoor Apparel, Camouflage, Military Footwear

J. ADKINS CORP. (MW)
427 E. Broadway (p)
Logansport, IN 46947
574-722-6200
JAMES ADKINS (President & G.M.M.) & Buys Men's Overcoats, Suits, Tailored Slacks, Tailored Jackets, Raincoats, Sportswear, Outer Jackets, Casual Slacks, Robes, Underwear, Hosiery, Gloves, Accessories, Big & Tall Men's Wear, Sweaters, Apparel, Footwear, Dress Shirts, Ties, Store Displays, Fixtures, Supplies

SHIRT SHACK (CLO)
524 E. Broadway (p)
Logansport, IN 46947
574-722-4349
LARRY JONES (Owner) & Buys Men's T-shirts, Shorts, Store Displays, Fixtures, Supplies

JOHN KNOEBEL & SONS, INC. (MW)
228 E. Main St. (p)
Madison, IN 47250
812-265-3728
JOE KNOEBEL (Owner) & Buys Men's Sportswear, Furnishings, Accessories, Store Displays, Fixtures, Supplies

ATHLETIC X-PRESS (SP-5)
(FOOT LOCKER)
1901 Southlake Mall
Merrillville, IN 46410
219-756-4303
Sales: $1 Million-$10 Million
Website: www.footlocker.com
JIMMY ADAMS (Mgr.) & Buys Men's Athletic Apparel, Activewear, Athletic Footwear, Licensed Apparel, Hiking Footwear

JOHN CICCO'S MENSWEAR (MW)
8250 Mississippi St. (b)
Merrillville, IN 46410
219-769-1744 / Fax: 219-769-1844
Sales: $100,001-$500,000
MARTA CICCO (President)
TINA POPP (Treasurer) & Buys Men's Overcoats, Suits, Tailored Slacks, Raincoats, Sweaters, Sport Shirts, Outer Jackets, Leather Apparel, Casual Slacks, Active Apparel, Dress Shirts, Robes, Ties, Underwear, Hosiery, Gloves, Headwear, Belts, Jewelry, Fragrances, Footwear, Big & Tall Men's Wear, Store Displays, Fixtures, Supplies

TRANS APPAREL GROUP (CLO-6)
(JAYMAR FACTORY OUTLET)
P.O. Box 700 (m-b-des)
5000 Ohio St.
Michigan City, IN 46360
219-879-7341 / Fax: 219-879-0388
Sales: $1 Million-$10 Million
ANDY NEAL (President) & Buys Leather Goods, Big & Tall Men's Wear, Men's Denim Apparel, Accessories, Outerwear, Sportswear, Suits

GOHN BROTHERS (MO)
P.O. Box 1110
105 Main St.
Middlebury, IN 46540
574-825-2400
JOHN SWARTZENTRUBER (President) & Buys Men's & Boys' Underwear, Hosiery, Store Displays, Fixtures, Supplies

AL-BAR RANCH (CLO)
55345 Fir Rd. (b)
Mishawaka, IN 46545
219-259-1188 / Fax: 219-258-1192
Sales: $500,000-$1 Million
JOHN EUBANK (President) & Buys Men's Western Wear, Raincoats, Sport Shirts, Outer Jackets, Active Apparel, Dress Shirts, Ties, Gloves, Headwear, Belts, Jewelry, Small Leather Goods, Footwear, 6 to 18 Boys' Western Wear, Big & Tall Men's Wear, Store Displays, Fixtures, Supplies

BLUE & GOLD SPORTS SHOP (GS & MO)
1605 N. Home St.
Mishawaka, IN 46565
574-255-9800 / Fax: 574-255-9700
Sales: $501,000-$1 Million
Website: www.blueandgold.com
LISA WEISSER (Dir.-Opers.) & Buys Licensed Apparel, Activewear, Store Displays, Fixtures, Supplies

WARD'S APPAREL (CLO-2)

1 E. Moore St.
Mooresville, IN 46158
317-831-3773 / Fax: 317-834-1749

WILLIAM WARD (Owner)

RAY MCGARY (Mgr.) & Buys Men's Wear, Sportswear, Furnishings, Accessories, Young Men's Wear, Urban Contemporary, Boys' Wear, Store Displays, Fixtures and Supplies

CARL'S DEPARTMENT STORE (MW)

3120 S. Madison St. (b)
Muncie, IN 47302
765-282-8112

ROBERT ETHERIDGE (Owner) & Buys Men's Denim, Dress Pants, Work Clothes, Robes, Underwear, Hosiery, Gloves, Belts, Wallets, Big & Tall Men's Wear, Store Displays, Fixtures, Supplies

FORD'S MENSWEAR (MW)

3000 N. Wheeling Ave. (m-b)
Muncie, IN 47303
765-282-5322 / Fax: 765-286-1598

MAX FORD (Owner) & Buys Men's Overcoats, Suits, Tailored Jackets, Tailored Slacks, Raincoats, Sportswear, Formalwear, Furnishings, Accessories, Footwear, Big & Tall Men's Wear, Store Displays, Fixtures, Supplies

K.B.C. BARGAIN CENTER, INC. (CLO-2)

(FACTORY CONNECTION)
(OFF-PRICE WORLD)
4201 N. State Rd. 3 (bud-p-m)
Muncie, IN 47303
765-284-1000 / Fax: 765-741-8857
Sales: $1 Million-$10 Million

RICHARD IRWIN (President) & Buys Boys' Apparel, Leather Goods, Big & Tall Men's Wear, Men's Casualwear, Denim Apparel, Formalwear, Accessories, Hosiery, Outerwear, Sleepwear, Sportswear, Suits, Swimwear, Underwear

LARRY CROSS-Boys' Apparel, Leather Goods, Big & Tall Men's Wear, Men's Casualwear, Denim Apparel, Formalwear, Accessories, Hosiery, Outerwear, Sleepwear, Sportswear, Suits, Swimwear, Underwear

NEW YORK NEW YORK (MW)

3501 Grandville Ave. (b)
Muncie, IN 47303
765-289-8433

WILLIAM F. CRAIG (Co-Owner) & Buys Young Men's Wear, Urban Contemporary, Store Displays, Fixtures, Supplies

JACKIE CRAIG (Co-Owner) & Buys Young Men's Wear, Urban Contemporary, Store Displays, Fixtures, Supplies

SMITTIES (MW)

1622 University Ave. (m-b)
Muncie, IN 47303
765-282-9851

DAVID OSBORNE (Owner) & Buys Men's Sportswear, Furnishings, Accessories, Footwear, Store Displays, Fixtures, Supplies

BRADLEY SCOTT SHOP (CLO)

1465 W. State Rd. 38 (p-m)
New Castle, IN 47362
765-529-4114

BILL DAVIS (Co-Owner) & Buys Men's Denim, Sport Shirts, Western Shirts, Belts, Footwear, Young Men's Denim, Store Displays, Fixtures, Supplies

OREDA DAVIS (Co-Owner) & Buys Men's Denim, Sport Shirts, Western Shirts, Belts, Footwear, Young Men's Denim, Store Displays, Fixtures, Supplies

YANCEY'S APPAREL (CLO)

68 N. 9th St. (m)
Noblesville, IN 46060
317-773-2973 / Fax: 317-773-2973

DAN YANCEY (Owner) & Buys Men's Wear, Sportswear, Furnishings, Accessories, Young Men's Wear, Store Displays, Fixtures, Supplies

HIGH 5 SPORTS (SP)

112 E. Main St.
North Manchester, IN 46962
260-982-4557
Sales: $100,001-$500,000

DON OSBORNE (Owner) & Buys Men's Activewear, Licensed Apparel, Athletic Apparel, Sports Apparel

NOTRE DAME COLLEGE BOOK STORE (SP)

P.O. Box 608
Bookstore Bldg.
Notre Dame, IN 46556
574-631-6316 / Fax: 574-631-7842
Website: www.nd.edu

LARRY RATLIFF-Activewear, Pants, Jackets, Hosiery, Shorts

JAS TOWNSEND & SON, INC. (CLO & MO)

P.O. Box 415 (bud-p-m)
133 N. 1st St.
Pierceton, IN 46582
219-594-5852 / Fax: 219-584-5580
Sales: $500,001-$1 Million
Website: www.jastown.com

DAN TOWNSEND (Co-Owner)

FRANCIS TOWNSEND (Co-Owner & V.P.-Opers.)

JOHN L. TOWNSEND (Co-Owner & Treas. & Gen. Mgr.) & Buys Boys' Apparel, Boys' Footwear, Men's Footwear, Leather Goods, Men's Apparel

TREAT'S SQUIRE SHOP, INC. (MW)

308 N. Michigan St. (m)
Plymouth, IN 46563
574-936-3669 / Fax: 574-936-3669

GARY TREAT (Owner) & Buys Men's & Young Men's Wear, Leather Apparel, Big & Tall Men's Wear, Footwear, Store Displays, Fixtures, Supplies

J.L. HIRSCH DEPARTMENT STORE (DEPT)

8 W. Main St. (m-b)
Poseyville, IN 47633
812-874-2719 / Fax: 812-874-2719

ROBERT HIRSCH (Co-Owner)

SUSAN WEATHERHOLT (Co-Owner) & Buys Men's Sportswear, Belts, Ties, Sweaters, Sport Shirts, Casual Slacks, Dress Shirts, Ties, Underwear, Hosiery, Jewelry, Small Leather Goods, Store Displays, Fixtures, Supplies

KESSLER'S SPORT SHOPS, INC. (SG-12)

930 E. Main St. (m-b)
Richmond, IN 47374
765-935-2595 / Fax: 765-935-1866
Sales: $1 Million-$10 Million

BOB DICKMAN (President) & Buys Men's Footwear, Big & Tall Men's Wear, Men's Casualwear, Accessories, Hosiery, Outerwear, Sportswear, Swimwear

PHILLIP DICKMAN (V.P. & Gen. Mgr.) & Buys Men's Footwear, Big & Tall Men's Wear, Men's Casualwear, Accessories, Hosiery, Outerwear, Sportswear, Swimwear

DANIEL BAKER (Treas.)

DENVER BAKER (Sls. Mgr.) & Buys Men's Sportswear

ROBERT DICKMAN (Mgr.-Real Estate)

KINGS MEN'S SHOP, INC. (MW)

724 E. Main St. (p-m)
Richmond, IN 47374
765-962-6735

HOWARD THOMAS (Owner) & Buys Men's Wear, Sportswear, Furnishings, Accessories, Store Displays, Fixtures, Supplies

B & B MEN'S & BOYS' WEAR (MW)

814 Main St. (m)
Rochester, IN 46975
574-223-2916

PHIL McCARTER (Owner) & Buys Men's Wear, Sportswear, Furnishings, Accessories, Young Men's Wear, Urban Contemporary, Boys' Wear, Formalwear, Store Displays, Fixtures and Supplies

JOHN McCARTER-Men's Wear, Sportswear, Furnishings, Accessories, Young Men's Wear, Urban Contemporary, Boys' Wear, Formalwear, Store Displays, Fixtures and Supplies

BENNETT'S (MW)

805 S. Main St. (p)
Salem, IN 47167
812-883-4502 / Fax: 812-883-6043

DONNA NORRIS (Owner) & Buys Men's Overcoats, Suits, Tailored Jackets, Tailored Slacks, Raincoats, Sweaters, Sport Shirts, Outer Jackets, Casual Slacks, Furnishings, Headwear, Accessories, Footwear, Big & Tall Men's Wear, 8 to 20 Boys' Wear, Urban Contemporary, Store Displays, Fixtures, Supplies

YODER DEPARTMENT STORE, INC. (DEPT)

P.O. Box 245 (bud-p-m)
300 S. Van Buren St.
Shipshewana, IN 46565
219-768-4887 / Fax: 219-768-7182
Sales: $500,000-$1 Million

JANET YODER (Owner)

LARRY YODER (Mgr.) & Buys Store Displays, Fixtures, Supplies

PAUL HOCHSTETLER-Men's Raincoats, Outer Jackets, Denim, Belts, Big & Tall Men's Wear

RICK PHILBROCK-Men's & Boys' Casual Shoes, Athletic Footwear, Slippers, Sandals, Boots, Work Shoes

JUDY MAST-Men's Sweaters, Sport Shirts, Dress Shirts, Ties, Robes, Underwear, Hosiery, Gloves, Boys' Sportswear

FAT DADDIES' OUTLET (MW)

503 S. Michigan St. (bud-p)
South Bend, IN 46601
574-287-6277

JOE GENDEL (Owner) & Buys Men's Work Clothing, Sportswear, Dress Shirts, Ties, Belts, Store Displays, Fixtures and Supplies, (Close Outs)

FUN TAN, INC. (CLO)

2258 S. Bend Ave.
South Bend, IN 46635
219-273-6227 / Fax: 219-273-6359

LARRY SKWARCAN (Co-Owner) & Buys Sunglasses, Men's Surf & Swimwear, Resortwear

LINDA SKWARCAN (Co-Owner) & Buys Sunglasses, Men's Surf & Swimwear, Resortwear

LOUIE'S TUX SHOP, INC. (MW-8)

(LOUIE'S TUX SHOP, INC.)
716 Lincoln Way West (bud-p-m-b)
South Bend, IN 46616
574-234-1061 / Fax: 574-234-1448

DONALD BUCZYNSKI (Owner) & Buys Men's Formalwear, Store Displays, Fixtures, Supplies

DAVID'S MEN'S CLOTHING (MW)

113 Lincolnway (m-b)
Valparaiso, IN 46383
219-462-0012 / Fax: 219-464-3516

DAVID SHURR (Owner) & Buys Men's Wear, Sportswear, Furnishings, Accessories, Store Displays, Fixtures, Supplies

BILSKIE TOWN & COUNTRY (CLO)

1107 Main St.
Vincennes, IN 47591
812-882-4222 / Fax: 812-882-6346

JOSEPH BILSKIE, JR. (Co-Owner) & Buys Men's Sportswear, Accessories, Footwear, Store Displays, Fixtures, Supplies

DONNA BILSKIE (Co-Owner) & Buys Men's Sportswear, Accessories, Footwear, Store Displays, Fixtures, Supplies

R.I. SPIECE (CLO)

306 Manchester Ave.
Wabash, IN 46992
260-563-8033 / Fax: 260-563-0358

TOM SPIECE (Owner) & Buys Store Displays, Fixtures, Supplies

DAVE SHANKLE-Men's Sweaters, Sport Shirts, Outer Jackets, Casual Slacks, Leather Apparel, Active Apparel, Athletic Hosiery, Headwear, Belts, Young Men's Wear

GARY GRIM-Men's Footwear

STEVE & BARRY'S UNIVERSITY SPORTWEAR (MO & SG)

316 State St.
West Lafayette, IN 47906
765-743-3044 / Fax: 765-746-3308
Sales: $1 Million-$10 Million

STEVEN SHORE (President) & Buys Men's Apparel, Skiwear, Licensed Apparel

BARRY PEVOR (V.P.) & Buys Men's Apparel, Skiwear, Licensed Apparel

DANESE MELLO (Mgr.) & Buys Men's Apparel, Skiwear, Licensed Apparel

THE UNIVERSITY BOOKSTORE (SP-2)

(PURDUE UNIVERSITY BOOKSTORE)
360 W. State St.
West Lafayette, IN 47096
765-743-9618 / Fax: 765-743-8659
Website: www.purdueu.com

STEVE BRIGGS-Men's Activewear, Pants, Jackets, Hosiery

MILLER'S DEPARTMENT STORE (DEPT)

(FRANK A. MILLER STORES, INC.)
115 N. Market St. (p-m)
Winamac, IN 46996
574-946-7604 / Fax: 574-946-7620
Sales: $100,001-$500,000

STEVE MILLER (Co-Owner) (@ 219-946-3544) & Buys Store Displays, Fixtures, Supplies

TOM MILLER (Co-Owner) & Buys Men's Overcoats, Tailored Jackets, Tailored Slacks, Raincoats, Sportswear, Sweaters, Sport Shirts, Outer Jackets, Leather Apparel, Casual Slacks, Active Apparel, Furnishings, Accessories, Footwear, 7 to 20 Boys' Wear, Urban Contemporary

HARRY E. MILLER (President)

DIAMONDS (MW)
104 State St. (p)
Algona, IA 50511
515-295-5595 / Fax: 515-295-9044
Sales: $100,001-$500,000
DAVE JANSEN (Owner) & Buys Men's Overcoats, Suits, Tailored Jackets, Raincoats, Tailored Slacks, Sportswear, Big & Tall Men's Wear, Sweaters, Sport Shirts, Outer Jackets, Casual Slacks, Active Apparel, Leather Apparel, Men's Work Shoes, Headwear, Accessories, Young Men's & Boys' Wear, Urban Contemporary, Store Displays, Fixtures, Supplies

ADVENTURELAND PARK, INC. (GS-13)
I-80 and Highway 65
Altoona, IA 50009
515-266-2121 / Fax: 515-266-9831
Sales: $1 Million-$10 Million
Website: www.adventurelandpark.com
JOHN KRANTZ (President)
DOUG CORNWELL (Mgr.-Opers.)
PENNY MADSEN (Mgr.-Retail Opers.) & Buys T-shirts, Sweats, Swimwear, Caps, Hats

DURLAM & DURLAM CLOTHING (CLO)
226 Main St. (m-b)
Ames, IA 50010
515-232-3261 / Fax: 515-663-8782
Sales: $500,001-$1 Million
Website: www.durlamanddurlam.com
DAVID DURLAM (President) & Buys Men's Overcoats, Suits, Tailored Jackets, Tailored Slacks, Raincoats, Sportswear, Sweaters, Sport Shirts, Outer Jackets, Leather Apparel, Casual Slacks, Active Apparel, Furnishings, Accessories, Big & Tall Men's Wear, Store Displays, Fixtures, Supplies

JOHN HUBER CLOTHIER (CLO)
404 Main St. (m-b)
Ames, IA 50010
515-233-4948
JOHN HUBER (Mgr.) & Buys Men's Sportswear, Furnishings, Store Displays, Fixtures, Supplies

SPORTS PAGE OF AMES (SG)
2801 Grand Ave. (p-m-b)
Ames, IA 50010
515-232-4111 / Fax: 515-232-0370
DAN SETTLE (Owner) & Buys Men's T-shirts, Sweatpants, Hosiery, Footwear

T. GALAXY RETAIL (CLO-3)
(NADLER BROTHERS)
P.O. Box 1786 (m)
206 Welch Ave.
Ames, IA 50014
515-292-1364 / Fax: 515-232-5557
Website: www.nadlerbros.com
BARRY NADLER (Co-Owner & President & C.E.O.)
JAMIE NADLER (Co-Owner & C.F.O.)
KERRY BISHOP (G.M.M.)
DONJA ESK-Men's Activewear, Big & Tall Men's Wear, Store Displays, Fixtures, Supplies

HOWARD'S (CLO)
415 Chestnut St. (m-b)
Atlantic, IA 50022
712-243-4982
MARK KRENGEL (Owner) & Buys Men's Sportswear, Furnishings, Accessories, Work Shoes, Dress Shoes, Boots, Store Displays, Fixtures, Supplies

KENNEDY BROTHERS CO. (DEPT)
P.O. Box 235 (p)
102 W. Ramsey St.
Bancroft, IA 50517
515-885-2284 / Fax: 515-885-2220
JANICE MOORE (G.M.M.) & Buys Men's Overcoats, Suits, Tailored Slacks, Raincoats, Big & Tall Men's Wear, Sportswear, Sweaters, Sport Shirts, Outer Jackets, Leather Apparel, Casual Slacks, Active Apparel, Furnishings, Belts, Fragrances, Boys' Sportswear, Furnishings

DAD & LAD CLOTHING (MW)
719 Story St. (m)
Boone, IA 50036
515-432-5281
Sales: $100,001-$500,000
BRAD CLARK (Owner) & Buys Men's & Young Men's Wear, Leather Apparel, Store Displays, Fixtures, Supplies

PEOPLES CLOTHING STORE (MW)
803 8th St. (m-b)
Boone, IA 50036
515-432-6637
JOHN NIEMANTS (Owner) & Buys Men's Sportswear, Furnishings, Accessories

WILSON'S CLOTHING (MW)
224 N. Main St. (p)
Buffalo Center, IA 50424
641-562-2434
Sales: $100,001-$500,000
MICHAEL WILSON (President) & Buys Men's Overcoats, Suits, Tailored Slacks, Raincoats, Big & Tall Men's Wear, Sportswear, Sweaters, Sport Shirts, Leather Apparel, Outer Jackets, Casual Slacks, Furnishings, Accessories, Headwear, Young Men's & Boys' Wear, Urban Contemporary, Store Displays, Fixtures, Supplies

BILLMEIER'S (MW)
513 N. Adams St. (m)
Carroll, IA 51401
712-792-3152
LOU BILLMEIER (Owner) & Buys Men's Sportswear, Furnishings, Accessories

WILKIE CLOTHIERS (MW)
125 W. 5th St. (m)
Carroll, IA 51401
712-792-9863
Sales: $100,001-$500,000
WADE WILKIE (Owner) & Buys Men's Overcoats, Suits, Tailored Jackets, Tailored Slacks, Raincoats, Sportswear, Sweaters, Sport Shirts, Outer Jackets, Leather Apparel, Casual Slacks, Furnishings, Belts, Jewelry, Fragrances, Store Displays, Fixtures, Supplies

PALACE CLOTHIERS, INC. (MW-2)
312 Main St. (m-b)
Cedar Falls, IA 50613
319-268-1958 / Fax: 319-273-8709
STEVE VOLZ (Owner) & Buys Men's Sportswear, Furnishings & Accessories, Footwear, Store Displays, Fixtures, Supplies

SAWYER CLOTHING, INC. (CLO)
106 Main St. (m-b)
Cedar Falls, IA 50613
319-277-1952
BOB SAWYER-Men's Sportswear, Furnishings & Accessories, Store Displays, Fixtures, Supplies

UNIVERSITY BOOK & SUPPLY, INC. (SP)
1009 W. 23rd St.
Cedar Falls, IA 50613
319-266-7581 / Fax: 319-277-1266
Website: www.panthersupply.com
ROSALYN LORENZ (President) & Buys Men's Activewear, Licensed Apparel

CLANCY'S LTD. (MW)

201 3rd Ave. SE (b)
Cedar Rapids, IA 52401
319-366-1116
Sales: $500,000-$1 Million

GARY LACOCK (President) & Buys Men's Sportswear, Furnishings, Headwear, Accessories, Store Displays, Fixtures, Supplies

HOLLEY'S, INC. (MW)

4444 1st Ave. NE, #12 (m-b)
Cedar Rapids, IA 52402
319-393-2310 / Fax: 319-378-7423
Sales: $1 Million-$10 Million

JAMES D. HOLLEY (President) & Buys Men's Sportswear, Furnishings, Headwear, Accessories, Big & Tall Men's Wear, Men's Footwear, Store Displays, Fixtures, Supplies

ROBERT J. HOLLEY (V.P.) & Buys Men's Sportswear, Furnishings, Headwear, Accessories, Big & Tall Men's Wear, Men's Footwear

JYM BAG CO. (CLO)

6015 Huntington Ct. NE
Cedar Rapids, IA 52402
319-393-3843 / Fax: 319-393-0917

JIM WAGNER (President) & Buys Active Apparel, Licensed Apparel

SIEBKE HOYT JEWELERS (JWLY & MO)

(SIEBKE HOYT JEWELERS & GALLERIA)
4800 1st Ave. NE
Cedar Rapids, IA 52402
319-363-2003 / Fax: 319-363-0344
Sales: $1 Million-$10 Million
Website: www.siebkehoyt.com

JAY HOYT (President)

JULIE LORIMER (G.M.) & Buys Jewelry

JIM IRELAN MENSWEAR (MW)

106 W. Jackson St. (p-m-b)
Centerville, IA 52544
641-856-3591
Sales: $100,001-$500,000

JIM IRELAN (Owner) & Buys Men's Overcoats, Suits, Raincoats, Sportswear, Furnishings, Headwear, Belts, Jewelry, Fragrances, Leather Apparel, Big & Tall Men's Wear, Urban Contemporary, Store Displays, Fixtures, Supplies

ROBERT HOUF (Asst. Mgr.) & Buys Men's Overcoats, Suits, Raincoats, Sportswear, Furnishings, Headwear, Belts, Jewelry, Fragrances, Leather Apparel, Big & Tall Men's Wear, Urban Contemporary, Store Displays, Fixtures, Supplies

BRIAN WILSON-Men's Overcoats, Suits, Raincoats, Sportswear, Furnishings, Headwear, Belts, Jewelry, Fragrances, Leather Apparel, Big & Tall Men's Wear, Urban Contemporary, Store Displays, Fixtures, Supplies

MR. G'S CLOTHING (MW)

220 W. Main St. (p-m)
Cherokee, IA 51012
712-225-2659

DALE GALLES (Owner) & Buys Men's Sportswear, Furnishings, Accessories, Boys' Wear, Leather Apparel, Store Displays, Fixtures, Supplies

WEIL'S CLOTHING (CLO)

114 N. 16th St. (p-m)
Clarinda, IA 51632
712-542-2213
Sales: $100,001-$500,000

LARRY BRIDIE (Co-Owner) & Buys Men's Overcoats, Suits, Tailored Jackets, Tailored Slacks, Raincoats, Sweaters, Sport Shirts, Outer Jackets, Casual Slacks, Furnishings, Headwear, Leather Apparel, Accessories, Young Men's & Boys' Shirts, Slacks, Jeans, Store Displays, Fixtures, Supplies, Footwear

SHIRA BRIDIE (Co-Owner) & Buys Men's Overcoats, Suits, Tailored Jackets, Tailored Slacks, Raincoats, Sweaters, Sport Shirts, Outer Jackets, Casual Slacks, Furnishings, Headwear, Leather Apparel, Accessories, Young Men's & Boys' Shirts, Slacks, Jeans, Store Displays, Fixtures, Supplies

MISTER G'S (CLO)

102 N. Main St.
Clarion, IA 50525
515-532-6583

LARRY GUTH (Owner) & Buys Men's Sportswear, Furnishings, Accessories

BOEGEL'S MENSWEAR (MW)

412 S. 2nd St. (m-b)
Clinton, IA 52732
563-242-3045
Sales: $100,001-$500,000

KARL BOEGEL (Co-Owner)

KARLEN BOEGEL MUELLER (Co-Owner)

BOBBI BOEGEL SCHERER (Co-Owner) & Buys Men's Sportswear, Furnishings, Headwear, Accessories, Young Men's Wear, Store Displays, Fixtures, Supplies

PARKER CASSIDY SUPPLY CO. (CLO-2)

1940 Lincoln Way (p-m)
Clinton, IA 52732
563-242-0683 / Fax: 563-242-0723

LEO VAN DEWALLE-Big & Tall Men's Wear, Men's Sportswear, Dress Shirts, Leather Apparel, Underwear, Hosiery, Belts, Young Men's & Boys' Sportswear, Store Displays, Fixtures, Supplies

A.B. TURNER & SON (DEPT)

P.O. Box 309 (p-m)
627 Davis Ave.
Corning, IA 50841
641-322-3950 / Fax: 641-322-3050
Sales: $100,001-$500,000

NANCY TURNER (Owner) & Buys Men's Sportswear, Furnishings, Accessories, Headwear, Leather Apparel, Footwear, Store Displays, Fixtures, Supplies

LEUTHOLD CLOTHING STORES (CLO)

202 N. Elm St. (m)
Cresco, IA 52136
563-547-4041 / Fax: 563-547-2829

ROY GORTER (G.M.M.) & Buys Men's Sportswear, Furnishings, Headwear, Accessories, Boys' Wear, Store Displays, Fixtures, Supplies

GENTRY SHOP, INC. (MW)

5515 Utica Ridge Rd. (b)
Davenport, IA 52807
563-324-6689 / Fax: 563-324-3759

GREG KAUTZ (Owner) & Buys Men's Sportswear, Furnishings, Headwear, Accessories, Leather Apparel, Store Displays, Fixtures, Supplies

RUNNING WILD (SP)

313 E. George Washington Blvd.
Davenport, IA 52803
563-323-7025

STEVE KILBURG (Owner) & Buys Activewear, Athletic Footwear

SYNDICATE HUB CLOTHING CORP. (MW)

2211 E. 52nd St. (m-b)
Davenport, IA 52807
563-354-5551

CURT BRUNSMA (Co-Owner) & Buys Men's Sportswear, Furnishings & Accessories, Store Displays, Fixtures, Supplies

MEREDITH BRUNSMA (Co-Owner) & Buys Men's Sportswear, Furnishings & Accessories, Store Displays, Fixtures, Supplies

SUE BRUNSMA (Co-Owner) & Buys Men's Sportswear, Furnishings & Accessories, Store Displays, Fixtures, Supplies

IOWA - Davenport

VON MAUR (DEPT-22)
6565 N. Brady St. (m-b)
Davenport, IA 52806
563-388-2200 / Fax: 563-388-2242
Sales: $10 Million-$50 Million
Website: www.vonmaur.com
Retail Locations: IL, IN, IA, KS, MN, NE, KY, MI
- CHARLES R. VON MAUR (Co-Chmn.)
- RICHARD B. VON MAUR (Co-Chmn.)
- JAMES VON MAUR (President)
- KENT MATHEWS (D.M.M.-Men's Clothing & Sportswear)
- CLIFF McDOW-Men's Outerwear, Slacks
- BRIAN FOWLER-Men's Active Apparel, Casual Slacks, Men's Better Sportswear, Young Men's Wear
- BRIAN SHELDON-Men's Sport Coats, Suits
- SCOTT GOLD (D.M.M.) & Buys Boys' Wear
- AMANDA SCHUSON-Men's Furnishings, Accessories, Men's Dress Shirts
- SHANNON McCOY-Men's Footwear
- LARRY ARMER (Visual Mdse. Mgr.) & Buys Store Displays, Fixtures, Supplies

AMUNDSON CLOTHING STORE (MW)
130 W. Water St. (m)
Decorah, IA 52101
563-382-5761
- RICHARD AMUDSON (Owner) & Buys Men's Sportswear, Furnishings, Accessories

SATURDAY NITE GUYS (MW)
1231 Broadway (m)
Denison, IA 51442
712-263-4421 / Fax: 712-463-4410
- AMY SCHULTZ (Owner) & Buys Men's Jeans, T-shirts, Dress Shirts, Underwear

BADOWERS (MW)
2817 Ingersoll Ave. (m-b)
Des Moines, IA 50312
515-283-2121 / Fax: 515-283-0995
- DAVE LEMONS (Mgr.) & Buys Men's Sportswear, Furnishings, Accessories, Dress Shoes, Boots, Store Displays, Fixtures, Supplies

BOND'S OF BEAVERDALE (CLO)
2821 Beaver Ave. (m)
Des Moines, IA 50310
515-274-3485 / Fax: 515-274-3486
- JEFFREY WATTS (Owner) & Buys Men's Sportswear, Furnishings, Accessories

FITNESS SPORTS LTD. (SP)
7230 University Ave.
Des Moines, IA 50311
515-277-4785 / Fax: 515-277-3854
Sales: $1 Million-$10 Million
Website: www.fitnesssports.com
- STEVEN BOBENHOUSE (Owner) & Buys Athletic Footwear
- SUSAN KOBLISKA (Mdse. Mgr.) & Buys Activewear

G & L CLOTHING CO. (MW & OL)
1801 Ingersoll Ave. (m)
Des Moines, IA 50309
515-243-7431 / Fax: 515-243-4527
Sales: $2 Billion
Website: www.gandlclothing.com
- DAVID MARCOVIS (President) & Buys Big & Tall Men's Wear, Men's Sportswear, Furnishings, Accessories, Sweaters, Leather Apparel, Casual Slacks, Activewear, Underwear, Gloves, Hosiery, Young Men's & Boys' Wear, Store Displays, Fixtures, Supplies
- JAMES MARCOVIS (C.E.O) & Buys Men's Overcoats, Suits, Tailored Jackets, Tailored Slacks, Raincoats, Sportswear, Outer Jackets, Dress Shirts, Robes, Big & Tall Men's Wear, Furnishings, Accessories, Store Displays, Fixtures and Supplies
- NASHI KHALASTCHI-Big & Tall Men's Wear, Men's Sportswear, Furnishings, Accessories
- JIM ANDERSON-Men's Ties
- BEN KAUFMANN-Footwear, Boots

MR. B. (CLO)
(REICHARDT'S, INC.)
(Div. of HICKMAN CO.)
1995 NW 86th St. (b)
Des Moines, IA 50325
515-276-8589 / Fax: 515-254-0806
Sales: $1 Million-$10 Million
Website: www.eclotheshorse.com
- WAYNE GRAHAM (Owner) & Buys Men's Wear, Leather Apparel
- TIM SITZMANN-Men's Wear, Leather Apparel

REICHARDT'S, INC. (MW)
847 42nd St. (m-b)
Des Moines, IA 50312
515-274-1558 / Fax: 515-274-6253
Sales: $1 Million-$10 Million
- WAYNE GRAHAM (President)
- JOHN REESE (Mgr.) & Buys Men's Overcoats, Suits, Tailored Jackets, Tailored Slacks, Raincoats, Casual Slacks, Sweaters, Sport Shirts, Outer Jackets, Activewear, Dress Shirts, Ties, Robes, Leather Apparel, Underwear, Hosiery, Gloves, Headwear, Belts, Jewelry, Small Leather Goods, Fragrances
- RENEE GIBSON (Office Mgr.) & Buys Store Displays, Fixtures, Supplies

S. JOSEPH & SONS, INC. (JWLY-3)
(JOSEPH'S JEWELRY)
317 6th Ave.
Des Moines, IA 50309
515-243-4148 / Fax: 515-283-0416
Sales: $10 Million-$50 Million
- BURTON JOSEPH, III (President)
- BILL BAUM (C.E.O.) & Buys Jewelry, Watches
- DEB JOSEPH-Watches
- SHELLY WEATHERBY-Jewelry

SKEFFINGTON'S (SP-6)
2453 SW 9th St. (m)
Des Moines, IA 50315
515-283-0453 / Fax: 515-282-4228
Website: www.skeffingtons.com
Retail Locations: IA, MO
- MARY JO HARTY (Owner) & Buys Men's & Boys' Tuxedos, Formalwear, Furnishings, Accessories, Footwear

VALLEY WEST UNIFORMS (SP)
8801 University Ave., #2B (m)
Des Moines, IA 50325
515-223-9090 / Fax: 515-223-9273
Sales: $100,001-$500,000
- TERRY DICKERSON (President) & Buys Men's Footwear, Men's Apparel, Men's Denim Apparel, Men's Formalwear, Men's Accessories, Men's Suits, Men's Uniforms

IOWA - Des Moines

YOUNKERS, INC. (DEPT-5)

(Div. of SAKS, INC.)
701 Walnut St.
Des Moines, IA 50309
414-421-0688 / Fax: 515-247-7182
Sales: $100 Million-$500 Million
Website: www.saksincorporated.com
Retail Locations: OR, NV, CA, AZ, HI, MT, WY, CO, TX, OK, KS, NE, SD, ND, MN, IA, MO, LA, MS, AL, CA, FL, SC, NC, VA, WV, KY, TN, IL, WI, MI, OH, PA, NY, MD, NJ, NY, CT, MA

MICHAEL MacDONALD (Chmn. & C.E.O.)
TORY BUCCINA (President)
PAUL RUBY (Sr. V.P. & Real Estate Contact) (@ 414-347-5306)
SANDY-Men's Belts, Underwear, Furnishings, Sleepwear, Accessories
WENDY NURRLADE-Men's Dress Shirts, Ties
SCOTT WINTERBOTTOM-Men's Suits, Outerwear, Sport Coats, Slacks, Clothing, London Fog, Suit Separates

ANNE OWEN (D.M.M.-Men's Sportswear)
DAVID OTTE-Men's Sweaters, Woven & Knit Shirts, Separates, Sportswear
MICHELLE WINGER-Men's Activewear, Young Men's Levis, Young Men's Bottoms & Tops
MATT KIRKE-Men's Better Sportswear, Ralph Lauren, Polo, Designer Sportswear, Liz Claiborne For Men, Denims

DONNA ROTHROCK (D.M.M.-Fragrances)
JAN COY-Men's Fragrances

MARK LESLIE (D.M.M.-Children's Wear)
SARA BIRIS-8 to 20 Boys' Clothing, Sportswear, Furnishings

TODD DREITH (D.M.M.-Footwear)
JOHN CORE-Men's Footwear

DOUG HANSEN (Div. V.P.-Visual Presentation) & Buys Store Displays, Fixtures

MEN'S CORNER (MW)

809 6th Ave. (m)
Dewitt, IA 52742
319-659-5771

BOB OWENS (Owner) & Buys Men's Sportswear, Furnishings, Accessories, Young Men's Wear, 8 to 20 Boys' Wear, Store Displays, Fixtures, Supplies

GRAHAM'S STYLE STORE (MW)

890 Main St. (m-b)
Dubuque, IA 52001
563-582-3760 / Fax: 563-556-6576
Sales: $500,000-$1 Million

JOSEPH GRAHAM (President & Owner) & Buys Men's Overcoats, Suits, Tailored Jackets, Tailored Slacks, Raincoats, Big & Tall Men's Wear, Sportswear, Casual Slacks, Sweaters, Sports Shirts, Outer Jackets, Leather Apparel, Activewear, Dress Shirts, Ties, Robes, Underwear, Gloves, Headwear, Accessorie
RON NOLTING-Tailored Slacks, Casual Slacks
HOWARD REIDEL-Hosiery

THEISEN SUPPLY, INC. (DEPT-12)

4949 Chavenelle Rd. (m)
Dubuque, IA 52002
563-556-4738 / Fax: 563-556-7959
Website: www.theisens.com

CHRIS THEISEN (Co-Owner)
TONY THEISEN (Co-Owner)
JIM THEISEN (President & Real Estate Contact) & Buys Store Displays
GREG CONWAY-Men's Sportswear, Underwear, Hosiery, Belts, Gloves, Headwear, Young Men's Wear, 8 to 20 Boys' Sportswear

WALSH STORES (DEPT-2)

P.O. Box 207 (p)
1301 Central Ave.
Dubuque, IA 52001
563-582-1869 / Fax: 563-582-1614
Sales: $1 Million-$10 Million

ANN LIDDLE (Co-Owner) & Buys Men's Raincoats, Big & Tall Men's Wear, Sportswear, Furnishings, Headwear, Belts, Boys' Wear, Urban Contemporary
MARK WALSH (President)
PAM WALSH (D.M.M.) & Buys Store Displays, Fixtures, Supplies

THEIS CLOTHING (CLO)

(P & H CLOTHING CO., INC.)
108 S. Main St.
Elkader, IA 52043
563-245-1405 / Fax: 563-245-2857

FLOYD POSSEHL (Partner) & Buys Men's Sportswear, Furnishings, Accessories, Young Men's Wear, Urban Contemporary, Leather Apparel, Store Displays, Fixtures, Supplies

RACINE'S MENSWEAR (MW)

614 Central Ave. (m)
Estherville, IA 51334
712-362-3302

JOHN RACINE (Owner) & Buys Men's Sportswear, Furnishings, Accessories

LEDERMAN'S, INC. (MW)

3524 Lafayette Rd. (p)
Evansdale, IA 50707
319-234-1222 / Fax: 319-235-8005

DAVID LEDERMAN (Owner) & Buys Men's Sportswear, Furnishings, Accessories

OVERLAND SHEEPSKIN (CLO-11 & OL & MO)

2096 Nutmeg Ave. (p-m-b)
Fairfield, IA 52556
641-472-8484 / Fax: 641-472-8474
Sales: $10 Million-$50 Million
Website: www.overland.com
Retail Locations: NM, CO, WY, CA, NE, IA, VT, UT

MARGE LEAHY (Co-Owner) & Buys Men's & Young Men's Outerwear, Sportswear, Sweaters, Leather Apparel, Headwear, Accessories
JERRY LEAHY (Co-Owner) & Buys Men's & Young Men's Outerwear, Sportswear, Sweaters, Leather Apparel, Headwear, Accessories
ROGER LEAHY (President)
AMBER LEAHY (V.P.) & Buys Coats
BECKY DODSON-Small Accessories

NOTE:-Buying of Store Displays, Fixtures, & Supplies Performed by Individual Store Managers

EDDIE QUINN CLOTHIER (MW)

820 Central Ave. (b)
Fort Dodge, IA 50501
515-576-1891

RICHARD WHITING (Owner) & Buys Men's Sportswear, Furnishings, Accessories

FOLEY CLOTHING CO., INC. (MW-2)

316 S. 25th St. (m-b)
Fort Dodge, IA 50501
515-573-3161
Sales: $500,000-$1 Million

JOHN JUNKMAN (President) & Buys Men's Sportswear, Furnishings, Headwear, Accessories, Urban Contemporary, Leather Apparel, Store Displays, Fixtures, Supplies

GLASGOW LTD. (MW)

724 Ave. G (b)
Fort Madison, IA 52627
319-372-5412

DOYLE HOYER (Owner) & Buys Men's Overcoats, Suits, Tailored Jackets, Tailored Slacks, Sportswear, Sweaters, Sport Shirts, Outer Jackets, Leather Apparel, Casual Slacks, Active Apparel
JEANNE HOYER (Mgr.) & Buys Men's Furnishings, Accessories, Men's Footwear, Store Displays, Fixtures, Supplies

J. McCOY & CO. (DEPT)
4502 Ave. O
Fort Madison, IA 52627
319-372-7829 / Fax: 319-372-7843
Sales: $100,001-$500,000
JOHN McCOY (Owner) & Buys Men's Apparel, Jeans
STEVE TEUFERT-Men's Apparel, Jeans

GOODNATURES STORE (DEPT)
314 State St. (m)
Garner, IA 50438
641-923-2761 / Fax: 641-923-2579
MARIE FREDRICK (Owner) & Buys Store Displays, Fixtures, Supplies, Men's Sportswear, 8 to 20 Boys' Wear, Urban Contemporary
LAURA ATHANASIOU-8 to 20 Boys' Wear

CROOKS CLOTHING CO. (MW)
226 Public Sq. (m)
Greenfield, IA 50849
641-743-8421
Sales: $100,001-$500,000
SHIRLEY MEISENHEIMER (Owner) & Buys Men's Overcoats, Suits, Tailored Slacks, Raincoats, Big & Tall Wear, Sweaters, Sportswear, Sport Shirts, Outer Jackets, Casual Slacks, Activewear, Furnishings, Headwear, Accessories, Boys' Clothing, Store Displays, Fixtures, Supplies

ESSER'S SHOES & CLOTHING (CLO & FW)
502 S. River Park Dr. (bud)
Guttenberg, IA 52052
319-252-2095
J. MATT ESSER (Owner) & Buys Men's Wear, Boys' Jeans, Tops, Underwear, Hosiery, Men's & Boys' Footwear
CONNIE ESSER-Men's Wear, Boys' Jeans, Tops, Underwear, Hosiery, Men's & Boys' Footwear

HARLAN CLOTHING (MW)
612 Market St. (m-b)
Harlan, IA 51537
712-755-5400 / Fax: 712-755-5970
LARRY MILLER (Owner) & Buys Men's Sportswear, Work Clothes, Furnishings, Headwear, Accessories, Young Men's Wear, Urban Contemporary, Store Displays, Fixtures, Supplies

GARY'S MENSWEAR (MW)
608 Sumner Ave.
Humboldt, IA 50548
515-332-3023
GARY MORITZ (Owner) & Buys Men's Sportswear, Furnishings, Headwear, Accessories, Footwear, Store Displays, Fixtures, Supplies

EWERS MEN'S STORE, INC. (MW)
28 S. Clinton St. (m)
Iowa City, IA 52240
319-337-3345
Sales: $500,000-$1 Million
ROBERT NOSER (Co-President) & Buys Men's Overcoats, Suits, Tailored Jackets, Tailored Slacks, Raincoats, Big & Tall Men's Wear, Sportswear, Sweaters, Sport Shirts, Outer Jackets, Casual Slacks, Wear, Furnishings, Headwear, Accessories, Footwear, Store Displays, Fixtures, Supplies
WILLIAM NOSER (Co-President) & Buys Men's Overcoats, Suits, Tailored Jackets, Tailored Slacks, Raincoats, Big & Tall Men's Wear, Sportswear, Sweaters, Sport Shirts, Outer Jackets, Casual Slacks, Wear, Furnishings, Headwear, Accessories, Footwear, Store Displays, Fixtures, Supplies
DWANE NOSER (C.E.O.)

JOHN WILSON'S SPORTING GOODS (SG-2)
Old Capital Town Ctr., #112 (p-m-b)
Iowa City, IA 52240
319-338-9291 / Fax: 319-338-9850
JOHN WILSON (Owner) & Buys Men's & Boys' Athletic Wear, Footwear, Accessories

PREFERRED STOCK (CLO)
114 S. Clinton St. (m)
Iowa City, IA 52240
319-351-7231 / Fax: 319-351-5312
VICTORIA GILPIN (Owner) & Buys Men's Casual Wear

UNIVERSITY OF IOWA BOOK STORE (SP)
Iowa Memorial Union
Iowa City, IA 52242
319-335-3179 / Fax: 319-335-3875
Website: www.book.uiowa.edu
GEORGE HERBERT (Mgr.) & Buys Fleece, Jackets, Hosiery

WESTERN WORLD, INC. (WW)
426 Hwy. 1 West (b)
Iowa City, IA 52246
319-351-8313 / Fax: 319-351-3242
WALLY ANDRUS (V.P.) & Buys Men's Sportswear, Furnishings, Headwear, Accessories, Boys' Wear, Store Displays, Fixtures, Supplies

WALLEN McADAMS CLOTHING, INC. (CLO)
604 Washington Ave. (m-b)
Iowa Falls, IA 50126
641-648-3371
NORMAN WALLEN (Owner) & Buys Men's & Young Men's Wear, Footwear, Store Displays, Fixtures, Supplies

JOHNSON - SCHMIDT, INC. (MW)
428 Main St. (m)
Keokuk, IA 52632
319-524-2505 / Fax: 319-524-2989
Sales: $100,001-$500,000
GARY L. JOHNSON (President) & Buys Men's Suits, Tailored Jackets, Tailored Slacks, Raincoats, Big & Tall Men's Wear, Sportswear, Sweaters, Sport Shirts, Casual Slacks, Headwear, Furnishings, Accessories, Leather Apparel, Store Displays, Fixtures, Supplies

BENZ CLOTHING (CLO)
113 Main St. (m-b)
Lake City, IA 51449
712-464-3361
SCOTT BENZ (Owner) & Buys Men's Sportswear, Footwear, Furnishings, Headwear, Accessories, Young Men's Wear, Store Displays, Fixtures, Supplies

STAG SHOP (MW)
115 E. Main St. (m)
Lamoni, IA 50140
641-784-6331
Sales: $100,001-$500,000
KEN COMBS (Owner) & Buys Men's Sportswear, Furnishings, Accessories, Store Displays

BILL MOLER'S (MW)
(SALMO, INC.)
113 S. Main St. (m)
Maquoketa, IA 52060
563-652-4383
JAKE BICKFORD (Owner) & Buys Men's Sportswear, Work Clothes, Furnishings, Headwear, Accessories, Store Displays, Fixtures, Supplies

GARMENT DESIGN (SP)
(GD & G Corp.)
1080 Lyons Ln.
Marion, IA 52302
319-377-4678 / Fax: 319-377-4679
JAMES HOFFMANN (Owner) & Buys Activewear, Licensed Apparel

IRWIN'S CLOTHING (MW)
1180 7th Ave. (m-b)
Marion, IA 52302
319-377-2200 / Fax: 319-377-0877
LEE LARSON (Owner) & Buys Men's Sportswear, Furnishings, Accessories

IOWA - Marshalltown

GILDNER'S (MW)
2628 E. Main St. (m-b)
Marshalltown, IA 50158
641-752-5477 / Fax: 641-754-4868
Sales: $500,001-$1 Million
DAVID SWANSON (Owner) & Buys Leather Goods, Men's Big & Tall Apparel, Men's & Boys' Apparel, Men's Casualwear, Men's Denim Apparel, Men's Formalwear, Men's Accessories, Men's Hosiery, Men's Outerwear, Men's Sportswear, Men's Suits, Men's Swimwear

DECKER SPORTING GOODS (SG-2)
4850 4th St. SW (m)
Mason City, IA 50401
641-423-7423 / Fax: 641-423-9324
BOB LEMON (Owner) & Buys Men's & Boys' Shirts, Fleece, Sweatpants, Hosiery, Footwear

MOORMAN CLOTHIERS LTD., INC. (MW-2)
2 S. Federal Ave. (m)
Mason City, IA 50401
641-423-5222 / Fax: 641-421-4188
Website: www.moormanclothiers.com
SCOTT MOORMAN (Owner) & Buys Men's Sportswear, Furnishings, Headwear, Accessories, Young Men's Wear, Store Displays, Fixtures, Supplies

RIVER JUNCTION TRADE CO. (CLO)
312 Main St. (b)
P.O. Box 275
McGregor, IA 52157
563-873-2387 / Fax: 563-873-3647
Sales: $1 Million-$10 Million
Website: www.riverjunction.com
JIM BOEKE (President) & Buys Men's Apparel
LINDA BOEKE (V.P.-Opers. & Gen. Mgr.) & Buys Men's Apparel

THE THREE SONS, INC. (DEPT)
P.O. Box 499 (b)
Financial District
Milford, IA 51351
712-338-2424 / Fax: 712-338-4322
Website: www.threesons.com
HERMAN RICHTER (Co-Owner) & Buys Men's & Boys' Sportswear, Furnishings, Accessories, Leather Apparel, Footwear, Store Displays, Fixtures, Supplies
PAULA RICHTER-Men's & Boys' Sportswear, Furnishings, Accessories, Leather Apparel, Footwear, Store Displays, Fixtures, Supplies

R & R CLOTHING (CLO)
304 E. Erie St. (m)
Missouri Valley, IA 51555
712-642-4185
RODNEY OLSEN (Owner) & Buys Men's Tailored Jackets, Tailored Slacks, Big & Tall Men's Sportswear, Furnishings, Headwear, Work Clothes, Accessories, Store Displays, Fixtures, Supplies

BAUMAN'S (MW)
(MT. VERNON CLOTHING CO., INC.)
124 1st St. West (m)
Mount Vernon, IA 52314
319-895-8692 / Fax: 319-895-9055
MIKE SMITH (Partner) & Buys Men's Sportswear, Furnishings, Headwear, Accessories, Footwear, Store Displays, Fixtures, Supplies

K & D CLOTHIERS (MW)
221 E. 2nd St. (b)
Muscatine, IA 52761
563-263-4901
Sales: $100,001-$500,000
DENNIS COCKSHOOT (Owner) & Buys Men's Overcoats, Tuxedos, Suits, Tailored Jackets, Tailored Slacks, Raincoats, Big & Tall Men's Wear, Sportswear, Sweaters, Sport Shirts, Outer Jackets, Casual Slacks, Tuxedo Sales/Rentals, Activewear, Furnishings, Young Men's Jeans, Accessories, Store Displays, Fixtures, Supplies

D.C. SPORTS (MW)
225 1st Ave. West (m-b)
Newton, IA 50208
641-792-6085 / Fax: 641-792-3906
Sales: Under $100,000
DOUG CUPPLES (Owner) & Buys Men's Sportswear, Furnishings, Accessories, Formal Boys' Apparel

LEUTHOLD'S (CLO)
115 W. 2nd St. North (p-m)
Newton, IA 50208
641-792-1067
DICK WENDEL (Owner) & Buys Men's Sportswear, Furnishings, Headwear, Accessories, Leather Apparel, Store Displays, Fixtures, Supplies

SAM'S CLOTHING (MW)
9 N. Frederick Ave. (m)
Oelwein, IA 50662
319-283-4728 / Fax: 319-283-1556
Sales: $100,001-$500,000
LARRY SCHWARTZ (Owner) & Buys Men's Sportswear, Furnishings, Headwear, Accessories, Store Displays, Fixtures, Supplies

L & K CLOTHING, INC. (MW)
107 Central Ave. NE (m)
Orange City, IA 51041
712-737-2941 / Fax: 712-737-2086
Sales: $500,000-$1 Million
LYLE HUISMAN (President & G.M.M.) & Buys Men's Overcoats, Suits, Tailored Jackets, Tailored Slacks, Raincoats, Big & Tall Men's Wear, Sportswear, Sweaters, Sport Shirts, Outer Jackets Casual Slacks Apparel Furnishings, Headwear, Leather Apparel, Accessories, Big & Tall Men's Wear, Store Displays

FLEMING'S CLOTHING (MW)
703 Main St. (p-m)
Osage, IA 50461
641-732-3582 / Fax: 641-732-3711
KEN EMERSON (Owner) & Buys Men's Sportswear, Furnishings, Accessories, Headwear, Leather Apparel, Big & Tall Men's, Urban Contemporary, Store Displays, Fixtures, Supplies

ROBINSON'S (MW)
(ROBINSON'S OF OSCEOLA, INC.)
127 S. Main St. (bud-p)
Osceola, IA 50213
641-342-2154 / Fax: 641-342-6166
Sales: $1 Million-$10 Million
BERNARD LINDER (Co-Owner)
DAVID M. THOMAS (Co-Owner) & Buys Store Displays, Fixtures, Supplies
DENNIS FOOTE (Assoc. Mgr.) & Buys Men's Sportswear, Furnishings, Headwear, Accessories, Young Men's Wear

SWIM'S SPORTS (SG)
208 1st Ave. East
Oskaloosa, IA 52577
641-673-6779
Sales: $100,001-$500,000
DOUG SWIM (Owner) & Buys Activewear, Licensed Apparel

FRANKLIN STREET CLOTHING (CLO)
612 Franklin St. (m)
Pella, IA 50219
641-628-3301
Sales: $100,001-$500,000
MIKE SCHURING (Owner) & Buys Men's Sportswear, Furnishings (No Robes), Big & Tall Wear, Belts, Small Leather Goods, Young Men's Wear, 8 to 20 Boys' Wear, Store Displays, Fixtures, Supplies

THE RED LOLLIPOP (KS)
617 Franklin St. (p-m)
Pella, IA 50219
641-628-4800 / Fax: 641-628-1579
EVA VANDELUNE (Owner) & Buys Boys' Wear, Sportswear, Furnishings, Accessories

WORMHOUDT & KEMPKES (MW)
816 Main (p-m-b)
Pella, IA 50219
641-628-4060 / Fax: 641-628-1065
MARY EDWARDS-Men's Sportswear & Suits, Dress Shoes, Big & Tall Men's, Classic Contemporary, Store Displays, Fixtures, Supplies

IOWA - Perry

LORD'S CLOTHING (MW)

1205 2nd St. (m)
Perry, IA 50220
515-465-2691 / Fax: 515-465-4238
Sales: $100,001-$500,000

TIM DeFORD (Owner) & Buys Men's Suits, Tailored Jackets, Tailored Slacks, Raincoats, Big & Tall Sweaters, Sport Shirts, Sportswear, Sweaters, Outer Jackets, Leather Apparel, Casual Slacks, Furnishings, Headwear, Accessories, 8 to 20 Boys' Wear, Store Displays, Fixtures, Supplies

HOWARD CLOTHING (MW)

600 W. Sheridan Ave. (m)
Shenandoah, IA 51601
712-246-2231 / Fax: 712-246-2237

DENNIS HOWARD (Owner) & Buys Men's Sportswear, Furnishings, Accessories, Boys' Wear Size 4 to 7 & 8 to 20

KARLTON'S, INC. (CLO)

515 4th St. (b)
Sioux City, IA 51101
712-255-4040 / Fax: 712-255-4099

KIM KLETSCHKE (Co-Owner) & Buys Men's Overcoats, Suits, Tailored Jackets, Tailored Slacks, Raincoats, Sportswear, Furnishings, Headwear, Young Men's Wear, Leather Apparel, Store Displays, Fixtures, Supplies

KAL KLETSCHKE (Co-Owner) & Buys Sportswear, Furnishings, Headwear, Young Men's Wear, Leather Apparel, Men's Accessories, Formal Wear, Store Displays, Fixtures, Supplies

REHAN'S UNIFORMS, INC. (SP)

2018 S. Saint AubinSt. (m-b)
Sioux City, IA 51106
712-276-1432 / Fax: 712-276-1672
Sales: $100,001-$500,000
Website: www.rehansuniforms.com

GEORGE RAHAN (Owner & Gen. Mgr.) & Buys Men's Uniforms

CINDY COOK (Store Mgr.) & Buys Men's Uniforms

SADOFF'S (MW)

(UP TO DATE STORE, INC.)
3023 Hamilton Blvd. (p)
Sioux City, IA 51104
712-234-7177

LESTER SADOFF (President) & Buys Men's Big & Tall Men's Wear, Sportswear, Dress Shirts, Underwear, Hosiery, Small Leather Goods, Store Displays, Fixtures, Supplies

SHOPPER'S SUPPLY (MW-3)

(Div. of SCHMIDT DISTRIBUTORS, INC.)
2912 Highway Blvd. (p-m)
Spencer, IA 51301
712-262-4583 / Fax: 712-580-4587
Sales: $1 Million-$10 Million
Website: www.weathershield.com

CHUCK SCHMIDT (President)

NANCY KRAMER-Men's Sport Shirts, Jeans, Footwear, Store Displays, Fixtures, Supplies

DEB JESSEN-Men's Sport Shirts, Jeans, Footwear, Store Displays, Fixtures, Supplies

SQUIRE SHOPPE (MW)

421 Grand Ave. (m)
Spencer, IA 51301
712-262-3627 / Fax: 712-262-0150
Sales: $100,001-$500,000

BOB VANDER TUIG (President) & Buys Men's Overcoats, Suits, Tailored Jackets, Tailored Slacks, Raincoats, Sportswear, Sweaters, Sport Shirts, Outer Jackets, Leather Apparel, Casual Slacks, Active Apparel, Dress Shoes, Boys' Wear, Store Displays, Fixtures, Supplies

EVAN'S CLOTHING (CLO)

1708 Hill Ave. (p)
Spirit Lake, IA 51360
712-336-2862

STEPHEN BALM (Owner) & Buys Men's Sportswear, Furnishings, Store Displays, Fixtures, Supplies, Footwear

FIELD'S MENSWEAR, INC. (MW)

106 E. 5th St. (p)
Tipton, IA 52772
563-886-2116

TOM PETITGOUT (President) & Buys Men's Sportswear, Furnishings, Headwear, Accessories, Footwear, Young Men's Wear, Store Displays, Fixtures, Supplies

T & M CLOTHING (CLO)

407 Cedar St. (m-b)
Tipton, IA 52772
563-886-2756 / Fax: 563-886-3056

GEORGE HEIN (Owner) & Buys Men's & Boys' Sportswear, Footwear

REUMAN'S CLOTHING (MW)

536 2nd St. (p)
Traer, IA 50675
319-478-8660
Sales: Under $100,000

MIKE REUMAN (Owner) & Buys Men's Sportswear, Furnishings, Accessories, Footwear

FRONTIER OUTFITTING, INC. (CLO)

3009 100th St.
Urbandale, IA 50322
515-278-5500 / Fax: 515-278-2316
Website: www.frontieroutfitting.com

PAT MARKS (Owner) & Buys Camouflage, Activewear, Outdoor Clothing, Ski Apparel, Footwear

MR. MARION MARKS (President)

CAMERON CLOTHING (CLO)

103 W. 4th St. (m)
Vinton, IA 52349
319-472-2520

KARI RIES (Owner) & Buys Men's Casual Wear, Urban Contemporary

CRAFT - COCHRAN ATHLETICS, INC. (SP)

1111 Ansborough Ave.
Waterloo, IA 50701
319-233-0243 / Fax: 319-233-9407
Sales: $1 Million-$10 Million
Website: www.craftcochran.com

STEVE MILES (Owner) & Buys Active Apparel, Athletics

PALACE CLOTHIERS (MW-2)

203 E. Tower Park Dr. (b)
Waterloo, IA 50701
319-234-7537 / Fax: 319-234-7539
Sales: $1 Million-$10 Million
Website: www.palaceclothiers.com

STEVEN J. VOLZ (President & G.M.M.) & Buys Men's Overcoats, Suits, Tailored Jackets, Big & Tall Men's Wear, Men's Slacks, Raincoats, Sportswear, Furnishings, Robes, Headwear, Accessories, Urban Contemporary, Footwear, Store Displays, Fixtures, Supplies

THE SPORTS CENTER (CLO)

2014 Byron Ave.
Waterloo, IA 50702
319-233-6803 / Fax: 319-233-0646

KEN LOWELL (Ofc. Mgr.) & Buys Activewear

TRI-CITY CLOTHING (MW)

713 Logan Ave. (p-m-b)
Waterloo, IA 50703
319-235-9659 / Fax: 319-235-2805

HARRY CARSON (Owner) & Buys Men's Sportswear, Furnishings, Accessories, Boys' Size 4 to 7 & 8 to 20, Footwear

SIECH'S BIG & TALL, INC. (MW)

824 La Porte Rd.
Waterlooo, IA 50702
319-235-6101 / Fax: 319-235-9901

CHRISTOPHER SIECH (Owner) & Buys Big & Tall Men's Wear, Furnishings, Headwear, Accessories, Store Displays, Fixtures, Supplies

IOWA - West Burlington

TURLEY'S (MW)

Westland Mall (m)
West Burlington, IA 52655
319-754-7766 / Fax: 319-754-4351

LARRY TURLEY (Owner) & Buys Men's Sportswear, Furnishings, Accessories, Leather Apparel, Store Displays, Fixtures, Supplies

SPORT ABOUT (SP)

1551 Valley West Dr.
West Des Moines, IA 50266
515-224-2344 / Fax: 515-457-1241

TIM CANNEY (Owner) & Buys Activewear, Athletic Footwear, Licensed Apparel

COUNTRY OUTLET (CLO)

1668 Hwy. 61 (m)
P.O. Box 204
Wever, IA 52658
319-372-1239 / Fax: 319-372-2892
Sales: $500,001-$1 Million

KATHY MABEUS (Owner) & Buys Men's Casualwear, Men's Outerwear

KANSAS - Arkansas City

JAN'S SPORT SHACK (CLO)
202 S. Summit Rd. (m-b)
Arkansas City, KS 67005
620-442-7425 / Fax: 620-442-7428
Sales: $500,001-$1 Million
JAN NITTLER (Owner) & Buys Men's & Boys' Sport Shirts, Active Apparel, Footwear, Store Displays, Fixtures, Supplies

GECHTER'S READY TO WEAR (CLO)
P.O. Box 576 (p)
103 S. Main St.
Cimarron, KS 67835
620-855-2269 / Fax: 620-855-3140
Sales: $100,001-$500,000
NORMA GECHTER (Co-Owner) & Buys Boys' Wear From 8 to 18, Urban Contemporary, Men's T-shirts, Jeans, Hosiery, Underwear, Store Displays, Fixtures and Supplies
JEANE ROHRBAUGH (Co-Owner) & Buys Boys' Wear From 8 to 18, Urban Contemporary, Men's T-shirts, Jeans, Hosiery, Underwear, Store Displays, Fixtures and Supplies

DREILINGS DEPARTMENT STORE (DEPT)
117 W. 6th (p-m-b)
Concordia, KS 66901
785-243-1121
Sales: $100,001-$500,000
GARY CASPERS (Owner) & Buys Men's Sportswear, Furnishings, Headwear, Accessories, Footwear, Western Wear, Store Displays, Fixtures, Supplies

JIM BELL & SON, INC. (MW)
P.O. Box D (p)
322 Broadway
Cottonwood Falls, KS 66845
620-273-6381 / Fax: 620-273-6125
Sales: $100,001-$500,000
BILL HAW (President)
DAVID KIRK (Mgr.) & Buys Men's Overcoats, Suits, Tailored Jackets, Tailored Slacks, Raincoats, Sportswear, Sweaters, Sport Shirts, Outer Jackets, Casual Slacks, Outdoor Wear, Furnishings, Headwear, Accessories, Boys' Wear, Footwear, Store Displays, Fixtures, Supplies

LASATER'S BY ROBIN (MW)
113 W. Central (p-m)
El Dorado, KS 67042
316-321-3280
Sales: $100,001-$500,000
ROBIN FORPAHL (Owner) & Buys Men's Sweaters, Sport Shirts, Outer Jackets, Casual Slacks, Knitwear, Swimwear, Outerwear, Store Displays, Fixtures, Supplies

POLZIN ENTERPRISES (MW)
(OUTFITTERS)
615 Commercial (m)
Emporia, KS 66801
620-342-2646
DIRK POLZIN (Owner) & Buys Men's Wear, Furnishings, Outerwear, Store Displays, Fixtures, Supplies

SHERAR WILLIAMS (CLO)
204 N. Main St. (p-m)
Eureka, KS 67045
620-583-6881
Sales: $500,001-$1 Million
PHYLLIS MILNER (Owner) & Buys Men's Sportswear, Furnishings, Accessories, 4 to 7 Boys' Wear, Store Displays, Fixtures, Supplies

CRAZY HOUSE (WW-2)
Rt. 1 (m-b)
Garden City, KS 67846
620-275-1417 / Fax: 620-275-8417
Sales: $500,001-$1 Million
Website: www.crazyhouse.com
GREG SHAW (Co-Owner) & Buys Men's & Boys' Western Wear, Outer Wear, Overcoats, Jackets, Sweaters, Jeans, Overalls, Jewelry, Boots, Store Displays, Fixtures, Supplies
BRIAN SHAW (Co-Owner) & Buys Men's & Boys' Western Wear, Outer Wear, Overcoats, Jackets, Sweaters, Jeans, Overalls, Jewelry, Boots, Store Displays, Fixtures, Supplies

FINLEY'S (MW)
(DARAT CORP.)
325 N. Main St. (m-b)
Garden City, KS 67846
620-276-3001
Sales: $100,001-$500,000
BOB FINLEY (Owner) & Buys Men's Sportswear, Furnishings, Accessories, Store Displays, Fixtures, Supplies

KEP'S (MW)
112 Grant St. (m)
Garden City, KS 67846
620-275-7687
Sales: $100,001-$500,000
KENDALL KEPLEY (Owner) & Buys Men's Overcoats, Suits, Tailored Slacks, Sportswear, Furnishings, Accessories, Big & Tall Men's Wear, Store Displays, Fixtures, Supplies

SQUIRE'S MEN'S & WOMEN'S WEAR (CLO)
304 N. Main St. (m-b)
Garden City, KS 67846
620-276-3701
Sales: $100,001-$500,000
KEN RAUHUT (Owner) & Buys Men's Sportswear, Furnishings, Accessories, Store Displays, Fixtures, Supplies

ATEN'S DEPARTMENT STORE (DEPT-2)
1103 Main (p-m)
Goodland, KS 67735
785-899-7101
Sales: $500,000-$1 Million
WAYNE ATEN (Owner) & Buys Men's Overcoats, Suits, Tailored Jackets, Tailored Slacks, Sportswear, Furnishings, Headwear, Belts, Small Leather Goods, Fragrances, Big & Tall Men's Wear, Young Men's & Boys' Wear, Store Displays, Fixtures, Supplies

MR. JIM'S HIS SHOP, INC. (MW)
1112 Main St. (p)
Goodland, KS 67735
785-899-5166 / Fax: 785-899-6278
JIM LUNSWAY (Owner) & Buys Men's Sportswear, Furnishings, Accessories, Footwear, Store Displays, Fixtures, Supplies

BRENTWOOD FOR MEN & WOMEN (CLO)
1523 Main St. (m)
Great Bend, KS 67530
620-792-3656 / Fax: 620-792-3658
Sales: $100,001-$500,000
MARK MINGENBACK (Co-Owner) & Buys Men's Sportswear, Furnishings, Accessories, Dress Shoes, Store Displays, Fixtures, Supplies
LESLIE MINGENBACK (Co-Owner) & Buys Men's Sportswear, Furnishings, Accessories, Dress Shoes, Store Displays, Fixtures, Supplies

LONG'S OF HUTCHINSON (CLO)
P.O. Box 2167 (m-b)
110 N. Main St.
Hutchinson, KS 67504
620-663-1561
WILLIAM D. LONG (President) & Buys Men's, Young Men's & Boys' Wear, Footwear, Urban Contemporary, Store Displays, Fixtures, Supplies

MAIN STREET MENSWEAR (MW & MO & OL)
115 N. Main St. (m-b)
Hutchinson, KS 67501
620-665-5221 / Fax: 620-665-5379
Sales: $100,001-$500,000
BILL LONG (Co-Owner) & Buys Men's Sportswear, Furnishings, Accessories, Store Displays, Fixtures, Supplies
J.R. LONG (Co-Owner) & Buys Men's Sportswear, Furnishings, Accessories, Store Displays, Fixtures, Supplies

McGINTY - WHITWORTH (CLO-2)
101 E. Madison Ave. (m-b)
Iola, KS 66749
620-365-3271 / Fax: 620-365-2702
JERRY WHITWORTH (Owner) & Buys Men's Sportswear, Furnishings, Accessories, Men's Big & Tall Wear, Young Men's Wear, Store Displays, Fixtures, Supplies

KANSAS - Junction City

TOM'S MENSWEAR (MW)
625 N. Washington St. (p)
Junction City, KS 66441
785-238-2024
Sales: $100,001-$500,000
TOM GOUDEY (Owner) & Buys Men's & Young Men's Sportswear, Furnishings, Accessories, Footwear, Store Displays, Fixtures, Supplies
MIKE GOUDEY (Mgr.) & Buys Men's & Young Men's Sportswear, Furnishings, Accessories, Footwear, Young Men's Size 36 & Up, Store Displays, Fixtures, Supplies

ANDERSON'S FORMAL WEAR (MW-30)
1401 Fairfax Trafficway, Bldg. C
Kansas City, KS 66115
913-321-7596 / Fax: 800-827-6161
Website: www.andersonsformalwear.com
Retail Locations: MN, KS, TX
DENNIS GERBER (Area Mgr.) & Buys Men's Formal Wear, Casual Shoes, Young Men's Formal Wear, Young Men's Footwear, Boys' Formal Wear, Boys' Footwear, Store Displays, Fixtures, Supplies

NIGRO'S WESTERN STORE (WW-2)
3320 Merriam Ln. (m-b)
Kansas City, KS 66106
913-262-7600 / Fax: 913-262-8066
Sales: $1 Million-$10 Million
TONY NIGRO (Owner) & Buys Men's Tailored Slacks, Sportswear, Dress Shirts, Accessories, Boys' Sportswear, Furnishings, Accessories, Urban Contemporary, Store Displays, Fixtures, Supplies

HOBBS (MW)
700 Massachusetts St.
Lawrence, KS 66044
785-331-4622 / Fax: 785-331-0512
MARK SWANSON-Men's Wear, Sportswear, Accessories, Footwear

JAYHAWK SPIRIT (SG-2)
935 Massachusetts St.
Lawrence, KS 66044
785-749-5194 / Fax: 785-749-5864
Website: www.jayhawkspirit.com
TOM WILKERSON (Owner) (@ 785-749-5858) & Buys Men's, Young Men's & Boys' Sportswear, Active Apparel, Store Displays, Fixtures, Supplies

K.U. BOOKSTORES (SP-2 & MO & OL)
University of Kansas
Kansas Union
Lawrence, KS 66045
785-864-4640 / Fax: 785-864-5264
Sales: $1 Million-$10 Million
Website: www.jayhawks.com
TIM NORRIS (Mgr.-Bookstore)
MARK TROMPETER-Athletic Apparel, Licensed Apparel, Bowling, Billiards

WEAVER'S, INC. (DEPT)
901 Massachusetts St. (m)
Lawrence, KS 66044
785-843-6360 / Fax: 785-843-6386
Sales: $1 Million-$10 Million
JOE FLANNERY (President & G.M.M.)
EARL REINEMAN (V.P.-Mdsg.) & Buys Men's Overcoats, Suits, Tailored Jackets, Tailored Slacks, Raincoats, Sportswear, Sweaters, Sport Shirts, Outer Jackets, Leather Apparel, Casual Slacks, Active Apparel, Furnishings, Dress Shirts, Ties, Robes, Underwear, Hosiery, Gloves, Headwear, Accessories, Belts, Jewelry, Small Leathers, Fragrances, Store Displays, Fixtures, Supplies

RUSELL - HAMPTON CO. (CLO & MO)
15440 W. 109th St. (m-b)
Lenexa, KS 66219
913-254-0500 / Fax: 913-559-3535
Sales: $1 Million-$10 Million
Website: www.ruh.com
ROBERT C. LOWE (President & Dir.-Opers.)
BRADLEY J. LOWE (V.P.)
TOM HANSEN (Treas.)
JEANNIE McCLUSKEY (Mgr.-Fin. & Acct.)
KATHY LOWE (Mgr.-HR & Info. Sys.)
LAUREN HUTSON-Boys' Apparel, Men's Apparel

STEVE'S SHOES, INC. (FW-74)
(SOLE OUTDOORS)
11333 Strang Line Rd. (m)
Lenexa, KS 66215
913-469-5535 / Fax: 913-469-5718
Retail Locations: KS, MO, TX, RI, TN, MI, WI, SD, IL, UT, AZ, NM, NV, WA
MIKE YEAGER (President)
LEN MORIZZO-Men's Dress Shoes, Casual Shoes, Athletic Footwear, Slippers
KENT KORSTAD-Boys' Dress Shoes, Casual Shoes, Athletic Footwear, Slippers, Hosiery, Belts, Accessories
JOHN PLANTENBERG (Real Estate Contact) & Buys Store Displays, Fixtures, Supplies

FINCHER'S FINDINGS (MW)
P.O. Box 289, Industrial Park (m)
Medicine Lodge, KS 67104
620-886-5952 / Fax: 620-886-3035
RON FINCHER (Owner) & Buys Licensed Men's Sportswear, Store Displays, Fixtures, Supplies, Screen printing T-shirts, Jackets, Headwear

HALLS CLOTHING (MW)
106 S. State (p)
Norton, KS 67654
785-877-2424
Sales: $100,001-$500,000
STEVE STRECK (Owner) & Buys All Men's, Young Men's & Boys' Wear, Footwear, Store Displays, Fixtures, Supplies

TOWN & COUNTRY (DEPT-2)
(ORSCHELN CORP.)
P.O. Box 697 (p)
2008 Princeton Rd.
Ottawa, KS 66067
785-242-3133 / Fax: 785-242-3525
REX CUMMINGS (Mgr.) & Buys Men's Jeans, Leather Apparel, Footwear, Outerwear, Accessories, Store Displays, Fixtures, Supplies

PETER CLOTHIERS (CLO)
7100 College Blvd. (m-b)
Overland Park, KS 66210
913-345-8700 / Fax: 913-345-0154
PETER ARVAN (Owner) & Buys Store Displays, Fixtures, Supplies
SPIRO ARVANITAKIS-Men's Sportswear, Furnishings, Accessories, Swimwear, Big & Tall Men's Wear

SWIM QUIK (MW)
7920 Santa Fe Dr. (m)
Overland Park, KS 66204
913-649-8456 / Fax: 913-381-7833
FRANCES WALTERS (Owner) & Buys Men's, Young Men's & Boys' Active Apparel, Store Displays, Fixtures, Supplies

SWIMWEAR SOLUTIONS, INC. (SP)
5053 W. 119th St.
Overland Park, KS 66209
913-345-1243 / Fax: 913-345-0997
LAUREL JONES (Owner) & Buys Accessories, Footwear, Hats, Swimwear, Resortwear, Men's Apparel

JOCK'S NITCH, INC. (CLO-6)
523 N. Broadway St. (m-b)
Pittsburg, KS 66762
620-231-9410 / Fax: 620-231-3514
Sales: $1 Million-$10 Million
Website: www.jocksnitch.com
PHIL MINTON (President & Dir.-Mktg. & Real Estate)
CATHY MINTON (Treas. & Mgr.-Fin.)
JOAN MINTON (Dir.-Info. Sys.) & Buys Boys' Apparel, Boys' Footwear, Men's Footwear, Men's Apparel, Men's Accessories, Men's Sportswear

SWISHER ENTERPRISES (WW)
E. Hwy. 54 (m)
Pratt, KS 67124
316-672-3641
HOWARD SWISHER (Owner) & Buys Men's Suits, Outerwear, Western Wear, Footwear, Boots, Headwear, Belts, Store Displays, Fixtures, Supplies

KANSAS - Salina

JOSEPH P. ROTH & SONS (MW)

1829 S. Ohio Ave. (b)
Salina, KS 67401
(DLS Outfitters)
785-825-8238 / Fax: 785-825-1915
Sales: $1 Million-$10 Million

CHARLES B. ROTH (President) & Buys Men's Overcoats, Suits, Tailored Jackets, Tailored Slacks, Raincoats, Sportswear, Sweaters, Furnishings, Sport Shirts, Outer Jackets, Accessories, Footwear, Store Displays, Fixtures, Supplies

FASHIONS UNLIMITED (CLO & SP)

503 Main St. (p)
Seneca, KS 66538
785-336-3655

SHARON ENNEKING (Owner) & Buys Men's Overcoats, Suits, Tailored Jackets, Tailored Slacks, Sport Coats, Sweaters, Sport Shirts, Outer Jackets, Casual Slacks, Dress Shirts, Underwear, Hosiery, Accessories, Young Men's Wear, Store Displays, Fixtures, Supplies

SPEARVILLE MERCANTILE CO. (GM)

P.O. Box 186 (p)
202 Main St.
Spearville, KS 67876
316-385-2311 / Fax: 316-385-2311

STEVE KNOEBER (Co-Owner) & Buys Men's & Boys' Jeans, Tops, Underwear, Hosiery, Sleepwear

JULIE KNOEBER (Co-Owner) & Buys Men's & Boys' Jeans, Tops, Underwear, Hosiery, Sleepwear, Store Displays, Fixtures and Supplies

THE PERUVIAN CONNECTION LTD. (MO-3)

Canaan Farm, Box 990 (b)
Tonganoxie, KS 66086
800-255-6429 / Fax: 913-845-2460
Website: www.peruvianconnection.com

ANNIE HURLBUT (Owner) & Buys Men's Imported Sweaters

PAYLESS SHOE SOURCE, INC. (FW-4964 & OL)

(PARADE OF SHOES)
P.O. Box 1189 (bud-p)
3231 SE 6th Ave.
Topeka, KS 66607
785-354-9026 / Fax: 785-368-7519
Sales: Over $1 Billion
Website: www.payless.com
Retail Locations: AZ, AK, AZ, AR, CA, CO, CT, DE, DC, FL, GA, HI, ID, IL, IN, IA, KS, KY, LA, ME, MD, MA, MI, MN, MS, MO, MT, NE, NV, NH, NJ, NM, NY, NC, ND, OH, OK, OR, PA, PR, RI, SC, SD, TN, TX, UT, VT, VA, WA, WV, WI, WY, Canada

KEN C. HICKS (President)

STEVEN J. DOUGLASS (C.E.O.)

DUANE L. CANTRELL (Exec. V.P.-Opers.)

STEVE GISH (Real Estate Contact) (@ 785-233-5171, Ext.: 7860)

MARY WEAVER (G.M.M.-Footwear) & Buys Men's Footwear

JEFFREY W. WAGNER (G.M.M.-Footwear) & Buys Boys' Footwear

BRIAN MCCALL-Watches, Men's Accessories, Hosiery, Leather Goods, Boys' Apparel

SPENCER'S MENSWEAR BIG & TALL (MW)

3300 S. Topeka Blvd., #2
Topeka, KS 66611
785-267-3104

ROSS SPENCER (Owner) & Buys Men's Sportswear, Furnishings, Accessories, Footwear, Store Displays, Fixtures, Supplies

SWAN'S FORMAL WEAR, INC. (SP-2)

2010 Ashworth Pl. SW (m-b)
P.O. Box 67179
Topeka, KS 66604
785-272-2272 / Fax: 785-272-4334
Sales: $1 Million-$10 Million

JOHN B. SWAN (President) & Buys Boys' Apparel, Boys' Footwear, Men's Footwear, Men's Apparel, Men's Formalwear, Men's Accessories, Men's Hosiery, Men's Suits

SHARON SWAN (Treas.) & Buys Boys' Apparel, Boys' Footwear, Men's Footwear, Men's Apparel, Men's Formalwear, Men's Accessories, Men's Hosiery, Men's Suits

GRAY & ROSEL (CLO)

111 N. Main (m)
Ulysses, KS 67880
620-356-1410 / Fax: 620-356-1465

MAY ROSEL (Owner) & Buys Men's & Boys' Wear, Footwear, Urban Contemporary, Store Displays, Fixtures, Supplies

BRICK'S (MW)

7732 E. Central (b)
Wichita, KS 67206
316-681-0361 / Fax: 316-681-0683
Sales: $1 Million-$10 Million

RUSSELL K. GORDON (President & G.M.M.) & Buys Men's Overcoats, Suits, Tailored Jackets, Tailored Slacks, Raincoats, Sportswear, Sweaters, Sport Shirts, Outer Jackets, Casual Slacks, Furnishings, Headwear, Accessories, Big & Tall Men's Wear, Footwear, Store Displays, Fixtures, Supplies

DANDALES WESTERN STORE (WW)

10929 E. Kellogg (m-b)
Wichita, KS 67207
316-683-8231 / Fax: 316-683-1761
Sales: $500,001-$1 Million

PAUL TREADWELL (Co-Owner)

VIRGINIA TREADWELL (Co-Owner) & Buys Men's Men's Big & Tall Wear, Men's Western Wear, Furnishings, Accessories, Young Men's Wear, Boys' Wear, Boots, Store Displays, Fixtures, Supplies

GENTRY LTD. (MW)

314 N. Rock Rd. (b)
Wichita, KS 67206
316-686-7821 / Fax: 316-686-2829
Sales: $1 Million-$10 Million

BRITT FULMER (Owner) & Buys Men's Robes, Fragrances, Underwear, Overcoats, Suits, Tailored Slacks, Raincoats, Tailored Jackets, Sweaters, Sport Shirts, Outer Jackets, Leather Apparel, Casual Slacks, Active Apparel, Dress Shirts, Ties, Robes, Underwear, Hosiery, Gloves, Headwear, Bel

JOHNSTON'S CLOTHIERS (MW & OL)

808 S. Hillside (m-b)
Wichita, KS 67211
316-682-1000 / Fax: 316-683-7308
Sales: $100,001-$500,000
Website: www.johnstonsonline.com

J.V. JOHNSTON (President & Co-Owner) & Buys Overcoats, Tailored Slacks, Raincoats, Suits, Tailored Jackets, Store Displays, Fixtures, Supplies, Casual Slacks

KEVIN EDMUNDSON (Co-Owner & G.M.M.) & Buys Sport Shirts, Outer Jackets, Leather Apparel, Dress Shirts, Ties, Robes, Active Apparel, Furnishings, Accessories, Big & Tall Wear, Sweaters

GARY BERNHARD-Underwear, Hosiery, Footwear

McPHAIL CLOTHIERS (MW)

7348 W. 21st St. North, #11
Wichita, KS 67205
316-729-1999 / Fax: 316-729-9040

MARK NORDYKE (Owner) & Buys Men's Casual Slacks, Furnishings, Accessories, Footwear

SHEPLER'S (WW-21 & OL & CAT)

6501 W. Kellogg Dr. (p-m)
Wichita, KS 67209
316-946-3838 / Fax: 316-946-3729
Sales: $100 Million-$500 Million
Website: www.sheplers.com
Retail Locations: AZ, CO, ID, KS, MO, NV, OK, TX, UT

MIKE ANOP (President & Real Estate Contact)
TOM TONGUE (Sr. V.P.)
BRENDA SCHAWE (G.M.M.)
JEFF PERICAN-Men's Jeans, Unbranded, Men's Dress Shirts, Men's Private Label Jeans
MIKE BURCHETT-Men's Casual Slacks, Dress Slacks, Outerwear, Dress Shirts
MARYANNE BRUGGEMAN-Men's Ties
SHEILA HUDSON-Men's Headwear, Accessories
JEFF PEARCE-Footwear (Machine Made)
TOM POTTER-Footwear (Hand Made)
DON STOUT (Displays Coord.) & Buys Store Displays, Fixtures

NOTE-Store Supplies Are Bought Individually at Each Location.

KENTUCKY - Ashland

AMERICAN APPAREL SHOPS, INC. (CLO)
(STARS & STRIPES CLOTHIERS)
115 6th St. (m-b)
P.O. Box 2496
Ashland, KY 41101
606-324-4848 / Fax: 606-326-0279
Sales: $1 Million-$10 Million
BRENT BECKETT (President & Mdse. Mgr.)
LINDA PRICE (G.M.M.) & Buys Boys' Apparel, Boys' Footwear, Men's Footwear, Leather Goods, Apparel, Big & Tall, Casualwear, Denim Apparel, Formalwear, Men's Accessories, Hosiery, Outerwear, Sleepwear, Sportswear, Suits, Swimwear, Underwear
DANNY CURTIS-Men's Footwear, Leather Goods, Men's Apparel, Mens's Big & Tall, Men's Casualwear, Denim Apparel, Formalwear, Accessories, Hosiery, Outerwear, Sleepwear, Sportswear, Suits, Swimwear, Underwear

ARMY & NAVY (AN)
236 16th St. (bud-p-m)
Ashland, KY 41101
606-324-0250
Sales: $100,001-$500,000
RICHARD DAMRON (Owner) & Buys Men's Work Clothing, Military Clothing, Furnishings, Undewear, Hosiery, Gloves, Belts, Headwear, Camouflage, Footwear, Store Displays, Fixtures, Supplies

HIS & HER SHOP (CLO)
2036 29th St. (p-m)
Ashland, KY 41101
606-324-7412
Sales: $100,001-$500,000
JOHN STAMBAUGH (Owner) & Buys Sportswear, Furnishings, Accessories, Store Displays, Fixtures and Supplies

STARS AND STRIPES CLOTHIERS (DEPT)
(AMERICAN APPAREL SHOPS, INC.)
P.O. Box 2496 (m-b)
2580 Winchester Ave.
Ashland, KY 41101
606-324-4848 / Fax: 606-326-0279
Sales: $1 Million-$10 Million
TOM WOLF (Owner)
DAN CURTIS (V.P.) & Buys Men's Overcoats, Suits, Tailored Jackets, Tailored Slacks, Raincoats, Sweaters, Sport Shirts, Outer Jackets, Leather Apparel, Casual Slacks, Active Apparel, Ties, Dress Shirts, Jewelry, Hosiery, Gloves, Robes, Underwear, Belts, Big & Tall Men's Wear, Young Men's Wear

ALL SWEATS (SP)
417 Knox St.
Barbourville, KY 40906
606-546-2195
Sales: $100,001-$500,000
CHARLES HILL (Owner) & Buys Apparel, Custom Apparel

RHODIE'S MEN'S SHOPPE (MW)
103 W. Flaget (m-b)
Bardstown, KY 40004
502-348-6456
Sales: $100,001-$500,000
RHODIE WHELER (Owner) & Buys Men's Sportswear, Furnishings & Accessories, Store Displays, Fixtures, Supplies

SPALDING & SONS, INC. (CLO)
122 N. 3rd St. (m-b)
Bardstown, KY 40004
502-348-3818
Sales: $100,001-$500,000
HAYDON SPALDING (Owner) & Buys Men's & Young Men's Wear, Boys' Wear

CONNECTIONS BIG & TALL CLOTHING (MW)
25806 US Hwy. 119 North
Belfry, KY 41514
304-235-3440
DAVID HATFIELD (Owner) & Buys Men's Wear, Men's Big & Tall, Accessories, Furnishings

TUCKER'S GATEWAY SHOP-O-RAMA (DEPT)
P.O. Box 937 (p-m)
112 US Hwy. 68 East
Benton, KY 42025
270-527-8361 / Fax: 270-527-5656
Sales: $100,001-$500,000
TERRY TUCKER (Owner) & Buys Men's & Boys' Sportswear, Furnishings, Accessories, Footwear, Store Displays, Fixtures, Supplies

GOLDEN-FARLEY, INC. (MW-2)
436 E. Main St. (m-b)
Bowling Green, KY 42101
270-842-6371 / Fax: 270-842-6372
Sales: $1 Million-$10 Million
SAM HALL (President) & Buys Men's Sportswear, Furnishings, Accessories, Young Men's Wear, Footwear, Store Displays, Fixtures, Supplies

JIM & GIL'S MEN'S SHOP, INC. (MW)
(JIM & GIL'S BIG & TALL)
1254 31 West Bypass (p)
Bowling Green, KY 42101
270-842-0827
Sales: $100,001-$500,000
JIM VOGLE (Co-Owner)
GIL COWLES (Co-Owner) & Buys Footwear, Store Displays, Fixtures, Supplies, Men's Formal Wear, Sportswear, Men's Big & Tall Wear, Furnishings, Accessories
MICHELLE COWLES-Men's Formal Wear, Sportswear, Men's Big & Tall Wear, Furnishings, Accessories

WESTERN KENTUCKY UNIVERSITY BOOKSTORE (SP)
1 Big Red Way
Bowling Green, KY 42101
270-745-2466 / Fax: 270-745-5336
Sales: $100,001-$500,000
GARY RANSDELL (President) & Buys Jackets, Hosiery, Licensed Apparel

MITCHELL'S MENSWEAR, INC. (MW)
221 E. Main St. (m)
Campbellsville, KY 42718
270-465-4461
Sales: $100,001-$500,000
LAURA WILDS (Co-Owner) & Buys Men's Sportswear, Urban Contemporary, Furnishings & Accessories, Footwear, Store Displays, Fixtures, Supplies

THE WALTER T. KELLEY CO., INC. (CLO & MO)
P.O. Box 240 (m-b)
3107 Elizabethtown Rd.
Clarkson, KY 42726
270-242-2012 / Fax: 270-242-4801
Sales: $1 Million-$10 Million
SARAH MANION (President & Gen. Mgr.)
EARL KING (V.P. & Treas.)
MAXINE EDWARDS-Leather Goods, Men's Apparel, Men's Accessories

FRANK'S MEN'S SHOP, INC. (MW)
32 W. Pike St. (m)
Covington, KY 41011
859-431-0667
Sales: Under $100,000
ED FRANK (Co-Owner) & Buys Men's Sportswear, Urban Contemporary, Furnishings & Accessories, Store Displays, Fixtures, Supplies
SID FRANK (Co-Owner) & Buys Men's Sportswear, Furnishings & Accessories, Store Displays, Fixtures, Supplies

M. GOLDBERG, INC. (MW)
138 S. Main St. (m)
Cynthiana, KY 41031
859-234-1833
Sales: $100,001-$500,000
JAMES A. BROWN (Owner)
SHIRLENE ASBURY-Men's Sportswear, Furnishings, Accessories, Footwear, Store Displays, Fixtures, Supplies

MURRELL'S MENSWEAR (MW)
120 Stockton (p-m)
P.O. Box 120
Edmonton, KY 42129
270-432-2585 / Fax: 270-432-2585
Sales: $100,001-$500,000
DIANE HARRIS (Mgr.) & Buys Men's Wear, Sportswear, Furnishings, Accessories, Young Men's Wear, Urban Contemporary, Boys' Wear, Store Displays, Fixtures and Supplies

RIDER'S, INC. (MW)
136 W. Dixie (m)
Elizabethtown, KY 42701
270-765-2233
AL RIDER (Owner) & Buys Men's Sportswear, Furnishings & Accessories, Headwear, Footwear, Store Displays, Fixtures, Supplies

MALLORY'S (CLO)
70 Public Sq. (m-b)
P.O. Box 576
Elkton, KY 42220
270-265-5352
Sales: $500,001-$1 Million
TERRY MALLORY (Co-Owner) & Buys Men's Footwear, Leather Goods, Men's Apparel, Mens's Big & Tall, Men's Casualwear, Men's Denim Apparel, Men's Accessories, Men's Hosiery, Men's Outerwear, Men's Sleepwear, Men's Sportswear, Men's Suits, Men's Underwear
JANE MALLORY (Co-Owner) & Buys Men's Footwear, Leather Goods, Men's Apparel, Mens's Big & Tall, Men's Casualwear, Men's Denim Apparel, Men's Accessories, Men's Hosiery, Men's Outerwear, Men's Sleepwear, Men's Sportswear, Men's Suits, Men's Underwear
SARAH SEAY (G.M.M.) & Buys Men's Footwear, Leather Goods, Men's Apparel, Mens's Big & Tall, Men's Casualwear, Men's Denim Apparel, Men's Accessories, Men's Hosiery, Men's Outerwear, Men's Sleepwear, Men's Sportswear, Men's Suits, Men's Underwear

RANDY'S CLOTHING & FOOTWEAR (CLO & FW)
205 W. Shelby (m)
Falmouth, KY 41040
859-654-8271
Sales: $100,001-$500,000
RANDY BASTIN (Owner) & Buys Men's Sportswear, Furnishings, Accessories, Footwear, Store Displays

MITCHELL'S CLOTHING (MW)
317 W. Broadway (m)
Frankfort, KY 40601
502-227-7758
Sales: $100,001-$500,000
CORINE CARPENTER (Owner)
PHILLIP KRING-Men's Sportswear, Furnishings, Belts, Leather Apparel, Men's Western Apparel, Work Clothes, Footwear, Young Men's Wear, Store Displays

SUIT CITY (MW)
1134 Old US 127 South (p)
Frankfort, KY 40601
502-223-5549
Sales: $100,001-$500,000
JACK BLACK (Owner) & Buys Men's Overcoats, Suits, Tailored Jackets, Tailored Slacks, Raincoats, Sweaters, Sport Shirts, Outer Jackets, Casual Slacks, Active Apparel, Furnishings, Headwear, Accessories, Leather Apparel, Store Displays

HOMESTEAD OF FRANKLIN, INC. (DEPT)
1075 S. Main St. (p)
Franklin, KY 42134
270-586-7111 / Fax: 270-586-5242
Sales: $100,001-$500,000
LOWELL COLLINS (President)
ANDY GREY (Mgr.) & Buys Men's & Boys' Jeans, Shirts, Furnishings, Accessories, Sportswear, Footwear, Store Displays, Fixtures, Supplies
ROBERT BRIGGS-Men's & Boys' Jeans, Shirts, Furnishings, Accessories, Sportswear, Footwear, Store Displays, Fixtures, Supplies

LEADER STORE (CLO)
410 Lake St. (m)
Fulton, KY 42041
270-472-3234 / Fax: 270-472-2112
Sales: $100,001-$500,000
MICHAEL HOMRA (Co-Owner) & Buys Footwear, Store Displays, Fixtures, Supplies

NOFFEL'S DEPARTMENT STORE (DEPT)
420 Lake St. (p)
Fulton, KY 42041
270-472-1182
Sales: Under $100,000
ALEX NOFFEL (Owner) & Buys Men's Sportswear, Furnishings, Accessories, Young Men's & Boys' Wear, Footwear

SCOTT COUNTY SPORTS, INC. (SP)
130 E. Main St.
Georgetown, KY 40324
502-863-3989
Sales: Under $100,000
NORMA GILLESPIE (Owner) & Buys Activewear, Athletic Footwear, Licensed Apparel

RUPERT'S DEPARTMENT STORE, INC. (DEPT)
132 E. Main St. (p-m-b)
Grayson, KY 41143
606-474-5341 / Fax: 606-474-0254
Sales: $500,000-$1 Million
TIMOTHY WILSON (President) & Buys Men's, Young Men's & Boys' Wear, Footwear, Store Displays, Fixtures, Supplies

POWERS & HORTON (MW)
116 S. Main St. (m-b)
Harlan, KY 40831
606-573-2525 / Fax: 606-573-7393
Sales: $500,000-$1 Million
BOYD BROWN (Partner & Mdse. Mgr.) & Buys Men's Overcoats, Suits, Tailored Jackets, Tailored Slacks, Sweaters, Sport Shirts, Outer Jackets, Sport Jackets, Active Apparel, Urban Contemporary, Furnishings, Accessories, Leather Apparel, Store Displays, Fixtures, Supplies

AGGIE SALE SPORT SHOP (SG)
US Hwy. 127 South (m)
Harrodsburg, KY 40330
606-522-3227 / Fax: 606-734-7483
Sales: $100,001-$500,000
BRUCE SPRINGATE (Owner) & Buys Active Apparel, T-shirts, Athletic Hosiery, Athletic Uniforms, Headwear, Store Displays, Fixtures, Supplies

BERNSTEIN'S (MW)
305 1st St. (m)
Henderson, KY 42420
270-826-3405
Sales: $100,001-$500,000
SHIRLEY BERNSTEIN (President)
JERRY LEE BERNSTEIN (G.M.M.) & Buys Men's Suits, Tailored Jackets, Tailored Slacks, Raincoats, Sweaters, Sport Shirts, Outer Jackets, Casual Slacks, Active Apparel, Furnishings, Belts, Small Leather Goods, Store Displays, Fixtures, Supplies

CRADLE 'N' TEEN SHOP (KS)
110 N. Main St. (m-b)
Henderson, KY 42420
270-826-2948 / Fax: 270-826-2350
Sales: $100,001-$500,000
BETTY O'DANIEL (Co-Owner) & Buys Boys' Wear to Size 20, Store Displays, Fixtures, Supplies
JIALENE O'NAN-Boys' Wear to Size 20, Store Displays, Fixtures, Supplies

KENTUCKY - Hopkinsville

ARTHUR - KLEIN (CLO)
110 E. 6th St. (m-b)
Hopkinsville, KY 42240
270-885-5556
Sales: $500,001-$1 Million
KATHERINE ARTHUR (Owner) & Buys Boys' Apparel, Men's Footwear, Men's Apparel, Men's Casualwear, Men's Denim Apparel, Men's Formalwear, Men's Accessories, Men's Hosiery, Men's Outerwear, Men's Sleepwear, Men's Sportswear, Men's Underwear
MACK ARTHUR (Store Mgr.) & Buys Boys' Apparel, Men's Footwear, Men's Apparel, Men's Casualwear, Men's Denim Apparel, Men's Formalwear, Men's Accessories, Men's Hosiery, Men's Outerwear, Men's Sleepwear, Men's Sportswear, Men's Underwear

HONCHELL'S (MW)
1266 Richmond Rd.
Irvine, KY 40336
606-723-7316
Sales: $100,001-$500,000
LARRY HONCHELL (Owner) & Buys Suits, Tailored Jackets, Tailored Slacks, Sportswear, Furnishings, Accessories, Young Men's Wear, Urban Contemporary, Boys' Wear, Store Displays, Fixtures, Supplies

JOHN B. ADAMS STORE, INC. (DEPT)
72 Isom Dr. (p-m)
Isom, KY 41824
606-633-4306
DANA RICHARDSON (Owner) & Buys Men's Casual Wear, Boys' Casual Wear, Furnishings, Accessories, Footwear, Urban Contemporary, Store Displays, Fixtures, Supplies

ROSE BROTHERS (DEPT-2)
P.O. Box 943 (p)
695 Hwy. 15 North
Jackson, KY 41339
606-666-2397 / Fax: 606-666-9842
Sales: $1 Million-$10 Million
Website: www.rosebros.com
DOUG ROSE (President & Co-Owner) & Buys Footwear, Men's Overcoats, Suits, Tailored Jackets, Tailored Slacks, Sportswear, Furnishings, Headwear, Belts, Small Leather Goods, Boys' Clothing, Sportswear, Accessories, Store Displays, Fixtures, Supplies
PHYLLIS ROSE (Co-Owner) & Buys Men's Overcoats, Suits, Tailored Jackets, Tailored Slacks, Sportswear, Furnishings, Headwear, Belts, Small Leather Goods, Boys' Clothing, Sportswear, Accessories, Store Displays, Fixtures, Supplies

DIZZY DAVE'S EAST (CLO)
102 E. Main St. (p-m)
La Grange, KY 40031
502-222-1400
Sales: $100,001-$500,000
PAUL GASSER (Owner) & Buys Men's Sweaters, Sport Shirts, Knit Sport Shirts, Outer Jackets, Casual Slacks, Jeans, Activewear, Underwear, Hosiery, Gloves, Belts, Work Clothes, Hunting Apparel, Footwear, Store Displays

NAPIER BROTHERS' CLOTHING (CLO)
35 Public Sq. (m-b)
Lancaster, KY 40444
859-792-2535
Sales: $100,001-$500,000
LONNIE NAPIER (Co-Owner) & Buys Men's Sportswear, Work Clothes, Furnishings, Accessories, Footwear, Store Displays, Fixtures, Supplies

ALL SPORTS, INC. (SG)
3401 Nicholasville Rd. (m)
Lexington, KY 40503
859-272-8656 / Fax: 859-271-0430
Sales: $1 Million-$10 Million
BLAINE ATKINS (Owner)
MARK MORFORD (Store Mgr.) & Buys Footwear, Headwear
MARK MONTGOMERY-Boys' Apparel, Men's Apparel, Mens's Big & Tall, Men's Casualwear, Men's Hosiery, Men's Sleepwear, Men's Sportswear, Men's Swimwear

BOB MICKLER'S, INC. (MW)
1093 W. High St. (m-b)
P.O. Box 1855
Lexington, KY 40508
859-254-3814 / Fax: 859-254-1889
Sales: $500,001-$1 Million
Website: www.bobmicklers.com
JULIE MICKLER (President) & Buys Men's Footwear, Leather Goods, Men's Big & Tall Apparel, Men's & Boys' Apparel, Men's Casualwear, Men's Denim Apparel, Men's Formalwear, Men's Accessories, Men's Outerwear, Men's Sportswear, Men's Suits
BOB MICKLER (C.E.O.)
JOHN HILER (Store Mgr.) & Buys Men's Footwear, Leather Goods, Men's Big & Tall Apparel, Men's & Boys' Apparel, Men's Casualwear, Men's Denim Apparel, Men's Formalwear, Men's Accessories, Men's Outerwear, Men's Sportswear, Men's Suits

DAWAHARE'S (CLO-26 & OL)
Gardenside Plz.
1845 Alexandria Dr.
Lexington, KY 40504
859-278-0422 / Fax: 859-514-3298
Website: www.dawahares.com
Retail Locations: KY, TN, WV
A.F. DAWAHARE (President)
JOE DAWAHARE (Dir.-Real Estate) (@ 859-514-3299, Ext.: 247)
RICHARD DAWAHARE (D.M.M.-Men's) & Buys Men's Suits
RANDY RAMEY-Men's Activewear, Licensed Apparel
GARY LASZEWSKI (@ 859-514-3232)-Young Men's Activewear, Boys' Activewear, Licensed Apparel

HOWARD & MILLER (MW)
127 N. Broadway (b-h)
Lexington, KY 40507
606-259-3926 / Fax: 606-259-3360
Sales: $100,001-$500,000
JEFF MILLER (Owner) & Buys Men's Wear, Sportswear, Furnishings, Accessories, Store Displays, Fixtures and Supplies

HOWARD - KNIGHT'S TALL & BIG (MW-2 & OL)
2216 Nicklesville Rd. (b)
Lexington, KY 40503
859-278-7005 / Fax: 859-276-1780
Sales: $100,001-$500,000
GEORGE HOWARD (Owner) & Buys Big & Tall Men's Wear, Furnishings, Sportswear, Accessories, Leather Apparel, Store Displays, Fixtures, Supplies

LOCKER ROOM, INC. (SG)
739 Lane Allen Rd. (p-m)
Lexington, KY 40504
859-276-1101 / Fax: 606-276-1112
Sales: $100,001-$500,000
SYLVIA MILBURN (Owner) & Buys Active Apparel, T-shirts, Shorts, Athletic Hosiery, Headwear, Supplies

MAD HATTER (CLO)
152 W. Main St. (p-m-b)
Lexington, KY 40507
859-252-6209
Sales: $100,001-$500,000
NORMAN GROSSMAN (Owner)
TERRY GROSSMAN (Mgr.) & Buys Men's, Boys', Urban Contemporary, Headwear, Store Displays, Fixtures, Supplies

MILL OUTLET (MW-2)
1066 E. New Circle Rd., #3 (bud)
Lexington, KY 40505
859-255-4576 / Fax: 859-281-6816
Sales: $100,001-$500,000
BOB DOLLINS (Co-Owner) & Buys Sportswear, Furnishings, Accessories, Young Men's Wear, Urban Contemporary, Boys' Wear
DAVE CAWOOD (Co-Owner) & Buys Sportswear, Furnishings, Accessories, Young Men's Wear, Urban Contemporary, Boys' Wear

PHILLIP GALL'S OUTDOOR SHOP (MW)
1555 E. New Circle Rd. (m-b)
Lexington, KY 40509
859-266-0469 / Fax: 859-269-5190
Sales: $1 Million-$10 Million
STEVEN GALL (President) & Buys Men's Sweaters, Sport Shirts, Outer Jackets, Casual Slacks, Skiwear, Outdoor Apparel, Leather Apparel, Belts, Young Men's Wear, Boys' Wear, Store Displays, Fixtures, Supplies
JOSH ISRAEL-Footwear

THE SPORTING TRADITION (SG)
410 W. Vine St. (p-m)
Lexington, KY 40507
859-255-8652
Sales: $100,001-$500,000
FRED PFISTER (Owner) & Buys Hunting & Clothing, Sportswear, Small Leather Goods, Outer Jackets, Leather Apparel, Hosiery, Gloves, Headwear, Belts, Store Displays, Fixtures and Supplies

T & T MEN'S FASHIONS (MW)
1509 Russell Cave Rd. (m)
Lexington, KY 40505
859-293-1017
Sales: $100,001-$500,000
SUAD DABIT (Owner) & Buys Men's Sportswear, Urban Contemporary, Furnishings, Accessories, 8 to 20 Boys' Suits, Store Displays, Fixtures, Supplies

WALLACE'S U.K. BOOKSTORE (SP-2)
(UNIVERSITY OF KENTUCKY)
106 Student Center Annex
Lexington, KY 40506
859-257-6304 / Fax: 859-257-5967
Sales: $5 Million-$10 Million
Website: www.ukbookstore.com
CHRIS LAWRANCE (Store Dir.)
LANA NORRIS-Activewear, Licensed Apparel

KING'S DEPARTMENT STORE (DEPT)
Middleburg St. (p-m)
Liberty, KY 42539
606-787-6688 / Fax: 606-787-2220
Sales: $100,001-$500,000
DAVID KING (Co-Owner) & Buys Footwear, Store Displays, Fixtures, Supplies
JERRY KING (Co-Owner) & Buys Men's Sportswear, Furnishings, Boys' Wear, Accessories, Store Displays, Fixtures and Supplies

BOB'S READY TO WEAR, INC. (CLO)
121 N. Main St. (p)
London, KY 40741
606-864-2134
Sales: $1 Million-$10 Million
JACK PARMAN (President) & Buys Big & Tall Men's Wear, Urban Contemporary, Furnishings, Headwear, Boys' Clothing, Store Displays, Fixtures and Supplies
ROBERT JOE PARMAN (Secy. & Treas.) & Buys Big & Tall Men's Wear, Urban Contemporary, Furnishings, Headwear, Boys' Clothing, Store Supplies, Men's Suits, Tailored Jackets, Tailored Slacks, Raincoats, Accessories, Sportswear, Boys' Sportswear, Furnishings, Accessories, Footwear

LOWE'S SPORTING GOODS (SG-2)
901 N. Main St. (m-b)
London, KY 40741
606-864-2207 / Fax: 606-864-2207
Sales: $1 Million-$10 Million
GLENN PROFFITT (Team Sls.) & Buys Boys' Apparel, Boys' Footwear, Men's Footwear, Men's Apparel, Men's Casualwear, Men's Hosiery, Men's Outerwear, Men's Sportswear, Men's Swimwear
ELAINE HELTON-Boys' Apparel, Boys' Footwear, Men's Footwear, Men's Apparel, Men's Casualwear, Men's Hosiery, Men's Outerwear, Men's Sportswear, Men's Swimwear

THE FASHION POST (CLO)
The Hurstbourne Forum
186 N. Hurstbourne Pkwy.
Louisville, KY 40222
502-423-6700 / Fax: 502-423-7217
Sales: $100,001-$500,000
STANLEY BAYERSDORFER (Owner) & Buys Men's Clothing, Suits, Sport Coats, Casual Wear, Sportswear, Furnishings, Accessories, Footwear

FASHION SHOP (SP-12)
11008 Decimal Dr.
Louisville, KY 40299
502-267-5415 / Fax: 502-267-0480
LARRY LEVINE (V.P.) & Buys Swimwear

GINGISS FORMAL WEAR (MW-4)
(SOUTH STANDARD ENTERPRISES)
Oxmoor Mall (bud-p-m-b-h)
Louisville, KY 40222
502-425-3962 / Fax: 502-425-1847
Sales: $100,001-$500,000
CHARLES MALKA (Co-Owner) & Buys Men's, Young Men's & Boys' Formal Wear, Accessories, Footwear, Furnishings
NOTE:-Buying of Store Displays, Fixtures, Supplies Performed at GINGISS FORMAL WEAR, Addison, Il - See Listing.

HUB DEPARTMENT STORE, INC. (DEPT)
1701 W. Market St. (p)
Louisville, KY 40203
502-584-8656 / Fax: 502-585-4440
Sales: $100,001-$500,000
MS. I. YOFFE (Owner) & Buys Footwear
HENRY YOFFE (Treasurer) & Buys Men's Sportswear, Furnishings, Accessories, Young Men's, 7 to 20 Boys' Wear, Store Supplies

KEN COMBS RUNNING STORE (SP)
4137 Shelbyville Rd.
Louisville, KY 40207
502-895-3410 / Fax: 502-895-3469
LARRY HOLT (Owner) & Buys Footwear
JUDY HOUSE (Mgr.) & Buys Running Apparel, Swimwear, Cycling Apparel

L. STRAUSS BIG & TALL MEN'S CLOTHING, INC. (MW & OL)
100 E. Market St. (m)
Louisville, KY 40202
502-582-3737 / Fax: 502-582-3738
Sales: $1 Million-$10 Million
Website: www.lstrauss.com
JOHN L. ORNSTEIN (President & Gen. Mgr.) & Buys Big & Tall Men's Wear, Accessories, Jeans, Underwear, Dress Shirts, T-shirts, Belts, Hosiery, Work Clothes, Furnishings, Store Displays, Fixtures, Supplies

PRESLAR'S WESTERN SHOP, INC. (WW-2)
(GRIZZLY CREEK OUTFITTERS)
4801 Outerloop Rd., #A104 (m)
Louisville, KY 40213
502-969-9019 / Fax: 502-969-8110
Sales: $100,001-$500,000
EDWARD PRESLAR (Owner) & Buys Store Displays, Fixtures, Supplies
DENNIS FOUSHEE (Gen. Mgr.) & Buys Men's Western Clothing, Sportswear, Furnishings, Accessories, Young Men's & Boys' Western Wear, Footwear, Store Displays, Fixtures, Supplies

KENTUCKY - Louisville

QUEST FOR THE OUTDOORS, INC. (CLO)
128 Breckenridge Ln. (m)
Louisville, KY 40207
502-893-5746 / Fax: 502-897-0556
Sales: $100,001-$500,000
DON BURCH (Owner) & Buys Footwear, Store Displays, Fixtures, Supplies
BARBARA BURCH-Men's Active Apparel, Sportswear, Boys' Active Apparel, Footwear

RODES CO. (DEPT-2 & OL)
(LITHGOW IND.)
461 4th Ave. (h)
Louisville, KY 40202
502-584-3112 / Fax: 502-584-8840
Sales: $1 Million-$10 Million
Website: www.rodes.com
LAWRENCE SMITH (Chmn. & C.E.O.)
SCOTT PRICE (V.P.) & Buys Men's Furnishings, Accessories
FRED TEALE (Dir.-Mktg. & Comms.)
JIM FRICKE-Sportswear
OPEN (Visual Dir.) & Buys Store Displays, Fixtures

SAM MEYER'S FORMAL WEAR (MW-11 & MO)
(SAM MEYERS, INC.)
3400 Bashford Ave.
Louisville, KY 40218
502-459-4885 / Fax: 502-473-1129
Sales: $100,001-$500,000
Website: www.sammeyers.com
JIM CORBETT (President)
SAM CORBETT (V.P.) & Buys Men's Formal Wear, Furnishings, Accessories, Footwear, Store Displays, Fixtures, Supplies

SHAHEEN'S (CLO-3)
994 Breakeridge Ln. (m-b)
Louisville, KY 40207
502-899-1550 / Fax: 502-899-5515
Sales: $1 Million-$10 Million
Website: www.shaheens.com
ELI SHAHEEN (Owner) & Buys Men's & Boys' Wear, Store Displays, Fixtures, Supplies

SMITH & LOGSDON, INC. (CLO)
(MARK DOWNS)
645 Bergman St. (bud)
Louisville, KY 40203
502-634-1212 / Fax: 502-634-1386
Sales: $500,000-$1 Million
LARRY VIRGIN (Owner) & Buys Men's Sportswear, Furnishings, Accessories, Headwear, Young Men's, 7 to 20 Boys' Wear, Store Displays, Fixtures, Supplies

YOUNG'S, INC. (CLO)
235 Madison Square Dr. (bud-p-m)
Madisonville, KY 42431
270-821-8861
Sales: $1 Million-$10 Million
WILLIAM H. YOUNG (Chmn. & President & Treas.) & Buys Men's Footwear, Leather Goods, Men's Apparel, Mens's Big & Tall, Men's Formalwear, Men's Accessories, Men's Outerwear, Men's Sportswear, Men's Suits, Men's Swimwear, Men's Uniforms
TRISH NOEL-Men's Footwear, Leather Goods, Men's Apparel, Mens's Big & Tall, Men's Formalwear, Men's Accessories, Men's Outerwear, Men's Sportswear, Men's Suits, Men's Swimwear, Men's Uniforms

MANCHESTER DRY GOODS CO., INC. (DG)
305 Bridge St. (m)
Manchester, KY 40962
606-598-2022
Sales: Under $100,000
MAUDE L. KEITH (President) & Buys Men's Sweaters, Sport Shirts, Outer Jackets, Leather Apparel, Dress Shirts, Robes, Underwear, Hosiery, Gloves, Belts, Store Displays, Fixtures, Supplies

MARION TOT 'N' TEEN (KS)
106 S. Main St. (m-b)
Marion, KY 42064
270-965-3635
Sales: $100,001-$500,000
LENORE DRENNAN (Owner) & Buys Infant to Size 7 Boys' Wear, Store Displays, Fixtures, Supplies

MESSER'S DEPARTMENT STORE (DEPT)
P.O. Box 826 (bud-p-m)
Main St.
Martin, KY 41649
606-285-3104 / Fax: 606-285-9672
TRUMAN MESSER (Owner) & Buys Men's Sportswear, Furnishings, Accessories, Young Men's Wear, Boys' Wear, Footwear, Store Displays, Fixtures, Supplies

BRUCE'S (DEPT)
(ROBERT K. BRUCE)
US 25
8430 Dixie Hwy.
Mason, KY 41054
859-824-4376 / Fax: 859-824-4779
Sales: $100,001-$500,000
SCOTT L. BRUCE (Owner)
BRENDA FORNASH-Men's Sportswear, Boys' Sportswear, Urban Contemporary, Furnishings, Accessories, Headwear, Footwear, Store Displays, Fixtures, Supplies

CASE'S MENSWEAR (MW)
17 E. 2nd St. (b)
Maysville, KY 41056
606-564-6107
Sales: $100,001-$500,000
OMAR CASE (Owner) & Buys Men's Wear, Sportswear, Furnishings, Accessories, Young Men's Wear, Store Displays, Fixtures, Supplies

MARTIN'S DEPARTMENT STORES, INC. (DEPT)
117 E. Main St. (p-m)
Morehead, KY 40351
606-784-4320 / Fax: 606-784-4320
Sales: $1 Million-$10 Million
BUD CORNETT (President)
MARGIE HUNTER-Men's Sportswear, Footwear, Furnishings, Accessories, Headwear, Young Men's Wear, 7 to 20 Boys' Wear, Store Displays, Fixtures, Supplies

THE CORN-AUSTIN CO., INC. (MW)
402 Main St. (m-b)
Murray, KY 42071
270-753-2472 / Fax: 270-753-8642
Sales: $1 Million-$10 Million
HAROLD McREYNOLDS (Owner) & Buys Men's Sportswear, Furnishings, Accessories, Headwear, Young Men's Wear, Footwear, Store Displays, Fixtures, Supplies

DAN'S OF MURRAY LTD. (MW)
1205 Chestnut St., #A (m)
Murray, KY 42071
270-753-0100 / Fax: 270-753-5631
Sales: $100,001-$500,000
DAN FOSTER (Owner) & Buys Men's Sportswear, Furnishings & Accessories, Young Men's Wear, Footwear, Store Displays, Fixtures, Supplies

ALBERT'S MEN'S SHOP (MW)
809 Monmouth St. (p)
Newport, KY 41071
859-261-9508 / Fax: 859-261-6678
Sales: $100,001-$500,000
FRED SCHILLING (Owner) & Buys Men's Uniforms, Store Displays, Fixtures, Supplies

SAUL'S VALUE STORE (MW)
817 Monmouth St. (p)
Newport, KY 41701
859-581-1304
Sales: $100,001-$500,000
MARVIN POLINSKY (Owner) & Buys Men's Raincoats, Tailored Jackets, Tailored Slacks, Sportswear, Furnishings, Small Leather Goods, Big & Tall Men's Wear, Young Men's & Boys' Wear, Footwear, Store Displays, Fixtures, Supplies

KENTUCKY - Nicholasville

LOGAN'S OF NICHOLASVILLE (CLO-2)
(MGM APPAREL, INC.)
114 N. Main St. (m-b)
Nicholasville, KY 40356
859-885-9632 / Fax: 859-255-6954
Sales: $500,001-$1 Million

MOLLY MUSGRAVE (Owner) & Buys Store Displays, Fixtures, Men's Sportswear, Furnishings, Accessories, Young Men's Wear

JUDY GRAHAM (Office Mgr.) & Buys Footwear, Store Supplies

EARLE OF RIVERMONT (MW)
2660 Frederica St. (m-b)
Owensboro, KY 42301
270-684-3111 / Fax: 270-684-4361
Sales: $100,001-$500,000

DAVID EPLING (Owner) & Buys Men's Wear, Sportswear, Furnishings, Accessories, Store Displays, Fixtures and Supplies

LARRY TACKETT'S MEN'S (MW)
145 W. Seminary St. (p-m)
Owenton, KY 40359
502-484-3437
Sales: $100,001-$500,000

LARRY TACKETT (Co-Owner) & Buys Men's Wear, Sportswear, Furnishings, Accessories, Store Displays, Fixtures and Supplies

DORIS TACKETT (Co-Owner) & Buys Men's Wear, Sportswear, Furnishings, Accessories, Store Displays, Fixtures and Supplies

HB & COMPANY (MW)
3128 Broadway (b)
Paducah, KY 42001
270-442-4377 / Fax: 270-444-7010
Sales: $100,001-$500,000

TODD ROSE (President) & Buys Men's Suits, Tailored Jackets, Tailored Slacks, Sportswear, Furnishings, Accessories, Leather Apparel, Footwear, Store Displays, Fixtures, Supplies

MICHELSON JEWELERS, INC. (JWLY-2 & OL)
P.O. Box 2680
1 Executive Blvd., #335
Paducah, KY 42001
270-444-0800 / Fax: 270-444-0806
Sales: $10 Million-$50 Million
Website: www.michelson-jewelers.com

BILL LENTZ (President)

LOUIS MICHELSON (C.E.O.)

OPEN (Sr. V.P.-Mdse.) & Buys Men's Jewelry, Watches

REIDLAND CLOTHING CO. (MW)
(J.T. CARNEAL ENTERPRISES)
5100 Reidland Rd. (p)
Paducah, KY 42003
270-898-6981 / Fax: 270-898-3032
Sales: $100,001-$500,000

J. T. CARNEAL (Owner) & Buys Men's Sportswear, Furnishings, Leather Apparel, Accessories, Big & Tall Men's Wear, Footwear, Store Displays, Fixtures, Supplies

SPIVEY'S, INC. (SP)
2232 Paris Bypass Rd.
Paris, KY 40361
859-987-2625 / Fax: 859-987-2627
Sales: $100,001-$500,000

BARBARA SPIVEY (Owner)

SUE PELFREY-Activewear, Athletic Footwear, Licensed Apparel

ANDERSON'S DEPARTMENT STORE (DEPT)
225 2nd St. (p)
Pikeville, KY 41501
606-437-7319
Sales: $100,001-$500,000

EDGAR ANDERSON (Owner) & Buys Men's Sportswear, Furnishings, Accessories, Headwear, Young Men's Wear, Boys' Wear, Footwear, Store Displays, Fixtures, Supplies

U.S. CAVALRY (AN-5 & MO & OL)
2855 Centennial Ave. (m-b)
Radcliff, KY 40160
270-351-1164 / Fax: 270-352-0266
Sales: $10 Million-$50 Million
Website: www.uscavalry.com

RANDY ACTON (President)

CHERYL HARDY (Dir.-Retail) & Buys Men's Athletic Wear, Outdoor Wear, T-shirts, Shorts, Jeans, Store Displays, Fixtures, Supplies

JEANINE MASON-T-shirts

JETT & HALL, INC. (MW)
200 W. Main St. (m)
Richmond, KY 40475
859-623-1975 / Fax: 859-626-8747
Sales: $100,001-$500,000

PAUL DAVID JETT (President) & Buys Men's Overcoats, Suits, Tailored Jackets, Tailored Slacks, Sweaters, Sport Shirts, Outer Jackets, Casual Slacks, Furnishings, Headwear, Accessories, Jeans, Leather Apparel, Footwear, Store Displays, Fixtures, Supplies

STEPPIN' OUT (WW-1)
729 Parkway Dr. (m)
Salyersville, KY 41465
606-349-6424 / Fax: 606-349-6424
Sales: $1 Million-$10 Million

JANICE CASTLE (Owner) & Buys Men's Sportswear, Shorts, T-shirts, Belts, Jewelry, Small Leather Goods, Store Displays, Fixtures, Supplies

W. CROMWELL (MW)
525 Washington St. (m-b)
Shelbyville, KY 40065
502-633-4440 / Fax: 502-633-2720
Sales: $100,001-$500,000

WILLIAM C. ANDROIT (Owner) & Buys Men's Sportswear, Furnishings & Accessories, Headwear, Store Displays, Fixtures, Supplies

HUGHES' DEPARTMENT STORE, INC. (DEPT)
116 S. Maple (m)
Somerset, KY 42501
606-678-5351

HELEN HUGHES (Owner)

INEZ CRISWELL (Asst. Mgr.) & Buys Men's Suits, Tailored Jackets, Tailored Slacks, Sweaters, Sport Shirts, Outer Jackets, Casual Slacks, Dress Shirts, Ties, Robes, Underwear, Hosiery, Headwear, Belts, Store Displays, Fixtures, Supplies

JIM HAWKINS ENTERPRISES, INC. (FW-5)
(B & H SHOES)
P.O. Box 42 (m)
210 E. Mount Vernon St.
Somerset, KY 42501
606-678-5611 / Fax: 606-679-7713
Sales: $1 Million-$10 Million

AMY BARNETT (Partner)

MARSHA BARNETT (Partner)

JAMES F. HAWKINS, III (Partner)

JUDY HOLTZCLAW (Partner)

DAN BARNETT (D.M.M.) & Buys Boys' Footwear, Men's Footwear

DAVID BARNETT-Boys' Footwear, Men's Footwear

HOLT'S DEPARTMENT STORE (DEPT)
525 Adams St. (m)
Sturgis, KY 42459
270-333-5559 / Fax: 270-333-5550
Sales: $100,001-$500,000

PHILIP HOLT (Owner) & Buys Men's Wear, Sportswear, Furnishings, Accessories, Footwear, Young Men's Wear, Store Displays, Fixtures, Supplies

SHIRT SHACK (CLO-2)
4685 Metropolis Lake Rd.
RR 4 Box 122A (p-m)
West Paducah, KY 42086
270-488-3114 / Fax: 270-488-2077
Sales: $100,001-$500,000

DAVID KELLY (Owner) & Buys Imprintable T-shirts, Shorts, Headwear, Sports Uniforms, Swimwear, Store Displays, Fixtures and Supplies

LOUISIANA - Abbeville

PHILS BOYS' & GIRLS' WEAR (KS)

316 S. State St. (p-m-b)
Abbeville, LA 70510
337-893-1724 / Fax: 337-893-8306
Sales: $100,001-$500,000

DENISE BOUDREAUX (President & G.M.M.) & Buys Boys' Sportswear, Accessories, Store Displays, Fixtures, Supplies

A & A WESTERN STORE (WW)

2813 S. MacArthur Dr. (p)
Alexandria, LA 71301
318-487-1961 / Fax: 318-487-1147

CORWYN ALDREDGE (President)

JASON ALDREDGE-Men's & Boys' Western Wear, Boots, Headwear, Related Furnishings & Accessories, Store Displays, Fixtures, Supplies

CAPLAN'S, INC. (CLO-2)

(GENESIS)
916 3rd St. (b)
P.O. Box 871
Alexandria, LA 71309
318-487-4231 / Fax: 318-443-8816
Sales: $1 Million-$10 Million

DAVID C. CAPLAN (President) & Buys Men's Footwear, Leather Goods, Men's Apparel, Mens's Big & Tall, Men's Casualwear, Men's Denim Apparel, Men's Formalwear, Men's Accessories, Men's Hosiery, Men's Outerwear, Men's Sleepwear, Men's Sportswear, Men's Suits, Men's Swimwear, Men's Underwear

ROBERT GINSBURGH (Controller)

BRENT CAPLAN (D.M.M.)

DONALD CAPLAN (Mgr.-Info. Sys.)

ECONOMY BOOTS, INC. (WW)

2100 Lee St. (m)
Alexandria, LA 71301
318-442-3172 / Fax: 318-442-0781

JERRY RUSHING (President) & Buys Men's & Boys' Western Wear, Headwear, Hats, Related Accessories, Work Shoes, Boots, Store Displays, Fixtures, Supplies

JERRY LEE & CO. (MW)

4005 Jackson St.
Alexandria, LA 71303
318-442-1870 / Fax: 318-449-1255

JERRY LEE (Owner) & Buys Men's Wear, Accessories, Furnishings, Footwear

WEISS & GOLDRING (DEPT)

P.O. Box 5813 (b)
3437 Masonic Dr., #1068
Alexandria, LA 71301
318-443-9200 / Fax: 318-445-2224
Sales: $1 Million-$10 Million

HARRY B. SILVER (Chmn.)

TED SILVER (President) & Buys Men's Overcoats, Suits, Tailored Jackets, Tailored Slacks, Raincoats

WILLIAM R. SILVER (V.P.) & Buys Men's Sportswear, Sweaters, Sport Shirts, Outer Jackets, Casual Slacks, Apparel, Furnishings, Headwear, Footwear

SELIGMAN'S DEPARTMENT STORE (DEPT)

129 S. Franklin St. (bud-m)
Bastrop, LA 71220
318-281-4701
Sales: $500,000-$1 Million

RON ISRAEL (Co-Owner) & Buys Men's Suits, Tailored Jackets, Tailored Slacks, Raincoats, Sportswear, Sweaters, Sport Shirts, Outer Jackets, Casual Slacks, Active Apparel, Furnishings, Headwear, Accessories, Big & Tall Men's Wear, Young Men's & Boys' Wear, Men's & Boys' Shoes, Store Di

SARA ISRAEL (Co-Owner) & Buys Men's Suits, Tailored Jackets, Tailored Slacks, Raincoats, Sportswear, Sweaters, Sport Shirts, Outer Jackets, Casual Slacks, Active Apparel, Furnishings, Headwear, Accessories, Big & Tall Men's Wear, Young Men's & Boys' Wear, Men's & Boys' Shoes, Store Di

ADOBE WESTERN & CASUAL (WW)

2015 Airline Hwy. (m)
Baton Rouge, LA 70815
225-928-7775 / Fax: 225-644-7547

SALLY DOSSETT (Owner) & Buys Men's Western Wear, Casual Wear, Young Men's & Boys' Wear, Western Furnishings, Accessories, Western Headwear, WesternBoots, Store Displays, Fixtures, Supplies

BATES & THIGPEN (MW)

P.O. Box 1506 (m)
335 3rd St.
Baton Rouge, LA 70821
225-387-0929 / Fax: 225-387-0920
Sales: $500,000-$1 Million

W. B. BATES, JR. (Co-Owner) & Buys Men's Overcoats, Suits, Tailored Jackets, Tailored Slacks, Raincoats, Sportswear, Sweaters, Sport Shirts, Outer Jackets, Casual Slacks, Furnishings, Headwear, Belts, Jewelry, Bostonian Shoes, Uniforms, Store Displays, Fixtures, Supplies

MITZI M. BATES (Co-Owner) & Buys Men's Overcoats, Suits, Tailored Jackets, Tailored Slacks, Raincoats, Sportswear, Sweaters, Sport Shirts, Outer Jackets, Casual Slacks, Furnishings, Headwear, Belts, Jewelry, Bostonian Shoes, Uniforms, Store Displays, Fixtures, Supplies

CARRIAGES FINE CLOTHIERS (CLO-2)

7622 Old Hammond Hwy. (bud-p-b-des)
Baton Rouge, LA 70809
225-926-6892 / Fax: 225-929-6070
Sales: $1 Million-$10 Million

LARRY ALLEN (Co-Owner) & Buys Boys' Apparel, Boys' Footwear, Men's Footwear, Leather Goods, Men's Apparel

JEFF DAQUANNO (Co-Owner) & Buys Boys' Apparel, Boys' Footwear, Men's Footwear, Leather Goods, Men's Apparel

RICHARD HILL (Co-Owner) & Buys Boys' Apparel, Boys' Footwear, Men's Footwear, Leather Goods, Men's Apparel

COHN-TURNER (MW-2)

8366 Jefferson Hwy. (b-h)
Baton Rouge, LA 70809
225-926-5909 / Fax: 225-926-5969
Sales: $1 Million-$10 Million

ED BERNSTEIN (Mgr.) & Buys Men's Overcoats, Suits, Tailored Jackets Tailored Slacks, Raincoats, Sportswear, Sweaters, Sport Shirts, Active Apparel, Outer Jackets, Casual Slacks, Furnishings, Accessories

DESIGNER'S DEN (MW-2)

(MALE IMAGE)
7319 Florida Blvd. (m-b)
Baton Rouge, LA 70806
225-926-2176 / Fax: 225-926-9940
Sales: $100,001-$500,000

WASSER SALAMEH (Owner) & Buys Men's Overcoats, Suits, Tailored Jackets, Tailored Slacks, Raincoats, Sportswear, Sweaters, Sport Shirts, Outer Jackets, Leather Apparel, Casual Slacks, Active Apparel, Dress Shirts, Ties, Robes, Underwear, Hosiery, Gloves, Headwear, Accessories, Footwear, Store Displays, Fixtures, Supplies

GINGISS FORMAL WEAR (MW-2)

(LOFTUS ENTERPRISES, INC.)
3114 College Dr., #G (m-b)
Baton Rouge, LA 70808
225-923-0880 / Fax: 225-291-5746

JOHN LOFTUS (Owner) & Buys Men's Formal Wear, Accessories, Men's & Boys' Formal Footwear, Store Displays, Fixtures, Supplies

HOT 'N' SPICY LINGERIE CO. (MO & OL)

11580 Perkins Rd.
Baton Rouge, LA 70884
225-757-8770 / Fax: 225-757-8644

DAVID ROSS (President)

ANNE ALEXANDER-Men's Robes, Furnishings, Underwear

MALE IMAGE (MW)

7301 Florida Blvd.
Baton Rouge, LA 70806
225-928-4720

YASSER SLEMEN (Owner) & Buys Men's Furnishings, Accessories, Footwear

MAYER COMPANY CLOTHIERS (MW)
5830 S. Sherwood Forest Blvd. (b)
Baton Rouge, LA 70816
225-293-5180 / Fax: 225-293-5140
Website: www.mayerco.com
JIM MAYER (Owner) & Buys Men's Wear, Young Men's Wear, Footwear, Sportswear, Tailored Jackets, Tailored Slacks

PAMPO'S DANCE EMPORIUM & SWIMWEAR (SP)
Mall of Louisiana
6400 Blue Bonnet Blvd.
Baton Rouge, LA 70836
225-769-3399 / Fax: 225-769-1551
MELANIE SAFER (Owner) & Buys Beach Cover Ups, Dance Wear, Swimwear, Headwear, Sandals, Dancing Shoes

SUN KISSED (CLO)
9622 Airline Hwy., #7
Baton Rouge, LA 70815
225-925-8775 / Fax: 225-925-8775
CINDY CHAPMAN (Owner) & Buys Swimwear
GLENDA CHAPMAN-Swimwear

SUPER STYLE FASHIONS (MW)
5151 Plank Rd. (m)
Baton Rouge, LA 70805
225-357-6222 / Fax: 225-357-6526
A. HAMIBEH (Owner) & Buys Men's Sportswear, Furnishings, Accessories, Footwear, Young Men's, Boys' Suits

YOUNG FASHIONS, INC. (CLO-13)
10300 Perkins Rd. (m)
P.O. Box 83258
Baton Rouge, LA 70810
225-766-1070 / Fax: 225-769-3282
Sales: $10 Million-$50 Million
Website: www.youngfashions.com
TANYA KENNEDY (Co-Owner) & Buys Boys' Apparel, Boys' Footwear, Men's Apparel, Mens's Big & Tall, Men's Casualwear, Men's Denim Apparel, Men's Accessories, Men's Hosiery, Men's Outerwear, Men's Sportswear, Men's Underwear, Men's Uniforms
GRANT KENNEDY (Co-Owner & Dir.-Mktg. & Real Estate)
ANDY PLAISANCE-Boys' Apparel, Boys' Footwear, Men's Apparel, Mens's Big & Tall, Men's Casualwear, Men's Denim Apparel, Men's Accessories, Men's Hosiery, Men's Outerwear, Men's Sportswear, Men's Underwear, Men's Uniforms

CAROLYN'S FAIRYLAND, INC. (KS & SP)
P.O. Box 6 (m-b)
Berwick, LA 70342
504-385-0231
Sales: $100,001-$500,000
CAROLYN PARRO (Owner) & Buys Boys' Clothing To Size 20, Boys' Sportswear, Furnishings, Accessories, Store Displays, Fixtures, Supplies

ROSENBLUM'S OF BOGALUSA (DEPT)
230 Cumberland St. (m)
Bogalusa, LA 70427
504-735-9397 / Fax: 504-732-3351
WALLY ROSENBLUM (Owner) & Buys Men's Sweaters, Sport Shirts, Outer Jackets, Leather Apparel, Casual Slacks, Active Apparel, Furnishings, Boys' Clothing, Men's & Boys' Footwear, Store Displays, Fixtures, Supplies

DAVIS' MEN'S STORE (MW)
2907 E. Texas St. (p-m)
Bossier City, LA 71111
318-742-2660 / Fax: 318-742-3731
B.J. DAVIS (Co-Owner)
LEE DAVIS (Co-Owner) & Buys Big & Tall Men's Wear, Leather Apparel, Warm-Up Suits, Furnishings, Accessories, Footwear, Store Displays, Fixtures, Supplies

POPE'S OF BOSSIER CITY, INC. (CLO-2)
(POPE'S LTD.)
P.O. Box 5549 (b)
526 Benton Rd.
Bossier City, LA 71111
318-746-0932 / Fax: 318-747-5956
Sales: $1 Million-$10 Million
WADE H. POPE (President & G.M.M.) & Buys Men's Sweaters, Sport Shirts, Outer Jackets, Leather Jackets, Casual Slacks, Active Apparel, Furnishings, Accessories, Footwear, Boys' Wear, Store Displays, Fixtures, Supplies

SQUIRES, INC. (SP-15)
4906 Shed Rd. (m)
Bossier City, LA 71111
318-746-2119 / Fax: 318-746-5040
Website: www.squirestux.com
WILLIAM SCHWARTZ (Owner) & Buys Men's Tuxedos, Furnishings, Accessories, Boys' Tuxedos, Men's & Boys' Footwear
JEFF HERNANDEZ (Opers. Mgr.) & Buys Store Displays, Fixtures, Supplies

SKOBELJ'S (CLO-2)
35451 Hwy. 11 (p)
Buras, LA 70041
985-657-7626
NANCY SCOBEL (Co-Owner) & Buys Men's Sportswear, Sweaters, Sport Shirts, Outer Jackets, Leather Jackets, Casual Slacks, Active Apparel, Furnishings, Accessories, Footwear, Store Displays
JOAN SPRINGER (Co-Owner) & Buys Men's Sportswear, Sweaters, Sport Shirts, Outer Jackets, Leather Jackets, Casual Slacks, Active Apparel, Furnishings, Accessories, Footwear, Store Displays

BEAU'S SPORTSWEAR (CLO)
812 E. Judge Perez Dr. (p-m-b)
Chalmette, LA 70043
504-277-6656
Sales: $100,001-$500,000
LYNDA CHATELAIN (Co-Owner) & Buys Men's Suits, Sweaters, Sport Shirts, Casual Slacks, Dress Shirts, Ties, Hosiery, Belts, Young Men's Wear, Boys' Clothing, Sportswear, Accessories, Store Displays, Fixtures, Supplies
PAULINE TROXCLAIR (Co-Owner) & Buys Men's Suits, Sweaters, Sport Shirts, Casual Slacks, Dress Shirts, Ties, Hosiery, Belts, Young Men's Wear, Boys' Clothing, Sportswear, Accessories, Store Displays, Fixtures, Supplies

FONTENOT & GUIDRY, INC. (CLO-2)
232 N. Main St. (p-m)
Church Point, LA 70525
337-684-5463
Sales: $500,000-$1 Million
DAVID G. WINN (Gen. Mgr.) & Buys Men's Suits, Big & Tall Wear, Sportswear, Dress Shirts, Ties, Robes, Underwear, Headwear, Belts, Fragrances, Boys' Clothing, Men's & Boys' Footwear
LORE LEE GUIDRY-Hosiery, Jewelry

McKNIGHT BROTHERS (CLO)
12321 St. Helena St. (m)
Clinton, LA 70722
225-683-8267 / Fax: 225-683-6839
ISAAC G. McKNIGHT Sr. (Owner) & Buys Men's Sweaters, Sport Shirts, Outer Jackets, Leather Apparel, Casual Slacks, Active Apparel, Furnishings, Accessories, Boys' Wear, Men's & Boys' Footwear, Store Displays, Fixtures, Supplies

CONTENDERS SPORTS (SP)
16249 E. Main St.
Cut Off, LA 70345
504-632-8868 / Fax: 504-632-8868
Sales: $100,001-$500,000
VAN GALJOUR (Co-Owner) & Buys Athletic Footwear, Athletics, Licensed Apparel
BOBBY GALJOUR (Co-Owner) & Buys Athletic Footwear, Athletics, Licensed Apparel

LOUISIANA - DeRidder

HEAD SOUTH (SP-2)
825 Mahlon St.
DeRidder, LA 70634
337-462-6910 / Fax: 337-462-5975
JAMES SEAMAN (Owner) (@ 337-238-4448) & Buys Activewear, Athletic Footwear, Athletics, Licensed Apparel

HOOKS' DEPARTMENT STORE, INC. (DEPT)
119 N. Washington St. (m)
DeRidder, LA 70634
337-463-4869 / Fax: 337-463-4869
BETTY HOOKS (Co-Owner) & Buys Boys' Apparel, Boys' Footwear, Leather Goods, Men's Apparel, Mens's Big & Tall, Men's Casualwear, Men's Denim Apparel, Men's Accessories, Men's Hosiery, Men's Outerwear, Men's Sportswear, Men's Suits
JIMMY HOOKS (Co-Owner) & Buys Boys' Apparel, Boys' Footwear, Leather Goods, Men's Apparel, Mens's Big & Tall, Men's Casualwear, Men's Denim Apparel, Men's Accessories, Men's Hosiery, Men's Outerwear, Men's Sportswear, Men's Suits
ERIC RAY (Store Mgr.) & Buys Boys' Apparel, Boys' Footwear, Leather Goods, Men's Apparel, Mens's Big & Tall, Men's Casualwear, Men's Denim Apparel, Men's Accessories, Men's Hosiery, Men's Outerwear, Men's Sportswear, Men's Suits

F.S. WILLIAMS STORE (DEPT)
5949 Hwy. 19 (p-m)
Ethel, LA 70730
225-683-8251 / Fax: 225-683-8392
Sales: $1 Million-$10 Million
MANSHIP WILLIAMS (Co-Owner) & Buys Men's Raincoats, Sweaters, Sport Shirts, Outer Jackets, Leather Apparel, Casual Slacks, Active Apparel, Furnishings, Headwear, Accessories, Big & Tall Men's Wear, Boys' Wear, Men's & Boys' Footwear, Boots, Store Displays, Fixtures, Supplies
RAY WILLIAMS (Co-Owner) & Buys Men's Raincoats, Sweaters, Sport Shirts, Outer Jackets, Leather Apparel, Casual Slacks, Active Apparel, Furnishings, Headwear, Accessories, Big & Tall Men's Wear, Boys' Wear, Men's & Boys' Footwear, Boots, Store Displays, Fixtures, Supplies

FREY OUTFITTERS (CLO)
1425 E. Laurel Ave. (m)
Eunice, LA 70535
337-546-0208 / Fax: 337-546-0209
SIDNEY FREY (Owner) & Buys Men's & Boys' Western Wear, Accessories, Boots, Sport Shirts, Men's Sportswear, Furnishings, Store Displays, Fixtures, Supplies
DONALD THIBODEAUX-Men's & Boys' Western Wear, Accessories, Boots, Sport Shirts, Men's Sportswear, Furnishings, Store Displays, Fixtures, Supplies

LOUIS WRIGHT STORE (DEPT)
P.O. Box 306 (m)
114 S. 2nd St.
Eunice, LA 70535
337-457-2616 / Fax: 337-457-3330
Sales: $100,001-$500,000
JOAN KERSTEIN (President & G.M.M.) & Buys Men's Suits, Tailored Jackets, Tailored Slacks, Raincoats, Sportswear, Sweaters, Sport Shirts, Outer Jackets, Casual Slacks, Furnishings, Headwear, Accessories, Young Men's Wear, Store Displays, Fixtures, Supplies

MANSHOP BY MYERS (MW)
127 S. 2nd St. (p-m)
Eunice, LA 70535
337-457-2051 / Fax: 337-457-8762
Sales: $100,001-$500,000
TOMMY MYERS (Owner) & Buys Men's Sportswear, Furnishings, Accessories, Leather Apparel, Young Men's Wear, Boys' School Uniforms, Men's & Boys' Footwear, Store Displays, Fixtures, Supplies

KELLEY'S CLOTHING (CLO)
203 N. Main St. (m)
Farmerville, LA 71241
318-368-3860
Sales: $100,001-$500,000
STEVEN KELLEY (Owner) & Buys Young Men's Wear, Footwear, Accessories, Tailored Jackets, Tailored Slacks, Men's Wear

RAMUS ARMY SURPLUS, INC. (AN)
12574 Hwy. 165 (p)
Glenmora, LA 71433
318-748-4883
VICTOR RAMUS (Owner) & Buys Men's Camouflage Clothing, Boots, Store Displays, Fixtures, Supplies

DADS & LADS CLOTHING (MW)
917 N. Bayou Dr. (m)
Golden Meadow, LA 70357
985-475-5830
MS. PAT DIZIER (Owner) & Buys Young Men's Wear, Footwear, Accessories, Tailored Jackets, Tailored Slacks, Men's Wear

COLLEGIATE SHOPPE, INC. (CLO)
310 Main St. (p-m-b)
Grambling, LA 71245
318-247-6151 / Fax: 318-247-8464
Sales: $100,001-$500,000
ASHTON WILKERSON (Owner) & Buys Men's Sweaters, Sport Shirts, Outer Jackets, Leather Apparel, Casual Slacks, Active Apparel, Furnishings, Headwear, Accessories, Footwear, Store Displays, Fixtures, Supplies

TIC-TOCK SHOPPE, INC. (KS)
2706 W. Thomas St. (p-m-b)
Hammond, LA 70401
985-542-0121
Sales: $100,001-$500,000
JOSEPH SCHIRO (President) & Buys Boys' Wear to Size 16, Store Displays, Fixtures, Supplies
CHERYL TALLIA (Office Mgr.) & Buys Sportswear
MARY COSTA (Floor Mgr.) & Buys Accessories

EARL WILLIAMS' STORE (CLO)
7873 Main St. (m-b)
Houma, LA 70360
985-868-1505 / Fax: 985-879-3737
EARL WILLIAMS (Co-Owner)
CHARLOTTE BLACK (Co-Owner) & Buys Men's Overcoats, Suits, Tailored Jackets, Tailored Slacks, Raincoats, Sportswear, Sweaters, Sport Shirts, Outer Jackets, Leather Apparel, Casual Slacks, Active Apparel, Furnishings, Dress Shirts, Ties, Robes, Underwear, Hosiery, Gloves, Accessories, Big & Tall Men's Wear, Men's Footwear
JOANN WILLIAMS (Co-Owner) & Buys Store Displays, Fixtures, Supplies

JOHNNY'S MEN'S SHOP (MW)
7816 Main (m)
Houma, LA 70360
985-872-3995
LUCAS TERRACINA (Mgr.) & Buys Men's Suits, Tailored Jackets, Tailored Slacks, Sportswear, Sport Shirts, Sweaters, Jeans, Casual Slacks, Leather Apparel, Furnishings, Dress Shirts, Ties, Hosiery, Gloves, Accessories, Belts, Small Leather Goods, Big & Tall Men's Shirts, Men's Footwear, Urban Contemporary, Store Displays, Fixtures, Supplies

SAADI HABERDASHERY (MW)
Southland Mall (b)
Houma, LA 70360
985-851-0130 / Fax: 985-853-0576
JAMES P. SAADI (President) & Buys Men's Overcoats, Suits, Tailored Jackets, Tailored Slacks, Raincoats, Sportswear, Furnishings, Headwear, Accessories, Big & Tall Men's Wear, Men's Footwear, Store Displays, Fixtures, Supplies

BRIAR PATCH (CLO-2)
(MARCEAUX'S)
918 N. Lake Arthur Ave. (m-b)
Jennings, LA 70546
337-824-7579 / Fax: 337-824-7684
Sales: $500,001-$1 Million
JOHN MARCEAUX (Owner)
JANET MARCEAUX-Men's Footwear, Leather Goods, Men's Apparel, Men's Hosiery, Men's Sportswear

LOUISIANA - Jennings

BROUSSARD'S MEN'S SHOP (MW)

126 S. Broadway St. (m)
Jennings, LA 70546
337-824-2975

BILLY BROUSSARD (Owner) & Buys Men's Wear, Furnishings, Accessories

C & C FEED (CLO)

P.O. Box 1213 (m-b)
Jennings, LA 70546
337-824-0445 / Fax: 337-616-3333

KEN CASSIDY (Co-Owner) & Buys Men's Western Wear, Western Furnishings, Accessories, Men's & Boys' Western Boots, Store Displays, Fixtures, Supplies

JIM CASSIDY (Co-Owner) & Buys Men's Western Wear, Western Furnishings, Accessories, Men's & Boys' Western Boots, Store Displays, Fixtures, Supplies

KEVIN CASSIDY (Co-Owner) & Buys Men's Western Wear, Western Furnishings, Accessories, Men's & Boys' Western Boots, Store Displays, Fixtures, Supplies

U.B. CARPENTER DEPARTMENT STORES (DEPT-2 & SG)

121 1st St. (p-m)
Jonesville, LA 71343
318-339-7143

SHERRI FLOYD (Mgr.) & Buys Men's Sportswear, Western Wear, Furnishings, Accessories, Store Displays, Fixtures, Supplies

ABDALLA'S (CLO)

P.O. Box 51348 (m-b)
Lafayette, LA 70505
337-262-7100 / Fax: 337-262-7199
Sales: $10 Million-$50 Million
Website: www.abdallas.com

BARABA BLACK (President)

TOM BLACK (V.P. & D.M.M.) & Buys Men's Overcoats, Suits, Tailored Jackets, Furnishings, Dress Shirts, Ties, Robes, Underwear, Hosiery, Gloves, Headwear, Accessories, Belts, Jewelry, Small Leathers

DAVID SMITH-Tailored Slacks, Raincoats, Sportswear, Sweaters, Sport Shirts, Outer Jackets, Leather Apparel, Casual Slacks, Athletic Apparel, Young Men's, 8 to 20 Boys' Clothing, Sportswear, Furnishings & Accesories

TIM BROUSSARD (Display Mgr.) & Buys Store Displays, Fixtures, Supplies

BROTHER'S (MW)

101 Arnould Blvd. (b)
Lafayette, LA 70506
337-984-7749 / Fax: 337-989-4466
Sales: $1 Million-$10 Million

EDWARD ABDALLA (President & Owner) & Buys Men's Wear, Overcoats, Tailored Jackets & Slacks, Raincoats, Sweaters, Sport Shirts, Outer Jackets, Leather Apparel, Casual Slacks, Dress Shirts, Ties, Robes, Underwear, Hosiery, Gloves, Belts, Jewelry, Small Leather Goods, Boys' Footwear, Store Displays, Fixtures, Supplies

JOSE MOSELEY-Men's Wear, Overcoats, Tailored Jackets & Slacks, Raincoats, Sweaters, Sport Shirts, Outer Jackets, Leather Apparel, Casual Slacks, Dress Shirts, Ties, Robes, Underwear, Hosiery, Gloves, Belts, Jewelry, Small Leather Goods, Boys' Footwear

CAL'S WESTERN STORE (WW)

4002 Johnston St. (p-m)
Lafayette, LA 70503
337-984-4308

CAL GAUTREAU (Owner)

JIM GAUTREAU (Mgr.) & Buys Men's Leather Apparel, Western Wear, Boys' Western Wear, Boots, Store Displays, Fixtures and Supplies

F. CAMALO (MW)

458 Heymann Blvd.
Lafayette, LA 70503
337-233-4984 / Fax: 337-233-4964

FRANK CAMALO (Owner) & Buys Men's Pants, Shirts, Accessories, Neckwear

GAIDRY'S MENSWEAR (MW-2)

902 Harding St. (b)
Lafayette, LA 70503
337-233-2730 / Fax: 337-237-7559
Sales: $1 Million-$10 Million

DAVID TRAHAN (President) & Buys Men's Overcoats, Suits, Tailored Jackets, Tailored Slacks, Raincoats, Sportswear, Sweaters, Sport Shirts, Outer Jackets, Leather Apparel, Casual Slacks, Active Apparel, Furnishings, Belts, Jewelry, Footwear, Store Displays, Fixtures, Supplies

PARTNERS LTD. (MW)

102 Arnould Blvd. (b)
Lafayette, LA 70506
337-984-9933 / Fax: 337-984-9944
Sales: $1 Million-$10 Million

DONALD USIE (Owner) & Buys Men's Sportswear, Furnishings, Accessories, Footwear

MAVIS USIE (Asst. Mgr.) & Buys Store Displays, Fixtures, Supplies

RIGHT ON FASHION (MW)

400 Jefferson St. (b)
Lafayette, LA 70501
337-237-5645

MAMDOUH QAMHAYEH (President & Owner)

TONY QAMHAYEH-Men's Wear, Young Men's Wear, Urban Contemporary, Accessories

SAM'S MENSWEAR (MW)

1800 NE Evangeline Thrwy. (m)
Lafayette, LA 70501
337-269-4049

SAM HODGES (Owner) & Buys Men's Wear, Footwear, Accessories, Sportswear

COTTEN'S BOOTS & WESTERN WEAR (WW)

2601 Ryan St. (m)
Lake Charles, LA 70601 (m)
337-436-5131 / Fax: 337-436-1365

JAMES COTTEN (President) & Buys Men's Western Wear, Tailored Jackets, Jeans, Sport Shirts, Accessories, Work Shoes, Boots, Boys' Western Wear Outer Jackets, Jeans, Sport Shirts, Accessories, Boots, Store Displays, Fixtures, Supplies

DONNA'S LINGERIE & SWIMWEAR, INC. (SP)

3518 Ryan St.
Lake Charles, LA 70605
337-477-1804 / Fax: 337-477-5431
Sales: $100,001-$500,000

DONNA MIER (Owner) & Buys Swimwear, Resort Wear

MEN'S DISCOUNT SHOP (MW-2)

331 W. Prien Lake Rd. (bud-p-m)
Lake Charles, LA 70601
337-478-4807 / Fax: 337-478-4808
Sales: $1 Million-$10 Million

FRANK ASSUNTO (Owner) & Buys Men's Overcoats, Suits, Tailored Jackets, Tailored Slacks, Raincoats, Sportswear, Furnishings, Headwear, Accessories, Big & Tall Men's Wear, Footwear

NED BROTHERS' CLOTHING (MW)

528 S. Martin Luther King Dr. (p)
Lake Charles, LA 70601
337-433-1462

DERVIS NED (Owner) & Buys Men's Wear, Footwear

NEW LOOK FASHION (MW)

728 Ryan St. (m)
Lake Charles, LA 70601
337-439-7875 / Fax: 337-439-7872

MITCH ABUSHANAB (Owner) & Buys Men's Wear, Young Men's Wear, Footwear, Accessories

LOUISIANA - Lake Charles

S & M BARGAIN CITY, INC. (CLO-4)
(LABELS)
(S & M FAMILY OUTLET)
826 3rd Ave. (b)
Lake Charles, LA 70601
337-433-2696 / Fax: 337-433-4618
Sales: $1 Million-$10 Million
JOE STOMA (President & Dir.-Fin. & Mktg. & Real Estate) & Buys Boys' Apparel, Boys' Footwear, Men's Footwear, Leather Goods, Men's Apparel, Men's Denim Apparel, Men's Accessories, Men's Hosiery, Men's Outerwear, Men's Sleepwear, Men's Sportswear, Men's Suits, Men's Swimwear
JANET STOMA (Treas.) & Buys Boys' Apparel, Boys' Footwear, Men's Footwear, Leather Goods, Men's Apparel, Men's Denim Apparel, Men's Accessories, Men's Hosiery, Men's Outerwear, Men's Sleepwear, Men's Sportswear, Men's Suits, Men's Swimwear
STEVE STOMA (V.P.) & Buys Boys' Apparel, Boys' Footwear, Men's Footwear, Leather Goods, Men's Apparel, Men's Denim Apparel, Men's Accessories, Men's Hosiery, Men's Outerwear, Men's Sleepwear, Men's Sportswear, Men's Suits, Men's Swimwear
LINDA N. THIBODEAUX (Dir.-HR)
FRED STOMA, Jr. (Mgr.-Warehouse)

SEL-MART OF LAKE CHARLES (CLO-2)
(DANOR, INC.)
3525 Ryan St. (p)
Lake Charles, LA 70605
337-477-6331 / Fax: 337-477-1617
DAVID SELF (Owner) & Buys Men's Raincoats, Sportswear, Sweaters, Sport Shirts, Outer Jackets, Casual Slacks, Active Apparel, Western Apparel & Accessories, Furnishings, Men's Western Boots, Work Boots, Boys' Western Wear, Sportswear, Store Displays, Fixtures, Supplies

STANDER'S YOUNG FASHIONS (KS)
325 W. Prien Lake Rd. (m-b)
Lake Charles, LA 70601
337-477-5294
MARY ANN JOHNSON (Owner) & Buys To Size 7 Boys' Wear, Furnishings, Accessories, Store Displays, Fixtures, Supplies

N.J. CARAWAY & CO., INC. (CLO)
P.O. Box 129 (m)
100 S. 2nd St.
Logansport, LA 71049
318-697-5540
JANET PALMER (Co-Owner) & Buys Men's Sportswear, Sweaters, Sport Shirts, Outer Jackets, Casual Slacks, Active Apparel, Ties, Dress Shirts, Belts, Underwear, Hosiery, Hats, Boys' Sportswear, Store Displays, Fixtures, Supplies
B. C. PALMER (Co-Owner) & Buys Men's Sportswear, Sweaters, Sport Shirts, Outer Jackets, Casual Slacks, Active Apparel, Ties, Dress Shirts, Belts, Underwear, Hosiery, Hats, Boys' Sportswear, Store Displays, Fixtures, Supplies

NICHOLS'S DRY GOODS (DG-10)
P.O. Box 1090 (p)
895 Sabine St.
Many, LA 71449
318-256-2300 / Fax: 318-256-9857
Sales: $10 Million-$50 Million
DEBBIE NICHOLS (Owner) & Buys Furnishings, Accessories, Boots, Store Displays, Fixtures, Supplies

RAYMOND'S DEPARTMENT STORE (DEPT)
317 N. Main St. (p)
Marksville, LA 71351
318-253-7125
Sales: $100,001-$500,000
RAYMOND J. LABORDE (Owner) & Buys Men's Sportswear, Furnishings, Accessories, Work Shoes, Boots, Store Displays

FERRARA'S BIG & TALL MEN (MW)
4210 Veterans Memorial Blvd.
Metairie, LA 70006
504-456-9991
AL FERRARA (Owner) & Buys Big & Tall Clothing, Sportswear, Formal Wear, Furnishings, Accessories, Men's Footwear, Store Displays, Fixtures, Supplies

PHIDIPPIDES (SP)
6601 Veterans Memorial Blvd.
Metairie, LA 70003
504-887-8900
SHIRLEY JACQUES (Owner) & Buys Activewear, Athletic Footwear

PORTER - STEVENS, INC. (MW)
3301 Veterans Memorial Blvd. (m-b)
Metairie, LA 70002
504-834-3771 / Fax: 504-834-3824
MELVIN GRODSKY (Owner)
WILLIAM CROCKETT-Men's Slacks, Sweaters, Sportswear, Active Apparel

BURT'S YOUNG FASHIONS (KS)
713 Main (b)
Minden, LA 71055
318-377-4320 / Fax: 318-377-6630
JANIS BRYAN (Owner) & Buys Boys' Sportswear to Size 7, Store Displays, Fixtures, Supplies

AVENUE KIDS (KS)
1823 Ave. of America (b)
Monroe, LA 71201
318-388-0505 / Fax: 318-388-0506
KATHERINE KELLEY (Owner) & Buys Boys' Wear, Footwear, Store Displays, Fixtures, Supplies
CAROLYN KOON (Mgr.) & Buys Boys' Wear, Footwear, Store Displays, Fixtures, Supplies

COTTON PATCH (CLO)
(RAY ENTERPRISES, INC.)
607 Louisville Rd. (m-b)
Monroe, LA 71207
318-387-0093 / Fax: 318-323-3804
CATHERINE RAY (Co-Owner) & Buys Men's Sportswear, Sweaters, Sport Shirts, Outer Jackets, Casual Slacks, Active Apparel, Belts, Ties, Store Displays, Fixtures, Supplies
BUD RAY (Co-Owner) & Buys Men's Sportswear, Sweaters, Sport Shirts, Outer Jackets, Casual Slacks, Active Apparel, Belts, Ties, Store Displays, Fixtures, Supplies

ELIAS' (CLO)
3126 Louisville Ave. (m-b)
Monroe, LA 71201
318-387-0126 / Fax: 318-387-0147
Sales: $1 Million-$10 Million
ALBERT ELIAS (President)
CHAD ELIAS (V.P.) & Buys Men's Footwear, Men's Apparel, Men's Casualwear, Men's Denim Apparel, Men's Accessories, Men's Hosiery, Men's Outerwear, Men's Sportswear, Men's Swimwear
MARCELLA ELIAS-Boys' Apparel, Boys' Footwear

LOUISIANA - Monroe

HADDAD'S, INC. (MW & OL)
1819 Ave. of America (b)
Monroe, LA 71201
318-323-4421 / Fax: 318-322-7669
Sales: $1 Million-$10 Million
Website: www.haddads.com
JOSEPH A. HADDAD (Co-Owner) & Buys Men's Sportswear, Overcoats, Suits, Tailored Jackets, Tailored Slacks, Sweaters, Sport Shirts, Outer Jackets, Active Apparel, Furnishings, Headwear, Belts, Small Leather Goods, Fragrances, Big & Tall Men's Wear, Men's Dress Shoes, Casual Shoes, Store Disp
WILLIAM D. HADDAD (Co-Owner) & Buys Men's Sportswear, Overcoats, Suits, Tailored Jackets, Tailored Slacks, Sweaters, Sport Shirts, Outer Jackets, Active Apparel, Furnishings, Headwear, Belts, Small Leather Goods, Fragrances, Big & Tall Men's Wear, Men's Dress Shoes, Casual Shoes, Store Disp

HANELINE'S MENSWEAR, INC. (MW)
2211 Louisville Ave. (b)
Monroe, LA 71201
318-323-9657 / Fax: 318-322-1294
Sales: $1 Million-$10 Million
RICHARD HANELINE (President & G.M.M.) & Buys Men's Big & Tall, Underwear, Tailored Slacks, Casual Shirts, Store Displays, Fixtures, Supplies
RONNIE HANELINE-Men's Big & Tall, Ties
ROLAND COATES-Men's Big & Tall, Overcoats, Suits, Tailored Jackets, Outer Jackets
DAVID ROARK-Men's Big & Tall, Sweaters, Sport Shirts, Apparel, Dress Shirts, Gloves, Headwear, Jewelry, Fragrances, Small Leather Goods, Footwear
ROGER HAMMOND-Men's Small Leather Goods, Footwear, Belts, Hosiery

JETSON, INC. (CLO)
(THE TOGGERY)
1400 N. 18th St. (b-h)
Monroe, LA 71201
318-388-4939 / Fax: 318-388-4986
Website: www.thetoggery.com
TOM BAKER (Owner) & Buys Men's Sportswear, Furnishings, Headwear, Accessories, Footwear, Store Displays, Fixtures, Supplies

SAL'S MEN'S & BOYS' FASHIONS (MW)
344 Desiard St. (m)
Monroe, LA 71201
318-322-9611
SALVADOR MILETELLO (Owner) & Buys Men's Sportswear, Jeans, Footwear, Furnishings, Headwear, Accessories, Young Men's Wear, 8 to 20 Boys' Wear
ESTELLE MILETELLO-Men's Sportswear, Jeans, Footwear, Furnishings, Headwear, Accessories, Young Men's Wear, 8 to 20 Boys' Wear

TOUCH OF STYLE (MW)
404 Desiard St. (p-m-b)
Monroe, LA 71201
318-387-6657
WON BYUN (Owner) & Buys Men's, Young Men's & Boys' Wear, Sportswear, Furnishings, Accessories, Men's & Boys' Footwear, Store Displays, Fixtures, Supplies

BEAR CREEK WESTERN STORE (WW-2)
35999 Hwy. 16 (p-m-b)
Montpelier, LA 70422
225-777-4578 / Fax: 225-777-4858
MELBA GIARDINA (President) & Buys Men's & Boys' Western Wear, Accessories, Boots, Moccasins, Store Displays, Fixtures, Supplies

ALUMNI SHOP FOR HIM & HER (CLO)
P.O. Box 2724 (m-b)
1035 9th St.
Morgan City, LA 70381
985-384-5338 / Fax: 985-384-2876
Sales: $100,001-$500,000
BILLY GIORDANO (President) & Buys Men's Sportswear, Overcoats, Suits, Tailored Jackets, Tailored Slacks, Sweaters, Sport Shirts, Outer Jackets, Casual Slacks, Furnishings, Headwear, Accessories, Young Men's & Boys' Wear, Men's & Boys' Footwear, Urban Contemporary, Store Displays, Fixtures, Supplies

BACKSTAGE, INC. (CLO)
700 E. Admiral Doyle Dr. (m)
New Iberia, LA 70560
337-365-2387
KERNIE BOUDREAUX (Owner) & Buys Men's Sport Shirts, Casual Shoes, Active Apparel, Belts, Jewelry, Store Displays, Fixtures, Supplies

GACHASSIN, INC. (MW)
P.O. Box 9068 (m)
956 S. Lewis St.
New Iberia, LA 70562
337-369-7000 / Fax: 337-364-2493
Website: www.gachassins.com
RICHARD D. GACHASSIN (Owner) & Buys Men's Uniforms, Work Clothes, Work Boots, Monogrammed Uniforms, Shirts, Jeans, Headwear, Store Displays, Fixtures, Supplies

GULOTTA'S, INC. (WW)
P.O. Box 9808 (m-b)
New Iberia, LA 70562
337-364-4140 / Fax: 337-364-7913
MARK GULOTTA (Owner) & Buys Men's Western Wear, Store Displays, Fixtures, Supplies

WORMSER'S MEN'S STORE (MW)
111 E. St. Peter St. (bud-p-m)
New Iberia, LA 70560
337-367-2526 / Fax: 337-367-2527
Sales: $500,000-$1 Million
JOHN WORMSER (Owner) & Buys Men's Sportswear, Furnishings, Accessories, Young Men's, Men's & Boys' Footwear, Store Displays, Fixtures, Supplies

AMERICAN FASHIONS (MW)
924 Canal St. (p-m)
New Orleans, LA 70112
504-528-9532 / Fax: 504-528-1848
MOHAMED SALEM (Owner) & Buys Men's Sportswear, Furnishings, Accessories, Footwear, Young Men's Levis, Store Displays, Fixtures, Supplies

AVALON BAZAAR (KS)
5741 Crowder Blvd. (b)
New Orleans, LA 70127
504-241-3332 / Fax: 504-241-8847
Sales: $500,001-$1 Million
DONNA ROUSSEL (Co-Owner) & Buys Boys' Wear to Size 14, Store Displays, Fixtures, Supplies
MONICA ROUSSEL (Co-Owner) & Buys Boys' Wear to Size 14, Store Displays, Fixtures, Supplies

BARRY MANUFACTURING (MW)
7300 Read Blvd. (b)
New Orleans, LA 70127
504-241-9033
BARRY ZEMAN (President & Owner)
JODY MARCHMAN-Men's Wear, Tailored Jackets, Footwear, Furnishings, Sportswear

CALIFORNIA DRAWSTRINGS (CLO & OL)
(SOUTHERN COMFORT COTTON)
812 Royal St. (m)
New Orleans, LA 70116
504-523-1371 / Fax: 504-523-8371
Website: www.californiadrawstrings.com
LINDA KEENAN (Owner) & Buys Cruise & Resort Wear, Shirts, Golf Apparel Shirts, Men's Hawaiian Shirts & Apparel

CASA ANGELO (DEPT)
212 Canal St. (p-m-b)
New Orleans, LA 70130
504-523-7814 / Fax: 504-581-7405
Sales: $100,001-$500,000
ANGELO PANTAZIS (Owner) & Buys Men's Sportswear, Furnishings, Accessories, Footwear, Store Displays, Fixtures, Supplies

COHEN'S FORMAL SHOP (MW)
714 N. Claiborne Ave. (m-b)
New Orleans, LA 70116
504-524-3322 / Fax: 504-524-9249
RUBIN COHEN (President & Owner) & Buys Tuxedo Rentals

LOUISIANA - New Orleans

COLEMAN'S (CLO-3)
(WM. B. COLEMAN CO., INC.)
4001 Earhart Blvd. (m)
New Orleans, LA 70125
504-822-1000 / Fax: 504-822-3152
Sales: $1 Million-$10 Million
WILLIAM B. COLEMAN, III (President)
WENDY LeGARDEUR (V.P.)
SARA GALASSI-Men's Wear, Overcoats, Sweaters, Sport Shirts, Dress Shirts, Gloves, Headwear, Boys' Wear, Sportswear, Furnishings, Accessories, Footwear, Store Displays, Fixtures, Supplies

DAMIN'S MENSWEAR (MW)
(LA VANTI)
3936 Dublin St. (m)
New Orleans, LA 70118
504-488-1241 / Fax: 504-482-9447
Sales: $1 Million-$10 Million
DAMIN HALUM (Owner) & Buys Men's Suits, Overcoats, Tailored Slacks, Sweaters, Sport Shirts, Outer Jackets, Leather Apparel, Casual Slacks, Active Apparel, Jeans, Furnishings, Headwear, Accessories, Footwear, Big & Tall Men's Wear, Urban Contemporary, Store Displays, Fixtures, Supplies, Footwear
RAED HALUM-Men's Suits, Overcoats, Tailored Slacks, Sweaters, Sport Shirts, Outer Jackets, Leather Apparel, Casual Slacks, Active Apparel, Jeans, Furnishings, Headwear, Accessories, Footwear, Big & Tall Men's Wear, Urban Contemporary, Store Displays, Fixtures, Supplies, Footwear

DOMINOES (CLO)
223 N. Peters St. (p-m)
New Orleans, LA 70130
504-561-8590 / Fax: 504-561-8599
Sales: $500,000-$1 Million
SHABI PERL (Owner) & Buys Men's & Young Men's Jackets, Jeans, Big & Tall Men's Wear, Boys' Clothing, Store Displays, Fixtures, Supplies
LINDA CHARLES-Men's Footwear

FASHION MAN, INC. (MW)
5700 Road Blvd. (m)
New Orleans, LA 70127
504-242-6666
VICTOR LARRY YATAK (Owner) & Buys Men's & Young Men's Suits, Tailored Jackets, Tailored Slacks, Raincoats, Sportswear, Sweaters, Sport Shirts, Outer Jackets, Leather Apparel, Casual Slacks, Men's Footwear, Active Apparel, Furnishings, Belts, Big & Tall Men's Wear, Store Displays, Fixtures, Supplies

GATOR'S DISCOUNT, INC. (CLO-6)
1506 O.C. Haley Blvd.
New Orleans, LA 70113
504-566-0910 / Fax: 504-566-7887
GREGORY ORTIZ (President) & Buys Men's & Boys' Apparel & Accessories

GENTLEMEN'S QUARTER LTD. (MW)
232 Royal St.
New Orleans, LA 70130
504-522-7139 / Fax: 504-596-3007
JERRY M. GRAVER (Owner) & Buys Furnishings, Accessories

GENTRY BIRKENSTOCK (MW)
Uptown Sq. (b)
200 Broadway, #108
New Orleans, LA 70118
504-866-8608 / Fax: 504-866-8609
Sales: $500,000-$1 Million
PAUL KULLMAN (Owner) & Buys Men's Sport Shirts, Comfort Footwear, Store Displays, Fixtures, Supplies

GEORGE BASS (MW)
201 Saint Charles Ave. (h)
New Orleans, LA 70170
504-582-1180 / Fax: 504-582-1181
Sales: $1 Million-$10 Million
Website: www.georgebass.com
GEORGE BASS (Owner & G.M.M.) & Buys Men's Wear, Tailored Jackets, Tailored Slacks, Sportswear, Furnishings, Footwear, Headwear, Accessories

JEFF'S HABERDASHERY (MW-2)
4100 General de Gaulle Dr., #D1B (b-h)
New Orleans, LA 70131
504-393-7074 / Fax: 504-393-1210
JEFF CHOUEST (Owner) & Buys Men's Sportswear, Sweaters, Sport Shirts, Outer Jackets, Leather Apparel, Casual Slacks, Active Apparel, Furnishings, Accessories, Belts, Men's Footwear, Store Displays, Fixtures, Supplies

M. GOLDBERG (MW)
Uptown Sq. (b)
200 Broadway., #121
New Orleans, LA 70118
504-866-1116 / Fax: 504-866-3818
Sales: $500,000-$1 Million
Website: www.mgoldbergclothier.com
MYRON GOLDBERG (Owner) & Buys Men's Overcoats, Suits, Tailored Jackets, Tailored Slacks, Raincoats, Sportswear, Sweaters, Sport Shirts, Outer Jackets, Leather Apparel, Casual Slacks, Active Apparel, Furnishings, Headwear, Accessories, Outdoor Wear, Men's Footwear, Boys' Wear, Store Di

MARCUS EVANS (MW)
4714 Paris Ave. (m-b)
New Orleans, LA 70122
504-284-6070 / Fax: 504-282-6085
WALTER DUPART (Owner) & Buys Men's Overcoats, Suits, Tailored Jackets, Tailored Slacks, Sportswear, Sweaters, Sport Shirts, Leather Apparel, Casual Slacks, Active Apparel, Furnishings, Pajamas, Accessories, Tuxedos, Footwear, Urban Contemporary, Store Displays, Fixtures, Supplies

MEYER THE HATTER (MW)
120 St. Charles Ave. (m-b)
New Orleans, LA 70130
504-525-1048 / Fax: 504-525-0259
Website: www.meyerthehatter.com
SAM H. MEYER (Co-Owner) & Buys Men's Headwear, Belts, Men's Embroidered Mexican Wedding Shirts, Store Displays, Fixtures, Supplies
WILLIAM MEYER (Co-Owner) & Buys Men's Headwear, Belts, Men's Embroidered Mexican Wedding Shirts, Store Displays, Fixtures, Supplies

MIRAGE FOR MEN (MW-2)
814 Canal St.
New Orleans, LA 70112
504-522-6376 / Fax: 504-522-9991
DAMIN HALUM (President)
SHADIA HALUM (Mgr.) & Buys Men's Sportswear, Furnishings, Accessories, Footwear

NEW YORK FASHIONS (CLO-3)
928 Canal St.
New Orleans, LA 70112
504-529-1361 / Fax: 504-486-9252
RICK MIRCHANDANI (Owner) & Buys Men's & Boys Apparel & Accessories, Footwear

PERLIS (CLO-4 & OL)
(CAJUN CLOTHING CO.)
6055 Magazine St. (b)
New Orleans, LA 70118
504-891-2073 / Fax: 504-896-9692
Sales: $1 Million-$10 Million
Website: www.perlis.com
DAVID W. PERLIS (President) & Buys Men's Sport Shirts, Casual Slacks, Shorts, Headwear, Cajun Clothing, Men's Suits, Tailored Jackets, Hosiery, Headwear, Belts, Fragrances, Big & Tall Men's Ties, Men's & Boys' Footwear, Men's Leather Apparel, Jewelry
DAVID G. PERLIS (C.E.O.) & Buys Men's Sweaters, Active Apparel, Robes
TOMMY BAKER (Dept. Mgr.) & Buys Men's Tailored Slacks, Raincoats, Sport Shirts, Outer Jackets, Casual Slacks, Dress Shirts, Gloves, Overcoats, Underwear, Big & Tall Men's Sport Shirts, Casual Slacks, Dress Shirts, Men's Leather Apparel, Jewelry
KELLEY LONG (Dept. Mgr.) & Buys Boys' Wear, Store Displays, Fixtures, Supplies
EDWIN ELY-Men's Accessories, Hosiery

LOUISIANA - New Orleans

RUBENSTEIN BROTHERS (CLO-2)

(ALL AMERICAN JEANS, INC.)
102 St. Charles St. (b)
New Orleans, LA 70130
504-581-6666 / Fax: 504-582-6982
Sales: $1 Million-$10 Million
Website: www.rubensteinbros.com

DAVID RUBENSTEIN (President) & Buys Men's Suits, Sportswear, Men's & Boys' Jeans, Sweaters, Slacks, Sport Shirts, Sport Coats, Footwear, Furnishings, Dress Shirts, Ties, Robes, Accessories, Belts, Underwear, Hosiery, Gloves, Jewelry, Small Leather Goods, Fragrances, Big & Tall Men's Wear, Store Displays, Fixtures, Supplies

NIKI RUBENSTEIN-Men's Sportswear, Dress Shirts, Ties

SHUSHAN LTD. (MW)

536 Saint Peter St. (m)
New Orleans, LA 70116
504-586-1188 / Fax: 504-586-1188
Website: www.shushans.com

SUSAN SHUSHAN (Owner) & Buys Sportswear, Furnishings, Accessories, Men's Wear

ELLIOT SHUSHAN-Sportswear, Furnishings, Accessories, Men's Wear

SOUL TRAIN FASHIONS (CLO-5)

131 Carondelet St. (m-b)
New Orleans, LA 70130
504-522-1000 / Fax: 504-522-1000

BALRAM MIRCHANDINI (Co-Owner) & Buys Men's Sportswear, Furnishings, Accessories, Young Men's, Boys' Wear, Store Displays, Fixtures, Supplies, Men's Footwear, Boys' Footwear

SOUTHERN RUNNER SPORTS (SP)

6112 Magazine St.
New Orleans, LA 70118
504-891-9999 / Fax: 504-891-9996
Sales: $100,001-$500,000
Website: www.southernrunner.com

MICHAEL ANDREWS (Owner) & Buys Activewear, Athletic Footwear

GEORGE OWEN-Athletic Clothing, Footwear

COUNTRY PACER, INC. (MW)

208 Main St. (m)
Oak Grove, LA 71263
318-428-8985 / Fax: 318-428-8949

CINDY CAPERS (Owner) & Buys Men's Wear, Urban Contemporary, Footwear, Accessories, Sportswear, Young Men's Wear

McCARTHY'S MENSWEAR (MW)

333 S. Main St. (h)
Opelousas, LA 70570
337-948-3325

BILLY McCARTHY (President) & Buys Men's Sportswear, Furnishings, Footwear, Accessories, Headwear, Young Men's Wear, Urban Contemporary, 8 to 20 Boys' Wear, Store Displays, Fixtures, Supplies

DAD & LAD TOGS, INC. (CLO)

1125 Main St.
Patterson, LA 70392
985-395-6587 / Fax: 985-395-6587

RAY RENTROP (Owner) & Buys Men's Sportswear, Furnishings, Accessories, Dress Shoes, Casual Shoes, Store Displays, Fixtures, Supplies

PIERRE PART STORE, INC. (GM)

P.O. Box 10 (p-m)
3421 Hwy. 70
Pierre Part, LA 70339
504-252-6261 / Fax: 504-252-6607

LOGI GUILLOT (Owner) & Buys Store Displays, Fixtures, Supplies

DeETTE KIVETT (Mgr.) & Buys Men's & Boys' Sport & Dress Shirts, Underwear, Sleepwear, Belts, Jeans, Men's Sportswear, Work Clothes, Work Boots, Boys' Wear

AUDREY GUILLOT (Mgr.) & Buys Men's & Boys' Sport & Dress Shirts, Underwear, Sleepwear, Belts, Jeans, Men's Sportswear, Work Clothes, Work Boots, Boys' Wear

FREMINS - JUST NEXT DOOR (DEPT)

P. O. Box 889 (p-m-b)
26275 Hwy. 23
Port Sulphur, LA 70083
985-564-2635 / Fax: 985-564-9139
Sales: $100,001-$500,000

DANNY FREMIN (Owner)

ROSE WISE-Men's & Boys' Sportswear, Furnishings, Accessories, Store Displays, Fixtures, Supplies

ALBERT'S (MW)

725 Louisa St. (m-b)
Rayville, LA 71269
318-728-6463 / Fax: 318-728-6464

CHARLES CHANEY (Owner) & Buys Men's Wear, Urban Contemporary, Footwear, Accessories, Men's Furnishings, Sportswear, Suits, Headwear

DELTA SALES CO. (DEPT)

P.O. Box 96 (m)
718 S. Louisa St.
Rayville, LA 71269
318-728-3501

GEORGE BOLTON (Owner) & Buys Men's Suits, Tailored Slacks, Sportswear, Sweaters, Sport Shirts, Outer Jackets, Casual Slacks, Active Apparel, Furnishings, Headwear, Belts, Big & Tall Men's Dress Shirts, Tailored Slacks, Work Clothes, Boys' Sportswear, Furnishings, Store Displays, Fixtures, Supplies

LEWIS & COMPANY LTD. (DEPT)

(LEWIS STAGG SHOP)
P.O. Box 340 (m-b)
110 N. Vienna St.
Ruston, LA 71273
318-255-3545 / Fax: 318-251-9905
Sales: $1 Million-$10 Million
Website: www.lewisfashions.com

W.A.J. LEWIS, III (President)

WILLIAM J. LEWIS (D.M.M.-Men's Wear) & Buys Store Supplies

RAY HARRIS-All Weather Coats, Suits, Tailored Jackets, Tailored Slacks, Raincoats, Sweaters, Sport Shirts, Outer Jackets, Casual Slacks, Active Apparel, Furnishings, Accessories, Young Men's Wear

ANN WHITE-Boys' Wear

LARRY GINN-Men's Dress Shoes, Athletic Footwear, Boots

LORI HAMILTON (Display Mgr.) & Buys Store Displays, Fixtures

KAMPER'S KORNER, INC. (CLO)

5848 Line Ave. (p)
Shreveport, LA 71106
318-861-6996 / Fax: 318-861-1782
Sales: $500,001-$1 Million
Website: www.kamperskorner.com

ANNETTE KNIGHT (Co-Owner) & Buys Men's Sportswear, Outdoor Wear, Sweaters, Sport Shirts, Outer Jackets, Casual Slacks, Active Apparel, Footwear, Boots, Young Men's Ski Wear, Store Displays, Fixtures, Supplies

JOHN KNIGHT (Co-Owner) & Buys Men's Headwear

JERRY COOK (Mgr.)

ON TIME FASHIONS (MW)

621 Texas St. (m)
Shreveport, LA 71101
318-221-6674 / Fax: 318-221-6610

SAM FASHHO (Owner) & Buys Men's Wear, Young Men's Wear, Tailored Jackets, Tailored Slacks, Footwear, Accessories, 8 to 20 Boys' Wear

LOUISIANA - Shreveport

OXFORD STREET (CLO-2)

8924 Jewella Dr. (m)
Shreveport, LA 71118
318-687-8054 / Fax: 318-687-8983
Sales: $100,001-$500,000

ISPEAR BROU (Owner) & Buys Men's Sportswear, Dress Shoes, Ties, Hosiery, Belts, Footwear, Jewelry, Small Leather Goods, Young Men's Wear, Urban Contemporary, 8 to 20 Boys' Wear, Easter Boys' Suits, Store Displays, Fixtures, Supplies

RANCHLAND SADDLES & RANCHWEAR (CLO)

3025 Bert Kouns Industrial Loop (m)
Shreveport, LA 71118
318-688-4291 / Fax: 318-688-4293
Sales: $500,000-$1 Million

JOHN WOODSON (President) & Buys Men's Leather Apparel, Western Wear, Boys' Western Wear, Furnishings, Accessories, Men's & Boys' Western Boots, Store Displays, Fixtures, Supplies

ROSENBLATH COMPANY, INC. (MW)

740 Azalea Dr. (m-b-h)
Shreveport, LA 71106
318-869-1926 / Fax: 318-869-0004

JOHN PICKENS (G.M.M.) & Buys Men's Overcoats, Suits, Tailored Jackets, Tailored Slacks, Rain Coats, Sweaters, Sport Shirts, Outer Jackets, Casual Slacks, Men's Dress Shoes, Furnishings, Accessories, Footwear, Store Displays, Fixtures, Supplies

SPORTSPECTRUM (SP)

7607 Youree Dr.
Shreveport, LA 71105
318-798-1241 / Fax: 318-798-1249
Website: www.sportspectrumusa.com

MATT BROWN (Owner) & Buys Activewear, Athletic Footwear, Licensed Apparel

YEARWOOD'S, INC. (CLO)

645 E. Bert Kouns Industrial Loop
Shreveport, LA 71118
318-688-1844 / Fax: 318-688-9997

PAT McGOVERN (Owner) & Buys Men's Uniforms, Headwear, Boots

CROSS GATES ATHLETIC CLUB (SP-2)

200 N. Military Rd.
Slidell, LA 70461
985-643-3500 / Fax: 985-643-9614
Website: www.crossgatesclub.com

MARYANN WELCH (Co-Owner)

LARRY WELCH (Co-Owner) & Buys Activewear, Athletic Footwear

HALLEY CO., INC. (MW)

150 Northshore Blvd., #4014 (b)
Slidell, LA 70460
985-641-7394 / Fax: 985-641-0306

GARY HALLEY (Partner) & Buys Men's Sportswear, Furnishings, Belts, Small Leather Goods, Jewelry, Young Men's Wear, Store Displays, Fixtures, Supplies, Accessories

JULIE HALLEY (Gen Mgr.) & Buys Men's Sportswear, Furnishings, Belts, Small Leather Goods, Jewelry, Young Men's Wear, Store Displays, Fixtures, Supplies, Accessories

THE PLACE (MW)

115 S. Main St. (m)
Springhill, LA 71075
318-539-5806 / Fax: 318-539-2899

BARBARA BRYAN (Owner) & Buys Men's Sportswear, Footwear, Furnishings, Accessories, Headwear, Young Men's Wear, Store Displays, Fixtures, Supplies

ROBERT C. BRYAN (G.M.M.) & Buys Men's Sportswear, Footwear, Furnishings, Accessories, Headwear, Young Men's Wear, Store Displays, Fixtures, Supplies

KHOURY'S (CLO)

1531 E. Napoleon St. (p-m-b)
Sulphur, LA 70663
337-528-2097 / Fax: 337-528-2073
Sales: $1 Million-$10 Million

STEVE KHOURY (Owner) & Buys Men's, Young Men's & Boys' Wear, Big & Tall Men's Wear, Men's & Boys' Footwear, Headwear, Accessories, Store Displays, Fixtures, Supplies

DIANNA KHOURY-Men's, Young Men's & Boys' Wear, Big & Tall Men's Wear, Men's & Boys' Footwear, Headwear, Accessories, Store Displays, Fixtures, Supplies

JAKE'S DEPARTMENT STORE, INC. (DEPT-2)

(MANGO'S TRADING CO. OF HOUMA)
P.O. Box 1871 (p-m)
508 St. Mary Hwy.
Thibodaux, LA 70301
985-447-4663 / Fax: 985-448-2282
Sales: $1 Million-$10 Million

RICHARD T. BOURGEOIS (President) & Buys Boys' Wear 8 to 20, Store Displays, Fixtures and Supplies

STEPHANIE TABOR (Mgr.) & Buys Men's Tailored Slacks, Sweaters, Sport Shirts, Casual Slacks, Active Apparel, Dress Shirts, Underwear, Hosiery, Small Leather Goods, Young Men's Wear, Urban Contemporary, Store Displays, Fixtures, Supplies

THE NEW STORE (MW)

607 W. 3rd St. (p)
Thibodaux, LA 70301
985-447-3155
Sales: $100,001-$500,000

FRANK TERRACINA (President) & Buys Store Displays, Fixtures, Supplies

THERESA LECHE (G.M.M.) & Buys Men's Overcoats, Tailored Slacks, Raincoats, Sportswear, Sweaters, Sport Shirts, Outer Jackets, Casual Slacks, Active Apparel, Furnishings, Headwear, Belts, Small Leather Goods, Big & Tall Men's Wear, Young Men's & Boys' Wear

DAD'S & LAD'S (MW)

652 LaSalle St. (m)
Ville Platte, LA 70586
337-363-6700 / Fax: 337-363-2235
Sales: $100,001-$500,000

FREDDIE PITRE (Owner) & Buys Men's Sportswear, Shoes, Furnishings, Accessories, Headwear, Young Men's Wear, 8 to 20 Boys' Wear, Store Displays, Fixtures, Supplies

TATE'S MEN'S & BOYS' SHOP, INC. (MW)

1756 W. Main St. (m-b)
Ville Platte, LA 70586
337-363-6607 / Fax: 337-363-6712
Sales: $100,001-$500,000

GREG TATE (President) & Buys Men's Overcoats, Suits, Tailored Jackets, Tailored Slacks, Raincoats, Big & Tall, Sweaters, Sportswear, Sport Shirts, Outer Jackets, Leather Apparel, Casual Slacks, Active Apparel, Furnishings, Headwear, Accessories, Boys' Wear, Men's & Boys' Shoes, Boots, Slippers, Store Displays, Fixtures, Supplies

HARPERS ARMY SURPLUS (AN)

117 N. Riverfront St. (p-m-b)
West Monroe, LA 71291
318-323-5590

KARL BAILEY (Owner) & Buys Work Boots, Sportswear, Outer Jackets, Active Apparel

J & H BOOTS & JEANS, INC. (CLO & WW)

5218 Cypress St. (p-m-b)
West Monroe, LA 71291
318-396-2407 / Fax: 318-396-9089

JAN JENTRY (Co-Owner) & Buys Men's & Boys' Western Wear, Sportswear, Dress Shirts, Ties, Underwear, Hosiery, Accessories, Boots, Store Displays, Fixtures, Supplies

JANELL JENTRY (Co-Owner) & Buys Men's & Boys' Clothing, Sportswear, Dress Shirts, Ties, Underwear, Hosiery, Accessories, Boots, Store Displays, Fixtures, Supplies

S & W WESTERN WEAR, INC. (WW-2)

101 Norris Ln. (m)
West Monroe, LA 71291
318-396-4212 / Fax: 318-397-1911
Sales: $1 Million-$10 Million

GEORGE WAGGONER (Owner) & Buys Men's Western Wear, Western Accessories & Furnishings, Boots

WESTERN & WORK WORLD (WW-2)

5129 Cypress St. (p-m)
West Monroe, LA 71291
318-396-8004 / Fax: 318-397-0863

JASON ALDRIDGE (Owner) & Buys Men's & Boys' Western Apparel, Accessories, Work Boots, Store Displays, Fixtures, Supplies

PRICE'S KNIGHT'S ARMOUR (MW)

(PRICE'S MEN'S STORE)
107 Main St. (m)
Winnfield, LA 71483
318-628-4481

LARRY PRICE (Owner)

GARLAND MILLER (Mgr.) & Buys Men's Sportswear, Footwear, Furnishings, Accessories, Headwear, Store Displays, Fixtures, Supplies

LAMAR TARBER (Asst.) & Buys Men's Sportswear, Footwear, Furnishings, Accessories, Headwear, Store Displays, Fixtures, Supplies

LOUIE'S CLOTHING & SHOE STORE (CLO & FW)

250 Center St.
Auburn, ME 04210
207-782-0341

MORRIS SILVERMAN (Owner) & Buys Men's Work Clothes, Big & Tall Wear, Sportswear, Leather Apparel, Young Men's Wear, Footwear, Store Displays, Fixtures & Supplies

THE BANGOR SKI RACK, INC. (CLO)

24 Longview Dr. (b)
Bangor, ME 04401
207-945-6474 / Fax: 207-945-6863
Sales: $500,000-$1 Million

JEFF PEET (Owner) & Buys Men's & Boys' Winter Outerwear, Ski Clothing, Furnishings, Headwear, Accessories, Young Men's Wear, Footwear, Store Displays, Fixtures, Supplies

DOUG OLIVER (Mgr.) & Buys Men's & Boys' Winter Outerwear, Ski Clothing, Furnishings, Headwear, Accessories, Young Men's Wear, Footwear, Store Displays, Fixtures, Supplies

NIMAN'S (MW)

25 Washington St., #B
Bangor, ME 04401
207-942-4980

NIMAN KARAM (Owner) & Buys Men's Big & Tall, Men's & Young Men's Pants, Shirts, Suits

SKLAR REGULAR BIG & TALL (MW-1)

(THE MAINE COAT TOWN)
(Div. of BEN SKLAR, INC.)
625 Broadway Shopping Center, #A (m-b)
Bangor, ME 04401
207-942-5323 / Fax: 207-942-5323
Sales: $500,000-$1 Million
Website: www.mainebigandtall.com

DAVID SKLAR (President) & Buys Men's Sportswear, Furnishings, Headwear, Belts, Big & Tall Men's Wear, Boys' Outerwear, Accessories, Store Displays, Fixtures, Supplies

JEKYLL & HYDE, INC. (AN)

70 Main St. (p-m)
Bar Harbor, ME 04609
207-288-3084 / Fax: 207-288-9687

STEVE RYAN (Co-Owner) & Buys Men's & Boys' Sweat Pants, Fleece, T-shirts, Fatigues, Khakis, Hosiery, Headwear, Urban Contemporary, Store Displays, Fixtures, Supplies

MARILYN RYAN (Co-Owner) & Buys Men's & Boys' Sweat Pants, Fleece, T-shirts, Fatigues, Khakis, Hosiery, Headwear, Store Displays, Fixtures, Supplies

LANGEVIN'S MEN'S & BOYS' WEAR (MW)

209 Main St. (m-b)
Biddeford, ME 04005
207-284-4963 / Fax: 207-284-4963

PETER LANGEVIN (President & G.M.M.) & Buys Men's Sportswear, Leather Apparel, Furnishings, Headwear, Accessories, Young Men's & Boys' Wear, Store Displays, Fixtures, Supplies

HOUSE OF LOGAN (CLO-2)

P.O. Box 387 (m-b)
20 Townsend Ave.
Boothbay Harbor, ME 04538
207-633-2293 / Fax: 207-633-5811
Sales: $500,000-$1 Million

SARAH WILCOX (President & G.M.M.) & Buys Boys' Wear, Store Displays, Fixtures, Supplies

ALEX LOGAN-Men's Tailored Jackets, Tailored Slacks, Raincoats, Sportswear, Furnishings, Headwear, Accessories, Store Displays, Fixtures and Supplies

PAINE'S CLOTHING STORE (CLO)

4 Commercial St. (m)
Boothbay Harbor, ME 04538
207-633-3262

TRAVIS S. PAINE (Co-Owner) & Buys Men's Raincoats, Sportswear, Footwear, Store Displays, Fixtures, Supplies

JUDY PAINE (Co-Owner) & Buys Men's Raincoats, Sportswear, Footwear, Store Displays, Fixtures, Supplies

W.S. EMERSON CO., INC. (DEPT-2)

15 Acme Rd. (bud-p)
Brewer, ME 04412
207-989-3410 / Fax: 207-989-8540

JOHN A. VICKERY, Sr. (President) & Buys Men's & Boys' Sportswear, Furnishings, Leather Apparel, Footwear, Store Displays, Fixtures, Supplies

WINTERPORT BOOT SHOP (FW)

264 State St. (b)
Brewer, ME 04412
207-989-6492 / Fax: 207-989-6496

MIKE ALLEN (President & Owner) & Buys Men's Boots, Footwear & Accessories

GRAND CITY (DEPT)

128 Main St. (bud)
Brunswick, ME 04011
207-725-8964 / Fax: 207-725-6801
Sales: $1 Million-$10 Million

SCOTT FENWICK (President & G.M.M.) & Buys Men's Sweaters, Furnishings, Accessories, Sportswear, Footwear, Young Men's Wear, Boys' Wear, Store Displays, Fixtures and Supplies

PENNELL'S, INC. (MW)

50 Main St. (m)
Brunswick, ME 04011
207-725-2443

DAVE GIRARDIN (Owner) & Buys Men's Big & Tall Clothing, Sportswear, Furnishings, Accessories, Work Clothes, Footwear, Store Displays, Fixtures, Supplies

ROSEN'S DEPARTMENT STORE (DEPT)

77 Main St. (p-m-b)
Bucksport, ME 04416
207-469-3306 / Fax: 207-469-2330

RICHARD ROSEN (Owner) & Buys Men's Raincoats, Sportswear, Dress Shirts, Underwear, Hosiery, Headwear, Swimwear, Small Leather Goods, Footwear, Young Men's & Boys' Wear, Urban Contemporary, Store Displays, Fixtures, Supplies

BOSTON SHOE STORE (FW)

(L. BERNARDINI CO., INC.)
261 Main St. (m)
Calais, ME 04619
207-454-2844 / Fax: 207-454-7330

LOUIS BERNARDINI (President) & Buys Men's Sportswear, Outerwear, Footwear, Young Men's Wear, Store Displays, Fixtures, Supplies

ADMIRAL'S BUTTONS (CLO)

36 Bayview St. (b)
Camden, ME 04843
207-236-2617 / Fax: 207-236-4475

CAROL EMANUEL (Co-Owner) & Buys Men's Sportswear & Casual Wear

BARTON EMANUEL (Co-Owner) & Buys Men's Sportswear & Casual Wear

BUZZELL'S CLOTHING STORE (CLO)

57 Sweden St. (m)
Caribou, ME 04736
207-493-4484
Sales: $100,001-$500,000

RONALD C. BUZZELL (Owner) & Buys Men's Overcoats, Sportswear, Leather Apparel, Headwear, Dress Shirts, Ties, Hosiery, Gloves, Belts, Footwear

LOIS GORDON-Store Displays, Fixtures, Supplies

JOSEPH SLEEPER & SONS, INC. (DEPT)

99 Linden St. (m)
Caribou, ME 04736
207-498-8181 / Fax: 207-498-8182
Sales: $1 Million-$10 Million

MARK SLEEPER (Co-Owner)

DAVID SLEEPER (Co-Owner)

JOSEPH SLEEPER, III (Co-Owner & Mgr.) & Buys Men's Sportswear, Leather Apparel, Furnishings, Accessories, Footwear, Young Men's & Boys' Wear, Urban Contemporary, Store Displays, Fixtures, Supplies

WILLEY'S (CLO-2)

248 State St., #18 (m)
Ellsworth, ME 04605
207-667-2511 / Fax: 207-667-8215
Sales: $1 Million-$10 Million

- ANN WILLEY GRANT (Co-Owner)
- ROSS GRANT (Co-Owner) & Buys Men's Sportswear, Leather Apparel, Furnishings, Accessories, Boys' Wear 8 to 20, Headwear, Young Men's Wear, Store Displays, Fixtures, Supplies
- ROGER GRANT-Men's Footwear

JOSEPH'S CLOTHING & SPORTING GOODS (MW & SG)

167 Main St. (b)
Fairfield, ME 04937
207-453-9756 / Fax: 207-453-6736
Sales: $1 Million-$10 Million
Website: www.josephssportinggoods.com

- HAROLD JOSEPH (Owner) & Buys Men's Golf Apparel
- JON EUSTIS (G.M.M.) & Buys Men's Footwear
- PAULA EUSTIS (Mgr.) & Buys Men's Golf Apparel, Sportswear, Denim Apparel, Headwear, Accessories, Boys' Wear, Leather Apparel, Young Men's Wear, Store Displays, Fixtures, Supplies

L.L. BEAN, INC. (MO & OL & CLO-2)

Casco St. (b)
Freeport, ME 04033
207-865-4761 / Fax: 207-552-2802
Sales: $500 Million-$1 Billion
Website: www.llbean.com

- CHRIS McCORMICK (President)
- (Sr. V.P. & Gen. Mgr.-L.L. Bean Men's)
- TOM ARMSTRONG (V.P. & Dir.-Activewear, Outerwear & Footwear)
- GREG HOUSER (D.M.M.) & Buys Men's & Boys' Wear
- (Prdt. Mgr.) & Buys Boys' Outerwear, Raincoats, Jackets, Vests, Leather Apparel
- DIANE SIMONDS (Prdt. Mgr.) & Buys Mens' Accessories & Sweaters, Footwear
- CAROLINE SINCLAIR (Prdt. Mgr.) & Buys Mens' Knits, Blazers
- SHARON COFFIN-Men's Knits, Blazers
- (Prdt. Dev.) & Buys Boys' Wear
- JIM GOTT-Woven Tops, Knits & Footwear
- BOBBY BERGE-Men's Outerwear
- PAUL MADDRELL (Supv.-Visual Mdsg.) & Buys Store Displays, Fixtures

MAINE-LY COUNTRY WESTERN WEAR (WW)

166 Yarmouth Rd. (m-b)
Gray, ME 04039
207-657-3412 / Fax: 207-657-5667

- ALLAN FOSTER (Co-Owner) & Buys Men's & Boys' Western Wear, All Related Accessories, Boots, Store Displays, Fixtures, Supplies
- ARLENE FOSTER (Co-Owner) & Buys Men's & Boys' Western Wear, All Related Accessories, Boots, Store Displays, Fixtures, Supplies

MARIERS MEN'S SHOP (MW)

33 Main St. (m)
Kennebunk, ME 04043
207-985-2122
Sales: $100,001-$500,000

- KARL HOOPER (Owner) & Buys Men's Sportswear, Furnishings & Accessories

MOUNTAIN TOPS, INC. (CLO-9)

401 Lafayette Ctr. (m)
Kennebunk, ME 04043
207-985-1919 / Fax: 207-985-1920

- DIANE FRAZIER (Owner) & Buys Men's Headwear, Young Men's Sweat Pants & Shirts, Boys' Wear, Store Displays, Fixtures, Supplies
- ROBERT G. FRAZIER (President)
- JAYNE COY-Men's Headwear, Young Men's Sweat Pants & Shirts, Boys' Wear, Store Displays, Fixtures, Supplies

DOCK SQUARE CLOTHIERS (CLO-3)

P.O. Box 650C (m-b)
Kennebunkport, ME 04046
207-967-5362 / Fax: 207-967-2918
Sales: $1 Million-$10 Million
Website: www.docksquareclothiers.com

- JOHN RINALDI (Owner) & Buys Men's Sportswear, Furnishings, Accessories, Young Men's Wear, Store Displays, Fixtures and Supplies
- BRIAN POWELL (G.M.M.) & Buys Men's Sportswear, Furnishings, Accessories, Young Men's Wear, Store Displays, Fixtures and Supplies

KITTERY TRADING POST (CLO & SG)

(TRADING POST OF KITTERY SPORTING GOODS)
P.O. Box 904 (p-m-b)
US Rt. 1
Kittery, ME 03904
207-439-2700 / Fax: 207-439-8001
Sales: $10 Million-$50 Million
Website: www.kitterytradingpost.com

- GARY ADAMS (President)
- SUSAN O'WIL-Big & Tall Wear, Sweaters, Sport Shirts, Casual Slacks, Active Apparel, Men's Overcoats, Tailored Jackets, Raincoats, Sweaters, Sport Shirts, Outer Jackets, Leather Apparel, Dress Shirts
- JIM BREWSTER-Overcoats, Raincoats, Big & Tall Wear, Outer Jackets, Hunting Apparel, Leather Apparel, Ties, Robes, Underwear, Headwear, Belts
- ANN BARBOUR-Small Leather Goods, Boys' Wear 7 & Up, Boys' Sportswear, Boys' Furnishings, Boys' Accessories
- KATINA YORK-Jewelry
- ERNIE DEMSEY-Men's Footwear
- KATHY BRODERICK-Store Displays, Fixtures, Supplies
- NANCY MATTHEWS-Store Displays, Fixtures, Supplies

BATES COLLEGE STORE (SP)

Chase Hall
56 Campus Ave.
Lewiston, ME 04240
207-786-6121 / Fax: 207-786-6119
Website: www.bates.edu/bookstore

- SARAH POTTER-Activewear, Outerwear

LAMEY-WELLEHAN (FW-6 & OL)

P.O. Box 1317 (b)
110 Lisbon St.
Lewiston, ME 04240
207-784-6595 / Fax: 207-784-9650
Sales: $1 Million-$10 Million
Website: www.lwshoes.com

- JAMES F. WELLEHAN (President)
- JACK SILKERMAN (Mdse. Mgr.)
- DON STOWELL-Men's & Boys' Footwear
- ANN HUMPHRIES-Men's Accessories, Hosiery

RENY'S (DEPT-12)

731 Rte. 1 (bud-p)
Newcastle, ME 04553
207-563-3177 / Fax: 207-563-5681
Sales: $10 Million-$50 Million

- ROBERT H. RENY (President) & Buys Footwear
- JOHN E. RENY (V.P.) & Buys Store Displays, Fixtures, Supplies
- MONICA KEMM-Men's & Boys' Wear, Urban Contemporary

MAINE - North Vassalboro

HEMPHILL'S, INC. (WW)
P.O. Box 74 (m-b)
Oak Grove Rd.
North Vassalboro, ME 04962
207-872-7964 / Fax: 207-873-6115

MARGARET HEMPHILL (Owner)

GRETA JOSEPH-Men's Riding & Western Wear, Belts, Native American Jewelry, Footwear, Store Displays, Fixtures, Supplies

THE HOLMES STORE (MW)
114 Main St. (m-b)
Northeast Harbor, ME 04662
207-276-3273 / Fax: 207-276-4096
Sales: $500,000-$1 Million

ANNE TUCKER (Owner) & Buys Tailored Jackets, Tailored Slacks, Raincoats, Sport Shirts, Outer Jackets, Leather Apparel, Casual Slacks, Dress Shirts, Ties, Robes, Underwear, Hosiery, Gloves, Headwear, Accessories, Men's Footwear, Store Displays, Fixtures, Supplies

L.F. PIKE & SON (MW)
339 Main St. (b)
Norway, ME 04268
207-743-6561
Sales: $100,001-$500,000

ARTHUR GOUIN (Owner) & Buys Men's Sportswear, Furnishings & Accessories

ATLANTIC SPORTSWEAR (CLO)
36 Waldron Way
Portland, ME 04103
207-797-5028 / Fax: 207-797-4729

JOHN FAY (Owner) & Buys Boys' Apparel, Footwear, Hats, Men's Apparel, Men's Surf & Swimwear, Resortwear, T-shirts, Imprinted Sportswear

DAVID WOOD (MW)
75 Market St. (b)
Portland, ME 04101
207-773-3906 / Fax: 207-773-3876
Website: www.davidwood.com

DAVID HODGKINS (Owner) & Buys Men's Wear, Footwear, Men's Furnishings, Accessories, Sportswear, and Suits

JOSEPH'S, INC. (CLO)
410 Fore St. (b)
Portland, ME 04101
207-773-1274 / Fax: 207-774-7217

JOSEPH REDMAN (Owner) & Buys Men's Sportswear, Furnishings & Accessories

LEVINSKY'S, INC. (CLO-2)
516 Congress St. (p-m)
Portland, ME 04101
207-774-0972 / Fax: 207-774-6091
Sales: $1 Million-$10 Million
Website: www.levinskys.com

ERIC LEVINSKY (President) & Buys Men's Tailored Jackets, Tailored Slacks, Raincoats, Sweaters, Casual Slacks, Dress Shirts, Sport Shirts, Outer Jackets, Active Apparel, Big & Tall Men's Wear, Ties, Robes, Belts, Small Leather Goods, Young Men's & Boys' Wear, Urban Contemporary, Men's & Boys' Footwear, Men's Furnishings, Headwear, Sportswear, Furnishings, Store Displays, Fixtures, Supplies

SUN CITY TANNING & SWIMWEAR (CLO)
1037 Forest Ave.
Portland, ME 04103
207-797-7410 / Fax: 207-797-7431

MIKE CARON (Co-Owner) & Buys Sunglasses, Fashion Accessories, Footwear, Hats, Apparel, Men's Surf & Swimwear, Resortwear, Men's Apparel, Men's Swimwear

DONNA CARON (Co-Owner) & Buys Sunglasses, Fashion Accessories, Footwear, Hats, Apparel, Men's Surf & Swimwear, Resortwear, Men's Apparel, Men's Swimwear

FRED P. STEVENS CO. (MW)
431 Main St. (m-b)
Presque Isle, ME 04769
207-762-1711
Sales: $100,001-$500,000

GALEN D. HATHAWAY (Owner & G.M.M.) & Buys Men's Overcoats, Suits, Tailored Jackets, Tailored Slacks, Raincoats, Sweaters, Sport Shirts, Outer Jackets, Casual Slacks, Active Apparel, Furnishings, Headwear, Belts, Jewelry, Small Leather Goods, Store Displays, Fixtures, Supplies

ROY'S ARMY & NAVY (AN)
710 Main St.
Presque Isle, ME 04769
207-768-3181

DANA PACKARD (Owner) & Buys Men's Apparel

EMBROIDERY SHOP (CLO & OL)
464 Main St. (m)
Rockland, ME 04841
207-594-8636 / Fax: 207-596-0256
Website: www.maineembroideryshop.com

JIM BRICKLE (Owner) & Buys Men's Sportswear & Outerwear, T-shirts

CARLISLES MEN'S STORE (CLO)
92 Congress St. (m-b)
Rumford, ME 04276
207-364-2581 / Fax: 207-364-2581

JOHN SOUCY (Owner) & Buys Men's Sportswear, Furnishings & Accessories, Boys' 4 to 20

HUSSEY'S GENERAL STORE (DEPT)
P.O. Box 81 (bud-p)
Rt. 32 & 105
Windsor, ME 04363
207-445-2511 / Fax: 207-445-3750

ROXANNE HUSSEY (Owner) & Buys Men's & Boys' Jeans, Tops, Fleece, Jackets, Work Clothes, Hunting Apparel, Rain Gear, Underwear, Hosiery, Hats, Belts, Suspenders, Footwear, Store Displays, Fixtures, Supplies

DALUCA, INC. (KS)
40 Flint Rock Dr.
York, ME 03909
804-762-4455 / Fax: 804-217-8999

D. DALUCA (Owner) & Buys Men's Activewear, Outerwear, Accessories, Footwear

SHELTON'S, INC. (CLO)
P.O. Box 10 (m-b)
Ocean Ave.
York, ME 03909
207-363-3810 / Fax: 207-363-0505

HAROLD ANDERSON (Owner) & Buys Men's Sweaters, Sport Shirts, Outer Jackets, Casual Slacks, Active Apparel, Swimwear, Young Men's Wear, Store Displays, Fixtures, Supplies

EVELYN COLBY (Mgr.)

IRA COLBY (Mgr.)

FIT TO A TEE SHIRT CO. (CLO-2)

107 Main St. (m-b)
Annapolis, MD 21401
410-268-6596
Sales: $500,001-$1 Million

PHILLIP WALSH (Co-Owner) & Buys Boys' & Men's Apparel, Casualwear, Denim Apparel, Accessories, Hosiery, Sleepwear, Sportswear

KAREN WALSH (Co-Owner) & Buys Boys' & Men's Apparel, Casualwear, Denim Apparel, Accessories, Hosiery, Sleepwear, Sportswear

HYDE PARK ANNAPOLIS HABERDASHERY (MW)

110 Dock St. (b)
Annapolis, MD 21401
410-269-0074 / Fax: 410-263-0074
Sales: $100,001-$500,000

DON GRIFFIN (Owner) & Buys Men's Sportswear, Furnishings, Accessories, Footwear, Store Displays, Fixtures, Supplies

JOHNSON'S, INC. (MW)

79 Maryland Ave. (m-b)
Annapolis, MD 21401
410-263-6390 / Fax: 410-263-9024
Sales: $1 Million-$10 Million

JEAN HELD (President & Owner) & Buys Men's Sportswear, Leather Apparel, Furnishings, Headwear, Accessories

HERB CUMMINS (V.P.) & Buys Men's Sportswear, Leather Apparel, Furnishings, Headwear, Accessories

NOTE-Store Displays, Fixtures & Supplies Are Handled by a Freelance Contractor.

ARMU PRODUCTS (CLO)

8322 Dalesford Rd. (bud-p-m)
Baltimore, MD 21234
410-661-6260 / Fax: 410-661-5581
Sales: $500,001-$1 Million
Website: www.armuproducts.com

ARNIE MUNOZ (Owner & Dir.-Fin.) & Buys Boys' Apparel, Men's Apparel

BRIAN LEFKO (MW)

303 Reistertown Rd. (m-b)
Baltimore, MD 21208
410-486-6788 / Fax: 410-602-1936
Sales: $1 Million-$10 Million

BRIAN LEFKO (Owner) & Buys Men's Sportswear, Furnishings & Accessories

CHANGES ENTERPRISES, LLC (MW-7)

409 Ensor St. (b)
Baltimore, MD 21202
410-727-1010 / Fax: 410-244-0720
Sales: $1 Million-$10 Million
Website: www.changes4you.com

ANDREW GOETZ (President)

STEWART SILBERMAN (Dir.-Fin. & Real Estate Contract) & Buys Men's Footwear, Leather Goods, Men's Big & Tall Apparel, Casualwear, Denim Apparel, Formalwear, Accessories, Hosiery, Outerwear, Sportswear, Suits, Swimwear

ANTONIO GRAY-Men's Footwear, Leather Goods, Men's Big & Tall Apparel, Casualwear, Denim Apparel, Formalwear, Accessories, Hosiery, Outerwear, Sportswear, Suits, Swimwear

HAROLD RUDO-Men's Footwear

DA-DA-DA (CLO-3)

2313 E. Monument St. (bud-p-m)
Baltimore, MD 21205
410-276-9063
Sales: $1 Million-$10 Million

MICHAEL MENDEZ (Owner) & Buys Men's Footwear, Leather Goods, Apparel, Casualwear, Hosiery, Outerwear, Sportswear

EDDIE JACOBS LTD. (MW)

10 Light St. (b)
Baltimore, MD 21202
410-752-2624 / Fax: 410-752-3395

EDDIE JACOBS, JR. (Owner) & Buys Men's Sportswear, Furnishings, Accessories

GAGE CLOTHES CO. (MW-2)

200 W. Baltimore St. (m-b)
Baltimore, MD 21201
410-727-0763 / Fax: 410-727-4174
Website: www.gagemens.com

WILLIAM GLAZER (President) & Buys Men's Overcoats, Suits, Tailored Jackets, Tailored Slacks, Raincoats, Big & Tall Men's Wear, Urban Contemporary, Men's Headwear, Sweaters, Sport Shirts, Outer Jackets, Casual Slacks, Active Apparel, Furnishings, Accessories, Boys' Tailored Clothing, Store Displays, Fixtures & Supplies

SHARI BASKIN (G.M.M.) & Buys Men's Overcoats, Suits, Tailored Jackets, Tailored Slacks, Raincoats, Big & Tall Men's Wear, Urban Contemporary, Men's Headwear, Sweaters, Sport Shirts, Outer Jackets, Casual Slacks, Active Apparel, Furnishings, Accessories, Boys' Tailored Clothing, Store Displays, Fixtures & Supplies

GEORGE HOWARD LTD. (MW)

Village of Cross Keys (b)
94 Village Sq.
Baltimore, MD 21210
410-532-3535 / Fax: 410-532-3087
Sales: $500,000-$1 Million

HOWARD SHAPIRO (Owner) & Buys Men's Overcoats, Suits, Tailored Jackets, Tailored Slacks, Raincoats, Sweaters, Men's Sportswear, Sport Shirts, Outer Jackets, Leather Apparel, Casual Slacks, Furnishings, Belts, Jewelry, Footwear

NOTE-Store Displays, Fixtures, Supplies Are Bought By a Freelance Contractor.

J.S. EDWARDS LTD. (MW)

1809 Reisterstown Rd.
Baltimore, MD 21208
410-653-2266 / Fax: 410-653-2677
Website: www.jsedwards.com

EDWARD STEINBERG (Owner) & Buys Men's Wear, Clothing, Furnishings, Accessories, Footwear

STAN GLEIMAN (G.M.M.) & Buys Men's Wear, Clothing, Furnishings, Accessories, Footwear

JERRY'S BARGAINS, INC. (KS & DISC)

605 W. Lexington St. (bud)
Baltimore, MD 21201
410-539-5860 / Fax: 410-385-2657
Sales: $500,000-$1 Million
Website: www.jerrysschooluniforms.com

GERALD M. SILVERMAN (President) & Buys Men's Sportswear, Boys' Wear to Size 20, Huskies, Footwear

ROBBIE SILVERMAN (G.M.M.) & Buys Men's Sportswear, Boys' Wear to Size 20, Huskies, Footwear

LEE'S PANTS HOUSE (MW)

116 N. Howard St. (m)
Baltimore, MD 21201
410-752-6082 / Fax: 410-752-9097

MISS LEE (Owner) & Buys Men's Sportswear, Furnishings, Accessories, Urban Contemporary

M & F FAMILY STORE (MW)

1800 Pennsylvania Ave. (m)
Baltimore, MD 21217
410-523-5875

SUNG WOO (Owner) & Buys Men's Casual Wear

MAN O MAN (MW)

2121 E. Monument St.
Baltimore, MD 21205
410-732-4793 / Fax: 410-531-1217

MR. KANG (Owner) & Buys Men's Sportswear, Furnishings, Accessories, Boys' 4 to 20 Sportswear

MARYLAND - Baltimore

THE MART (CLO-2)
321 W. Lexington St. (bud-p-m)
Baltimore, MD 21201
410-752-1535 / Fax: 410-752-7338
HYMAN CHABBOTT (Owner) & Buys Men's Sportswear, Dress Shirts, Ties, Underwear, Hosiery, Belts, Headwear, Young Men's & Boys' Wear, Urban Contemporary, Store Displays, Fixtures, Supplies

MARYLAND SCREEN PRINTERS, INC. (CLO)
180 Portal St. (p-m)
Baltimore, MD 21224
410-633-3333 / Fax: 410-633-3761
Website: www.mdscreen.com
GARRETT PFEIFER (Owner) & Buys Men's, Young Men's & Boys' T-shirts, Urban Contemporary, Sport Shirts, Shorts, Store Displays, Fixtures, Supplies

MATERIALISTIK, INC. (CLO)
2217 Harford Rd.
Baltimore, MD 21218
410-235-2864 / Fax: 410-235-9252
MICHAEL MOORE (Owner) & Buys Men's Wear, Urban Contemporary, Men's Accessories, Furnishings

N. SCHLOSSBERG & SON (CLO)
(SINGER SALES LTD.)
8007 Liberty Rd. (bud)
Baltimore, MD 21244
410-521-2445 / Fax: 410-521-2488
Sales: $1 Million-$10 Million
ELLIOTT SINGER (Owner) & Buys Men's Sportswear, Dress Shirts, Underwear, Hosiery, Jewelry, Small Leather Goods, Young Men's & Boys' Wear, Store Displays, Fixtures, Supplies

OUTLINE MEN'S FASHIONS (MW)
207 Mondawmin Mall (b)
Baltimore, MD 21215
410-225-0409 / Fax: 410-225-0071
NISSIM KAVIN (Owner & Store Mgr.) & Buys Men's Sportswear, Furnishings, Headwear, Accessories, Footwear, Store Displays, Fixtures, Supplies

RED FOX (CLO-2)
307 N. Howard St.
Baltimore, MD 21201
410-728-0090 / Fax: 410-837-4612
Sales: $500,001-$1 Million
DAVID DUKE (Owner) & Buys Men's Footwear, Leather Goods, Casualwear, Denim Apparel, Sportswear

TOTAL MALE (MW)
2330 E. Monument St. (m-b)
Baltimore, MD 21205
410-327-5182 / Fax: 410-522-7182
Sales: $500,001-$1 Million
JOHN BATES (Owner) & Buys Small Leather Goods, Men's Big & Tall Apparel, Casualwear, Denim Apparel, Formalwear, Accessories, Hosiery, Outerwear, Sportswear, Suits
AL FORD (Store Mgr.) & Buys Small Leather Goods, Men's Big & Tall Apparel, Casualwear, Denim Apparel, Formalwear, Accessories, Hosiery, Outerwear, Sportswear, Suits

TUXEDO ZONE, INC. (MW-2)
3320 Eastern Ave.
Baltimore, MD 21224
410-534-1000 / Fax: 410-534-2334
CLEVELAND HORTON (Owner) & Buys Men's and Boys' Tuxedos, Footwear

VALET FORMAL WEAR (MW-2)
P.O. Box 11046 (h)
Baltimore, MD 21212
410-433-4999 / Fax: 410-433-5965
Website: www.valetformalwear.com
GEORGE WHARTON (Gen. Mgr.) & Buys Men's Wear, Young Men's & Boys' Formal Wear, Complete Wedding Apparel, Store Supplies

BEL AIR ATHLETIC (SP)
658 Boulton St.
Bel Air, MD 21014
410-838-2670 / Fax: 410-893-0278
Sales: $100,001-$500,000
JOHN GORMAN (Mgr.) & Buys Activewear, Athletic Footwear, Boys' Dancewear
RENEE TAYLOR-Activewear, Athletic Footwear, Boys' Dancewear

HIRSCH'S MEN'S STORE, INC. (MW)
9 S. Main St. (m)
Bel Air, MD 21014
410-838-2828
DAVID COHEN (Owner & President) & Buys Men's Sportswear, Leather Apparel, Dress Shirts, Ties, Underwear, Hosiery, Headwear, Belts, Young Men's Wear, Store Displays, Fixtures, Supplies

THE T-SHIRT PEOPLE (SP)
10722 Hanna St.
Beltsville, MD 20705
301-937-4843 / Fax: 301-937-2916
Website: www.thet-shirtpeople.com
GERRY FLAIGG (Owner) & Buys Activewear

SOUTH MOON UNDER (CLO-8 & OL)
619 Franklin Ave. (m)
Berlin, MD 21811
410-641-1644 / Fax: 410-641-3032
Website: www.southmoonunder.com
FRANK GUNION (President)
CHARLIE GROOM-Men's Sportswear, Hosiery, Casual Shoes, Young Men's Wear, Urban Contemporary, Store Displays, Fixtures, Supplies

JAMES LTD. (MW-2)
7101 Democracy Blvd. (m-b)
Bethesda, MD 20817
301-365-2913 / Fax: 301-365-4911
MR. JAMES (Owner) & Buys Men's Sportswear, Furnishings, Accessories

P.J.'S SPORT (SP)
10466 Auto Park Dr.
Bethesda, MD 20817
301-365-0355 / Fax: 301-365-5949
Sales: $500,001-$1 Million
PHIL GALIPO (President) & Buys Activewear, Athletic Footwear, Licensed Apparel

WINN BROTHERS (MW)
7101 Democracy Blvd. (b)
Bethesda, MD 20817
301-365-9466
STEVEN WINNICK (Owner) & Buys Men's Sportswear, Furnishings & Accessories, Store Displays, Fixtures, Supplies

BIRD 33 SPORTSWEAR (CLO)
620 Cherry Hill Rd.
Brooklyn, MD 21225
410-355-5535 / Fax: 410-355-5527
ALONZO BROWN (Owner) & Buys Men's and Boys' Clothing, Denim Jean Sets, Fleece Sets, Shirts, Hats, Headwear, Sweaters, Shorts, Hosiery, Accessories, Belts, Fitted Headwear, Coats, Leather Accessories, and Boots

BAY COUNTRY SHOP (CLO)
2709 Ocean Gateway (b)
Cambridge, MD 21613
410-221-0700 / Fax: 410-221-0441
Sales: $100,001-$500,000
Website: www.baycountryshop.com
CONNIE TUBMAN (Owner) & Buys Men's Sportswear, Dress Shirts, Headwear, Jewelry, Small Leather Goods, Urban Contemporary, Store Displays, Fixtures, Supplies

CY'S TOGGERY (CLO)
719 Frederick Rd. (m-b)
Catonsville, MD 21228
410-747-8760 / Fax: 410-747-8949
MARVIN MEYER (President & Owner)
PAUL DELIVUK-Men's & Boys' Formal Wear

COHEN'S CLOTHIERS FOR MEN (MW)
6466 Cranbrook Rd. (m)
Cockeysville, MD 21030
410-666-8020 / Fax: 410-666-3952
MR. COHEN (Owner) & Buys Men's Sportswear, Furnishings, Accessories, Boys' 4 to 22

UNIVERSITY BOOK CENTER (SP)
(UNIVERSITY OF MARYLAND)
Stamp Student Union Bldg.
College Park, MD 20742
301-314-2665 / Fax: 301-403-8326
Website: www.ubc.umd.edu
PAUL MALONI (Dir.)
PAM VIANDS (Mgr.) & Buys Fleece, Jackets, Hosiery, Licensed Apparel

HYATT & CO. (MW-3)
10300 Patuxent Pkwy. (m-b)
Columbia, MD 21044
410-730-8060 / Fax: 410-995-1133
EDWARD HYATT (Co-Owner)
HARVEY HYATT (Co-Owner) & Buys Men's Sportswear, Formal Wear, Footwear, Store Displays, Fixtures, Supplies

PRINCETON SPORTS (SG-2 & OL)
10730 Little Patuxent Pkwy.
Columbia, MD 21044
410-995-1894 / Fax: 410-992-9082
Website: www.princetonsports.com
ALAN DAVIS (Owner) & Buys Men's & Boys' Athletic Apparel, Apparel, Ski Apparel, Swimwear

BURTON'S, INC. (MW)
800 Frederick St. (p)
Cumberland, MD 21502
301-777-3866 / Fax: 301-777-3709
Sales: $1 Million-$10 Million
REX W. BURTON (President & G.M.M.) & Buys Men's Sportswear, Furnishings, Belts, Accessories

CHERRY'S, INC. (SP)
26 W. Dover St.
Easton, MD 21601
410-822-4750 / Fax: 410-822-4751
Sales: $100,001-$500,000
MICHAEL CHERRY (Owner) & Buys Athletic Footwear, Hunting Apparel, Hiking Shoes
DAVID CHERRY (President) & Buys Athletic Footwear, Hunting Apparel, Hiking Shoes
NANCY EASON-Athletic Footwear, Hunting Apparel, Hiking Shoes

SUNNY'S GREAT OUTDOORS (AN-15)
7540 Washington Blvd. (m)
Elkridge, MD 21075
410-799-4900 / Fax: 410-799-4907
Website: www.sunnysonline.com
JOHN SULLIVAN (President & Mdse. Mgr.)
SHARA TERJUNG-Men's Sportswear, Gloves, Belts, Underwear, Hosiery, Jeans, Footwear, Small Leather Goods, Big & Tall Men's Wear, Raincoats, Shirts, Sweaters

EDWARD'S FASHIONS (MW)
116 W. Main St. (m)
Elkton, MD 21921
410-398-7007 / Fax: 410-398-0345
EDWARD KIOMALL (Owner) & Buys Men's Sportswear, Formal Wear, Furnishings, Accessories, Big & Tall Men's Wear, Store Displays, Fixtures, Supplies

RASCALS EXTREME SPORTS (SG)
8480 Baltimore National Pike
Ellicott City, MD 21043
410-480-2002 / Fax: 410-480-2003
JOANNE KROHN (Owner) & Buys Men's Beachwear, Casual Shoes, Accessories, Jewelry, Store Displays, Fixtures, Supplies

C-MART DISCOUNT WAREHOUSE (CLO)
1503 Rockspring Rd. (p-m-b-des)
Forest Hill, MD 21050
410-879-7858 / Fax: 410-893-0916
Sales: $1 Million-$10 Million
Website: www.cmartdiscount.com
DOUGLAS CARTON (Owner & President) & Buys Men's Sportswear, Furnishings, Accessories, Boys' Suits
KEITH SELBERG-Men's Sportswear, Furnishings, Accessories, Boys' Suits

KING'S MENSWEAR (MW)
11 S. Market St. (b)
Frederick, MD 21701
301-663-5322 / Fax: 301-663-5796
Sales: $500,000-$1 Million
DICK KESSLER (Owner) & Buys Men's Overcoats, Suits, Tailored Jackets, Tailored Slacks, Raincoats, Sportswear, Sweaters, Sport Shirts, Outer Jackets, Casual Slacks, Leather Apparel, Dress Shirts, Ties, Belts, Dress Shoes, Footwear, Furnishings, Accessories
NOTE-Store Displays, Fixtures, Supplies Bought By Outside Contractor

RUGGED WEARHOUSE (CLO-10)
417 S. Jefferson St. (bud)
Frederick, MD 21701
301-631-0303 / Fax: 301-631-2162
Website: www.ruggedwearhouse.com
RON GABRIEL (Owner)
PAUL GABRIEL (C.E.O.)
KEVIN CRAWFORD-Men's Wear
MONIQUE DeCLERICO-Men's Wear
DIANA HUTCHINSON-Boys' Wear

CRESTMONT MEN'S CLOTHING (MW)
7 W. Main St. (b)
Frostburg, MD 21532
301-689-5777 / Fax: 301-689-2733
Sales: $100,001-$500,000
JIM BARNES (Owner) & Buys Men's Footwear, Sportswear, Furnishings, Headwear, Accessories, Leather Apparel, Store Displays, Fixtures, Supplies

HUDSON TRAIL OUTFITTERS CO. (SG-9)
(HUDSON TRAIL OUTFITTERS LTD.)
401 N. Frederick Ave.
Gaithersburg, MD 20879
301-948-2474 / Fax: 301-977-8971
Website: www.hudsontrail.com
HANK COHEN (Owner) & Buys Men's Outdoor Apparel, Footwear, Boys' Outdoor Apparel & Footwear

SWIM PRO, INC. (SP)
P.O. Box 736
10831 Lanham Severn Rd.
Glen Dale, MD 20769
301-464-6923 / Fax: 301-464-4507
Sales: $100,001-$500,000
LINDA HOFFMAN (G.M.M.) & Buys Athletic Wear

KURLY'S MEN'S & BOYS' CLOTHING (MW)
6124 Greenbelt Rd. (m)
Greenbelt, MD 20770
301-345-8643 / Fax: 301-345-8643
Sales: $100,001-$500,000
RAMESH PATEL (Owner) & Buys Men's Sportswear, Furnishings, Belts, Jewelry, Fragrances, Young Men's Sportswear, Urban Contemporary, Store Displays, Fixtures, Supplies

MARYLAND - Hagerstown

DEXTER SHOE CO. (FW-22 & OL)
(DEXTER SHOE FACTORY OUTLET)
(BERKSHIRE HATHAWAY GROUP, INC.)
(Macro Retail)
(Burrow's Safety Shoes)
(Super Shoes)
601 Dual Hwy.
Hagerstown, MD 21740
301-766-7513 / Fax: 301-393-3923
Sales: $100 Million-$500 Million
Website: www.dexteroutlets.com
Retail Locations: VT, VA, WY, WV, AL, AK, AZ, AR, CA, CO, CT, DE, DC, FL, GA, HI, ID, IL, IN, IA, NM, NY, NC, ND, SC, SD, TN, WI, KS, KY, LA, ME, MD, MA, MI, MN, MS, MO, MT, NE, NV, NH, NJ, OH, OK, OR, PA, RI, TX, UT,

- TERRY TIERNEY (President)
- STEVE LEWIS (G.M.-Retail Opers.) & Buys Footwear
- ALAN LAFFERIERE (Purch.-Dexter Outlet Stores) & Buys Footwear

H.H. BROWN RETAIL, INC. (FW-19)
(SUPER SHOE STORE)
(H.H. BROWN SHOE CO., INC.)
601 Dual Hwy. (m)
Hagerstown, MD 21740
301-766-7513 / Fax: 301-393-3923
Sales: $10 Million-$50 Million
Website: www.hhbrown.com

- TERRY TIERNEY (President)
- GREG GOODREAU (G.M.M.)
- TOM SEIDENSTRICKER-Men's Casual Sportswear
- JAY RANKIN-Men's Athletic Footwear, Sportswear, Men's Work & Hiking Shoes

HOFFMAN CLOTHIERS, INC. (MW)
15 N. Potomac St. (m-b)
Hagerstown, MD 21740
301-739-0700 / Fax: 301-739-0708
Sales: $100,001-$500,000
Website: www.hoffmanclothiers.com

- JAMES E. BAKER (Owner) & Buys Men's Sportswear, Furnishings, Accessories, Dress Shoes, Casual Shoes, Young Men's Sportswear, Store Displays, Fixtures

INGRAM'S MEN'S SHOP (MW)
36 N. Jonathan St. (m-b)
Hagerstown, MD 21740
301-739-3494 / Fax: 301-766-4253
Sales: $1 Million-$10 Million

- FRANK FEARNOW, JR. (President & Owner) & Buys Men's Overcoats, Suits, Tailored Jackets, Tailored Slacks, Footwear, Sportswear, Sweaters, Sport Shirts, Outer Jackets, Leather Apparel, Casual Slacks, Furnishings, Headwear, Accessories, Young Men's Wear, Big & Tall Men's Wear, Dress Shoes, Work Boots, S

JOS. A. BANK CLOTHIERS, INC. (MW-260 & MO)
500 Hanover Pike (b)
Hampstead, MD 21074
410-239-2700 / Fax: 410-239-5700
Sales: Over $1 Billion
Website: www.josbank.com
Retail Locations: DE, PA, MD, VA, DC, IL, MN, MO, OH, IN, KS, MI, WI, AL, LA, FL, MS, NC, GA, SC, TN, KY, CO, TX, UT

- ROBERT WILDRICK (C.E.O. & President)
- JIM THORNE (V.P.-Men's Clothing) & Buys Men's Suits, Men's Raincoats, Topcoats, Outerwear, Blazers, Sportcoats, Formal Wear, Dress Shoes, Sweaters, Knits, Men's Wovens, Casual Pants, Leather or Suede Apparel
- PETER SATTEN (Visual Div. V.P. Merchandising) & Buys Store Displays, Fixtures, Supplies
- TOM TERES (V.P. & G.M.M.-Sportswear & Furnishings) & Buys Activewear, Sportswear, Outerwear, Dress Shirts, Sweaters, Outerwear, Leather or Suede Apparel
- CHUCK FRAZIER (Real Estate Contact) (@ 410-239-5730)
- NOTE-50 Additional Stores Will Open by the End of 2004.

LEVTRAN ENTERPRISES, INC. (FW-30 & AP)
(DOWNTOWN LOCKER ROOM)
P.O. Box 958
Hanover, MD 21076
410-850-5900 / Fax: 410-850-5915
Website: www.dtlrlive.com
Retail Locations: MD, DC

- GLEN GAYNOR (President & Co-Owner)
- ANTHONY TRANTAS (Co-Owner)
- JIM SANDERS-Work Shoes, Rubber Footwear, Athletic Footwear, Boys' Dress Shoes, Shoe Related Accessories.
- TOD KIRSSIN-Work Shoes, Rubber Footwear, Athletic Footwear, Boys' Dress Shoes, Shoe Related Accessories.
- RICK LEVIN (Real Estate Contact)

SAVVI FORMAL WEAR (MW-4)
(DISTRICT FORMAL WEAR, INC.)
8839 Annapolis Rd. (m)
Lanham, MD 20706
301-731-0230 / Fax: 301-731-4713
Website: www.savviformalwear.com

- FRANK GUARNIERI (Co-Owner) & Buys Men's Formal Wear, Accessories, Men's Dress Shoes, Store Displays, Fixtures, Supplies
- GENE LUPI (Co-Owner) & Buys Accessories, Men's Dress Shoes, Urban Contemporary, Store Displays, Fixtures, Supplies

TUXEDO HOUSE (MW)
2135 Greenspring Dr. (m-b)
Lutherville Timonium, MD 21093
410-252-6220 / Fax: 410-560-3233
Website: www.tuxedohouse.com

- SCOTT FURMAN (Owner) & Buys Men's & Boys' Formal Wear

BRUNO CIPRIANI (MW)
(A & E NAPOLI, LTD.)
11301 Rockville Pike (m-b)
North Bethesda, MD 20895
301-468-0483 / Fax: 301-770-5957
Website: www.brunocipriani.com

- EDUARDO DEPANDI (Owner) & Buys Store Displays, Fixtures, Supplies, Men's Sportswear, Furnishings, Accessories
- ALEX ABBASZADEH (Mgr.) & Buys Men's Sportswear, Furnishings, Accessories

MARVIN'S MENSWEAR (MW)
200 E. Alder St. (m-b)
Oakland, MD 21550
301-334-9211 / Fax: 301-334-2499
Sales: $100,001-$500,000

- MARVIN JONES (Owner) & Buys Men's Sportswear, Urban Contemporary, Furnishings & Accessories, Store Displays, Fixtures, Supplies
- BLAIR GLASS-Men's Sportswear, Urban Contemporary, Furnishings & Accessories, Store Displays, Fixtures, Supplies

RUDY'S (CLO-2)
P.O. Box 86 (m)
115 S. 2nd St.
Oakland, MD 21550
301-334-2654 / Fax: 301-334-2692

- ROBERT RUDY (President & Owner)
- AMY RUDY-Men's Sportswear, Swimwear, Outerwear, Furnishings, Accessories, Footwear, Store Displays, Fixtures, Supplies

HATLAND.COM (SP)
11429 Crystal Hwy.
Ocean City, MD 21842
410-524-7399 / Fax: 410-524-4791
Website: www.hatland.com

- RAMON ORTIZ (Mgr.) & Buys Activewear, Headwear, Licensed Apparel

MODERN ATHLETE (SP)
P.O. Box 1968
Ocean City, MD 21842
410-723-3977 / Fax: 410-723-1337

- MARY ANN DILLARD (Owner) & Buys Activewear, Athletic Footwear, Athletics

J. S. EDWARDS (MW)

Woodholme Shopping Ctr.
1809 Reisterstown Rd.
Pikesville, MD 21208
410-653-2266 / Fax: 410-653-2677

EDWARD STEINBERG (Owner) & Buys Menswear, Footwear, Accessories, Furnishings

DOUBLE D'S FITNESS & ACTIVEWEAR (SP)

1010 Theater Dr.
Prince Frederick, MD 20678
410-257-3141

JOYCE DICKERSON (Owner) & Buys Activewear, Athletic Footwear, Athletics

ALAN FURMAN & CO., INC. (JWLY & OL & MO)

12250 Rockville Pike, #270
Rockville, MD 20852
301-762-4606 / Fax: 301-881-0810
Sales: $10 Million-$50 Million
Website: www.alanfurman.com

ALAN FURMAN (President) & Buys Jewelry

MR. CURLEY, INC. (MW)

652 S. Salisbury Blvd. (p)
Salisbury, MD 21801
410-749-1099

MR. CURLEY (Owner) & Buys Men's Sportswear, Furnishings & Accessories, Headwear, Dress Shoes, Boots, Young Men's Wear, Boys' Wear, Store Displays, Fixtures, Supplies

PHILLIP'S MEN'S SHOP (CLO)

325 Civic Ave. (m-b)
P.O. Box 209
Salisbury, MD 21804
410-749-1216 / Fax: 410-742-3292
Sales: $500,001-$1 Million

HAROLD PHILLIPS, Jr. (President & Gen. Mgr.) & Buys Men's Footwear, Leather Goods, Big & Tall, Casualwear, Denim Apparel, Formalwear, Accessories, Hosiery, Outerwear, Sleepwear, Sportswear, Suits, Swimwear, Underwear

DAVID PHILLIPS (V.P.) & Buys Men's Footwear, Leather Goods, Big & Tall, Casualwear, Denim Apparel, Formalwear, Accessories, Hosiery, Outerwear, Sleepwear, Sportswear, Suits, Swimwear, Underwear

DEBBIE WILLEY (Store Mgr.) & Buys Men's Footwear, Leather Goods, Big & Tall, Casualwear, Denim Apparel, Formalwear, Accessories, Hosiery, Outerwear, Sleepwear, Sportswear, Suits, Swimwear, Underwear

ARTHUR'S CLOTHIERS (MW)

560 Ritchie Hwy., #H (p)
Severna Park, MD 21146
410-544-3016 / Fax: 410-544-3017

ARTHUR GAUTHIER (Owner) & Buys Men's Sportswear, Furnishings & Accessories, Headwear, Footwear, Young Men's Wear, Boys' Wear, Urban Contemporary, Store Displays, Fixtures, Supplies

CAVALIER MEN'S SHOP, INC. (MW-12)

3847 Branch Ave., #119 (m)
Temple Hills, MD 20748
/ Fax: 301-899-9420
Website: www.cavalierman.com

NORM ORLEANS (Owner) & Buys Men's Sportswear, Furnishings & Accessories

LARRY FINK-Urban Contemporary, Store Displays, Fixtures, Supplies

LAWRENCE REED (MW)

Iverson Mall (p-m-b)
3849 Branch Ave.
Temple Hills, MD 20748
301-423-8383 / Fax: 301-899-1744

ALVIN ATLAS (Owner) & Buys Men's Sportswear, Leather Apparel, Accessories, Footwear, Store Displays, Fixtures, Supplies

J.W.'S WESTERN WEAR (WW)

2090 Crane Hwy. (b)
Waldorf, MD 20601
301-645-3144 / Fax: 301-645-0806

JEAN WAGER (Owner) & Buys Men's & Boys' Western Wear, Related Accessories, Men's & Boys' Boots, Store Displays, Fixtures, Supplies

BENN'S, INC. (MW)

140 Village Shopping Ctr. (m)
Westminster, MD 21157
410-848-8020 / Fax: 410-751-9998

MIKE CRICHTEN (Owner) & Buys Men's Sportswear, Furnishings & Accessories, Store Displays, Fixtures, Supplies

SHOE CITY SPORTS (CLO-20)

(ESCO LTD.)
1800 Woodlawn Dr. (p-m-b)
Woodlawn, MD 21207
410-944-1666 / Fax: 410-944-1665
Website: www.shoecityonline.com

EARL FREEDMAN (Owner) & Buys Store Displays, Fixtures, Supplies

TED GREENBERG (President)

DON HEASLEY (Mdse. Mgr.)

SEAN CONNOR-Headwear, Accessories, Belts, Jewelry, Small Leathers, Young Men's Wear, Boys' Wear Accessories

MIKE JESSUP-Tailored Slacks, Raincoats, Big & Tall Wear, Sweaters, Sport Shirts, Outer Jackets, Leather Apparel, Casual Slacks, Active Apparel, Dress Shirts, Robes, Boys' Wear Sportswear

DAN GALLAGHER-Men's Footwear

BOB SOVOCA-Boys' Footwear

MASSACHUSETTS - Acton

GOULD'S OF ACTON, INC. (CLO-2)

260 Great Rd. (b)
Acton, MA 01720
978-263-0374 / Fax: 978-263-5923
Website: www.gouldsclothing.com

MARVIN GOULD (G.M.M.) & Buys Men's Overcoats, Suits, Tailored Jackets, Leather Apparel, Tailored Slacks, Raincoats, Sportswear, Sweaters, Sport Shirts, Outer Jackets, Casual Slacks, Furnishings, Headwear, Accessories, Big & Tall Men's Wear, Store Displays, Fixtures, Supplies

RICHARD POWDERLY (Mgr.) & Buys Men's Overcoats, Suits, Tailored Jackets, Leather Apparel, Tailored Slacks, Raincoats, Sportswear, Sweaters, Sport Shirts, Outer Jackets, Casual Slacks, Furnishings, Headwear, Accessories, Big & Tall Men's Wear, Store Displays, Fixtures, Supplies

MAIN STREET FORMAL (MW)

320 N. Main St. (m)
Acushnet, MA 02743
508-995-0200 / Fax: 508-995-3511

JACK BENEDITO (Owner) & Buys Men's & Boys' Formal Wear, Dress Shoes, Accessories, Store Displays, Fixtures, Supplies

BEN'S UNIFORMS (SP)

20 Main St. (m)
Amesbury, MA 01913
978-388-0471 / Fax: 978-388-7878
Sales: $500,001-$1 Million
Website: www.bensuniforms.com

SUSAN KARAS (Co-Owner) & Buys Men's Footwear, Leather Goods, Men's Apparel, Men's Big & Tall, Men's Casualwear, Men's Denim Apparel, Men's Formalwear, Men's Accessories, Men's Hosiery, Men's Outerwear, Men's Sleepwear, Men's Sportswear, Men's Swimwear, Men's Underwear, Men's Uniforms

HERBERT KARAS (Co-Owner) & Buys Men's Footwear, Leather Goods, Men's Apparel, Men's Big & Tall, Men's Casualwear, Men's Denim Apparel, Men's Formalwear, Men's Accessories, Men's Hosiery, Men's Outerwear, Men's Sleepwear, Men's Sportswear, Men's Swimwear, Men's Underwear, Men's Uniforms

W.E. FULLER & CO. (MW)

45 Main St. (p-m)
Amesbury, MA 01913
978-388-0287

RON J. FULLER (Owner) & Buys Men's Overcoats, Suits, Tailored Jackets, Tailored Slacks, Raincoats, Sportswear, Sweaters, Sport Shirts, Outer Jackets, Casual Slacks, Active Apparel, Furnishings, Belts, Jewelry, Fragrances, Big & Tall Men's Wear, Store Displays, Fixtures, Supplies

UNIVERSITY BOOK STORE (SP)

(UNIVERSITY OF MASSACHUSETTS-AMHERST)
Campus Center Bldg.
Amherst, MA 01003
413-545-2619 / Fax: 413-545-4396

JOHN KUSISTO (Mgr.) & Buys Fleece, Jackets, Hosiery, Athletic Footwear

ANDOVER SHOP, INC. (MW-3)

P.O. Box 5127 (b-des)
127 Main St.
Andover, MA 01810
978-475-2252 / Fax: 978-475-7138
Sales: $1 Million-$10 Million
Website: www.theandovershop.com

VIRGIL MARSON (Owner & Treas.) & Buys Men's Sportswear, Accessories, Furnishings, Footwear, Young Men's, Boys' Wear, Store Displays, Fixtures, Supplies

CHARLES DAVIDSON (President) & Buys Men's Sportswear, Accessories, Furnishings, Footwear, Young Men's, Boys' Wear, Store Displays, Fixtures, Supplies

DAVID MARSON-Men's Sportswear, Accessories, Furnishings, Footwear, Young Men's, Boys' Wear, Store Displays, Fixtures, Supplies

KAPS, INC. (CLO-4)

5 Main St. (m, b, h)
Andover, MA 01810
978-475-3905 / Fax: 978-475-9119
Sales: $1 Million-$10 Million

RICHARD KAPELSON (President)

JON KAPELSON-Men's Overcoats Tailored Jackets, Suits, Tailored Slacks, Raincoats, Sweaters, Sport Shirts, Outer Jackets, Sportswear, Casual Slacks, Headwear, Big & Tall Men's Wear, University Shop, Accessories, Footwear, Store Displays, Fixtures, Supplies

PRIVITERA CLOTHING DESIGN (MW)

77 Main St. (b)
Andover, MA 01810
978-475-9727

GUISEPPE PRIVITERA (Owner) & Buys Men's Sportswear, Furnishings & Accessories, Store Displays, Fixtures, Supplies

PARADISE JEWELERS (JWLY-2 & OL)

(PARADISE FAMILY JEWELERS)
424 Main St.
Athol, MA 01331
978-249-5944 / Fax: 508-943-3881
Sales: $500,001-$1 Million
Website: www.paradisefamilyjewelers.com

SUSAN PARADISE (Owner)

MIKE PARADISE (Dir. - e-Commerce) & Buys Jewelry, Watches

DAVID M. PARADISE-Jewelry

FLETCHER'S, INC. (CLO)

49 Main St. (m)
Ayer, MA 01432
978-772-3693

RICHARD FLETCHER (Owner) & Buys Men's Formal Wear, Sportswear, Furnishings, Accessories, Store Displays, Fixtures, Supplies

P.N. LAGGIS' STORE (MW)

67 Main St. (m, b)
Ayer, MA 01432
978-772-2619

NICHOLAS LAGGIS (Owner) & Buys Men's Sportswear, Men's Big and Tall, Footwear, Store Displays, Furnishings, Accessories

***BARRINGTON OUTFITTERS (CLO & FW & OL)**

289 Main St. (m)
Barrington, MA 01230
413-528-0021 / Fax: 413-528-6857
Sales: $1 Million-$10 Million
Website: www.gbshoes.com

RICHARD DRUCKER-Men's Sportswear, Furnishings, Headwear, Accessories, Young Men's Wear, Boys' Wear, Big & Tall Men's Wear, Men's & Boys' Footwear, Store Displays, Fixtures, Supplies

PETER DRUCKER-Men's Sportswear, Furnishings, Headwear, Accessories, Young Men's Wear, Boys' Wear, Big & Tall Men's Wear, Men's & Boys' Footwear, Store Displays, Fixtures, Supplies

ALAN BILZERIAN (CLO-2)

34 Newbury St. (m-b-h)
Boston, MA 02116
617-536-1001 / Fax: 617-236-4770
Sales: $1 Million-$10 Million

ALAN BILZERIAN (Owner) & Buys Men's Overcoats, Suits, Tailored Jackets, Tailored Slacks, Sportswear, Furnishings, Accessories, Footwear, Urban Contemporary, Store Displays, Fixtures, Supplies

BIG MEN STOUT MEN'S SHOP (MW)

59 Temple Pl. (p-m)
Boston, MA 02111
617-542-5397 / Fax: 617-542-5762
Website: www.bigmen.com

HERBERT BROWN (Co-Owner) & Buys Men's Big & Tall Clothing, Sportswear, Hunting Apparel, Work Wear, Leather Apparel, Furnishings, Headwear, Footwear, Young Men's Wear, Store Displays, Fixtures, Supplies

CHARLES BROWN (Co-Owner) & Buys Men's Big & Tall Clothing, Sportswear, Urban Contemporary, Hunting Apparel, Work Wear, Leather Apparel, Furnishings, Headwear, Footwear, Young Men's Wear, Store Displays, Fixtures, Supplies

MASSACHUSETTS - Boston

BUY OR DYE, INC. (CLO-2)
348 Newbury St. (m)
Boston, MA 02115
617-421-1222 / Fax: 617-421-1515
Sales: $1 Million-$10 Million
CRAIG LEONARD (Owner) & Buys Men's Sportswear, Leather Apparel, Footwear, Young Men's Wear, Store Displays, Fixtures, Supplies

EL PULY FASHIONS (MW)
146 South St., #A (h)
Boston, MA 02130
617-524-1057 / Fax: 617-524-2054
SANTO MELO (Owner) & Buys Men's Sportswear, Accessories, Footwear, Store Displays, Fixtures, Supplies

ERIC SCHAPERO CO., INC. (MW)
98 Union Park (bud-h)
Boston, MA 02118
617-423-2842 / Fax: 617-426-6314
ERIC SHAPERO (Owner) & Buys Men's & Boys' Sportswear, Shirts, Footwear, Store Displays, Furnishings, Accessories
DANIEL SWANSON (G.M.M.) & Buys Men's & Boys' Sportswear, Shirts, Footwear, Store Displays, Furnishings, Accessories

FILENE'S (DEPT-44)
(Div. of MAY DEPARTMENT STORES)
426 Washington St. (m-b-h)
Boston, MA 02108
(May Merchandising Corp.)
617-357-2100 / Fax: 617-357-2594
Sales: $1.6 Billion
Website: www.filenes.com
Retail Locations: MA, CT, RI, NY, VT, ME, NH
TOM KINGSBURY (President)
RODNEY HANES (Real Estate Contact) (@ 314-342-6609)
JEFF KANTOR (Sr. V.P. & G.M.M.)
PAUL METCALF (D.M.M.)
TOM NYSTROM-Men's Traditional and Contemporary Suits, Men's Raincoats, Overcoats
ANDY BIXBY-Men's Dress Shirts
JOE SANNELLA-Men's Ties
MERIDITH ROSOF-Men's Underwear, Hosiery, Pajamas, Robes
BOB BURENNING (D.M.M.-Men's Collections & Sportswear)
TOM NYSTROM-Men's Collections, Nautica, Perry Ellis, Liz Claiborne, Tommy Hillfiger, Jones New York, DKNY, Men's Active Apparel, Swimwear, Shorts
PETER MEYER-Men's Sweaters, Knits, Greg Norman, Izod
DAVID LECLAIR-Men's Sports Shirts- Chaps, Polo
BABAK TAGHIZADEH-Men's Suits, Separates, Moderate Sport Coats, Outerwear, Casual Pants
FRED MASS-Men's Accessories, Gifts, Weather Acccessories
GREG LEMBO-Men's Jeans, Nautica, Polo, Guess, Calvin Klein, Tommy

RICK HENRY (D.M.M.-Young Men's)
MARTIN BOUDREAU-Young Men's Active Apparel, Urban Contemporary, Fubu, Mecca, Wovens, Sweaters, Levi Tops
LUKE FRASER-Boys' Furnishings, Young Men's and Boys' Pants, Young Men's Levi Pants, Young Men's Jeans
GREG LEVBO-Boys' Collections, Tops, Activewear, Outerwear

BILL WHALEY (D.M.M.-Fragrances)
MIRIAM FEENY-Men's Fragrances

ELLIOT ROSENFIELD (D.M.M.) & Buys Footwear
WILLIAM BROWN-Men's Casual Shoes, Dress Shoes, Athletic Footwear, Boys' Footwear

FRED HAND (Sr. V.P.-Visual Mdsg.)
ELLEN KUPPENS (Div. V.P.-Visual Mdsg.) & Buys Store Displays, Fixtures, Supplies

HELENE'S LEATHER (CLO)
110 Charles St. (b-h)
Boston, MA 02114
617-742-2077
GREG BOURNAZOS (Mgr.) & Buys Men's Leather Jackets, Western Boots, Store Displays, Fixtures, Supplies

KIM'S MENSWEAR, INC. (MW)
505 Washington St. (m)
Boston, MA 02111
617-426-5590 / Fax: 781-729-3214
FOO KIM (Owner) & Buys Men's Sportswear, Urban Contemporary, Boys' Wear, Accessories, Furnishings, Store Displays, Fixtures, Supplies

LOUIS BOSTON (CLO)
234 Berkeley St. (b-h)
Boston, MA 02116
617-262-6100 / Fax: 617-266-4586
Sales: $10 Million-$50 Million
Website: www.louisboston.com
MURRAY PEARLSTEIN (President & G.M.M.) & Buys Men's Sportswear, Furnishings, Accessories, Dress & Casual Footwear, Store Displays, Fixtures, Supplies

MR. ALAN, INC. (MW)
608 Washington St. (m)
Boston, MA 02111
617-426-0333
Sales: $100,001-$500,000
AL KELLY (Owner) & Buys Men's Furnishings, Sportswear, Accessories, Store Displays

NEW YORK MEN, INC. (MW)
2179 Washington St. (p-m-b)
Boston, MA 02119
617-427-5399
MR. SU HUNG (Owner) & Buys Men's Sportswear, Sweaters, Sport Shirts, Outer Jackets, Leather Apparel, Casual Slacks, Active Apparel, Accessories, Belts, Small Leather Goods, Young Men's Wear, Urban Contemporary, Boys' Wear, Store Displays, Fixtures, Supplies

NORTHEASTERN UNIVERSITY BOOKSTORE (SP)
(BARNES & NOBLE #656)
360 Huntington Ave.
Boston, MA 02115
617-373-2000 / Fax: 617-373-5977
Sales: $5 Million-$10 Million
Website: www.bkstore.com/northeastern
TOM MEISEL (Gen. Mgr.)
RICHARD FREELAND (President) & Buys Jackets, Hosiery, Licensed Apparel

MASSACHUSETTS - Boston

RICCARDI (CLO)
(A. RICCARDI LTD.)
116 Newbury St. (b-h)
Boston, MA 02116
617-266-3158 / Fax: 617-266-8405
Sales: $1 Million-$10 Million
RICCARDO DALLAI (Owner) & Buys Men's Sportswear, Furnishings, Small Leather Goods, Dress & Designer Footwear, Store Displays, Fixtures, Supplies

SEA BOSTON, USA (MW-2)
150 Market St., #Z (m)
Boston, MA 02109
617-367-8208 / Fax: 978-887-7058
ARTHUR MERRY (Co-Owner) (@ 978-887-0945) & Buys Men's Activewear, Shirts, Shorts, Hats, Store Displays, Fixtures, Supplies
SHERRY MERRY (Co-Owner) & Buys Men's Activewear, Shirts, Shorts, Hats, Store Displays, Fixtures, Supplies

SIMON'S MEN'S CLOTHING (MW)
(STATE STREET CLOTHING, INC.)
220 Clarendon St. (b)
Boston, MA 02116
617-266-2345 / Fax: 617-266-7108
Sales: $1 Million-$10 Million
Website: www.simonsclothing.com
DAVID SIMON (Owner)
NORMAN SWARTZ (G.M.M.) & Buys Men's Suits, Sportswear, Accessories, Furnishings, Jewelry, Fragrances, Leather Apparel, Store Displays, Fixtures, Supplies

STOUT MEN'S SHOP (MW)
59 Temple Pl.
Boston, MA 02111
617-542-5397 / Fax: 617-542-5762
CHUCK BROWN (Owner) & Buys Men's Big & Tall, Furnishings, Accessories

THE TANNERY (FW-2)
402 Boylston St. (m-b)
Boston, MA 02116
617-267-0899 / Fax: 617-267-1681
JOHN PIERRE (Owner) & Buys Men's Dress Shoes, Casual Boots, Leather Jackets, Belts, Hosiery, Small Leather Goods, Store Displays, Fixtures, Supplies

ZAREH, INC. (MW)
1 Liberty Sq. (b)
Boston, MA 02109
617-350-6070 / Fax: 617-350-6072
Sales: $1 Million-$10 Million
GREGORY THOMAJAN (Owner) & Buys Men's Wear, Suits, Sportswear, Furnishings, Robes, Accessories, Footwear, Store Displays, Fixtures, Supplies

HUB FORMAL WEAR (MW-45)
141 Campanelli Dr.
Braintree, MA 02184
781-848-2200 / Fax: 781-848-5770
Website: www.mrtux.com
Retail Locations: CT, MA, ME, RI, NH, FL
MARK ATKIN (Owner) & Buys Men's & Boys' Tuxedos, Formal Footwear, Related Furnishings, Accessories, Store Displays, Fixtures, Supplies

MILTON'S, INC. (CLO-6)
250 Granite St. (m-b)
Braintree, MA 02184
781-848-1880 / Fax: 781-848-1090
Sales: $10 Million-$50 Million
Website: www.miltons.com
DANA KATZ (President & G.M.M.) & Buys Men's Sportswear, Sweaters, Sport Shirts, Men's Casual Slacks, Active Apparel, Men's Furnishings & Accessories, Men's Overcoats, Raincoats, Outer Jackets, Leather Apparel, Suits, Tailored Jackets, Tailored Slacks, Big & Tall Men's Wear
GRACE LEVA (C.O.O. & C.F.O) & Buys Men's Sportswear, Sweaters, Sport Shirts, Men's Casual Slacks, Active Apparel, Men's Furnishings & Accessories, Men's Overcoats, Raincoats, Outer Jackets, Leather Apparel, Suits, Tailored Jackets, Tailored Slacks, Big & Tall Men's Wear
WILLIAM LEVA (Dir.-Stores) & Buys Men's Sportswear, Sweaters, Sport Shirts, Men's Casual Slacks, Active Apparel, Men's Furnishings & Accessories, Men's Overcoats, Raincoats, Outer Jackets, Leather Apparel, Suits, Tailored Jackets, Tailored Slacks, Big & Tall Men's Wear

SIMON & SONS OF BRAINTREE (MW)
250 Granite St. (b-h)
Braintree, MA 02184
781-848-2746 / Fax: 781-848-0838
Sales: $1 Million-$10 Million
ARTHUR SIMON (President)
PAUL SIMON (V.P.) & Buys Men's Sportswear, Accessories. Furnishings, Leather Apparel, Boys' Wear 8-20, Store Displays, Fixtures, Supplies

HABITAT EAST (CLO)
P.O. Box 1633
Brewster, MA 02631
508-487-4447
STEVEN ABRAMS (Owner) & Buys Boys' Apparel, Hats, Men's Apparel, Men's Surf & Swimwear, Outdoor Gear & Apparel, Resortwear, T-shirts, Imprinted Sportswear, Swimwear

VILLAGE UNIFORMS (SP-2)
200 Westgate Dr., #S25 (m)
Brockton, MA 02301
508-584-1170 / Fax: 508-580-9918
Sales: $1 Million-$10 Million
FAYE SILVA (President) & Buys Men's Footwear, Men's Apparel, Men's Accessories, Men's Outerwear, Men's Sportswear, Men's Uniforms
GARY KESSEL (V.P.) & Buys Men's Footwear, Men's Apparel, Men's Accessories, Men's Outerwear, Men's Sportswear, Men's Uniforms

OSTUNI FACTORY OUTLET (MW)
21 Cambridge (m-b)
Burlington, MA 01803
781-272-2650
Sales: $500,001-$1 Million
GASPAR OSTUNI (Owner) & Buys Men's Sportswear, Sweaters, Sports Shirts, Casual Slacks, Dress Shirts, Big and Tall Wear, Hosiery, Belts, Furnishings, Dress Shoes, Store Displays, Fixtures, Supplies

PATTERSON'S BACKBAY DANCEWEAR, INC. (SP-2)
185 Cambridge St.
Burlington, MA 01803
781-273-3089 / Fax: 781-221-5607
Sales: $100,001-$500,000
Website: www.backbaydancewear.com
FERN PATTERSON (Co-Owner) & Buys Activewear, Athletic Footwear, Dancewear, Dance Shoes

AMERICAN IMAGE SPORTS (SP)
13 Dunster St.
Cambridge, MA 02138
617-547-1688 / Fax: 617-547-4105
HEZI GADAI (Owner) & Buys Activewear, Athletic Footwear

ANDOVER SHOP, INC. (MW-3)
22 Holyoke St. (b-h)
Cambridge, MA 02138
617-876-4900 / Fax: 617-876-3789
Sales: $1 Million-$10 Million
CHARLES DAVIDSON (Owner) & Buys Men's Sportswear, Furnishings & Accessories, Store Displays, Fixtures, Supplies

MASSACHUSETTS - Cambridge

BRINE'S SPORTING GOODS (SG-3 & OL)

(JAMES F. BRINE, INC.)
29 Brattle St. (p-m)
Cambridge, MA 02138
617-876-4218 / Fax: 617-491-1097
Sales: $1 Million-$10 Million
Website: www.brinessports.com

JAMES BRINE (Co-Owner) & Buys Men's & Boys' Active Wear, T-shirts, Casual Sportswear, Athletic Footwear, Hats, Store Displays, Fixtures, Supplies

MAURA ALLEN (Co-Owner) & Buys Men's & Boys' Active Wear, T-shirts, Casual Sportswear, Athletic Footwear, Hats, Store Displays, Fixtures, Supplies

CRAIG CONWAY-Athletic Footwear

HARVARD CO-OP (GS-6)

1400 Massachusetts Ave. (m)
Cambridge, MA 02238
617-499-2000 / Fax: 617-547-2768
Sales: $50 Million-$100 Million
Website: www.thecoop.com

JEREMIAH P. MURPHY, JR. (President)

JOSEPH KING-Men's Licensed Apparel, Men's Accessories

NOTE-This Store Sells Harvard University Licensed Apparel Only.

KEEZERS (MW)

140 River St. (m-b)
Cambridge, MA 02139
617-547-2455 / Fax: 617-547-2888
Website: www.keezers.com

LEONARD GOLDSTEIN (Owner) & Buys Men's Overcoats, Suits, Tailored Jackets, Tailored Slacks, Raincoats, Sweaters, Outer Jackets, Dress Shirts, Ties, Headwear, Formal Wear, Men's Big and Tall, Footwear

STONESTREETS, INC. (MW)

1276 Massachusetts Ave. (b)
Cambridge, MA 02138
617-547-3245 / Fax: 617-547-0529
Sales: $1 Million-$10 Million

WILLIAM HOOTSTEIN (Owner) & Buys Men's Sportswear, Furnishings, Accessories, Casual & Dress Footwear, Store Displays, Fixtures, Supplies

GARY DRINKWATER-Men's Sportswear, Furnishings, Accessories, Casual & Dress Footwear, Store Displays, Fixtures, Supplies

CASUAL MALE CORP. (MW-472 & OL & MO)

(CASUAL MALE BIG & TALL)
(CASUAL MALE OUTLET STORE)
555 Turnpike St. (m)
Canton, MA 02021
781-821-2500 / Fax: 781-821-7650
Sales: $500 Million-$1 Billion
Website: www.casualmale.com
Retail Locations: AL, AZ, AR, CA, CO, CT, DE, DC, FL, GA, ID, IL, IN, IA, KS, KY, LA, ME, MO, MA, MI, MN, MS, MO, MT, NE, NV, NH, NJ, NM, NY, NC, ND, OH, OK, OR, PA, RI, SC, SD, TN, TX, UT, VT, VA, WA, WV, WI

SEYMOUR HOLTZMAN (Chmn.)

DAVID I. LEVIN (President & C.E.O.)

DENNIS HERNREICH (C.F.O.)

STEPHEN GATSIK (President - Casual Male Big & Tall)

JOEL SCHREIBMAN (Sr. V.P. - e-Commerce/Catalog)

DICK DEROIS (Sr. V.P. & Dir.-Opers.)

JOHN BAHRET (Dir.-Store Planning) & Buys Store Displays, Fixtures

JOSEPH CORNELY (Sr. V.P. & Dir.-Real Estate)

ROBERT SCHOEN (Real Estate Contact-East Coast) (@ 718-828-9300, Ext.: 2076)

MANDY ANDERSEN (Real Estate Contact-Midwest) (@ 630-916-1349)

BARBARA SHERRY (Purch. Mgr.) & Buys Store Supplies

DALE ROSEMAN-Big & Tall Men's Dress Shirts, Ties, Furnishings

KAREN MARTIN-Big & Tall Men's Accessories, Underwear, Hosiery

DON MAHONEY-Big & Tall Men's Jeans, Denim Shorts

DIANE PETRUSKY-Active Casual Male

MEG LEUNG-Big & Tall Men's Woven Sports Shirts and Vests

MICHEAL LEIGHTON-Big & Tall Men's Dress Slacks, Big & Tall Men's Outerwear, Tops, Bottoms

CHRIS GRIDLEY-Big & Tall Men's Sweaters, Knits

KAREN MARTIN-Big & Tall Men's Shoes

ROBERT MURPHY-Footwear, Small Leather Goods, Accessories

NOTE-Store plans on opening 40 new stores each year, until reaching 800 total units.

A.L. AVERY & SONS (DEPT)

127 Main St. (p)
Charlemont, MA 01339
413-339-4915 / Fax: 413-339-0156
Sales: $1 Million-$10 Million

DENNIS AVERY (Co-Owner) & Buys Men's Sweaters, Work Clothes, Underwear, Hosiery, Headwear, Work Shoes, Boots, Boys' Clothing, Sportswear, Store Displays, Fixtures, Supplies

KAREN HOGNESS (Co-Owner) & Buys Men's Sweaters, Work Clothes, Underwear, Hosiery, Headwear, Work Shoes, Boots, Boys' Clothing, Sportswear, Store Displays, Fixtures, Supplies

JACK'S MEN'S SHOP (MW-2)

402 Broadway (h)
Chelsea, MA 02150
617-889-3246 / Fax: 617-884-1921

RON SILVERSTEIN (Owner) & Buys Men's Sportswear, Furnishings & Accessories, Urban Contemporary, Footwear, Store Displays, Fixtures, Supplies

BOSTON COLLEGE BOOKSTORE (SP)

McElroy Commons
Chestnut Hill, MA 02467
617-552-3520 / Fax: 617-552-2808
Website: www.bc.edu/bookstore.html

RACHEL GANNON-Fleece, Jackets, Licensed Apparel

KULIG'S CLOTHING (MW)

328 Front St. (p-m-b)
Chicopee, MA 01013
413-592-6600

WES KULIG (Owner) & Buys Men's & Boys' Tuxedos, Related Accessories, Footwear, Furnishings, Store Displays, Fixtures, Supplies

GIBELEY'S, INC. (MW)

85 Andover St. (b)
Danvers, MA 01923
978-774-4080 / Fax: 978-774-4087
Sales: $1 Million-$10 Million
Website: www.gibleys.com

ROBERT GIBELEY (Owner)

ALLEN GIBELEY-Men's Sportswear, Accessories, Furnishings, Footwear, Store Displays, Fixtures, Supplies

UGO'S, INC. (MW)

60 Shaker Rd. (b-des)
East Longmeadow, MA 01028
413-525-4274
Sales: $100,001-$500,000

UGO GUARNA (Owner) & Buys Men's Sportswear, Furnishings & Accessories, Store Displays, Fixtures, Supplies

MASSACHUSETTS - Edgartown

GREAT PUT-ON (CLO)

P.O. Box 532 (b)
1 Dock St.
Edgartown, MA 02539
508-627-5495 / Fax: 508-627-5098

KEN BILZERIAN (Co-Owner)
NICOLE BILZERIAN (Co-Owner) & Buys Men's Sportswear, Swimwear, Furnishings, Small Leather Goods, Leather Apparel, Casual Shoes, Dress Shoes, Store Displays, Fixtures and Supplies

SUNDOG, INC. (MW)

P.O. Box 604 (m-b)
41 Main St.
Edgartown, MA 02539
508-693-3482
Sales: $500,001-$1 Million

BEVERLY FOLTS (Co-Owner) & Buys Men's Sportswear, Furnishings & Accessories, Footwear, Store Displays, Fixtures, Supplies
FRANKLIN FOLTS (Co-Owner) & Buys Men's Sportswear, Furnishings & Accessories, Footwear, Store Displays, Fixtures, Supplies

BABY WORLD (KS)

428 S. Main St. (b)
Fall River, MA 02721
508-672-7491 / Fax: 508-677-1474
Sales: $100,001-$500,000

NOEMIA DeMELLO (Owner) & Buys Boys' Wear to Size 14, Dress Shoes, Related Accessories, Furnishings, Store Displays, Fixtures, Supplies

BAY STATE TRADING (CLO)

(TAG APPAREL CO., INC.)
420 Quequechan St. (m-b)
Fall River, MA 02723
508-673-2811

TED GAVRILUK (Owner) & Buys Men's Sportswear, Dress Shirts, Underwear, Hosiery, Dress Shoes, Boys' Sportswear, Store Displays, Fixtures, Supplies

EDDIE'S MEN'S & BOYS' CLOTHING (MW)

227 S. Main St. (m-b)
Fall River, MA 02721
508-679-3622
Sales: $500,001-$1 Million

EDDIE BORGES (Owner) & Buys Men's Sportswear, Furnishings, Men's Casual Shoes, Dress Shoes, Belts, Urban Contemporary, Store Displays, Fixtures, Supplies

NEXT GENERATION (MW)

1435 Pleasant St. (m)
Fall River, MA 02723
508-672-5491
Sales: $500,001-$1 Million

FERNANDA VIEIRA (Owner) & Buys Leather Goods, Men's Apparel, Accessories, Outerwear, Sleepwear, Sportswear, Suits, Footwear, Young Men's Apparel

STUFFCO INTERNATIONAL (CLO-4)

315 Pleasant St. (m-b-des)
P.O. Box 3287
Fall River, MA 02722
508-674-8459 / Fax: 508-672-9348
Sales: $1 Million-$10 Million

BRIAN JOINSON (President)
IRVING LEVINE (Owner & Dir.-Fin.) & Buys Leather Goods, Men's Apparel, Men's Accessories, Men's Hosiery, Men's Outerwear
LOU MELLO (Sr. V.P.-Real Estate)

MAXWELL & CO., INC. (CLO)

200 Main St. (b)
Falmouth, MA 02540
508-540-8752 / Fax: 508-540-1089
Website: www.maxwell-co.com

DAN MAXWELL (Owner) & Buys Men's Sportswear, Leather Apparel, Accessories, Furnishings, Men's Footwear, Store Displays, Fixtures, Supplies

MARIO'S (MW)

779 Main St. (b)
Fitchburg, MA 01420
978-342-9245

MARIO D'ONFRO (Owner) & Buys Men's Sportswear, Furnishings, Store Displays, Fixtures, Supplies

K. CLOTHES, INC. (MW)

1 N. Main St. (m)
Florence, MA 01062
413-584-3380

KEVIN COX (Owner) & Buys Men's & Young Men's Work Wear, Work Boots, Store Displays

THE T.J.X. COMPANIES (CLO-1105)

(MARSHALLS)
(T.J. MAXX)
770 Cochituate Rd. (bud-p)
Framingham, MA 01701
508-390-3000 / Fax: 508-390-2439
Sales: Over $7 Billion
Website: www.tjx.com
Retail Locations: All 50 States

JEROME ROSSI (President)
CAROL MEYOWITZ (President.-Mdsg.)
TIM MINOR (V.P. & G.M.M.-Men's)
DEBBIE MESSIER (Mgr.-Purch.) & Buys Store Supplies
LIZ NOYES (Fix. Purch. Agent) & Buys Store Displays, Fixtures
JIM CUTONE (Mdse. Mgr.-Men's Contemporary & Activewear)
MARK CORCORAN (Mdse. Mgr.) & Buys Men's Traditional, Better Brands
MARK DeOLIVEIRA-Traditional Tops, Best Brands
GENEVIEVE BARRETT-Traditional Tops, Knits, Wovens
CLAIRE CARROLL-Sweaters
RICK KESTLER-Best Brands & Sweaters
FRANK DeMARCO-Men's Active Apparel, Licensed Apparel
MELODY SCHILLER-Contemporary Tops & Bottoms
BILL HIRSCH (Mdse. Mgr.-Men's Traditional & Specialty)
CHUCK THOMPSON-Men's Outerwear, Tailored Jackets, Tailored Slacks
STEVE CORMIER-Men's Bottoms, Tailored Jackets, Tailored Slacks, Men's Big and Tall
PETER BENJAMIN (Mdse. Mgr.-Men's Furnishings)
PATTY MASLANSKI-Men's Dress Shirts
SUE PRIESS-Men's Basic Furnishings
CHRISTINIA YANKEE-Men's Underwear, Small Leather Goods
BOB BECKER-Neckwear, Hosiery
BILL BUFALINO-Men's Underwear, Sleepwear, Winter Accessories
DAN CLINE (V.P. & G.M.M.-Children's)
CHERYL OUTFIELD-Boys' Fashion Clothing
MARK DeOLIVIERA (Mdse. Mgr.-Boys' Basics)
MARY LEE GREEN-8 to 20 Boys' Suits, Dresswear, Coordinates, Polo, Duckhead
ROBIN RUSH-Boys' Outerwear
JAY CUNNINGHAM-8 to 20 Boys' Tops, Sweaters, Turtlenecks
TIM SCOTT-8 to 20 Boys' Activewear
EILEEN BURNIVAL-Tops, Bottoms
DENISE BEGIN-8 to 20 Boys' Sleepwear, Pajamas, Robes, Hosiery
OPEN-Athletic Footwear
LYNN GIBSON (Real Estate Contact-West Coast) (@ 650-903-2253)

(THE T.J.X. COMPANIES Cont. on

(THE T.J.X. COMPANIES Cont.)

DEB HOLMSEN (Real Estate Contact-Southwest) (@ 949-719-1163)

DON SMITH (Real Estate Contact-Southeast) (@ 770-980-1197)

BILL LEHMAN (Real Estate Contact-Midwest) (@ 816-523-7760)

MARK WALKER (Real Estate Contact-Northeast Div.) (@ 508-390-2230)

MIKE CALLAHAN (Real Estate Contact-Northeast Div.)

BILL VRTTAS (Real Estate Contact- Northern Div.)

DENISE DOWNING (Real Estate Contact-Northern Div.)

CAROL HUGGIN (Real Estate Contact-Northern Div.)

ALAMO STYLES (WW & OL)

305 Union St. (p-m-b)
Franklin, MA 02038
508-528-0860
Sales: $100,001-$500,000
Website: www.alamostyles.com

CAROL KOCH (Owner) & Buys Men's Western Wear & Related Accessories, Dance Boots, Shoes, Store Displays, Fixtures, Supplies

GEORGETOWN SHOE & CLOTHING (CLO & FW)

64 Central St. (m)
Georgetown, MA 01833
978-352-8572
Sales: $100,001-$500,000

JAMES RAUSEO (Partner) & Buys Men's & Boys' Urban Contemporary, Sportswear, Furnishings, Accessories, Shoes, Store Displays, Fixtures, Supplies

ARTHUR RAUSEO (Partner) & Buys Men's & Boys' Urban Contemporary, Sportswear, Furnishings, Accessories, Shoes, Store Displays, Fixtures, Supplies

NELSON'S (MW)

248 Main St. (p-m)
Gloucester, MA 01930
978-283-5675
Sales: $500,001-$1 Million

JAMES H. NELSON, JR. (Owner) & Buys Men's Sportswear, Sweaters, Sport Shirts, Outer Jackets, Leather Apparel, Casual Slacks, Active Apparel, Underwear, Hosiery, Gloves, Headwear, Belts, Work & Casual Footwear, Store Displays, Fixtures, Supplies

GATSBY'S (CLO)

25 Railroad St. (m-b)
Great Barrington, MA 01230
413-528-9455 / Fax: 413-528-9454

PHYLIS FINK (Owner) & Buys Men's Sportswear, Men's and Boys' Footwear, Furnishings, Accessories, Boys' Wear, Store Displays

JACK'S COUNTRY SQUIRE (CLO)

316 Main St. (m-b)
Great Barrington, MA 01230
413-527-1390 / Fax: 413-528-5111
Sales: $500,001-$1 Million

DAVID PEVZNER (President) & Buys Boys' Apparel, Boys' Footwear, Men's Footwear, Leather Goods, Men's Apparel, Men's Big & Tall, Men's Casualwear, Men's Denim Apparel, Men's Formalwear, Men's Accessories, Men's Hosiery, Men's Outerwear, Men's Sleepwear, Men's Sportswear, Men's Suits, Men'

OLDE VILLAGE MONOGRAMMING (CLO)

2 Stillwell St. (p-m)
Great Barrington, MA 01230
413-528-3904 / Fax: 413-528-3904

NEIL NOURSE (Owner) & Buys Men's & Boys' Shirts, Jackets, T-shirts, Sportswear, Activewear, Hats, Store Displays

THE OUTLET STORE (MW)

12 Chapman St. (p)
Greenfield, MA 01301
413-773-3996
Sales: $500,001-$1 Million

DONALD F. WHITE (Owner) & Buys Men's Sportswear, Furnishings, Robes, Headwear, Accessories, Footwear, Fragrances, Store Displays, Fixtures and Supplies

ROONEY'S (CLO)

231 Main St. (m)
Greenfield, MA 01301
413-774-3381
Sales: $100,001-$500,000

DAVE ROONEY (Co-Owner) & Buys Men's Tailored Clothing, Sportswear, Leather Apparel, Accessories, Furnishings, Footwear, Boys' Wear, Men's Big and Tall, Store Displays, Fixtures, Supplies

BRENDA ROONEY (Co-Owner) & Buys Men's Tailored Clothing, Sportswear, Leather Apparel, Accessories, Furnishings, Footwear, Boys' Wear, Men's Big and Tall, Store Displays, Fixtures, Supplies

WILSON'S, INC. (DEPT)

258 Main St. (m-b)
Greenfield, MA 01301
413-774-4326 / Fax: 413-774-2878

KEVIN O'NEIL (President)

DEBRA DLY (D.M.M.) & Buys Men's Overcoats, Tailored Jackets, Tailored Slacks, Raincoats, Sportswear, Furnishings, Robes, Headwear, Accessories, Dress & Casual Footwear, Young Men's Wear, Boys' Wear

TAMMARA BEAUREGARD-Store Displays, Fixtures, Supplies

TALBOT'S MENS' (MW-3)

1 Talbots Dr.
Hingham, MA 02043
781-749-7600 / Fax: 781-741-4369

ARNOLD B. ZETCHER (Chmn., President & C.E.O.)

HAL BOSWORTH (Sr. V.P. & G.M.)

JOHN PHILLIPS (Dir.-Men's Prod. Div.)

DAVID DIRIENZO (Dir.-Men's Merch.)

EDWARD LARSEN (C.F.O. & Sr. V.P. of Finance)

AUDREY BASBAS-Men's Apparel, Sportswear, Outerwear, Accessories, Furnishings

LISA DINALLO-Men's Casual Apparel

ELLEN MAYER-Men's Footwear

BECKER'S (MW)

323 Main St. (p-m)
Holyoke, MA 01040
413-532-5797
Sales: $100,001-$500,000

HAROLD BECKER (President) & Buys Men's, Boys' & Urban Contemporary Jeans, Casual Wear, Work Clothes, Furnishings & Accessories, Store Displays

E.S. SPORTS CORP. (CLO)

47 Jackson St.
Holyoke, MA 01040
413-534-5634 / Fax: 413-538-8648

FRANK SUHER-Men's & Boys' Screen Printable T-shirts, Active Apparel, Headwear

MASS BAY CO. (CLO-2)

595 Main St. (p)
Hyannis, MA 02601
508-771-2114 / Fax: 508-771-4515

BILL JEFFRIES (Owner) & Buys Men's Sportswear, Furnishings, Accessories, Footwear, Workwear, Store Displays, Fixtures, Supplies

SHELBY MACKIE (Mgr.) & Buys Urban Contemporary, Streetwear

PURITAN CLOTHING CO. (MW-5)

P.O. Box 730 (m-b)
408 Main St.
Hyannis, MA 02601
508-775-2400 / Fax: 508-771-3277
Sales: $10 Million-$50 Million

MILTON PENN (Chmn.) & Buys Men's Overcoats, Suits, Tailored Jackets

RICHARD PENN (President) & Buys Contemporary Clothing, Tailored Slacks

HOWARD PENN (V.P.) & Buys Men's Footwear

LINDA GRICE (Display Mgr.) & Buys Store Displays, Fixtures, Supplies

ROBERT HARRISON-Men's Outer Jackets, Casual Slacks, Raincoats, Collections, Jeans, Sweaters, Sport Shirts, Furnishings

MASSACHUSETTS - Hyannis

SUITS YOU SWIMWEAR, INC. (SP-2)
556 Main St.
Hyannis, MA 02601
508-771-1617 / Fax: 508-790-1314
NELLY LYONS (Owner) & Buys Men's & Boys' Swimwear

VASALLO'S MEN'S FASHIONS (MW)
362 Centre St., #C (m)
Jamaica Plain, MA 02130
617-522-0005
VICTOR LOPEZ (Owner) & Buys Men's Sportswear, Furnishings, Accessories, Store Displays, Fixtures, Supplies

AL MAGOON'S (MW)
130 S. Broadway (p)
Lawrence, MA 01843
978-686-6676
Sales: $100,001-$500,000
DAVE O'SHEA (Owner) & Buys Men's Raincoats, Sweaters, Sport Shirts, Outer Jackets, Casual Slacks, Active Apparel, Dress Shirts, Underwear, Hosiery, Gloves, Belts, Work Shoes, Casual Shoes, Boys' Clothing, Sportswear, Store Displays, Fixtures, Supplies

MIA BAMBINI (MO & KS)
360 Merrimack St. (m)
Riverwalk Building
Lawrence, MA 01843
978-682-3600 / Fax: 978-682-3131
Website: www.miabambini.com
MIA ANTOGNONI (President & Mdsg. Dir.) & Buys Infant to Size 7 Boys' Wear, Footwear

NED'S, INC. (MW)
355 Essex St. (m-b)
Lawrence, MA 01840
978-687-7512
Sales: $100,001-$500,000
NED SABBAGH (President & Owner)
MILDRED MONTANAZ (G.M.M.) & Buys Men's Sportswear, Furnishings, Accessories, Young Men's Wear

PARLY CORP. (MW)
(LA MODA)
407 Essex St. (m)
Lawrence, MA 01840
978-685-8703
PAUL TSANG (Owner) & Buys Men's Sportswear, Furnishings & Accessories, Footwear, Urban Contemporary, Store Displays, Fixtures, Supplies

ZABIAN'S, INC. (MW)
19 Main St. (m-b-h)
Lee, MA 01238
413-243-0136 / Fax: 413-243-8284
MIKE ZABIAN (Owner) & Buys Men's Sportswear, Leather Apparel, Accessories, Urban Contemporary, Men's Footwear, Furnishings, Store Displays, Fixtures, Supplies

THE WILLIAM A. ALLEN CO., INC. (CLO)
(ALLEN'S)
26 Main St. (m-b)
P.O. Box 329
Leominster, MA 01453
978-534-3111 / Fax: 978-534-3112
Sales: $1 Million-$10 Million
TUCKER ALLEN (President) & Buys Boys' Apparel, Men's Footwear, Leather Goods, Men's Apparel, Men's Big & Tall, Men's Casualwear, Men's Accessories, Men's Hosiery, Men's Outerwear, Men's Sportswear, Men's Swimwear, Men's Underwear
WILLIAM A. ALLEN (Treas.)
THOMAS C. ALLEN (G.M.M.)

MICHELSON'S SHOES (SP-2)
1780 Massachusetts Ave.
Lexington, MA 02173
781-862-1034 / Fax: 781-861-6780
Sales: $501,000-$1 Million
Website: www.michelsonshoes.com
RICHARD MICHELSON (Owner) & Buys Men's & Boys' Footwear
ERIC MICHELSON-Men's & Boys' Footwear

THE STRIDE RITE CORP. (FW-200 & OL)
(STRIDE RITE)
(STRIDE RITE FAMILY FOOTWEAR)
P.O. Box 9191 (m-b)
191 Spring St.
Lexington, MA 02421
617-824-6000 / Fax: 617-864-1372
Sales: $500 Million-$1 Billion
Website: www.strideritecorp.com
Retail Locations: MA, CT, NJ, NY, PA, VA, MD, NC, SC, GA, FL, AZ, TN, KY, OH, IN, MI, IA, MN, ND, IL, LA, OK, TX, AZ, NM, CA, RI, NH, WV, WI, KS, NV, OR, WA, NE
DAVID CHAMBENLAIM (C.E.O.)
JIM HARTE (Real Estate Contact) (@ 617-824-6237)
MARY ELLEN TURNER (Dir.) & Buys Boys' Footwear

A.O. WHITE SPORT, INC. (CLO)
702 Bliss Rd. (b-des)
Longmeadow, MA 01106
413-567-1706 / Fax: 412-567-1731
Sales: $1 Million-$10 Million
LEWIS WHITE (President & C.F.O.) & Buys Men's Big & Tall, Men's Casualwear, Men's Denim Apparel, Men's Accessories, Men's Hosiery, Men's Sportswear, Men's Suits

SCHULMAN'S (AN)
1488 Middlesex St. (p)
Lowell, MA 01851
978-452-0694
Sales: $100,001-$500,000
GEORGE SCHULMAN (Owner) & Buys Men's Military Clothing

J.B. SIMONS, INC. (MW)
(SIMONS UNIFORM)
329 Lynnway (p-m-b)
Lynn, MA 01901
781-595-2644 / Fax: 781-596-1950
Sales: $1 Million-$10 Million
AL SIMONS-Store Displays, Fixtures, Supplies, Men's Police, Fire, & Postal Uniforms, Footwear, Related Accessories
LESLIE GORDON-Store Displays, Fixtures, Supplies, Men's Police, Fire, & Postal Uniforms, Footwear, Related Accessories

PENNYWORTH'S, INC. (MW-2 & SG)
136 Boston Ave., #A (m-b-h)
Lynn, MA 01904
781-595-6710 / Fax: 781-593-0120
LOWELL BLITT (Owner)
BARRY GALER (Mgr.) & Buys Men's Casual Wear, Sportswear, Hoisery, Headwear, Accessories, Footwear, Store Displays

JERRY'S ARMY & NAVY (AN)
P.O. Box 14 (p)
Malden, MA 02148
781-324-6990 / Fax: 781-324-6997
Sales: $1 Million-$10 Million
MARIO EISEN (Owner) & Buys Men's Work Wear, Sportswear, Outerwear, Jackets, Casual Wear, Underwear, Hoisery, Gloves, Belts, Boots, Accessories, Store Displays

SPARKS' DEPARTMENT STORES, INC. (DEPT)
90 Pleasant St. (m)
Malden, MA 02148
781-321-0400 / Fax: 781-397-8310
ALBERT SPARKS (Co-Owner) & Buys Men's Sportswear, Boys' Clothing, Sportswear, Urban Contemporary, Accessories, Store Displays, Furnishings
AMY SPARKS (Co-Owner) & Buys Men's Sportswear, Boys' Clothing, Sportswear, Urban Contemporary, Accessories, Store Displays, Furnishings

BRADY'S MENSWEAR (MW)
152 Main St. (b)
Marlborough, MA 01752
508-485-0346 / Fax: 508-490-7829
Sales: $500,001-$1 Million
PAUL BRADY (Owner) & Buys Men's Sportswear, Furnishings, Accessories, Men's Footwear, Store Displays

THE SPORTING LIFE (SG)
12 Steeple St.
Mashpee, MA 02649
508-539-0007 / Fax: 508-539-0008
CURTIS JESSUP (Owner) & Buys Men's Sportswear, Sports Shirts, Accessories, Furnishings, Headwear, Footwear

MELTING POT (MW)
1647 Bluehill Ave. (m-b)
Mattapan, MA 02126
617-298-2288 / Fax: 617-689-9820
WAN SHIN (Owner) & Buys Men's Sportswear, Urban Contemporary, Store Displays, Fixtures, Supplies

MAYNARD OUTDOOR STORE, INC. (DEPT)
24 Nason St. (m)
Maynard, MA 01754
978-897-2133 / Fax: 978-897-9449
AMY CAO (Co-Owner) & Buys Men's, Young Men's & Boys' Active Apparel, Sportswear, Outdoor Clothing, Accessories, Furnishings, Store Displays, Fixtures, Supplies
GEORGE CAO (Co-Owner) & Buys Men's, Young Men's & Boys' Active Apparel, Sportswear, Outdoor Clothing, Accessories, Furnishings, Store Displays, Fixtures, Supplies
FRED BASTONE-Footwear

LORD'S DEPARTMENT STORE (DEPT)
446 Main St. (m)
Medfield, MA 02052
508-359-2361 / Fax: 508-359-2375
NANCY KELLY-LAVIN (President) & Buys Men's Sportswear Tops, Accessories, Furnishings, Boys' Wear, Store Displays, Fixtures, Supplies

LEE ELLIOT FORMAL WEAR (SP)
23 Riverside Ave. (des)
Medford, MA 02155
781-395-3365 / Fax: 781-396-0952
Sales: $1 Million-$10 Million
Website: www.misterg.net
LEE ELLIOT (Owner) & Buys Leather Goods, Men's Formalwear, Men's Accessories

MELROSE ARMY NAVY STORE (AN)
488 Main St. (p-m)
Melrose, MA 02176
781-665-9729 / Fax: 781-665-0472
Sales: $500,001-$1 Million
MICHAEL WHITE (Owner) & Buys Men's Work Clothes, Jeans, Tops, Jackets, Fleece, Boys' Pants & Shirts, Combat Boots, Work Boots, Store Displays

SPALLONE & SON (MW)
90 Main St. (m-b-h)
Milford, MA 01757
508-473-4920
Sales: $500,001-$1 Million
JOSEPH SPALLONE (Owner) & Buys Men's Overcoats, Suits, Tailored Jackets, Tailored Slacks, Raincoats, Sweaters, Sport Shirts, Outer Jackets, Leather Apparel, Active Apparel, Furnishings, Belts, Fragrances, Men's Footwear, Store Displays, Fixtures, Supplies

ISLAND PURSUIT (CLO-8)
2 Straight Wharf (b)
Nantucket, MA 02554
508-228-5117 / Fax: 941-383-5865
MICHAEL VALENTINO (Owner) & Buys Men's Wear, Sportswear, Urban Contemporary, Accessories, Furnishings, Men's Footwear, Store Displays, Fixtures, Supplies

MARINA CLOTHING CO. (MW)
P.O. Box 2697 (m-b)
Nantucket, MA 02584
508-228-6868 / Fax: 508-228-6606
MICHEL BECAAS (Owner) & Buys Seasonal Men's Sportswear, Accessories, Furnishings, Store Displays, Fixtures, Supplies

MURRAY'S TOGGERY SHOP, INC. (CLO-2)
(Div. of NANTUCKET REDS)
62 Main St. (m-b)
Nantucket, MA 02554
508-228-0437 / Fax: 508-228-8732
Sales: $1 Million-$10 Million
Website: www.nantucketreds.com
PHILIP MURRAY (President)
JOHN MURRAY (V.P.) & Buys Men's Overcoats, Raincoats, Casual Slacks, Suits, Tailored Jackets, Tailored Slacks, Sportswear, Sport Shirts, Outer Jackets, Leather Apparel, Furnishings, Dress Shirts, Accessories, Ties, Robes, Men's Active Apparel, Hosiery, Gloves, Underwear, Store Displays, Fixtures, Supplies
GILLES BRIDIER (G.M.M.) & Buys Men's Overcoats, Raincoats, Casual Slacks, Suits, Tailored Jackets, Tailored Slacks, Sportswear, Sport Shirts, Outer Jackets, Leather Apparel, Furnishings, Dress Shirts, Accessories, Ties, Robes, Men's Active Apparel, Hosiery, Gloves, Underwear, Footwear, Store Displays, Fixtures, Supplies
TRISH BRIDIER-Boys' Wear to Size 20

NANTUCKET SPORTS LOCKER (SP)
30 Main St.
Nantucket, MA 02554
508-228-5669 / Fax: 508-228-8141
MARSHA KOTALAC (Owner) & Buys Athletic Footwear, Activewear

NOBBY CLOTHES SHOPS, INC. (CLO)
P.O. Box 538 (m-b)
17 Main St.
Nantucket, MA 02554
508-228-1030 / Fax: 508-228-6568
SAM LIMPERIS (Mgr.) & Buys Men's Sportswear, Big & Tall Men's Wear, Accessories, Furnishings, Footwear, Boys' Footwear, Store Displays, Fixtures, Supplies

S. COTTON CO., INC. (SG)
(OUTDOOR STORE)
38 North Ave. (bud-m)
Natick, MA 01760
508-653-9400 / Fax: 508-651-3030
Sales: $1 Million-$10 Million
Website: www.natickoutdoor.com
HENRY KANNER (Mgr.) & Buys Men's & Boys' Wear, Activewear, Hosiery, Headwear
MIKE KRZYMINSKI-Men's & Boys' Footwear, Athletic Footwear

CARTER'S CLOTHING STORE (CLO-2)
55 William St. (b)
New Bedford, MA 02740
508-993-8221 / Fax: 508-992-2400
Sales: $1 Million-$10 Million
STEPHEN CARTER (Owner) & Buys Men's Sportswear, Work Clothes, Furnishings, Belts, Students Jeans, Corduroy Casual Pants, Shirts, Jean Jackets, Leather Apparel, Urban Contemporary, Men's Footwear, Work Boots, Accessories, Store Displays, Fixtures, Supplies

PEPIN'S MEN'S APPAREL (MW)
1263 Acushnet Ave. (m)
New Bedford, MA 02746
508-992-9141
Sales: $100,001-$500,000
MARIO OLIVERA (Owner) & Buys Men's Sportswear, Furnishings & Accessories, Men's Footwear, Store Displays, Fixtures, Supplies

SULLIVAN BROTHERS CLOTHING, INC. (CLO)
1765 Acushnet Ave. (m)
New Bedford, MA 02746
508-999-6251
Sales: $500,001-$1 Million
JIM SULLIVAN (Owner) & Buys Young Men's & Boys' Formal Wear, Related Accessories, Footwear, Furnishings, Store Displays, Fixtures, Supplies

JOHN FARLEY CLOTHIERS (MW)
31 Water St. (b)
Newbury Port, MA 01950
978-462-5401 / Fax: 978-462-5402
JOHN ALLISON (Owner) & Buys Men's Sportswear, Furnishings & Accessories, Store Displays, Fixtures, Supplies

MASSACHUSETTS - Newburyport

HYMAN'S - PENNYWORTH'S, INC. (CLO-2)

45 Storey Ave.
Port Plaza
Newburyport, MA 01950
978-462-2711 / Fax: 978-463-1731
Sales: $1 Million-$10 Million
Website: www.hymanspennyworths.com

LOWELL BLITT (President)

BOB GILMAN (Gen. Mgr.) & Buys Boys' Apparel, Boys' Footwear, Men's Footwear, Men's Casualwear, Men's Accessories, Men's Outerwear, Men's Sportswear

MOSHER'S (MW)

1221 Centre St. (b)
Newton Centre, MA 02459
617-527-3121 / Fax: 617-527-7568
Sales: $1 Million-$10 Million

DANA MOSHER (Owner) & Buys Men's Sportswear, Furnishings, Belts, Accessories, Men's Footwear, Store Displays, Fixtures, Supplies

MR. SID (MW-2)

1211 Centre St. (b)
Newton Centre, MA 02459
617-969-4540 / Fax: 617-969-3650
Sales: $1 Million-$10 Million
Website: www.mrsid.com

IRA SEGEL (President) & Buys Men's Sportswear, Leather Apparel, Accessories, Furnishings, Footwear, Store Displays, Fixtures, Supplies

J. RICH CLOTHING (MW)

22 Masonic St.
Northampton, MA 01060
413-586-6336 / Fax: 413-585-5705

JOSEPH RICH (Owner) & Buys Men's Wear, Sportswear, Furnishings, Accessories

RUNNERSHOP, INC. (SP)

114 Main St.
Northampton, MA 01060
413-586-1971 / Fax: 413-586-7071

STEVE SNOVER (Owner) & Buys Running Apparel, Footwear

TAYLOR MEN (CLO-1)

(STRADA)
150 Main St. (b)
Northampton, MA 01606
413-585-0130 / Fax: 413-582-0084
Sales: $1 Million-$10 Million

DAVID CASALI (Owner) & Buys Men's Footwear, Leather Goods, Men's Apparel, Men's Casualwear, Men's Denim Apparel, Men's Accessories, Men's Outerwear, Men's Sleepwear, Men's Sportswear, Men's Suits, Men's Swimwear, Men's Underwear

MELISSA PERRY (Reg. Mgr.) & Buys Men's Footwear, Leather Goods, Men's Apparel, Men's Casualwear, Men's Denim Apparel, Men's Accessories, Men's Outerwear, Men's Sleepwear, Men's Sportswear, Men's Suits, Men's Swimwear, Men's Underwear

WEAR-GUARD CORP. (MO & OL & CLO)

(Div. of ARAMARK CORP.)
141 Longwater Dr. (p)
Norwell, MA 02061
781-871-4100 / Fax: 781-982-0119
Sales: $1 Million-$10 Million
Website: www.wearguard.com

DAVID GOLD (President)

JUDY DUNNING (V.P. - Mdsg.) & Buys Knit Shirts, T-shirts, Work Clothing, Rainwear, Men's Winter Outerwear, Footwear

TAKE IT EASY BABY (CLO)

35 Circuit Ave. (m-b)
Oak Bluffs, MA 02557
508-693-2864 / Fax: 508-693-2899

LAURENCE E. BILZERIAN (Owner) & Buys Men's Overcoats, Suits, Raincoats, Sport Coats, Sport Shirts, Outer Jackets, Casual Slacks, Active Apparel, Dress Shirts, Hosiery, Headwear, Footwear, Young Men's Wear, Urban Contemporary, Boys' Wear, Store Displays, Fixtures, Supplies

CANTERBURY LEATHER SHOP (CLO-2)

P.O. Box 874 (m-b-h)
Orleans, MA 02653
508-255-4542 / Fax: 508-255-4542
Sales: $1 Million-$10 Million

SCOTT RILEY (Owner)

BARBARA GRANT (Gen. Mgr.) & Buys Men's Leather Outerwear, Sportswear, Footwear, Store Displays, Fixtures, Supplies

WATSON'S MEN'S (MW)

(H.C. CLOTHING CORP.)
P.O. Box 2724 (p-m)
34 Main St., #A
Orleans, MA 02653
508-255-3003 / Fax: 508-255-3410
Sales: $1 Million-$10 Million

HENRY V. COLLERAN (President) & Buys Men's Overcoats, Raincoats, Tailored Jackets, Tailored Slacks, Sportswear, Furnishings, Headwear, Accessories, Big & Tall Men's Wear, Young Men's, Urban Contemporary, Store Displays, Fixtures, Supplies

STEVEN VALENTI, INC. (MW)

157 North St. (b)
Pittsfield, MA 01201
413-443-2569 / Fax: 413-499-4029

STEVEN VALENTI (President) & Buys Men's Sportswear, Furnishings, Accessories, Footwear, Store Displays, Fixtures, Supplies

M & M SPORTING GOODS CO. (SG)

2 Main St. (p)
Plymouth, MA 02360
508-746-1915 / Fax: 508-746-5225

PETER MacCAFERRI (Owner) & Buys Men's T-shirts, Active Wear, Licensed Apparel, Athletic Footwear, Boys' T-shirts, Accessories, Store Displays, Fixtures, Supplies

PILGRIM'S PROGRESS (CLO)

13 Court St. (b-h)
Plymouth, MA 02360
508-746-6033 / Fax: 508-747-0388
Website: www.pilgrimsprogressclothing.com

PETER BRIGIDA (Owner) & Buys Men's Sportswear, Furnishings & Accessories, Men's Footwear, Store Displays, Fixtures, Supplies

BODYBODY (CLO)

P.O. Box 562 (m-b)
Provincetown, MA 02657
508-487-6332 / Fax: 508-487-9153

RICHARD TREAT (Owner) & Buys Men's Wear, Sportswear, Accessories, Furnishings, Store Displays, Fixtures, Supplies

CAPE TIP SPORTSWEAR (SP)

P.O. Box 1346
224 Commercial St.
Provincetown, MA 02657
508-487-3736 / Fax: 508-487-3874
Sales: $100,001-$500,000

DAVE OLIVER (Owner) & Buys Activewear, Athletic Footwear, Licensed Apparel

HAJJAR'S CLOTHING COMPANIES (MW-5)
513 Quincy Ave. (m)
Quincy, MA 02169
617-479-3251 / Fax: 617-479-9450
Sales: $500,000-$1 Million
Website: www.big-tall.com
TOUFIC HAJJAR (Owner) & Buys Big & Tall Men's Wear, Overcoats, Suits, Tailored Jackets, Leather Apparel, Tailored Slacks, Raincoats, Sweaters, Sport Shirts, Outer Jackets, Casual Slacks, Active Apparel, Dress Shirts, Ties, Robes, Underwear, Hosiery, Gloves, Belts
STEVEN HAJJAR (G.M.M.) & Buys Big & Tall Men's Wear, Overcoats, Suits, Tailored Jackets, Leather Apparel, Tailored Slacks, Raincoats, Sweaters, Sport Shirts, Outer Jackets, Casual Slacks, Active Apparel, Dress Shirts, Ties, Robes, Underwear, Hosiery, Gloves, Belts

STARTING LINE (SP)
310 Revere St.
Revere, MA 02151
781-284-8300 / Fax: 781-284-8300
DENNIS TOTO (Co-Owner) & Buys Activewear, Athletic Footwear
JOYCE TOTO (Co-Owner) & Buys Activewear, Athletic Footwear

JOHN TARR STORE (CLO)
49 Main St. (m-b)
Rockport, MA 01966
978-546-6524
Sales: $500,001-$1 Million
BETHANY CARLSON (Owner) & Buys Men's Sportswear, Footwear, Boots, Accessories, Furnishings, Boys' Knitwear, Store Displays, Fixtures, Supplies

J.B. APPAREL, INC. (MW)
300 Martin Luther King Blvd. (p)
Roxbury, MA 02119
617-445-6044 / Fax: 617-445-6815
PAUL ZALVAN (Owner) & Buys Men's & Boys' Sportswear, Furnishings & Accessories, Footwear, Store Displays, Fixtures, Supplies

JERRY'S ARMY & NAVY STORE (AN-2)
301 Essex St. (p)
Salem, MA 01970
978-744-1547 / Fax: 978-744-5974
Sales: $1 Million-$10 Million
Website: www.jerrysarmynavy.com
STEVEN SAXE (Co-Owner)
RICHARD SAXE (Co-Owner)
WALTER GREEN (Store Mgr.) & Buys Men's Work Clothes, Casual Clothing, Active Wear, T-shirts, Footwear, Combat Boots, Store Displays
WILLIAM LAZDOWSKI-Military Clothing, Camouflage

TRIPPI'S UNIFORM (MW)
268 Boston Tpke. (bud-b)
Shrewsbury, MA 01545
508-755-4721 / Fax: 508-792-3354
Sales: $500,001-$1 Million
MICHAEL TRIPPI (Co-Owner) & Buys Men's Footwear, Men's Apparel, Men's Uniforms & Workclothes
ANTHONY TRIPPI (Co-Owner) & Buys Men's Footwear, Men's Apparel, Men's Uniforms & Workclothes

BAY VIEW MEN'S SHOP (CLO)
473 W. Broadway (m)
South Boston, MA 02127
617-269-7375 / Fax: 617-269-3272
Sales: $1 Million-$10 Million
WALTER BAVINEAU (Owner) & Buys Men's & Boys' Sportswear, Furnishings, Accessories, Store Displays, Fixtures, Supplies

JONES' DEPARTMENT STORE (CLO)
673 E. Broadway (p-m)
South Boston, MA 02127
617-268-0358 / Fax: 617-268-1207
Sales: $500,000-$1 Million
JERRY HERSCH (Owner) & Buys Jackets, Tailored Slacks, Footwear, Sportswear, Headwear, Belts, Big Men's Wear, Young Men's Wear, Activewear

DAVENPORT & CO. (CLO & MO)
146 Bowdoin St.
Springfield, MA 01109
413-781-1505
Sales: $500,001-$1 Million
Website: www.davenportandco.com
DEE DAVENPORT (President) & Buys Men's Footwear, Men's Apparel, Men's Casualwear, Men's Formalwear, Men's Suits, Men's Swimwear

FASHION CITY (MW)
1220 Main St. (bud)
Springfield, MA 01103
413-732-7760
KUMJALE LEE (Owner) & Buys Men's Sportswear, Headwear, Belts, Urban Contemporary, Store Displays, Fixtures, Supplies

FENTON'S ATHLETIC SUPPLIES, INC. (SG-2)
826 Main St. (m)
Springfield, MA 01105
413-732-6700 / Fax: 413-737-2755
Sales: $1 Million-$10 Million
JAMES FENTON-Men's & Boys' T-shirts, Shorts, Activewear, Hosiery, Accessories, Store Displays

LAVENE'S (MW)
1163 Main St. (m-b)
Springfield, MA 01103
413-737-9213
Sales: $1 Million-$10 Million
KHALID ANSARI (Owner) & Buys Men's Sportswear, Men's Footwear, Store Displays, Furnishings & Accessories

SCHILLACI'S FASHIONS (MW)
1087 State St. (m)
Springfield, MA 01109
413-732-7558 / Fax: 413-731-9171
Sales: $1 Million-$10 Million
Website: www.schillacis.com
CHARLES CLARK (Owner) & Buys Men's Wear, Boys' Wear, Sportswear, Belts, Hosiery, Footwear, Urban Contemporary, Accessories, Furnishings, Store Displays, Fixtures, Supplies

TONY'S TAILORING (MW)
1158 Main St. (m)
Springfield, MA 01103
413-732-0353
Sales: $500,001-$1 Million
TONY D'ANGELO (Owner) & Buys Men's & Young Men's Suits, Sweaters, Sport Shirts, Outer Jackets, Casual Slacks, Dress Shirts, Ties, Formal Wear, Store Displays, Fixtures, Supplies

STOUGHTON ARMY NAVY CENTER (AN)
763 Washington St.
Stoughton, MA 02072
781-341-0769
Sales: $500,001-$1 Million
ROBERT KUSHNER (President) & Buys Men's Apparel, Footwear, Licensed Apparel

COLOR, INC. (CLO-50)
490 Boston Post Rd. (m)
Sudbury, MA 01776
978-443-1970 / Fax: 978-443-1712
Sales: $1 Million-$10 Million
Website: www.thecolorstores.com
LUCY MACKALL (Chmn. & C.E.O. & Real Estate Contact)
AL SHAMEKLIS (President & Dir.-Store Opers.)
TOM EMMONS (V.P.)
TINA REID (Controller)
CHERYL MARCHETTI (Mgr.-H.R.)
PHYLLIS ROCHE-Boys' Apparel, Men's Casualwear, Men's Sportswear, T-shirts

MASSACHUSETTS - Vineyard Haven

BLACK DOG TAVERN CO., INC. (CLO-12)
P.O. Box 2219
Beach St. Ext.
Vineyard Haven, MA 02568
508-540-4409 / Fax: 508-540-4496
Sales: $10 Million-$50 Million
Website: www.theblackdog.com
ROBERT DOUGLAS (President)
ROBERT DOUGLAS, Jr. (C.O.O. & Gen. Mgr.)
NANNO GUTIERREZ (President - Ret. Opers.) & Buys Men's Apparel, Men's Casualwear, Men's Accessories, Men's Sportswear, Men's Underwear

BRICKMAN'S (CLO-2)
8 Main St. (m)
Vineyard Haven, MA 02568
508-693-0047 / Fax: 508-693-5622
BRUCE LEVETT (President) & Buys Men's & Boys' Sportswear, Furnishings, Accessories, Footwear, Store Displays, Fixtures, Supplies

THE GREEN ROOM (CLO-3)
P.O. Box 1297 (b)
71 Main St.
Vineyard Haven, MA 02568
508-693-6463 / Fax: 508-693-6081
Website: www.vineyardsurf.com
ELAINE BARSE (Owner) & Buys Men's Sportswear, Denim, Men's Formal Wear, Accessories, Furnishings, Footwear, Store Displays, Fixtures, Supplies

NAT FALK, INC. (MW)
64 Main St. (m-b)
Ware, MA 01082
413-967-6721 / Fax: 413-967-5264
Sales: $500,001-$1 Million
CHARLES LASK (Owner) & Buys Men's Big and Tall, Sportswear, Furnishings & Accessories, Footwear, Urban Contemporary, Store Displays, Fixtures, Supplies

WILTON CHILDREN'S STORE (KS)
(WILTON MANUFACTURING CO., INC.)
P.O. Box 329 (m)
Ware, MA 01082
413-967-5811 / Fax: 413-967-6047
Sales: $1 Million-$10 Million
ROBERT K. McLEAN (Owner) & Buys Store Displays, Fixtures, Supplies
ROBERT WILTON-Men's Sweaters, Sport Shirts, Casual Slacks, Active Apparel
SUSAN FINOCCHIO-Men's Underwear, Boys' 8 to 20 Clothing, Sportswear, Furnishings, Accessories, Men's & Boys' Footwear
THERESA ROBERT-Men's Belts

EASTERN CLOTHING (MW & OL)
(EASTERN COAT CO., INC.)
76 Coolidge Hill Rd. (m-b)
Watertown, MA 02472
617-924-8240 / Fax: 617-924-4872
Website: www.easternclothing.com
JOHN AIRASIAN (Co-Owner) & Buys Men's Suits, Tailored Jackets, Tailored Slacks, Raincoats, Sweaters, Sport Shirts, Casual Slacks, Active Apparel, Dress Shirts, Ties, Store Displays, Fixtures, Supplies
PAUL AIRASIAN (Co-Owner) & Buys Men's Suits, Tailored Jackets, Tailored Slacks, Raincoats, Sweaters, Sport Shirts, Casual Slacks, Active Apparel, Dress Shirts, Ties, Store Displays, Fixtures, Supplies
NOTE:-This Store Specializes in Hard-To-Fit & Athletic Cut Suits.

A PIECE OF WORK (MW)
117 E. Main St. (p-m)
Webster, MA 01570
508-949-3639
JUNE CARPENTER (Owner) & Buys Men's Work Clothes, Knit Shirts, Formalwear, Footwear, Store Displays, Fixtures, Supplies

LEBOW CLOTHING FOR MEN & BOYS (MW)
178 Linden St. (m-b)
Wellesley, MA 02482
781-431-7194 / Fax: 781-431-7588
Sales: $100,001-$500,000
Website: www.lebowclothing.com
JOEL H. LEBOW (President & G.M.M.) & Buys Men's Overcoats, Suits, Tailored Jackets, Tailored Slacks, Raincoats, Sportswear, Sweaters, Sport Shirts, Outer Jackets, Casual Slacks, Furnishings, Accessories, Active Apparel, Dress Shirts, Ties, Robes, Headwear, Better Imported & Domestic Young Men's & Boys' Dress Clothing, Sizes 8 to 20 Boys' Prep Clothing, Sportswear, Special Sizes, Store Displays, Fixtures, Supplies

CHADWICK'S OF BOSTON (MO & OL)
(BRYLANE)
(REAL COMFORT)
(JESSICA LONDON)
35 United Drive
West Bridgewater, MA 02379
508-583-8110 / Fax: 508-583-4879
Sales: Over $1 Billion
Website: www.cataloglink.com
KEVIN DOYLE (Exec. V. P.)
MARY HAITE (Sr. V.P.-Mdse)
JOHN POWER (D.M.M.) & Buys Men's and Young Men's Wear, Men's Footwear
ROBERT FRENCH-Accessories

HANNOUSH JEWELERS, INC. (JWLY-71)
(GOLDSTEIN SWANK & GORDON)
(HARSTANS JEWELERS)
(LENOX JEWELERS)
134 Capital Dr.
West Springfield, MA 01089
413-846-4640 / Fax: 413-788-7588
Sales: $50 Million-$100 Million
Website: www.hannoush.com
Retail Locations: CT, FL, MA, MS, NH, NY, VT
TONY HANNOUSH (President)
NABIL HANNOUSH (V.P.) & Buys Jewelry
PETER HANNOUSH (V.P.) & Buys Precious Stones, Diamonds
GEORGE HANNOUSH (V.P.-Planning) & Buys Jewelry, Watches
NORMAN HANNOUSH (Real Estate Contact) (@ 413-788-7588, Ext.: ext. 116)

T-SHIRT STATIONS, INC. (CLO)
1458 Riverdale St. (p-m-b)
West Springfield, MA 01089
413-732-5271 / Fax: 413-731-5502
FRED AARON-Screen Printable T-shirts, Shorts, Store Displays, Fixtures, Supplies

YALE GENTON, INC. (CLO)
400 Riverdale St. (b)
West Springfield, MA 01089
413-781-1834 / Fax: 413-788-0171
Sales: $1 Million-$10 Million
MILTON R. BERMAN (Chmn.) & Buys Store Displays, Fixtures, Supplies
MARK BERMAN (President) & Buys Men's Overcoats, Suits, Tailored Jackets, Tailored Slacks, Raincoats, Big & Tall Men's Wear, Sportswear, Sweaters, Sport Shirts, Outer Jackets, Leather Apparel, Casual Slacks, Furnishings, Dress Shirts, Ties, Robes, Underwear, Hosiery, Gloves, Accessories, Belts, Jewelry, Small Leathers, Fragrances, Sportswear, Furnishings

D & L HOUSE OF LEATHER, INC. (MW & OL)
350 Main St. (m)
West Yarmouth, MA 02763
508-778-4055 / Fax: 508-771-1571
Website: www.houseofleather.com
DENISE DONAHUE (Owner) & Buys Men's & Boys' Motorcycle Leather Jackets, Gloves, Footwear, Store Displays, Fixtures, Supplies
MICHELLE ATCHISON-Men's & Boys' Motorcycle Leather Jackets, Gloves, Footwear, Store Displays, Fixtures, Supplies

BURTON UNIFORM CORP. (MW & OL)

246 Washington St. (m)
Weymouth, MA 02188
781-335-3903 / Fax: 781-335-3940
Sales: $1 Million-$10 Million
Website: www.burtonuniform.com

JEFFERY WINER (Owner) & Buys Men's Work Shirts, Uniforms, Pants, Jackets, Footwear, Store Displays, Fixtures, Supplies

DOVER BARGAIN STORE (SP)

20 Old Colony Dr.
Weymouth, MA 02188
617-423-0031

MILTON KAMENIDIES (Owner) & Buys Activewear, Athletic Footwear

JOUBERT'S, INC. (CLO)

611 Washington St. (m-b)
Whitman, MA 02382
781-447-6617 / Fax: 781-447-0706
Sales: $1 Million-$10 Million

EDWARD JOUBERT (Owner & G.M.M.) & Buys Store Displays, Fixtures, Supplies

MIKE WINIEWICZ-Men's Jeans, Sportswear, Dress Shirts, Robes, Underwear, Gloves, Headwear, Footwear

ANN HILL-Boys' Wear, Boys' Footwear, Related Sportswear, Accessories, Furnishings

UNIFIRST CORP. (CLO)

68 Jonspin Rd. (m)
Wilmington, MA 01887
800-347-7888 / Fax: 301-925-8826
Website: www.unifirst.com

RONALD D. CROATTI (President)

TIM FRAUMAN (Dir.-Sales) & Buys Men's Rental Uniforms, Store Displays, Fixtures, Supplies

ARMANDO'S, INC. (MW)

254 Grafton St. (m)
Worcester, MA 01604
508-757-1530 / Fax: 508-757-0745

ARMANDO SODANO (Owner) & Buys Men's Wear, Sportswear, Work Shirts, Pants, Jackets, Footwear, Store Displays, Fixtures, Supplies, Accessories, Furnishings

LUJON MEN'S CLOTHING, INC. (MW)

35 Pleasant St. (m-b-h)
Worcester, MA 01609
508-752-3289 / Fax: 508-752-1002
Sales: $500,001-$1 Million
Website: www.lujons.com

JOHN ISRAELIAN (President) & Buys Men's Sportswear, Furnishings, Headwear, Accessories, Footwear, Urban Contemporary, Store Displays, Fixtures, Supplies

ANDRE THIBEAULT (V.P. & Store Mgr.) & Buys Men's Sportswear, Furnishings, Headwear, Accessories, Footwear, Urban Contemporary, Store Displays, Fixtures, Supplies

SHACK'S, INC. (MW-3)

403 Main St. (m-b)
Worchester, MA 01608
508-753-8188 / Fax: 508-757-0250
Sales: $1 Million-$10 Million

MICHAEL SHACK (Co-Owner) & Buys Men's Sportswear, Furnishings & Accessories, Dress Shoes, Casual Shoes, Store Displays, Fixtures, Supplies

JEFFERY SHACK (Co-Owner) & Buys Men's Sportswear, Furnishings & Accessories, Dress Shoes, Casual Shoes, Store Displays, Fixtures, Supplies

PHIL SHACK (Co-Owner) & Buys Men's Sportswear, Furnishings & Accessories, Dress Shoes, Casual Shoes, Store Displays, Fixtures, Supplies

JONES NEW YORK MEN (MW & OT)

(Div. of JONES APPAREL GROUP)
1 Premium Outlet Blvd. (m-b)
Wrentham, MA 02093
508-384-7396

HOWARD BUERKLE (President)

JENNIFER MATS (Dir.-Opers. & Mktg.)

GASPER VULTAGGIO (Merchandiser) & Buys Men's Sportswear, Furnishings, Accessories

MICHIGAN - Ada

AMWAY CORP. (MO)
7575 E. Fulton Rd. (p)
Ada, MI 49355
616-787-6000 / Fax: 616-787-5163
Sales: Over $7 Billion
Website: www.amway.com

STEVEN VAN ANDEL (Chairman)
DICK DEVOS (President)
KIM BOND (D.M.M.)
DENNIS SCHULTZ-Men's Wear Sportswear, Dress Shirts, Ties, Men's Footwear, Furnishings, Robes, Underwear, Hosiery, Headwear
TED KIMBLE-Boys' Wear, Store Displays, Fixtures and Supplies

YOUNG'S APPAREL CORP. (MW)
111 S. Superior St. (m)
Albion, MI 49224
517-629-8752

CHARLES YOUNG (Owner) & Buys Men's Sportswear, Footwear, Furnishings, Accessories, Displays, Fixtures, Supplies

BRENNAN JEWELRY, INC. (JWLY-14)
(SEARS WATCH & JEWELRY REPAIR)
7627 Allen Rd.
Allen Park, MI 48101
313-388-1140 / Fax: 313-388-1754
Sales: $1 Million-$10 Million

STEVEN WALTERS (President) & Buys Jewelry, Watches

STACEY'S MEN'S SHOP, INC. (MW)
120 E. Superior St. (m-b)
Alma, MI 48801
989-463-4220

DUANE STACEY (Owner) & Buys Men's Sportswear, Furnishings, Accessories, Store Displays, Fixtures, Supplies

ANN ARBOR BIVOUAC, INC. (CLO)
336 S. State St. (b)
Ann Arbor, MI 48104
734-761-6207 / Fax: 734-761-7179
Website: www.a2biv.com

ED DAVIDSON (Owner) & Buys Men's Raincoats, Sweaters, Sport Shirts, Outer Jackets, Casual Slacks, Active Apparel, Underwear, Headwear, Small Leather Goods, Footwear, Young Men's Wear, Boys' Wear, Swimwear, Store Displays, Fixtures, Supplies

THE M DEN (CLO-6)
315 S. Main St. (m)
Ann Arbor, MI 48104
734-997-8000 / Fax: 734-761-8289
Sales: $1 Million-$10 Million
Website: www.mden.com

DAVE HIRTH (Co-Owner & Gen. Mgr.) & Buys Boys' Apparel, Leather Goods, Men's Apparel, Men's Outerwear, Men's Sportswear
DOUG HORNING (Co-Owner & Gen. Mgr.) & Buys Boys' Apparel, Leather Goods, Men's Apparel, Men's Outerwear, Men's Sportswear

MOE SPORTS SHOPS, INC. (CLO & OL-2)
711 N. University Ave. (p)
Ann Arbor, MI 48104
734-668-6915 / Fax: 734-741-2596
Website: www.moesportshops.com

BUD VANDEWEGE (Owner) & Buys Men's T-shirts, Fleece & Sweat Pants, Team Licensed Apparel, Outerwear, Headwear, Sweaters, Activewear

RENAISSANCE (MW)
350 S. Main St. (m-b)
Ann Arbor, MI 48104
734-769-8511 / Fax: 734-769-9927

ROGER POTHUS (Owner) & Buys Men's Suits, Sportswear, Outerwear, Formal Wear, Furnishings, Accessories, Dress Shoes, Casual Shoes, Store Displays, Fixtures, Supplies

SAM'S STORE, INC. (CLO)
207 E. Liberty St. (m-b)
Ann Arbor, MI 48104
734-663-8611
Sales: $500,001-$1 Million

DUNCAN COLE (President) & Buys Boys' Footwear, Men's Footwear, Men's Apparel, Mens's Big & Tall, Men's Accessories, Men's Outerwear, Men's Sportswear, Men's Swimwear
ARI MORRIS (Store Mgr.) & Buys Boys' Footwear, Men's Footwear, Men's Apparel, Mens's Big & Tall, Men's Accessories, Men's Outerwear, Men's Sportswear, Men's Swimwear

SHAHIN CUSTOM TAILORING (CLO)
212 S. Main St. (b)
Ann Arbor, MI 48104
734-665-7698

MR. SHAHIN (Owner) & Buys Men's Sportswear, Furnishings, Accessories

VAHAN'S CLOTHING & TAILORING (MW)
311 E. Liberty St. (b)
Ann Arbor, MI 48104
734-662-7888
Sales: $100,001-$500,000

VAHAN BASMAJIAN (Owner) & Buys Men's Sportswear, Furnishings, Accessories

VAN BOVEN, INC. (MW)
326 S. State St. (b)
Ann Arbor, MI 48104
734-665-7228 / Fax: 734-665-1355
Sales: $1 Million-$10 Million
Website: www.vanboven.com

JAMES A. ORR (President)
PETER ORR-Men's Sportswear, Furnishings, Accessories, Store Displays, Fixtures, Supplies
GARY CLARK-Men's Sportswear, Furnishings, Accessories, Store Displays, Fixtures, Supplies

CORBISHLEY'S (MW)
229 E. Huron St. (m)
Bad Axe, MI 48413
989-269-8441 / Fax: 989-269-8498

CHARLES CORBISHLEY (Owner) & Buys Men's Wear, Formalwear, Furnishings, Accessories, Store Displays, Fixtures, Supplies

CLAIR'S TUX SHOP (MW-2)
590 W. Columbia (b)
Battle Creek, MI 49015
616-962-0826 / Fax: 616-345-4450
Sales: $100,001-$500,000

JIM CLAIR (Owner) & Buys Men's & Boys' Tuxedos, Furnishings, Accessories, Footwear

JACK PEARL'S TEAM SPORTS (SG)
26 W. Michigan Ave. (m)
Battle Creek, MI 49017
616-964-9476 / Fax: 616-964-7082
Website: www.pearlsports.com

JACK PEARL (President & Owner) & Buys Team Clothing

NEW YORK COLLECTION (MW)
30 Michigan Ave. East (m-b)
Battle Creek, MI 49017
616-964-1283

MR. SAMIR (Owner) & Buys Men's Wear, Sportswear, Footwear, Furnishings, Accessories, Store Displays, Fixtures, Supplies

STYLES 'N' PLAY (CLO-4)
5775 Beckley Rd.
Battle Creek, MI 49017
269-979-0428 / Fax: 517-882-1592

NORMAN NGUYEN (Owner) & Buys Men's Wear, Sportswear, Furnishings, Footwear, Boots
JAMES LEWIS-Men's Wear, Sportswear, Furnishings, Footwear, Boots

J-B MEN'S APPAREL SHOP (MW)
1306 Columbus Ave. (m)
Bay City, MI 48708
989-895-8716

BILL KEIPER (Owner) & Buys Men's Sportswear, Furnishings, Accessories, Store Displays, Fixtures, Supplies

MILL END (MW-4)
103 Center Ave (m)
Bay City, MI 48708
989-893-6791 / Fax: 989-893-3745
ROBERT FOLKERT (Co-Owner) & Buys Men's Denim, Tops, Outerwear, Boys' Apparel & Footwear
JACKIE FOLKERT (Co-Owner) & Buys Men's Denim, Tops, Outerwear, Boys' Apparel & Footwear

NORMAN CORP. (CLO-6)
4177 S. Three Mile Rd. (bud)
Bay City, MI 48706
989-684-1900 / Fax: 989-684-1979
STANLEY FIRKSER (President) & Buys Men's Wear, Boys' Wear, Urban Contemporary, Accessories, Furnishings, Footwear, Store Displays, Fixtures, Supplies

VILLAGE BOUTIQUE (CLO)
P.O. Box 838
109 Bridge St.
Bellaire, MI 49615
231-533-6419 / Fax: 231-533-6087
JILL SCHNEIDER (Co-Owner) & Buys Resortwear, Swimwear, Headwear, Sandals
MARK SCHNEIDER (Co-Owner) & Buys Resortwear, Swimwear, Headwear, Sandals

THE ABELMAN CO. (CLO)
P.O. Box 75 (p)
327 Sophie St.
Bessemer, MI 49911
906-663-4411 / Fax: 906-663-4242
Sales: $1 Million-$10 Million
Website: www.abelmansclothing.com
ROBERT ABELMAN (Owner) & Buys Men's Overcoats, Suits, Tailored Jacket, Tailored Slacks, Raincoats, Sportswear, Sweaters, Sport Shirts, Outer Jackets, Casual Slack, Active Apparel, Furnishings, Accessories, Big & Tall Men's Wear, Footwear, Young Men's Wear, Store Displays, Fixtures, Supplies

CLAYMORE SHOP, INC. (CLO)
908 S. Adams (b)
Birmingham, MI 48009
248-642-7755 / Fax: 248-642-7632
Website: www.claymoreshop.com
BOB BENKERT (President & Owner)
ALAN SKIBA (Sales) & Buys Men's Sportswear, Dress Shoes, Casual Shoes, Furnishings, Accessories, Polo Boys', Leather Apparel, Urban Contemporary, Store Displays, Fixtures, Supplies

DURUS CUSTOM TAILOR (CLO-3)
(GOWANI CORP.)
4087 W. Maple Rd. (m)
Birmingham, MI 48301
248-642-6662
MR. GOWANI (President) & Buys Men's Overcoats, Suits, Tailored Jackets, Tailored Slacks, Big & Tall Men's Wear, Sportswear, Sport Shirts, Dress Shirts, Ties, Store Displays, Fixtures & Supplies

IT'S THE RITZ, INC. (CLO-3)
(CARUSO, CARUSO)
(FRANKIE & DEBBIE'S)
193 W. Maple Rd. (b)
Birmingham, MI 48009
248-645-5151 / Fax: 248-645-0706
Sales: $1 Million-$10 Million
FRANK CARUSO (Co-Owner & Real Estate Contact)
COLLEEN POZZVOLI-Leather Goods, Men's Apparel, Men's Casualwear, Men's Denim Apparel, Men's Outerwear, Men's Sportswear

LARRY BARKHOUSE TRADITIONAL CLOTHIERS (MW)
55 W. Maple Rd. (b)
Birmingham, MI 48009
248-644-7060 / Fax: 248-646-3308
Sales: $100,001-$500,000
LARRY BARKHOUSE (Owner) & Buys Men's Suits, Tailored Jackets, Tailored Slacks, Casual Slacks, Ties, Belts, Fragrances

VARSITY SHOP, INC. (SG)
277 Pierce St. (p)
Birmingham, MI 48009
248-646-4466 / Fax: 248-646-9428
VINCE SECONTINE (Owner) & Buys Men's & Boys' Team Clothing, Footwear, Accessories

THE YACHTSMAN, INC. (CLO)
1105 S. Adams
Birmingham, MI 48009
248-723-9838 / Fax: 248-723-9841
MICHAEL CLOW (Owner) & Buys Outdoor Clothing, Boots
TOM SHINN (Mgr.) & Buys Outdoor Clothing, Boots

L'UOMO VOGUE (MW)
6520 Telegraph Rd. (m-b)
Bloomfield, MI 48301
248-855-7788 / Fax: 248-855-9495
BRUCE GOLDMAN (Owner) & Buys Men's Suits, Formal Wear, Sportswear, Outerwear, Furnishings, Footwear, Accessories, Store Displays, Fixtures, Supplies

CARL STERR, INC. (MW)
3621 W. Maple Rd. (b-h)
Bloomfield Hills, MI 48301
248-645-6675 / Fax: 248-645-1422
CARL STERR (Owner) & Buys Men's Sportswear, Furnishings, Footwear, Accessories, Store Displays, Fixtures, Supplies

J & J WESTERN STORE (WW)
14241 US Hwy. 12 (p)
Brooklyn, MI 49230
517-592-2813 / Fax: 517-592-4244
MADELON FLOER (Owner) & Buys Men's & Boys' Western Wear, Furnishings, Accessories, Footwear, Store Displays, Fixtures, Supplies

ROCKY'S OUTDOOR OUTFITTERS (DEPT)
4014 S. Saginaw St. (m)
Burton, MI 48529
810-742-5420 / Fax: 810-742-8999
CHARLIE HERMAN (G.M.M.) & Buys Sport Shirts, Leather Apparel, Outer Jackets, Footwear, Store Displays, Fixtures, Supplies

BAKER'S WESTERN STORE (WW)
7403 E. Boon Rd. (p)
Cadillac, MI 49601
231-775-5432 / Fax: 231-775-5151
JENNIFER JEWETT (Owner) & Buys Men's Western Clothing, Sportswear, Headwear, Boots, Accessories, Boys' Western Shirts, Jeans, Leather Apparel, Store Displays, Fixtures & Supplies

MONKEY BUSINESS, INC. (CLO-6)
400 5th St. (m)
Calumet, MI 49913
906-337-5555 / Fax: 906-337-3167
Sales: $1 Million-$10 Million
Website: www.monkbiz.com
DENNIS SLIVA (Owner) & Buys Boys' Apparel, Men's Apparel, Men's Accessories, Men's Sportswear
KRISTINA OLSON-Boys' Apparel, Men's Apparel, Men's Accessories, Men's Sportswear

VAN DYKE CLOTHIERS, INC. (MW-3)
25730 Van Dyke (b)
Center Line, MI 48015
586-757-7517 / Fax: 586-757-2847
Sales: $1 Million-$10 Million
DONALD ROSS (Owner) & Buys Store Displays, Fixtures, Supplies
SERENA CRISAN-Men's Suits, Tailored Jackets, Tailored Slacks, Raincoats, Leather Apparel, Sportswear, Sweaters, Sport Shirts, Outer Jackets, Casual Slacks, Active Apparel, Footwear, Furnishings, Accessories, Urban Contemporary

MICHIGAN - Charlotte

SMITH'S MENSWEAR, INC. (MW)

145 Cochran St. (b)
Charlotte, MI 48813
517-543-1470 / Fax: 517-543-1490

SCOTT COOPER (Co-Owner) & Buys Men's Sportswear, Furnishings, Footwear, Accessories, Store Displays, Fixtures, Supplies

JIM DeMUTH (Co-Owner) & Buys Men's Sportswear, Furnishings, Footwear, Accessories, Store Displays, Fixtures, Supplies

NEPHEW'S OF MACKINAC (CLO-2)

400 N. Main St. (b)
P.O. Box 460
Cheboygan, MI 49721
231-627-7054 / Fax: 906-847-3932
Sales: $500,001-$1 Million

NANCY NEPHEW-PORTER (Owner) & Buys Men's Footwear, Leather Goods, Men's Apparel, Men's Casualwear, Men's Denim Apparel, Men's Accessories, Men's Hosiery, Men's Outerwear, Men's Sportswear, Men's Swimwear, Men's Underwear

KATE NYE (Gen. Mgr.) & Buys Men's Footwear, Leather Goods, Men's Apparel, Men's Casualwear, Men's Denim Apparel, Men's Accessories, Men's Hosiery, Men's Outerwear, Men's Sportswear, Men's Swimwear, Men's Underwear

SUE BROWN (Store Mgr.) & Buys Men's Footwear, Leather Goods, Men's Apparel, Men's Casualwear, Men's Denim Apparel, Men's Accessories, Men's Hosiery, Men's Outerwear, Men's Sportswear, Men's Swimwear, Men's Underwear

VIAU'S MEN'S SHOPS (CLO)

404 N. Main St. (m-b)
Cheboygan, MI 49721
231-627-2610 / Fax: 231-627-5952
Sales: $100,001-$500,000

JOHN VIAU (Owner)

STEVE VIAU (President) & Buys Men's Sportswear, Furnishings, Accessories, Footwear, Store Displays, Fixtures, Supplies

VOGEL & FOSTER'S, INC. (CLO)

109 S. Main St. (p)
Chelsea, MI 48118
734-475-1606 / Fax: 734-475-7480
Sales: $1 Million-$10 Million

MICHAEL JACKSON (President) & Buys Men's Sportswear, Furnishings, Boots, Accessories, Store Displays, Fixtures, Supplies

ED REHMANN & SONS (MW)

151 W. Broad St. (m-b)
Chesaning, MI 48616
989-845-6761 / Fax: 989-845-5216
Sales: $500,000-$1 Million

ROB REHMANN (Co-Owner) & Buys Men's Ties, Hosiery, Belts

RIC REHMANN (Co-Owner) & Buys Men's Men's Sportswear, Shirts, Jeans, Leather Apparel

RICH REHMANN-Men's Tailored Suits, Robes, Underwear, Gloves, Store Displays, Fixtures, Supplies

AL REHMANN-Men's Headwear, Footwear

ALLEN & BELL'S DEPARTMENT STORE (DEPT)

420 McEwan (m)
Clare, MI 48617
989-386-9521 / Fax: 989-386-7220

JOHN BLICK (Owner) & Buys Men's & Boys' Tuxedos, Sportswear, Footwear, Furnishings, Accessories, Store Displays, Fixtures, Supplies

CHESTER'S MENSWEAR (MW)

39323 Garfield Rd. (m)
Clinton Township, MI 48038
586-263-1880 / Fax: 586-263-7858

STEVE JABLAOUI (Owner) & Buys Men's Sportswear, Furnishings, Accessories, Store Displays, Fixtures, Supplies

WAREHOUSE & ARMY SURPLUS (AN)

248 Washington (m-b)
Coloma, MI 49038
616-468-5900 / Fax: 616-468-5904

ANDREW KENDALL (Owner) & Buys Men's Military Style Clothing, Footwear, Furnishings, Accessories, Store Displays, Fixtures, Supplies

BACHELOR'S (MW-5)

(CECIL B)
(CITY MAN)
(BACHELORS)
(THAT GUY)
124 Fairlane Town Ctr., #J (b)
Dearborn, MI 48126
313-271-0302 / Fax: 313-336-7294
Sales: $1 Million-$10 Million

AMRAT BHAGWAN (Co-Owner) & Buys Men's Wear, Furnishings, Accessories, Footwear

PRAVIN BHAGWAN (Co-Owner) & Buys Men's Wear, Furnishings, Accessories, Footwear, Store Displays, Fixtures and Supplies

SUREN BHAGWAN (Co-Owner) & Buys Men's Wear, Furnishings, Accessories, Footwear, Store Displays, Fixtures and Supplies

CITY SHINE (CLO)

13240 Michigan Ave
Dearborn, MI 48126
313-582-2500 / Fax: 313-582-2400
Sales: $1 Million-$10 Million

NEDAL HATEM (Owner) & Buys Sportswear, Athletic Footwear

NOTE-This Store Buys Closeouts Only.

HARRY'S ARMY SURPLUS, INC. (AN-2)

2050 N. Telegraph Rd. (p)
Dearborn, MI 48128
313-565-6605 / Fax: 313-565-4530
Sales: $1 Million-$10 Million
Website: www.harrysurplus.com

IRV ZELTZER (Owner) & Buys Men's Sportswear, Sweaters, Men's Sport Shirts, Outer Jackets, Casual Slacks, Leather Apparel, Active Apparel, Hosiery, Gloves, Headwear, Belts, Boots, Store Displays, Fixtures, Supplies

MANNO CLOTHING & TAILORING (CLO)

23810 Michigan Ave., #101 (m)
Dearborn, MI 48124
313-561-1419 / Fax: 313-561-5113

PAT MANNO (Owner) & Buys Men's Overcoats, Suits, Tailored Jackets, Tailored Slacks, Raincoats, Sportswear, Sweaters, Sport Shirts, Outer Jackets, Casual Slacks, Furnishings, Dress Shirts, Ties, Hosiery, Accessories, Belts, Footwear, Fragrances, Store Displays, Fixtures, Supplies

NEW YORK COLLECTION (MW)

12824 W. Warren (bud)
Dearborn, MI 48126
313-581-6100

ABDUL HASSAN (Owner) & Buys Men's Tuxedos, Dress Shoes, Sportswear, Furnishings, Accessories, Store Displays, Fixtures, Supplies

NICHOLS SKI & PATIO, INC. (SG-2)

21938 Michigan Ave (m)
Dearborn, MI 48124
313-565-0044 / Fax: 313-565-3938
Sales: $1 Million-$10 Million
Website: www.nicholskiandpatio.com

KAREN NICHOLS (Owner) & Buys Men's & Boys' Ski Wear

PRICE'S MENSWEAR (MW)

22263 Michigan Ave. (m-b)
Dearborn, MI 48124
313-563-8866 / Fax: 313-563-8975
Sales: $1 Million-$10 Million
Website: www.pricesmenswear.com

FRANK MANCHEL (President) & Buys Men's Sportswear, Footwear

JIM MANCHEL (G.M.M.) & Buys Men's Sportswear, Footwear

JOHN TOROSIAN-Men's Dress Shirts, Hats, Accessories, Store Displays, Fixtures, Supplies

MICHIGAN - Dearborn

RAGS (MW)
(EUROPEAN CLOTHIERS LTD., INC.)
18900 Michigan Ave. (b)
Dearborn, MI 48126
313-240-4889 / Fax: 313-240-7760
ROBERT GRUMET (Owner) & Buys Men's Sportswear, Furnishings, Accessories, Footwear, Store Displays, Fixtures, Supplies

MID LAKES SCREEN PRINTING & ACTIVEWEAR (CLO)
P.O. Box 407
121 E. Orchard St.
Delton, MI 49046
616-623-8340 / Fax: 616-623-4740
KATIE DOLFMAN (Owner) & Buys Activewear

BEL-AIR BIG & TALL (MW)
8820 8th Mile
Detroit, MI 48234
313-893-2878 / Fax: 313-893-2878
TIMOTHY SONG (Owner) & Buys Men's Big & Tall, Men's Wear, Accessories, Furnishings, Store Displays, Fixtures, Supplies

THE BROADWAY (MW-2)
1247 Broadway (b)
Detroit, MI 48226
313-963-2171 / Fax: 313-963-7326
Sales: $1 Million-$10 Million
RICHARD MARTIN (Co-Owner) & Buys Men's Sportswear, Furnishings, Accessories, Leather Apparel, Dress Shoes, Young Men's Wear, Urban Contemporary
MARC CLARKE (Co-Owner) & Buys Men's Sportswear, Furnishings, Accessories, Leather Apparel, Dress Shoes, Young Men's Wear, Urban Contemporary
LARRY WASH (Mgr.) & Buys Men's Sportswear, Furnishings, Accessories, Leather Apparel, Dress Shoes, Young Men's Wear, Urban Contemporary

CITY SLICKER SHOES (FW)
164 Monroe St.
Detroit, MI 48226
313-963-1963 / Fax: 313-963-7326
MARK CLARK-Men's & Boys' Footwear, Hosiery

CUSMANO TUXEDO, INC. (MW-2)
16703 Mack Ave. (m-b)
Detroit, MI 48224
313-881-3530 / Fax: 313-881-3531
JOSEPH CUSMANO (Owner) & Buys Men's & Boys' Tuxedos, Furnishings, Accessories, Footwear, Store Displays, Fixtures, Supplies

FASHION MENSWEAR CORP. (MW)
15354 Grand River Rd. (p)
Detroit, MI 48227
313-273-0001 / Fax: 313-836-3621
CHARLES YANG (Owner) & Buys Men's Sportswear, Furnishings, Accessories, Store Displays, Fixtures, Supplies

H & H APPAREL (CLO)
1065 Woodward Ave. (p)
Detroit, MI 48226
313-963-7870
BOB WHITBREAD (Co-Owner) & Buys Men's Furnishings, Accessories, Big & Tall Men's Wear, Dress Shoes, Store Displays, Fixtures, Supplies
JAMES SCHENK (Co-Owner) & Buys Men's Furnishings, Accessories, Big & Tall Men's Wear, Dress Shoes, Store Displays, Fixtures, Supplies

HENRY THE HATTER (MW-3)
1307 Broadway
Detroit, MI 48226
313-962-0970 / Fax: 313-962-0855
PAUL WASSERMAN (Owner) & Buys Men's Headwear, Accessories, Store Displays, Fixtures, Supplies

HOT SAM'S QUALITY CLOTHES, INC. (MW)
1317 Brush (m-b)
Detroit, MI 48226
313-961-6779 / Fax: 313-961-6919
Sales: $1 Million-$10 Million
TONY STOVALL (Co-Owner) & Buys Men's Overcoats, Suits, Tailored Jackets, Tailored Slacks, Raincoats, Sportswear, Leather Apparel, Trench Coats, Boys' Suits, Ties, Dress Shoes, Store Displays, Fixtures, Supplies
CLIFF GREEN (Co-Owner) & Buys Men's Overcoats, Suits, Tailored Jackets, Tailored Slacks, Raincoat, Sportswear, Leather Apparel, Trench Coats, Boys' Suits, Ties, Dress Shoes, Store Displays, Fixtures, Supplies

J.L. STONE CO., INC. (MW)
1231 Broadway (m-b)
Detroit, MI 48226
313-961-1656 / Fax: 313-964-0335
Sales: $500,000-$1 Million
SHELDON STONE (Owner) & Buys Men's, Young Men's & Boys' Wear, Urban Contemporary, Furnishings, Accessories, Store Displays, Fixtures

NATIONAL DRY GOODS CO. (DG)
1200 Trumbull Ave. (b)
Detroit, MI 48216
313-961-3656 / Fax: 313-961-8684
Sales: $1 Million-$10 Million
Website: www.nationaldrygoods.com
JUDY EPSTEIN (Owner)
BRIAN KLAYMAN (G.M.M.) & Buys Men's Wear, Big & Tall Men's Wear, Footwear, Urban Contemporary, Accessories, Furnishings, Store Displays, Fixtures, Supplies

PRINCE'S MENSWEAR (MW)
6549 Woodward (p)
Detroit, MI 48202
313-871-0229 / Fax: 313-822-1877
JOHN SUH (Owner) & Buys Men's Sportswear, Furnishings, Accessories, Store Displays, Fixtures, Supplies

QUEEN'S FASHION BOUTIQUE (SP)
20500 Conant St.
Detroit, MI 48234
313-891-9081
MARY TURNER (Owner) & Buys Men's Urban Contemporary, Accessories
NOTE:-Carries primarily Afrocentric styles and fashions.

RAGE MEN'S SHOP (MW)
15401 Grand River (p)
Detroit, MI 48227
313-273-2100 / Fax: 313-273-2100
CHI YEO (Mgr.) & Buys Men's Sportswear, Belts, Accessories, Store Displays, Fixtures, Supplies

SERMAN'S, INC. (MW)
1238 Randolph (m)
Detroit, MI 48226
313-964-1335 / Fax: 313-964-5727
Sales: $1 Million-$10 Million
STEVEN ROSS (President & G.M.M.) & Buys Men's Sportswear, Furnishings, Footwear, Accessories, Boys' Sportswear, Store Displays, Fixtures, Supplies

SPECTACLES (MW)
230 E. Grand River (m-b)
Detroit, MI 48226
313-963-6886 / Fax: 313-963-5408
Website: www.spectaclesdetroit.com
DIANE SMITH (Owner) & Buys Men's & Young Men's Sweaters, Sport Shirts, Casual Slacks, Jeans, T-shirts, Fleece Wear, Headwear, Belts, Jewelry, Small Leather Goods, Urban Contemporary, Store Displays, Fixtures, Supplies

SUNNY'S PLACE (MW)
(SUN USA CORP.)
10767 Grand River Ave. (m)
Detroit, MI 48204
313-834-6609 / Fax: 313-834-8428
MR. AHN (Owner)
MILES ADOLPH (Mgr.) & Buys Men's Sportswear, Furnishings, Accessories, Young Men's Wear, Urban Contemporary, Footwear, Store Displays, Fixtures, Supplies

MICHIGAN - Detroit

T.K. MENSWEAR, INC. (MW)
8824 Greenfield rd. (m)
Detroit, MI 48238
313-836-1880 / Fax: 313-836-1880
LARRY TUFTS (Owner) & Buys Men's Footwear, Sportswear, Furnishings, Accessories, Store Displays, Fixtures, Supplies

UNDERGROUND MENSWEAR, INC. (MW)
1860 Finkell (b)
Detroit, MI 48223
313-837-4350 / Fax: 313-837-4351
Sales: $500,001-$1 Million
AALIYAH SALAAM (Owner) & Buys Men's Sportswear, Furnishings, Accessories, Boys' Wear, Store Displays, Fixtures, Supplies
ED JORDEN (Mgr.) & Buys Men's Sportswear, Furnishings, Accessories, Boys' Wear, Store Displays, Fixtures, Supplies

UNITED MENSWEAR (MW)
11976 E. Warren (p)
Detroit, MI 48214
313-824-3910
GAJO KIM (Owner) & Buys Men's Casual Wear, Sportswear, Furnishings, Accessories, Store Displays, Fixtures, Supplies

WASHINGTON CLOTHIERS, INC. (MW)
3044 W. Grand Blvd., #1160 (b)
Detroit, MI 48202
313-871-6060 / Fax: 313-871-2640
Sales: $1 Million-$10 Million
Website: www.wcapparel.com
ALBERT KABAK (President)
MARY HATCHER-Men's Overcoats, Suits, Tailored Jackets, Tailored Slacks, Raincoats, Sweaters, Sport Shirts, Outer Jackets, Casual Slacks, Furnishings, Headwear, Accessories, Top Coats, Store Displays, Fixtures, Supplies
LARRY FIFER-Men's Overcoats, Suits, Tailored Jackets, Tailored Slacks, Raincoats, Sweaters, Sport Shirts, Outer Jackets, Casual Slacks, Furnishings, Headwear, Accessories, Top Coats, Store Displays, Fixtures, Supplies

THE CARRIAGE HOUSE (GS)
265 Lighthouse Rd. (p-m)
Eagle Harbor, MI 49950
906-289-4581
ANNE KIPFER (Owner) & Buys Lighthouse Clothing, T-shirts, Active Wear, Headwear

M.S.U. BOOKSTORE (SP)
(MICHIGAN STATE UNIVERSITY)
International Ctr.
East Lansing, MI 48824
517-355-3450 / Fax: 517-353-9827
BILL KIRCHINGER (Mgr.) & Buys Activewear, Pants, Jackets, Hosiery, Shorts, Licensed Apparel

PLUM PIT SHOPS, INC. (CLO)
24953 Gratiot Ave. (b)
East Point, MI 48021
586-773-1910
MR. PIOSEAK (Mgr.) & Buys Men's Tops, Retro Clothing

O'CONNOR'S, INC. (MW)
116 Newman (m-b)
East Tawas, MI 48730
989-362-3437 / Fax: 989-362-7944
JOHN O'CONNOR (Co-Owner) & Buys Men's Overcoats, Suits, Tailored Jackets, Tailored Slacks, Raincoats, Sportswear, Dress Shoes, Furnishings, Headwear, Accessories, Store Displays, Fixtures, Supplies
TIM O'CONNOR (Co-Owner) & Buys Men's Overcoats, Suits, Tailored Jackets, Tailored Slacks, Raincoats, Sportswear, Dress Shoes, Furnishings, Headwear, Accessories, Store Displays, Fixtures, Supplies

SUPPLY SERGEANT (AN)
1115 Ludington St. (p)
Escanaba, MI 49829
906-786-7861 / Fax: 906-786-6803
JEAN BRANDENBURG (Owner) & Buys Work Wear, Outdoor Wear & Accessories, Hunting Apparel & Supplies, Military Surplus, Workboots, Raincoats

WHIFFLETREE (MW)
1220 Ludington St. (m)
Escanaba, MI 49829
906-786-2777 / Fax: 906-789-9025
Website: www.thewhiffletree.com
DAN YOUNG (Owner) & Buys Men's Suits, Sportswear, Furnishings, Accessories, Footwear, Store Displays, Fixtures, Supplies,Young Men's Clothing

YOUNG'S FORMAL WEAR (MW)
112 N. 22nd St. (m-b)
Escanaba, MI 49829
906-786-2526 / Fax: 906-786-2403
RON YOUNG-Men's Formalwear, Accessories, Footwear, Furnishings
GINA YOUNG-Men's Formalwear, Accessories, Footwear, Furnishings

EBELS' FAMILY CENTER, INC. (CLO)
420 Prosper Rd. (m)
Falmouth, MI 49632
231-826-3333 / Fax: 231-826-4243
BERNICE EBELS (Co-Owner) & Buys Men's Sportswear, Furnishings, Boots, Casual Shoes, Headwear, Accessories, Young Men's Wear, Boys' Wear, Store Displays, Fixtures, Supplies

RECREATIONAL LEISURE CORP. (CLO)
31506 Grand River (p)
Farmington, MI 48336
248-477-0212 / Fax: 248-477-1340
Website: www.recleisure.com
RAY MICHRINA (Owner)
LAURA BURCH-Men's Outer Jackets, Leather Apparel, Active Apparel, Boys' Sportswear

THE SHIRT BOX (MW)
32500 Northwestern Hwy.
Farmington Hills, MI 48334
248-851-6770 / Fax: 248-851-6835
RON ELKUS (Owner) & Buys Men's Sportswear, Furnishings, Accessories, Active Wear, Dress Shirts, Casual Shirts, Store Displays, Fixtures, Supplies

THC/BARON'S, INC. (MW)
(BARON'S)
27888 Orchard Lake Rd. (b-des)
Farmington Hills, MI 48334
248-865-9959 / Fax: 248-865-9265
Sales: $10 Million-$50 Million
PHILIP L. ELKUS (President) & Buys Men's Apparel, Men's Big & Tall Apparel, Men's Casualwear, Men's Outerwear, Men's Accessories, Men's Sleepwear, Men's Suits, Men's Activewear
DAVID ELKUS (V.P.) & Buys Men's Apparel, Men's Big & Tall Apparel, Men's Casualwear, Men's Outerwear, Men's Accessories, Men's Sleepwear, Men's Suits, Men's Activewear
ESTELLE ELKUS (Treas.) & Buys Men's Apparel, Men's Big & Tall Apparel, Men's Casualwear, Men's Outerwear, Men's Accessories, Men's Sleepwear, Men's Suits, Men's Activewear

BAUMAN'S RUNNING & FITNESS (SP)
1453 W. Hill Rd.
Flint, MI 48507
810-238-5981 / Fax: 810-234-9072
Sales: $100,001-$500,000
MARK BAUMAN (Owner) & Buys Activewear, Athletic Footwear

COMPLETE RUNNER (SP)
915 S. Dort Hwy., #F
Flint, MI 48503
810-233-8851 / Fax: 810-233-8857
Website: www.completerunner.com
JESSIE GRIFFITH (Owner) & Buys Activewear, Athletic Footwear

JAMES GLOVE & SUPPLY, INC. (SP)
3422 W. Pasadena Ave.
Flint, MI 48504
810-733-5780 / Fax: 810-733-5969
GAIL McKONE-BURNS (Owner)
JUDY McKONE-Men's & Boys' Gloves, Men's Jackets

MALEK DABAJA'S NEEDLE (CLO)

3402 Corunna Rd (m-b)
Flint, MI 48503
810-234-6261
Sales: $100,001-$500,000

MALEK DABAJA (Owner) & Buys Men's Wear, Sportswear, Furnishings, Accessories

PARVIZI (MW)

3387 S. Linden Rd. (m-b)
Flint, MI 48507
810-230-1788 / Fax: 810-230-1788
Website: www.parviziclothing.com

PARVIZ PARVIZI (Co-Owner) & Buys Men's Suits, Formal Wear, Sportswear, Dress Shoes, Outerwear, Accessories, Men's Big & Tall Wear, Store Displays, Fixtures, Supplies

FRED PARVIZI (Co-Owner) & Buys Men's Suits, Formal Wear, Sportswear, Dress Shoes, Outerwear, Accessories, Men's Big & Tall Wear, Store Displays, Fixtures, Supplies

SEVEN-O-SEVEN MEN'S STORE (MW-3)

134 W. Puritan (m-b)
Flint, MI 48505
810-789-3429 / Fax: 810-789-7582

GENE SUK (Owner) & Buys Men's Suits, Sportswear, Dress Shoes, Furnishings, Accessories, Boys' Wear, Store Displays, Fixtures, Supplies

DECATO'S MENSWEAR (MW)

357 Central St. (m-b)
Franklin, MI 03235
603-934-4919
Sales: $100,001-$500,000

DICK WISER (Owner) & Buys Men's Sportswear, Furnishings & Accessories

FREEPORT ELEVATOR (MW)

223 Division St. (m-b)
Freeport, MI 49325
616-765-8421 / Fax: 616-765-3588
Sales: $100,001-$500,000

JIM DECKER (Owner) & Buys Men's Jeans, Work Clothes, Work Shoes

BLUE STAR SPORTSWEAR (SP)

8244 Embury Rd.
Grand Blanc, MI 48439
800-694-8415 / Fax: 810-694-8200
Website: www.bluestarsportswear.com

DAVID BARTELS (Owner) & Buys Activewear

LAURIES (KS)

11346 S. Saginaw (b)
Grand Blanc, MI 48439
810-694-3110 / Fax: 810-694-0049

GEORGE BEERS (Co-Owner) & Buys To Size 20 Boys' Wear, Footwear, Accessories, Furnishings, Store Displays, Fixtures, Supplies

TIMOTHY BEERS (Co-Owner) & Buys To Size 20 Boys' Wear, Footwear, Accessories, Furnishings, Store Displays, Fixtures, Supplies

BIG & TALL WAREHOUSE (MW)

785 Center Dr. NW, #B2 (m-b)
Grand Rapids, MI 49544
616-785-0165 / Fax: 616-785-1290
Sales: $1 Million-$10 Million

GREG ALVESTEFFER (Owner) & Buys Fragrances, Leather Goods, Men's Apparel, Men's Big & Tall Apparel, Men's Casualwear, Men's Denim Apparel, Men's Designer Apparel, Men's Accessories, Men's Hosiery, Men's Outerwear, Men's Sleepwear, Men's Sportswear, Men's Suits, Men's Swimwear, Men's Underwear

F. DAVID BARNEY, INC. (MW)

125 Ottawa Ave. NW (b)
Grand Rapids, MI 49503
616-458-6118 / Fax: 616-458-5713
Sales: $500,001-$1 Million
Website: www.fdbarney.com

DAVID BARNEY (Owner) & Buys Men's Wear, Sportswear, Footwear, Furnishings, Accessories, Store Displays, Fixtures, Supplies

FITZGERALD'S MENSWEAR (MW)

1870 Breton Rd. (b)
Grand Rapids, MI 49506
616-957-2220 / Fax: 616-957-0517
Website: www.fitzs.com

JERRY GIROD (Owner) & Buys Men's Sportswear, Formal Wear, Furnishings, Accessories, Dress Shoes, Store Displays, Fixtures, Supplies

HOUSE OF STYLES (MW-2)

645 Jefferson Ave. (m)
Grand Rapids, MI 49503
616-243-8585 / Fax: 616-243-4223
Sales: Under $100,000

EARNEST MATHIS (President) & Buys Men's Overcoats, Tailored Jackets, Tailored Slacks, Suits, Dress Shirts, Sweaters, Ties, Headwear, Belts, Leather Apparel, Urban Contemporary, Store Displays, Fixtures, Supplies

JURGENS & HOLTVLUWER (MW)

1054 Leonard St. NW (m-b)
Grand Rapids, MI 49504
616-459-3117 / Fax: 616-459-0350

RICH BISHOP (Co-Owner) & Buys Men's Sportswear, Furnishings, Headwear, Accessories, Dress Shoes

CURT HOLTVLUWER (Co-Owner) & Buys Men's Sportswear, Furnishings, Headwear, Accessories, Dress Shoes

KLEIMAN'S (MW)

424 S. Division (m)
Grand Rapids, MI 49503
616-456-9505 / Fax: 616-456-9506

LAWRENCE KLEIMAN (Owner) & Buys Men's Sportswear, Furnishings, Accessories, Dress Shoes, Store Displays, Fixtures, Supplies

MC SPORTING GOODS, INC. (SG-70 & OL)

3070 Shaffer Ave. SE (m)
Grand Rapids, MI 49512
616-942-2600 / Fax: 616-942-1973
Website: www.mcsports.com
Retail Locations: KS, MO, IL, IN, OH, MI, WI

JERRY KLEIN (Exec. V.P. Mdse. & Real Estate Contact)

MARK LUNDVICK (G.M.M.) & Buys Licensed Goods Products

ROB HENDERHAM-Men's & Boys' Activewear & Athletic Apparel, Footwear, Licensed Products

MEIJER, INC. (DEPT-156)

2929 Walker Ave. NW (p)
Grand Rapids, MI 49544
616-453-6711 / Fax: 616-453-6067
Website: www.meijer.com
Retail Locations: MI, IL, IN, OH, KY

PAUL BOYER (President)
HANK MEIJER (C.E.O.)
SCOTT NOWAKOWSKI (Real Estate Contact-KY, MI, OH, IN)
MIKE KINSTLE (Real Estate Contact-IL)
HARRY MULL-Men's Slacks, Fleecewear, Sleepwear, Hosiery, Underwear
TRICIA WESTING-Men's Woven Sportshirts & Knit Sportshirts, Headwear
RICK KAREL-Men's Outerwear
RAY MOULDEN-Men's Dress Shoes, Casual Shoes
SCOTT KOLQUITT-Boys' Sportswear
SAM KRAUSE-Boys' Footwear, Athletic Footwear, Seasonal Merchandise

THE NEW YORKER (MW)

1511 Wealthy St. SE (m-b)
Grand Rapids, MI 49506
616-459-5805 / Fax: 616-459-7128

MOHHAMED JAMAL (Owner) & Buys Men's Wear, Sportswear, Footwear, Furnishings, Accessories, Store Displays, Fixtures, Supplies

ROGERS' DEPARTMENT STORE (DEPT)

1001 28th St. SW
Grand Rapids, MI 49509
616-538-6000 / Fax: 616-538-0613
Website: www.rogersdepartmentstore.com

DAN HURWITZ (President)

HICKEY'S WALTON-PIERCE (MW)

17140 Kercheval Ave. (b)
Grosse Pointe, MI 48230
313-882-8970 / Fax: 313-882-0342
Sales: $1 Million-$10 Million

WILLIAM P. HUNTINGTON (President) & Buys Men's Overcoats, Suits, Tailored Jackets, Tailored Slacks, Raincoats, Headwear, Sportswear, Sweaters, Sport Shirts, Outer Jackets, Furnishings, Accessories, Footwear, Store Displays, Fixtures, Supplies

MICHIGAN - Hamtramck

BENSON BROTHERS SPORTSWEAR (MW)
9720 Joseph Campau (m)
Hamtramck, MI 48212
313-972-1150 / Fax: 313-871-3303
Sales: $100,001-$500,000
SANGMIN AHN (Owner) & Buys Men's Wear, Boys' Wear, Store Displays, Fixtures, Supplies

CAMPAU CLOTHING CO., INC. (MW)
9643 Joseph Campau (m)
Hamtramck, MI 48212
313-871-8112 / Fax: 313-871-4059
Sales: $1 Million-$10 Million
ARNOLD LANTOR (President & G.M.M.) & Buys Men's Big & Tall Men's Wear, Sweaters, Sport Shirts, Outer Jackets, Casual Slacks, Dress Shirts, Ties, Underwear, Hosiery, Belts, Big & Tall Men's Wear, Footwear, Store Displays, Fixtures, Supplies

G-MART (MW)
10012 Joseph Campau (p)
Hamtramck, MI 48212
313-874-4666 / Fax: 313-874-4666
JADWIGA PALAC (Owner) & Buys Men's & Boys' Wear, Urban Contemporary, Leather Apparel, Footwear, Store Displays, Fixtures, Supplies

HAMTRAMCK MENSWEAR (MW)
9531 Joseph Campau (m)
Hamtramck, MI 48212
313-872-0800
CHONG HAGGART (Owner) & Buys Men's Sportswear, Furnishings, Accessories, Store Displays, Fixtures, Supplies

GARTNER'S DEPARTMENT STORE (DEPT)
P.O. Box 240 (p-m)
102 Quincy
Hancock, MI 49930
906-482-4000 / Fax: 906-482-7327
Sales: $500,000-$1 Million
ROBERTA KAHN (Co-Owner) & Buys Store Displays, Fixtures, Supplies
RICHARD KAHN (Co-Owner) & Buys Store Displays, Fixtures, Supplies
DAVE PLEIMLING-Men's Sportswear, Furnishings, Accessories, Young Men's Wear

BRENNAN'S MENSWEAR (MW)
308 State St. (m-b)
Harbor Beach, MI 48441
989-479-3305 / Fax: 989-479-9802
WALLY BRENNAN (Owner) & Buys Men's Wear, Sportswear, Urban Contemporary, Footwear, Furnishings, Accessories, Store Displays, Fixtures, Supplies

APRON STRINGS (KS-2)
141 State St. (b)
Harbor Springs, MI 49740
231-526-0500 / Fax: 231-526-5205
GREG BALOK (Co-Owner) & Buys To Size 7 Boys' Wear, Store Displays, Fixtures, Supplies
KIM BALOK (Co-Owner) & Buys Store Displays, Fixtures, Supplies
AMY BALOK (Co-Owner) & Buys Store Displays, Fixtures, Supplies

VIRGIL W. POWERS & SONS, INC. (DEPT-2)
28 State St. (m)
Hart, MI 49420
231-873-2088 / Fax: 231-873-2896
MICHAEL POWERS (President) & Buys Men's & Boys' Wear, Footwear, Store Displays, Supplies

JR. MENSWEAR BIG & TALL (MW)
24918 John R. St. (m)
Hazel Park, MI 48030
248-543-4646 / Fax: 248-543-4646
JERRY SOROKA (Owner) & Buys Men's Wear, Big & Tall Men's Wear, Store Displays, Fixtures, Supplies

HUTCHINSON'S STORES FOR CHILDREN (KS)
16 W. 8th St. (m-b)
Holland, MI 49423
616-392-1682 / Fax: 616-392-2100
Sales: $500,001-$1 Million
SUE HUTCHINSON (President & G.M.M.) & Buys Boys' Clothing, Sportswear, Furnishings, Accessories To Size 7, Store Displays, Fixtures, Supplies

LOKKER - RUTGERS CO. (MW)
39 E. 8th St. (m)
Holland, MI 49423
616-392-3237 / Fax: 616-392-9947
Sales: $1 Million-$10 Million
JEROME KOBES (President) & Buys Men's Overcoats, Suits, Tailored Jackets, Raincoats, Sportswear, Sweaters, Outer Jackets, Activewear, Ties, Robes, Headwear, Accessories, Fragrances, Underwear, Hosiery, Gloves, Belts
RONALD LUGTEN (G.M.M.) & Buys Men's Big & Tall Wear, Footwear, Sport Shirts, Dress Shirts, Casual Slacks, Dress Pants

OUTPOST (CLO)
25 E. 8th St. (p-m-b)
Holland, MI 49423
616-396-5556 / Fax: 616-396-9494
Website: www.hollandoutpost.com
RICH MOSER (Owner) & Buys Men's Sportswear, Footwear, Store Displays, Fixtures, Supplies

STEKETEE'S (DEPT-2)
12339 James (bud-p-m-b)
Holland, MI 49424
616-393-0022 / Fax: 616-393-8949
Sales: $10 Million-$50 Million
TWILA McINTOSH (V.P. & G.M.M.) & Buys Men's Furnishings, Belts, Jewelry, Small Leather Goods, Men's Suits, Sportswear, Raincoats, Men's Fragrances

SCHENK'S DEPARTMENT STORE (MW)
15213 N. Holly Rd. (p)
Holly, MI 48442
248-634-4951 / Fax: 248-634-0647
DAVID SCHENK (Owner) & Buys Men's Tailored Jackets, Tailored Slacks, Raincoats, Sportswear, Furnishings, Headwear, Belts, Jewelry, Small Leather Goods, Boys' Sportswear, Urban Contemporary, Furnishings, Accessories, Store Displays, Fixtures, Supplies

COUNTRY SQUIRE (MW)
408 Sheldon Ave. (m)
Houghton, MI 49931
906-482-9938 / Fax: 906-483-0771
JOHN LEHTO (Owner) & Buys Men's Sportswear, Furnishings, Accessories, Footwear
ERIK LEHTO (Mgr.) & Buys Store Displays, Fixtures, Supplies

KEEGSTRA DEPARTMENT STORE (DEPT)
3499 Kelly St. (p)
Hudsonville, MI 49426
616-669-9752 / Fax: 616-669-5447
JOEL KEEGSTRA (Owner) & Buys Store Displays, Fixtures, Supplies
PAT PIKE-Men's Wear, Boys' Wear, Furnishings, Accessories

McCLUTCHEY'S, INC. (CLO-2)
P.O. Box 306 (m)
3510 S. Strait Hwy.
Indian River, MI 49749
231-238-7712
Sales: $100,001-$500,000
KATHY WHITENER (Mgr.) & Buys Men's Tailored Clothing, Sportswear, Furnishings, Footwear, Belts, Boys' Clothing & Sportswear, Store Displays, Fixtures, Supplies

STREETWEAR (CLO)
(CRAIG OLSON ENTERPRISES, INC.)
1070 S. Stephenson Ave.
Iron Mountain, MI 49801
906-774-1980 / Fax: 906-774-9927
Sales: $500,001-$1 Million
CRAIG OLSON (President) & Buys Activewear, Athletic Footwear
MARSHA OLSON (G.M.M.) & Buys Activewear, Athletic Footwear

MICHIGAN - Jackson

ACTION SPORTS SUPPLIES (CLO)
1515 Horton Rd. (m-b)
Jackson, MI 49202
517-789-6166 / Fax: 517-789-6168
DAVE KENNEDY (Owner) & Buys Men's & Boys' Athletic Wear, T-shirts, Shorts, Hosiery, Store Displays, Fixtures, Supplies

ETERNAL SUN (CLO)
3322 Francis St.
Jackson, MI 49203
517-783-4786 / Fax: 517-529-4492
CONNIE VINSON (Co-Owner) & Buys Men's Surf & Swimwear
GEORGE VINSON (Co-Owner) & Buys Men's Surf & Swimwear

FURMAN'S, INC. (MW)
141 E. Michigan Ave. (m-b)
Jackson, MI 49201
(Kreiss & Gordon)
517-782-0502 / Fax: 517-782-3076
Sales: $1 Million-$10 Million
WOODY FURMAN (Owner) & Buys Men's, Young Men's & Boys' Wear, Footwear, Store Displays, Fixtures, Supplies

ACORN (DEPT-2)
210 Farmers Alley (m-b)
Kalamazoo, MI 49007
269-345-3541 / Fax: 269-345-0212
Sales: $10 Million-$50 Million
STEVEN PHILLIPS (President) & Buys Men's Wear

GOLDEN NEEDLE TAILOR (MW)
228 E. Michigan Ave. (b)
Kalamazoo, MI 49007
269-349-3434 / Fax: 269-349-3122
MOUNIR FAHS (Owner) & Buys Men's Sportswear, Footwear, Furnishings, Accessories, Store Displays, Fixtures, Supplies
FRANK FAHS (Mgr.) & Buys Men's Sportswear, Footwear, Furnishings, Accessories

KALAMAZOO REGALIA (SP-2 & MO)
(KALAMAZOO SPORTSWEAR)
728 W. Michigan Ave. (m)
Kalamazoo, MI 49007
269-344-4299 / Fax: 269-344-2227
Sales: $1 Million-$10 Million
Website: www.kazoosports.com
JIM BELLINGER (Owner) & Buys Men's Apparel, Men's Accessories, Furnishings
TERRY SQUIRES (Mgr.-Sales)
LORRIE KELLY (Ofc. Mgr.) & Buys Men's Apparel, Men's Accessories, Furnishings

LIBIN'S (MW)
1028 E. Cork St. (m)
Kalamazoo, MI 49001
269-381-0746 / Fax: 269-381-0711
Sales: $1 Million-$10 Million
FRED LIBIN (President) & Buys Men's Store Displays, Fixtures, Supplies
SCOTT RHULAND-Men's Furnishings
BRENDA PIERCE-Men's Sportswear, Ties, Jeans

THE TOT TO TEEN VILLAGE (KS)
229 W. Kilgore Rd. (m-b)
Kalamazoo, MI 49002
269-381-7800 / Fax: 269-381-7803
Sales: $1 Million-$10 Million
DAVID PENNING (President)
RONALD KLOOSTERMAN (G.M.M.) & Buys Store Displays, Fixtures, Supplies
MARY VAN DYKE-To Size 7 Boys' Wear

NORTHLAND FASHION FOOTWEAR (FW)
Northland Plaza Mall (m-b)
Kalkska, MI 49646
231-258-9114 / Fax: 231-258-4449
JANET ASCIONE (Owner) & Buys Men's & Boys' Casual Wear, Footwear Furnishings, Accessories, Hosiery

DELTA EMBROIDERY (SP)
1611 N. Grand River
Lansing, MI 48906
517-482-6565 / Fax: 517-482-6463
KIM LITTLE (President) & Buys Activewear

HOLDEN - REID CORP. (CLO-2)
522 Frandor (m-b)
Lansing, MI 48912
517-351-6969 / Fax: 517-351-2953
WAYNE HOLDEN (Chmn.) & Buys Young Men's & Boys' Wear, Store Displays, Fixtures, Supplies, Men's Sportswear, Furnishings, Swimwear, Accessories
ROBERT REID-Men's Sportswear, Furnishings, Swimwear, Accessories
BILL WOLL-Men's Sportswear, Furnishings, Swimwear, Accessories
ROBERT HOLDEN-Men's Footwear

KOSITCHEK'S (MW)
113 N. Washington Sq. (b)
Lansing, MI 48933
517-482-1171 / Fax: 517-482-1177
Sales: $1 Million-$10 Million
DAVID KOSITCHEK (President) & Buys Men's Suits, Overcoats. Sweaters, Active Apparel, Sport Shirts, Dress Shirts, Ties, Robes, Tailored Jackets, Tailored Slacks, Raincoats, Casual Slacks, Outer Jackets, Underwear, Hosiery, Gloves, Belts, Jewelry, Fragrances, Footwear, Store Displays, Fixtures, Supplies

THORNE'S PENDELTON SHOP (CLO)
232 W. Nepessing St. (b)
Lapeer, MI 48446
810-664-8212
JOSEPH WENZLICK (Owner) & Buys Men's Wear, Footwear, Furnishings, Accessories, Store Displays, Fixtures, Supplies

JACK'S PLACE NORTH LTD. (MW)
27881 Southfield (m-b)
Lathrup Village, MI 48076
248-569-5405 / Fax: 248-569-5518
Sales: $1 Million-$10 Million
GARY KAPPY (President)
IRA KAPPY (G.M.M.) & Buys Men's Sportswear, Leather Apparel, Furnishings, Accessories, Store Displays, Fixtures, Supplies
ARNOLD SIEGEL (D.M.M.) & Buys Men's Sportswear, Leather Apparel, Furnishings, Accessories, Men's Footwear, Store Displays, Fixtures, Supplies

MITCHELL'S DEPARTMENT STORE (DEPT)
P.O. Box 576 (p)
101 S. Main St.
Leslie, MI 49251
517-589-8701
Sales: $100,001-$500,000
JIM MITCHELL (Owner) & Buys Men's Leather Apparel, Sportswear, Furnishings, Headwear, Accessories, Footwear, Big & Tall Men's Wear, Young Men's Wear, Boys' Wear, Store Displays, Fixtures, Supplies

ALLIE BROTHERS TAILORS (MW & OL)
20295 Middlebelt Rd. (m)
Livonia, MI 48152
248-477-4434 / Fax: 248-477-1416
Website: www.alliebrothers.com
JOHN ALLIE (Owner) & Buys Men's Slacks, Police & Fire Uniforms, Footwear

J.R.'S TANNING & SURFWEAR (SP)
28422 Five Mile Rd.
Livonia, MI 48154
734-261-6666 / Fax: 734-261-6699
JEFF REININK (Owner) & Buys Sunglasses, Accessories, Footwear, Swimwear, Men's Apparel, Men's Surf & Swimwear, Outdoor Gear & Appparel, Resortwear, Skate Apparel, T-shirts, Imprinted Sportswear, Urban Streetwear

KLEIN'S OF LIVONIA, INC. (CLO)
37205 W. Six Mile Rd. (m)
Livonia, MI 48152
734-591-9244 / Fax: 734-591-9209
Sales: $1 Million-$10 Million
HOWARD KLEIN (Owner) & Buys Men's Sportswear, Furnishings, Accessories, Store Displays, Fixtures, Supplies

LAND & SEAS, INC. (CLO)
37652 W. Six Mile Rd.
Livonia, MI 48152
734-464-5589
MARY HIGGINS (Owner) & Buys Men's Sweaters, T-shirts

SCOTT COLBURN SADDLERY, INC. (WW)
20411 Farmington Rd. (m)
Livonia, MI 48152
248-476-1262 / Fax: 248-476-3406
SARAH COLBURN (Owner) & Buys Men's Western Wear, Accessories, Footwear, Boys' Western Wear

STEVE PETIX CLOTHIER, INC. (MW)
27565 Grand River Rd. (b)
Livonia, MI 48152
248-474-1190 / Fax: 248-645-5913
Sales: $1 Million-$10 Million
TONY VETTRAINO (President) & Buys Men's & Boys' Tuxedos
JIM PETIX (V.P.) & Buys Men's & Boys' Tuxedos

RAVENS MENSWEAR (MW-2)
(RAVEN INVESTMENT PROPERTIES)
117 E. Ludington Ave. (p-m-b)
Ludington, MI 49431
231-843-4560
CHRIS RAVEN (Co-Owner) & Buys Men's Sportswear, Furnishings, Accessories, Urban Contemporary, Footwear, Store Displays, Fixtures, Supplies
VICKI RAVEN (Co-Owner) & Buys Men's Sportswear, Furnishings, Accessories, Men's Footwear, Store Displays, Fixtures, Supplies

MACKINAW CLOTHING (CLO)
319 Central Ave. (m-b)
Mackinaw City, MI 49701
231-436-8411 / Fax: 231-436-7342
Sales: $100,001-$500,000
RICHARD WEICK (Owner) & Buys Men's Sportswear, Furnishings, Headwear, Accessories, Footwear, Store Displays, Fixtures, Supplies

PEOPLES STORE (CLO)
239 S. Cedar (p-m)
Manistique, MI 49854
906-341-2779
Sales: Under $100,000
SALLY STRAM (Mgr.) & Buys Men's Tailored Clothing, Sportswear, Furnishings, Footwear, Boys' Wear, Store Displays, Fixtures, Supplies

GETZ'S, INC. (DEPT)
218 S. Front St. (m-b)
Marquette, MI 49855
906-226-3561 / Fax: 906-226-3022
Sales: $1 Million-$10 Million
ROBERT ALLAN GETZ (Co-Owner & G.M.M.) & Buys Men's & Boys' Wear, Footwear
RICHARD CADEN (Co-Owner & President) & Buys Store Displays, Fixtures, Supplies
DENNIS MINTAY (G.M.M.) & Buys Men's & Boys' Wear, Footwear

BARINGER'S MEN'S SHOP (MW)
129 E. Main St. (m-b)
Midland, MI 48640
989-832-8651
Sales: $100,001-$500,000
NORMA BARINGER (Owner) & Buys Men's Sportswear, Furnishings, Accessories, Store Displays, Fixtures, Supplies

THOMAS TRADING POST, INC. (WW)
2292 N. Eastman Rd. (m-b)
Midland, MI 48642
989-631-1104 / Fax: 989-631-7171
Sales: $500,000-$1 Million
DAVE THOMAS (Owner) & Buys Men's Western Wear, Big & Tall Men's Wear, Men's Casual Wear, Gloves, Accessories, Footwear, Store Displays, Fixtures, Supplies

ARMS BROTHERS' STORE FOR MEN (MW)
361 N. Main St. (b)
Milford, MI 48381
248-685-8449
Sales: $100,001-$500,000
THOMAS S. MOTLEY (Owner) & Buys Men's Footwear, Men's Wear, Young Men's Wear, Furnishings, Accessories, Store Displays, Fixtures and Supplies
RON BARNETTE (Mgr.) & Buys Men's Footwear, Men's Wear, Young Men's Wear, Furnishings, Accessories, Store Displays, Fixtures and Supplies

JONES FOR MEN, INC. (MW)
10 E. Front St. (b)
Monroe, MI 48161
734-241-9444 / Fax: 734-241-8755
TODD JONES (Owner) & Buys Men's Sportswear, Furnishings, Accessories, Footwear, Store Displays, Fixtures, Supplies

FACTORY SURPLUS SALES (CLO-2)
10112 US Hwy. 31 (p)
Montague, MI 49437
231-894-6633 / Fax: 231-896-2233
GLEN NAGHTIM (Owner) & Buys Men's & Boys' Casual Wear, Accessories

GEBRAN'S APPAREL (MW)
81 Macomb Pl.
Mount Clemens, MI 48043
586-465-5410 / Fax: 586-783-0545
PETE COLLIAS (Owner) & Buys Men's Suits, Sportswear, Accessories, Furnishings, Footwear

NEW YORKER (KS)
117 S. Main St. (p-m)
Mount Pleasant, MI 48858
989-773-7619
JOHN R. KARR (Owner) & Buys Boys' Outerwear, Up to Size 8 Sportswear, Store Displays, Fixtures, Supplies

THE QUALITY STORES (DG-200)
P.O. Box 3315
455 E. Ellis Rd.
Muskegan, MI 49443
231-798-0218 / Fax: 231-798-0023
Website: www.farmandcountry.com
PETER FITZSIMMONS (President)
KEN BUSCH (Store Planner) & Buys Store Displays, Fixtures, Supplies
PAT HORSFELL-Men's Work Clothes, Denim Jeans, Casual Shirts, Sportswear, Underwear, Hosiery, Headwear, Gloves, Belts

SHOPPERS' WORLD, INC. (DEPT-5)
21675 Coolidge (bud-p)
Oak Park, MI 48237
248-399-5252 / Fax: 248-399-0127
Sales: $10 Million-$50 Million
MAX GENDELMAN (Owner)
FRANK BRADBURN (President) & Buys Store Displays, Fixtures, Supplies
MICHAEL GENDELMAN-Men's Sweaters, Sport Shirts, Outer Jackets, Casual Slacks, Active Apparel, Dress Shirts, Ties, Robes, Underwear, Hosiery, Gloves, Belts, Jewelry, Young Men's Wear, 7 & Up Boys' Wear, Sportswear, Furnishings, Accessories
NOTE-Footwear is a Leased Department.

BARYAMES' TUX SHOP (MW-2)
2421 W. Grand River (m)
Okemos, MI 48864
517-349-6555 / Fax: 517-349-9010
Website: www.baryamestux.com
KATINA BARYAMES (Owner) & Buys Men's Tuxedos, Formal Accessories, Dress Shoes, Store Displays, Fixtures, Supplies

PLAYMAKERS (SP)
2299 W. Grand River
Okemos, MI 48864
517-349-3803 / Fax: 517-349-8627
Sales: $1 Million-$10 Million
Website: www.playmakers.com
CURT MUNSON (Owner)
DAVE GRAF (General Mgr.) & Buys Activewear, Licensed Apparel
JOHN BENEDICT (Mgr.)
KLAUS MEINGAST-Athletic Footwear

STORRER'S CLOTHING (MW)
110 N. Washington St. (m)
Owosso, MI 48867
989-725-2800
JAMES A. STORRER (Co-Owner) & Buys Men's Sportswear, Furnishings, Accessories
FAYENNE STORRER (Co-Owner) & Buys Men's Sportswear, Furnishings, Accessories

BAHNOF SPORT (SG-4)
P.O. Box 677 (b)
Petoskey, MI 49770
231-347-1040 / Fax: 231-347-4909
Website: www.bahnofs.com
LINNELL SMITH (Owner) & Buys Men's & Boys' Ski Clothing, Footwear
RYAN SMITH-Accessories, Boots

CIRCUS SHOP, INC. (KS)
323 E. Mitchell St. (b)
Petoskey, MI 49770
231-347-3433 / Fax: 231-347-0390
Sales: $100,001-$500,000
Website: www.circusshop.com
LYNN DUSE (Owner & Mgr.) & Buys Boys' Clothing, Furnishings, Headwear, Accessories
MARNIE DUSE (G.M.M.)

CLOTHES POST, INC. (MO & CLO)
326 E. Mitchell St. (m-b)
Petoskey, MI 49770
231-347-4562 / Fax: 231-347-4590
JEFF PAGEL (Owner) & Buys Men's Wear, Sportswear, Furnishings, Accessories

COUNTRY CASUALS, INC. (CLO-8)
(EXPRESSIONS)
(J. PHILLIPS)
311 E. Mitchell St. (m-b)
Petoskey, MI 49770
231-347-6501
Sales: $1 Million-$10 Million
RODNEY PHILLIPS (President)
STEVE BAKER (Controller)
JUDY PHILLIPS (Dir.-Purch.) & Buys Boys' Apparel, Leather Goods, Men's Sleepwear, Men's Swimwear

LEATHER BARN (CLO)
325 East Lake (b)
Petoskey, MI 49770
231-347-5120 / Fax: 231-347-5120
JACKIE LERCH (Owner) & Buys Men's Leather Jackets, Coats, Small Leather Goods, Belts

H.T.C., INC. (SP)
(PITTSFORD SPORTSWEAR, INC.)
P.O. Box 217
Pittsford, MI 49271
517-523-2167 / Fax: 517-523-2167
DANIEL L. McCLOREY (President) & Buys Insulated Snowsuits, Outerwear

B.J. BENJIM'S (MW)
225 W. Centre Ave. (m)
Portage, MI 49024
269-329-3230 / Fax: 269-329-3385
JIM GERESY (Co-Owner) & Buys Big & Tall Men's Wear, Urban Contemporary, Store Displays, Fixtures, Supplies
STEVE BAUM (Co-Owner) & Buys Big & Tall Men's Wear, Urban Contemporary, Store Displays, Fixtures, Supplies

MITZELFELD'S, INC. (DEPT)
312 Main St. (b)
Rochester, MI 48307
248-651-8171 / Fax: 248-651-0724
Sales: $1 Million-$10 Million
LAMONT MITZELFELD (President) & Buys Men's Sportswear, Furnishings, Robes, Headwear, Clothing, Accessories,Young Men's Wear, Leather Apparel, Boys' Wear
SUE BENEDIX (Store Designer) & Buys Store Displays, Fixtures, Supplies
BRAD MITZEFELD-Footwear

LECONTE LTD. (MW)
3086 Walton Blvd. (b)
Rochester Hills, MI 48309
248-375-5577 / Fax: 248-375-2051
MICHAEL BROWE (Owner) & Buys Men's Sportswear, Footwear, Furnishings, Accessories

RICHARD'S CLOTHING (CLO)
245 N. 3rd St. (m)
Rogers City, MI 49779
989-734-3676
RICHARD VOLGELHEIM (Owner)
VAL VOGELHEIM-Men's Overcoats, Suits, Tailored Jackets, Tailored Slacks, Raincoats, Big & Tall Men's Wear, Sportswear, Sweaters, Sport Shirts, Outer Jackets, Leather Apparel, Casual Slacks, Active Apparel, Furnishings, Dress Shirts, Ties, Robes, Underwear, Hosiery, Gloves, Headwear, Accessories, Belts, Small Leather Goods, Fragrances, Footwear, Young Men's Wear, Store Displays, Fixtures, Supplies

CORKY'S (CLO-2)
(AQUA BAY CONCEPTS, INC.)
26451 Gratiot Ave. (p)
Roseville, MI 48066
586-775-8270 / Fax: 586-775-8256
KEVIN ANGER (President) & Buys Men's Wear, Urban Contemporary, Footwear, Accessories

EDWARD'S MEN'S SHOPS, INC. (MW)
4670 State St. (m-b)
Saginaw, MI 48603
989-793-4523 / Fax: 989-793-4524
Sales: $1 Million-$10 Million
JIM SILK (Chmn.) & Buys Men's Overcoats, Suits, Tailored Jackets, Tailored Slacks, Raincoats, Men's Sweaters, Sportswear, Sport Shirts, Outer Jackets, Casual Slacks, Furnishings, Leather Apparel, Headwear, Accessories, Men's Footwear
GARY SILK (President) & Buys Men's Overcoats, Suits, Tailored Jackets, Tailored Slacks, Raincoats, Men's Sweaters, Sport Shirts, Outer Jackets, Casual Slacks, Furnishings, Leather Apparel, Headwear, Accessories

SCHAEFER HAT STORE, INC. (MW)
128 N. Washington St.
Saginaw, MI 48607
989-752-5404 / Fax: 989-752-5404
MRS. WILBUR HOFFMAN (Owner) & Buys Men's Sportswear, Furnishings, Accessories, Headwear, Store Displays, Fixtures, Supplies
ROGER B. BORCHARD-Men's Sportswear, Furnishings, Accessories, Headwear, Store Displays, Fixtures, Supplies

CONNIE'S CHILDREN SHOP (KS)
23200 Greater Mack (p-m)
Saint Clair Shores, MI 48080
586-777-8020 / Fax: 586-777-4255
MAXINE KORT (Owner) & Buys Young Men's Wear, To Size 20 Boys' Wear, Footwear, Store Displays, Fixtures, Supplies
DENISE KORT (Mgr.) & Buys Young Men's Wear, To Size 20 Boys' Wear, Footwear, Store Displays, Fixtures, Supplies

VAN DUSEN CLOTHING (CLO-4)
(CLYDE'S KIDS, INC.)
419 N. State St.
Saint Ignace, MI 49781
906-643-9947 / Fax: 906-632-7877
CLYDE VAN DUSEN (President) & Buys Men's & Boys' Active Apparel
GREG VAN DUSEN (President) & Buys Men's & Boys' Active Apparel

REHMANN'S (MW)
122 N. Clinton Ave. (m)
Saint Johns, MI 48879
989-224-7139
BOB REHMANN (Owner) & Buys Men's Sportswear, Furnishings, Accessories

MICHIGAN - Saint Joseph

FISCHER - LANDIS CLOTHING CO. (MW)

321 State St. (m-b)
Saint Joseph, MI 49085
616-983-7848 / Fax: 616-982-7082
Website: www.fischer-landis.com

DOUG LANDIS (Owner) & Buys Men's Suits, Sportswear, Outerwear, Accessories, Footwear, Men's Big & Tall Wear, Store Displays, Fixtures, Supplies

CASUAL MAN, INC. (MW)

740 Lake St. (b)
Saugatuck, MI 49453
616-857-2665 / Fax: 616-857-4576

RICK MELAHN (Owner) & Buys Men's Sportswear, Store Displays, Fixtures, Supplies, Accessories

SAUGATUCK TRADERS (CLO)

214 Butler (m-b)
Saugatuck, MI 49453
616-857-4005 / Fax: 616-857-3545

MARSHA BURD (Owner) & Buys Men's Casual Wear, Furnishings, Footwear, Accessories, Store Displays, Fixtures, Supplies

MR. B'S WEARHOUSE (MW)

(MAX 10)
12033 US 131 (bud-m)
Schoolcraft, MI 49087
616-679-2580 / Fax: 616-679-2611
Sales: $10 Million-$50 Million
Website: www.offpricebermo.com

ED BERNARD (Owner)
SUSAN REILLY-Men's Wear Clothing, Small Leather Goods, Boys' Wear Sportswear
MICHELLE FOLITIO-Ties, Gloves, Headwear, Belts, Jewelry, Boys' Wear Accessories
JENNY SOWELL-Men's Wear Clothing, Small Leather Goods, Boys' Wear Sportswear

M. HALE CO., INC. (DEPT)

257 Center St. (m)
South Haven, MI 49090
616-637-8456
Sales: $100,001-$500,000

GEORGE HALE (President)
JIM HALE (G.M.M.) & Buys Men's Sportswear, Leather Apparel, Furnishings, Headwear, Accessories, Young Men's Wear, Boys' Wear, Store Displays, Fixtures, Supplies

N & R DEPARTMENT STORE, INC. (CLO)

432 Phoenix St. (bud-m)
South Haven, MI 49090
616-637-2003

RUTH NOVAK (Owner)
TOM McREERY-Men's Sportswear, Furnishings, Accessories, Store Displays, Fixtures, Supplies

C'EST LA VIE SPORTSWEAR (CLO-3)

Northland Center, #J-21 (p)
Southfield, MI 48075
248-557-6070 / Fax: 248-557-7420

JIM SEBA (Co-Owner) (@ 248-552-9525) & Buys Men's & Young Men's Sportswear, Accessories, Store Displays, Fixtures, Supplies
BETH KRANYAK (Co-Owner) & Buys Men's & Young Men's Sportswear, Accessories, Store Displays, Fixtures, Supplies

GIANNI'S (MW)

Northland Mall, #J5 (b)
Southfield, MI 48075
248-559-8841 / Fax: 248-737-6679

JOHN YIM (Owner) & Buys Men's Sportswear, Dress Shoes, Ties, Belts, Footwear

MAX GREEN'S MENSWEAR, INC. (MW-4)

(MAX GREEN'S KIDS)
Northland Center (p-m-b)
Southfield, MI 48075
248-569-1710 / Fax: 248-569-2937
Sales: $1 Million-$10 Million
Website: www.maxgreens.com

ROBERT GREEN (President) & Buys Men's Wear, Sportswear, Furnishings, Accessories, Footwear, Store Displays, Boys' Wear & Footwear, Fixtures, Supplies

SUN'S CLOTHING CO., INC. (MW-2)

Northland Mall, #334 (m-b)
21500 Northwestern Hwy.
Southfield, MI 48075
248-443-5432 / Fax: 248-443-0040

CHARLES HONG (Owner) & Buys Men's Furnishings, Accessories, Store Displays, Fixtures, Supplies

TOTAL RUNNER (SP-2)

29207 Northwestern Hwy.
Southfield, MI 48034
248-354-1177 / Fax: 248-354-2245
Sales: $500,001-$1 Million
Website: www.totalrunner.com

DAVID J. HOWELL (Owner)
BOB BARIL (Mgr.) & Buys Athletic Footwear
DEBORAH CIOSEK HAAPALA-Activewear

LUDWICK'S MENSWEAR (MW)

37390 Van Dyke Ave. (m-b)
Sterling Heights, MI 48312
586-939-6616 / Fax: 586-939-1413
Sales: $100,001-$500,000

LUDWICK LABAJ (Owner) & Buys Men's Sportswear, Footwear, Furnishings, Accessories

UNITED SPORTS APPAREL (SP)

2650 John Beers Rd.
Stevensville, MI 49127
616-429-3194 / Fax: 616-429-3204
Sales: $500,001-$1 Million
Website: www.usa-apparel.com

VICKI KATZ (Co-Owner) & Buys Activewear, Licensed Apparel
JEANNE KATZ (Co-Owner) & Buys Activewear, Licensed Apparel

SPORTSARAMA, INC. (MW)

114 W. Chicago Rd. (p-m-b)
Sturgis, MI 49091
616-651-5382 / Fax: 616-659-4191
Website: www.sportsarama.com

GARY STEWART (Owner) & Buys Men's Athletic Wear, Athletic Footwear
BONNIE STEWART-Men's Athletic Wear, Athletic Footwear

BAHLE'S DEPARTMENT STORE (DEPT)

210 St. Joseph St. (m-b)
Suttons Bay, MI 49682
231-271-3841 / Fax: 231-271-4211

KARL BAHLE (Co-Owner) & Buys Men's Sportswear, Furnishings, Big & Tall Men's Wear, Leather Apparel, Footwear, Store Displays, Fixtures, Supplies
LOIS BAHLE (Co-Owner) & Buys Men's Sportswear, Furnishings, Big & Tall Men's Wear, Leather Apparel, Footwear, Store Displays, Fixtures, Supplies

CUDA UNIFORM (SP)

24559 Van Born (bud-p-m)
Taylor, MI 48180
313-292-7422 / Fax: 313-292-8539
Sales: $500,001-$1 Million

JOHN BRANCHEAU (Owner & Real Estate Contact) & Buys Men's Footwear, Leather Goods, Men's Apparel, Mens's Big & Tall, Men's Accessories, Men's Uniforms

JEAN & TOP (CLO)

23600 Eureka (p)
Taylor, MI 48180
734-287-8230 / Fax: 734-287-2190

DANNY SONG (Owner) & Buys Men's & Young Men's Jeans, Tops, Belts, Hosiery, Boys' Sportswear, Urban Contemporary, Store Displays, Fixtures, Supplies

CAPTAIN'S QUARTERS (MW)

151 E. Front St. (m-b)
Traverse City, MI 49684
231-946-7066 / Fax: 231-946-7071
Website: www.captainsquarters.net

MAURICE ALLEN (Owner) & Buys Men's Suits, Formal Wear, Sportswear, Outerwear, Accessories, Store Displays, Fixtures, Supplies
JASON ALLEN-Men's Suits, Formal Wear, Sportswear, Outerwear, Accessories, Store Displays, Fixtures, Supplies

SCHIEBER'S TALL & BIG (MW)

2034 S. Airport Rd.
Traverse City, MI 49686
231-941-4421 / Fax: 231-941-8634

BILL SCHIEBER (Owner) & Buys Men's Wear, Big & Tall Men's Sportswear, Outerwear, Western Wear, Suits, Furnishings, Accessories

THE SHIRTERY (CLO)

2345 West Rd. (p)
Trenton, MI 48183
734-675-3888 / Fax: 734-675-0779

DEBBIE GRASSA (Owner) & Buys Men's & Boys' Urban Contemporary, T-shirts, Fleece, Polo Shirts, Accessories

COREY'S JEWELERS, INC. (JWLY-41)

(COREY'S JEWEL BOX)
(CJI)
(THE LOOP)
1301 Combermere Dr.
Troy, MI 48083
248-585-1848 / Fax: 248-585-4770
Sales: $10 Million-$50 Million
Website: www.coreysjewelbox.com
Retail Locations: OH, IN, MI, MA, NY, NC, GA, FL, MT, OK, TX, CO

AL FOLAND (President) & Buys Jewelry, Watches

ELI OF TROY MENSWEAR, INC. (MW)

5067 Rochester Rd. (p-m-b-des)
Troy, MI 48085
248-689-2010 / Fax: 248-689-4131
Sales: $500,001-$1 Million

RANDY NORMAN (Owner) & Buys Men's Sportswear, Furnishings, Headwear, Accessories, Young Men's Wear, Footwear

THAT GUY BY TEEN MAN (MW)

Oakland Mall (m)
340 W. Fourteen Mile Rd.
Troy, MI 48083
248-588-2858 / Fax: 248-588-4199
Sales: $1 Million-$10 Million

SUREN BHAGWAN (Owner) & Buys Men's Suits, Raincoats, Sweaters, Outer Jackets, Leather Apparel, Casual Slacks, Active Apparel, Dress Shirts, Ties, Belts, Footwear, Store Displays, Fixtures, Supplies

VIA ROMA MEN'S CLOTHIER (MW-2)

Oakland Mall (p-m-b)
618 W. Fourteen Mile Rd.
Troy, MI 48083
248-585-7100 / Fax: 248-585-7172

MO ORAM-Men's Sportswear, Furnishings, Accessories, Footwear, Store Displays, Fixtures, Supplies

JEAN RIDGE, INC. (MW)

45101 Cass Ave. (b)
Utica, MI 48317
586-739-8347

TOM STEEH (Owner) & Buys Men's and Boys' Sportswear, Belts, Hosiery, Footwear, Store Displays, Fixtures, Supplies

PRESIDENT TUXEDO RENTAL (MW-40)

32185 Hollingsworth Ave. (p-m-b)
Warren, MI 48092
800-837-8897 / Fax: 586-264-5141
Website: www.presidenttuxedo.com
Retail Locations: IL, MI, OH

MICHAEL SBORCCA (Owner & Real Estate Contact)

KATHLEEN HENDERSON-Men's & Boys' Tuxedos, Shirts, Accessories, Jewelry, Shoes

BACHELORS USA, INC. (MW)

Summit Place Mall
315 N. Telegraph Rd., #129
Waterford, MI 48327
248-682-8810

OPEN-Men's Formal Wear, Urban Contemporary, Sportswear, Accessories

DUNHAM'S ATHLEISURE CORP. (CLO-123)

5000 Dixie Hwy. (p-m)
Waterford, MI 48329
248-674-4991 / Fax: 248-674-4980
Retail Locations: MI, PA, WI, OH, IN, IA, NY, MN, IL, WV, MA, SD

MICHELE LEMERE-Boys' T-shirts, Shorts, Fleece, Athletic Apparel

JIM HALL-Licensed Apparel

JEFF BLOOM-Athletic Footwear

STEVE STEINMAN-Athletic Footwear

JOHN PALMER (Real Estate Contact)

HARDWOOD, INC. (MW)

908 W. Huron St. (b)
Waterford, MI 48328
248-681-2300 / Fax: 248-681-8232

RONALD CLARKE (Owner) & Buys Men's & Boys' Tuxedos, Furnishings, Accessories, Work Uniforms

JOE'S ARMY NAVY SURPLUS CO. (AN-2)

981 W. Huron St. (bud)
Waterford, MI 48328
248-681-5277 / Fax: 248-681-9367

HERMAN GOLDSMITH (Co-Owner) & Buys Men's Sportswear, Leather, Furnishings, Headwear, Accessories, Young Men's Wear, Boys' Wear, Store Displays, Fixtures and Supplies

JEFF GOLDSMITH (Co-Owner) & Buys Men's Sportswear, Leather, Furnishings, Headwear, Accessories, Young Men's Wear, Boys' Wear, Men's & Young Men's Footwear

RUNNIN' GEAR (SP-2)

5390 Dixie Hwy.
Waterford, MI 48329
248-623-7296
Sales: $100,001-$500,000

PAUL COUGHLIN (Co-Owner) & Buys Activewear, Athletic Footwear

LINDA COUGHLIN (Co-Owner) & Buys Activewear, Athletic Footwear

SHIFMAN MENSWEAR (MW)

5630 Dixie Hwy. (p)
Waterford, MI 48329
248-623-2172
Sales: $500,000-$1 Million

STEWART SHIFMAN (Owner) & Buys Men's & Boys' Wear, Leather Apparel, Footwear, Store Displays, Fixtures, Supplies

JACKSON'S WESTERN STORE, INC. (WW)

1110 W. Superior (m-b)
Wayland, MI 49348
269-792-2550 / Fax: 269-792-4550
Sales: $1 Million-$10 Million

MARY JACKSON (Owner) & Buys Men's Western Apparel, Footwear, & Accessories

DESIGNER WEARHOUSE CENTER (CLO)

35028 Michigan Ave. (b)
Wayne, MI 48184
734-595-7445 / Fax: 734-595-7474

ZANA CLARK (Owner) & Buys Men's Designer Denim, Footwear, Store Displays, Fixtures, Supplies

FORMAL AFFAIR (MW)

(THE NADEAU CO.)
32449 Michigan Ave. (p)
Wayne, MI 48184
734-728-2222 / Fax: 734-728-8199
Sales: $500,001-$1 Million
Website: www.nadeauco.com

RICHARD NADEAU (Owner) & Buys Men's Formal Wear, Boys' Formal Wear, Hosiery, Ties, Gloves, Dress Shirts, Headwear, Jewelry, Footwear

BRODY'S BOYS' & YOUNG MEN'S WEAR (MW & OL)

6690 Orchard Lake Rd. (m-b)
West Bloomfield, MI 48322
248-851-6232 / Fax: 248-851-4792
Website: www.brodysonline.com

LESTER BRODY (Co-Owner) & Buys Men's Sportswear, Furnishings, Small Leather Goods, Footwear, Young Men's Wear, Boys' Wear, Store Displays, Fixtures, Supplies

MARK BRODY (Co-Owner) & Buys Men's Sportswear, Furnishings, Small Leather Goods, Footwear, Young Men's Wear, Boys' Wear, Store Displays, Fixtures, Supplies

MICHIGAN - Westland

LOVERS' LANE (CLO-23)

37816 Ford Rd.
Westland, MI 48185
734-728-5646 / Fax: 734-728-0119
Website: www.loverslane.com

MERILYN KING (Owner) & Buys Men's Surf & Swimwear, Resortwear
MIKE ALLMAN (Real Estate Contact)

BARRETT'S (MW)

111 W. Grand River Ave. (m)
Williamston, MI 48895
517-655-1766

TOM MITCHELL (Owner) & Buys Men's Sportswear, Footwear, Furnishings, Accessories, Young Men's & Boys' Wear

THE CHELSEA GROUP (MW)

2944 Biddle Ave. (m)
Wyandotte, MI 48192
734-285-7020 / Fax: 734-285-0895
Sales: $1 Million-$10 Million

GILBERT ROSE (President) & Buys Men's Outerwear
PETER ROSE (V.P.) & Buys Men's Outerwear, Urban Contemporary, Men's Sportswear, Furnishings, Headwear, Accessories, Footwear, Store Displays, Fixtures, Supplies

MINNESOTA - Aitkin

BUTLER'S PROMOTIONS, INC. (CLO)

301 Minnesota Ave. North (bud)
Aitkin, MN 56431
218-927-2185 / Fax: 218-927-2186
Sales: $100,001-$500,000

CHUCK BUTLER (Owner) & Buys Men's Sportswear, Sweaters, Sport Shirts, Outer Jackets, Casual Slacks, Active Apparel, Furnishings, Young Men's Wear, Boys' Wear

LEUTHOLD'S (CLO)

North Bridge Mall, #E4
Albert Lea, MN 56007
507-373-3142 / Fax: 507-373-3230
Sales: Under $100,000
Website: www.leutholds.com

WILLIAM HERTLING (Owner) & Buys Men's Sportswear, Furnishings, Accessories, Leather Apparel, Young Men's Wear, Urban Contemporary, Boys' Wear

RANDY'S MENSWEAR (MW)

418 Broadway (m)
Alexandria, MN 56308
320-762-2475 / Fax: 320-762-2157
Sales: Under $100,000

RANDY SPODEN (Owner) & Buys Men's Sportswear, Furnishings, Accessories, Urban Contemporary

JENSON'S DEPARTMENT STORE (DEPT)

112 E. Main St. (m)
Anoka, MN 55303
612-421-5343 / Fax: 763-421-5343
Sales: $100,001-$500,000
Website: www.jensonsclothing.com

TOM JENSON (Owner) & Buys Men's Sportswear, Leather Apparel, Accessories, Footwear, Store Displays, Fixtures, Supplies

JEFF LYNCH (Mgr.) & Buys Men's Sportswear, Leather Apparel, Accessories, Footwear, Store Displays, Fixtures, Supplies

PURM-ART (GM)

202 Main St. (p-m)
Anoka, MN 55303
763-427-7797 / Fax: 763-427-3767

JOHN STADDER (Co-Owner) & Buys Active Apparel, Leather Apparel, T-shirts, Fleece & Shorts, Hats, Athletic Hosiery, Store Displays, Fixtures and Supplies

JUDY STADDER (Co-Owner) & Buys Active Apparel, Leather Apparel, T-shirts, Fleece & Shorts, Hats, Athletic Hosiery, Store Displays, Fixtures and Supplies

GAMES PEOPLE PLAY (SP-2)

701 18th Ave. NW
Austin, MN 55912
507-433-7593 / Fax: 507-433-9791

LANCE R. POGONES (Partner) & Buys Activewear, Athletic Footwear

KEENAN'S MENSWEAR (MW)

500 N. Main St. (m-b)
Austin, MN 55912
507-433-3921
Sales: $100,001-$500,000

JACK KEENAN (President) & Buys Men's Overcoats, Suits, Tailored Jackets, Tailored Slacks, Formalwear, Raincoats, Sweaters, Sport Shirts Outer Jackets, Casual Slacks, Formalwear, Active Apparel, Leather Apparel, Furnishings, Accessories, Headwear, Belts

LEUTHOLD'S (CLO)

417 N. Main St. (m)
Austin, MN 55912
507-437-4294 / Fax: 507-437-4294
Sales: $100,001-$500,000

PHIL TURVOLD (Owner) & Buys Men's Sportswear, Furnishings, Dress Shirts, Accessories, Store Displays, Fixtures

BEMIDJI WOOLEN MILLS (CLO)

P.O. Box 277 SG (m-b)
Bemidji, MN 56619
218-751-5166 / Fax: 218-751-4659
Sales: $1 Million-$10 Million

WILLIAM BATCHELDER (Owner) & Buys Men's Sportswear & Outerwear, Furnishings, Headwear, Accessories, Casual Shoes

CIRCLE D'S (CLO)

107 Nature Rd. NW (m)
Bemidji, MN 56601
218-751-5130 / Fax: 218-754-0408

DOREEN HALVERSON (Owner) & Buys Men's Apparel, Footwear, Western Apparel, Accessories, Furnishings, Jewelry, Headwear, Belts

PATTERSON'S MENSWEAR (MW-3)

P.O. Box 220 (m)
200 3rd St.
Bemidji, MN 56601
218-751-4743 / Fax: 218-751-0228
Sales: $1 Million-$10 Million

STEVE PATTERSON (President) & Buys Men's Work Clothes, Sportswear, Leather Apparel, Furnishings, Headwear, Accessories, Young Men's Wear, Boys' Wear, Footwear

GARY'S MENSWEAR (MW)

1317 Pacific Ave. (m)
Benson, MN 56215
320-842-5811

DAVID FROMLING (Co-Owner) & Buys Men's Clothing Sportswear, Furnishings, Accessories, Young Men's Wear, Urban Contemporary, Formal Wear, Related Furnishings & Accessories

CINDY FROMLING (Co-Owner) & Buys Men's Clothing Sportswear, Furnishings, Accessories, Young Men's Wear, Urban Contemporary, Formal Wear, Related Furnishings & Accessories

BREKKEN'S MEN'S STORE (MW)

1232 Hwy. 210 West (m-b)
Brainerd, MN 56401
218-829-3874 / Fax: 218-829-0433
Sales: $500,000-$1 Million

MARK PARRISH (Co-Owner) & Buys Men's Sportswear, Furnishings, Accessories, Footwear

ROBERT A. BREKKEN-Men's Sportswear, Furnishings, Accessories, Footwear

GREG LARSON SPORTS (SG & OL)

P.O. Box 567 (m)
Brainero, MN 56401
218-829-5358 / Fax: 218-829-0162
Website: www.glssports.com

GREG LARSON (Owner) & Buys Active Apparel, T-shirts, Shorts, Athletic Hosiery, Headwear

WILSON'S - THE LEATHER EXPERTS (CLO-513)

7401 Boone Ave. North (m-b)
Brooklyn Park, MN 55428
763-391-4000 / Fax: 763-391-4486
Sales: $100 Million-$500 Million
Website: www.wilsonsleather.com
Retail Locations: AL, AZ, AR, CA, CO, CT, DE, FL, GA, ID, IL, IN, IA, KS, KY, LA, ME, MD, MA, MI, MN, MO, NE, NV, NH, NJ, NM, NC, ND, NY, OH, OK, OR, PA, RI, SC, SD, TN, TX, UT, VA, WA, WV, WI, ON

DAVID ROGERS (President)

JOEL WALLER (C.E.O.)

TERESA WRIGHT (V.P. - Mdse.)

BILL HUTCHISON (Mdse. Mgr.) & Buys Men's Motorcycle Wear, Men's Outerwear, Fashion Jackets, Sportswear, Long Coats, Casual Jackets, Men's, Young Men's & Big & Tall Men's Wear, Overcoats, Raincoats

RANDY STERN-Small Leather Goods, Handbags, Travel, Gloves, Shoes

DUNN'S RETAIL GRAND JUNCTION (CLO & MO)

2800 Southcross Dr. (b)
Burnville, MN 55306
800-431-2904 / Fax: 800-517-9452
Sales: $10 Million-$50 Million

DON KOTULA (President) & Buys Men's Hunting Clothing, 8 to 16 Boys' Hunting Clothing, Store Displays, Fixtures, Supplies

LEADER DEPARTMENT STORE (DEPT)

P.O. Box 351 (p)
133 S. Main
Cambridge, MN 55008
763-689-1025 / Fax: 763-689-5600

NEIL JOHNSON (Owner) & Buys Men's Sportswear, Leather Apparel, Accessories, Furnishings, Headwear, Big & Tall Wear, Young Men's Wear, Urban Contemporary, Boys' Wear, Store Displays, Fixtures, Supplies

ADVANCED SPORTSWEAR, INC. (SP-2)
8700 E. Point Douglas Rd., #108
Cottage Grove, MN 55016
651-459-5002 / Fax: 651-459-0843
TERRY THOMPSON (Owner) & Buys Activewear

BRUUN'S FOR MEN, INC. (MW)
107 S. Broadway (m-b)
Crookston, MN 56716
218-281-5808 / Fax: 218-281-5828
Sales: $100,001-$500,000
KENT BRUUN (Owner) & Buys Men's Suits, Coats, Sportswear, Furnishings, Accessories, Footwear, Store Displays, Fixtures, Supplies

FOUR SEASONS (DEPT & CLO-3)
(FOUR SEASONS DEPT. STORE)
101 N. Broadway (m)
Crookston, MN 56716
218-281-5049 / Fax: 218-281-4056
JIM CHANDLER (Owner) & Buys Men's Sportswear, Furnishings, Headwear, Accessories, Big & Tall Men's Wear, Boys' Wear, Urban Contemporary, Store Displays, Fixtures, Supplies

JIM'S CLOTHING & SPORTGOODS (DEPT)
789 6th St. (m-b)
Dawson, MN 56232
320-769-2317 / Fax: 320-769-4455
Sales: $500,001-$1 Million
JIM PRESTHOLDT (Owner) & Buys Men's Wear, Sportswear, Furnishings, Accessories, Young Men's Wear, Urban Contemporary, Boys' Wear, Store Displays, Fixtures and Supplies
MONICA BOTHUN-Men's Wear, Sportswear, Furnishings, Accessories, Young Men's Wear, Urban Contemporary, Boys' Wear, Store Displays, Fixtures and Supplies

L.J. NORBY CO. (DEPT)
823 Washington Ave. (m)
Detroit Lakes, MN 56501
(Henry Doneger)
218-847-5665 / Fax: 218-847-5661
Sales: $1 Million-$10 Million
Website: www.norbysonline.com
MICHAEL NORBY (President & G.M.M.) & Buys Store Displays, Fixtures, Supplies
RONALD ZEMAN (V.P.) & Buys Men's, Boys' & Students Clothing, Leather Apparel, Sportswear, Accessories, Footwear, Urban Contemporary, Big and Tall

AUSTIN-JARROW, INC. (SP-2)
123 W. Superior St.
Duluth, MN 55802
218-722-1185
Sales: $1 Million-$10 Million
BILL AUSTIN (President) & Buys Activewear, Athletic Footwear, Licensed Apparel

BARBO'S COLUMBIA CLOTHING CO. (MW)
303 W. Superior St. (m-b)
Duluth, MN 55802
218-722-3339 / Fax: 218-722-8048
Sales: $1 Million-$10 Million
ED BARBO (Owner) & Buys Men's & Young Men's Overcoats, Suits, Tailored Jackets, Tailored Slacks, Sportswear, Furnishings, Accessories, Leather Apparel, Headwear, Footwear, Store Displays, Fixtures, Supplies

CIMARRON OF DULUTH, INC. (CLO-2)
(PALLADIO'S)
2206 Mountain Shadow Dr.
Duluth, MN 55811
218-727-7576 / Fax: 218-727-3545
TOM CRASSWELLER (President) & Buys Men's Suits, Sportswear, Outerwear, Young Men's Wear, Furnishings, Accessories, Store Displays, Fixtures, Supplies

HARRY ALLEN FALL, INC. (CLO)
Medical Arts Bldg. (b)
Duluth, MN 55802
218-722-1711 / Fax: 218-722-1712
Sales: $1 Million-$10 Million
LEO J. SPOONER (C.E.O.)
ALAN E. MARKHAM (V.P. & G.M.M.) & Buys Men's Furnishings, Small Leather Goods, Sportswear, Accessories, Fragrances, Footwear, Swimwear, Store Displays, Fixtures, Supplies
JOHN MOHN-Men's Furnishings, Small Leather Goods, Sportswear, Accessories, Fragrances, Footwear, Swimwear, Store Displays, Fixtures, Supplies

MAINSTREAM FASHIONS FOR MEN (MW)
125 W. Superior (m)
Duluth, MN 55802
218-723-1970 / Fax: 218-723-8189
Website: www.mainstreamformen.com
DOUG MELANDER (Co-Owner) & Buys Men's & Young Men's Sportswear, Furnishings, Accessories, Footwear, Store Displays, Fixtures, Supplies
TOM HENDERSON (Co-Owner) & Buys Men's & Young Men's Sportswear, Furnishings, Accessories, Footwear, Store Displays, Fixtures, Supplies

MAURICE'S, INC. (CLO-437)
(AMERICAN RETAIL GROUP)
105 W. Superior St. (m)
Duluth, MN 55802
(Arkin California)
218-727-8431 / Fax: 218-720-2102
Sales: $50 Million-$100 Million
Retail Locations: AZ, AR, CO, GA, ID, IL, IN, IA, KS, KY, MD, MI, MN, MS, MO, MT, NE, NV, NY, NC, ND, OH, OK, OR, PA, SC, SD, TN, TX, UT, VA, WA, WV, WI, WY
ROLAND BRENNINKMEYER (President & C.E.O.)
LISA RHODES (V.P. & G.M.M.)
TOM KARIS (Real Estate Contact)
MELISSA MORIARTY (D.M.M.-Young Men's)
THERESA DUMAIS-Young Men's Tops, Outerwear
JUIIE ANDERSON-Young Men's Bottoms
DON SCHRODER (V.P.-Mktg.) & Buys Store Displays, Fixtures and Supplies

MINNESOTA SURPLUS AND OUTFITTERS (MW-2)
(Div. of MINNESOTA SURPLUS, INC.)
218 W. Superior St. (p)
Duluth, MN 55802
218-727-3133 / Fax: 218-722-2042
Sales: $1 Million-$10 Million
PETER FURO (Co-Owner) & Buys Men's Sportswear, Leather Apparel, Underwear, Hosiery, Headwear, Belts, Outerwear, Young Men's Wear, Urban Contemporary, Boys' Wear, Store Displays, Fixtures, Supplies
DAVID FURO (Co-Owner) & Buys Men's Sportswear, Leather Apparel, Underwear, Hosiery, Headwear, Belts, Outerwear, Young Men's Wear, Boys' Wear, Store Displays, Fixtures, Supplies
FRED ROGERS (Co-Owner) & Buys Footwear

TNT OUTFITTERS (MW)
211 Demers Ave. (m)
East Grand Forks, MN 56721
218-773-8683
Sales: Under $100,000
TIM TWETEN (Owner) & Buys Sweaters, Sport Shirts, Outer Jackets, Casual Slacks, Denim, Underwear, Hosiery, Gloves, Headwear, Belts, Footwear, Work & Western Boots, Store Displays, Fixtures and Supplies

RACQUET RAGS, INC. (SP)
755 Prairie Center Dr.
Eden Prairie, MN 55344
952-941-5632 / Fax: 952-829-2631
Sales: $100,001-$500,000
MICHAEL PICKERT (Mgr.) & Buys Activewear, Athletic Footwear, Racquets

CEDRIC'S DEPARTMENT STORE (DEPT-2)
3660 Galleria (b-h)
Edina, MN 55435
952-854-8833 / Fax: 952-925-4553
Website: www.cedricsformen.com
CEDRIC KIRCHNER (Owner) & Buys Men's Overcoats, Suits, Tailored Jackets, Tailored Slacks, Sportswear, Dress Shirts, Ties, Accessories, Store Displays, Fixtures, Supplies
KENT KIRCHNER-Men's Overcoats, Suits, Tailored Jackets, Tailored Slacks, Sportswear, Dress Shirts, Ties, Accessories, Store Displays, Fixtures, Supplies

EDINA COUNTRY CLUB (SG)
5100 Woodale Ave.
Edina, MN 55424
952-927-5775
Website: www.edinacountryclub.org
MICHELLE LASS-Men's Golf Apparel

TRAIL MARK (CLO)
3265 Galleria
Edina, MN 55435
952-929-1950
MARK THOMPSON-Men's Active Apparel

J. D. MILLS CO. (CLO)
230 E. Sheridan (m)
Ely, MN 55731
218-365-3376 / Fax: 218-365-3376
Sales: $100,001-$500,000
JOHN MILLS (Owner) & Buys Men's Sportswear, Furnishings, Accessories, Footwear, Store Displays, Fixtures, Supplies

ENDERSON CLOTHING (MW)
220 Downtown Plz. (p-m)
Fairmont, MN 56031
507-238-2342 / Fax: 507-238-2760
Sales: $100,001-$500,000
BRIAN SANDBERG (Owner) & Buys Men's Sportswear, Leather Apparel, Furnishings, Headwear, Accessories, Footwear, Boys' Wear, Store Displays, Fixtures, Supplies

FARIBO WOOLENS RETAIL (CLO)
1819 2nd Ave. N.W. (p)
Faribault, MN 55021
507-334-1644 / Fax: 507-334-9431
Website: www.faribowool.com
EILEEN MIKKALSON-Men's Casual Wear, Furnishings, Scarves, Blankets, Gloves

JIM & JOE CLOTHING CO. (MW)
P.O. Box 796 (m)
316 Central Ave.
Faribault, MN 55021
507-334-6619 / Fax: 507-334-6619
Sales: $500,000-$1 Million
GARY LAZARZ (President & G.M.M.) & Buys Men's Sportswear, Furnishings, Headwear, Accessories, Footwear, Young Men's Wear, Store Displays, Fixtures, Supplies
JOSH SOLBERG (G.M.M.) & Buys Men's Sportswear, Furnishings, Headwear, Accessories, Footwear, Young Men's Wear, Store Displays, Fixtures, Supplies

GARY'S CLOTHING (MW)
114 W. 1st St. (p-m)
Fosston, MN 56542
218-435-1676
Sales: $100,001-$500,000
GARY STORRUSTEN (Owner) & Buys Men's Sportswear, Furnishings, Leather Apparel, Accessories, Footwear, Store Displays, Fixtures, Supplies

BEAR TRACK OUTFITTING CO. (SP)
P.O. Box 937
Grand Marais, MN 55604
218-387-1162
Website: www.bear-track.com
DAVID WILLIAMS (Owner) & Buys Activewear, Pro Fly Skiing, Kayaking, Canoes, Snowboarding

RYDEN'S BORDER STORE (DEPT)
Hwy. 61 (p)
Grand Portage, MN 55605
218-475-2330 / Fax: 218-475-2607
SAM BOOMER (Co-Owner) & Buys Men's Work Clothes, T-shirts, Sweaters, Shirts, Outer Jackets, Store Displays, Fixtures, Supplies
SHANNON HICKS-Men's Footwear

BRIER CLOTHING & SHOE (MW)
413 N. 1st Ave. West (m)
Grand Rapids, MN 55744
218-326-2553
Sales: $100,001-$500,000
BILL BRIER (Owner) & Buys Men's Sportswear, Furnishings, Headwear, Belts, Jewelry, Big & Tall Men's Wear, Footwear, Store Displays, Fixtures, Supplies
WENDY GREEN-Men's Sportswear, Furnishings, Headwear, Belts, Jewelry, Big & Tall Men's Wear, Footwear, Store Displays, Fixtures, Supplies

GLEN'S ARMY & NAVY STORE (AN)
701 NW 4th St.
Grand Rapids, MN 55744
218-326-1201 / Fax: 218-326-9437
HOWARD EICHORN (Co-Owner) & Buys Activewear, Athletic Footwear, Skiing Apparel, Licensed Apparel
MITCH EICHORN (Co-Owner) & Buys Activewear, Athletic Footwear, Skiing Apparel, Licensed Apparel
RUSTY EICHORN (Co-Owner) & Buys Activewear, Athletic Footwear, Skiing Apparel, Licensed Apparel

YELLOW BRICK ROAD CO., INC. (CLO-2)
212 S. 1st St. (p)
Hackensack, MN 56452
218-675-6377 / Fax: 218-675-6377
JOHN NELSON (Owner) & Buys Men's Raincoats, Sweaters, Sport Shirts, Outer Jackets, Casual Slacks, Active Apparel, Underwear, Hosiery, Headwear, Young Men's Wear, Boys' Wear, Store Displays, Fixtures, Supplies

WINNICK'S CLOTHING, INC. (CLO)
16345 Hwy. 65 NE (p)
Ham Lake, MN 55304
763-434-9147 / Fax: 763-434-9147
Sales: $500,000-$1 Million
Website: www.winnicksclothing.com
DAN WINNICK (V.P.) & Buys Men's Outer Jackets, Leather, Casual Slacks, Robes, Underwear, Hosiery, Gloves, Belts, 8 to 20 Boys' Clothing, Store, Displays, Fixtures, Supplies, Big & Tall Men's Wear, Men's Small Leathers
SCOTT WINNICK-Big & Tall Men's Wear, Men's Small Leathers, Men's Headwear, Jewelry, Fragrances, Footwear

MEYER CO. (DEPT)
113 E. 2nd St. (m)
Hastings, MN 55033
651-437-9811
JIM SCHNEIDER (Owner)
TOM SCHNEIDER (Mgr.) & Buys Men's Outerwear, Sportswear, Headwear, Accessories, Boys' Wear, Store Displays
GAYLE SCHNEIDER (Mgr.) & Buys Men's Outerwear, Sportswear, Headwear, Accessories, Boys' Wear, Store Displays

LEUTHOLD JACOBSON (CLO)
212 E. Howard St. (m)
Hibbing, MN 55746
218-263-5972 / Fax: 218-263-6824
Sales: $500,001-$1 Million
STEVE JACOBSON (Owner) & Buys Men's Sportswear, Leather Apparel, Furnishings, Headwear, Accessories, Young Men's Wear, Footwear, Store Displays, Fixtures, Supplies

MINNESOTA - Hibbing

MEN'S SHOP (MW)

117 E. Howard (m)
Hibbing, MN 55746
218-263-9575

MR. WILSON (Owner) & Buys Men's Sportswear, Furnishings, Accessories, Footwear, Store Displays, Fixtures, Supplies

T-SHIRT FACTORY & ODD SHOP (CLO)

2630 1st Ave. (p-m)
Hibbing, MN 55746
218-262-4224 / Fax: 218-262-6380
Sales: $100,001-$500,000

JOHN FILLMAN (Owner) & Buys Boys' Apparel, Men's Apparel, Men's Accessories, Men's Outerwear, Men's Sportswear

B JAMES (CLO)

1060 Hwy. 15 (m)
Hutchinson, MN 55350
320-587-7100 / Fax: 320-587-7132
Sales: $1 Million-$10 Million

DAVE MINEA (Owner) & Buys Leather Goods, Men's Apparel, Mens's Big & Tall, Men's Casualwear, Men's Denim Apparel, Men's Formalwear, Men's Accessories, Men's Hosiery, Men's Outerwear, Men's Sportswear, Men's Suits, Men's Swimwear, Men's Underwear

MASONS MEN'S SHOP (MW)

339 3rd St.
International Falls, MN 56649
218-283-9750

DONALD MASON (Owner) & Buys Men's Formal Wear, Sportswear, Furnishings, Accessories, Footwear, Urban Contemporary, Store Displays, Fixtures, Supplies

STROM CLOTHING CO. (CLO)

409 2nd St. (m-b)
Jackson, MN 56143
507-847-2110 / Fax: 507-847-4901
Sales: $100,001-$500,000

BRAD STROM (Owner) & Buys Men's Formal Wear, Sportswear, Furnishings, Accessories, Young Men's Wear, Store Displays, Fixtures and Supplies

LUTSEN MOUNTAIN SHOP (CLO)

P.O. Box 190
452 Ski Hill Rd.
Lutsen, MN 55612
218-663-7842 / Fax: 218-663-7858
Sales: $100,001-$500,000

MARY JUNNILA (Owner) & Buys Men's Sportswear, Outdoor Wear, Ski Apparel, Active Apparel, Sweater, Gloves, Headwear, Footwear, Store Displays, Fixtures, Supplies

COOK'S, INC. (CLO)

217 E. Main St. (m)
Luverne, MN 56156
507-283-8224 / Fax: 507-283-8514
Website: www.cookclothing.net

ROBERT COOK (Owner) & Buys Men's Sportswear, Furnishings, Accessories, Young Men's Wear, Urban Contemporary, Boys' Wear, Store Displays, Fixtures and Supplies

C & S SUPPLY CO., INC. (MW)

1951 N. Riverfront Dr. (p)
Mankato, MN 56001
507-387-1171 / Fax: 507-387-2481

DAN CORCORAN (Owner)

ROBIN SCHENDEL (Asst. Mgr.) & Buys Men's Sportswear, Accessories, Furnishings, Footwear, Young Men's Wear, Boys' Wear, Store Displays, Fixtures, Supplies

MATT J. GRAIF, INC. (MW)

3 Civic Court Plz. (b)
Mankato, MN 56001
507-345-3000 / Fax: 507-345-3001
Sales: $500,000-$1 Million

GARY KRATZKE (President & G.M.M.) & Buys Men's Overcoats, Suits, Tailored Jackets, Tailored Slacks, Raincoats, Big & Tall Wear, Sportswear, Sweaters, Sport Shirts, Outer Jackets, Leather Apparel, Casual Slacks, Active Apparel, Dress Shirts, Ties, Robes, Underwear, Hosiery, Gloves, Belts, Jewelry

STAGE CLOTHES USA (CLO)

P.O. Box 1178 (m)
Maple Grove, MN 55311
763-425-6946 / Fax: 763-425-5355
Sales: $1 Million-$10 Million
Website: www.stageclothes.com

MIKE SHARE (President) & Buys Men's Footwear, Leather Goods, Men's Apparel, Men's Accessories

MISTER COOL'S CLOTHING (MW)

337 W. Main St. (p-m)
Marshall, MN 56258
507-532-9520 / Fax: 507-537-1502
Sales: $100,001-$500,000

JOE COOL (Owner) & Buys Men's Sportswear, Furnishings, Accessories, Young Men's Wear, Store Displays, Fixtures, Supplies

POOR BORCH'S, INC. (MW)

1309 E. College Dr. (m)
Marshall, MN 56258
507-532-4880 / Fax: 507-532-9018
Sales: $500,000-$1 Million
Website: www.borchs.com

CHAD WYFFELS (Owner) & Buys Men's Raincoats, Work & Ski Jackets, Hunting Clothes, Sport Shirts, Underwear, Gloves, Headwear, Accessories, Footwear, Store Displays, Fixtures, Supplies

RUNNINGS (DG-28)

(RUNNING SUPPLY, INC.)
1401 E. Main St. (p)
Marshall, MN 56258
507-532-9566 / Fax: 507-532-6543
Website: www.runnings.doitbest.com

DENNIS REED (Co-Owner) & Buys Store Displays, Fixtures, Supplies

BILL JONES (Co-Owner)

LEON WARNER-Men's Overcoats, Suits, Sweaters, Outer Jackets, Work Clothes, Denim Slacks, Underwear, Hosiery, Headwear, Belts, Ties, Footwear, Young Men's Wear, Urban Contemporary, Boys' Wear

WEE MODERNS (SP)

252 W. Main St.
Marshall, MN 56258
507-532-6625
Sales: $100,001-$500,000

REINHOLD KEHREN (President) & Buys Store Displays, Fixtures, Supplies

LAURA KEHREN (G.M.M.) & Buys Infants, Toddlers 4 to 16 Boys' Wear

YOUNG'S GENERAL MERCHANDISE (DEPT)

P.O. Box 190 (m)
Middle River, MN 56737
218-222-3513
Sales: $100,001-$500,000

STEVE HOLM (V.P.) & Buys Work Clothes, Sweaters, Sport Shirts, Casual Slacks, Active Apparel, Dress Shirts, Robes, Underwear, Hosiery, Gloves, Headwear, Belts, Jewelry, Footwear, Young Men's Wear, Big & Tall Men's Wear, Outer Jackets, Boys' Clothing, Sportswear, Store Displays, Fixtures, Supplies

ALFRED OLSON CO. (DEPT)

P.O. Box 127 (bud)
195 2nd Ave. S.W.
Milaca, MN 56353
320-983-3193 / Fax: 320-983-6135
Sales: $1 Million-$10 Million

TOM OLSON (Owner & G.M.M.) & Buys Men's Sportswear, Furnishings, Headwear, Accessories, Young Men's Wear, Urban Contemporary, Footwear, Boys' Wear, Store Displays, Fixtures, Supplies

ABRAM'S CUSTOM TAILORING (MW)

3829 W. 50th St. (b-h)
Minneapolis, MN 55410
612-920-2275 / Fax: 612-952-2930
Sales: Under $100,000

ABRAM AYAZ (Owner) & Buys Men's Sportswear, Furnishings, Accessories, Store Displays, Fixtures, Supplies

MINNESOTA - Minneapolis

AL JOHNSON (MW)
3922 W. 50th St. (b)
Minneapolis, MN 55424
952-920-5450 / Fax: 952-922-3873
- WALTER REA (Owner) & Buys Men's Sportswear, Leather Apparel, Furnishings, Headwear, Accessories, Footwear, Store Displays, Fixtures, Supplies
- BECKY REA (Mgr.) & Buys Men's Sportswear, Leather Apparel, Furnishings, Headwear, Accessories, Footwear

BELLESON'S, INC. (MW)
3908 W. 50th St. (b)
Minneapolis, MN 55424
612-927-4694 / Fax: 612-927-8473
Sales: $1 Million-$10 Million
- JOHN NOVACHIS (President) & Buys Leather Goods, Men's Big & Tall Apparel, Men's Apparel, Men's Casualwear, Men's Denim Apparel, Men's Formalwear, Men's Accessories, Men's Hosiery, Men's Outerwear, Men's Sportswear, Men's Suits, Men's Swimwear, Men's Sleepwear, Men's Underwear

BURWICK 'N' TWEED (MW)
JACK McGUIRE ASSOCIATES (m-b)
3940 W. 50th St.
Minneapolis, MN 55424
952-926-9551 / Fax: 952-922-1642
Sales: $500,000-$1 Million
- MARVIN SILVER (Owner) & Buys Men's Overcoats, Suits, Tailored Jackets, Tailored Slacks, Raincoats, Men Sportswear, Sweaters, Sports Shirts, Outer Jackets, Leather Apparel, Casual Slacks, Active Apparel

GAVIIDAE PENDLETON SHOP (CLO)
651 Nicollet Mall (m-b)
125 Gaviidae Common
Minneapolis, MN 55402
612-340-0771
Website: www.pendleton-usa.com
- MARY MEYERS (Mgr.) & Buys Men's Shirts, Sweaters, Sportswear, Tailored Jackets, Tailored Slacks, Ties, Hosiery, Store Displays, Fixtures, Supplies

GOLD COUNTRY (CLO-2)
400 14th Ave. SE
Minneapolis, MN 55414
612-331-3354 / Fax: 612-935-9515
- RON LEAFBLAD (President & Owner) & Buys Store Displays, Fixtures, Supplies
- TROY AMUNDSON (Gen. Mgr.)
- ERICA LEAFBLAD-Men's Outer Jackets, Active Apparel, Licensed Headwear

HUBERT WHITE, INC. (MW)
IOS Ctr. (b)
747 Nicollet Ave.
Minneapolis, MN 55402
612-339-8236 / Fax: 612-339-9320
Sales: $1 Million-$10 Million
Website: www.hubertwhite.com
- ROBERT J. WHITE (President) & Buys Men's Wear
- BRADLEY SHERMAN (V.P.) & Buys Men's Furnishings, Accessories, Footwear, Store Displays, Fixtures, Supplies
- CHUCK SIMPKINS-Men's Sportswear

JJ FLASH (CLO)
13 S. 7th St. (m-b-des)
Minneapolis, MN 55402
612-371-4775 / Fax: 612-333-5236
Sales: $500,001-$1 Million
Website: www.nightwear.com
- DEBBIE ERICKSON (Store Mgr.)
- ARNOLD ODESSKY (President) & Buys Men's Footwear, Leather Goods, Men's Apparel, Men's Casualwear, Men's Denim Apparel, Men's Accessories, Men's Hosiery, Men's Outerwear, Men's Sportswear, Men's Suits, Men's Underwear

KAPLAN BROS, INC. (MW-2)
1414 E. Lake St.
Minneapolis, MN 55407
612-729-9465 / Fax: 612-729-9514
Sales: $100,001-$500,000
- JERRY KAJANDER (President) & Buys Men's Work Clothes, Sweaters, Sport Shirts, Outer Jackets, Casual Slacks, Dress Shirts, Ties, Store Displays, Fixtures, Supplies
- DAN GRANT (V.P.) & Buys Men's Underwear, Hosiery, Belts, Gloves, Headwear, 8 to 16 Boys' Wear, Footwear, Urban Contemporary

MAIN STREET OUTFITTERS (SP)
3001 Hennepin Ave.
Minneapolis, MN 55408
612-822-4385 / Fax: 612-822-4508
- JUDI TICE (Owner) & Buys Activewear
- RICHARD TICE (President) & Buys Activewear

MARATHON SPORTS (SP)
2312 W. 50th St.
Minneapolis, MN 55410
612-920-2606 / Fax: 612-927-4876
Sales: $1 Million-$10 Million
- STEVE HOAG (Owner) & Buys Athletic Footwear, Running Apparel

MARSHALL FIELD'S (DEPT-64 & MO & OL)
(Div. of TARGET CORPORATION)
(Formerly DAYTON'S)
(Formerly HUDSON'S)
33 S. 6th St. (m-b-h)
Minneapolis, MN 55402
(Associated Mdsg. Corp.)
612-304-6073 / Fax: 612-375-3879
Sales: Over $3 Billion
Website: www.marshallfields.com
Retail Locations: IL, VA, MN, MI, NY, ND, CA, IN, ND, WI, OH, SD
- ROBERT J. ULRICH (Chairman & C.E.O.)
- LINDA AHLERS (President- Marshall Field's) (@ 612-375-3239)
- DALE NITSCHKE (G.M.M.-Men's & Boys' & Real Estate Contact)
- ERTUGRUL TUZCU (Exec. V.P.-Store Opers.) (@ 612-375-2743)
- MIKE LITWIN (Real Estate Contact)
- DOUG COOKSEY (D.M.M.-Men's Wear & Furnishings) (@ 612-375-2735)
- RICK JOHNS (Sr. Buyer) & Buys Men's Underwear, Hosiery, Sleepwear, Robes, Dress Shirts, Neckwear
- MARK McNEILL-Men's Suits, Overcoats, Tailored Jackets, Raincoats
- PHIL PRICE-Men's Belts, Small Leather Goods, Gloves, Suspenders, Accessories
- BROOKE CUNDIFF-Designer & Better Sportswear
- PAM ANDERSON-Men's Outerwear, Jackets
- ROBERT PAINE (Sr. Buyer) & Buys Men's Tops, Knits, Sweaters, Swimwear
- MISTY STOFFREGEN-Men's Casual Slacks, Dockers
- CHRIS SHERER (Sr. Buyer) & Buys Traditional Collections
- ANDY GALLAHER (Sr. Buyer) & Buys Young Men's Shop
- BROOKE IVERSON-Young Men's Shop
- KELLY GEADELMAN (D.M.M.-Children's)
- STACIA THOMPSON-Boys' Wear 8 to 20
- JAMIE BECKER (V.P.-Visual Displays) & Buys Store Displays, Fixtures, Supplies

MINNEAPOLIS METRODOME (GS)
900 S. 5th St.
Minneapolis, MN 55415
612-332-0386 / Fax: 612-332-8334
Sales: $1 Million-$10 Million
Website: www.msfc.com
- ANNE VISTODEAU (Mgr.) (@ 612-335-3397) & Buys Licensed Apparel

MINNESOTA - Minneapolis

MINNESOTA VIKING NOVELTY STORE (SP)
(VOLUME SERVICES AMERICA)
900 S. 5th St.
Minneapolis, MN 55415
612-340-0403 / Fax: 612-340-1626
Sales: $500,001-$1 Million
ANDREW FLODIN (Mgr.) & Buys Licensed Apparel

NATE'S CLOTHING CO. (MW)
27 N. 4th St. (m-b)
Minneapolis, MN 55401
612-333-1401 / Fax: 612-333-3909
Sales: $1 Million-$10 Million
SHELDON WITEBSKY (Owner) & Buys Men's Sportswear, Overcoats, Suits, Tailored Jackets, Tailored Slacks, Raincoats
STEPHEN WITEBSKY (V.P.) & Buys Men's Sportswear, Overcoats, Suits, Tailored Jackets, Tailored Slacks, Raincoats
ALAN WITEBSKY-Men's Furnishings, Accessories, Belts, Store Displays, Fixtures, Supplies

NORTHERN SUN MERCHANDISING (CLO)
2916 E. Lake St. (m-b)
Minneapolis, MN 55406
612-729-2001 / Fax: 612-729-0149
Sales: $1 Million-$10 Million
Website: www.northernsun.com
SCOTT CRAMER (Owner) & Buys Boys' Apparel, Men's Apparel
ROXANNE-Boys' Apparel, Men's Apparel

ST. CROIX SHOP (MW)
651 Nicollet Mall (b)
Minneapolis, MN 55402
612-339-0128
Website: www.stcroixshop.com
JIM TIFFANY (Owner)
KAREN NELSON (Mgr.) & Buys Men's Sportswear, Store Displays, Fixtures, Supplies

TOP SHELF (CLO)
3040 Lyndale Ave. South (h)
Minneapolis, MN 55408
612-824-2800 / Fax: 612-824-7370
Website: www.topshelfinc.com
JOHN MEEGAN (Owner) & Buys Men's Custom Suits, Shirts, Ties, Belts, Hosiery, Suspenders, Store Displays, Fixtures, Supplies

FANBUZZ.COM (CLO-2 & OL)
10729 Bren Rd., #E
Minnetonka, MN 55343
952-852-8802
Sales: $10 Million-$50 Million
Website: www.fanbuzz.com
SCOTT KILLIAN (Co-Owner & President)
TIM BRULE (Co-Owner)
MICHAEL KOVACH (Mgr.-Opers.)
BRYAN PULLMAN-Boys' Apparel, Men's Apparel, Men's Accessories

STAHLKE STORES (DEPT-2)
116 S. Union (m)
Mora, MN 55051
320-679-1533 / Fax: 320-679-3461
Sales: $100,001-$500,000
BILL STAHLKE (Owner) & Buys Men's Sportswear, Furnishings, Headwear, Accessories, Young Men's Wear, Footwear, 8 to 20 Boys' Wear, Footwear, Store Displays, Fixtures, Supplies
SUE STAHLKE-Men's Sportswear, Furnishings, Headwear, Accessories, Young Men's Wear, Footwear, 8 to 20 Boys' Wear, Footwear, Store Displays, Fixtures, Supplies
JOHN STAHLKE-Men's Sportswear, Furnishings, Headwear, Accessories, Young Men's Wear, Footwear, 8 to 20 Boys' Wear, Footwear, Store Displays, Fixtures, Supplies

KEARNEY'S, INC. (CLO)
(CITY CENTER KIDS STORE)
City Center Mall
Morris, MN 56267
320-589-2644 / Fax: 320-589-9018
Sales: $100,001-$500,000
FLOYD SCHMIDTALL (President)
PAM SUTTER (Co-Owner) & Buys Men's Sportswear, Sweaters, Sport Shirts, Outer Jackets, Casual Slacks, Active Apparel, Dress Shirts, Hosiery, Swimwear, Footwear, Young Men's Wear, Ties, Gloves, Belts, 8 to 20 Boys' Wear, Store Displays, Fixtures, Supplies
RUTH KEARNEY (Co-Owner) & Buys Men's Sportswear, Sweaters, Sport Shirts, Outer Jackets, Casual Slacks, Active Apparel, Dress Shirts, Hosiery, Swimwear, Footwear, Young Men's Wear, Ties, Gloves, Belts, 8 to 20 Boys' Wear, Store Displays, Fixtures, Supplies

JACOBSEN'S DEPARTMENT STORE, INC. (DEPT)
419 Division St. (p)
Northfield, MN 55057
507-645-4672 / Fax: 507-645-0783
Sales: $500,000-$1 Million
Website: www.jacobsens-family-store.com
ROLAND A. JACOBSEN (President) & Buys Men's Wear, Young Men's & Boys' Wear, Footwear, Store Displays, Fixtures, Supplies

RARE PAIR (CLO)
401 Division St. South
Northfield, MN 55057
507-645-4257 / Fax: 507-645-3191
Website: www.rarepair.com
KRIN FINGER (Owner) & Buys Men's Sportswear, Sweaters, Sport Shirts, Casual Slacks, Active Apparel, Jeans, T-shirts, Shorts, Glove, Headwear, Belts, Hosiery, Footwear, Outerwear, Store Displays, Fixtures and Supplies

DUEBER'S, INC. (DEPT-28)
P.O. Box 779 (bud-m)
300 Industrial Blvd.
Norwood, MN 55368
952-467-3085 / Fax: 952-467-3001
Sales: $1 Million-$10 Million
Retail Locations: MN, OR
CHARLES DUEBER (President & Real Estate Contact) & Buys Men's Sportswear, Furnishings, Accessories, Footwear, 8 to 18 Boys' Wear, Urban Contemporary, Store Displays, Fixtures, Supplies

JO FARHO'S BRIDAL & TUXEDO (SP)
7141 10th St. North (m-b)
Oakdale, MN 55128
651-735-3298
Sales: $1 Million-$10 Million
DEBBIE SZYBATKA (Co-Owner) & Buys Men's Apparel, Mens's Big & Tall, Men's Formalwear, Men's Accessories, Men's Hosiery
MARCIE SZYBATKA (Co-Owner) & Buys Men's Apparel, Mens's Big & Tall, Men's Formalwear, Men's Accessories, Men's Hosiery

SAINT CLAIR'S FOR MEN (MW)
117 N. Cedar St. (m-b)
Owatonna, MN 55060
507-451-2406 / Fax: 507-446-9206
GREGORY KRUEGER (Owner) & Buys Men's Formal Wear, Outerwear, Sportswear, Suits, Big & Tall Men's Wear, Store Displays, Fixtures, Supplies

BISHOP CO. (CLO)
101 S. Main St. (bud-m)
Park Rapids, MN 56470
218-732-5277 / Fax: 218-732-7599
Sales: $100,001-$500,000
ROLLIS J. BISHOP (President & G.M.M.)
ANN ROBERTS (V.P. & Mgr.) & Buys Tailored Slacks, Raincoats, Sweaters, Sport Shirts, Outer Jackets, Casual Slacks, Active Apparel, Furnishings, Accessories, Boys' Wear

ZAPF'S LEATHER & WESTERN WEAR (WW)

114 W. James St. (m)
Paynesville, MN 56362
320-243-3797

CHUCK KOISHEL (Owner) & Buys Western Clothing, Related Furnishings & Accessories, Leather Apparel, Store Displays, Fixtures and Supplies

RICHTER'S MEN'S (MW)

137 W. Main St. (m)
Perham, MN 56573
218-346-5575 / Fax: 218-346-5681

STEVE RICHTER (Owner) & Buys Men's Wear, Sportswear, Furnishings, Accessories, Young Men's Wear, Urban Contemporary, Store Displays, Fixtures and Supplies

JOSEPHSON CLOTHING STORE (MW)

215 Bush St. (p-m)
Red Wing, MN 55066
651-388-4261 / Fax: 651-388-6038
Sales: $500,000-$1 Million

THOMAS L. WITHERS (Owner) & Buys Men's Sportswear, Leather Apparel, Furnishings, Headwear, Accessories, Store Displays, Fixtures, Supplies

RED WING SHOE CO., INC. (FW-465)

(RED WING SHOE)
(RED WING SHOE & REPAIR)
(WORK OUTFITTERS)
314 Main St. (b)
Red Wing, MN 55066
651-388-8211 / Fax: 651-385-0897
Sales: $100 Million-$500 Million
Website: www.redwingshoe.com
Retail Locations: MN, OK, CO, ID, UT, AZ, NM, NV, CA, HI, OR, WA, AK, IL, KY, MO, WI, TX, MD, OH, VA, NY, MA, RI, NH, ME, VT, CT, NJ, NE, PA, DE, NC, SC, GA, FL, AL, TN, MS, IN, MI, IA, SD, ND, MT, KS, LA

WILLIAM SWEASY (Chmn.)

GREG SKEEN (V.P.-Tech.) & Buys Men's Footwear, Leather Goods, Men's Accessories, Men's Apparel, Hosiery

JANE HICKOK (Real Estate Contact) (@ 651-385-1766)

WILSON'S OF REDWOOD FALLS, INC. (CLO)

153 E. 2nd St. (b)
Redwood Falls, MN 56283
507-637-8512
Sales: $1 Million-$10 Million

PETER DE WOLFE (Owner) & Buys Men's Footwear, Leather Goods, Men's Apparel, Mens's Big & Tall, Men's Casualwear, Men's Denim Apparel, Men's Formalwear, Men's Accessories, Men's Hosiery, Men's Outerwear,Men's Sleepwear, Men's Sportswear, Men's Suits, Men's Swimwear, Men's Underwear, Men's Uniforms

DAVE KUEHL (Store Mgr.)

FAMILY TREE (CLO)

P.O. Box 306 (p-m-b)
Richmond, MN 56368
320-597-3700

LYNN PIRAM (Owner) & Buys Men's Sportswear, Accessories, Store Displays, Fixtures, Supplies

ANDERSON'S FORMAL WEAR (MW-39)

1945 3rd Ave. SE
Rochester, MN 55902
507-282-8828 / Fax: 507-282-2582
Website: www.andersons.com
Retail Locations: MN, NY, MA, ME, NJ, PA, MD, AL, OH, IA, WI, IL, KS, TX, CO, NM, CA, ID

DAVID FRANA (V.P.) & Buys Men's Formal Wear, Young Men's & Boys', Suits, Formal Accessories, Formal Furnishings, Dress Shoes, Store Displays, Fixtures, Supplies

RICK PAULSON (Mgr.-Opers. & Real Estate Contact) (@ 507-292-6102) & Buys Men's Formal Accessories, Young Men's & Boys' Formal Wear, Suits, Formal Furnishings, Dress Shoes, Store Displays, Fixtures, Supplies

HANNY'S, INC. (MW-4)

19 1st Ave. SW (b)
Rochester, MN 55902
507-289-4077 / Fax: 507-289-8840
Sales: $1 Million-$10 Million

VINCENT BERG (Co-Owner & President)

TIM BERG (Co-Owner) & Buys Men's Outerwear, Headwear, Footwear, Store Displays, Fixtures, Supplies

BETTE FERSCHWEILER-Men's Sweaters, Casual Slacks, Sport Shirts, Furnishings, Accessories, Leather Apparel

TYROL SKI & SPORTS, INC. (SG)

1923 2nd St. NW
Rochester, MN 55902
507-288-1683 / Fax: 507-281-0132

JERRY SCHLIEP (Owner) & Buys Active Apparel, T-shirts, Fleece & Shorts, Footwear, Athletic Hosiery, Headwear, Store Displays, Fixtures and Supplies

PLEASANT HILLS SADDLE SHOP (CLO-2)

20750 Roger Dr. (p-m)
Rogers, MN 55374
763-428-8636 / Fax: 763-428-4534
Website: www.phsaddle.com

PAUL GROSSER (Co-Owner) & Buys Men's Sportswear, Dress Shirts, Ties, Hosiery, Gloves, Headwear, Belts, Jewelry, Small Leather Goods, Fragrances, Young Men's Wear, 8 to 20 Boys' Clothing, Sportswear, Furnishings, Accessories, Footwear

KATY GROSSER (Co-Owner) & Buys Men's Sportswear, Dress Shirts, Ties, Hosiery, Gloves, Headwear, Belts, Jewelry, Small Leather Goods, Fragrances, Young Men's Wear, 8 to 20 Boys' Clothing, Sportswear, Furnishings, Accessories, Footwear

HALBERSTADT'S CLOTHIERS, INC. (MW-7)

Crossroads Center
Saint Cloud, MN 56301
320-251-2100

JEFF HALBERSTADT (Co-Owner) & Buys Men's Sportswear, Leather Apparel, Furnishings, Accessories, Footwear, Store Displays, Fixtures, Supplies

TIM HALBERSTADT (Co-Owner) & Buys Men's Sportswear, Leather Apparel, Furnishings, Accessories, Footwear, Urban Contemporary, Store Displays, Fixtures, Supplies

KNIGHT'S CHAMBER, INC. (MW-5)

Crossroads Ctr. (p)
4201 W. Division St.
Saint Cloud, MN 56301
320-253-7030 / Fax: 320-253-0171
Sales: $1 Million-$10 Million

MIKE BITZAN (President & G.M.M.) & Buys Men's Overcoats, Suits, Tailored Jackets, Tailored Slacks, Raincoats, Sportswear, Sweaters, Leather Apparel, Dress Shirts, Ties, Belts, Jewelry, Footwear, Store Displays, Fixtures, Supplies

JIM LONG-Men's Overcoats, Suits, Tailored Jackets, Tailored Slacks, Raincoats, Sportswear, Sweaters, Leather Apparel, Dress Shirts, Ties, Belts, Jewelry, Footwear, Urban Contemporary, Store Displays, Fixtures, Supplies

MARK PAUL'S BIG & TALL MEN'S (MW)

(MD CLOTHIERS, INC.)
3415 W. Division St. (m-b)
Saint Cloud, MN 56301
320-253-0535

MARK LATZKA (Owner) & Buys Store Displays, Fixtures, Supplies, Big & Tall Men's Wear

BRET LATZKA-Big & Tall Men's Wear

PATRICIA LATZKA-Big & Tall Men's Wear

MIMBACH FLEET SUPPLY, INC. (MW)

755 Mayhew Lake Rd. NE (m-b)
Saint Cloud, MN 56304
320-252-1682 / Fax: 320-252-0045
Sales: $1 Million-$10 Million
Website: www.mimbachfleet.com

STEVE GUMIELA-Men's Work Clothes, Big & Tall Wear, Footwear

HOIGAARD'S, INC. (CLO)

3550 Hwy. 100 South (m)
Saint Louis Park, MN 55416
952-929-1351 / Fax: 952-929-2669
Website: www.hoigaards.com

CONRAD HOIGAARD (President & Owner)

JILL BREWER-Men's Wear, Outdoor Clothing

SOX APPEAL (CLO-15)
5821 Cedar Lake Rd. South
Saint Louis Park, MN 55416
952-943-1011 / Fax: 612-934-5665
SUE SCHNECK (V.P.-Mdsg.) & Buys Men's, Young Men's & Boys' Hosiery, Hosiery, Store Displays, Fixtures, Supplies

DONALD'S, INC. (CLO)
972 Payne Ave. (p)
Saint Paul, MN 55101
651-776-2723 / Fax: 651-776-2880
Website: www.donaldsuniform.com
LARRY LAUGHLIN (President) & Buys Store Displays, Fixtures, Supplies
BARBRA WILLIAMSON-Men's Sportswear, Furnishings, Accessories, Boys' Wear, Young Men's Wear, Urban Contemporary

MIDWAY UNIFORMS, INC. (SP)
1625 University Ave. West (m)
Saint Paul, MN 55104
651-644-6476 / Fax: 651-644-2439
Sales: $500,001-$1 Million
JORDAN ANDERSON (Owner & G.M.M.)
JENNIFER ROONEY (Store Mgr.) & Buys Men's Footwear, Men's Apparel, Men's Accessories, Men's Outerwear, Men's Sportswear, Men's Suits, Men's Uniforms

MILBÊRN CLOTHING CO. (MW & OL)
1685 University Ave. (p-m-b)
Saint Paul, MN 55104
651-645-2922 / Fax: 651-645-2922
Sales: $500,000-$1 Million
Website: www.milbern.com
HERBERT BERNICK (President) & Buys Men's Overcoats, Suits, Tailored Jackets, Tailored Slacks, Raincoats, Big & Tall Men'sWear, Sportswear, Sweaters, Sport Shirts, Outer Jackets, Casual Slacks, Active Apparel, Dress Shirts, Ties, Belts, Store Display, Fixtures, Supplies
STEVEN BERNICK (V.P. & G.M.M.) & Buys Men's Sportswear, Leather Apparel, Dress Shirts, Ties, Hats, Belts, Urban Contemporary, Store Displays, Fixtures, Supplies

BILL'S TOGGERY (MW)
138 Lewis St. S (m-b)
Shakopee, MN 55379
952-445-3735 / Fax: 952-445-6567
BILL WERMERSKIRCHEN (Owner) & Buys Men's Sportswear, Furnishings, Accessories, Young Men's Wear, Store Displays, Fixtures and Supplies

MIDWEST SUPPLY (DG-2)
2117 Maple Ave. (bud-p)
Slayton, MN 56172
507-836-8238 / Fax: 507-836-6567
MYRON TRULOCK (Co-Owner) & Buys Men's Western Wear & Outer Jackets, Dress Shirts, Belts, Jeans, Work Clothes, Underwear, Headwear, Young Men's Wear
KEN SHILLER (Co-Owner) & Buys Men's Wear, Store Displays, Fixtures, Supplies

B & G CROSSING (CLO)
(MARIE AVE. DRY GOODS, INC.)
601 Marie Ave. (m-b)
South Saint Paul, MN 55075
651-451-8563
DAVE GERKOVICH (Owner) & Buys Men's Sportswear, Leather, Furnishings, Headwear, Accessories, Footwear, Young Men's Wear, Store Displays, Fixtures, Supplies

THE SPORTSMAN'S GUIDE (MO)
411 Farwell Ave.
South Saint Paul, MN 55075
651-451-3030 / Fax: 651-450-6130
Sales: $10 Million-$50 Million
Website: www.sportsmansguide.com
GREG BINKLEY (President)
JOHN CASLER (V.P.- Mdse.)
ROBERT KIMMEL (Sr. Dir.) & Buys Men's Footwear
MIKE LEE-Sport Shirts, Leather Apparel, Outer Jackets, Casual Slacks, Athletic Apparel, Underwear, Hosiery, Gloves, Headwear, Belts

ALTO'S, INC. (MW)
235 Chestnut St. (m-b)
Virginia, MN 55792
218-741-7430
CLIFFORD ALTO (Owner) & Buys Men's Wear, Footwear, Urban Contemporary, Store Displays, Fixtures, Supplies

LUNDRIGAN'S (CLO-4)
P.O. Box 699 (m-b)
Walker, MN 56484
218-547-1041 / Fax: 218-547-2041
NANCY FREEMAN (Owner) & Buys Men's Young Men's Outewear, Tailored Jackets, Tailored Slacks, Leather, Sportswear, Furnishing, Accessories, Footwear, Store Diaplays, Fixtures, Supplies

THE FOURSOME (CLO-5)
841 E. Lake St. (m-b)
Wayzata, MN 55391
952-473-4667 / Fax: 952-473-9731
Sales: $10 Million-$50 Million
Website: www.thefoursome.com
RON ENGEL (Chmn.)
GORDY ENGEL (President) & Buys Men's Footwear, Leather Goods, Men's Accessories, Men's Apparel, Hosiery
MARY COOK (G.M.M.) & Buys Men's & Boys' Wear, Footwear
JEFF TILLOTSON-Men's Sportswear, Big & Tall Men's Wear, Men's Casual Accessories, Hosiery, Sleepwear, Underwear, Tailored Slacks, Tailored Clothing, Shirts, Ties, Accessories
JOHN HERZOG-Men's Footwear

LAKE COUNTRY OUTFITTERS, INC. (MW)
631 E. Lake St. (m-b)
Wayzata, MN 55391
952-476-6044
DARRYL WINTERNHEIMER (Owner) & Buys Men's Sportswear, Footwear

SPORTS HUT (CLO & OL)
(MIDWEST SPORTS, INC.)
1175 E. Wayzata Blvd. (m)
Wayzata, MN 55391
952-473-8843 / Fax: 952-473-9292
Website: www.sportshut.com
JAMES McWETHY (Owner) & Buys Store Displays, Fixtures, Supplies
ANDREW HOLMBERG (Gen. Mgr.) & Buys Store Displays, Fixtures, Supplies
KATHLEEN BURNS-Men's Overcoats, Sweaters, Outer Jackets, Urban Contemporary
DAVE DANIELS-Footwear

KEN'S CASUALS (MW)
Center Point Mall (p-m)
321 W. 5th St.
Willmar, MN 56201
320-235-2425
Sales: $100,001-$500,000
JAN SHELTENS (Co-Owner) & Buys Men's Suits, Slacks, Sportswear, Furnishings, Accessories, Store Displays, Fixtures, Supplies
PAM KLEIN (Co-Owner) & Buys Men's Suits, Slacks, Sportswear, Accessories

THE STAG (WW-2)
(RAW, INC.)
328 10th St. (m)
Windom, MN 56101
507-831-1922 / Fax: 507-376-4411
STAN WENDLAND (Co-Owner) & Buys Men's Western Shirts, Store Displays, Fixtures, Supplies
DALE RYAN (Co-Owner) & Buys Men's Western Shirts, Store Displays, Fixtures, Supplies

GREAT ARMY & NAVY SURPLUS STORES, INC. (MW-3)

P.O. Box 918 (bud)
113 Liberty St.
Winona, MN 55987
507-452-1348 / Fax: 507-452-1349

RICH AHRENS, JR. (President) & Buys Men's Jeans, Work Clothing, Big & Tall Men's Wear, Outer Jackets, Underwear, Hosiery, Gloves, Headwear, Footwear, Store Displays, Fixtures, Supplies

SHARON AHRENS (V.P.) & Buys Men's Jeans, Work Clothing, Big & Tall Men's Wear, Outer Jackets, Underwear, Hosiery, Gloves, Headwear, Footwear, Store Displays, Fixtures, Supplies

TARGET DIRECT (MO & OL)

(SIGNALS CATALOG)
(WIRELESS CATALOG)
(SEASONS CATALOG)
(Div. of TARGET CORPORATION)
9501 Hudson Rd. (p)
Woodbury, MN 55125
(Associated Mdsg. Corp.)
651-578-6101 / Fax: 651-578-6161
Sales: $200 Million
Website: www.signals.com

DALE NITHSCHKE (President)

JOHN OLLMANN-Men's T-shirts, Ties, Underwear, Hosiery, Footwear

MICHAEL INSKEEP-Men's T-shirts, Ties, Underwear, Hosiery

FLEET OF WORTHINGTON, INC. (MW)

P.O. Box 875 (p-m)
Hwy. 59 North
Worthington, MN 56187
507-372-7456 / Fax: 507-372-4798
Sales: $10 Million-$50 Million

NORM GALLAGHER (Owner) & Buys Men's Raincoats, Sportswear, Dress Shirts, Robes, Underwear, Hosiery, Gloves, Headwear, Belts, Jewelry, Small Leather Goods, Big & Tall Men's Wear, Young Men's Wear, Boys' Wear, Clothing, Sportswear, Footwear, Store Displays, Fixtures, Supplies

COVERED BRITCHES (MW)

308 Main St.
Zumbrota, MN 55992
507-732-7388

DAVID BABBITT (Owner) & Buys Tailored Jackets, Tailored Slacks, Sweaters, Sport Shirts, Outer Jackets, Leather Apparel, Casual Slacks, Work Clothing, Furnishings, Accessories, Store Displays, Fixtures and Supplies

LOCHNER'S, INC. (CLO)

340 Main St. (p-m)
Zumbrota, MN 55992
507-732-5555 / Fax: 507-732-4555
Sales: $100,001-$500,000

PEGGY LOCHNER (Co-Owner) & Buys Men's Sweaters, Sport Shirts, Casual Slacks, Active Apparel, Dress Shirts, Ties, Hosiery, Belts, Young Men's Wear, Sportswear, Furnishings, Accessories

DON LOCHNER (Co-Owner) & Buys Men's Sweaters, Sport Shirts, Casual Slacks, Active Apparel, Dress Shirts, Ties, Hosiery, Belts, Young Men's Wear, Sportswear, Furnishings, Accessories

MISSISSIPPI - Amory

ANTHONY'S MEN'S SHOP (MW)
P.O. Box 465 (m)
218 N. Main St.
Amory, MS 38821
662-256-2911
Sales: $100,001-$500,000
DOROTHY HANEY (Co-Owner)
JOHN HANEY (Co-Owner) & Buys Men's Sportswear, Furnishings, Footwear, Accessories, Store Displays, Fixtures, Supplies

TOMMY'S MENSWEAR (MW)
128 N. Main St. (m-b)
Amory, MS 38821
662-256-2134
BARRY SWAN (Owner) & Buys Men's Wear, Footwear, Big & Tall Men's Wear, Store Displays, Fixtures, Supplies

SIMS CLOTHING (CLO)
113 Public Sq.
Batesville, MS 38606
662-563-2390
Sales: $100,001-$500,000
BILLY DOWNS (Owner) & Buys Men's Sportswear, Leather Apparel, Furnishings, Headwear, Accessories, Footwear, Young Men's Wear, Store Displays, Fixtures, Supplies

STUBB'S (DEPT & MW)
(WILLIAMS DEPARTMENT STORE)
133 Public Sq. (p-m)
Batesville, MS 38606
662-563-7362
SMITTY WILLIAMS (Co-Owner) & Buys Men's Sport Coats, Suits, Tailored Jackets, Tailored Slacks, Raincoats, Dress Shirts, Casual Slacks, Sportswear, Ties, Belts, Footwear, Young Men's Wear, Boys' Wear, Store Displays, Fixtures, Supplies

ANTHONY'S MEN'S STORE (MW)
501 Main St. (b)
Bay Saint Louis, MS 39520
228-467-7731 / Fax: 228-467-7731
PAM LOIACAINO (Owner) & Buys Men's Sportswear, Footwear, Furnishings, Accessories, Store Displays, Fixtures, Supplies

GOLDBERG'S DEPARTMENT STORE (DEPT)
121 N. Hayden St. (m)
Belzoni, MS 39038
662-247-3111 / Fax: 662-247-3112
CHARLES GOLDBERG (Owner) & Buys Men's Sportswear, Leather Apparel, Furnishings, Headwear, Accessories, Footwear, Young Men's Wear, 8 to 20 Boys' Wear, Store Displays, Fixtures, Supplies

GRAY DEPARTMENT STORE, INC. (DEPT)
206 Market St. (p)
Booneville, MS 38829
662-728-5741
Sales: $100,001-$500,000
JIMMY JONES (Owner) & Buys Men's Suits, Sportswear, Furnishings, Accessories, Urban Contemporary, Store Displays, Fixtures

MEN'S QUARTERS, INC. (MW)
605 E. Church St. (m)
Booneville, MS 38829
662-728-3933
P. HALE AUST (Owner) & Buys Men's Sportswear, Furnishings, Accessories, Store Displays, Fixtures, Supplies

BUSICK & SON, INC. (MW)
P.O. Box 247 (m)
300 Government St.
Brandon, MS 39042
601-825-5902
Sales: $100,001-$500,000
R. N. BUSICK (President) & Buys Men's Sportswear, Sweaters, Sport Shirts, Outer Jackets, Casual Slacks, Active Apparel, Furnishings, Belts, Fragrances, Leather Apparel, Headwear, Footwear, Young Men's Wear, Boys' Wear, Big & Tall Men's Wear, Store Displays, Fixtures, Supplies

CHILDREN'S WORLD (KS)
714 Brookway Blvd. (m-b)
Brookhaven, MS 39601
601-833-1444 / Fax: 601-833-3549
Sales: $100,001-$500,000
IVOLENE COKER (Owner) & Buys 8 to 20 Boys' Wear, Clothing, Sportswear, Furnishings, Headwear, Belts, Jewelry, Footwear, Store Displays, Fixtures, Supplies
CATHY NORTON-8 to 20 Boys' Wear, Clothing, Sportswear, Furnishings, Headwear, Belts, Jewelry, Footwear
VICKIE GOZA-8 to 20 Boys' Wear, Clothing, Sportswear, Furnishings, Headwear, Belts, Jewelry, Footwear

HODGES MEN'S SHOP (MW)
P.O. Box 288 (m)
101 W. Cherokee St.
Brookhaven, MS 39602
601-833-6351
Sales: $100,001-$500,000
BRUCE RICHARDSON (Owner) & Buys Men's Overcoats, Suits, Raincoats, Sweaters, Sport Shirts, Outer Jackets, Leather Apparel, Casual Slacks, Furnishings, Accessories, Footwear, Store Displays, Fixtures, Supplies

LOCKER ROOM MEN'S SHOP (MW)
117 W. Cherokee St. (m)
Brookhaven, MS 39601
601-833-7731
Sales: $100,001-$500,000
LES BUMGARNER (Owner) & Buys Men's Overcoats, Suits, Tailored Jackets, Tailored Slacks, Raincoats, Sweaters, Sport Shirts, Outer Jackets, Casual Slacks, Active Apparel, Leather Apparel, Furnishings, Headwear, Accessories, Footwear, Urban Contemporary, Store Displays, Fixtures, Supplies

CALHOUN COUNTY COOPERATIVE (CLO)
110 E. Railroad Ave. (m)
Calhoun City, MS 38916
662-628-6682 / Fax: 662-628-6026
Sales: Under $100,000
EDDIE HELMS (Mgr.) & Buys Men's Overcoats, Raincoats, Sport Shirts, Outer Jackets, Boots, Shorts, Casual Slacks, Denim, Headwear, Store Displays, Fixtures, Supplies

STUBBS' DEPARTMENT STORE (DEPT)
P.O. Box 690 (p)
104 S. Main St.
Calhoun City, MS 38916
662-628-5753
GEORGE SIMON (Owner) & Buys Men's Suits, Tailored Slacks, Sportswear, Underwear, Hosiery, Dress Shirts, Small Leather Goods, Footwear, Young Men's Wear, Swimwear, Store Displays, Fixtures, Supplies

BUTTROSS DEPARTMENT STORE (DEPT)
P.O. Box 545 (m)
115 W. Peace St.
Canton, MS 39046
601-859-2892
Sales: $100,001-$500,000
ERNEST BUTTROSS (Owner)
MIRIAM BUTTROSS (G.M.M.) & Buys Men's Sportswear, Furnishings, Headwear, Accessories, Footwear, Young Men's Wear, Boys' Wear, Store Displays, Fixtures, Supplies

THE PLAYERS OF MISSISSIPPI (MW)
239 W. Peace St. (m)
Canton, MS 39046
601-859-7290 / Fax: 601-859-7225
Sales: $100,001-$500,000
ROD HALTEH (Owner) & Buys Men's & Boys' Wear, Urban Contemporary, Footwear, Store Displays, Fixtures, Supplies

CHIPLEY'S (DEPT)

P.O. Box 191 (m)
107 N. Pearl
Carthage, MS 39051
601-267-3281 / Fax: 601-267-3425
Sales: $100,001-$500,000
Website: www.chipleys.com

RACHEL CHIPLEY (Owner)
MARY ANN EDGAR (Mgr.) & Buys Men's Sportswear, Sweaters, Sport Shirts, Casual Slacks, Active Apparel, Furnishings, Accessories, Belts, Small Leather Goods, Young Men's & Boys' Wear, Store Displays, Fixtures, Supplies

COGHLAN FASHIONS FOR MEN (MW)

(ALAN'S)
103 Hwy. 16 West (m)
Carthage, MS 39051
601-267-3955

CORRINA PIERCE (Owner) & Buys Men's Sportswear, Leather Apparel, Hosiery, Ties, Dress Shirts, Small Leather Goods, Fragrances, Accessories, Underwear, Headwear, Young Men's Wear, Boys' Suits, Store Displays, Fixtures, Supplies

SUPER SOUL SHOP (MW)

258 Yazoo Ave. (m)
Clarksdale, MS 38614
662-624-6794

GEORGE DAHO (Owner) & Buys Men's Wear, Accessories, Furnishings

ABRAHAM'S MEN'S SHOPPE (MW-1)

136 N. Sharpe Ave. (b)
Cleveland, MS 38732
662-843-4541 / Fax: 662-843-2650

DANNY ABRAHAM (Owner) & Buys Men's Sportswear, Furnishings, Accessories, Footwear, Young Men's Wear, Urban Contemporary, Boys' Wear, Leather Apparel, Store Displays, Fixtures, Supplies

ALLAN REYNOLDS' SHOES (SP)

421 N. Davis Ave.
Cleveland, MS 38732
662-846-7222 / Fax: 662-846-6222
Sales: $501,000-$1 Million

ALLAN REYNOLDS (Owner) & Buys Athletic Footwear, Outdoor Footwear

JAY'S DEPARTMENT STORE (DEPT)

110 N. Sharpe Ave. (m)
Cleveland, MS 38732
662-843-4201 / Fax: 662-843-4202
Sales: $1 Million-$10 Million

MARGIE BRUNNER (Owner) & Buys Store Displays, Fixtures, Supplies
BOB McCARTY (G.M.M.) & Buys Men's, Boys' & Students' Wear
TERESA KITCHENS-Footwear

POPE CO., INC. (CLO)

P.O. Box 1627 (m)
Collins, MS 39428
601-765-6736

JOHNNY POPE (President) & Buys Store Displays, Fixtures and Supplies
GAYLE POPE (Co-Owner) & Buys Men's Suits, Sport Shirts, Casual Slacks, Sportswear, Furnishings, Small Leather Goods, Footwear, Young Men's Wear, Boys' Wear

UPTON'S DEPARTMENT STORE (DEPT)

P.O. Box 566 (m)
114 E. Main St.
Collins, MS 39428
601-765-4922

PAUL UPTON (Co-Owner) & Buys Men's, Young Men's & 8 to 20 Boys' Suits, Tailored Jackets, Tailored Slacks, Sportswear, Furnishings, Headwear, Accessories, Footwear, Store Displays, Fixtures, Supplies
DENISE UPTON-WILLIAMSON (Co-Owner) & Buys Men's, Young Men's & 8 to 20 Boys' Suits, Tailored Jackets, Tailored Slacks, Sportswear, Furnishings, Headwear, Accessories, Footwear, Store Displays, Fixtures, Supplies
STEVEN WILLIAMSON (Co-Owner) & Buys Men's, Young Men's & 8 to 20 Boys' Suits, Tailored Jackets, Tailored Slacks, Sportswear, Furnishings, Headwear, Accessories, Footwear, Store Displays, Fixtures, Supplies

THE GLOBE (CLO)

424 Main St. (p)
Columbus, MS 39701
662-328-6465

LEON GORDON (Owner) & Buys Men's Sportswear, Leather Apparel, Headwear, Accessories, Dress Shirts, Hosiery, Gloves, Footwear, Young Men's Wear, Boys' Wear, Store Displays, Fixtures, Supplies
GARY GORDON (Asst. Mgr.) & Buys Men's Sportswear, Leather Apparel, Headwear, Accessories, Dress Shirts, Hosiery, Gloves, Footwear, Young Men's Wear, Boys' Wear, Store Displays, Fixtures, Supplies

JIM'S CLOTHING, INC. (MW)

1301 Hwy. 45 North, #A (m-b)
Columbus, MS 39701
662-328-8816 / Fax: 662-328-9607

JIM DAVIS (Owner) & Buys Men's Wear, Store Displays, Fixtures, Supplies

LOOKING GOOD (MW-2)

119 5th St. South (b)
Columbus, MS 39701
662-328-3431 / Fax: 662-328-3431
Sales: $100,001-$500,000

DANNY MELVANI (Owner) & Buys Men's & Boys' Wear, Urban Contemporary, Footwear, Store Displays, Fixtures, Supplies

REED'S OF COLUMBUS, INC. (CLO-4)

2013 Hwy. 45 North (m-b)
Columbus, MS 39701
662-327-2684 / Fax: 662-328-0080
Website: www.columbusmississippi.com

LEX JACKSON (President) & Buys Men's Sportswear, Furnishings, Accessories, Footwear, Young Men's Wear, Urban Contemporary, Boys' Wear, Store Displays, Fixtures, Supplies

CASEY'S (CLO)

P.O. Box 389 (m)
312 E. Railroad Ave.
Crystal Springs, MS 39059
601-892-3771
Sales: $100,001-$500,000

ALTON FUNCHESS, JR. (Owner) & Buys Men's Suits, Tailored Jackets, Tailored Slacks, Sportswear, Furnishings, Big & Tall Men's Wear, Headwear, Belts, Small Leather Goods, Footwear, Young Men's Wear, Boys' Wear

CHILDREN'S SHOP (KS)

102 N. Cumming St. (p-m-b)
Fulton, MS 38843
662-862-3641
Sales: $100,001-$500,000

MARGARET SENTER CRITZ (Owner) & Buys Infant to Size 16 Boys' Wear, Store Displays, Fixtures, Supplies

COUNTRY GENTLEMAN (CLO)

1644 Hwy. 1 South (b)
Greenville, MS 38701
662-332-1356 / Fax: 662-334-6515
Sales: $1 Million-$10 Million

DON MORRIS (Co-Owner & Dir.-Fin. & Real Estate) & Buys Men's Footwear, Leather Goods, Big & Tall, Casualwear, Denim Apparel, Formalwear, Accessories, Hosiery, Outerwear, Sleepwear, Sportswear, Suits, Swimwear, Underwear
TINA MORRIS (Co-Owner & Dir.-Info. Sys. & HR) & Buys Men's Footwear, Leather Goods, Big & Tall, Casualwear, Denim Apparel, Formalwear, Accessories, Hosiery, Outerwear, Sleepwear, Sportswear, Suits, Swimwear, Underwear

LOOKING GOOD (CLO-16)

(JEAN JOINT)
300 Washington Ave. (b)
Greenville, MS 38701
662-335-1017 / Fax: 662-334-9354
Sales: $1 Million-$10 Million

BOBBY DADLANI (Owner) & Buys Men's Overcoats, Suits, Tailored Jackets, Tailored Slacks, Sportswear, Dress Shirts, Underwear, Headwear, Jewelry, Small Leather Goods, Footwear, Young Men's Wear, Boys' Wear, Store Displays, Fixtures, Supplies

MISSISSIPPI - Greenville

MANSOUR'S CLOTHING (MW)

1630 Hwy. 1 South (b-h)
Greenville, MS 38701
662-378-3000 / Fax: 662-378-3063
Sales: $1 Million-$10 Million

JOHN MANSOUR, SR. (Co-Owner) & Buys Headwear, Big & Tall Men's Wear, Men's Sport Shirts, Outer Jackets, Leather Apparel, Casual Slacks, Active Apparel, Dress Shirts, Ties, Robes, Belts, Footwear, Store Displays, Fixtures, Supplies

GEORGE MANSOUR JR. (Co-Owner) & Buys Men's Sport Shirts, Outer Jackets, Leather Apparel, Casual Slacks, Active Apparel, Dress Shirts, Ties, Robes, Belts, Footwear, Men's Underwear, Jewelry, Small Leather Goods, Fragrance, Store Displays, Fixtures, Supplies

S. GOODMAN'S, INC. (DEPT)

731 Washington Ave. (p)
Greenville, MS 38701
662-332-2658 / Fax: 662-332-0337

SIDNEY M. GOODMAN (President & G.M.M.)

SAM GOODMAN (V.P.) & Buys Men's Sportswear, Work Clothes, Furnishings, Accessories, Big & Tall Men's Wear, Young Men's Wear, Boys' Wear, Store Displays, Fixtures, Supplies

REBECCA GOODMAN-Store Displays, Fixtures, Supplies

DEBBIE CARTER-Footwear

GOLDBERG'S, INC. (SP-4)

501 Howard St.
Greenwood, MS 38930
662-453-8503 / Fax: 662-453-8504

MIKE GOLDBERG (Mgr. & Buyer) & Buys Active Apparel, Athletic Footwear

KORNFELD'S, INC. (DEPT)

318 Johnson (p-m-b)
Greenwood, MS 38930
662-453-1352
Sales: $100,001-$500,000

LESLIE KORNFELD (Co-Owner) & Buys Store, Displays, Fixtures, Supplies, Men's Wear, Sportswear, Furnishings, Accessories, Big & Tall Men's Wear, Footwear

MURRAY B. KORNFELD (Co-Owner) & Buys Men's Wear, Sportswear, Furnishings, Accessories, Big & Tall Men's Wear, Footwear

PHIL'S SQUIRE SHOPPE (MW)

(SQUIRE SHOPPE)
705 W. Park Ave. (m-b)
Greenwood, MS 38930
662-453-8256 / Fax: 662-453-8883
Sales: $500,000-$1 Million

PHIL ELLIS, JR. (President) & Buys Men's Overcoats, Suits, Sportscoats, Tailored Slacks, Sweaters, Sportshirts, Outer Jackets, Leather Apparel, Casual Slacks, Dress Shirts, Ties, Robes, Underwear, Hosiery, Headwear, Belts, Gloves, Young Men's Wear, Store Displays, Fixtures and Supplies

STANLEY'S DEPARTMENT STORE, INC. (DEPT)

P.O. Box 674 (bud)
218 E. Johnson St.
Greenwood, MS 38930
662-453-3623 / Fax: 662-453-3623

DANNY RATLIFF (V.P.) & Buys Men's Overcoats, Suits, Raincoats, Sweaters, Sport Shirts, Outer Jackets, Leather Apparel, Casual Slacks, Dress Shirts, Ties, Robes, Underwear, Hosiery, Gloves, Belts, Small Leather Goods, Boys' Clothing, Sportswear, Accessories, Big & Tall Men's Wear, Footwear, Store Displays, Fixtures, Supplies

DENIS RATLIFF-Men's Overcoats, Suits, Raincoats, Sweaters, Sport Shirts, Outer Jackets, Leather Apparel, Casual Slacks, Dress Shirts, Ties, Robes, Underwear, Hosiery, Gloves, Belts, Small Leather Goods, Boys' Clothing, Sportswear, Accessories, Big & Tall Men's Wear, Footwear, Store Displays, Fixtures, Supplies

SUPER SOUL SHOP (CLO)

409 Howard St. (m)
Greenwood, MS 38930
662-455-2915 / Fax: 662-455-2915

HILDA RUSTOM (Partner) & Buys Men's Wear, Boys' Suits, Jeans, Pants, Urban Contemporary, Headwear, Footwear, Store Displays, Fixtures, Supplies

ABRAHAM RUSTOM (Partner) & Buys Men's Wear, Boys' Suits, Jeans, Pants, Urban Contemporary, Headwear, Footwear, Store Displays, Fixtures, Supplies

STAG SHOP, INC. (MW & OL)

1730 Commerce (b)
Grenada, MS 38901
662-226-4213
Website: www.siegfriedshirts.com

BILL BRUNSON (Owner) & Buys Men's Wear, Pants, Sport Coats, Store Displays, Fixtures, Supplies

TRUSTY'S, INC. (MW)

113 1st St. (b)
Grenada, MS 38901
662-226-2732 / Fax: 662-226-2732

ED PENN (Co-Owner) & Buys Men's Wear, Footwear, Headwear, Accessories, Belts, Ties, Hosiery, Store Displays, Fixtures, Supplies

TERRY LYON (Co-Owner) & Buys Men's Wear, Footwear, Headwear, Accessories, Belts, Ties, Hosiery, Store Displays, Fixtures, Supplies

ELLIS SALLOUM'S (CLO)

1409 24th Ave. (m)
Gulfport, MS 39501
228-863-0972
Sales: $100,001-$500,000

KALEEL SALLOUM (Co-Owner) & Buys Store Supplies, Men's Tailored Clothing, Sportswear, Furnishings, Accessories, Dress Shoes

ELLIS SALLOUM (Co-Owner) & Buys Men's Tailored Clothing, Sportswear, Furnishings, Accessories, Dress Shoes, Store Displays, Fixtures and Supplies

MOSES' DEPARTMENT STORE (DEPT)

1612 25th Ave. (m-b)
Gulfport, MS 39501
228-863-6814 / Fax: 228-868-9147
Sales: $1 Million-$10 Million

FRANK MOSES (Co-Owner)

ANNEAS MOSES, JR. (Co-Owner)

DAVID MOSES (Mgr.) & Buys Men's Sportswear, Sweaters, Sport Shirts, Outer Jackets, Casual Slacks, Active Apparel, Furnishings, Accessories, Footwear, Young Men's Wear, Urban Contemporary, 8 to 14 Boys' Wear, Store Displays, Fixtures, Supplies

S.F. ALMAN LTD. (CLO)

452 Court House Rd., #A (b)
Gulfport, MS 39507
228-896-6474 / Fax: 228-896-2244

FERRELL ALMAN (Owner & President) & Buys Men's Suits, Raincoats, Tailored Jackets, Tailored Slacks, Sportswear, Furnishings, Accessories, Swimwear, Footwear, Store Displays, Fixtures, Supplies

WARR'S MEN'S CLOTHING (MW-1)

(WARR'S)
767 16th St. (m-b)
Gulfport, MS 39507
228-896-3919 / Fax: 228-896-3925
Sales: $100,001-$500,000

BRENT WARR (Owner) & Buys Men's Suits, Tailored Jackets, Tailored Slacks, Sportswear, Furnishings, Belts, Fragrances, Leather Apparel, Store Displays, Fixtures, Supplies

PRICE & CO. (MW)

1000 Turtle Creek Dr. (m-b)
Hattiesburg, MS 39402
601-264-9454 / Fax: 601-264-9466
Sales: $1 Million-$10 Million
Website: www.randyonline.com

RANDY PRICE (President & G.M.M.) & Buys Men's Overcoats, Suits, Tailored Jackets, Tailored Slacks, Sweaters, Sport Shirts, Outer Jackets, Casual Slacks, Leather Apparel, Furnishings, Headwear, Belts, Small Leather Goods, Fragrances, Footwear, Store Displays, Fixtures, Supplies

T.J.'S WESTERN WARE, INC. (WW-2)

6424 Hwy. 49 (p-m-b)
Hattiesburg, MS 39401
601-582-9378 / Fax: 601-582-2079

RONALD JEFCOAT (Owner) & Buys Men's & Boys' Western Wear, Footwear, Store Displays, Fixtures, Supplies

BOOTS & SPURS RANCH SUPPLIES (CLO)

3926 Hwy. 178 West (p)
Holly Springs, MS 38635
662-252-6965 / Fax: 662-252-6965
Sales: $100,001-$500,000

DOTTIE CHUMNEY (Owner) & Buys Men's & Boys' Western Wear, Footwear, Belts, Hosiery, Gloves, Headwear, Store Displays, Fixtures, Supplies

LINWOOD'S (CLO)

125 S. Market St. (p-m-b)
Holly Springs, MS 38635
662-252-1322 / Fax: 662-252-1656

GRAHAM MILLER (Owner) & Buys Store Displays, Fixtures, Men's Sportswear, Furnishings, Headwear, Belts, Jewelry, Small Leather Goods, Dress Shoes, Young Men's & Boys' Wear

JOEY MILLER-Men's Sportswear, Furnishings, Headwear, Belts, Jewelry, Small Leather Goods, Dress Shoes, Young Men's & Boys' Wear

MILLER DEPARTMENT STORE (DEPT)

107 S. Market St. (p-m)
Holly Springs, MS 38635
662-252-2661
Sales: $1 Million-$10 Million

GRAHAM MILLER (Owner) & Buys Men's Sportswear, Leather Apparel, Furnishings, Headwear, Accessories, Footwear, Young Men's Wear, Boys' Wear, Store Displays, Fixtures

MARK MILLER (G.M.M.) & Buys Men's Sportswear, Leather Apparel, Furnishings, Headwear, Accessories, Footwear, Young Men's Wear, Urban Contemporary, Boys' Wear, Store Displays, Fixtures

ABRAHAM'S (CLO)

115 Front St. (b)
Indianola, MS 38751
662-887-2026
Sales: $500,000-$1 Million

MICHAEL ABRAHAM (Owner) & Buys Men's Overcoats, Suits, Men's Tailored Clothing, Raincoats, Sweaters, Sport Shirts, Outer Jackets, Leather Apparel, Casual Slacks, Active Apparel, Furnishings, Headwear, Accessories, Big & Tall Men's Wear, Footwear, Store Displays, Fixtures, Supplies

HELEN ABRAHAM (G.M.M.) & Buys Men's Overcoats, Suits, Men's Tailored Clothing, Raincoats, Sweaters, Sport Shirts, Outer Jackets, Leather Apparel, Casual Slacks, Active Apparel, Furnishings, Headwear, Accessories, Big & Tall Men's Wear, Footwear, Store Displays, Fixtures, Supplies

YOUNG IDEAS (KS)

422 Hwy. 82 East (m-b)
Indianola, MS 38751
662-887-5539 / Fax: 662-887-5543

ALAN SILVERBLATT (Co-Owner) & Buys 8 to 20 Boys' Wear, Footwear, Store Displays, Fixtures, Supplies

LEANNE SILVERBLATT (Co-Owner) & Buys 8 to 20 Boys' Wear, Footwear, Store Displays, Fixtures, Supplies

ENCORE PRODUCTS (CLO)

P.O. Box 571 (m)
119 S. Fulton
Iuka, MS 38852
662-423-3484 / Fax: 662-424-0205

CHARLES EMMONS (Owner) & Buys Imprintable T-shirts, Headwear, Store Displays, Fixtures, Supplies

BUFFALO PEAK OUTFITTERS (MW & SG)

115 Highland Vlg. (b)
Jackson, MS 39211
601-366-2557 / Fax: 601-982-1645
Website: www.buffalopeak.net

ROBERT McCAIN (President & Owner) & Buys Men's Wear, Sportswear, Outerwear, Outdoor Apparel, Footwear

FASHION CORNER (MW)

101 E. Capital St. (m)
Jackson, MS 39201
601-355-4007
Sales: $100,001-$500,000

SALIBA DABIT (Owner) & Buys Men's Sweaters, Sport Shirts, Suits, Dress Shirts, Ties, Hosiery, Belts, Urban Contemporary, Store Displays, Fixtures, Supplies

GREAT SCOTT (MW)

4400 Old Canton Rd. (b)
Jackson, MS 39211
601-984-8855
Sales: $1 Million-$10 Million

STEVE SCOTT (Owner) & Buys Men's & Young Men's Wear, Sportswear, Furnishings, Accessories, Footwear, Store Displays, Fixtures, Supplies

HOUSE OF BRAND, INC. (MW)

(THE SANDERS CO.)
2023 Hwy. 80 West (m-b)
Jackson, MS 39204
601-353-2715 / Fax: 601-352-1096
Sales: $500,000-$1 Million

AUDREY BRAND (President)

SAM BRAND (V.P.) & Buys Big & Tall Men's Wear, Footwear, Urban Contemporary, Store Displays, Fixtures, Supplies

IN STYLE, INC. (MW-2)

955 Ellis Ave. (m-b)
Jackson, MS 39209
601-355-8187 / Fax: 601-355-0325

HARESH CHATLANI (Owner) & Buys Men's Sportswear, Furnishings, Headwear, Accessories, Footwear, Young Men's Wear, Urban Contemporary, Boys' Wear, Store Displays, Fixtures, Supplies

JOE'S HIGH FASHION (MW)

925 Ellis Ave. (m)
Jackson, MS 39209
601-352-8410 / Fax: 601-352-8448

JOE KHALAS (President & Owner) & Buys Men's Wear

LATEST FASHION (MW)

1700 Terry Rd. (m)
Jackson, MS 39204
601-944-1419 / Fax: 601-922-1181

STELLA ERHABOR (Owner) & Buys Men's & Boys' Wear, Urban Contemporary, Store Displays, Fixtures, Supplies

MISSISSIPPI - Jackson

McRAE'S (DEPT-30)
(SAKS INCORPORATED)
P.O. Box 20080
3455 Hwy. 80 West
Jackson, MS 39289
601-352-8029 / Fax: 601-968-5300
Sales: $100 Million-$500 Million
Website: www.mcraes.com
Retail Locations: AL, FL, LA, MS
- TONI BROWNING (President & C.E.O.)
- JOE SHERMAN (V.P.- Exec. Mdsg.)
- HARRY CUNNINGHAM (Dir.-Visual Mdsg.) & Buys Store Displays, Fixtures
- BRIAN KORLITZ (Dir.-Purchasing) & Buys Store Supplies
- BOB SEARS (V.P. & G.M.M.-Men's) (@ 865-981-6206)
- JIM HARRANG-Sportswear
- OPEN-Men's Moderate Sportswear, Active Tops, Sportswear, Modorate Collections
- DAVID LUTHER-Men's Shirts, Ties
- DON CHIZK (D.M.M.-Boys')
- JEFF USEFORGE-Men's Accessories, 8 to 20 Boys' Updated Sportswear, Clothing, Furnishings
- TIM FRANKLIN-Boys' Wear 4 to 7
- OPEN-Boys' Footwear, Men's Footwear
- JIM BAKER-Men's Pants, Separates, Better Sportswear, Suits, Outerwear
- PHIL GODBOLD-Young Men's Wear, Men's Denim, Urban Contemporary

OXFORD STREET (MW-47)
1131 Metro Ctr. (b)
Jackson, MS 39209
601-354-3151 / Fax: 601-354-3152
- ELIE KARAM (Co-Owner) & Buys Men's & Boys' Wear, Dress Shoes, Casual Shoes, Footwear, Store Displays, Fixtures, Supplies
- ISPEAR BROU (Co-Owner) & Buys Men's Sportswear, Dress Shoes, Ties, Hosiery, Belts, Footwear, Jewelry, Small Leather Goods, Young Men's Wear, Urban Contemporary, 8 to 20 Boys' Wear, Easter Boys' Suits, Store Displays, Fixtures, Supplies
- ELIAS DABIT (Co-Owner) & Buys Men's Overcoats, Suits, Tailored Jackets, Tailored Slacks, Raincoats, Sportswear, Furnishings, Leather Apparel, Headwear, Belts, Jewelry, Small Leather Goods, Footwear, Store Displays, Fixtures, Supplies

THE ROGUE (MW)
4450 I 55 North (b)
Jackson, MS 39211
(DLS OUTFITTERS)
601-362-6383 / Fax: 601-362-9248
Sales: $1 Million-$10 Million
Website: www.therogue.com
- JIMMY KEITHS-Men's Suits, Swimwear, Accessories, Hosiery, Footwear
- WILLIAM NEVILLE (Owner) & Buys Men's Wear, Leather Apparel, Footwear, Store Displays, Fixtures, Supplies

T-SHIRTS LTD. (CLO)
1274 Metro Ctr. (p-m)
Jackson, MS 39209
601-969-1040
- AZIM JALADIN (Owner) & Buys Men's & Boys' Imprintable T-shirts, Sportswear, Store Displays, Fixtures, Supplies

CLAUDE JULIAN'S, INC. (CLO)
141 Madison St. (b)
Kosciusko, MS 39090
662-289-4821 / Fax: 662-289-4418
- CLAUDE JULIAN (Owner) & Buys Men's Suits, Tailored Jackets, Tailored Slacks, Sportswear, Sweaters, Sport Shirts, Outer Jackets, Casual Slacks, Active Apparel, T-shirts, Furnishings, Accessories, Footwear, Store Displays, Fixtures, Supplies

LEONARD'S (DEPT)
(W.C. LEONARD & CO.)
P.O. Box 649 (m)
131 W. Jefferson St.
Kosciusko, MS 39090
662-289-5211 / Fax: 662-289-5279
Sales: $1 Million-$10 Million
Website: www.leonardsdepartmentstore.com
- ALLEN MASSEY (President) & Buys Men's Wear, Store Displays, Fixtures, Supplies
- JAY PRICE-Men's Wear, Footwear
- PETTY CRITTENDEN-Boys' Wear

U-SHOP POPULAR FASHIONS (MW)
146 S. Jackson St. (p-m)
Kosciusko, MS 39090
662-289-9211
Sales: Under $100,000
- MARTIN UKPABY (Owner) & Buys Men's Sportswear, Urban Contemporary, Dress Shirts, Footwear, Store Displays, Fixtures, Supplies

ANGIE BYRD WESTERN WEAR (WW)
286 Poole Creek Rd. (bud)
Laurel, MS 39443
601-428-7981 / Fax: 601-428-7981
Sales: $100,001-$500,000
- ANGIE BYRD (Owner) & Buys Men's Western Wear, Young Men's Western Wear, Boys' Western Wear, Western Furnishings, Accessories, Footwear, Store Displays, Fixtures, Supplies

ARTHUR'S CLOTHES SHOP (MW)
P.O. Box 1216 (m)
313 Central Ave.
Laurel, MS 39440
601-426-6637
Sales: $100,001-$500,000
- ARTHUR FROHMAN (Owner) & Buys Men's Suits, Tailored Jackets, Tailored Slacks, Big & Tall Men's Wear, Sportswear, Sweaters, Sport Shirts, Outer Jackets, Furnishings, Dress Shirts, Accessories, Ties, Robes, Underwear, Hosiery, Headwear, Belts, Leather Apparel, Footwear, Store Displays, Fixtures, Supplies

PLAZA CHILDREN'S SHOPPE (KS)
904 Parkside Plz. (m-b)
Laurel, MS 39440
601-426-9500
- IRENE WELLS (Owner) & Buys 8 to 20 Boys' Wear, Footwear, Boys' Urban Contemporary, Store Displays, Fixtures, Supplies

SMITH & SON, INC. (CLO)
316 Front St. (p-m)
Laurel, MS 39440
601-426-9744 / Fax: 601-426-9743
Sales: $100,001-$500,000
- MARTHA McCRANEY (Co-Owner) & Buys Men's Sportswear, Furnishings, Accessories, Footwear, Young Men's Wear, Urban Contemporary, Boys' Wear, Store Displays, Fixtures, Supplies
- SAM McCRANEY (Co-Owner) & Buys Men's Sportswear, Furnishings, Accessories, Footwear, Young Men's Wear, Urban Contemporary, Boys' Wear, Store Displays, Fixtures, Supplies
- WAYNE McCRANEY (Co-Owner) & Buys Buy Men's Sportswear, Furnishings, Accessories, Footwear, Young Men's Wear, Urban Contemporary, Boys' Wear, Store Displays, Fixtures, Supplies

TOM CAT, INC. (CLO)
(CALICO CAT)
P.O. Box 2633 (m-b)
Laurel, MS 39442
601-425-2505 / Fax: 601-425-2506
Sales: $1 Million-$10 Million
- CHUCK EDWARDS (Owner) & Buys Men's Sportswear, Sweaters, Sport Shirts, Coats, Outer Jackets, Leather Apparel, Casual Slacks, Ties, Underwear, Hosiery, Belts, Fragrances, Store Displays, Fixtures, Supplies

COHEN'S DEPARTMENT STORE (DEPT)
224 Court Sq. (m)
Lexington, MS 39095
662-834-2083
Sales: $100,001-$500,000
PHIL COHEN (Owner) & Buys Men's, Young Men's & Boys' Wear, Sportswear, Furnishings, Footwear, Big & Tall Men's Wear, Store Displays, Fixtures, Supplies

PERRY'S DEPARTMENT STORE (DEPT)
112 S. Church (p-m-b)
Louisville, MS 39339
662-773-5353 / Fax: 662-773-8200
Sales: $500,000-$1 Million
ODIE R. KEEN (Co-Owner) & Buys Men's Sportswear, Leather Apparel, Furnishings, Headwear, Accessories, Footwear, Young Men's & Boys' Wear, Store Displays, Fixtures, Supplies

VINCENT'S CLOTHIER (MW-4)
5154 Main St. (m-b)
Lucedale, MS 39452
601-947-7462 / Fax: 601-947-7402
CRAIG VINCENT (Owner) & Buys Men's Sportswear, Furnishings, Headwear, Accessories, Footwear, Young Men's Wear, 8 to 20 Boys' Wear, Store Displays, Fixtures, Supplies
LISA SMITH (Mgr.) & Buys Men's Sportswear, Furnishings, Headwear, Accessories, Footwear, Young Men's Wear, 8 to 20 Boys' Wear, Store Displays, Fixtures, Supplies

SPRINGER DRY GOODS (DG)
P.O. Box 189 (p-m)
Hwy. 15
Maben, MS 39750
662-263-8144 / Fax: 662-263-4611
J. O. SPRINGER, SR. (Owner) & Buys Store Displays, Fixtures, Supplies
J.O. SPRINGER, JR. (Mgr.) & Buys Western Wear, Men's Work Clothes, Furnishings, Accessories, Footwear

MEADOR'S (MW)
111 S. Main St. (m-b-h)
Magee, MS 39111
601-849-3521 / Fax: 601-849-3521
TOMMY MEADOR (Owner) & Buys Men's Formal Wear, Custom Suits, Sportswear, Furnishings, Accessories, Store Displays, Fixtures & Supplies

DELTA UNIFORM CO. (SP)
225 E. Main St. (m-b)
P.O. Box 348
Marks, MS 38646
662-326-4321 / Fax: 662-326-4320
Sales: $500,001-$1 Million
MINDY LIPSON (President)
ALVA CLARK-Men's Footwear, Leather Goods, Apparel, Accessories, Suits, Uniforms

POCKET PLEASERS (KS)
(PANG ENTERPRISES)
250 Main St. (m-b)
Marks, MS 38646
662-326-6097
Sales: $100,001-$500,000
TEDFORD PANG (Co-Owner) & Buys 8 to 20 Boys' Wear, Sportswear, Headwear, Hosiery, Footwear, Store Displays, Fixtures, Supplies
STACY PANG (Co-Owner) & Buys 8 to 20 Boys' Wear, Sportswear, Headwear, Hosiery, Footwear, Store Displays, Fixtures, Supplies

HI-FASHIONS (MW)
1722 Smithdale (p-m-b)
McComb, MS 39648
601-684-5099 / Fax: 601-684-5099
JIM KHALAF (Owner) & Buys Men's Wear, Footwear, Headwear, Accessories, Store Displays, Fixtures, Supplies
ELIZABETH KHALAF-Men's Wear, Footwear, Headwear, Accessories, Store Displays, Fixtures, Supplies

OUR GANG (CLO)
Edgewood Mall (m-b)
1722 Smithfield Rd.
McComb, MS 39648
601-684-7302 / Fax: 601-684-7347
PHILLIP PATRICK (Co-Owner) & Buys Men's Wear, Sportswear, Furnishings, Leather Apparel, Footwear, Headwear, Accessories, Young Men's Wear, Store Displays, Fixtures and Supplies
KATHY PATRICK (Co-Owner) & Buys Men's Wear, Sportswear, Furnishings, Leather Apparel, Footwear, Headwear, Accessories, Young Men's Wear, Store Displays, Fixtures and Supplies

PIKE COUNTY CO-OP (DG)
P.O. Box 937 (m)
McComb, MS 39649
601-684-1651 / Fax: 601-684-0057
Sales: $1 Million-$10 Million
THOMAS TULAR (Mgr.)
AMGELA FAIRCHILD-Men's Work Clothes, Western Wear, Gloves, Hats, Belts, Overcoats, Footwear, Store Displays, Fixtures, Supplies

STEPHENS' (CLO)
210 N. Main St. (m)
Mendenhall, MS 39114
601-847-2611 / Fax: 601-847-6637
LLOYD STEPHENS (Owner) & Buys Men's Wear, Sportswear, Leather Apparel, Furnishings, Accessories, Casual Shoes, Dress Shoes, Young Men's Wear, Urban Contemporary, Store Displays, Fixtures, Supplies

HARRY MAYER, INC. (MW)
P.O. Box 2827 (b)
2115 5th St.
Meridian, MS 39302
601-693-1135 / Fax: 601-693-1158
Sales: $1 Million-$10 Million
HARRY MAYER, JR. (President) & Buys Men's & Young Men's Wear, Sportswear, Furnishings, Accessories, Leather Apparel, Footwear, Store Displays, Fixtures, Supplies

LOEB'S, INC. (MW)
2209 Front St. (m-b)
Meridian, MS 39301
601-482-4004 / Fax: 601-482-7599
ROBERT LOEB (Owner) & Buys Men's Wear, Footwear, Accessories, Store Displays, Fixtures, Supplies

SAM'S FASHION (MW)
2301 5th St. (m)
Meridian, MS 39301
601-693-2731 / Fax: 601-581-4555
Sales: $500,000-$1 Million
SAM DABIT (Owner) & Buys Men's Overcoats, Suits, Tailored Jackets, Tailored Slacks, Sweaters, Sport Shirts, Outer Jackets, Leather Apparel, Casual Slacks, Active Apparel, Dress Shirts, Ties, Underwear, Gloves, Belts, Big & Tall Men's Wear, Urban Contemporary, Footwear, Headwear
TERRE BARFIELD (Mgr.) & Buys Men's Overcoats, Suits, Tailored Jackets, Tailored Slacks, Sweaters, Sport Shirts, Outer Jackets, Leather Apparel, Casual Slacks, Active Apparel, Dress Shirts, Ties, Underwear, Gloves, Belts, Big & Tall Men's Wear, Urban Contemporary, Footwear, Headwear

SAPPINGTON'S, INC. (MW)
102 W. Bankhead (m)
New Albany, MS 38652
662-534-4041 / Fax: 662-534-4041
TOMMY SAPPINGTON (Owner) & Buys Men's Jeans, Shirts, Belts, Boys' Jeans, Shirts, Store Displays, Fixtures, Supplies

VAN-ATKINS OF NEW ALBANY (CLO-2)
100 W. Bankhead St. (bud-m)
New Albany, MS 38652
662-534-5012 / Fax: 662-534-5012
Sales: $1 Million-$10 Million
CHUCK COOPER (Owner) & Buys Men's Jewelry

MISSISSIPPI - Newton

FELDMAN'S, INC. (CLO-10)

109 S. Main St. (p)
Newton, MS 39345
601-683-2864 / Fax: 601-683-7001

DAVID FELDMAN (Partner) & Buys Men's, Young Men's & Boys' Outerwear, Sportswear, Furnishings, Headwear, Accessories, Footwear, Store Displays, Fixtures, Supplies

LEE FELDMAN (Partner) & Buys Men's, Young Men's & Boys' Outerwear, Sportswear, Furnishings, Headwear, Accessories, Footwear, Store Displays, Fixtures, Supplies

GORDON FASHION (CLO)

2144 W. Jackson Ave. (m)
Oxford, MS 38655
662-234-7315 / Fax: 662-234-7315

TIMOTHY GORDON (Owner) & Buys Men's & Boys' Wear, Urban Contemporary, Store Displays, Fixtures, Supplies

THE J.E. NEILSON CO. (DEPT)

119 Court House Sq. (m)
Oxford, MS 38655
662-234-1161 / Fax: 662-234-1167
Sales: $1 Million-$10 Million
Website: www.neilsons1839.com

WILL LEWIS (Owner & Gen. Mgr.) & Buys Store Displays, Fixtures and Supplies

LARRY BRYSON-Men's Sportswear, Furnishings, Accessories

PAT MONTGOMERY-Infant to Size 20 Boys' Wear

NOEL MONTGOMERY-Footwear

NATIONAL MENSWEAR OF OXFORD (MW)

2313 Jackson Ave. West
Oxford, MS 38655
662-234-4204 / Fax: 662-236-9659

JERRY FRANKLIN (Owner) & Buys Men's Accessories, Hosiery, Ties, Furnishings

BARGAIN ANNEX (MW)

733 Delmas Ave. (b)
Pascagoula, MS 39567
228-762-9199 / Fax: 228-762-3071
Website: www.theclothingplace.com

JOE STOUT (President & Owner) & Buys Men's Wear, Accessories, Furnishings, Headwear, Hosiery, Underwear, 8 to 20 Boys' Wear

MONTIE'S SPORTING GOOD, INC. (SG)

2147 Market St. (h)
Pascagoula, MS 39567
228-762-7534 / Fax: 228-762-7405

MONTIE RICHARDS (President & Owner)

BILL DENTON (G.M.M.) & Buys Men's Wear, Sportswear, Active Apparel

CAPITAL MENSWEAR (MW-2)

3040 Hwy. 80 (m)
Pearl, MS 39208
601-932-2323 / Fax: 601-932-3743

BOB POLLARD (Owner)

RON MARTIN (Mgr.) (@ 601-957-3700) & Buys Men's Wear, Sportswear, Big & Tall Men's Wear, Furnishings, Headwear, Accessories, Young Men's Wear, Store Displays, Fixtures, Supplies

MIKE POLLARD-Men's Wear, Sportswear, Big & Tall Men's Wear, Furnishings, Headwear, Accessories, Young Men's Wear, Store Displays, Fixtures, Supplies

STEVE'S ON THE SQUARE (MW)

415 Center Ave. (h)
Philadephia, MS 39350
601-656-5056 / Fax: 601-656-9309

STEVE WILKERSON (President & Owner) & Buys Men's Wear

MICHAEL'S (DEPT)

29 S. Main St. (m-b)
Pontotoc, MS 38863
662-489-4311 / Fax: 662-489-4343
Sales: $100,001-$500,000

MICHAEL SIMON (President) & Buys Men's Wear, Sportswear, Furnishings, Headwear, Accessories, Leather Apparel, Young Men's & Boys' Wear, Accessories, Footwear, Store Displays, Fixtures, Supplies

WILLIAM WHITE (Mgr.) & Buys Men's Wear, Sportswear, Furnishings, Headwear, Accessories, Leather Apparel, Young Men's & Boys' Wear, Accessories, Footwear, Store Displays, Fixtures, Supplies

APPLES LTD., INC. (CLO)

512 S. Main St. (m-b)
Poplarville, MS 39470
601-795-4546 / Fax: 601-795-4941

ROBERT APPLEWHITE (Owner) & Buys Men's Sportswear, Leather Jackets, Furnishings, Accessories, Footwear, Young Men's & Boys' Wear, Store Displays, Fixtures, Supplies

TRADITIONAL JEWELERS, INC. (JWLY-5)

1200 E. County Line Rd., Suite 224
Ridgeland, MS 39157
601-956-2388 / Fax: 601-956-4495
Sales: $1 Million-$10 Million

ROBERT MONTGOMERY (President) & Buys Jewelry, Watches

DAVID CAPTON-Jewelry, Watches

VERNON MONTGOMERY-Jewelry, Watches

R.L. AARON'S, INC. (DEPT-3)

1005 Broadway (bud-p)
Shelby, MS 38774
662-398-5191 / Fax: 662-398-7470
Sales: $1 Million-$10 Million

R. L. AARON (Owner)

SAM M. ROSENTHAL-Men's, Young Men's & Boys' Wear, Sportswear, Leather Apparel, Furnishings, Headwear, Accessories, Footwear, Store Displays, Fixtures, Supplies

ROYAL'S WESTERN STORE (WW)

P.O. Box 520 (p)
1135 Hwy. 28
Soso, MS 39480
601-729-2143 / Fax: 601-729-2143
Sales: $100,001-$500,000

REON WAED (Owner) & Buys Men's Western Wear, Young Men's Western Wear, Boys' Western Wear, Accessories, Footwear, Headwear, Store Displays, Fixtures, Supplies

COWBOY CORNER SADDLERY & WESTERN WEAR (WW)

3698 Goodman Rd. East (m-b)
South Haven, MS 38672
662-349-3267 / Fax: 662-890-3987
Website: www.thecowboycorner.com

CHARLES TACKETT (Co-Owner) & Buys Men's Western Wear & Sportswear, Western Dress Shirts, Hosiery, Western Headwear, Accessories, Footwear, Young Men's Wear, Boys' Wear, Store Displays, Fixtures, Supplies

TERESA TACKETT (Co-Owner) & Buys Men's Western Wear & Sportswear, Western Dress Shirts, Hosiery, Western Headwear, Accessories, Footwear, Young Men's Wear, Boys' Wear, Store Displays, Fixtures, Supplies

GEORGE SHERMAN CLOTHIERS, INC. (MW)

100 Russell St. (b)
Starkville, MS 39759
662-323-2324 / Fax: 662-323-2326
Sales: $500,000-$1 Million

GEORGE SHERMAN (Owner) & Buys Men's Sportswear, Furnishings, Leather Apparel, Accessories, Urban Contemporary, Footwear, Headwear, Store Displays, Fixtures, Supplies

THE LODGE (SP)

408 S. Dale Ctr.
Starkville, MS 39759
662-324-1597 / Fax: 662-324-6923
Website: www.thelodgeonline.com

JOHN HENDRICKS (Owner) & Buys Active Apparel, Athletic Footwear, Licensed Apparel, Headwear, Underwear, Hosiery

SMITH & BYARS (MW)

122 Main St. (p)
Starkville, MS 39759
662-323-5793

SAMMY SMITH (Owner) & Buys Men's Sportswear, Leather Apparel, Furnishings, Accessories, Footwear, Store Displays, Fixtures, Supplies

McCULLAR, LONG & McCULLOUGH (MW)

108 S. Spring (b)
Tupelo, MS 38801
662-842-4165 / Fax: 662-844-9512
Website: www.mlmclothiers.com

JIMMY LONG (President) & Buys Men's Wear, Sportswear, Furnishings, Small Leather Goods, Fragrances, Accessories, Footwear, Store Displays, Fixtures, Supplies

JOE YARBER (V.P.) & Buys Men's Wear, Sportswear, Furnishings, Small Leather Goods, Fragrances, Accessories, Footwear, Store Displays, Fixtures, Supplies

R.W. REED CO., INC. (CLO-4)

P.O. Box 230 (m-b)
110 Elizabeth St.
Tupelo, MS 38801
662-840-0224 / Fax: 662-844-8254
Sales: $1 Million-$10 Million

JACK R. REED (President)

JOHN RUSH-Men's Apparel, Accessories

MORRIS MCCAIN-Boys' Footwear, Men's Footwear

TOM GREEN-Men's Apparel

KRISTA BLANDARD-Jewelry

RAGS FOR MEN, INC. (CLO)

807 Harrison (b)
Tupelo, MS 38801
662-842-3061 / Fax: 662-844-3199

JILL ESTES (Owner) & Buys Men's Wear, Sportswear, Leather Apparel, Furnishings, Accessories, Footwear, Store Displays, Fixtures, Supplies

SIMMONS' DEPARTMENT STORE (DEPT)

737 Beulah Ave. (m)
Tylertown, MS 39667
601-876-3636 / Fax: 601-876-6808
Sales: $100,001-$500,000

J. W. CRAFT (Owner) & Buys Men's Wear, Leather Apparel, Sportswear, Furnishings, Headwear, Accessories, Young Men's & Boys' Wear, Footwear, Store Displays, Fixtures, Supplies

CHARLES' DEPARTMENT STORE (DEPT)

1314 Washington St. (m)
Vicksburg, MS 39180
601-636-2725
Sales: $500,000-$1 Million

CHARLES ABRAHAM (Owner) & Buys Men's Suits, Tailored Jackets, Tailored Slacks, Raincoats, Sportswear, Sweaters, Sport Shirts, Outer Jackets, Casual Slacks, Active Apparel, Furnishings, Accessories, Big & Tall Men's Wear, Young Men's Leather Apparel, Footwear, Store Displays, Fixtures

THE HUB, INC. (CLO)

P.O. Box 1026 (b)
1312 Washington St.
Vicksburg, MS 39180
601-636-5011 / Fax: 601-636-5159
Sales: $1 Million-$10 Million

JOHN WAYNE JABOUR (President & Co-Owner) & Buys Men's & Young Men's Wear, Footwear, Accessories, Hosiery, Outerwear, Sportswear, Activewear, Store Displays, Fixtures, Supplies

AMZI TAHMES (Co-Owner) & Buys Men's & Young Men's Wear, Footwear, Accessories, Hosiery, Outerwear, Sportswear, Activewear, Store Displays, Fixtures, Supplies

ON-TIME FASHIONS OF VICKSBURG (MW)

1411 Washington St. (m)
Vicksburg, MS 39188
601-638-3493 / Fax: 601-638-3493

ELLIS RANTISI (Owner) & Buys Men's Wear, Boys' Pants & Suits, Shirts, Footwear, Store Displays, Fixtures, Supplies

LOLLY POP SHOP (KS)

703 Station St. (m-b)
Waynesboro, MS 39367
601-735-3411
Sales: $100,001-$500,000

BARBARA SIGLER (Owner) & Buys To Size 7 Boys' Wear, Footwear, Store Displays, Fixtures, Supplies

NU LOOK FASHIONS (CLO)

211 E. Main St. (m-b)
West Point, MS 39773
662-494-8254 / Fax: 662-494-7427

BILAL KADOOS (Owner) & Buys Men's & Boys' Wear, Footwear, Store Displays, Fixtures, Supplies

BLACK & WHITE STORES, INC. (CLO-4)

236 S. Main St. (bud-p-m)
Yazoo City, MS 39194
662-746-1671 / Fax: 662-746-2571
Sales: $1 Million-$10 Million

JAMES CHISOLM (President) & Buys Store Displays, Fixtures, Supplies

JOHN CHISHOLM (V.P.) & Buys Men's Suits, Big & Tall Men's Wear, Furnishings, Belts, Small Leather Goods, Sportswear, Men's Sweaters, Sport Shirts, Outer Jackets, Casual Slacks, Accessories, Footwear, Boys' Wear, Footwear, Store Displays, Fixtures and Supplies

NELDA CHISHOLM (Secy. & Treas.) & Buys Men's Suits, Big & Tall Men's Wear, Furnishings, Belts, Small Leather Goods, Sportswear, Men's Sweaters, Sport Shirts, Outer Jackets, Casual Slacks, Accessories, Footwear, Boys' Wear, Footwear, Store Displays, Fixtures and Supplies

RICHARD TURNER MENSWEAR (MW)
1504 Main St. (m)
Bethany, MO 64424
660-425-8162
Sales: $100,001-$500,000
RICHARD K. TURNER (Owner) & Buys Men's Suits, Tailored Jackets, Tailored Slacks, Sportswear, Sweaters, Sport Shirts, Outer Jackets, Leather Apparel, Furnishings, Accessories, Casual Slacks, Active Apparel, Dress Shirts, Ties, Underwear, Hosiery, Gloves, Belts, Footwear, Young Men's Wear, Urban Contemporary, 8 & Up Boys' Wear, Store Displays, Fixtures, Supplies

HORTON'S, INC. (CLO-3)
110 E. Jackson St. (p-m)
Bolivar, MO 65613
417-326-7194 / Fax: 417-777-7290
Sales: $100,001-$500,000
CAROLYN HORTON (V.P.) & Buys Men's Sweaters, Sport Shirts, Outer Jackets, Casual Slacks, Active Apparel, Furnishings, Belts, Small Leather Goods, Young Men's Wear, Boys' Wear, Big & Tall Men's Wear
JERRY HORTON (Co-Owner) & Buys Store Displays, Fixtures, Supplies

DULANEY FARMERS' STORE, INC. (DEPT)
209 Kansas Ave. (p)
Bosworth, MO 64623
660-534-7719
Sales: $100,001-$500,000
SUE DULANEY (Owner) & Buys Men's Work Clothes, Underwear, Belts, Footwear, Store Displays, Fixtures, Supplies

REISH (CLO)
120 S. Commercial St. (bud-p-m)
Branson, MO 65616
417-334-3634
Sales: $100,001-$500,000
JOE REISH (Co-Owner)
BARBARA REISH (Co-Owner) & Buys Men's Footwear, Boys' Footwear, Store Displays, Fixtures, Supplies

H. TOOEY MERCANTILE CO., INC. (MW)
304 N. Main St. (m)
Brookfield, MO 64628
660-258-2542 / Fax: 660-258-2716
Sales: $100,001-$500,000
WILLIAM J. DORSEY (President) & Buys Men's Overcoats, Suits, Tailored Jackets, Tailored Slacks, Raincoats, Sportswear, Sweaters, Sport Shirts, Outer Jackets, Casual Slacks, Active Apparel, Furnishings, Dress Shirts, Ties, Robes, Underwear, Hosiery, Gloves, Headwear, Belts, Accessories, Small Leather Goods, Men's Big & Tall Wear, Young Men's Wear, Footwear, Store Displays, Fixtures, Supplies

R & J SHOES & APPAREL, INC. (MW & FW)
1008 W. Dallas St. (p-m-b)
Buffalo, MO 65622
417-345-2720
Sales: $100,001-$500,000
RALPH ROLLER, JR. (Co-Owner) & Buys Sport Shirts, Outer Jackets, Casual Shirts, Active Apparel, Dress Shirts, Belts, Western Wear, Dress Shoes, Casual Shoes, Athletic Footwear, Slippers, Boots, Moccasins, Store Displays, Fixtures, Supplies
SHEILA ROLLER (Co-Owner) & Buys Sport Shirts, Outer Jackets, Casual Shirts, Active Apparel, Dress Shirts, Belts, Western Wear, Dress Shoes, Casual Shoes, Athletic Footwear, Slippers, Boots, Moccasins, Store Displays, Fixtures, Supplies

SMITH'S READY TO WEAR (CLO)
212 W. Grand Ave. (p)
Campbell, MO 63933
573-246-2241
Sales: $100,001-$500,000
BETTY SMITH (Co-Owner) & Buys Men's Sportswear, Sweaters, Sport Shirts, Outer Jackets, Casual Slacks, Active Apparel, Furnishings, Small Leather Goods, Store Displays, Fixtures, Supplies
COY SMITH (Co-Owner) & Buys Men's Sportswear, Sweaters, Sport Shirts, Outer Jackets, Casual Slacks, Active Apparel, Furnishings, Small Leather Goods, Store Displays, Fixtures, Supplies

GARBER'S MENSWEAR (MW)
Town Plaza Shopping Ctr. (b)
Cape Girardeau, MO 63703
573-335-2837
Sales: $500,000-$1 Million
RODNEY BRIDGES (Owner) & Buys Men's Overcoats, Suits, Tailored Jackets, Tailored Slacks, Tuxedos, Sportswear, Accessories, Furnishings, Footwear, Young Men's Wear, Store Displays, Fixtures, Supplies

GUY'S BIG & TALL, INC. (MW)
2136 William St. (m-b)
Cape Girardeau, MO 63703
573-334-0007 / Fax: 573-335-6657
Sales: $100,001-$500,000
CURT JOHNS (President) & Buys Men's Big & Tall Clothing, Store Displays, Fixtures, Supplies

CARL'S MENSWEAR, INC. (CLO)
20 S. Folger St. (p-m-b)
Carrollton, MO 64633
660-542-2344 / Fax: 660-542-2244
CARL MAIS (Owner) & Buys Men's & Young Men's Wear, Tuxedos, Footwear, Store Displays, Fixtures, Supplies

GLOBE CLOTHING STORE (MW)
315 Ward Ave. (m)
Caruthersville, MO 63830
573-333-4006
JOHN SELLERS (Owner) & Buys Men's Wear, Footwear, Store Displays, Fixtures, Supplies

JAN'S FASHION (SP)
105 W. 8th St.
Cassville, MO 65625
417-847-4671
JAN SHORE (Co-Owner) & Buys Men's & Boys' Active Apparel, Accessories, Footwear, Store Displays, Fixtures & Supplies
CHARLES SHORE (Co-Owner) & Buys Men's & Boys' Active Apparel, Accessories, Footwear, Store Displays, Fixtures & Supplies
EVELYN RIDDLE (Co-Owner) & Buys Men's & Boys' Active Apparel, Accessories, Footwear, Store Displays, Fixtures & Supplies
VERDAYNE RIDDLE (Co-Owner) & Buys Men's & Boys' Active Apparel, Accessories, Footwear, Store Displays, Fixtures & Supplies

ANGELL'S WESTERN WEAR AND MORE (WW)
107 N. Allen St. (m-b)
Centralia, MO 65240
573-682-2555
Sales: $500,000-$1 Million
LUTHER ANGELL (Owner) & Buys Men's Western Wear, Overcoats, Suits, Tailored Jackets, Tailored Slacks, Raincoats, Sweaters, Sport Shirts, Outer Jackets, Leather Apparel, Casual Slacks, Active Apparel, Dress Shirts, Ties, Underwear, Hosiery, Gloves, Headwear, Belts, Jewelry, Footwear

KNICKERBOCKER CLOTHING (MW)
14358 S. Outer 40 (m)
Chesterfield, MO 63017
314-439-1700 / Fax: 314-439-1701
DAVID KARNEY (Owner) & Buys Men's Big & Tall Apparel, Men's Boys' Apparel, Men's Formalwear, Men's Accessories, Men's Hosiery, Men's Suits

LIFE UNIFORM SHOPS, INC. (SP-291)
(ANGELICA Corp.)
424 S. Woods Rd. (bud-p-m-b)
Chesterfield, MO 63017
314-854-3800 / Fax: 314-889-1140
Sales: $50 Million-$100 Million
Website: www.lifeuniform.com
DENIS RAAB (President)
JOAN DIETRICH (V.P. & G.M.M.)
BRUCE DAVIDSON (V.P.-Opers.)
MARK DUVE (V.P.-Real Estate)
DIANE PILGRIM (Controller)
STEVE BORGMEYER (Dir.-HR)
MIKE JULIAN (Mgr.-Info. Sys.)
DONNA PAGE-Footwear
DENISE PAGANO-Men's Apparel, Men's Uniforms
DONNA PAGE-Men's Apparel, Men's Uniforms

MARATHON SPORTS (SP)
13453 Chesterfield Plz.
Chesterfield, MO 63017
314-434-9577 / Fax: 314-434-9193
Sales: $100,001-$500,000
JERRY KOKESH (Owner) & Buys Running Gear, Running Shoes, Accessories

BEEMER'S (MW)
605 Locust St. (m)
Chillicothe, MO 64601
660-646-1306
JAMES BEEMER (Owner) & Buys Men's Overcoats, Suits, Raincoats, Tailored Slacks, Sportswear, Dress Shirts, Underwear, Hosiery, Accessories, Swimwear, Store Displays, Fixtures, Supplies

CUMMINGS' MENSWEAR, INC. (MW)
113 W. Franklin St. (m)
Clinton, MO 64735
660-885-8322 / Fax: 660-885-6810
DAVID CUMMINGS (Owner) & Buys Men's Overcoats, Suits, Tailored Jackets, Tailored Slacks, Raincoats, Sportswear, Furnishings, Accesssories, Big & Tall Men's Wear, Store Displays, Fixtures, Supplies

PUCKETTS SPORTSMAN'S OUTFITTER (MW & SP)
906 E. Broadway (m-b)
Columbia, MO 65201
573-443-8777 / Fax: 573-875-3960
DALE PUCKETT (Owner) & Buys Men's Wear, Sportswear, Dress Shirts, Underwear, Hosiery, Accessories, Swimwear, Footwear, Store Displays, Fixtures, Supplies

TIGER SPIRIT (SP)
(T & T Enterprises)
111 S. 9th St.
Columbia, MO 65201
573-449-0608 / Fax: 573-875-2625
MICHELLE DILLARD (Owner) & Buys Active Apparel

PIONEER WESTERN WEAR & MORE (WW & OL)
130 E. Main St.
Fredericktown, MO 63645
573-783-2821
SHIRLEY ASLINGER-Men's Western Wear, Hats, Boots, Suits, Sport Coats, Formalwear

ZIM'S CLOTHING (MW)
525 Court St. (m-b)
Fulton, MO 65251
573-642-6466
Sales: $100,001-$500,000
J.W. ZIMMERMAN (Owner) & Buys Footwear
DEBBIE McINTIRE-Men's Wear, Boys' Jeans, Casual Shirts, Store Displays, Fixtures, Supplies

CURTIS DEPARTMENT STORE (DEPT-4)
26 Court Sq. (m-b)
Gainesville, MO 65655
417-679-3913 / Fax: 417-683-6460
Sales: $100,001-$500,000
Website: www.curtisstore.com
DAVID QUACKENBUSCH (Co-Owner) (@ 417-683-4554) & Buys Men's Sportswear, Footwear, Jeans, Boys' Jeans, Tops, Underwear, Hosiery, Urban Contemporary, Store Displays, Fixtures, Supplies
KEREY QUACKENBUSCH (Co-Owner) (@ 417-683-4554) & Buys Men's Sportswear, Footwear, Jeans, Boys' Jeans, Tops, Underwear, Hosiery, Urban Contemporary, Store Displays, Fixtures, Supplies

ELBERT DEPARTMENT STORE (DEPT)
104 W. Grand Ave. (p-m)
Gallatin, MO 64640
660-663-3541
Sales: $100,001-$500,000
SPENCE ELBERT (President) & Buys Men's Sportswear, Furnishings, Footwear, Store Displays, Fixtures, Supplies
JUDY ELBERT (V.P.) & Buys Men's Sportswear, Furnishings, Footwear, Store Displays, Fixtures, Supplies

TREEHOUSE (CLO)
418 N. Main St. (p)
Granby, MO 64844
417-472-6325 / Fax: 417-472-7158
JOHN STYRON (Co-Owner) & Buys Men's & Boys' Jeans, Shirts, T-shirts, Active Wear, Footwear, Store Displays, Fixtures, Supplies
BETH STYRON (Co-Owner) & Buys Men's & Boys' Jeans, Shirts, T-shirts, Active Wear, Footwear, Store Displays, Fixtures, Supplies

HICKMAN MILLS OUTDOOR SALES (MW)
1327 Main St. (p)
Grandview, MO 64030
816-761-0200 / Fax: 816-761-0214
Sales: $1 Million-$10 Million
JAMES KENNEDY (President) & Buys Footwear, Store Displays, Fixtures, Supplies
DIAN POUSH-Men's Work Clothes, Underwear, Hosiery, Gloves, Belts

ALL SPORT (SP)
2713 Cantrell Rd.
Harrisonville, MO 64701
816-380-3339 / Fax: 816-887-4717
Sales: $100,001-$500,000
JOHN ABNOS (Owner) & Buys Activewear, Athletic Footwear, Athletic Apparel, Licensed Apparel, Team Uniforms

KRAMER'S CLOTHING (MW)
1915 Main St. (m)
Higginsville, MO 64037
660-584-2352
BETTY KRAMER (President) & Buys Men's Overcoats, Suits, Tailored Jackets, Tailored Slacks, Raincoats, Sportswear, Sweaters, Sport Shirts, Outer Jackets, Casual Slacks, Active Apparel, Furnishings, Headwear, Accessories, Men's Big & Tall Wear, Young Men's Wear, Boys' Jeans, Store Displays, Fixtures, Supplies
KRIS KRAMER (G.M.M.) & Buys Men's Overcoats, Suits, Tailored Jackets, Tailored Slacks, Raincoats, Sportswear, Sweaters, Sport Shirts, Outer Jackets, Casual Slacks, Active Apparel, Furnishings, Headwear, Accessories, Men's Big & Tall Wear, Young Men's Wear, Boys' Jeans, Store Displays, Fixtures, Supplies
BOB BECK (Mgr.) & Buys Men's Overcoats, Suits, Tailored Jackets, Tailored Slacks, Raincoats, Sportswear, Sweaters, Sport Shirts, Outer Jackets, Casual Slacks, Active Apparel, Furnishings, Headwear, Accessories, Men's Big & Tall Wear, Young Men's Wear, Boys' Jeans, Store Displays, Fixtures, Supplies

C & H WESTERN WEAR (WW)
2914 High Ridge Blvd. (m)
High Ridge, MO 63049
636-677-0000
Sales: $100,001-$500,000
CONNIE JETER (President & Owner) & Buys Men's, Young Men's & 8 & Up Boys' Western Wear, Urban Contemporary, Related Furnishings, Headwear, Accessories, Boots, Moccasins, Store Displays, Fixtures, Supplies

MISSOURI - Independence

WESTERN ARMY STORE (AN)
103 W. Lexington Ave. (m)
Independence, MO 64050
816-252-4038 / Fax: 816-836-5666
ABE YODLER (Owner) & Buys Men's & Boys' Jeans, Shirts, Hosiery, Footwear, Work Wear, Boots, Store Displays, Fixtures, Supplies
BRIAN YODLER-Men's & Boys' Jeans, Shirts, Hosiery, Footwear, Work Wear, Boots, Store Displays, Fixtures, Supplies

HOUSE OF BARGAINS (DEPT)
5505 Bus. 50 West (p)
Jefferson City, MO 65109
573-893-2020 / Fax: 573-893-5831
Sales: $1 Million-$10 Million
CAREY BOGG (President) & Buys Men's Sweaters, Sport Shirts, Outer Jackets, Leather Apparel, Casual Slacks, Active Apparel, Furnishings, Headwear, Accessories, Store Displays, Fixtures, Supplies
CAROL OTT-Men's Sweaters, Sport Shirts, Outer Jackets, Leather Apparel, Casual Slacks, Active Apparel, Furnishings, Headwear, Accessories, Store Displays, Fixtures, Supplies
DEBBIE SMITH-Footwear

ANDERSON'S WESTERN WEAR (WW)
505 N. Range Line Rd. (m-b)
Joplin, MO 64801
417-623-3066 / Fax: 417-206-9973
JOANNE ANDERSON (Owner) & Buys Men's & Boys' Western Wear, Footwear, Store Displays, Fixtures, Supplies

THE CLOSET (MW-3 & OL & MO)
(ELAN CLOTHIERS)
(THE ATTIC)
(THE DUDS SHOP)
2724 Main St. (b)
Joplin, MO 64804
417-624-2197 / Fax: 417-624-9131
ROB EDMOND (Co-Owner) & Buys Men's Overcoats, Suits, Sweaters, Sport Shirts, Casual Slacks, Active Apparel, Dress Shirts, Ties, Hosiery, Belts, Young Men's & Boys' Wear, Footwear, Store Displays, Fixtures, Supplies
ELAINA EDMOND (Co-Owner) & Buys Men's Overcoats, Suits, Sweaters, Sport Shirts, Casual Slacks, Active Apparel, Dress Shirts, Ties, Hosiery, Belts, Young Men's & Boys' Wear, Footwear, Store Displays, Fixtures, Supplies

AMERICAN FORMAL & BRIDAL (CLO)
1331 Main St.
Kansas City, MO 64105
816-221-7971 / Fax: 816-421-1717
Website: www.kctux.com
BEN PENNER (Owner) & Buys Men's Tuxedos & Formal Accessories, Footwear, Store Displays, Fixtures, Supplies

GARRY GRIBBLE'S SPORTS (SP-2)
8600 Ward Pkwy.
Kansas City, MO 64114
816-363-4800 / Fax: 816-822-0101
Sales: $1 Million-$10 Million
GARRY GRIBBLE (Owner) & Buys Athletic Footwear, Running Apparel

HALL'S FINE GIFTS (CLO-2)
200 E. 25th St. (m-b-h)
Kansas City, MO 64108
816-274-8111 / Fax: 816-274-4471
Sales: $10 Million-$50 Million
ROBERT LEITSTEIN (President & C.E.O.)
DON RODGERS (Display Mgr.) & Buys Store Displays, Fixtures, Supplies
AL LEINEN-Men's Overcoats, Suits, Tailored Jackets, Tailored Slacks, Raincoats, Young Men's
TODD EPPERLEY-Men's Sportswear, Furnishings, Headwear, Accessories, Belts, Small Leather Goods
STEFFENIE YATES-Fragrances
SUSY DAMON-Footwear

HAROLD PENER MENSWEAR (MW-24)
1801 E. 63rd St. (p-m)
Kansas City, MO 64130
816-363-6262 / Fax: 816-822-8038
HAROLD PENER (President) & Buys Men's Wear, Sportswear, Accessories, Furnishings, Young Men's & Boys' Wear
DAVID PENER (V.P.) & Buys Men's Wear, Sportswear, Accessories, Furnishings, Young Men's & Boys' Wear, Urban Contemporary
BARRY PENER (V.P. & Real Estate Contact) & Buys Footwear

IMAGERY, INC. (CLO)
4117 Pennsylvania Ave. (m-b)
Kansas City, MO 64111
816-531-8222 / Fax: 816-756-1441
AL CRUMLY (Owner) & Buys Men's Overcoats, Sport Coats, Sweaters, Sport Shirts, Casual Slacks, Active Apparel, Hosiery, T-shirts, Ties, Belts, Fragrances, Jewelry, Small Leather Goods, Store Displays, Fixtures, Supplies

JACKSON TRENT (MW)
(PINSTRIPES)
601 W. 48th St.
Kansas City, MO 64112
816-531-3355 / Fax: 816-531-3389
JACK RING (Owner) & Buys Men's Wear, Furnishings, Accessories, Footwear

KANSAS CITY POLO PARTNERS, INC. (CLO)
410 Nichols Rd. (b)
Kansas City, MO 64112
816-753-5010 / Fax: 816-931-5771
RICK BREHM (Mgr.) & Buys Men's Overcoats, Suits, Tailored Jackets, Tailored Slacks, Raincoats, Sportswear, Furnishings, Accessories, Boys' Sweats, Sport Shirts, Casual Slacks, T-shirts, Leather Apparel, Active Apparel, Dress Shirts, Tailored Jackets, Outer Jackets, Hosiery, Footwear, Store Displays, Fixtures, Supplies
NOTE-Store Carries Only Ralph Lauren Apparel

MICHAEL'S CLOTHING CO., INC. (MW)
1830 Main St. (b-des)
Kansas City, MO 64108
816-221-0000 / Fax: 816-221-0014
Sales: $1 Million-$10 Million
Website: www.michaelsclothing.com
EUGENE L. NOVORR (Chmn.)
KEITH NOVORR (President) & Buys Men's Wear, Sweaters, Sportshirts, Outer Jackets, Fragrances, Ties, Robes, Footwear, Belts, Boys' Suits, Store Displays, Fixtures, Supplies
BOB MOORE-Dress Shirts, Hosiery
DAVE JOHNSON-Underwear, Shoes
LES NICHOLS-Headwear

UNIVERSITY OF MISSOURI - KANSAS CITY BOOKSTORE (SP)
(UNIVERSITY OF MISSOURI)
5000 Rock Hill Rd.
Kansas City, MO 64110
816-235-2665 / Fax: 816-235-1443
Sales: Under $100,000
CHAD STIPH (Mgr.) & Buys Activewear, Fleece, Jackets, Hosiery

DOYNE'S MENSWEAR (MW)
107 South Side Sq. (m)
Kennett, MO 63857
573-888-9656
DOYNE GATEWOOD (Owner) & Buys Men's Suits, Tailored Jackets, Tailored Slacks, Sportswear, Furnishings, Hardware, Accessories, Footwear, Store Displays, Fixtures, Supplies

SIEREN'S PALACE (CLO-8)
(OLD TOWNE CLOTHING)
(MELISSA'S CLOSET)
202 1/2 S. Franklin St. (m-b)
Kirksville, MO 63501
660-665-6820 / Fax: 660-665-3064
HERBERT SIEREN (President) & Buys Men's Sportswear, Outerwear, Boys' Sportswear, Outerwear, Store Displays, Fixtures, Supplies

MISSOURI - Kirksville

TROESTER'S CLOTHING (MW)
120 S. Franklin St. (m-b)
Kirksville, MO 63501
660-665-6416 / Fax: 660-665-0977
Sales: $500,000-$1 Million
KENT TROESTER (Co-Owner) & Buys Men's Overcoats, Suits, Tailored Jackets, Tailored Slacks, Raincoats, Sportswear, Sweaters, Sport Shirts, Outer Jackets, Leather Apparel, Casual Slacks, Active Apparel, Furnishings, Dress Shirts, Ties, Robes, Underwear, Hosiery, Gloves, Headwear, Accessor
JOHN TROESTER (Co-Owner) & Buys Men's Overcoats, Suits, Tailored Jackets, Tailored Slacks, Raincoats, Sportswear, Sweaters, Sport Shirts, Outer Jackets, Leather Apparel, Casual Slacks, Active Apparel, Furnishings, Dress Shirts, Ties, Robes, Underwear, Hosiery, Gloves, Headwear, Accessor

ALPINE SHOP LTD. (CLO-3 & SG & OL)
440 N. Kirkwood Rd. (m-b)
Kirkwood, MO 63122
314-962-7715 / Fax: 314-962-7718
Website: www.alpineshop.com
RUSSELL HOLLENBECK (Owner) & Buys Men's Sweaters, Sport Shirts, Outer Jackets, Casual Slacks, Active Apparel, Thermal Underwear, Headwear, Young Men's Wear, Boys' Ski Wear, Footwear, Store Displays, Fixtures, Supplies

ROBERTS' DEPARTMENT STORE (DEPT)
1019 Gulf St. (m)
Lamar, MO 64759
417-682-2237 / Fax: 417-682-2237
Sales: $100,001-$500,000
DAVID ROBERTS (Owner) & Buys Men's Sportswear, Dress Shirts, Underwear, Hosiery, Jewelry, Small Leather Goods, Boys' Wear, Store Displays, Fixtures, Supplies

SUN & FUN (CLO)
213 Hwy. 5 North (m)
Laurie, MO 65038
573-374-6226
JAN LEE (Owner) & Buys Men's Sport Shirts, Swimwear, Shorts, Store Displays, Fixtures, Supplies

CLARKS MENSWEAR (MW)
P.O. Box 151 (m)
102 N. Jefferson St.
Lebanon, MO 65536
417-532-6560
RICHARD CLARK (Owner) & Buys Men's Sportswear, Furnishings, Store Displays, Fixtures, Supplies

BRANTS' MEN'S & BOYS' WEAR (MW)
15 E. Kansas Ave. (p)
Liberty, MO 64068
816-781-6234 / Fax: 816-781-6235
RALPH BRANT, JR. (Owner) & Buys Men's Overcoats, Suits, Tailored Jackets, Tailored Slacks, Raincoats, Sportswear, Sweaters, Sport Shirts, Outer Jackets, Leather Apparel, Furnishings, Casual Slacks, Active Apparel, Dress Shirts, Ties, Robes, Underwear, Hosiery, Gloves, Headwear, Accessories, Belts, Jewelry, Small Leather Goods, Boys' Wear, Store Displays, Fixtures, Supplies

SICKREY'S DEPARTMENT STORE (DEPT)
205 Main St. (m)
Lilbourn, MO 63862
573-688-2541
ROGER SICKREY (Owner) & Buys Men's Sweaters, Sport Shirts, Outer Jackets, Casual Slacks, Active Apparel, Furnishings, Boys' Wear, Urban Contemporary, Store Displays, Fixtures, Supplies

UNCLE SAM'S SAFARI OUTFITTERS, INC. (AN-3 & OL)
14218 Manchester Rd.
Manchester, MO 63011
636-394-2888 / Fax: 636-394-6927
Website: www.unclesams.com
MIKE DYER-Hunting Apparel, Boots

WALLIS FAMILY STORE (CLO)
P.O. Box 918 (p-m-b)
130 1st St.
Marble Hill, MO 63764
573-238-4485
Sales: $100,001-$500,000
MARY E. WALLIS (Owner) & Buys Men's Wear, Boys' Tops, Jeans, Underwear, Men's Workwear, Hosiery, Footwear, Store Displays, Fixtures, Supplies

MURRAY'S STORE (DEPT)
118 N. Kansas Ave. (m)
Marceline, MO 64658
660-376-3332
Sales: $100,001-$500,000
VEDA WHITE (Owner) & Buys Men's Tailored Jackets, Tailored Slacks, Raincoats, Sweaters, Sport Shirts, Outer Jackets, Casual Slacks, Active Apparel, Dress Shirts, Ties, Robes, Underwear, Hosiery, Gloves, Headwear, Belts, 7 & Up Boys' Wear, Sportswear, Footwear, Store Displays, Fixtures, Supplies

FIELDS CLOTHING OF MARYVILLE (MW)
103 E. 4th St. (m)
Maryville, MO 64468
660-582-2861 / Fax: 660-582-3367
SUE HILSABECK (Co-Owner) & Buys Men's Overcoats, Suits, Tailored Jackets, Tailored Slacks, Raincoats, Sportswear, Furnishings, Accessories, Big & Tall Men's Wear, Store Displays, Fixtures, Supplies

COOK'S MEN'S STORE (MW)
116 S. Market St. (b)
Memphis, MO 63555
660-465-2511 / Fax: 660-465-8905
Sales: $500,001-$1 Million
JOHN S. COOK (Owner) & Buys Men's Overcoats, Suits, Tailored Jackets, Tailored Slacks, Raincoats, Big & Tall Men's Wear, Sportswear, Sweaters, Sport Shirts, Outer Jackets, Leather Apparel, Casual Slacks, Active Apparel, Dress Shirts, Ties, Robes, Underwear, Hosiery, Gloves, Belts

HAGAN CLOTHING CO., INC. (MW)
100 N. Jefferson Ave. (m)
Mexico, MO 65265
573-234-1115 / Fax: 573-581-3032
Sales: $500,000-$1 Million
JOHN HAGAN (President) & Buys Men's Overcoats, Suits, Tailored Jackets, Tailored Slacks, Raincoats, Leather Apparel, Sweaters, Sport Shirts, Outer Jackets, Casual Slacks, Active Apparel, Dress Shirts, Ties, Robes, Underwear, Hosiery, Gloves, Headwear, Belts, Jewelry, Small Leather Goo

DUVAL - REID CLOTHING CO., INC. (MW)
318 W. Reed St. (p-m)
Moberly, MO 65270
660-263-6326 / Fax: 660-263-6724
Sales: $100,001-$500,000
BILL REID, JR (President) & Buys Men's Overcoats, Suits, Tailored Jackets, Tailored Slacks, Raincoats, Sportswear, Furnishings, Headwear, Accessories, Footwear, Store Displays, Fixtures, Supplies
REGINA REID (Secy. & Treas.) & Buys Men's Overcoats, Suits, Tailored Jackets, Tailored Slacks, Raincoats, Sportswear, Furnishings, Headwear, Accessories, Footwear, Store Displays, Fixtures, Supplies

BROWNSBERGER'S (CLO)
313 Broadway (p-m)
Monett, MO 65708
417-235-7227 / Fax: 417-235-1155
Sales: $100,001-$500,000
MICHAEL J. BROWNSBERGER (Owner) & Buys Men's Tuxedos, Footwear, Store Displays, Fixtures, Supplies

MANSFIELD'S CLOTHING (MW)
P.O. Box 3 (p)
316 Broadway
Monett, MO 65708
417-235-3143
CHARLES ROWELL (Owner) & Buys Men's Wear, Furnishings, Store Displays, Fixtures, Supplies

CIRCLE M WESTERN STORE (WW-3 & OL)

(CIRCLE C WESTERN STORE)
9805 E. 20th St. (b)
Mountain Grove, MO 65711
417-926-3320 / Fax: 417-926-3037
Website: www.cmdwesternwear.com

DON ANDERSON (Owner) & Buys Men's & Boys' Western Wear, Footwear, Boots, Store Displays, Fixtures, Supplies

RICHARDS BROTHERS OF MOUNTAIN GROVE (DEPT)

P.O. Box 866 (b)
Mountain Grove, MO 65711
417-926-4168 / Fax: 417-926-6303

WELLS RICHARDS (Owner) & Buys Men's Overalls, Jeans, Store Displays, Fixtures, Supplies

FELDMAN BROTHERS, INC. (CLO-4)

304 N. 2nd St.
Odessa, MO 64076
816-633-5538 / Fax: 816-230-8374

DAN FELDMAN (Owner) (@ 816-792-3348) & Buys Men's Work Clothes, Jeans, Western Wear, Footwear, Store Displays, Fixtures and Supplies

BLAIR'S LANDING (CLO-1)

5845 Hwy. 54
Osage Beach, MO 65065
573-348-5101 / Fax: 573-348-2260
Sales: $500,000-$1 Million

JUDY BLAIR (Co-Owner) & Buys Men's Small Leather Goods, Fragrances, Footwear, Store Displays, Fixtures and Supplies

ALAN BLAIR (Co-Owner) & Buys Men's Overcoats, Sportswear, Robes, Ties, Belts, Young Men's Wear, Footwear, Store Displays, Fixtures, Supplies

BUCHHEIT, INC. (DEPT-5 & OL)

(CENTRAL STATE WHOLESALE DISTRIBUTORS)
33 PCR 540 (bud)
Perryville, MO 63775
573-547-1010 / Fax: 573-547-1689
Website: www.buchheitonline.com

TIM BUCHHEIT (President)

ANGIE GEILE-Men's Sportswear, Furnishings, Accessories, Footwear, Boys' Wear, Young Men's Wear, Store Displays, Fixtures, Supplies

ROZIER MERCANTILE CO., INC. (DEPT)

P.O. Box 150 (p)
2 E. St. Marie's St.
Perryville, MO 63775
573-547-6521 / Fax: 573-547-8090

JOHN W. LOTTES (Mgr. & Corp. Secy.) & Buys Store Displays, Fixtures, Supplies

JIM LOTTES (Mgr.) & Buys Men's, Young Men's & Boys' Wear, Footwear, Store Displays, Fixtures, Supplies

SKIP LOTTES-Store Displays, Fixtures, Supplies

COLEMAN'S SHOE & CLOTHING (CLO & FW)

101 N. Main St. (b)
Piedmont, MO 63957
573-223-7530 / Fax: 573-223-3201
Sales: $100,001-$500,000

AL R. COLEMAN (Owner) & Buys Men's Suits, Tailored Jackets, Tailored Slacks, Sportswear, Sweaters, Sport Shirts, Leather Apparel, Furnishings, Belts, Jewelry, Small Leather Goods, Young Men's & Boys' Clothing, Sportswear, Furnishings, Accessories, Footwear, Store Displays, Fixtures, Supplies

PINE VALLEY WESTERN STORE (CLO)

P.O. Box 73600 (p)
Rt. 3
Potosi, MO 63664
573-438-3210

DORIS BOURBAN (Owner) & Buys Men's Western Shirts, Store Displays, Fixtures, Supplies

H.E. WARREN & SONS, INC. (CLO)

P.O. Box 686 (p-m)
Pine & McClurg
Richland, MO 65556
573-765-3381
Sales: $100,001-$500,000

MARGARET WARREN (Owner) & Buys Men's Sweaters, Sport Shirts, Outer Jackets, Casual Slacks, Active Apparel, Furnishings, Boys' Wear, Footwear, Store Displays, Fixtures, Supplies

THRO CLOTHING CO. (MW)

229 N. Main St. (p-m)
Saint Charles, MO 63301
636-724-0132 / Fax: 636-724-1777

J. MAURICETHRO, JR. (President) & Buys Men's Overcoats, Suits, Tailored Jackets, Tailored Slacks, Raincoats, Sportswear, Sweaters, Sport Shirts, Outer Jackets, Leather Apparel, Casual Slacks, Active Apparel, Furnishings, Headwear, Belts, Men's Big & Tall Suits, Boys' Wear, Footwear, Store Displays, Fixtures, Supplies

FRANK NETSCH (Secy.) & Buys Men's Overcoats, Suits, Tailored Jackets, Tailored Slacks, Raincoats, Sportswear, Sweaters, Sport Shirts, Outer Jackets, Leather Apparel, Casual Slacks, Active Apparel, Furnishings, Headwear, Belts, Men's Big & Tall Suits, Boys' Wear, Footwear, Store Displays, Fixtures, Supplies

LEIBOWITZ, INC. (MW)

3831 Frederick Ave. (m-b)
Saint Joseph, MO 64506
816-279-7481 / Fax: 816-279-7471
Sales: $500,000-$1 Million

MARSHALL WRIGHT (President) & Buys Men's Overcoats, Suits, Tailored Jackets, Tailored Slacks, Raincoats, Sportswear, Apparel, Furnishings, Headwear, Accessories, Footwear, Store Displays, Fixtures, Supplies

ST. JOE BOOT CO., INC. (CLO)

3749 Pacific St. (b)
Saint Joseph, MO 64507
816-232-8128 / Fax: 816-279-9678

CAROL CROWSER (Owner)

KELLY SMITH (Mgr.) & Buys Men's, Young Men's, 8 to 20 Boys' Wear, Western Wear, Related Furnishings, Accessories, Headwear, Boots, Moccasins, Store Displays, Fixtures, Supplies

ST. JOSEPH TENNIS & SWIM CLUB (SP)

3107 N. Belt Hwy.
Saint Joseph, MO 64506
816-233-0261
Sales: $500,001-$1 Million

RON SELKIRK (Mgr.) & Buys Tennis Apparel, Related Footwear

OBBIE BARRY-Tennis Apparel

ASHER'S CLOTHING & SHOE CO. (MW & FW)

2907 N. Kingshighway Blvd. (b)
Saint Louis, MO 63115
314-367-5100 / Fax: 314-361-6562
Sales: $1 Million-$10 Million

ASH ROHRA (President) & Buys Men's Sportswear, Furnishings, Accessories, Young Men's Wear, Urban Contemporary, Boys' Wear, Footwear

ANGELA ASH (G.M.M.) & Buys Men's Sportswear, Furnishings, Accessories, Young Men's Wear, Urban Contemporary, Boys' Wear, Footwear

MISSOURI - Saint Louis

B & L STYLE SHOP (MW)

5635 Delmar Blvd. (m)
Saint Louis, MO 63112
314-361-1398

FRANK BARBER (Co-Owner)
LOUIS OXENHANDLER (Co-Owner) & Buys Men's Suits, Tailored Jackets, Tailored Slacks, Sportswear, Furnishings, Headwear, Accessories, Footwear, Store Displays, Fixtures, Supplies

BOXERS (MW)

310 N. Euclid Ave. (m-b)
Saint Louis, MO 63108
314-454-0209

BEVERLY RUSSINA (Owner) & Buys Men's Furnishings, Store Displays, Fixtures, Supplies

BROWN SHOE COMPANY, INC. (FW-1300 & OL)

(F.X. LASALLE)
(FACTORY BRAND SHOE)
(FAMOUS FOOTWEAR)
(NATURALIZER)
P.O. Box 29 (bud-p-m-b-des)
8300 Maryland Ave.
Saint Louis, MO 63105
314-854-4000 / Fax: 314-854-4274
Sales: Over $1 Billion
Website: www.brownshoe.com
Retail Locations: MO, NY, AL, AZ, AR, CA, CO, CT, DE, FL, GA, ID, IL, IN, IA, KS, KY, LA, ME, MD, MA, MI, MN, MS, MO, MT, NE, NV, NJ, NM, NY, NC, ND, OH, OK, OR, PA, RI, SC, SD, TN, TX, VA, WA, WV, WI

RONALD A. FROMM (Chairman & C.E.O.)
JOE WOOD (President-Famous Footwear)
BRYON D. NORFLEET (President-Naturalizer Div.)
GARY M. RICH (Pres.-Brown Shoe Wholesale Div.)
ANDREW M. ROSEN (C.F.O. & Treas. Brown Shoe)
DAVID HANNEBRINK (Sr. V.P. & G.M.M.-Men's Footwear)
DAVID H. SCHWARTZ (Sr. V.P.-Opers., Brown Shoe/Brown Intl.)
MICHAEL L. OBEFLANDER (V.P. & Gen. Counsel)
TOM TALBOT (V.P., & Real Estate Contact-Naturalizer) (@ 314-854-4035)
RICHARD SCHUMACHER (V.P. & Controller)
PAUL SHAPIRO, SR. (V.P. & G.M.) & Buys Boys' Footwear

CRUISIN' USA (CLO & MO & OL)

10285 Bach Blvd. (bud-p-m)
Saint Louis, MO 63132
314-426-4886 / Fax: 314-426-1713
Sales: $1 Million-$10 Million
Website: www.cruisinusa.com

ALAN SPETNER (President)
HELEN SPETNER (V.P.-Opers.)
ROB SPETNER (Sls. Mgr.)

DILLARD'S DEPARTMENT STORES, INC. - ST. LOUIS DIV. (DEPT-70 & MO & OL)

145 Crestwood Plz. (m-b)
Saint Louis, MO 63126
314-968-5890 / Fax: 314-301-6796
Website: www.dillards.com
Retail Locations: MA, ID, UT, CO, OK, NE, IA, IL, IN, KS, TX, CA, NV, AZ, NM, AR, WY, MI, FL, AL, MS, LA, TN, SC, NC, VA, OH, KY

JOE BRENNAN (President)
JOSEPH STORY (V.P. & Const. Mgr. & Real Estate Contact)
RON WIGGINS (G.M.M.-Men's)
MIKE SHIELDS (D.M.M.-Men's Clothing & Furnishings)
MICHAEL GASTMAN-Denim Shorts, Levi's, Tommy Hilfiger, Polo, Guess & Nautica Denim
STACEY ALBRACHT-Big & Tall Men's Wear, Men's Coordinates
WENDY TAGGART-Men's Advanced Sportswear, Perry Ellis, Claiborne For Men, Guess Classics, Calvin Klein, Joseph Abboud, Esprit, Golf Wear
ANGIE SKRIVIN-Men's Collections, Polo, Nautica, Private Label
MARTIN WARREN-Men's Outerwear, Activewear, Leather Apparel, Sportswear, Logo Swimwear, Sweaters, Outdoor Apparel, Knit Sport Shirts, Shorts & Casual Slacks
JAMIE SCHERER (@ 480-736-2030)-Belts, Accessories, Small Leather Goods
KAY WHITE (@ 501-301-3945)-Men's Gloves, Scarves
JOANIE HOUX (@ 817-831-5166)-Men's Robes, Pajamas

MIKE BOWMAN (D.M.M.) & Buys Children's Wear
CAREY FILER (@ 314-301-6890)-8 to 20 Boys' Moderate Clothing, Sportswear, Furnishings
MICHELLE HENDRIX-Accessories
HENRY BERRY-3 to 7 Boys

NOTE:-Men's Suits & Tailored Wear, Dress Shirts, Ties, Underwear, Hosiery Are Bought at DILLARD'S, Little Rock, AR-See Listing

FAMOUS - BARR (DEPT-43)

(L. S. AYRES)
(THE JONES STORE)
(MAY DEPARTMENT STORES)
601 Olive St. (bud-p-m-b-h)
Saint Louis, MO 63101
(May Merchandising Corp.)
314-444-3111 / Fax: 314-444-3401
Sales: $1.2 Billion
Website: www.maycompany.com
Retail Locations: AZ, AK, AZ, AR, CA, CO, CT, DE, DC, FL, GA, HI, ID, IL, IN, IA, KS, KY, LA, ME, MD, MA, MI, MN, MS, MO, MT, NE, NV, NH, NJ, NM, NY, NC, ND, OH, OK, OR, PA, RI, SC, SD, TN, TX, UT, VT, VA, WA, WV, WI, WY

IRA PICKELL (President & C.E.O.)
DWAYNE VAUGHN (Real Estate Contact-Famous - Barr & Foley's) (@ 314-342-6798)
PAUL GRZYMKOWSKI (Sr. V.P. & G.M.M.-Men's & Boys')

RICK McCLEW (D.M.M.-Men's Furnishings, Clothing & Pants)
OPEN-Men's Slacks, Sports Coats, Overcoats, Tailored Jackets, Tailored Slacks, Raincoats, Footwear
JIM ROCCO-Men's Dress Shirts
HACKER PLOTKIN-Men's Sport Shirts, Outer Jackets, Leather Apparel
DAN PALAS-Men's Suits, Neckwear
OPEN-Men's Robes, Underwear, Hosiery
MIKE LIBBIE-Men's Accessories, Small Leathers, Sunglasses, Headwear

JOHN FROELICH (D.M.M.-Men's Sportswear) & Buys Collections
DAVE KNIPPLE-Men's Sport Shirts, Outer Jackets, Leather Apparel
CHARLIE HOLMES-Men's Sweaters, Men's Wear, Knit Sport Shirts
ANDREW DAVIS-Modern & Denim Collection
JOE ALEXANDER-Men's Active Apparel, Active Sportswear

PHIL SALVATO (D.M.M.-Young Men's & Boys') (@ 314-444-2689)
HOLLY SESTAK-Size 8 to 20 Boys' Active Tops Collections
JESSICA ROCH-Size 8 to 20 Boys' Furnishings, Accessories, Outer Jackets, Casual Slacks
KRISTIN KOZOR-Young Men's Active Apparel, Knits, Sportswear, Urban Contemporary, Boys' 8 to 20 Denim

SANDY FLANNIGIN (V.P.-Visual Mdse.) & Buys Store Displays, Fixtures, Supplies

MISSOURI - Saint Louis

GELBER'S MENSWEAR, INC. (MW)

1001 Washington Ave. (p)
Saint Louis, MO 63101
314-421-6698
Sales: $100,001-$500,000

BEN GELBER (Owner) & Buys Men's Wear, Urban Contemporary, Store Displays, Fixtures, Supplies

GOODMAN MERCANTILE CO. (MW)

1314 Washington Ave. (p-m)
Saint Louis, MO 63103
314-231-1363 / Fax: 314-231-1365
Sales: $1 Million-$10 Million

SAM GOODMAN (Owner) & Buys Men's Boys' Wear
HARTLEY GOODMAN-Men's Sportswear, Furnishings, Footwear, Store Displays, Fixtures, Supplies

JOE'S CLOTHING (MW)

5757 Natural Bridge Rd. (m-b)
Saint Louis, MO 63120
314-389-8200 / Fax: 314-381-9480
Sales: $1 Million-$10 Million

RANDY KENT (President)
JON MILLER (V.P.) & Buys Footwear, Store Displays, Fixtures, Supplies, Men's & Young Men's Wear

LEE J. CLOTHING (CLO)

389 N. Euclid Ave.
Saint Louis, MO 63108
314-367-2303 / Fax: 314-361-4810

LEE JOHNSON (Owner) (@ 314-614-4849) & Buys Men's Casual Wear, Belts, Ties, Hosiery, Sunglasses, Jewelry

MAY DEPARTMENT STORES CO. (DEPT-428)

(FAMOUS-BARR)
(FILENE'S)
(FOLEY'S)
(HECHT'S)
(KAUFMANN'S)
(L.S. AYERS)
(MEIER & FRANK)
(ROBINSONS-MAY)
(STRAWBRIDGE)
611 Olive St.
Saint Louis, MO 63101
314-342-6300 / Fax: 314-342-4461
Sales: Over $1 Billion
Website: www.maycompany.com
Retail Locations: AZ, AK, AZ, AR, CA, CO, CT, DE, DC, FL, GA, HI, ID, IL, IN, IA, KS, KY, LA, ME, MD, MA, MI, MN, MS, MO, MT, NE, NV, NH, NJ, NM, NY, NC, ND, OH, OK, OR, PA, RI, SC, SD, TN, TX, UT, VT, VA, WA, WV, WI, WY

EUGENE KAHN (Chmn. & C.E.O.)
CAROL WILLIAMS (President - May Dept. Stores Intl.)
JAY LEVITT (President-May Mdse. Co.)
JUDITH K. HOFER (C.E.O.-May Mdse. Co.)
DWAYNE VAUGHN (Real Estate Contact) (@ 314-342-6798)
RODNEY HANES (Real Estate Contact) (@ 314-342-6609)

MAY MERCHANDISING CORP. (CBO-439)

(MAY DEPARTMENT STORES CO.)
615 Olive St.
Saint Louis, MO 63101
314-554-7100 / Fax: 314-554-7650
Website: www.maycompany.com

EUGENE S. KAHN (Chmn. & C.E.O.-May Cos.)
JAY H. LEVITT (C.E.O.-MMC/MDSI)
JAY LEVITT (President)
GARY BOYSON (Sr. V.P. & G.M.M.) & Buys Men's, Young Men's, Boys' Sportswear
JASON STEVENS-Men's Collections
GREG KREDELL-Men's & Women's Sweaters
DION PULLAM-Men's Knitwear
MARK ZION-Men's Pants
JIM LEAHY (D.M.M.-Men's Sportswear)
RON KATANICK-Men's Activewear
TOM WINEBRENNER-Dress Shirts & Neckwraps
DEBBIE MURTHA (Sr. V.P. & G.M.M.-Fragrances/Cosmetics)
ANN JOOS-Men's Fragrances
KIRK HANSELMAN-Furnishings & Men's Clothing
TOM STOFFEL (D.M.M.-Footwear)
CURT EASTER-Boys' Footwear, Men's Footwear
MARK CLARK (D.M.M.-Young Men's)
JOHN KRUEGER-Jeans Collections
DAVID FLOOD-Young Men's Apparel & Tops
SARAH LAVELLE-Boys' 8 to 20
TIM SAMSAL-Boys' 8 to 20 Bottoms & Young Men's Bottoms

ROBERTS' BOYS' SHOP, INC. (KS)

9733 Clayton Rd. (m)
Saint Louis, MO 63124
314-997-1770 / Fax: 314-997-3518

DAVE ROBERTS (Owner) & Buys Boys' 4 to 20 Sportswear, Outerwear, Knitwear, Hosiery, Furnishings, Footwear, Store Displays, Fixtures, Supplies

RUNNING CENTER OF ST. LOUIS, INC. (SP)

9430 Manchester Rd.
Saint Louis, MO 63119
314-961-2647 / Fax: 314-961-0454
Sales: $500,001-$1 Million
Website: www.runningcenterstl.com

KENT BOHLING (Owner) & Buys Activewear, Athletic Footwear

MISSOURI - Saint Louis

SAM CAVATO, INC. (MW)
265 Plaza Frontenac (b)
Saint Louis, MO 63131
314-997-1100 / Fax: 314-997-1904
SAM CAVATO (Owner) & Buys Men's Suits, Tailored Jackets, Tailored Slacks, Sportswear, Furnishings, Accessories, Footwear, Store Displays, Fixtures, Supplies
PAUL JOSEPH (Mdse. Mgr.) & Buys Men's Suits, Tailored Jackets, Tailored Slacks, Sportswear, Furnishings, Accessories, Footwear, Store Displays, Fixtures, Supplies

SPORTSPRINT, INC. (SP-3)
6197 Bermuda Dr.
Saint Louis, MO 63135
314-521-9000 / Fax: 314-521-0395
Sales: $2 Million-$5 Million
Website: www.sportsprint.com
RALPH ROCKAMANN, JR. (President & G.M.M.) & Buys Licensed Apparel, Activewear, Athletics

SUPERDOME (MW-4)
(MJP ENTERPRISES CORP.)
29 N. Oaks Plz. (p)
Saint Louis, MO 63121
314-383-3484 / Fax: 314-383-0367
GARY PAK (President) & Buys Men's Suits, Tailored Slacks, Raincoats, Sportswear, Big & Tall Men's Wear, Sweaters, Sport Shirts, Leather Apparel, Casual Slacks, Active Apparel, T-shirts, Dress Shirts, Ties, Underwear, Hosiery, Gloves, Headwear, Belts, Jewelry, Small Leather Goods, Fragrances, Footwear, Size 7 & Up Boys' Wear, Shorts, Urban Contemporary

TCC CLOTHIERS (MW)
(MISTER GUY)
9817 Clayton Rd.
Saint Louis, MO 63124
314-991-5262 / Fax: 314-692-2041
TERRY FELUMB (Co-Owner) & Buys Men's Wear, Clothing, Furnishings, Accessories, Footwear
CARLA FELUMB (Co-Owner) & Buys Men's Wear, Clothing, Furnishings, Accessories, Footwear

VURRO CLOTHIERS, INC. (MW)
209 Kirkwood (b)
Saint Louis, MO 63122
314-965-1878 / Fax: 314-965-4946
MICHAEL VURRO (Owner) & Buys Men's Wear, Store Displays, Fixtures, Supplies

WOODY'S, INC. (MW)
10411 Clayton Rd., #104 (b)
Saint Louis, MO 63131
314-569-3272 / Fax: 314-569-3572
Sales: $500,001-$1 Million
MAURICE ERWIN (President) & Buys Leather Goods, Men's Apparel, Men's Big & Tall Apparel, Men's Casualwear, Men's Designer Apparel, Men's Formalwear, Men's Accessories, Men's Hosiery, Men's Outerwear, Men's Sportswear, Men's Suits, Men's Swimwear

WELLER'S MENSWEAR, INC. (MW)
3113 W. Broadway (m-b)
Sedalia, MO 65301
660-826-4719 / Fax: 660-827-3250
KENNETH WELLER (President) & Buys Men's Formal Wear, Suits, Sportswear, Outerwear, Western Wear, Footwear, Men's Big & Tall Wear, Store Displays, Fixtures, Supplies
CAROL WELLER (V.P.) & Buys Men's Formal Wear, Suits, Sportswear, Outerwear, Western Wear, Footwear, Men's Big & Tall Wear, Store Displays, Fixtures, Supplies

FALKOFF'S OF SIKESTON, INC. (MW)
118 E. Front St. (p-m)
Sikeston, MO 63801
573-471-9331 / Fax: 573-471-1325
Sales: $500,000-$1 Million
DAVID FRIEDMAN (Treasurer) & Buys Men's Overcoats, Suits, Tailored Jackets, Tailored Slacks, Raincoats, Sweaters, Sport Shirts, Outer Jackets, Casual Slacks, Active Apparel, Furnishings, Headwear, Accessories, Big & Tall Men's Wear, Young Men's Wear, Footwear, Store Displays, Fixtures, Su

LINDA'S WESTERN STORE (WW)
483 Western Dr. (m-b)
Sikeston, MO 63801
573-471-4677
LINDA WEST (Owner) & Buys Men's & Boys' Western Wear, Footwear, Store Displays, Fixtures, Supplies

BUSY BEE DEPARTMENT STORE (DEPT & OL)
2920 S. Glenstone Ave. (p)
Springfield, MO 65804
417-823-7410 / Fax: 417-823-7411
Website: www.busybeestores.com
MARK ROSEN (Owner)
BRENDA GARDNER (Gen. Mgr.) & Buys Men's Wear, Boys' Bottoms, Tops, Underwear, Store Displays, Fixtures and Supplies
JULIE WHITE (Mgr.) & Buys Men's Wear, Tops, Underwear

E.B. & ASSOCIATES (DEPT)
(FM STORES, INC.)
1368 E. Sunshine St. (bud)
Springfield, MO 65804
417-882-9244
Sales: $100,001-$500,000
BILL ARBEITMAN (Owner) & Buys Men's Suits, Tailored Jackets, Tailored Slacks, Big & Tall Wear, Sportswear, Sweaters, Sport Shirts, Leather Apparel, Casual Slacks, Active Apparel, Dress Shirts, Ties, Underwear, Hosiery, Belts, Boys' Sportswear, Store Displays, Fixtures, Supplies

MEN'S SUIT MART, INC. (MW)
2730 S. Glenstone Ave. (m-b)
Springfield, MO 65804
417-889-7848
SANDY WHITE (Owner) & Buys Men's Suits, Overcoats, Raincoats, Tailored Jackets, Tailored Slacks, Ties, Belts, Footwear

MR. BLACKWELL'S (MW)
(MBA)
1907 S. Glenstone, #C (m-b)
Springfield, MO 65804
417-887-8200 / Fax: 417-887-5968
REX BLACKWELL (Owner) & Buys Men's Wear, Footwear

P & J BIG & TALL MEN'S SHOP (MW-3)
2738 S. Campbell Ave. (m-b)
Springfield, MO 65807
417-882-6503 / Fax: 417-882-6578
PHIL BARE (Co-Owner) & Buys Big & Tall Men's Wear, Store Displays, Fixtures, Supplies
JEAN BARE (Co-Owner) & Buys Big & Tall Men's Wear, Store Displays, Fixtures, Supplies

PFI WESTERN STORE (WW & OL)
2816 S. Ingram Mill Rd. (m-b)
Springfield, MO 65804
417-889-2668 / Fax: 417-889-7204
Sales: $1 Million-$10 Million
Website: www.pfiwestern.com
JOHNELLE LITTLE (G.M.M.) & Buys Men's Overcoats, Suits, Tailored Jackets, Tailored Slacks, Raincoats, Men's Big & Tall Wear, Sportswear, Sweaters, Sport Shirts, Outer Jackets, Leather Apparel, Casual Slacks, Active Apparel, Dress Shirts
SUIE DIECK-MEYER-Ties, Belts, Jewelry, Small Leather Goods, Fragrances, Boys' Wear
LARRY BURKS-Headwear, Saddles & Tack
PAUL PATTERSON-Footwear

RIDGE RUNNER SPORTS (SP)
3057 S. Fremont Ave.
Springfield, MO 65804
417-882-5590 / Fax: 417-881-8490
Sales: $100,001-$500,000
MARY GOSS (Owner) & Buys Athletic Footwear, Activewear

MISSOURI - Springfield

TOWN & COUNTY, INC. (CLO)

2660 S. Glenstone Ave. (b)
Springfield, MO 65804
417-883-6131 / Fax: 417-883-7271
Sales: $1 Million-$10 Million

BOB LOWE (President) & Buys Men's Overcoats, Suits, Tailored Jackets, Tailored Slacks, Raincoats, Sportswear, Sweaters, Sport Shirts, Outer Jackets, Leather Apparel, Casual Slacks, Active Apparel, Furnishings, Accessories, Footwear, Store Displays, Fixtures, Supplies

ADAM'S WESTERN STORE (WW)

P.O. Box 33 (p)
Hwys. 63 & 19 North
Thayer, MO 65791
417-264-3215

PHYLLIS ADAMS (Owner) & Buys Men's & Boys' Western Shirts, Sport Jackets, Pants, Jeans, Sport Shirts, Hosiery, Belts, Boots, Store Displays, Fixtures, Supplies

DICKEY - BUB FARM & HOME (CLO-2)

1 Union Village Shopping Ctr. (p-m)
Union, MO 63084
636-583-1177 / Fax: 636-583-6778

STEVE DICKEY (Co-Owner) & Buys Men's Wear, Sportswear, Swimwear, Furnishings, Small Leather Goods, Belts, Jewelry, Young Men's Wear & Boys' Wear, Store Displays, Fixtures, Supplies

CHAMBERS STORE (DEPT)

P.O. Box 216 (p-m)
Hwy. 63
Vienna, MO 65582
573-422-3617

ANN BAX (Owner) & Buys Men's Jeans, T-shirts, Sport Shirts, Casual Slacks, Belts, Small Leather Goods, Fragrances, Footwear, Boys' Wear, Footwear, Store Displays, Fixtures, Supplies

Q & R ENTERPRISES, INC. (CLO)

(FARM & HOME OF WARRENSBURG)
P.O. Box 63 (p-m)
Warrensburg, MO 64093
660-747-9196 / Fax: 660-747-9441
Sales: $1 Million-$10 Million

JODI TROTTER (Asst. Mgr.) & Buys Men's Jeans, Western Suits, Tailored Slacks, Raincoats, Big & Tall Men's Wear, T-shirts, Sportswear, Dress Shirts, Underwear, Hosiery, Gloves, Headwear, Belts, Small Leather Goods, Footwear, Boys' Wear, Footwear, Store Displays, Fixtures, Supplies

TAYLOR'S MENSWEAR, INC. (MW)

112 N. Main St. (m)
Webb City, MO 64870
417-673-3863
Sales: $500,000-$1 Million

TOM TAYLOR (Owner) & Buys Men's Wear, Footwear, Store Displays, Fixtures, Supplies

C & K CLOTHING (CLO)

1211 Parkway (m)
West Plains, MO 65775
417-256-6793 / Fax: 417-256-1670

JO BETH MONTGOMERY (Owner) & Buys Men's & Boys' Sportswear, Jeans, Casualwear, Accessories, Hosiery, Small Leather Goods, Belts, Store Displays, Fixtures, Supplies

MACINTYRE'S (CLO)

205 E. Park Ave. (m)
Anaconda, MT 59711
406-563-3731 / Fax: 406-563-7796
Sales: $500,001-$1 Million

STEVE FRANCISCO (Co-Owner) & Buys Men's Wear, Sportswear, Furnishings, Headwear, Accessories, Leather Apparel, Boots, Dress Shoes, Store Displays, Fixtures, Supplies

GUST'S OF BIG TIMBER (DEPT)

P.O. Box 1169 (m)
200 McLeod St.
Big Timber, MT 59011
406-932-5451 / Fax: 406-932-6310
Sales: $100,001-$500,000

VIRGIL GUST (Owner) & Buys Men's Dress Shirts, Ties, Robes, Underwear, Hosiery, Glovers, Headwear, Young Men's Wear & 8 to 20 Boys' Wear, Western Wear All Sizes, Footwear

ED GUST-Sweaters, Shorts, Shirts, Outer Jackets, Casual Slacks, Active Apparel

JANE GUST-Men's Belts, Jewelry, Small Leather Goods, Store Displays, Fixtures, Supplies

JASON'S CLOTHING STORE (MW)

2564 King Ave. West (b)
Billings, MT 59102
406-655-4300 / Fax: 406-651-4376
Sales: $500,000-$1 Million

DON ALWEIS (Owner) & Buys Men's Apparel, Footwear Store Displays, Fixtures, Supplies

SHIPTON'S BIG R (WW-3)

P.O. Box 30477 (m)
1411 3rd Ave. North
Billings, MT 59107
406-252-0503 / Fax: 406-252-7298
Website: www.shiptonsbigr.com

JAY R. CARROL (Co-Owner) & Buys Store Displays, Fixtures, Supplies

JANE DEVITT-Men's & Boys' Western Wear, Footwear

SUTTONS (CLO)

(SHALDE, INC.)
1844 Broadwater Ave. (m-b)
Billings, MT 59102
406-656-2702 / Fax: 406-656-4821

SHANNA NASON (Co-Owner) & Buys Men's Sportswear, Furnishings, Accessories, Store Displays, Fixtures, Supplies

ALLISON MICHELOTTI (Co-Owner) & Buys Men's Sportswear, Furnishings, Accessories, Store Displays, Fixtures, Supplies

TIME OUT SPORTS, INC. (SP)

1603 Grand Ave.
West Park Plz.
Billings, MT 59102
406-245-9735 / Fax: 406-245-9735

CINDY THOMPSON (Owner) & Buys Activewear, Athletic Footwear

MATT ROBERTS (G.M.M.) & Buys Activewear, Athletic Footwear

MONTANA WOOLEN SHOP LTD. (CLO)

8703 Huffine Ln. (m)
Bozeman, MT 59718
406-587-8903
Website: www.montanawoolenshop.com

PEG (Co-Owner) & Buys Slippers, Store Displays, Fixtures, Supplies, Men's & Boys' Sportswear, Furnishings

TOM (Co-Owner) & Buys Men's & Boys' Sportswear, Furnishings

NORTHERN LIGHTS TRADING CO. (CLO)

1716 W. Babcock St. (m-b-des)
Bozeman, MT 59715
406-586-2225 / Fax: 406-586-7544
Sales: $1 Million-$10 Million

MIKE GARCIA (Owner)

GREG CARACCIOLO (Gen. Mgr.) & Buys Boys' Apparel, Boys' Footwear, Men's Footwear, Leather Goods, Men's Apparel, Men's Casualwear, Men's Denim Apparel, Men's Accessories, Men's Outerwear, Men's Sportswear

DEBRA TAVERNITI (M.M.) & Buys Boys' Apparel, Boys' Footwear, Men's Footwear, Leather Goods, Men's Apparel, Men's Casualwear, Men's Denim Apparel, Men's Accessories, Men's Outerwear, Men's Sportswear

SCHNEE'S BOOTS, INC. (FW-2 & MO & OL)

(SCHNEE'S BOOTS & SHOES)
(SUNDANCE SHOES)
121 W. Main St. (m)
Bozeman, MT 59715
406-587-0981 / Fax: 406-587-2172
Sales: $1 Million-$10 Million
Website: www.schnees.com

STEVE SCHNEE (President) & Buys Boys' Footwear, Men's Footwear, Leather Goods, Men's Accessories, Men's Apparel, Hosiery

WILD WEST SHIRT CO., INC. (WW)

1400 N. Rouse Ave. (bud-p)
Bozeman, MT 59715
406-587-5133 / Fax: 406-587-5347
Sales: $1 Million-$10 Million

DON COWLES (President & Dir.-Real Estate)

LEONARD BALUSKI (Controller)

BRUCE HUNTSMAN (Mgr.-Admin.) & Buys Boys' Apparel, Men's Apparel, Men's Casualwear, Men's Sportswear

LINDA BAREFILED (Mgr.-Retail Opers.) & Buys Boys' Apparel, Men's Apparel, Men's Casualwear, Men's Sportswear

FAUGHTS, INC. (CLO)

P.O. Box 670 (p)
133 W. Central Ave.
Browning, MT 59417
406-338-2275 / Fax: 406-338-7609
Sales: $500,000-$1 Million

BRIAN ELLIOTT (Owner) & Buys Store Displays, Fixtures, Supplies

ANN ELLIOTT (G.M.M.) & Buys Men's Sportswear, Furnishings, Accessories, Boys' Wear

JILL HEIL-Footwear

MOSES FOR MEN, INC. (MW)

Butte Plaza Mall (b)
3100 Harrison St.
Butte, MT 59701
406-494-5168

JOE MOSES (Owner) & Buys Men's Wear, Young Men's Wear, Store Displays, Fixtures, Supplies

RICHARDS & ROCHELLE MEN'S STORE, INC. (MW)

17 N. Main St. (m)
Butte, MT 59701
406-782-1761 / Fax: 406-782-1761
Sales: $100,001-$500,000

ERNEST C. RICHARDS, JR. (President) & Buys Men's Wear, Sportswear, Furnishings, Accessories

ERNEST C. RICHARDS, SR.-Men's Wear, Sportswear, Furnishings, Accessories, Store Displays, Fixtures and Supplies

THOMAS FAMILY APPAREL (CLO)

3636 Harrison Ave. (b)
Butte, MT 59701
406-494-2959 / Fax: 406-494-1744
Sales: $1 Million-$10 Million

PAUL F. THOMAS (President) & Buys Men's Sportswear, Furnishings, Headwear, Accessories, Young Men's Wear, Urban Contemporary, Boys' Wear 6 & Up, Infant Footwear, Store Displays, Fixtures, Supplies

MONTANA - Butte

WEIN'S, INC. (MW)
37 W. Park St. (m)
Butte, MT 59701
406-782-1208 / Fax: 406-782-1209
Sales: $500,000-$1 Million
Website: www.weinsonline.com
JOEL A. BROUDY (President) & Buys Men's Sportswear, Furnishings, Robes, Accessories, Headwear, Footwear, Store Displays, Fixtures, Supplies

KITSON'S (CLO)
100 1st St. North (m-b)
Cascade, MT 59421
406-468-2721
GLEN KITSON (Owner) & Buys Men's Sweaters, Sport Shirts, Outer Jackets, Casual Slacks, Active Apparel, Western Wear, Belts, Underwear, Hosiery

NORMAN'S WESTERN WEAR, INC. (WW)
601 W. Main St. (m)
Cutbank, MT 59427
406-873-5313 / Fax: 406-873-5317
DOUG NORMAN (Owner) & Buys Men's & Boys' Western Wear, Boots, Store Displays, Fixtures, Supplies

YANKEE JIM TRADING POST (WW)
P.O. Box 127 (m-b-h)
Gardner, MT 59030
406-848-7234
WADE LAUBACH (Co-Owner) & Buys Men's Western Wear, Sportswear, Furnishings, Headwear, Accessories, Young Men's Wear, 8 to 20 Boys' Wear, Big & Tall Men's Wear, Leather Apparel, Footwear, Store Displays, Fixtures, Supplies
KIRK LAUBACH (Co-Owner) & Buys Store Displays, Fixtures, Supplies

C.S.W.W. (CLO-4)
(BIG R STORES)
P.O. Box 6430 (p)
4800 10th Ave. South
Great Falls, MT 59405
406-761-6623 / Fax: 406-761-1504
CHARLES SCHMIDT (Owner)
GENE WIKE (G.M.M.) & Buys Men's Work Clothes, Boots

KAUFMAN'S MENSWEAR CENTRE (MW)
411 Central Ave. (b)
Great Falls, MT 59401
406-761-5010 / Fax: 406-761-5013
Sales: $500,001-$1 Million
IRA M. KAUFMAN, JR. (Owner)
BRIAN KAUFMAN-Men's Sportswear, Furnishings, Headwear, Accessories, Footwear, Store Displays, Fixtures, Supplies

MONTANA ATHLETIC SUPPLY, INC. (SG)
515 2nd Ave. South (m)
Great Falls, MT 59405
406-453-5649 / Fax: 406-453-5678
Sales: $100,001-$500,000
Website: www.mtathletic.com
MARK O'LOUGHLIN (Owner) & Buys Boys' Apparel, Men's Apparel, Men's Denim Apparel, Men's Hosiery, Men's Outerwear, Men's Sportswear

FORD'S (DEPT)
P.O. Box 1737 (m)
Hamilton, MT 59840
406-363-2251 / Fax: 406-375-9330
Sales: $1 Million-$10 Million
ALAN FORD (President) & Buys Men's Sportswear, Furnishings, Headwear, Accessories, Young Men's & Boys' Wear, Store Displays, Fixtures, Supplies

HART OF THE WEST (WW)
P.O. Box 1128 (p)
Hwy. 2 West
Harlem, MT 59526
406-353-2251 / Fax: 406-353-4251
HEATHER SCHWENKE (Co-Owner) & Buys Men's Western Wear, T-shirts, Active Apparel, Western Belts, Footwear

RAY'S SPORTS & WESTERN WEAR (WW)
(RAY & ALMA HINAND, INC.)
P.O. Box 306 (m-b)
Hwy. 12 East
Harlowton, MT 59036
406-632-4320 / Fax: 406-632-4328
ALMA HINAND (Owner) & Buys Men's Western Wear, Boys' Western Wear, Footwear
RICK HINAND-Men's Western Wear, Boys' Western Wear, Footwear

CAVALIERS, INC. (MW)
321 3rd St. (b)
Havre, MT 59501
406-265-1224 / Fax: 406-265-1225
DOUG ROSS (Owner) & Buys Men's & Students' Wear, Footwear, Store Displays, Fixtures, Supplies

MASTER SPORTS (SG-2)
301 1st St. (m)
Havre, MT 59501
406-265-4712 / Fax: 406-265-7019
Sales: $500,001-$1 Million
BOB EVANS, Jr. (Owner) & Buys Boys' Apparel, Men's Footwear, Men's Apparel, Men's Casualwear, Men's Denim Apparel, Men's Hosiery, Men's Outerwear, Men's Sportswear
BOB EVANS, Sr. (V.P.) & Buys Boys' Apparel, Men's Footwear, Men's Apparel, Men's Casualwear, Men's Denim Apparel, Men's Hosiery, Men's Outerwear, Men's Sportswear

NORMAN'S RANCHWEAR (WW)
P.O. Box 1286 (m-b)
114 3rd Ave.
Havre, MT 59501
406-265-4523 / Fax: 406-265-4523
Sales: $100,001-$500,000
SCOTT YOUNG (Co-Owner) & Buys Men's & Boys' Western Wear, Leather Apparel, Footwear
KAY YOUNG (Co-Owner) & Buys Store Displays, Fixtures, Supplies

BY GEORGE SHEILA'S (CLO)
320 N. Last Chance Gulch (b-h)
Helena, MT 59601
406-442-2720 / Fax: 406-442-2531
Sales: $100,001-$500,000
GEORGE GREGORY ALLEN (President) & Buys Men's Overcoats, Suits, Tailored Slacks, Tailored Jackets, Raincoats, Sweaters, Sport Shirts, Outer Jackets, Casual Slacks, Active Apparel, Furnishings, Headwear, Accessories, Young Men's Wear, Footwear, Store Displays, Fixtures, Supplies

CAPITAL SPORTS & WESTERN WEAR (WW & SG)
1092 Helena Ave. (m)
Helena, MT 59601
406-443-2978 / Fax: 406-442-8136
Sales: $1 Million-$10 Million
ED BEALL (Co-Owner) & Buys Boys' Apparel, Men's Footwear, Men's Apparel, Men's Denim Apparel
ART KEELER (Co-Owner) & Buys Boys' Apparel, Men's Footwear, Men's Apparel, Men's Denim Apparel

DeVORE'S SADDLERY (WW)
4 W. Lawrence Ave. (m)
Helena, MT 59601
406-442-2150
Sales: $100,001-$500,000
KENT DeVORE (Owner) & Buys Men's Western Wear, Dress Shirts, Ties, Tailored Jackets, Sweaters, Leather Apparel, Belts, Boots

DON'S, INC. (CLO)
P.O. Box 780 (p-m)
120 2nd Ave. South
Lewistown, MT 59457
406-538-9408 / Fax: 406-538-9461
Sales: $1 Million-$10 Million
Website: www.dons-store.com
DALE PFAU (Owner)
DON PFAU (President) & Buys Store Displays, Fixtures, Supplies
PENNY PHILIP-Men's Sweaters, Sport Shirts, Outer Jackets, Casual Slacks, Western Wear, Dress Shirts, Robes, Underwear, Hosiery, Gloves, Headwear, Belts, Jewelry, Small Leather Goods, Young Men's & Boys' Wear, Sportswear, Accessories
CHARLIE PFAU-Footwear, Men's Wear

SPORTS, INC. (SG)
333 2nd Ave. North
Lewistown, MT 59457
406-538-3496 / Fax: 406-538-2801
Website: www.sportsinc.com
DAVE SALVI (President & C.E.O.)
KENT NARDQUIST (Dir.-Mktg.) & Buys Men's Footwear, Men's Sportswear, Men's Activewear, Sporting Goods

GARLAND'S TOWN & COUNTRY (CLO)
P.O. Box 249 (bud-p-m-b)
Lincoln, MT 59639
406-362-4244 / Fax: 406-362-4667
Sales: $100,001-$500,000
TERESA GARLAND (Owner & Mgr.) & Buys Men's, Young Men's & Boys' Outerwear, Active Apparel, Footwear, Store Displays, Fixtures, Supplies

BOB'S OUTDOOR (CLO)
114 N. Main St. (m)
Livingston, MT 59047
406-222-1954
SHELLY CHAPEL (Owner) & Buys Men's Sweaters, Outer Jackets, Leather Apparel, Gloves, Headwear, Footwear, Store Displays, Fixtures and Supplies

MILES CITY SADDLERY (WW)
808 Main St. (m-b)
Miles City, MT 59301
406-232-2512
Website: www.milescitysaddlery.com
JACK DEIBEL (Owner) & Buys Men's Suits, Sportswear, Western Wear, Big & Tall Men's Wear, Boys' Wear, Mocassins, Store Displays, Fixtures, Supplies
DEBBIE LaBREE (Mgr.) & Buys Men's Suits, Sportswear, Western Wear, Big & Tall Men's Wear, Boys' Wear, Moccasins, Store Displays, Fixtures, Supplies
DIANA DAVIS (Asst. Mgr.) & Buys Men's & Boys' Overalls

ARMY & NAVY ECONOMY STORE (AN)
322 N. Higgins Ave. (bud-p)
Missoula, MT 59802
406-721-1315 / Fax: 406-549-8690
Sales: $1 Million-$10 Million
JAMES McGUIRL (Owner) & Buys Activewear, Athletic Footwear, Licensed Apparel, Golf Apparel, Snowboards, Skiwear, Jeans, Flannel Shirts, Outerwear
TOBY McGUIRL-Footwear, Activewear, Athletic Footwear, Licensed Apparel, Golf Apparel, Snowboards, Skiwear, Jeans, Flannel Shirts, Outerwear

BRADY'S SPORTSMAN'S SURPLUS (SG & WW)
(HIGH COUNTRY)
(WESTERN OUTFITTERS)
(WESTERN SPORTSMAN)
P.O. Box 4166 (p)
Trempers Shopping Ctr.
Missoula, MT 59806
406-721-5500 / Fax: 406-728-1112
Sales: $1 Million-$10 Million
TERRY BRADY (Owner)
BRYAN HARMON (Mgr.) & Buys Men's Skiwear, Shorts, Active Apparel, Men's Active Apparel, Work Clothes, Fleecewear, Footwear
BARBARA WESTOVER-Men's Western Shirts, Sweaters, Sport Shirts, Outer Jackets, Casual Slacks, Leather Apparel, Underwear, Belts, Small Leather Goods, Store Displays, Fixtures & Supplies

DESMOND'S OF MONTANA (MW)
129 N. Higgins Ave. (b)
Missoula, MT 59802
406-728-8233 / Fax: 406-728-7400
Sales: $500,000-$1 Million
BILL CHAVEZ (Owner) & Buys Men's Wear, Footwear, Store Displays, Fixtures, Supplies

QUALITY SUPPLY, INC. (CLO-4)
P.O. Box 17110
2801 W. Broadway
Missoula, MT 59808
406-549-2355 / Fax: 406-542-2355
DAVID R. PETERSON (President)
SUZANNE PETERSON-Men's Work Clothes, Western Wear, Footwear, Store Displays, Fixtures, Supplies

MOUNTAIN WEST CLOTHING, INC. (WW)
P.O. Box 999 (m-b)
Plains, MT 59859
406-826-3513
Sales: $100,001-$500,000
LAURA REHBEIN (Mgr.) & Buys Men's Western Wear, Footwear, Store Displays, Fixtures, Supplies

THE FIRST RESORT (CLO)
(JAMES W. DUFORD)
219 Main St. (b)
Polson, MT 59860
406-883-2129 / Fax: 406-883-2398
Website: www.firstresortclothing.com
JAMES W. DUFORD (Owner & President) & Buys Men's Sportswear, Furnishings, Headwear, Accessories, Young Men's Wear, Boys' Wear
TALI DUFORD (Secy. & Treas. & Mgr.) & Buys Men's Sportswear, Furnishings, Headwear, Accessories, Young Men's Wear, Boys' Wear

THE VILLAGE SHOP (CLO)
118 S. Broadway
Red Lodge, MT 59068
406-446-2020 / Fax: 406-446-2023
BETH STEEN (Owner) & Buys Shoes, Hiking Boots, Hunting Apparel

WATERS' MEN'S & LADIES' STORE (CLO)
P.O. Box 190 (p-m)
Red Lodge, MT 59068
406-446-2018
BETTY WATERS (Owner) & Buys Men's Wear, Sportswear, Accessories, Urban Contemporary, Store Displays, Fixtures & Supplies

RONAN SPORTS & WESTERN (MW)
204 Hwy. 93 South (p-m)
Ronan, MT 59864
406-676-3701 / Fax: 406-676-3703
ROBERT SCHREIDER (President) & Buys Men's Raincoats, Active Apparel, Gloves, Sweaters, Sport Shirts, Outer Jackets, Casual Slacks, Dress Shirts, Underwear, Hosiery, Hats, Belts, Footwear, Boys' Wear, Leather Apparel, Western Wear, Boys' Sportswear, Store Displays, Fixtures, Supplies
MARLENE MILTON-Men's Raincoats, Active Apparel, Gloves, Sweaters, Sport Shirts, Outer Jackets, Casual Slacks, Dress Shirts, Underwear, Hosiery, Hats, Belts, Footwear, Boys' Wear, Leather Apparel, Western Wear, Boys' Sportswear, Store Displays, Fixtures, Supplies

TANDE TOGGERY (CLO-2)
122 Main St. (m)
Scobey, MT 59263
406-487-2414 / Fax: 406-487-2414
CRAIG TANDE (Owner) & Buys Men's Suits, Sportswear, Furnishings, Accessories, Young Men's Wear, Urban Contemporary, Footwear, Boys' Wear, Store Displays, Fixtures, Supplies

LARSON CLOTHING CO. (MW)
159 Main St. (m)
Shelby, MT 59474
406-434-5112
PAUL STEINER (Owner) & Buys Men's Sportswear, Furnishings, Headwear, Accessories, Leather Apparel, Footwear, Store Displays, Fixtures, Supplies

YELLOWSTONE MERCANTILE CO. (DEPT)

102 N. Central Ave. (m-b)
Sidney, MT 59270
406-488-1201 / Fax: 406-488-1251
Sales: $500,000-$1 Million

KATHRYN VARCO SMITH (President)
TOM PAVEK (G.M.M.) & Buys Men's Overcoats, Suits, Tailored Jackets, Tailored Slacks, Raincoats, Sweaters, Sport Shirts, Outer Jackets, Casual Slacks, Leather Apparel, Furnishings, Robes, Headwear, Accessories, Boys' Wear, Urban Contemporary, Store Displays, Fixtures, Supplies
JOYCE CALLEN-Footwear

EAGLE'S STORE (DEPT)

P.O. Box 280 (p-m)
3 Canyon St.
West Yellowstone, MT 59758
406-646-9300 / Fax: 406-646-4217

KAREN EAGLE (Partner) & Buys Men's Western Sportswear, Footwear, Store Displays, Fixtures, Supplies
WALTER EAGLE (Partner) & Buys Men's Western Sportswear, Footwear, Store Displays, Fixtures, Supplies
FRANKIE EAGLE (Partner) & Buys Men's Western Sportswear, Footwear, Store Displays, Fixtures, Supplies

THE VILLAGE SHOP, INC. (CLO)

201 Central Ave. (m-b)
Whitefish, MT 59937
406-862-3200 / Fax: 406-862-9444
Sales: $500,001-$1 Million

TAMI YUNCK (Co-Owner) & Buys Men's Footwear, Leather Goods, Men's Apparel, Men's Casualwear
NANCY SCENNUNGSEN (Co-Owner) & Buys Men's Footwear, Leather Goods, Men's Apparel, Men's Casualwear

BRYAN'S (CLO)

(H & K , INC.)
P.O. Box 818 (p)
202 Main St.
Wolf Point, MT 59201
406-653-1450 / Fax: 406-653-2709
Sales: $100,001-$500,000

KEITH BRYAN (President)
JAN HIGGINS-Men's Wear, Sportswear, Furnishings, Headwear, Accessories, Footwear, Boys' & Students Wear, Urban Contemporary, Store Displays, Fixtures, Supplies

SMITH'S DEPARTMENT STORE (DEPT)
P.O. Box 595 (bud-p)
112 S. Main St.
Atkinson, NE 68713
402-925-5255 / Fax: 402-925-5255
Sales: $100,001-$500,000

RICK SMITH (Owner) & Buys Men's Headwear, Accessories, Boys' Wear, Suits, Tailored Jackets, Tailored Slacks, Sweaters, Sport Shirts, Outer Jackets, Casual Slacks, Footwear, Store Displays, Fixtures, Supplies

LEONA SMITH-Men's Headwear, Accessories, Boys' Wear, Suits, Tailored Jackets, Tailored Slacks, Sweaters, Sport Shirts, Outer Jackets, Casual Slacks, Footwear, Store Displays, Fixtures, Supplies

THE DOUBLETREE (CLO)
424 S. 8th Ave. (p)
Broken Bow, NE 68822
308-872-5352
Sales: $100,001-$500,000

MARLENE McGAUGHEY (Owner) & Buys Overcoats, Suits, Sweaters, Dress Shirts, Ties, Underwear, Hosiery, Gloves, Belts, Jewelry, Small Leather Goods, Fragrances, Boys' Clothing, Boots, Store Displays, Fixtures, Supplies

ANDERSON'S, INC. (CLO-3)
141 W. 3rd St. (p-m-b)
Chadron, NE 69337
308-432-3285 / Fax: 308-432-2538
Sales: $100,001-$500,000

WILLIAM GIESELER, JR. (President) & Buys Men's Sportswear, Furnishings, Boys' Wear 8 to 20, Urban Contemporary, Store Displays, Fixtures, Supplies

RICHARD GIESELER (Mgr.) & Buys Activewear, Athletic Footwear, Licensed Apparel

BORDY'S CLOTHING, INC. (WW)
2419 11th St. (m)
Columbus, NE 68601
402-564-0011 / Fax: 402-563-1110
Sales: $100,001-$500,000

JOE BORDY (Co-Owner) & Buys Store Displays, Fixtures, Supplies

STEVE BORDY (Co-Owner & G.M.M.) & Buys Men's Western Wear, Overcoats, Suits, Tailored Jackets, Tailored Slacks, Raincoats, Sweaters, Sport Shirts, Outer Jackets, Casual Slacks, Dress Shirts, Ties, Underwear, Belts, Urban Contemporary, Store Displays, Fixtures, Supplies

GERALD SAMPTER CLOTHIER, INC. (MW & OL)
517 N. Main St. (p-m-b)
Fremont, NE 68025
402-727-1531 / Fax: 402-727-1921
Sales: $500,001-$1 Million
Website: www.sampters.com

ROBERT MISSEL (President & Owner) & Buys Men's Overcoats, Suits, Tailored Jackets, Tailored Slacks, Tuxedos, Raincoats, Sportswear, Furnishings, Headwear, Belts, Jewelry, Fragrances, Big & Tall Men's Wear, Store Displays, Fixtures, Supplies

MORRIS CLOTHING CO. (MW)
125 N. Main St. (m)
Gordon, NE 69343
308-282-1010
Sales: $100,001-$500,000

TOM H. MORRIS (President) & Buys Men's & Boys' Clothing, Furnishings, Sportswear, Headwear, Accessories, Footwear, Urban Contemporary, Store Displays, Fixtures, Supplies

GRAND ISLAND WESTERN SHOP (WW)
111 Diers Ave. (bud-p-m-b)
P.O. Box 1065
Grand Island, NE 68803
308-382-5679 / Fax: 308-382-2045
Sales: $1 Million-$10 Million

DAVE VOSS (President) & Buys Boys' Apparel, Boys' Footwear, Men's Apparel, Men's Big & Tall, Men's Casualwear, Men's Denim Apparel, Men's Accessories, Men's Suits

LONGRIN'S FOR MEN (MW-2)
223 W. 3rd St. (m-b)
Grand Island, NE 68801
308-382-9048
Sales: $100,001-$500,000
Website: www.canfitu.com

DICK LONGRIN (Owner) & Buys Men's Big & Tall, Casual Wear, Knits, Suits, Tuxedos

WHITEAKER STORE (CLO)
P.O. Box 278 (m)
265 Main St.
Harrison, NE 69346
308-668-2251 / Fax: 308-668-2251
Sales: $50 Million-$100 Million

JOE WHITEAKER (Owner) & Buys Men's, Young Men's Western Wear, Sweaters, Ties, Robes, Underwear, Hosiery, Gloves, Western Hats, Belts, Small Leather Goods, Headwear, Footwear, Store Displays, Fixtures, Supplies

ALLEN'S OF HASTINGS (DEPT)
P.O. Box 987 (m)
1115 W. 2nd St.
Hastings, NE 68902
402-463-5633 / Fax: 402-463-5730
Sales: $500,000-$1 Million

ROBERT ALLEN (President)

ERIK ALLEN (Mgr.) & Buys Store Displays, Fixtures, Supplies

ELAINE LAUX-Men's Wear, Sportswear, Furnishings, Headwear, Hosiery, Underwear

THE BUCKLE, INC. (CLO-300)
P.O. Box 1480 (m)
2407 W. 24th St.
Kearney, NE 68845
308-236-8491 / Fax: 308-236-4493
Sales: $338 Million
Website: www.buckle.com
Retail Locations: WA, OR, CA, MI, ID, UT, AZ, NM, TX, OK, WY, CO, KS, NE, SD, ND, MN, IA, MO, AR, LA, MS, AL, GA, FL, SC, NC, VA, WV, PA, OH, MI, IN, IL, WI

DAN HIRSCHFELD (Chmn.)

DENNIS H. NELSON (President & C.E.O.)

BRETT MILKIE (V.P. & Real Estate Contact)

JASON SCHINER (V.P.-Men's Mdsg.) & Buys Men's Sportswear, Young Men's Wear, Sizes 8 to 14 Boys' Sportswear, Shirts, T-shirts, Outerwear, Sweaters, Jeans, Shorts, Footwear, Sandles, Headwear, Urban Contemporary

LORI KOEPPKE (Dir.-Opers.) & Buys Store Displays, Fixtures, Supplies

LORRON DEPARTMENT STORE (DEPT)
112 E. 2nd St. (m)
Kimball, NE 69145
308-235-4011
Sales: $100,001-$500,000

LORNA EVELYN (Co-Owner)

RONALD EVELYN (Co-Owner) & Buys Men's & Boys' Wear, Footwear, Store Displays, Fixtures, Supplies

LOUDON'S FOR MEN (MW)
504 N. Washington (m-b)
Lexington, NE 68850
308-324-3451 / Fax: 308-324-3451
Sales: $100,001-$500,000
Website: www.loudons.com

STEVE LOUDON (Owner) & Buys Men's Suits, Formal Wear, Sportswear, Big & Tall Men's Wear, Furnishings, Accessories, Western Wear, Dress Shoes, Store Displays, Fixtures, Supplies

NEBRASKA - Lincoln

THE FORT, INC. (CLO-2)
5601 S. 56th St., #4 (p-m-b)
Lincoln, NE 68516
402-423-9341 / Fax: 402-423-9369
Sales: $1 Million-$10 Million
Website: www.headforthefort.com
CARL WOHLFARTH (Chmn.)
KEITH SCHOMERUS (President) & Buys Men's Western Headwear, Belts, Boots
LINDA SCHOMERUS (Mdse. Mgr.) & Buys Men's Western Suits, Tailored Jackets, Tailored Slacks, Raincoats, Sweaters, Sport Shirts, Outer Jackets, Leather Apparel, Casual Slacks, Active Apparel, Dress Shirts, Ties, Young Men's Western Wear, Big & Tall Men's Western Wear, Boys' Western Wear, Store Displays, Fixtures, Supplies
ANN PERCEVAL-Underwear, Hosiery, Gloves, Small Leather Goods, Fragrances

GARY MICHAEL'S CLOTHIERS (MW)
3520 Village Dr., #600
Lincoln, NE 68516
402-423-7848
Website: www.garymichaels.com
GARY NOVOTNY (Owner) & Buys Men's Wear, Men's Accessories, Furnishings, Footwear

HOLWAY FORMAL WEAR, INC. (MW-2)
1228 P St. (m)
Lincoln, NE 68508
402-476-2262 / Fax: 402-476-1388
Sales: $100,001-$500,000
Website: www.holwayformalwear.com
JIM KOPETKA (Owner) & Buys Men's Tuxedos & Formal Accessories, Store Displays, Fixtures, Supplies

KNIGHT'S FAMILY STORES, INC. (CLO)
Van Dorn Plaza (p-m)
2600 S. 48th
Lincoln, NE 68506
402-488-6900 / Fax: 402-488-8787
Sales: $500,000-$1 Million
DEAN KNIGHT (President) (@ 402-488-8787) & Buys Store Displays, Fixtures, Supplies, Men's Wear, Sportswear, Furnishings, Headwear, Accessories
LANNE DRAKE-Store Displays, Fixtures, Supplies, Men's Wear, Sportswear, Furnishings, Headwear, Accessories

THE POST & NICKLE (CLO-2)
(HITCHIN POST OF LINCOLN, INC.)
144 N. 14th St. (m-b)
Lincoln, NE 68508
402-476-3432 / Fax: 402-476-3454
Sales: $100,001-$500,000
GALE SUP (Owner)
DAVID BERGO-Men's Overcoats, Tailored Jackets, Tailored Slacks, Raincoats, Sportswear, Furnishings, Headwear, Accessories, Leather Apparel, Footwear, Store Displays, Fixtures, Supplies

DENIM & DUDS (CLO)
(C & K DISTRIBUTORS, INC.)
W. Hwy. 6 & 34 (p-m)
RR 3, P.O. Box 9
McCook, NE 69001
308-345-3590 / Fax: 308-345-3593
Sales: $100,001-$500,000
JERRY COYLE (Owner)
BECKY FUNK (Mgr.) & Buys Men's Jeans & Tops, Boots, Store Displays, Fixtures, Supplies

LARSON FLORINE (MW)
P.O. Box 483 (b)
425 Norfolk Ave.
Norfolk, NE 68701
402-371-2148
Sales: $100,001-$500,000
NORM GEYER (Owner) & Buys Men's Sportswear, Furnishings, Headwear, Accessories, Leather Apparel, Footwear, Store Displays, Fixtures, Supplies

HIRSCHFELD'S (MW)
401 N. Dewey St. (m-b)
North Platte, NE 69101
308-534-8700 / Fax: 308-532-0983
Sales: $1 Million-$10 Million
ALAN HIRSCHFELD (President & G.M.M.) & Buys Men's Suits, Tailored Jackets, Tailored Slacks, Raincoats, Sweaters, Sport Shirts, Outer Jackets, Leather Apparel, Casual Slacks, Furnishings, Headwear, Accessories, Young Men's Wear, Footwear, Store Displays, Fixtures, Supplies

SPORT SHOPPE, INC. (CLO-3)
1000 S. Dewey St. (m-b)
North Platte, NE 69101
308-534-4450 / Fax: 308-534-4455
Sales: $100,001-$500,000
TIM O'CONNOR (Owner) & Buys Men's Sportswear, Dress Shirts, Hosiery, Headwear, Young Men's Wear & Boys' Wear, Footwear, Store Displays, Fixtures, Supplies
SANDRA LENZ (Mgr.) & Buys Men's Sportswear, Dress Shirts, Hosiery, Headwear, Young Men's Wear & Boys' Wear, Footwear, Store Displays, Fixtures, Supplies

BEL AIR (MW)
717 N. 114th St.
Omaha, NE 68154
248-656-1325 / Fax: 402-493-5160
SHELDON LERNER-Men's Wear, Accessories, and Footwear
RICHARD LERNER-Men's Wear, Accessories, and Footwear

BRODKEY BROTHERS, INC. (JWLY-10)
(BRODKEY JEWELRY)
12165 W. Center Rd., #73
Omaha, NE 68144
402-330-9800 / Fax: 402-697-0603
Sales: $10 Million-$50 Million
Website: www.brodkey.com
SHERMAN F. BRODKEY (President) & Buys Jewelry, Watches
MARC BRODKEY-Jewelry, Watches

CANFIELD'S, INC. (MW)
8457 W. Center Rd. (p-m)
Omaha, NE 68124
402-393-3363 / Fax: 402-393-2221
Sales: $100,001-$500,000
Website: www.canfields.com
LEROY CANFIELD (President) & Buys Men's Sportswear, Furnishings, Footwear, Store Displays, Fixtures, Supplies
RICK CANFIELD (V.P.) & Buys Men's Sportswear, Furnishings, Footwear, Store Displays, Fixtures, Supplies

DICK'S WESTERN WEAR, INC. (WW-2)
4315 S. 120th St. (m-b)
Omaha, NE 68137
402-697-0737
Sales: $100,001-$500,000
SUSAN HEARD (Mgr.) & Buys Men's & Boys' Western Wear, Footwear, Headwear, Furnishings

FITNESS GEAR (SP)
156 E. 3rd St.
Omaha, NE 68144
402-397-2000
DAVID KUTLER (Owner) & Buys Active Apparel

NEBRASKA - Omaha

GORDMAN'S, INC. (CLO-42)
12100 W. Center Rd. (p-m-b)
Omaha, NE 68144
402-691-4000 / Fax: 402-691-4269
Sales: $100 Million-$500 Million
Website: www.gordmans.com
JEFFREY GORDMAN (President & C.E.O.)
NORM FARRINGTON (C.I.O., V.P., & Dir.-Info. Sys.)
JEFFREY BYAL (V.P.-Fin.)
RON HALL (V.P.-Opers.)
JIM COOKE (V.P.-Store Opers.)
DEAN WILLIAMSON (V.P.-HR)
GENE KAPLAN (Dir.-Property Mgmt.)
STAN TREVINO (Dir.-Info. Sys.)
MICHAEL HAMMOND (Dir.-Mktg.)
RICH PALMER (Dir.-Loss Prevention)
WILL CHAMPENOY (Dir.-Visuals)
CHRIS MAHER (Mgr.-HR)
SCOTT DAVIS (D.M.M.) & Buys Boys' Apparel, Men's Apparel, Men's Sportswear
Andre Zapy-Boys' Apparel, Men's Apparel
STEVE SIREF-Young Men's & Boys' Apparel

JERRY RYAN GENTLEMEN'S APPAREL, INC. (MW)
7806 Dodge St. (b)
Omaha, NE 68114
402-330-6614 / Fax: 402-330-6619
Sales: $1 Million-$10 Million
JOHN RYAN (President) & Buys Men's Overcoats, Tailored Jackets, Tailored Slacks, Big & Tall Men's Wear, Store Displays, Fixtures and Supplies
DAN RYAN (V.P.) & Buys Big & Tall Men's Wear, Men's Sportswear, Furnishings, Accessories, Headwear, Footwear, Store Displays, Fixtures and Supplies

LINDLEY CLOTHING STORE (MW-2)
707 N. 132nd St. (b)
Omaha, NE 68154
402-491-4000 / Fax: 402-491-3344
Sales: $100,001-$500,000
JOHN LINDLEY (Co-Owner) & Buys Men's Sportswear, Furnishings, Headwear, Accessories, Store Displays, Fixtures, Supplies
MIKE LINDLEY (Co-Owner) & Buys Men's Sportswear, Furnishings, Headwear, Accessories, Store Displays, Fixtures, Supplies

NEBRASKA CLOTHING CO. (MW)
1012 Howard St.
Omaha, NE 68102
402-346-6114 / Fax: 402-346-2356
Website: www.bugeaters.com
BRAD ASHFORD (Owner) & Buys Men's Wear, Men's Accessories, Furnishings
EMILY LUKAS-Men's Wear, Men's Accessories, Furnishings

PARSOW'S, INC. (MW)
120 Regency Pkwy. (b)
Omaha, NE 68114
402-397-7900 / Fax: 402-397-7903
Sales: $1 Million-$10 Million
Website: www.parsows.com
SOL PARSOW (President)
DAVID PARSOW (G.M.M.) & Buys Men's Wear, Leather Apparel, Footwear, Store Displays, Fixtures, Supplies
STEVE PARSOW (G.M.M.) & Buys Men's Wear, Leather Apparel, Footwear, Store Displays, Fixtures, Supplies
LARRY GINSBURG (G.M.M.) & Buys Men's Wear, Leather Apparel, Footwear, Store Displays, Fixtures, Supplies

ROSSI CLOTHIERS (MW)
11032 Elm St.
Omaha, NE 68144
402-397-3608 / Fax: 402-397-9695
CHARLIE ROSSI (Owner) & Buys Men's Wear, Men's Accessories, Furnishings, Footwear

STEWART'S TOPS & BOTTOMS (MW)
2423 N. 24th St. (bud-p-des)
Omaha, NE 68110
402-341-8216
Sales: $500,001-$1 Million
EVERETT STEWART (Owner) & Buys Jewelry, Boys' Footwear, Men's Footwear, Leather Goods, Men's Apparel, Men's Formalwear, Men's Accessories, Men's Hosiery, Men's Outerwear, Men's Sleepwear, Men's Suits, Watches
EVERETT STEWART, JR. (Mgr.-Sales) & Buys Jewelry, Boys' Footwear, Men's Footwear, Leather Goods, Men's Apparel, Men's Formalwear, Men's Accessories, Men's Hosiery, Men's Outerwear, Men's Sleepwear, Men's Suits, Watches

UNO BOOKSTORE (SP)
(UNIVERSITY OF NEBRASKA)
6001Dodge St.
Omaha, NE 68182
402-554-2336 / Fax: 402-554-3220
Sales: $100,001-$500,000
Website: www.unobookstore.com
MICHAEL SCHMIDT-Activewear, Fleecewear, Jackets, Hosiery, Shorts

WOLF BROTHERS WESTERN (WW-3 & OL)
7001 Dodge St. (m-b)
Omaha, NE 68132
402-558-3005 / Fax: 402-558-3006
Sales: $100,001-$500,000
Website: www.wolfbrothers.com
JOE KIRSHENBAUM (Owner)
TOM KIRSHENBAUM-Men's & Boys' Western Wear, Footwear, Accessories, Headwear, Store Displays, Fixtures, Supplies

MOYER'S (CLO-2)
(ROMAR, INC.)
1511 M St. (p-m-b)
Ord, NE 68862
308-728-5750 / Fax: 308-728-5750
Sales: $100,001-$500,000
BOB MOYER (Owner) & Buys Men's Wear, Casual Wear, Accessories, Boys' Wear, Work Shoes, Urban Contemporary, Store Displays, Fixtures, Supplies

BRYAN JENSON CLOTHING, INC. (MW)
622 Howard Ave. (p)
Saint Paul, NE 68873
308-754-4813
Sales: $100,001-$500,000
MR. LOREN STUDLEY (Owner) & Buys Clothing, Sportswear, Furnishings

THE BOUTIQUE, INC. (CLO)
1818 Broadway (m-b)
Scottsbluff, NE 69361
308-632-3621 / Fax: 308-632-7721
Sales: $100,001-$500,000
Website: www.scottsbluff.net/boutique
ALEX PESTER (President)
DOROTHY PESTER (V.P. & G.M.M.) & Buys Men's Apparel, Men's Formalwear
JERRA PESTER (Store Mgr.) & Buys Men's Apparel, Men's Formalwear

KROGER SHOELAND, INC. (FW)
518 Seward St.
Seward, NE 68434
402-643-3283
Website: www.krogershoeland.metroville.com
CHERYL KROGER (Co-Owner) & Buys Men's & Boys' Footwear, Accessories
DAVE KROGER (Co-Owner) & Buys Men's & Boys' Footwear, Accessories

YOUNG'S WESTERN WEAR (WW)

(RED FRONT MERCANTILE CO.)
143 N. Main St. (p-m)
Valentine, NE 69201
402-376-1281 / Fax: 402-376-2281
Sales: $1 Million-$10 Million
Website: www.discountwesternwear.com

MARY YOUNG (Co-Owner) & Buys Men's Western Overcoats, Tailored Jackets, Tailored Slacks, Raincoats, Sweaters, Outer Jackets, Leather Apparel, Ties, Underwear, Hosiery, Gloves, Headwear, Belts, Jewelry, Small Leather Goods, Fragrances, Boys' Western Wear, Footwear, Store Displays, Fixtures, Supplies

MIKE YOUNG (Co-Owner) & Buys Men's Western Overcoats, Tailored Jackets, Tailored Slacks, Raincoats, Sweaters, Outer Jackets, Leather Apparel, Ties, Underwear, Hosiery, Gloves, Headwear, Belts, Jewelry, Small Leather Goods, Fragrances, Boys' Western Wear, Footwear, Store Displays, Fixtures, Supplies

CORK YOUNG (Co-Owner) & Buys Men's Western Overcoats, Tailored Jackets, Tailored Slacks, Raincoats, Sweaters, Outer Jackets, Leather Apparel, Ties, Underwear, Hosiery, Gloves, Headwear, Belts, Jewelry, Small Leather Goods, Fragrances, Boys' Western Wear, Footwear, Store Displays, Fixtures, Supplies

SCHMITT CLOTHING STORE (CLO)

P.O. Box 225 (m-b)
106 S. Main St.
West Point, NE 68788
402-372-2171 / Fax: 402-372-2171
Sales: $500,000-$1 Million

GENE PEATROWSKY (Owner) & Buys Overcoats, Suits, Tailored Jackets, Tailored Slacks, Raincoats, Big & Tall Wear, Sweaters, Sport Shirts, Outer Jackets, Leather Apparel, Casual Slacks, Active Apparel, Furnishings, Accessories, Young Men's Wear, Footwear, Store Displays, Fixtures, Supplie

WESTERN EDGE (CLO)

(RYAN, INC.)
701 Lincoln Ave. (p-m)
York, NE 68467
402-362-4881 / Fax: 402-362-4887
Sales: $500,001-$1 Million

BRYAN BECHTEL (Mgr.) & Buys Men's Sportswear, Jeans, T-shirts, Dress Shirts, Ties, Hosiery, Gloves, Headwear, Belts, Jewelry, Small Leather Goods, Western Wear, Young Men's Wear, Western Wear, Sizes 8 to 20 Boys' Jeans, T-shirts, Western Wear, Footwear

MOUNTAIN MERCANTILE TRUE VALUE (DEPT)

169 Clover St. (bud-p-m)
Caliente, NV 89008
775-726-3891 / Fax: 775-726-3894

KEVIN PHILLIPS (Partner)

TERI PHILLIPS (Partner) & Buys Men's, Boys' & Students Wear, Footwear, Store Displays, Fixtures, Supplies

MURDOCK'S OF CARSON CITY, INC. (MW)

1811 N. Carson (m-b)
Carson City, NV 89701
775-882-5551

ROGER MURDOCK (Owner) & Buys Men's Wear, Store Displays, Fixtures, Supplies

CAPRIOLA'S (WW & MO)

(J. M. CAPRIOLA, INC.)
500 Commercial St. (b)
Elko, NV 89801
775-738-5816 / Fax: 775-738-8980
Website: www.capriolas.com

DOUG WRIGHT (Owner) & Buys Men's Western Wear, Boys' Western Wear, Store Displays, Fixtures, Supplies

PAULA WRIGHT-Men's Western Wear, Boys' Western Wear, Store Displays, Fixtures, Supplies

CEDAR CREEK CLOTHING (MW)

(BOB'S TOGS, INC.)
453 Idaho St. (p-m-b)
Elko, NV 89801
775-738-3950 / Fax: 775-738-3960
Sales: $500,000-$1 Million
Website: www.cedarcreekclothing.com

DUANE H. JONES (President & G.M.M.) & Buys Men's Overcoats, Suits, Tailored Jackets, Tailored Slacks, Leather Apparel, Sportswear, Casual Slacks, Active Apparel, Furnishings, Headwear, Belts, Small Leather Goods, Footwear, Fragrances, Big & Tall Men's Wear, Store Displays, Fixtures, Supplies

ELKO GENERAL MERCHANDISE (GM)

416 Idaho St. (p)
Elko, NV 89801
775-738-3295 / Fax: 775-738-9382
Sales: $100,001-$500,000
Website: www.rabbitbrush.com/anacabe

ELKO ANACABE (Owner)

ANITA FRANZOIA (Owner) & Buys Men's Overcoats, Raincoats, Work Clothes, Underwear, Hosiery, Gloves, Headwear, Belts, Small Leather Goods, Footwear, Store Displays, Fixtures, Supplies

ANDY'S WESTERN WEAR (WW)

501 11th St. (p-m)
Ely, NV 89301
775-289-2504

LEE ANDERSON (Partner) & Buys Men's & Boys' Western Wear, Jeans, Outer Jackets, Furnishings, Headwear, Accessories, Boots (Casual & Work), Store Displays, Fixtures, Supplies

FIDEL'S CLOTHING CENTER (CLO)

581 Sierra Way (m)
Hawthorne, NV 89415
775-945-2652 / Fax: 775-945-3017

JOSEPHINE GOMEZ (Owner) & Buys Men's & Boys' Wear, Footwear, Store Displays, Fixtures, Supplies

GREAT OUTDOOR CLOTHING (SP-12 & MO)

341 Ski Way, #201
Incline Village, NV 39451
775-832-9100 / Fax: 775-832-8088
Website: www.greatoutdoors.com

STEPHEN MEYERS (Owner)

JENNIFER McCAIN (Mgr.)

BONNIE MYERS (V.P.) & Buys Apparel, Skiwear, Athletic Footwear, Outdoor Footwear, Bicycle Apparel, Outdoor Apparel

LOIS BEDIENT-Apparel, Skiwear, Athletic Footwear, Outdoor Footwear, Bicycle Apparel, Outdoor Apparel

DIANE STANBURY-Apparel, Skiwear, Athletic Footwear, Outdoor Footwear, Bicycle Apparel, Outdoor Apparel

INCLINE OUTFITTERS (SP)

930 Tahoe Blvd., #204
Incline Village, NV 89451
775-831-0432 / Fax: 775-201-0262
Website: www.inclineoutfitters.com

SUSAN LYNNES (Owner) & Buys Men's Apparel, Footwear & Accessories

ADAM'S WESTERN STORE (WW)

1415 Western Ave. (b)
Las Vegas, NV 89102
702-384-6077 / Fax: 702-477-0170

VICKI PAULBICK (Owner) & Buys Men's Western Wear, Boots, Sneakers, Leather Apparel, Store Displays, Fixtures, Supplies

BIANCA OF NEVADA, INC. (FW-15)

(WEST COAST & PARTNERS)
3485 W. Harman, Suite 125 (des)
Las Vegas, NV 89103
702-736-2444 / Fax: 702-736-6020
Sales: $10 Million-$50 Million

SAL CARSELLO (President)

CHARLES GREER (Controller)

JEANNE MARKEL (@ 702-736-1309)-Boys' Apparel, Boys' Footwear, Men's Footwear, Leather Goods, Men's Accessories, Men's Apparel, Hosiery, Watches

PATTY MELE-Boys' Apparel, Boys' Footwear, Men's Footwear, Leather Goods, Men's Accessories, Men's Apparel, Hosiery, Watches

PATTY OLIVA-Boys' Apparel, Boys' Footwear, Men's Footwear, Leather Goods, Men's Accessories, Men's Apparel, Hosiery, Watches

SANDRA TUCCELLI-Boys' Apparel, Boys' Footwear, Men's Footwear, Leather Goods, Men's Accessories, Men's Apparel, Hosiery, Watches

DEBBIE DUMLAC-Boys' Apparel, Boys' Footwear, Men's Footwear, Leather Goods, Men's Accessories, Men's Apparel, Hosiery, Watches

BKOZ (CLO)

3632 S. Maryland Pkwy. (p)
Las Vegas, NV 89109
702-893-3078 / Fax: 702-796-0392
Website:
www.bkozclothing.nv.switchboard.com

DANNY KAY (Co-Owner) & Buys Men's Boys' Wear, Urban Contemporary, Footwear, Jeans, and T-shirts

CELLINI'S (MW)

2600 W. Sahara Blvd., #114 (m-b)
Las Vegas, NV 89102
702-251-8233 / Fax: 702-251-0393

JOE ETTEDGUI (Owner) & Buys Men's Wear, Dress Shoes, Store Displays, Fixtures, Supplies

CUZZENS, INC. (MW-3)

101 Convention Center Dr. (b-h)
Las Vegas, NV 89101
702-732-1326 / Fax: 702-732-1060
Sales: $10 Million-$50 Million

STEVE VIETHS (President & G.M.M.) & Buys Men's Wear, Leather Apparel, Footwear, Store Displays, Fixtures, Supplies

NEVADA - Las Vegas

D. FINE MEN'S STORE (MW)
(D. FINE, INC.)
3400 Las Vegas Blvd. South (m-b)
Mirage Hotel
Las Vegas, NV 89109
702-792-7760 / Fax: 702-792-7686
DON FINE (Owner) & Buys Men's Sportswear, Furnishings, Headwear, Accessories, Footwear, Store Displays, Fixtures, Supplies
PETER HOROWITZ-Men's Sportswear, Furnishings, Headwear, Accessories, Footwear, Store Displays, Fixtures, Supplies
MIKE MARTIN-Men's Sportswear, Furnishings, Headwear, Accessories, Footwear, Store Displays, Fixtures, Supplies

DEALERS ROOM CASINO CLOTHIERS (CLO-2)
3507 S. Maryland Pkwy. (b)
Las Vegas, NV 89103
702-732-3932 / Fax: 702-732-3932
JANE JULIUS (Owner) & Buys Men's Suits, Tailored Jackets, Tailored Slacks, Big & Tall Men's Wear, Sportswear, Sweaters, Sport Shirts, Outer Jackets, Casual Slacks, Active Apparel, Dress Shirts, Ties, Gloves, Footwear, Young Men's & Boys' Tuxedos

FLAMINGO APPAREL (CLO-2)
3555 Las Vegas Blvd. South (m-b)
Flamingo Hilton Hotel
Las Vegas, NV 89109
702-734-8337 / Fax: 702-734-6615
Sales: $1 Million-$10 Million
RUTH MASSARANI (President & G.M.M.)
JACKI HEFETZ-Boys' Wear, Store Displays, Fixtures, Supplies
TOMMY WISE-Sweaters, Men's Sportswear, Sport Shirts, Leather Apparel Casual Slacks Active Apparel, Furnishings, Accessories, Headwear, Store Displays, Fixtures and Supplies

FOUR ACES MENSWEAR (MW)
124 S. 1st St. (b)
Las Vegas, NV 89101
702-383-6994 / Fax: 702-383-6995
HOWARD BOCK (Owner) & Buys Men's Suits, Tailored Jackets, Tailored Slacks, Big & Tall Men's Wear, Furnishings, Dress Shirts, Hosiery, Jewelry, Small Leather Goods, Dress Shoes, Store Displays, Fixtures and Supplies

FRONT ROW SPORTS (SG-2)
4300 Meadows Ln., #270 (m)
Las Vegas, NV 89107
702-878-2468 / Fax: 702-878-8404
Sales: $1 Million-$10 Million
JIM SIMONSON (President) & Buys Boys' Apparel, Leather Goods, Men's Apparel, Mens's Big & Tall, Men's Outerwear, Men's Sportswear
TOM SIMONSON (V.P.) & Buys Boys' Apparel, Leather Goods, Men's Apparel, Mens's Big & Tall, Men's Outerwear, Men's Sportswear

GIGATT (CLO)
1600 Brooks Ave.
Las Vegas, NV 89030
702-631-5927
BOBBIE ELLIOT (Owner) & Buys Men's & Boys' African Attire, Suits, Headwear, Accessories

GQ CLOTHIERS (MW)
(GY ENTERPRISES, INC.)
3333 S. Maryland Pkwy. (bud-h)
Las Vegas, NV 89109
702-731-4717 / Fax: 702-731-9474
Website: www.gqclothier.com
GEORGE YAGHI (Owner) & Buys Men's Wear, Custom Clothing, Suits, Footwear, Store Displays, Fixtures, Supplies

GRAY FIFTH AVENUE (MW)
Fashion Show Mall (p)
4503 Paradise Rd., #P
Las Vegas, NV 89109
702-731-6670 / Fax: 702-731-6959
SALIM MERHI (Owner) & Buys Big & Tall Men's Wear, Men's Sweaters, Sport Shirts, Outer Jackets, Casual Slacks, Dress Shirts, Ties, Jewelry, Fragrances, Store Displays, Fixtures, Supplies

HARRIS & FRANK, INC. (MW-2)
3200 Las Vegas Blvd. South (m-b)
Las Vegas, NV 89109
702-737-7545 / Fax: 702-737-7545
Sales: $10 Million-$50 Million
JACK KAMINSKI (C.E.O. & Real Estate Contact)
ROBERT MARINOFF (V.P.-Opers.)
ROBERT FISHER (V.P.-Mdsg.) & Buys Men's Wear, Store Displays, Fixtures, Supplies

THE JOCK SHOP (SP)
5785 W. Sahara Ave.
Las Vegas, NV 89102
702-871-4910 / Fax: 702-871-1933
Sales: $1 Million-$10 Million
DEAN WEIBLE (Owner) & Buys Activewear, Athletic Footwear

MARSHALL-ROUSSO (SP-44)
(Marshall Retail Group)
2330 Industrial Rd. (m-b)
Las Vegas, NV 89102
702-385-5233 / Fax: 702-385-2842
Retail Locations: NV
MICHAEL WILKINS (President)
JENNIFER McLAUGHLIN-Men's Wear, Footwear

MELWANI'S (MW)
(CLOTHES HORSE, INC.)
3200 Las Vegas Blvd. South (b)
Las Vegas, NV 89109
702-733-6676 / Fax: 702-733-6019
MURLI MELWANI (Owner) & Buys Men's Wear, Store Displays, Fixtures, Supplies

MORT WALLIN OF LAKE TAHOE (MW)
Bally's Grand Hotel (b-h)
3645 S. Las Vegas Blvd.
Las Vegas, NV 89109
702-736-1313
BRAD WALLIN (Owner) & Buys Men's Wear, Footwear

RAUL VEGAS LTD. (MW)
252 Convention Center Dr., #5 (bud-p)
Las Vegas, NV 89109
702-734-8264
RAUL MOYA (Owner) & Buys Men's Suits, Tailored Jackets, Tailored Slacks, Sportswear, Sweaters, Sport Shirts, Outer Jackets, Casual Slacks, Accessories, Dress Shirts, Ties, Hosiery, Belts, Store Displays, Fixtures and Supplies

SPORTS LOGO (SG)
3500 Las Vegas Blvd. South
Las Vegas, NV 89109
702-792-2338 / Fax: 702-792-2338
Sales: $1 Million-$10 Million
BRUCE SMITH (Owner) & Buys Boys' Apparel, Men's Apparel, Men's Hosiery, Men's Outerwear, Men's Sportswear
STEVE ZURITA (Store Mgr.) & Buys Boys' Apparel, Men's Apparel, Men's Hosiery, Men's Outerwear, Men's Sportswear

TUXEDO JUNCTION WEST (MW-2)
(TUXEDO JUNCTION, INC.)
(TUXEDO JUNCTION EAST)
3540 W. Sahara (m)
Las Vegas, NV 89102
702-873-8830 / Fax: 702-876-5231
Sales: $100,001-$500,000
Website: www.tuxedojunction-lv.com
ROBERT MOON (Owner) & Buys Men's & Boys' Formal Wear, Store Displays, Fixtures, Supplies

TUXEDO PALACE (MW-2 & OL)
(BRIDAL SALON AT TUXEDO PALACE)
4001 S. Decatur (m-b)
Las Vegas, NV 89103
702-367-4433 / Fax: 702-367-8453
Website: www.tuxedopalace.com
LAWRENCE SMITH (Co-Owner) & Buys Men's Formal Wear, Store Displays, Fixtures, Supplies

READ'S GOLDEN RULE STORE (DEPT)
P.O. Box 88 (p)
Mountain City, NV 89831
775-763-6616 / Fax: 775-763-6060
Sales: $100,001-$500,000
CHARLES E. READ (Owner & Mdse. Mgr.) & Buys Store Displays, Fixtures, Supplies
NORMA READ-Men's & Boys' Wear

HOLLYWOOD STAR (MW)
2201 Civic Center Dr. (m)
North Las Vegas, NV 89030
702-642-3534
Sales: $100,001-$500,000
SAM KIM (Owner) & Buys Men's Sportswear, Furnishings, Headwear, Accessories, Urban Contemporary

CLOWN'S CLOSET (KS)
The Reno Hilton Hotel (b)
Reno, NV 89595
775-322-2311 / Fax: 775-323-5111
LINDA DETOMASO (Owner) & Buys to Size 14 Boys' Wear, Store Displays, Fixtures, Supplies

PARADIES SHOPS (SP-5)
2001 E. Plumb Ln.
Reno, NV 89502
775-329-6021 / Fax: 775-329-9125
CATHY PIERSON (Mgr.) & Buys Active Apparel, Golf Apparel Apparel

RENO SUPER T'S (SP)
436 N. Virginia St.
Reno, NV 89501
775-323-2643 / Fax: 775-323-2643
FRANK SCIBILIA (Owner) & Buys Active Apparel

STEAMBOAT WESTERN WEAR (WW)
16960 S. Virginia St. (m)
Reno, NV 89511
775-849-2400 / Fax: 775-849-2440
Sales: $100,001-$500,000
R. ANGELO TOGLIATTI (Owner) & Buys Men's, Young Men's & Boys' Western Wear, Leather Apparel

TWIN CITY SURPLUS, INC. (DEPT & OL)
1675 E. 4th St. (p)
Reno, NV 89512
775-323-5630 / Fax: 775-323-7814
Website: www.twincitysurplus.com
SHAWN SLITER (G.M.M.) & Buys Men's Work Clothing, Jeans, Underwear, Work Boots, Store Displays, Fixtures, Supplies

CUSTOM CAPS & SHIRTS (SP & MO)
52 E. Glendale Ave.
Sparks, NV 89431
775-356-5353 / Fax: 775-356-5399
Sales: $100,001-$500,000
MIKE BASS (Owner) & Buys Custom Apparel, Hunting Apparel, Footwear

SPORTIF USA (CLO & MO & OL)
1415 Greg St., #101 (b)
Sparks, NV 89431
775-359-6400 / Fax: 775-353-3400
Sales: $10 Million-$50 Million
Website: www.sportif.com
JOHN KIRSCH (President)
DOUG MOIR (C.F.O.)
MICHELLE HAYDEN (Mgr.-Purch.) & Buys Men's Footwear, Men's Apparel, Men's Accessories

TAHOE T-SHIRTERY (SP)
P.O. Box 6118
Tahoe City, NV 96145
530-583-7495
MARK LANZ (Owner) & Buys Active Apparel

TIP'S WESTERN WEAR (WW)
185 Melarkey (m)
Winnemucca, NV 89445
775-623-3300 / Fax: 775-623-3909
KEN TIPTON (Co-Owner) & Buys Men's Western Wear, Boys' Western Wear
CATHY TIPTON (Co-Owner) & Buys Store Displays, Fixtures and Supplies

GOLDEN RULE STORE (CLO)
42 N. Main St. (m)
Yerington, NV 89447
775-463-3811 / Fax: 775-463-3811
DEANNE ROTCHY (Owner) & Buys Men's Sportswear, Footwear, Store Displays, Fixtures, Supplies

ZEPHYR COVE RESORT (SP)
760 Hwy. 50
Zephyr Cove, NV 89448
775-588-6644 / Fax: 775-588-9627
Website: www.tahoedixie2.com
NANCY McMASTERS (Mgr.) & Buys Active Apparel
CHUCK SHAPIRO (Mgr.) & Buys Active Apparel

NEW HAMPSHIRE - Concord

BRITCHES OF CONCORD, INC. (CLO)
1 Eagle Sq. (b)
Concord, NH 03301
603-225-4184 / Fax: 603-882-5012
Website: www.britchesofconcord.com
RAY BOUCHER (President) & Buys Men's Sportswear, Furnishings, Headwear, Accessories

EDWARD FINE & SON (MW)
5 S. Main St. (b)
Concord, NH 03301
603-228-8461
Sales: $100,001-$500,000
EDWARD FINE, JR. (Owner) & Buys Men's Wear, Store Displays, Fixtures, Supplies
SUSAN E. FINE (G.M.M.) & Buys Men's Wear, Store Displays, Fixtures, Supplies

JOE KING'S SHOE SHOP, INC. (FW)
45 N. Main St. (bud-p-b-des)
Concord, NH 03301
603-225-6012 / Fax: 603-225-0032
Sales: $1 Million-$10 Million
TOM KING (President)
JEFF ROBERGE (Mgr.) & Buys Boys' Footwear, Licensed Apparel, Watches, Men's Accessories, Men's Apparel, Hosiery, Men's Footwear

GEORGE & PHILLIP'S (SP-2)
173 Water St.
Exeter, NH 03833
603-772-3156 / Fax: 603-772-8631
SELMA M. FREEDMAN (President)
BERT FREEDMAN (V.P.) & Buys Activewear, Athletic Footwear, T-shirts, Shorts, Caps

GARNET HILL (MO & OL & CLO-2)
231 Main St. (b)
Franconia, NH 03580
603-823-5545 / Fax: 603-823-7034
Website: www.garnethill.com
RUSS GAITSKILL (President)
JOANNE MOGREN-Men's Robes, Underwear, Sleepwear, Slippers

DECATO'S MENSWEAR, INC. (CLO)
357 Central St. (m)
Franklin, NH 03235
603-934-4919
Sales: $100,001-$500,000
DICK WISER (Owner) & Buys Men's Sportswear, Dress Shirts, Headwear, Accessories, Store Displays, Fixtures, Supplies

DUPUIS COUNTRY STORE, INC. (GM)
P.O. Box 27
Rt. 3
Groveton, NH 03582
603-636-1462
BERNARD DUPUIS (Owner) & Buys Men's Coats, Sportswear, Headwear, Accessories, Furnishings, Footwear, Young Men's Wear, to Size 14 Boys' Wear, Store Displays, Fixtures, Supplies

DORR MILL STORE (CLO & OL)
(DORR FABRICS, INC.)
P.O. Box 88 (m-b)
Hale St.
Guild, NH 03754
603-863-1197 / Fax: 603-863-7458
Website: www.dorrmillstore.com
TERRY DORR (Owner) & Buys Men's Sweaters, Sport Shirts, Casual Slacks, Active Apparel, Dress Shirts, Ties, Hosiery, Gloves, Belts, Jewelry

BIB & CRIB (KS)
440 Lafayette Rd. (m-b)
Hampton, NH 03842
603-926-5455
Website: www.bibandcrib.com
KAMA GEORGE (Owner) & Buys Boys' Wear Up To Size 7, Store Displays, Fixtures & Supplies

CHURCH'S CHILDREN'S CLOTHES (KS-2)
(KAFRAN, INC.)
2 E. South St. (b)
Hanover, NH 03755
603-643-4205
Sales: $100,001-$500,000
Website: www.churchschildrensclothes.com
FRANCIS WHITE (Owner)
PETER WHITE-Store Displays, Fixtures, Supplies, 8 to 20 Boys' Wear, Footwear
DANIEL WHITE-8 to 20 Boys' Wear, Footwear

DARTMOUTH CO-OP SOCIETY (SG & CLO & OL)
25 S. Main St. (m-b)
Hanover, NH 03755
603-643-3100 / Fax: 603-643-2718
Sales: $1 Million-$10 Million
Website: www.dartmouthcoop.com
DON POWERS (G.M.M.) & Buys Men's Active Apparel, Sweaters, Sport Shirts, Outer Jackets, Casual Slacks, Headwear, Belts, Small Leather Goods, Footwear, Young Men's Wear, Apparel, Store Displays, Fixtures, Supplies

ROSEY JEKES, INC. (CLO)
15 Lebanon St. (b)
Hanover, NH 03755
603-643-3693 / Fax: 603-643-6339
KENNETH FABRIKANT (Owner) & Buys Men's Dress Coats, Suits, Raincoats, Sportswear, Dress Shirts, Headwear, Store Displays, Fixtures, Supplies

GREAT WEST TRADING (WW)
1158 Hooksett Rd. (p)
Hooksett, NH 03106
603-627-2531 / Fax: 603-627-6955
Website: www.gwtco.com
ROGER LETENDRE (President)
PAM THORNTON (Mgr.) & Buys Men's Western Wear, Related Accessories, Furnishings, Footwear, Store Displays, Fixtures, Supplies

THE WOODEN SOLDIER (CLO)
Hwy. 16-302 (b)
P.O. Box 800
Intervale, NH 03845
603-356-5643 / Fax: 603-356-3530
Sales: $1 Million-$10 Million
DAVID MENNELLA (President) & Buys Boys' Apparel, Boys' Footwear, Men's Apparel

JACK FROST SHOP (CLO-2)
Main St. (m)
P.O. Box F
Jackson, NH 03846
603-383-4391 / Fax: 603-383-4331
Website: www.jackfrostshop.com
BILL TINKHAM (Owner) & Buys Men's Sportswear, Furnishings, Small Leather Goods, Footwear, Store Displays, Fixtures, Supplies

MILLER BROTHERS-NEWTON, INC. (MW-2)
105 Main St. (m-b)
Keene, NH 03431
603-352-3039
Website: www.mbnmenswear.com
ROBERT WICHLAND (Co-Owner) & Buys Men's Sportswear, Footwear, Furnishings & Accessories
DAVID WICHLAND (Co-Owner) & Buys Men's Sportswear, Footwear, Furnishings & Accessories
JOHN WICHLAND (Co-Owner) & Buys Men's Sportswear, Footwear, Furnishings & Accessories

MELNICK'S (SP-2)
574 Main St.
Laconia, NH 03246
603-524-1276 / Fax: 603-527-0893
Website: www.melnicksshoe.com
KEVIN SULLIVAN (Owner) & Buys Activewear, Athletic Footwear, Licensed Apparel

ESSENTIALS FOR MEN (MW-3)
River Mill Complex, #350 (b)
85 Mechanic St.
Lebanon, NH 03766
603-448-6750 / Fax: 603-448-6950
LYNN KOCHANEK (Co-Owner)
WALTER KOCHANEK (Co-Owner) & Buys Men's Wear, Sportswear, Furnishings, Small Leather Goods, Accessories, Footwear, Store Displays, Fixtures, Supplies

HIRSCH'S (MW)
59 Hanover St. (p)
Lebanon, NH 03766
603-448-2454 / Fax: 603-448-2117
Sales: $100,001-$500,000
EDWARD HIRSCH (Gen. Mgr.) & Buys Men's Wear, Furnishings, Accessories, Footwear
RAPHAEL HARRIS (Display Mgr.) & Buys Store Displays, Fixtures, Supplies

RARE ESSENTIALS (CLO)
85 Mechanic St.
Lebanon, NH 03766
603-448-6750 / Fax: 603-448-6950
WALT KOCHANEK (@ 603-448-6750)-Men's Wear, Accessories, Furnishings

LAHOUT'S COUNTRY CLOTHING & SKI SHOP (CLO-7 & SG)
245 Union St. (bud-p)
Littleton, NH 03561
603-444-5838 / Fax: 603-444-0545
Website: www.lahouts.com
RON LAHOUT (Co-Owner) & Buys Tailored Jackets, Tailored Slacks, Raincoats, Sportswear, Outerwear, Outdoor Wear, Ski Wear, Shirts, Shorts, Furnishings, Headwear, Belts, Jewelry, Small Leather Goods, Boys' Wear (7 & Up), Store Displays, Fixtures & Supplies
JOE LAHOUT (Co-Owner) & Buys Tailored Jackets, Tailored Slacks, Raincoats, Sportswear, Furnishings, Headwear, Belts, Jewelry, Small Leather Goods, Boys' Wear (7 & Up), Footwear, Outerwear

GEORGE'S APPAREL, INC. (MW & OL)
675 Elm St. (m-b)
Manchester, NH 03101
603-622-5441 / Fax: 603-627-8055
Website: www.georgesapparel.com
GEORGE ANGELOPOULOS (President)
BERNIE MARCHEWSKY-Men's Sportswear, Store Displays, Fixtures, Supplies
GARY MARINO-Belts, Ties, Accessories
DENNIS LABBE-Dress Shirts, Dress Pants

DICK AVARD'S HABERDASHERY (MW & OL)
117 Main St.
Nashua, NH 03060
603-889-0305
RICHARD AVARD (President) & Buys Men's Sportswear, Ties, Robes, Hosiery, Gloves, Belts, Store Displays, Fixtures, Supplies

HUBERT'S DEPARTMENT STORE, INC. (DEPT-5)
4654 Main St. (p-m-b)
Newport, NH 03773
603-863-0659 / Fax: 603-863-0827
Website: www.hubertsstores.com
KATHLEEN HUBERT (Co-Owner)
GUENTER HUBERT (Co-Owner) & Buys Men's Furnishings, Sportswear, Swimwear, Accessories, Young Men's & Boys' Wear, Footwear, Store Displays, Fixtures, Supplies
TOM HUBERT (Co-Owner) & Buys Boys' Wear, Young Men's Wear, Furnishings, Accessories

JOE JONES SKI & SPORTS SHOP, INC. (SG-9)
P.O. Box 920 (p-m-b)
2709 White Mountain Hwy.
North Conway, NH 03860
603-356-9411 / Fax: 603-356-6474
Website: www.joejonessports.com
CHUCK WAGENHEIM (President)
ESTHER WAGENHEIM-Men's Sweaters, Outer Jackets, Active Apparel, Headwear, Accessories, Ski Apparel, Swimwear, Young Men's Wear, 8 to 18 Boys' Swimwear, Ski Apparel
DAVID DETHLEFT-Footwear

THE SCOTTISH LION IMPORT SHOP (MO & CLO & OL)
P.O. Box 1700 (m-b)
Main St.
North Conway, NH 03860
603-356-6383 / Fax: 603-356-9032
Sales: $1 Million-$10 Million
Website: www.scottishlion.com
JOHN R. HURLEY (Owner)
JUDITH HURLEY (G.M.M.) & Buys Scottish & Irish Imported Men's Tailored Jackets, Sport Jackets, Headwear, Jewelry, Fragrances, Kilts, Store Displays, Fixtures, Supplies

EASTERN MOUNTAIN SPORTS, INC. (SG-64 & OL)
P.O. Box 850 (p-m-b)
1 Vose Farm Rd.
Peterborough, NH 03458
603-924-9571 / Fax: 603-924-9138
Website: www.emsonline.com
Retail Locations: CO, CT, DE, IL, ME, MD, MA, MI, NH, NJ, NY, OH, PA, RI, VT, VA
WILL MANZER (President & G.M.M.)
BOB DOWNY (V.P. & Real Estate Contact)
HARRY McPHERSON-Men's Outerwear
OPEN-Men's Accessories, Boys' Wear, Men's Underwear, Men's Pants, Shorts, Sweaters, Knit & Woven Shirts
MARSHALL MERRIAN-Men's & Boys' Footwear

OCEAN PROPERTIES LTD. (CLO)
1000 Market St., Bldg. 1, #300
Portsmouth, NH 03801
603-559-2165 / Fax: 306-559-2194
AMANDA-Boys' Apparel, Boys' Swimwear, Accessories, Hats, Men's Apparel, Men's Surf & Swimwear, Resortwear, T-shirts, Imprinted Sportswear

STUART SHAINES (MW)
123 Congress St. (b)
Portsmouth, NH 03801
603-436-2513 / Fax: 603-436-4363
Sales: $500,001-$1 Million
STUART N. SHAINES (President)
RICHARD A. MARTUSCELLO (Exec. V.P. & C.E.O. & G.M.M.) & Buys Men's Urban Contemporary, Store Displays, Fixtures, Supplies

WHOLLY MACRO (CLO-2 & OL)
(MACRO POLO, INC.)
89 Market St. (m)
Portsmouth, NH 03801
603-436-8338 / Fax: 603-436-8878
Website: www.macropolo.com
WILL BERLINER (Owner)
ANGELA GEORGE (Mgr.) & Buys Men's Sportswear, Sweaters, Sport Shirts, Outer Jackets, Casual Slacks, T-shirts, Headwear, Jewelry, Footwear, Urban Contemporary, Store Displays, Fixtures, Supplies

MICHAEL'S OF MAIN ST. LTD. (CLO)
34 N. Broadway
Salem, NH 03079
603-898-1540
SHAWN MacLEAN (Owner) & Buys Men's Suits, Sportswear, Outerwear, Leather Apparel, Accessories, Footwear, Store Displays, Fixtures, Supplies

HOWARD'S LEATHER STORES (CLO)

Rt. 9 (p-m)
Spofford, NH 03462
603-363-4325 / Fax: 603-363-8016
Sales: $100,001-$500,000

JOE PLANTE (Co-Owner) & Buys Men's Tailored Jackets, Outer Jackets, Gloves, Leather Apparel, Headwear, Accessories, Boots, Supplies

JANE PLANTE (Co-Owner) & Buys Men's Tailored Jackets, Outer Jackets, Gloves, Leather Apparel, Headwear, Accessories, Boots, Supplies

THE TIMBERLAND CO. (CLO-72)

200 Domain Dr. (b)
Stratham, NH 03885
603-772-9500 / Fax: 603-773-1640
Sales: Over $1 Billion
Website: www.timberland.com

SIDNEY SWARTZ (Chmn.)
JEFFREY SWARTZ (C.E.O. & President)
BRIAN McKEON (C.F.O. & Sr. V.P.-Fin. & Admin.)
KENNETH PUCKER (C.O.O.& Sr. V.P. & Gen. Mgr.)
JOHN CAMMONS (C.A.O. & V.P.-Fin.)
CAROL YANG (Chief Mktg. Ofcr.)
GARY SMITH (Sr. V.P.)
SCOTT BRIGGS (Sr. V.P.-Sls.)
MARC SCHNEIDER (V.P.)
GREG SALTZBERG (V.P. & Treas.)
BRUCE JOHNSON (V.P.)
DANETTE WINEBERG (V.P. & Gen. Counsel)
STEVEN BRIGHAM (V.P.-Info. Sys.)
BONNIE MONAHAN (V.P.-Bus. Dev.)
DOUG CLARK (V.P.-Prdt. Dev.)
MALCOLM GRAY (Sr. Dir.-Mktg.)
JOHN ANDRELIUNAS (Sr. Dir.-Prdt. Dev.)
AMY MARZEC-Leather Goods, Men's Accessories, Hosiery, Watches
TIM FOLEY-Men's Footwear, Sportswear, Casualwear, Denim, Designer Apparel, Outerwear, Young Men's Wear

BIRTH OF THE BLUES (CLO)

(SUNDANCE JEANS OF BERLIN, INC.)
K-Mart Plz.
Rt. 12-A
West Lebanon, NH 03784
603-298-7848

DAVID HEIMBERG (Owner) & Buys Men's Jeans, Sport Shirts, Store Displays, Fixtures, Supplies

SOLOMON'S STORE (DEPT)

P.O. Box 189 (p)
Main St.
West Stewartstown, NH 03597
603-246-8822 / Fax: 603-246-3672
Sales: $100,001-$500,000

PAULINE S. DALEY (G.M.M.) & Buys Men's Raincoats, Overcoats, Sweaters, Sport Shirts, Casual Slacks, Active Apparel, Dress Shirts, Ties, Underwear, Hosiery, Gloves, Headwear, Belts, Footwear, Store Displays, Fixtures, Supplies

BARRON GENTLEMAN (MW-3)
(ESSENELL CORP.)
175 Whitehorse Pike (m-b)
Absecon, NJ 08201
609-383-1344 / Fax: 609-283-1356
TED LISCHIN (Owner) & Buys Men's Wear, Footwear, Store Displays, Fixtures, Supplies

BILL'S WORK & CASUAL WEAR (MW)
P.O. Box 125 (p)
2369 Hwy. 34
Allenwood, NJ 08720
732-528-6828 / Fax: 732-528-6274
Sales: $1 Million-$10 Million
BARRIE SIEGEL (President) & Buys Men's Sportswear, Work Clothing & Uniforms, Underwear, Hosiery, Gloves, Headwear, Belts, Big & Tall Men's Wear, Boys' Jeans, Corduroys, Tops, Swimwear, T-shirts, Beachwear, Footwear, Store Displays, Fixtures, Supplies

MR. FASHION, INC. (MW)
540 Cookman Ave. (m)
Asbury Park, NJ 07712
732-775-5151
Sales: $100,001-$500,000
CARL WILLIAMS (Owner) & Buys Men's Wear, Footwear, Hats, Store Displays, Fixtures, Supplies

CASINO MALE (MW)
1026 Atlantic Ave. (bud-p-b)
Atlantic City, NJ 08401
609-344-1766 / Fax: 609-345-7552
Sales: $1 Million-$10 Million
DAVID HOFELD (President & Owner) & Buys Men's Wear Clothing, Suits, Tailored Jackets & Slacks, Raincoats, Outer Jackets, Leather Apparel
FRANK TETI-Ties, Underwear, Hosiery, Gloves, Headwear, Accessories
RENA HOFELD-Sweaters, Sport Shirts

ELEGANZA (CLO)
3107 Boardwalk
Atlantic City, NJ 08401
609-348-4894 / Fax: 609-344-6144
Sales: $1 Million-$10 Million
GINO IOVINO (Owner) & Buys Men's Footwear, Leather Goods, Big & Tall Men's Wear, Casualwear, Denim, Formalwear, Accessories, Outerwear, Sportswear, Suits, Swimwear
ROBERT MORICCI (Store Mgr.)

GRIMALDI'S (MW)
2100 Boardwalk, #181
Atlantic City, NJ 08401
609-344-8422
MAXINE SPECTOR (Owner) & Buys Store Displays, Fixtures, Supplies
GILLIAN MAY-Men's Overcoats, Suits, Tailored Jackets, Tailored Slacks, Sportswear, Furnishings, Headwear, Belts, Jewelry, Small Leather Goods, Big & Tall Men's Wear, Footwear, Urban Contemporary, Store Displays, Fixtures and Supplies

HI-FIVE FASHIONS (MW)
1718 Atlantic Ave. (m-b)
Atlantic City, NJ 08401
609-345-1741 / Fax: 609-345-1119
MIKE RHAS (Mgr.) & Buys Men's & Boys' Wear, Urban Contemporary, Store Displays, Fixtures, Supplies
MALCOM STEWARD (Mgr.) & Buys Men's & Boys' Wear, Urban Contemporary, Store Displays, Fixtures, Supplies

ITALIAN DIMENSION, INC. (MW)
2307 Atlantic Ave. (b-h)
Atlantic City, NJ 08401
609-348-1662
PAT Di PALMA (Owner) & Buys Men's Wear, Domestic & Italian Imports, Footwear, Store Displays, Fixtures, Supplies

JAY'S DESIGNER TEES (SP)
3030 Ocean Dr.
Avalon, NJ 08202
609-368-3042
JAY SCHWARTZ (Owner) & Buys Activewear, Licensed Activewear

THE ISLANDERS STORE (DEPT)
(PROCO, INC.)
7th & Broadway (m-b)
Barnegat Light, NJ 08006
609-494-1753 / Fax: 609-494-6805
DAVID PROUSE (Mgr.) & Buys Men's Swimwear, Shorts, Sport Shirts, 8 to 20 Boys' Swimwear, Shorts, Sport Shirts, Footwear, Store Displays, Fixtures, Supplies

HERBERT'S (AN)
468 Broadway (p-m)
Bayonne, NJ 07002
201-437-7904 / Fax: 201-437-7906
ALAN SCHINASI (Owner) & Buys Men's Work Clothes, Jeans, Shirts, Footwear, Store Displays, Fixtures, Supplies

VALENZUELA'S MEN'S SHOP (MW)
(MODA ULTIMA, INC.)
796 Broadway (m-b)
Bayonne, NJ 07002
201-823-2007
ALDO BENAVIDES (Owner) & Buys Men's Wear, Footwear, Urban Contemporary, Store Displays, Fixtures, Supplies

SINK 'R SWIM SHOP (CLO)
11117 Long Beach Blvd. (m)
Beach Haven, NJ 08008
609-492-4554 / Fax: 609-492-4281
JOHN COYLE (Owner) & Buys Store Displays, Fixtures, Supplies
MICHAEL BELL (Mgr.-Men's Dept.) & Buys Men's Suits, Tailored Jackets, Tailored Slacks, Raincoats, Sweaters, Sport Shirts, Windbreakers, Casual Slacks, Active Apparel, Swimwear, Dress Shirts, Ties, Robes, Underwear, Hosiery, Headwear, Belts, Jewelry, Small Leather Goods, Footwear

CHRIS & CO. (MW)
9 S. Washington Ave. (b)
Bergenfield, NJ 07621
201-387-8889 / Fax: 201-439-0829
CHRIS POULOS (Owner) & Buys Men's Regular & Big & Tall Size Clothing, Footwear, Store Displays, Fixtures, Supplies

BEN & MOLLY (MW-2)
(POLSKYS)
P.O. Box 38 (p)
41 Clementon Rd.
Berlin, NJ 08009
856-767-7616 / Fax: 856-845-6530
SCOTT LUPOW (President) & Buys Men's Sportswear, Furnishings, Belts, Store Displays, Fixtures, Supplies

PAUL'S FASHIONS, INC. (MW)
41 Clements Ave. (m)
Berlin, NJ 08009
856-767-5266
PAUL COHEN (Owner) & Buys Men's Wear, Footwear, Store Displays, Fixtures, Supplies

SNEAKER WORLD (SP)
(ECONOMY SHOES)
539 Bloomfield Ave.
Bloomfield, NJ 07003
973-743-7994 / Fax: 973-743-2186
ALAN RAPPAPORT (Mgr.) & Buys Activewear, Athletic Footwear, Licensed Apparel

NEW JERSEY - Boonton

BOB'S MEN'S SHOP (MW)
P.O. Box 481 (m)
602 Main St.
Boonton, NJ 07005
973-334-1496
JAMES SWEYNOR (Owner) & Buys Men's Overcoats, Raincoats, Tailored Jackets, Suits, Sportswear, Accessories, Big & Tall Men's Wear, Store Displays, Fixtures, Supplies

MILLER & MAGOWAN, INC. (MW)
P.O. Box 69 (m-b)
210 Farnsworth Ave.
Bordentown, NJ 08505
609-298-1524 / Fax: 609-298-3100
Sales: $100,001-$500,000
D. SCOTT MAGOWAN (V.P.) & Buys Men's Overcoats, Suits, Tailored Jackets, Tailored Slacks, Raincoats, Sweaters, Sport Shirts, Outer Jackets, Casual Slacks, Active Apparel, Furnishings, Headwear, Accessories, Store Displays, Fixtures, Supplies

B & B DEPARTMENT STORE (DEPT-7)
254 Drum Point Rd. (m-b)
Brick, NJ 08723
732-920-3300 / Fax: 732-920-1323
Sales: $1 Million-$10 Million
JEFF DAVIDSON (Co-Owner)
PHILIP BERTOLE (Co-Owner) & Buys Men's Tailored Slacks, Sweaters, Sport Shirts, Outer Jackets, Leather Apparel, Casual Slacks, Apparel, Furnishings, Headwear, Big & Tall Men's Wear, Store Displays, Fixtures, Supplies
BERDETTE TOLGAN-8 to 20 Boys' Wear, Young Men's Wear, Boys' Footwear
Linda SCILLIA-Men's Footwear

BURLINGTON COAT FACTORY (CLO-414 & OL)
(COHOES FASHIONS, INC.)
1830 Rt. 130 North (bud-p)
Burlington, NJ 08016
609-387-7800 / Fax: 609-387-7071
Sales: $2.2 Billion
Website: www.coat.com
Retail Locations: WA, OR, CA, NV, AZ, TX, NM, CO, ID, KS, OK, FL, SC, NC, VA, PA, NY, NJ, MN, MA, NE
MONROE MILSTEIN (President & C.E.O.)
STEPHEN MILLSTEIN (V.P. & G.M.M.)
TARA NEWHALL (V.P. - Men's & Boys' Outerwear) & Buys Men's Outerwear, Wool Outerwear, Wool Overcoats, Leather Apparel, Raincoats
BRIAN SHAFFER-Wool Outerwear, Tailored Outerwear, Raincoats, Ski Coats
OPEN-Light-weight Coats
LINDA SMALL-Boys' Coats
STEVE KOSTER (President - Men's Div.)
GREG SOSONKA (Mdse. Mgr.-Men's Clothing)
LINDA LePELIS-Men's Contemporary Collections
SHERRI AIRHEART-Men's Active Apparel, Swimwear, Young Men's Sportswear, Basic Jeans, Suits, Denim Jackets, Bottoms, Slacks
DEBBIE PALMAR-Men's Ties, Handkerchiefs, Belts, Suspenders, Young Men's Ties
ROYA MOHSENIAN-Men's Suits, Tailored Suit Separates, Tailored Slacks, Sportcoats, Blazers, Young Men's Street Wear
DEBBIE GREENBERG (Mdse. Mgr.-Men's)
ERIC RELLSA-Men's Woven Shirts, Big & Tall Wovens & Knits
LINDA LEPELIS-Men's Sweaters, Robes, Pajamas
ZACHARY PADGETT-Men's Underwear, Robes, Pajamas, Woven & Knit Shirts
DEBBIE KAUFMAN-Men's Big & Tall Dress Shirts
DANA KADY-Men's Casual Pants, Jeans, Corduroy Bottoms, Slacks
LAURIE HALL-Men's Hosiery
BETH TROVATO-7-16 Boys' Apparel
ROB GRAPSKI (Real Estate Contact)

CHILDREN'S SAMPLE SHOP, INC. (KS)
Liberty Sq. (p-m)
Burlington, NJ 08016
609-387-7100 / Fax: 609-387-7102
Sales: $1 Million-$10 Million
ED MUCHNICK (President) & Buys 4 to 7 Boys' Wear, Boys' Footwear, Outwerwear, Sportswear, Store Displays, Fixtures, Supplies

LEGENDARY ARMS, INC. (SP)
P.O. Box 197
Califon, NJ 07830
800-528-2767
Sales: $500,001-$1 Million
Website: www.legendaryarms.com
SUDHA GUPTA (Owner) & Buys Men's Uniforms

DOUBLE S MARKETING, INC. (CLO)
214 S. Broadway (bud)
Camden, NJ 08103
856-966-6221 / Fax: 856-966-0093
IN SONG (Owner) & Buys Men's Underwear & Hosiery, Boys' Wear, Urban Contemporary, Store Displays, Fixtures, Supplies

TOMORROW MEN'S SHOP, INC. (MW)
220 S. Broadway (p)
Camden, NJ 08103
856-963-1353
ANDY CHOI (Owner) & Buys Men's Sportswear, Furnishings, Small Leather Goods, Fragrances, Young Men's Wear, Store Displays, Fixtures, Supplies

GREAT WHITE SHARK (MW-2)
410 Washington St.
Cape May, NJ 08204
609-884-1811 / Fax: 609-884-5233
TONY RANTUCCIO (Owner) & Buys Big & Tall Menswear, Furnishings, Accessories

TAPPIN'S, INC. (JWLY-3)
(FREDERIC GOODMAN JEWELERS)
452 Pompton Ave.
Cedar Grove, NJ 07009
973-239-6201 / Fax: 973-239-6208
Sales: $1 Million-$10 Million
Website: www.goodmanjewelers.com
FRANK GOODMAN (President)
GAIL GOODMAN-Jewelry, Watches

DAVISON'S MEN'S SHOP (MW)
107 Haddonfield-Berlin Rd. (b)
Cherry Hill, NJ 08034
856-795-0070 / Fax: 856-795-3484
ANTHONY GARIANO (Co-Owner)
LAWRENCE GARIANO (Co-Owner) & Buys Men's & Boys' Suits, Sportswear, Accessories, Footwear, Store Displays, Fixtures, Supplies

LEE NEWMAN CLOTHING (MW)
(H. S. MANAGEMENT CO., INC.)
(LEE NEWMAN FINE MENS CLOTHING)
P.O. Box 3524 (b)
2076 E. State Hwy. 70 North
Cherry Hill, NJ 08034
856-424-8388 / Fax: 856-424-6717
HARRY SHIROFF (President) & Buys Men's Sportswear, Furnishings, Accessories, Store Displays, Fixtures, Supplies

NEW JERSEY - Chester

MARS STORES OF CHESTER, INC. (DEPT-3)
(MARS RJ)
179 Rt. 206 South (m)
Chester, NJ 07930
908-879-7577 / Fax: 908-879-5929
ROBERT APPLEBAUM (Owner) & Buys Men's Sportswear, Furnishings, Belts, Boys' Wear, Young Men's Wear, Store Displays, Fixtures, Supplies

COUNTRY SQUIRE MEN'S SHOP (MW)
1075 Raritan Rd. (m-b)
Clark, NJ 07066
732-382-6063 / Fax: 732-382-6760
ARTIE LaLUAN (Owner) & Buys Men's Sportswear, Furnishings, Accessories, Tuxedos

BIKERLEATHER.COM (OL)
(EXTREME BIKER WEAR)
45 E. Madison Ave., #B
Clifton, NJ 07011
973-253-2820 / Fax: 973-253-2824
Website: www.bikerleather.com
ASAD AHMED (Owner) & Buys Men's and Boys' Leather Wear, Motorcycle Jackets, Bomber Jackets, Dusters, Vests, Shirts, Chaps, Pants, Flag Jackets, Gloves, and Saddlebags
ASAD BASHARAT (G.M.M.) & Buys Men's and Boys' Leather Wear, Motorcycle Jackets, Bomber Jackets, Dusters, Vests, Shirts, Chaps, Pants, Flag Jackets, Gloves, and Saddlebags

ROWE - MANSE EMPORIUM (CLO)
1065 Bloomfield Ave.
Clifton, NJ 07012
973-472-8170 / Fax: 973-472-8866
CARMEN MAGGIO (Owner)
SIBBI THOMPSON-Men's Wear & Boys' Wear
FRANZ EBERTZ (Visual Mdsr.) & Buys Store Displays, Fixtures, Supplies

STEVE 19 (CLO-2)
280 Norwood Ave. (m-b)
Deal, NJ 07723
732-531-9299 / Fax: 732-531-4396
Sales: $1 Million-$10 Million
STEVE EITELBURG (Owner) & Buys Men's Footwear, Casualwear, Suits

RICKY'S ARMY-NAVY STORE (AN)
2925 Rt. 130 South
Delran, NJ 08075
856-461-6666 / Fax: 856-786-6679
Sales: $100,001-$500,000
PHIL JOSEPHS (Owner) & Buys Work Wear, Footwear

CLOTHING CENTER, INC. (CLO)
645 Rt. 18 (p-m-b)
East Brunswick, NJ 08816
732-254-0870 / Fax: 732-651-1404
STEVE WORBY (Owner) & Buys Men's & Boys' Wear, Footwear, Store Displays, Fixtures, Supplies
GREG LEVYASH (Store Mgr.) & Buys Men's & Boys' Wear, Footwear, Store Displays, Fixtures, Supplies

BRADDOCK'S, INC. (MW)
180 State Rt. 35 South, #2004 (m-b)
Eatontown, NJ 07724
732-542-0615 / Fax: 732-542-0888
Sales: $1 Million-$10 Million
ROBERT BRUDNER (Co-Owner)
PETER BRUDNER (Co-Owner) & Buys Store Displays, Fixtures, Supplies, Men's Wear, Leather Apparel, Footwear
STEVEN BRUDNER (Co-Owner) & Buys Men's Wear, Leather Apparel, Footwear, Urban Contemporary

SPENCER GIFTS, INC. (GS-700 & OL)
(SPENCER GIFTS EXPRESS)
(DAPY)
(GLOW)
(SPIRIT)
(AMERICA'S HALLOWEEN HEADQUARTERS)
6826 Black Horse Pike (m)
Egg Harbor Township, NJ 08234
609-645-3300 / Fax: 609-645-8062
Website: www.spencergifts.com
Retail Locations: AL, AZ, AR, CA, CO, CT, DE, FL, GA, HI, ID, IL, IN, IA, KS, KY, LA, ME, MD, MA, MI, MN, MS, MO, MT, NE, NV, NH, NJ, NM, NY, NC, ND, OH, OK, OR, PA, RI, SC, SD, TN, TX, UT, VT, VA, WA, WV, WI, WY
STEVE SILVERSTEIN (President & C.E.O.)
ROZ HAYDEN (Purch. Agent) (@ 609-645-5605) & Buys Store Displays, Fixtures, Supplies
PATTY CATANZARO
JOHN NEWMAN-Boxer Shorts, Men's & Boy's T-Shirts
SUSAN WALLDMAN (Real Estate Contact)

ELITE MEN'S APPAREL, INC. (MW)
201 Broad St. (m)
Elizabeth, NJ 07201
908-558-7414
LARRY BETHAEA (Owner) & Buys Men's Wear, Store Displays, Fixtures, Supplies

GQ MENSWEAR (MW)
221 Broad St. (m)
Elizabeth, NJ 07201
908-351-5150 / Fax: 908-289-1974
Sales: $500,000-$1 Million
SYUNG YOO (Owner) & Buys Men's Sportswear, Furnishings, Accessories, Urban Contemporary, Store Displays, Fixtures, Supplies

MANNING'S (SP)
64 Broad St.
Elizabeth, NJ 07201
908-352-4219 / Fax: 908-352-0283
MR. ALI (Owner) & Buys Activewear, Athletic Footwear, Licensed Apparel

SHOPPER'S WORLD (DEPT-9)
100 Broad St. (m-b)
Elizabeth, NJ 07201
908-351-3488 / Fax: 908-351-9077
ABE Dushey (President) & Buys Men's Sportswear, Dress Shirts, Ties, Underwear, Hosiery, Headwear, Belts, Leather Apparel, T-shirts, 8 to 18 Boys' Wear, Urban Contemporary, Store Displays, Fixtures, Supplies
RAOUL AGUILLAR (Mgr.) & Buys Men's Sportswear, Dress Shirts, Ties, Underwear, Hosiery, Headwear, Belts, Leather Apparel, T-shirts, 8 to 18 Boys' Wear, Urban Contemporary, Store Displays, Fixtures, Supplies

SOUL FASHION NUMBER ONE (MW-2)
101 Broad St. (bud-p)
Elizabeth, NJ 07201
908-352-9229
CHON LIM (Owner) & Buys Men's Wear, Sportswear, Furnishings, Store Displays, Fixtures and Supplies

THREE GUYS MEN'S & BOYS' OUTLET (MW)
1170 Elizabeth Ave. (bud-p-m-b-h)
Elizabeth, NJ 07201
908-527-0888 / Fax: 908-352-0445
PETER ZWETKOW (Owner) & Buys Overcoats, Big & Tall Men's Wear, Sportswear, Underwear, Hosiery, Young Men's Wear, Urban Contemporary, Store Displays, Fixtures and Supplies

BEN DANIELS, INC. (MW)
11 Grand Ave. (m-b)
Englewood, NJ 07631
201-569-4845
BEN DANIELS (Mgr.) & Buys Men's Wear, Store Displays, Fixtures, Supplies

CASUAL PLUS, INC. (MW)
70 W. Palisades Ave. (p)
Englewood, NJ 07631
201-567-6066
Sales: $1 Million-$10 Million
SAMSON PARK (Owner)
SIMON LEE-Men's T-shirts, Urban Contemporary, Store Displays, Fixtures, Supplies

NEW JERSEY - Englewood

FRANK OF ROMA (MW)
126 Engle St. (p-m)
Englewood, NJ 07631
201-567-7640
TONY ROMA (Owner) & Buys Men's Wear, Sportswear, Furnishings, Accessories, Young Men's Wear, Boys' Wear, Store Displays, Fixtures and Supplies

KEN'S FASHIONS (MW)
1604 Plaza Rd. (m-b)
Fair Lawn, NJ 07410
201-964-2624
Sales: $1 Million-$10 Million
KEN EHRMAN (Owner) & Buys Leather Goods, Big & Tall Men's Wear, Casualwear, Denim, Formalwear, Hosiery, Outerwear, Sportswear, Suits, Swimwear

MARTIN PROCESS CO. (MW-4)
(MAR PROWEAR CORP.)
10 Commerce Rd. (m)
Fairfield, NJ 07004
973-227-3440 / Fax: 212-695-5049
Sales: $10 Million-$50 Million
MARTIN RIBACK (President)
DAVE LAPIDOS (V.P.)
MITCHELL RIBACK (V.P.)
NORMAN RIBACK (V.P.) & Buys Men's Apparel, Men's Big & Tall Apparel, Men's Casualwear, Men's Accessories, Men's Outerwear, Men's Sportswear, Men's Suits, Men's Swimwear, Young Men's Apparel, Boys' Apparel, Casualwear, Accessories, Outerwear, Swimwear

FEET FIRST, INC. (FW-8)
5142 W. Harley Pond Rd. (bud-p-m-b)
Farmingdale, NJ 07727
732-751-0077 / Fax: 732-751-1129
Sales: $1 Million-$10 Million
Website: www.feetfirstsneakers.com
TIM CONHEENEY (President & C.O.O.) & Buys Boys' Apparel, Men's & Boys' Footwear, Leather Goods, Licensed Apparel, Watches, Men's Accessories, Men's Apparel, Hosiery
CATHY LOWING (Dir.-Adv.)
JACK FORBES (Mgr.) & Buys Boys' Apparel, Men's & Boys' Footwear, Leather Goods, Licensed Apparel, Watches, Men's Accessories, Men's Apparel, Hosiery
MICHELE SEIP (Mgr.) & Buys Boys' Apparel, Men's & Boys' Footwear, Leather Goods, Licensed Apparel, Watches, Men's Accessories, Men's Apparel, Hosiery
SCOTT PRIOLA (Mgr.) & Buys Boys' Apparel, Men's & Boys' Footwear, Leather Goods, Licensed Apparel, Watches, Men's Accessories, Men's Apparel, Hosiery

FLEMINGTON DEPARTMENT STORE (DEPT & OL)
151 Rt. 31 (m-b-h)
Flemington, NJ 08822
908-782-7662 / Fax: 908-782-7859
Sales: $10 Million-$50 Million
Website: www.flemingtondeptstore.com
MARTIN RESNICK (Owner) & Buys Store Displays, Fixtures, Supplies, Men's & Boys' Jeans, Tops, Hosiery, Underwear, Footwear
MICHAEL WILBUR-Men's & Boys' Jeans, Tops, Hosiery, Underwear, Footwear, Urban Contemporary

SNEAKERS PLUS (SP-3)
(CHRIS GACOS ASSOC.)
295 Hwy. 202
Flemington, NJ 08822
908-788-2921 / Fax: 908-788-9497
Website: www.sneakersplus.com
CHRIS GACOS (Owner) & Buys Licensed Apparel & Footwear, Activewear
BARBARA HERMLINGER-Licensed Apparel & Footwear, Activewear

HARDEN BOUTIQUE (MW)
(LA NAISSANCE CORP.)
1538 Le Moine (m-b)
Fort Lee, NJ 07024
201-592-0444 / Fax: 201-592-0419
Sales: $100,001-$500,000
HARDEN HAYENPOUR (Owner) & Buys Men's Wear, Footwear, Store Displays, Fixtures, Supplies

HMG SALES EXCHANGE (MW)
2486 8th St., #B
Fort Lee, NJ 00000
201-947-7777 / Fax: 201-944-8909
Sales: $1 Million-$10 Million
MITCHELL GREENBLATT (President) & Buys Men's Activewear, Pants, Shirts, Skirts, Dresses, Blouses, Accessories, Hosiery, Underwear, Sleepwear, Swimwear, Casualwear
MARISA GREENBLATT (V.P.) & Buys Children's Activewear, Pants, Shirts, Skirts, Dresses, Blouses, Accessories, Hosiery, Underwear, Sleepwear, Swimwear, Casualwear

L.J. TOTAL MEN (MW-2)
8535 Rt. 9 North (m)
Freehold, NJ 07728
732-431-5770 / Fax: 732-431-5771
Sales: $100,001-$500,000
LARRY JOHN (Owner) & Buys Men's Wear, Accessories, Footwear, Store Displays, Fixtures, Supplies

MALE IMAGE LTD. (MW)
3710 US Hwy. 9, #2811 (m)
Freehold, NJ 07728
732-780-3486
MORRIS GRYSMAN (Owner) & Buys Men's Wear, Sportswear, Furnishings, Accessories, Young Men's Wear, Footwear, Store Displays, Fixtures and Supplies

HUGS & KISSES, LLC (KS)
319 Jim Leeds Rd. (m)
Galloway, NJ 08201
609-404-0049
DOREE JONES (Co-Owner) & Buys Boys' Wear Up to 14
TARA JONES (Co-Owner) & Buys Boys' Wear Up to 14

POPULAR CLUB PLAN (MO)
(FEDERATED DEPARTMENT STORES, INC.)
22 Lincoln Pl. (m)
Garfield, NJ 07026
973-471-4300 / Fax: 973-472-3249
Website: www.popularclub.com
WAYNE GARTER (President)
KATHY WELLS (V.P. & G.M.M.)
SHERRIE ZIMMERMAN-Men's Outerwear, Leather Apparel, Sport Coats, Dress Furnishings, Accessories
JOHN SUNDBACK-Size 3 to 18 Boys' Wear, Men's Tops, Men's Bottoms
JANINE BARTON-Men's Jewelry

FINISH LINE, INC. (SP)
4 Vernon Crossing Rd.
Glenwood, NJ 07418
973-764-5020 / Fax: 973-764-5027
GERALD SICILIANO (Mgr.) & Buys Athletic Apparel, Athletic Footwear, Licensed Apparel

ONORE (MW)
100 Riverside Sq.
Hackensack, NJ 07601
201-343-0110 / Fax: 201-343-2597
RICHARD CINTRON (President) & Buys Men's Big & Tall Clothing, Sportswear, Furnishings, Accessories, Shoes

PAPILLON CLOTHING, INC. (MW-2)
241 Riverside Sq. (h)
Hackensack, NJ 07601
201-489-2122 / Fax: 201-871-3478
Sales: $1 Million-$10 Million
JOSEPH SOLEIMANI (Owner) & Buys Men's Sportswear, Accessories, Suits, Tailored Jackets, Tailored Slacks, Furnishings, Store Displays, Fixtures, Supplies

PROZY'S ARMY & NAVY (AN-2)
121 Main St. (bud-p-m)
Hackensack, NJ 07601
201-489-9191 / Fax: 201-489-0918
Sales: $1 Million-$10 Million
TED PROSNITZ (Co-Owner) & Buys Men's Sportswear, Furnishings, Headwear, Accessories, Leather Apparel, T-shirts, Footwear, Urban Contemporary, Store Displays, Fixtures and Supplies
MILTON PROSNITZ (Co-Owner) & Buys Men's Sportswear, Furnishings, Headwear, Accessories, Leather Apparel, T-shirts, Footwear, Urban Contemporary, Store Displays, Fixtures and Supplies

SOME'S UNIFORMS, INC. (SP)
314 Main St. (m-b)
Hackensack, NJ 07601
201-843-1199 / Fax: 201-843-3014
Sales: $1 Million-$10 Million
Website: www.somes.com
JEROME SOME (President) & Buys Men's Footwear, Leather Goods, Sportswear, Uniforms

SUPERIOR TAILORING CO. (MW)
683 Main St.
Hackensack, NJ 07601
201-343-8348
SAM AZZOLLINI (Owner) & Buys Jackets, Suits, Pants

DAD & LAD (MW)
147 Main St. (m)
Hackettstown, NJ 07840
908-852-4808 / Fax: 908-852-2534
MICHAEL WEISS (Owner) & Buys Men's Wear, Sportswear, Furnishings

RICHARD BENNETT (MW)
207 E. Kings Hwy. (b)
Haddonfield, NJ 08033
856-795-5885 / Fax: 856-795-3734
Sales: $1 Million-$10 Million
BENJAMIN SANTORO (President)
REGINALD ROGERS (Dir.-Visual Mdsg.) & Buys Store Displays, Fixtures, Supplies
SUSAN BERG-Men's Sportswear, Furnishings, Accessories

JACK 'N' JULES MEN'S SHOP, INC. (MW)
2633 Whitehorse Hampton Sq. Rd. (m-b)
Hamilton, NJ 08690
609-586-8808 / Fax: 609-586-7415
JACK D'AGOSTINO (Owner) & Buys Men's Wear, Store Displays, Fixtures, Supplies

STEPH'S, INC. (MW)
111 Frank Rodgers Blvd. (m-b)
Harrison, NJ 07029
973-481-9168 / Fax: 973-481-0978
STEVE McCORMICK (Owner) & Buys Men's Sportswear, Furnishings, Store Displays, Fixtures, Supplies

CARROLL'S FASHIONS (CLO)
(MR. CARROLL)
197 Boulevard (m)
Hasbrouck Heights, NJ 07604
201-288-2130 / Fax: 201-288-6033
GEORGE EGGERS (Owner) & Buys Men's Tailored Jackets, Tailored Slacks, Coats, Suits, Hosiery, Underwear, Accessories, Store Displays, Fixtures, Supplies

GARMANY (MW-2)
1 Bethany Rd. (h)
Hazlet, NJ 07730
732-888-2127 / Fax: 732-888-6290
Website: www.garmany.com
JOHN GARMANY-Men's Overcoats, Suits, Tailored Slacks & Jackets, Raincoats, Sportswear, Sweaters, Sport Shirts, Outer Jackets, Leather Apparel, Casual Slacks, Active Apparel, Furnishings, Dress Shirts, Ties, Robes, Underwear, Hosiery, Gloves, Headwear
LARRY GARMANY-Men's Overcoats, Suits, Tailored Slacks & Jackets, Raincoats, Sportswear, Sweaters, Sport Shirts, Outer Jackets, Leather Apparel, Casual Slacks, Active Apparel, Furnishings, Dress Shirts, Ties, Robes, Underwear, Hosiery, Gloves, Headwear
LAUREANO GARMANY-Men's Overcoats, Suits, Tailored Slacks & Jackets, Raincoats, Sportswear, Sweaters, Sport Shirts, Outer Jackets, Leather Apparel, Casual Slacks, Active Apparel, Furnishings, Dress Shirts, Ties, Robes, Underwear, Hosiery, Gloves, Headwear

J & M MEN'S & BOYS' APPAREL (MW)
Airport Plz. (m-b)
1350 Hwy. 36
Hazlet, NJ 07730-1701
732-739-0118 / Fax: 732-332-9299
JERRY GREEN (Owner) & Buys Men's Sportswear, Boys' Sportswear, Big & Tall Men's Sportswear, Shirts, Store Displays, Fixtures, Supplies

BARNEY'S BARGAIN STORE (CLO-2)
1327 Liberty Ave. (m)
Hillside, NJ 07205
973-926-1188 / Fax: 973-923-4242
Sales: $1 Million-$10 Million
EUGENE DARKE (President) & Buys Boys' Apparel, Boys' Footwear, Men's Footwear, Leather Goods, Big & Tall Men's Wear, Casualwear, Formalwear, Hosiery, Outerwear, Sportswear, Suits, Swimwear, Underwear, Uniforms

HOUSE OF CHARLES MENSWEAR (MW)
404 Washington St. (m-b)
Hoboken, NJ 07030
201-659-3270
Sales: $100,001-$500,000
CHARLES LALLO (Owner) & Buys Men's Wear, Sportswear, Furnishings, Accessories, Store Displays, Fixtures, Supplies

FAST BREAK (SP)
(1021 SPRINGFIELD AVENUE CORP.)
1021 Springfield Ave.
Irvington, NJ 07111
973-374-8116
JOSEPH BRAHA (Mgr.) & Buys Athletic Footwear, Athletic Apparel, Licensed Apparel

JOE'S INCITTI CLOTHING (CLO)
11 Mill Rd. (p-m)
Irvington, NJ 07111
973-371-8322 / Fax: 973-371-4469
GLEN INCITTI (Mgr.) & Buys Men's & Boys' Denim, Shirts, T-shirts, Fleecewear, Outer Jackets & Work Clothes, Footwear, Store Displays, Fixtures, Supplies

BENEL CLOTHES, INC. (MW)
2829 Kennedy Blvd. (p-m)
Jersey City, NJ 07306
201-333-2226
MIKE RAUSCH (Owner) & Buys Men's Wear, Men's & Boys' Tuxedos, Store Displays, Fixtures, Supplies

HEIR'S MEN'S SHOP (MW)
525 Westside Ave. (bud-p-m)
Jersey City, NJ 07304
201-435-9031 / Fax: 201-435-8831
Sales: $500,000-$1 Million
JEFF HEIR (Owner) & Buys Sweaters, Sport Shirts, Outer Jackets, Leather Apparel, Casual Slacks, Active Apparel, Work Clothes, Dress Shirts, Ties, Underwear, Hosiery, Gloves, Headwear, Big & Tall Men's Wear, Young Men's Wear, Urban Contemporary, Boys' Wear, Footwear, Store Display

KING'S SON, INC. (MW)
309 Central Ave. (p)
Jersey City, NJ 07307
201-656-6055 / Fax: 201-656-7625
MORRIS ULL (Owner)
SCOTT ULL-Men's Wear, Sportswear, Furnishings, Young Men's Wear, Urban Contemporary, Store Displays, Fixtures and Supplies
MARK ULL-Men's Wear, Sportswear, Furnishings, Young Men's Wear, Urban Contemporary, Store Displays, Fixtures and Supplies

NEW JERSEY - Jersey City

LORD'S MEN'S SHOP (MW-3)

(LORD'S CHILDREN'S SHOP)
(LORD'S, INC.)
2869 Kennedy Blvd. (m-b)
Jersey City, NJ 07306
201-795-1900 / Fax: 201-795-2181

ELLIOT BRAHA (Co-Owner) (@ 201-795-1040) & Buys Size 8 to 20 Boys' Wear, Urban Contemporary, Related Accessories & Furnishings, Store Displays, Fixtures, Supplies

ROBERT BRAHA (Co-Owner) & Buys Men's Wear, Footwear, Related Accessories & Furnishings, Store Displays, Fixtures, Supplies

LORSCH, INC (MW)

911 Bergen Ave. (b)
Jersey City, NJ 07306
201-659-8819 / Fax: 201-659-8820
Sales: $500,000-$1 Million

JON SANFORD (Owner) & Buys Men's Suits, Tailored Jackets, Tailored Slacks, Overcoats, Raincoats, Sportswear, Accessories, Footwear, Store Displays, Fixtures, Supplies

MACABE'S (AN-2)

306 Central Ave. (m)
Jersey City, NJ 07307
201-659-2167

JEFF BAUM (Owner) & Buys Men's & Young Men's Formal Wear

MORLEE'S MEN SHOP, INC. (CLO)

160 Newark Ave. (p)
Jersey City, NJ 07302
201-435-2759

LENNY MORLEE (Owner) & Buys Active Apparel, Urban Contemporary, Store Displays, Fixtures and Supplies

NU-LOOK FASHIONS (CLO)

905 Bergen Ave. (bud-p)
Jersey City, NJ 07306
201-792-0476

KIYOUNG JANG (Owner) & Buys Men's Wear, Sportswear, Furnishings, Young Men's Wear, Urban Contemporary, Boys' Wear, Store Displays, Fixtures and Supplies

STANLEY CLOTHES, INC. (MW)

346 Grove St. (p)
Jersey City, NJ 07302
201-332-3927

LUCY WOLFF (Co-Owner) & Buys Tailored Slacks, Big & Tall Men's Wear, Dress Shirts, Underwear, Hosiery, Belts, Store Displays, Fixture and Supplies

STANLEY WOLFF (Co-Owner) & Buys Tailored Slacks, Big & Tall Men's Wear, Dress Shirts, Underwear, Hosiery, Belts, Store Displays, Fixtures and Supplies

PINCH PENNY & DRESSWELL (CLO)

10 Bridge St. (p-m-b)
Lambertville, NJ 08530
609-397-2229 / Fax: 609-397-8373
Sales: $500,001-$1 Million

MARTIN LUTHER (President) & Buys Leather Goods, Men's Casualwear, Denim, Accessories, Hosiery, Outerwear, Sleepwear, Sportswear

MARCIA CHAPMAN (Treas.)

MARTIN'S CASUALS (CLO)

P.O. Box 8 (m)
703 Grand Central Ave.
Lavallette, NJ 08735
732-830-1188 / Fax: 732-793-8582
Sales: $1 Million-$10 Million

BARBARA HESSLEIN (Partner) & Buys Men's Sweaters, Sport Shirts, Outer Jackets, Casual Slacks, Active Apparel, Footwear, Urban Contemporary

NATHAN HESSLEIN (Partner) (@ 908-830-1188) & Buys Store Displays, Fixtures, Supplies

JIGGER SHOP (KS-2)

Noyes Bldg. (p)
Lawrenceville School
Lawrenceville, NJ 08648
609-896-0620 / Fax: 609-924-9651

DAVID ANTIS-8 to 20 Boys' Sportswear, Urban Contemporary

NOTE:-Buying of Store Displays, Fixtures, Supplies Performed at PRINCETON UNIVERSITY STORE, Princeton, NJ - See Listing.

STEPHEN'S LEATHER GOODS (CLO)

682 Whitehead Rd. (m-b)
Lawrenceville, NJ 08648
609-394-3663 / Fax: 609-989-0052

NICK KOULCOTES-Leather Apparel, Small Leathers

DANTE ZELLER TUXEDO (SP-30)

277 W. Saint Georges Ave. (m-b-des)
Linden, NJ 07036
908-486-2829 / Fax: 908-486-1642
Sales: $1 Million-$10 Million
Website: www.dantetuxedos.com

DANIEL IAMMATTEO (President) & Buys Boys' Apparel, Boys' Footwear, Men's Footwear, Apparel, Formalwear, Accessories

JULIEN'S ARMY-NAVY STORE (AN)

316 N. Wood Ave. (m-b)
Linden, NJ 07036
908-486-8012 / Fax: 908-486-5282
Sales: $100,001-$500,000

ALAIN JULIEN (Owner) & Buys Men's Denim Tops, Work Clothes, Casual Wear, Footwear, Hosiery, Boys' Denim Tops, Underwear & Hosiery

LINGERIE BY SEENA (SP)

2 W. Northfield Rd.
Livingston, NJ 07039
973-992-4909

HELEN KIRSCH (Owner) & Buys Beach Apparel, Swimwear, Headwear, Beach Shoes

ROWMA MEN'S SHOP (MW)

161 S. Livingston Ave. (b)
Livingston, NJ 07039
973-994-0034 / Fax: 973-994-4451
Sales: $500,000-$1 Million

MARESA ZUCCA (Owner) & Buys Men's Wear, Sportswear, Furnishings, Accessories

SAM'S CLOTHING FOR MEN & BOYS (MW)

(Div. of HYMAN COHEN & SONS, INC.)
555 S. Livingston Ave. (b-h)
Livingston, NJ 07039
973-422-1000 / Fax: 973-422-0516
Sales: $500,000-$1 Million

JEFFREY COHEN-Men's Wear, Leather Apparel, T-shirts, 8 to 20 Boys' Wear, Footwear, Urban Contemporary, Store Displays, Fixtures, Supplies

MAURICE COHEN-Men's Wear, Leather Apparel, T-shirts, 8 to 20 Boys' Wear, Footwear, Urban Contemporary, Store Displays, Fixtures, Supplies

SPORTS EXPRESS (SP)

Livingston Mall
112 Eisenhower Pkwy.
Livingston, NJ 07039
973-535-6477 / Fax: 973-535-1772

RON KURZWILL (Owner) & Buys Licensed Apparel

LYNDHURST MEN'S SHOP (MW)

298 Stuyvesant Ave. (p)
Lyndhurst, NJ 07071
201-438-2121
Sales: $500,000-$1 Million

ROSE LaFASO (Owner)

JIM LaFASO-Men's Tailored Slacks, Sportswear, Dress Shirts, Ties, Underwear, Robes, Hosiery, Accessories, Store Displays, Fixtures, Supplies

JOHN LaFASO-Men's Tailored Slacks, Sportswear, Dress Shirts, Ties, Underwear, Robes, Hosiery, Accessories, Store Displays, Fixtures, Supplies

PRIMA ON MAIN (MW)
44 Main St. (m)
Madison, NJ 07940
973-377-9256 / Fax: 973-377-1878
DENISE LUCIANO (Co-Owner) & Buys Sportswear, Dress Shirts, Ties, Underwear, Hosiery, Accessories, Store Displays, Fixtures and Supplies
MARK CONNY (Co-Owner) & Buys Sportswear, Dress Shirts, Ties, Underwear, Hosiery, Accessories, Store Displays, Fixtures and Supplies

MELDISCO (FW-2500)
(FOOTSTAR, INC.)
933 MacArthur Blvd. (bud-p-m)
Mahwah, NJ 07430
201-934-2000 / Fax: 201-934-0398
Sales: Over $1 Billion
Website: www.footstar.com
Retail Locations: AL, AK, AZ, CA, CO, CT, DC, DE, FL, GA, HI, ID, IL, IN, IA, KS, KY, LA, ME, MD, MA, MI, MN, MS, MO, MT, NE, NV, NH, NJ, NM, NY, NC, ND, OH, OK, OR, PA, PR, RI, SC, SD, TN, TX, UT, VT, VA, WA, WV, WI
JEFFREY SHEPARD (President & C.E.O.)
MARK STARACE (V.P. & Mdse. Mgr.) & Buys Boys' Footwear
MICHAEL HILLS (V.P. & G.M.M.)
CHRISTINE ALBANESE-Men's Footwear, Hosiery
ALLEN JONES (Real Estate Contact)

DAVE'S MEN'S & BOYS' SHOP (MW)
41 S. Main St.
Manville, NJ 08835
908-725-9027 / Fax: 908-725-5606
DAVID HABER (Co-Owner) & Buys Men's Suits, Formal Wear, Outerwear, Sportswear, Furnishings, Accessories, Swimwear, Western Wear, Big & Tall Men's Wear, Footwear, Store Displays, Fixtures, Supplies
ALICE HABER (Co-Owner) & Buys Men's Suits, Formal Wear, Outerwear, Sportswear, Furnishings, Accessories, Swimwear, Western Wear, Big & Tall Men's Wear, Urban Contemporary, Footwear, Store Displays, Fixtures, Supplies

THE KID'S CLOSET (KS)
1785 Springfield Ave.
Maplewood, NJ 07040
973-763-4934 / Fax: 973-761-5942
CLARENCE WILLIAMS (Owner) & Buys Boys' Wear, Sportswear, Furnishings, Accessories, Footwear

MAGUIRE'S OF MAPLEWOOD (MW)
167 Maplewwod Ave (m-b)
Maplewood, NJ 07040
973-762-4062 / Fax: 973-762-4060
GLENN MAGUIRE-Men's Sportswear, Furnishings, Accessories

MODERN CLOTHES (MW)
1607 Springfield Ave. (b)
Maplewood, NJ 07040
973-761-1800
A. J. RAMESH (Owner) & Buys Men's Suits, Sports Jackets, Slacks & Tuxedos

MIDDLESEX ARMY & NAVY (AN)
315 Bound Brook Rd. (m)
Middlesex, NJ 08846
732-968-2848 / Fax: 732-968-8646
BARBARA LALLY (President & Owner) & Buys Sportswear, Furnishings, Accessories, Young Men's Wear, Urban Contemporary, Boys' Wear, Store Displays, Fixtures and Supplies

RIVERSIDE JEANS (CLO)
780 Frenchtown Rd. (p)
Milford, NJ 08848
908-996-3223 / Fax: 908-996-3224
SANDY DESAPIO (Co-Owner) & Buys Men's Work Clothes, Sweaters, Sport Shirts, Outer Jackets, Leather Apparel, Casual Slacks, Active Apparel, Ties, Underwear, Hosiery, Gloves, Belts, Young Men's Wear, Urban Contemporary, 8 to 20 Boys' Wear, Footwear, Store Displays, Fixtures, Supplies
CARMINE DESAPIO (Co-Owner) & Buys Men's Work Clothes, Sweaters, Sport Shirts, Outer Jackets, Leather Apparel, Casual Slacks, Active Apparel, Ties, Underwear, Hosiery, Gloves, Belts, Young Men's Wear, Urban Contemporary, 8 to 20 Boys' Wear, Footwear, Store Displays, Fixtures, Supplies

FREEMAN INTERNATIONAL (FW & OL)
(FRENCHSHRINER.COM)
136 Summit Ave. (b-des)
Montvale, NJ 07645
201-930-9399 / Fax: 201-930-9392
Website: www.frenchshriner.com
DAVID MASUR-Men's Fine Leather Footwear

THE SOCK CO. (FW-4)
P.O. Box 112 (p-m)
153 N. Kinderkamack Rd.
Montvale, NJ 07645
201-307-0675 / Fax: 201-307-0358
Sales: $1 Million-$10 Million
Website: www.sockcompany.com
EILEEN TABANO (President)
JENNIFER TABANO (Exec. V.P.) & Buys Boys' Apparel, Boys' Footwear, Men's Footwear, Casualwear, Accessories, Hosiery, Sportswear, Underwear
JIM TABANO (Exec. V.P.) & Buys Boys' Apparel, Boys' Footwear, Men's Footwear, Casualwear, Accessories, Hosiery, Sportswear, Underwear
VINCENT TABANO (Exec. V.P.) & Buys Boys' Apparel, Boys' Footwear, Men's Footwear, Casualwear, Accessories, Hosiery, Sportswear, Underwear
RICHARD TABANO (Treas.) & Buys Boys' Apparel, Boys' Footwear, Men's Footwear, Casualwear, Accessories, Hosiery, Sportswear, Underwear

RESSA'S MEADOWLAND CLEANERS (MW)
82 Moonachie Rd. (b)
Moonachie, NJ 07074
201-641-0068
NICK RESSA (Owner) & Buys Men's Wear, Store Displays, Fixtures, Supplies

ANSON NEWTON LTD. (CLO)
Mt. Kemble Ave. (m-b)
Morristown, NJ 07960
973-539-1117
PAT PARILLO (Owner) & Buys Men's Sportswear, Accessories, Outerwear, Knitwear, Hosiery, Store Displays, Fixtures, Supplies

EPSTEIN'S (DEPT)
P.O. Box 902 (m-b)
32 Park Pl.
Morristown, NJ 07963
973-267-5111 / Fax: 973-538-6442
Sales: $10 Million-$50 Million
JEFF LEVY (V.P. & G.M.M.)
BOB DIERING (Mdse. Mgr.) & Buys Men's Sportswear, Dress Shirts, Basic Furnishings, Men's Headwear, Accessories, Ties, Activewear, Young Men's Wear, Leather Apparel, Collections, Casual Slacks, Boys' Wear, Footwear
MEG TOPOLSKI-Store Displays, Fixtures, Supplies

CAMPUS CLASSICS (SP)
P.O. Box 757
3019 Marne Hwy.
Mount Laurel, NJ 08054
856-234-7474 / Fax: 856-722-8036
Sales: $500,001-$1 Million
GERALD DUNCAN (Owner) & Buys Activewear

NEW JERSEY - New Brunswick

J.C. MENSWEAR (MW)
369 George St. (m)
New Brunswick, NJ 08901
732-545-2520 / Fax: 732-545-5057
Sales: $100,001-$500,000
HYEOP CHA (Owner) & Buys Men's Sportswear, Furnishings, Headwear, Accessories, Young Men's Wear, Store Displays, Fixtures, Supplies

NATELSON (CLO)
10 Jules Ln.
New Brunswick, NJ 08901
732-249-5300 / Fax: 732-249-0355
DAVID NATELSON (Owner) & Buys Men's Sportswear, Boys' Wear, Boys' Sportswear, Boys' Furnishings, Boys' Active Apparel

ADAM'S HABERDASHERS (MW)
1275 Springfield Ave.
New Providence, NJ 07974
908-665-0800 / Fax: 908-464-6394
Website: www.adamsmada.com
JOSEPH SAVINO (Owner) & Buys Men's Wear, Men's Furnishings, Sportswear, Accessories, Headwear

AMERICA'S FASHIONS (MW)
150 Ferry St. (p-m-b)
Newark, NJ 07105
973-344-8813 / Fax: 973-344-7311
ALEJANDRO HERNANDEZ (Owner) & Buys Men's Wear, Sportswear, Resortwear, Outerwear, Footwear, Headwear, Knitwear, Underwear, Accessories, Hosiery, Furnishings, Store Displays, Fixtures, Supplies

CLINTON MEN'S SHOP (MW)
494 Clinton Ave. (bud-p-m-b-h)
Newark, NJ 07108
973-824-9013 / Fax: 973-824-0235
STEPHEN STEINER-Men's Wear, Big & Tall Men's Wear, Sportswear, Furnishings, Footwear, Young Men's Wear, Urban Contemporary, Boys' Wear, Store Displays, Fixtures and Supplies
JOSEPH STEINER-Men's Wear, Big & Tall Men's Wear, Sportswear, Furnishings, Young Men's Wear, Urban Contemporary, Boys' Wear, Store Displays, Fixtures and Supplies
DANNY STEINER-Men's Wear, Big & Tall Men's Wear, Sportswear, Furnishings, Young Men's Wear, Urban Contemporary, Boys' Wear, Store Displays, Fixtures and Supplies

EBONY FASHIONS (MW)
212 Market St. (m)
Newark, NJ 07102
973-242-8830 / Fax: 973-242-7057
Sales: $100,001-$500,000
PAUL NAM (Owner) & Buys Men's Sport Shirts, Outer Jackets, Urban Contemporary, Casual Shoes, Active Apparel, Underwear, Hosiery, Gloves, Headwear, Belts, Jewelry, Small Leather Goods

GREEN'S TUXEDO SHOP (MW)
38 Branford Pl. (m)
Newark, NJ 07102
973-622-5395
DAVID PATERSON (Owner) & Buys Men's & Boys' Tuxedos, ac, Furnishings, Hosiery

J & J BIG & TALL MEN, INC. (MW)
889 Broad St. (p-m-b)
Newark, NJ 07102
973-624-4638 / Fax: 973-575-1536
JOHN OH (Owner) & Buys Men's Clothing Sportswear, Furnishings, Accessories, Big & Tall Men's Wear

JEAN'S PLACE, INC. (MW)
744 Broad St. (b-h)
Newark, NJ 07102
973-622-5652 / Fax: 973-622-3408
Sales: $1 Million-$10 Million
GILBERT PALK (Owner) & Buys Men's Sportswear, Jeans, Furnishings, Belts, Young Men's Wear, Boys' Sportswear

JOE FISCHMAN, INC. (MW)
20 Branford Pl. (m)
Newark, NJ 07102
973-642-8235 / Fax: 973-642-8236
Sales: $100,001-$500,000
JOSEPH MANTO (Owner) & Buys Men's Sportswear, Furnishings, Accessories, Dress Shoes, Ties, Hosiery, Belts, Young Men's Wear

MEIGA (MW)
101 Ferry St.
Newark, NJ 07105
973-589-4708 / Fax: 973-589-1730
MANUEL YGLESIAS (Owner)
HARVEY WILKS-Men's Wear, Accessories

MR. MAN (MW)
10 Branford Pl.
Newark, NJ 07102
973-642-5853
JIMMY SMITH (Mgr.) & Buys Men's Sportswear, Furnishings, Accessories, Urban Contemporary

NATE KUPPERMAN (MW)
130 South St. (m)
Newark, NJ 07114
973-589-8461
Sales: $100,001-$500,000
STEWART KUPPERMAN (President) & Buys Men's Sportswear, Dress Shirts, Ties, Hosiery, Belts

NEWARK SLIP CO. (DEPT-2)
75 1st St. (bud-p-m-b)
Newark, NJ 07107
973-484-6300 / Fax: 973-484-8803
Sales: $1 Million-$10 Million
ROBERT COHEN (Owner) & Buys Men's Wear, Sportswear, Furnishings, Young Men's Wear, Urban Contemporary, Boys' Wear, Store Displays, Fixtures and Supplies
JOE PETITO-Men's Wear, Sportswear, Furnishings, Young Men's Wear, Urban Contemporary, Boys' Wear, Store Displays, Fixtures and Supplies
WALTER CIENKI-Men's Wear, Sportswear, Furnishings, Young Men's Wear, Urban Contemporary, Boys' Wear, Store Displays, Fixtures and Supplies

ROCCO'S URBAN FASHIONS (CLO)
1097 Bergen St. (p-m)
Newark, NJ 07112
973-282-2902 / Fax: 973-282-2802
JAMES ROBERTSON (Owner) & Buys Men's Urban Contemporary, Sportswear, Casual Slacks, Active Apparel, Furnishings, Headwear, Accessories, Footwear

SHOUT, INC. (CLO-5)
149 Ferry St. (m)
Newark, NJ 07105
973-466-1064 / Fax: 973-466-1070
Sales: $1 Million-$10 Million
JONATHAN NEMEROW (Owner) & Buys Overcoats, Suit, Tailored Jackets, Tailored Slacks, Sportswear, Furnishings, Footwear, Store Displays, Fixtures and Supplies
JOE CORSETTO (V.P.) & Buys Overcoats, Jackets, Slacks, Sportswear, Furnishings, Footwear, Store Displays, Fixtures and Supplies

T. J. STORES, INC. (DEPT-2)
181 Ferry St. (p)
Newark, NJ 07105
973-344-4080 / Fax: 973-344-6729
Sales: $1 Million-$10 Million
TED SERURE (Owner) & Buys Men's Sportswear, Furnishings, Accessories, Footwear, Store Displays, Fixtures, Supplies

TREK TRADING, INC. (CLO-2)
192 Market St. (m-b-des)
Newark, NJ 07102
973-648-3500 / Fax: 973-623-1404
Sales: $1 Million-$10 Million
J. LEE (Owner & Real Estate Contact) & Buys Men's Leather Jackets, Outerwear, Sportswear, Store Displays, Fixtures, Supplies

UNIQUE DESIGN (MW)
1125 Branford Pl. (h)
Newark, NJ 07102
973-565-0085 / Fax: 973-242-2518
DENNIS INCI (Owner) & Buys Men's Footwear, Accessories

STYLE SHOP (MW)
178 Spring St. (m-b)
Newton, NJ 07860
973-383-2220
JOE TOLERICO (Co-Owner) & Buys Men's Sportswear, Furnishings, Accessories, Store Displays, Fixtures, Supplies
DONNA MARION (Co-Owner) & Buys Men's Sportswear, Furnishings, Accessories, Store Displays, Fixtures, Supplies

CLAIBORNE FOR MEN (MW-13)
(Div. of LIZ CLAIBORNE, INC.)
1 Claiborne Ave. (m-b)
North Bergen, NJ 07047
201-295-6000 / Fax: 201-295-7850
Website: www.lizclaiborne.com
PAUL CHARRON (Chmn. & C.E.O. & President)
KAREN MURRAY (President-Men's Apparel)
ROBERT NEGRON (President-Retail)
ED BUCCIARELL (President-Small Leather Goods)
MICHAEL SCARPA (C.F.O.)
ELAINE GOODELL (C.A.O. & V.P. & Controller)
JOHN SELLVAN (C.I.O.)
LARRY McCLURE (Sr. V.P.-H.R.)
ALBERT SHAPIRO (V.P.-Mktg.)
ANGELA AHRENDTS (V.P.-Mdsg.)
BRAD LENZ (V.P.-Store Planning & e-Commerce)

TUXEDOS BY ROSE (MW & OL)
7727 Bergenline Ave. (m-b)
North Bergen, NJ 07047
201-869-4010 / Fax: 201-869-8523
Website: www.uniformality.com
JOE MILLER (Owner) & Buys Men's & Boys' Tuxedos

FORUM FOR MEN, INC. (MW)
11 Bloomfield Ave. (m-b)
North Caldwell, NJ 07006
973-226-0100
A. BRUCCHIERI (President) & Buys Men's Formal Wear, Clothing, Sportswear
JAMES MAFFEI (V.P.-Opers.) & Buys Store Displays, Fixtures, Supplies
VICTOR ROWTONDA-Footwear

LUCAS MENSWEAR, INC. (MW)
900 Tilton Rd. (h)
Northfield, NJ 08225
609-641-2088 / Fax: 609-641-2169
Sales: $500,000-$1 Million
LOU MARCHIANO (President) & Buys Men's Sportswear, Dress Shirts, Ties, Hosiery, Belts
SHARON ATKIN (Office Mgr.) & Buys Men's Sportswear, Dress Shirts, Ties, Hosiery, Belts

FRANKLIN MEN'S SHOP (MW)
228 Franklin Ave. (m)
Nutley, NJ 07110
973-667-0189 / Fax: 973-667-4049
Sales: $500,000-$1 Million
JAY PIRO (Owner) & Buys Men's Wear, Outerwear, Headwear, Knitwear, Underwear, Accessories, Hosiery, Furnishings, Leather Apparel, Store Displays, Fixtures, Supplies

NUTLEY FASHIONS, INC. (MW)
(CHARLES DANIELS LTD.)
381 Centre St. (des)
Nutley, NJ 07110
973-667-4440
Sales: $100,001-$500,000
CHARLES MCLAUGHLIN (President) & Buys Jewelry, Men's Footwear, Fragrances, Men's Apparel, Men's Casualwear, Men's Denim Apparel, Men's Accessories, Men's Hosiery, Men's Outerwear, Men's Sleepwear, Men's Suits, Men's Sportswear, Men's Swimwear, Men's Underwear, Watches

SWANK MEN'S SHOP (MW)
171 Franklin Ave. (m-b-des)
Nutley, NJ 07110
973-667-6244 / Fax: 973-667-7286
Sales: $500,001-$1 Million
SAM CIARAMELLO (President) & Buys Men's Footwear, Men's Apparel, Fragrances, Leather Goods, Men's Casualwear, Men's Denim Apparel, Men's Designer Apparel, Men's Formalwear, Men's Accessories, Men's Hosiery, Men's Outerwear, Men's Sleepwear, Men's Sportswear, Men's Suits, Men's Swimwear
RICK SICO-Men's Footwear, Men's Apparel, Fragrances, Leather Goods, Men's Casualwear, Men's Denim Apparel, Men's Designer Apparel, Men's Formalwear, Men's Accessories, Men's Hosiery, Men's Outerwear, Men's Sleepwear, Men's Sportswear, Men's Suits, Men's Swimwear

HABAND COMPANY (MO & OL)
112 Bauer Dr.
Oakland, NJ 07436
201-651-1000 / Fax: 201-405-7774
Website: www.haband.com
DUKE HABERNICKEL (President) & Buys Men's Suits, Blazers, Sportswear, Slacks, Shorts, Shirts, Outerwear, Jackets, Accessories, Belts, Footwear, Dress Shoes

KABAT MEN'S SHOP (MW)
720 Asbury Ave. (m-b-h)
Ocean City, NJ 08226
609-399-1625 / Fax: 609-399-5986
RICHARD KABAT (President & Owner) & Buys Men's Wear, Sportswear, Furnishings, Accessories, Store Displays, Fixtures and Supplies

LEON'S MEN'S SHOP (MW)
756 Asbury Ave. (p)
Ocean City, NJ 08226
609-399-2768 / Fax: 609-601-0511
Sales: $100,001-$500,000
NICK PALERMO (President & Owner) & Buys Sportswear, Furnishings, Accessories, Young Men's Wear, Urban Contemporary, Boys' Wear, Store Displays, Fixtures and Supplies

SEA OATS (KS-3)
710 Asbury Ave. (b)
Ocean City, NJ 08226
609-398-8399 / Fax: 609-398-6930
SKIP TOLOMEO (President) & Buys Boy's Swimwear, Dresswear, Outerwear, Footwear, Related Accessories & Furnishings, Store Displays, Fixtures, Supplies

CR TRADING, INC. (MW)
242 Main St. (p)
Orange, NJ 07050
973-678-4500 / Fax: 973-678-4504
MRS. LIM (Owner) & Buys Men's Sportswear, Furnishings, Headwear, Accessories

PETER NAGY ENTERPRISES, INC. (MW)
(STEPP'N OUT)
219 Main St., #223 (m)
Orange, NJ 07050
973-678-2225 / Fax: 973-678-9050
Sales: $1 Million-$10 Million
PETER NAGY (Owner) & Buys Boys' Apparel, Men's Footwear, Fragrances, Leather Goods, Men's Apparel, Men's Big & Tall Apparel, Men's Casualwear, Men's Denim Apparel, Men's Designer Apparel, Men's Formalwear, Men's Accessories, Men's Outerwear, Men's Sleepwear, Men's Sportswear, Men's Suits, Men's Swimwear, Men's Underwear, Young Men's Apparel

WEBER'S MEN'S SHOP (MW)
310 Broad Ave. (m)
Palisades Park, NJ 07650
201-944-0820
REBA WEBER (Owner) & Buys Men's Wear, T-shirts, Sportswear, Resortwear, Outerwear, Headwear, Knitwear, Underwear, Accessories, Furnishings, Store Displays

HE-MAN BIG & TALL MEN'S SHOP (MW-2)
255 Rt. 4 West (p-m)
Paramus, NJ 07652
201-845-8494 / Fax: 201-845-5279
Website: www.he.qpg.com
JEROME DEMPSEY (President) & Buys Men's Big & Tall Clothing, Sportswear, Furnishings, Headwear, Accessories

NEW JERSEY - Paramus

RAMSEY OUTDOOR STORE, INC. (MW-3)
P.O. Box 1689 (b)
Rt. 17 North
Paramus, NJ 07652
201-261-5000 / Fax: 201-261-2742
Sales: $10 Million-$50 Million
Website: www.ramseyoutdoor.com
STUART LEVINE (President) & Buys Men's Sportswear, Outerwear, T-shirts, Footwear
MARVIN STEIN (Mgr.) & Buys Store Displays, Fixtures & Supplies

CANAL MENSWEAR (MW)
185 Jefferson St. (m-b-h)
Passaic, NJ 07055
973-472-3930 / Fax: 973-472-1665
PHIL CANAL (Owner) & Buys Store Displays, Fixtures, Supplies
ALEX CANAL-Men's & Young Men's Wear, Urban Contemporary, Knitwear, Accessories, Outerwear, Leather Apparel

LEONARD MEN'S SHOP (MW)
704 Main Ave. (m)
Passaic, NJ 07055
973-778-7437
PETER KIM (Owner) & Buys Men's Sportswear, Furnishings, Accessories

OLYMPIC TOWN (SP-5)
(K.S.N. SPORTING GOODS & FOOTWEAR, INC.)
(C.D.N. SPORTS, INC.)
168 Jefferson St.
Passaic, NJ 07055
973-777-1125 / Fax: 973-777-3654
KYONG SU NOH (Owner) & Buys Activewear, Athletic Footwear

YO-YO, INC. (CLO-2)
P.O. Box 2120 (m)
680 Main Ave.
Passaic, NJ 07055
973-471-1990 / Fax: 973-471-1986
Sales: $1 Million-$10 Million
YOURI COHEN (President) & Buys Leather Goods, Men's Casualwear, Denim, Accessories, Outerwear, Sportswear, Underwear

EMS FASHIONS (MW)
99 Main St. (m)
Paterson, NJ 07505
973-523-4861
HEIK AHN (Owner) & Buys Men's Wear, Sportswear, Young Men's Wear, Urban Contemporary, Boys' Wear, Furnishings, Accessories, Footwear
SANG AHN-Men's Wear, Sportswear, Young Men's Wear, Urban Contemporary, Boys' Wear, Furnishings, Accessories, Footwear

MATARIS' MEN'S CLOTHING (MW)
86 Main St.
Paterson, NJ 07505
07505
973-279-4000 / Fax: 973-279-0007
AHMAD MATARIS (Owner) & Buys Men's Wear, Sportswear, Furnishings, Accessories, Young Men's Wear, Urban Contemporary, Store Displays, Fixtures and Supplies

PATERSON MEN'S SHOP, INC. (MW)
139 Main St. (m)
Paterson, NJ 07505
973-742-4326
MICHAEL ROSENTHAL (Owner) & Buys Men's Wear, Sportswear, Furnishings, Accessories, Store Displays, Fixtures and Supplies

YES MEN FASHIONS (MW)
161 Main St.
Paterson, NJ 07505
973-345-1819
MR. NAM (Owner) & Buys Men's & Boys' Sportswear, Sport Shirts, Casual Shoes, Furnishings, Accessories

PALMYRA PANTS CO. (MW)
9370 Crescent Blvd. (p-m)
Pennsauken, NJ 08110
856-662-0398 / Fax: 856-662-4791
Sales: $100,001-$500,000
HOWARD EISENBERG (Owner) & Buys Men's Overcoats, Suits, Raincoats, Sportswear, Dress Shirts, Ties, Robes, Hosiery, Belts, Big & Tall Men's Wear, Footwear, Slacks, Jeans, Store Displays, Fixtures, Supplies

ROCHESTER FORMAL WEAR (MW)
Hwy. 38 & Airport Cir. (m-b)
Pennsauken, NJ 08109
856-662-6644 / Fax: 856-662-6618
MR. LENORD (Owner) & Buys Formalwear

FORMAN MILLS (CLO-15)
1070 Thomas Busch Memorial Hwy.
Pennsauker, NJ 08110
856-486-1447 / Fax: 856-488-9641
Website: www.formanmills.com
RICHARD FORMAN (President)
BOB SHANK (V.P.) & Buys Store Displays, Fixtures, Supplies
HAL LIFSHITZ-Men's Sweaters, Sport Shirts, Casual Slacks, Sportswear, Big & Tall Men's Wear
SOPHIE GURF-Accessories, Underwear
DWIGHT KING-Underwear, Hosiery
RANDY WOODEN-Licensed Apparel, Branded Athletic Wear, Active Apparel, Fleece, Outerwear, Jackets

DULI FASHIONS (MW)
185 Smith St., #A (m)
Perth Amboy, NJ 08861
732-826-5817
Sales: $500,000-$1 Million
YUN H. LEG (Co-Owner) & Buys Men's Wear, Urban Contemporary, Store Displays, Fixtures, Supplies
TONY LEE (Co-Owner) & Buys Men's Wear, Urban Contemporary, Store Displays, Fixtures, Supplies

FERTIG'S (CLO)
195 New Brunswick Ave. (m)
Perth Amboy, NJ 08861
732-442-1079 / Fax: 732-442-0054
Website: www.fertigs.com
RICHARD FERTIG (President & Owner) & Buys Sweaters, Sport Shirts, Outer Jackets, Casual Slacks, Active Apparel, Jeans, Work Clothes, Boys' School Uniforms, Dress Shirts, Ties, Underwear, Hosiery, Gloves, Belts, Young Men's Wear, Urban Contemporary, Footwear, Store Displays, Fixtures and Supplies

JOY FASHIONS (MW)
141 Smith St. (m)
Perth Amboy, NJ 08861
732-826-0822
MR. JEON (Owner) & Buys Men's & Young Men's Wear, Accessories, Store Displays, Fixtures, Supplies

PONZI TAILOR SHOP (MW)
356 S. Main St. (m)
Phillipsburg, NJ 08865
908-845-3913 / Fax: 908-454-3913
PONZI ROMANO (President & Owner) & Buys Suits, Tailored Jackets, Tailored Slacks, Big & Tall Men's Wear, Dress Shirts, Ties, Belts

HANS' CLOTHING (MW)
148 E. Front St. (m)
Plainfield, NJ 07060
908-561-2196
MR. HANS (Owner) & Buys Men's Wear

PARK GENTRY, INC. (MW)
168 E. Front St.
Plainfield, NJ 07060
908-756-2112 / Fax: 908-226-0728
TOM ALJIAN (Owner) & Buys Men's Suits, Formal Wear, Sportswear, Outerwear, Footwear, Store Displays, Fixtures, Supplies

PLAINFIELD DANDY (MW)
147 E. Front St. (m-b)
Plainfield, NJ 07060
908-753-3949
KONG PARK (Owner) & Buys Men's Wear, Urban Contemporary, Store Displays, Fixtures, Supplies

NEW JERSEY - Point Pleasant Beach

BRAVE NEW WORLD (CLO-3)
1208 Richmond Ave. (m-b)
Point Pleasant Beach, NJ 08742
732-899-8220 / Fax: 732-899-7205
Website: www.bravesurf.com

BILL LAMMERS (Owner) & Buys Store Displays, Fixtures, Supplies

PHYLLIS HORSTING (@ 732-899-7844, Ext.: 12)-Men's Sportswear

BETH SOLK (@ 732-899-7874)-Footwear, Boys' Sportswear

McLAUGHLIN'S (SP)
637 Arnold Ave.
Point Pleasant Beach, NJ 08742
732-899-2700 / Fax: 732-899-2702
Sales: $500,001-$1 Million

SCOTT McLAUGHLIN (Co-Owner) & Buys Men's Overcoats, Tailored Jackets, Tailored Slacks, Suits, Raincoats, Sportswear, Furnishings, Belts, Small Leather Goods, Young Men's Wear, 8 to 20 Boys' Wear, Footwear

KEVIN McLAUGHLIN (President) & Buys Athletic Apparel, Licensed Apparel, Team Products

LANDAU'S (MO & CLO)
102 Nassau St. (b)
Princeton, NJ 08542
609-924-3494 / Fax: 609-924-3680
Sales: $1 Million-$10 Million

ROBERT LANDAU (President) & Buys Men's Sweaters, Store Displays, Fixtures, Supplies

HENRY LANDAU (V.P.) & Buys Store Displays, Fixtures, Supplies

PANTS SALOON (MW)
301 N. Harrison St.
Princeton, NJ 08540
609-924-6276

JIM CLOEN (President & Owner) & Buys Sportswear, Belts, Young Men's Wear, Footwear, Outerwear, Knitwear, Urban Contemporary, Boys' Wear, Store Displays, Fixtures and Supplies

PRINCETON ARMY & NAVY SUPPLY STORE (AN)
14 1/2 Witherspoon St. (p-m)
Princeton, NJ 08542
609-924-0994 / Fax: 609-924-8593

MIKE BONIN (Owner) & Buys Men's & Boys' Jeans, Denims Shirts, Underwear, Hosiery, Belts, Outer Jackets, Footwear, Urban Contemporary, Store Displays, Fixtures, Supplies

PRINCETON UNIVERSITY STORE (MW-2 & OL & MO)
36 University Pl. (m-b)
Princeton, NJ 08540
609-921-8500 / Fax: 609-924-9651
Sales: $1 Million-$10 Million
Website: www.pustore.com

JAMES SYKES (President) & Buys Store Displays, Fixtures & Supplies

TONI KLEIN (H.R. Mgr.) & Buys Sport Shirts, Dress Shirts, Robes, Underwear, Hosiery, Gloves, Belts, Jewelry, Small Leather Goods, Fragrances, Ties

DAVID ANTIS-Men's Overcoats, Suits, Tailored Jackets, Tailored Slacks, Raincoats, Sweaters, Outer Jackets, Casual Slacks, Ties, Active Apparel, Urban Contemporary, Active Apparel

MAGNO MODA WEAR TAILORS (MW)
6 S. Maple Ave. (m-b)
Ridgewood, NJ 07450
201-445-1331

FRANK MAGNO (Owner) & Buys Suits, Tailored Jackets, Tailored Slacks, Dress Shirts, Ties

HARRY'S ARMY & NAVY (AN)
(Div. of MEHR'S TEXTILE, INC.)
691 Rt. 130
Robbinsville, NJ 08691
609-585-5450 / Fax: 609-585-4440
Sales: $1 Million-$10 Million
Website: www.harrys.com

ERIC MEHR (President)

MARK WORWIT (Purch. Mgr.) & Buys Coveralls, Accessories, Work Clothing, Hunting Apparel, Military Apparel

PAUL BUCK-Work Shoes, Safety Shoes, Hunting Boots

ESQUIRE BIG & TALL, INC. (MW-2)
238 Rockaway Town Square Mall (m-b)
Rockaway, NJ 07866
973-366-6005 / Fax: 973-366-2330

DEBBIE YELLIN (Owner) & Buys Big & Tall Men's Wear, Urban Contemporary, Store Displays, Fixtures, Supplies

FLIP SIDE (CLO)
907 St. George Ave. (m)
Roselle, NJ 07203
908-241-2710

LARRY MILLER (Co-Owner) & Buys Men's Hats, Accessories, Furnishings, Store Displays, Fixtures, Supplies

ROBERTA MILLER (Co-Owner) & Buys Men's Hats, Accessories, Furnishings, Store Displays, Fixtures, Supplies

BILTMORE TUXEDOS (MW)
4 Station Sq. (m-b)
Rutherford, NJ 07070
201-438-6636 / Fax: 201-438-7638

GREG AFARIAN (Owner) & Buys Men's & Boys' Tuxedos

BOB GOLDSTEIN, INC. (MW)
51 Park Ave. (b)
Rutherford, NJ 07070
201-935-5058

TOM STEIMLE (Owner) & Buys Men's Wear, Store Displays, Fixtures, Supplies

SERETI (CLO-10)
225 Highland Cross Rd.
Rutherford, NJ 07070
201-438-5800 / Fax: 201-438-7717
Sales: $10 Million-$50 Million

FRED MARGULIES-Men's Leather Coats, Jackets, Vests, Pants, Sportswear, Store Displays, Fixtures, Supplies

ISLAND STYLE, INC. (CLO)
1032 Ocean Ave. (m-b)
Sea Bright, NJ 07760
732-842-0909 / Fax: 732-842-5854

DERF McTIGHE (Owner) & Buys Men's Sportswear, Bathing Suits, Boys' Sportswear, Bathing Suits, Footwear, Store Displays, Fixtures, Supplies

R.J. FURLONG & CO., INC. (MW)
2150 Hwy. 35 (b)
Sea Girt, NJ 08750
732-974-2353 / Fax: 732-974-2316
Sales: $1 Million-$10 Million

R. J. FURLONG (Owner) & Buys Men's & Young Men's Wear, Sportswear, Swimwear, Outerwear, Footwear, Headwear, Knitwear, Underwear, Accessories, Hosiery, Furnishings, Store Displays, Fixtures, Supplies

HERITAGE SURF & SPORT (SG-3)
3700 Landis Ave. (m)
Sea Isle City, NJ 08243
609-263-3033 / Fax: 609-263-9696
Website: www.heritagesurf.com

BARBARA HERITAGE (Owner) & Buys Men's & Boys' Surf Apparel, Swimwear

ATHLETE'S OUTLET, INC. (CLO)
20 Enterprise Ave. (p-m)
Secaucus, NJ 07039
201-866-8779 / Fax: 201-903-1036

LARRY KUPER (Owner) & Buys Men's Fleecewear, T-shirts, Footwear, Store Displays, Fixtures, Supplies

NEW JERSEY - Secaucus

DAFFY'S (CLO-16)

Daffy's Way (m)
Secaucus, NJ 07094
201-902-0800 / Fax: 201-902-9015
Website: www.daffys.com

- IRVING SHULMAN (President)
- CHRIS FREELANDER (Exec. V.P. & G.M.M.-Men's Wear)
- LISA KOCH-Men's Sportswear, Clothing, Leather Apparel
- MARGIE TUCKER-COLE-Men's Accessories, Furnishings, Footwear
- OLGA GELANN-Boys' Wear 8-20
- ELIDA BEHAR-Boys' Footwear

DR. JAYS (MW-17)

(JOSEPH BETESH, INC.)
101 County Ave. (p)
Secaucus, NJ 07094
201-864-4300 / Fax: 201-864-1119
Website: www.drjays.com

- ELLIOT BETESH (President) & Buys Men's Wear, Related Accessories & Furnishings, Store Displays, Fixtures, Supplies
- MADDY EPSTEIN-Boys' Sportswear, Furnishings, Urban Contemporary
- KARIM WAZANI-Footwear

LOVE CLOTHES (CLO)

3 Millcreek Dr.
Secaucus, NJ 07094
201-330-9424 / Fax: 201-392-0570
Website: www.loveclothesltd.com

- ALAN KAMINOW (Owner)
- RANDY KAMINOW-Swimwear, Underwear

MARTY SHOES, INC. (FW-85 & OL)

(MARTY'S WAREHOUSE SHOE OUTLET)
60 Enterprise Ave. North (m-b-des)
Secaucus, NJ 07094
201-319-0500 / Fax: 201-319-1446
Sales: $50 Million-$100 Million
Website: www.martyshoes.com
Retail Locations: CT, FL, NV, NY

- MARTIN SAMOWITZ (Chmn.)
- JOHN ADAMS (President)
- ROBERT SCHMIDT (V.P.-Opers. & Real Estate Contact)
- JOHN ADAMS-Men's Footwear, Hosiery
- JACK SCACCO-Boys' Footwear, Hosiery

SYMS CORP. (CLO-41)

Syms Way (m)
Secaucus, NJ 07094
201-902-9600 / Fax: 201-902-9874
Website: www.syms.com
Retail Locations: CT, FL, GA, IL, MA, MD, MI, MO, NC, NJ

- SY SYMS (Chmn.)
- MARCY SYMS (C.E.O.)
- ALLEN BRAILLSFORD (Real Estate Contact) (@ 201-902-9600)
- RON ZINDMAN (Exec. V.P. & G.M.M.)
- MYRA BUTENSKY (V.P. & D.M.M.) & Buys Men's Suits, Overcoats & Formal Wear
- PETER HUNT-Men's Outerwear, Leather Jackets, Jeans, Activewear, Neckwear, Sportshirts, Raincoats, Overcoats, Leather Coats
- JIM WILKS-Men's Dress Shirts, Furnishings
- SUE FLAUM-Men's Hosiery, Underwear, Mufflers, Scarves, Shorts, Small Leather Goods, Hats, Gloves, Belts, Accessories

JWT STORES, INC. (CLO-4 & OL)

(HANDS)
(DELLA'S)
P.O. Box 609 (m)
Ship Bottom, NJ 08008
609-494-6780 / Fax: 609-494-8509
Website: www.handstores.com

- CHARLES TIER (President) (@ 609-597-5233) & Buys Store Displays, Fixtures, Supplies
- MARY ELLENDER-Men's Sportswear, Furnishings, Accessories, Outerwear, Swimwear, Headwear, Knitwear, Hosiery, Boys' Wear, Footwear, Urban Contemporary

BILL'S ARMY & NAVY STORE (AN)

(BILL'S OF MILLBURN, INC.)
666 Morris Tnpk. (p-m)
Short Hills, NJ 07078
973-467-0086 / Fax: 973-467-8429
Website: www.billsarmynavy.com

- LEE LUCAS (Owner) & Buys Men's Sportswear, Jeans, Underwear, Work Clothes, Urban Contemporary, Store Displays, Fixtures, Supplies

BOBBIE'S (MW)

732 Morris Tnpk. (b-h)
Short Hills, NJ 07078
973-376-7770 / Fax: 973-379-2770
Sales: $1 Million-$10 Million

- DAVID STERN (Owner) & Buys Men's & Boys' Sportswear, Furnishings, Leather Apparel
- DAVID PEREZ-Store Displays, Fixtures, Supplies

TUX INTERNATIONAL (MW)

Short Hills Mall
1200 Morris Tnpk., #C113
Short Hills, NJ 07078
973-564-9009 / Fax: 973-761-7188
Website: www.zellertuxedo.com

- JASON CAMARET-Men's & Boys' Formal Wear, Urban Contemporary, Store Displays, Fixtures, Supplies

WOLFHEAD ATHLETIC (CLO)

720 Morris Tnpk.
Short Hills, NJ 07078
973-376-1112 / Fax: 973-379-2770
Website: www.wolfheadathletic.com

- DAVID STERN (Owner) & Buys Licensed Apparel, Activewear

THE RUNNING STORE (SP)

Grove Shopping Plz.
595 State Hwy. 35
Shrewsbury, NJ 07702
732-758-8008

- SALLY McLOONE (Owner) & Buys Activewear, Athletic Footwear

THE HUB (MW)

(F & C ENTEPRISES)
273 New Rd. (m-b)
Somers Point, NJ 08244
609-926-0688 / Fax: 609-926-9305
Sales: $100,001-$500,000
Website: www.thehubclothing.com

- FRED DODD (Owner) & Buys Men's Sportswear, Furnishings, Big & Tall Men's Wear, Raincoats, Belts, Footwear, Store Displays, Fixtures, Supplies

JOHN'S, INC. (MW)

720 Hamilton St. (m-b)
Somerset, NJ 08873
732-249-8800 / Fax: 732-249-8903
Sales: $1 Million-$10 Million

- BEATRICE LEVY (Owner) & Buys Store Displays, Fixtures, Supplies, Men's Sportswear, Jeans, Furnishings, Activewear, Outerwear, Uniforms, Work Clothing, Safety Shoes & Boots
- LOU BASSKSIN-Footwear

SOMERVILLE BIG & TALL, INC. (MW)

79 W. Main St. (m-b)
Somerville, NJ 08876
908-725-8887

- ED ZADOURIAN (Owner) & Buys Big & Tall Men's Wear, Store Displays, Fixtures, Supplies

JUSTIN (MW)

6 S. Orange Ave. (m-b)
South Orange, NJ 07079
973-762-0824 / Fax: 973-762-7631
Website: www.justin.com

- JEAN CHARLES (Owner) & Buys Men's Wear, Footwear, Store Displays, Fixtures, Supplies

VILLAGE TWEED, INC. (MW)
1213 3rd Ave. (b)
Spring Lake, NJ 07762
732-449-2723 / Fax: 732-449-2725
ROGER PASQUARIELLO (Owner) & Buys Men's Wear, Footwear, Store Displays, Fixtures, Supplies

VALLEY SPORTS, INC. (SG-2)
1106 Valley Rd. (b)
Stirling, NJ 07980
908-580-1188 / Fax: 908-580-1884
Sales: $1 Million-$10 Million
BILLY CHAO (Owner) & Buys Men's Footwear, Casualwear, Accessories, Hosiery, Outerwear, Sportswear
REGINA CHAO (Store Mgr.) & Buys Men's Footwear, Casualwear, Accessories, Hosiery, Outerwear, Sportswear
SELENA CHAO (Store Mgr.) & Buys Men's Footwear, Casualwear, Accessories, Hosiery, Outerwear, Sportswear

B.J. STORES, INC. (DEPT-4)
260 97th St. (bud)
Stone Harbor, NJ 08247
609-368-6066 / Fax: 609-368-1080
DAVID HOY (President) & Buys Store Displays, Fixtures, Supplies
JOHN P. GARNIEWSKI (G.M.M.) & Buys Men's Sport Shirts, Active Apparel, Underwear, Hosiery, Gloves, Headwear, Belts, Fragrances, 8 to 20 Boys' Clothing, Sportswear, Accessories, Summer Type Shoes, Sandals

SUNCATCHER SURF SHOP (CLO & MW)
(MARKLE'S, INC.)
9425 2nd Ave. (m-b)
Stone Harbor, NJ 08247
609-368-3488 / Fax: 609-368-7829
TOM MARKLE (Owner) & Buys Men's & Boys' Sportswear, Footwear, Fixtures, Supplies
PETE LENGLE-Men's & Boys' Sportswear, Footwear, Fixtures, Supplies
BRIAN MARKLE-Men's & Boys' Sportswear, Footwear, Fixtures, Supplies

SEALFONS (CLO-2)
490 Springfield Ave. (m-b)
Summit, NJ 07871
908-277-1777 / Fax: 908-277-3054
Sales: $10 Million-$50 Million
BERT MODELL (President)
ERIC MODELL-Men's Wear, Footwear, Accessories, Furnishings
SHARON MODELL-Boys' Wear, T-shirts, Accessories, Furnishings

BOB KISLIN'S OUTDOOR SPORT (SG)
1214 Rt. 37 East, #18 (p)
Toms River, NJ 08753
732-929-9300 / Fax: 732-270-8654
RONALD KISLIN (President & Owner) & Buys Sports Related Clothing, Sweaters, Sport Shirts, Outer Jackets, Active Apparel

HARRIS CLOTHING STORE (CLO)
31 Main St. (m-b)
Toms River, NJ 08753
732-349-1068
GLENN HARRIS (President & Owner) & Buys Men's Wear, Sportswear, Furnishings, Accessories, Young Men's Wear, Store Displays, Fixtures and Supplies

RED THE UNIFORM TAILOR, INC. (CLO-2)
2161 Whitesville Rd. (m-b)
Toms River, NJ 08755
732-901-7772 / Fax: 932-901-7337
Sales: $1 Million-$10 Million
Website: www.rtut.com
HARVEY KLEIN (President)
BRUCE KLEIN (Mgr.-Retail Opers.) & Buys Men's Footwear, Apparel, Accessories, Hosiery, Underwear, Uniforms
BARRY KLEIN (Mgr.-Wrhs. Opers.)

ROGERS' CLOTHES (MW)
1201 Hooper Ave. (m)
Toms River, NJ 08753
732-240-6262
Sales: $1 Million-$10 Million
ROBERT ST. LIFER (Owner) & Buys Men's & Boys' Sweaters, Sport Shirts, Outer Jackets, Leather Apparel, Ties, Hosiery, Casual Slacks, Store Displays, Fixtures, Supplies

BYER'S MEN'S SHOP (MW)
129 N. Broad St. (p)
Trenton, NJ 08608
609-392-7049 / Fax: 609-695-7240
MARK BYER (Co-Owner) & Buys Men's Wear, Store Displays, Fixtures, Supplies
MICHAEL BYER (Co-Owner) & Buys Men's Wear, Store Displays, Fixtures, Supplies

CARELLA'S (FW)
(CARELLA SHOE)
2431 Nottingham Way (m-b)
Trenton, NJ 08619
609-587-5823
Sales: $1 Million-$10 Million
FREDERICK CARELLA (President) & Buys Boys' Footwear
TOM CARELLA (G.M.) & Buys Men's Footwear
JIMMY CARELLA-Hosiery

CENTER CITY SPORTS (SP-2)
43 E. State St.
Trenton, NJ 08608
609-394-1919 / Fax: 609-394-5553
WILLIE WANG (Owner) & Buys Licensed Activewear, Activewear, Athletic Footwear
CHRIS EVANS (Mgr.) & Buys Licensed Activewear, Activewear, Athletic Footwear

CLOTHING COMPANY (CLO)
731 Hwy. 33 (p-m-b)
Trenton, NJ 08690
609-586-2332 / Fax: 609-588-8827
RICHARD COX (Owner) & Buys Men's Overcoats, Suits, Tailored Jackets, Tailored Slacks, Raincoats, Sportswear, Furnishings, Headwear, Accessories, Store Displays, Fixtures, Supplies

THE PREP FACTORY OUTLET (CLO)
1700 Nottingham Way
Trenton, NJ 08619
609-588-9659 / Fax: 609-584-1610
Sales: $1 Million-$10 Million
ROGER CONSTABLE (Co-Owner) & Buys Boys' Apparel, Boys' Footwear, Men's Footwear, Leather Goods, Big & Tall Men's Wear, Formalwear, Accessories, Hosiery, Outerwear, Sportswear, Suits, Uniforms
ED DIESON (Co-Owner) & Buys Boys' Apparel, Boys' Footwear, Men's Footwear, Leather Goods, Big & Tall Men's Wear, Formalwear, Accessories, Hosiery, Outerwear, Sportswear, Suits, Uniforms
JAMES REA (Co-Owner) & Buys Boys' Apparel, Boys' Footwear, Men's Footwear, Leather Goods, Big & Tall Men's Wear, Formalwear, Accessories, Hosiery, Outerwear, Sportswear, Suits, Uniforms

REISS MEN'S & BOY'S SHOP (MW-2)
(SUIT WORLD)
141 N. Broad St.
Trenton, NJ 08608
609-695-2949
GARY REISS (Owner) & Buys Men's Suits, Formal Wear, Sportswear, Outerwear, Accessories, Young Men's Wear, Boys' Wear, Footwear, Store Displays, Fixtures, Supplies

SIMON'S DISCOUNT STORE (MW)
1611 N. Olden Ave.
Trenton, NJ 08638
609-394-2606 / Fax: 609-394-4943
CHUL LEE (Co-Owner) & Buys Men's Wear, Store Displays, Fixtures, Supplies
HYE LEE (Co-Owner) & Buys Men's Wear, Urban Contemporary, Store Displays, Fixtures, Supplies

NEW JERSEY - Tuckerton

H.G. MARSHALL & CO. (MW)
116 S. Green St.
Tuckerton, NJ 08087
609-296-6565
STEVE CLIFTON (Owner) & Buys Men's Wear, Men's Big & Tall, Work Clothing, Footwear, Accessories, Furnishings

SOLDIER CITY (AN & OL & MO)
P.O. Box 1105
Turnersville, NJ 08012
856-582-1360 / Fax: 856-582-1365
Website: www.soldiercity.com
ROY RACER (G.M.M.) & Buys Men's and Boys' Camouflage, Military Apparel, Footwear, Boots, Combat Boots, Headwear

BATTLE HILL CENTER (CLO)
1037 Stuyvesant ave. (m)
Union, NJ 07083
908-687-0886 / Fax: 908-688-1197
Sales: $500,001-$1 Million
ROBERT LEVY (Owner) & Buys Leather Goods, Men's Sportswear, Men's Underwear

DUGOUT, INC. (MW)
1035 Stuyvesant Ave. (p-m-b)
Union, NJ 07083
908-964-9545 / Fax: 908-688-1197
JOHN PALLATTO (Owner) & Buys Men's Sportswear, Furnishings, Accessories

DAVID BURR, INC. (MW-3)
3900 Bergenline Ave. (b)
Union City, NJ 07087
201-867-2545 / Fax: 201-867-0496
Sales: $1 Million-$10 Million
Website: www.davidburruniformco.com
JAMIE BURR (President) & Buys Store Displays, Fixtures, Supplies, Men's Wear & 8 to 20 Boys' Wear
JODY BURR-Men's Wear & 8 to 20 Boys' Wear, Urban Contemporary

EL WATERLOO, INC. (CLO)
4500 Bergenline Ave. (p-m)
Union City, NJ 07087
201-864-4084 / Fax: 201-348-8175
Sales: $1 Million-$10 Million
FRANCISCO BAS (Owner) & Buys Store Displays, Fixtures, Supplies, Men's & Young Men's Leather Apparel
VICTOR BAS-Men's & Young Men's Leather Apparel, Urban Contemporary

FASHION HOUSE, INC. (MW)
4705 Bergenline Ave. (p)
Union City, NJ 07087
201-864-0063
SY ENGEBWY (Owner) & Buys Men's Sportswear, Furnishings, Accessories

OLYMPIC SHOP (CLO)
622 Valley Rd. (m-b)
Upper Montclair, NJ 07043
973-744-0044 / Fax: 973-744-1962
Sales: $1 Million-$10 Million
VINCE NICASTRO-Men's Suits, Tailored Slacks, Tailored Jackets
JIM FRANCIOSE-Sportswear, Robes, Underwear, Hosiery, Accessories, Footwear
LYNN CIALLELLA-Boys' Tailored Slacks, Tailored Jackets, Sportswear

BERNIE'S ARMY & NAVY STORE (AN)
709 E. Landis Ave. (p)
Vineland, NJ 08360
856-691-4747
BERNIE FLICK (Owner) & Buys Men's Work Clothing, Sportswear, Furnishings, Headwear, Belts, Big & Tall Men's Wear, Footwear, Robes, Underwear, Hosiery, Gloves, Store Displays, Fixtures, Supplies

BONANZA ARMY NAVY (AN)
165 N. Delsea Dr. (p)
Vineland, NJ 08360
856-696-4888 / Fax: 856-692-0400
Sales: $500,000-$1 Million
RAY FRIEDMAN (Owner) & Buys Men's Raincoats, Sweaters, Sport Shirts, Outer Jackets, Casual Slacks, Active Apparel, T-shirts, Dress Shirts, Ties, Underwear, Hosiery, Gloves, Headwear, Belts, Small Leather Goods, Young Men's Wear, Urban Contemporary, Footwear

G STREET (CLO)
Cumberland Mall, #B12 (m)
3849 S. Delsea Dr.
Vineland, NJ 08360
856-327-2636 / Fax: 856-327-0178
Sales: $500,001-$1 Million
ANTHONY MAGUERI (President)
JAMES DYCH (Store Mgr.) & Buys Young Men's Overcoats, Tailored Slacks, Sportswear, Dress Shirts, Ties, Hosiery, Gloves, Headwear, Belts, Footwear, Store Displays, Fixtures, Supplies

FRANK'S BIG & TALL MEN'S SHOP (MW-6)
1000 Rt. 35, #C (p-m-b)
Wanamassa, NJ 07712
732-922-1525 / Fax: 732-922-0706
Sales: $1 Million-$10 Million
Website: www.franksbigandtall.com
KEN MAROWITZ (Owner) & Buys Big & Tall Men's Outerwear, Footwear
JOE MAROWITZ-Big & Tall Men's Sportswear

FRANTONI FASHIONS (MW)
(FTG, INC.)
10 E. Washington Ave. (m)
Washington, NJ 07882
908-689-5477
BOB SARLITT (Owner) & Buys Men's Wear, Footwear, Store Displays, Fixtures, Supplies

Babies 'R' Us (KS-336)
(Div. of TOYS 'R' US)
1 Geoffrey Way
Wayne, NJ 07470
973-617-3500
Sales: Over $11 Billion
Website: www.toysrus.com
Retail Locations: AL, AR, AL, CA, CO, FI, GA, IL, IN, KS, KY, LA, MI, MN, MS, MO, NE, NV, NH, NJ, NY, NC, OH, OR, TX, UT, WA, OK, SC, TN, VA, WV, SD, WI, PA
ELLIOTT WAHLE (President)
DAVID PICOT (V.P.)
CAROL CALHAND (Real Estate Contact)
PAMELA WALLACK (Sr. V.P. & G.M.M.)
DEBBIE SCHNEIDER-Newborn & Infant Boys' Wear
PAT MOSCA-Infant & Newborn Layettes
CARI SHAPIRO (D.M.M.-Boys' Wear)
SUE STRANDSKOV-Boys' Wear 2 to 16
LINDA WINE-4 to 7 Boys' Wear
LISA COOPER-Boys' Sleepwear, Robes
LARRY SMITH-Boys' Footwear
JAMES MALATESTA-Store Displays, Fixtures and Supplies

ESQUIRE BIG & TALL (MW)
1528 Willowbrook Mall (m-b)
Wayne, NJ 07470
973-785-9812
ANDREW YELLIN (Owner) & Buys Men's Big & Tall Sizes, Footwear, Urban Contemporary, Store Displays, Fixtures, Supplies

AL JAKE, INC. (CLO)
P.O. Box 207 (bud-p-m)
5528 Bergenline Ave.
West New York, NJ 07093
201-864-3036 / Fax: 201-864-2546
Sales: $100,001-$500,000
AL BRAGIN (President & G.M.M.)
MORRIS BRAGIN-Boys' Apparel, Boys' Footwear, Men's Footwear, Leather Goods, Licensed Apparel, Big & Tall Men's Wear, Casualwear, Denim, Accessories, Hosiery, Outerwear, Sleepwear, Sportswear, Suits, Swimwear, Underwear
JOHANNA NEWSOME-Boys' Apparel, Boys' Footwear, Men's Footwear, Leather Goods, Licensed Apparel, Big & Tall Men's Wear, Casualwear, Denim, Accessories, Hosiery, Outerwear, Sleepwear, Sportswear, Suits, Swimwear, Underwear

CITY LOOK (MW)
(HOURIES BROTHERS)
5701 Bergenline Ave. (b)
West New York, NJ 07093
201-867-4212
Sales: $500,000-$1 Million
ATA HOURIZADEH (Partner) & Buys Men's Italian Clothing, Sportswear, Italian Leather Apparel, Furnishings, Accessories, Footwear, Urban Contemporary, Store Displays, Fixtures, Supplies

HUDSON TAILORING CO. (MW)
6321 Bergenline Ave. (m)
West New York, NJ 07093
201-869-0555
MR. JERRY (Owner) & Buys Men's & Boys' Tuxedos

LITTLE MARCY'S, INC. (CLO)
6600 Bergenline Ave. (m-b)
West New York, NJ 07093
201-861-2050 / Fax: 201-861-0535
ROBERT COLE (President)
MAXINE COLE (V.P.) & Buys 8 to 20 Boys' Sportswear

PRATO FASHIONS (MW-11)
5613 Bergenline Ave.
West New York, NJ 07093
201-330-3352 / Fax: 201-330-8798
Website: www.pratooutlets.com
MOHAMAD ASHMAWAY (Owner) & Buys Men's Clothing, Accessories, Furnishings, Footwear

VIHAN CUSTOM TAILORS (MW)
6010 Bergenline Ave. (m-b)
West New York, NJ 07093
201-865-7010
MR. VIHAN (Owner) & Buys Men's Sportswear, Furnishings, Accessories

WALTER BAUMAN JEWELERS, INC. (JWLY-5 & MO & OL)
643 Eagle Rock Ave.
West Orange, NJ 07052
973-731-3155 / Fax: 973-731-9705
Sales: $10 Million-$50 Million
Website: www.walterbauman.com
WALTER BAUMAN (President)
EDWARD BAUMAN (V.P.-Purch.)
FREDDIE BAUMAN-Jewelry, Watches

WARDROBE WAGON, INC. (CLO & MO & OL)
555 Valley Rd. (bud)
West Orange, NJ 07052
973-736-5500 / Fax: 973-669-1578
Sales: $1 Million-$10 Million
Website: www.wardrobewagon.com
JERRY OPPENBERG (Owner) & Buys Men's Wear, Footwear, Store Displays, Fixtures, Supplies

FRANCOLINO CLOTHIER (MW)
129 Elm St.
Westfield, NJ 07090
908-233-1273
JOSEPH FRANCOLINO (President & Co-Owner) & Buys Men's Formal Wear, Suits, Sportswear, Big & Tall Men's Wear, Store Displays, Fixtures, Supplies
ROSETTA FRANCOLINO (V.P. & Co-Owner) & Buys Men's Formal Wear, Suits, Sportswear, Big & Tall Men's Wear, Store Displays, Fixtures, Supplies

LEADER STORE (MW)
(WESTFIELD LEADER STORE)
109 E. Broad St. (p-m-b)
Westfield, NJ 07090
908-233-5609 / Fax: 908-233-3441
JOE SPECTOR (Owner) & Buys Men's Sportswear, Tops, Furnishings, Big & Tall Men's Wear, Boys' Activewear, Store Displays, Fixtures, Supplies

SHERRY'S DISTINCTIVE CLOTHING (MW)
111 Quimby St. (b)
Westfield, NJ 07090
908-232-0065
JOE SHERRY (Owner) & Buys Men's Wear, Urban Contemporary, Store Displays, Fixtures, Supplies

DAVID WILSON MEN'S SHOP (MW)
164 Haddon Ave. (m-b-des)
Westmont, NJ 08108
856-858-4146
Sales: $1 Million-$10 Million
DAVID WILSON (President) & Buys Men's Footwear, Leather Goods, Casualwear, Denim, Formalwear, Accessories, Hosiery, Outerwear, Sportswear, Suits, Swimwear, Sleepwear
MARTHA WILSON (V.P.)
DENISE PINGON (Store Mgr.)

PELICAN SWIM & SKI (SP-4)
P.O. Box 36
Rt. 22
Whitehouse, NJ 08888
908-534-2400 / Fax: 908-534-6337
Sales: $10 Million-$50 Million
Website: www.pelicanski.com
BILL WAGNER (Controller) & Buys Skiing & Snowboarding Apparel

DEJA VU, INC. (CLO-2)
P.O. Box 1442 (m)
5212 Boardwalk
Wildwood, NJ 08260
609-522-1220 / Fax: 609-729-4909
MR. DROR (Owner) & Buys Men's & Boys' Sportswear, Store Displays, Fixtures, Supplies

SILEN'S SHOES & RESORT WEAR (CLO)
5000 Pacific Ave. (p-m)
Wildwood, NJ 08260
609-522-2155 / Fax: 609-522-3831
Sales: $500,001-$1 Million
BARRY RASMUSSEN (Owner) & Buys Men's Casual & Resort Wear, Footwear, Store Displays, Fixtures, Supplies

AGAINST ALL ODDS USA (MW-32)
269 Woodbridge Ctr.
Woodbridge, NJ 07095
732-855-6950 / Fax: 201-641-8133
Website: www.aao-usa.com
KENNY KIM (Owner) & Buys Urban Contemporary, Footwear, Sportswear, Accessories

POLSKY'S, INC. (CLO-2)
164 S. Broad St. (p-m)
Woodbury, NJ 08096
856-845-4780 / Fax: 856-845-6530
Sales: $1 Million-$10 Million
SCOTT LUPOW (Owner) & Buys Young Men's & Boys' Sportswear, Furnishings, Accessories, Footwear, Work Uniforms
JUSTIN LUPOW-Store Displays, Fixtures, Supplies

FARRIER SPORTING GOODS (SG)
Godwin & Crescent Ave. (m-b)
Wyckoff, NJ 07481
201-891-9520 / Fax: 201-891-6608
Sales: $500,001-$1 Million
CHARLES COLEMAN (President) & Buys Boys' Apparel, Men's Footwear, Hosiery, Outerwear, Sportswear, Swimwear, Underwear
TOM McDONALD (V.P.)
TIM GARTNER (Store Mgr.)

WYCKOFF IVY SHOP (CLO)
386 Franklin Ave. (b)
Wyckoff, NJ 07481
201-891-2210 / Fax: 201-891-4833
Sales: $1 Million-$10 Million
ROBERT ABBIATI (Owner) & Buys Men's Suits, Tailored Jackets, Tailored Slacks, Sweaters, Sport Shirts, Outer Jackets, Leather Apparel, Casual Slacks, Active Apparel, Furnishings, Headwear, Accessories, 8 to 20 Boys' Wear, Store Displays, Fixtures, Supplies

NEW MEXICO - Alamogordo

DOLLAR BOOTS & JEANS (CLO)
2850 N. White Sand Blvd. (p)
Alamogordo, NM 88310
505-437-4721 / Fax: 505-434-6540
Sales: $100,001-$500,000
RON GRISAK (Co-Owner) & Buys Men's Outerwear, Western Shirts, Jeans, Belts, Leather Apparel, Hats, Accessories, Young Men's Wear, Boys' Wear, Footwear
KIM GRISAK (Co-Owner) & Buys Men's Outerwear, Western Shirts, Jeans, Belts, Leather Apparel, Hats, Accessories, Young Men's Wear, Boys' Wear
LINDA CONNELLY-Men's Outerwear, Western Shirts, Jeans, Belts, Leather Apparel, Hats, Accessories, Young Men's Wear, Boys' Wear

AMERICAN MAN BIG & TALL (MW)
2828 Carlisle Blvd. NE (p-m-b)
Albuquerque, NM 87110
505-883-5554
JAY (Owner) & Buys Men's Wear, Big & Tall Men's Wear, Sportswear, Furnishings, Accessories

GINGISS FORMALWEAR (MW)
6600 Menaul Blvd. NE, #343 (m)
Albuquerque, NM 87120
505-883-6620 / Fax: 505-883-6827
Website: www.gingiss.com
DAVID McKINNEY (Owner) & Buys Formal Wear & Related Furnishings, Accessories

KAUFMAN'S WEST (MW)
1660 Eubank NE (m)
Albuquerque, NM 87112
505-293-2300 / Fax: 505-275-1441
NATE KORN (Owner) & Buys Men's Uniforms, Footwear

LOBO MEN'S SHOP (MW)
2120 Central Ave. SE (p-m)
Albuquerque, NM 87106
505-243-6954 / Fax: 505-842-0533
Sales: $500,000-$1 Million
B. N. NELLOS (Secy.) & Buys Men's Sportswear, Leather Apparel, Furnishings, Headwear, Accessories, Young Men's Wear, Footwear, Store Displays, Fixtures, Supplies

MR. CASUAL & SUITS UNLIMITED, INC. (MW)
5406 Menaul Blvd. NE (m)
Albuquerque, NM 87110
505-883-1060 / Fax: 505-883-6239
Sales: $500,000-$1 Million
Website: www.flash.net/~mrcasual
LARRY GARCIA (Co-Owner) & Buys Men's Sportswear, Furnishings, Accessories, Store Displays, Fixtures, Supplies
MANNY GARCIA (Co-Owner) & Buys Men's Sportswear, Furnishings, Accessories, Footwear, Store Displays, Fixtures, Supplies

ROBERT BAILEY CORP. (MW-2)
4900 Cutler Ave. (b)
Albuquerque, NM 87110
505-881-2750 / Fax: 505-881-2752
MARK BAILEY (Owner) & Buys Men's Sportswear, Furnishings, Accessories, Shoes
JAMES TORRES (Controller) & Buys Store Displays, Fixtures, Supplies

STROMBERG'S, INC. (MW)
6640 Indian School Rd. NE (m-b)
Albuquerque, NM 87110
505-268-7477 / Fax: 505-883-6036
Sales: $1 Million-$10 Million
GRETCHEN STROMBERG (President)
RAY McKENZIE (G.M.M.) & Buys Men's Overcoats, Suits, Tailored Jackets, Tailored Slacks, Raincoats, Men's Sweaters, Sport Shirts, Outer Jackets, Casual Slacks, Big & Tall Wear
LISA KEFLER-Men's Sweaters, Sport Shirts, Outer Jackets, Casual Slacks, Big & Tall Wear, Men's Furnishings, Small Leather Goods
GEORGE HARTZELL-Footwear

UNIVERSITY OF NEW MEXICO BOOKSTORE (SP-2)
University of New Mexico
Albuquerque, NM 87131
505-277-5451 / Fax: 505-277-6330
Sales: $5 Million-$10 Million
MELANIE SPARKS (Director)
VIRGINIA MARTINEZ (Opers. Mgr.) & Buys Fleece, Jackets, Hosiery, Licensed Apparel
MARIAN SCANLON (Mgr.) & Buys Active Apparel, Licensed Apparel

WESTERN MERCANTILE, INC. (WW-5)
(WESTERN MERCANTILE OLD MILL)
(WESTERN MERCANTILE SOUTH VALLEY)
(WESTERN MERCANTILE VALENCIA)
(DAN'S WESTERN STORE, INC.)
111 Rio Bravo Blvd. SE (m)
Albuquerque, NM 87105
505-877-1504 / Fax: 505-877-8687
Sales: $1 Million-$10 Million
ALLAN TRUELOCK (President)
JAY CHRISTINSON (V.P. & Dir.-Real Estate)
LARRY CHRISTINSON (V.P.) & Buys Boys' Footwear, Men's Footwear, Leather Goods, Men's Apparel, Men's Denim Apparel
GREG ARTZ-Leather Goods

WESTERN WAREHOUSE (WW-30 & OL)
(Div. of COOPERS, INC.)
11205 Montgomery Blvd. (m-b)
Albuquerque, NM 87111
505-559-5000 / Fax: 505-296-0278
Sales: $10 Million-$50 Million
Website: www.westernwarehouse.com
Retail Locations: AZ, CA, CO, NM
JERRY KRUMM (C.E.O. & President & Real Estate Contact)
PAT ROONEY (D.M.M.) & Buys Men's Western Wear, Leather Apparel, Hosiery, Young Men's Wear, Boys' Wear
LINDA BRANDENBERG-Small Leather Goods, Jewelry, Men's Headwear, Belts
TONY BROCK-Footwear
BILL WAKLEY-Store Displays, Fixtures, Supplies

BENNIE'S WESTERN WEAR (WW)
205 W. Main St. (m)
Artesia, NM 88210
505-746-2542 / Fax: 505-748-2695
Website: www.bennieswestern.com
BENNIE MASON (Partner) & Buys Men's & Boys' Western Wear, Related Accessories, Furnishings, Headwear, Boots, Store Displays, Fixtures, Supplies
JIMMY MASON-Men's & Boys' Western Wear, Related Accessories, Furnishings, Headwear, Boots, Store Displays, Fixtures, Supplies

CULP'S WESTERN WEAR (WW)
P.O. Box 42 (p)
204 N. 2nd St.
Belen, NM 87002
505-864-8660
Sales: $100,001-$500,000
JOE FISHER (Co-Owner)
GLENDA FISHER (Co-Owner) & Buys Men's Western Wear, Dress Shirts, Outer Jackets, Sweaters, Big & Tall Men's Wear, Gloves, Hats, Belts, Boys' Western Clothing, Boots, Store Displays, Fixtures, Supplies

DAVID'S MEN'S & BOYS' WEAR (MW)
233 N. Main St. (p)
Belen, NM 87002
505-864-8563
DAVID CORDOVA (Owner) & Buys Men's Sportswear, Furnishings, Accessories, Young Men's Wear, Store Displays, Fixtures and Supplies

DUNLAP (DEPT)
2302 W. Pierce St. (m)
Carlsbad, NM 88220
505-234-9909 / Fax: 505-234-9927
LONNY SOUTER (Asst. Mgr.) & Buys Men's Wear & Footwear

PHILLIPS COWBOY SHOP (WW)

802 W. Mermod St. (p-m)
Carlsbad, NM 88221
505-885-2568 / Fax: 505-887-6829
Sales: $500,000-$1 Million

BILL PHILLIPS (Owner) & Buys Men's & Boys' Western Wear, Headwear, Accessories, Young Men's Jeans, Footwear, Store Displays, Fixtures, Supplies

CIMARRON WEST (WW)

P.O. Box 201 (m)
256 10th St.
Cimarron, NM 87714
505-376-2423

CASEY JEFFERS (Owner) & Buys Men's & Young Men's Western Wear, Related Furnishings, Headwear, Accessories, Boots, Moccasins, Store Displays, Fixtures, Supplies

TANKERSLEY'S, INC. (CLO)

306 N. Main St. (m-b-h)
Clovis, NM 88101
505-762-0362 / Fax: 505-763-0082

HOMER TANKERSLEY (Co-Owner) & Buys Men's Sportswear, Accessories, Big & Tall Men's Wear, Store Displays, Fixtures, Supplies

PAUL TANKERSLEY (Co-Owner) & Buys Men's Sportswear, Accessories, Big & Tall Men's Wear, Footwear, Young Men's Wear, Store Displays, Fixtures, Supplies

RAY'S UNITED (CLO)

P.O. Box 956 (p-m)
113 S. Gold Ave.
Deming, NM 88030
505-546-9822

RAY TREJO (Owner) & Buys Western Wear, Men's Sportswear, Furnishings, Accessories, Young Men's Wear, Urban Contemporary, Boys' Wear, Store Displays, Fixtures and Supplies

TRICE'S WESTERN WEAR (WW)

210 W. Cole Ave. (b)
Gallup, NM 87301
505-863-4631

TRICE GREEN (Owner) & Buys Western Wear, Related Furnishings, Accessories, Boots, Store Displays, Fixtures, Supplies

ZIMMERMAN'S DEPARTMENT STORE, INC. (DEPT)

216 W. 66th Ave. (p-m)
Gallup, NM 87301
505-863-3142
Sales: $100,001-$500,000

ARNOLD HUDGEONS (Owner) & Buys Men's & Boys' Wear, Footwear, Store Displays, Fixtures, Supplies

HATCH MERCANTILE CO. (CLO)

P.O. Box 310 (m)
111 W. Hall St.
Hatch, NM 87937
505-267-4411

ALBITA LARA (Co-Owner) & Buys Footwear, Men's Western Wear, T-shirts, Active Apparel, Sweaters, Sport Shirts, Outer Jackets, Dress Shirts, Underwear, Hosiery, Headwear, Belts, Small Leather Goods, Fragrances, Young Men's Wear, 7 to 20 Boys' Wear

KATRINA WINDER (Co-Owner) & Buys Men's Western Wear, T-shirts, Active Apparel, Sweaters, Sport Shirts, Outer Jackets, Dress Shirts, Underwear, Hosiery, Headwear, Belts, Small Leather Goods, Fragrances, Young Men's Wear, 7 to 20 Boys' Wear

BOOTSIE'S WESTERN STORE (WW)

108 E. Broadway St.
Hobbs, NM 88240
505-393-6862 / Fax: 505-393-3995

BUCK JONES (Co-Owner) & Buys Men's Western Wear, Leather Apparel, Headwear, Accessories, Young Men's Western Wear, 8 to 20 Boys' Western Wear, Boots, Store Displays, Fixtures, Supplies

MARTIN BOOT CO. (WW)

201 E. Broadway St. (p-m-b)
Hobbs, NM 88240
505-397-2668

RICHARD MARTIN (Owner) & Buys Western Wear, Headwear, Furnishings, Related Accessories, Work Boots, Casual Boots, Dress Boots, Store Displays, Fixtures, Supplies

THE MODEL (CLO)

Broadmoor Mall (b)
1401 N. Turner St.
Hobbs, NM 88240
505-393-0044 / Fax: 505-393-5300

RANDY FIELDS (Co-Owner) & Buys Men's Sportswear, Furnishings, Headwear, Accessories, Young Men's Wear, Jeans, T-shirts, Store Displays, Fixtures, Supplies

MARC FIELDS (Co-Owner) & Buys Men's Sportswear, Furnishings, Headwear, Accessories, Young Men's Wear, Jeans, T-shirts, Store Displays, Fixtures, Supplies

WORKHORSE BOOT & JEANS (CLO)

206 W. Broadway St. (p)
Hobbs, NM 88240
505-397-4605
Sales: $100,001-$500,000

LARRY HARDIMAN (Owner) & Buys Men's Sportswear, Underwear, Hosiery, Belts, Small Leather Goods, Western Wear, Dress Boots, Work Boots, Moccasins, Store Displays, Fixtures, Supplies

S & H MEN'S MART (MW)

2182 N. Main St. (b)
Las Cruces, NM 88001
505-526-5096 / Fax: 505-526-1276
Sales: $500,000-$1 Million

CHARLES HILL (President) & Buys Men's Sweaters, Outer Jackets, Leather Apparel, Sport Shirts, Active Apparel, Furnishings, Headwear, Accessories, Big & Tall Men's Wear, Young Men's Wear, Boys' Wear, Footwear, Store Displays, Fixtures, Supplies

POPULAR DRY GOODS (DG)

119 Bridge St. (p)
Las Vegas, NM 87701
505-425-7272

HELEN HILLSON (Owner)

DENNIS LUJAN-Men's Western Wear, Leather Jackets, Western Ties, Hats, Accessories, 4 to 16 Boys' Western Wear Boots, Store Displays, Fixtures, Supplies

CB FOX, INC. (DEPT)

P.O. Box 1119 (p-m-b)
1735 Central Ave.
Los Alamos, NM 87544
505-662-2285 / Fax: 505-662-0983
Sales: $1 Million-$10 Million

TOM HALL (President) & Buys Men's Casual Slacks, Suits, Tailored Jackets, Tailored Slacks, Raincoats, Sweaters, Sport Shirts, Outer Jackets, Overcoats, Dress Shirts, Ties, Robes, Underwear, Hosiery, Gloves, Belts, Jewelry, Small Leather Goods, Fragrances, Sportswear, Furnishings, Leather Apparel, Young Men's & Boys' Wear

DAVID V. FOX (C.E.O.) & Buys Men's Casual Slacks, Suits, Tailored Jackets, Tailored Slacks, Raincoats, Sweaters, Sport Shirts, Outer Jackets, Overcoats, Dress Shirts, Ties, Robes, Underwear, Hosiery, Gloves, Belts, Jewelry, Small Leather Goods, Fragrances, Sportswear, Furnishings, Leather Apparel, Young Men's & Boys' Wear

ANDY FOX (G.M.M.) & Buys Footwear, Store Displays, Fixtures, Supplies

OLD MILL WESTERN MERCANTILE, INC. (WW)

19763 Hwy. 314
Los Lunas, NM 87002
505-865-5432 / Fax: 505-865-8426

CORKY MORRISON-Men's & Boys' Western Wear, Boots, Store Displays, Fixtures, Supplies

VALENCIA WESTERN MERCANTILE (WW)

3469 Hwy. 47 (m)
Los Lunas, NM 87031
505-865-1515 / Fax: 505-865-3606

MIKE WRIGHT (Mgr.) & Buys Western Wear, Related Furnishings, Headwear, Accessories, Boots, Store Displays, Fixtures, Supplies

NEW MEXICO - Los Ranchos de Albuquerque

DAN'S BOOTS & SADDLES (WW & OL)

6903 4th St. NW (b)
Los Ranchos de Albuquerque, NM 87107
505-345-2220 / Fax: 505-344-0436
Website: www.dansbootsandsaddles.com

LARRY CHRISTENSEN (President)

MARTY NORLIN-Footwear, Men's Outerwear, Leather Apparel, Western Wear, Furnishings, Headwear, Accessories, Young Men's Wear, Boys' Wear, Store Displays, Fixtures, Supplies

ADELO'S TOWN & COUNTRY STORE (DEPT)

P.O. Box 517 (p)
Main St. & Hwy. 63
Pecos, NM 87552
505-757-8565

GEORGE ADELO (Mgr.) & Buys Men's & Boys' Jeans, T-shirts, Sportswear, Furnishings, Store Displays, Fixtures, Supplies

SKINNER'S WESTERN WEAR (WW)

P.O. Box 638 (m)
112 S. Ave. A
Portales, NM 88130
505-356-5072
Sales: $100,001-$500,000

SANDY SKINNER (President) & Buys Men's Suits, Overcoats, Raincoats, Sweaters, Outer Jackets, Casual Slacks, Active Apparel, Ties, Underwear, Gloves, Headwear, Accessories, Young Men's & Boys' Wear, Boots, Store Displays, Fixtures, Supplies

MAIN STREET (SP)

201 W. Main St.
Red River, NM 87558
505-754-6414 / Fax: 505-754-3358

TED CALHOUN (Co-Owner)

LINDA CALHOUN (Co-Owner) & Buys Active Apparel

MILLER'S CROSSING (CLO)

P.O. Box 219 (bud-p-m)
212 W. Main St.
Red River, NM 87558
505-754-2374 / Fax: 505-754-2375
Sales: $100,001-$500,000

JUDY MILLER (Co-Owner) & Buys Men's Raincoats, Sweaters, Sport Shirts, Outer Jackets, Active Apparel, Headwear, Footwear, Store Displays, Fixtures, Supplies

JOHN MILLER (Co-Owner) & Buys Men's Raincoats, Sweaters, Sport Shirts, Outer Jackets, Active Apparel, Headwear, Store Displays, Fixtures, Supplies

PATRICK'S OF RED RIVER (CLO)

P.O. Box 547 (p-m)
508 E. Main St.
Red River, NM 87558
505-754-2912

ANN TOMPKINS (Owner) & Buys Men's Sportswear, Headwear, Furnishings, Accessories, Boys' Wear, Store Displays, Fixtures, Supplies

CORSINI (MW)

107 W. San Francisco St. (m-b-h)
Santa Fe, NM 87501
505-820-2300 / Fax: 505-820-2300

FABRIZIO GIOVANNINI (Owner) & Buys Men's Sportswear, Accessories, Store Displays, Fixtures and Supplies

HARRY'S, INC. (CLO)

202 Galisteo Ave.
Santa Fe, NM 87501
505-988-1959 / Fax: 505-995-8118

GREG VOIDA (Owner) & Buys Men's Sportswear, Furnishings, Headwear, Accessories, Young Men's Wear, Shoes, Store Displays, Fixtures, Supplies

PINKOYOTE (CLO)

330 Old Santa Fe Trl. (bud-p-m)
Santa Fe, NM 87501
505-983-3030 / Fax: 505-988-2363
Sales: $500,001-$1 Million

PATRICIA KEMPE (Owner) & Buys Men's Apparel, Men's Casualwear, Men's Accessories, Men's Outerwear, Men's Sportswear, Men's Suits

SIMPLY SANTA FE (CLO)

72 E. San Francisco St. (b)
Santa Fe, NM 87501
505-988-3100 / Fax: 505-988-9292
Sales: $1 Million-$10 Million

ARMAND ORTEGA (Co-Owner) & Buys Leather Goods, Men's Apparel, Men's Casualwear, Men's Denim Apparel, Men's Accessories, Men's Outerwear, Men's Sportswear

SARAH WILSON (Co-Owner)

TEES & SKIS (SP)

107 Washington Ave.
Santa Fe, NM 87501
505-983-5637 / Fax: 505-680-1225

JOHN KINSOLVING (Owner) & Buys Men's Apparel

WENDY KINSOLVING-Men's Apparel

O.K. CLOTHIERS (MW)

133 S. 4th St. (m)
Santa Rosa, NM 88435
505-472-3790
Sales: Under $100,000

ARTHUR A. GALLEGOS (Owner) & Buys Men's Tailored Jackets, Sweaters, Sport Shirts, Outer Jackets, Casual Slacks, Leather Apparel, Active Apparel, Dress Shirts, Robes, Underwear, Hosiery, Gloves, Small Leather Goods, Headwear, Belts, Fragrances, Young Men's & Boys' Sportswear, Underwear, Gloves, Belts, Footwear, Store Displays, Fixtures, Supplies

TOWN & COUNTRY CLOTHES, INC. (CLO)

105 4th St. (p)
Santa Rosa, NM 88435
505-472-3951
Sales: Under $100,000

E. M. LUCERO (Owner) & Buys Men's Footwear, Store Displays, Fixtures, Supplies, Men's Overcoats, Suits, Tailored Jackets, Tailored Slacks, Sweaters, Sport Shirts, Outer Jackets, Active Apparel

MARY F. VIA-Men's Wear, Overcoats, Suits, Tailored Jackets, Tailored Slacks, Sweaters, Sport Shirts, Outer Jackets, Active Apparel

CLARKE & CO. (MW)

120 E. Bent St. (p)
Taos, NM 87571
505-758-2696 / Fax: 505-758-2696

CLARKE SHERER (Owner) & Buys Tailored Jackets, Tailored Slacks, Sweaters, Sport Shirts, Outer Jackets, Leather Apparel, Casual Shirts, Ties, Robes, Hosiery, Gloves, Belts, Small Leather Goods, Fragrances, Store Displays, Fixtures, Supplies

GON-MAR CLOTHES STORE (DEPT)

101 Camino de La Placita, #A (bud-p)
Taos, NM 87571
505-758-2972

NICK F. MARTINEZ (Owner) & Buys Men's Sportswear, Furnishings, Headwear, Accessories, Young Men's Wear, Big & Tall Men's Wear, 6 to 20 Boys' Wear, Footwear, Store Displays, Fixtures, Supplies

PAUL'S MEN'S SHOP (MW)

304 N. Pueblo Rd. (p-m)
Taos, NM 87571
505-758-3877

PAUL MARTINEZ (Owner) & Buys Men's Western Wear, Formal Wear, Sportswear, Furnishings, Accessories, Store Displays, Fixtures and Supplies

RIPS WESTERN WEAR (WW)

P.O. Box 297 (m-b)

314 Wheeler St.

Texico, NM 88135

505-482-3363 / Fax: 505-482-9427

Sales: $100,001-$500,000

ROY SNODGRASS (Owner) & Buys Boots, Men's & Boys' Western Wear, Leather Apparel, Furnishings, Headwear, Accessories, Store Displays, Fixtures, Supplies

KAREN SNODGRASS-Men's & Boys' Western Wear, Leather Apparel, Furnishings, Headwear, Accessories, Store Displays, Fixtures, Supplies

TOMMY SNODGRASS-Men's & Boys' Western Wear, Leather Apparel, Furnishings, Headwear, Accessories, Store Displays, Fixtures, Supplies

AMIN'S, INC. (CLO-2)

P.O. Box 467

400 N. Broadway

Truth or Consequences, NM 87901

505-897-2200

Sales: $1 Million-$10 Million

JOHN AMIN (President)

GEORGE AMIN (V.P.)

CARL AMIN (D.M.M.) & Buys Men's Footwear, Leather Goods, Men's Apparel, Men's Casualwear, Men's Denim Apparel, Men's Accessories, Men's Hosiery, Men's Outerwear, Men's Sleepwear, Men's Sportswear, Men's Swimwear, Men's Underwear

NEW YORK - Albany

B. LODGE CORPORATION (CLO)

75 N. Pearl (bud)
Albany, NY 12207
518-463-4646 / Fax: 518-463-0565
Sales: $1 Million-$10 Million

JACK YONALLY (Owner) & Buys Men's Sportswear, Urban Contemporary, Furnishings, Accessories, Store Displays, Fixtures, Supplies

CARUSO'S CUSTOM CLOTHIER (MW)

1823 Western Ave. (m-b)
Albany, NY 12203
518-464-6097 / Fax: 518-464-6098
Sales: $500,000-$1 Million
Website: www.carusoscustomclothier.com

MIKE CARUSO (Owner) & Buys Men's Wear, Furnishings, Accessories, Store Displays, Fixtures, Supplies

CHOPPA FORMAL WEAR (MW)

1020 Central Ave. (p)
Albany, NY 12205
518-453-2202 / Fax: 518-935-2003
Website: www.choppatux.com

TONY CHOPPA, SR. (Owner) & Buys Men's, Young Men's & Boys' Formal Wear, Footwear, Furnishings, Accessories

TONY CHOPPA, JR. (Mgr.) & Buys Store Displays, Fixtures, Supplies

CHRISTOPHER'S MEN'S STORE (MW-3)

90 State St., #511 (h)
Albany, NY 12207
518-689-0014 / Fax: 518-689-0018
Website: www.christophersclothing.com

VINCE RUA (Owner)

LES SCHWARTZBERG (V.P.-Mrch) & Buys Men's Suits, Men's Big & Tall, Accessories, Furnishings, Footwear, Store Displays

MORRIS MEN'S SHOP (MW)

181 Central Ave. (p)
Albany, NY 12206
518-462-4647

HAL MORRIS (Owner) & Buys Men's Wear, Furnishings, Accessories, Store Displays, Fixtures, Supplies

SPECTOR'S APPAREL (CLO)

233 Central Ave. (b)
Albany, NY 12206
518-434-0187 / Fax: 518-434-0902

ROBERT S. KAYNE (President) & Buys Men's Sweaters, Sport Shirts, Outer Jackets, Leather Apparel, Casual Slacks, Active Apparel, Furnishings, Boys' Wear, Footwear, Store Displays, Fixtures, Supplies

A BAY INTERNATIONAL (CLO)

(S. DAVOD IMDAD)
23 James St.
Alexandria Bay, NY 13607
315-482-4031 / Fax: 315-482-7045

DAVID IMDAD (Owner) & Buys Men's Sportswear, Dress Shirts, Gloves, Headwear, Accessories, Young Men's Wear, Boys' Wear 7 & Up, Store Displays, Fixtures, Supplies

KAMPUS KAVE (SP)

11 N. Main St. (p-m)
Alfred, NY 14802
607-587-9233

MARC RAWADY (Owner) & Buys Men's & Young Men's College Clothing, T-shirts, Fleece, Shorts, Active Apparel, Headwear, Store Displays, Fixtures and Supplies

ALDO'S UOMO (MW-2)

(CLOTHING FASHION OUTLET LTD.)
(ALDO'S MENSWEAR)
4224 Maple Rd. (p-m-b)
Amherst, NY 14226
716-834-3378 / Fax: 716-834-3436
Sales: $1 Million-$10 Million

DON CANNIZZARO (Co-Owner) & Buys Footwear, Men's Overcoats, Suits, Tailored Jackets, Tailored Slacks, Raincoats, Sweaters, Sport Shirts, Outer Jackets, Casual Slacks, Dress Shirts, Ties, Underwear, Hosiery, Accessories, Leather Apparel, Headwear, Store Displays, Fixtures, Supplies

ALDO DIVENCENZO (Co-Owner) (@ 716-675-7120) & Buys Men's Overcoats, Suits, Tailored Jackets, Tailored Slacks, Raincoats, Sweaters, Sport Shirts, Outer Jackets, Casual Slacks, Dress Shirts, Ties, Underwear, Hosiery, Accessories, Leather Apparel, Headwear, Footwear, Store Displays, Fixtures, Supplies

AMITYVILLE MEN'S SHOP, INC. (MW)

184 Park Ave. (m)
Amityville, NY 11701
631-264-2916
Sales: $100,001-$500,000

WAREN COHN (Owner) & Buys Men's Wear, Store Displays, Fixtures, Supplies

ARCADE MEN'S SHOP (MW)

263 Main St. (p-m-b)
Arcade, NY 14009
585-492-4040
Sales: $100,001-$500,000

JAY MAY (Co-Owner) & Buys Men's Wear, Sportswear, Furnishings, Accessories, Store Displays, Fixtures and Supplies

KATHY MAY (Co-Owner) & Buys Men's Wear, Sportswear, Furnishings, Accessories, Store Displays, Fixtures and Supplies

HICKORY & TWEED, INC. (CLO)

410 Main St. (m-b-des)
Armonk, NY 10504
914-273-3397 / Fax: 914-273-3849
Sales: $1 Million-$10 Million
Website: www.hickorytweed.com

SKIP BEITZEL (President)

MICHAELA BEITZEL (V.P.) & Buys Boys' Apparel, Boys' Footwear, Men's Footwear, Men's Apparel, Men's Casualwear, Men's Accessories, Men's Outerwear, Men's Sleepwear, Men's Sportswear, Men's Swimwear, Men's Underwear

KAREN TOPP-Boys' Apparel, Boys' Footwear, Men's Footwear, Men's Apparel, Men's Casualwear, Men's Accessories, Men's Outerwear, Men's Sleepwear, Men's Sportswear, Men's Swimwear, Men's Underwear

LILLIES & LACE (CLO)

480 Main St.
Armonk, NY 10504
914-273-2253 / Fax: 914-273-2253

ANNA GUEBLIA (Owner) & Buys Beach Cover-Ups, Swimwear

BOB NOLAN'S SPORTING GOODS CO. (SG)

39 Genesee St.
Auburn, NY 13021
315-252-7249 / Fax: 315-258-8762
Website: www.nolansports.com

BOB NOLAN (Owner) & Buys Active Apparel, Swimwear, Athletic Footwear

LIBERTY STORE (MW & OL)

5 E. Genesee St. (m)
Auburn, NY 13021
315-252-1761 / Fax: 315-252-1761
Sales: $1 Million-$10 Million
Website: www.thelibertystore.com

MARTY GOLDMAN (President) & Buys Men's Wear, Sweaters, Sport Shirts, Outer Jackets, Leather Apparel, Casual Slacks, Active Apparel, Furnishings, Accessories, Footwear, Store Displays, Fixtures, Supplies

LO-MAN OUTDOOR STORE LTD. (MW)

140 Deer Park Ave. (m)
Babylon, NY 11702
631-669-2064 / Fax: 631-669-0552
Sales: $1 Million-$10 Million

LOUIS E. FRIEDMAN (Owner) & Buys Men's Raincoats, Sweaters, Sport Shirts, Outer Jackets, Casual Slacks, Active Apparel, Furnishings, Headwear, Belts, Small Leather Goods, Young Men's Wear, Footwear

VINCENT NOTARSTEFANO (Mgr.) & Buys Men's Raincoats, Sweaters, Sport Shirts, Outer Jackets, Casual Slacks, Active Apparel, Furnishings, Headwear, Belts, Small Leather Goods, Young Men's Wear, Footwear

DOUBLE M WESTERN STORE (WW)
678 Rt. 67 (b)
Ballston Spa, NY 12020
518-885-9543 / Fax: 518-885-9895
Website: www.doublemwestern.com
KATHLEEN MARTIN (Owner) & Buys Men's & Boys' Western Wear, Related Furnishings, Headwear, Accessories, Western Boots, Work Boots, Moccasins, Store Displays, Fixtures, Supplies
CINDY MARTIN-Men's & Boys' Western Wear, Related Furnishings, Headwear, Accessories, Western Boots, Work Boots, Moccasins, Store Displays, Fixtures, Supplies

CHARLES MEN'S SHOP, INC. (MW)
200 E. Main St. (p-m)
Batavia, NY 14020
585-343-2086 / Fax: 585-343-2086
DAVE HOWE (Owner) & Buys Men's Wear, Sportswear, Furnishings, Accessories, Store Displays, Fixtures and Supplies

MILITARY COLLECTION (AN)
954 Montauk Hwy.
Bayport, NY 11705
631-447-6289 / Fax: 631-363-9226
MICHAEL KULAK (Owner) & Buys Men's Sportswear, Accessories, Footwear, Boys' Wear, Boys' Accessories, Boys' Footwear

FANWEAR.COM (OL & SG)
176 Harris Rd.
Bedford Hills, NY 10507
914-242-7014 / Fax: 914-242-7015
Sales: $501,000-$1 Million
Website: www.fanwear.com
BOB LITWIN (President)
JENNIFER JONES (Mgr.) & Buys Licensed Apparel
ROBIN LITWIN-Licensed Apparel

ROBERTO ANZALONE (MW)
195 Main St. (p)
Binghamton, NY 13905
607-797-9549
ROBERTO ANZALONE (Owner) & Buys Men's Ties, Belts, Store Displays, Fixtures, Supplies

SALL-STEARN'S, INC. (MW)
52 Court St. (b)
Binghamton, NY 13901
607-722-7780 / Fax: 607-722-0482
Sales: $500,000-$1 Million
RON SALL (President) & Buys Men's Overcoats, Suits, Tailored Jackets, Tailored Slacks, Raincoats, Sweaters, Sport Shirts, Outer Jackets, Leather Apparel, Casual Slacks, Active Apparel, Furnishings, Headwear, Accessories, Big & Tall Men's Wear, Footwear, Store Displays, Fixtures, Supplies

VALET SHOP, INC. (MW)
84 Front St. (m-b)
Binghamton, NY 13905
607-723-9024 / Fax: 607-723-7323
PASQUAL PALOMBARO (Owner) & Buys Store Displays, Fixtures, Supplies
JOHN PALOMBARO-Men's Wear, Furnishings, Accessories

WOODS MEN'S & BOYS' WEAR (MW & OL)
658 Suffolk Ave. (m)
Brentwood, NY 11717
631-273-0212 / Fax: 631-273-0230
Sales: $500,001-$1 Million
Website: www.woodsmenwear.com
RICK WOODS (President) & Buys Men's Wear, Sportswear, Leather Apparel, Furnishings, Headwear, Accessories, Big & Tall Men's Wear, Footwear, Urban Contemporary, Store Displays, Fixtures, Supplies

O'CONNELL, LUCAS & CHELF, INC. (CLO)
3240 Main St. (m-b)
Buffalo, NY 14214
716-836-4140 / Fax: 716-832-6355
Sales: $1 Million-$10 Million
Website: www.oconnells.biz
JOHN HUBER (President) & Buys Men's Sweaters, Sport Shirts, Outer Jackets, Active Apparel, Robes, Headwear, Store Displays, Fixtures, Supplies, Footwear, Accessories
BERNHARD J. HUBER (C.E.O.) & Buys Men's Overcoats, Suits, Tailored Jackets, Tailored Slacks, Raincoats, Big & Tall Men's Wear, Leather Apparel, Young Men's & Boys' Wear, Footwear, Accessories

RIVERSIDE MEN'S QUALITY SHOP, INC. (MW)
(RIVERSIDE MEN'S SHOP)
783 Tonawanda St. (m-b)
Buffalo, NY 14207
(DLS Outfitters)
716-875-8400 / Fax: 716-875-9916
Sales: $1 Million-$10 Million
TIMOTHY H. HARE (President)
JOE JACOBI (V.P.) & Buys Men's Sweaters, Sport Shirts, Furnishings, Accessories, Footwear
STAN ROOK-Men's Raincoats, Outer Jackets, Leather Apparel, Casual Slacks

UNITED MEN'S FASHIONS (MW)
3082 Bailey Ave. (m-b)
Buffalo, NY 14215
716-837-0100 / Fax: 716-837-0670
Website: www.unitedmens.com
BOB COHEN (Owner) & Buys Men's Wear, Footwear, Store Displays, Fixtures, Supplies

WASHINGTON SURPLUS CENTER, INC. (AN & SG)
(TENT CITY)
674 Main St. (p-m)
Buffalo, NY 14202
716-853-1515 / Fax: 716-853-1517
Sales: $1 Million-$10 Million
Website: www.tentcitybuffalo.com
CHARLES B. KUSHNER (President) & Buys Overcoats, Men's Big & Tall Wear, Leather Apparel, Casual Slacks, Active Apparel, Footwear, Hiking Boots
ED STANDISH (G.M.M.) & Buys Headwear, Belts

WORD UP FASHIONS (CLO)
1337 Jefferson Ave.
Buffalo, NY 14208
716-884-5844
Website: www.wordupfashions.qpg.com
DEREK FOSTER (Owner) & Buys Men's Urban Contemporary, Accessories, Casual Slacks, Ties, Gloves, Suits, Jewelry, Footwear, Boys' Wear up to 7, Boys Furnishings and Accessories

DICK ANTHONY LIMITED (MW)
166 S. Main St. (p)
Canandaigua, NY 14424
585-394-4876 / Fax: 585-394-2488
Website: www.dickanthonyltd.com
JEFF ANTHONY (Owner) & Buys Men's Wear, Sportswear, Furnishings, Accessories, Store Displays, Fixtures and Supplies

DAVIDSON SHOES (SP & MO)
153 S. Main St.
Canandaiqua, NY 14424
585-394-5417 / Fax: 585-394-8071
Website: www.shoestoboot.com
MARK HOGAN (Owner) & Buys Athletic Footwear, Outdoor Footwear

BOYS' WORLD OF CEDARHURST (KS)
375 Rugby Rd. (b)
Cedarhurst, NY 11516
516-295-5328 / Fax: 516-295-2223
Sales: $500,000-$1 Million
SHARON BADER (Co-Owner) & Buys 4 to 22 Boys' Dress Wear, Sportswear, Furnishins, Accessories
GARY BADER (Co-Owner) & Buys 4 to 22 Regular, Slim & Husky Boys' Wear, Furnishings, Accessories

NEW YORK - Cedarhurst

JERRIE SHOP (CLO-2)
404 Central Ave. (b)
Cedarhurst, NY 11516
516-569-1144 / Fax: 516-569-1761
Sales: $1 Million-$10 Million
TAMI SHANKMAN (President & C.E.O.) & Buys Men's Wear, Big & Tall Apparel, Outerwear, Sportswear, Swimwear
AMY VOGEL (V.P.) & Buys Men's Sportswear
MARNA HANN-Men's Swimwear

MORTON'S ARMY & NAVY (AN)
108 Cedarhurst Ave. (p-m)
Cedarhurst, NY 11516
516-569-6366 / Fax: 516-569-8258
Sales: $1 Million-$10 Million
STEVEN SILVERMAN (Owner) & Buys Men's Young Men's & Boys' Sportswear, Accessories, Leather Outerwear, Footwear, Store Displays, Fixtures, Supplies

RICO'S CLOTHING (MW)
16 Railroad Ave. (m-b)
Center Moriches, NY 11934
631-878-1022 / Fax: 631-878-1098
Website: www.ricosclothing.com
RICHARD MAAG (Mgr.) & Buys Men's Suits, Tailored Jackets, Tailored Slacks, Accessories, Formalwear, Leather Apparel, Footwear, Furnishings, Store Displays, Fixtures, Supplies

CENTEREACH WORK N' PLAY, INC. (CLO)
2149 Middle Country Rd. (m)
Centereach, NY 11720
631-585-7767 / Fax: 631-585-7768
Website: www.shopworkandplay.com
KENNY LEHRER (Owner) & Buys Men's Work Clothes, Casual Wear, Footwear, Urban Contemporary, Furnishings, Accessories, Store Displays, Fixtures, Supplies

CLINTON SHOE CENTER (SP)
16 W. Park Row
Clinton, NY 13323
315-853-5615 / Fax: 315-853-1544
Sales: $100,001-$500,000
JACK LANE (Owner) & Buys Athletic Footwear, Outdoor Footwear, Apparel

EDWARD ALAN (MW)
(CARL & BOB'S)
102 Jericho Tpke.
Commack, NY 11725
631-864-4830 / Fax: 631-864-4831
ALAN SCHLOFFER (Owner) & Buys Men's Wear, Accessories, Furnishings, Men's Big & Tall

WILLIAM ARONOW CO. (RB)
12 Sartoga St. (bud-p-m-b)
Commack, NY 11725
631-858-0244
WILLIAM ARONOW (Owner) & Buys Men's Wear, Size 8 to 18 Boys' Wear

FRAN'S BRIDAL SHOP, INC. (SP-2)
75 Denison Pkwy. East (b-des)
Corning, NY 14830
607-962-6122 / Fax: 607-962-6122
Sales: $500,001-$1 Million
FRANCES BATES (Owner) & Buys Men's Wear, Formalwear, Footwear
CANDACE BATES-WEICKMAN-Men's Wear, Formalwear, Footwear

BERNARD'S CLOTHIERS FOR MEN (MW)
107 Main St. (m-b)
Cortland, NY 13045
607-756-5951 / Fax: 607-662-0909
Sales: $500,000-$1 Million
BERNARD WINEBURG (Owner) & Buys Men's Overcoats, Suits, Tailored Jackets, Tailored Slacks, Raincoats, Big & Tall Wear, Sweaters, Sport Shirts, Outer Jackets, Leather Apparel, Casual Slacks, Active Apparel, Furnishings, Accessories, Footwear, Young Men's Wear, Urban Contemporary, Store Displays, Fixtures, Supplies

WEBCLOTHES.COM (OL)
165 S. Main St. (p)
Cortland, NY 13045
607-662-0141 / Fax: 607-662-0144
Website: www.webclothes.com
SUE CATANOSO-Boys' Wear, Furnishings, Accessories

STEWART'S DEPARTMENT STORE (MW)
85 Main St. (p-m)
Delhi, NY 13753
607-746-2254 / Fax: 607-746-2254
Sales: $100,001-$500,000
GEORGE B. STEWART (Owner) & Buys Men's Wear, Sportswear, Furnishings, Belts, Small Leather Goods, Boys' Sportswear, Furnishings, Accessories, Store Displays, Fixtures, Supplies

CHARNEY'S, INC. (MW-2)
3150 Erie Blvd. East (m-b)
DeWitt, NY 13214
315-463-6011 / Fax: 315-433-1220
Sales: $1 Million-$10 Million
MEL CHARNEY (President & G.M.M.) & Buys Men's Wear, Suits, Tailored Jackets & Slacks, Raincoats, Big & Tall Wear, Sweaters, Sports Shirts, Outer Jackets, Leather Apparel, Dress Shirts, Ties, Robes, Underwear, Hosiery, Gloves, Headwear, Belts, Jewelry, Sportswear, Furnishings, Big & Tall Men's Wear, Boys' Suits, Sportcoats, Shirts, Ties, Pants, Store Displays, Fixtures, Supplies

DAN'S SPORT CENTER, INC. (SG)
16 Cedar St. (m)
Dobbs Ferry, NY 10522
914-693-1754 / Fax: 914-693-4981
DANIEL ZIMKIN (Owner) & Buys Men's Active Apparel, Team Uniforms, Underwear, Hosiery, Belts, Headwear, T-shirts, Fleecewear, Shorts, Store Displays, Fixtures and Supplies

FIELD OF TEAMS (GS)
501 Columbia Plz.
Rtes. 9 & 20
East Greenbush, NY 12061
518-479-3009 / Fax: 518-479-2476
LESLIE KACZOR (Owner) & Buys Licensed Apparel, Footwear
KATHY LUCHNER (Mgr.) & Buys Athletic Footwear, Outdoor Footwear

SPRINGER'S CLOTHING CO., INC. (MW)
39 Newtown Ln.
East Hampton, NY 11937
631-324-8840 / Fax: 631-324-8892
JUDY SPRINGER (Owner) & Buys Men's Wear, Accessories, Furnishings, Store Displays

EAST NORTHPORT ARMY & NAVY STORE (AN)
(M & B STORES, INC.)
275 Larkfield Rd. (m)
East Northport, NY 11731
631-261-2950 / Fax: 631-754-5142
Sales: $100,001-$500,000
PAUL WILKOW (Owner) & Buys Men's Jeans, Shirts, Work Clothes, Underwear, Hosiery, Belts, Footwear, Urban Contemporary, Store Displays, Fixtures, Supplies

SCHWAB'S 2ND WIND, INC. (SP)
1371 Rte. 25A
East Setauket, NY 11733
631-751-5534 / Fax: 631-751-5592
Sales: $100,001-$500,000
HAROLD SCHWAB (Owner) & Buys Activewear, Athletic Footwear

H. STRAUSS, INC. (MW)
363 W. Church St.
Elmira, NY 14901
607-733-7475 / Fax: 413-778-8459
Website: www.hstrauss.com
BRUCE CHALMERS (Owner) & Buys Men's Suits, Sportcoats, Outerwear, Footwear

PAL'S SPORTS CENTER (SG)
142 W. Water St. (m)
Elmira, NY 14901
607-732-8367 / Fax: 607-733-7149
GEORGE MALONEY (Owner) & Buys Men's & Boys' T-shirts, Fleece, Shorts, Active Apparel, Athletic Hosiery, Headwear, Athletic Footwear, Store Displays, Fixtures and Supplies
JAMES PROPER (Mgr.) & Buys Men's & Boys' T-shirts, Fleece, Shorts, Active Apparel, Athletic Hosiery, Headwear, Athletic Footwear, Store Displays, Fixtures and Supplies

PANOSIAN'S, INC. (FW)
(MR. PANOSIAN'S)
303 N. Main St. (p)
Elmira, NY 14901
607-734-8133 / Fax: 607-737-5287
Sales: $100,001-$500,000
DAVID PANOSIAN (President)
RICHARD PIROZZOLO (G.M.M.) & Buys Athletic Footwear, Dress Footwear, Casual Footwear, Slippers

PRINCETON SKI SHOP (SG-4)
380 Saw Mill River Rd. (b-des)
Elmsford, NY 10523
914-592-4141 / Fax: 914-592-6110
Sales: $10 Million-$50 Million
Website: www.princetonski.com
RICK CARP (Co-Owner, Dir. - Finance & Real Estate) & Buys Boys' Wear, Men's & Boys' Footwear,Men's Wear, Accessories, Hosiery
JORDAN CARP (Co-Owner)

S & B CLOTHING INDUSTRIES (MW)
120 Milbar Blvd. (m)
Farmingdale, NY 11735
631-293-4848 / Fax: 631-293-4839
STEVEN BRAUSTEIN (Owner) & Buys Men's Wear, Furnishings, Accessories, Store Displays, Fixtures, Supplies

RETAIL APPAREL, INC. (MW-38)
(SID'S PANTS)
(EPIC)
146 Hanse Ave. (p-m)
Freeport, NY 11526
516-867-6200 / Fax: 516-867-6278
Retail Locations: FL, MA, NJ, NY, PA
AL COHEN (Real Estate Contact)
ALAN BECKER-All Young Men's Wear, Men's Furnishings, Men's Accessories

CLAPPER'S MEN'S SHOP ROOSEVELT (MW)
Roosevelt Field Mall (b-h)
Garden City, NY 11530
516-747-5000 / Fax: 516-747-5550
MARIO LICHTENSTEIN (Owner) & Buys Men's Wear, Footwear, Store Displays, Fixtures, Supplies

SUPER CASUALS (MW)
52 Seneca (p)
Geneva, NY 14456
315-789-1933 / Fax: 315-789-1933
Website: www.supercasuals.com
JOSEPH FRAGNOLI (Owner)
STEVE FRAGNOLI (V.P.) & Buys Men's Sweaters, Sport Shirts, Outer Jackets, Casual Slacks, Active Apparel, Dress Shirts, Ties, Robes, Underwear, Hosiery, Gloves, Headwear, Belts, Big & Tall Men's Wear, Footwear, Boys' Wear, Urban Contemporary, Store Displays, Fixtures, Supplies

JONATHAN REID LTD. (MW-5)
166 Glen St. (m-b)
Glens Falls, NY 12801
518-793-5678 / Fax: 518-793-5678
Sales: $1 Million-$10 Million
JON SEGAN (Owner & President) & Buys Men's Overcoats, Suits, Tailored Jackets, Tailored Slacks, Raincoats, Sweaters, Sport Shirts, Outer Jackets, Leather Apparel, Casual Slacks, Furnishings, Headwear, Belts, Small Leather Goods, Store Displays, Fixtures, Supplies

DUNDAY'S CLOTHIER CORP. (MW)
49 N. Main St. (m)
Gloversville, NY 12078
518-725-4213 / Fax: 518-725-4213
Sales: $500,001-$1 Million
JOE GILLIS (Owner) & Buys Men's Wear, Furnishings, Accessories, Store Displays, Fixtures, Supplies

CHLOE'S CLEANERS, CLOTHES & MORE (CLO)
20 Jamestown St. (p-m-b)
Gowanda, NY 14070
716-532-4444 / Fax: 716-532-4444
BARB BELSCHER (Mgr.) & Buys Men's Suits, Tailored Jackets, Tailored Slacks, Sweaters, Sport Shirts, Outer Jackets, Casual Slacks, Active Apparel, Furnishings, Headwear, Belts, Big & Tall Men's Wear, Store Displays, Fixtures, Supplies

GARMEX (MW)
14 Hen Hawk Rd. (bud-p-m-b)
Great Neck, NY 11024
516-829-1000
Website: www.garmex.com
BRUCE POLATNICK (President)
MARISOL URDANETA (V.P.)
JO ALEXA-All Men's, Young Men's & Boys' Wear

THE ANNEX SHOPPE, INC. (CLO)
330 Wheatley Plz. (b-des)
Greenvale, NY 11548
516-621-1840 / Fax: 516-621-1806
Sales: $1 Million-$10 Million
Website: www.annexshoppe.com
GLENN WERNER (President)
BOB MORGAN (Store Mgr.) & Buys Boys' Wear, Men's & Boys' Footwear, Men's Wear, Sportswear, Formalwear, Denim, Accessories, Hosiery, Outerwear, Sleepwear, Swimwear, Uniforms, Suits, ym apparel
ROBERT WERNER-Boys' Wear, Men's & Boys' Footwear, Men's Wear, Sportswear, Formalwear, Denim, Accessories, Hosiery, Outerwear, Sleepwear, Swimwear, Uniforms, Suits, ym apparel

BROWSERS (CLO)
P.O. Box 431 (m)
33 Sheather St.
Hammondsport, NY 14840
607-569-2497 / Fax: 607-569-3119
Sales: $100,001-$500,000
PAMELA KNAPP (Owner) & Buys Men's Sweaters, Sport Shirts, Active Apparel, Footwear

D. J. MARINO (SG)
95 E. Front St. (m)
Hancock, NY 13783
607-637-3573
Sales: $100,001-$500,000
DONALD MARINO (Owner) & Buys Men's Hunting Clothes, Dress Pants, Sport Coats, Active Apparel, Footwear, Boots, Store Displays, Fixtures, Supplies

HARRIMAN CLOTHING CO. (AN)
(HARRIMAN ARMY & NAVY, INC.)
186 Rte. 17M
Harriman, NY 10926
845-783-6053 / Fax: 845-783-5150
Sales: $100,001-$500,000
Website: www.ruggedstuff.com
MADELYN GOLDBERG (Owner) & Buys Hunting Apparel, Military Apparel, Footwear, Boots, Sportswear

BEN-LEE DISTRIBUTORS, INC. (DEPT-3)
270 Halstead Ave. (p-m-b)
Harrison, NY 10528
914-939-7272 / Fax: 914-835-0710
GLEN ROTKER (Owner) & Buys Men's & Boys' Wear, Footwear, Underwear, Hosiery, Store Displays, Fixtures, Supplies

NEW YORK - Hempstead

HARLEY DAVIDSON OF HEMPSTEAD (SP)
4 Laurel Ave. (m-b)
Hempstead, NY 11550
516-481-7100 / Fax: 516-481-7106
Sales: $500,001-$1 Million

MARTIN AHOLTZ (Partner) & Buys Boys' Wear, Men's Footwear, Men's Sportswear, Men's Accessories, Men's Furnishings, Men's Outerwear

RICHARD CRISTANI (Partner, Dir.- Finance, Mktg., Real Estate & HR) & Buys Store Fixtures & Displays

JEANNIE SMITH-Boys' Wear, Boys' Footwear, Men's Footwear, Men's Sportswear, Furnishings, Accessories, Outerwear

HOFSTRA UNIVERSITY BOOKSTORE (SP)
200 Hofstra University
Hempstead, NY 11549
516-463-6654 / Fax: 516-463-4827
Sales: $500,001-$1 Million
Website: www.hofstra.bkstore.com

MICHELLE DURAN (Mdse. Mgr.) & Buys Activewear, Athletics

STREET GEAR, INC. (SP)
245 Fulton Ave.
Hempstead, NY 11550
516-538-1603 / Fax: 516-538-0453

DAVE TANZMAN (Mgr.) & Buys Athletic Footwear, Activewear

RUDY'S MENSWEAR (MW)
216 S. Main St. (p-m-b)
Herkimer, NY 13350
315-866-3270 / Fax: 315-866-5044
Sales: $1 Million-$10 Million

RUDY DONATO (President)

GINA HARTMAN-Men's Overcoats, Suits, Tailored Jackets, Tailored Slacks, Raincoats, Sweaters, Sport Shirts, Outer Jackets, Casual Slacks, Active Apparel, Headwear, Accessories, Big & Tall Men's Wear, Footwear, Store Displays, Fixtures, Supplies

GOLDMAN BROTHERS, INC. (MW)
183 S. Broadway (m-b)
Hicksville, NY 11801
516-931-0441 / Fax: 516-931-1062
Website: www.goldmanbros.com

HOWARD GOLDMAN (Co-Owner)

ELIZABETH GOLDMAN (Co-Owner) & Buys Men's Sportswear, Furnishings, Accessories, Footwear, Store Displays, Fixtures, Supplies

WORLD BRANDS, INC. (MW-2)
(MEN'S WORLD)
108 New South Rd. (m)
Hicksville, NY 11801
516-937-0400 / Fax: 516-937-1342
Sales: $1 Million-$10 Million

GARY CALMENSON (Owner) & Buys Men's Apparel, Men's Big & Tall Apparel, Men's Designer Apparel, Men's Formalwear, Men's Accessories, Men's Hosiery, Men's Outerwear, Men's Sleepwear, Men's Sportswear, Men's Suits, Men's Swimwear, Men's Uniforms, Young Men's Apparel, Footwear

HOMER MEN'S & BOYS' STORE, INC. (MW)
9 S. Main St. (p)
Homer, NY 13077
607-749-3314 / Fax: 607-749-4304
Sales: $500,000-$1 Million

ROLAND FRAGNOLI (Owner) & Buys Men's, Young Men's & Boys' Wear, Urban Contemporary, Footwear, Accessories, Furnishings, Store Displays, Fixtures, Supplies

ULTA MODA FASHIONS (MW)
461 Rte. 376
Grand Union Plz.
Hopewell Junction, NY 12533
845-227-4119

ARMANDO PERUSSINO (Owner) & Buys Men's Wear, Footwear, Urban Contemporary, Store Displays, Fixtures, Supplies

THOMAS F. KINNEY, INC. (MW)
30 Broadway (m)
Hornell, NY 14843
607-324-2833

THOMAS KINNEY (Owner) & Buys Men's Wear, Sportswear, Furnishings, Accessories, Young Men's Wear, Store Displays, Fixtures and Supplies

DIAMOND'S ARMY & NAVY, INC. (AN)
344 New York Ave. (m)
Huntington, NY 11743
631-427-1012 / Fax: 631-427-1052

SID PERCYZ (Owner) & Buys Men's Work Clothes, Jeans, Underwear, Hosiery, Outer Jackets, Footwear, Store Displays, Fixtures, Supplies

MR. IZIU (President)

MARSH'S MEN'S SHOP, INC. (MW)
270 Main St. (b-des)
Huntington, NY 11743
631-423-1660 / Fax: 631-423-1670
Sales: $1 Million-$10 Million
Website: www.marshs.com

DANIEL MARSH (President & Partner) & Buys Men's Footwear, Fragrances, Leather Goods, Men's Apparel, Men's Big & Tall Apparel, Men's Casualwear, Men's Denim Apparel, Men's Designer Apparel, Men's Formalwear, Men's Accessories, Men's Hosiery, Men's Outerwear, Men's Sleepwear, Men's Sportswear, Men's Suits, Men's Swimwear, Men's Underwear, Footwear

RONALD MARSH (V.P. & Partner) & Buys Men's Footwear, Fragrances, Leather Goods, Men's Apparel, Men's Big & Tall Apparel, Men's Casualwear, Men's Denim Apparel, Men's Designer Apparel, Men's Formalwear, Men's Accessories, Men's Hosiery, Men's Outerwear, Men's Sleepwear, Men's Sportswear, Men's Suits, Men's Swimwear, Men's Underwear, Footwear

MARVIN MARSH (Partner) & Buys Men's Footwear, Fragrances, Leather Goods, Men's Apparel, Men's Big & Tall Apparel, Men's Casualwear, Men's Denim Apparel, Men's Designer Apparel, Men's Formalwear, Men's Accessories, Men's Hosiery, Men's Outerwear, Men's Sleepwear, Men's Sportswear, Men's Suits, Men's Swimwear, Men's Underwear, Footwear

SUPER RUNNERS SHOP, INC. (FW-6)
(NEW BALANCE NEW YORK)
355 New York Ave. (b)
Huntington, NY 11743
631-549-3006 / Fax: 631-549-3336
Sales: $1 Million-$10 Million
Website: www.superrunnersshop.com

JANE MUHRCKE (President) & Buys Boys' Footwear, Men's Footwear, Watches, Men's Accessories, Men's Apparel, Hosiery

GARY MUHRCKE (V.P.) & Buys Boys' Footwear, Men's Footwear, Watches, Men's Accessories, Men's Apparel, Hosiery

CORNELL STORE (GM)
(STATLER LOBBY SHOP)
Central Ave. (p)
Ithaca, NY 14853
607-255-4927 / Fax: 607-254-4577
Sales: $10 Million-$50 Million
Website: www.thecornellstore.com

TOM ROMANTIC (Dir.)

JOAN MANHEIM (Adv. Mgr.) & Buys Store Displays, Fixtures, Supplies

SAM BONANNI-Men's Sweaters, Sport Shirts, Outer Jackets, Active Apparel, Ties, Underwear, Hosiery, Gloves, Headwear, Belts, Licensed Apparel, Boys' Wear

MORRIS' MENSWEAR (CLO)
134 The Commons (m-b)
Ithaca, NY 14850
607-272-3761 / Fax: 607-272-3761
Sales: $500,001-$1 Million
CHRISTEN LEWIS (President) & Buys Men's Suits, Sportswear, Sweaters, Sport Shirts, Outer Jackets, Casual Slacks, Active Apparel, Big & Tall Men's Wear, Store Displays, Fixtures, Supplies

LANDER'S MEN'S STORE (MW)
215 N. Main St. (p)
Jamestown, NY 14701
716-483-5400
CLIFFORD POWERS, JR. (Co-Owner) & Buys Men's Wear, Footwear, Furnishings, Accessories, Store Displays, Fixtures, Supplies
ANN POWERS (Co-Owner) & Buys Men's Wear, Footwear, Furnishings, Accessories, Store Displays, Fixtures, Supplies

BERNIE'S (MW)
255 Main St. (bud)
Johnson City, NY 13790
607-797-6955
Sales: $100,001-$500,000
FREDERIC DASZEWSKI (Owner) & Buys Footwear, Store Displays, Fixtures, Supplies, Men's Overcoats, Big & Tall Men's Wear, Sportswear, Furnishings, Headwear, Belts, Jewelry, Small Leather Goods, Young Men's Wear
VANESSA DASZEWSKI (Mgr.) & Buys Men's Overcoats, Big & Tall Men's Wear, Sportswear, Furnishings, Headwear, Belts, Jewelry, Small Leather Goods, Young Men's Wear

CHARLES DEPARTMENT STORE (DEPT)
113 Katonah Ave. (b-h)
Katonah, NY 10536
914-232-5200 / Fax: 914-232-1951
Website: www.charlesdeptstore.com
JIM RANERI (Co-Owner) & Buys Men's Sportswear, Furnishings, Accessories, Footwear, Store Displays, Fixtures and Supplies
DAVID RANERI (Co-Owner) & Buys Men's Sportswear, Furnishings, Accessories, Footwear, Store Displays, Fixtures and Supplies

SQUIRES (MW-2)
193 Katonah Ave. (b)
Katonah, NY 10531
914-232-0212 / Fax: 914-232-7385
LLOYD KUSHNER (Owner) & Buys Men's Sportswear, Western Wear, Furnishings, Accessories, Formal Wear, Swim Wear, Men's Big & Tall Wear, Sizes 8 to 20 Boys' Wear, Footwear, Store Displays, Fixtures, Supplies

NAPOLIS (MW-2)
2761 Delaware Ave. (m-b)
Kenmore, NY 14217
716-874-2727 / Fax: 716-874-0312
JOSEPH NAPOLIS (Owner) & Buys Men's Wear, Sportswear, Furnishings, Accessories, Young Men's Wear, Urban Contemporary, Footwear, Store Displays, Fixtures and Supplies

SUN QUEST TANNING (CLO)
P.O. Box 189
Lafayette, NY 13084
315-677-9647 / Fax: 315-677-9647
WAYNE MOORE (Co-Owner) & Buys Sunglasses, Footwear, Men's Swimwear, Men's Surf & Swimwear
BARBARA MOORE (Co-Owner) & Buys Sunglasses, Footwear, Men's Swimwear, Men's Surf & Swimwear

GREAT RANGE OUTFITTERS (MW)
71 Main St.
Lake Placid, NY 12946
518-523-1650 / Fax: 518-523-7578
BILL O'LEARY (Owner) & Buys Men's Wear, Men's Accessories, Furnishings, Store Displays

RUTHIE'S RUN (CLO)
(C & W JOHNSTON, INC.)
11 Main St. (m-b)
Lake Placid, NY 12946
518-523-3271 / Fax: 518-523-7272
Sales: $500,000-$1 Million
Website: www.ruthiesrun.com
WAYNE JOHNSTON (Co-Owner)
CATHERINE JOHNSTON (Co-Owner) & Buys Men's Sportswear, Furnishings, Belts, Jewelry, Footwear, Store Displays, Fixtures, Supplies
CHANTAL GREGG (Mgr.) & Buys Men's Sportswear, Furnishings, Belts, Jewelry, Footwear, Store Displays, Fixtures, Supplies

C.L. CARNAHAN CORP. (MW-2)
(CARNAHAN CLOTHING CO.)
373 E. Fairmount Ave. (m-b)
Lakewood, NY 14750
716-763-5102 / Fax: 716-763-5109
Sales: $1 Million-$10 Million
DALE A. SANDBERG (President) & Buys Men's Overcoats, Raincoats, Outer Jackets, Gloves, Headwear, Casual Slacks, Suits, Tailored Jackets, Tailored Slacks, Big & Tall Men's Wear, Formal Wear, Sweaters, Sport Shirts, Casual Slacks, Active Apparel
JUDY THURBER-Men's Overcoats, Raincoats, Outer Jackets, Gloves, Headwear, Casual Slacks, Suits, Tailored Jackets, Tailored Slacks, Big & Tall Men's Wear, Formal Wear, Sweaters, Sport Shirts, Casual Slacks, Active Apparel

NEW YORK STORE CORP. (MW)
(THE LANCASTER)
16 Central Ave. (m-b)
Lancaster, NY 14086
716-683-4374 / Fax: 716-684-4594
SHELDON L. KURTZMAN (President) & Buys Men's Sportswear
ALAN KURTZMAN-Men's Sportswear, Store Displays, Fixtures and Supplies

MANCINO CUSTOM TAILORS (MW)
(PALMER AVE. CORP.)
1931 Palmer Ave. (b-h)
Larchmont, NY 10538
914-834-9373 / Fax: 914-834-2280
Sales: $500,000-$1 Million
TONY MANCINO (Co-Owner) & Buys Men's Suits, Sport Coats, Slacks, Shirts, Ties, Accessories
MARY ANN MANCINO (Co-Owner) & Buys Men's Suits, Sport Coats, Slacks, Shirts, Ties, Accessories

HUCK FINN CLOTHES, INC. (CLO-60)
(LABEL SHOPPER)
(PRICELESS KIDS)
(PETER HARRIS CLOTHES)
952 Troy Schenectady Rd. (bud-p-m-b)
Latham, NY 12110
518-785-1650 / Fax: 518-785-0100
Sales: $1 Million-$10 Million
Retail Locations: CT, MA, NH, NY, OH, RI
PETER H. ELITZAR (President & G.M.M.)
HELEN HOUSER (Controller & Mgr.- Finance)
JUDY THIESEN (Dir.- Opers. & Mktg.) & Buys Store Displays & Fixtures
KENDRA WEBER-Men's Wear, Men's Big & Tall, Furnishings, Accessories, Outerwear, Sportswear, Suits, Swimwear

KELLY CLOTHES (MW)
579 Troy-Schenectady Rd., #223 (m)
Latham, NY 12110
518-785-3796 / Fax: 518-785-0334
DONALD C. REUTEMANN (President)
ANNE BERRUYER-Men's Wear, Sportswear, Leather Apparel, Furnishings, Headwear, Accessories, Big & Tall Men's Wear, Young Men's Wear, Boys' Wear, Store Displays, Fixtures, Supplies

PETER HARRIS (CLO-11)
(HUCK FINN CLOTHES, INC.)
952 Troy-Schenectady Rd. (m-b)
Latham, NY 12110
518-785-1650 / Fax: 518-785-0100
Sales: $10 Million-$50 Million
PETER ELITZER (President)
KENDRA WEBER-Men's Sportswear, Ties, Dress Shirts, Footwear
CAROL PRENDERGAST-Boys' & Students' Dress Pants, Sport Shirts, Jeans, Dress Shirts, Urban Contemporary

NEW YORK - Levittown

TRI-FRAN, INC. (MW)

(EVAN'S)
128 Gardiners Ave. (p-m)
Levittown, NY 11756
516-796-8353 / Fax: 516-796-8353
Sales: $100,001-$500,000

IRV WOLFOWITZ (Owner) & Buys Men's Jeans, Outer Jackets, T-shirts, Dress Shirts, Underwear, Hosiery, Footwear, Store Displays, Fixtures, Supplies

LERCH & DALY CLOTHIERS (MW)

58 Main St. (p)
Lockport, NY 14094
716-434-8700 / Fax: 716-434-9795
Sales: $1 Million-$10 Million

CHARLES GRAY (Owner) & Buys Men's Overcoats, Suits, Tailored Jackets, Tailored Slacks, Raincoats, Big & Tall Wear, Furnishings, Accessories, Leather Apparel, Footwear, Urban Contemporary, Store Displays, Fixtures, Supplies

LOCKPORT SURPLUS CENTER (MW)

5943 S. Transit Rd. (p-m-b)
Lockport, NY 14094
716-433-8991 / Fax: 716-433-9044

LILLIAN KUSHNER (Co-Owner)

JIM KUSHNER (Co-Owner) & Buys Men's Sweaters, Sport Shirts, Outer Jackets, Leather Apparel, Casual Slacks, Active Apparel, Dress Shirts, Underwear, Hosiery, Gloves, Headwear, Belts, Small Leather Goods, Big & Tall Men's Wear, Students' Wear, Footwear, Urban Contemporary, Store Displays, Fixtures, Supplies

CASEY'S MEN'S & BOYS' WEAR (MW)

28 Atlantic Ave. (m)
Lynbrook, NY 11563
516-593-9533

IRWIN MESSINGER (Owner) & Buys Men's & Boys' Jeans, Casual Pants, Tops, Outerwear, Urban Contemporary, Store Displays, Fixtures, Supplies

MUR-LEE, INC. (MW)

24 Atlantic Ave. (b)
Lynbrook, NY 11563
516-599-7777 / Fax: 516-593-0549
Sales: $1 Million-$10 Million

BRUCE LEVITT (Co-Owner) & Buys Overcoats, Suits, Tailored Jackets, Tailored Slacks, Big & Tall Men's Wear, Sweaters, Sport Shirts, Outer Jackets, Leather Apparel, Casual Slacks, Activewear, Furnishings, Dress Shirts, Ties, Robes, Underwear, Hosiery, Headwear, Accessories, Belts, Jewelry, Boys' Wear, Sportswear, Boys' Footwear, Store Displays, Fixtures and Supplies

HARRY LEVITT (Co-Owner) & Buys Overcoats, Suits, Tailored Jackets, Tailored Slacks, Big & Tall Men's Wear, Sweaters, Sport Shirts, Outer Jackets, Leather Apparel, Casual Slacks, Activewear, Furnishings, Dress Shirts, Ties, Robes, Underwear, Hosiery, Headwear, Accessories, Belts, Jewelry, Boys' Wear, Sportswear, Boys' Footwear, Store Displays, Fixtures and Supplies

SUITS WEARHOUSE (MW-5)

9 Lincoln Pl. (m-b)
Lynbrook, NY 11563
516-596-6660 / Fax: 516-596-6661

EZRA KARKO (Owner) & Buys Men's Sportswear, Furnishings, Accessories, Footwear, Store Displays, Fixtures, Supplies

F1 MARKETING GROUP, INC. (MO)

707 Fenimore Rd. (p-m)
Mamaroneck, NY 10543
914-381-3274 / Fax: 914-381-3270
Website: www.speedgear.com

GARY LOW (President)

CAROLINE HENRY-Men's & Boys' T-shirts, Polo Shirts

ROBERT'S DEPARTMENT STORE (DEPT)

342 Mamaroneck Ave. (m)
Mamaroneck, NY 10543
914-698-0969 / Fax: 914-698-0969

MANNY ENES (Owner) & Buys Sportswear, Jeans, Furnishings, Accessories, Young Men's Wear, Urban Contemporary, Footwear, Store Displays, Fixtures and Supplies

HIRSHLEIFER'S ETC. (SP & OL)

2080 Northern Blvd. (h)
Manhasset, NY 11030
516-627-3566 / Fax: 516-627-3579
Website: www.hirshleifers.com

PAUL HIRSHLEIFER (President) & Buys Men's Furnishings, Accessories, Footwear

EAGLE'S MENSWEAR (MW)

(A. E. OUTFITTERS, INC.)
890 Sunrise Mall (m-b)
Massapequa, NY 11758
516-795-4151 / Fax: 516-799-9088
Sales: $500,001-$1 Million

ALAN EAGLE (Co-Owner) & Buys Men's Wear, Young Men's Wear, Furnishings, Accessories, Footwear, Store Displays, Fixtures, Supplies

MARVIN TURNER (Co-Owner) & Buys Men's Wear, Young Men's Wear, Furnishings, Accessories, Footwear, Store Displays, Fixtures, Supplies

JOHNEY'S (MW)

Sunrise Mall, Upper Level
Massapequa, NY 11758
516-795-4566

OPEN-Men's & Young Men's Tailored Jackets, Tailored Slacks, Suits, Overcoats, Sportswear, Ties, Belts, Leather Apparel, Footwear, Store Displays, Fixtures, Supplies

LONNY'S WARDROBE, INC. (CLO-15)

(BRIEF ESSENTIALS)
2031 Merrick Rd. (m-b)
Merrick, NY 11566
516-223-4420 / Fax: 516-223-4428
Sales: $10 Million-$50 Million

WALTER GOLDSTEIN (President)

GARY GOLDSTEIN (V.P., Dir.- Finance, Mktg., Real Estate & HR) & Buys Store Displays, Fixtures & Supplies, Men's Sportswear, Big & Tall Apparel, Denim, Swimwear, Underwear, Uniforms, Accessories, Furnishings

ROGUE INTERNATIONAL (MW)

2161 Merrick Rd. (b)
Merrick, NY 11566
516-623-6262 / Fax: 516-623-0326

BEN FLEISCHER (President) & Buys Men's Suits, Sportswear, Furnishings, Accessories, Store Displays, Fixtures, Supplies

FOELLER MEN'S SHOP, INC. (MW)

88 Dunning Rd., #12 (m-b)
Middletown, NY 10940
845-343-7727 / Fax: 845-342-2563

KEITH MOULTON (Owner) & Buys Men's Wear, Footwear, Furnishings, Accessories, Store Displays, Fixtures, Supplies

H & G WEBER'S, INC. (MW)

171 Dolson Ave. (m-b)
Middletown, NY 10940
845-343-5220 / Fax: 845-343-5220
Sales: $500,000-$1 Million

GREGORY GILMAN (Owner) & Buys Men's Work Clothes, Jeans, Hosiery, Gloves, Headwear, Belts, Footwear, Store Displays, Fixtures, Supplies

SAPERSTEIN'S (MW)
P.O. Box 492 (p)
41 Main St.
Millerton, NY 12546
518-789-3365 / Fax: 518-789-4041
Sales: $1 Million-$10 Million
LEWIS SAPERSTEIN (President) & Buys Men's Tailored Jackets, Tailored Slacks, Big & Tall Men's Wear, Sport Shirts, Outer Jackets, Casual Slacks, Active Apparel, Furnishings, Belts, Young Men's Wear, Urban Contemporary, Boys' Wear, Footwear, Store Displays, Fixtures, Supplies

TERNI'S STORE (GM)
46 Main St. (m-b)
Millerton, NY 12546
518-789-3474 / Fax: 518-789-3474
Sales: $100,001-$500,000
PHIL TERNI (Owner) & Buys Men's Wear, Sportswear, Ties, Robes, Hosiery, Gloves, Headwear, Belts, Small Leather Goods, Store Displays, Fixtures and Supplies

FORESTO MEN'S SHOP, INC (MW)
309 Willis Ave. (b)
Mineola, NY 11501
516-746-1410 / Fax: 516-747-8192
Sales: $500,001-$1 Million
DOMINICK FORESTO (President) & Buys Men's Wear, Sportswear, Furnishings, Accessories, Store Displays, Fixtures, Supplies

ROBERT'S (MW)
152 Jericho Tpke. (m-b)
Mineola, NY 11501
516-746-7234
ROBERT SEEWALDT (Owner) & Buys Men's Wear, Footwear, Furnishings, Accessories, Store Displays, Fixtures, Supplies

THE FACTORY STORE (CLO-3)
(MHB INDUSTRIES, INC.)
100 E. Main St.
Mohawk, NY 13407
315-866-5150 / Fax: 315-866-5253
RON BROWN (Gen. Mgr.) & Buys Men's Sweaters, Sport Shirts, Outer Jackets, Leather Apparel, Casual Slacks, Active Apparel, Dress Shirts, Ties, Underwear, Hosiery, Gloves, Headwear, Belts, Jewelry, Small Leather Goods, Fragrances, Footwear, Urban Contemporary

JULES MENSWEAR, INC. (MW)
9 Lake St. (m-b)
Monroe, NY 10950
845-783-3521
BARRY GROSSARTH (Owner) & Buys Men's Wear, Sportswear, Furnishings, Accessories, Footwear, Store Displays, Fixtures and Supplies

PIER GROUP (MW)
P.O Box 2209 (m-b)
Montauk, NY 11954
631-668-4319 / Fax: 631-688-3199
TOM BOGDAN (President) & Buys Store Displays, Fixtures, Supplies
BARBARA KALLE-Men's Sportswear, Furnishings, Accessories

JENNINGS DEPARTMENT STORE (DEPT)
147 Main St. (m)
Moravia, NY 13118
315-497-1341
Sales: $100,001-$500,000
CLAUDE STOKER (Owner) & Buys Men's, Young Men's & Boys' Ski Jackets, Sportswear, Furnishings, Headwear, Accessories, Footwear, Store Supplies
PAT STOKER-Boys' Wear

CHAMBERS ARMY & NAVY STORE, INC. (AN)
65 S. 4th Ave. (m)
Mount Vernon, NY 10550
914-664-4650 / Fax: 914-664-2879
Sales: $1 Million-$10 Million
JOHN LEE (President/Gen. Mgr.) & Buys Men's Footwear, Men's Apparel, Men's Casual Wear, Men's Denim Apparel, Men's Formalwear, Men's Accessories, Men's Hosiery, Men's Outerwear, Men's Sportswear, Men's Underwear, Men's Uniforms

JOSEPH BASHAN CORP. (MW)
64 S. 4th Ave. (m)
Mount Vernon, NY 10550
914-699-3293 / Fax: 914-699-3293
IL KYU KIM (Owner) & Buys Men's Wear, Furnishings, Accessories, Store Displays, Fixtures, Supplies

TWO FASHION CORP. (MW)
32 S. 4th Ave. (m)
Mount Vernon, NY 10550
914-664-4643
MS. LEE (Owner) & Buys Men's Wear, Furnishings, Accessories, Store Displays, Fixtures, Supplies

EKIZIAN TUXEDOS (MW)
78 S. Middletown Rd. (m-b)
Nanuet, NY 10954
845-624-8686 / Fax: 845-624-2618
MEG FRANCO (Mgr.) & Buys Men's, Young Men's & 8 & Up Boys' Formal Wear, Formal Shirts, Ties, Accessories, Headwear, Footwear, Store Displays, Fixtures, Supplies

THE SUTTON CO. (DEPT)
P.O. Box 444 (p)
120 S. Main St.
Naples, NY 14512
716-374-2628
Sales: $100,001-$500,000
JAMES E. STAFFORD (Owner) & Buys Men's Raincoats, Sweaters, Sport Shirts, Outer Jackets, Active Apparel, Underwear, Hosiery, Gloves, Headwear, Belts, Big & Tall Men's Wear, Footwear, Store Displays, Fixtures, Supplies

KHAKI'S, INC. (CLO-2)
188 Main St. (m-b-h)
New City, NY 10956
845-634-1119 / Fax: 845-634-1213
PAUL SHINDER (Owner) & Buys Men's & Young Men's Wear, Urban Contemporary, Furnishings, Accessories, Footwear, Store Displays, Fixtures, Supplies

NEISNER'S MEN'S SHOP OF NEW CITY (MW)
24 N. Main St. (p-m)
New City, NY 10956
845-634-4669 / Fax: 845-634-4669
Sales: $500,001-$1 Million
CHARLES MEYERS (Owner) & Buys Men's & Boys' Wear, Furnishings, Accessories, Store Displays, Fixtures, Supplies

A. VITULLO, INC. (MW)
New Hartford Shopping Ctr. (b)
New Hartford, NY 13413
315-724-2169 / Fax: 315-797-5902
Sales: $1 Million-$10 Million
RONALD VITULLO (Owner) & Buys Men's Overcoats, Suits, Tailored Jackets, Tailored Slacks, Raincoats, Sweaters, Sport Shirts, Leather Coats, Casual Slacks, Active Apparel, Furnishings, Headwear, Belts, Tuxedos, Store Displays, Fixtures, Supplies

SCHECTER'S MENSWEAR, INC. (MW)
New Hartford Shopping Ctr. (m)
New Hartford, NY 13413
315-724-5383
Sales: $1 Million-$10 Million
PAUL SCHECTER (Owner) & Buys Men's Sportswear, Furnishings, Accessories, Big & Tall Men's Wear, Store Displays, Fixtures, Supplies

TWEEDS CLOTHING (MW)
(URBAN APPAREL LTD.)
1472 Union Tpke. (p-m)
New Hyde Park, NY 11040
718-347-1744 / Fax: 516-328-3912
LARRY LABEL (President) & Buys Store Displays, Fixtures, Supplies
MARTY BROWN-Men's Wear, Furnishings, Accessories

NEW YORK - New Rochelle

BALLY, INC. (CLO-39 & OL)

1 Bally Pl. (b-des)
New Rochelle, NY 10801
914-632-4444 / Fax: 914-632-8264
Sales: $10 Million-$50 Million
Website: www.bally.com
Retail Locations: CA, FL, GA, HI, IL, LA, MA, MI, NV, NJ, NY, WA, VA, TX

CAROL BRADY (Real Estate Contact)
BROOKS UYEDA (Mdse. Mgr.) & Buys Men's Leather Coats, Jackets, Pants, Vests, Leather & Fabric Knitwear
TONY STRIPPOLI-Men's Accessories, Men's Footwear

DOMENIC MEN'S SHOP (MW)

486 Main St. (p-m)
New Rochelle, NY 10801
914-632-9411

NICK MAZZA (Co-Owner) & Buys Men's Wear, Store Displays, Fixtures, Supplies
ADDISON CORNELIUS (Co-Owner) & Buys Men's Wear, Urban Contemporary, Store Displays, Fixtures, Supplies

I. B. COHEN (CLO)

525 Main St. (m-b)
New Rochelle, NY 10801
914-632-7100 / Fax: 914-632-7101
Sales: $500,000-$1 Million

LEWIS COHEN (Owner) & Buys Men's Wear, Footwear, Furnishings, Accessories, Store Displays, Fixtures, Supplies

The Following Section Comprises the Five Boroughs of NEW YORK CITY

Bronx

Brooklyn

New York City

Queens

Staten Island

NEW YORK - Bronx

B & G CLOTHES (MW)
586 E. 187th St. (b-h)
Bronx, NY 10458
718-367-5508 / Fax: 718-367-5508
Sales: $500,001-$1 Million
VINCENT BORGESE (Owner) & Buys Men's Sportswear, Furnishings, Accessories, Store Displays, Fixtures, Supplies

CEDAR - DALE ARMY & NAVY STORE, INC. (AN)
216 W. 231st St.
Bronx, NY 10463
718-548-1750 / Fax: 718-548-2305
BARRY FRIEDMAN (President) & Buys Activewear, Athletic Footwear, Athletic Apparel, Casual Sportswear, Licensed Apparel, Store Displays

EAGLE MEN'S FASHIONS CO. (MW)
2995 3rd Ave. (bud-p)
Bronx, NY 10455
718-292-2067
SUNG YOUNG (Owner) & Buys Men's Wear, Sportswear, Furnishings, Accessories, Young Men's Wear, Urban Contemporary, Footwear, Boys' Wear, Store Displays, Fixtures and Supplies

FORDHAM BOYS' SHOP, INC. (MW)
2381 Grand Concourse (p)
Bronx, NY 10468
718-933-3965 / Fax: 718-933-3965
SAM LEE (Owner) & Buys Men's Wear, Sportswear, Furnishings, Accessories, Young Men's Wear, Urban Contemporary, Boys' Wear, Store Displays, Fixtures and Supplies

FOX MENSWEAR (MW)
2076 White Plains Rd. (m-b)
Bronx, NY 10462
718-792-2015 / Fax: 718-792-2016
EDWARD FOX (President) & Buys Men's Wear, Footwear, Furnishings, Accessories, Store Displays, Fixtures, Supplies

FRANK'S SPORT SHOP, INC. (SG)
430 E. Tremont Ave. (p)
Bronx, NY 10457
718-299-9628 / Fax: 718-583-1652
Website: www.frankssports.com
MOSES STEIN (Owner) & Buys Men's Sportswear, Active Apparel, T-shirts, Fleece & Shorts, Accessories, Headwear, Footwear

JAY'S SPORTING GOODS (SP)
19 W. Fordham Rd.
Bronx, NY 10468
718-295-4055
JANG CHOI (Owner) & Buys Activewear, Athletic Footwear

JEANS PLUS, INC. (MW-3)
151 E. Burnside Ave.
Bronx, NY 10453
718-733-8182 / Fax: 718-733-7534
MARTIN COHEN (Owner) & Buys Men's Jeans, Tops, Coats, Boys' Wear, Urban Contemporary, Footwear, Store Displays, Fixtures, Supplies

JEANS STAR CORP. (CLO-5)
1041 E. 163rd St. (m)
Bronx, NY 10459
718-617-0555 / Fax: 718-617-2615
HANAN SHOSHANI (President)
SHOLOMO SHOSHANI-Men's & Boys' T-shirts, Active Apparel, Headwear, Jeans, Footwear, Urban Contemporary, Store Displays, Fixtures, Supplies

KAHN'S MEN'S APPAREL (MW & AN)
4396 White Plains Rd. (p-m)
Bronx, NY 10466
718-994-6503
Sales: $500,001-$1 Million
RICHARD SAFFER (Owner) & Buys Men's Work Clothing, Sportswear, Furnishings, Accessories, Young Men's Wear, Urban Contemporary, Store Displays, Fixtures and Supplies

KEYMAN'S FASHIONS, INC. (MW)
2484 Grand Concourse (p)
Bronx, NY 10458
718-220-4929
JAMES KIM (Owner) & Buys Men's Wear, Sportswear, Furnishings, Accessories, Young Men's Wear, Urban Contemporary, Footwear, Store Displays

LOEHMANN'S, INC. (CLO-44)
2500 Halswy St. (bud-p-m-b-des)
Bronx, NY 10461
718-409-2000 / Fax: 718-518-2766
Sales: Over $1 Billion
Website: www.loehmanns.com
ROBERT N. FRIEDMAN (Chmn. & C.E.O.)
ROBERT GLASS (President & C.O.O.)
FRANK LAMOLINO (C.I.O. & Sr. V.P.)
BETH WONSKI (Sr. V.P. -Planning Alloc.)
ANTHONY D'ANNIBALE (Sr. V.P.-Mdsg.)
JOHN MAINS (Sr. V.P.-Mdsg.)
FRED FORCELLATI (V.P.-Mktg.)
NANCY STRAFACE (V.P.-HR)
MICHELE SCHNITZEL (Dir.-Store Opers.)
TERESA PETRILLI (Dir.-Info. Sys.)
CHARLES BROWN (Dir.-Mktg.)
DEBBIE BARTON-Leather Goods
SUZI CARTLIDGE-Jewelry, Watches
JULIA FELBIN-Men's Accessories, Men's Outerwear
BRENDA LOWE-Men's Suits, Sportswear
KELLY O'CONNER-Men's Apparel, Men's Casualwear, Men's Outerwear, Men's Swimwear

MANFIX MEN'S FASHIONS (MW-2)
2893 3rd Ave. (p)
Bronx, NY 10455
718-993-8526 / Fax: 201-865-5267
Sales: $500,001-$1 Million
ROGELIO ALVAREZ (Owner) & Buys Men's Wear, Overcoats, Suits, Tailored Jackets & Slacks, Raincoats, Big & Tall Wear, Sportswear, Sweaters, Sport Shirts, Outer Jackets, Leather Apparel, Dress Shirts, Ties, Robes, Underwear, Gloves, Belts, Furnishings, Accessories, Young Men's Wear, Footwear

PHILIP KOENIG (MW)
3448 E. Tremont Ave. (p)
Bronx, NY 10465
718-829-5248 / Fax: 718-829-5248
Sales: $500,001-$1 Million
VINNY-Men's Wear, Sportswear, Furnishings, Accessories, Young Men's Wear, Urban Contemporary, Footwear, Store Displays, Fixtures and Supplies

PLANET EARTH (CLO-3)
361 W. Fordham Rd. (b-des)
Bronx, NY 10468
718-584-5104 / Fax: 718-584-5104
Sales: $1 Million-$10 Million
Website: www.planetearthclothing.com
ALBERT YEDID (Owner)
RAFY YEDID-Leather Goods, Licensed Apparel, Men's Apparel, Men's Casualwear, Men's Denim Apparel, Men's Formalwear, Men's Accessories, Men's Outerwear, Men's Sportswear, Men's Underwear

RAY DEPARTMENT STORE (DEPT)
2825 3rd Ave. (m)
Bronx, NY 10455
718-665-7691 / Fax: 718-292-3372
ELIE SAAD (President) & Buys Store Displays, Fixtures, Supplies
LEON SAAD-Men's & Young Men's Sportswear, Furnishings, Accessories, 7 to 14 Boys' Wear, Footwear, Urban Contemporary

S. K. POTTER, INC. (MW)
(POTTER'S MEN'S SHOP)
1239 Castle Hill Ave. (m)
Bronx, NY 10462
718-829-7670
Sales: $500,001-$1 Million
ROBERT BUSTARD (Owner) & Buys Men's Wear, Suits, Sportswear, Furnishings, Accessories, Store Displays, Fixtures and Supplies

WALTON FASHIONS (MW-3)
49 E. 170th St.
Bronx, NY 10452
718-293-6721 / Fax: 718-579-9464
GEHAD IGBADRA (Owner) & Buys Men's Wear, Urban Contemporary, Footwear, Accessories, Sportswear

NEW YORK - Brooklyn

1538 TRADING CORP. (MW)
538 Pitkin Ave. (m)
Brooklyn, NY 11212
718-485-1016
YOUNG KANG (Owner) & Buys Men's Wear, Suits, Sportswear, Furnishings, Accessories, Store Displays, Fixtures, Supplies

AL'S MEN'S SHOP (MW)
1140 Fulton St. (m)
Brooklyn, NY 11216
718-622-7106 / Fax: 718-622-2804
AL FRIEDMAN (Owner)
ERIC BULLEM-Men's Wear, Suits, Accessories, Footwear, Men's Work Clothes, Store Displays, Fixtures, Supplies

ALEX'S MR. ESQUIRE, INC. (MW-3)
513 Nostrand Ave. (p-m-b)
Brooklyn, NY 11216
718-398-1179 / Fax: 718-783-9094
ADAM ABRAHAM (Owner) & Buys Men's Wear & Boys' Suits, Footwear, Furnishings, Accessories, Store Displays, Fixtures, Supplies

AVENUE J STORES (KS-2)
1405 Ave. J
Brooklyn, NY 11230
718-258-8571 / Fax: 718-258-8579
JOSEPH NEIMAR (Owner) & Buys Boys' Wear, Furnishings, Accessories, Store Displays, Fixtures and Supplies

BENCRAFT HATTERS (MW-2)
(BESDOR, INC.)
236 Broadway (m-b)
Brooklyn, NY 11211
718-384-5517 / Fax: 718-972-1788
Sales: $1 Million-$10 Million
Website: www.bencrafthats.com
STAN GOLDSTEIN (Owner) (@ 718-972-3784) & Buys Men's Hats, Ties, Belts, Store Displays, Fixtures, Supplies

BERTA STORES (CLO-2)
2207 Coney Island Ave. (p-m)
Brooklyn, NY 11223
718-645-3351 / Fax: 718-645-3377
Sales: $10 Million-$50 Million
RONALD WEINISCH (Owner) & Buys Store Displays, Fixtures, Supplies, Men's Sportswear, Accessories, Footwear
BARBARA WEINISCH-Men's Sportswear, Accessories, Footwear
NADER MOHAMED-8 to 16 Boys' Sportswear, Accessories

BOHM ENTERPRISES (RB)
1299 Coney Island Ave.
Brooklyn, NY 11230
718-377-6515
ANDY BOHM-Men's & Boys' Sportswear, Outerwear, Activewear

BORO PARK BEST FASHION CORP. (MW)
4810 16th Ave. (m-b)
Brooklyn, NY 11204
718-437-1020
Website: www.boroparkbestfashion.com
RACHEL MAYER (Owner) & Buys Men's & Boys' Sportswear, Furnishings, Accessories, Urban Contemporary, Store Displays, Fixtures, Supplies

BRACH SPORTSWEAR (MW)
4211 13th Ave. (b)
Brooklyn, NY 11219
718-871-6060
ELI BRACH (Owner) & Buys Men's Sportswear, Accessories, Furnishings, Store Displays, Fixtures, Supplies

BROOKLYN PLANET KIDS (CLO)
5002 Church Ave. (m-b)
Brooklyn, NY 11203
718-346-7700 / Fax: 718-346-7800
Sales: $1 Million-$10 Million
EZRA FALACK (Owner) & Buys Boys' Wear, Boys' Footwear, Store Displays, Fixtures, Supplies

BROOKVILLE MENSWEAR (MW)
1606 Pitkin Ave. (m-b)
Brooklyn, NY 11212
718-342-0499 / Fax: 718-342-0499
Sales: $500,000-$1 Million
FELIX RIVERA (Owner) & Buys Men's Sportswear, Furnishings, Accessories, Footwear, Store Displays, Fixtures, Supplies

CASTLE CLOTHES (MW)
6203 18th Ave. (p)
Brooklyn, NY 11204
718-331-2379 / Fax: 718-621-5309
Sales: $500,000-$1 Million
Website: www.castleclothes.com
STANLEY CASTLE (Owner) & Buys Store Displays, Fixtures, Supplies, Men's Wear, Young Men's Wear, Big & Tall Wear, Furnishings, Accessories
RYAN MORANCIK-Men's Wear, Young Men's Wear, Big & Tall Wear, Urban Contemporary, Furnishings, Accessories

CATO ARMY & NAVY STORE (AN)
654 Manhattan Ave. (p-m)
Brooklyn, NY 11222
718-383-3004
MARION VENEZIANO (Owner) & Buys Men's Work Clothes, Active Apparel, Jeans, T-shirts, Hosiery, Underwear, Urban Contemporary, Camouflage, Military Clothing

CENTRAL SPORTS, INC. (SG)
2436 McDonald Ave.
Brooklyn, NY 11223
718-946-6006 / Fax: 718-946-2915
MIKE SEDA (Owner) & Buys Sportswear, Athletic Footwear

CHEVY'S MEN'S SHOP (MW)
2077 86th St. (m-b)
Brooklyn, NY 11214
718-372-4333
Sales: $500,000-$1 Million
MICHAEL SHEVELOV (Owner)
YURY FINKELSTEYN (Mgr.) & Buys Men's Wear, Accessories, Footwear, Furnishings, Store Displays, Fixtures, Supplies

CHUCKY DESIGNER SHOES LTD. (FW)
1304 Kings Hwy. (m-b-des)
Brooklyn, NY 11229
718-376-1003 / Fax: 718-998-8061
CHARLES ERANI (President) & Buys Men's Dress Shoes, Casual Shoes, Boots, Work Shoes, Belts, Small Leather Goods, Store Displays, Fixtures, Supplies

E & J LAWRENCE CORP. (DEPT-44)
(JIMMY JAZZ)
43 Hall St., 7th Fl. (m)
Brooklyn, NY 11205
718-596-1414 / Fax: 718-596-7288
Website: www.jimmyjazzstores.com
Retail Locations: NJ, NY
JOE KEZRI (Owner) & Buys Store Displays, Fixtures, Supplies
ABE HANAM (Real Estate Contact)
ALBERT HARRARY-Sportswear, Boys' Sportswear, Urban Contemporary
ROBERT SHAPIRO-Sportswear, Boys' Sportswear, Urban Contemporary
MITCH BERSON-Athletic Footwear
LOUIS Oscar-Men's Shoes

ENGLANDER'S, INC. (MW)
1218 Ave. J (p-m-b)
Brooklyn, NY 11230
718-756-6634 / Fax: 718-756-6634
Sales: $100,001-$500,000
ROSE ENGLANDER (Co-Owner) & Buys Men's, Young Men's & Boys' Clothing, Sportswear, Furnishings, Accessories, Store Displays, Fixtures, Supplies
ALLEN ENGLANDER (Co-Owner) & Buys Men's Sportswear, Furnishings, Accessories, Young Men's Wear, Boys' Wear, Store Displays, Fixtures and Supplies

NEW YORK - Brooklyn

EXQUISITE SHOP, INC. (CLO)
29 Graham Ave. (p-b)
Brooklyn, NY 11206
718-599-6602
MR. PARK (Owner) & Buys Men's Sportswear, Dress Shirts, Gloves, Headwear, Belts, Store Displays, Fixtures and Supplies

F & M SPORTSWEAR (MW)
4915 13th Ave. (p-m-b)
Brooklyn, NY 11219
718-436-2442
MARTY GOLDBERG (Owner) & Buys Men's & Boys' Sportswear, Accessories, Footwear, Furnishings, Store Displays, Fixtures, Supplies

THE FAMILY DRY GOODS (DG)
5021 13th Ave. (m)
Brooklyn, NY 11219
718-436-8372
ARON GOLD (Owner) & Buys Men's & Boys' Wear, Furnishings, Accessories, Store Displays, Fixtures, Supplies

FAMOUS FAMILY SHOP (CLO)
1430 Coney Island Ave. (p-m-b)
Brooklyn, NY 11230
718-252-7292 / Fax: 718-252-1411
JACOB FREUND (Owner) & Buys Men's Dress Shirts, Sports Shirts, Tailored Slacks, Casual Slacks, Underwear, Hosiery, Store Displays, Fixtures, Supplies

FRANCISCO LEE FASHIONS OF NY (MW)
375 Jay St. (p)
Brooklyn, NY 11201
718-624-6489
FRANCISCO LEE (Owner) & Buys Men's Sportswear, Furnishings, Accessories, Store Displays, Fixtures, Supplies

FREEMAN'S SHOP (MW)
4714 5th Ave. (bud)
Brooklyn, NY 11220
718-439-8620
Sales: $500,000-$1 Million
THERESE CREIDY (Co-Owner) & Buys Men's, Young Men's & Boys' Wear, Furnishings, Accessories, Store Displays, Fixtures, Supplies
JOHN CREIDY (Co-Owner) & Buys Men's, Young Men's & Boys' Wear, Furnishings, Accessories, Store Displays, Fixtures, Supplies

FULTON SNEAKS (SP)
515 Fulton St.
Brooklyn, NY 11201
718-237-1506 / Fax: 718-330-0980
JONG WON (Owner) & Buys Activewear, Athletic Footwear, Licensed Apparel

G & G QUALITY CLOTHING (MW-4)
165 Division Ave.
Brooklyn, NY 11211
718-384-7686 / Fax: 718-388-3210
ARON GLAUBER (Owner) & Buys Winter Coats, Suits, Furnishings, Accessories, Dress Shirts, Dress Pants

GENTLEMAN'S BOUTIQUE (MW)
4714 16th Ave. (b)
Brooklyn, NY 11204
718-853-5313 / Fax: 718-437-1477
JOSEPH WEINSTOCK (Co-Owner) & Buys Men's Sportswear, Furnishings, Accessories, Footwear, Store Displays, Fixtures, Supplies
EDITH WEINSTOCK (Co-Owner) & Buys Men's Sportswear, Furnishings, Accessories, Footwear, Store Displays, Fixtures, Supplies

GEORGE MICHAEL MEN'S SUITS OUTLET (MW)
5424 5th Ave. (p-m-b)
Brooklyn, NY 11220
718-439-0333 / Fax: 718-768-1120
GEORGE MICHAEL (Owner) & Buys Men's & Boys' Wear, Accessories, Furnishings, Store Displays, Fixtures, Supplies

GET SET (MW)
2131 Nostrand Ave. (m)
Brooklyn, NY 11210
718-859-2720 / Fax: 718-859-0965
RONNIE YOUFFAN (Owner) & Buys Men's Active Wear, Casual Wear, Men's Dress & Sports Footwear, Urban Contemporary, Store Displays, Fixtures, Supplies

HANDSOME AT 5TH AVE. (MW)
7316 5th Ave. (m)
Brooklyn, NY 11209
718-630-5029 / Fax: 718-630-5048
JABER JEBELI (Owner) & Buys Men's Sportswear, Furnishings, Accessories, Footwear, Urban Contemporary, Store Displays, Fixtures, Supplies

HANDSOME BOUTIQUE (MW-2)
1595 Pitkin Ave. (m)
Brooklyn, NY 11212
718-342-4177
PAUL SINGH (Owner) & Buys Men's Wear, Furnishings, Sportswear, Accessories, Young Men's Wear, Urban Contemporary, Footwear, Store Displays, Fixtures and Supplies

HARRY'S BELMONT, INC. (MW)
84 Belmont Ave. (p)
Brooklyn, NY 11212
718-498-7390 / Fax: 718-346-9186
Sales: $1 Million-$10 Million
GERALD MINZER (Owner)
NEIL BURKE-Men's Sportswear, Furnishings, Accessories, 8 to 20 Boys' Wear, Urban Contemporary, Athletic Footwear, Boots, Store Displays, Fixtures, Supplies

HARTSTEIN'S CLOTHING (MW)
5513 New Utrecht Ave. (m)
Brooklyn, NY 11219
718-871-8440
SHULA HARTSTEIN (Owner) & Buys Men's Hasidic Clothing, Related Furnishings & Accessories, Store Displays, Fixtures, Supplies

HOUSE OF JEANS (CLO-3)
2118 Ave. U (m)
Brooklyn, NY 11229
718-891-3758 / Fax: 718-332-0700
HOWARD SMALL (Owner)
ROBERT PRESS-Men's Jeans, T-shirts, Active Apparel, Hosiery, Underwear, Belts, Urban Contemporary

I MAX FASHIONS (MW-2)
1466 Rockaway Pkwy. (m-b)
Brooklyn, NY 11201
718-272-0196 / Fax: 718-272-6613
IZZY STEINBERG (Co-Owner)
SIMONE DUNCAN (Co-Owner) & Buys Men's Wear, Young Men's Wear, Accessories, Footwear, Furnishings, Store Displays, Fixtures, Supplies

ISA (CLO)
88 N. 6th St.
Brooklyn, NY 11211
718-387-3363 / Fax: 718-387-3464
ISA SAALABI (Owner) & Buys Apparel

JUST MEN'S FASHION, INC. (MW)
753 Manhattan Ave. (p-m-b)
Brooklyn, NY 11222
718-784-2969
Sales: $500,000-$1 Million
TAE LEE (Owner) & Buys Men's Sportswear, Furnishings, Accessories, Store Displays, Fixtures, Supplies
JAE LEE-Men's Sportswear, Furnishings, Accessories, Store Displays, Fixtures, Supplies

NEW YORK - Brooklyn

KBM MEN'S & BOYS' SHOP, INC. (MW)
(KNICKERBOCKER BOYS' & MEN'S)
370 Knickerbocker Ave. (p-m)
Brooklyn, NY 11237
718-452-8000 / Fax: 718-452-8002
Sales: $500,000-$1 Million
ARIE BUCHEISTER (President) & Buys Men's & Boys' Wear, Men's Footwear, Furnishings, Accessories
RAYMOND ROSA (G.M.M.) & Buys Men's & Boys' Wear, Men's Footwear, Furnishings, Accessories
BETH BUCHEISTER-Men's Store Displays, Fixtures, Supplies, Men's & Boys' Wear, Men's Footwear, Furnishings, Accessories

KING DAVID'S MENSWEAR, INC. (MW-2)
4018 13th Ave. (m)
Brooklyn, NY 11218
718-851-9865 / Fax: 718-437-1786
ISAAC SHOUELA (Owner) & Buys Men's Wear, Urban Contemporary, Accessories, Furnishings, Store Displays, Fixtures, Supplies

LBJ JEANS CORP. (MW)
1510 Neptune Ave. (m)
Brooklyn, NY 11224
718-449-4552 / Fax: 718-449-4573
Sales: $500,000-$1 Million
ROBERT REISS (Owner) & Buys Store Displays, Fixtures, Supplies, Men's & Boys' Jeans, Sport Shirts, Underwear, Jackets, Accessories
JOSEPH HECHT-Men's & Boys' Jeans, Sport Shirts, Underwear, Jackets, Accessories, Urban Contemporary

LEADING MALE CONCEPTS OF KINGS PLAZA (MW-2)
1220 Kings Hwy. (p-m-b)
Brooklyn, NY 11229
718-253-5002 / Fax: 718-376-3312
Sales: $500,001-$1 Million
ALLEN FROST (Owner) & Buys Men's Wear, Men's Furnishings, Accessories, Leather Apparel, Men's Dress Footwear, Store Displays, Fixtures, Supplies
ADAM FROST-Men's Wear, Men's Furnishings, Accessories, Leather Apparel, Men's Dress Footwear, Store Displays, Fixtures, Supplies

LEE AVE. CLOTHING CENTER (MW)
122 Lee Ave. (p-m)
Brooklyn, NY 11211
718-522-6792 / Fax: 718-834-1699
MR. BRACH (Owner) & Buys Hasidic Religious Clothing, Related Furnishings, Accessories

LEO'S DEPARTMENT STORE, INC. (DEPT)
7913 13th Ave. (m)
Brooklyn, NY 11228
718-256-8915 / Fax: 718-256-2022
Website: www.brafitters.com
ELLEN BOCHNER (President) & Buys Men's & Boys' Underwear, Hosiery, Robes, Slippers, Sleepwear, Store Displays, Fixtures, Supplies

LESTAN FASHIONS (SP)
1902 Ralph Ave. (m-b)
Brooklyn, NY 11234
718-531-0800 / Fax: 718-531-0005
Sales: $1 Million-$10 Million
Website: www.lestanbridal.com
WALT LESSMAN (President & Gen. Mgr.) & Buys Men's Formalwear
TAMMY WERNER (Dir. - Opers.)
HARRIET LESSMAN (Treas.) & Buys Men's Formalwear

LESTER'S (CLO-11)
2411 Coney Island Ave. (m-b)
Brooklyn, NY 11223
718-375-7337 / Fax: 718-627-3974
LESTER KRONSFELD (Owner)
PERRY SCHOOR (V.P.)
HOWARD HIRSCHMAN-Men's Sportswear, Furnishings, Accessories, Men's Footwear
TONI COHN-Boys' Clothing, Sportswear, Footwear, Furnishings, Accessories
CARLOS POWELL-Boys' Footwear

M & M HEALTH CARE APPAREL COMPANY (SP)
1541 60th St. (bud-p-m-b)
Brooklyn, NY 11219
718-871-8188 / Fax: 718-436-2067
Sales: $1 Million-$10 Million
Website: www.fashionease.com
ABRAHAM KLEIN (President & C.F.O.) & Buys Men's Scrubs, Uniforms, Footwear
FAYE JUSTIN-Men's Scrubs, Uniforms, Footwear

MAC'S MEN'S SHOP (MW)
1977 Flatbush Ave. (p)
Brooklyn, NY 11234
718-377-5127 / Fax: 718-377-3422
ANTHONY BALZOFIORE (President) & Buys Civil Service Uniforms, Men's Sportswear, Store Displays, Fixtures & Supplies

MAFERBO CLOTHING CORP. (CLO)
162 Flushing Ave. (m)
Brooklyn, NY 11205
718-624-5387
WILLIAM ESPINOZA (Owner) & Buys Men's Casual Wear, Sports Wear, Store Displays, Fixtures, Supplies

MALE ATTITUDE, INC. (MW)
2084 86th St. (b)
Brooklyn, NY 11214
718-449-7518
Sales: $500,001-$1 Million
GEORGE HENNING (Owner) & Buys Men's Sportswear, Furnishings, Accessories, Footwear, Store Displays, Fixtures, Supplies

MALE EGO (MW-2)
(RUMBER CORP.)
2040 86th St. (m-b)
Brooklyn, NY 11212
718-266-2020
Sales: $500,000-$1 Million
BERNARD KLEIN (Owner) & Buys Men's Sportswear, Furnishings, Accessories, Store Displays, Fixtures, Supplies

MARCY CLOTHING CORP. (MW)
4409 13th Ave. (m-b)
Brooklyn, NY 11219
718-854-3977 / Fax: 718-853-7503
GARY STERN (Owner) & Buys Men's & Boys' Wear, Accessories, Furnishings, Store Displays, Fixtures, Supplies

MAURICIO'S CLOTHING, INC. (MW)
37 Graham Ave. (m-b)
Brooklyn, NY 11206
718-388-9418 / Fax: 718-388-9418
Sales: $100,001-$500,000
MAURICE TAUBENFELD (Owner) & Buys Men's Wear, Boys' Suits, Accessories, Furnishings, Store Displays, Fixtures, Supplies

MURRAY'S CORNER, INC. (SP)
590 Nostrand Ave.
Brooklyn, NY 11216
718-771-8668 / Fax: 718-493-1992
SASSON SAWDAYEE (Owner) & Buys Activewear, Athletic Footwear, Licensed Apparel

NEW KEYMAN'S CORP. (MW)
822 Flatbush Ave. (m)
Brooklyn, NY 11226
718-287-8947
MRS. KIM (Co-Owner) & Buys Men's Wear, Furnishings, Accessories, Footwear, Store Displays, Fixtures, Supplies
YOUNG KIM (Co-Owner) & Buys Men's Wear, Furnishings, Accessories, Footwear, Store Displays, Fixtures, Supplies

P.R. GRAND STORE, INC. (DEPT)
1935 86th St. (m)
Brooklyn, NY 11214
718-265-6330 / Fax: 718-265-6331
P. REBENSTOCK (Owner) & Buys Men's Sleepwear, Slippers, Underwear, Hosiery, Boys' Underwear, Store Displays, Fixtures, Supplies

NEW YORK - Brooklyn

RAINBOW APPAREL CO., INC. (CLO-1000)
(FOXMOOR)
(UPS N DOWNS)
1000 Pennsylvania Ave. (bud-p-m)
Brooklyn, NY 11207
718-485-3000 / Fax: 718-485-3807
Sales: $500 Million-$1 Billion
Website: www.rainbowshops.com
Retail Locations: AL, AZ, AR, CA, CO, CT, DE, DC, FL, GA, IL, IN, KS, KY, LA, MD, MA, MI, MN, MS, MO, NH, NJ, NY, NM, NC, OH, OK, PA, RI, SC, TN, TX, UT, VA, WA, WV, WI, PR
JOSEPH CHEHEBAR (Owner)
ALBERT CHEHEBAR (President)
KEN KIRK (C.I.O.)
ISSAC CHEHEBAR (Treas.)
LOU LAIKEN (Controller)
KEVIN COHEN (Dir. - Store Opers.)
MICHAEL GRAZI (Dir. - Purch. & Sales) & Buys Store Supplies & Fixtures
TOM MAGILL (Merch. Mgr.) & Buys Boys' Wear, Footwear
EZRA JEMAL-Boys' Wear
THOMAS STEIN-Footwear

REFRESH SPORTS, INC. (MW)
1585 Pitkin Ave. (p-m-b)
Brooklyn, NY 11212
718-345-8012
SO YO (Co-Owner) & Buys Men's Sportswear, Furnishings, Accessories, Store Displays, Fixtures, Supplies
RAY YO (Co-Owner) & Buys Men's Clothing. Sportswear, Furnishings, Accessories, Store Displays, Fixtures, Supplies

REISER MENSWEAR CORP. (MW)
51 Graham Ave. (m)
Brooklyn, NY 11206
718-388-3232
JOE REISER (Owner) & Buys Men's Wear, Urban Contemporary, Furnishings, Accessories, Store Displays, Fixtures, Supplies

RELIABLE NAVAL TAILORING (MW)
106 Flushing Ave. (p-m-b)
Brooklyn, NY 11205
718-858-6033
VINCENT FAIELLA (Owner) & Buys Military Men's, Young Men's & Boys' Wear, Men's, Young Men's & Boys' Military Footwear, Furnishings, Accessories, Store Displays, Fixtures, Supplies

THE RUNNING START (SP)
2113 Ave. U
Brooklyn, NY 11229
718-934-9113 / Fax: 718-615-1774
LILA KAPLAN (Owner) & Buys Activewear, Athletic Footwear, Running Apparel

S & M CHILDREN'S CENTER INC. (CLO-9)
(BRUNSWICK SHOPPERS)
(GOLDEN SHOPPERS)
(PITKIN BARGAIN CENTER)
(SHPPERS JAMAICA)
(SHOPPERS WORLD)
(S D CENTER)
60 Graham Ave. (bud-p-b)
Brooklyn, NY 11206
718-388-1255 / Fax: 718-486-7651
Sales: $1 Million-$10 Million
MIKE MAHAN (Co-Owner) & Buys Boys' Wear, Footwear, Men's Outerwear, Sleepwear, Sportswear, Swimwear, Hosiery, Underwear
ABE DUSHY (President, Real Estate Contact & HR Mgr.) & Buys Boys' Wear, Footwear, Men's Outerwear, Sleepwear, Swimwear, Swimwear, Hosiery, Underwear

SELECTIONS SPORTS (SP)
854 Flatbush Ave.
Brooklyn, NY 11226
718-287-2283
JOSEPH HANONO (Owner) & Buys Activewear, Athletic Footwear, Licensed Apparel

SESIN CLOTHING, INC. (MW)
366 Knickerbocker Ave. (m-b)
Brooklyn, NY 11237
718-443-5722
RAYMOND SESIN (Owner) & Buys Men's & Boys' Clothing, Sportswear, Furnishings, Accessories, Store Displays, Fixtures, Supplies

SHANGRI-LA SPORTS (SP)
(GAL ASSOCIATES OF NY, INC.)
1708 Sheepshead Bay Rd.
Brooklyn, NY 11235
718-934-0095
LISA FERRANTI (Owner) & Buys Activewear, Athletic Footwear, Licensed Apparel

SHERBROOK GUILO, INC. (MW)
(OLYMPIC)
1 DeKalb Ave. (m)
Brooklyn, NY 11201
718-237-1224
JAS SADINA (Owner) & Buys Men's Jeans, Outer Jackets, T-shirts, Active Wear, Shorts, Footwear, Store Displays, Fixtures, Supplies

SHERIDAN MEN'S SHOP (MW)
1146 Liberty Ave. (p-m)
Brooklyn, NY 11208
718-277-6480
ALLEN SCHACHTER (Owner) & Buys Men's Wear, Sportswear, Furnishings, Accessories, Footwear, Young Men's Wear, Urban Contemporary, Boys' Wear, Store Displays, Fixtures and Supplies

SHIRTS & MORE (MW)
10 Lee Ave. (p-m)
Brooklyn, NY 11211
718-384-3442
ZEVIE WEINBAUM-Dress Shirts, Hosiery, Underwear, Gloves, Umbrellas, Scarves, Robes, Sleepwear, Small Leather Goods, Belts, Furnishings, Accessories

SHIRTS PLUS, INC. (MW)
1374 Coney Island Ave. (b)
Brooklyn, NY 11230
718-252-4488
Sales: $100,001-$500,000
TOBY GOLDBERG (Owner) & Buys Men's Slacks, Raincoats, Blazers, Shirts, Sweaters, Accessories

SHOUELA STORES, INC. (MW-2)
6228 18th Ave. (m-b)
Brooklyn, NY 11204
718-232-6303
JACK SHOUELA (Owner) & Buys Men's Wear, Men's Sports & Dress Footwear, Urban Contemporary, Furnishings, Accessories, Store Displays, Fixtures, Supplies

SONG'S CLOTHING (MW)
1069 Flatbush Ave. (m-b)
Brooklyn, NY 11226
718-284-5801
MR. SONG (Owner) & Buys Men's Wear, Furnishings, Accessories, Store Displays, Fixtures, Supplies

THE SPORTSWEAR DEPOT (SP)
6521 18th Ave.
Brooklyn, NY 11204
718-259-1186 / Fax: 718-234-0690
ALLAN DETELBAUM (Owner) & Buys Activewear, Athletic Footwear, Licensed Apparel

STAR DISCOUNT (MW)
60 Belmont Ave. (bud-p)
Brooklyn, NY 11212
718-385-5445 / Fax: 718-385-5445
SHOHLMO SHAH (Owner) & Buys Men's Wear, Sportswear, Furnishings, Accessories, Young Men's Wear, Store Displays, Fixtures and Supplies

THAT'S MY BOY, INC. (KS)
2909 Clinton Rd. (m)
Brooklyn, NY 11229
718-338-4616
HELEN GREENBATT (Co-Owner) & Buys 8 to 20 Boys' Wear, Furnishings, Accessories, Store Displays, Fixtures, Supplies
SONYA TRAGER (Co-Owner) & Buys 8 to 20 Boys' Wear, Furnishings, Accessories, Store Displays, Fixtures, Supplies

NEW YORK - Brooklyn

TRIANGLE SPORTS (SG)
182 Flatbush Ave. (p)
Brooklyn, NY 11217
718-638-5300 / Fax: 718-638-4335
Sales: $1 Million-$10 Million

BILL SHAPIRO (President & Mdse. Mgr.) & Buys Men's Work Clothes, T-shirts, Men's Footwear (Work Shoes), Urban Contemporary, Active Wear

UNIQUE FASHIONS (MW)
1396 Fulton St. (m)
Brooklyn, NY 11216
718-636-0090 / Fax: 718-636-3120

MR. YOO (Owner) & Buys Men's Sportswear, Furnishings, Accessories, Young Men's Wear, Urban Contemporary, Boys' Wear, Store Displays, Fixtures and Supplies

VICTOR'S (MW)
(IDY BROTHERS, INC.)
1214 Kings Hwy. (b)
Brooklyn, NY 11229
718-627-2187 / Fax: 718-627-0158

VICTOR IDY (Owner) & Buys Men's Sportswear, Furnishings, Accessories, Footwear

VINNIE'S CLOTHING (MW)
307 Utica Ave. (m-b)
Brooklyn, NY 11213
718-773-2364 / Fax: 718-636-9066

VINNIE ROBERTSON (Owner) & Buys Men's Sportswear, Furnishings, Accessories, Urban Contemporary, Store Displays, Fixtures, Supplies

WALLACH'S MEN'S & BOYS' WEAR (MW)
4113 13th Ave. (m)
Brooklyn, NY 11219
718-438-1454
Sales: $500,000-$1 Million

NATHAN WALLACH (Owner) & Buys Men's & Boys' Clothing, Sportswear, Furnishings, Accessories, Urban Contemporary, Store Displays, Fixtures, Supplies

WOLF'S SPORTSWEAR (MW)
1119 Ave. J (bud-p)
Brooklyn, NY 11230
718-253-7501

SLIG WOLF (Owner) & Buys Men's Sportswear, Furnishings, Accessories, Store Displays, Fixtures and Supplies

ZEKO MENSWEAR, INC. (MW)
4106 13th Ave. (p-m)
Brooklyn, NY 11219
718-851-9865

ISAAC SHOUELA (Owner) & Buys Men's Regular Sizes, Big & Tall Sizes, Boys' Wear, Urban Contemporary, Furnishings, Accessories, Store Displays, Fixtures, Supplies

ZOLDAN'S FOR MEN & BOYS (MW-2)
4709 13th Ave. (m)
Brooklyn, NY 11219
718-854-8448

MICHAEL FREIDMAN (Owner) & Buys Men's & Boys' Wear, Furnishings, Accessories, Store Displays, Fixtures, Supplies

NEW YORK - New York

A. T. HARRIS FORMALWEAR, LTD. (MW)
11 E. 44th St. (m-b)
New York, NY 10017
212-682-6325 / Fax: 212-682-6148
Website: www.atharris.com
PERCY SOTOMAYO (Mgr.) & Buys Men's & Boys' Tuxedos, Related Furnishings, Accessories & Footwear, Store Displays, Fixtures, Supplies

ADDISON ON MADISON (MW)
698 Madison Ave. (b)
New York, NY 10021
212-308-2660 / Fax: 212-750-4444
Sales: $1 Million-$10 Million
BRIAN HALL (President) & Buys Men's Shirts, Ties, Accessories, Store Displays, Fixtures, Supplies

ADVANTAGE SALES (RB)
1333 Broadway
New York, NY 10018
212-868-3100 / Fax: 212-868-3112
MEL KAYE-Men's Sportswear, Furnishings, Accessories, Young Men's, Men's Big & Tall, Boys' Apparel & School Uniforms
ROBERT BRODHERSON-Men's Sportswear, Furnishings, Accessories, Young Men's, Men's Big & Tall, Boys' Apparel & School Uniforms

AEROPOSTALE, INC. (CLO-500)
112 W. 34th St. (b)
New York, NY 10120
646-485-5398 / Fax: 646-485-5440
Website: www.aeropostale.com
Retail Locations: AL, AZ, CA, CT, DE, DC, FL, GA, IL, IN, IA, KS, KY, LA, ME, MD, MA, MI, MN, MO, NE, NH, NJ, NY, NC, OH, PA, RI, SC, TN, VT, VA, WV, WI
JULIAN GEIGER (Chmn. & C.E.O.)
JOHN MILLS (President) (@ 877-872-5630, Ext.: 5661)
MICHAEL CAVALLARO (Visual Msdg.) & Buys Store Displays, Fixtures & Supplies
CHRIS FINAZZO (G.M.M.)
MARK CIECKO-Men's Sportswear, Active Wear, Accessories, Young Men's
JESSICA LINDAUER-Men's Footwear
NOTE:-Plans to open 80 - 100 stores per year for the next 5 years, increasing from 335 to 900 stores.

ALAN DAVID (MW)
170 Broadway (b)
New York, NY 10038
212-577-2747 / Fax: 212-577-6098
ALAN HOROWITZ (Owner) & Buys Men's Sportswear, Furnishings, Accessories, Urban Contemporary, Leather Apparel, Footwear, Store Displays, Fixtures, Supplies

ALLOY (OL)
151 W. 26th St., 11th Fl.
New York, NY 10001
212-244-4307 / Fax: 212-244-4311
Website: www.donscomp.com
SUSAN VAN ARSDALE-Beachwear, Activewear, Surf & Swimwear, Wet Suits, Headwear, Sandals

ASSOCIATED MERCHANDISING CORP. (RB)
(Div. Of TARGET CORP.)
500 7th Ave. (bud-p-m-b-h)
New York, NY 10018
212-819-6600 / Fax: 212-819-6701
RICHARD KUZMICH (President & C.E.O.)
GEORGE MICHELETTI (Sr. V.P. & G.M.M.-Men's)
DOUGLAS BERTSCH (Sr. V.P.-Target Corp. & Overseas Mdsg. Svcs. Div.)
LARRY AZAR (V.P.-Marshal Fields)
JAME DAVINE (V.P.-Target Soft Line)
LORI JACOBS (Div. Mgr.-Target Soft Line)
STEPHANIE MASJONI (Div. Mgr.-Mervyn's)
RACHEL REICHENBACH (Div.-Target) & Buys Men's Woven Bottoms
TEO TAYLOR (V.P.-Mdse.)

ATHLETIC STYLE (SP)
118 E. 59th St.
New York, NY 10022
212-838-2564 / Fax: 212-888-9184
Sales: $2 Million-$5 Million
VICTOR FAVUZZA (Owner) & Buys Activewear, Athletic Footwear

BARNEY'S NEW YORK (CLO-7 & OT-9)
575 5th Ave. (m-b-h)
New York, NY 10017
212-450-8700 / Fax: 212-450-8694
Sales: $100 Million-$500 Million
Website: www.barneys.com
HOWARD SOCOL (President & C.E.O.)
TOM KALENDERIAN (Exec. V.P. & G.M.M.-Men's Wear)
WANDA COLON (V.P. & G.M.M.) & Buys Men's Sportswear, International Clothing, Outerwear
JAY BELL-Men's Sportswear, Designer Wear, Casual Wear
BILL COURNOYER (V.P. & D.M.M.) & Buys Men's Tailored Jackets, Suits
BILL COURNOYER-Men's Suits
MELISSA GALLAGHER (V.P. & D.M.M.-Accessories) & Buys Men's Footwear
GABRIELA VASSALLO-Men's Accessories, Umbrellas
WANDA COHEN (V.P.) & Buys Men's Sportswear, Furnishings, Accessories, Footwear
DAVID NEW (V.P.-Display) & Buys Store Displays, Fixtures, Supplies

BEAU BRUMMEL (MW)
421 W. Broadway (b-des)
New York, NY 10012
212-219-2666 / Fax: 212-925-4064
Website: www.beaubrummel.com
STEVE GUTMAN (President)
AVRAM GOLDMAN (Exec. V.P.-Mdsg.) & Buys Men's Suits, Tailored Jackets, Tailored Slacks, Overcoats, Sportswear, Casual Slacks, Sweaters, Sport Shirts, Outer Jackets, Furnishings, Dress Shirts, Ties, Hosiery, Accessories, Belts, Leather Apparel, Urban Contemporary, Store Displays, Fixtures, Supplies

BEN FREEDMAN GENT'S FURNISHINGS (MW)
137 Orchard St. (p-m)
New York, NY 10002
212-674-0854 / Fax: 212-260-3562
Sales: $500,000-$1 Million
AVI SAKS (Owner) & Buys Men's Sportswear, Furnishings, Accessories, Leather Apparel, Store Displays, Fixtures, Supplies (Closeouts), Urban Contemporary

BERGDORF GOODMAN (CLO & MO)
(Div. of THE NEIMAN MARCUS GROUP)
745 5th Ave. (b-h)
New York, NY 10019
212-753-7300 / Fax: 212-872-8886
Sales: $100 Million-$500 Million
Website: www.neimanmarcus.com
RONALD FRASCH (Chmn. & C.E.O.)
RICHARD BOWES (V.P.-Fashion Director)
MARGARET SPANILLIO (Sr. V.P. & G.M.M.-Men's)
FRED SANTANGELO (D.M.M.-Men's Clothing) & Buys Private Label
MICHAEL ISAAC-Oxford Dept., Men's Suits, Separates, Turnbull
YUKIHRO KATSUTA (D.M.M.-Men's Sportswear)
LOUISA CHUINARD-Men's Sportswear
BRUCE WELDON-Men's Designer Sportswear Boutiques, Men's Sportswear, Domestic Designer, European Collection, Private Label
RICHARD BOWES (D.M.M.-Men's Furnishings, Accessories)
JENNIFER SLAFF-Men's Accessories
ANNETTE DeBUIS-Men's Furnishings
LINDA FARGO (Dir.-Visual Mdsg.) & Buys Store Displays, Fixtures, Supplies

BILLY MARTIN'S WESTERN WEAR (WW)
220 E. 60th St. (m-b)
New York, NY 10022
212-861-3100 / Fax: 212-308-6381
Website: www.billymartins.com
DOUG NEWTON (Owner)
CINDY FOWLER-Men's Western Wear, Boots, Furnishings, Accessories, Store Displays, Fixtures, Supplies

NEW YORK - New York

BLOOMINGDALE'S (DEPT-23 & OL)

(Div. Of FEDERATED DEPT. STORES, INC.)
919 3rd Ave. (b)
New York, NY 10022
(Federated Merchandising Group)
212-705-2000 / Fax: 212-705-5746
Sales: Over $1 Billion
Website: www.bloomingdales.com

EDWIN J. HOLMAN (President)
DAVID FISHER (Sr. V.P. & G.M.M.-Men's and Children's)
FRANK DINAPOLI (D.M.M.-Men's Tailored Clothing/Designers)
LORI SWERSKY-Men's Classic Designer
ANGELA JANEVSKI (Sr. Assistant) & Buys Men's Classic Designer
MIMI FUKUYOSHI-Men's European/ Trend Designer
MARC HUNTER (Sr. Assistant) & Buys Men's European/ Trend Designer
MARK KATZ-Mens' Suits & Sportscoats
LAURA GRUMAN (Sr. Assistant) & Buys Mens' Suits & Sportcoats
JESSICA STRASSBERG-Mens' Trousers
KATIE PRATICO (Sr. Assistant) & Buys Mens' Trousers
SUSAN BRESLIN-Mens' Overcoats, Raincoats & Outerwear
TROY McERLAIN-Men's Dress & Casual Shoes

DAN LEPPO (D.M.M.-Men's Dress Furnishings)
TOMAS KINDLER-Mens' Polo Dress Shirts, Bridge Designers, Private Label, Designer
RACHEL KATZ (Sr. Assistant) & Buys Mens' Polo Dress Shirts, Bridge Designers, Private Label, Designer
CHERYL SHAPIRO-Men's Neckwear, Belts & Braces
LAURA NEST-Men's Neckwear, Belts & Braces
BRIAN SMALL-Men's Underwear Loungewear, Sleepwear, Robes & Hosiery
LISA STRAUSS-Men's Underwear Loungewear, Sleepwear, Robes & Hosiery
ROSALIA BUCARO-Mens' Leather Goods, Gifts, Jewelry & Seasonal Accessories

SCOTT POLWORTH (D.M.M.-Men's Collections)
LISA VERGA-Mens' DKNY Jeans, Claiborne, Polo Jeans, Nautica Jeans, DKNY, Wilke Rodriquez
CHRISTINA BYNO (Sr. Assistant) & Buys Men's Nautica
DOREEN MINCH-Men's Trend Denim, Contemporary, Tommy Jeans, Kenneth Cole, Reaction, Calvin Klein Jeans
DIANA PON-Men's Golf Apparel, Polo, Swiss Army
DEIRDRE MALONEY-Men's Active/Streetwear, Modern Dressing, Young Men's Active, Young Men's Sportswear, Contemporary Denim

FRANK DINAPOLI (D.M.M.-Men's Sportswear)
KARA SIDELL-Mens' Wovens, Pants
SARAH GOLDEN (Asst. Buyer) & Buys Mens' Wovens
SHANA BERG (Sr. Assistant) & Buys Mens' Casual Dress Slacks, Casual Pants, Branded Pants, Tommy Bahama, Swim, Walking Shorts
SARAH KELLAMS (Asst. Buyer) & Buys Mens' Denims
AMY DALTON (Asst. Buyer) & Buys Mens' Knits
ELIZABETH GUNN (Asst. Buyer) & Buys Mens' Sweaters

LIZ BAILEY (D.M.M.-Children's) (@ 212-705-5606)
BETH HARVEY (@ 212-705-5980)-8-20 Boys' Tops, Bottoms, Activewear, Basic Bottoms, Polo, Collection

RACHAEL ARNOLD (Creative Dir.) & Buys Store Displays, Fixtures & Supplies

BLUEFLY.COM (OL)

(BLUEFLY, INC.)
42 W. 39th St., 9th Fl. (bud-p-m-b-h)
New York, NY 10018
212-944-8000 / Fax: 212-354-3400
Website: www.bluefly.com

KEN SEIFF (C.E.O.)
PATRICK BARRY (Exec V.P. & C.F.O.)
JONATHAN MORRIS (Exec V.P.)
ALEX MONICA (V.P.-Men's Dept.)
ALTON LOCK-Men's Men's Furnishings, Accessories, Footwear
JONAS SHAPIRO-Men's Sportswear

BOUNTY TRADING CORP. (CLO)

1370 Broadway
New York, NY 10018
212-279-5900 / Fax: 212-564-5950
Website: www.bountytrading.com

ROBERT WAX (Owner)
SAM BLOCK-Men's Swimwear
MAC ALBERT-Men's Apparel

BRIONI (MW-2)

(BRIONI ROMAN LOOK LTD.)
57 E. 57th St. (b-h)
New York, NY 10022
212-376-5777 / Fax: 212-376-5778
Website: www.brioni.com

ETTORA PERRONE (President)
MICHAEL RESLAN (Mgr.) & Buys Italian Imported Men's Wear, Men's Dress Footwear, Accessories, Furnishings, Store Displays, Fixtures, Supplies

BRITISH AMERICAN HOUSE (MW)

488 Madison Ave. (b)
New York, NY 10022
212-752-5880 / Fax: 212-644-9005

PAUL GREEN (Owner) & Buys Men's Sportswear, Furnishings, Accessories, Leather Apparel, Urban Contemporary, Store Displays, Fixtures, Supplies

BROOKS BROTHERS (MW-152 & MO & OL)

(Div. Of MARKS & SPENCER, PLC.)
346 Madison Ave. (b)
New York, NY 10017
212-682-8800 / Fax: 212-687-8308
Sales: $500 Million-$1 Billion
Website: www.brooksbrothers.com
Retail Locations: AL, AZ, CA, CO, CT, DC, FL, GA, HI, IA, IL, IN, KY, LA, MA, MD, ME, MI, MN, MO, NC, NH, NJ, NM, NV, NY, OH, OR, PA, PR, RI, SC, TN, TX, UT, VA, VT, WA, WI

JOSEPH GROMEK (President & C.E.O.)
LOU AMENDOLA (President & G.M.M.-Men's)
PAUL DELEONE (Real Estate Contact)
CLAUDIA SCALA (V.P. & D.M.M.-Tailored & Sportswear) (@ 212-309-7325)
PATRICK THORTON (Sr. Buyer) (@ 212-309-7280) & Buys Suits, Tuxedos, Raincoats, Overcoats
SCOTT HOFFMAN-Tailored Jackets, Sportscoat, Tailored Slacks
JEFF BLEE-Dress Shirts, Neckwear, Formal Wear, Basics, Robes, Accessories, Small Leathers, Jewelry
BROOK FELDMAN (Sr. Buyer) & Buys Casual Slacks, Shorts, Outerwear, Woven Shirts
ALISHA WEINER (Sr. Buyer) & Buys Sweaters, Knits, Boys' Wear, Young Men's Wear
PAUL SADOWSKI (V.P.-Creative Dir.) & Buys Store Displays, Fixtures and Supplies
GUY VOGLINO (V.P. & D.M.M.-Furnishings & Accessories) & Buys Store Displays, Fixtures & Supplies

BURBERRY (CLO-38)

1350 Ave. of the Americas (b)
New York, NY 10019
212-757-3700 / Fax: 212-246-9449
Website: www.burberry.com
Retail Locations: CA, CO, CT, GA, HI, IL, MA, MI, NJ, NY, PA, TX

EUGENIA ULASEWICZ (President)
DAVID THARP (G.M.M.)
MICHAEL ISAAC-Men's Sportswear, Leather Apparel
MARIA YENTIS-Men's Furnishings
STACEY BERMAN-Accessories & Footwear
SAL LENCO (Visual Mdse. Mgr.) & Buys Store Displays, Fixtures, Supplies

NEW YORK - New York

CAMOUFLAGE CLOTHING (MW-2)
241 W. 13th St. (b)
New York, NY 10011
212-691-1750 / Fax: 212-691-1751
Sales: $1 Million-$10 Million
NORMAN USIAK (Owner) & Buys Men's Apparel, Men's Casualwear, Men's Denim Apparel, Men's Designer Apparel, Men's Formalwear, Men's Accessories, Men's Hoisery, Men's Outerwear, Men's Sportswear, Men's Suits, Men's Swimwear

CANAL JEAN CO., INC. (SP)
504 Broadway
New York, NY 10012
212-226-1130 / Fax: 212-226-8084
IRA RUSSACK (Owner)
MET GILLIAM-Activewear, Athletic Footwear

CHICABADI WEAR, INC. (CLO)
1149 Broadway (p-m-b)
New York, NY 10001
212-532-5488 / Fax: 212-532-9272
Sales: $1 Million-$10 Million
ALI ABADI (Owner) & Buys Men's Sportswear, Urban Contemporary, Belts, Store Displays, Fixtures, Supplies

CONWAY STORES (CLO-18)
1333 Broadway (m-b)
New York, NY 10018
212-967-5300 / Fax: 212-967-6740
ABE COHEN (President & Owner)
ED GOLDEN-Men's Wear, Sportswear, Furnishings, Accessories, Young Men's Wear
DEBBIE CURE-Boys' Wear, Urban Contemporary

DAVE'S ARMY & NAVY, INC. (AN)
581 Ave. of the Americas (m)
New York, NY 10011
212-989-6444 / Fax: 212-627-5244
BOB LEVY (Owner) & Buys Men's & Boys' Jeans, Shirts, Furnishings, Accessories, Men's Dress & Sport Footwear, Store Displays, Fixtures, Supplies

DETOUR (MW & SP-2)
425 W. Broadway (m)
New York, NY 10012
212-979-2692 / Fax: 212-995-1301
Website: www.detoursoho.com
AVI MIZERAH (Owner) & Buys Men's Wear, Sportswear, Furnishings, Accessories, Young Men's Wear, Footwear, Urban Contemporary, Boys' Wear, Store Displays, Fixtures and Supplies

DICKENS FOR MEN LTD. (MW)
1326 3rd Ave. (m-b-des)
New York, NY 10021
212-249-6455 / Fax: 212-249-4281
D. FERRARI (President & Owner)
JOYCE FERRARI-Men's Sportswear, Footwear, Furnishings, Accessories, Young Men's Wear

DINO BALDINI (MW)
444 Madison Ave. (m-b)
New York, NY 10022
212-486-8920 / Fax: 212-486-3277
EDDIE ADELI (Owner) & Buys Men's Outercoats, Tailored Jackets, Tailored Slacks, Suits, Sportswear Furnishings, Accessories, Formal Wear, Footwear, Store Displays, Fixtures, Supplies

DLS OUTFITTERS (RB-150)
(GET REAL CLOTHES.COM)
44 W. 55th St (b)
New York, NY 10019
212-399-0750 / Fax: 212-399-0916
Sales: $50 Million-$100 Million
Website: www.getrealclothes.com
Retail Locations: CA, FL, IA, IL, LA, MA, MD, ME, MI, MO, MS, NC, NE, NH, NJ, NY, OH, OK, PA, SC
FRED DERRING (C.E.O.) & Buys Men's Apparel, Footwear
LEE LEONARD-Men's Apparel, Furnishings
MELISSA QUINLIVAN-Men's Acessories

DRIMMER INDUSTRIES (MW)
122 W. 27th St., 4th Fl. (m)
New York, NY 10001
212-675-5496 / Fax: 212-627-4973
BERNARD DRIMMER (President)
MITCH DRIMMER (V.P.) & Buys All Men's, Young Men's & Boys' Wear (For Export)

EISENBERG & EISENBERG, INC. (MW)
16 W. 17th St. (bud-p-m-b)
New York, NY 10011
212-627-1290 / Fax: 212-627-1293
Sales: $1 Million-$10 Million
ERIC EISENBERG (Co-Owner) & Buys Men's Wear, Store Displays, Fixtures, Supplies
GLENN EISENBERG (Co-Owner) & Buys Men's Furnishings, Accessories

ERMENEGILDO ZEGNA CORP. (MW-10 & OL)
(ZEGNA OUTLET)
730 5th Ave. (b)
New York, NY 10019
212-246-2244 / Fax: 212-246-2266
Sales: $1 Million-$10 Million
Website: www.ezegna.com
ROBERT ACKERMAN (President & C.E.O.)
ANDREW GROSSMAN-Fragrances, Leather Goods, Men's Apparel, Men's Big & Tall Apparel, Men's Denim Apparel, Men's Casualwear, Men's Designer Apparel, Men's Formalwear, Men's Accessories, Men's Outerwear, Men's Sleepwear, Men's Sportswear, Men's Suits, Men's Swimwear, Men's Underwear, Men's Uniforms
DIANE McNULTY-Men's Shoes

FINLAY FINE JEWELRY CORP. (JWLY-1040)
529 5th Ave.
New York, NY 10017
212-808-2800 / Fax: 212-808-2946
Sales: $500 Million-$1 Billion
Website: www.finlayenterprises.com
Retail Locations: AZ, AR, CA, CO, CT, DE, DC, FL, GA, HI, ID, IL, IN, IA, KS, KY, LA, ME, MD, MA, MI, MN, MS, MO, MT, NE, NV, NH, NJ, NM, NY, NC, ND, OH, OK, OR, PA, RI, SC, TN, TX, VT, VA, WA, WV, WI
JOE E. MELVIN (President)
ARTHUR E. REINER (C.E.O.)
LESLIE PHILIP (V.P.-Mdse.) & Buys Jewelry, Watches
NICOLE ANDERSON (Real Estate Contact)

FOWAD TRADING CO., INC. (CLO)
2558 Broadway (m-b)
New York, NY 10025
212-222-8000 / Fax: 212-222-2888
Sales: $500,000-$1 Million
FOWAD ELLESMAWY (Owner) & Buys Men's Wear, Urban Contemporary, Leather Apparel, Furnishings, Accessories, Store Displays, Fixtures, Supplies

FRENCH CONNECTION (CLO-25)
512 7th Ave., 25th Fl.
New York, NY 10018
212-221-3157 / Fax: 212-302-6839
Website: www.frenchconnection.com
Retail Locations: AZ, NY, NJ, CT, LA, VA, MA, FL, PA, WA, IL
GUS MEHAN (Exec V.P.-Wholesale)
DINA McCAFFREY (V.P.-Men's Wear Sales)
ADAM SINGER (V.P.-Men's Wear) & Buys Bodywear, Accessories, Footwear

NEW YORK - New York

GIDDON ENTERPRISES, INC. (MW)
(ROTHMAN'S)
200 Park Ave. S. (m)
New York, NY 10003
212-777-7400 / Fax: 212-979-2216
Website: www.rothmansny.com
KENNETH GIDDON (Owner) & Buys Store Displays, Fixtures, Supplies, Men's Sportswear, Furnishings, Accessories, Footwear
JIM GIDDON-Men's Sportswear, Furnishings, Accessories, Footwear

GRAND SLAM STORE (CLO)
1557 Broadway (p-m)
New York, NY 10036
212-398-6388 / Fax: 212-398-6502
AARON COHEN (President) & Buys Men's Sportswear, Store Displays, Fixtures, Supplies
ELLIOT COHEN (V.P.) & Buys Men's Sportswear, Store Displays, Fixtures, Supplies

GREENMAN ASSOCIATES (RB)
5 W. 36th St., 5th Fl. (bud-p-m)
New York, NY 10001
212-564-0080 / Fax: 212-268-1165
Sales: $10 Million-$50 Million
Website: www.greenmanonline.com
KENNETH SCHIFF (Co-Owner) & Buys Men's & Boys' Wear
NORMAN MORELL (Co-Owner) & Buys Men's & Boys' Wear, Urban Contemporary

GUY & GAL (MW)
278 W. 125th St. (p-m)
New York, NY 10027
212-222-1944
WON TUCK KIM (Owner) & Buys Men's Wear, Clothing, Sportswear, Footwear, Furnishings, Accessories

HENRY DONEGER (RB)
(DONEGER GROUP)
(DONEGER KIDS'-MEN'S)
463 7th Ave. (bud-p-m-b-h)
New York, NY 10018
212-564-1266 / Fax: 212-564-3971
Website: www.doneger.com
ABBEY DONEGER (President)
MARK MENSKY (G.M.M.-Men's & Kids)
WENDY GOLD-4 to 20 Boys' Wear, Boys' Outerwear, Young Men's
KATHY ROZEWSKI-Boys' Sleepwear, Newborn, Toddler Boys'
LIZ SWATORY-Men's Accessories, Largewear, Outerwear, Activewear
SHARON HAUSNER-Men's Sportswear, Collections, Activewear, Outerwear, Lounging, Accessories

HIGH VOLTAGE STORES, INC. (CLO-8)
(BANG BANG BOUTIQUE)
1375 Broadway, 4th Fl. (p)
New York, NY 10018
212-730-0927 / Fax: 212-730-1044
JACK MENASHE (Owner & Real Estate Contact) & Buys Men's Suits, Outerwear, Sportswear, Accessories
ROBERT THOMPSON-Store Displays, Fixtures, Supplies

HOWARD SPORTSWEAR (CLO)
85 Orchard St. (m-b)
New York, NY 10002
212-226-4307 / Fax: 212-226-4307
Website: www.brasandhosiery.com
HOWARD MARKOWITZ (President) & Buys Men's Sleepwear, Hosiery, Underwear, Store Displays, Fixtures, Supplies

J. CREW GROUP, INC. (CLO-150 & MO & OL)
(Div. of POPULAR CLUB PLAN)
(CLIFFORD & WILLS)
770 Broadway (p-m-b)
New York, NY 10003
212-209-2500 / Fax: 212-209-2666
Sales: $100 Million-$500 Million
Website: www.jcrew.com
Retail Locations: AL, AZ, CA, CO, CT, DE, DC, FL, GA, IL, IN, KS, ME, MD, MA, MI, MN, MO, NV, NH, NJ, NM, NY, NC, OH, OR, PA, RI, SC, TN, TX, UT, VT, VA, WA, WI
MILLARD DREXLER (C.E.O.)
TRUDY SULLIVAN (C.O.O.-Retail & Mail)
OPEN (Exec. V.P.-Men's) & Buys Men's Apparel
CAROL SHARPE (Exec. V.P.-Mdse. Mail Order & Retail/G.M.M.)
SCOTT HYATT (Sr. V.P.-Prod.)
NANCY HOLCEKER (D.M.M.) & Buys Footwear, Accessories
STEVE BARTHA (Real Estate Contact)

J. McLAUGHLIN (CLO-25)
1343 3rd Ave. (b-h)
New York, NY 10021
212-472-1934 / Fax: 212-472-1967
Website: www.jmclaughlin.com
JAY McLAUGHLIN (Co-Owner) & Buys Men's Urban Contemporary, Store Displays, Fixtures, Supplies
KEVIN McLAUGHLIN (Co-Owner) & Buys Men's Sportswear, Leather Outerwear, Store Displays, Fixtures, Supplies

J. PRESS, INC. (MW-4)
530 7th Ave. (m-b)
New York, NY 10018
212-997-3600 / Fax: 212-997-5515
Sales: $1 Million-$10 Million
Website: www.jpressonline.com
MR. SUMI (V.P.)
HIRO KINOSHITA (Mgr.) & Buys Men's Wear, Sportswear, Accessories, Furnishings, Store Displays, Fixtures, Supplies

J.J. HAT CENTER, INC. (SP & MO)
310 5th Ave. (m-b)
New York, NY 10001
212-239-4368 / Fax: 212-971-0406
Sales: $1 Million-$10 Million
Website: www.jjhatcenter.com
IDA J. O'TOOLE (President) & Buys Men's Accessories
MARK WILLIAMSON (Gen. Mgr.) & Buys Headwear

JEFFREY NEW YORK (MW)
449 W. 14th St.
New York, NY 10014
212-206-3928 / Fax: 212-220-8647
DAVID RUBENSTEIN-Men's Designer Sportswear

JIL SANDER (CLO-20)
212 5th Ave.
New York, NY 10010
212-447-9200 / Fax: 212-447-9696
Website: www.jilsander.com
ADRIA CARPIANO-Men's Suits, Accessories

JODAMO INTERNATIONAL LTD. (MW)
321 Grand St. (b)
New York, NY 10002
212-219-0552 / Fax: 212-219-0041
JOSE MASRI (President)
MORRIS MASRI-Men's Wear, Furnishings, Accessories, Leather Apparel, Men's Dress Shoes, Store Displays, Fixtures, Supplies

KAUFMAN'S (AN)
319 W. 42nd St. (m)
New York, NY 10036
212-757-5670 / Fax: 212-757-9686
JIM KORN (Owner) & Buys Men's Outdoor Apparel, Outerwear, Boots, Store Displays, Fixtures, Supplies

NEW YORK - New York

KENNETH COLE PRODUCTIONS, INC. (FW-61 & OL & MO)

(KENNETH COLE)
(KENNETH COLE OUTLET)
603 W. 50th St. (m-b-des)
New York, NY 10019
212-265-1500 / Fax: 212-713-6633
Sales: $100 Million-$500 Million
Website: www.kennethcole.com
Retail Locations: NY, AZ, CA, CO, CT, DC, FL, GA, HI, FL, IL, LA, MA, MI, NV, NJ, NY, PA, TX, VA

KENNETH D. COLE (President & C.E.O.)
PAUL BLUM (Exec. V.P.)
TINA GUMINA (V.P.- Mdse.) & Buys Boys' Footwear, Men's Footwear, Leather Goods, Licensed Apparel, Watches, Men's Accessories, Hosiery
DENISE TANZMAN (V.P.-Catalog)
COURTNEY CLARK (V.P.-E-commerce)
CHRISTINE RUSSO (Real Estate Contact)

KIDS TOWN (KS-5)

450 7th Ave., Suite 1401 (p-m)
New York, NY 10123
212-564-1616 / Fax: 212-630-0502

JOSEPH SUTTON (Owner) & Buys 8 to 20 Boys' Wear, Urban Contemporary, Store Displays, Fixtures, Supplies

KINGSIZE (MO & OL)

(BRYLANE)
463 7th Ave.
New York, NY 10018
212-613-9500 / Fax: 212-502-8819
Sales: Over $1 Billion
Website: www.kingsizedirect.com

GINA PICCIO (V.P. & G.M.M.)
GILDA CASPER-Sportcoats, Dress Slacks
JEFF BORGHI-Woven Shirts, Furnishings
SUSAN WILCOX-Casual Bottoms, Shorts, Sweaters, Jeans, Licensed Apparel
TONY LAFEVER-Sleepwear, Accessories
BILL MASON-Footwear

L.S. MENSWEAR (MW)

49 W. 45th St., 3rd Fl. (b)
New York, NY 10036
212-575-0933 / Fax: 212-944-2589

RACHEL SHEINBAUM (President) & Buys Men's Suits, Tailored Jackets, Tailored Slacks, Ties, Dress Shirts, Accessories, Store Displays, Fixtures, Supplies

THE LEATHER MAN, INC. (CLO)

111 Christopher St. (m)
New York, NY 10014
212-243-5339 / Fax: 212-243-5372
Website: www.theleatherman.com

CHARLES MUELLER (President & Owner)
MAX GREGORY (Mgr.) & Buys Leather Jackets, Leather Gloves

LORD & TAYLOR (DEPT-86)

(Div. Of MAY DEPARTMENT STORES)
424 5th Ave. (b)
New York, NY 10018
212-382-7800 / Fax: 212-827-5084
Sales: $2 Billion
Website: www.lordandtaylor.com
Retail Locations: CO, CT, DC, DE, FL, GA, IL, KY, LA, MA, MD, MI, MO, NC, NJ, NY, OH, PA, RI, TX, VA

RICH O. CLAUSING (Chmn.)
JANE T. ELFERS (President & C.E.O.)
ARTHUR SNOZNICK (V.P.-Construction)
ROBERT BEFFA (Real Estate Contact) (@ 314-342-6466)
MARY BETH SHERRIDAN (Sr. V.P. & G.M.M.-Men's & Boys' Wear)
EARL F. SLUSS (Exec. V.P.-Mdsg.)

KEN SIDE (V.P. & D.M.M.-Men's Sportswear Collections) (@ 212-391-3647) & Buys Seasonal Sportswear, Knits, Shorts, Sweaters, Cut & Sewn Sport Shirts, Active Sportswear
TOM ECHRICH-Men's Suits, Outerwear, Rainwear, Top Coats, Leather Apparel, Men's Dress Slacks, Casual Slacks, Sport Coats
RICHARD GUALITERI-Men's Perry Ellis, Gant, Reunion, Guess Denim, Nautica
JONATHON GRELLER-Polo, Claiborne, Men's Active Wear, Nike, Izod, Nautica Competition, Nautica Collection, Chaps, Golf Apparel Wear, Greg Norman Collection, Nautica, Calvin Klein, D.K.N.Y., Tommy Hilfiger, Timberland

TOM WHITNEY (D.M.M.-Men's Dress & Personal Furnishings)
GLENN WICHERN-Men's Dress Shirts, Belts, Small Leather Goods, Jewelry, Slippers, Ties, Leather Goods, Luggage, Accessories
ANDREW DOLE-Men's Underwear, T-shirts, Hosiery, Robes, Pajamas
DEBBY BRANCO (D.M.M.-Men's Footwear)
ANTHONY PERRY-Men's Shoes

MICHAEL SALINAS (V.P.-Visual Mdsg.) & Buys Store Displays, Fixtures, Supplies

LOUIS CHOCK, INC. (MW & MO & SP)

74 Orchard St. (b)
New York, NY 10002
212-473-1929 / Fax: 212-473-6273
Sales: $500,001-$1 Million
Website: www.chockcatalog.com

ZALMAN ZELL (Owner) & Buys Men's Underwear, Hosiery, Sleepwear, Slippers, Store Displays, Fixtures, Supplies

LOUTIE (MW-2)

1775 Broadway (b)
New York, NY 10019
212-265-2299 / Fax: 217-265-2207

NORY HOUR (Owner) & Buys Men's Sportswear, Furnishings, Accessories, Urban Contemporary, Store Displays, Fixtures, Supplies

NEW YORK - New York

MACY'S EAST (DEPT-114 & OL)

(Div. Of FEDERATED DEPT. STORES)
151 W. 34th St. (m-b-h)
New York, NY 10001
(Federated Merchandising Group)
212-695-4400 / Fax: 212-494-1547
Sales: Over $1 Billion
Website: www.macys.com
Retail Locations: AL, CT, DE, FL, GA, LA, MA, MD, ME, MA, NH, NJ, NY, PA, PR, RI, VA

JAMES E. GRAY (President)
HARVEY SAMUELSON (V.P.-Store Dev.) (@ 212-494-4360)
KEVIN MORRISSEY (Exec. V.P. & G.M.M.) (@ 212-494-3243)
PHIL RUTMAN (V.P. & D.M.M.-Men's Collections)
MELINDA ISRAEL (@ 212-494-3912)-Perry Ellis, Reunion, Claiborne
BONNIE GOLN-Polo, Timberland, LaCoste
MARTINE DeMARTINE (@ 212-494-3917)-American & European Designers, Tommy Hilfiger, Nautica, DKNY, Kenneth Cole

LES STEIGER (V.P. & D.M.M.- Men's Tailored Wear) (@ 212-494-3929)
PHIL MARKERT (@ 212-414-2234)-Sports Coats, Dress Slacks
JIM EDELMAN (@ 212-494-5190)-Men's Suits, Overcoats, Raincoats, Designer Suits

ROBERT NAYLOR (D.M.M.-Men's Sportswear) (@ 212-494-4445) & Buys Men's Contemporary Collections, Girbaud, Guess Sportswear, Calvin Klein Sportswear
KAREN MCKELVIE (@ 212-494-4685)-Men's Activewear & Swimwear
LISE LEMIUX (@ 212-494-3918)-Men's Walking Shorts, Outerwear
KURT MEISTER-Men's Knit, Izod, Golf Apparel
JODY MILLER (@ 212-494-1792)-Men's Sweaters, Woven, Collections

FRANK CHELLEW (D.M.M.-Men's Furnishings & Accessories) (@ 212-494-3178)
STEPHANIE SCHMIDT-Men's Polo Dress Shirts, Fashion Dress Shirts, Solid Dress Shirts
HOLLY CURP-Men's Belts, Small Leathers
YUSSEF MAHMOUD-Men's Underwear, Hosiery, Robes, Pajamas
MICHAEL TERISI-Men's Ties
MICHAEL GIURICI-Hats, Gloves, Mufflers, Sunglasses, Jewelry

MR. CARY FRIEDMAN (V.P. & D.M.M.- Young Men's & Boys' Wear)
ED LANNING (@ 212-494-3649)-Young Men's Casual Jeans, Levi's, Casual Pants
JENNIFER SPAULDING-Young Men's Activewear, Knits, Wovens, Levi's, Tops, Accessories
CHRIS THORN (@ 212-494-3910)-8 to 20 Boys', Outer Jackets, Sweaters, Accessories
BRET BARTLEY (@ 212-494-3753)-8 to 20 Boys' Contemporary & Traditional Collections, Polo, Tommy Hilfiger Bottoms
JANE RUTHMAN (@ 212-494-3908)-Young Men's Urban Collection
MICHELINE JORDAN (V.P.-Fragrances) (@ 212-494-4231)
MARTI MOORE-Men's Fragrances

RICHARD ARNSTEIN (G.M.M.-Jewelry & Accessories)
LIYA SHATASHVILI-Men's Jewelry
RANDALL OKEY (Dir.-Watches) (@ 212-494-4530) & Buys Fine Watches
NANCY PIKRAMENOS-Moderate Watches

MARK MINICIELLO (V.P.-Visual Mdsg.) (@ 212-494-2809) & Buys Store Displays, Fixtures and Supplies

MANTWEL (MW)

118 Orchard St. (b)
New York, NY 10002
212-505-9664 / Fax: 212-473-7938
Sales: $1 Million-$10 Million
Website: www.moshoes.com

SIMON LITVIN (President & Owner) & Buys Sweaters, Sport Shirts, Outer Jackets, Leather Apparel, Casual Slacks, Dress Shirts, Belts, Hosiery, Footwear
STEVEN LITVIN-Sweaters, Sport Shirts, Outer Jackets, Leather Apparel, Casual Slacks, Dress Shirts, Belts, Hosiery, Footwear

MARDANA (MW)

132 7th Ave. S. (b)
New York, NY 10014
212-620-8108 / Fax: 212-989-7988

TONY WALIA (Owner) & Buys Sweaters, Sport Shirts, Outer Jackets, Casual Slacks, Active Apparel, Jeans, Ties, Underwear, Hosiery, Belts, Jewelry, Small Leathers

MARPROWEAR (RB)

990 Ave. of the Americas (p)
New York, NY 10018
212-279-3606 / Fax: 212-695-5049
Sales: $10 Million-$50 Million

NORMAN RIBACK (President & G.M.M.) & Buys Young Men's & Boys' Sportswear, Leather Outerwear

MARTIN BAYER ASSOCIATES (RB)

171 W. 57th St. (b)
New York, NY 10019
212-586-4766 / Fax: 212-586-4768

MARTIN J. BAYER (President) & Buys Men's Sportswear, Furnishings, Leather Apparel, Urban Contemporary
JEANNE BAYER (V.P.) & Buys Men's Accessories

MAXWELL (FW)

(JOAN & DAVID)
4 W. 58th St. (des)
New York, NY 10019
212-371-8250 / Fax: 212-751-2688
Sales: $50 Million-$100 Million

MARK M. COCOZZA (President & C.E.O.) & Buys Leather Goods, Men's Accessories, Men's Apparel, Hosiery

MEN'S WALKER, INC. (FW)

100 West 125th St. (m)
New York, NY 10027
212-666-2621 / Fax: 914-377-1146

KEVIN McGILL (Owner) & Buys Men's Dress Shoes, Headwear, Accessories, Hosiery

THE MERCHANDISE NETWORK (RB)

1333 Broadway, #1720 (p-m)
New York, NY 10018
646-674-1044 / Fax: 212-564-8320
Sales: $10 Million-$50 Million

PENNY ROSENBERGER (President)
MURRAY BERK-All Coats & Suits
SUSAN CAMILLIERE-Better Sportswear, Active Apparel, Knits, Sweaters

MODELL'S SPORTING GOODS (SG-109)

498 7th Ave., 20th Fl.
New York, NY 10018
212-822-1000 / Fax: 212-822-1596
Sales: $10 Million-$50 Million
Website: www.modells.com
Retail Locations: DE, DC, MD, NJ, NY, PA, VA

WILLIAM MODELL (Chmn.)
MITCHEL MODELL (C.E.O.)
WILLIE KAPLAN (V.P.-Mdsg.)
CATHY DRIMALAS (Real Estate Contact)
JEFF KARTEN-Outer Jackets, Casual Slacks, Men's & Boys' Work Clothes, Sportswear, Furnishings, Hats, Robes, Gloves, Young Men's Wear, 8 to 20 Boys' Wear, Men's & Boys' Heavy Outerwear, Rainwear, 8 to 20 Boys' Underwear, Hosiery
JEFF SHAFFER-Accessories, Furnishings, Casual Shoes, Boots
RON BRUNETT-Store Displays, Fixtures, Supplies

MOE PENN HATS (SP)

395 Grand St. (m-b)
New York, NY 10002
212-475-4156 / Fax: 212-871-2044

NATHAN WEISS (President & Owner) & Buys Men's Headwear

NEW YORK - New York

MORRIS BROTHERS (MW)
2322 Broadway (m-b)
New York, NY 10024
212-724-9000 / Fax: 212-724-3505
Sales: $1 Million-$10 Million
PHILIP KRUMHOLTZ (Owner) & Buys Men's & Young Men's Tailored Jackets, Tailored Slacks, Suits, Sportswear, Dress Shirts, Ties, Accessories, 8 to 20 Boys' Wear, Store Displays, Fixtures, Supplies

MR. NED, INC. (MW)
137 5th Ave. (b)
New York, NY 10003
212-924-5042 / Fax: 517-534-1238
NED MATEOSIAN (Co-Owner) & Buys Store Displays, Fixtures, Supplies, Men's Shirts, Ties (Suits & Slacks Custom Made)
BERT MATEOSIAN (Co-Owner) & Buys Men's Shirts, Ties (Suits & Slacks Custom Made)

N. PEAL (CLO)
5 W. 56th St.
New York, NY 10019
212-333-3500 / Fax: 212-489-6881
JERRY BUTLER (Owner) & Buys Men's Clothing, Furnishings, Accessories, Store Displays

NAPOLEON, INC. (MW-4)
1048 3rd Ave. (m-b)
New York, NY 10021
212-308-3000 / Fax: 212-688-2195
Website: www.napoleonfashions.com
DANIEL OURSHALIMAN (President) & Buys Men's Wear, Furnishings, Accessories, Footwear, Store Displays, Fixtures, Supplies

NEW YORK ATHLETIC CLUB (SP)
180 Central Park S.
New York, NY 10019
212-247-5100 / Fax: 212-767-7014
FRANK CASTRO (Mgr.) & Buys Activewear, Athletic Footwear

NEW YORK UNIVERSITY BOOK CENTERS (SP)
18 Washington Pl.
New York, NY 10003
212-998-4667 / Fax: 212-995-4118
Sales: $1 Million-$10 Million
Website: www.bookc.nyu.edu
JO ANN McGREEVY (Exec. Dir.)
JAMES OWES (G.M.M.) & Buys Fleece, Jackets, T-shirts

OFF 5TH (OT-51)
(SAKS INCORPORATED)
362 9th Ave., 17th Fl.
New York, NY 10001
212-320-4700 / Fax: 212-320-4850
Website: www.saksfifthavenue.com
Retail Locations: AZ, CA, CO, CT, FL, GA, HI, IL, LA, MA, MI, MO, NC, NJ, NV, NY, OH, OK, OR, PA, SC, TN, TX, VA
MIKE WOLKOFF (G.M.M.-Men's Division)
ANNE ASSANTE (D.M.M.) & Buys Men's Furnishings, Outerwear
JOHN CURSIN-Men's Sportswear
JIM SONTAG-Men's Clothing
CONNIE LIEBERMAN-Boys'
ERIC FAIRER (Real Estate Contact)

P & H IMPORTS (CLO-3)
(JR. VANITY)
1201 Broadway (p-m)
New York, NY 10001
212-725-1511 / Fax: 212-741-2232
Sales: $1 Million-$10 Million
DEEPAK KHUBCHANDAN (Partner) & Buys Men's Sportswear, Store Displays, Fixtures, Supplies
HIRO C. DASANI (Partner) & Buys Men's Sportswear, Store Displays, Fixtures, Supplies
DEEPAK SHIVNANI (Partner) & Buys Men's Sportswear, Urban Contemporary, Store Displays, Fixtures, Supplies

PANTS AND ..! (GS)
(GREATER NY PANTS COMPANY)
61 W. 49th St. (p)
New York, NY 10112
212-757-8550
DANIEL MERIMS (President) & Buys Men's T-shirts, Jackets, Store Displays, Fixtures, Supplies
WILLIAM SIGAL (V.P.) & Buys Men's T-shirts, Jackets, Store Displays, Fixtures, Supplies

PARAGON SPORTING GOODS (SG)
871 Broadway (p-m)
New York, NY 10003
212-255-8036 / Fax: 212-929-1831
Website: www.paragonsports.com
BRUCE BLANK (President & Owner)
PERRY EPSTEIN (G.M.M.)
KURT ROSENQUIST-Men's Active Apparel, T-shirts, Fleece & Shorts, Headwear
BERT HOLLAND-Men's Athletic Footwear

PAUL SMITH, INC. (MW)
108 5th Ave. (b-h)
New York, NY 10011
212-627-9770 / Fax: 212-627-9773
Website: www.paulsmith.co.uk
PAUL SMITH (President & Owner)
CLIFF HUNT (G.M.M.) & Buys Men's Wear, Sportswear, Furnishings, Footwear, Accessories, Young Men's Wear

PAUL STUART (MW-2 & MO)
Madison Ave. at 45th St. (b)
New York, NY 10017
212-682-0322 / Fax: 212-983-2742
Sales: $10 Million-$50 Million
Website: www.paulstuart.com
CLIFFORD GRODD (President)
PAUL OSTROVE (V.P.)
MICHAEL OSTROVE (Mdse. Mgr.)
MARTIN GUREWITZ-Men's Sportswear
MICHELLE SCHWARTZ-Sweaters, Knits
BILL FREEMAN-Outer Jackets, Leather Apparel, Raincoats
JOSEPH PACHECO-Men's Ties, Handkerchiefs, Formal Wear, Links, Studs
MATTHEW KORNER-Men's Pajamas, Underwear, Dress Shirts, Slippers
NORMAN KORNER-Men's Footwear

PETER ELLIOT (MW)
1070 Madison Ave. (b-des)
New York, NY 10028
212-570-2300 / Fax: 212-570-4636
Website: www.peterelliotny.com
ELLIOT RABIN (Owner) & Buys Men's Wear, Clothing, Sportswear, Furnishings, Accessories, Store Displays, Fixtures, Supplies
ARINA-Boys' Wear, Accessories, Furnishings

PORTA BELLA (MW-20 & OL)
38 W. 34th St., 3rd Fl.
New York, NY 10001
212-239-7380 / Fax: 212-239-4380
Website: www.portabellastores.com
Retail Locations: NY
ANDY ASHMAWY (President) & Buys Men's Suits, Tailored Jackets, Tailored Slacks, Dress Shirts, Sportcoats
KARL ASHMAWY-Men's Accessories & Footwear

PRATO MENSWEAR OUTLETS (MW-10)
28 West 34th St. (p)
New York, NY 10001
212-629-4730 / Fax: 212-465-9312
Sales: $10 Million-$50 Million
Website: www.pratooutlets.com
MOHAMED ASHMAWY (V.P.)
ALLEN HYMOWITZ (V.P.) & Buys Men's Wear, Outerwear, Leather Apparel, Tailored Suits
PAUL SEIDEN-Leather Apparel, Men's Sportswear, Store Displays, Fixtures, Supplies

NEW YORK - New York

PROFESSIONAL BOOK STORES (SP)
530 La Guardia Pl.
New York, NY 10012
212-998-4680 / Fax: 212-505-6514
Website: www.bookc.nyu.edu
DAWN GROSS (Mgr.) & Buys Fleece, Jackets, T-shirts

RICHIE'S CLOTHING (SP)
(PHYSICAL ACTIVEWEAR)
122 Delancey St.
New York, NY 10002
212-529-1472 / Fax: 212-614-4818
DAVID MIZRAHI (Mgr.) & Buys Sweatsuits, Activewear, Athletic Footwear

RIFLESSI (MW & OL)
260 Madison Ave. (b)
New York, NY 10016
212-679-4875 / Fax: 212-532-5375
Sales: $1 Million-$10 Million
Website: www.riflessinyc.com
ALDO TRUSELLO (Partner) & Buys Jewelry, Leather Goods, Men's Apparel, Men's Casualwear, Men's Designer Apparel, Men's Formalwear, Men's Accessories, Men's Outerwear, Men's Suits
LORI BENAYOUN (Partner) & Buys Jewelry, Leather Goods, Men's Apparel, Men's Casualwear, Men's Designer Apparel, Men's Formalwear, Men's Accessories, Men's Outerwear, Men's Suits
AVI BENAYOUN (Partner) & Buys Jewelry, Leather Goods, Men's Apparel, Men's Casualwear, Men's Designer Apparel, Men's Formalwear, Men's Accessories, Men's Outerwear, Men's Suits

ROBERTO CAVALLI (MW)
711 Madison Ave.
New York, NY 10021
212-755-7722 / Fax: 212-755-7477
Website: www.robertocavalli.it
ROBERTO CAVALLI (Owner) & Buys Men's Casual Slacks, Designer Jeans, Footwear, Furnishings, Accessories

ROSS STORES, INC. (CLO-409)
1372 Broadway, 10th Fl. (bud-p)
New York, NY 10018
212-382-2700 / Fax: 212-730-1139
Sales: Over $1 Billion
Website: www.rossstores.com
Retail Locations: AZ, CA, CO, DC, FL, GA, GU, HI, ID, MD, MT, NV, NJ, NM, NC, OK, OR, PA, SC, TX, UT, VA, WY, WA
MICHAEL BALMUTH (Vice Chmn. & C.E.O.)
JAMES C. PETERS (President & C.O.O.)
MICHAEL WILSON (Sr. V.P.-Distribution)
MICHAEL HAMILTON (Sr. V.P.-Stores)
JIM SASSIO (Sr. V.P. & Real Estate Contact) (@ 510-505-4484)
BARRY GLUCK (Sr. V.P./G.M.M.-Men's, Boys' & Footwear)
DAN McPHEE (V.P./D.M.M.-Better Sportswear)
KEITH GOODMAN (D.M.M.-Sportswear, Outerwear, & Swimwear)
COURTNEY PICCONE-Men's Bottoms
TERRI THOMAS-Dress Shirts
DAVID WACKMAN-Men's Wovens & Sweaters
SUSAN CHIN-Men's Denim Collection
HAL WALLACE-Accessories, Ties
ELSIE SANBRIA-Loungewear, Sleepwear
BILL LOESCH-Hats & Bags
JOHN BYKOWSKI-Men's Active & Licensed
CYNTHIA HENRY-Underwear
BRIDGET FERRARA-Men's Furnishings
ARLENE PATEMOSTRO-Better Traditional & Update Sportswear
MARV SADOWSKY-Knitwear, Golfwear, & Chaps

ABE MINDE (V.P./D.M.M.-Young Men's)
RUSS CAPUTO-Young Men's Outerwear
MICHELE GOLDBERG-EC Young Men's Bottoms & Swim
KELLEY O'CONNOR-EC Young Men's Tops
TRACY RUSSELL-Better Young Men's, Urban

ELLEN SHAMASKIN (V.P./D.M.M.-Boys')
CARL MATTEO (D.M.M.-Boys')
STEVEN BAUMANN-Boys' 4-7 Moderate Sportswear & Boy's Sportswear Sets
BARRY GALFAND-Boys' 8 to 20
ALAN RUBIN-Boys' 4 to 20
BETTY BRIX (@ 213-623-2640)-Boys' 4 to 20
CLAIRE ARBITER-Boys' 4 to 20
SHIELA BRENNAN-Boys' 4 to 20

JAMES VAN CLEEF-Athletic Shoes
SCOTT KOLSKY-Men's Footwear
DEBORAH LOVE (@ 510-505-4400)-Store Displays, Fixtures and Supplies

ROTHMAN'S (MW-3)
200 Park Ave. South (m-b)
New York, NY 10003
212-777-7400 / Fax: 212-979-2216
Website: www.rothmansny.com
KEN GIDDON (President)
JIM GIDDON (V.P.) & Buys Men's Sportswear, Furnishings, Footwear, Accessories, Store Displays, Fixtures, Supplies
MARK RUBENSTEIN (Mgr.) & Buys Men's Tailored Clothing, Slacks, Outerwear, Sportswear, Furnishings, Accessories

RUNAWAY BOUTIQUE, INC. (MW)
418 S. Park Ave. (m-b)
New York, NY 10016
212-686-8502 / Fax: 212-686-8502
AHMED ADAM (Owner) & Buys Men's Sportswear, Dress Shirts, Ties, Jewelry, Small Leather Goods, Footwear, Store Displays, Fixtures, Supplies

SAINT LAURIE LTD. (CLO)
22 W. 32nd (m)
New York, NY 10001
212-643-1916 / Fax: 212-695-4709
Website: www.saintlaurie.com
ANDREW KOZINN (Owner) & Buys Men's Wear, Sportswear, Furnishings, Accessories, Store Displays, Fixtures and Supplies

NEW YORK - New York

SAKS FIFTH AVENUE (DEPT-60 & MO-2)

(SAKS FIFTH AVENUE ENTERPRISES)
(FOLIO CATALOG)
(BULLOCK & JONES CATALOG)
12 E. 49th St. (b-h)
New York, NY 10017
212-753-4000 / Fax: 212-940-4109
Sales: Over $1 Billion
Website: www.saksfifthavenue.com
Retail Locations: AZ, CA, CO, CT, FL, GA, IL, LA, MD, MA, MI, MN, MO, NV, NJ, NY, OH, OK, OR, PA, TX, SC, VA

CHRISTINA JOHNSON (President & C.E.O.)
BRIAN MARTIN (Exec. V.P. - Real Estate)
CAROLYN BIGGS (Exec. V.P. - Store Opers.)
HARVEY ROSENBLOOM (Sr. V.P. & Dir. - Store Opers.)
CODY KONDO (G.M.M.-Men's) (@ 212-940-5868)
DAN McCAMPBELL (D.M.M. - Men's Denim & Swimwear)
TOM OTT (D.M.M. - Men's Designers Apparel, Formalwear, Suits)
MARY COSTANZO-Men's Sportswear & Activewear
MICHAEL LEVY-Modern Suits, Sport Coats
LOUIS DIGIACOMO-Swimwear, Polo
PETER HARRIS-Men's Traditional Clothing
BRIAN BESSEMER-European & American Designer Clothing, Formals, Outer Coats, Sportcoats, Trousers, Outerwear, Leather, Suede, Shearling, Men's Raincoats
DOMINIQUE BURNET-Men's Sweaters & Knits, Private Label Casual Slacks, Active Apparel
BETH GOODMAN-Boys' Apparel

JILL LOUIS (D.M.M.-Men's Dress Furnishings) (@ 212-940-5901)
SUE ANN NEWBERG (D.M.M.-Watches)
KIM BECKER (@ 212-940-5965)-Men's Dress Shirts
LINDSEY GORDON-Men's Pajamas, Hosiery, Underwear, Robes, Men's Neckwear
ALLISON ROSS-Accessories, Belts, Small Leathers
DONA DAVID-Men's & Boys' Footwear
CARYN NEARY-Men's & Boys' Footwear
SUZANNE SCARAMUCICH-Men's Footwear

DEBRA WALTERS (D.M.M.-Cosmetics) (@ 212-940-5858)
MICHAEL HAWLEY (@ 212-940-5870)-Men's Fragrances
JACKIE KEEHAN-Men's Collections

TERRY JACOBS (Dir.-Visual Mdse.) (@ 212-940-4841) & Buys Store Displays
ERIC FAIRES (Real Estate-Saks Fifth Avenue) (@ 901-937-2113)
PAUL RUBY (Real Estate-SDSG) (@ 414-347-4595)

SAKURA SHOJI, INC. (CLO)

3 E. 44th St. (b)
New York, NY 10017
212-661-3880 / Fax: 212-661-3881

NEKO MITSUNAKA (Owner) & Buys Men's Suits, Coats, Sportswear, Leather Apparel, Dress Shoes, Footwear, Store Displays, Fixtures & Supplies
PETER TOSHI-Men's Suits, Coats, Sportswear, Leather Apparel, Dress Shoes, Footwear, Urban Contemporary

SCOOP MEN (MW)

1277 3rd Ave.
New York, NY 10021
212-744-3380
Website: www.scoopnyc.com

STEFANI GREENFIELD (Co-Owner) & Buys Men's Footwear, Pants, Shirts

SILVER TRADING (MW-10)

(CACTUS TRADING, INC.)
485 7th Ave., #501 (p-m-b)
New York, NY 10018
212-643-8500 / Fax: 212-643-8573
Sales: $1 Million-$10 Million

NORMAN SILVER (V.P.) & Buys Men's, Young Men's & Boys' Clothing, Furnishings, Accessories, Leather Apparel (Closeouts)

SOPHISTICATED BUYS (RB)

1411 Broadway, #431
New York, NY 10018
212-819-9080 / Fax: 212-819-1976

NORMAN HUROWITZ (Co-Owner) & Buys Men's Wear (Off Price)
BRENDA SIMOWITZ (Co-Owner) & Buys Men's Wear (Off Price)

SOSINSKY, INC. (MW)

143 Orchard St. (b)
New York, NY 10002
212-254-2307

SAM WEISS (Owner) & Buys Men's Sweaters, Sport Shirts, Dress Shirts, Ties, Robes, Hosiery, Gloves, Belts, Store Displays, Fixtures and Supplies

SPEED JEANS & SPORTS (MW)

3582 Broadway
New York, NY 10031
212-234-8700 / Fax: 212-234-8700

SAM KALIM (Owner) & Buys Men's Sportswear, Jeans, Urban Contemporary, Accessories

THE STARTING LINE (SP)

180 8th Ave.
New York, NY 10011
212-691-4729 / Fax: 212-675-9410

JOE SALCE (Co-Owner) & Buys Activewear, Athletic Footwear
GUS SALCE (Co-Owner) & Buys Activewear, Athletic Footwear

SUNRISE BUYING, INC. (RB)

450 7th Ave., #2206 (bud-p-m)
New York, NY 10123
212-594-0170 / Fax: 212-465-9267
Sales: $10 Million-$50 Million

FRANK TAVELLA (Owner) & Buys Men's Wear (Off-Price Only)

TAKASHIMAYA (DEPT)

693 5th Ave., 8th Fl. (b)
New York, NY 10022
212-350-0100 / Fax: 212-350-0192

VIRGINIA HAYGOOD (G.M.M.) & Buys Men's Fragrances
ANDREW MANDELL-Men's Furnishings, Leather Jackets, Accessories, Coats, Knits

TANINO CRISCI AMERICA (FW & OL & MO)

(TANINO CRISCI)
795 Madison Ave. (des)
New York, NY 10021
212-535-1014 / Fax: 212-535-1125
Sales: $1 Million-$10 Million
Website: www.taninocrisci.com

TANINO CRISCI (President)
SERGIO PIERGIOVANNI (G.M.) & Buys Men's Footwear, Leather Goods, Watches, Men's Accessories, Men's Apparel
FIORE GUGLIELMI-Men's Footwear, Leather Goods, Watches, Men's Accessories, Men's Apparel

TINO COSMA (MW)

30 W. 57th St., #F14 (b-des)
New York, NY 10019
212-541-8120 / Fax: 212-956-3767
Sales: $1 Million-$10 Million
Website: www.tinocosma.com

TINO COSMA (President)
ANGELO LIBANI (Gen. Mgr.) & Buys Jewelry, Fragrances, Leather Goods, Men's Apparel, Men's Designer Apparel, Men's Formalwear, Men's Accessories

TOBALDI LTD. (MW)

83 Rivington St. (m)
New York, NY 10002
212-260-4330 / Fax: 212-260-4331
Sales: $500,001-$1 Million

MORRIS TOBALDI (Owner) & Buys Men's Wear, Sportswear, Furnishings, Accessories, Store Displays, Fixtures and Supplies

TURNBALL & ASSER CUSTOM CLOTHIERS (CLO-2)

42 E. 57th St.
New York, NY 10022
212-752-5700 / Fax: 212-319-8577
Website: www.turnballandasser.com

SIMON HOBBS (Mgr.) & Buys Men's Furnishings, Accessories

NEW YORK - New York

UNDER WARES FOR HIM (MW & OL)
210 E. 58th St. (m-b)
New York, NY 10022
212-838-1200 / Fax: 212-838-2449
Website: www.underwaresforhim.com

RON LEE (Owner) & Buys Men's Swimwear, Pajamas, Underwear, Robes, Hosiery

UNION (MW-2)
172 Spring St. (m-b)
New York, NY 10012
212-226-8493 / Fax: 212-226-8495
Sales: $500,001-$1 Million

MARYANN FUSCO (Owner) & Buys Men's Footwear, Leather Goods, Men's Apparel, Men's Casualwear, Men's Denim Apparel, Men's Accessories, Men's Outerwear, Men's Sportswear

UNTITLED (CLO)
26 W. 8th St.
New York, NY 10011
212-505-9725 / Fax: 212-505-9375

GAPU SURI (Owner) & Buys Clothing, Sportswear, Furnishings, Headwear, Accessories, Footwear, Store Displays, Fixtures, Supplies

UPLAND TRADING CO. (MW)
236 E. 13th St.
New York, NY 10003
212-673-4994

ARMANDO NEGRON (Owner) & Buys Men's Wear, Men's Accessories, Furnishings, Footwear

VIA SPIGA (SP-14)
156 W. 56th St., #15
New York, NY 10019
212-489-9770 / Fax: 212-459-9635
Website: www.viaspiga.com

TED DeGRACIA-Men's Footwear, Accessories

VICTOR STORES, INC. (CLO)
119 Dyckman St.
New York, NY 10040
212-567-8212 / Fax: 212-304-8349

VICTOR ABRAHAM (Owner) & Buys Men's Sportswear, Furnishings, Belts, Small Leathers, Young Mens Shop, Urban Contemporary, Store Displays, Fixtures & Supplies

LUE RODRIGUES-Men's Sportswear, Furnishings, Belts, Small Leathers, Young Mens Shop, Urban Contemporary, Store Displays, Fixtures & Supplies

WALID MENSWEAR, INC. (MW)
230 E. 14th St. (m-b)
New York, NY 10003
212-673-5638 / Fax: 212-673-5638

SALEH DOUBAN (Owner) & Buys Men's Wear, Sportswear, Furnishings, Accessories, Young Men's Wear, Store Displays, Fixtures and Supplies

WEBER - ARIES (MW)
141 W. 36th St., 18th Fl. (bud-p-m-b)
New York, NY 10018
212-563-5731 / Fax: 212-563-5828

NORMAN PIERSON (President) & Buys Men's Suits, Tailored Slacks, Sport Coats, Overcoats, Raincoats

WEISS & MAHONEY, INC. (CLO)
142 5th Ave. (m)
New York, NY 10011
212-675-1915 / Fax: 212-633-8573
Website: www.wmarmynavy.com

IRA WEISS (Owner) & Buys Jeans, Outerwear, Clothing, Military Clothing, Work Shoes, Belts, Headwear, Urban Contemporary, Store Displays, Fixtures and Supplies

WEST SIDE APPAREL, INC. (MW-2)
(FRANK STELLA LTD.)
440 Columbus Ave. (b)
New York, NY 10024
212-877-5566 / Fax: 212-765-4053

JOHN HELLINGS (Owner) (@ 212-957-1600) & Buys Men's Sportswear, Furnishings, Accessories, Leather Apparel, Store Displays, Fixtures, Supplies

WESTEND RESIDENT BUYERS (RB)
11 Riverside Dr. (m-b-h)
New York, NY 10023
212-724-6350

MARILYN COHEN (President) & Buys Men's Sportswear, Furnishings, Accessories

WORTH & WORTH LTD. (SG)
101 W. 55th St., #3N (b)
New York, NY 10019
212-265-2887 / Fax: 212-265-2998
Sales: $1 Million-$10 Million
Website: www.hatshop.com

HARRY ROSENHOLTZ (President) & Buys Men's Apparel, Men's Accessories

ORLANDO PALACIOS (Mgr.-Mdse.) & Buys Headwear

Y & K MERCHANDISE CORP. (MW)
8 W. 28th St.
New York, NY 10001
212-696-0457 / Fax: 212-213-6823

ZOUHIR JAAFAR (Owner) & Buys Men's Wear, Sportswear, Urban Contemporary, Jeans, T-shirts, Sweats

YOHJI YAMAMOTO USA, INC. (CLO)
103 Grand St. (b-h)
New York, NY 10013
212-966-9066 / Fax: 212-966-9144
Website: www.yohjiyamamoto-usa.com

MINORI SHIRONISHI (G.M.M.) & Buys Men's Wear, Sportswear, Furnishings, Accessories, Footwear

ZELLER TUXEDO, INC. (SP-22)
421 7th Ave. (m-b-des)
New York, NY 10001
212-290-0217 / Fax: 212-290-0428
Sales: $1 Million-$10 Million
Website: www.zellertuxedo.com
Retail Locations: NJ, NY

GARY STICKLES (Chmn.)

AARON CHAMPAGNE (President) & Buys Boys' Apparel, Men's Footwear, Men's Apparel, Men's Formalwear, Men's Accessories

THOMAS EPSTEIN (V.P.)

BRIAN MILLER (Real Estate Contact)

NEW YORK - Queens

ACTIVE WEARHOUSE, INC. (CLO-8)
(SPORTLANE)
(TRANSIT)
(N.Y.C. CLOTHING)
1940 Hazen St. (m-b)
East Elmhurst, NY 11370
718-850-7290 / Fax: 718-850-7802
Sales: $10 Million-$50 Million
Website: www.transitnyc.com
HAIM KEDMI (President, Dir.- Finance, Mktg.& Real Estate) & Buys Men's Footwear, Men's Wear, Sportswear
MIRON SWARTZ (V.P.) & Buys Men's Footwear, Men's Wear, Outerwear, Sportswear

AVIREX USA (CLO-3)
(AVIREX OUTLET)
(THE COCKPIT)
3300 47th Ave. (m-b)
Long Island, NY 11101
212-575-1616 / Fax: 212-575-1636
Sales: $1 Million-$10 Million
Website: www.avirex.com
JEFF CLYMAN (President)
JACKY CLYMAN (Exec. V.P. & Dir.- Finance, Mktg. & Fullfillment) & Buys Boys' Wear, Men's Wear, Men's & Boys' Footwear

BAR-TED ARMY & NAVY STORE (AN & OL)
3025 Steinway St., #1
Astoria, NY 11103
718-278-2443 / Fax: 718-274-2273
RUSSELL BROOKS (Owner) & Buys Sportswear, Work Clothes, Uniforms, T-shirts, Active Apparel, Furnishings, Accessories, Young Men's Wear, Work Shoes, Urban Contemporary, Store Displays, Fixtures and Supplies

BEN-RIC FASHIONS (SP)
(BEN-RIC FURS)
18614 Union Tnpk. (m-b-des)
Flushing, NY 11366
718-454-0320 / Fax: 718-454-3865
Sales: $500,001-$1 Million
JERRY COLA (President) & Buys Men's Wear, Outerwear
CHRISTINA KYROW (Store Mgr.)

BOB'S SNEAKER CORNER (SP)
9441 Liberty Ave.
Ozone Park, NY 11417
718-843-8452 / Fax: 718-843-8453
BOB GAGLIARDI (Owner) & Buys Athletic Footwear, Activewear, Licensed Apparel
JERRY MINICHIELLO (Mgr.) & Buys Athletic Footwear, Activewear, Licensed Apparel

BROADLEY'S (MW)
(BROADLEY & RALEIGH'S, INC.)
3206 Broadway (p)
Astoria, NY 11106
718-728-5143 / Fax: 718-274-6942
PAUL TARADASH (Owner) & Buys Men's Wear, Urban Contemporary, Furnishings, Accessories, Store Displays, Fixtures, Supplies
RON WOODSON (Mgr.) & Buys Men's Wear, Urban Contemporary, Furnishings, Accessories, Store Displays, Fixtures, Supplies

CENTRAL SKIN DIVERS (SP)
16009 Jamaica Ave. (b)
Jamaica, NY 11432
718-739-5772 / Fax: 718-739-3679
Sales: $500,001-$1 Million
SETH ORENSTEIN (Partner/Mgr.) & Buys Leather Goods, Men's Apparel, Men's Casualwear, Men's Denim Apparel, Men's Designer Apparel, Men's Accessories, Men's Outerwear, Men's Sleepwear, Men's Sportswear, Men's Swimwear, Men's Underwear, Men's Uniforms
ARTHUR ORENSTEIN (Partner) & Buys Leather Goods, Men's Apparel, Men's Casualwear, Men's Denim Apparel, Men's Designer Apparel, Men's Accessories, Men's Outerwear, Men's Sleepwear, Men's Sportswear, Men's Swimwear, Men's Underwear, Men's Uniforms

DAN DIAMOND (MW)
3076 Steinway St. (b)
Astoria, NY 11103
718-728-5562 / Fax: 718-728-0178
Sales: $500,001-$1 Million
LESTER DIAMOND (President) & Buys Leather Goods, Men's Big & Tall Apparel, Men's & Boys' Apparel, Men's Casualwear, Men's Denim Apparel, Men's Formalwear, Men's Accessories, Men's Hosiery, Men's Outerwear, Men's Sportswear, Men's Suits, Men's Swimwear, Men's Underwear

DIVINE ROBE SUPREME (SP)
8606 Parsons Blvd.
Jamaica, NY 11432
718-523-2082 / Fax: 718-523-0216
RANJANA GHOSE (Owner) & Buys Activewear, T-shirts, Shorts

DOMINO MEN'S SHOP OF BAY SHORE (MW)
5825 Myrtle Ave. (m-b)
Ridgewood, NY 11385
718-497-8896
RICH BRANCATO (Owner) & Buys Men's Wear, Footwear, Suits, Furnishings, Accessories, Store Displays, Fixtures, Supplies

EMPIRE STATE CLOTHIERS (MW)
16616 Jamaica Ave. (p)
Jamaica, NY 11432
718-523-1150 / Fax: 718-523-0911
Sales: $500,001-$1 Million
ALAN MARKOWITZ (Owner) & Buys Men's Wear, Sportswear, Furnishings, Accessories, Young Men's Wear, Urban Contemporary, Store Displays, Fixtures and Supplies

GOODY'S MEN'S SHOP, INC. (MW)
8209 153rd Ave. (p-m-b)
Howard Beach, NY 11414
718-322-1200 / Fax: 718-738-9128
Sales: $1 Million-$10 Million
FRED FORSTADT (Owner) & Buys Men's Wear, Leather Apparel, Store Displays, Fixtures, Supplies

HENRY'S MENSWEAR INC (MW)
7007 Grand Ave (m-b)
Flushing, NY 11378
718-898-5452
ROBERT McCORD (Owner) & Buys Men's Wear, Sportswear, Furnishings, Accessories, Store Displays, Fixtures and Supplies

KIM'S FASHIONS (MW)
14734 Jamaica Ave.
Jamaica, NY 11435
718-526-1867
MR. HAN (Owner) & Buys Men's Wear, Sportswear, Furnishings, Accessories, Store Displays, Fixtures and Supplies

KING BOULEVARD MEN'S SHOP (MW)
4724 Greenpoint Ave. (m-b)
Long Island City, NY 11104
718-784-8995 / Fax: 718-472-9239
MICHAEL PEREZ (President) & Buys Men's Wear, Urban Contemporary, Footwear, Furnishings, Accessories, Store Displays, Fixtures, Supplies

MAN O MAN MENSWEAR LTD., INC. (MW-2)
8902 165th St. (m-b)
Jamaica, NY 11432
718-523-0999 / Fax: 718-297-4337
ORIN SCHILLER (Owner) & Buys Men's Wear, Footwear, Store Displays, Fixtures, Supplies

MARTY'S MEN'S FASHIONS (MW)
3116 Steinway St.
Astoria, NY 11103
718-726-1356 / Fax: 718-726-9156
MARTY EISNER (Owner) & Buys Men's Wear, Footwear, Furnishings, Accessories, Store Displays, Fixtures, Supplies

NEW YORK - Queens

MEDUSA BOUTIQUE (CLO)
3751 82nd St. (b)
Jackson Heights, NY 11372
718-507-6544 / Fax: 718-507-6570
Website: www.medusaboutique.qpg.com
JULIAN LOPEZ (Owner) & Buys Men's Wear, Furnishings, Accessories, Footwear

METROPOLITAN FASHIONS, INC. (MW)
16210 Jamaica Ave. (m)
Jamaica, NY 11432
718-526-5555 / Fax: 718-526-5557
Sales: Under $100,000
CLAY WU (Owner) & Buys Men's Wear, Footwear, Furnishings, Accessories, Store Displays, Fixtures, Supplies

MIKE'S FASHION & IMPORT, INC. (MW)
3724 Junction Blvd., #A (m-b)
Corona, NY 11368
718-429-0933
MIKE NASTLI (Owner) & Buys Men's Wear, Furnishings, Footwear, Accessories, Young Men's Wear, Boys' Wear, Store Displays, Fixtures and Supplies

MIKE'S STEINWAY FORMAL (MW)
3158 Steinway (m-b)
Astoria, NY 11103
718-545-5682 / Fax: 718-545-5682
MIKE HARTOFILIS (Owner) & Buys Men's Wear, Formalwear, Furnishings, Accessories, Footwear, Store Displays, Fixtures, Supplies

THE OUTLET (CLO)
(BLUE RIBBON SHIRT CO.)
3217 Steinway (p-m-b)
Long Island City, NY 11103
718-274-3848 / Fax: 718-274-3909
Sales: $100,001-$500,000
BOB WEINBROWN (Co-Owner) & Buys Store Displays, Fixtures, Supplies, Men's Tailored Slacks, Sportswear, Dress Shirts, Ties, Robes, Underwear, Hosiery, Belts, Small Leather Goods, Footwear
EDWARD WEINBROWN (Co-Owner) & Buys Men's Tailored Slacks, Sportswear, Dress Shirts, Ties, Robes, Underwear, Hosiery, Belts, Small Leather Goods
JOE MACALUSO-Men's Tailored Slacks, Sportswear, Dress Shirts, Ties, Robes, Underwear, Hosiery, Belts, Small Leather Goods

R & S ARMY NAVY SHOP (AN)
9113 Jamaica Ave.
Woodhaven, NY 11421
718-441-4670 / Fax: 718-805-1213
Website: www.armynavyusa.com
SIMON STRUM (Owner) & Buys Military Clothing, Work Clothing, Work Uniforms, Sportswear, Jeans, Furnishings, Accessories, Work Shoes, Young Men's Wear, Boys' Jeans, Store Displays, Fixtures and Supplies

RALEIGH MEN'S CLOTHING (MW)
3206 Broadway
Long Island City, NY 11106
718-278-7521
PAUL TEREDASH-Men's Sportswear, Accessories, Furnishings

ROCKAWAY BEACH SURF SHOP (SP)
177 Beach 116th St.
Far Rockaway Beach, NY 11694
718-474-9345 / Fax: 718-474-1936
TOM SENA (Owner) & Buys Wet Suits, Active Apparel & Accessories

SNEAKER CIRCLE (SP)
(TRINIL SPORTS, INC.)
9725 Queens Blvd.
Rego Park, NY 11374
718-896-4535 / Fax: 718-896-4535
NILESH PATEL (Owner) & Buys Athletic Footwear

SUNHILL FASHIONS INC (MW)
16334 Jamaica Ave. (p-m)
Jamaica, NY 11432
718-297-6737
MYONG CHANG (Owner) & Buys Men's Wear, Furnishings, Accessories, Store Displays, Fixtures and Supplies

THEO & THEO'S, INC. (MW)
3283 Steinway St. (p-m)
Long Island City, NY 11103
718-932-7290 / Fax: 718-274-2694
Sales: $100,001-$500,000
JOHN TSIFORIS (Owner) & Buys Footwear, Men's & Boys' Wear, Sportswear, Furnishings, Accessories, Store Displays, Fixtures and Supplies

TREAD CONCOURSE (SP-3)
(METRIPOLITAN UNIFORMS)
(PREMIERE UNIFORMS)
(TREAD EASY SHOES)
16210 Jamaica Ave. (m-b)
Jamaica, NY 11432
718-526-5555 / Fax: 718-526-5557
Sales: $1 Million-$10 Million
CLAY WU (President) & Buys Men's Footwear, Uniforms, Outerwear, Uniform Accessories
GINA WU (Store Mgr.)

VIM STORES (CLO-30)
(FAMOUS HORSE, INC.)
164-01 Jamaica Ave. (p-m-b)
Jamaica, NY 11432
718-387-3777 / Fax: 718-388-2721
Sales: $10 Million-$50 Million
Website: www.vim.com
Retail Locations: NY
JOSEPH JOSEPH (President) & Buys Store Displays, Fixtures, Supplies, Men's & Boys' Sportswear, Furnishings, Accessories, Men's & Boys' Footwear
KATHY TIEMA-Men's & Boys' Sportswear, Furnishings, Accessories, Men's & Boys' Footwear, Urban Contemporary
VIKRAD PATEL-Men's & Boys' Footwear
ELAZAR JOSEPH (Real Estate Contact)

VINCCI (MW)
(VINCCI AUSTIN CORP.)
70-39 Austin St. (m-b)
Forest Hills, NY 11375
718-261-1588 / Fax: 718-374-0039
Sales: $100,001-$500,000
MIKE MITAROTONDA (President) & Buys Men's Wear, Furnishings, Accessories, Footwear, Store Displays, Fixtures, Supplies
MARIO MITAROTONDA (V.P.) & Buys Men's Wear, Furnishings, Accessories, Footwear, Store Displays, Fixtures, Supplies

VONS, INC. (SP)
106-11 Northern Blvd.
Corona, NY 11368
718-898-1113 / Fax: 718-898-1553
ORTNER MURRAY (Owner) & Buys Athletic Footwear, Activewear, Licensed Apparel

NEW YORK - Staten Island

BOZO'S RETAIL ARMY & NAVY (AN)

2742 Hylan Blvd. (m-b)
Staten Island, NY 10306
718-351-8465 / Fax: 718-351-0659
Sales: Under $100,000

MIKE PARENTI (Owner) & Buys Men's Wear, Boys' Jeans, Jackets, Sweat Pants, Underwear, Leather Apparel, Footwear, Store Displays, Fixtures, Supplies

C.H. MARTIN, INC. (DEPT-4)

156 Port Richmond Ave. (p)
Staten Island, NY 10302
718-273-2350 / Fax: 718-273-6873
Sales: $1 Million-$10 Million

CHARLES GOLDMAN (President)

DAVID GOLDMAN-Jeans, Active Apparel, Furnishings, Belts, Sportswear, Ties, Shoes, Store Displays, Fixtures, Supplies

NAT'S MEN'S SHOP (MW)

81 Port Richmond Ave. (m)
Staten Island, NY 10302
718-442-1698 / Fax: 718-442-1698
Sales: $100,001-$500,000

PAT SILVESTRI (Owner) & Buys Work Clothes, Sportswear, Underwear, Hosiery, Gloves, Headwear, Belts, Store Displays, Fixtures and Supplies

JAMES RUSSELL (Mgr.) & Buys Work Clothes, Sportswear, Underwear, Hosiery, Gloves, Headwear, Belts, Store Displays, Fixtures and Supplies

BRIAN'S SPORT SHOP (SP)

386 Broadway

Newburgh, NY 12550

845-562-4615 / Fax: 845-562-4615

Sales: $500,001-$1 Million

HAI NA (Owner) & Buys Activewear, Athletic Footwear, Licensed Apparel

McLAUGHLIN'S (DEPT)

27 S. Broad St. (m)

Norwich, NY 13815

607-334-7040 / Fax: 607-334-7030

SCOTT McLAUGHLIN (Co-Owner) & Buys Men's Overcoats, Tailored Jackets, Tailored Slacks, Suits, Raincoats, Sportswear, Furnishings, Belts, Small Leather Goods, Young Men's Wear, 8 to 20 Boys' Wear, Footwear

A SUMMER PLACE LTD. (CLO)

P.O. Box 317 (b)

Bay Walk

Ocean Beach, NY 11770

631-583-9696

Sales: $100,001-$500,000

RON SMITH (Co-Owner)

ROBERTA SMITH (Co-Owner) & Buys Men's Sportswear, Belts, Hosiery, Headwear, Footwear, Store Displays, Fixtures, Supplies

NEMO'S ARMY & NAVY STORE (AN-4)

3232 Long Beach Rd. (m)

Oceanside, NY 11572

516-764-8706 / Fax: 516-766-4065

Sales: $500,000-$1 Million

Website: www.nemos.com

MARTIN ISAACSON (President) & Buys Men's & Boys' Sportswear, Furnishings, Store Displays, Fixtures, Supplies

CARL ISAACSON-Footwear, Activewear, Accessories, Furnishings, Boots, T-shirts, Shorts, Camping

UDELCO, INC. (CLO)

103 S. Greenbush Rd.

Orangeburg, NY 10962

845-359-4885

CHARLES UDELSMAN (Owner)

SUSAN UDELSMAN-Men's Active Wear, Sportswear, Outerwear, Accessories, Footwear, Store Displays, Fixtures, Supplies

RUNNERS ROOST (SP)

4190 N. Buffalo Rd.

Orchard Park, NY 14127

716-662-1331

DAVE BORODZIK (Owner) & Buys Athletic Footwear, Activewear, T-shirts, Shorts, Related Accessories

BOB'S ARMY & NAVY STORE (AN)

159 Main St.

Ossining, NY 10562

914-762-8900 / Fax: 914-923-3614

NEIL WOOLF (Owner) & Buys Activewear, Athletic Footwear, Athletics, Licensed Apparel

TALLMAN'S DEPARTMENT STORE (DEPT)

150 Village Sq. (m)

Painted Post, NY 14870

607-962-2033 / Fax: 607-936-1815

DAVID TALLMAN (Owner) & Buys Men's Sportswear, Furnishings, Headwear, Accessories, Footwear, Store Displays, Fixtures, Supplies

CARL & BOB'S MEN'S STORE (MW)

41 E. Main St (m-b)

Patchogue, NY 11772

631-475-3808 / Fax: 631-475-1578

ED SCHLESSER-Men's Big & Tall, Furnishings, Sportswear, Accessories, Young Men's Wear, Urban Contemporary, Store Displays, Fixtures and Supplies

MEL'S ARMY & NAVY CENTER (AN)

25 S. William St. (m)

Pearl River, NY 10965

845-735-3321 / Fax: 845-735-4944

Sales: $500,001-$1 Million

MEL LIEBMANN (Owner) & Buys Men's Outerwear, Sweaters, Sport Shirts, Outer Jackets, Leather Apparel, Casual Slacks, Active Apparel, Furnishings, Headwear, Accessories, Young Men's Wear, Boys' Sportswear, Footwear, Store Displays, Fixtures, Supplies

SAGAN'S MEN'S SHOP (MW)

10 S. Main St. (m)

Port Henry, NY 12974

518-546-7212

Sales: $500,001-$1 Million

JACK WOODS (Owner) & Buys Men's Wear, Sportswear, Furnishings, Accessories, Young Men's Wear, Urban Contemporary, Store Displays, Fixtures and Supplies

KAMICK'S FINE TAILORING (MW)

150 Shore Rd. (b)

Port Washington, NY 11050

516-944-9436 / Fax: 516-944-2420

ROBIN KAMICK (Owner) & Buys Men's & Boys' Wear, Store Displays, Fixtures, Supplies

COWEN'S COUNTRY STORE (CLO)

65 Market St. (m)

Potsdam, NY 13676

315-265-3950

Sales: $100,001-$500,000

DANIEL COWEN (Owner) & Buys Men's Tailored Jackets, Tailored Slacks, Work Clothes, Sweaters, Sport Shirts, Casual Slacks, Furnishings, Belts, Young Men's Wear, Urban Contemporary, Boys' Wear, Store Displays, Fixtures and Supplies

M & M ARMY & NAVY STORE (AN)

460 Main St. (m)

Poughkeepsie, NY 12601

845-452-5220

STEVE WARREN (Owner) & Buys Men's Jeans, Work Clothes, Uniforms, Outerwear, Hosiery, Underwear, Headwear, Gloves, Sweaters, Outer Jackets, Active Apparel, Urban Contemporary, Work Shoes, Boots, Store Displays, Fixtures and Supplies

ADRIAN JULES LTD. - CUSTOM TAILOR (MW)

P.O. Box 17260 (m-b)

1392 Ridge Rd. East

Rochester, NY 14617

585-342-7160 / Fax: 585-342-0345

Website: www.adrianjules.com

ADRIAN ROBERTI (President & Owner)

PETER ROBERTI-Ties, Belts, Furnishings, Accessories, Footwear, Store Displays, Fixtures and Supplies

GOLDSTEIN'S CLOTHING MARKET (MW)

128 W. Main St. (p-m)

Rochester, NY 14614

716-454-7715

STAN KRAVITZ (Owner) & Buys Men's Wear, Sportswear, Furnishings, Accessories, Dress Shoes, Store Displays, Fixtures and Supplies

KREISS & GORDON (RB)

481 South Wood Rd.

Rockville Center, NY 11570

516-223-0888 / Fax: 516-223-9746

Website: www.kreissandgordon.com

KENNETH GORDON (President & Owner) & Buys Men's Sportswear, Suits, Accessories

SUNRISE SPORTS (SG)

314 Sunrise Hwy. (m)

Rockville Centre, NY 11570

516-766-5328 / Fax: 516-766-3218

Sales: $500,001-$1 Million

Website: www.sunrisesportsinc.com

TOM VELLA (Owner) & Buys Men's T-shirts, Fleece, Shorts, Active Apparel, Headwear, Accessories, Footwear, Store Displays, Fixtures and Supplies

HERB PHILIPSON ARMY & NAVY STORE (AN-5)

300 W. Dominick St. (m)

Rome, NY 13440

315-336-1300 / Fax: 315-337-5840

Sales: $1 Million-$10 Million

GARY PHILIPSON (Owner)

MAUREEN BAUER-Men's & Boys' Sportswear, Work Clothes, Footwear, Outerwear, Furnishings, Accessories, Camouflage

RESIDENT SHOPPERS SERVICE, INC. (CLO)
Rome Industrial Park (p-m)
Rome, NY 13440
315-336-6870 / Fax: 315-336-0778
Sales: $1 Million-$10 Million
Website: www.shoppersservice.com
MARY ANN ROSEN (Owner) & Buys Men's Sweaters, Sport Shirts, Outer Jackets, Casual Slacks, Jogging Suits, Shorts, Ties, Robes, Underwear, Hosiery, Gloves, Headwear, Belts, Footwear, Store Displays, Fixtures and Supplies
WILLIAM YEAGER-Men's Sweaters, Sport Shirts, Outer Jackets, Casual Slacks, Jogging Suits, Shorts, Ties, Robes, Underwear, Hosiery, Gloves, Headwear, Belts, Footwear, Store Displays, Fixtures, Supplies

DRESSER (MW)
3 Bryant Ave (m-b-des)
Roslyn, NY 11576
516-484-4845 / Fax: 516-625-6213
GERALD BALLIN (Owner) & Buys Men's Wear, Sportswear, Furnishings, Accessories, Footwear, Store Displays, Fixtures and Supplies

TYRONE (MW)
1432 Old Northern Blvd.
Roslyn, NY 11576
516-484-3330
NORMAN BUKSBAUM-Men's Pants, Shirts, Accessories
RICHARD BUKSBAUM-Men's Pants, Shirts, Accessories

LEE'S FOUR SEASONS (MW)
428 State St
Schenectady, NY 12305
518-370-1966
CHUWON LEE (Owner) & Buys Sweaters, Sport Shirts, Casual Slacks, Active Apparel, Underwear, Hosiery, Gloves, Headwear, Belts, Young Men's Wear, Urban Contemporary, Store Displays, Fixtures and Supplies

RUDNICK'S (MW)
(SCHENECTADY RUDNICK CORP.)
P.O. Box 716 (p-m)
308 State St.
Schenectady, NY 12301
518-372-6486 / Fax: 518-372-0198
Sales: $1 Million-$10 Million
LYNDA TOLOKONSKY (President)
NORMAN TOLOKONSKY-Men's Work Clothes, Dress Shirts, Ties, Robes, Footwear, Store Displays, Fixtures, Supplies

SIMON'S MENSWEAR (MW)
(RUBERSI SALES, INC.)
1671 Union St. (m)
Schenectady, NY 12309
518-377-1182 / Fax: 518-377-1159
MIKE BERNSTEIN (Owner) & Buys Men's Sportswear, Furnishings, Headwear, Accessories, Footwear, Store Displays, Fixtures, Supplies

MARSHALL BROTHERS (CLO)
50 E. Genesse St. (b)
Skaneateles, NY 13152
315-685-2213 / Fax: 315-685-2214
Sales: $500,000-$1 Million
JAMES MARSHALL (Owner) & Buys Men's Overcoats, Suits, Tailored Jackets, Tailored Slacks, Raincoats, Men's Sweaters, Sport Shirts, Outer Jackets, Casual Slacks, Active Apparel, Furnishings, Headwear, Accessories, Store Displays, Fixtures & Supplies

EDWARD ARCHER (MW)
85 Main St.
South Hampton, NY 11968
631-283-2668
EDWARD ARCHER-Men's Sportswear, Footwear, Furnishings

BERGAN'S MEN'S SHOP, INC. (MW)
328 S. Salina St. (bud-p-m)
Syracuse, NY 13202
315-471-9162 / Fax: 315-422-9852
Website: dreamscape.com/berganshoes
DAVID BERGAN (Co-Owner) & Buys Footwear, Men's Sweaters, Sport Shirts, Outer Jackets, Leather Apparel, Casual Slacks, Active Apparel, Men's Formal Wear, Furnishings, Headwear, Accessories, Young Men's Wear, Store Displays, Fixtures, Supplies
MICHAEL BERGAN (Co-Owner) & Buys Men's Sweaters, Sport Shirts, Outer Jackets, Leather Apparel, Casual Slacks, Active Apparel, Men's Formal Wear, Furnishings, Headwear, Accessories, Young Men's Wear, Urban Contemporary, Store Displays, Fixtures, Supplies

CENTORES TUXEDOS (MW-2)
3328 W. Genesee St. (p-m-b)
Syracuse, NY 13219
315-488-1525 / Fax: 315-484-7842
Website: www.centorestuxedos.com
KEVIN KELLY (Owner) & Buys Formal Wear, Related Furnishings, Accessories, Footwear, Store Displays, Fixtures and Supplies

DE JULIO'S ARMY & NAVY STORE (AN)
666 Burnet Ave. (p)
Syracuse, NY 13203
315-479-8170 / Fax: 315-479-5329
Sales: $100,001-$500,000
DAN DeJULIO (Owner) & Buys Men's Outer Jackets, Casual Slacks, Active Apparel, Footwear, Work Clothes, Big & Tall Men's Wear, Store Displays, Fixtures, Supplies
RICK DeJULIO-Men's Outer Jackets, Casual Slacks, Active Apparel, Footwear, Work Clothes, Big & Tall Men's Wear, Store Displays, Fixtures, Supplies

KOOLAKIAN & MANRO MEN'S WEAR (MW)
132 E. Genesee St. (m-b)
Syracuse, NY 13202
315-471-7410 / Fax: 315-471-3835
Sales: $100,001-$500,000
CHARLES MANRO (Co-Owner) & Buys Men's Wear, Sportswear, Footwear, Furnishings, Accessories, Store Displays, Fixtures and Supplies
ED KOOLAKIAN (Co-Owner) & Buys Men's Wear, Sportswear, Footwear, Furnishings, Accessories, Store Displays, Fixtures and Supplies

LEARBURY FACTORY OUTLET STORE (MW)
401 N. Salina St. (m)
Syracuse, NY 13203
315-422-2267 / Fax: 315-422-9770
Sales: $1 Million-$10 Million
VINCENT RUA (Owner) & Buys Men's Overcoats, Raincoats, Sportswear, Furnishings, Headwear, Accessories, Store Displays, Fixtures, Supplies
BRUCE MAYBERRY-Footwear

MANNY'S ON S.U. CAMPUS, INC. (CLO & OL)
151 Marshall St. (p)
Syracuse, NY 13210
315-472-8863
Sales: $500,000-$1 Million
Website: www.mannysonline.com
MICHAEL RUBENSTEIN (Owner) & Buys Men's Outer Jackets, Active Apparel, Ties, Underwear, Hosiery, Gloves, Accessories
BILL NESTER-Men's Outer Jackets, Active Apparel, Ties, Underwear, Hosiery, Gloves, Accessories, Footwear, Store Displays, Fixtures & Supplies

NEW YORK - Syracuse

MISTER SHOP (MW)
(SHAPIRO BROTHERS CO., INC.)
259 W. Fayette St. (b)
Syracuse, NY 13202
315-471-6367 / Fax: 315-422-3251
Sales: $500,000-$1 Million
Website: www.mistershopsyracuse.com
JOEL SHAPIRO (President) & Buys Men's Overcoats, Suits, Tailored Jackets, Tailored Slacks, Raincoats, Sweaters, Sport Shirts, Outer Jackets, Leather Apparel, Casual Slacks, Dress Shirts, Ties, Hosiery, Belts, Fragrances, Footwear, Store Displays, Fixtures, Supplies

SYRACUSE UNIVERSITY BOOKSTORES (SP-5)
(SYRACUSE UNIVERSITY)
303 University Pl.
Syracuse, NY 13244
315-443-9900 / Fax: 315-443-1683
Sales: $10 Million-$20 Million
Website: www.syr.edu/bkst
BETSY ENGLISH (Dir.)
GALE YOUMELL-Activewear, Pants, Jackets, Hosiery, Shorts, Licensed Apparel

BURNS BROTHERS' MENSWEAR (MW)
2786 Sheridan Dr. (p-m)
Tonawanda, NY 14150
716-838-2300
JOHN BURNS (Owner) & Buys Men's Suits, Formal Wear, Footwear, Furnishings, Accessories, Store Displays, Fixtures and Supplies

CAHILL'S SPORTING GOODS (SG)
26 4th St. (p-m)
Troy, NY 12180
518-272-0991
DANIEL CAHILL (Owner) & Buys Men's Sweaters, Sport Shirts, Outer Jackets, Active Apparel, Headwear, Accessories, Footwear, Store Displays, Fixtures, Supplies

RODINOS, INC. (MW)
348 Congress St. (m)
Troy, NY 12180
518-274-1151
Sales: $100,001-$500,000
JOSEPH RODINO (Owner) & Buys Men's Wear, Footwear, Furnishings, Accessories, Store Displays, Fixtures, Supplies

MAIN BEACH SURF & SPORT, INC. (SP)
P.O. Box 1359
Montauk Hwy.
Wainscott, NY 11975
631-537-2716 / Fax: 631-537-6310
LARS SVANBERG (Owner) & Buys Ski Wear, Activewear, Athletic Footwear

JOHN'S TAILOR & MEN'S SHOP (MW)
19 Main St. (m-b)
Walden, NY 12586
845-778-7692 / Fax: 845-778-5790
CHRIS STANOS (Owner) & Buys Men's Wear, Sportswear, Furnishings, Accessories, Store Displays, Fixtures and Supplies

WEBB'S CLOTHING (MW)
146 Delaware (b)
Walton, NY 13856
607-865-4302
BETSY MUNN (Owner) & Buys Men's Overcoats, Raincoats, Sweaters, Sport Shirts, Outer Jackets, Casual Slacks, Active Apparel, Dress Shirts, Ties, Underwear, Hosiery, Gloves, Belts, Store Displays, Fixtures, Supplies

ABC BUYING GROUP (RB)
P.O. Box 156 (b-des)
Wantagh, NY 11793
516-520-1207 / Fax: 516-520-2066
Sales: $10 Million-$50 Million
LOU ARGYROPOULOS (President & Owner) & Buys Men's & Boys' Apparel, Accessories

APEX ARMY & NAVY (AN)
103 Public Sq. (p-m-b)
Watertown, NY 13601
315-782-2321 / Fax: 315-782-9493
Sales: $500,001-$1 Million
EDWARD KRUPKIN (Owner) & Buys Men's Work Clothes, Uniforms, Jeans, Casual Slacks, Sport Shirts, Outer Jackets, Leather Apparel, Active Apparel, Underwear, Hosiery, Gloves, Headwear, Belts, Urban Contemporary, Store Displays, Fixtures and Supplies

SCOTT-DEL CHILDREN'S WEAR (KS)
1020 Union Rd. (m-b)
West Seneca, NY 14224
716-674-1162
Sales: $100,001-$500,000
DORIAN E. BEMBENISTA (Owner) & Buys Boys' Clothing, Sportswear, Furnishings, Accessories, Store Displays, Fixtures, Supplies

FRANK ADAMS MENSWEAR (MW)
132-9 Main St. (b)
Westhampton Beach, NY 11959
631-288-1341
WILLIAM SEXTON (President) & Buys Men's Tailored Jackets, Young Men's Wear, Sportswear, Furnishings, Accessories, Store Displays, Fixtures & Supplies
PEGGY SEXTON-Men's Tailored Jackets, Young Men's Wear, Sportswear, Furnishings, Accessories, Store Displays, Fixtures & Supplies

LUBIN'S MAN'S WORLD (MW)
63 Tarrytown Rd. (m-b)
White Plains, NY 10607
914-965-6004 / Fax: 914-965-4817
Sales: $1 Million-$10 Million
BARRY KIRSCHNER (Owner) & Buys Domestic & European Men's Wear, Accessories, Furnishings

WESTCHESTER ROAD RUNNER (SP)
179 E. Post Rd.
White Plains, NY 10601
914-682-0637 / Fax: 914-949-4166
ANDY KIMERLING (Owner) & Buys Athletic Footwear, Activewear

WINDSOR TUXEDOS (SP)
181 Mamaroneck Ave., #A (b-des)
White Plains, NY 10601
914-948-8330
Sales: $500,001-$1 Million
H. STANLEY CORD (President) & Buys Jewelry, Men's Designer Apparel, Men's Formalwear, Men's Hosiery
LARRY CORD (V.P.) & Buys Jewelry, Men's Designer Apparel, Men's Formalwear, Men's Hosiery
PAUL CORD (V.P.-Opers.) & Buys Jewelry, Men's Designer Apparel, Men's Formalwear, Men's Hosiery

BRENNAN'S MENSWEAR, INC. (MW)
5522 Main St. (p-m)
Williamsville, NY 14221
716-565-3848
Sales: $500,000-$1 Million
Website: www.brennans.com
ROBERT GOULDING, JR. (President) & Buys Men's Wear, Big & Tall Men's Wear, Footwear, Furnishings, Accessories, Store Displays, Fixtures, Supplies

THE ORVIS SHOP (SG)
(REED & SON ENTERPRISES, INC.)
5655 Main St. (m)
Williamsville, NY 14221
716-631-513 / Fax: 716-633-8903
Sales: $500,001-$1 Million
JIM GUIDA (Owner) & Buys Men's Casual & Outdoor Clothing, Footwear, Store Displays, Fixtures, Supplies

TUXEDO JUNCTION (MW-35)
120 Earhart Dr. (b)
Williamsville, NY 14231
716-633-2400 / Fax: 716-633-1719
Website: www.tuxedojunction.com
Retail Locations: NY
BARRY SNYDER (Owner)
MIKE BRISTOL (V.P.-Prod.) & Buys Men's, Young Men's & Boys' Formal Wear, Footwear, Urban Contemporary, Related Formal Accessories, Store Displays, Fixtures, Supplies

NATIONAL JEAN (CLO)

(JSK SALES, INC.)
650 Willis Ave. (m)
Williston Park, NY 11596
516-742-2999 / Fax: 516-742-4720
Website: www.nationaljeancompany.com

JIMMY GURRIERI (Owner) & Buys Men's Jeans, Shirts, Store Displays, Fixtures, Suppies

GALLO'S (CLO-3)

12056 Main St. (bud-p-m)
Wolcott, NY 14590
315-594-2171 / Fax: 315-594-9244
Sales: $500,000-$1 Million

JOSEPH GALLO (Owner) & Buys Men's Suits, Tailored Jackets, Tailored Slacks, Sweaters, Sport Shirts, Outer Jackets, Overcoats, Raincoats, Dress Shirts, Ties, Robes, Underwear, Hosiery, Gloves, Leather Apparel, Casual Slacks, Active Apparel, Furnishings, Headwear, Belts, Jewelry, Smal

JOHN GALLO (G.M.M.) & Buys Men's Suits, Tailored Jackets, Tailored Slacks, Sweaters, Sport Shirts, Outer Jackets, Overcoats, Raincoats, Dress Shirts, Ties, Robes, Underwear, Hosiery, Gloves, Leather Apparel, Casual Slacks, Active Apparel, Furnishings, Headwear, Belts, Jewelry, Smal

THOMAS MILLER MEN'S STORE (MW)

8285 Jericho Tpke. (h)
Woodbury, NY 11797
516-367-3590 / Fax: 516-367-4890
Sales: $1 Million-$10 Million

THOMAS MILLER (President & Owner) & Buys Men's Wear, Sportswear, Dress Shirts, Footwear, Ties, Hosiery, Gloves, Accessories, Store Displays, Fixtures and Supplies

CHANGES, INC. (MW)

19 Tinker St. (p-m-b)
Woodstock, NY 12498
845-679-4750

LOU DERRING (Owner) & Buys Sportswear, Dress Shirts, Ties, Underwear, Hosiery, Gloves, Headwear, Belts, Small Leathers, Footwear, Store Displays, Fixtures and Supplies

ELAINE COHEN (Mgr.) & Buys Sportswear, Dress Shirts, Ties, Underwear, Hosiery, Gloves, Headwear, Belts, Small Leathers, Store Displays, Fixtures and Supplies

MS. FORTUNA-Sportswear, Dress Shirts, Ties, Underwear, Hosiery, Gloves, Headwear, Belts, Small Leathers, Store Displays, Fixtures and Supplies

PACKER'S (SP)

189 Ashburton Ave.
Yonkers, NY 10701
914-965-4290

M. PACKER (Owner)

SUSAN PACKER-Athletic Footwear, Activewear, Licensed Apparel

JAY TALBERT, INC. (MW)

102 S. 2nd St. (m-b)
Albemarle, NC 28001
704-983-0905 / Fax: 704-983-0905
Sales: $100,001-$500,000

JERRY TALBERT (Owner) & Buys Men's Sportswear, Furnishings, Accessories, Headwear, Store Displays, Fixtures, Supplies

CLASSIC BREED (CLO)

610 Randolph Mall (p)
Asheboro, NC 27203
336-626-5170 / Fax: 336-626-5170
Sales: $100,001-$500,000

DAVID WHITAKER (Owner) & Buys Men's Sportswear, T-shirts, Shorts, Store Displays, Fixtures, Supplies

CLOTHES WAREHOUSE (CLO-2)

Hwy. 64 West (b)
Asheboro, NC 27203
336-629-5164 / Fax: 336-629-0396
Sales: $1 Million-$10 Million

CRAIG BRANSON (President & Co-Owner) & Buys Urban Contemporary

LARRY McKENZIE (Co-Owner) & Buys Men's Overcoats, Suits, Tailored Jackets, Tailored Slacks, Raincoats, Big & Tall Men's Wear, Sportswear, T-shirts, Dress Shirts, Ties, Underwear, Hosiery, Gloves, Headwear, Belts, Small Leather Goods, 8 to 20 Boys' Wear, Store Displays, Fixtures, Supplies

CHRISTY McKENZIE (Co-Owner, Secy. & Treas.) & Buys Men's Overcoats, Suits, Tailored Jackets, Tailored Slacks, Raincoats, Big & Tall Men's Wear, Sportswear, T-shirts, Dress Shirts, Ties, Underwear, Hosiery, Gloves, Headwear, Belts, Small Leather Goods, 8 to 20 Boys' Wear, Store Displays, Fixtures, Supplies

JOHN MERRILL'S MENSWEAR (MW-2)

1457 N. Fayetteville St. (m-b)
Asheboro, NC 27203
336-672-2899 / Fax: 336-672-2570
Sales: $100,001-$500,000

GILBERT INGOLD (President, G.M.M. & Owner) & Buys Men's Overcoats, Suits, Tailored Jackets, Sweaters, Sport Shirts, Casual Slacks, Furnishings, Belts, Underwear, T-shirts, Dress Shirts, Tuxedos, Store Displays, Fixtures, Supplies

BENJAMIN LEWIS TUXEDOS (MW)

555 Merrimon Ave. (m-b)
Asheville, NC 28804
828-258-2245

SANDY AUSTIN (Owner) & Buys Men's & Boys' Formal Wear

JACKSON TRADING CO., INC. (CLO)

641 Patton Ave. (m)
Asheville, NC 28806
828-254-1812 / Fax: 828-254-3758
Sales: $1 Million-$10 Million

CHARLES JACKSON (President & Owner) & Buys Men's Western Wear, Sport Shirts, Outer Jackets, Leather Apparel, Casual Slacks, Active Apparel, Hosiery, Headwear, Belts, Jewelry, Small Leather Goods, Footwear, Store Displays, Fixtures, Supplies

ATLANTIC BEACH SURF SHOP (CLO)

515 W. Fort Macon Rd. (m)
Atlantic Beach, NC 28512
252-726-9382 / Fax: 252-726-1200
Website: www.absurfshop.com

TOMMY MORROW (Owner) & Buys Men's & Boys' Sportswear, Belts, Footwear, Urban Contemporary, Swim Suits, Store Displays, Fixtures, Supplies

BERT'S SURF SHOPS (CLO-12)

(Div. of PEARSON'S DEPARTMENT STORES)
P.O. Box 3010
304 W. Fort Macon Rd.
Atlantic Beach, NC 28512
252-726-1730 / Fax: 252-726-1562

CURTIS PEARSON (G.M.M. & Co-Owner) & Buys Men's Sportswear, Headwear, Belts, Dress Shirts, Boys' Wear, Footwear, Urban Contemporary, Store Displays, Fixtures, Supplies

BETTY PEARSON (Co-Owner) & Buys Men's Jewelry, Small Leather Goods, Fragrances

NOTE:-For Balance of Buyers & Lines Carried See Listing For PEARSON'S DEPARTMENT STORES, Kinston, NC.

DAVIS BEACHWEAR SHOP (CLO)

P.O. Box 456 (bud-p-m-b)
119 Atlantic Blvd.
Atlantic Beach, NC 28512
252-726-2204

KATHERINE CROWE (Owner)

BUDDY DAVIS-Men's Beachwear, Store Displays, Fixtures, Supplies

SUGAR MOUNTAIN SPORTS (SP)

P.O. Box 369
1009 Sugar Mountain Resort Dr.
Banner Elk, NC 28604
828-898-4521 / Fax: 828-898-6820
Sales: $100,001-$500,000
Website: www.skisugar.com

MS. GERRI WOODY (Owner) & Buys Ski Apparel, Sportswear, Footwear

FABRICATE, INC. (CLO)

431 Front St. (m-b)
Beaufort, NC 28516
252-728-7950 / Fax: 252-728-7950

BARBARA PEARL (Owner) & Buys Men's Shirts

FRED'S GENERAL MERCANTILE (DEPT)

501 Beach Mountain Pkwy. (m)
Beech Mountain, NC 28604
828-387-4838 / Fax: 828-387-4042
Sales: $1 Million-$10 Million
Website: www.fredsgeneral.com

MARJORIE PFOHL (Co-Owner)

FRED PFOHL (Co-Owner & President)

APRIL CLOWGH (Mgr.) & Buys Men's Sportswear, Accessories, Footwear, Boys' Wear, Store Displays, Fixtures, Supplies

THERESA'S FASHIONS (CLO-2)

P.O. Box 175 (m)
114 E. Main St.
Beulaville, NC 28518
910-298-3924 / Fax: 910-298-5162
Sales: $100,001-$500,000

THERESA HUSSEY (Co-Owner) & Buys Footwear, Men's Sportswear, Furnishings, Accessories, Young Men's Wear, Store Displays, Fixtures, Supplies

WILBUR HUSSEY (Co-Owner) & Buys Men's Sportswear, Furnishings, Accessories, Young Men's Wear, Store Displays, Fixtures, Supplies

J.W. TWEEDS (DEPT)

447 Laurel Chase Dr.
Blowing Rock, NC 28605
828-898-6166 / Fax: 828-898-5859

CAROL DICKERSON (Owner) & Buys Men's Wear, Clothing, Overcoats, Suits, Furnishings, Accessories, Footwear

SPORTS FANATIC (SP)

1180 Blowing Rock Rd.
Boone, NC 28607
828-264-1141
Sales: $100,001-$500,000

JODY PRUESS (Owner) & Buys Athletics, Activewear, Golf Apparel, Licensed Apparel

BURLINGTON BRANDS (CLO-9)

P.O. Box 1023 (m)
1266 Plaza Dr.
Burlington, NC 27215
336-229-5155 / Fax: 336-227-3788
Sales: $1 Million-$10 Million
Website: www.burlingtonbrands.com

KEVIN FITZGERALD (President & G.M.M.) & Buys Men's Sportswear, Urban Contemporary

BLAKE WAGGONER (V.P.) & Buys Men's Ties, Belts, Accessories

ELLIS McCULLOCH-Accessories, Store Displays, Fixtures, Supplies

NORTH CAROLINA - Burlington

JEFFERIES SOCKS (MO)

P.O. Box 1680 (m)
1176 N. Church St.
Burlington, NC 27216
336-226-7316 / Fax: 336-226-8217
Sales: $500,000-$1 Million
Website: www.monarchhosiery.com

KEN HAMBY (Gen. Mgr.) & Buys Men's & Boys' Hosiery, Store Displays, Fixtures, Supplies
RUTH MORGAN (G.M.M.) & Buys Men's & Boys' Hosiery, Store Displays, Fixtures, Supplies

R.E. BELL CO., INC. (CLO)

711 E. Davis St. (p)
Burlington, NC 27215
336-226-3422 / Fax: 336-226-3222
Sales: $1 Million-$10 Million

MELISSA BELL (President & Owner) & Buys Men's Tailored Slacks, Raincoats, Sportswear, Dress Shirts, Ties, Robes, Underwear, Gloves, Headwear, Belts, Small Leather Goods, Footwear, Big & Tall Men's Wear, Men's Work Clothes, Hosiery, Store Displays, Fixtures, Supplies

DAVID'S LTD. (MW)

105 Main St. (b)
Burnsville, NC 28714
828-682-6542 / Fax: 828-682-1155

DAVID McINTOSH (Owner)
CRISTAL RANDOLPH (G.M.M.) & Buys Men's Sportswear, Furnishings, Accessories, Footwear, Store Displays, Fixtures, Supplies

DAYDREAMS ACTIVEWEAR & HATTERAS OUTDOORS (SP)

P.O. Box 947
Rt. 12
Buxton, NC 27920
252-995-5548 / Fax: 252-995-5469
Sales: $501,000-$1 Million

CAROL DAWSON (President) & Buys Apparel, Footwear

MARINE CORPS EXCHANGE 0131 (PX-20)

Marine Corps Base, Bldg. #895 (m-b)
Camp Lejeune, NC 28542
910-451-2481 / Fax: 910-353-4105
Sales: $10 Million-$50 Million
Website: www.mccs.lejeune.com/www.mccs.usmc.com

TERESA CONOVER-Men's Sportswear, Activewear, Casualwear, Outerwear, Footwear, Furnishings, Accessories
JUDY WHITE-Store Displays, Fixtures, Supplies

O'NEILL'S CLOTHING (MW)

Carr Mill Mall (b)
200 N. Greensboro St.
Carrboro, NC 27510
919-967-3100 / Fax: 919-967-3100

JOHN O'NEILL (Owner) & Buys Men's Sportswear, Furnishings, Accessories

TRAIL SHOP (CLO & OL)

308 W. Franklin St.
Chapel Hill, NC 27516
919-929-7626 / Fax: 919-942-1468
Website: www.thetrailshop.com

JOE COATES (Owner) & Buys Men's Outdoor Clothing

UNC STUDENT STORE (SP)

(UNIVERSITY OF NORTH CAROLINA)
CB #1530
Daniels Bldg.
Chapel Hill, NC 27599
919-962-5066 / Fax: 919-962-7392
Sales: $100,001-$500,000
Website: www.store.unc.edu

JOHN JONES (Dir. Operations) & Buys Licensed Activewear, Pants, Shorts, Jackets, Hosiery, Headwear
GREG MORTON (Assoc. Dir.) & Buys Licensed Activewear, Pants, Shorts, Jackets, Hosiery, Headwear

BELK STORES SERVICES (CBO-210 & OL)

2801 W. Tyvola Rd. (bud-p-m-b-h)
Charlotte, NC 28217
704-357-1000 / Fax: 704-357-3952
Sales: $2 Billion
Website: www.belk.com
Retail Locations: FL, TX, AR, MS, AL, GA, SC, NC, VA, MD, WV, KY, TN

JOHN M. BELK (C.E.O.)
McKAY BELK (President-Mdsg.)
TIM BELK (Co-President)
JOHNNY BELK (Co-President)
SCOTT HINSON (Real Estate Contact)
DENNIS MYER (Sr. V.P.-Mdsg. & G.M.M.-Men's & Boys')
DAVID ZANT (G.M.M. - Men's)
RON MELLOTT (D.M.M.-Clothing, Furnishings, & Young Men)
PETER PRICE (D.M.M.-Men's Sportswear, Young Men's Wear)
JAN CLEVENGER (D.M.M.-Sportswear)
JOHN PADGETT-Men's Moderate to Better Dress Shirts, Neckwear
BOB LUSK-Hilfiger, Polo, Nautica, Golf
MIKE HART-Moderate Collections
JERRY YODER-Clothing & Tailored Bottoms
TOM BURNS-Suits, Tailored Jackets, Tailored Slacks, Casual Slacks
DAVID PRITCHETT-Better Collections, Activewear
THOMAS JACOBER-Men's Sweaters, Sport Shirts, Outer Jackets, Leather Apparel
BETH BROWN-Signature Sportswear, Collections
DAN MADAY-Signature Active Apparel, Better Denim
TOM BURNS-Outerwear & Casual Bottoms
THOMAS JACOBER-Big & Tall Men's Wear, Men's Overcoats, Raincoats
SELENA HANKS-Big & Tall
SCOTT DROMMS-Young Men's Wear, Urban Contemporary
SCOTT DROMMS-Young Men's Collections
AUDRA ATKINSON-Young Men's Classifications
BETH LINGLE-Urban Contemporary, Furnishings, Accessories
EDDIE JANKINSON-Furnishings & Accessories
ANNE BRYAN (D.M.M.-Boys' Wear)
STEVE LaBATT-Size 8 to 20 Boys' Active Apparel, Collections, Clothing, Private Label Sportswear, Furnishings, Accessories, 4 to 7 Clothing
MARY JANE GREER-Boys' 4 to 7

FRED BROWN-Men's Footwear
GREG JONES-Children's Shoes

KAY MANNINO (V.P.-Visual Mdsg.) & Buys Store Displays
DENNIS CAUDLE (Interior Construction Mgr.) & Buys Store Fixtures

(BELK STORES SERVICES Cont. on

(BELK STORES SERVICES Cont.)

JIM WHITE (Purch. Agent) & Buys Store Supplies

NOTE:-Also See Central Division, Charlotte, NC & Northern Division, Raleigh, NC.

CAMPUS SPORTS (SP)

9620 University City Blvd., #A
Charlotte, NC 28213
704-548-8622
Website: www.minergear.com

ALLEN ISLEY (Mgr.) & Buys Licensed Apparel, Activewear

CASUALS PLUS (CLO)

2048 N. Graham St. (m)
Charlotte, NC 28206
704-339-0111 / Fax: 704-339-0145

ESTHER PARK (Co-Owner)

HEE PARK (Co-Owner) & Buys Men's Suits, Tailored Jackets, Tailored Slacks, Sweaters, Sport Shirts, Outer Jackets, Leather Apparel, Active Apparel, Casual Slacks, Dress Shirts, Ties, Hosiery, Small Leather Goods, Belts, Gloves, Jewelry, Fragrances, Footwear, Store Displays, Fixtures, Supplies

ESQUIRE BIG & TALL (MW)

3014 Eastway Dr. (b)
Charlotte, NC 28205
704-536-6505 / Fax: 704-536-6819

FRED LOWE (Co-Owner) & Buys Big & Tall Men's Wear, Urban Contemporary, Related Accessories & Furnishings, Footwear Store Displays, Fixtures, Supplies

JASON LOWE (Co-Owner) & Buys Big & Tall Men's Wear

FAIRCLOUGH & CO., INC. (MW)

102 Middleton Dr. (b)
Charlotte, NC 28207
704-331-0001 / Fax: 704-332-5854
Website: www.faircloughonline.com

PAUL HADDOCK (Owner) & Buys Store Displays, Fixtures, Supplies, Men's Sportswear, Furnishings, Accessories, Footwear

JOHN BRYANT (Mgr.) & Buys Men's Sportswear, Furnishings, Accessories, Footwear

THE FAMOUS MART (DEPT-2)

(CHARLOTTE SALVAGE)
P.O. Box 220268 (b)
300 Rampart St.
Charlotte, NC 28222
704-333-5157 / Fax: 704-333-5158
Sales: $1 Million-$10 Million
Website: www.famousmart.com

LOUIS SINKOE (President & Owner) & Buys Men's Suits, Tailored Jackets, Tailored Slacks, Sportswear, Furnishings, Headwear, Accessories, Young Men's & Boys' Wear, Store Displays, Fixtures and Supplies

HOLLOWAY'S MEN'S SHOP, INC. (MW-2)

5430 N. Tryon St., #15 (m-b)
Charlotte, NC 28213
704-597-8153 / Fax: 704-597-7753
Sales: $100,001-$500,000

JAMES HOLLOWAY (Owner) & Buys Men's Sportswear, Accessories, Young Men's Wear, 8 to 20 Boys' Wear, Urban Contemporary, Store Displays, Fixtures, Supplies

BETTY LITTLE (Mgr.) & Buys Men's Sportswear, Accessories, Young Men's Wear, 8 to 20 Boys' Wear, Footwear, Store Displays, Fixtures, Supplies

JESSE BROWN'S OUTDOORS (CLO-2 & OL)

Sharon Corners, #2M (b)
4732 Sharon Rd.
Charlotte, NC 28210
704-556-0020 / Fax: 704-556-9447
Sales: $1 Million-$10 Million
Website: www.jessebrown.com

BILL DARTEE (President)

CHIP RATTEREE-Men's Raincoats, Footwear, Active Apparel, Outdoor Wear

SUZY JOHNSON-Men's Sweaters

LEBO'S SHOE STORE, INC. (FW-6 & MO)

(LEBO'S)
2321 Crown Centre Dr. (bud-p-m-b)
Charlotte, NC 28227
704-321-5000 / Fax: 704-321-5100
Sales: $1 Million-$10 Million
Website: www.lebos.com

JEROME LEVIN (Chmn.)

GAYLE HENDERSON (Controller & Mgr.)

DEREK CRITCHER-Men's Footwear

MILTON'S CLOTHING CUPBOARD OF CHARLOTTE (MW)

8128 Providence Rd. (m-b)
Charlotte, NC 28277
704-364-8686 / Fax: 704-366-1292
Website: www.brucejulian.com

BRUCE JULIAN (President) & Buys Men's Sportswear, Dress Shirts, Ties, Hosiery, Gloves, Headwear, Accessories, Footwear, Store Displays, Fixtures, Supplies

NEW STYLE SETTER (MW)

2313 Lasalle St. (m)
Charlotte, NC 28216
704-399-0324 / Fax: 704-399-0324

MR. GOINGS (Owner) & Buys Men's Sportswear, Furnishings, Accessories

NIGHT DREAMS OF CHARLOTTE (CLO)

(ADAM & EVE)
5309 E. Independence Blvd., #F
Charlotte, NC 28212
704-567-5515 / Fax: 704-567-6007

PAUL WILLIAMS (Owner) & Buys Swimwear

OUTFITTERS (MW)

3205 Freedom Dr., #35B (m-b)
Charlotte, NC 28208
704-391-8837

LARRY GUNRAJ (Owner) & Buys Men's Sportswear, Furnishings, Accessories, Boys' 4 to 7 & 8 to 20

PAUL SIMON CO. (MW-2)

1027 Providence Rd. (b)
Charlotte, NC 28207
704-372-6842 / Fax: 704-372-3201
Website: www.paulsimonco.com

PAUL SIMON (Owner) & Buys Men's Sweaters, Sport Shirts, Casual Slacks, Outer Jackets, Active Apparel, Leather Apparel, Accessories, Footwear, Store Displays, Fixtures, Supplies

RACK ROOM SHOES, INC. (FW-320)

(THE DEISCHMANN GROUP)
8310 Technology Dr. (m-b)
Charlotte, NC 28262
704-547-9200 / Fax: 704-547-8153
Sales: $100 Million-$500 Million
Website: www.rackroomshoes.com
Retail Locations: FL, GA, KY, MO, NC, OH, SC, TN, TX, VA

DJOERN GULDEN (President & C.E.O.)

DEREK BORDEAUX (V.P.-Mdse.)

BOBBY RAMMER-Men's Footwear

JUDY LEMMUN-Children's Footwear

JERRY APPLE-Accessories

JIM SHERRILL-Accessories

DAVE OSTERHUS (Real Estate Contact)

RUN FOR YOUR LIFE (SP)

2422 Park Rd.
Charlotte, NC 28203
704-358-0713 / Fax: 704-347-8102

LARRY FREDERICK (Owner) & Buys Running Related Activewear, Athletic Footwear

TAPACO, INC. (MW-2)

(TAYLOR, RICHARDS & CONGER)
6401 Morrison Blvd. (b)
Charlotte, NC 28211
704-366-9092 / Fax: 704-364-1152
Website: www.trcstyle.com

GLEN TAYLOR (Partner) & Buys Men's Footwear, Men's Sportswear, Furnishings, Accessories, Headwear, Young Men's Wear, 8 to 20 Boys' Wear, Store Displays, Fixtures, Supplies

RICHARD PATTISON (Partner) & Buys Men's Sportswear, Furnishings, Accessories, Headwear, Young Men's Wear, 8 to 20 Boys' Wear, Store Displays, Fixtures, Supplies

NORTH CAROLINA - Charlotte

TAYLOR, RICHARDS & CONGER (MW-2)
6401 Morrison Blvd.
Charlotte, NC 28211
704-366-9092 / Fax: 704-364-1152
Website: www.trcstyle.com
GLEN TAYLOR-Men's Apparel, Accessories

TOM JAMES CO. (CLO)
1200 E. Morehead St., #190 (m)
Charlotte, NC 28204
704-334-5301 / Fax: 704-334-5304
Website: www.tomjamesretail.com
KARL HAM (Owner) & Buys Men's Sportswear, Furnishings, Accessories, Boys' 8 to 20

BOOT HILL LEATHER SHOP (CLO)
P.O. Box 208 (m-b)
Hwy. 19
Cherokee, NC 28719
828-497-7981 / Fax: 828-497-7981
MARY JACOBS (Mgr.) & Buys Men's Leather Jackets, Small Leather Goods, Belts, Footwear, Accessories

MARINE CORPS EXCHANGE 0220 (PX-5)
Marine Corps Air Station, Bldg. 3918
Cherry Point, NC 28533
252-447-7041 / Fax: 252-447-2922
Sales: $10 Million-$50 Million
Website: www.aafes.com
PARAN WHEELER (Retail Officer)
DEBRA GARNER (Purch. Agent) & Buys Store Displays, Fixtures, Supplies
KAYE HARVEY-Men's Wear, Boys' Wear

ALPHA & OMEGA (CLO)
111 Wall St.
Clinton, NC 28328
910-590-2889
PAQUITA SMITH-Business, Formal and Religious Men's Wear, Sportswear, Furnishings, & Accessories
LONNIE SMITH-Business, Formal and Religious Men's Wear, Sportswear, Furnishings, Accessories

BIG BLUE STORE OF CLINTON, INC. (CLO)
149 Martin Luther King Blvd. (p-m)
Clinton, NC 28328
910-592-6707 / Fax: 910-592-1289
Sales: $1 Million-$10 Million
DELMAR POLLERT (President) & Buys Men's Work Clothes, Hosiery, Underwear, Footwear, Store Displays, Fixtures, Supplies

NETA'S, INC. (KS & SP)
27 Union St. South (bud)
Concord, NC 28025
704-782-2913
Sales: $500,000-$1 Million
NETA B. HELMS (Owner) & Buys 8 to 20 Boys' Wear, Store Displays, Fixtures, Supplies
KATHERINE PETREA (Mgr.) & Buys 8 to 20 Boys' Wear, Store Displays, Fixtures, Supplies

PHIDIPPIDES SPORTS CENTER (SP)
1400 Hwy. 29 North, #55
P.O. Box 1284
Concord, NC 28026
704-786-3312 / Fax: 704-786-3311
KEITH ALLEY (Owner) & Buys Athletic Footwear
EDDIE BONDS-Activewear, Athletics, Licensed Apparel

SHOE SHOW, INC. (FW-880)
(SHOE SHOW)
(SHOE DEPARTMENT)
2201 Trinity Church Rd. (p)
Concord, NC 28026
704-782-4143 / Fax: 704-782-3411
Website: www.shoeshow.com
Retail Locations: TX, OK, KS, WI, IA, MO, AK, LA, MS, TN, KY, IN, MI, OH, GA, FL, SC, NC, VA, WV, PA, MD, NJ, NY, CT, MA, VT, ME, NH, RI
ROBERT TUCKER (Owner)
DAVE KIMBALL-Men's Dress Footwear (Shoe Show)
ART HOGGE-Men's Athletic Footwear (Shoe Show)
CARL ROE-Men's Dress Footwear (Shoe Department)
BOB SEVOKEA-Men's Athletic Footwear (Shoe Department)
DWAYNE NEWELL-Boys' Dress Shoes, Casual Shoes, Slippers, Boots
JACQUELINE SNIPES-Men's Hosiery
KIRK KRULL (Real Estate Contact)

SHIRMARRO'S FASHIONS (MW)
1555 Lake Rd. (m-b)
Creedmoor, NC 27522
919-528-0364 / Fax: 919-528-0364
RON ELLIOT (Owner) & Buys Men's Sportswear, Leather Apparel, Accessories, Store Displays, Fixtures, Supplies

LOUIS BAER DEPARTMENT STORE, INC. (DEPT)
P.O. Box 399 (bud-p)
E. Broad St.
Dunn, NC 28334
910-892-3336
Sales: $100,001-$500,000
RONALD M. KIMMEL (President) & Buys Footwear
ANN NELSON-Men's Suits, Sportswear, Headwear, Furnishings, Accessories, Young Men's Wear, Boys' Wear
ELIZABETH WILLIFORD-Men's Wear

THE QUALITY SHOP, INC. (CLO)
201 E. Broad St. (bud-p-m)
Dunn, NC 28334
910-892-3593 / Fax: 910-892-3593
Sales: $500,000-$1 Million
CALLIE E. LEWIS (Co-Owner) & Buys Men's Footwear, Men's Sweaters, Sport Shirts, Outer Jackets, Casual Slacks, Leather Apparel, Active Apparel, Furnishings, Headwear, Boys' Wear, Urban Contemporary, Store Displays, Fixtures, Supplies
RONALD W. LEWIS (Co-Owner) & Buys Men's Sweaters, Sport Shirts, Outer Jackets, Casual Slacks, Leather Apparel, Active Apparel, Furnishings, Headwear, Boys' Wear, Store Displays, Fixtures, Supplies

RICHARD'S (CLO)
1903 West Cumberland St., #B (p-m)
Dunn, NC 28334
910-892-5510 / Fax: 910-892-5510
Sales: $100,001-$500,000
RICHARD BAER (Owner) & Buys Men's & Boys' Sportswear, Formal Wear, Footwear, Store Displays, Fixtures, Supplies

PEOPLES CLOTHING STORE (CLO)
345 W. Main St. (m)
Durham, NC 27701
919-688-6265
COFTON JOHNSON (Owner) & Buys Men's Sportswear, Footwear, Furnishings, Accessories

THARRINGTON'S CLOTHIERS (MW)
1103 W. Club Blvd. (b)
Durham, NC 27701
919-286-2216
Sales: $1 Million-$10 Million
Website: www.tharringtons.citysearch.com
PERRY R. THARRINGTON, III (President) & Buys Men's Overcoats, Suits, Tailored Jackets, Tailored Slacks, Raincoats, Sweaters, Sport Shirts, Outer Jackets, Casual Slacks, Leather Apparel, Dress Shirts, Ties, Robes, Underwear, Hosiery, Gloves, Headwear, Belts, Small Leather Goods, Footwear, Big & Tall Men's Wear, Store Displays, Fixtures, Supplies

VICKER'S CLOTHING, INC. (MW)
1821 Hillandale Rd. (p)
Durham, NC 27705
919-309-1169 / Fax: 919-383-1788
MACK VICKERS (Owner) & Buys Men's Sportswear, Furnishings, Accessories, Footwear

E.S. CHESSON & SON, INC. (DEPT)
P.O. Box 372 (p-m)
E. Main St.
Elizabeth City, NC 27909
252-335-4180 / Fax: 252-335-5312
Sales: $100,001-$500,000
BRANTLEY REDDING (President & Mdse. Mgr.) & Buys Men's & Students Wear, Footwear, Store Displays, Fixtures, Supplies

SUITS, INC. (MW & MO)
213 Piondexter St., #A (m-b)
Elizabeth City, NC 27909
252-335-9025 / Fax: 252-335-9564
TONY ROYAL (Owner) & Buys Men's Suits, Dress Shirts, Ties, Furnishings, Accessories

LEINWANDS, INC. (DEPT)
132 Broad St. (p-m-b)
Elizabethtown, NC 28337
910-862-3772 / Fax: 910-862-7346
RICHARD A. LEINWAND (President) & Buys Men's Sportswear, Leather Apparel, Accessories, Young Men's Wear, Urban Contemporary, 7 to 20 Boys' Wear, Footwear, Store Displays, Fixtures, Supplies

FAIRMONT DEPARTMENT STORE (DEPT)
203 S. Main St. (m)
Fairmont, NC 28340
910-628-7547 / Fax: 910-628-7547
Sales: $500,000-$1 Million
J. C. CAPPS (Owner)
JAY CAPPS (Mgr.) & Buys Men's Overcoats, Suits, Tailored Jackets, Tailored Slacks, Sportswear, Furnishings, Headwear, Belts, Jewelry, Small Leather Goods, Big & Tall Men's Wear, Young Men's & Boys' Clothing, Sportswear, Footwear, Store Displays, Fixtures, Supplies

CASTLE UNIFORMS (CLO-2 & MO)
1834 Owen Dr., #B
Fayetteville, NC 28304
910-485-4126 / Fax: 910-485-1825
Website: www.castleuniforms.com
HECTOR BLACK (Owner) & Buys Men's Medical Uniforms, Store Displays, Fixtures, Supplies
MISTI BASKETT-Men's Medical Uniforms, Store Displays, Fixtures, Supplies

FLEISHMAN'S TINY TOWN (KS)
P.O. Box 53447 (m-b-h)
3015 Fort Bragg Rd.
Fayetteville, NC 28305
910-323-1991 / Fax: 910-323-3940
MARILYN FLEISHMAN (Owner) & Buys Infants, Young Men's, 8 to 14 Boys' Wear, Boys' Footwear

LEON SUGAR'S, INC. (MW)
320 N. McPherson Church Rd. (h)
Fayetteville, NC 28303
910-864-2230 / Fax: 910-868-9829
Sales: $1 Million-$10 Million
MITCH SUGAR (Owner)
WILLIE EDGE (D.M.M.) & Buys Men's Sportswear, Furnishings, Headwear, Belts, Footwear, Store Displays, Fixtures, Supplies

SUNNY MENSWEAR (MW-2)
200 Hay St. (p-m-b)
Fayetteville, NC 28301
910-323-5724 / Fax: 910-323-8634
MR. SUNNY CHO (Owner) & Buys Men's Suits, Tailored Jackets, Tailored Slacks, Sweaters, Sport Shirts, Outer Jackets, Casual Slacks, Leather Apparel, Active Apparel, Headwear, Belts, Small Leather Goods, Jewelry, Fragrances, Footwear, Store Displays, Fixtures, Supplies

PEOPLES DEPARTMENT STORES, INC. (DEPT)
35 E. Main St. (p)
Franklin, NC 28734
828-524-3115 / Fax: 828-524-2800
Sales: $1 Million-$10 Million
JAMES C. JACOBS (President)
STEPHEN LONG (Gen. Mgr.) & Buys Men's & Boys' Wear, Leather Apparel, Footwear, Store Displays, Fixtures, Supplies

ASHWORTH'S, INC. (MW)
210 S. Main St. (m-b)
Fuquay-Varina, NC 27526
919-552-5201 / Fax: 919-552-7801
JAMES B. ASHWORTH (President & Owner) & Buys Men's Wear, Footwear, Store Displays, Fixtures, Supplies
STEVE ASHWORTH (V.P.) & Buys Men's Wear, Footwear, Store Displays, Fixtures, Supplies

BROADWAY FASHIONS (MW-2)
103 W. Main Ave. (m-b)
Gastonia, NC 28052
704-867-1161 / Fax: 704-861-1161
Website: www.kennymahtani.com
KENNY MAHTANI (Owner) & Buys Men's Sportswear, Furnishings, Accessories

GENTLEMEN'S CLOTHIERS LTD. (MW)
P.O. Box 1415 (m-b)
218 S. Railroad St.
Gastonia, NC 28053
704-730-9800
Sales: $500,000-$1 Million
ROY MOORE (Owner) & Buys Men's Overcoats, Suits, Tailored Jackets, Tailored Slacks, Raincoats, Sweaters, Sport Shirts, Outer Jackets, Casual Slacks, Furnishings, Headwear, Accessories, Boys' Clothing, Big & Tall Men's Wear, Store Displays, Fixtures, Supplies

MANHATTAN FASHIONS BIG & TALL (MW)
2956 Franklin Square Shopping Ctr.
Gastonia, NC 28054
704-854-3776
NEIL CHOPRA (Owner) & Buys Men's Big & Tall, Furnishings, Accessories

MERCHANT (CLO-2)
P.O. Box 5242 (m-b)
143 Eastridge Mall, #G
Gastonia, NC 28054
704-865-7841 / Fax: 704-853-2262
Sales: $1 Million-$10 Million
SALIM L. MERCHANT (President) & Buys Young & Progressive Suits, Men's Sweaters, Outer Jackets, Casual Slacks, Active Apparel, Dress Shirts, Ties, Sportswear, Leather, Footwear, Store Displays, Fixtures, Supplies

MR. K STORES, INC. (DEPT)
128 E. Main St. (p)
Gastonia, NC 28052
704-864-0721 / Fax: 704-854-9490
Sales: $500,000-$1 Million
MS. FRANKIE GARDIN (Owner) & Buys Big & Tall Men's Suits, Tailored Jackets, Tailored Slacks, Raincoats, Sweaters, Sport Shirts, Outer Jackets, Leather Apparel, Casual Slacks, Active Apparel, Furnishings, Headwear, Accessories, Footwear, Young Men's Wear, Store Displays, Fixtures, Supplies

ARIES FORMAL WEAR (MW)
319 N. Spence Ave. (m-b)
Goldsboro, NC 27534
919-778-8444
DEBRA HODGIN (Owner) & Buys Men's & Boys' Formal Wear

ATHLETE'S CHOICE (SP)
(M.I.S. HEEN ENTERPRISES, INC.)
625 E. Berkley Mall
Goldsboro, NC 27534
919-778-2690 / Fax: 919-778-2514
MIKE HANEY (Owner) & Buys Athletic Footwear, Activewear, Licensed Apparel

NORTH CAROLINA - Goldsboro

BEST & SAUL'S MEN'S SHOP (MW)
Sunrise Shopping Ctr. (m-b)
1725 E. Ash St.
Goldsboro, NC 27530
919-734-0866 / Fax: 919-734-8951
Sales: $100,001-$500,000
JERRY G. BEST (Owner) & Buys Men's Wear, Leather Apparel, Young Men's Wear, Store Displays, Fixtures, Supplies

CANNON'S MEN'S SHOP (MW-3)
(WILSON, INC.)
P.O. Box 10457 (m)
1803 Wayne Memorial Dr., #D
Goldsboro, NC 27530
919-734-0740 / Fax: 919-778-5896
GROVER CANNON (Owner) & Buys Men's & Boys' Wear, Footwear, Related Accessories & Furnishings, Store Displays, Fixtures, Supplies

COUNTRY VIEW WESTERN STORE (WW)
4070 US 70 East
Goldsboro, NC 27534
919-778-2452 / Fax: 919-778-1690
Website: www.country-view.com
MARVIN WORRELL, JR. (Co-Owner) & Buys Men's Western Wear, Leather Apparel, 8 to 16 Boys' Western Wear, Footwear, Store Displays, Fixtures, Supplies
EARLENE WORRELL (Co-Owner) & Buys Men's Western Wear, Leather Apparel, 8 to 16 Boys' Western Wear, Footwear, Store Displays, Fixtures, Supplies

NEW YORK FASHIONS (CLO)
121 E. Walnut St. (m-b)
Goldsboro, NC 27530
919-731-2550
ANDY BULCHANDANI (Owner) & Buys Men's Sportswear, Furnishings, Accessories

SPORTSMAN'S WORLD, INC. (MW-3)
200 W. Holly St. (m)
Goldsboro, NC 27530
919-731-7321 / Fax: 919-731-7356
Website: www.sportsmansworld.com
JIM BRYAN (Co-Owner)
RICHARD NARRON (Co-Owner)
KAY GOULDING-Men's & Boys' Athletic Apparel, Licensed Apparel

BLUMENTHAL'S, INC. (CLO-2)
358 S. Elm St. (p-m)
Greensboro, NC 27401
336-272-6363 / Fax: 336-272-4712
Sales: $1 Million-$10 Million
ROBERT L. BLUMENTHAL (President) & Buys Men's Sweaters, Sport Shirts, Outer Jackets, Casual Slacks, Leather Apparel, Furnishings, Headwear, Belts, Young Men's & Boys' Wear, All Footwear, Store Displays, Fixtures, Supplies

G.Q. FASHIONS (MW)
1022 Summit Ave.
Greensboro, NC 27405
336-274-1665 / Fax: 336-272-9255
YOUNG T. YU (Owner) & Buys Men's & Young Men's Wear, Footwear, Store Displays, Fixtures, Supplies

GORDON'S (MW)
3702 Lawndale Dr.
Greensboro, NC 27455
336-286-2620 / Fax: 336-286-2665
GORDON TURNER (Owner) & Buys Menswear, Mens Clothing, Furnishings, Footwear, Accessories

THE HUB LTD. (MW)
3900 W. Market St., #C (m-b)
Greensboro, NC 27407
336-292-6882 / Fax: 336-292-6938
Website: www.thehubltd.com
PEGGY TAGER (Owner)
KENT TAGER (President) & Buys Men's Sportswear, Accessories, Store Displays, Fixtures, Supplies
KEITH TAGER-Men's Sportswear, Accessories, Store Displays, Fixtures, Supplies

J. S. MEIER MEN'S STORE (MW)
803 Friendly Ctr. Rd., #A (m-b)
Greensboro, NC 27408
336-378-0006 / Fax: 336-852-6606
RONDA BENTS (Owner) & Buys Men's Casual Wear, Hosiery, Footwear

MITCHELL'S CLOTHING STORE (MW)
311 E. Market St. (m)
Greensboro, NC 27401
336-272-7002 / Fax: 336-272-6976
JOHN MITCHELL (Owner) & Buys Men's Sportswear, Furnishings, Accessories

RANKIN'S CLOTHING (CLO)
206 S. Elm St. (bud-p)
Greensboro, NC 27401
336-274-6310 / Fax: 336-334-0172
ROBERT RANKIN, JR. (Co-Owner) & Buys Men's Overcoats, Suits, Tailored Jackets, Tailored Slacks, Raincoats, Sweaters, Sport Shirts, Casual Slacks, Leather Apparel, Dress Shirts, Ties, Hosiery, Hats, Belts, Big & Tall Men's Wear, Boys' Jeans, T-shirts, Active Apparel, All Footwear, Store Displays, Fixtures, Supplies
ROBERT RANKIN, SR. (Co-Owner) & Buys Men's Overcoats, Suits, Tailored Jackets, Tailored Slacks, Raincoats, Sweaters, Sport Shirts, Casual Slacks, Leather Apparel, Dress Shirts, Ties, Hosiery, Hats, Belts, Big & Tall Men's Wear, Boys' Jeans, T-shirts, Active Apparel, All Footwear, Store Displays, Fixtures, Supplies

SCHIFFMAN'S, INC. (JWLY-7)
(KELLER & GEORGE)
(SHREVE & CO.)
(SYLVAN'S)
P.O. Box 1079
225 S. Elm St.
Greensboro, NC 27401
336-272-5146 / Fax: 336-272-5326
Sales: $10 Million-$50 Million
Website: www.schiffmans.com
ARNOLD SCHIFFMAN, JR. (President)
H. VANCE SCHIFFMAN (V.P.-Opers.) & Buys Loose Diamonds
ARNOLD SCHIFFMAN, III-Jewelry, Watches

SHOWFETY'S, INC. (MW)
116 E. Market St. (m)
Greensboro, NC 27401
336-272-7040 / Fax: 336-272-7805
MICHEL SHOWFETY (Owner) & Buys Men's Raincoats, Headwear, Belts, Work Uniforms, Footwear, Store Displays, Fixtures, Supplies

COFFMAN'S MENSWEAR, INC. (MW)
P.O. Box 854 (b)
505 Red Banks Rd.
Greenville, NC 27834
252-756-8237 / Fax: 252-756-6854
Sales: $1 Million-$10 Million
Website: www.coffmanmenswear.com
WILLIAM COFFMAN (Co-President) (@ 919-756-8237) & Buys Men's Suits, Sportswear, Furnishings, Accessories, Footwear, Store Displays, Fixtures, Supplies
JOHN COFFMAN (Co-President) & Buys Men's Suits, Sportswear, Furnishings, Accessories, Footwear, Store Displays, Fixtures, Supplies

FORT HENRY ARMY & NAVY STORE (AN)
1501 S. Evans St. (m)
Greenville, NC 27834
252-756-8781
Sales: $100,001-$500,000
MRS. HEATH (Owner) & Buys Military Apparel, Men's Sportswear, Leather Apparel, Furnishings, Headwear, Accessories, Big & Tall Men's Wear, Young Men's & Boys' Wear, Footwear, Store Displays, Fixtures, Supplies

OVERTON'S, INC. (MO & CLO-3 & OL)
111 Red Banks Rd.
Greenville, NC 27835
800-334-6541 / Fax: 252-355-2923
Website: www.overtons.com
V. PARKER OVERTON (President & Owner) & Buys Men's Sportswear, Underwear, Hosiery, Men's Accessories, Footwear
H. L. NORRIS (V.P.) & Buys Men's Sportswear, Underwear, Hosiery, Men's Accessories, Footwear

ANDERSON'S UNIFORM CO. (CLO)

P.O. Box 850 (m)
5630 Hwy. 49 North
Harrisburg, NC 28075
704-455-2102 / Fax: 704-455-1522

NORWOOD ANDERSON (Owner) & Buys Men's Medical & Civil Uniforms, Work Clothes, Footwear, Store Displays, Fixtures, Supplies

VANCE ATHLETIC SUPPLY CO., INC. (SP-8)

104 Market St.
Henderson, NC 27537
252-492-2321 / Fax: 252-492-1686
Sales: $2 Million-$5 Million

BOB NELSON (Co-Owner)

KURT MEADOWS (Co-Owner) & Buys Activewear, Athletic Footwear, Licensed Apparel

JOSEPH LAUGHTER CLOTHIER (MW)

1727 Brevard Rd., #C (m-b-des)
Hendersonville, NC 28791
828-697-7781

JOSEPH LAUGHTER (Owner) & Buys Men's Sportswear, Furnishings, Accessories

BROWN SHED (MW)

1734 N. Center St. (m)
Hickory, NC 28601
828-322-3869 / Fax: 828-324-2068

JIMMY BROWN (Owner) & Buys Men's Suits, Sportswear, Furnishings, Accessories, Footwear

LEE 'N' ANN'S, INC. (KS & SP)

1040 2nd St. NE (m-b)
Hickory, NC 28601
828-327-3532
Sales: $500,001-$1 Million

JANE H. MILLER (V.P.) & Buys Infants, Boys' Clothing, Young Men's, 8 to 20 Boys' Wear, Urban Contemporary, Boys' Footwear, Store Displays, Fixtures, Supplies, Shoes

MISTER TUXEDO OF HICKORY (MW)

336 Lenoir Rhyne Blvd. SE
Hickory, NC 28601
828-323-9181 / Fax: 828-328-9598

GREG LUCAS (Owner) & Buys Men's Tuxedos, Suits, Footwear, Accessories

LINDSAY ODOM LTD. (CLO)

1501 N. Main St. (p-m-b)
High Point, NC 27262
336-885-8500 / Fax: 336-885-9643

LINDSAY ODOM (Owner) & Buys Men's Sweaters, Sport Shirts, Outer Jackets, Tailored Clothing, Casual Slacks, Leather Apparel, Active Apparel, Furnishings, Accessories, Footwear, Store Displays, Fixtures, Supplies

SIGMON'S FASHIONS, INC. (CLO)

2730 Hickory Blvd. (bud-p-m)
Hudson, NC 28638
828-728-6725 / Fax: 828-726-0536
Sales: $1 Million-$10 Million

RUPERT SIGMON (President) & Buys Men's Sportswear, Leather Apparel, Belts, Small Leather Goods, Ties, 8 to 20 Boys' Wear, Men's Shoes, Store Displays, Fixtures, Supplies

TIM SIGMON-Men's Sportswear, Leather Apparel, Belts, Small Leather Goods, Ties, 8 to 20 Boys' Wear, Urban Contemporary, Men's Shoes, Store Displays, Fixtures, Supplies

MARGOLIS MEN'S STORE (MW)

Westwood Village Shopping Ctr. (b)
1140 Western Blvd.
Jacksonville, NC 28546
910-455-3797 / Fax: 910-455-3969

LLOYD KOONCE (Owner) & Buys Men's Sportswear, Furnishings, Footwear, Store Displays, Fixtures, Supplies

COTTON GIN, INC. (DEPT)

Deep Creek Farm (p-m)
Jarvisburg, NC 27947
252-491-2387 / Fax: 252-491-8668
Website: www.cottongin.com

THOMAS WRIGHT (Owner) & Buys Men's Sportswear, Footwear, Furnishings & Accessories, Store Displays, Fixtures, Supplies

J & J APPAREL STORE, INC. (CLO)

7384 NC 222 West (m)
Kenly, NC 27542
919-284-4002 / Fax: 919-284-2924

STEVE JOHNSON (Co-Owner)

CHRIS JOHNSON (Co-Owner) & Buys Men's & Boys' Sportswear, Urban Contemporary, Furnishings, Store Displays, Fixtures, Supplies

BIRTHDAY SUITS (CLO-4)

P.O. Box 2436
2000 S. Croatan Hwy.
Kill Devil Hills, NC 27948
252-441-5338 / Fax: 252-449-8428
Website: www.birthday-suits.com

GREG BENNETT (Co-Owner) & Buys Boys' Swimwear, Sunglasses, Accessories, Footwear, Hats, Men's Apparel, Men's Surf & Swimwear, Resortwear, T-shirts, Imprinted Sportswear

JILL BENNETT (Co-Owner) & Buys Boys' Swimwear, Sunglasses, Accessories, Footwear, Hats, Men's Apparel, Men's Surf & Swimwear, Resortwear, T-shirts, Imprinted Sportswear

McGINNIS DEPARTMENT STORE (DEPT)

243 S. Battleground Ave.
Kings Mountain, NC 28086
704-739-3116 / Fax: 704-730-0056

JOHN McGINNIS (Owner) & Buys Men's Sportswear, T-shirts, Dress Shirts, Ties, Robes, Underwear, Hosiery, Gloves, Headwear, Belts, Small Leather Goods, Young Men's Wear, Urban Contemporary, 8 to 20 Boys' Wear, Men's & Boys' Athletic Footwear, Store Displays, Fixtures, Supplies

SAGESPORT, INC. (CLO-7 & OL)

P.O. Box 1129 (m)
815 Floyd St.
Kings Mountain, NC 28086
704-739-2366 / Fax: 704-739-7059
Website: www.sagesport.com

CORKY FULTON (G.M.M.) & Buys Men's Athletic Apparel, Licensed Apparel, Shoes, Urban Contemporary, Store Displays, Fixtures, Supplies

STEVE McCACHREN-Men's Wear, Young Men's Wear, Boys' Wear

H. STADIEM, INC. (MW)

P.O. Box 338 (m)
124 N. Queen St.
Kinston, NC 28501
252-527-1166 / Fax: 252-527-3240
Sales: $1 Million-$10 Million

HYMAN STADIEM (President) & Buys Men's Sportswear, Footwear, Store Displays, Fixtures, Supplies

SUE MADSEN-Boys' Wear, Footwear, Urban Contemporary

JOSH ALLEN MENSWEAR (MW)

225 E. New Bern Rd. (b)
Kinston, NC 28501
252-527-9675 / Fax: 252-527-9675

BOB SMITH (Owner) & Buys Men's Suits, Tailored Jackets, Tailored Slacks, Big & Tall Men's Wear, Sweaters, Sport Shirts, Casual Slacks, Active Apparel, Dress Shirts, Ties, Hosiery, Belts, Store Displays, Fixtures, Supplies

PEARSON'S DEPARTMENT STORES (DEPT)

(BERT'S SURF SHOP)
P.O. Box 96 (p-m-b)
210 New Bern Rd.
Kinston, NC 28501
252-527-0845 / Fax: 252-527-3161

BERTRAM PEARSON (Co-Owner) & Buys Men's Wear, Boys' Wear, Urban Contemporary, Men's & Boys' Footwear, Store Displays, Fixtures, Supplies

GLORIA PEARSON (Co-Owner) & Buys Men's Wear, Boys' Wear, Men's & Boys' Footwear, Store Displays, Fixtures, Supplies

TOPS-BOTTOMS-SOULS (MW)

135 N. Queen St. (m)
Kinston, NC 28501
252--523-7466 / Fax: 252-527-9441

ALPHONZO BRIGGERS (Owner) & Buys Men's Sportswear, Furnishings, Accessories, Boys' 4 to 7 & 8 to 20

GRAY'S, INC. (DEPT-6 & OL)

P.O. Box 1097 (m-b)
Kitty Hawk, NC 27949
800-382-5006 / Fax: 252-261-1792
Sales: $1 Million-$10 Million
Website: www.grays-sportswear.com

JULIE GRAY (Co-Owner)
LARRY GRAY (Co-Owner)
RONNIE GRAY (Co-Owner) & Buys Men's Sweaters, Sportswear, Leather Apparel, Active Apparel, Sport Shirts, Casual Slacks, Belts, Outer Jackets, Jewelry, Boys' Sportswear, Urban Contemporary, Young Men's Wear, Boys' Wear

JUST FOR THE BEACH (DEPT-3)

P.O. Box 8004 (bud-m)
Kitty Hawk, NC 27969
252-453-2393 / Fax: 252-261-5653
Website: www.justforthebeach.com

BETTY HALL (Co-Owner) & Buys Footwear, Men's, Young Men's & Boys' Beachwear, Store Displays, Fixtures, Supplies
KEN HAGOOD (Co-Owner) & Buys Men's, Young Men's & Boys' Beachwear, Store Displays, Fixtures, Supplies

THE MEN'S DEN (MW)

(SUTTON SHOES)
7943 Hwy. 70 West (m)
La Grange, NC 28551
252-566-4230 / Fax: 252-566-4523

DARRELL SUTTON (Owner) & Buys Men's Overcoats, Suits, Tailored Jackets, Tailored Slacks, Sweaters, Sport Shirts, Outer Jackets, Leather Apparel, Casual Slacks, Activewear, Dress Shirts, Ties, Underwear, Hosiery, Headwear, Accessories, Footwear, Big & Tall Men's Wear, Young Men's Wear, Urban Contemporary, Store Displays, Fixtures, Supplies

BARRON'S MENSWEAR (MW)

131 S. Main St. (p)
Laurinburg, NC 28352
910-276-3483 / Fax: 910-276-3484

DAVID STONE (Owner) & Buys Men's Suits, Sportswear, Leather Apparel, Furnishings, Headwear, Accessories, Footwear, Big & Tall Men's Wear, Young Men's & Boys' Wear, Urban Contemporary, Footwear, Store Displays, Fixtures, Supplies

J.E. WOMBLE & SON, INC. (GM)

805 Front St.
Lillington, NC 27546
910-893-5753 / Fax: 910-893-6420

RAY WOMBLE, JR. (Owner) & Buys Men's, Young Men's & Boys' Work Clothes, Boots, Store Displays, Fixtures, Supplies
CAMERON MARTIN (Mgr.) & Buys Men's, Young Men's & Boys' Work Clothes, Boots, Store Displays, Fixtures, Supplies

ROWE'S MEN'S SHOP, INC. (MW)

136 Shannon Village Shopping Ctr.
Louisburg, NC 27549
919-496-3573 / Fax: 919-496-0101

MIKE ROWE (Owner) & Buys Men's Apparel, Footwear, Accessories

WASHINGTON MEN'S STORE (MW)

P.O. Box 339 (m)
302 N. Elm St.
Lumberton, NC 28358
910-738-7712 / Fax: 910-738-8198

W. C. WASHINGTON (Co-Owner) & Buys Men's Overcoats, Suits, Tuxedos, Tailored Jackets, Tailored Slacks, Raincoats, Sweaters, Sport Shirts, Outer Jackets, Leather Apparel, Casual Slacks, Active Apparel, Dress Shirts, Ties, Robes, Underwear, Hosiery, Gloves, Headwear, Belts, Jewelry, Small Leather Goods, Footwear, Urban Contemporary, Store Displays, Fixtures, Supplies
JOAN WASHINGTON (Co-Owner) & Buys Men's Overcoats, Suits, Tuxedos, Tailored Jackets, Tailored Slacks, Raincoats, Sweaters, Sport Shirts, Outer Jackets, Leather Apparel, Casual Slacks, Active Apparel, Dress Shirts, Ties, Robes, Underwear, Hosiery, Gloves, Headwear, Belts, Jewelry, Small Leather Goods, Footwear, Store Displays, Fixtures, Supplies

PENLAND & SONS DEPARTMENT STORE (DEPT)

P.O. Box 272 (p-m-b)
Main St.
Marshall, NC 28753
828-649-2811

BARBARA PENLAND (Owner) & Buys Boys' Swimwear, Sunglasses, Accessories, Footwear, Hats, Men's Apparel, Men's Surf & Swimwear, Resortwear, T-shirts, Imprinted Sportswear

BENJAMIN'S (CLO)

100 N. Sterling St. (m)
Morganton, NC 28655
828-437-7272 / Fax: 828-437-7393
Website: www.intermezzocollection.com

BEN BELTON (Owner) & Buys Men's Sportswear, Furnishings, Accessories

LIM'S MENSWEAR (MW-15)

(J.H.D. ENTERPRISES LTD.)
100 Center St., Suite 600 (bud-p-m-b-h)
Morrisville, NC 27560
919-465-2024 / Fax: 919-465-2021
Sales: $10 Million-$50 Million

YUL LIM (C.O.O. & Co-Owner) & Buys Store Displays, Fixtures, Supplies, Men's Suits, Overcoats, Sportswear, Accessories, Footwear, Big & Tall Men's Wear
BOBBY LIM (V.P. & Co-Owner) & Buys Men's Suits, Overcoats, Sportswear, Accessories, Footwear, Big & Tall Men's Wear, Urban Contemporary

BRINTLE'S TRAVEL STORE (CLO)

125 Plaza Ln.
Mount Airy, NC 27030
336-352-3161 / Fax: 336-352-3167
Sales: $1 Million-$10 Million
Website: www.brintles.com

THOMAS BRINTLE (Owner)
SUSAN EDWARDS (Mgr.) & Buys Raincoats, Sportswear, Furnishings, Accessories, Footwear, Young Men's & Boys' Wear, Store Displays, Fixtures, Supplies

F. REES CO., INC. (MW)

198 N. Main St. (b)
Mount Airy, NC 27030
336-786-6121 / Fax: 336-786-5391
Sales: $1 Million-$10 Million

F. EUGENE REES, JR. (President) & Buys Men's Overcoats, Suits, Tailored Jackets, Tailored Slacks, Raincoats, Sportswear, Dress Shirts, Ties, Robes, Underwear, Hosiery, Gloves, Tuxedos, Accessories, Footwear, Big & Tall Men's Wear

ROBBY'S SALES, INC. (DEPT)

457 N. Main St. (m)
Mount Airy, NC 27030
336-786-8017 / Fax: 336-786-8599

JAKE ROBERTSON (President & Owner) & Buys Men's Jeans, T-shirts, Leather Jackets, Underwear, Gloves, Headwear, Belts, Small Leather Goods, Active Apparel, Footwear, Store Displays, Fixtures, Supplies
DANNY LEDFORD-Men's Jeans, T-shirts, Leather Jackets, Underwear, Gloves, Headwear, Belts, Small Leather Goods, Active Apparel, Footwear, Store Displays, Fixtures, Supplies

SCENIC OUTLET (CLO)

113 Scenic Outlet Ln. (p)
Mount Airy, NC 27030
336-352-4500 / Fax: 336-352-3387
Sales: $1 Million-$10 Million

GROVER HAYMORE (Owner) & Buys Men's Overcoats, Tailored Jackets, Tailored Slacks, Raincoats, Big & Tall Men's Wear, Sweaters, Sport Shirts, Outer Jackets, Leather Apparel, Casual Slacks, Active Apparel, T-shirts, Dress Shirts, Ties, Underwear, Hosiery, Headwear, Belts, Young Men's Wear, 8 to 20 Boys' Wear

WHALEBONE SURF SHOP (SG-2)

2214 S. Croatan Hwy. (p)
Nags Head, NC 27949
252-441-6747 / Fax: 252-261-6024
Website: www.whalebonesurfshop.com

JIM VAUGHAN (Co-Owner) & Buys Men's Swimwear, T-shirts, Surf Gear, Active Apparel, Headwear

APRIL VAUGHAN (Co-Owner) & Buys Men's Swimwear, T-shirts, Surf Gear, Active Apparel, Headwear

WORLD FASHIONS (CLO)

2701 Neuse Blvd. (bud)
New Bern, NC 28560
252-638-6151 / Fax: 252-636-3678

NANCY WHEELER (Owner) & Buys Men's Suits, Sportswear, Furnishings, Accessories, Young Men's Wear, Urban Contemporary, 8 to 20 Boys' Wear, Men's & Boys' Footwear, Store Displays, Fixtures, Supplies

MARSHA & CO. (CLO)

P.O. Box 298 (m)
Newton Grove, NC 298
910-594-0502 / Fax: 910-594-2235
Sales: Under $100,000

JUNE HAIRR (Owner) & Buys Men's Casual Wear

J.R. PRIESTER'S CLOTHES (CLO)

903 Main St. (b)
North Wilkesboro, NC 28659
336-838-2531 / Fax: 336-838-2132

J. R. PRIESTER, SR. (President)

JIM PRIESTER, JR. (Secy. & Treas.) & Buys Men's Wear, Footwear, Store Displays, Fixtures, Supplies

SMITHEY'S OF NORTH WILKESBORO (DEPT-2)

319 10th St. (m)
North Wilkesboro, NC 28659
336-838-4012
Sales: $100,001-$500,000

CLYDE HOLLAND (President) & Buys Men's Overcoats, Suits, Tailored Jackets, Tailored Slacks, Raincoats, Sportswear, Sweaters, Sport Shirts, Outer Jackets, Active Apparel, Furnishings, Belts, Small Leather Goods, Young Men's & Boys' Wear, Store Displays, Fixtures, Supplies

FLAMINGO ROW (CLO)

13 E. 1st St. (p)
Ocean Isle Beach, NC 28469
910-579-3126 / Fax: 910-597-3035

SIMON CHITRIT (Owner) & Buys Men's Western Wear, Swimwear, Beach Shoes, Store Displays, Fixtures, Supplies

INLAND WATERWAY TREASURE CO. (CLO)

P.O. Box 850 (p-m)
Hodges St.
Oriental, NC 28571
252-249-1797 / Fax: 252-249-3099
Website: www.inlandwaterwayonline.com

J.H. WINSTON (Co-Owner) & Buys Men's T-shirts, Sweaters, Active Apparel, Gloves, Belts, Headwear, Outer Jackets, Casual Shoes, Store Displays, Fixtures, Supplies

PAULA WINSTON (Co-Owner) & Buys Men's T-shirts, Sweaters, Active Apparel, Gloves, Belts, Headwear, Outer Jackets, Casual Shoes, Store Displays, Fixtures, Supplies

GENTLEMAN'S CORNER, INC. (MW)

P.O. Box 1377 (b)
Village Sq.
Pinehurst, NC 28374
910-295-2011 / Fax: 910-295-0429

CHRIS DALRYMPLE (Owner) & Buys Tailored Jackets, Sportswear, Furnishings, Store Displays, Fixtures, Supplies

NEW YORK HI STYLE (MW-2)

111 Washington St. (p)
Plymouth, NC 27962
252-946-2599 / Fax: 252-793-4177

ANDY LALWANI (Owner) & Buys Men's Tuxedos, Sportswear, Furnishings, Accessories, Young Men's, Boys' Wear, Footwear, Urban Contemporary, Store Displays, Fixtures, Supplies

CHOCKEY'S (MW)

1641 N. Market Dr. (h)
Raleigh, NC 27609
919-872-3166 / Fax: 919-850-3261
Sales: $500,001-$1 Million
Website: www.chockeysmensfashion.com

CHOCKEY KASSEM (Owner) & Buys Men's Sportswear, Furnishings, Accessories, Headwear, Footwear, Store Displays, Fixtures & Supplies

CITY IN THE SOUTH, INC. (CLO)

1404 New Bern Ave.
Raleigh, NC 27610
919-839-0888 / Fax: 919-839-0705
Website: www.cityinthesouth.com

JAMES McCULLOUGH (Co-Owner)

TRAUNL CARTER (Co-Owner) & Buys Urban Contemporary, Hats, Belts, Cologne and Gold Tooth Fronts

GINGISS FORMAL WEAR (MW-2)

(THALGURL, INC.)
7106 Glenwood Ave. (m)
Raleigh, NC 27612
919-783-8911 / Fax: 919-783-8912
Website: www.gingiss.com/raleigh

DENISE MAEYAERT (Owner) & Buys Men's Formal Wear, Store Displays, Fixtures, Supplies

GREAT OUTDOOR PROVISION CO. (CLO-7)

2017 Cameron St. (m)
Raleigh, NC 27605
919-833-1741 / Fax: 919-839-2011
Website: www.greatoutdoorprovision.com

TOM VALONE (President & Owner)

SHEILA BROWN-Men's Sportswear, Men's Casual Wear, Outdoor Apparel, Shoes, Belts

ISAACS' MEN'S STORE (MW)

309 S. Wilmington St. (m-b)
Raleigh, NC 27601
919-834-4978 / Fax: 919-834-8535

SHALOM ROKACH (Owner) & Buys Men's Sportswear, Furnishings, Accessories

LIBERTY FASHIONS (MW)

333 S. Wilmington St. (m-b)
Raleigh, NC 27601
919-821-1787

MR. ILUNG JOE (Owner) & Buys Men's Casual Wear

NCSU BOOKSTORES (SP)

(NORTH CAROLINA STATE UNIVERSITY)
P.O. Box 7224
Raleigh, NC 27695
919-515-2161 / Fax: 919-515-2618
Website: www.fis.ncsu.edu/ncsubookstores

RICHARD HAYES (Mgr.)

MELANIE WALL (Mdsg. & Mktg. Mgr.)

CASEY PETERS-Licensed Activewear, Pants, Jackets, Hosiery

NORTH CAROLINA - Raleigh

NOWELL'S CLOTHING CO., INC. (MW)
P.O. Box 10005 (b-h)
435 Daniel St.
Raleigh, NC 27605
919-828-7285 / Fax: 919-828-8118
Sales: $1 Million-$10 Million
Website: www.nowellsclothing.com
SCHOONER NOWELL (Owner) & Buys Men's Suits, Formalwear, Sportswear, Sweaters, Furnishings, Dress Shirts, Accessories, Belts, Footwear
MS. LUBET NOWELL-Store Displays, Fixtures, Supplies

V.I.P. FORMAL WEAR, INC. (MW-7)
3801 S. Wilmington St. (p-m-b-des)
Raleigh, NC 27603
919-772-7215 / Fax: 919-662-8562
Website: www.vipformalwear.com
FRED MILLER (Owner) & Buys Men's Formal Wear, Accessories, Big & Tall Men's Formal Wear, 8 to 18 Boys' Formal Wear, Men's & Boys' Footwear, Related Furnishings & Accessories

VARSITY MENSWEAR (MW)
4325 Glenwood Ave., #2152 (b)
Raleigh, NC 27622
919-782-2570 / Fax: 919-782-5129
Sales: $1 Million-$10 Million
Website: www.varsitymenswear
HARRY POLLOCK (President) & Buys Men's Overcoats, Suits, Tailored Jackets, Tailored Slacks, Raincoats, Sweaters, Sport Shirts, Outer Jackets, Leather Apparel, Dress Shirts, Ties, Underwear, Hosiery, Belts, Small Leather Goods, Jewelry, Fragrances, Footwear, Urban Contemporary, Store Displays, Fixtures, Supplies

ALEXANDREA'S (CLO)
2026 Cameron St.
Raleight, NC 27605
919-832-0005
SANDRA WORKMAN (Owner) & Buys Boys' Apparel, Boys' Swimwear, Men's Apparel, Swimwear

FREID'S, INC. (CLO)
1100 Roanoke Ave. (m)
Roanoke Rapids, NC 27870
252-537-9675
ROBERT BROWN (Owner) & Buys Men's Overcoats, Suits, Tailored Jackets, Tailored Slacks, Raincoats, Sweaters, Sport Shirts, Outer Jackets, Casual Slacks, Leather Apparel, Active Apparel, Headwear, Footwear, Big & Tall Men's Wear, Store Displays, Fixtures, Supplies

NEW YORK FASHIONS (MW)
1005 Roanoke Ave. (m)
Roanoke Rapids, NC 27870
252-535-3434 / Fax: 252-535-3434
Sales: $100,001-$500,000
KENNY LAKHIANI (Owner) & Buys Men's Sportswear, Furnishings, Accessories, Headwear, Young Men's Wear, Urban Contemporary, 8 to 20 Boys' Wear, Men's & Boys' Footwear, Store Displays, Fixtures, Supplies

SNIDER'S DEPARTMENT STORE (DEPT)
P.O. Box 457 (bud)
Main St.
Robbinsville, NC 28771
828-479-3414
Sales: $100,001-$500,000
CAROL S. WARD (Owner) & Buys Men's Sportswear, Furnishings, Boys' Wear, Accessories, Men's & Boys' Footwear, Store Displays, Fixtures, Supplies

R.W. GOODMAN CO., INC. (CLO)
119 S. Lee St. (p)
Rockingham, NC 28379
910-895-6342 / Fax: 910-895-1507
Sales: $1 Million-$10 Million
KENNETH GOODMAN (V.P. & Owner) & Buys Store Displays, Fixtures, Supplies
R. W. GOODMAN (V.P.)
KEVIN GARDNER-Men's Suits, Sportswear, Sports Shirts, Furnishings, Ties, Accessories

BULL'S EYE WESTERN WEAR (CLO)
(DURLEN, INC.)
1220 S. Wesleyan Blvd. (m)
Rocky Mount, NC 27803
252-977-1448 / Fax: 252-977-1448
Sales: $100,001-$500,000
WANDA PARKER (Co-Owner) & Buys Men's & Boys' Western Wear, Men's & Ladies Western Wear, Headwear, Men's & Boys' Footwear, Childrens Footwear, Store Displays, Fixtures, Supplies
TIM PARKER (Co-Owner) & Buys Men's & Boys' Western Wear, Men's & Ladies Western Wear, Headwear, Men's & Boys' Footwear, Childrens Footwear, Store Displays, Fixtures, Supplies

MANHATTAN MEN'S CLOTHING (MW-4)
1944 Stone Rose Ave.
Rocky Mount, NC 27804
252-972-9889 / Fax: 252-972-9708
FRANK YI (Owner)
DAVID SHIN (V.P.) & Buys Men's Suits, Sportswear, Furnishings, Accessories, Urban Contemporary, Boots, Footwear, Store Displays, Fixtures, Supplies

H.G. GREENE STORE (DEPT)
3203 Clingman Rd. (bud-p-m)
Ronda, NC 28670
336-984-3481
ROBERT GREENE (President) & Buys Men's Work Clothes, Hosiery, Headwear, Young Men's Work Clothes, Boys' Work Clothes, Men's & Boys' Work Shoes, Store Displays, Fixtures, Supplies

FOGLEMAN'S MEN'S SHOP (MW-2)
111 N. Main St.
Roxboro, NC 27573
336-599-2733 / Fax: 336-599-2733
CARL BOWES (Owner) & Buys Men's Suits, Sportswear, Footwear, Furnishings, Accessories

FOOTWEAR PLUS (WW)
2744 Durham Rd. (p-m)
Roxboro, NC 27573
336-597-8075 / Fax: 336-597-3895
C. W. CHAMBERS (Owner) & Buys Store Displays, Fixtures, Supplies
MIKE CHAMBERS (Mgr.) & Buys Men's Western Style Apparel, Leather Apparel, Western Headwear, Big & Tall Men's Wear, Boys' Western Wear, Men's & Boys' Boots, Store Displays, Fixtures and Supplies

HENRY DANIEL CLOTHIER (MW)
P.O. Box 278 (b)
117 S. Main St.
Roxboro, NC 27573
336-599-4182 / Fax: 336-599-4182
Sales: $500,000-$1 Million
HENRY S. DANIEL, JR. (President) & Buys Men's & Young Men's Wear Suits, Sportswear, Furnishings, Accessories, Store Displays, Fixtures, Supplies

THE THREAD SHED FAMILY CLOTHING (CLO)
(LOFLIN'S ENTERPRISES, INC.)
133 S. Main St. (m)
Salisbury, NC 28144
704-633-1159 / Fax: 704-633-1162
DAVE LOFLIN (V.P.) & Buys Men's Suits, Tailored Jackets, Tailored Slacks, Big & Tall Men's Wear, Men's Sweaters, Sport Shirts, Outer Jackets, Casual Slacks, Active Apparel, T-shirts, Dress Shirts, Ties, Underwear, Hosiery, Gloves, Headwear, Belts, Small Leather Goods, Young Men's Wear, 8 to 20 Boys' Wear, Store Displays, Fixtures, Supplies

AVENT & THOMAS (DEPT)
124 E. Main St. (p)
Sanford, NC 27332
919-776-2311 / Fax: 919-777-2771
Sales: $100,001-$500,000
LYNWOOD JONES (President & Owner) & Buys Men's Sportswear, Young Men's & Boys' Jeans, Tops, Accessories, Store Displays, Fixtures, Supplies

A.V. WRAY & 6 SONS, INC. (CLO)

P.O. Box 65 (bud-p-m-b-des)
913 N. Lafayette St.
Shelby, NC 28150
704-482-3883 / Fax: 704-482-4355
Sales: $500,001-$1 Million

STOUGH WRAY, JR. (President)
SHELLY WRAY ROBERTS (Mgr.-Adv.) & Buys Men's Apparel, Boys' Apparel, Men's Footwear, Boys' Footwear, Accessories
LOU WRAY-Men's Apparel

BISH MILITARY SURPLUS (AN)

(BISH ENTERPRISES, INC.)
P.O. Box 451 (p)
277 Bish Rd.
Siler City, NC 27344
919-663-3336 / Fax: 919-663-2820

JOHN McSWEEN (President) & Buys Military Oriented Men's, Young Men's & Boys' Wear, Store Displays, Fixtures, Supplies

FARMER'S ALLIANCE STORE, INC. (GM)

134 S. Chatham Ave. (m)
Siler City, NC 27344
919-742-3020

ED CLAPP (President)
NANCY TYSOR (Mgr.) & Buys Men's Wear, Work Wear, Sportswear, Footwear, Young Men's & Boys' Wear, Store Displays, Fixtures, Supplies

HUGH AUSTIN'S STORE (MW)

237 E. Market St. (b)
Smithfield, NC 27577
919-934-8401

MARK AUSTIN (Owner) & Buys Men's Suits, Sportswear, Footwear, Furnishings, Accessories

MATCH PLAY OF PINEHURST (MW)

695 SW Broad St. (p-m-b)
Southern Pines, NC 28387
910-692-3741 / Fax: 910-695-1097

FRANCES SMITH (Co-Owner)
DOUGLAS SMITH (Co-Owner)
PAT GRADY (President)
PAT EASTER-Men's Golf Apparel

WELLBORN'S FOR MEN & BOYS (MW-2)

P.O. Box 129 (m)
209 Locust Ave.
Spruce Pine, NC 28777
828-765-2866 / Fax: 828-765-0928
Sales: $1 Million-$10 Million

JOHN WELLBORN (Co-Owner & G.M.M.) & Buys Men's Overcoats, Suits, Tailored Jackets, Tailored Slacks, Raincoats, Sweaters, Sport Shirts, Outer Jackets, Casual Slacks, Leather Apparel, Active Apparel, Dress Shirts, Ties, Robes, Underwear, Hosiery, Gloves, Headwear, Belts, Small Leather Goods, Jewelry, Fragrances, Workclothes, Footwear, Big & Tall Men's Wear, Store Displays, Fixtures, Supplies
SCOTTIE WELLBORN (Co-Owner) & Buys Sportswear, Furnishings, Accessories, Footwear, Store Displays, Fixtures and Supplies

PLYLER MEN'S STORE, INC. (MW)

101 W. Broad St. (m-b)
Statesville, NC 28677
704-873-6021 / Fax: 704-871-8873
Sales: $500,000-$1 Million

JOE PLYLER (President & G.M.M.) & Buys Men's Overcoats, Suits, Tailored Jackets, Tailored Slacks, Raincoats, Sweaters, Sport Shirts, Outer Jackets, Casual Slacks, Headwear, Dress Shirts, Ties, Robes, Belts, Jewelry, Footwear, Big & Tall Men's Wear, Store Displays, Fixtures, Supplies
LE ROY PLYLER (V.P.) & Buys Underwear, Hosiery, Small Leather Goods, Fragrances, Gloves

SURFSIDE SPORTSWEAR & GIFTS, INC. (SP)

P.O. Box 2220
314 N. New River Dr.
Surf City, NC 28445
910-328-4141 / Fax: 910-328-4460
Sales: $501,000-$1 Million
Website: www.surfsidesportswear.com

LORI HOWARD (Owner)
ELIZABETH FUSSELL-Swimwear, Beachwear, Beach Footwear

ZACK'S OF TOPSAIL (CLO)

P.O. Box 2675
Surf City, NC 28445
910-328-5904 / Fax: 910-328-5905

SANDY MINNICH (Owner) & Buys Fashion Accessories, Footwear, Men's Apparel, Men's Surf & Swimwear, Resorts Wear, T-shirts, Imprinted Sportswear

SCHULMAN'S DEPARTMENT STORE (DEPT)

P.O. Box 7 (p-m-b)
35 E. Main St.
Sylva, NC 28779
828-586-2716

SOL SCHULMAN (Owner) & Buys Men's Suits, Formal Wear, Sweaters, Sport Shirts, Outer Jackets, Casual Slacks, Leather Apparel, Active Apparel, Furnishings, Headwear, Accessories, Footwear, Young Men's & Boys' Wear, Store Displays, Fixtures, Supplies

MAST GENERAL STORE, INC. (GM-5)

(OLD BOONE MERCANTILE)
(MAST STORE ANNEX)
Hwy. 194 South (m)
Valle Crucis, NC 28691
828-963-6511 / Fax: 828-963-1883
Sales: $10 Million-$50 Million
Website: www.mastgeneralstore.com

FAYE COOPER (Co-Owner)
JOHN COOPER (Co-Owner)
FRED MARTIN (G.M.M. & V.P.) & Buys Men's Sweaters, Sport Shirts, Casual Slacks, Active Apparel, T-shirts, Jeans, Dress Shirts, Ties, Gloves, Hats, Small Leather Goods, Belts, Young Men's Wear
WILLIAM WILSON-Men's Sweaters, Sport Shirts, Casual Slacks, Active Apparel, T-shirts, Jeans, Dress Shirts, Ties, Gloves, Hats, Small Leather Goods, Belts, Young Men's Wear
KAREN HOFFMAN-Gloves, Hats, Accessories, Belts
MICHELLE MILLER-Boys' Footwear
JIM BROWN-Boys' Footwear

HILTON'S MEN'S SHOP (MW)

P.O. Box 831 (m)
111 W. Main St.
Washington, NC 27889
252-946-5951
Sales: $100,001-$500,000

HILTON E. SAWYER (President & G.M.M.) & Buys Men's Overcoats, Suits, Tailored Jackets, Tailored Slacks, Raincoats, Big & Tall Men's Wear, Sweaters, Sport Shirts, Outer Jackets, Leather Apparel, Casual Slacks, Dress Shirts, Ties, Robes, Underwear, Hosiery, Gloves, Belts, Jewelry, Small Leather Goods, Hats, Footwear, Fragrances, Store Displays, Fixtures, Supplies

RUSSELL'S MEN'S SHOP (MW)

118 W. Main St. (m)
Washington, NC 27889
252-946-2120

RUSSELL SMITH (Owner) & Buys Men's Suits, Sportswear, Furnishings, Accessories
NORWOOD CHERRY-Men's Suits, Sportswear, Furnishings, Accessories

KANNON'S CLOTHING, INC. (CLO)

P.O. Box 1540 (b)
10 Main St.
Wendell, NC 27591
919-365-7074 / Fax: 919-365-0370
Sales: $1 Million-$10 Million

GEORGE KNUCKLEY (President, G.M.M. & Co-Owner) & Buys Men's Overcoats, Suits, Tailored Jackets, Tailored Slacks, Raincoats, Sweaters, Sport Shirts, Outer Jackets, Casual Slacks, Leather Apparel, Active Apparel, Furnishings, Headwear, Accessories, Footwear, Store Displays, Fixtures, Supplies

BOO JEFFERSON (G.M.M. & Co-Owner) & Buys Men's Overcoats, Suits, Tailored Jackets, Tailored Slacks, Raincoats, Sweaters, Sport Shirts, Outer Jackets, Casual Slacks, Leather Apparel, Active Apparel, Furnishings, Headwear, Accessories, Footwear, Store Displays, Fixtures, Supplies

JOE ANN WRIGHT (G.M.M. & Co-Owner) & Buys Men's Overcoats, Suits, Tailored Jackets, Tailored Slacks, Raincoats, Sweaters, Sport Shirts, Outer Jackets, Casual Slacks, Leather Apparel, Active Apparel, Furnishings, Headwear, Accessories, Footwear, Store Displays, Fixtures, Supplies

McNEILL'S DEPARTMENT STORE (DEPT)

P.O. Box 727 (p-m-b)
2 N. Jefferson Ave.
West Jefferson, NC 28694
336-246-7362 / Fax: 336-246-7362
Sales: $100,001-$500,000

ROBBIN L. McNEILL (Owner) & Buys Men's Suits, Sportswear, Furnishings, Accessories, Store Displays, Fixtures, Supplies

BRANDON LEMLY-Men's Suits, Sportswear, Furnishings, Accessories, Store Displays, Fixtures, Supplies

KRAMER'S (CLO)

707 S. Madison Ave. (b)
Whiteville, NC 28472
910-642-2006 / Fax: 910-642-2006

H. KRAMER (President)

MICHAEL KRAMER (V.P.) & Buys Men's Suits, Sportswear, Furnishings, Accessories, Leather Apparel, Footwear, Young Men's Wear, Store Displays, Fixtures, Supplies

MOSKOW'S, INC. (CLO)

729 S. Madison St. (p-m)
Whiteville, NC 28472
910-642-2320

A. H. MOSKOW (President) & Buys Men's Suits, Tailored Jackets, Tailored Slacks, Sweaters, Sport Shirts, Outer Jackets, Casual Slacks, Leather Apparel, Active Apparel, Headwear, Furnishings, Accessories, Footwear, Young Men's & Boys' Wear

STEVE MOSKOW (V.P.) & Buys Men's Suits, Tailored Jackets, Tailored Slacks, Sweaters, Sport Shirts, Outer Jackets, Casual Slacks, Leather Apparel, Active Apparel, Headwear, Furnishings, Accessories, Footwear, Young Men's & Boys' Wear, Urban Contemporary

MARTIN SUPPLY CO., INC. (DEPT)

217 Washington St. (m)
Williamston, NC 27892
252-792-2123 / Fax: 252-792-2976
Sales: $100,001-$500,000

GEORGE GRIFFIN, III (Mgr.) & Buys Men's Work Clothes, Sport Shirts, Sweaters, Outer Jackets, Gloves, Headwear, Belts, Work Shoes, Store Displays, Fixtures, Supplies

ANDERSON CLOTHING CO. (CLO)

4107 Oleander Dr.
Wilmington, NC 28403
910-794-4448 / Fax: 910-313-3323

STEVE ANDERSON (Owner) & Buys Sportswear, Sport Shirts, Active Wear, Headwear, Athletic Footwear

B. LEONARD (MW)

32 N. Front St. (b-des)
Wilmington, NC 28401
910-343-1899 / Fax: 910-762-8609

BENJAMIN L. D'LUGIN, JR. (President) & Buys Men's Overcoats, Suits, Tailored Jackets, Tailored Slacks, Raincoats, Sweaters, Sport Shirts, Outer Jackets, Casual Slacks, Active Apparel, Furnishings, Headwear, Belts, Small Leather Goods, Leather Apparel, Store Displays, Fixtures, Supplies

CANADY'S SPORTS CENTER, INC. (SG)

3220 Wrightsville Ave. (m)
Wilmington, NC 28403
910-791-6280 / Fax: 910-791-0034

ROBERT ORRELL (V.P.)

JAMIE WILSON-Men's Sportswear, Hunting Apparel

FLEISHMAN'S FINE CLOTHIERS (CLO)

3500 Oleander Dr., #F6 (b)
Wilmington, NC 28403
910-799-4861 / Fax: 910-799-4867

NEAL FLEISHMAN (Owner) & Buys Men's Suits, Sweaters, Sport Shirts, Outer Jackets, Leather Apparel, Casual Slacks, Active Apparel, Furnishings, Footwear, Store Displays, Fixtures, Supplies

GENTRY HOUSE (MW)

3500 Oleander Dr., #2B (m-b)
Wilmington, NC 28403
910-392-1338 / Fax: 910-392-2857

KENDAL REGISTER (Owner) & Buys Men's Sportswear, Furnishings, Accessories

ISAAC'S MEN'S STORE (MW)

102 N. Front St. (p-m)
Wilmington, NC 28401
910-763-8185 / Fax: 910-763-8185

ISAAC LAZARO (Owner) & Buys Men's Sportswear, Furnishings, Accessories, Boys' 8 to 20

R. BRYAN & CO. (MW)

1908 Eastwood Rd., #231 (m-b)
Wilmington, NC 28403
910-509-1331 / Fax: 910-509-3002

RICHARD BRYAN (Owner) & Buys Men's Sportswear, Furnishings, Accessories

TOP TOAD (CLO & OL)

362 Nutt St.
Wilmington, NC 28401
910-343-9245 / Fax: 910-763-6494

DIANA PELLINGTON (Owner) & Buys Men's T-shirts, Hats, Footwear, Hosiery, Store Displays, Fixtures, Supplies

GEORGE RICE'S FORMAL & SPECIALTIES (MW)

P.O. Box 3695 (m)
Centura Village Shopping Ctr.
Wilson, NC 27893
252-243-6957

GEORGE RICE (Owner) & Buys Men's Suits, Formal Wear, Tuxedos, Formal Footwear

RUBY RICE (President) & Buys Men's Suits, Formal Wear, Tuxedos, Formal Footwear

SKI & TENNIS STATION (CLO-2)

119 S. Stratford Rd. (m-b)
Winston Salem, NC 27104
336-722-6111 / Fax: 336-727-8648
Website: www.skiandtennisstation.com

DOUG ROBERT (President & Owner)

MELI RUCKER-Men's & Boys' Ski Wear, Apparel, Active Apparel, Gloves, Swimwear

STEPHEN TUTTLE'S MENSWEAR (MW)

205 S. Stratford Rd. (b)
Winston Salem, NC 27103
336-727-0207 / Fax: 336-727-0207

STEPHEN TUTTLE (Owner) & Buys Men's Suits, Sportswear, Furnishings, Accessories, Footwear

NORTH CAROLINA - Winston-Salem

CAHILL & SWAIN, INC. (MW-2)

3255 Healy Dr. (b)
Winston-Salem, NC 27103
336-765-4423 / Fax: 336-767-0787
Sales: $1 Million-$10 Million

MICHAEL R. SWAIN (President & G.M.M.) & Buys Men's Furnishings, Headwear, Accessories, Store Displays, Fixtures, Supplies

DAN MOTSINGER (V.P.) (@ 910-767-0731) & Buys Men's Sportswear, Sweaters, Sport Shirts, Outer Jackets, Leather Apparel, Casual Slacks, Active Apparel, Apparel, Footwear, Store Displays, Fixtures and Supplies

MILLER'S VARIETY STORE, INC. (CLO)

622 N. Trade St. (p-m-b)
Winston-Salem, NC 27101
336-722-0549 / Fax: 336-722-1800
Sales: $100,001-$500,000

NATALIE MILLER (Owner) & Buys Men's Overcoats, Suits, Tailored Jackets, Tailored Slacks, Raincoats, Sweaters, Sport Shirts, Outer Jackets, Leather Apparel, Casual Slacks, Active Apparel, Dress Shirts, Ties, Underwear, Hosiery, Gloves, Shorts, Jeans, Headwear, Belts, Jewelry, Small Leather Goods, Big & Tall Men's Wear, Young Men's & Boys' Wear, Men's & Boys' Footwear, Store Displays, Fixtures, Supplies

NATHAN MILLER-Men's Overcoats, Suits, Tailored Jackets, Tailored Slacks, Raincoats, Sweaters, Sport Shirts, Outer Jackets, Leather Apparel, Casual Slacks, Active Apparel, Dress Shirts, Ties, Underwear, Hosiery, Gloves, Shorts, Jeans, Headwear, Belts, Jewelry, Small Leather Goods, Big & Tall Men's Wear, Young Men's & Boys' Wear, Men's & Boys' Footwear, Store Displays, Fixtures, Supplies

ROBERT MILLER-Men's Overcoats, Suits, Tailored Jackets, Tailored Slacks, Raincoats, Sweaters, Sport Shirts, Outer Jackets, Leather Apparel, Casual Slacks, Active Apparel, Dress Shirts, Ties, Underwear, Hosiery, Gloves, Shorts, Jeans, Headwear, Belts, Jewelry, Small Leather Goods, Big & Tall Men's Wear, Young Men's & Boys' Wear, Urban Contemporary, Men's & Boys' Footwear, Store Displays, Fixtures, Supplies

NORMAN STOCKTON, INC. (MW-2)

P.O. Box 5066 (b)
249 S. Stratford Rd.
Winston-Salem, NC 27113
336-723-1079 / Fax: 336-722-5457
Sales: $1 Million-$10 Million

HILL STOCKTON (President, G.M.M. & Owner) & Buys Store Displays, Fixtures, Supplies

STEVE STEELMAN-Men's Overcoats, Suits, Tailored Jackets, Tailored Slacks, Raincoats, Sweaters, Sport Shirts, Casual Slacks, Footwear

CHARLES THOMPSON-Men's Sportswear, Furnishings, Accessories, Footwear

REDIX STORE, INC. (CLO)

120 Causeway Dr. (p-m-b)
Wrightsville Beach, NC 28480
910-256-2201 / Fax: 910-256-2295

GORDON REDDICK (Owner) & Buys Men's Sportswear, Sweaters, Sport Shirts, Leather Apparel, Casual Slacks, Active Apparel, Furnishings, Boys' Sport Shirts, Shorts, Hosiery, Footwear, Beachwear, Swimwear, Store Displays, Fixtures, Supplies

FRANK WATERS-Men's Sportswear, Sweaters, Sport Shirts, Leather Apparel, Casual Slacks, Active Apparel, Furnishings, Boys' Sport Shirts, Shorts, Hosiery, Footwear, Beachwear, Swimwear, Store Displays, Fixtures, Supplies

SUE REDDICK-Men's Sportswear, Sweaters, Sport Shirts, Leather Apparel, Casual Slacks, Active Apparel, Furnishings, Boys' Sport Shirts, Shorts, Hosiery, Footwear, Beachwear, Swimwear, Store Displays, Fixtures, Supplies

JACKIE CHADWICK-Men's Sportswear, Sweaters, Sport Shirts, Leather Apparel, Casual Slacks, Active Apparel, Furnishings, Boys' Sport Shirts, Shorts, Hosiery, Footwear, Beachwear, Swimwear, Store Displays, Fixtures, Supplies

SWEETWATER SURF SHOP (SG & OL)

10 N. Lumina Ave.
Wrightsville Beach, NC 28480
910-256-3821 / Fax: 910-256-1004
Website: www.sweetwatersurfshop.com

CHUCK BOURGEOIS (Owner)

TONY BULTER (G.M.M.) & Buys Men's Swimwear & Surfwear

NORTH DAKOTA - Bismarck

HANSEN'S MENSWEAR (MW)

2700 State St., #M3
Bismarck, ND 58503
701-222-8205

BARRY HANSEN (Owner) & Buys Men's Sportswear, Furnishings, Accessories, Tuxedos, Big & Tall Men's Wear

DALE'S CLOTHING (CLO)

P.O. Box 44
14 N. Main St.
Bowman, ND 58623
701-523-3620 / Fax: 701-523-3810

DALE HOCHHALTER (Owner) & Buys Men's Urban Contemporary, Sportswear, Furnishings, Headwear, Accessories, Leather Apparel, 8 to 20 Up Boys' Wear, Footwear

MARCIA HOCHHALTER-Men's Sportswear, Furnishings, Headwear, Accessories, Leather Apparel, 8 to 20 Up Boys' Wear, Footwear

LYLE'S WESTERN WEAR (WW-2)

448 W. 21st St., #B
Dickinson, ND 58601
701-227-0349
Website: www.lyleswestern.com

KAY CARLSON (Mgr.) & Buys Men's Western Apparel, Boots, Furnishings, Accessories

NODAK SUPPLY, INC. (CLO-2)

P.O. Box 9258 (m)
3515 W. Main St.
Fargo, ND 58103
701-293-1155 / Fax: 701-235-8288

GREG YANISH-Men's Raincoats, Sweaters, Sport Shirts, Outer Jackets, Leather Apparel, Casual Slacks, Active Apparel, T-shirts, Dress Shirts, Underwear, Hosiery, Gloves, Headwear, Belts, Small Leather Goods, Footwear, Big & Tall Men's Wear, Young Men's Wear, Urban Contemporary, 7 to 20 Boys' Wear

STRAUS CO. (MW-2 & OL)

P.O. Box 9466 (m)
3223 13th Ave. SW
Fargo, ND 58103
701-235-7593 / Fax: 701-235-6724
Sales: $1 Million-$10 Million
Website: www.strausclothing.com

EDWARD R. STERN (President)

JOHN STERN (G.M.M.) & Buys Men's Sportswear

RICK H. STERN-Men's Furnishings, Overcoats, Suits, Tailored Jackets, Tailored Slacks, Raincoats

DON HOVDEN-Big & Tall Men's Wear, Belts, Footwear

THE SQUIRE SHOP (CLO)

519 Hill Ave. (m-b)
Grafton, ND 58237
701-352-2640 / Fax: 701-352-0048

RITA AMIOT (Owner) & Buys Men's Sportswear, Furnishings, Accessories

GERRELL'S SPORT CENTER (SG)

1004 S. Washington St. (m)
Grand Forks, ND 58201
701-775-0553 / Fax: 701-775-0209

BRAD WESTRUM (Owner) & Buys Active Apparel, T-shirts, Fleece & Shorts, Athletic Hosiery, Licensed Apparel, Men's Team Wear

HOME OF ECONOMY (CLO-5)

1508 N. Washington St. (p)
Grand Forks, ND 58203
701-772-6611 / Fax: 701-772-6521

JEAN KIESAU (President)

WADE PEARSON (V.P.-Opers.) & Buys Store Displays, Fixtures

LINDA ERICKSON-Men's Jeans, Sportswear, Casual Wear, Outer Jackets, Work Clothes, Underwear, Boots, Boys' Jeans

SILVERMAN'S, INC. (MW-2)

P.O. Box 13135 (p-m)
3001 S. Columbia Rd.
Grand Forks, ND 58201
701-775-2521 / Fax: 701-775-9016
Sales: $1 Million-$10 Million

STEPHEN M. SILVERMAN (President)

JIM DAHLEN (G.M.M.) & Buys Men's Overcoats, Suits, Tailored Jackets, Tailored Slacks, Raincoats, Sweaters, Sport Shirts, Outer Jackets, Casual Slacks, Leather Apparel, Active Apparel, Furnishings, Headwear, Accessories, Dress Shoes, Big & Tall Men's Wear, Store Displays, Fixtures, Supplies

MILLER'S CLOTHING (MW)

716 Lincoln Ave. (m)
Harvey, ND 58341
701-324-2341
Sales: $100,001-$500,000

PAUL MILLER (Owner) & Buys Men's Overcoats, Suits, Tailored Jackets, Tailored Slacks, Raincoats, Sweaters, Sport Shirts, Outer Jackets, Casual Slacks, Leather Apparel, Active Apparel, Furnishings, Accessories, Dress Shoes, Boots, Big & Tall Men's Wear, 8 to 20 Boys' Wear, Store Displays, Fixtures, Supplies

HABERDASHERY (CLO)

805 3rd St. (m)
Langdon, ND 58249
701-256-3243 / Fax: 701-256-3316

JEFF FISK (Owner) & Buys Men's Wear, Sportswear, Furnishings, Accessories, Young Men's Wear, Urban Contemporary, Boys' Wear, Store Displays, Fixtures and Supplies

LYLE'S WESTERN WEAR (WW-2)

2121 N. Broadway
Minot, ND 58701
701-852-5144 / Fax: 701-852-5144
Website: www.lyleswestern.com

CAROL WAHLSTROM (Owner) & Buys Men's Western Wear, Boots, Furnishings, Accessories

THE GOLDEN RULE (CLO)

P.O. Box 609 (p-m)
108 Main Ave. East
Rolla, ND 58367
701-477-3891 / Fax: 701-477-3025

TODD MEARS (Owner) & Buys Men's Sportswear, Furnishings, Headwear, Accessories, Footwear, Boys' Wear, Store Displays, Fixtures, Supplies

ROSS SIVERTSON-Men's Sportswear, Furnishings, Headwear, Accessories, Footwear, Boys' Wear, Urban Contemporary, Store Displays, Fixtures, Supplies

HARRIS CLOTHING STORE (CLO)

P.O. Box 640 (m-b)
111 Main Ave. E.
Rolla, ND 58367
701-477-5186 / Fax: 701-477-5186
Sales: $100,001-$500,000

JEANNETE HARRIS (Owner) & Buys Men's Sweaters, Sport Shirts, Outer Jackets, Casual Slacks, Leather Apparel, Active Apparel, Dress Shirts, Ties, Underwear, Hosiery, Gloves, Headwear, Belts, Small Leather Goods, Footwear, Western Wear, Big & Tall Men's Wear, Boys' Wear, Store Displays, Fixtures, Supplies

SYDNEY HARRIS (Mgr.) & Buys Men's Sweaters, Sport Shirts, Outer Jackets, Casual Slacks, Leather Apparel, Active Apparel, Dress Shirts, Ties, Underwear, Hosiery, Gloves, Headwear, Belts, Small Leather Goods, Footwear, Western Wear, Big & Tall Men's Wear, Boys' Wear, Urban Contemporary, Store Displays, Fixtures, Supplies

BORTH'S DEPARTMENT STORE (DEPT-5)

(ZINCK, INC.)
116 2nd St. SE (m)
Rugby, ND 58368
701-776-5007 / Fax: 701-776-2597
Sales: $100,001-$500,000

GEORGE ZINCK (Co-Owner) & Buys Men's Sweaters, Sport Shirts, Outer Jackets, Casual Slacks, Active Apparel, Headwear, Accessories, Footwear, Big & Tall Men's Wear, Young Men's & Boys' Wear, Store Displays, Fixtures, Supplies

DYVONNE ZINCK (Co-Owner) & Buys Men's Sweaters, Sport Shirts, Outer Jackets, Casual Slacks, Active, Young Men's & Boys' Wear, Urban Contemporary, Store Displays, Fixtures, Supplies

STOCKMAN'S SUPPLY, INC. (WW)

P.O. Box 756 (m)

802 W. Main Ave.

West Fargo, ND 58078

701-282-3255 / Fax: 701-282-3545

KARN JAMESON (Clothing Mgr.) & Buys Men's Western Wear, Sport Shirts, Outer Jackets, Leather Apparel, Dress Shirts, Ties, Gloves, Headwear, Belts, Jewelry, Small Leather Goods, Fragrances, Boots, Young Men's Wear, 7 to 20 Boys' Wear (All Western Wear)

OHIO - Ada

REICHERT'S DEPARTMENT STORE (MW)
111 S. Main St. (p)
Ada, OH 45810
419-634-2881 / Fax: 419-634-2881
FRED REICHERT (Owner) & Buys Men's Sportswear, Furnishings, Headwear, Accessories, Belts, Footwear, Store Displays, Fixtures, Supplies

BODY & SOLE FITNESS & APPAREL (SP)
1488 N. Portage Path
Akron, OH 44313
330-864-7858
Sales: $100,001-$500,000
LAURA HYLAND (Owner) & Buys Activewear, Athletic Footwear

BOUMADI CLOTHIER (MW-2)
3999 W. Market St. (m)
Akron, OH 44333
330-666-3000 / Fax: 330-666-3000
SAMMY BOUMADI (Owner) & Buys Men's Sportswear, Furnishings, Accessories, Footwear, Urban Contemporary, Store Displays, Fixtures & Supplies

CANTERBURY CLOTHIERS LTD., INC. (CLO)
117 Merz Blvd. (b)
Akron, OH 44333
330-869-8600 / Fax: 330-869-6910
Sales: $1 Million-$10 Million
EARL SEITZINGER (Co-Owner & President)
GEORGE FRANKINO (Co-Owner & V.P.) & Buys Men's Wear, Store Displays, Fixtures & Supplies

JABBOUR'S (MW)
1454 N. Portage Path (b)
Akron, OH 44313
330-836-9653 / Fax: 330-836-7467
MRS. JABBOUR (Co-Owner) & Buys Men's Sportswear, Big & Tall, Furnishings, Accessories, Store Displays, Fixtures, Supplies
HUDA JABBOUR (Co-Owner) & Buys Men's Footwear

KENMORE TAILORS & CLOTHIERS (MW)
966 Kenmore Blvd. (m)
Akron, OH 44314
330-745-5122 / Fax: 330-753-7200
Sales: $500,000-$1 Million
HOWARD KENT (Owner) & Buys Men's Overcoats, Suits, Tailored Jackets, Tailored Slacks, Raincoats, Sweaters, Sport Shirts, Outer Jackets, Casual Slacks, Furnishings, Headwear, Accessories, Young Men's Wear, Big & Tall Men's Wear, Store Displays, Fixtures, Supplies

LEODY'S CLOTHIERS (MW)
30 Sand Run Rd. (b)
Akron, OH 44333
330-835-3000 / Fax: 835-867-3338
LEO CORNACCHIONE (Owner) & Buys Men's Sportswear, Footwear, Furnishings, Accessories, Store Displays, Fixtures & Supplies

OJ'S MEN'S & BOYS' WEAR (MW-4)
(HEA SANG KIM)
1589 Plaza Dr. (p-m)
Akron, OH 44320
330-836-2056 / Fax: 330-864-0840
Sales: $1 Million-$10 Million
HEA SANG KIM (Owner) & Buys Store Displays, Fixtures, Supplies
MEAS HAN-Men's Overcoats, Suits, Raincoats, Sportswear, Dress Shirts, Ties, Underwear, Gloves, Headwear, Belts, Jewelry, Small Leathers, Footwear, Young Men's Wear, Urban Contemporary, Boys' Wear, Big & Tall Men's Wear, Store Displays, Fixtures & Supplies

SPORTS & SHIRTS (SP)
3925 Clover Hill Rd.
Akron, OH 44313
330-869-6767 / Fax: 330-665-1797
TERRY ABRAMOVICH (Owner) & Buys Activewear

SUIT WORLD, INC. (MW)
943 N. Main St. (m-b)
Akron, OH 44310
330-434-0924 / Fax: 330-434-0924
Sales: $100,001-$500,000
ODY FRANGIOUDAKIS (Owner) & Buys Men's Sportswear, Slacks, Sportcoats, Suits, Ties, Shorts, Belts, Hosiery, Store Displays, Fixtures & Supplies

WIND SONG WESTERN WORLD, INC. (WW)
8713 Worthington Rd. SW (p)
Alexandria, OH 43001
740-924-2522 / Fax: 740-924-9521
JUDY BALTHROP (Owner) & Buys Men's & Boys' Western Wear, Footwear, Headwear

LAUBER CLOTHING (CLO)
221 N. Defiance St. (m-b)
Archbold, OH 43502
419-445-2421 / Fax: 419-446-0294
TIM SMITH (Owner) & Buys Men's Wear, Sportswear, Furnishings, Belts, Small Leathers, Store Displays, Fixtures and Supplies

OUTDOOR ARMY STORE OF ASHTABULA (AN)
4420 Main Ave.
Ashtabula, OH 44004
440-992-8791 / Fax: 440-992-0552
Sales: $1 Million-$10 Million
WILLIAM HYLAND (Owner) & Buys Activewear, Athletic Footwear, Outerwear, Headwear

BARON'S MEN'S SHOP (MW)
67 S. Court St. (m)
Athens, OH 45701
740-592-5205 / Fax: 740-594-8080
Sales: $100,001-$500,000
FRED CLUFF (Owner) & Buys Men's Sportswear, Leather Coats, Furnishings, Headwear, Accessories, Store Displays, Fixtures, Supplies
JIM WEAVER-Men's Sportswear, Leather Coats, Furnishings, Headwear, Accessories, Store Displays, Fixtures, Supplies

MAC'S THRIFTY STORE (MW)
940 E. State St.
Athens, OH 45701
740-592-3773
JIM McLEARN (Owner) & Buys Men's Accessories, Footwear

WALTER THOMAS STORE (MW)
P.O. Box 104 (b)
115 E. Main St.
Barnesville, OH 43713
740-425-1132 / Fax: 740-425-1132
Sales: $100,001-$500,000
ERROL BRILL (President) & Buys Men's Wear, Store Displays, Fixtures, Supplies
TOM BRILL (Mgr.) & Buys Men's Wear, Footwear, Store Displays, Fixtures, Supplies

HUBER-BUCHENROTH (CLO)
120 W. Columbus St.
Bellefontaine, OH 43311
937-592-7936 / Fax: 937-593-2831
Sales: $100,001-$500,000
JAMES GREER (Co-Owner) & Buys Men's Wear, Leather Apparel, Footwear, Headwear, Store Displays, Fixtures, Supplies

CLOTHES HANGER (CLO)
141 E. Main St. (m)
Bellevue, OH 44811
419-483-5612
LYNN MIDDLESWARTH (Owner) & Buys Athletic Apparel, T-shirts, Shorts, Hosiery, Headwear, Licensed Apparel

HAWK'S CLOTHING, INC. (MW-3)
105 S. Main St. (p)
Bryan, OH 43506
419-636-1240 / Fax: 419-636-6330
Sales: $500,000-$1 Million
JACK JOHNSON (Chmn.) & Buys Men's & Young Men's Suits, Sportswear, Leather Apparel, Footwear, Shirts, Pants

ROBERT'S MEN'S SHOP (MW)
711 Wheeling Ave. (p-m-b)
Cambridge, OH 43725
740-432-5837 / Fax: 740-432-5837
ROBERT LEY (Owner) & Buys Men's Sportswear, Furnishings, Accessories, Young Men's Wear, Store Displays, Fixtures & Supplies

OHIO - Canton

ADAM'S MEN'S CLOTHIER (CLO)
4597 Beldon Village St. NW (m)
Canton, OH 44718
330-493-0117 / Fax: 330-493-0791
ADAM GOLDMAN (Owner) & Buys Men's Sportswear, Furnishings, Accessories, Headwear, Young Men's Wear, Store Displays, Fixtures & Supplies
TED GOLDMAN-Men's Sportswear, Furnishings, Accessories, Young Men's Wear, Store Displays, Fixtures & Supplies

DICKSON'S MENSWEAR, INC. (MW)
410 Market Ave. North (p)
Canton, OH 44702
330-453-0581
JACK DICKSON (Owner) & Buys Men's Sportswear, Footwear, Headwear, Furnishings, Accessories, Store Displays, Fixtures and Supplies

HUB VICTOR (SP)
710 30th St. NE
Canton, OH 44714
330-452-4179 / Fax: 330-452-1933
DON STAMBAUGH (Owner) & Buys Activewear, Headwear, Athletic Apparel, Shorts, Socks, Belts

MR. HYDE'S LEATHER (CLO)
3778 Cleveland Ave. NW (m-b)
Canton, OH 44709
330-492-2320 / Fax: 330-492-1232
PATRICK GURGANUS (Co-Owner) & Buys Men's Leather Jackets, Leather Coats, Headwear, Leather Apparel, Leather Accessories, Store Displays, Fixtures & Supplies
LINDA GURGANUS (Co-Owner) & Buys Men's Leather Jackets, Leather Coats, Headwear, Leather Apparel, Leather Accessories, Urban Contemporary, Footwear, Store Displays, Fixtures & Supplies

QUONSET HUT, INC. (CLO-5)
3235 Cleveland Ave. NW (p)
Canton, OH 44709
330-492-1293 / Fax: 330-492-4351
Website: www.qhut.com
PETE OLSON (Owner) & Buys Store Displays, Fixtures, Supplies
DANA MANIST-Men's & Boys' T-shirts

UNNER'S SUPPLY SHOP (SP-3)
1134 30th St. NW
Canton, OH 44709
330-493-4588
Website: www.runnerssupply.com
TERRY LEWIS (Owner) & Buys Activewear, Athletic Footwear

OVISCO SPORTS (SP)
800 Grand Lake Rd.
Celina, OH 45822
419-586-1255 / Fax: 419-586-1355
Sales: $100,001-$500,000
KEVIN SMITH (Owner) & Buys Activewear, Licensed Apparel

CUFFS (CLO)
18 E. Orange St.
Chagrin Falls, OH 44022
440-247-2828 / Fax: 440-247-1087
Website: www.cuffsclothing.com
ROGER KOWALL (Owner) & Buys Men's Sportswear, Furnishings, Accessories

PETER'S STORE FOR MEN, INC. (MW)
40 N. Main St. (b)
Chagrin Falls, OH 44022
440-247-8462 / Fax: 440-247-6549
PETER DiBLASI (Owner) & Buys Men's Overcoats, Suits, Tailored Jackets, Tailored Slacks, Sportswear, Furnishings, Accessories, Footwear, Store Displays, Fixtures, Supplies

TOUCH OF LACE (CLO)
31 N. Main St.
Chagrin Falls, OH 44022
440-247-7117 / Fax: 440-247-7355
ANN CRUMP (Owner) & Buys Swimwear

ACTION SPORTSWEAR OUTLET (CLO)
1725 W. Galbraith Rd. (m)
Cincinnati, OH 45239
513-522-4455
ED BLAMER (Owner) & Buys Men's & Boys' Sportswear, T-shirts, Headwear, Shorts, Store Displays, Fixtures & Supplies

ADAM SHOPS, INC. (MW)
(HOUSE OF ADAM)
622 Vine St. (p-m)
Cincinnati, OH 45202
513-241-2697 / Fax: 513-241-5656
Sales: $500,000-$1 Million
STANLEY GRAY (President & G.M.M.)
UGO PERROTTA-High Fashion Men's Overcoats, Suits, Tailored Jackets, Tailored Slacks, Raincoats, Sweaters, Sport Shirts, Outer Jackets, Casual Slacks, Dress Shirts, Ties, Underwear, Hosiery, Gloves, Headwear, Accessories, Footwear, Boys' Wear, Young Men's Wear, Store Displays
GEORGE PARASKA-High Fashion Men's Overcoats, Suits, Tailored Jackets, Tailored Slacks, Raincoats, Sweaters, Sport Shirts, Outer Jackets, Casual Slacks, Dress Shirts, Ties, Underwear, Hosiery, Gloves, Headwear, Accessories, Footwear, Boys' Wear, Store Displays, Fixtures

CASTLE HOUSE (KS)
3435 Edwards Rd. (b)
Cincinnati, OH 45208
513-871-2458 / Fax: 513-561-2005
JOAN STAMM (Owner) & Buys 8 To 20 Boys' Wear, Urban Contemporary, Store Displays, Fixtures, Supplies

THE CINCY SHOP (CLO-3)
(ROGER STAPLETON)
55 W. 5th St. (p)
Cincinnati, OH 45202
513-621-0003 / Fax: 513-241-7550
Website: www.cincyshop.com
ROGER STAPLETON (Owner) & Buys Men's & Boys' Active Apparel, Store Displays, Fixtures, Supplies

DINO'S OF KENWOOD, INC. (MW)
28 W. 4th St.
Cincinnati, OH 45202
513-984-0660 / Fax: 513-984-2770
Sales: $1 Million-$10 Million
DR. J. J. ASGHEAR (President)
SHOAIB ASGHER (C.E.O.) & Buys Store Displays, Fixtures, Supplies
ALBERT LOEB-Men's Overcoats, Suits, Tailored Jackets, Tailored Slacks, Raincoats, Sweaters, Sport Shirts, Outer Jackets, Casual Slacks, Active Apparel, Furnishings, Headwear, Accessories

FEDERATED DEPARTMENT STORES, INC. (DEPT-440)
(BLOOMINGDALE'S)
(BURDINES)
(GOLDSMITH'S)
(LAZARUS)
(MACY'S EAST)
(MACY'S WEST)
(RICH'S)
(STERN'S)
(BON MARCHE)
(LIBERTY HOUSE)
7 W. 7th St.
Cincinnati, OH 45202
513-579-7000 / Fax: 513-579-7555
Sales: Over $1 Billion
Website: www.federated-fds.com
Retail Locations: PR, AL, CT, DE, FL, GA, LA, ME, MD, MA, NH, NJ, NY, PA, RI, VA, AZ, CA, MN, NV, NM, TX, SC, IN, KY, OH, WV, TN, PA
JAMES M. ZIMMERMAN (Chmn.)
TERRY J. LUNDGREN (C.E.O.)
LEONARD MARCUS (President-Federated Mdse. Group)
KAREN M. HOGUET (C.F.O. & Sr. V.P.)
GARY NAY (Real Estate Contact)
NOTE-See Each Division for Buyer Information.

OHIO - Cincinnati

GREAT LOOK FASHIONS (CLO-3)
927 E. McMillan St. (p)
Cincinnati, OH 45206
513-281-8006 / Fax: 513-281-8006

PAUL AHN (Owner) & Buys Men's Sportswear, Furnishings, Accessories, Footwear, Young Men's Wear, 8 to 20 Boys' Wear, Store Displays, Fixtures & Supplies

HUNT CLUB CLOTHIERS (MW)
Fountain Square Plz. (m-b)
Cincinnati, OH 45202
513-721-2004 / Fax: 513-345-6602
Sales: $1 Million-$10 Million
Website: www.huntclubclothiers.com

JEFF BESECKER (Owner) & Buys Men's Footwear, Store Displays, Fixtures, Supplies
DAVE HALL-Men's Wear

KAST-A-WAY SWIMWEAR (SP-5 & MO)
9356 Cincinnnati Columbus Rd.
Cincinnati, OH 45241
513-777-7967 / Fax: 513-777-1062
Sales: $501,000-$1 Million
Website: www.kastawayswimwear.com

PATTY KAST (Owner)
BARBARA FERRARA-Swimwear
NANCY PALM-Swimwear

KOCH SPORTING GOODS (SG)
131 W. 4th St. (m)
Cincinnati, OH 45202
513-621-2352 / Fax: 513-621-5977

EDWARD KOCH (Owner)
GREG KOCH-Active Apparel, T-shirts, Shorts, Team Uniforms

McHAHN'S FASHIONS CO. (CLO)
(McHAHN'S, INC.)
703 Race St.
Cincinnati, OH 45202
513-421-4246 / Fax: 513-421-0216

MR. DAVID HAN (Owner) & Buys Men's & Boys' Wear, Urban Contemporary, Footwear, Store Displays, Fixtures, Supplies

MIKE & CAROL TROTTA, INC. (CLO)
406 Walnut St.
Cincinnati, OH 45202
513-621-2930 / Fax: 513-621-8566

MIKE TROTTA (Co-Owner) & Buys Men's Sportswear, Furnishings, Accessories
CAROL TROTTA (Co-Owner) & Buys Men's Sportswear, Furnishings, Accessories, Store Displays, Fixtures and Supplies

NADLER'S (CLO)
(MELVIN NADLER, INC.)
813 Forest Fair Dr. (m)
Cincinnati, OH 45240
513-671-2400 / Fax: 513-346-4742
Sales: $500,000-$1 Million

MELVIN NADLER (President)
JERRY SACKS (G.M.M.) & Buys Men's Overcoats, Suits, Tailored Jackets, Tailored Slacks, Footwear, Jackets, Coats, Raincoats, Furnishings, Sportswear, Store Supplies, Displays, Fixtures

NOBBY CUSTOM TAILORS, INC. (CLO)
14 W. 7th St. (b-h)
Cincinnati, OH 45202
513-621-2613 / Fax: 513-621-2640

ANTHONY BIANCO (Owner) & Buys Sweaters, Sport Shirts, Dress Shirts, Ties, Hosiery, Belts, Store Displays, Fixtures and Supplies

SCOTT'S STORES, INC. (CLO-2)
(BIG DOLLAR)
1436 Vine St. (bud-p-m)
Cincinnati, OH 45210
513-721-7811 / Fax: 513-721-7811
Sales: $500,001-$1 Million

STEVEN ROTHCHILDS (President) & Buys Men's Footwear
LOUIS ROTHCHILDS (V.P.)
FRANCES ROTHCHILDS (V.P.-Opers.) & Buys Jewelry

SMITH'S TOGGERY SHOP, INC. (MW)
1425 Vine St. (p)
Cincinnati, OH 45202
513-721-7335 / Fax: 513-721-7379

LARRY ASHFORD (Owner) & Buys Men's Sportswear, Headwear, Footwear, Accessories, Furnishings, Boys' Wear

SOUL FASHION (MW)
224 Swifton Commons
Cincinnati, OH 45237
513-631-3798 / Fax: 513-631-3022

VICTOR AILDASANI (Owner) & Buys Men's Sportswear, Accessories, Big & Tall, Footwear, Young Men's Wear, Urban Contemporary, Size 8 to 20 Boys' Wear, Store Displays, Fixtures, Supplies

GENTRY CLOTHIERS, INC. (MW-2)
6475 E. Galbraith Rd. (m-b)
Cincinnatti, OH 45236
513-791-5900 / Fax: 513-791-9905

DAN BRAEUER (President) (@ 513-791-9800) & Buys Store Displays, Fixtures, Supplies
JERRY BAHR-Men's Overcoats, Suits, Tailored Jackets, Tailored Slacks, Raincoats, Sportswear, Furnishings, Headwear, Accessories, Footwear

ADESSO (MW)
19920 Detroit Rd.
Cleveland, OH 44116
440-333-4778 / Fax: 440-333-5655

DAN VARNADER-Men's Apparel, Accessories

ALBERT'S PROSPECT (MW)
(MR. ALBERT'S MEN'S WORLD)
618 Prospect Ave. SE (p)
Cleveland, OH 44115
216-696-3359 / Fax: 216-696-0887

ALBERT WASSERMAN (Owner) & Buys Men's Sportswear, Young Men's Wear, Furnishings, Accessories, Footwear, Store Displays, Fixtures & Supplies

BELKIN'S MEN'S SHOP (MW)
3095 W. 25th St. (p)
Cleveland, OH 44113
216-621-2205 / Fax: 216-621-5026

LEONARD HOICOWITZ (Owner) & Buys Men's Sportswear, Furnishings, Accessories, Big & Tall, Store Displays, Fixtures, Supplies

CAPITAL CLOTHES (MW-2)
11706 Buckeye Rd. (m)
Cleveland, OH 44120
216-561-5500 / Fax: 216-561-6501

MARTIN ALTMAN (Owner) & Buys Men's Wear, Sportswear, Furnishings, Accessories, Young Men's Wear, Urban Contemporary, Boys' Wear, Store Displays, Fixtures and Supplies
BARRY KOLIN (President) & Buys Men's Footwear, Men's Dress Wear, Furnishings, Headwear, Accessories, Jeans, Young Men's Suits, Dress Shirts, Boys' Wear, Urban Contemporary, Leather Apparel, Store Displays, Fixtures, Supplies

CHRISTOPHER'S TRADITIONAL CLOTHING BROKERS (CLO)
(CHRISTOPHER'S CLOTHIERS)
200 Public Sq. (m-b)
Cleveland, OH 44114
216-621-6333 / Fax: 216-621-9641
Sales: $500,001-$1 Million

ROBERT GENOVESE (President) & Buys Men's Footwear, Apparel, Big & Tall Apparel, Leather Goods, Fragrances, Casualwear, Formalwear, Accessories, Hosiery, Outerwear, Sportswear, Suits, Uniforms
PETER TARNAY (V.P.) & Buys Men's Footwear, Apparel, Big & Tall Apparel, Leather Goods, Fragrances, Casualwear, Formalwear, Accessories, Hosiery, Outerwear, Sportswear, Suits, Uniforms

OHIO - Cleveland

FASHION RETAIL, INC. (MW-5)

(T & T)
8013 Euclid Ave. (p)
Cleveland, OH 44103
216-229-2909 / Fax: 216-229-2921

MR. HAN (Owner) & Buys Men's Sportswear, Furnishings, Accessories, Headwear, Young Men's, 8 to 20 Boys' Wear, Store Displays, Fixtures & Supplies

FORD'S CLOTHIER (MW)

19821 Detroit Rd. (b)
Cleveland, OH 44116
440-333-2355 / Fax: 440-333-4777
Website: www.fordsclothier.com

JEFF FORD (Owner) & Buys Men's Sportswear, Furnishings, Accessories, Store Displays, Fixtures and Supplies

GALCO SALES CO., INC. (MO & MW)

(GALCO ARMY STORE)
4004 E. 71st St. (bud-p)
Cleveland, OH 44105
216-883-2770 / Fax: 216-883-2770
Sales: $100,001-$500,000

ALAN LANDY (Owner) & Buys Men's Work Clothing, Outerwear, Military Apparel, Underwear, Hosiery, Gloves, Headwear, Belts, Big & Tall Men's Sportswear, Store Displays, Fixtures, Supplies

MICHAEL LANDY (G.M.M.) & Buys Men's Sweaters, Sport Shirts, Outer Jackets, Military Apparel, Leather Jackets, Casual Slacks, Active Apparel, Footwear, Store Displays, Fixtures and Supplies

GENTLEMAN'S QUARTERS (MW)

(LARCHMERE CLOTHIERS, INC.)
12807 Larchmere Blvd. (b-h)
Cleveland, OH 44120
216-229-7083

WALTER THOMPSON (Owner) & Buys Men's Wear, Sportswear, Dress Shirts, Ties, Robes, Underwear, Hosiery, Belts, Jewelry, Store Displays, Fixtures and Supplies

GOLDFISH UNIFORM (CLO)

200 Prospect Ave. East (bud-p-m)
Cleveland, OH 44115
216-861-4244 / Fax: 216-861-1136

JEFF ALPERN (President & Owner)

CHRIS DEPENTI-Uniforms For Men & Related Furnishings, Accessories

GOLLAND SHOES FOR MEN (FW)

230 Heeron Rd. (b-h)
Cleveland, OH 44122
216-623-1750 / Fax: 216-623-0662

MARK GOLLAND (Owner) & Buys T-shirts, Shorts, Active Apparel, Hosiery, Headwear, Belts, Store Displays, Footwear, Fixtures and Supplies

GREAT LOOK (MW)

14331 Euclid Ave. (m)
Cleveland, OH 44112
216-681-1433 / Fax: 216-681-1434

K.C. CHO (Owner) & Buys Men's Sportswear, Furnishings, Accessories, Young Men's, 8 to 20 Boys' Wear, Urban Contemporary, Store Displays, Fixtures & Supplies

JAY-VEE MEN'S CLOTHING CENTER (MW)

1266 W. 6th St. (m)
Cleveland, OH 44113
216-241-4536 / Fax: 216-241-0042

DON BROOKS (President) & Buys Men's Wear, Men's Footwear, Store Displays, Fixtures, Supplies

KILGORE TROUT (CLO)

(S & N, INC.)
28601 Chagrin Blvd. (b)
Cleveland, OH 44122
216-831-0488 / Fax: 216-831-6553

WALLY NAYMON (Owner) & Buys Men's Wear, Urban Contemporary, Footwear, Store Displays, Fixtures, Supplies

LEKARA, INC. (MW)

(RHETT'S)
13592 Euclid Ave.
Cleveland, OH 44112
216-541-8659 / Fax: 216-541-2424

LES KINGS (Owner) & Buys Men's Sportswear, Furnishings, Accessories, Store Displays, Fixtures & Supplies

JIM FLEMMING-Men's Men's Footwear, Urban Contemporary, Sportswear, Furnishings, Accessories, Store Displays, Fixtures & Supplies

M & M CLOTHIERS (MW-3)

1300 W. 6th St. (p-m-b)
Cleveland, OH 44113
216-861-1040 / Fax: 216-861-5558

MIKE ABOUMERHI (President) & Buys Men's Sportswear, Footwear, Furnishings, Accessories, Headwear, Young Men's, Sizes 8 to 20 Boys' Wear, Store Displays, Fixtures & Supplies

MARTIN'S MENSWEAR, INC. (MW)

696 185th St. (m)
Cleveland, OH 44119
216-481-4949
Sales: $100,001-$500,000

FRANK BARRESI (Owner) & Buys Men's Sportswear, Headwear, Footwear, Furnishings, Accessories, Young Men's Wear, Store Displays, Fixtures & Supplies

MEN'S DESIGNER OUTLETS (MW)

1104 Euclid Ave. (b)
Cleveland, OH 44115
216-861-7848 / Fax: 216-861-1320

MIKE YASSEN (Owner) & Buys Men's Wear, Custom Tailored Outerwear, Coats, Store Displays, Fixtures, Supplies

The Net Master Co., Inc. (MW-21)

(CRICKET-WEST)
(CHRISTIAN ST. JOHN)
28790 Chagrin Blvd., #345 (m-b)
Cleveland, OH 44122
440-473-1968 / Fax: 216-831-0470
Sales: $10 Million-$50 Million
Website: www.netmaster.com

NORMAN DIAMOND (President & Owner)

RICK DIAMOND (V.P.) & Buys Men's & Young Men's Wear, Store Displays, Fixtures, Supplies

RANDY DIAMOND (V.P. & Real Estate Contact) & Buys Men's & Young Men's Wear, Men's Footwear, Store Displays, Fixtures, Supplies

KEVIN VAN ORDAR (Cricket-West D.M.M.) & Buys Young Men's Contemporary Wear

DAVID KOHLER-Young Men's Wear, Urban Contemporary, Boys' Wear

R R TRADING CO., INC. (MW)

19300 Detroit Rd. (b)
Cleveland, OH 44116
440-356-0100 / Fax: 440-356-4000

RICHARD RASGAITIS (Owner) & Buys Men's Sportswear, Furnishings, Accessories, Footwear, Store Displays, Fixtures & Supplies

ROBERT'S CLOTHES, INC. (MW)

(BILL TAYLOR HATS)
425 Prospect Ave. East (p)
Cleveland, OH 44115
216-241-3544
Website: www.billtaylorthemadhatter.com

GEORGE ZOLIS (Owner) & Buys Men's Sportswear, Furnishings, Accessories, Footwear, Store Displays, Fixtures & Supplies

SHORT SIZES, INC. (MW & MO & OL)

6051 Mayfield Rd. (m)
Cleveland, OH 44124
440-605-1000 / Fax: 440-605-1065
Sales: $1 Million-$10 Million
Website: www.shortsizes.com

ROBERT STERN (President & G.M.M.) & Buys Men's Short Size Suits, Tailored Jackets, Tailored Slacks, Raincoats, Sportswear, Dress Shirts, Ties, Robes, Underwear, Hosiery, Headwear, Accessories

TOM SCHWAB (Gen. Mgr.) & Buys Men's Short Size Suits, Tailored Jackets, Tailored Slacks, Raincoats, Sportswear, Dress Shirts, Ties, Robes, Underwear, Hosiery, Headwear, Accessories, Footwear

OHIO - Cleveland

SILVERMAN'S (CLO-3)
(SILVERMAN BROTHERS, INC.)
6601 Harvard Ave. (p-m-b)
Cleveland, OH 44105
216-429-1600 / Fax: 216-429-2010
Sales: $1 Million-$10 Million
- ALAN SILVERMAN (President)
- STEVE KAPLAN (G.M.M.) & Buys Men's & Boys' Sportswear, Men's Footwear, Furnishings, Accessories, Uniforms

TNT APPAREL & SHOES (MW-17 & FW)
(TNT MEN'S FASHIONS)
502 Euclid Ave. (p-m-b)
Cleveland, OH 44114
216-575-0517 / Fax: 216-575-0568
Sales: $1 Million-$10 Million
- MICHAEL HAN (Owner) & Buys Men's Overcoats, Suits, Tailored Slacks, Raincoats, Sweaters, Sport Shirts, Outer Jackets, Casual Slacks, Active Apparel, Furnishings, Headwear, Accessories, Footwear, Boys' Wear, Urban Contemporary, Store Displays, Fixtures, Supplies
- TYRONE CARR (G.M.M.) & Buys Men's Overcoats, Suits, Tailored Slacks, Raincoats, Sweaters, Sport Shirts, Outer Jackets, Casual Slacks, Active Apparel, Furnishings, Headwear, Accessories, Footwear, Boys' Wear, Urban Contemporary, Store Displays, Fixtures, Supplies

WORK SMART, INC. (MW-3)
11645 Lorain Ave. (bud)
Cleveland, OH 44111
216-941-9603
- NICK KATSAROS (Owner) & Buys Men's & Young Men's Wear, Work Clothes, Urban Contemporary, Activewear, Big & Tall Men's Work Clothes, Activewear, Footwear, Store Displays, Fixtures, Supplies

DSW SHOE WAREHOUSE, INC. (FW-101)
(VALUE CITY DEPT. STORES, INC.)
1675 Watkins Rd. (m-b)
Columbus, OH 43207
614-237-7100 / Fax: 614-497-1356
Sales: $100 Million-$500 Million
Website: www.dswshoe.com
Retail Locations: OH, OK, VA
- MIKE TANNER (President)
- DEBBIE FERREE (V.P.-Mdse.)
- BECKY SAYRE (Coordinator-Mdse.)
- TRACY SNOW (Real Estate Contact)
- LARRY CARPENTER-Family Rubber Shoes
- LARRY CAMERON-Men's Dress Shoes, Sandals
- SALLY WILLIAMS-Boys' Shoes, Family Slippers
- RICK SMITH-Men's Footwear
- KIM PARTRIDGE-Men's Footwear
- ANGELIQUE LINDSLEY-Hosiery

EASTON SHOES (SP)
2052 Crown Plaza Dr.
Columbus, OH 43235
614-457-6662
- MARCIA COMERAS (Co-Owner) & Buys Men's Shoes, Hosiery, & Accessories
- LENNY COMERAS (Co-Owner) & Buys Men's Shoes, Hosiery, & Accessories

EXPRESS MEN'S (MW-469)
(Div. of THE LIMITED, INC.)
Egston Town Centre (m)
Columbus, OH 43230
614-472-3891 / Fax: 614-415-5205
Sales: $600 Million
Website: www.limited.com
Retail Locations: AL, AZ, AR, CA, CO, CT, DE, DC, FL, GA, HI, IL, IN, IA, KS, KY, LA, ME, MD, MA, MI, MN, MO, NE, NH, NJ, NM, NY, NC, ND, OH, OR, PA, RI, SC, TN, TX, UT, VA, WA, WV, WI
- MICHAEL A. WEISS (President & C.E.O.)
- JAMIE BERSANI (Real Estate Contact) (@ 614-415-7456)
- PAUL RAFFIN (Exec. V.P. Mdse.) & Buys Men's Shirts, Casual Wear, Accessories

FRONT RUNNER (SP)
1344 W. Lane Ave.
Columbus, OH 43221
614-486-0301 / Fax: 614-486-0568
Sales: $1 Million-$10 Million
- KEVIN O'GRADY-Apparel, Skiwear, Outdoor Apparel, Athletic Footwear
- RICHIE COHEN-SMITH-Apparel, Skiwear, Outdoor Apparel, Athletic Footwear

HAT & SOLE (SP)
2378 E. Main St.
Columbus, OH 43209
614-235-2719
- SHOOKI (Owner) & Buys Men's Shoes & Headwear

K. C. MEN'S CLOTHING (MW)
3385 Cleveland Ave. (m)
Columbus, OH 43224
614-267-7171 / Fax: 614-267-7173
- DAVID WON (Owner) & Buys Men's Sportswear, Furnishings, Accessories, Footwear, Store Displays, Fixtures & Supplies

LEE'S STYLE SHOP (CLO)
1009 Mt. Vernon Ave. (m)
Columbus, OH 43203
614-253-1816 / Fax: 614-253-0414
- KENNETH COHEN (President) & Buys Men's Sportswear, Leather Apparel, Furnishings, Headwear, Accessories, Footwear, Young Men's & Boys' Wear
- THOMAS CAMPBELL (Mgr.) & Buys Urban Contemporary, Store Displays, Fixtures, Supplies

OXLEY'S CLOTHIERS, INC. (MW)
9681 Sawmill Rd. (m-b)
Columbus, OH 43065
614-760-1940 / Fax: 614-326-0085
Sales: $500,000-$1 Million
- LEE REEVES (Owner) & Buys Men's Sportswear, Furnishings, Accessories, Footwear, Store Displays, Fixtures & Supplies

ROD'S WESTERN PALACE, INC. (WW & OL & MO)
3099 Silver Dr. (m)
Columbus, OH 43224
614-268-8200 / Fax: 614-268-8203
Website: www.rods.com
- SCOTT HARTLE (Owner) & Buys Store Supplies
- KIM KONRAD (Visual Merchandiser) & Buys Store Displays, Fixtures
- JANET JEANKS-Men's, Young Men's & Boys' Western Wear, Infant to 20 Boys', Leather Apparel, Related Furnishings, Headwear & Accessories, Big & Tall Men's Western Wear

SCHOTTENSTEIN STORES CORP. (DEPT-114)
(VALUE CITY DEPARTMENT STORES)
3241 Westerville Rd. (bud-p-m)
Columbus, OH 43224
614-471-4722 / Fax: 614-237-9421
Sales: Over $1 Billion
Website: www.valuecity.com
Retail Locations: DE, GA, IL, IN, KY, MD, MI, MO, NC, NJ, OH, PA, TN, VA, WV
- JOHN ROSSLER (President)
- ED PRUITT (V.P.-Men's Div. Mdse.) & Buys Men's Wear
- LARRY MARCELLO (@ 617-245-5806)-Men's Suits, Tailored Jackets
- OPEN (@ 213-688-0906)-Men's Wear, Young Men's Wear, Sportswear, 8 to 20 Boys', Footwear
- CHUCK CADLI-Men's Accessories
- PAUL EMMOS-Men's Active Apparel, Ties, Belts, Outerwear
- JOSEPH SOFSAYRE-Young Men's Wear, Accessories
- PAUL EMMONS-Men's Dress Shirts, Sweaters
- RON FINESTON (Mdse. Mgr.-Children's) & Buys Sizes 8 to 20 Boys' Wear, Branded & Non-Branded Apparel, Coordinates, Boys' Basics, Sleepwear
- JEFF GORSKY-Boys' Bottoms, 8 to 20 Boys' Activewear

VALUE CITY STORES (DEPT-116)

(Div. Of RETAIL VENTURES, INC.)
4290 E. 5th St. (bud-p-m)
Columbus, OH 43219
614-473-9541 / Fax: 614-239-9605
Sales: Over $1 Billion
Website: www.valuecity.com
Retail Locations: DE, GA, IL, IN, KY, MD, MI, MS, NC, NJ, OH, PA, TN, VA, WV

STUART GLASSER (President & C.E.O.)
DAVID LAZOVIC (G.M.M. & D.M.M)
PETER McCOSKEI-Big & Tall Men's Wear, Outer Wear
CHUCK CADILI-Belts, Underwear, Hosiery, Accessories
LARRY MARCELLO-Men's Suits, Sportswear, Better Slacks, Raincoats, Top Coats
MICHELE WALEN-Men's Budget & Moderate Tops, Sweaters, Knits
TERESA PADRO-DEAN-Better & Designer Sportswear, Knits, Sweaters
JOE SOFFAYER-Young Men's Wear, Urban Contemporary
ALAN SCHLESINGER (Real Estate Contact)
NOTE-Buying Also Performed at SCHOTTENSTEIN STORES, Columbus, OH - See Listing.

WOODHOUSE LYNCH CLOTHIERS, INC. (MW)

146 E. Broad St. (b-h)
Columbus, OH 43215
614-228-7200

TOM LYNCH, SR. (Owner) & Buys Men's Sportswear, Furnishings, Accessories, Store Displays, Fixtures & Supplies
THOMAS LYNCH, JR. (V.P.-Mdse. Mgr.) & Buys Men's Sportswear, Furnishings, Accessories, Store Displays, Fixtures & Supplies

CARROLL'S MEN'S SHOP (MW)

541 Main St. (m)
Coshocton, OH 43812
740-622-4935 / Fax: 740-622-8248

STEVEN MURRAY (Owner) & Buys Men's Wear, Sportswear, Headwear, Furnishings, Accessories, Store Displays, Fixtures and Supplies

LEVINSON'S (MW-2)

2231 Front St. (m)
Cuyahoga Falls, OH 44221
330-923-8888 / Fax: 330-922-0911

BILL BURCH (Owner) & Buys Police, Fire, Industrial & Work Uniforms, Related Furnishings, Accessories

THE ELDER - BEERMAN STORES CORP. (DEPT-67)

P.O. Box 1448 (p-m-b)
3155 El-Bee Rd.
Dayton, OH 45401
937-296-2800 / Fax: 937-296-2885
Sales: $500 Million-$1 Billion
Website: www.elder-beerman.com
Retail Locations: IL, IN, KY, MI, OH, PA, WV, WI

STEVEN C. MASON (Chmn.)
BYRON L. BERGREN (President & C.E.O.)
EDWARD TOMECHKO (Exec. V.P., C.F.O., Secy. & Treas.)
STEVEN LIPTON (Sr. V.P. & Controller)
MARK ZWERNER (Sr. V.P. & G.M.M.)
MIKE AZAD (V.P.-Planning)
JOHN LUPO (Exec. V.P.-Merch. & Mktg.)
JAMES ZAMBERLAN (Exec. V.P.-Stores)

LISA YETTER-BROWN (D.M.M.-Men's Tailored & Furnishings)
GREG WAYTON-Men's Suits, Top Coats, Raincoats, Sports Coats, Tailored Jackets, Outerwear
TERRY COONER-Men's Sleepwear, Robes, Underwear, Hosiery, Men's Accessories, Headwear, Scarves
STEVE MILLER-Casual Slacks, Shorts

GARY HOWARD (D.M.M.-Men's Sportswear, Active Apparel, Young Men's Wear & Outerwear)
DAVID NESBITT-Men's Better Collections
MARSHA CUMBERLEDGE-Men's Better Collections
GREG WRIGHTON-Men's & Young Men's Active Apparel, Outer Jackets, Young Men's Bottoms & Collections
DOUG DAVIS-Men's Sportswear, Accessories, Sport Shirts, Big & Tall Men's Wear, Tops, Sweaters, Izod

STEVE SPINKS (D.M.M.-Children's) & Buys Boys' Accessories
SUSAN ROGERS-8 to 20 Boys' Sportswear, Active Apparel, Casual Slacks, Knits & Woolens
LORRAINE GEBHART-Boys' Accessories
DAVID McDONALD (Real Estate Contact) (@ 937-296-1776)

FIFTH AVENUE MENSWEAR, INC. (MW)

5200 Salem Ave. (p)
Dayton, OH 45426
937-854-0555 / Fax: 937-854-0555

MI JANG (Owner) & Buys Men's Sportswear, Furnishings, Accessories, Store Displays, Fixtures & Supplies
YOUNG JANG (Mgr.) & Buys Men's Sportswear, Furnishings, Accessories, Store Displays, Fixtures & Supplies

HENRY'S DISCOUNT (SP)

6267 W. 3rd St. (m-b)
Dayton, OH 45427
937-263-3242
Sales: $500,001-$1 Million

YOUNG G. KIM (President) & Buys Men's Footwear, Fragrances, Apparel, Casualwear, Denim Apparel, Accessories, Hoisery, Outerwear, Sportswear, Suits, Underwear

JEANS GLORY (CLO)

46 S. Main St. (bud-p-m)
Dayton, OH 45402
937-461-1105

SUNNY KIM (Owner) & Buys Sportswear, Jeans, T-shirts, Shorts, Young Men's Wear, Urban Contemporary, Store Displays, Fixtures and Supplies

LONDON WEST, INC. (MW)

6133 Far Hills Ave. (b)
Dayton, OH 45459
937-435-0245 / Fax: 937-435-3471

GREG KELLER (Owner) & Buys Men's Footwear, Men's Sportswear, Furnishings, Accessories, Store Displays, Fixtures & Supplies

PRICE STORES (MW)

52 S. Jefferson Ave. (b)
Dayton, OH 45402
937-224-7631 / Fax: 937-224-8431
Website: www.pricestores.com

ED WIMSATT (Co-Owner)
NANCY WIMSATT (Co-Owner)
GARY POULIOT (Gen. Mgr.) & Buys Men's Sportswear, Leather, Formal Wear, Headware, Furnishings, Footwear, Young Men's Wear, 8 to 20 Boys' Wear, Store Displays, Fixtures, Supplies

STECK & STEVENS CUSTOM LETTERING (SP)

4014 E. Patterson Rd.
Dayton, OH 45430
937-426-3116 / Fax: 937-426-4125

MIKE BLANKENSHIP (Owner) & Buys Activewear, Headwear

STEP-N-STYLE (SP)
3217 W. Siebenthaler Ave. (m-b-des)
Dayton, OH 45406
937-276-5552 / Fax: 937-276-5552
Sales: $500,001-$1 Million
RANI KISHINCAND (President) & Buys Boys' Footwear, Men's Footwear, Apparel, Leather Goods, Fragrances, Casualwear, Designer Apparel, Accessories, Hosiery, Outerwear, Sportswear, Suits, Young Men's Apparel
ASHOK KISHINCAND (V.P.) & Buys Boys' Footwear, Men's Footwear, Apparel, Leather Goods, Fragrances, Casualwear, Designer Apparel, Accessories, Hosiery, Outerwear, Sportswear, Suits, Young Men's Apparel
DANNY KISHINCAND-Boys' Footwear, Men's Footwear, Apparel, Leather Goods, Fragrances, Casualwear, Designer Apparel, Accessories, Hosiery, Outerwear, Sportswear, Suits, Young Men's Apparel

TNT FASHIONS (MW-3)
(HAHN'S SPORTSWEAR)
(HAHN'S FASHION, INC.)
32 S. Main St. (m-b)
Dayton, OH 45402
937-223-5541 / Fax: 937-223-8584
ROBERT HAHN (Owner) & Buys Men's Wear, Footwear, Store Displays, Fixtures, Supplies

LION CLOTHING, INC. (MW)
206 N. Main St. (m-b)
Delphos, OH 45833
419-692-9981
JOHN ODEMWELLER (Owner) & Buys Men's Wear, Sportswear, Furnishings, Accessories, Young Men's Wear, Store Displays, Fixtures and Supplies

KING'S SHOES (FW)
13592 Euclid Ave. (m-b)
East Cleveland, OH 44112
216-541-8659 / Fax: 216-541-2424
Sales: $100,001-$500,000
LESLIE KING (President) & Buys Men's Footwear, Leather Goods, Men's Apparel, Men's Accessories, Men's Hosiery
JIM FLEMING (Mgr.) & Buys Men's Footwear, Leather Goods, Men's Apparel, Men's Accessories, Men's Hosiery

PAUL ARROW'S PANTS SHOP, INC. (MW)
520 Market St. (bud-p-m-b)
East Liverpool, OH 43920
330-385-1835 / Fax: 330-385-6649
Sales: $100,001-$500,000
PAUL BRASLAWSCE (Owner & Mgr.) & Buys Men's Sportswear, Furnishings, Accessories, Store Displays, Fixtures & Supplies

LOUIS COHN'S MENSWEAR (MW)
(S & J CLOTHING CORP.)
4610 Midway Mall
Elyria, OH 44035
440-324-5758 / Fax: 440-324-5758
TOM MAZUR (President & Owner) & Buys Men's Sportswear, Furnishings, Accessories, Big & Tall Men's Wear, Men's Footwear, Urban Contemporary, Store Displays, Fixtures and Supplies

WAGONER STORES, INC. (DEPT-6)
324 Union Blvd. (p-m)
Englewood, OH 45322
937-836-3636 / Fax: 937-832-0336
Sales: $100,001-$500,000
CARL WAGONER (Owner) & Buys Men's Jeans, Outerwear, Suits, Raincoats, Headwear, Small Leather Goods, Underwear, Hosiery, T-shirts, Footwear

LOWRY'S (KS)
2731 W. Market St. (m-b)
Fairlawn, OH 44333
330-836-2246 / Fax: 330-836-2247
RICK LOWRY (Owner) & Buys 8 to 16 Boys' Wear, Urban Contemporary, Store Displays, Fixtures, Supplies

HOCHSTETTLER'S OLD MILL (CLO)
428 W. Main Cross St. (p-m)
Findlay, OH 45840
419-422-1951 / Fax: 419-425-1954
MARK HOCHSTETTLER (Owner)
BONNIE HOCHSTETTLER-CarHart Brand of Men's Work Clothes

TOGGERY (MW)
Market Square Shopping Center (p-m-b)
Findlay, OH 45840
419-422-7171 / Fax: 419-422-0891
RICHARD ALIC (Owner) & Buys Men's Wear, Suits, Dress Shirts, Ties, Hosiery, Belts, Young Men's Wear, Store Displays, Fixtures and Supplies

FRANKFORT SUPPLY CENTER, INC. (CLO)
(IMC AGRIBUSINESS)
9217 Westfall Rd. (m)
Frankfort, OH 45628
740-998-5851 / Fax: 740-998-2505
KAREN DEWITT-Men's & Boys' T-shirts, Jeans, Shorts, Footwear, Store Displays, Fixtures, Supplies

HOME FIELD ADVANTAGE (SG)
82 Mill St.
Gahanna, OH 43230
614-337-1990 / Fax: 614-337-1791
JOE CALVARIO (Owner) & Buys Men's and Boys' Sportswear, Sport Shirts, Active Apparel, Headwear, Athletic Footwear

THE JAMES STORE (KS)
124 E. Broadway
Granville, OH 43023
740-587-3061 / Fax: 740-587-3062
NANCY GRAHAM (Owner) & Buys Infant to 7 Boys' Wear, Accessories, Store Displays, Fixtures, Supplies

THE WORKINGMAN'S STORE (MW)
502 Heaton St. (m)
Hamilton, OH 45011
513-893-0282
Sales: $100,001-$500,000
PAUL M. JEWELL (Owner) & Buys Men's Jackets, Slacks, Raincoats, Sport Shirts, Outer Jackets, Casual Slacks, Active Apparel, Windbreaker Jackets, Furnishings, Western Wear, Denim Wear, Headwear, Belts, Clothing, Big & Tall Men's Wear, Sweaters, Dress Shirts, Ties, Robes, Underwear, Hosiery, Gloves, Footwear

SPIECH MEN'S & BOYS' WEAR (MW)
44 N. Main St. (p-m)
Hubbard, OH 44425
330-534-5295
Sales: Under $100,000
RICHARD SPIECH (Owner) & Buys Men's Sportswear, Furnishings, Accessories, Footwear, Big & Tall Men's Wear, Young Men's Wear, Urban Contemporary, Store Displays, Fixtures & Supplies

COUNTRY BLUES, INC. (CLO)
134 N. Main St. (m)
Hudson, OH 44236
330-656-3032
Sales: $500,000-$1 Million
MARC PENNER (Owner) & Buys Men's Sweaters, Sport Shirts, Outer Jackets, Casual Slacks, Active Apparel, Young Men's & Boys' Wear, Store Displays, Fixtures, Supplies

RILEY'S CLOTHIERS (CLO)
100 N. Main St. (b)
Hudson, OH 44236
330-656-3343 / Fax: 216-655-0776
JEFF RILEY (Co-Owner) & Buys Men's Sportswear, Furnishings, Accessories, Footwear, Store Displays, Fixtures, Supplies
BRIAN RILEY (Co-Owner) & Buys Men's Sportswear, Furnishings, Accessories, Footwear, Store Displays, Fixtures, Supplies
ROY RILEY (Co-Owner) & Buys Men's Sportswear, Furnishings, Accessories, Footwear, Store Displays, Fixtures, Supplies

1887 SHOP (CLO)
(SAWMILL CREEK SHOPS)
200 Sawmill Creek Dr. West (b)
Huron, OH 44839
419-433-5402 / Fax: 419-433-6088
Sales: $500,000-$1 Million
HOLLY McGORY (Gen. Mgr.) & Buys Men's Sweaters, Sport Shirts, Outer Jackets, Leather Apparel, Casual Slacks, Active Apparel, Dress Shirts, Ties, Robes, Hosiery, Gloves, Belts, Jewelry
DIXIE VERMEEREN (Gen. Mgr.)

BOB LINN SPORTING GOODS (SG)
212 N. 2nd St. (p-m)
Ironton, OH 45638
740-532-4872 / Fax: 740-532-5497
JEFF LINN (Owner) & Buys Active Apparel, T-shirts, Athletic Apparel, Team Apparel

UNIVERSITY BOOKSTORE (SP)
(KENT STATE UNIVERSITY)
Student Center
Summit St.
Kent, OH 44242
330-672-2762 / Fax: 330-672-3758
Sales: $100,001-$500,000
MILL MARGUARDT (Mgr.)
TIM SCHUPPENHAUER-Fleecewear, Jackets

KENTON SURPLUS (MW)
201 W. Franklin St.
Kenton, OH 43326
419-673-5173 / Fax: 419-675-3493
LAVERNE DICK (Co-Owner) & Buys Men's Work Clothing
JOSEPH DICK (Co-Owner) & Buys Men's Work Clothing

CHARLEY GEIGER'S HABERDASHERY (MW)
14710 Detroit Ave. (m-b)
Lakewood, OH 44107
216-521-1771 / Fax: 216-521-2614
Website: www.shopgeigers.com
CHARLEY GEIGER (Owner) & Buys Men's Sportswear, Leather Apparel, Furnishings, Headwear, Accessories, Big & Tall Men's Wear, Young Men's Wear, Store Displays, Fixtures, Supplies
GORDON GEIGER-Men's Footwear

HAMMOND'S CLOTHIERS (MW)
203 S. Broad St. (b)
Lancaster, OH 43130
740-653-0663 / Fax: 740-653-4113
SHERRY LOVELL (Co-Owner)
DAVID BEHRENS (Co-Owner) & Buys Men's Sportswear, Furnishings, Headwear, Accessories, Leather Apparel, Footwear, Store Displays, Fixtures, Supplies

LANCASTER SALES CO. (MW-3)
P.O. Box 578 (p)
Rt. 33 South
Lancaster, OH 43130
740-653-5334 / Fax: 740-653-2783
Sales: $1 Million-$10 Million
FRED HILLMAN (Co-Owner) & Buys Men's & Boys' Wear, Footwear, Store Displays, Fixtures, Supplies
FRED HILLMAN (Co-Owner) & Buys Men's & Boys' Apparel, Furnishings, Footwear & Accessories

HOFELLER, HIATT & CLARK, INC. (MW)
237 N. Main St. (b)
Lima, OH 45801
419-228-5621 / Fax: 419-222-1978
Sales: $500,000-$1 Million
Website: www.hofellerhiattclark.com
PHILLIP C. OSMON (President) & Buys Men's Sportswear, Leather Apparel, Big & Tall Men's, Young Men's Clothing & Sportswear, Store Displays, Fixtures, Supplies

MABE'S CLOTHING (CLO)
18 S. Main St. (m)
London, OH 43140
740-852-1262 / Fax: 740-852-0666
Sales: $100,001-$500,000
MARTHA MABE (Owner)
DAVID MABE (Mgr.) & Buys Men's Sportswear, Furnishings, Accessories, Footwear, Store Displays, Fixtures, Supplies

JAX STORE FOR MEN & WOMEN (CLO)
149 E. Erie Ave. (b)
Lorain, OH 44052
440-246-5288
SCOTT BEYERS (Owner) & Buys Men's Sportswear, Furnishings, Accessories, Footwear, Fixtures & Supplies

RAKICH & RAKICH, INC. (MW)
506 Broadway (m-b)
Lorain, OH 44052
440-244-5685 / Fax: 440-244-1016
Sales: $1 Million-$10 Million
RANDY RAKICH (Owner) & Buys Men's Wear, Better Sweaters, Dress Shirts, Ties, Belts, Uniforms, Formal Wear, Formal Accessories, Store Displays, Fixtures and Supplies

ARNHOLT'S CLOTHING (CLO)
215 W. Main St. (p)
Loudonville, OH 44842
419-994-4531
Sales: $100,001-$500,000
ROGER ARNHOLT (Owner) & Buys Men's Sportswear, Furnishings, Accessories, Headwear, Young Men's, Store Displays, Fixtures & Supplies

VANCE'S STORE (CLO)
37 E. 2nd St. (p-m)
Manchester, OH 45144
937-549-2188
Sales: $100,001-$500,000
MARILYN SCOTT (Co-Owner) & Buys Men's, Young Men's & Boys' Casual Wear & Jeans, Urban Contemporary, Footwear, Store Displays, Fixtures, Supplies

DON NASH LTD. (CLO)
23 E. 3rd St. (b-h)
Mansfield, OH 44902
419-524-8238 / Fax: 419-524-0526
DON NASH (Owner) & Buys Men's Sportswear, Footwear, Furnishings, Accessories, Headwear, Big & Tall Men's Wear, Store Displays, Fixtures & Supplies

ROSENBLUM'S, INC. (CLO)
20650 Libby Rd. (m-b)
Maple Heights, OH 44137
216-662-7907
Sales: $500,000-$1 Million
ROBERT D. SOBEL (President) & Buys Men's Sportswear, Leather Apparel, Furnishings, Headwear, Footwear, Accessories, Big & Tall Men's, Young Men's Wear, Store Displays, Fixtures, Supplies

SCHAFER LEATHER STORE (WW)
140 Front St.
Marietta, OH 45750
740-373-5101 / Fax: 740-373-5373
ROBERT SCHAFER (Owner) & Buys Western Wear, Accessories, Store Displays, Fixtures and Supplies

WORKINGMAN'S STORE, INC. (MW-2)
113 Putnam St. (m)
Marietta, OH 45750
740-373-5648 / Fax: 740-373-5691
Sales: $1 Million-$10 Million
Website: www.workingmanstore.com
DAVID SCHRAMM (President) & Buys Men's Casual Slacks, Active Apparel, Dress Shirts, Gloves, Headwear, Belts, Men's Footwear

TOGGERY (MW)
1441 Marion Waldo Rd. (m)
Marion, OH 43302
740-389-3336 / Fax: 740-389-3336
MIKE ALIC (Owner) & Buys Men's Wear, Sportswear, Furnishings, Accessories, Store Displays, Fixtures and Supplies

HOWARD'S TIGER RAGS (MW)
(JOEL RUBIN, INC.)
125 Lincoln Way West
Massillion, OH 44647
330-833-4303 / Fax: 330-833-4303
JOEL RUBIN (Owner) & Buys Men's Sportswear, Footwear, Big & Tall, Young Men's & Boys' Wear, Store Displays, Fixtures, Supplies

OHIO - Maumee

THE CUSTOM SHOP CLOTHIERS (MW-4)

6475 Wheatstone Ct. (m-b)
Maumee, OH 43537
419-861-2400 / Fax: 419-861-2401
Website: www.customshop.com
Retail Locations: TX, MI, CA, DC

MICHAEL SMITH (Owner) & Buys Men's Wear, Furnishings, Accessories, Footwear

TERRIACO TAILORING SUITS (CLO)

8837 Mentor Ave. (b-h)
Mentor, OH 44060
440-974-9119 / Fax: 440-974-9371

ALEX TERRIACO (Owner) & Buys Men's Wear, Sportswear, Dress Shirts, Ties, Hosiery, Belts, Jewelry, Small Leathers, Store Displays, Fixtures and Supplies

SUTTMAN'S MEN'S & BOYS' WEAR (MW)

P.O. Box 244 (p)
26 S. Main St.
Miamisburg, OH 45342
937-866-3251
Sales: $500,000-$1 Million

BEN SUTTMAN (Owner) & Buys Men's Sweaters, Sport Shirts, Outer Jackets, Leather Jackets, Casual Slacks, Active Apparel, Furnishings, Headwear, Footwear, Accessories, Young Men's & Boys' Wear, Urban Contemporary, Store Displays, Fixtures, Supplies

MIDDLEPORT DEPARTMENT STORE, INC. (DEPT)

107 Mill St. (bud-p)
Middleport, OH 45760
740-992-3148 / Fax: 740-992-0104
Sales: $100,001-$500,000

TOM DOOLEY (Co-Owner) & Buys Men's Suits, Sportscoats, Furnishings, Accessories, Sweaters, Sport Shirts, Casual Slacks

BRUCE FISHER (Co-Owner) & Buys Men's Suits, Sportscoats, Furnishings, Accessories, Sweaters, Sport Shirts, Casual Slacks

WORTHMORE CLOTHES (CLO)

(KRUMBEIN'S, INC.)
(WORTHMORE LADIES' SHOP)
327 City Center Mall (p-m)
Middletown, OH 45042
513-422-7762 / Fax: 513-422-1107
Sales: $500,000-$1 Million

MARK KRUMBEIN (Co-Owner) & Buys Store Displays, Fixtures, Supplies

MILTON KRUMBEIN (Co-Owner) & Buys Men's Suits, Tailored Slacks, Raincoats, Sweaters, Sport Shirts, Outer Jackets, Casual Slacks, Furnishings, Footwear, Headwear, Accessories, Store Displays, Fixtures, Supplies

CHRIS KRUMBEIN (Co-Owner) & Buys Store Displays, Fixtures, Supplies

MAXWELL BROTHERS, INC. (CLO)

45 W. Jackson St. (p-m)
Millersburg, OH 44654
330-674-4936
Sales: $100,001-$500,000

JOHN F. MAXWELL (Owner) & Buys Men's Sportswear, Furnishings, Accessories, Big & Tall Men's to Size 2X, Young Men's, Store Displays, Fixtures & Supplies

BOWMAN CLOTHING STORE (CLO)

3726 Snook Rd. (m-b)
Morrow, OH 45152
513-494-2872

JUNE BOWMAN (Owner) & Buys Men's Suits, Sweaters, Sport Shirts, Outer Jackets, Casual Slacks, Active Apparel, Footwear, Furnishings, Headwear, Belts, Jewelry, Small Leather Goods, Young Men's Wear, 8 to 20 Boys' Wear, Store Displays, Fixtures, Supplies

COLONIAL MENSWEAR, INC. (MW)

101 S. Main St. (m-b)
Mount Vernon, OH 43050
740-397-7380 / Fax: 740-397-5762
Sales: $100,001-$500,000

RICHARD LASLO (Owner) & Buys Men's Sportswear, Furnishings, Accessories, Belts, Young Men's, Small Leather Goods, Store Displays, Fixtures & Supplies

ROCKY SHOES & BOOTS, INC. (FW-2)

39 E. Canal St. (m-b)
Nelsonville, OH 45764
740-753-9100 / Fax: 740-753-4024
Sales: $50 Million-$100 Million

MICHAEL BROOKS (President & C.E.O.)

DAVID SHARP (Sr. V.P.-Sales)

ANNETTE WINDLAND (Co-Mgr.) & Buys Boys' Apparel, Boys' Footwear, Leather Goods, Men's Footwear, Men's Accessories, Hosiery, Men's Apparel

KEVEN DOTSON (Co-Mgr.) & Buys Boys' Apparel, Boys' Footwear, Leather Goods, Men's Footwear, Men's Accessories, Hosiery, Men's Apparel

HOLLISTER CO. (MW-49)

(Div. of ABERCROMBIE & FITCH)
6301 Fitch Path
New Albany, OH 43054
614-283-6500 / Fax: 614-283-8121
Website: www.hollisterco.com

MIKE JEFFRIES (Chmn. & C.E.O.) & Buys Men's Casualwear, Jeans, Shirts, Accessories

SETH JOHNSON (C.O.O.)

ROBERT'S MEN'S SHOP (MW)

130 W. High Ave.
New Philadelphia, OH 44663
330-364-6773 / Fax: 330-364-8702

MICHAEL LYE (Owner) & Buys Men's Sportswear, Suits, Accessories, Sportcoats, Furnishings, Footwear

CORNELL-WELLESLEY LTD. (CLO)

(CORNELL CLOTHING CO., INC.)
22 N. Park Pl. (b)
Newark, OH 43055
740-345-8410
Sales: $100,001-$500,000

RAMONA PIERCE (Chmn.)

ROBIN PIERCE (President) & Buys Men's Sweaters, Sport Shirts, Outer Jackets, Leather Apparel, Casual Slacks, Active Apparel, Furnishings, Headwear, Accessories, Boy Scout Uniforms, Store Displays, Fixtures, Supplies

AMY PIERCE-Young Men's Wear

KEN'S HIS & HERS SHOP (CLO)

8 W. Broad St. (p)
Newton Falls, OH 44444
330-872-3190 / Fax: 330-872-7712

KEN LAYSHOCK (Owner) & Buys Men's Wear, Sportswear, Furnishings, Accessories, Store Displays, Fixtures and Supplies

MONTY'S TAILORS (MW)

51 E. Park Ave. (m-b)
Niles, OH 44446
330-652-2664

PHILIP MONTEVIDEO-Suits, Tailored Jackets, Tailored Slacks, Dress Shirts, Ties, Casual Slacks, Hosiery

JON'S CLOTHIER, INC. (MW)

1111 S. Main St. (p-m)
North Canton, OH 44720
330-499-0090 / Fax: 330-499-6198
Sales: $100,001-$500,000

JON SYNDER (Owner) & Buys Men's Sportswear, Furnishings, Accessories, Headwear, Footwear, Store Displays, Fixtures & Supplies

BIGFELLA'S INC. (MW)

4601 Northfield Rd.
North Randall, OH 44128
216-475-6623 / Fax: 216-475-6624

THOMAS BAEK (Owner) & Buys Men's Big & Tall Wear, Furnishings, Accessories, Footwear

WRIGHT'S BIG & TALL SUITS (MW)

(PONG WRIGHT, INC.)
953 Hanson St. (m-b)
Northwood, OH 43619
419-691-5951 / Fax: 419-691-5960

PONG WRIGHT (Owner) & Buys Big & Tall Men's Wear, Footwear, Sportswear, Furnishings, Accessories, Store Displays, Fixtures, Supplies

HAMMER - HUBER, INC. (CLO-2)
210 Milan Ave. (p-m)
Norwalk, OH 44857
419-668-9417 / Fax: 419-626-0122
DORIS HAMMER-HUBER-Men's Overcoats, Big & Tall Wear, Sweaters, Sport Shirts, Outer Jackets, Leather Apparel, Casual Slacks, Active Apparel, Dress Shirts, Ties, Robes, Underwear, Hosiery, Gloves, Headwear, Belts, Small Leather Goods, Boys' Footwear, Men's Footwear
RICHARD HAMMER-HUBER-Men's Overcoats, Big & Tall Wear, Sweaters, Sport Shirts, Outer Jackets, Leather Apparel, Casual Slacks, Active Apparel, Dress Shirts, Ties, Robes, Underwear, Hosiery, Gloves, Headwear, Belts, Small Leather Goods, Boys' Footwear, Men's Footwear

WOODVILLE SURPLUS (AN-2)
2172 Woodville Rd. (m)
Oregon, OH 43616
419-691-4636 / Fax: 419-691-7074
Sales: $1 Million-$10 Million
MICHAEL FELSTEIN (President) & Buys Store Displays, Fixtures, Supplies
KIMBERLY ROVITO (V.P.) & Buys Men's Casual Wear, Work Clothes, Sweaters, Sport Shirts, Leather Jackets, Gloves, Hosiery, Underwear, Headwear, Belts, Small Leather Goods, Footwear, Young Men's Wear, Urban Contemporary

GUSTWILLER'S (CLO)
116 W. Main St. (m)
Ottawa, OH 45875
419-523-6395 / Fax: 419-523-6394
Sales: $1 Million-$10 Million
TOM GUSTWILLER (Owner) & Buys Men's, Young Men's & Boys' Suits, Sportswear, Footwear, Big & Tall Men's, Urban Contemporary, Store Displays, Fixtures, Supplies

MIAMI UNIVERSITY BOOKSTORE (SP)
Shriver Ctr.
Oxford, OH 45056
513-529-2600 / Fax: 513-529-2625
Sales: $500,001-$1 Million
FRANK KOONTZ (Mgr.)
MARY NEASUS-Licensed Activewear, Golf Apparel, Fleecewear, Jackets, Hosiery, Shorts

BUCKEYE SPORTS CENTER, INC. (SG)
4610 State Rd. (m-b)
Peninsula, OH 44264
330-929-3366 / Fax: 330-929-8836
JIM ARMINGTON (Owner) & Buys Ski Wear

JAME'S CLOTHIERS (CLO)
30679 Pine Tree Rd. (b)
Pepper Pike, OH 44124
216-831-6470 / Fax: 216-831-6471
JAMES BRADLIN (Owner) & Buys Men's Sportswear, Furnishings, Accessories, Store Displays, Fixtures & Supplies
JOE PASTER-Men's Footwear, Men's Sportswear, Furnishings, Accessories, Store Displays, Fixtures & Supplies

LEIST'S DEPARTMENT STORE (DEPT)
P.O. Box 337 (m)
West St.
Piketon, OH 45661
740-289-2049 / Fax: 740-289-4587
Sales: $100,001-$500,000
PAUL LEIST (Owner & President) & Buys Men's & Boys' Clothing, Sportswear, Footwear, Big & Tall Men's, Store Displays, Fixtures, Supplies
EMERSON LEIST (V.P.) & Buys Men's & Boys' Clothing, Sportswear, Footwear, Big & Tall Men's, Urban Contemporary, Store Displays, Fixtures, Supplies

BARCLAY'S MEN'S & WOMEN'S (CLO)
314 N. Main St. (p-m)
Piqua, OH 45356
937-773-5928 / Fax: 937-773-5462
STANLEY HARRISON (Owner) & Buys Men's Wear, Sportswear, Furnishings, Accessories, Store Displays, Fixtures and Supplies

MARTING'S (DEPT)
P.O. Box 441 (m-b)
515 Chillicothe St.
Portsmouth, OH 45662
740-354-4511 / Fax: 740-353-3685
Sales: $1 Million-$10 Million
LARRY L. LEITER (President & C.E.O.) & Buys Men's Sportswear, Footwear, Furnishings, Headwear, Accessories, Young Men's & Boys' Wear, Store Displays
SCOTT SCHULTZ (Opers. Mgr.) & Buys Store Fixtures, Supplies

WOLFF CLOTHING (MW & OL)
320 Chillicothe St. (m-b)
Portsmouth, OH 45662
740-353-6110
Sales: $100,001-$500,000
AGNES COLLINS (Co-Owner) & Buys Men's Sportswear, Furnishings, Headwear, Accessories, Young Men's Wear, Big & Tall Men's Wear, Store Displays, Fixtures, Supplies

ABERCROMBIE & FITCH CO. (SP-250 & MO & OL)
(LIMITED, INC., THE)
(HOLLISTER CO.)
4 Limited Pkwy. East
Reynoldsburg, OH 43068
614-577-6500 / Fax: 614-577-6565
Sales: $100 Million-$500 Million
Website: www.abercrombie.com
Retail Locations: AL, AK, AZ, CA, CO, CT, DE, DC, FL, GA, HI, ID, IL, KS, KY, LA, ME, MD, MA, MI, MN, MS, PA, RI, SC, SD, TN, TX, MT, VA, WA, WI
MIKE JEFFRIES (President & C.E.O.)
JOHN FISKE (V.P.-H.R.)
JEFF SINKY (Real Estate Contact)
JAMIE SCHISLER-Men's Apparel, Accessories, Footwear

FORD'S CLOTHIER (MW)
19821 Detroit Rd. (b)
Rocky River, OH 44116
440-333-2355 / Fax: 440-333-4777
Sales: $1 Million-$10 Million
Website: www.fordsclothier.com
JEFF FORD (Owner) & Buys Men's Sportswear, Furnishings, Accessories, Store Displays, Fixtures and Supplies

RR FREESTYLE FOR MEN (MW)
19300 Detroit Rd. (b)
Rocky River, OH 44116
440-356-0100 / Fax: 440-356-4000
Sales: $100,001-$500,000
Website: www.rrfreestyle.com
RICHARD RASGAITIS, JR. (Owner) & Buys Men's Overcoats, Suits, Tailored Jackets, Tailored Slacks, Raincoats, Sweaters, Sport Shirts, Outer Jackets, Leather Apparel, Casual Slacks, Active Apparel, Dress Shirts, Ties, Robes, Hosiery, Gloves, Belts, Jewelry

KELLERMEYER'S MENSWEAR (MW)
143 W. Spring St. (m)
Saint Marys, OH 45885
419-394-4424 / Fax: 419-394-7564
VIRGIL BEHR (Owner) & Buys Boys' & Men's Sportswear, Furnishings, Accessories, Store Displays, Fixtures and Supplies

MOFFETT'S MENSWEAR (MW)
396 E. State St. (p-m)
Salem, OH 44460
330-332-5425
Sales: $100,001-$500,000
GARY MOFFETT (Owner) & Buys Men's Overcoats, Suits, Tailored Jackets, Tailored Slacks, Raincoats, Sportswear, Sweaters, Sport Shirts, Outer Jackets, Leather Apparel, Casual Slacks, Furnishings, Headwear, Accessories, Footwear, Big & Tall Men's, Young Men's Wear, Store Displays, Fixtures, Supplies

OHIO - Salem

TENNILLE'S (KS)
635 E. State St. (m)
Salem, OH 44460
330-332-9424 / Fax: 330-332-9424
GARY ABRAMS (Co-Owner) & Buys 8 to 16 Boys' Wear, Store Displays, Fixtures, Supplies
BETTY J. ABRAMS (Co-Owner) & Buys 8 to 16 Boys' Wear, Urban Contemporary, Store Displays, Fixtures, Supplies

TODD'S MEN'S & BOYS' WEAR (MW)
P.O. Box 544
Shreve, OH 44676
330-567-2101
ARTHUR TODD (Owner) & Buys Formal Wear, Related Furnishings, Accessories

MYER & STONE CO. (MW)
100 Mall Dr. (p)
Steubenville, OH 43952
740-266-6181 / Fax: 740-266-6183
Sales: $500,000-$1 Million
MORT SLAVEN (Owner) & Buys Men's Overcoats, Suits, Tailored Jackets, Tailored Slacks, Raincoats, Sportswear, Sweaters, Sport Shirts, Outer Jackets, Leather Apparel, Casual Slacks, Active Apparel, Furnishings, Dress Shirts, Ties, Robes, Hosiery, Gloves, Headwear, Accessories, Big &
FRANK COLLIER (G.M.M.) & Buys Young Men's Wear, Urban Contemporary, Boys' Clothing, Sportswear, Furnishings, Accessories

JABBOUR'S CLOTHING (MW)
(Stow Tailoring)
3310 Kent Rd. (m-b)
Stow, OH 44224
330-686-1776
Sales: $100,001-$500,000
MIKE JABBOUR (Owner) & Buys Men's Footwear, Sportswear, Furnishings, Accessories, Store Displays, Fixtures & Supplies

ENDURANCE SPORTS (SP)
(STARTING LINE)
6056 Wilmington Pike
Sugarcreek, OH 45459
937-848-6250
Sales: $100,001-$500,000
JOE SARGENT (President) & Buys Activewear, Athletic Footwear

ROBERT'S MENSWEAR, INC. (MW)
5131 S. Main St. (m-b)
Sylvania, OH 43560
419-882-3894 / Fax: 419-882-0395
Sales: $500,000-$1 Million
THOMAS E. LINDSLEY (President) & Buys Men's Overcoats, Suits, Tailored Jackets, Tailored Slacks, Raincoats, Sportswear, Furnishings, Headwear, Footwear, Accessories, Leather Apparel, Store Displays, Fixtures, Supplies

DIAMOND'S MEN'S SHOP (MW)
466 Southwyck Mall (p-b)
Toledo, OH 43614
419-865-1211 / Fax: 419-865-7848
PAUL STARK (Owner) & Buys Men's Sportswear, Big & Tall, Furnishings, Young Men's, Accessories, Footwear, Urban Contemporary, Store Displays, Fixtures, Supplies

JACK'S MENSWEAR (MW)
3402 Dorr St. (m)
Toledo, OH 43607
419-536-1551 / Fax: 419-536-8510
JEFF CONN (Owner) & Buys Men's Sportswear, Footwear, Furnishings, Accessories, Boys' Wear, Young Men's, Urban Contemporary, Store Displays, Fixtures & Supplies

M-D LIMITED, INC. (MW)
(MICHAEL DAVID LTD.)
405 Madison Ave. (b)
Toledo, OH 43604
419-255-1039 / Fax: 419-255-7649
MICHAEL BRINKER (Owner) & Buys Men's Sportswear, Dress Shirts, Ties, Hosiery, Belts, Jewelry, Small Leather Goods, Store Displays, Fixtures & Supplies, Men's Footwear
JIM DOWLING-Men's Footwear

NEIL'S MEN'S SHOP (MW)
4326 W. Central Ave. (b)
Toledo, OH 43615
419-531-9781 / Fax: 419-531-9772
FRANK KAHLE (Owner) & Buys Men's Overcoats, Suits, Tailored Jackets, Tailored Slacks, Raincoats, Sweaters, Sport Shirts, Outer Jackets, Casual Slacks, Active Apparel, Furnishings, Accessories, Footwear, Urban Contemporary, Store Displays, Fixtures, Supplies

PEPE'S MENSWEAR & TAILOR SHOP (MW)
5950 Airport Hwy. (m-b)
Toledo, OH 43615
419-865-0035 / Fax: 419-865-8604
PEPE SANTORO (Owner) & Buys Men's Sportswear, Furnishings, Accessories, Store Displays, Fixtures & Supplies

SZAR'S MEN'S SHOP (MW)
4743 N. Summit St. (p-m)
Toledo, OH 43611
419-726-2226
JOHN SZAR (Owner)
WILLIAM SZAR-Suits, Tailored Jackets, Tailored Slacks, Raincoats, Sportswear, Dress Shirts, Ties, Underwear, Hosiery, Belts, Store Displays, Fixtures and Supplies

L & N CLOTHING (CLO)
228 N. Water St. (bud-p-m)
Uhrichsville, OH 44683
740-922-5861 / Fax: 740-922-5861
Sales: $100,001-$500,000
LEE NOVAK (Owner) & Buys Men's Sportswear, Footwear, Boys' Jeans, Store Displays, Fixtures, Supplies

CHILDREN'S VILLAGE (KS & SP)
110 N. Sandusky Ave. (m-b)
Upper Sandusky, OH 43351
419-294-2664
Sales: $100,001-$500,000
GENEVA DILLON (Owner) & Buys 8 to 20 Boys' Wear, Men's Sport Shirts, Urban Contemporary, Store Displays, Fixtures, Supplies

MARTIN & SON, INC. (CLO)
5359 Liberty St. (m-b)
Vermillion, OH 44089
440-967-4256 / Fax: 440-967-9599
Sales: $1 Million-$10 Million
JAMES FRIEDMAN (President & G.M.M.)
MARTIN M. FRIEDMAN (C.E.O.)
DICK FRIEDMAN (V.P.) & Buys Men's Overcoats, Sportswear, Leather Apparel, Casual Slacks, Active Apparel, Underwear, Hosiery, Belts, Headwear, Footwear, Urban Contemporary, Store Displays, Fixtures, Supplies

ARMY NAVY STORE (AN-6)
125 W. Market St. (bud)
Warren, OH 44481
330-395-6752 / Fax: 330-392-0303
NICK LUFTIG (Owner) & Buys Men's Overcoats, Sport Shirts, Outer Jackets, Casual Slacks, Active Apparel, Leather Jackets, Furnishings, Headwear, Accessories, Footwear, Young Men's & Boys' Wear, Store Displays, Fixtures, Supplies

CHESTERFIELD TAILORS, INC. (MW)
153 E. Market St. (p)
Warren, OH 44481
330-395-4392
SAM JACON (Owner) & Buys Men's Sportswear, Furnishings, Accessories, Footwear, Store Displays, Fixtures & Supplies
PHIL ADAMS (Mgr.) & Buys Men's Sportswear, Furnishings, Accessories, Footwear, Store Displays, Fixtures & Supplies

OHIO - Warren

MICKEY'S ARMY & NAVY STORE, INC. (AN)
239 Main Ave. SW (m)
Warren, OH 44481
330-392-2525 / Fax: 330-395-4324
Sales: $1 Million-$10 Million
MARTIN L. COHEN (Owner) & Buys Men's Jeans, Tops, Leather Jackets, Store Displays, Fixtures, Supplies, Men's Footwear
DAVE KELLER-Men's Footwear
LARRY MARKS-Men's Footwear

SHAW'S CLOTHING (CLO)
137 N. Fulton St. (m)
Wauseon, OH 43567
419-335-8041 / Fax: 419-335-8029
DOUG SHAW (Owner) & Buys Men's Formal Wear, Sportswear, Furnishings, Accessories, Young Men's Wear, Urban Contemporary, Store Displays, Fixtures and Supplies

ADAMS COUNTY DEPARTMENT STORE (DEPT)
11142 State Rt. 41 (p-m)
West Union, OH 45693
937-544-2913 / Fax: 937-544-8816
ANNETTE McKEE (Co-Owner) & Buys Sweaters, Sport Shirts, Dress Shirts, Casual Slacks, Underwear, Hosiery, Gloves, Jeans, Headwear, Young Men's Wear, Urban Contemporary, Boys' Wear, Store Displays, Fixtures and Supplies
ESTHER GREENE (Co-Owner) & Buys Sweaters, Sport Shirts, Dress Shirts, Casual Slacks, Underwear, Hosiery, Gloves, Jeans, Headwear, Young Men's Wear, Urban Contemporary, Boys' Wear, Store Displays, Fixtures and Supplies

DAYE'S DEPARTMENT STORE (DEPT)
P.O. Box 396 (m)
121 N. Cross St.
West Union, OH 45693
937-544-2743
Sales: $100,001-$500,000
WILLIAM G. HACKWORTH (Owner) & Buys Men's, Young Men's & Boys' Sport Jackets, Jeans, Dress Shirts, Sport Shirts, Ties, Underwear, Hosiery, Headwear, Accessories, Footwear, Store Displays, Fixtures, Supplies

JUMPS CLOTHING (MW)
118 Myrtle Ave. (m-b)
Willard, OH 44890
419-935-6203 / Fax: 419-935-6055
Sales: $100,001-$500,000
JERRY STACKHOUSE (Owner)
RHONDA MONTGOMERY (G.M.M.) & Buys Men's Sweaters, Sport Shirts, Outer Jackets, Leather Apparel, Casual Slacks, Active Apparel, Furnishings, Headwear, Accessories, Store Displays, Fixtures, Supplies

H. FREEDLANDER CO. (DEPT)
125 W. Liberty St. (p-m)
Wooster, OH 44691
330-262-4010 / Fax: 330-263-0880
Sales: $1 Million-$10 Million
MARY STREETER (President)
STEVE HUTTIE (C.E.O. & G.M.M.) & Buys Men's Overcoats, Suits, Tailored Jackets, Tailored Slacks, Raincoats, Headwear, Sweaters, Sport Shirts, Outer Jackets, Leather Apparel, Casual Slacks, Active Apparel, Big & Tall Men's Wear, Young Men's Wear, Boys' Wear, Men's Furnishings, Belts, Jewelry

OLDER BROTHERS, INC. (AN-4)
123 E. Liberty St. (m-b)
Wooster, OH 44691
330-262-5457 / Fax: 330-264-2051
PATY BLACKBURN (Owner) & Buys Men's, Young Men's & Boys' Sportswear, Footwear, Store Displays, Fixtures, Supplies

GODFRY'S (MW)
92 Worthington Mall (b)
Worthington, OH 43085
614-433-0101 / Fax: 614-433-7112
Sales: $1 Million-$10 Million
HEINZ ELLROD (President) & Buys Men's Overcoats, Suits, Tailored Jackets, Tailored Slacks, Raincoats, Sweaters, Sport Shirts, Outer Jackets, Leather Apparel, Casual Slacks, Active Apparel, Dress Shirts, Ties, Robes, Hosiery, Gloves, Headwear, Belts, Fragrances, Footwear, Store Displays

FAST FASHIONS (MW)
45 E. Main St. (p-m)
Xenia, OH 45385
937-372-2429 / Fax: 937-372-5997
Website: www.fast-fashions.com
RONALD DECUIR (Owner) & Buys Men's Sportswear, Furnishings, Accessories, Store Displays, Fixtures and Supplies

CAPPELLI MEN'S STORE (MW)
(MISTER TUXEDO)
66 Boardman-Poland Rd. (p-m)
Youngstown, OH 44512
330-758-4855
MARK JACOBSON (Owner) & Buys Suits, Tailored Jackets, Tailored Slacks, Dress Shirts, Ties, Belts, Store Displays, Fixtures and Supplies

DI NELLO MEN'S SHOP (MW)
7050 Market St., #103 (m)
Youngstown, OH 44512
330-758-1278
JOHN DiNELLO (Owner) & Buys Men's Sportswear, Furnishings, Accessories, Store Displays, Fixtures and Supplies

DIFFERENCE (MW)
7098 Lockwood Blvd. (b)
Youngstown, OH 44512
330-726-1960
KELLENE MAVAR (Owner)
RANDY KOSTEK-Men's Sportswear, Footwear, Furnishings, Accessories, Big & Tall Men's, Store Displays, Fixtures & Supplies

LORD CHESTERFIELD MENSWEAR (MW)
7110 Market St. (m-b)
Youngstown, OH 44512
330-758-4521 / Fax: 330-758-3155
Sales: $500,000-$1 Million
NICK POLITO (Co-Owner)
JEFF MANUEL (Co-Owner) & Buys Men's Sportswear, Furnishings, Accessories, Footwear, Leather Apparel, Store Displays, Fixtures, Supplies

MASTERS TUXEDO & DRY CLEANING (SP-34 & MO)
4328 New Rd. (m-b)
Youngstown, OH 44515
330-793-4224 / Fax: 330-788-4011
Sales: $10 Million-$50 Million
Website: www.masterstuxedo.cm
Retail Locations: VT, PA, VA, MD, WV, AL, OH
MARK JACOBSON (President, Gen. Mgr. & Real Estate Contact) & Buys Jewelry, Men's Footwear, Men's Formalwear, Men's Accessories, Men's Hosiery

SILVER'S VOGUE SHOP (MW)
27 Federal Pl. West (m)
Youngstown, OH 44503
330-744-7819 / Fax: 330-744-4747
Sales: $100,001-$500,000
BARRY SILVER (Owner) & Buys Men's Overcoats, Suits, Tailored Jackets, Tailored Slacks, Raincoats, Sportswear, Sweaters, Outer Jackets, Leather Apparel, Casual Slacks, Furnishings, Footwear, Headwear, Accessories, Young Men's Wear, Urban Contemporary, Big & Tall Men's Wear

TWO GUYS CLOTHING (MW)
107 Federal Plz. (p-m)
Youngstown, OH 44503
330-743-2833
SOO YOUNG (Owner) & Buys Men's Sportswear, Furnishings, Accessories, Footwear, Young Men's, 8 to 20 Boys' Wear, Store Displays, Fixtures & Supplies

OHIO - Zanesville

WADE'S CLOTHING (MW)

(LARRY WADE LTD., INC.)

Colony Center (m-b)

3546 N. Maple Ave.

Zanesville, OH 43701

740-452-9394 / Fax: 740-452-7318

Sales: $500,000-$1 Million

Website: www.wadesclothing.com

LARRY WADE (Owner) & Buys Men's Overcoats, Suits, Tailored Jackets, Tailored Slacks, Raincoats, Sportswear, Sweaters, Sport Shirts, Outer Jackets, Leather Apparel, Casual Slacks, Apparel, Footwear, Furnishings, Headwear, Accessories, Urban Contemporary, Store Displays, Fixtures, S

OKLAHOMA - Ada

BLACK'S MEN'S & LADIES' (MW)
109 W. Main St. (m-b)
Ada, OK 74820
580-436-3000 / Fax: 580-436-3001
Sales: $500,000-$1 Million
JOE LANDRUM (Owner) & Buys Men's Sportswear, Furnishings, Accessories, Footwear, Big & Tall Men's Wear, Store Displays, Fixtures, Supplies
CHRIS FEILER-Men's Sportswear, Furnishings, Accessories, Footwear, Big & Tall Men's Wear, Store Displays, Fixtures, Supplies

KATZ DEPARTMENT STORE (DEPT)
P.O. Box 176 (p-m)
832 Arlington Ctr.
Ada, OK 74820
580-436-1744
Sales: $100,001-$500,000
HENRY KATZ (Partner) & Buys Men's Sportswear, Furnishings, Accessories, Store Displays, Fixtures, Supplies

AUSTIN'S MEN'S STORE (MW)
108 W. Broadway (m-b)
Altus, OK 73521
580-482-4562 / Fax: 580-477-0128
Sales: $500,000-$1 Million
LESLIE BRISCOE (Owner) & Buys Men's Sportswear, Leather Apparel, Accessories, Footwear, Young Men's Wear, Store Displays, Fixtures, Supplies

THE FAMOUS (CLO)
P.O. Box 711 (p-m)
106 W. Broadway
Anadarko, OK 73005
405-247-3441
Sales: $100,001-$500,000
GRADY DULWORTH (Co-Owner) & Buys Men's Furnishings, Sportswear, Footwear, Store Displays, Fixtures, Supplies
GAYLA TALLI (Co-Owner & Mgr.) & Buys Men's Furnishings, Sportswear, Footwear, Store Displays, Fixtures, Supplies

GEORGE'S DEPARTMENT STORE (DEPT)
124 W. Broadway (p)
Anadarko, OK 73005
405-247-5291
Sales: $100,001-$500,000
GEORGE SALAMY (Partner) & Buys Men's Sportswear, Furnishings, Accessories, Headwear, Young Men's, 8 to 20 Boys' Wear, Footwear, Store Displays, Fixtures & Supplies

JIMMY'S WESTERN WEAR (WW)
32 Tiffany Plz. (m)
Ardmore, OK 73401
580-223-0002
Sales: $100,001-$500,000
JIM OWEN (Owner) & Buys Young Men's & Boys' Clothing, Western Wear, Men's Footwear, Leather Apparel, Headwear, Accessories, Store Displays, Fixtures, Supplies

NOEL DATIN'S MENSWEAR, INC. (MW)
9 W. Main St.
Ardmore, OK 73401
580-223-0579
Sales: $100,001-$500,000
JOHN TODD (Owner) & Buys Men's Sportswear, Furnishings, Accessories, Young Men's, Store Displays, Fixtures & Supplies
PHILLIP TODD (Mgr.) & Buys Men's Sportswear, Furnishings, Accessories, Young Men's, Store Displays, Fixtures & Supplies

ATOKA WESTERN WEAR (WW)
1807 S. Mississippi Ave. (m)
Atoka, OK 74525
580-889-3166
Sales: $100,001-$500,000
MELBA MOBBS (Owner) & Buys Men's Western Wear, Sportswear, Furnishings, Accessories, Young Men's, 8 to 20 Boys' Wear, Headwear, Store Displays, Fixtures & Supplies
SHERRI HARDEN-Men's Footwear

MAY BROTHERS (MW)
100 W. Frank Phillips Blvd. (b)
Bartlesville, OK 74003
918-336-6855 / Fax: 918-336-6856
Sales: $500,000-$1 Million
H. M. MAY (President) & Buys Men's Wear, Footwear, Store Displays, Fixtures, Supplies

STYLE SHOPPE (CLO)
110 N. Cimarron Ave. (m)
P.O. Box 487
Boise City, OK 73933
580-544-3231
Sales: $100,001-$500,000
LANE REYNOLDS (Co-Owner)
AUDREY COCHRAN (Co-Owner) & Buys Men's Sportswear, Furnishings, Accessories, Young Men's, 8 to 20 Boys' Wear, Store Displays, Fixtures & Supplies

BRUTON'S DRY GOODS (DG)
102 N. Broadway (p)
Broken Bow, OK 74728
580-584-3858 / Fax: 580-584-9436
Sales: $100,001-$500,000
WILL E. BRUTON (Owner) & Buys Men's Wear, 8 to 20 Young Men's & Boys' Sportswear, Urban Contemporary, Western Headwear, Belts, Footwear, Store Displays, Fixtures, Supplies

SHARPE DRY GOODS CO., INC. (DG-25)
P.O. Box 328 (p)
200 N. Broadway
Checotah, OK 74426
918-473-2233 / Fax: 918-473-0346
Sales: $1 Million-$10 Million
Website: www.sharpeclothing.com
Retail Locations: OK, AR, LA
LOGAN SHARPE (G.M.M.) & Buys Men's Tailored Jackets, Tailored Slacks, Sweaters, Sport Shirts, Outer Jackets, Casual Slacks, Active Apparel, Furnishings, Headwear, Accessories, Footwear, Young Men's Wear, Boys' Wear, Big & Tall Wear, Overcoats, Store Displays, Fixtures, Supplies
CURTIS SOUTHERN-Men's Wear, Footwear
GARY UTLEY-Men's Wear, Footwear
LUKE SHARPE (Real Estate Contact)

DOTTIE'S SPORT & WESTERN WEAR (WW-2)
1114 S. Lynn Riggs Blvd. (m)
Claremore, OK 74017
918-342-4544
Sales: $100,001-$500,000
DOTTIE FUSIK (Owner) & Buys Store Displays, Fixtures, Supplies, Western Wear, Related Furnishings, Accessories, Headwear, Boots
DIANE RHOADES (Mgr.) & Buys Western Wear, Related Furnishings, Accessories, Headwear, Boots

MEN'S SHOP (MW)
987 W. Will Rogers Blvd. (m-b)
Claremore, OK 74017
918-341-6433
Sales: $100,001-$500,000
JERRY FEESE (Owner) & Buys Men's Sportswear, Furnishings, Accessories, Western Wear, Footwear, Store Displays, Fixtures, Supplies

KING'S STORE (CLO)
P.O. Box 23 (p-m)
1st St.
Clayton, OK 74536
918-569-4187
Sales: $100,001-$500,000
DEWITT KING (Owner) & Buys Men's & Boys' Jeans, Tops, Underwear, Sleepwear, Hosiery, Footwear, Store Displays, Fixtures, Supplies
GINGER KING-Men's & Boys' Jeans, Tops, Underwear, Sleepwear, Hosiery, Footwear, Store Displays, Fixtures, Supplies

LEN'S MENSWEAR (MW)
522 Frisco Ave. (m)
Clinton, OK 73601
580-323-2167
Sales: $100,001-$500,000
LEN RAHHAL (Owner) & Buys Men's Wear, Tailored Slacks, Footwear, Accessories

OKLAHOMA - Crescent

CRESENT CLOTHING, LLC (CLO)
P.O. Box 428 (p-m)
103 N. Grand St.
Crescent, OK 73028
405-969-3773 / Fax: 405-969-3773
Sales: $100,001-$500,000
DEBRA BLADES (President) & Buys Men's & Boys' Suits, Tailored Jackets, Tailored Slacks, Raincoats, Sweaters, Sport Shirts, Outer Jackets, Casual Slacks, Active Apparel, Footwear, Store Displays, Fixtures, Supplies

WOODWARD DEPARTMENT STORE, INC. (DEPT)
P.O. Box 500 (m)
Cyril, OK 73029
580-464-3371 / Fax: 580-464-2617
Sales: $100,001-$500,000
CHRIS WOODWARD (Owner) & Buys Men's & Boys' Sportswear, Urban Contemporary, Footwear, Store Displays, Fixtures, Supplies

CRUTCHER'S WESTERNWEAR (WW-2)
1503 N. Hwy. 81 (m)
Duncan, OK 73533
580-252-3220 / Fax: 580-255-8924
Sales: $500,000-$1 Million
MARK CRUTCHER (Co-Owner) & Buys Men's, Young Men's & Boys' Western Wear, Store Displays, Fixtures, Supplies
BOB CRUTCHER (Co-Owner) & Buys Men's Footwear, Men's, Young Men's & Boys' Western Wear, Store Displays, Fixtures, Supplies

McCALL'S (CLO)
(H. GIBB & SON, INC.)
21 S. Broadway (b)
Edmond, OK 73034
405-348-2400 / Fax: 405-348-8030
Sales: $1 Million-$10 Million
STEVE GIBSON (President) & Buys Men's Overcoats, Suits, Tailored Jackets, Tailored Slacks, Raincoats, Sportswear, Furnishings, Headwear, Accessories, Footwear, Store Displays, Fixtures, Supplies
KARIE SCOT-Young Men's & Boys' Wear

PARKWAY, INC. (MW)
140 E. 5th St. (b)
Edmond, OK 73034
405-341-3211 / Fax: 405-341-3831
Sales: $1 Million-$10 Million
MARK NEIGHBORS (Owner) & Buys Men's Overcoats, Suits, Tailored Jackets, Tailored Slacks, Raincoats, Sweaters, Sport Shirts, Outer Jackets, Casual Slacks, Furnishings, Headwear, Accessories, Leather Apparel, Big & Tall Men's Wear, Store Displays, Fixtures, Supplies
BRIAN NEIGHBORS-Men's Overcoats, Suits, Tailored Jackets, Tailored Slacks, Raincoats, Sweaters, Sport Shirts, Outer Jackets, Casual Slacks, Furnishings, Headwear, Accessories, Leather Apparel, Big & Tall Men's Wear, Store Displays, Fixtures, Supplies
PAM NEIGHBORS-Men's Footwear

CIRCLE A WESTERN WEAR (WW)
3000 W. 3rd St. (b)
Elk City, OK 73644
580-225-7363
Sales: $100,001-$500,000
RAYMOND ALBERT (Co-Owner) & Buys Men's Sportswear, Furnishings, Accessories, Footwear, Boys' Wear, Store Displays, Fixtures, Supplies
EDWARD ALBERT (Co-Owner) & Buys Men's Sportswear, Furnishings, Accessories, Footwear, Boys' Wear, Store Displays, Fixtures, Supplies

JONES' MENSWEAR (CLO)
(BUTCHER & CO.)
109 N. Main St.
Elk City, OK 73644
580-225-3187 / Fax: 580-225-3188
LARRY BUTLER (Owner) & Buys Men's Wear, Boys' Wear, Accessories, Footwear

SIMPSON'S MERCANTILE (DEPT)
228 E. Randolph Ave. (p)
Enid, OK 73701
580-234-4998 / Fax: 580-234-5227
Sales: $1 Million-$10 Million
LARRY SIMPSON (Co-Owner) & Buys Men's Sportswear, Western Wear, Footwear, Boys' Clothing, Store Displays, Fixtures, Supplies
RICK SIMPSON (Co-Owner) & Buys Men's Raincoats, Underwear, Gloves, Belts

WAY OUT WEST LEATHER & WESTERN WEAR (WW)
4800 W. Garriott
Enid, OK 73703
580-233-5186 / Fax: 580-233-5186
Sales: $100,001-$500,000
DON PERRY (Co-Owner) & Buys Men's Wear, Young Men's & Boys' Western Wear, Footwear, Store Displays, Fixtures, Supplies

BOB'S CLOTHING STORE (MW)
413 W. Main St. (m)
Henryetta, OK 74437
918-652-3355 / Fax: 918-652-3355
Sales: $100,001-$500,000
RICK THOMPSON (Owner) & Buys Men's Overcoats, Suits, Tailored Jackets, Tailored Slacks, Raincoats, Sweaters, Sport Shirts, Outer Jackets, Casual Slacks, Leather Apparel, Furnishings, Small Leather Goods, Fragrances, Belts, Footwear, Young Men's & Boys' Wear, Big & Tall Men's Wear, Urban Contemporary, Store Displays, Fixtures, Supplies

JOE ANN SHOP (KS)
P.O. Box 300 (b)
416 W. Main St.
Henryetta, OK 74437
918-652-3742 / Fax: 918-652-3742
Sales: $100,001-$500,000
CLAIRE HAYNES (Owner) & Buys 8 to 16 Boys' Wear, Footwear, Store Displays, Fixtures, Supplies

PAUL'S WESTERN STORE, INC. (CLO)
Rt. 2 (p)
P.O. Box 104
Henryetta, OK 74437
918-652-9210 / Fax: 918-652-7159
Sales: $100,001-$500,000
DICK WEST (Co-Owner) & Buys Men's Raincoats, Western Suits, Tailored Jackets, Tailored Slacks, Leather Apparel, Dress Shirts, Ties, Gloves, Accessories, Headwear, Store Displays, Fixtures, Supplies
GAIL WEST (Co-Owner) & Buys Men's Raincoats, Western Suits, Tailored Jackets, Tailored Slacks, Leather Apparel, Dress Shirts, Ties, Gloves, Accessories, Headwear, Footwear, Store Displays, Fixtures, Supplies

LEVINE'S MAINFAIR (MW)
P.O. Box 884 (p-m-b)
313 S. Main St.
Hobart, OK 73651
580-726-5686 / Fax: 580-726-5003
Sales: $500,000-$1 Million
JERRY LEVINE (Owner) & Buys Men's Sportswear, Accessories, Footwear, Boys' Wear, Store Displays, Fixtures, Supplies

THE PIONEER STORE (DEPT)
P.O. Box 128 (p-m)
102 E. Main St.
Hominy, OK 74035
918-885-2151 / Fax: 918-885-2152
Sales: $500,000-$1 Million
CHARLES FAIRWEATHER (President) & Buys Men's Overcoats, Suits, Tailored Jackets, Tailored Slacks, Raincoats, Sweaters, Sport Shirts, Outer Jackets, Casual Slacks, Furnishings, Robes, Headwear, Accessories, Boys' Wear, Store Displays, Fixtures, Supplies

J'S WESTERN WEAR (WW)
1804 E. Jackson St. (p)
Hugo, OK 74743
580-326-7504 / Fax: 580-326-7505
Sales: $100,001-$500,000
J.D. STANFIELD (Partner) & Buys Men's, Young Men's & Boys' Western Wear, Related Furnishings, Headwear, Accessories, Boots, Store Displays, Fixtures, Supplies
LACINDA STANFIELD (Partner) & Buys Men's, Young Men's & Boys' Western Wear, Related Furnishings, Headwear, Accessories, Boots, Store Displays, Fixtures, Supplies

S & H DEPARTMENT STORE, INC. (DEPT)
2 W. Main St. (m)
Idabel, OK 74745
580-286-3442
Sales: $100,001-$500,000
EUAL E. HILL (Owner)
CHARLIE HILL-Men's Overcoats, Suits, Tailored Jackets, Tailored Slacks, Raincoats Apparel, Furnishings, Headwear, Sweaters, Sport Shirts, Outer Jackets, Casual Slacks, Active Apparel, Accessories, Boys' Wear, Big & Tall Men's Wear, Store Displays, Fixtures, Supplies

KELLY'S, INC. (DEPT)
P.O. Box 1200 (m)
417 Main St.
Jay, OK 74346
918-253-8395 / Fax: 918-253-4878
Sales: $100,001-$500,000
MARY ANN KELLY (President) & Buys Men's Suits, Tailored Jackets, Tailored Slacks, Sportswear, Furnishings, Belts, Jewelry, Small Leather Goods, Boys' Clothing, Sportswear, Furnishings, Accessories, Footwear, Store Displays, Fixtures, Supplies

J & K OUTFITTERS (CLO)
HC 67 (b)
P.O. Box 9-1
Kansas, OK 74347
918-868-3857 / Fax: 918-868-2589
Sales: $100,001-$500,000
KAREN HUSONG (Co-Owner) & Buys Men's Western Apparel, Furnishings, Accessories, Store Displays, Fixtures & Supplies
JIM HUSONG (Co-Owner) & Buys Men's Western Apparel, Furnishings, Accessories, Footwear, Store Displays, Fixtures & Supplies

EDWARD & SON CLOTHIERS (MW)
(EDWARD'S MEN'S WEAR)
P.O. Box 106 (p-m-b)
405 SW C Ave.
Lawton, OK 73501
580-353-5800 / Fax: 580-353-5888
Sales: $1 Million-$10 Million
Website: www.edwardsmenswear.com
EDWARD HAMRA (President)
EDWARD E. HAMRA, JR. (V.P.)
MARK RAMMING (G.M.M.) & Buys Men's Overcoats, Suits, Tailored Jackets, Tailored Slacks, Raincoats, Sweaters, Sport Shirts, Outer Jackets, Leather Apparel, Casual Slacks, Active Apparel, Furnishings, Headwear, Accessories, Footwear, Big & Tall Men's Wear, Store Displays, Fixtures, Supplies

P.R. WILLIAMSON CO., INC. (DEPT)
P.O. Box 188 (m)
322 S. Main St.
Lindsay, OK 73052
405-756-2021
Sales: $100,001-$500,000
MARY HARRISON (Owner) & Buys Men's Sportswear, Furnishings, Accessories, Footwear, Store Displays, Fixtures, Supplies

BEANE WESTERN WEAR (WW)
P.O. Box 354 (m-b)
405 Hwy. 70 West
Lone Grove, OK 73443
580-657-4090
Sales: $100,001-$500,000
BRAD BEANE (President & Owner) & Buys Men's Suits, Outer Jackets, Tailored Jackets, Western Shirts, Gloves, Western Hats, Belts, Small Leather Goods, Footwear, Jewelry, Fragrances, Boys' Clothing, Store Displays, Fixtures, Supplies, Sport Shirts, Leather Apparel, Dress Shirts, Headwear, Boys' Clothing

HARPER'S WESTERN STORE (WW)
100 Chuck Sewell Dr. (m-b)
Marietta, OK 73448
580-276-5000
Sales: $100,001-$500,000
JERRY HARPER (Co-Owner) & Buys Men's & Boys' Western Wear, Men's Footwear, Store Displays, Fixtures, Supplies
LINDA HARPER (Co-Owner) & Buys Men's & Boys' Western Wear, Men's Footwear, Store Displays, Fixtures, Supplies

THE MEETING PLACE (SP)
(MALE QUARTERS)
116 E. Choctow St. (b)
McAlester, OK 74501
918-426-6148 / Fax: 918-423-2107
Sales: $100,001-$500,000
ZONA ROGERS (Owner) & Buys Young Men's & Boys' Sportswear, Furnishings, Accessories, Store Displays, Fixtures, Supplies

HUNT'S MEN'S FASHIONS (SP)
11 N. Main St.
Miami, OK 74354
918-542-5454
BOB HUNT (Owner) & Buys Coats & Sportswear

BALFOUR (MW)
(OBALCO, INC.)
319 W. Boyd St. (b)
Norman, OK 73069
405-321-6539 / Fax: 405-364-3841
Sales: $100,001-$500,000
Website: www.collegegear.com
GROVER OZMUM (Owner) & Buys Men's Golf Apparel Shirts, Outer Jackets, Active Apparel, Boys' T-shirts, Store Displays, Fixtures, Supplies

CAYMAN'S CLOTHIERS, INC. (CLO)
2001 W. Main St.
Norman, OK 73069
405-360-3913 / Fax: 405-579-3914
Sales: $100,001-$500,000
CAYLON COLEMAN (Co-Owner)
PATSY COLEMAN (Co-Owner) & Buys Men's Footwear
SHELLEY COX (Co-Owner) & Buys Men's Sportswear, Furnishings, Young Men's & Boys' Wear, Store Displays, Fixtures, Supplies

UNIVERSITY BOOK STORE (SP-2)
(UNIVERSITY OF OKLAHOMA)
731 Elm Ave., Rm 125
Norman, OK 73019
405-325-3511 / Fax: 405-325-1482
Sales: $100,001-$500,000
Website: www.oklahoma.bkstr.com
GARY MADOLE (Mgr.) & Buys Activewear, Fleece, Jackets, Hosiery, Shorts, Sport Hats

AMBASSADOR SHOP (MW)
1001 W. Memorial Rd., #1 (b)
Oklahoma City, OK 73114
405-755-1588 / Fax: 405-751-4490
Sales: $100,001-$500,000
Website: www.ambassadorshop.com
MO JAVAHERI (Owner) & Buys Men's Sportswear, Furnishings, Footwear, Accessories, Store Displays, Fixtures & Supplies

BUD BOSTIC'S MENSWEAR (MW)
3629 NW 22nd St. (m)
Oklahoma City, OK 73107
405-947-2957
Sales: $500,000-$1 Million
BUD BOSTIC (Owner) & Buys Men's Suits, Tailored Jackets, Tailored Slacks, Sport Shirts, Dress Shirts, Ties, Hosiery, Belts, Footwear, Store Displays, Fixtures, Supplies

OKLAHOMA - Oklahoma City

DICK RENO SPORTSWEAR (MW)

9340 N. May Ave. (m)
Oklahoma City, OK 73120
405-755-4033
Sales: $100,001-$500,000

DICK RENO (Co-Owner) & Buys Men's Sweaters, Tailored Jackets, Robes, Sport Shirts, T-shirts, Casual Slacks, Headwear, Boys' Sportswear, Store Displays, Fixtures, Supplies

MARYANN RENO (Co-Owner) & Buys Men's Sweaters, Tailored Jackets, Robes, Sport Shirts, T-shirts, Casual Slacks, Headwear, Boys' Sportswear, Store Displays, Fixtures, Supplies

GIL'S, INC. (MW-3)

P.O. Box 14749 (b)
7644 North Western Ave.
Oklahoma City, OK 73154
405-848-0334 / Fax: 405-848-1630

GIL MITCHELL (Owner) & Buys Men's Sportswear, Furnishings, Headwear, Accessories, Store Displays, Fixtures & Supplies

TERESA WILEY-Men's Sportswear, Furnishings, Headwear, Accessories, Store Displays, Fixtures & Supplies

HYROOPS - THE BIG TALL PLACE (MW-5)

(BIG & TALL, INC.)
2747 NW Expressway St. (b)
Oklahoma City, OK 73112
405-840-1801 / Fax: 405-848-9480
Sales: $1 Million-$10 Million

ROBERT R. BROWNS (Owner) & Buys Men's Sportswear, Furnishings, Headwear, Big & Tall Men's Wear, Accessories, Belts, Small Leather Goods

JAY STEVENS APPAREL FOR BIG OR TALL MEN (MW-3 & OL)

(GELLMAN'S, INC.)
2747 NW Expressway (m)
Oklahoma City, OK 73112
866-823-4546 / Fax: 405-848-9480
Website: www.jaystevens.com

STEVEN GELLMAN (President & G.M.M.) & Buys Big & Tall Men's Sportswear, Furnishings, Belts, Accessories

LANGSTON CO. (DG-3)

P.O. Box 83138 (p)
2224 Exchange Ave.
Oklahoma City, OK 73108
405-235-9536 / Fax: 405-235-1645
Sales: $1 Million-$10 Million
Website: www.langstons.com

R. MICHAEL BARBER (President) & Buys Men's, Boys' & Students' Wear, Store Displays, Fixtures, Supplies

MR. JOHN'S (MW)

6609 N. May Ave.
Oklahoma City, OK 73116
405-842-1137 / Fax: 405-842-6828
Sales: $100,001-$500,000

JOHN ANGELIDIS (Owner) & Buys Men's Sweaters, Sport Shirts, Outer Jackets, Leather Apparel, Casual Slacks, Tailored Slacks, Dress Shirts, Ties, Belts, Fragrances, Boys' Sportswear

MR. OOLEY'S (MW)

1901 NW Expwy., #1023
Oklahoma City, OK 73118
405-879-0888 / Fax: 405-843-6798
Website: www.mrooleys.com

DAVID OOLEY (Owner) & Buys Men's Suits, Furnishings, Accessories, Footwear

THE OLD BALL PARK (MW)

3114 NW 23rd St. (m)
Oklahoma City, OK 73107
405-949-2255 / Fax: 520-447-5148

MR. TERRY HANNAH (President & Owner)

LES SPRINGS-Sportswear with Sports Memorabilia Themes

SAM'S BEST BUYS (MW)

2409 S. Agnew Ave. (bud)
Oklahoma City, OK 73108
405-636-1486 / Fax: 405-636-1487
Sales: $100,001-$500,000

PAULINE GOLDSTEIN (Co-Owner) & Buys Men's Sportswear, Belts, Leather Apparel, Big & Tall Men's Wear, Boys' Wear, Store Displays, Fixtures, Supplies

GENE GOLDSTEIN (Co-Owner) & Buys Men's Sportswear, Belts, Leather Apparel, Big & Tall Men's Wear, Boys' Wear, Store Displays, Fixtures, Supplies

BERNICE GOLDSTEIN (Co-Owner) & Buys Men's Sportswear, Belts, Leather Apparel, Big & Tall Men's Wear, Boys' Wear, Store Displays, Fixtures, Supplies

SEABROOK'S FORMAL WEAR, INC. (MW)

1838 NW 1st St.
Oklahoma City, OK 73106
800-880-3577 / Fax: 405-232-6241
Sales: $100,001-$500,000

PATRICIA LINSENBARTH (Owner) & Buys Men's Formal Wear, Store Displays, Fixtures, Supplies

TRACEY BARTNETT-Men's Formal Wear, Store Displays, Fixtures, Supplies

TARTAN CLOTHING CO. (SP)

413 N. Meridian Ave.
Oklahoma City, OK 73107
405-946-6850 / Fax: 405-946-6276

SUSAN SUTHERLAND (Co-Owner) & Buys Men's Wear, Accessories, Furnishings

TENER'S WESTERN OUTFITTERS (WW-4)

4320 W. Reno Ave.
Oklahoma City, OK 73107
405-946-5500 / Fax: 405-948-7746
Sales: $100,001-$500,000

ANDY HUGHES (President) & Buys Men's Western Wear & Accessories, Footwear, 8 to 20 Boys' Western Wear, Store Displays, Fixtures, Supplies

JAY SHUMATE'S APPAREL (MW)

204 W. Paul Ave. (p-m-h)
Pauls Valley, OK 73075
405-238-2569
Sales: $100,001-$500,000

JAY SHUMATE (Owner) & Buys Men's Wear, Sportswear, Suits

STEPPIN' OUT (WW-3)

P.O. Box 208 (m)
Pauls Valley, OK 73075
405-238-2123 / Fax: 405-238-6523
Sales: $500,000-$1 Million

ANN MARCUM (Owner) & Buys Men's, Young Men's & Boys' Western Wear, Store Displays, Fixtures, Supplies

ERMY'S MENSWEAR (MW)

(CHEATHAM)
529 Harrison St. (m)
Pawnee, OK 74058
918-762-2530
Sales: $100,001-$500,000

KEITH CHEATHAM (Owner) & Buys Sportswear, Men's Wear

McVAY'S (CLO)

108 N. 1st St. (p-m-b)
Ponca City, OK 74601
580-765-9350 / Fax: 580-765-1601
Sales: $100,001-$500,000

GARY E. McVAY (Owner) & Buys Men's Western Wear, Leather Apparel, Down Jackets, Coats, Sportswear, Underwear, Hosiery, Accessories, Footwear, Size 8 to 20 Young Men's & Boys' Wear, Big & Tall Men's Wear, Store Displays, Fixtures, Supplies

MOORE'S APPAREL, INC. (CLO)

2101 N. 14th St., #124 (m-b)
Ponca City, OK 74601
580-765-4345 / Fax: 580-765-0156
Sales: $100,001-$500,000

TED IMPSON (Owner) & Buys Men's Wear, Store Displays, Fixtures, Supplies

BROWN'S DRY GOODS (DG)
P.O. Box 575 (m)
161 W. Broadway
Pond Creek, OK 73766
580-532-4967
Sales: Under $100,000
MARY PHILBRICK (Owner) & Buys Men's Sportswear, Work Clothes, Furnishings, Accessories, Young Men's Wear, Store Displays, Fixtures, Supplies

BERNARD'S NEW IMAGE, INC. (CLO-2)
P.O. Box 936 (m-b)
Poteau, OK 74953
918-647-8585 / Fax: 918-647-2170
Sales: $100,001-$500,000
DAVID BERNARD (President) & Buys Men's Wear, Footwear, Boys' Western Wear, Store Displays, Fixtures, Supplies

R-BAR WESTERN (WW)
5021 N. Broadway
Poteau, OK 74953
918-647-9586
Sales: $100,001-$500,000
ELSIE LAWRENCE (Co-Owner) & Buys Men's Footwear, Men's Western Wear, Furnishings, Accessories, Store Displays, Fixtures and Supplies

CIRCLE W WESTERN WEAR (WW)
218 W. Main St. (m)
Purcell, OK 73080
405-527-6788 / Fax: 405-527-8138
Sales: $100,001-$500,000
Website: www.circlew.com
GAROLD DUNCAN (Co-Owner) & Buys Men's Footwear, Men's, Young Men's & Boys' Casual Western Wear, Furnishings, Accessories, Store Displays, Fixtures & Supplies
DARLENE DUNCAN (Co-Owner) & Buys Men's, Young Men's & Boys' Casual Western Wear, Furnishings, Accessories, Store Displays, Fixtures & Supplies

LAKE COUNTRY SPORTING GOODS (SP)
31 W. 41st St.
Sand Springs, OK 74063
918-245-2104 / Fax: 918-245-2718
STEVE McBRIDE (Owner) & Buys Activewear, Athletic Footwear, Athletics

MOCK BROTHERS SADDLERY, INC. (WW)
17941 W. 9th St. (p-m-b)
Sand Springs, OK 74063
918-245-7259 / Fax: 918-245-5234
Sales: $100,001-$500,000
ALBERT R. MOCK (Owner) & Buys Store Displays, Fixtures, Supplies
BRETT MOCK-Men's & Boys' Western Wear

SHEPHERD'S (MW)
116 E. Main St. (b)
Shawnee, OK 74801
405-275-2280
Sales: $100,001-$500,000
TOM SHEPHERD (Co-Owner)
NICK SHEPHERD (Co-Owner) & Buys Men's Sportswear, Accessories, Big & Tall Men's Wear, Store Displays, Fixtures, Supplies

BAYOUTH'S DEPARTMENT STORE (DEPT-2)
P.O. Box 277 (p)
110 E. Rogers Blvd.
Skiatook, OK 74070
918-396-2211 / Fax: 918-396-3102
Sales: $100,001-$500,000
A. B. BAYOUTH (President) & Buys Men's Sportswear, Furnishings, Accessories, Boys' Wear, Store Displays, Fixtures, Supplies

BATES BROTHERS, INC. (MW)
704 S. Main St. (b)
Stillwater, OK 74074
405-372-8158 / Fax: 405-377-3613
Sales: $1 Million-$10 Million
RICHARD EASTER (Owner) & Buys Men's Sportswear, Furnishings, Headwear, Accessories, Footwear, Store Displays, Fixtures, Supplies

KATZ DEPARTMENT STORE (DEPT)
(Div. of DUNLAP CO.)
P.O. Box 2467 (b)
701 S. Main St.
Stillwater, OK 74076
405-372-4225 / Fax: 405-743-8123
DENNIS SILVERS (Store Mgr.) & Buys Men's Men's Wear, Store Displays, Fixtures and Supplies

UNIVERSITY SPIRIT (SP)
244 S. Knoblock St.
Stillwater, OK 74074
405-377-0555 / Fax: 405-377-2204
CHRIS NORRIS (Owner) & Buys Activewear

WOODEN NICKEL (CLO)
225 S. Knoblock St. (m-b)
Stillwater, OK 74074
405-377-8808 / Fax: 405-377-8814
Sales: $500,000-$1 Million
K. COHLMIA (Owner) & Buys Men's Sportswear, Leather Apparel, Furnishings, Footwear, Store Displays, Fixtures, Supplies

KIMBERLY'S BOUTIQUE (CLO)
105 N. Muskogee Ave. (m-b)
Tahlequah, OK 74464
918-456-7766
Sales: $100,001-$500,000
KIM BUTLER (Owner) & Buys Men's & Boys' Formal Wear, Store Displays, Fixtures, Supplies

WORKMAN DEPARTMENT STORE, INC. (DEPT)
235 N. Muskogee Ave. (m)
Tahlequah, OK 74464
918-456-6931 / Fax: 918-456-6454
Sales: $1 Million-$10 Million
CHARLES WORKMAN (Owner) & Buys Men's Sportswear, Furnishings, Headwear, Accessories, Leather Apparel, Boys' Wear, Store Displays, Fixtures, Supplies

ABERSON'S MEN'S (MW)
(CABERSON'S COMPANIES, INC.)
3509 S. Peoria Rd.
Tulsa, OK 74105
918-742-2421 / Fax: 918-744-0621
Sales: $100,001-$500,000
STEVE ABERSON (Owner) & Buys Men's Sportswear, Outerwear, Accessories, Footwear, Store Displays, Fixtures, Supplies

BRENNER'S LTD. (MW)
427 S. Boston Ave., #250 (m-b)
Tulsa, OK 74103
918-583-8555 / Fax: 918-583-4780
Sales: $100,001-$500,000
SAM BRENNER (Owner) & Buys Men's Wear, Suits, Sportswear, Footwear, Furnishings

CAMBRIDGE LTD. (CLO)
6808 S. Memorial, #155 (p)
Tulsa, OK 74133
918-252-9120 / Fax: 918-252-0423
Sales: $100,001-$500,000
N. K. BHOJWANI (Owner) & Buys Men's Sportswear, Furnishings, Accessories, Footwear, Store Displays, Fixtures, Supplies

COJUIS (CLO)
5073 N. Peoria Rd. (p)
Tulsa, OK 74126
918-425-1104 / Fax: 918-425-5130
Sales: $100,001-$500,000
FERDINE WILLIS (Owner) & Buys Men's Sportswear, Urban Contemporary, Furnishings, Accessories, Young Men's & Boys' Wear, Store Displays, Fixtures & Supplies

OKLAHOMA - Tulsa

DRYSDALE'S, INC. (CLO)

3220 S. Memorial Dr. (m-b)
Tulsa, OK 74145
918-664-6481 / Fax: 918-664-1431

JIM McCLURE (President) & Buys Store Displays, Fixtures, Supplies

SIGMUND SCHWIER-Men's Overcoats, Suits, Tailored Jackets & Slacks, Raincoats, Sweaters, Outer Jackets, Big & Tall Men's Wear, Leather Apparel, Casual Slacks, Ties, Robes, Underwear, Hosiery, Belts, Headwear, Young Men's Shop, Men's Sport Shirts

DAVE SOMERS-Men Gloves, Jewelry, Small Leather Goods, Fragrances, Men's Footwear

TINA SMITH-Men's Headwear

TAMMY MOODY-Boys' Clothing, Sportswear, Furnishings, Accessories

ED BESHARA'S FINE CLOTHING (MW)

3539 S. Harvard Ave. (b-h)
Tulsa, OK 74135
918-743-6416 / Fax: 918-744-9255
Sales: $100,001-$500,000

ED BESHARA, JR. (Owner) & Buys Men's Wear, Footwear, Store Displays, Fixtures, Supplies

GINGISS FORMAL WEAR (MW)

8125 E. 51st St., #O (m-b)
Tulsa, OK 74145
918-664-4080 / Fax: 918-664-4199
Sales: $100,001-$500,000

SCOTT RYAN (Owner) & Buys Men's & Boys' Formal Wear

MARK-IT STORES OF TULSA, INC. (MW)

4107 S. Yale Ave. (m)
Promenade Mall
Tulsa, OK 74135
918-622-8711 / Fax: 208-293-9970
Sales: $100,001-$500,000

EDDIE TAYLOR (Owner) & Buys Men's Sportswear, Urban Contemporary, Furnishings, Accessories, Headwear, Young Men's, Sizes 7 & Up Boys' Wear, Store Displays, Fixtures & Supplies

NAME BRANDS, INC. (CLO-17)

4705 S. Memorial Dr. (bud-p-m-b)
Tulsa, OK 74145
918-665-4138 / Fax: 918-664-2808
Sales: $10 Million-$50 Million

STEVE HARRISON-Men's & Boys' Wear, Footwear

RUNNER'S WORLD (SP)

3346 E. 51st St.
Tulsa, OK 74135
918-749-7557
Sales: $100,001-$500,000

BOB HOENIG (Owner) & Buys Athletic Footwear, Activewear

WOODWARD DEPARTMENT STORE, INC. (DEPT)

P.O. Box 276
108 S. Broadway St.
Walters, OK 73572
580-875-2172
Sales: $100,001-$500,000

DAVID WOODWARD (Owner) & Buys Men's Sweaters, Sport Shirts, Outer Jackets, Dress Shirts, Ties, Robes, Underwear, Hosiery, Belts, Footwear, Young Men's & Boys' Wear, Store Displays, Fixtures, Supplies

FRANKS DEPARTMENT STORE (DEPT)

109 E. Cecil Ave. (m)
Waynoka, OK 73860
580-824-5351
Sales: $100,001-$500,000

KAMEL COHLMIA (Owner) & Buys Men's Sportswear, Furnishings, Headwear, Accessories, Young Men's & Boys' Wear, Leather Apparel, Store Displays, Fixtures, Supplies

BUTCHER'S MENSWEAR (MW)

106 W. Main St. (m-b)
Weatherford, OK 73096
580-772-1444 / Fax: 580-772-1460
Sales: $500,000-$1 Million

JIM BUTCHER (Co-Owner) & Buys Men's Sportswear, Furnishings, Accessories, Headwear, Young Men's Wear, Store Displays, Fixtures & Supplies

FARRELL BUTCHER (Co-Owner) & Buys Men's Sportswear, Furnishings, Accessories, Headwear, Young Men's Wear, Store Displays, Fixtures & Supplies

O.K. BOOT (WW)

111 E. Main St. (m-b)
Weatherford, OK 73096
580-772-1953 / Fax: 580-772-0302
Sales: $100,001-$500,000

DIANE WRIGHT (Owner) & Buys Men's Sportswear, Western Wear, Headwear, Accessories, Footwear, Big & Tall Men's Wear, Store Displays, Fixtures, Supplies

B & M FAMILY STORE (CLO)

P.O. Box 394 (m)
225 W. Main St.
Wilburton, OK 74578
918-465-3669
Sales: $100,001-$500,000

MARGIE HAMMONS (Owner) & Buys Men's Casual Western Wear, Jeans, Belts, T-shirts, Footwear, Young Men's & Boys' Wear, Store Displays, Fixtures & Supplies

MASHORE'S DEPARTMENT STORE (DEPT)

P.O. Box 148 (m-b)
107 W. Main St.
Wilson, OK 73463
580-668-2196
Sales: $100,001-$500,000

JERRY MASHORE (Co-Owner) & Buys Men's Sportswear, Furnishings, Footwear, Accessories, 8 to 20 Young Men's & Boys' Wear, Store Displays, Fixtures & Supplies

JOHN D'S SADDLERY (WW)

2630 Oklahoma Ave. (p-m)
Woodward, OK 73801
580-256-2680
Sales: $100,001-$500,000

JOHN D. MARSTON (Owner) & Buys Men's & Boys' Western Wear, Footwear, Store Displays, Fixtures, Supplies

METTRY'S (DEPT)

P.O. Box 308 (p-m)
101 S. Dean A. McGee Ave.
Wynnewood, OK 73098
405-665-2230 / Fax: 405-665-5703
Sales: $100,001-$500,000

CRAIG S. METTRY (President) & Buys Men's, Young Men's & 8 to 20 Boys' Sportswear, Furnishings, Headwear, Accessories, Western Wear, Footwear, Big & Tall Men's Wear, Store Displays, Fixtures, Supplies

NIMBUS (CLO)
25 E. Main St. (b)
Ashland, OR 97520
541-482-3621 / Fax: 541-482-3898
Website: www.hisfavoriteshirts.com
KEN SILVERMAN (Owner) & Buys Men's Wear, Sportswear, Dress & Casual Shirts, Furnishings, Accessories, Store Displays, Fixtures and Supplies

STEVEN'S FINE CLOTHING (CLO)
1197 Commercial St. (p)
Astoria, OR 97103
503-325-1421 / Fax: 503-325-1421
STEVEN KUSTURA (Owner) & Buys Men's Wear, Young Men's & 8 to 20 Boys' Wear, Sportswear, Furnishings, Accessories, Store Displays, Fixtures, Supplies

ATHLETIC DEPARTMENT (SP-2)
(FIVE STAR SPORTS)
3275 SW Cedar Hills Blvd.
Beaverton, OR 97005
503-646-0691 / Fax: 503-646-0692
Sales: $1 Million-$10 Million
DANNY ADAMS (Owner) & Buys Activewear, Athletic Footwear

MOHAN CUSTOM CLOTHIERS (CLO & OL)
(MOHAN, INC.)
16270 SW Cormorant Ct. (b-des)
Beaverton, OR 97007
503-579-2900 / Fax: 503-579-5600
Sales: $100,001-$500,000
Website: www.mohanclothiers.com
PIERRE MOHAN (President) & Buys Men's Custom Suits, Tailored Jackets, Tailored Slacks, Casual Slacks, Ties
R. MOHAN (V.P.) & Buys Men's Custom Suits, Tailored Jackets, Tailored Slacks, Casual Slacks, Ties

NIKE, INC. (FW-88 & OL)
(NIKE FACTORY STORE)
(NIKE STORE)
(NIKE TOWN)
1 Bowerman Dr. (m-b)
Beaverton, OR 97005
503-641-6453 / Fax: 503-671-6300
Sales: Over $1 Billion
Website: www.nike.com
Retail Locations: NH, CT, NJ, NY, PA, DE, VA, MD, NC,SC, GA, FL AL TN, MS, KY, OH, IN, MI, IA, WI, MN,IL, MD, TX CO, UT, AZ, NV, CA, OR, WA, MA, HI
PHILIP H. KNIGHT (C.E.O. & President)
MARY KATE BUCKLEY (V.P.-E-Commerce)
PAUL MIGAKI (V.P. & G.M. (U.S. Equipment)
CRAIG ZANON (V.P. & G.M. (U.S. Footwear)
ROB GROSCUP (Real Estate Contact)
SONJA WEBB-Boys' Apparel, Boys' Footwear, Leather Goods, Licensed Apparel, Men's Footwear, Men's Apparel, Watches, Men's Accessories, Hosiery

COLUMBIA SPORTSWEAR (SP)
Primeout Mall
61316 S. Hwy. 97
Bend, OR 97701
541-389-5008 / Fax: 541-389-6152
RICHARD FREUND (Store Mgr.) & Buys Activewear, Athletic Footwear

LOCAL JOE (CLO)
929 NW Wall St.
Bend, OR 97701
541-385-7137 / Fax: 541-385-7415
A.J. CHOEN (Owner) & Buys Men's Wear, Young Men's Wear, Sportswear, Footwear, Accessories, Hosiery, Furnishings, Denim

ROBERT'S CLOTHES (CLO)
945 NW Wall St. (b-h)
Bend, OR 97701
541-382-2391 / Fax: 541-382-2758
ROBERT OLSON (Owner) & Buys Men's Wear, Sportswear, Footwear, Headwear, Furnishings, Accessories, Store Displays, Fixtures and Supplies
MARK OLSON (Mgr.) & Buys Men's Wear, Sportswear, Footwear, Furnishings, Accessories, Store Displays, Fixtures, and Supplies

SPOTTED MULE SADDLERY & WESTERN WEAR (WW)
2221 NE 3rd Ave. (m-b)
Bend, OR 97701
541-389-9144 / Fax: 541-389-6861
MONT WEST (Owner)
CINDY PARSONS-Men's & Boys' Western Wear, Furnishings, Accessories, Footwear

CANNON BAY BEACH CLUB (SP)
198 N. Hemlock
Cannon Beach, OR 97110
503-436-1919 / Fax: 503-436-1919
DAVID DASSE (Owner) & Buys Activewear, Swimwear

CANNON BEACH OUTDOOR WEAR (CLO & OL)
239 N. Hemlock (p-m)
Cannon Beach, OR 97110
503-436-2832 / Fax: 503-436-2832
WHITNEY GREENAWALD (Owner) & Buys Men's Outerwear, Raincoats, Shorts, Sweaters, Sport Shirts, Outer Jackets, Casual Slacks, Underwear, Hosiery, Headwear, Gloves, Belts, Sandals, Store Displays, Fixtures, Supplies

EL MUNDO FOR MEN (MW-2 & OL)
P.O. Box 164 (m-b)
Cannon Beach, OR 97110
503-436-1002 / Fax: 503-436-1003
Website: www.elmundo.com
GEORGE VETTER (Owner) & Buys Men's Sportswear, Headwear, Furnishings, Accessories, Men's, Young Men's & Boys' Novelty T-shirts, Boxer Shorts, Men's and Boys' Formal Wear, Tuxedos, Furnishings, Accessories, Store Displays, Fixtures, Supplies

HENRY'S (CLO)
P.O. Box 430 (m)
Cannon Beach, OR 97110
503-436-2618 / Fax: 503-436-2769
Sales: $100,001-$500,000
PAUL DUEBER (Owner) & Buys Men's & Boys' T-shirts, Sweaters, Pants, Footwear, Store Displays, Fixtures, Supplies

NICK ALLAN'S MENSWEAR (MW)
250 SW 3rd St. (m)
Corvalis, OR 97333
541-753-3717 / Fax: 541-753-1157
NICK BONOMO (Owner) & Buys Men's Sportswear, Furnishings, Headwear, Accessories, Shoes, Dress Boots, Young Men's Wear, Store Displays, Fixtures, Supplies

SEDLAK'S BOOTS & SHOES (FW)
225 SW 2nd St. (b)
Corvalis, OR 97333
541-752-1498 / Fax: 541-752-1498
PAUL MUMFORD (President) & Buys Men's Work & Hiking Boots, Casual Shoes, Dress Shoes, Hosiery, Hosiery, Headwear, Outdoor Clothing, Sweaters, Outer Jackets, Store Displays, Fixtures, Supplies

OREGON - Corvallis

MEHLHAF'S STORE FOR MEN (MW)
300 SW Madison (m-b)
Corvallis, OR 97333
541-757-8070
Sales: $500,000-$1 Million
RICHARD C. MEHLHAF (President) & Buys Men's Overcoats, Suits, Tailored Jackets, Tailored Slacks, Raincoats, Sportswear, Sweaters, Sport Shirts, Outer Jackets, Casual Slacks, Active Apparel, Furnishings, Headwear, Accessories, Footwear, Store Displays, Fixtures, Supplies

SCHWEITZER CASUAL MENSWEAR (CLO)
730 Main St. (m)
Cottage Grove, OR 97424
541-942-4249
AL SCHWEITZER (Co-Owner)
TIM SCHWEITZER (Co-Owner) & Buys Men's Work Clothes, Western Wear, Related Furnishings, Furnishings, Headwear, Accessories, Men's, Young Men's & Boys' Boots, Store Displays, Fixtures, Supplies

HARRY RITCHIE'S JEWELERS, INC. (JWLY-28)
(DON RINGMAKER)
956 Willamette St.
Eugene, OR 97401
541-686-1787 / Fax: 541-485-8841
Sales: $10 Million-$50 Million
Website: www.harryritchies.com
Retail Locations: OR, WA, CA, ID
HARRY RITCHIE (Chmn.)
DONALD RITCHIE (President)
DEBBIE VEUM-Jewelry, Watches
GENERAL GROWTH (Real Estate Contact)

McKENZIE OUTFITTERS (CLO-2)
475 Valley River Ctr. (b)
Eugene, OR 97401
541-343-2300 / Fax: 541-344-7351
Sales: $100,001-$500,000
JERRY GODFREY (President) & Buys Men's Sweaters, Sport Shirts, Outer Jackets, Dress Shoes, Gloves, Belts, Headwear, T-shirts, Shorts, Boots, Athletic Footwear, Store Displays, Fixtures, Supplies

RUN PRO (SP)
525 High St.
Eugene, OR 97401
541-343-1842 / Fax: 541-868-2083
GENE SOLOMON (Owner) & Buys Activewear, Athletic Footwear

TROUTMAN'S EMPORIUM, INC. (DEPT-35)
P.O. Box 5467 (p-m)
86776 McVay Hwy.
Eugene, OR 97405
(ARKIN CALIFORNIA)
541-746-9611 / Fax: 541-747-7891
Sales: $100 Million-$500 Million
Website: www.emporiumonline.com
Retail Locations: OR, WA, ID, CA, NV
DALLAS TROUTMAN (Chmn.)
RON SCHIFF (President & Real Estate Contact)
RON TROUTMAN (G.M.M.)
KITTY BATES-Men's Overcoats, Suits, Tailored Jackets, Tailored Slacks, Raincoats, Casual Slacks, Furnishings, Dress Shirts, Ties, Big & Tall Men's Wear, Men's Leather Apparel, Outerwear, Robes, Headwear, Gloves, Underwear, Belts, Small Leather Goods, Jewelry, Fragrances, Active Apparel
JANE MCMAHON-Men's Sweaters, Sport Shirts
RALPH MATTESON-Men's Basic Jeans, Jackets, Levis & Work Clothes, Western Wear
MICHAEL RANGELOFF-Young Men's Wear
OPEN-Boys' Wear
BOB CRAWFORD-Men's Footwear, Athletic Footwear
VAUGH GLENN-Store Displays, Fixtures & Supplies

RLK & CO. (CLO)
(TIMBERLINE LODGE GIFT SHOP)
Timberline Lodge Ski Area
Government Camp, OR 97028
503-272-3311 / Fax: 503-622-0710
Sales: $100,001-$500,000
Website: www.timberlinelodge.com
JEFF KOHNSTAMM (Owner)
BARBARA TAYLOR-Casual Apparel, Skiwear

FITNESS STUFF, INC. (OL & MO)
478 NE 219th St.
Gresham, OR 97030
503-661-5560 / Fax: 503-669-9519
Sales: $500,001-$1 Million
Website: www.fitnessstuffusa.com
CAROL WOODY (Owner) & Buys Men's Activewear, Athletic Footwear, Fitness & Exercise Clothing

GARDNER'S MENSWEAR (MW)
193 N. Main St. (p)
Heppner, OR 97836
541-676-9218
Website: www.heppner.net
LEROY GARDNER (Owner) & Buys Men's Wear, Sportswear, Furnishings, Accessories, Young Men's Wear, Urban Contemporary, Boys' Dress Shirts, Store Displays, Fixtures and Supplies

ROEMARKS MENSWEAR, INC. (MW)
201 E. Main St. (b)
Hermiston, OR 97838
541-567-3831 / Fax: 541-567-3619
ROE GARDNER (Co-Owner)
MARILYN GARDNER (Co-Owner) & Buys Men's Sportswear, Western Wear, Furnishings, Headwear, Shoes, Boots, Accessories, Young Men's Wear, Urban Contemporary, Store Displays, Fixtures, Supplies

BOOT HILL (WW & OL)
2139 N. Cornell Rd. (m)
Hillsboro, OR 97124
503-648-7925 / Fax: 503-693-6689
Website: www.boot-hill.com
LOREN BENNETT (Owner) & Buys Men's, Young Men's & Boys' Western Wear, Related Furnishings, Headwear, Boots, Accessories, Store Displays, Fixtures, Supplies

LA HAIE'S MAN'S SHOP, INC. (MW)
277 E. Main (m-b)
Hillsboro, OR 97124
503-648-2341 / Fax: 503-648-2342
Sales: $500,000-$1 Million
Website: www.lahaies.com
GREG LaHAIE (Owner) & Buys Men's Sportswear, Leather Jackets, Furnishings, Headwear, Accessories, Young Men's Wear, Big & Tall Men's Wear, Footwear, Store Displays, Fixtures, Supplies

NORM THOMPSON (CLO-6 & OL & MO)
3188 NW Aloclek Dr.
Hillsboro, OR 97124
503-614-4600 / Fax: 503-614-4637
Website: www.normthompson.com
REBECCA JEWLETT (President)
ANN HJEMBOE (V.P.-Mdse.) & Buys Store Display, Fixtures, Supplies
ELLIOT WAHBA-Men's Casual Slacks, Tailored Slacks, Sweaters, Outerwear, Underwear
FRANK KRAMHMAN-Men's Robes, Sleepwear, Sport Shirts, Sport Coats
BETH GRUNFIELD-Men's Footwear

MATTERHORN SWISS VILLAGE (CLO-2)
59950 Wallowa Lake Hwy. (m-b)
Joseph, OR 97846
541-432-4071 / Fax: 541-432-4071
Website: www.matterhornswissvillage.com
MARK THORNBERG (Co-Owner) & Buys Men's, Young Men's & Boys' Raincoats, Outer Jackets, T-shirts, Sweaters, Dress Shirts, Active Apparel, Hosiery, Headwear, Accessories, Store Displays, Fixtures, Supplies
GWEN THORNBERG (Co-Owner) & Buys Men's, Young Men's & Boys' Raincoats, Outer Jackets, T-shirts, Sweaters, Dress Shirts, Active Apparel, Hosiery, Headwear, Accessories, Urban Contemporary, Store Displays, Fixtures, Supplies

OREGON - Joseph

SPORTS CORRAL, INC. (CLO)
P.O. Box 58 (p-m-b)
Joseph, OR 97846
541-432-4363 / Fax: 541-432-4363

LARRY SNOOK (Owner) & Buys Men's & Boys' Sportswear, Furnishings, Western Wear, Footwear, Store Displays, Fixtures, Supplies

BIG R RANCH, FARM & HOME (DG-3)
6225 S. 6th St. (p)
Klamath Falls, OR 97603
541-882-5548 / Fax: 541-882-2199

STEVE TYRHOLM (Owner)

SHAYNE HANSEN (@ 541-830-0415)-Men's Sportswear, Dress Shirts, Ties, Underwear, Gloves, Headwear, Accessories, Young Men's & Boys' Wear, Footwear

BOGATAY'S TUXEDO RENTALS (MW)
119 8th St. (b)
Klamath Falls, OR 97601
541-884-8811 / Fax: 541-850-5934
Sales: $500,001-$1 Million

THOMAS GOLDEN (President) & Buys Men's Formalwear, Men's Hosiery, Furnishings, Accessories

MICHELLE GOLDEN (V.P.) & Buys Men's Formalwear, Men's Hosiery, Furnishings, Accessories

DREW'S MEN'S & WOMEN'S APPAREL (CLO)
733 Main St. (p-m-b)
Klamath Falls, OR 97601
541-884-4121 / Fax: 541-883-2539
Website: www.drewsboots.com

PATRICK CAVANAUGH (Owner) & Buys Men's Sportswear, Leather Apparel, Furnishings, Headwear, Accessories, Footwear, Store Displays, Fixtures, Supplies

STEVE MORROW (Asst. Mgr.) & Buys Men's Sportswear, Leather Apparel, Furnishings, Headwear, Accessories, Footwear, Store Displays, Fixtures, Supplies

GLASS BUTTERFLY (KS)
140 A Ave. (m-b)
Lake Oswego, OR 97034
503-636-9043 / Fax: 503-635-9754

PHILLIP CHIZUM (President)

LINDA PARSONS-8 to 20 Boys' Wear, Urban Contemporary, Store Displays, Fixtures, Supplies

FETSCH'S (MW)
15 N. E St.
Lakeview, OR 97630
541-947-2223

CARTER FETSCH (Owner) & Buys Men's, Young Men's & Boys' Clothing, Sportswear, Furnishings, Headwear, Accessories, Shoes, Store Displays, Fixtures, Supplies

CORNER CLOSET (CLO)
2147 Broadway (m)
Malin, OR 97632
541-723-2455 / Fax: 541-723-2443

JANICE KALINA (Owner) & Buys Men's, Young Men's, Boys' Shorts, T-shirts, Sport Shirts, Dress Shoes, Underwear, Hosiery, Gloves, Belts, Small Leather Goods

BLACK BIRD SHOPPING CENTER (MW & OL)
1810 W. Main St. (p-m-b)
Medford, OR 97501
541-779-5431 / Fax: 541-779-4151
Sales: $1 Million-$10 Million
Website: www.b-bird.com

BILL QUITT (President & Gen. Mgr.) & Buys Store Displays, Fixtures, Supplies

RANDY HALL-Men's & Boys' Clothing, Sportswear, Furnishings, Accessories

TOM MAYER-Footwear

JACKSON'S MEN'S STORE (MW)
621 Medford Ctr. (m-b)
Medford, OR 97504
541-773-6260 / Fax: 541-773-3082

RAY JACKSON (Owner) & Buys Men's Sportswear, Furnishings, Accessories, Store Displays, Fixtures and Supplies

NORRIS SHOE CO. (FW)
221 E. Main St. (m)
Medford, OR 97501
541-772-2123 / Fax: 541-772-9373
Website: www.norrisshoes.com

JOHN NORRIS (Owner) & Buys Men's Work Shoes, Dress Shoes, Casual Shoes, Boots, Athletic Footwear, Slippers, Sandals, Hosiery, Belts

SPORTSTER (MW)
412 N. Main St. (m-b)
Milton-Freewater, OR 97862
541-938-3607 / Fax: 541-938-3607

ROYAL HANSEN (Owner) & Buys Men's Sportswear, Furnishings, Footwear, Accessories, Young Men's Wear, Store Displays, Fixtures, Supplies

QUISENBERRY'S (MW)
207 S. Oregon St., #2109 (m-b)
Ontario, OR 97914
541-889-5114 / Fax: 541-889-4512

WINSTON QUISENBERRY (Owner) & Buys Men's Western Clothing, Sportswear, Furnishings, Headwear, Accessories, Big & Tall Men's Western & Traditional Wear, Footwear, Store Displays, Fixtures, Supplies

GRANT GRIGG (Mgr.) & Buys Men's Western Clothing, Sportswear, Furnishings, Headwear, Accessories, Big & Tall Men's Western & Traditional Wear, Footwear, Urban Contemporary, Store Displays, Fixtures, Supplies

RED'S CLOTHING CO. (SP)
233 S. Main St.
Pendleton, OR 97801
541-278-1404
Sales: $100,001-$500,000
Website: www.redsclothingco.com

MIKE WALLIS (Owner) & Buys Hunting Boots, Western Wear, Furnishings, Accessories

ANDY & BAX SURPLUS (CLO)
(B & A DISTRIBUTING)
324 SE Grand Ave. (bud-p-m)
Portland, OR 97214
503-234-7538 / Fax: 503-239-8817
Sales: $1 Million-$10 Million
Website: www.andyandbax.com

DAN BAXTER (Owner)

TED SCHOPF (Mgr.) & Buys Men's Cold Weather Outerwear, Raincoats, Sweaters, Outer Jackets, Active Apparel, Hosiery, Gloves, Headwear, Belts, Footwear, Store Displays, Fixtures, Supplies

ESTES MEN'S CLOTHING (MW)
2328 W. Burnside (b)
Portland, OR 97210
503-227-0275 / Fax: 503-227-0273
Sales: $500,000-$1 Million
Website: www.estesmens.com

TONY SPEAR (Owner) & Buys Men's Sportswear, Leather Apparel, Furnishings, Headwear, Accessories, Footwear, Store Displays, Fixtures, Supplies

OREGON - Portland

FRED MEYER, INC. (DEPT-134)

(Div. of THE KROGER CO.)
P.O. Box 42121 (p)
3800 SE 22nd Ave.
Portland, OR 97242
503-232-8844 / Fax: 503-797-7435
Sales: $15 Billion
Website: www.fredmeyer.com
Retail Locations: AZ, CA, ID, IL, OH, OR, UT, WA, WI

DARRELL WEBB (President) (@ 503-797-7417)
SAM K. DUNCAN (C.E.O.)
DAVID CAMPISI (Sr. V.P. - Apparel)
PAMELA CRANE (Real Estate Contact)
MARY FITZPATRICK (Visual Mdsg. Mgr.) & Buys Store Displays, Fixtures & Supplies

KELLY PERRY (V.P. & D.M.M. - Men's)
ANITA WINT-Men's Dress Shirts, Ties, Dress Slacks, Headwear, Sweaters, Outerwear, Sportshirts, Casual Slacks, Big & Tall Wear
TINA CAUTHORN-Men's Basic, Robes, Underwear, Hosiery, Luggage
KRISTI HOLCHOULS-Men's Casualwear
JODI ROBERTS-Men's Sportswear
MATT HALEY-Big & Tall Men's Wear
HEATHER GAIGER-Men's Outwerwear
BRENT BEEBE-Young Men's Wear
MOLLY BASSETT-Sportswear, Activewear, Belts, Accessories

RICK HOALST (V.P. - Children's Mdse.)
SUSAN SUNASALEI-Boys' 4 to 20
AMY BRENELMAN-Toddlers' 4 to 7
MICHELLE VANESS-8 to 18 Boys' Sportswear & Outerwear, Toddlers' & Boys' 4 to 20

BETH ARKO (V.P. - Children's Footwear)
MICHAEL MACCHIONE-Boys' Footwear

JOHN HELMER HABERDASHER (MW & OL)

969 SW Broadway (b)
Portland, OR 97205
503-223-4976 / Fax: 503-223-8451
Sales: $500,000-$1 Million
Website: www.johnhelmer.com

JOHN HELMER, III (President) & Buys Men's Sportswear, Furnishings, Headwear, Accessories, Young Men's Wear, Store Displays, Fixtures, Supplies

JOWER'S, INC. (MW)

8801 N. Lombard St. (bud-p)
Portland, OR 97203
503-286-1818 / Fax: 503-285-9781
Sales: $500,001-$1 Million

MARILYN KORENAGA (President) & Buys Men's Footwear, Men's Apparel, Men's Hosiery, Work Clothing

THE LION'S DEN, INC. (MW)

(THE MAN'S SHOP)
8511 N. Lombard St. (m)
Portland, OR 97203
503-286-3514
Sales: $500,000-$1 Million

JERRY A. LEVETON (Co-Owner) & Buys Men's Sportswear, Leather Apparel, Furnishings, Headwear, Accessories, Footwear, Young Men's Wear, Store Displays, Fixtures, Supplies
ROBERT J. LEVETON (Co-Owner) & Buys Men's Sportswear, Leather Apparel, Furnishings, Headwear, Accessories, Footwear, Young Men's Wear, Urban Contemporary, Store Displays, Fixtures, Supplies

MARIO'S, INC. (MW & CLO-2)

833 SW Broadway (b)
Portland, OR 97205
503-241-5034 / Fax: 503-299-6277
Sales: $1 Million-$10 Million
Website: www.marios.com

MARIO BISIO (Owner) & Buys Men's Sportswear, Leather Apparel, Footwear, Urban Contemporary, Accessories
MARK JENSEN-Men's Clothing,Sportswear, Leather Apparel, Urban Contemporary, Accessories, Footwear
PATRICK ANGUS-Store Displays, Fixtures, Supplies

MEIER & FRANK (DEPT-21)

(ZCMI - ZION'S CO-OPERATIVE MERCANTILE INSTITUTION)
(Div. of MAY DEPARTMENT STORES COMPANY)
621 SW 5th Ave. (bud-p-m-b-h)
Portland, OR 97204
503-223-0512 / Fax: 503-241-2671
Sales: $399 Million
Website: www.meierandfrank.com
Retail Locations: OR, UT, WA

CRAIG ISRAEL (President & C.E.O.)
JIM WEINBERG (V.P. & G.M.M.)
KEVIN SHOENER (D.M.M.-Men's & Boys' Wear)
ROBIN CROWELL (D.M.M.- Men's Sportswear & Collections)
FRANK COCONATO (D.M.M.-Men's Sportswear & Collections)
STEVE HAAS (D.M.M.-Men's Furnishings)
JENNIFER DUNAJSKI-Men's Knit Shirts, Lauren, Golf Knits, Sweaters
RALPH COLLINS-Men's Fashion Accessories, Furnishings, Hosiery, Loungewear, Underwear, Gloves
STEVE CORVI-Men's Sportshirts, Izod, Carribean Joe, Izod Jeans, Ralph Lauren Chaps
JEFF STEINBERG-Men's MDSI, Active Separates, Swimwear, Russell Athletic, Nike, Licensed Apparel, Outerwear, Walkshorts, Designer Shorts, Dockers Walkshorts, Izod
JAY MORRISON-Men's Collections, Quiksilveredition, Polo Belts, Tommy Hilfiger, Polo, Nautica
HENRY MONTALVO-Men's Suits, Suit Separates, Pant Suits, Rainwear/Topcoats
BETH WHITE-Men's Dress Slacks, Slates/Levi Pants, Designer Dress Pants, Dockers Pants, Casual Slacks, Lauren Pants, Designer Casual Pants
CHRIS GRATTAN-Denim Collections, Tommy Jeans, Polo Jeans Co., Nautica Jeans, Guess Jeans, Calvin Klein Jeans, DKNY Jeans, Lucky Brand Jeans, French Connection, Trend
CHARLIE CONOVER-Guys 8-20 Separates, Furnishings, Casual Pants, Levi Bottoms, Shorts & Young Men's Levi Jeans/Pants, Levi Shorts, Levi Knits, Levi Wovens
LIZ FISKE-AMELUXEN-Guys 8-20 Woven Tops, Russell, Knit Tops, Active, Sweaters, Outerwear, Ocean Pacific, Guess, Ecko, Quiksilver, Lucky Brand Jeans, Other Collections, Nautica, Hilfiger
KIRK LOHMOLDER-Men's Better Sportscoats, Blazers, Better Dress Slacks
LYNN SARVER-Men's Collections, Perry Ellis, Claiborne, Kenneth Cole, DKNY
KARA AYERS-Men's Underwear, Hosiery, Jockey, Sleepwear, Robes
SUE KIEFER-Men's Belts, Sunglasses, Small Leather Goods, Gifts, Seasonal, Accessories, Personal Electronics
RICK HLAD-Men's Furnishings, Izod, Private Label, Van Heusen, Better Dress, G. Beene, R.L. Dress Shirts

(MEIER & FRANK Cont. on next page)

OREGON - Portland

(MEIER & FRANK Cont.)

SHAWN SALAS-Neckwear
LINDA MOHOLT-Updated Footwear
MELISSA RAPP-Men's Fragrances
KIM SIMPSON (D.M.M.-Footwear)
GLEN STENSRUD-Athletic Footwear
KIM SHORT-Better Footwear
CHRIS HAMPSON (Design & Construction Mgr.) & Buys Store Displays, Fixtures, Supplies
CHRIS MANSON (Real Estate Contact)

PHILLIP STEWART CUSTOM (MW)

1202 19th Ave. SW (b)
Portland, OR 97205
503-226-3589 / Fax: 503-226-6719
Sales: $500,001-$1 Million

JIM MAER (Owner) & Buys Leather Goods, Men's Big & Tall Apparel, Men's & Boys' Apparel, Men's Casualwear, Men's Denim Apparel, Men's Formalwear, Men's Accessories, Men's Hosiery, Men's Outerwear, Men's Sportswear, Men's Suits, Men's Swimwear

SIZES UNLIMITED (MW-5)

2523 SE 9th St. (p)
Portland, OR 97202
503-230-9510 / Fax: 503-230-8035

TONY ODIERNO (President) & Buys Big & Tall Men's Sportswear, Furnishings, Accessories, Urban Contemporary, Store Displays, Fixtures, Supplies

THE TUX SHOP (MW-65)

(MR. FORMAL, INC.)
1205 SE Grand Ave. (bud-p-m-b-h)
Portland, OR 97214
503-239-8838 / Fax: 503-239-8883
Sales: $1 Million-$10 Million
Website: www.mrformaltuxedos.com
Retail Locations: OR, WA, ID, CA

ED HONEYCUTT (President)
VICKI KEITH (G.M.M.) & Buys Men's Formal Wear, Dress Shirts, Ties, Jewelry, Accessories, Hosiery, Gloves, Headwear

PRINEVILLE'S MENSWEAR (MW)

231 Main St. (p)
Prineville, OR 97754
541-447-6580 / Fax: 541-447-5179
Sales: $100,001-$500,000
Website: www.prinevillesmesnwear.com

EDDIE LANE (Co-Owner)
MARIE LANE (Co-Owner)
JIM LANE (Co-Owner) & Buys Men's Suits, Tailored Slacks, Leather Apparel, Raincoats, Sportswear, Furnishings, Headwear, Accessories, Western Wear, Work Clothes, Footwear, Store Displays, Fixtures, Supplies

ANTIDOTE (CLO)

446 SW 6th St. (p-m)
Redmond, OR 97756
541-504-1807 / Fax: 541-504-1856

KENNY MARKS (Owner) & Buys Boys' Wear Up to 7, Urban Contemporary, Street Wear, Boys' Footwear, Boys' Accessories, Boys' Furnishings, and Young Men's Clothing
DEBBIE EARP-Boys' Wear Up to 7, Urban Contemporary, Street Wear, Boys' Footwear, Boys' Accessories, Boys' Furnishings, and Young Men's Clothing

FORMALLY YOURS (SP)

519 SE Jackson St. (p)
Roseburg, OR 97470
541-672-8233 / Fax: 541-672-4607

RAMON COMELLAS (Owner) & Buys Formal Wear, Related Furnishings, Accessories, Store Displays, Fixtures and Supplies
ROBERT COMELLAS-Formal Wear, Related Furnishings, Accessories, Store Displays, Fixtures and Supplies

HARRINGTON CLOTHING (MW)

1817 Columbia Blvd. (m)
Saint Helens, OR 97051
503-397-4052 / Fax: 503-366-3788

DON-Men's Wear, Sportswear, Furnishings, Accessories, Young Men's Wear, Urban Contemporary, Boys' Wear, Store Displays, Fixtures and Supplies

DOUBLE H WESTERN WEAR (WW)

4198 Silverton Rd. NE (p-m)
Salem, OR 97305
503-362-4973 / Fax: 503-362-3150
Website: www.doublehwesternwear.com

MIKE HODGES (Owner) & Buys Men's & Boys' Western Wear, Footwear, Store Displays, Fixtures, Supplies

LES NEWMAN'S WORK & OUTDOOR CLOTHING (CLO)

(C. L. NEWMAN CO., INC.)
179 Commercial NE (m-b)
Salem, OR 97301
503-363-5508 / Fax: 503-588-2637

GREG SYVERSON (Owner) & Buys Men's Outerwear, Sportswear, Furnishings, Accessories, Footwear, Store Displays, Fixtures, Supplies

MORRY'S LTD. (MW)

(MORRY'S MEN'S STORE, INC.)
554 Ferry St. SE (b)
Salem, OR 97301
503-370-9744 / Fax: 503-370-7501

MORRY RAGLE (Partner) & Buys Men's Clothing
JIM ADAMS (Partner) & Buys Men's Sportswear, Leather Apparel, Furnishings, Headwear, Accessories, Store Displays, Fixtures, Supplies

SHRYOCK'S APPAREL (MW)

290 Commercial St. NE (m-b)
Salem, OR 97301
503-363-9292 / Fax: 503-363-9294
Sales: $1 Million-$10 Million

MARK MESSMER (President) & Buys Men's Sportswear, Furnishings, Accessories, Footwear
KIRK MESSMER-Men's Sportswear, Furnishings, Accessories, Footwear

VAN'S OUTDOOR STORE (WW)

831 Lancaster Dr. NE (m)
Salem, OR 97301
503-399-7096 / Fax: 503-589-8058

JOHN WELLS (Owner)
WENDY MOREY-Men's Jeans, Outdoor Clothing, Belts, T-shirts, Fleece, Formal Wear

TERHARS, INC. (CLO)

P.O. Box 8 (p-m)
27 Broadway
Seaside, OR 97138
503-738-5515 / Fax: 503-738-7532

PETER TERHAR (Partner) (@ 503-738-5516) & Buys Footwear, Sandals, Men's Sportswear, Leather Apparel, Headwear, Accessories, Young Men's & Boys' Wear, Urban Contemporary, Store Displays, Fixtures, Supplies
JEFF TERHAR (Partner) & Buys Men's Sportswear, Leather Apparel, Headwear, Accessories, Young Men's & Boys' Wear, Store Displays, Fixtures, Supplies

LEAVITT'S WESTERN WEAR (WW)

100 E. Cascade (p-m)
Sisters, OR 97759
541-549-6451 / Fax: 541-549-4771

JOHN LEAVITT (Owner) & Buys Men's & Boys' Western Wear, Store Displays, Fixtures, Supplies

LAXTON'S BIG AND TALL (MW)

505 S. A St.
Springfield, OR 97477
541-747-9412 / Fax: 541-747-2348

KENT LAXTON (Owner) & Buys Big & Tall Men's Wear, Men's Accessories, Furnishings

JENSEN-KREITZER CLOTHING (DEPT)

351 N. 3rd Ave. (m)
Stayton, OR 97383
503-769-5572 / Fax: 503-769-5572

TODD JENSEN (Owner) & Buys Sportswear, Furnishings, Accessories, Store Displays, Fixtures and Supplies

DAN-DEE SALES (MW)

610 Main St. (p)
Sweet Home, OR 97386
541-367-5544 / Fax: 541-367-5197

JACK LEGG (Owner) & Buys Work Clothes, Underwear, Hosiery, Gloves, Headwear, Belts, Jeans, Store Displays, Fixtures and Supplies

OREGON - The Dalles

TONY'S TOWN & COUNTRY, INC. (MW)

401 E. 2nd St. (bud-p-m-b)
The Dalles, OR 97058
541-296-5230 / Fax: 541-296-1820
Sales: $500,000-$1 Million

JIM DAY (Owner) & Buys Big & Tall Men's Wear, Men's Sportswear, Boys' Wear, Sweaters, Sport Shirts, Outer Jackets, Leather Apparel, Casual Slacks, Active Apparel, Furnishings, Dress Shirts, Ties, Robes, Underwear, Hoisery, Gloves, Headwear, Store Displays, Fixtures, Supplies

WOODBURN DEPARTMENT STORE, INC. (DEPT)

P.O. Box 191 (m)
979 N. Pacific Hwy.
Woodburn, OR 97071
503-982-0091
Sales: $500,000-$1 Million

AYESH SHANAH (Owner) & Buys Men's & Boys' Wear, Store Displays, Fixtures, Supplies

RUN AROUND, INC. (FW-2)
1351 Easton Rd. (p)
Abington, PA 19001
215-886-6937 / Fax: 215-886-9512
Sales: $1 Million-$10 Million
HANK DE VINCENT (President) & Buys Men's & Boys' Dress Shoes, Casual Shoes, Slippers, Hiking Boots, Hosiery, Store Displays, Fixtures, Supplies

BIG APPLE FASHIONS (CLO & FW)
806 E. Hamilton St.
Allentown, PA 18101
610-820-5353 / Fax: 610-820-5535
VICTOR KAPOOR (Owner) & Buys Men's & Boys' Athletic Footwear, Boots

C.E. ROTH FORMAL WEAR (MW)
208 N. 10th St. (m-b)
Allentown, PA 18102
610-432-9452 / Fax: 610-432-6176
MARTIN SEMMEL (Owner) & Buys Men's & Boys' Formal Wear

FINISH LINE RUNNING STORE (SP)
17 S. 12th St.
Allentown, PA 18102
610-432-9939 / Fax: 610-434-3422
Sales: $501,000-$1 Million
Website: www.finishlinerunningstore.com
CHRIS SCHMIDT (Owner) & Buys Men's Activewear, Athletic Footwear

N. LANDAU HYMAN JEWELERS (JWLY-62)
(THE LANDAU COLLECTION OF COSTUME JEWELRY)
Village W. Shopping Court
Allentown, PA 18101
610-435-9755 / Fax: 610-433-2790
Sales: $10 Million-$50 Million
Website: www.landaujewelry.com
Retail Locations: AZ, CA, CT, FL, GA, IL, MD, MA, MI, NV, NY, PA, TX, VA, DC, England
NAT L. HYMAN (Owner & Real Estate Contact)
NICK BAXEVANE (V.P.-Mdse.)
MINA HYMAN (@ 610-740-1086)-Jewelry, Watches

NATIONAL FOOTWEAR (FW-2 & OL)
4571 Tilghman St.
Allentown, PA 18104
610-398-3900 / Fax: 610-398-8199
Website: www.nationalfootwear.com
JOHN DAWSON (Owner) & Buys Men's Casual Shoes, Work Shoes, Boots, Slippers, Store Displays, Fixtures, Supplies

PARK'S MENSWEAR (MW-2)
744 Hamilton Mall (m-b)
Allentown, PA 18101
610-434-5347
JONG KIM (Owner) & Buys Men's & Boys' Footwear

KEITH'S COUNTRY CASUALS (CLO)
2606 Old Rt. 220 North (m-b)
Altoona, PA 16601
814-944-7233 / Fax: 814-944-7282
Sales: $100,001-$500,000
VIRGIL CANNARSA (President) & Buys Men's Leather Apparel, Raincoats, Big & Tall, Outer Jackets, Casual Slacks, Belts, Jewelry, Small Leather Goods, Footwear, Boys' Wear, Store Displays, Fixtures, Supplies

JACKETS 'N' THINGS (MW)
42 E. Butler Ave. (m)
Ambler, PA 19002
215-542-9705 / Fax: 215-542-3991
BARBARA RUGGIERO (Owner) & Buys Men's & Boys' Sportswear, Sportshirts, Outer Jackets, Casual Slacks, Hosiery, Gloves, Belts, Headwear, Store Displays, Fixtures, Supplies

TONY LAGUDA FORMAL WEAR (MW-1)
48 Butler Ave.
Ambler, PA 19002
215-646-2651
TONY LAGUDA (Owner) & Buys Men's & Boys' Formal Wear

CHARLES' MEN'S STORE, INC. (MW)
541 Merchant St. (m)
Ambridge, PA 15003
724-266-2618 / Fax: 724-251-9643
Sales: $100,001-$500,000
NORMAN DiCLEMENTE (President) & Buys Men's Sportswear, Furnishings, Headwear, Accessories, Big & Tall Men's Wear

LOCUST GROVE COUNTRY SHOP (WW)
3153 Garvers Ferry Rd.
Apollo, PA 15613
724-478-1846 / Fax: 724-478-5223
RICHARD LACRONE (Co-Owner) & Buys Men's Western Wear, Outer Jackets, Casual Slacks, Active Apparel
ERIN LACRONE (Co-Owner) & Buys Men's Western Wear, Outer Jackets, Casual Slacks, Active Apparel

STAR ARMY & NAVY, INC. (AN-1)
3414 Pennell Rd. (bud)
Aston, PA 19014
610-497-5845
Sales: $500,000-$1 Million
JOE VALENT (Owner) & Buys Men's & Boys' Jeans, Work Clothing, Sweatsuits, Footwear, Army Surplus

KATANA SPORTS (SP)
1711 Chestnut Ave.
Barnesboro, PA 15714
814-948-9182
JOHN KATANA, JR. (Mgr.) & Buys Activewear, Athletic Footwear

ZEIDEN'S (MW)
1508 7th Ave.
Beaver Falls, PA 15010
724-846-6400 / Fax: 724-846-8496
Sales: $500,000-$1 Million
RICHARD HOWARD (Owner) & Buys Men's Sportswear, Furnishings, Accessories

AMERICAN OUTFITTERS (CLO-25)
Rt. 2 (p)
Box 91
Bedford, PA 15522
814-623-6417 / Fax: 814-623-1255
Website: www.americanoutfitters.com
Retail Locations: PA, MD, WV, GA, FL, CH, TX, IL
ROBERT TURKOVICH, SR. (President & Real Estate Contact) & Buys Store Displays, Fixtures, Supplies
ROBERT TURKOVICH, JR. (Real Estate Contact) & Buys Men's Sportswear, Urban Contemporary, Furnishings, Accessories
DAVE TURKOVICH-Footwear

AL GAUDIO'S (MW)
1198 Postraven Rd.
Belle Vernon, PA 15012
724-929-4953
AL GAUDIO (Owner) & Buys Men's Leather Apparel, Store Displays, Fixtures, Supplies

PEIGHT'S COUNTRY STORE (GM-2)
(PEIGHT SUPPLY)
136 Peight's Ln. (p)
Belleville, PA 17004
717-935-2922 / Fax: 717-935-2662
BEN PEIGHT (Owner) & Buys Men's Jeans, Underwear, Hosiery, Footwear, Store Displays, Fixtures, Supplies

AMERICAN PANTS CO. (CLO-3)
3466 Progress Dr., #111
Bensalem, PA 19020
215-244-7941 / Fax: 215-244-9581
MARTIN BRAIT (President & G.M.M.) & Buys Urban Contemporary, Headwear
WILLIAM SCHWARTZ (Secy. & Treas.) & Buys Men's & Young Men's Wear, Headwear, Store Displays, Fixtures, Supplies

EDCO MEN'S & BOYS' CLOTHING (MW)
104 Neshaminy Mall (p-m-b)
Bensalem, PA 19020
215-322-7373
Sales: $500,000-$1 Million
MATTHEW J. SMITH (Owner) & Buys Men's, Young Men's & Boys' Wear, Leather Apparel, Accessories, Store Displays, Fixtures, Supplies

PENNSYLVANIA - Berwick

CAPITA'S CLOTHING OUTLET (CLO)
1331 Rear Ave.
Berwick, PA 18603
570-752-4320
MIKE CAPITA (Owner) & Buys Men's Sportswear, Furnishings, Belts, Dress Shoes, Store Displays, Fixtures, Supplies

HARRY'S (SP)
112 W. Front St.
Berwick, PA 18603
570-752-5212
Sales: $100,001-$500,000
JOHN SABATINO (Owner) & Buys Activewear, Athletic Footwear

VINCENT VILLAGE EXPRESS (CLO & DISC)
114 E. Front St. (m)
Berwick, PA 18603
570-752-3633 / Fax: 570-752-1226
Sales: Under $100,000
VINCENT Di AUGUSTINO (Owner) & Buys Tuxedos & Accessories

AARDVARK SPORT SHOP, INC. (SP)
571 Main St.
Bethlehem, PA 18018
610-866-8300 / Fax: 610-868-2697
Sales: $500,001-$1 Million
Website: www.vark.com
BRUCE HAINES (Owner) & Buys Activewear, Athletic Footwear, Headwear

BOOTH'S CORNER SHOES (FW)
1362 Naamans Creek Rd. (b)
Bootwyn, PA 19061
610-485-7280 / Fax: 610-497-0919
ANDREW WEISS (Owner) & Buys Men's & Boys' Dress Shoes, Casual Shoes, Athletic Footwear, Boots, Store Displays, Fixtures, Supplies

EVANS' (CLO)
(JAMES R. EVANS CO., INC.)
80 Main St. (p)
Bradford, PA 16701
814-368-4916
Sales: $100,001-$500,000
JOHN SHATARA (Co-Owner) & Buys Men's Sportswear, Leather Apparel, Young Men's Wear, Furnishings, Headwear, Accessories, Store Displays, Fixtures, Supplies

MAN'S WORLD (MW)
105 Main St. (m)
Bradford, PA 16701
814-368-6520
JOE BUTLER (Owner) & Buys Men's Sportswear, Furnishings, Accessories, Casual Shoes, Athletic Footwear, Store Displays, Fixtures, Supplies

MAYER BRAUSER STORE (MW)
90 Main St. (m-b)
Bradford, PA 16701
814-368-3555 / Fax: 814-368-3555
JOSEPH BRAUSER (Owner) & Buys Men's Sportswear, Work Clothes, Furnishings, Belts, Men's & Boys' Dress Shoes, Casual Boots, Athletic Footwear, Urban Contemporary, Store Displays, Fixtures, Supplies

BRYN MAWR RUNNING CO. (SP)
828 W. Lancaster Ave.
Bryn Mawr, PA 19010
610-527-5510 / Fax: 610-527-3241
Website: www.runbmrc.org
BOB SCHWELM (Owner) & Buys Athletic Footwear, Activewear, Headwear, Accessories

MILLER'S SHOES (FW)
215 S. Main St. (b)
Butler, PA 16001
724-287-7751 / Fax: 724-287-6329
JAMES CHIPREAN (Owner) & Buys Men's & Boys' Dress Shoes, Casual Shoes, Athletic Footwear, Slippers, Boots, Accessories

WORKINGMAN'S STORE (MW)
257 S. Main St. (m-b)
Butler, PA 16001
724-287-5572
ALAN ROSENBERG (Owner) & Buys Men's Work Clothes, Belts, Hosiery, Work Shoes, Work Boots, Rubber Boots, Store Displays, Fixtures, Supplies

ROSELLE SHOP (DEPT)
36 N. Main St. (p)
Carbondale, PA 18407
570-282-5614
SAM COLLURA (President) & Buys Men's, Young Men's & Boys' Sportswear, Furnishings, Accessories, Store Displays, Fixtures, Supplies

DUTREY SHOES (FW)
26 N. Hanover St. (m)
Carlisle, PA 17013
717-249-4839 / Fax: 717-249-9584
JOHN DUTREY (Owner) & Buys Men's & Boys' Dress Shoes, Casual Shoes, Athletic Footwear, Slippers, Boots, Related Accessories, Store Displays, Fixtures, Supplies

TOWER ONE SAFETY SUPPLY (MW)
420 E. North St. (m-b)
Carlisle, PA 17013
717-243-8722 / Fax: 717-243-8621
ALLEN GRACE (Owner) & Buys Men's & Boys' Dress Shoes, Casual Shoes, Work Boots, Hunting & Hiking Boots, Hosiery, Belts, Small Leather Goods, Store Displays, Fixtures, Supplies

WARDECKER'S (MW)
32 N. Hanover St. (m-b)
Carlisle, PA 17013
717-249-2114
FRED WARDECKER (President & Owner)
BARRY SLEAR-Men's Sportswear, Furnishings, Accessories

BURKHOLDER FABRICS (CLO)
1910 St. Thomas Edenville Rd.
Chambersburg, PA 17201
717-369-3155
ROY BURKHOLDER (Owner) & Buys Men's & Boys' Clothing, Accessories, Footwear Headwear, Store Displays, Fixtures, Supplies

LYONS & CO. (MW)
P.O. Box 363 (b)
83 S. Main St.
Chambersburg, PA 17201
717-263-9254 / Fax: 717-263-9255
Sales: $500,000-$1 Million
L. GREGG LYONS (President) & Buys Men's Dress Shirts, Robes, Gloves, Headwear, Men's Sportswear, Leather Apparel, Accessories, Store Displays, Fixtures, Supplies
DENNIS THOMPSON-Men's Sportswear, Leather Apparel, Store Displays, Fixtures, Supplies
JOHN BUHRMAN-Men's Ties, Underwear, Footwear

COLLARS 'N' CUFFS (MW)
506 Ave. of the States (m-b)
Chester, PA 19013
610-874-1537 / Fax: 610-874-0789
SCOTT BROWN (Owner) & Buys Men's Sportswear, Furnishings, Accessories

TOPPS SPORTSWEAR (SP)
515 Ave. of the States
Chester, PA 19013
610-872-7574
CHONG HUISOO (Owner) & Buys Activewear, Athletic Footwear

SKAPIK'S DEPARTMENT STORE (DEPT)
552 Miller Ave. (p-m)
Clairton, PA 15025
412-233-5151
Sales: $100,001-$500,000
MARY LOU McCULLUM (Co-Owner & G.M.M.) & Buys Men's Wear, Headwear, Store Displays, Fixtures, Supplies

PENNSYLVANIA - Clarion

CROOKS' CLOTHING CO. (CLO)

P.O. Box 487 (m)
539 Main St.
Clarion, PA 16214
814-226-8020 / Fax: 814-226-8026
Website: www.flcrooks.com

JIM CROOKS (President) & Buys Men's Overcoats, Suits, Tailored Jackets, Tailored Slacks, Raincoats, Sweaters, Sport Shirts, Outer Jackets, Casual Slacks, Active Apparel, Furnishings, Headwear, Accessories, Leather Apparel, Footwear, Young Men's Wear, Store Displays, Fixtures, Supplies

WEIN'S (CLO-2)

622 Main St. (m)
Clarion, PA 16214
814-226-7401 / Fax: 814-226-7400
Sales: $500,001-$1 Million

ALAN WEIN (President & G.M.M.) & Buys Store Displays, Fixtures, Supplies

ERIC FAULK-Men's, Young Men's & Boys' Wear, Footwear

COATESVILLE ARMY & NAVY, INC. (AN)

228 E. Lincoln Hwy. (p)
Coatesville, PA 19320
610-384-1683 / Fax: 610-384-3594
Sales: $100,001-$500,000

JUDY SKOLNIK (President) & Buys Men's Raincoats, Overcoats, Leather Apparel, Dress Shirts, Ties, Robes, Small Leather Goods, Footwear, Young Men's Shop, Boys' Accessories, Big & Tall Men's Wear, Men's Sweaters, Sport Shirts, Outer Jackets, Casual Slacks, Active Apparel, Underwear, Hosiery, Gloves, Belts, Boys' Clothing, Sportswear, School Uniforms 3 to 38 Husky Boys', Furnishings

TUCK APPAREL SHOP (MW)

211 E. Lincoln Hwy. (m)
Coatesville, PA 19320
610-384-1111

RICHARD TUCK (Owner) & Buys Men's Sportswear, Furnishings, Accessories

UNIQUE HANDBAGS AND FASHIONS (SP)

236 Lincoln Hwy.
Coatesville, PA 19320
610-384-8232

DARIUS GREEN (Owner) & Buys Men's Accessories, Fragrances

FLOCCO'S SHOES & CLOTHING (CLO & FW)

110 Fayette St. (m)
Conshohocken, PA 19428
610-828-5544 / Fax: 610-828-5195
Sales: $500,000-$1 Million
Website: www.floccos.com

DON FLOCCO (President) & Buys Big & Tall Men's Wear, Sportswear, Furnishings, Headwear, Accessories, Footwear, Young Men's & Boys' Wear 6 to 20, Store Displays, Fixtures, Supplies

JOE FLOCCO-Big & Tall Men's Wear, Sportswear, Furnishings, Headwear, Accessories, Footwear, Young Men's & Boys' Wear 6 to 20, Store Displays, Fixtures, Supplies

BENETT STORES, INC. (MW)

857 Main St. (p-m)
Darby, PA 19023
610-583-1000 / Fax: 610-583-1024
Sales: $500,000-$1 Million

PAUL FELDMAN (President) & Buys Men's Overcoats, Suits, Tailored Jackets, Tailored Slacks, Raincoats, Sportswear, Sweaters, Sport Shirts, Outer Jackets, Leather Apparel, Casual Slacks, Footwear, Athletic Apparel, Furnishings, Headwear, Accessories, Big & Tall Men's Wear, 5 & Up Boys' Wear, Store Displays, Fixtures, Supplies

GUS VALERIO-Men's Overcoats, Suits, Tailored Jackets, Tailored Slacks, Raincoats, Sportswear, Sweaters, Sport Shirts, Outer Jackets, Leather Apparel, Casual Slacks, 5 & Up Boys' Wear

BUD TEAFORD-Footwear, Athletic Apparel, Furnishings, Headwear, Accessories, Big & Tall Men's Wear

WEAVER'S STORE, INC. (CLO)

1011 Dry Tavern Rd. (p)
Denver, PA 17517
717-445-6791 / Fax: 717-445-8211

IRVIN WEAVER, SR. (Owner) & Buys Men's Sportswear, Furnishings, Headwear, Accessories, Footwear, Young Men's & Boys' Wear, Store Displays, Fixtures, Supplies

IRVIN WEAVER, JR.-Men's Sportswear, Furnishings, Headwear, Accessories, Footwear, Young Men's & Boys' Wear, Store Displays, Fixtures, Supplies

MODERN MALE (MW)

581 McKean Ave. (p-m)
Donora, PA 15033
724-379-5599

JOHN CUPPER (Owner) & Buys Men's Sportswear, Furnishings, Accessories, Young Men's Wear, Urban Contemporary, Boys' Wear, Store Displays, Fixtures and Supplies

LISA MARTIN (Mgr.) & Buys Men's Sportswear, Furnishings, Accessories, Young Men's Wear, Urban Contemporary, Boys' Wear, Store Displays, Fixtures and Supplies

ARNOLD'S FAMILY SHOES (FW)

478 N. Main St. (m)
Doylestown, PA 18901
215-345-5451 / Fax: 215-345-9224

STEVE ARNOLD (Owner) & Buys Men's & Boys' Dress Shoes, Casual Shoes, Slippers, Boots, Hosiery

PAT ARNOLD-Men's & Boys' Dress Shoes, Casual Shoes, Slippers, Boots, Hosiery

BEACON UNIFORMS (CLO)

505 S. Blakely St.
Dunmore, PA 18512
570-344-2822 / Fax: 570-969-9095

NICHOLAS CAPRIO (Owner) & Buys Men's Tuxedos, Work Wear, Accessories, Footwear

FRIEDMAN'S MENSWEAR & SHOES (MW)

220 E. Drinker St. (b)
Dunmore, PA 18512
570-343-1759 / Fax: 570-343-5589

PHILIP FRIEDMAN (Owner) & Buys Men's Suits, Overcoats, Sportswear, Blazers, Slacks, Leather Apparel, Furnishings, Ties, Dress Shirts, Accessories, Belts, Men's Dress Shoes, Casual Shoes, Store Displays, Fixtures, Supplies

KATHY KAREN CHILDREN'S SHOPPE (KS & OL)

201 E. Drinker St. (b)
Dunmore, PA 18512
570-343-1383

WALTER PACHUK (Co-Owner)

KATHY PACHUK (Co-Owner) & Buys Infant to 20 Boys' Wear, Prep School Sizes, Swimwear, Store Displays, Fixtures, Supplies

TALLY-HO TRADING POST (WW)

RR 4
P.O. Box 4252
Dushore, PA 18614
570-928-7392

SCOTT MENE (Owner) & Buys Men's Western Apparel, Footwear

SNYDER'S (FW)

112 Washington St. (b)
E. Stroudsburg, PA 18301
570-421-0610 / Fax: 570-421-0610

WADE SNYDER (Owner) & Buys Men's Footwear

GOOD'S STORE, INC. (CLO-3)
1338 Main St. (p)
East Earl, PA 17519
717-354-4026 / Fax: 717-355-2230
Sales: $10 Million-$50 Million
KENNETH B. BURKHOLDER (President)
JERRY ROGGIE (D.M.M.-Sportswear, Accessories, Footwear, Boys' Wear) & Buys Overcoats, Suits, Tailored Jackets, Tailored Slacks, Raincoats, Big &Tall Men's Wear, Men's Sweaters, Sport Shirts, Outer Jackets, Casual Slacks, Furnishings, Belts, Boys' Clothing, Sportswear
RON SIEGRIST-Overcoats, Suits, Tailored Jackets, Tailored Slacks, Raincoats, Big & Tall Men's Wear, Men's Sweaters, Sport Shirts, Outer Jackets, Casual Slacks, Furnishings, Belts, Boys' Clothing, Sportswear
ERNEST MARTIN (Mgr.) & Buys Store Displays, Fixtures, Supplies

SUBURBAN ARMY & NAVY (AN)
2826 Dekalb Pike
East Norriton, PA 19401
610-275-3716 / Fax: 610-275-5786
Sales: $501,000-$1 Million
Website: www.suburban-army-navy.com
NELSON PRICE (Owner) & Buys Activewear, Hiking Apparel, Related Footwear, Accessories

CROMPTON'S MENSWEAR (MW)
156 Berwick Heights Rd.
East Stroudsburg, PA 18360
570-424-1869 / Fax: 570-424-5449
JAMES CROMPTON (Owner) & Buys Men's Big & Tall, Footwear, Accessories, Furnishings

AMERICAN HEALTH CARE APPAREL (DEPT & MO)
302 Towncenter Blvd. (p-m)
Easton, PA 18040
610-250-0584 / Fax: 610-250-1226
Sales: $1 Million-$10 Million
HOWARD GORDON (President) & Buys Store Displays, Fixtures, Supplies
SUZANNE CHECK (Purch. Mgr.) & Buys Men's Tailored Slacks, Sweaters, Sport Shirts, Casual Slacks, Active Apparel, Dress Shirts, Ties, Robes, Underwear, Hosiery, Belts, Big & Tall Men's Wear, Footwear

THE LONDON SHOP, INC. (CLO)
339 Northampton St. (b)
Easton, PA 18042
610-258-0161 / Fax: 610-258-2368
Sales: $1 Million-$10 Million
MIKE CUSANO (President) & Buys Men's Sportswear, Furnishings, Accessories, Leather Apparel, Headwear, Store Displays, Fixtures, Supplies

NEW YORK TAILORS (CLO)
407 Northampton St. (b)
Easton, PA 18042
610-252-1345
JOSEPH R. RADOGNA (Owner) & Buys Men's Sportswear, Furnishings, Accessories, Urban Contemporary

FRENCH CREEK SHEEP & WOOL CO. (MO & OL)
P.O. Box 110 (b)
Elverson, PA 19520
610-286-5700 / Fax: 610-286-0324
Website: www.frenchcreeksheep.com
JEAN FLAXENBURG (Owner) & Buys Men's Overcoats, Sweaters, Outer Jackets, Leather Apparel, Dress Shirts

CAPPY'S CLOTHES (CLO)
5 E. 4th St. (m)
Emporium, PA 15834
814-486-0421
EVELYN ACKMAN (Owner) & Buys Men's Sportswear, Active Apparel, Furnishings, Accessories

JASPER HARRIS & SONS (MW)
26 E. 4th St. (p-m)
Emporium, PA 15834
814-486-1127
MARVIN HARRIS (Owner) & Buys Men's Sportswear, Furnishings, Accessories, Dress Shoes, Casual Shoes, Slippers, Boots, Store Displays, Fixtures, Supplies

DONECKER'S, INC. (CLO & OL)
409 N. State St. (m-b)
Ephrata, PA 17522
717-738-9500 / Fax: 717-738-9523
Sales: $10 Million-$50 Million
Website: www.doneckers.com
H. WILLIAM DONECKER (President)
ELLEN MOWRER (G.M.M.)
BARRY GARL-Men's Overcoats, Suits, Tailored Jackets, Tailored Slacks, Raincoats, Big & Tall Men's Wear, Furnishings, Accessories, Dress Shirts, Ties, Footwear, Sportswear, Sweaters, Sport Shirts, Outer Jackets, Leather Apparel, Casual Slacks, Activewear, Robes, Underwear, Hosiery, Gloves, Accessories
KAREN HEMMERICH-Boys' Wear
CYNTHIA GEASLARD (Display Dir.) & Buys Store Displays, Fixtures, Supplies

ISAAC BAKER & SON, INC. (MW)
1001 State St. (b)
Erie, PA 16501
814-454-7144 / Fax: 814-454-7146
Sales: $100,001-$500,000
Website: www.isaacbaker.com
S. SAMUEL SHERMAN (President)
DAVID SHERMAN-Men's Overcoats, Suits, Tailored Jackets, Tailored Slacks, Raincoats, Sportswear, Sweaters, Sport Shirts, Outer Jackets, Leather Apparel, Casual Slacks, Footwear, Store Displays, Fixtures, Supplies

KRAUS' DEPARTMENT STORE (DEPT)
810 Parade St. (m)
Erie, PA 16503
814-453-4314 / Fax: 814-452-3967
Sales: $1 Million-$10 Million
LOU ANN NOWOSIELSKI (President) & Buys Men's Accessories, Outerwear, Activewear & Hosiery
THOMAS NOWOSIELSKI (Dir.-Purch.) & Buys Men's Accessories, Outerwear, Activewear & Hosiery

L. PRESS & CO. (MW)
1216 State St. (m)
Erie, PA 16501
814-459-7213 / Fax: 814-452-0519
Sales: $500,000-$1 Million
ARTHUR PRESS (Owner) & Buys Men's Sportswear, Furnishings, Big & Tall Men's Wear, Footwear, Store Displays, Fixtures, Supplies
AARON PRESS-Men's Sportswear, Furnishings, Big & Tall Men's Wear, Footwear, Store Displays, Fixtures, Supplies

TOM KARLE & SONS (MW)
3424 Peach St.
Erie, PA 16508
814-864-0525 / Fax: 814-866-7282
TOM KARLE (Owner)
TOM KARLE, JR.-Men's Wear, Footwear & Accessories, Furnishings

PAUL FREDRICK (MO & OL)
(PAUL FREDRICK MEN'S STYLE)
223 W. Poplar St. (m)
Fleetwood, PA 19522
610-944-0909 / Fax: 610-944-7600
Sales: $10 Million-$50 Million
Website: www.mensstyle.com
PAUL SACHER (President)
ED GILGALLON (V.P.-Mdse.) & Buys Men's Apparel, Accessories, Watches
LARRY SCHECTERMAN-Men's Jewelry, Apparel, Accessories, Watches

J.H. SHOOP & SONS (CLO)
P.O. Box 126 (m-b)
Freeport, PA 16229
724-295-4126
JOHN E. SHOOP (Owner) & Buys Men's Sportswear, Furnishings, Accessories, Footwear, Big & Tall Men's Wear, Store Displays, Fixtures, Supplies

T & S MENSWEAR, INC. (MW)
17 Chambersburg St. (m)
Gettysburg, PA 17325
717-334-7575
SUSAN TROFTLE (Owner) & Buys Men's Sportswear, Furnishings, Accessories

ALICE'S WONDERLAND (MW)
1581 Rt. 6
Greeley, PA 18425
570-226-4251 / Fax: 570-226-6990
JOHN KARPICK (Owner) & Buys Men's Big & Tall, Furnishings, Accessories

E.L.M. DEPARTMENT STORE (CLO)
12 Center Sq. (p)
Greencastle, PA 17225
717-597-3710 / Fax: 717-597-5486
N. HAROLD MARTIN (Owner)
JAN MARTIN-Men's Sportswear, Furnishings, Accessories

PITTMAN'S WESTERN WEAR & TACK SHOP (WW)
13775 Molly Pitcher Hwy. (p)
Greencastle, PA 17225
717-597-3094
HENRY PITTMAN (President) & Buys Men's, Young Men's & Boys' Western Wear, Accessories, Furnishings, Headwear, Boots, Store Displays, Fixtures, Supplies

HUB (MW)
181 Main St. (m)
Greenville, PA 16125
724-588-7850 / Fax: 724-588-8297
RAY STUBERT (Owner) & Buys Men's Sportswear, Furnishings, Accessories

BURDICK'S, INC. (CLO)
151 S. Broad St. (b)
Grove City, PA 16127
724-458-8665 / Fax: 724-458-8110
Sales: $500,001-$1 Million
TOM BURDICK (President) & Buys Men's & Young Men's Wear, Suits, Jeans, Footwear, Swimwear, Accessories

DIETRICH MEN'S SHOP (MW)
320 State St. (m-b)
Hamburg, PA 19526
610-562-7548 / Fax: 610-562-8044
LESLIE WERLEY (Owner) & Buys Men's Sportswear, Headwear, Footwear, Furnishings, Accessories

HANOVER CLOTHING CO. (MW)
(KEA, INC.)
4244 Carlisle St. (m-b)
Hanover, PA 17331
717-632-3323 / Fax: 717-632-8518
Sales: $1 Million-$10 Million
Website: www.bigandtall.com
COURTNEY BRICKMAN (Owner) & Buys Men's Overcoats, Suits, Tailored Jackets, Tailored Slacks, Raincoats, Sportswear, Big & Tall Sweaters, Sport Shirts, Outer Jackets, Casual Slacks, Leather Apparel, Dress Slacks, Ties, Robes, Underwear, Hosiery, Gloves, Headwear, Belts, Jewelry, Small Leather Goods

INSTANT REPLAY (SP)
715 Carlisle St.
Hanover, PA 17331
717-637-0258 / Fax: 717-637-2755
Sales: $500,001-$1 Million
JACK GARRETT-Activewear, Athletic Footwear, Licensed Apparel

KLEFFEL'S, INC. (CLO)
1000 Carlisle St. (m)
Hanover, PA 17331
717-632-3133 / Fax: 717-632-1677
Sales: $1 Million-$10 Million
STEVE LAWRENCE (President) & Buys Store Displays, Fixtures, Supplies
BRIAN LIPPY-Men's Overcoats, Suits, Tailored Jackets, Tailored Slacks, Raincoats, Sportswear, Furnishings, Headwear, Accessories, Young Men's & 4 to 20 Boys' Wear, Leather Apparel

BROAD ST. ARMY NAVY STORE (AN)
1316 N. 3rd St. (p)
Harrisburg, PA 17102
717-234-4948 / Fax: 717-238-4818
Website: www.quartermasters.com
ARLENE ROSS (Owner) & Buys Men's Pants, Shirts, Work Apparel, Underwear, Hosiery

EDDIE'S MEN'S SHOP (MW)
313 Market St. (m)
Harrisburg, PA 17101
717-232-7676 / Fax: 717-232-7676
Website: www.eddiesonline.com
EDDIE RUTH (Owner) & Buys Men's Sportswear, Furnishings, Headwear, Accessories, Footwear, Big & Tall Men's Wear, Leather Apparel, Young Men's & Boys' Wear, Store Displays, Fixtures, Supplies

SWEATERMILL, INC. (CLO)
115 S. York Rd. (b-h)
Hatboro, PA 19040
215-441-8966 / Fax: 215-441-4248
Sales: $500,000-$1 Million
YVETTE KORNFIELD (President)
JOE KORNFIELD (V.P.) & Buys Men's Sportswear, Furnishings, Accessories, Special Order Footwear

M.L. LAWRENCE CO. (CLO)
385 Lancaster Ave. (m-b)
Haverford, PA 19041
610-649-8899 / Fax: 610-649-4311
LARRY PEARLMAN (Owner) & Buys Men's Sportswear, Furnishings, Accessories

WHARTON'S, INC. (MW-3)
552 Lancaster Ave.
Haverford, PA 19041
610-525-5700 / Fax: 610-526-1800
Website: www.whartoncleaners.com
PAUL HAROOTOUNIAN (Owner) & Buys Men's Formal Wear, Footwear, Jewelry, Accessories

DOTTE'S DEPARTMENT STORE (DEPT-2)
9 E. Broad St. (bud-p)
Hazleton, PA 18201
570-454-5971
DAVID DOTTE (Co-Owner) & Buys Men's & Boys' Wear, Store Displays, Fixtures, Supplies
MARIA DOTTE (Co-Owner) & Buys Men's & Boys' Wear, Store Displays, Fixtures, Supplies

WHEATON & SONS (MW)
3651 E. State St. (m-b)
Hermitage, PA 16148
724-346-3301
BOB WHEATON (Owner) & Buys Men's Sportswear, Furnishings, Accessories

LESTER'S (MW)
219 Alleghany St. (p)
Hollidaysburg, PA 16648
814-695-7579
Sales: $100,001-$500,000
GERALD SACKS (Owner) & Buys Men's Suits, Tailored Jackets, Tailored Slacks, Raincoats, Sportswear, Furnishings, Belts, Jewelry, Small Leather Goods, Store Displays, Fixtures, Supplies

CLOTHES QUARTERS, INC. (MW)
McDade Mall (p-m-b)
Holmes, PA 19043
610-522-1412 / Fax: 610-534-8417
DAVE WIESEN (Owner) & Buys Men's Wear, Urban Contemporary, School Uniforms, Headwear, Swimwear, Knitwear, Store Displays, Fixtures, Supplies

ART'S APPAREL FOR HIM (CLO)
843 Main St. (m-b)
Honesdale, PA 18431
570-253-3080 / Fax: 570-253-3228
THOMAS FASSHAUER (President) & Buys Men's Sportswear, Furnishings, Accessories

PENNSYLVANIA - Honesdale

SULLUM'S, INC. (MW)
564 Main St. (p)
Honesdale, PA 18431
570-253-3641 / Fax: 570-253-3686
Sales: $1 Million-$10 Million
HAROLD SULLUM (President) & Buys Men's Gloves, Footwear, Store Displays, Fixtures, Supplies
SHEILA SULLUM (G.M.M.) & Buys Men's Sportswear, Accessories, Young Men's Wear, 8 to 20 Boys' Wear

WOODLOCH WOOLENS, INC. (CLO-4)
216 Willow Ave. (p-m-b)
Honesdale, PA 18431
570-253-6072 / Fax: 570-253-9076
HARRY KIESENDAHL (Owner) & Buys Headwear, Accessories, Store Displays, Fixtures, Supplies
CONNIE MIKULAK-Men's & Boys' Wear & Accessories

700 SHOP (MW-2)
700 Philadelphia St. (m)
Indiana, PA 15701
724-465-8411
RAY STANKIEWICZ (Owner) & Buys Men's Wear, Footwear, Store Displays, Fixtures, Supplies

BERK'S MEN'S STORE (MW)
12210 Rt. 30 (m-b)
Irwin, PA 15642
724-863-6201 / Fax: 724-863-5546
BRUCE BERK (Owner) & Buys Men's Sportswear, Furnishings, Accessories

BOTWINICK'S (CLO)
479 Old York Rd. (b)
Jenkintown, PA 19046
215-884-9762 / Fax: 215-884-9763
GERALD BOTWINICK (Owner) & Buys Store Displays, Fixtures, Supplies
PHYLISS GURALNICK-Men's Dress Shirts, Ties, Hosiery, Tailored Jackets, Tailored Slacks, Casual Slacks, Boys' Wear
KEN SCHULMAN-Men's Sweaters, Sport Shirts, Urban Contemporary

JENKINTOWN RUNNING CO. (SP)
Baederwood Shopping Ctr.
1661 The Fairway
Jenkintown, PA 19046
215-887-2848 / Fax: 215-887-2868
Website: www.jenkrun.com
BOB GAMBERG (Partner) & Buys Athletic Footwear & Apparel

BROGIE'S MEN'S CLOTHING OUTLET (MW)
932 Bedford St. (p)
Johnstown, PA 15902
814-536-7553
Website: www.brogies.com
JERRY BROGDEN (Owner) & Buys Men's Sportswear, Big & Tall Men's Wear, Headwar, Footwear, Furnishings, Accessories

MILLER'S OF JOHNSTOWN, INC. (MW)
P.O. Box 638 (b)
525 Main St.
Johnstown, PA 15907
814-536-5341 / Fax: 814-536-0200
Sales: $500,000-$1 Million
H. JAY CLARK (Owner & G.M.M.) & Buys Men's Sportswear, Headwear, Men's Furnishings, Robes, Accessories, Footwear, Store Displays, Fixtures, Supplies

KEEFER'S ARMY & NAVY (AN)
270 Wyoming Ave. (m)
Kingston, PA 18704
570-287-2511 / Fax: 570-288-1232
DON KEEFER (Owner) & Buys Men's Sportswear, Furnishings, Headwear, Belts, Footwear, Big & Tall Men's Wear, Store Displays, Fixtures, Supplies

JOE'S ATHLETICS & APPAREL (AN)
124 Market St.
Kittanning, PA 16201
724-548-5815 / Fax: 724-548-5814
Sales: $500,001-$1 Million
ARNOLD MOSS (Owner) & Buys Activewear, Athletic Footwear

S. BLUHM'S (GM)
Rt. 6 (p-m)
Laceyville, PA 18623
570-869-1287 / Fax: 570-869-1477
KEITH BLUHM (Owner) & Buys Men's Sportswear, Boys' Wear, Store Displays, Fixtures, Supplies

DAVID W. MENSWEAR (MW)
1659 Litiz Pike (p-m-b)
Lancaster, PA 17601
717-397-5422 / Fax: 717-367-1959
Sales: $1 Million-$10 Million
DAVID HOWELL (President & G.M.M.) & Buys Men's Sportswear, Furnishings, Headwear, Footwear, Store Displays, Fixtures, Supplies

FILLING'S MEN'S SHOP (MW)
(FILLING'S TRADITIONAL CLOTHING FOR MEN & WOMEN)
401 W. Lemon St.
Lancaster, PA 17603
717-397-2480 / Fax: 717-295-4765
Website: www.fillingsclothing.com
JOHN JAY FILLING (President) & Buys Men's Sportswear, Formal Wear, Accessories, Footwear

JASON'S, INC. (CLO)
43 W. King St. (m)
Lancaster, PA 17603
717-392-0471 / Fax: 717-392-0784
GLEN QUINN (Mgr.) & Buys Men's Sportswear, Furnishings, Footwear, Urban Contemporary

TMB (CLO)
36 N. Queen St. (m-b)
Lancaster, PA 17603
717-394-8842 / Fax: 717-393-9245
Website: www.tmbclothing.com
LARRY HELICHER (Owner) & Buys Men's Suits, Men's Big and Tall, Sportswear, Leather Apparel, Furnishings, Dress Shirts, Accessories, Footwear, Store Displays, Fixtures, Supplies

PURITAN'S MEN'S SHOP (MW)
321 W. Main St. (p)
Lansdale, PA 19446
215-855-6862 / Fax: 215-855-9029
Sales: $500,000-$1 Million
EDWARD DiBLASI, JR. (Owner) & Buys Men's Wear, Store Displays, Fixtures, Supplies

HENRY'S MEN'S SHOP (MW)
130 W. Ridge St. (m-b)
Lansford, PA 18232
570-645-3336
JOE YANACEK (Owner) & Buys Men's Sportswear, Furnishings, Accessories

CASSEL'S MEN'S CLOTHING (MW)
756 Cumberland St. (b)
Lebanon, PA 17042
717-273-5422 / Fax: 717-273-5162
JAMES G. CASSEL (President & Owner)
DEL ROTH-Men's Sportswear, Furnishings, Accessories

FEATHERHILL WESTERN SHOP (WW & OL)
19 Featherhill Rd. (m-b)
Lenhartsville, PA 19534
610-562-5000 / Fax: 610-562-5877
Website: www.featherhill.com
KARLENE MINNICH (Owner) & Buys Men's Western Clothing, Leather Apparel, Furnishings, Headwear, Accessories, Footwear, Store Displays, Fixtures, Supplies

THE CHILDREN'S CENTER (KS)
(ENCK, INC.)
428 Market St. (m)
Lewisburg, PA 17837
570-524-9243
Sales: $100,001-$500,000
JOAN E. LEE (Owner) & Buys Newborn to 7X Boys' Wear, Store Displays, Fixtures, Supplies

POST & RAIL MEN'S SHOP (MW)
106 E. Main St. (m-b)
Ligonier, PA 15658
724-238-9235 / Fax: 724-238-4762
Sales: $100,001-$500,000
DAVID A. PURNELL (Owner) & Buys Men's Wear, Men's Accessories, Furnishings, Footwear
CINDY PURNELL-Men's Wear, Men's Accessories, Furnishings, Footwear

ENGLUND'S APPAREL FOR MEN (MW-2)
115 W. King St. (b)
Malvern Shopping Ctr.
Malvern, PA 19355
610-644-9315 / Fax: 610-695-9659
Sales: $1 Million-$10 Million
Website: www.englundsapparel.com
FRANK ENGLUND (President) & Buys Men's & Young Men's Sportswear, Dress Shirts, Robes, Ties, Headwear, Accessories, Footwear, Store Displays, Fixtures, Supplies
DAVID PHILLIPS-Men's & Young Men's Underwear, Hosiery, Gloves

FRANK KLINE CLOTHING (MW)
1 S. Kennedy Dr. (b)
McAdoo, PA 18237
570-929-1030 / Fax: 570-929-0300
SANFORD KLINE (Owner) & Buys Men's Work Clothing, Jeans & Tops

B. GROSS MENSWEAR (MW)
2 E. State St. (b)
Media, PA 19063
610-566-7990 / Fax: 610-892-7968
WILLIAM GROSS (Owner)
BRUCE MIDDLEMAN (Mgr.) & Buys Men's Wear, Leather Apparel, Footwear, Store Displays, Fixtures, Supplies

MAC'S CLOTHING (MW)
P.O. Box 194 (p)
10 Industrial Park Rd.
Mifflintown, PA 17059
717-436-2440 / Fax: 717-436-6714
Sales: $500,000-$1 Million
C. W. McLAUGHLIN (Owner) & Buys Men's Sweaters, Sport Shirts, Outer Jackets, Casual Slacks, Dress Shirts, Accessories, Ties, Underwear, Hosiery, Robes, Gloves, Big & Tall Men's Sportswear, Belts, Store Displays, Fixtures, Supplies

KNABE SWIM & TROPHY, INC. (SP)
2526 Monroeville Blvd.
Monroeville, PA 15146
412-824-6540 / Fax: 412-824-6551
Sales: $100,001-$500,000
LINDA KELLY (Co-Owner) & Buys Men's Swimwear
DENNIS KELLY (Co-Owner) & Buys Men's Swimwear

MATLOW'S MEN'S STORE (MW)
141 S. Oak St. (p-m)
Mount Carmel, PA 17851
570-339-1420 / Fax: 570-339-1420
Sales: $500,000-$1 Million
PAUL KAMINSKI (President) & Buys Men's Sportswear, Boys' Wear, Urban Contemporary, Store Displays, Fixtures, Supplies
MARK KOVELESKI (G.M.M.) & Buys Men's Ties, Gloves, Robes, Underwear, Clothing

D. L. STEVICK CLOTHIERS (MW)
300 Bridge St. (b)
New Cumberland, PA 17070
717-920-5050 / Fax: 717-763-5205
D. L. STEVICK (Owner) & Buys Men's Sportswear, Furnishings, Accessories
JOE BAKER (Mgr.) & Buys Men's Sportswear, Furnishings, Accessories

BARTOLACCI BROTHERS' SUITS (MW)
940 5th Ave. (b)
New Kensington, PA 15068
724-337-3938
GUIDO BARTOLACCI (Owner) & Buys Men's Sportswear, Furnishings, Accessories

PATI'S FORMAL WEAR (MW-2)
816 5th Ave. (m-b)
New Kensington, PA 15068
724-337-4751 / Fax: 724-334-7726
ANTONIO GACCETTA-Men's & Boys' Formal Wear

HASSIS MEN'S SHOP (MW)
3533 W. Chester Pike (m-b)
Newtown Square, PA 19073
610-353-3115 / Fax: 610-353-8525
KEVIN SEGAR (Owner) & Buys Men's Sportswear, Furnishings, Accessories, Footwear

MANE CHANGES BOUTIQUE (CLO)
114 E. Main St. (m-b)
Norristown, PA 19401
610-277-3354
MARGARET DELLISANTI (Owner) & Buys Men's Sportswear, Furnishings, Accessories

PAGNONI (MW)
123 W. Germantown Pike (m-b)
Norristown, PA 19401
610-275-8323
MARCO PAGNONI (Owner) & Buys Men's & Boys' Formal Wear

LA ROCCA'S MEN'S STORE (MW)
12 Clinton St. (p)
North East, PA 16428
814-725-3305 / Fax: 814-725-2580
Sales: $100,001-$500,000
WALTER BARCZYK (Owner) & Buys Men's Overcoats, Suits, Raincoats, Tailored Jackets, Tailored Slacks, Sportswear, Furnishings, Belts, Big & Tall Men's Wear, Workwear, Accessories, Footwear, Store Displays, Fixtures, Supplies

M. GUBIN & SON (MW)
P.O. Box 31 (m)
90 Queen St.
Northumberland, PA 17857
570-473-7870 / Fax: 570-473-1870
Sales: $500,000-$1 Million
CHARLES SNYDER (President) & Buys Men's Overcoats, Suits, Tailored Slacks, Tailored Jackets, Raincoats, Sportswear, Sweaters, Sport Shirts, Outer Jackets, Leather Apparel, Casual Slacks, Active Apparel, Furnishings, Accessories, Footwear, Store Displays, Fixtures, Supplies

SCHWARTZ'S MEN'S SHOP (MW)
103 N. Main St. (p)
Old Forge, PA 18518
570-457-4071
Sales: $100,001-$500,000
BURT SCHWARTZ (President) & Buys Men's Furnishings, Footwear
MEL SCHWARTZ (Mdse. Mgr.) & Buys Men's Headwear, Accessories
RICHARD SCHWARTZ-Men's Sportswear, Leather Apparel, Store Displays, Fixtures, Supplies

STUTZ SPECIALTY SHOP (KS-2)
115 Delaware Ave. (p-m-b)
Olyphant, PA 18447
570-383-2997 / Fax: 570-383-2834
Sales: $100,001-$500,000
MIKE STUTZ (Owner) & Buys Men's Overcoats, Suits, Tailored Jackets, Tailored Slacks, Raincoats, Sportswear, Sweaters, Sport Shirts, Outer Jackets, Leather Apparel, Casual Slacks, Active Apparel, Furnishings, Dress Shirts, Accessories, Ties, Robes, Underwear, Hosiery, Gloves, Belts, Young Men's Wear, Urban Contemporary, 8 to 20 Boys' Clothing, Sportswear, Furnishings, 8 to 20 Boys' Parochial School Uniforms, Boy Scout Uniforms

FRED'S HABERDASHERY (MW)
324 Delaware Ave. (p-m)
Palmerton, PA 18071
610-826-2330
Sales: $100,001-$500,000
FRED J. NOTHSTEIN (Owner) & Buys Men's Overcoats, Suits, Tailored Jackets, Tailored Slacks, Raincoats, Sportswear, Sweaters, Sport Shirts, Outer Jackets, Leather Apparel, Casual Slacks, Active Apparel, Furnishings, Headwear, Accessories, Store Displays, Fixtures, Supplies

PENNSYLVANIA - Philadelphia

A MAN'S IMAGE (MW)
(ABE MANDEL & SONS, INC.)
1709 E. Passyunk Ave., #17 (p-m-b)
Philadelphia, PA 19148
215-755-7100 / Fax: 215-462-3616
Sales: $1 Million-$10 Million
ABE MANDEL (President & G.M.M.) & Buys Men's Overcoats, Suits, Clothing, Sportswear, Furnishings, Footwear, Young Men's Wear, Urban Contemporary, Store Displays, Fixtures, Supplies

ALLURE (MW & OL)
4255 Main St. (b)
Philadelphia, PA 19127
215-482-5299 / Fax: 215-509-6317
Website: www.allureonline.com
ROBERT PALIDORA (Owner) & Buys Men's Wear, Leather Apparel, Urban Contemporary, Store Displays, Fixtures, Supplies

***ALPHA SHIRT CO. (CLO-14 & MO)**
401 E. Hunting Park Ave. (b)
Philadelphia, PA 19124
215-291-0300 / Fax: 800-845-4970
Sales: $100 Million-$500 Million
Website: www.alphashirt.com
VINCE TYRA (President)
HOWARD MOROF (C.F.O.)
MICHAEL BRODE (V.P.)
PAUL ROGERS (V.P.-Sls.)
LINDA MACELLVEN (Dir.-HR)
PAM FISHMAN (Mgr.-Mktg. & Prod. Dev.)
JULIE STOLIGROSZ (Dir.-Mdsg.) & Buys Men's Apparel
KIRT SCHLOSS (Mgr.-Purch.) & Buys Men's Apparel

BECKER MEN'S STORE (MW)
6310 Woodland Ave. (bud-p-m-b)
Philadelphia, PA 19142
215-729-4725 / Fax: 215-729-5587
STAN NELSON (President) & Buys Men's Sportswear, Leather Apparel, Furnishings, Headwear, Accessories, Footwear, Young Men's Wear, Urban Contemporary, Store Displays, Fixtures, Supplies
SCOTT NELSON (Mgr.) & Buys Men's Sportswear, Leather Apparel, Furnishings, Headwear, Accessories, Footwear, Young Men's Wear, Urban Contemporary, Store Displays, Fixtures, Supplies

BOYD'S (CLO)
1818 Chestnut St. (m-b)
Philadelphia, PA 19103
215-564-9000 / Fax: 215-564-2876
Sales: $10 Million-$50 Million
Website: www.boydsphiladelphia.com
GERALD GUSHNER (President & G.M.M.) & Buys Store Displays, Fixtures, Supplies
MARK GUSHNER (D.M.M.)
KENT GUSHNER-Men's Overcoats, Suits, Tailored Jackets, Tailored Suits, Raincoats, Outer Jackets, Casual Slacks, Big & Tall Men's Wear
PAUL GATTI-Men's Overcoats, Suits, Tailored Jackets, Tailored Suits, Raincoats, Outer Jackets, Casual Slacks, Big & Tall Men's Wear
TOM STAUNTON-Men's Sweaters, Active Apparel, Sport Shirts
MIKE CUTONE-Men's Furnishings, Accessories
JOE JAFFE-Footwear

CADET NECKWEAR TIE CORNER (MW-3)
300 Market St. (p-m)
Philadelphia, PA 19106
215-627-5829 / Fax: 215-592-0257
Sales: $500,000-$1 Million
JERRY GINSBERG (Owner) & Buys Men's Overcoats, Tailored Jackets, Raincoats, Sweaters, Sportswear, Sport Shirts, Outer Jackets, Leather Apparel, Casual Slacks, Active Apparel, Furnishings, Dress Shirts, Accesssories, Ties, Underwear, Hosiery, Gloves, Belts, Jewelry, Store Displays, Fixtures, Supplies

CITY BLUE, INC. (CLO-20)
1106 Chestnut St. (m)
Philadelphia, PA 19107
215-922-7505 / Fax: 215-496-9881
Retail Locations: NJ, GA, DE, OH, CT, IL
JOE NADAV (President & Real Estate Contact) & Buys Men's Sportswear, Headwear, Accessories, Leather Apparel, Footwear, Young Men's Wear, Urban Contemporary, Store Displays, Fixtures, Supplies

D'AMBROSIO CLOTHES, INC. (MW)
6405 N. Broad St. (m)
Philadelphia, PA 19126
215-927-0485 / Fax: 215-927-0488
J. D'AMBROSIO (Owner) & Buys Men's Sportswear, Furnishings, Accessories

DIGULIO'S (MW-2)
5904 Torresdale Ave. (m-b)
Philadelphia, PA 19135
215-288-2128 / Fax: 215-288-6273
STEPHEN DiGULIO (Co-Owner) & Buys Men's Sportswear, Furnishings, Accessories
MICHAEL DiGULIO (Co-Owner) & Buys Men's Sportswear, Furnishings, Accessories

EDCO MENSWEAR OF COTTMAN (MW)
2339 Cottman Ave. (p)
Philadelphia, PA 19149
215-333-7300
MATT SMITH (Owner) & Buys Men's Sportswear, Furnishings, Accessories, Boys' 8 to 20

FRANK SUSSMAN CO. (CLO)
28 N. 3rd St. (m)
Philadelphia, PA 19106
215-627-3221 / Fax: 215-627-7359
Sales: $10 Million-$50 Million
Website: www.franksussman.com
LAWRENCE H. BURSTEIN (President) & Buys Men's Sportswear, Surfwear, Underwear, Hosiery, T-shirts, Headwear, Young Men's Wear
PETER PRINICK (Opers. Mgr.) & Buys Store Displays, Fixtures, Supplies

GOLDEN BELL MENSWEAR (MW)
5636 N. 5th St.
Philadelphia, PA 19120
215-224-5798
JONG KIM (Owner) & Buys Men's Sportswear, Furnishings, Accessories

GUIDO'S, INC. (MW)
6728 Castor Ave. (m-b)
Philadelphia, PA 19149
215-722-1585 / Fax: 215-722-1585
Sales: $500,001-$1 Million
MIKE VISCO (President) & Buys Leather Goods, Men's Big & Tall Apparel, Men's Apparel, Men's Casualwear, Men's Denim Apparel, Men's Formalwear, Men's Accessories, Men's Hosiery, Men's Outerwear, Men's Sportswear, Men's Suits, Men's Swimwear
RITA VISCO (Treas.) & Buys Leather Goods, Men's Big & Tall Apparel, Men's Apparel, Men's Casualwear, Men's Denim Apparel, Men's Formalwear, Men's Accessories, Men's Hosiery, Men's Outerwear, Men's Sportswear, Men's Suits, Men's Swimwear

HART'S WORK CLOTHES (MW)
2563 Germantown Ave. (p-m)
Philadelphia, PA 19133
215-225-5050 / Fax: 215-225-5050
Sales: $500,000-$1 Million
SAMMY HAHN (Owner) & Buys Men's Sportswear, Work Clothes, Underwear, Hosiery, Footwear, Urban Contemporary, Store Displays, Fixtures, Supplies

PENNSYLVANIA - Philadelphia

HARVARD INDUSTRIES (MW)
6401 Vine St.
Philadelphia, PA 19139
877-687-8437 / Fax: 610-853-2263
Sales: $1 Million-$10 Million
Website: www.thetieguys.com
JACK SANFT (President & C.O.O.) & Buys Men's Big & Tall Apparel, Men's Casualwear, Men's Denim Apparel, Men's Formalwear, Men's Accessories, Men's Hosiery, Men's Outerwear, Men's Sportswear, Men's Suits, Men's Swimwear

ISAAC GOLDBERG CO., INC. (AN)
902 Chestnut St.
Philadelphia, PA 19107
215-925-9393 / Fax: 215-925-2955
Sales: $1 Million-$10 Million
CHARLES GOLDBERG (President) & Buys Footwear
NANA GOLDBERG (V.P.) & Buys Men's Sportswear, Work Clothes
HOWARD SOLOMON-Men's Outerwear
SID GOLDBERG-Men's Belts, Underwear, Hosiery

JEANS WORLD (MW-2)
46 S. 52nd St.
Philadelphia, PA 19139
215-747-5488
CHUNG CHOI (Owner) & Buys Men's Sportswear, Furnishings, Accessories

JOSEPH'S SPORTING GOODS (SP)
4652 Frankford Ave.
Philadelphia, PA 19124
215-535-2335 / Fax: 215-535-8675
SANG KOO PARK (President) & Buys Activewear, Athletic Footwear, Licensed Apparel

KAY'S TOGGERY SHOP (MW)
3631 Germantown Ave. (m)
Philadelphia, PA 19140
215-225-5948 / Fax: 215-228-7600
GARY SANDROW (Owner) & Buys Men's Sportswear, Furnishings, Accessories, Boys' 12 to 18

KIM'S CLOTHING (MW)
154 W. Chelten Ave. (p-m-b)
Philadelphia, PA 19144
215-843-1510 / Fax: 215-843-2620
BENJAMIN KIM (Owner) & Buys Men's Wear, Footwear, Boys' Suits, Store Displays, Fixtures, Supplies

KRASS BROTHERS, INC. (MW)
901 South St. (p)
Philadelphia, PA 19147
215-923-5080
Sales: $1 Million-$10 Million
BEN KRASS (President) & Buys Men's & Young Men's Wear, Store Displays, Fixtures, Supplies

LEO'S APPAREL FOR MEN & BOYS (MW)
2705 Germantown Ave. (p)
Philadelphia, PA 19133
215-223-1683 / Fax: 215-223-4430
Sales: $1 Million-$10 Million
DAVID ROSENBLUM (Co-Owner) & Buys Men's Overcoats, Suits, Tailored Jackets, Tailored Slacks, Raincoats, Sportswear, Sweaters, Sport Shirts, Outer Jackets, Casual Slacks, Activewear, Furnishings, Hats, Accessories, Young Men's & Boys' Wear, Big & Tall Men's Wear, Leather Apparel
JAMES SINGLETON (Mgr.) & Buys Store Displays, Fixtures, Supplies

LIPMAN'S ARMY & NAVY (AN)
5837 Germantown Ave. (p-m)
Philadelphia, PA 19144
215-848-0159
MICHAEL YAZDI (Owner) & Buys Men's Work Clothes, Jeans, Tops, Underwear, Hosiery, Belts

MITCHELL & NESS SPORTS (SP)
1229 Walnut St.
Philadelphia, PA 19107
215-592-6512 / Fax: 215-592-1180
Sales: $500,001-$1 Million
PETER CAPOLINO (President) & Buys Activewear, Licensed Apparel

NET BY DENIM (MW-10)
1136 Market St.
Philadelphia, PA 19107
215-564-2767 / Fax: 215-564-2984
ILAN AZKEN (Owner) & Buys Men's Wear, Footwear, Designer Urban Contemporary, Sportswear
YANIV ZAKEN-Men's Wear, Footwear, Designer Urban Contemporary, Sportswear

OK'S KIDDIE SHOP (KS)
2626 Germantown Ave.
Philadelphia, PA 19133
215-229-9599
Sales: $100,001-$500,000
CHANG KIM (Owner) & Buys 8 to 20 Boys' Wear, Urban Contemporary, Store Displays, Fixtures, Supplies

OLYMPIA SPORTS (SG-12)
(J'S PANTS & SHIRTS)
3134 Kensington Ave. (m)
Philadelphia, PA 19134
215-423-7437 / Fax: 215-423-6361
Website: www.olympiasports.com
DAN KIM (President & Owner) & Buys Men's Athletic Apparel, Team Clothing, Licensed Apparel, Footwear

PARK'S MENSWEAR (MW)
2635 Germantown Ave. (m-b)
Philadelphia, PA 19133
215-225-2112
Sales: $100,001-$500,000
KIM SUNG HO (Owner) & Buys Men's, Young Men's & Boys' Wear, Footwear, Store Displays, Fixtures, Supplies
MRS. KIM-Men's, Young Men's & Boys' Wear, Urban Contemporary, Footwear, Store Displays, Fixtures, Supplies

PENN-DEL MANAGEMENT CO. (MW)
(GIGOLO'S, INC.)
1817 E. Passyunk Ave. (b)
Philadelphia, PA 19148
215-465-4565 / Fax: 215-271-9853
Sales: $500,000-$1 Million
TONY MIGERY (Owner) & Buys Men's Wear, Footwear, Store Displays, Fixtures, Supplies

PHILLY'S KIDS (SP-2)
1020 Market St.
Philadelphia, PA 19107
215-925-4737 / Fax: 215-925-2925
Sales: $500,001-$1 Million
JACOB ABRAHAM (President) & Buys Activewear, Athletic Footwear, Licensed Apparel, Infant to 20 Boys' Wear & Footwear

SHIRLEY'S FOR KIDS (KS)
3620 Germantown Ave. (m-b)
Philadelphia, PA 19140
215-228-8550 / Fax: 215-228-8879
JACOB GEVURTZ (Owner) & Buys 8 to 20 Boys' Wear, Urban Contemporary, Leather Apparel, Store Displays, Fixtures, Supplies

SHIRT CORNER PLUS (MW)
251 Market St. (m)
Philadelphia, PA 19106
215-925-1724 / Fax: 215-627-5188
Sales: $1 Million-$10 Million
MARVIN GINSBERG (Owner) & Buys Men's Sportswear, Big & Tall Men's Wear, Men's Furnishings, Accessories
SOL HARTMAN (D.M.M.) & Buys Men's Sportswear, Big & Tall Men's Wear, Men's Furnishings, Accessories

SOUL FASHION (MW)
10 S. 52nd St. (p-m)
Philadelphia, PA 19139
215-471-6464
Sales: $100,001-$500,000
WON SONG (Owner) & Buys Men's Wear, Urban Contemporary, Store Displays, Fixtures, Supplies

PENNSYLVANIA - Philadelphia

SPORTS FAVORITES, INC. (SP-4)
2201 Cottman Ave.
Philadelphia, PA 19149
215-725-7186 / Fax: 215-725-8153
LARRY GLAUSER (President) & Buys Activewear, Licensed Apparel, Hosiery

SUNSHINE BLUES (CLO-14)
501 Adams Ave. (b)
Philadelphia, PA 19120
215-722-3240 / Fax: 215-856-7400
Sales: $10 Million-$50 Million
G. T. CHAWLA (President)
JIM IMBROGNIO (G.M.M.) & Buys Men's Overcoats, Outer Jackets, Leather Apparel, Sportswear, Casual Slacks, Active Apparel, Sweaters, Sport Shirts, Dress Shirts, Footwear, Urban Contemporary, Store Displays, Fixtures, Supplies

SUPER PRO (SP)
2963 N. 22nd St.
Philadelphia, PA 19132
215-225-1120
STEVE LEE (Owner) & Buys Athletic Footwear

SUPER SNEAKER, INC. (SP-1)
6228 Woodland Ave.
Philadelphia, PA 19142
215-727-1400 / Fax: 215-726-0364
RICHARD LIPPO (Co-Owner)
CONRAD PETRONGOLO (Co-Owner) & Buys Activewear, Athletic Footwear, Licensed Apparel

TIES TO YOU (SP)
835 N. Preston St.
Philadelphia, PA 19104
215-386-7081 / Fax: 215-549-0950
SAM JONES (Owner) & Buys Men's Ties, Belts, Wallets, Watches, Shirts, Accessories

TODAY'S STYLES (MW-4)
1800 E. Passyunk Ave. (b)
Philadelphia, PA 19148
215-462-0624 / Fax: 215-271-9853
Sales: $500,000-$1 Million
ANTHONY MAUGERI (President & G.M.M.) & Buys Men's Sportswear, Footwear, Furnishings, Headwear, Accessories

TOP MAN (MW-4)
2316 N. Front St. (p-m-b)
Philadelphia, PA 19133
215-423-8615 / Fax: 215-423-3383
JOON LEE (Owner) & Buys Men's & Boys' Wear, Urban Contemporary, Store Displays, Fixtures, Supplies

TOPS 'N' BOTTOMS OF NEW YORK, INC. (CLO-25)
(Div. of DEB SHOPS)
9401 Blue Grass Rd. (m)
Philadelphia, PA 19114
215-676-6000 / Fax: 215-676-6665
Website: www.debshops.com
Retail Locations: MA, RI, NH, ME, VT, CT, NJ, NY, PA, DE, VA, MD, WV, NC, TN, KY, OH, IN, MI, IA, WI, MN, SD, ND, IL, MO, KS, NE, OK, TX, CO, WY, ID, UT, AZ, NM, CA, OR, WA
MARVIN ROUNICK (President)
WARREN WEINER (V.P. & Corp. Counsel)
DAVID ROUNICK (G.M.M.) & Buys Young Men's Outerwear, Sportswear
STANLEY UHR (Real Estate Contact) (@ 215-676-6600)

TORRE CLOTHES (MW)
(VICTORY CLOTHES CO., INC.)
1217 S. Broad St. (p-m-b)
Philadelphia, PA 19147
215-468-7272 / Fax: 215-468-7353
Website: www.torrebigandtall.com
MARK ROSENFELD (President) & Buys Men's Sportswear, Big & Tall Leather Outerwear, Furnishings, Accessories, Store Displays, Fixtures, Supplies
JEANETTE BREEN (G.M.M.) & Buys Men's Sportswear, Big & Tall Leather Outerwear, Furnishings, Accessories, Store Displays, Fixtures, Supplies
VICTOR MILLER-Footwear

TRIPLE PLAY SPORTS (SP-2)
827 S. 9th St.
Philadelphia, PA 19147
215-923-5466 / Fax: 215-923-4197
Sales: Under $100,000
Website: www.tripleplaysports.com
FRANK LAROSA (Mgr.) & Buys Activewear, Athletic Footwear, Athletics, Licensed Apparel

URBAN OUTFITTERS, INC. (CLO-50 & OL)
1809 Walnut St. (m-b)
Philadelphia, PA 19103
215-564-2313 / Fax: 215-557-4706
Sales: $100 Million-$500 Million
Website: www.urbanoutfitters.com
Retail Locations: NY, PA, MA, DC, FL, IL, OH, MN, WA, OR, CA, TX , AZ, NY, RI, CT, VT, MI, IN, WI, KS, CO, Europe, London, Dublin
RICHARD A. HAYNE (President)
SUSAN OTTO (Creative Dir.) & Buys Store Displays, Fixtures, Supplies
WADE MCDEVITT (Real Estate Contact) (@ 215-564-4011)
CHRIS COLBY (D.M.M-Men's)
CANDACE FERRANDERO-Men's Sportswear, Young Men's Wear, Urban Contemporary
PATRICIA ASSUI-Accessories, Footwear
JESSE GOLDMAN-Tops
MICHAEL HOFFMAN-Bottoms

VIZURI (MW)
329 South St. (b)
Philadelphia, PA 19147
215-592-4844 / Fax: 215-592-4845
Sales: $1 Million-$10 Million
M DEVON MORRISON (President) & Buys Leather Goods, Men's Big & Tall Apparel, Men's & Boys' Apparel, Men's Casualwear, Men's Denim Apparel, Men's Formalwear, Men's Accessories, Men's Hosiery, Men's Outerwear, Men's Sportswear, Men's Suits, Men's Swimwear
LISA STRICKLAND (V.P.) & Buys Leather Goods, Men's Big & Tall Apparel, Men's & Boys' Apparel, Men's Casualwear, Men's Denim Apparel, Men's Formalwear, Men's Accessories, Men's Hosiery, Men's Outerwear, Men's Sportswear, Men's Suits, Men's Swimwear

WAYNE EDWARD'S (MW)
1521 Walnut St. (b)
Philadelphia, PA 19102
215-563-6801 / Fax: 215-563-4984
Website: www.wayne-edwards.com
WAYNE GLASSMAN (President) & Buys Men's Sportswear, Furnishings, Accessories, Footwear, Leather Apparel, Store Displays, Fixtures, Supplies

YOUNG'S FASHIONS (MW)
114 S. 52nd St. (p-m)
Philadelphia, PA 19139
215-472-3100 / Fax: 215-472-3100
YOUNG KIM (Owner) & Buys Men's Sportswear, Furnishings, Accessories
KYONG S. KIM-Men's Sportswear, Furnishings, Accessories

ROTHROCKS' (CLO)
126 N. Front St. (m)
Philipsburg, PA 16866
814-342-4742
Sales: $100,001-$500,000
RONALD ROTHROCKS (Co-Owner & President) & Buys Men's Sportswear, Furnishings, Accessories, Footwear, Store Displays, Fixtures, Supplies
JUDITH ROTHROCKS (Co-Owner) & Buys Footwear, Store Displays, Fixtures, Supplies

ABE BERNSTEIN (MW)
807 E. Carson St. (p)
Pittsburgh, PA 15203
412-431-0912 / Fax: 412-431-8861
Website: www.usabe.com
BILL BERNSTEIN (Partner) & Buys Men's Sportswear, Workboots, Headwear, Furnishings, Accessories

THE BOOK CENTER (SP-2)
(UNIVERSITY OF PITTSBURGH)
4000 5th Ave.
Pittsburgh, PA 15213
412-648-1455 / Fax: 412-648-1902
Sales: $100,001-$500,000
Website: www.pitt.edu/bookcenter
ROSEMARIE SLEZAK (Exec. Dir.) & Buys Activewear, Fleecewear, Jackets, Headwear, Footwear, Hosiery, Shorts, Licensed Apparel
DENNIS CROVELLA-Activewear, Fleecewear, Jackets, Headwear, Footwear, Hosiery, Shorts, Licensed Apparel

BROADWAY OUTDOORS (MW)
(BROADWAY ARMY & NAVY)
909 Liberty Ave. (bud-p)
Pittsburgh, PA 15222
412-391-3331 / Fax: 412-261-3441
Website: www.warsurplus.com
ROBERT MORRIS (Owner) & Buys Men's Leather Apparel, Casual Slacks, Active Apparel, Furnishings, Headwear, Accessories, Sweaters, Outer Jackets, Military Apparel

CHARLES SPIEGEL (MW)
5841 Forbes Ave. (h)
Pittsburgh, PA 15217
412-421-9311 / Fax: 412-421-9315
CHARLES SPIEGEL (Owner) & Buys Men's Sportswear, Headwear, Footwear, Furnishings, Accessories

DICK'S CLOTHING & SPORTING GOODS (SG-136 & OL)
200 Industry Dr. (p)
Pittsburgh, PA 15275
412-809-0100 / Fax: 412-809-0724
Sales: $500 Million-$1 Billion
Website: www.dickssportinggoods.com
Retail Locations: AL, CT, DE, GA, IL, IN, IA, KS, KY, MD, MA, MI, MO, NJ, NY, NC, OH, PA, SC, TN, VT, VA, WV, WI
EDWARD STACK (C.E.O.)
GARY STERLING (Sr. V.P.-Mdse)
JOSEPH QUERI (Real Estate Contact) (@ 412-788-6066)
JOHN PAGE (G.M.M.)
DAVE ASWALD (Golf Mgr.)
LESLIE BRISCOE-Men's Casual Wear
RAY KURPE-Running Shoes
JILL MARTIN-Men's Active Wear
SHERYL SANCTIS-Men's Apparel

FORREST OUTDOOR SPORTS ARMY/NAVY (AN)
3300 Sawmill Run Blvd.
Pittsburgh, PA 15227
412-881-4774
Sales: $500,001-$1 Million
MARY JANE FORREST (Owner) & Buys Apparel, Activewear, Licensed Apparel

HEINZ HEALEY'S (MW)
1 Station Sq.
Pittsburgh, PA 15219
412-281-5115 / Fax: 412-281-2065
CHAS SCHALDENBRAND-Men's Wear, Suits, Sportswear, Accessories

J & B SALES CO. (MW)
1025 5th Ave. (bud-p)
Pittsburgh, PA 15219
412-566-1491 / Fax: 412-566-1492
Sales: $500,000-$1 Million
JULIAN ELBING (Owner) & Buys Men's Sportswear, Sweaters, Active Apparel, Dress Shirts, Robes, Underwear, Hosiery, Gloves, Belts, Store Displays, Fixtures, Supplies

JOSEPH ORLANDO, INC. (MW)
606 Liberty Ave. (b)
Pittsburgh, PA 15222
412-765-1726 / Fax: 412-765-1950
Website: www.josephorlando.com
JOSEPH ORLANDO (President) & Buys Men's Tailored Suits, Sweaters, Sport Shirts, Casual Slacks, Active Apparel, Outerwear, Furnishings, Dress Shirts, Ties, Hosiery, Belts, Jewelry, Footwear

KAUFMANN'S (DEPT-52)
(Div. Of MAY DEPARTMENT STORES)
400 5th Ave. (p-m)
Pittsburgh, PA 15219
(May Mdsg. Corp.)
412-232-2000 / Fax: 412-232-2546
Sales: Over $1.5 Billion
Website: www.kaufmanns.com
Retail Locations: NY, OH, PA, WV
ANDREW PICKMAN (President & C.E.O.)
BOB BESFA (Real Estate Contact) (@ 314-342-6466)
JOHN GUNNERSON (Sr. V.P. & G.M.M.-Men's & Boys')
STEPHEN EVANS (V.P. & D.M.M.-Men's Furnishings, Tailored Sportswear)
OPEN-Men's Casual Slacks, Dockers, Hager Slacks, Tailored Slacks, Sport Coats
JASON ROUSH (@ 412-232-6173)-Men's Ties, Designer Neckwear
MICHAEL BARNES-Men's Robes, Hosiery, Underwear
TIMOTHY REID-Dress Shirts
KIRK HANSELMAN (V.P. & D.M.M.-Men's Sportswear & Collections) (@ 412-232-2823)
GREG KREDELL-Men's Collections, Polo, Tommy Hilfiger, Jones New York
BRIAN NOSAL-Men's Moderate Sport Shirts, Nautica, Calvin Klein, Sport Shirt Collections
ROXANNE HUMES-Men's Knits, Sweaters
KIRK STILLMACK-Men's Active Apparel

TERRY SINGER (D.M.M.-Men's, Young Men's & Boys' Clothing)
KURT JOHNSON-Men's Overcoats, Raincoats, Outerwear, Suits
RICK BROWN-Young Men's Tops
SALLY KANE-Young Men's Bottoms & Denim
SHAWN WURTZBACHER-Boys' Wear Size 8 to 20

SALLY GIUNTINT (D.M.M.-Footwear)
MITCH BARCASKY-Men's Footwear
JOSH SAXMAN-Boys' Footwear

JIM APRUDZESE (V.P.-Visual Mdsg.) & Buys Store Displays, Fixtures and Supplies

KING SPORTSWEAR (SG-2)
2701 Robinson Blvd.
Pittsburgh, PA 15235
412-371-4643 / Fax: 412-371-5427
KAANG KO (Owner) & Buys Men's & Boys' Sportswear & Footwear

PENNSYLVANIA - Pittsburgh

LARRIMOR'S (MW-2)
501 Grant St. (b)
Pittsburgh, PA 15219
412-471-5727 / Fax: 412-471-3404
Website: www.larrimors.com
J. CARL SLESINGER (President)
TED PFORR (V.P. & G.M.M.) & Buys Men's Store Displays, Fixtures, Supplies
LISA MICHAEL-Men's Sportswear, Furnishings, Accessories
ED REESE-Footwear

LITTLE'S OF PITTSBURGH (SP)
5850 Forbes Ave.
Pittsburgh, PA 15217
412-521-3530 / Fax: 412-521-3870
JOEL SIGAL (Owner) & Buys Athletic Footwear, Casual Footwear, Dress Footwear, Activewear

LONDON DOCK (CLO-3)
5842 Forbes Ave. (b)
Pittsburgh, PA 15217
412-421-5710 / Fax: 412-421-8553
Sales: $1 Million-$10 Million
DENNIS WOLK (Co-Owner)
BRENT WOLK (Co-Owner)
SHELDON B. WOLK (Co-Owner) & Buys Men's, Young Men's & Boys' Wear, Store Displays, Fixtures, Supplies

LYDELL'S FOR MEN (MW)
120 5th Ave., #111
Pittsburgh, PA 15222
412-281-9098 / Fax: 412-281-9099
MR. BLANKS (Owner) & Buys Men's Wear, Men's Accessories, Furnishings, Ties, Belts, Suits, Casual Slacks

MT. OLIVER MEN'S SHOP (MW)
201 Brownsville Rd. (p)
Pittsburgh, PA 15210
412-431-3057
MR. RALPH-Men's Casual Wear

NEWMAN'S (KS-2)
(NEWMAN LONDON YOUTH CENTER, INC.)
5834 Forbes Ave. (m-b)
Pittsburgh, PA 15217
412-421-5000 / Fax: 412-421-8721
Sales: $1 Million-$10 Million
MITCHELL L. TOIG (President) & Buys 8 to 20 Boys' Wear, Leather Apparel, Store Displays, Fixtures, Supplies

REED SPORTS (SG-2)
2377 Noblestown Rd. (p)
Pittsburgh, PA 15205
412-921-9800 / Fax: 412-921-3904
Website: www.reedsports.com
THOMAS REED (Co-Owner) & Buys Men's Suits, Sportswear, Accessories, Footwear, Young Men's Wear, Size 8 to 20 Boys' Wear
JIM REED (Co-Owner) & Buys Store Displays, Fixtures, Supplies

SPECIALTY CLOTHING CO. (MW)
1023 5th Ave. (m-b)
Pittsburgh, PA 15219
412-391-1288 / Fax: 412-391-1486
LARRY RUBIN (Owner) & Buys Men's Suits, Tailored Jackets, Tailored Slacks, Raincoats, Sportswear, Leather Apparel, Dress Shirts, Ties, Hosiery, Belts, Big & Tall Men's Wear, Young Men's & Boys' Wear, Store Displays, Fixtures, Supplies

SPORTS DELI (SP)
Parkway Center Mall
1165 McKenny Ln.
Pittsburgh, PA 15220
412-919-5880
Sales: $500,001-$1 Million
MICHAEL AUTIERI (Owner) & Buys Men's & Boys' Activewear, Licensed Apparel, Athletic Footwear, Athletic Apparel, Ski Wear, Golf Apparel

WILLI'S SKI & SNOWBOARDSHOPS (CLO-6)
3738 Library Rd. (m)
Pittsburgh, PA 15234
412-882-5660 / Fax: 412-881-5027
Sales: $1 Million-$10 Million
Website: www.skiandboard.net
LINDA KLEIN (President) & Buys Men's, Young Men's & Boys' Active Apparel, Ski & Snowboard Apparel, Tennis Apparel, Helmets, Footwear, Store Displays, Fixtures, Supplies

DUCHESS & DUKE CLOTHING (CLO)
75 William St. (m-b)
Pittston, PA 18640
570-654-3851
PAULA CAPRI (President) & Buys Men's Outer Jackets, Leather Apparel, Casual Slacks, Active Apparel
PAUL CAPRI (G.M.M.) & Buys Men's Outer Jackets, Leather Apparel, Casual Slacks, Active Apparel

A. WEITZENKORN'S SONS (MW-2)
145 E. High St. (m)
Pottstown, PA 19464
610-323-8810 / Fax: 610-970-6839
Sales: $1 Million-$10 Million
Website: www.netjunction.com/weitzenkorn
GREGG J. WEITZENKORN (C.E.O.) & Buys Big & Tall Men's Wear, Store Displays, Fixtures, Supplies
WILLIAM CONRAD-Men's Overcoats, Suits, Tailored Jackets, Tailored Slacks, Raincoats, Big & Tall Men's Wear, Footwear
CURT FREY-Men's Sport Shirts, Active Apparel, Furnishings, Headwear, Accessories
SANDY-Young Men's Wear, Urban Contemporary
SANDRA RICHARDS-Ties, Men's Sweaters

ARMY & NAVY STORE (AN)
(DIRECT BROTHERS, INC.)
229 High St. (m-b)
Pottstown, PA 19464
610-323-8000 / Fax: 610-970-9000
Sales: $100,001-$500,000
UNG SOK CHON (Owner) & Buys Men's Work Clothes, Jeans, Hunting Clothing, Leather Jackets, Underwear, Headwear, Hosiery, Gloves, Belts, Boys' Work Clothes, Jeans, Hunting Clothing, Underwear, Headwear, Hosiery, Gloves, Footwear, Store Displays, Fixtures, Supplies

BOHORAD'S, INC. (CLO)
6 N. Centre St. (m)
Pottsville, PA 17901
570-622-7930 / Fax: 570-628-2733
LEE BOHORAD (President) & Buys Men's Sportswear, Furnishings, Headwear, Accessories, Store Displays, Fixtures, Supplies

ROMAN TAILORS & CLOTHIERS (MW)
308 W. Market St. (b)
Pottsville, PA 17901
570-622-1214
ROMOLO LAURETI (Owner) & Buys Men's Sportswear, Furnishings, Accessories

ARMY & NAVY STORE (AN)
3400 Plaza Dr. (p)
Reading, PA 19605
610-921-0251 / Fax: 610-921-8488
SHEILA BLATT (Owner) & Buys Men's Work Clothes, Outerwear, Shorts, Shirts, Hosiery, Underwear, Belts

PENNSYLVANIA - Reading

BILL'S KHAKIS (MO & OL)

(Div. of W. THOMAS CO., INC.)
531 Canal St., #201
Reading, PA 19602
610-372-9765 / Fax: 610-373-1499
Sales: $1 Million-$10 Million
Website: www.billskhakis.com

BILL THOMAS (Owner) & Buys Men's Casual Slacks

BOSCOV'S DEPARTMENT STORE, INC. (DEPT-34 & OL)

4500 Perkiomen Ave. (bud-p-m-b)
Reading, PA 19606
610-779-2000 / Fax: 610-370-3789
Sales: $500 Million-$1 Billion
Website: www.boscovs.com
Retail Locations: DE, MD, NJ, NY, PA

ALBERT BOSCOV (Chmn.)
EDWIN LAKIN (President)
JOHN HILS (Real Estate Contact) (@ 610-370-3808)
ROBERT OPPENHEIMER (Sr. V.P. & G.M.M.-Men's)
GERALD BOWDREN (Sr. V.P.) & Buys Men's Separates, Slacks
MIKE BUZAN (D.M.M.-Men's)
ROGER FRAZIER-Men's Suits, Outerwear, Leather Apparel
MIKE MULLINS-Men's Moderate Sportswear, Leather Apparel
BILL RAPLEY-Better Sportswear
BRIAN NUGENT (D.M.M.-Young Men's & 8 to 20 Boys' Wear, Athletic Apparel)
SUE DEL ELMO-Young Men's Tops, Sportswear
CHARLIE WEBER-Boys' Footwear
MICHAEL SCHIRMER (Dir.-Visual Mdsg.) & Buys Store Displays, Fixtures, Supplies

MAZZO'S (CLO)

48 S. 6th St.
Reading, PA 19602
610-375-7192 / Fax: 610-375-4656

JOHN MAZZO (Owner) & Buys Men's Sportswear, Accessories, Footwear, Store Displays, Fixtures, Supplies

SUPER SHOES (FW-20)

(H.H. BROWN)
1800 Kutztown Rd. (m-b)
Reading, PA 19604
610-929-9766 / Fax: 610-929-2963
Website: www.superstoes.com
Retail Locations: PA, CA, VA, MD

JAMES ISSLER (C.E.O.)
TERRY TIERNEY (Real Estate Contact) (@ 301-722-6563) & Buys Store Displays, Fixtures, Supplies
GREG GOODRUE-Men's & Boys' Dress Shoes, Casual Shoes, Work Boots, Western Boots, Hiking Boots, Athletic Footwear, Slippers, Moccasins, Rain Gear

CAPE HORN CORNER (WW)

3040 Windsor Rd. (p-m-b)
Red Lion, PA 17356
717-244-6425 / Fax: 717-244-8565

SKIP SEIFERT (Owner) & Buys Men's & Boys' Western Wear, Store Displays, Fixtures, Supplies

ROARING SPRING DEPARTMENT STORE (DEPT)

Rt. 36 South
Roaring Spring, PA 16673
814-224-2157 / Fax: 814-224-2421

DOUG MINGLE (Owner) & Buys Men's & Boys' Jeans, Shirts, Sweaters, Footwear, Store Displays, Fixtures, Supplies

PHYLLIS' JEANS & APPAREL (CLO)

177 Airport Rd. (m)
Rostrauer, PA 15012
412-384-5247

ISADORE SMALL (Owner) & Buys Men's Levis, Belts, Store Supplies

IVAN'S MENSWEAR & WOMEN'S APPAREL (CLO)

29 N. St. Mary's St. (p-m-b)
Saint Marys, PA 15857
814-834-3460 / Fax: 814-834-7871
Sales: $100,001-$500,000

MICHAEL L. FAULK (President & G.M.M.) & Buys Men's Suits, Tailored Jackets, Raincoats, Outer Jackets, Small Leather Goods, Sportswear, Sport Shirts, Big & Tall Men's Wear, Active Apparel, Furnishings, Belts, Jewelry, Footwear, Young Men's Wear, Store Displays, Fixtures, Supplies
DEAN HANES-Men's Suits, Tailored Jackets, Raincoats, Outer Jackets, Small Leather Goods, Sportswear, Sport Shirts, Big & Tall Men's Wear, Active Apparel, Furnishings, Belts, Jewelry, Footwear, Young Men's Wear, Store Displays, Fixtures, Supplies

NESSER'S CLOTHING (MW)

137 Pittsburgh St.
Scottsdale, PA 15683
724-887-3323 / Fax: 724-887-4270

ISAAC NESSER (Owner) & Buys Men's Wear, Men's Big & Tall, Accessories, Furnishings

COUNTRY CLUB MEN'S SHOP (MW-2)

138 Penn Ave. (b)
Scranton, PA 18503
570-343-1888 / Fax: 570-343-2210
Sales: $500,000-$1 Million

TOM KELLY (Owner) & Buys Men's Sportswear, Furnishings, Accessories, 8 to 20 Boys' Wear

LA SALLE - THE IMAGE MAKERS (MW)

830 S. Webster Ave. (b)
Scranton, PA 18505
570-344-0727 / Fax: 570-344-6852
Sales: $500,000-$1 Million

RITA D'ANGELO, SR. (President & G.M.M.) & Buys Men's Clothing, Overcoats, Suits, Tailored Jackets, Tailored Slacks, Raincoats, Leather Apparel, Young Men's Wear
JEFF D'ANGELO (V.P.) & Buys Men's Sportswear, Sweaters, Sport Shirts, Outer Jackets, Casual Slacks, Active Apparel, Furnishings, Accessories, Footwear, Young Men's Wear, Urban Contemporary, Store Displays, Fixtures, Supplies

QUINT'S ARMY & NAVY STORE (AN-2)

P.O. Box 20039 (bud)
107 Lackawanna Ave.
Scranton, PA 18501
570-342-3848 / Fax: 570-347-8468
Sales: $100,001-$500,000

DONALD H. KEEFER (Owner) & Buys Men's Outer Jackets, Underwear, Belts, Big & Tall Wear, Casual Slacks, Hosiery, Footwear, Store Displays, Fixtures, Supplies
EARL S. QUINT-Men's Gloves

SUBURBAN CASUALS (MW)

832 Scanton-Carbondale Hwy. (m-b)
Scranton, PA 18508
570-343-9886 / Fax: 570-343-0165

CAROL SELIGE (Co-Owner) & Buys Men's Sportswear, Store Displays, Fixtures, Supplies
JOHN SICKLER-Men's Coats, Suits, Dress Shirts, Ties, Sport Jackets, Accessories
CAROLINE JOHN-Footwear

TUCK'S CLOTHING STORE (MW)

125 Penn Ave. (p)
Scranton, PA 18503
570-342-5222

MARSHALL TUCK (Owner) & Buys Men's, Young Men's & Boys' Wear, Urban Contemporary, Footwear, Store Displays, Fixtures, Supplies

J. KLEINBAUER, INC. (CLO & OL)
28 N. Market St. (m-b)
Selinsgrove, PA 17870
570-374-8824 / Fax: 570-374-6381
Sales: $1 Million-$10 Million
Website: www.jkleinbauer.com
JOE W. KLEINBAUER (Owner)
JUDD WILLIAMS-Men's Wear
CANDI BYLER-Boys' Wear

CRICKLEWOOD (MW)
417 Beaver St. (m)
Sewickley, PA 15143
412-741-7414 / Fax: 412-741-7414
C. B. HAYS-Men's Casual Wear

REYER'S SHOE STORE (FW-2 & OL)
40 S. Water Ave. (bud-p-m-b-des)
Sharon, PA 16146
724-981-2200 / Fax: 724-983-8269
Sales: $10 Million-$50 Million
Website: www.reyers.com
MARK JUBELIRER (President) & Buys Men's Footwear
STEVEN JUBELIRER (V.P.) & Buys Boys' Footwear
RENEE FRANEK-Boys' Footwear
NINA KOSTAS-Leather Goods, Men's Accessories, Hosiery

ACTIVE FOOTWEAR (FW)
(TRES K'S, INC.)
236 Calder Way
State College, PA 16801
814-234-0304
Sales: $100,001-$500,000
DON KASSAB (Mgr.) & Buys Athletic Footwear
KERRY KASSAB-Athletic Footwear

BOSTONIAN LTD. (CLO)
106 S. Allen St. (b)
State College, PA 16801
814-238-8655
SCOTT KRESGE (Owner) & Buys Men's Sportswear, Furnishings, Accessories

COLLEGIATE PRIDE, INC. (SP-2)
(LION'S PRIDE)
3019 Enterprise Dr.
State College, PA 16801
814-237-4377 / Fax: 814-237-6638
GARY MOYER (President)
JOHN SHAEFFER-Activewear

JACK HARPER'S YOUNG MEN'S SHOP (CLO)
114 W. College Ave.
Ave. (m-b)
State College, PA 16801
814-237-8900 / Fax: 814-238-5797
Website: www.yms.com
CHARLES KRANICH (Co-Owner) & Buys Men's Sportswear, Young Men's Wear, Furnishings, Accessories
CHRIS KOPAC (Co-Owner) & Buys Men's Sportswear, Young Men's Wear, Furnishings, Accessories

O.W. HOUTS & SONS, INC. (DEPT)
120 N. Buckhout St. (p)
State College, PA 16801
814-238-6701 / Fax: 814-238-6700
Sales: $1 Million-$10 Million
LARRY HOUTS (President)
DORSEY HOUTS (Gen. Mgr.) & Buys Men's & Students Clothing, Sportswear, Furnishings, Headwear, Footwear, Store Displays, Fixtures, Supplies

SICKAFUS SHEEPSKINS (CLO & MO)
Rts. 183 & 78
Strausstown, PA 19559
610-488-1782 / Fax: 610-488-1576
Website: www.sheepskinvsa.com
PAT SICKAFUS (President) & Buys Men's Sportswear, Outerwear, Accessories, Big & Tall, Slippers, Store Displays, Fixtures, Supplies

CHARLES X. BLOCK, INC. (MW)
251 W. Broad St. (m)
Tamaqua, PA 18252
570-668-1112 / Fax: 570-668-1112
THEODORE BLOCK (Owner) & Buys Men's Sportswear, Furnishings, Accessories
RICH GIBSON (Mgr.) & Buys Men's Sportswear, Furnishings, Accessories

HARRISON'S (MW)
408 Corbet (m-b)
Tarentum, PA 15084
724-226-2123
PATRICK GOULD (Mgr.) & Buys Men's Sportswear, Furnishings, Accessories

VELTRIS MEN'S SHOP (MW)
310 George St. (b)
Throop, PA 18512
570-489-4301
JOHN VELTRI (Owner) & Buys Men's Sportswear, Furnishings, Accessories

TITUSVILLE BARGAIN STORE (CLO & OL)
(Keystone Merean Tote Co.)
101 N. Franklin St. (p-m)
Titusville, PA 16354
814-827-7132 / Fax: 814-827-2464
Website: www.bigandtallguys.com
SCOTT LINNON (Owner) & Buys Men's Sportswear, Footwear, Furnishings, Accessories

NOLAN'S DEPARTMENT STORE (DEPT)
P.O. Box 175 (m)
Topton, PA 19562
610-682-2447
Sales: $100,001-$500,000
STANLEY NOLAN (Owner) & Buys Men's Sportswear, Furnishings, Headwear, Belts, Small Leather Goods, Young Men's Wear, Overcoats, Suits, Tailored Jackets, Tailored Slacks, Raincoats, Footwear, Big & Tall Men's Wear, Store Displays, Fixtures, Supplies

PENN STATE BOOK STORE ON CAMPUS (SP-26 & MO & OL)
(PENN STATE UNIVERSITY)
Book Store Bldg.
University Park, PA 16802
814-863-3611 / Fax: 814-863-1233
Sales: $2 Million-$5 Million
Website: www.bkstore.com.psu
TOM BAURER (G.M.M.)
MARILYN LEWIS (Asst. Gen. Mgr.) & Buys Fleecewear, Jackets, Hosiery, Shorts

MALCOM QUALITY CLOTHING (MW)
146 Grant Ave. (m-b)
Vandergrift, PA 15690
724-568-3261
MICHAEL NICHOLAS (Owner) & Buys Men's Sportswear, Furnishings, Accessories

BLAIR CORP. (MO & OL)
220 Hickory St. (p-m)
Warren, PA 16366
814-723-3600 / Fax: 814-726-6208
Sales: $100 Million-$500 Million
Website: www.blair.com
JOHN ZAWACKI (President)
ROBERT D. CROWLEY (V.P. & G.M.M.-Men's)
ROBERT BROWN-Men's Overcoats, Raincoats, Sweaters, Sport Shirts, Outer Jackets, Dress Shirts, Ties
TERRY L. MOLDOVAN-Men's Suits, Tailored Jackets, Tailored Slacks, Casual Slacks
PATRICIA BLACKWELL-Men's Robes, Underwear, Hosiery, Gloves, Belts, Activewear, Footwear

AMERICAN EAGLE OUTFITTERS (CLO-654 & OL)

(BLUE HOTS)
(THRIFTY'S)
150 Thorn Hill Industrial
Warrendale, PA 15086
724-776-4857 / Fax: 724-779-5585
Sales: $500 Million-$1 Billion
Website: www.ae.com
Retail Locations: WA, MT, NV, NS, NB, UT, AZ, NM, CO, TX, OK, KS, NE, SD, ND, IA, MD, OR, LA, MS, TN, AL FL, GA, NC, SC, VA, ID, MN, WV, OH, IN, MI PA NY, NJ, DE, CT, RI, MA, VT, NH, ME, WI, IL

JAY SCHOTTENSTEIN (Chmn. & C.E.O.)
ROGER MARKFIELD (President & Chief Mdsg. Officer)
LAURA WEIL (Exec. V.P. & C.F.O.)
JAMES O'DONNELL (C.O.O.)
JOSEPH KERIN (Exec. V.P. & Dir.-Store Opers.)
GEORGE SAPPENFIELD (Exec. V.P.-Real Estate)
JEFF SMITH (V.P. & Real Estate Contact)
CHRISTEN NIEHL (Real Estate Contact-East)
DORA SCERTZER (Real Estate Contact-West)
WENDY RICH (D.M.M.-Men's) & Buys Men's Sweaters
ALEXANDRA BASSO-Men's Woven Shirts
MICHAEL SULLIVAN (D.M.M.-Footwear) & Buys All Athletic Footwear
CHRIS NAGELSON-Men's Denim Bottoms, Asst. Bottoms, Shorts, Men's Knit Shorts, Activewear

DAVID'S LTD., INC. (CLO)

50 N. Main St. (b)
Washington, PA 15301
724-228-1884 / Fax: 724-229-3357

TOM ZIMMARO (Owner) & Buys Men's Sportswear, Furnishings, Accessories

HAYNES' TRIANGLE SPORTSWEAR (MW)

Oak Spring Rd. (m-b)
Washington Mall
Washington, PA 15301
724-222-6950 / Fax: 724-222-6950
Sales: $1 Million-$10 Million

LEE HAYNES (President) & Buys Leather Goods, Men's Big & Tall Apparel, Men's & Boys' Apparel, Men's Casualwear, Men's Denim Apparel, Men's Formalwear, Men's Accessories, Men's Hosiery, Men's Outerwear, Men's Sportswear, Men's Suits, Men's Swimwear
KENNY DUCKWORTH (Sls. Mgr.) & Buys Leather Goods, Men's Big & Tall Apparel, Men's & Boys' Apparel, Men's Casualwear, Men's Denim Apparel, Men's Formalwear, Men's Accessories, Men's Hosiery, Men's Outerwear, Men's Sportswear, Men's Suits, Men's Swimwear

LOWRY'S WESTERN SHOP (WW)

935 Henderson Ave. (b)
Washington, PA 15301
724-228-1225 / Fax: 724-228-4704

BILL LOWRY (Co-Owner) & Buys Men's Western Wear, Leather Apparel, Ties (Western Only), Headwear, Accessories, Footwear, Young Men's & Boys' Wear, Store Displays, Fixtures, Supplies
DONNA LOWRY (Co-Owner) & Buys Men's Western Wear, Leather Apparel, Ties (Western Only), Headwear, Accessories, Footwear, Young Men's & Boys' Wear, Store Displays, Fixtures, Supplies

TRAPUZZANO'S (MW)

27 W. Chestnut St. (m-b)
Washington, PA 15301
724-222-8613 / Fax: 724-222-7216
Website: www.trapuzzanos.com

ROBERT JOHNS (Owner) & Buys Men's & Boys' Formal Wear, Police Uniforms

GARRISON'S MEN'S SHOP (MW)

89 Main St. (m)
Wellsboro, PA 16901
570-724-3497 / Fax: 570-724-5811
Sales: $100,001-$500,000

ALAN GARRISON (Owner) & Buys Men's Overcoats, Suits, Tailored Jackets, Tailored Slacks, Raincoats, Sportswear, Sweaters, Sport Shirts, Outer Jackets, Leather Apparel, Casual Slacks, Active Apparel, Furnishings, Accessories, Footwear, Big & Tall Men's Wear, Urban Contemporary, Store Displays, Fixtures, Supplies

R.J. DUNHAM, INC. (DEPT)

(R.J. DUNHAM DEPARTMENT STORE)
45 Main St. (p-m)
Wellsboro, PA 16901
570-724-1905 / Fax: 570-724-2221
Sales: $100,001-$500,000

R. JAMES DUNHAM (President & Mdse. Mgr.) & Buys Store Displays, Fixtures, Supplies
NANCY DUNHAM-Store Displays, Fixtures, Supplies
JOHN DUNHAM-Men's Sportswear, Furnishings, Accessories, Footwear, Young Men's Wear, Big & Tall Men's Wear, Men's Utility Wear

AFTER HOURS (MW-241)

1340 Enterprise Dr.
West Chester, PA 19380
610-692-6624 / Fax: 610-692-3826
Website: www.afterhours.com
Retail Locations: AL, ME, NJ, NY, PA, MD, OH, IA, WI, IL, KS, TX, CO, NM, CA, ID

JOSEPH DOYLE (President) & Buys Men's Formalwear, Footwear, Accessories
BARRY REICHERT (Mgr.) & Buys Men's Formalwear, Footwear, Accessories
STEVE ENGLISH (Real Estate Contact)

M & M CLOTHIERS (CLO)

3535 Mountainview Dr., #C
West Mifflin, PA 15122
412-650-6400 / Fax: 412-650-6554
Sales: $100,001-$500,000

MOSES FATFAT (Owner) & Buys Men's Sportswear, Accessories, Young Men's Wear, Urban Contemporary, Leather Apparel, Formal Wear, Store Displays, Fixtures, Supplies

ACKLEY & SON (DEPT)

311 W. Main St. (bud-p)
Westfield, PA 16950
814-367-2732 / Fax: 814-367-5502

GERALD BLISS (Co-Owner)
JOAN BLISS (Co-Owner) & Buys Men's Work Clothes, Sweaters, Sport Shirts, Outer Jackets, Active Apparel, Underwear, Hosiery, Belts, Sportswear, Footwear, Store Displays, Fixtures, Supplies

ARMY NAVY (AN & OL)

(KAYTON CO.)
1045 Grape St. (p)
Whitehall, PA 18052
610-266-1045 / Fax: 610-266-0622

HENRY KURLANSIK (Owner) & Buys Store Displays, Fixtures, Supplies
SANDRA SILFIES-Men's Jeans
JAMES GATES-Men's & Boys' Furnishings
JOHN BENOWITZ-Footwear

TOP HAT FORMAL WEAR (MW)

1809 MacArthur Rd. (m-b)
Whitehall, PA 18052
610-821-9525 / Fax: 610-821-8755
Website: www.tophatformalwear.com

RON KAHN (Owner) & Buys Men's & Boys' Formal Wear

KRANSON CLOTHES, INC. (MW & OL)

145 Mundy St. (p-m-b)
Wilkes-Barre, PA 18702
570-823-8612 / Fax: 570-823-8624
Website: www.kransonuniform.com

DOUG KRANSON (President) & Buys Men's Uniforms, Footwear
SAUL KRANSON (V.P.) & Buys Men's Sweaters, Sport Shirts, Outer Jackets, Leather Apparel, Casual Slacks, Active Apparel, Furnishings, Boys' Wear, Store Displays, Fixtures, Supplies

OUTLET ARMY & NAVY STORE (AN)

113 S. Main St. (p)
Wilkes-Barre, PA 18701
570-822-4305 / Fax: 570-970-0740

SHELDON BLOCK (Co-Owner) & Buys Men's Sportswear, Leather Apparel, Footwear, Young Men's & Boys' Wear
JOE BLOCK-Men's Raincoats, Big & Tall Men's Wear, Furnishings, Headwear, Belts, Small Leather Goods, Urban Contemporary

PENNSYLVANIA - Williamsport

CLOTHIER (MW)
134 W. 4th St. (m-b)
Williamsport, PA 17701
570-322-5707 / Fax: 570-322-5721
FRANCIS CICCARELLI (Owner) & Buys Men's Wear, Leather Apparel, Big & Tall Men's Wear, Footwear, Store Displays, Fixtures, Supplies

VICARY'S WEST (MW)
76 Commerce Dr. (m-b)
Wyomissing, PA 19610
610-375-7848 / Fax: 610-376-7848
NICK MORROW (Owner) & Buys Men's Furnishings, Accessories

BOB'S TAILOR SHOP (MW)
1033 E. Market St. (m)
York, PA 17403
717-854-6990
Sales: $100,001-$500,000
BOB HEINER (Owner) & Buys Men's Sport Coats, Pants, Ties

BON-TON STORES, INC. (DEPT-73)
(Div. of S. GRUMBACHER & SON)
P.O. Box 2821 (m-b)
2801 E. Market St.
York, PA 17405
717-757-7660 / Fax: 717-751-3196
Sales: $500 Million-$1 Billion
Website: www.bonton.com
Retail Locations: CT, MA, MD, NH, NJ, NY, PA, VT, WV
FRANK TWORECKE (President & C.O.O.)
CHRISTINE PAKACS-Men's Suits, Tailored Jackets, Tailored Slacks
LANCE ITKOFF-Men's Knits, Young Men's Sweaters, 8 to 20 Boys' Wear, Accessories

GRIFFITH SMITH CO. (MW)
45 W. Market St. (p-b)
York, PA 17401
717-854-8128 / Fax: 717-852-3163
Website: www.griffithsmith.com
DAVID SMITH (Owner) & Buys Men's Sportswear, Furnishings, Accessories

RIGBY'S (MW)
106 S. Main St. (b)
Zelienople, PA 16063
724-452-7810 / Fax: 724-452-7091
DAVID HOUSEHOLDER (Owner) & Buys Men's Sportswear, Furnishings, Accessories

PUERTO RICO - Adjuntas

TIENDA LA UNICA (CLO-2)
Munoz Riviera, #12 (p)
Adjuntas, PR 00601
787-829-0010
Sales: $100,001-$500,000
DOMINGO MELENDEZ (Owner) & Buys Men's Sportswear, Furnishings, Boys' Sportswear, Jewelry, Footwear, Urban Contemporary, Store Displays, Fixtures, Supplies

LA GRAN VIA (MW-14)
Ave. Jose de Diego, #167 (p)
Arecibo, PR 00612
787-878-3396 / Fax: 787-879-3334
Sales: $1 Million-$10 Million
MAURICIO NORIEGA-Men's & Boys' Wear

LA IDEAL (MW)
54 Mariano Vidal (h)
Arecibo, PR 00612
787-878-5930
ANGEL LUIS TERRON (Owner) & Buys Men's & Boys' Wear, Urban Contemporary, Footwear, Store Displays, Fixtures, Supplies

BLANCO VELEZ STORES, INC. (MW-41)
P.O. Box 1619 (p-m-b)
Rd. #5, K Point M55 Luchetta Industrial Park
Bayamon, PR 00960-1619
787-740-2400 / Fax: 787-740-2452
Sales: $10 Million-$50 Million
PERFECTO MASSO (President)
ELIAS LUIS BLANCO (G.M.M.)
MARCELO CHINNI (D.M.M.) & Buys Men's Suits, Big & Tall Men's Wear, Sportswear, Dress Shirts, Ties, Hosiery, Belts, Fragrances, Boys' Wear, Store Displays, Fixtures, Supplies
MARTIN AYALA-Men's & Boys' Wear
FRANCISCO LOPEZ-Men's Suits, Big & Tall Men's Wear, Sportswear, Dress Shirts, Ties, Hosiery, Belts, Fragrances, Boys' Wear, Store Displays, Fixtures, Supplies
CARMELO BURGOS-Men's Suits, Big & Tall Men's Wear, Sportswear, Dress Shirts, Ties, Hosiery, Belts, Fragrances, Boys' Wear, Store Displays, Fixtures, Supplies

OLAZABAL & CIA, INC. (CLO)
P.O. Box 2926 (p-m)
Bayamon, PR 00960
787-740-1414 / Fax: 787-798-8989
Sales: $1 Million-$10 Million
ANTONIO OLAZABAL (President) & Buys Store Displays, Fixtures, Supplies
EMILIO OLAZABAL-Men's & Boys' Wear

THE GRAND STORE (DEPT-10)
61 Petances St.
Caguas, PR 00725
787-743-3200 / Fax: 787-743-1017
NADIR ALKATEB (Owner) & Buys Men's & Boys' Wear, Store Displays, Fixtures, Supplies

METHOD, INC. (MW-12)
San Patricio Plz., #118
Caparra Heights, PR 00920
787-792-6450
OSCAR JUELLE (Owner) & Buys Men's & Boys' Wear, Store Displays, Fixtures, Supplies
LOUIS SANTORI-Young Men's Wear

LEONARDO 5TH AVE., INC. (MW-12)
869 Km 1.0 Balmas Industrial Park (des)
P.O. Box 8781
Catano, PR 00962
787-788-9000 / Fax: 787-788-2120
Sales: $1 Million-$10 Million
Website: www.leonardos.com
LEONARDO CORDERO, Sr. (President) & Buys Men's & Boys' Apparel, Men's Casualwear, Men's Denim Apparel, Men's Formalwear, Men's Accessories, Men's Hosiery, Men's Outerwear, Men's Sportswear, Men's Suits
ANNIE CORDERO (V.P.-Fin.)
LEONARDO CORDERO, Jr. (V.P.-Opers.)

BADRAN STORE (DEPT-11)
53 Ave. Jose de Diego
Cayey, PR 00736
787-738-5131 / Fax: 787-842-1443
EZZAT HASSAN BADRAN (Owner) (@ 787-841-8221) & Buys Men's & Boys' Wear, Urban Contemporary, Store Displays, Fixtures, Supplies

DAN'S MEN'S SHOP (MW-2)
Ave. Jose de Diego, #106E (p)
Cayey, PR 00736
787-738-2483
JOSE LOPEZ (Owner) & Buys Men's Suits, Sweaters, Sport Shirts, Leather Apparel, Casual Slacks, Belts, Dress Shirts, Ties, Robes, Underwear, Hosiery

FERNANDEZ & CORRIPIO, INC. (MW-32)
(TIENDA FERCO)
1 Ave. Munoz Rivera North (bud-p-m-b-des)
Cayey, PR 00736
787-263-4242 / Fax: 787-263-4242
Sales: $10 Million-$50 Million
MATIAS FERNANDEZ (President) & Buys Boys' Apparel, Leather Goods, Men's Apparel, Men's Big & Tall Apparel, Men's Casualwear, Men's Denim Apparel, Men's Formalwear, Men's Hosiery, Men's Outerwear, Men's Suits, Men's Underwear, Men's Uniforms, Watches, Young Men's Apparel
JOSE CORRIPIO (Treas.) & Buys Boys' Apparel, Leather Goods, Men's Apparel, Men's Big & Tall Apparel, Men's Casualwear, Men's Denim Apparel, Men's Formalwear, Men's Hosiery, Men's Outerwear, Men's Suits, Men's Underwear, Men's Uniforms, Watches, Young Men's Apparel
HECTOR BONILLA (Gen. Mgr.) & Buys Boys' Apparel, Leather Goods, Men's Apparel, Men's Big & Tall Apparel, Men's Casualwear, Men's Denim Apparel, Men's Formalwear, Men's Hosiery, Men's Outerwear, Men's Suits, Men's Underwear, Men's Uniforms, Watches, Young Men's Apparel
TOMAS MORA (Gen. Mgr.) & Buys Boys' Apparel, Leather Goods, Men's Apparel, Men's Big & Tall Apparel, Men's Casualwear, Men's Denim Apparel, Men's Formalwear, Men's Hosiery, Men's Outerwear, Men's Suits, Men's Underwear, Men's Uniforms, Watches, Young Men's Apparel
JOSE BELILLIA-Boys' Apparel, Leather Goods, Men's Apparel, Men's Big & Tall Apparel, Men's Casualwear, Men's Denim Apparel, Men's Formalwear, Men's Hosiery, Men's Outerwear, Men's Suits, Men's Underwear, Men's Uniforms, Watches, Young Men's Apparel

LOS MAHONES UNISEX (CLO-3)
P.O. Box 331 (p-m)
Cayey, PR 00737
787-738-4612 / Fax: 787-738-1480
Sales: $500,000-$1 Million
ELADIO RODRIGUEZ VAZQUEZ (Owner)
WETTE ZAYAS-Men's Sweaters, Casual Slacks, Active Apparel, Dress Shirts, Headwear, Boys' Sportswear, Footwear, Store Displays, Fixtures, Supplies

TIENDA CASTRODAD (CLO-2)
32 De Diego (b)
Cidra, PR 00739
787-739-3781
Sales: $100,001-$500,000
SIXTO RAFAEL CASTRODAD (Owner) & Buys Men's Suits, Tailored Jackets, Tailored Slacks, Big & Tall Men's Wear, Sportswear, Furnishings, Dress Shirts, Ties, Robes, Underwear, Hosiery, Headwear, Accessories, Belts, Boys' Wear, Urban Contemporary, Store Displays, Fixtures, Supplies

PUERTO RICO - Fajardo

EL MILITAR (MW)
Calle Iglesias, #52
Fajardo, PR 00738
787-863-5350
JORGE LUIS LOPEZ (Owner) & Buys Men's Wear, Footwear, Store Displays, Fixtures, Supplies

ROBERTMAN STORES (CLO)
4 Garrido Morales
Fajardo, PR 00738
787-863-2303
JOSE ANTONIORIVERA QUINONES (Owner) & Buys Men's Wear, Store Displays, Fixtures, Supplies

LA COBACHA, INC. (MW-2)
San Patricio Shopping Center (m-b)
Guaynabo, PR 00968
787-792-6002 / Fax: 787-782-6693
Sales: $1 Million-$10 Million
LUIS RODRIGUEZ (President) & Buys Leather Goods, Men's Big & Tall Apparel, Men's & Boys' Apparel, Men's Casualwear, Men's Denim Apparel, Men's Formalwear, Men's Accessories, Men's Hosiery, Men's Outerwear, Men's Sportswear, Men's Suits, Men's Swimwear
MARGARITA RODRIGUEZ (Treas.)
OMAIRA SANTO (Store Mgr.)

J.C. PENNEY CO. DE PUERTO RICO (DEPT-7)
Plaza Las Americas
Hato Rey, PR 00918
787-758-1919 / Fax: 787-752-5539
KERRY COOK (President)
MANUEL GONZALEZ (G.M.M.-Men's) & Buys Footwear
CARMEN ROVLES-Boys' Wear
FRANSCIO ROIG-Ties, Underwear, Accessories, Men's Wear
MANUEL GONZDEZ-Young Men's Wear

TIENDAS DONATO (MW-36)
Ave. Balbosa, #268
Hato Rey, PR 00918
787-753-0730 / Fax: 787-250-0116
DONATO FERNANDEZ (President & Real Estate Contact) & Buys Men's Sportswear, Urban Contemporary, Store Displays, Fixtures, Supplies

ANGEL STORE (MW)
P.O. Box 495
Dr. Vidal, #10
Humacao, PR 00792
787-852-2290
ANGEL LUIS ARROYO (Owner) & Buys Men's Sportswear, Sweaters, Sport Shirts, Casual Slacks, Active Apparel, Dress Shirts, Ties, Underwear, Belts, Store Displays, Fixtures and Supplies

DISCOPRINT (SP)
Carreras St., #50
Humacao, PR 00791
787-852-5450 / Fax: 787-852-5450
GUIRRLLERMO MONTERRBY (Owner) & Buys Active Apparel, Athletic Footwear, Licensed Apparel

EL TRIUNFO (MW)
P.O. Box 8061
Humacao, PR 00792
787-852-5711
Sales: $100,001-$500,000
CRESENSEO ARROYO (Owner) & Buys Men's Wear, Store Displays, Fixtures, Supplies

TIENDA JUNELBA (CLO-3)
10 Union (p)
Lajas, PR 00667
787-899-4787 / Fax: 787-899-4787
ANTONIO BAYON (Owner) & Buys Men's Sportswear, Sport Shirts, Casual Slacks, Active Apparel, Hosiery, Accessories, Young Men's & Boys' Wear, Urban Contemporary, Footwear, Store Displays, Fixtures, Supplies

ALLEN'S OF SAN JUAN (MW-2)
(COLLAY'S MEN'S SHOP)
12 Calle Post S (bud-p-m)
Mayaguez, PR 00680
787-832-8230 / Fax: 787-832-0065
Sales: $1 Million-$10 Million
ANDY BEAUCHAMP (President) & Buys Leather Goods, Men's Big & Tall Apparel, Men's & Boys' Apparel, Men's Casualwear, Men's Denim Apparel, Men's Formalwear, Men's Accessories, Men's Hosiery, Men's Outerwear, Men's Sportswear, Men's Suits, Men's Swimwear

EL SPORTSMAN DE MAYAGUEZ, INC. (CLO-2)
Calle Post #5 (p)
Mayaguez, PR 00680
787-833-4590 / Fax: 787-832-6737
Sales: $1 Million-$10 Million
JUAN DORESTE (Owner) & Buys Men's Wear, Urban Contemporary, Store Displays, Fixtures, Supplies

LAS GANGAS, INC. (CLO)
P.O. Box 1530 (p-m)
Mayaguez, PR 00681
787-832-1364 / Fax: 787-834-3749
Sales: $1 Million-$10 Million
MR. VELIGMAN (Owner) & Buys Boys' Clothing, Sportswear, Furnishings, Accessories, Urban Contemporary, Store Displays, Fixtures, Supplies

MADRID MODAS CORP. (KS)
Mayaguez Mall
975 Hosdos Ave.
Mayaguez, PR 00680
787-834-7792 / Fax: 787-834-7792
FRANK NG (Owner) & Buys 2 to 20 Boys' Wear, Urban Contemporary, Store Displays, Fixtures, Supplies

LA NUEVA ESQUINA (MW)
Apt. #222, Calle Principal
Morovis, PR 00687
787-862-3655
SIXTO ORTIZ (Owner) & Buys Men's Wear, Urban Contemporary, Footwear, Store Displays, Fixtures, Supplies

CASA LOPEZ (CLO-2)
(OSVALDO L. DEDOS, INC.)
Isabel 70 y Leon (m-b)
Ponce, PR 00730
787-842-0174 / Fax: 787-841-1891
Sales: $1 Million-$10 Million
OSVALDO L. DEDOS (President) & Buys Men's Suits, Big & Tall Men's Wear, Sport Shirts, Casual Slacks, Active Apparel, 8 to 20 Boys' Clothing, Footwear, Urban Contemporary, Store Displays, Fixtures, Supplies

BIG CORNER (MW)
Ave. Jose de Diego, #503 (m)
Puerto Nuevo, PR 00920
787-783-1108 / Fax: 787-273-1280
Sales: $100,001-$500,000
ELENA ZAYAS (President) & Buys Men's Overcoats, Suits, Tailored Jackets, Tailored Slacks, Big & Tall, Sweaters, Sport Shirts, Outer Jackets, Casual Slacks, Active Apparel, Dress Shirts, Belts, Urban Contemporary, Store Displays, Fixtures, Supplies

SANTINI (CLO-2)
P.O. Box 43
Rio Grande, PR 00745
787-887-2145 / Fax: 787-887-6810
HECTOR DIAZ SANTINI (Owner)
HECTOR DIAZ FERRER-Men's Wear, Footwear, Store Displays, Fixtures, Supplies

ALMACENES RIVIERA (CLO-8)
101 Ave. Jose de Diego
Rio Piedras, PR 00925
787-758-1616 / Fax: 787-758-2847
MEIFY PEREZ (Owner)
ANA VICTORIA CRUZ-Men's & Boys' Sportswear, Urban Contemporary, Pants, Underwear, Hosiery, Accessories, Store Displays, Fixtures, Supplies

PUERTO RICO - San Juan

EUROMODA (MW)
P.O. Box 362635
San Juan, PR 00935
787-753-7134 / Fax: 787-756-5916

JESUS CASTIEL, SR. (Owner)
JESUS CASTIEL, JR.-Men's Wear
JUAN CARLOS CASTIEL-Men's Footwear

S. FERNANDEZ & CO., INC. (CLO-2)
262 San Francisco St.
San Juan, PR 00902
787-724-8085 / Fax: 787-725-1097
Sales: $100,001-$500,000

CARLOS GONZALES (Owner) & Buys Men's Wear, Store Displays, Fixtures, Supplies
LEO RODRIQUEZ-Men's Wear, Store Displays, Fixtures, Supplies
CARLOS PEREZ-Men's Footwear, Urban Contemporary

WILLIAM'S STORE (CLO)
Calle Ruiz Belves, #279
San Sebastian, PR 00685
787-896-2783 / Fax: 787-896-0300

WILLIAM CRUZ (Owner) & Buys Men's Wear, Urban Contemporary, Store Displays, Fixtures, Supplies

LA ISLA (DEPT)
8-Celis Aguilera
Santa Isabel, PR 00757
787-845-4130 / Fax: 787-845-4130

PEDRO BARED (President) & Buys Men's Wear, Store Displays, Fixtures, Supplies

CLUBMAN, INC. (MW-12)
(LE CLUB)
P.O. Box 9164 (b)
1116 Ponce de Leon Ave.
Santurce, PR 00908
787-725-3680 / Fax: 787-721-3680
Sales: $1 Million-$10 Million

ALFREDO RAMIREZ (V.P.)
ANGEL RAMIREZ-Men's Suits, Tailored Jackets, Tailored Slacks, Sport Shirts, Casual Slacks, Active Apparel, Furnishings, Accessories, Footwear, Store Displays, Fixtures, Supplies

GENTLEMAN, INC. (MW)
1672 Ponce de Leon (b)
Santurce, PR 00909
787-727-1523 / Fax: 787-723-1268
Sales: $1 Million-$10 Million

SALOMON BENDER (Owner) & Buys Men's Suits, Tailored Jackets, Tailored Slacks, Raincoats, Dress Shirts, Belts, Big & Tall Men's Wear, Sweaters, Sport Shirts, Outer Jackets, Casual Slacks, Active Apparel, Ties, Robes, Underwear, Accessories, Store Displays, Fixtures, Supplies

MARTINEZ ARIAS & CO. (MW-27)
P.O. Box 9374 (b)
Santurce, PR 00908
787-275-2880 / Fax: 787-275-2550
Sales: $10 Million-$50 Million

LUIS MARTINEZ (President & G.M.M.) & Buys Men's Wear, Urban Contemporary, Footwear, Store Displays, Fixtures, Supplies

BLACKTON (MW)
P.O. Box 50971
Toabaja, PR 00950
787-783-6760 / Fax: 787-783-6760

CARLOS NEGRON (Owner) & Buys Big & Tall Men's Suits, Sportswear, Furnishings, Accessories, Footwear, Urban Contemporary, Store Displays, Fixtures, Supplies

RHODE ISLAND - Barrington

MILAN FINE MEN'S CLOTHIER (MW)
270 County Rd. (h)
Barrington, RI 02806
401-247-9209 / Fax: 401-247-5940
RICHARD DARAKIAN (Partner)
JERRY DARAKIAN (Partner) & Buys Men's Sportswear, Furnishings, Shoes, Accessories, Store Displays, Fixtures, Supplies

THE SHORELINE (CLO)
238 Ocean Ave.
Block Island, RI 02807
401-466-5800 / Fax: 401-466-5410
DANIELLE DUFFY (Owner) & Buys Men's Wear, Store Displays, Fixtures, Supplies

STAR DEPARTMENT STORE, INC. (CLO)
P.O. Box 190 (p)
Water St.
Block Island, RI 02807
401-466-5541 / Fax: 401-466-2503
JAMES ERNST (Owner) & Buys Men's, Young Men's & Boys' Sportswear, Footwear, Store Displays, Fixtures, Supplies

JANE'S OUTLET (CLO)
116 Tupelo St. (m)
Bristol, RI 02809
401-253-5660 / Fax: 401-253-5660
Sales: $100,001-$500,000
STEVE KURLAN (Owner) & Buys Men's Sportswear, Sweaters, Sport Shirts, Outer Jackets, Casual Slacks, Active Apparel, Furnishings, Accessories, Dress Shirts, Ties, Hosiery, Gloves, Hats, Belts, Jewelry, Urban Contemporary, Store Displays, Fixtures, Supplies

CANTERBURY (CLO)
650 Oaklawn Ave. (b-h)
Cranston, RI 02920
401-944-4757 / Fax: 401-944-3458
Sales: $500,001-$1 Million
Website: www.ecanterbury.com
RONALD GARAFANO (President) & Buys Men's Suits, Tailored Jackets, Tailored Slacks, Formal Wear, Sportswear, Active Apparel, Accessories, Urban Contemporary, Store Displays, Fixtures, Supplies

JOE'S PLACE (CLO)
1744 Cranston St. (p)
Cranston, RI 02920
401-946-5050 / Fax: 401-942-5762
JOSEPH McFADDEN (Co-Owner) & Buys Men's, Young Men's & Boys' Clothing, Sportswear, Furnishings, Headwear, Accessories, Urban Contemporary, Store Displays, Fixtures, Supplies
LORI RICE (Co-Owner) & Buys Men's, Young Men's & Boys' Clothing, Sportswear, Furnishings, Headwear, Accessories, Store Displays, Fixtures, Supplies

ANN & HOPE (GM-2)
1 Ann & Hope Way
Cumberland, RI 02864
401-722-1000 / Fax: 401-725-7190
Sales: $100 Million-$500 Million
Website: www.annhope.com
IRWIN CHASE (President)
FRED LOONEY (C.E.O.)
SAM CHASE (Exec. V.P.)
KATHLEEN McCONAGHY-Men's Sportswear, Furnishings, Accessories, Boys' Wear, Footwear, Store Displays, Fixtures and Supplies
KIM BELASCO-Men's Sportswear, Furnishings, Accessories, Young Men's Wear, Boys' Wear, Big & Tall Men's Wear, Footwear, Store Displays, Fixtures and Supplies

ATTITUDES (MW)
Lincoln Mall (m)
Lincoln, RI 02865
401-333-6230 / Fax: 401-333-6230
STEVE MINICUCCI (Owner) & Buys Men's, Young Men's & Boys' Clothing, Urban Contemporary, Sportswear, Dress Shirts, Ties, Hosiery, Gloves, Headwear, Belts, Shoes, Boots, Store Displays, Fixtures, Supplies

T-SHIRT HUT (CLO-4)
38 Pier Market Pl., #A (p)
Narragansett, RI 02882
401-782-4945 / Fax: 401-364-6441
MIKE RYAN (Co-Owner)
KATHY RYAN (Co-Owner) & Buys T-shirts, Shorts, Tank Tops, Sport Shirts, Sandals, Store Displays, Fixtures, Supplies

ARMY & NAVY SURPLUS STORE (AN)
262 Thames St. (p)
Newport, RI 02840
401-847-3073 / Fax: 401-847-3079
Sales: $500,000-$1 Million
Website: www.newportarmynavy.com
RICHARD BACKMAN (Owner) & Buys Men's Sportswear, Sweaters, Sport Shirts, Casual Slacks, Outer Jackets, Active Apparel, Underwear, Hosiery, Gloves, Belts, Small Leather Goods, Headwear, Leather Apparel, Deck Shoes, Athletic Footwear, Outer Shoes, Urban Contemporary, Store Displays, Fixtures, Supplies

BEACH PARTY SWIMWEAR (CLO)
P.O. Box 1
135 Swinburne Row, Brick Market Pl.
Newport, RI 02840
401-847-9730 / Fax: 407-847-9730
KATHERINE WEDGE (Co-Owner) & Buys Boys' Swimwear, Men's Surf & Swimwear
SYLVIA WEDGE (Co-Owner) & Buys Boys' Swimwear, Men's Surf & Swimwear

MICHAEL HAYES CO. (MW-3)
204 Bellevue Ave. (m-b)
Newport, RI 02840
401-846-3090 / Fax: 401-848-7224
MICHAEL HAYES (Owner)
CHRISTOPHER HAYES-Men's Sportswear, Furnishings & Accessories, Men's Footwear

THE NARAGANSETT (MW)
1 Bannister's Wharf (b-h)
Newport, RI 02840
401-847-0303 / Fax: 401-849-5455
FRANK GLADDING (Owner) & Buys Men's Sportswear, Sweaters, Sport Shirts, Outer Jackets, Leather Jackets, Casual Slacks, Active Apparel, Furnishings, Accessories, Dress Shirts, Ties, Underwear, Hosiery, Gloves, Headwear, Belts, Small Leather Goods, Store Displays, Fixtures, Supplies

NEWPORT BREEZE, INC. (CLO)
1 Bannister Wharf (p)
Newport, RI 02840
401-849-4381 / Fax: 401-849-4381
LINDA PICKENS (Co-Owner) & Buys Men's & Boys' T-shirts, Shorts, Store Displays, Fixtures, Supplies
STEVE PICKENS (Co-Owner) & Buys Men's & Boys' T-shirts, Shorts, Store Displays, Fixtures, Supplies

POTTER CLOTHING CO., INC. (CLO)
(POTTER & CO.)
172 Thames St. (m)
Newport, RI 02840
401-847-0392 / Fax: 401-847-4530
HAROLD WERNER (Owner) & Buys Store Displays, Fixtures, Supplies
BARBARA HELMBRECHT-Men's Sportswear, Furnishings, Accessories, Footwear, Young Men's Wear, 8 to 20 Boys' Wear
WAYNE STEPALAVICH-Men's Sportswear, Furnishings, Accessories, Footwear, Young Men's Wear, 8 to 20 Boys' Wear

TEAM ONE NEWPORT (MO & CLO & OL)
P.O. Box 1443 (m-b-h)
561 Thames St.
Newport, RI 02840
401-847-2368 / Fax: 401-849-8460
Sales: $1 Million-$10 Million
Website: www.team1newport.com
MARTHA F. PARKER (President) & Buys Men's Shorts, Shirts, Hats & Foul Weather Gear, Footwear
PEGGY KOPELCHECK-Men's Shorts, Shirts, Hats & Foul Weather Gear
ROBIN MERRILL-Men's Furnishings, Accessories, Footwear

THE TRADING COMPANY (CLO-2)

27 Bowens Wharf (p)
Newport, RI 02840
401-848-2539

DAVID FERNANDEZ (President) & Buys Men's T-shirts, Tank Tops, Shorts, Sweaters, Sport Shirts, Outer Jackets, Hats, Accessories, Young Men's Wear, Boys' Wear, Store Displays, Fixtures, Supplies

WILSON'S OF WICKFORD (CLO)

(WILSON'S, INC.)
35 Brown St. (b)
North Kingstown, RI 02852
401-294-9514 / Fax: 401-294-1519

PAUL WILSON (President) & Buys Store Displays, Fixtures, Supplies

CRAIG WILSON (V.P.) & Buys Men's Footwear, Leather Apparel, Sportswear, Outerwear, Sweaters, Big & Tall Men's Wear, Accessories

JIM WILSON (V.P.) & Buys Men's Wear, Suits, Sportcoats, Dress Slacks, Furnishings

APEX, INC. (DEPT-1 & OL)

100 Main St. (p-m-b)
Pawtucket, RI 02862
401-723-3500 / Fax: 401-723-9452
Sales: $10 Million-$50 Million
Website: www.apexstores.com

ANDREW GATES (President)

MICHAEL DVORIN (V.P. & G.M.M.)

MICHAEL DVORIN (Mgr.-Purch.) & Buys Store Displays, Fixtures, Supplies

MICHAEL DVORIN-Young Men's Wear, Collections, 8 to 20 Boys' Wear, Sporting Wear, Urban Contemporary, Mens Footwear

SPIRIT RECOGNITION, INC. (CLO)

639 Central Ave. (p-m)
Pawtucket, RI 02861
401-722-0500 / Fax: 401-722-0252
Website: www.spirit.cc

BOB MARSHALL (Partner) & Buys Men's T-shirts, Active Apparel, Shorts, Headwear, Store Displays, Fixtures, Supplies

JILL MARSHALL (Partner) & Buys Men's T-shirts, Active Apparel, Shorts, Headwear, Store Displays, Fixtures, Supplies

NOTE-This Store Sells Primarily College & Fraternity Wear.

BRIGGS PROVIDENCE (MW)

200 S. Main St. (b)
Providence, RI 02903
401-453-0025 / Fax: 401-521-5525
Sales: $1 Million-$10 Million
Website: www.briggstheshop.com

PAULA D. DOHERTY (President)

BRIGGS A. DOHERTY, JR. (G.M.M.) & Buys Men's Sportswear, Furnishings, Headwear, Store Displays, Fixtures, Supplies

CONTINENTAL MENSWEAR LTD. (MW)

130 Washington St. (m)
Providence, RI 02903
401-421-4721

KEN NORIGIAN (Owner) & Buys Men's Sportswear, Leather Apparel, Headwear, Accessories, Young Men's & Boys' Wear, Urban Contemporary, Store Displays, Fixtures, Supplies

ELMWOOD FASHION DISCOUNT (CLO)

489 Elmwood Ave. (p-m)
Providence, RI 02907
401-461-7939 / Fax: 401-467-4559

PEDRO TEJADA (Owner) & Buys Men's Sportswear, Furnishings, Dress Shirts, Ties, Underwear, Shoes, Belts, Young Men's Wear, Urban Contemporary, 8 to 20 Boys' Wear, Store Displays, Fixtures, Supplies

FRANKLIN ROGERS LTD. (MW)

142 Westminster St. (m-b)
Providence, RI 02903
401-454-8170 / Fax: 401-454-4380

ROGER GROSS (President) & Buys Men's Sportswear, Furnishings, Headwear, Accessories, Store Displays, Fixtures, Supplies

HARVEY LTD. (MW)

114 Waterman St. (p-m-b)
Providence, RI 02906
401-331-5950

HARVEY LAPIDES (Owner) & Buys Men's Sportswear, Furnishings, Headwear, Accessories, Store Displays, Fixtures and Supplies

HANK LESPERANCE (Mgr.) & Buys Men's Sportswear, Furnishings, Headwear, Accessories, Store Displays, Fixtures and Supplies

HONORBILT FASHIONS (MW)

106 Washington (bud)
Providence, RI 02903
401-331-5422

JOHN GERVORIAN (Owner) & Buys Men's Sportswear, Furnishings, Headwear, Accessories, Young Men's Wear, Store Displays, Fixtures, Supplies

PHILIP WOLFE HABERDASHER, INC. (MW)

84 Dorrance St. (b)
Providence, RI 02908
401-331-6532 / Fax: 401-454-8149
Sales: $500,000-$1 Million

PEGGY ANN KERWIN (Owner) & Buys Men's Overcoats, Suits, Tailored Jackets, Tailored Slacks, Leather Apparel, Raincoats, Sportswear, Furnishings, Accessories, Belts, Urban Contemporary, Small Leather Goods, Fragrances, Footwear, Store Displays, Fixtures and Supplies

ZUCCOLO, INC. (MW)

200 Atwells Ave. (b)
Providence, RI 02903
401-521-0646

JOSEPH A. ZUCCOLO (Owner) & Buys Men's Sportswear, Furnishings & Accessories, Store Displays, Fixtures and Supplies

BURKHARDT'S (MW)

1086 Willet Ave. (m-b)
Riverside, RI 02915
401-433-1460
Sales: $100,001-$500,000

WALTER BURKHARDT (Partner) & Buys Men's Sportswear, Furnishings, Shoes, Headwear, Accessories, Young Men's Wear, Store Displays, Fixtures, Supplies

MABEL BURKHARDT (Partner)

CAMIRE'S ATHLETIC SOLES & LEVIS (SG)

20 Main St., #B (m)
Wakefield, RI 02879
401-782-8353
Sales: $100,001-$500,000

ROGER CAMIRE (Owner) & Buys Men's Jeans, T-shirts, Active Apparel, Shorts, Sport Shirts, Outer Jackets, Hosiery, Athletic Footwear, Hiking Boots, Store Displays, Fixtures, Supplies

MARY CAMIRE-Men's Jeans, T-shirts, Active Apparel, Shorts, Sport Shirts, Outer Jackets, Hosiery, Athletic Footwear, Hiking Boots, Store Displays, Fixtures, Supplies

DIVERSIFIED RETAILERS, INC. (CLO-2)

153 Old Tower Hill Rd. (p)
Wakefield, RI 02879
401-783-3613 / Fax: 401-783-3227

GERALD RICHMOND (Partner) & Buys Men's Sportswear, Hosiery, Belts, Accessories, Small Leather Goods, Casual Footwear, Slippers, Boots, Store Displays, Fixtures, Supplies

KEN RICHMOND (Partner) & Buys Men's Sportswear, Hosiery, Accessories, Belts, Small Leather Goods, Casual Footwear, Slippers, Boots, Store Displays, Fixtures, Supplies

GOB SHOP (MW)

(JLJ SALES)
465 Main St. (p)
Warren, RI 02885
401-245-4800 / Fax: 401-247-0080

ROBERT ESTRELLA, SR. (Owner) & Buys Men's Sportswear, Leather Apparel, Furnishings, Headwear, Accessories, Footwear, Young Men's Wear, Store Displays, Fixtures, Supplies

RHODE ISLAND - Warren

JAMIEL'S SHOE WORLD, INC. (FW-2)

471 Main St. (bud-p-m-b)
Warren, RI 02885
401-245-4389 / Fax: 401-247-7765
Sales: $1 Million-$10 Million

LILY JAMIEL (President) & Buys Leather Goods
DOUGLAS JAMIEL-Watches
FRANCIS JAMIEL-Boys' Apparel, Boys' Footwear
SUSAN JAMIEL-Men's Footwear
MARY J. TAVARES-Men's Footwear, Men's Accessories, Hosiery

GIAN, INC. (MW)

200 Bald Hill Rd. (b)
Warwick, RI 02886
401-739-5400 / Fax: 401-739-2648
Sales: $500,000-$1 Million

TOM ALTIERI (Owner) & Buys Men's Sportswear, Furnishings, Accessories, Headwear, Store Displays, Fixtures, Supplies

JOSEPH DAVID BIG & TALL, INC. (MW)

757 Airport Rd. (m)
Warwick, RI 02886
401-739-0530
Website: www.josephdavid.com

DAVID GAROFALO (Co-Owner) & Buys Big & Tall Men's Sportswear, Furnishings, Accessories, Store Displays, Fixtures, Supplies
JOSEPH SCIANNA (Co-Owner) & Buys Big & Tall Men's Sportswear, Furnishings, Accessories, Store Displays, Fixtures, Supplies

WALDORF TUXEDO CO. (MW-5)

1222 Warwick Ave. (b-h)
Warwick, RI 02888
401-463-3336 / Fax: 401-463-5828
Website: www.waldorftux.com

ROBERT QUIRK (Partner) & Buys Men's & Boys' Tuxedos, Footwear

GARA'S MEN'S SHOP, INC. (MW)

23 Washington St. (bud)
West Warwick, RI 02893
401-828-1005
Sales: $100,001-$500,000

ROBERT GARAFANO (President) & Buys Men's Sportswear, Furnishings, Accessories, Footwear, Store Displays, Fixtures, Supplies

THE PARAGON GIFTS, INC. (MO)

89 Tom Harvey Rd. (m)
Westerly, RI 02891
401-596-0929 / Fax: 401-596-6142
Sales: $10 Million-$50 Million
Website: www.paragongifts.com

MARY JANE SPOONER (Mdse. Mgr.) & Buys Men's Ties, Belts, Small Leather Goods, Gloves, Boys' Wear, T-shirts

TOSCANO'S MEN'S SHOP, INC. (MW)

9 Canal St. (p-m)
Westerly, RI 02891
401-596-2584
Sales: $100,001-$500,000

PAUL GENCARELLA (V.P.) & Buys Men's Sportswear, Furnishings, Footwear

LANOIE MENSWEAR, INC. (MW)

P.O. Box 158 (b)
273 Social St.
Woonsocket, RI 02895
401-762-3385
Sales: $100,001-$500,000

ROGER G. LANOIE (President) & Buys Men's Overcoats, Suits, Tailored Jackets, Leather Apparel, Tailored Slacks, Raincoats, Sportswear, Sweaters, Sport Shirts, Outer Jackets, Casual Slacks, Active Apparel, Furnishings, Headwear, Accessories, Belts, Store Displays, Fixtures, Supplies

LIONEL SMITH LTD. (MW)
132 Laurens St. SW (b)
Aiken, SC 29801
803-648-2100 / Fax: 803-643-4142
VAN SMITH (Owner) & Buys Men's Sportswear, Furnishings, Accessories, Store Displays, Fixtures, Supplies

NEW IMAGE (CLO)
(NEW ESQUIRE FASHIONS)
109 Laurens St. (p)
Aiken, SC 29801
803-642-5152
SUN KIM (Owner) & Buys Men's, Young Men's & Boys' Wear, Footwear, Store Displays, Fixtures, Supplies

KARAMCHANDANI BROTHERS (MW-2)
104 E. Benson St. (m)
Anderson, SC 29624
864-224-2092 / Fax: 864-224-0727
BOBBY KARAM (Owner) & Buys Men's Sportswear, Furnishings, Accessories, Footwear, Urban Contemporary, Store Displays, Fixtures, Supplies

McCALL'S, INC. (MW)
102 Miracle Mile Dr. (b)
Anderson, SC 29621
864-226-8211
Sales: $500,001-$1 Million
DAVID F. McCALL, JR. (President & G.M.M.) & Buys Men's Sportswear, Furnishings, Accessories, Footwear, Store Displays, Fixtures, Supplies

KENNEDY'S (MW)
132 N. Oak St. (p)
Batesburg-Leesville, SC 29006
803-532-4081
RALPH S. KENNEDY (Co-Owner) & Buys Men's Sportswear, Furnishings, Footwear, Store Displays, Fixtures, Supplies
DAN HEAD (Co-Owner) & Buys Men's Sportswear, Furnishings, Footwear, Store Displays, Fixtures, Supplies

5TH AVENUE (MW)
330 Robert Smalls Pkwy., #15B (m)
Beaufort, SC 29902
843-524-0744
Sales: $500,001-$1 Million
SAM ADDASSI (Owner) & Buys Men's Sportswear, Furnishings, Accessories, Footwear, Urban Contemporary, Store Displays, Fixtures, Supplies

LIPSITZ DEPARTMENT STORE (DEPT-2)
(LIPSITZ ENTERPRISES, INC.)
P.O. Box 369 (m-b)
825 Bay St.
Beaufort, SC 29901
843-524-0124
NEIL LIPSITZ (President) (@ 843-524-2330) & Buys Men's Footwear, Casual Footwear, Dress Boots, Athletic Footwear, Store Displays, Fixtures, Supplies
LUCILLE LIPSITZ (V.P.) & Buys Men's & Young Men's Sweaters, Sport Shirts, Outer Jackets, Casual Slacks, Active Apparel, Furnishings, Headwear, Accessories, Big & Tall Men's Wear, Urban Contemporary, Leather Apparel, 8 to 20 Boys' Wear, Store Displays, Fixtures, Supplies
JOE LIPSITZ-Men's & Young Men'sSweaters, Sport Shirts, Outer Jackets, Casual Slacks, Active Apparel, Furnishings, Headwear, Accessories, Big & Tall Men's Wear, Urban Contemporary, Leather Apparel, 8 to 20 Boys' Wear, Store Displays, Fixtures, Supplies

JEAN SHOP SPORTSWEAR, INC. (MW)
222 Public Sq. (m)
Belton, SC 29627
864-338-6328
EUNICE FIELDS (Owner) & Buys Men's Sport Shirts, Urban Contemporary, Jeans, T-shirts, Shorts, Belts, Store Displays, Fixtures, Supplies

GQ FASHIONS (CLO-3)
1026 Broad St. (bud-p)
Camden, SC 29020
803-432-9169
YUSEF HAMEEN (Owner) & Buys Boys' Clothing, Men's Sportswear, Furnishings (No Underwear), Accessories, Headwear, Footwear, Urban Contemporary, Store Displays, Fixtures, Supplies

319 MEN (MW)
(T. BRADSHAW, INC.)
321 King St. (h)
Charleston, SC 29401
843-577-8807 / Fax: 843-720-1840
Sales: $500,000-$1 Million
TIM SHAW (Owner) & Buys Men's Sportswear, Furnishings, Headwear, Accessories, Boys' Clothing, Men's Footwear, Store Displays, Fixtures, Supplies

A.J. DAVIS & CO. (CLO)
296 King St. (b-des)
Charleston, SC 29401
843-577-3088 / Fax: 843-853-8461
Sales: $500,001-$1 Million
Website: www.ajdavis.net
SALLY DAVIS (Co-Owner) & Buys Men's Sportswear, Furnishings, Accessories, Store Displays, Fixtures, Supplies
ALAN DAVIS (Co-Owner) & Buys Men's Sportswear, Furnishings, Accessories, Store Displays, Fixtures, Supplies

THE BEN SILVER CORP. (MO & CLO & OL)
149 King St. (b)
Charleston, SC 29401
843-577-4556 / Fax: 843-723-1543
Website: www.bensilver.com
ROBERT PRENNER (Co-Owner) & Buys Men's Blazers, Shirts, Ties, Headwear, Sweaters, Suspenders, Footwear, Store Displays, Fixtures, Supplies
SUE PRENNER (Co-Owner) & Buys Men's Blazers, Shirts, Ties, Headwear, Sweaters, Suspenders, Footwear, Store Displays, Fixtures, Supplies

BERLIN'S (CLO)
114 King St. (b-h)
Charleston, SC 29401
843-722-1665 / Fax: 843-577-0077
Sales: $1 Million-$10 Million
STEVE BERLIN (President) & Buys Men's Wear, Leather Apparel, Accessories, Footwear
HENRY BERLIN (C.E.O.) & Buys Men's Wear, Leather Apparel, Accessories, Footwear
ELAINE BERLIN (V.P.) & Buys Store Displays, Fixtures, Supplies

BLUESTEIN'S MENSWEAR (MW)
494 King St. (p)
Charleston, SC 29403
843-722-1738 / Fax: 843-722-1195
Sales: $1 Million-$10 Million
NICKY BLUESTEIN (Owner) & Buys Men's Overcoats, Suits, Tailored Jackets, Raincoats, Sweaters, Sport Shirts, Outer Jackets, Leather Apparel, Casual Slacks, Active Apparel, Dress Shirts, Ties, Hosiery, Gloves, Headwear, Belts, Jewelry, Formal Shirts, Big & Tall Men's Wear, Young Men's Wear, Urban Contemporary, 8 to 20 Boys' Suits, Footwear, Store Displays, Fixtures, Supplies

BOB ELLIS SHOES, INC. (FW-3)
332 King St. (m-b)
Charleston, SC 29401
843-723-2945 / Fax: 843-723-5214
Website: www.bobellisshoes.com
MORRIS KALINSKY (Owner) & Buys Men's Dress Shoes, Casual Shoes, Boots, Belts, Hosiery, Store Displays, Fixtures, Supplies

HI FASHION OF N.Y. (MW)
375 18th St. (bud)
Charleston, SC 29401
843-577-3021 / Fax: 843-571-4311
RODGER SAHIJRAM (Owner) & Buys Men's Sportswear, Furnishings, Accessories, Urban Contemporary, Footwear, Store Displays, Fixtures, Supplies

SOUTH CAROLINA - Charleston

HIPBONE (CLO)
7095 N. Kenwood Dr.
Charleston, SC 29406
843-813-1807 / Fax: 843-813-3050
JEROME DELAIN-Boys' Apparel, Boys' Swimwear, Accessories, Footwear, Men's Swimwear, Skate Apparel
ERNEST VERA-Boys' Apparel, Boys' Swimwear, Accessories, Footwear, Men's Swimwear, Skate Apparel

J.J.W. LUDEN & CO., INC. (GM)
78 Alexander St.
Charleston, SC 29403
843-723-7829 / Fax: 843-723-7433
Website: www.ludensoutfitters.com
SHEILA BUTLER (Owner) & Buys Men's Sportswear, Headwear, Footwear, Store Displays, Fixtures, Supplies

M. DUMAS & SONS (CLO)
294 King St. (p-m-b)
Charleston, SC 29401
843-723-8603 / Fax: 843-723-8604
Sales: $1 Million-$10 Million
Website: www.locountry.com/dumas
CLAIRE DUMAS (Owner)
LARRY DUMAS-Men's Sportswear, Leather Apparel, Furnishings, Headwear, Accessories, Young Men's Wear, 8 to 20 Boys' Wear, Store Displays, Fixtures, Supplies
DAVID DUMAS-Men's Sportswear, Leather Apparel, Furnishings, Headwear, Accessories, Young Men's Wear, 8 to 20 Boys' Wear, Store Displays, Fixtures, Supplies
TOPPER SCHACTE-Footwear, Dress Shoes, Casual Shoes, Athletic Footwear, Sandals, Work Shoes

MAX'S MEN'S STORE (MW)
328 King St. (b-des)
Charleston, SC 29401
843-722-4024 / Fax: 843-722-4025
Sales: $1 Million-$10 Million
ERIC KRAWCHECK (Co-Owner) & Buys Men's Overcoats, Suits, Tailored Jackets, Tailored Slacks, Raincoats, Sweaters, Sport Shirts, Outer Jackets, Leather Apparel, Casual Slacks, Active Apparel, Outer Jackets, Furnishings, Headwear, Belts, Footwear, Store Displays, Fixtures, Supplies
MAURICE KRAWCHECK (Co-Owner) & Buys Men's Overcoats, Suits, Tailored Jackets, Tailored Slacks, Raincoats, Sweaters, Sport Shirts, Outer Jackets, Leather Apparel, Casual Slacks, Active Apparel, Outer Jackets, Furnishings, Headwear, Belts, Footwear, Store Displays, Fixtures, Supplies

MR. JOHN'S BEACH STORE (SP)
P.O. Box 28
Charleston, SC 29403
843-588-9150
PAUL CHRYSOSTOM (Owner) & Buys Swimwear, Headwear, Sandals
PATTY CHRYSOSTOM-Swimwear, Headwear, Sandals

THE PEOPLES STORE OF CHARLESTON, INC. (CLO)
472 Meeting St., #E (bud-p-m)
Charleston, SC 29403
843-723-8097 / Fax: 843-722-7616
Sales: $500,001-$1 Million
M. E. WYLAND (President & G.M.M.) & Buys Men's Overcoats, Suits, Tailored Slacks, Raincoats, Sweaters, Sport Shirts, Outer Jackets, Casual Slacks, Furnishings, Belts, Small Leather Goods, Young Men's & Boys' Wear, Footwear, Store Displays, Fixtures, Supplies

SUPER BAD MEN'S CLOTHING (MW-3)
532 King St. (b)
Charleston, SC 29403
843-577-0132 / Fax: 843-577-0132
ABRAHAM DABIT (Owner) & Buys Men's Clothing, Sportswear, Furnishings, Accessories, Footwear, Urban Contemporary, Boys' Clothing, Store Displays, Fixtures, Supplies

YOUNG'S FASHIONS (CLO)
5619 Rivers Ave. (p)
Charleston, SC 29406
843-747-6041 / Fax: 843-722-1940
SONG YUN (Owner) & Buys Men's Sportswear, Urban Contemporary, Accessories, Store Displays, Fixtures, Supplies

B.C. MOORE & SONS (DEPT-78)
P.O. Drawer 1108 (m)
45 Powe St.
Cheraw, SC 29520
843-537-5211 / Fax: 843-537-3416
Sales: $10 Million-$50 Million
JAMES C. CRAWFORD III (President)
RON CROWFORD (V.P. & G.M.M.)
TIM POLITER-Men's Wear, Leather Apparel
STEVEN HUMPHRIES-Men's Wear, Leather Apparel
DAVID GREENE-Boys' Wear
BOBBY BOUSMAN-Footwear, Store Displays, Fixtures, Supplies

BIG APPLE FASHIONS (MW)
143 Market St. (m-b)
Cheraw, SC 29520
843-537-4279 / Fax: 843-537-4279
Sales: $500,001-$1 Million
PAM MEHRA (Co-Owner) & Buys Men's Sportswear, Dress Shirts, Ties, Gloves, Headwear, Belts, Jewelry, Small Leather Goods, Footwear, Urban Contemporary, Store Displays, Fixtures, Supplies
VICTOR KAPOOR (Co-Owner) & Buys Men's & Boys' Athletic Footwear, Boots

THE FAMILY FASHION (MW)
P.O. Box 772 (m)
128 Market St.
Cheraw, SC 29520
843-537-9262
DOROTHY DANKINS (Owner)
VALERIE DAWKINS (Mgr.) & Buys Men's Sportswear, Furnishings, Accessories, Footwear, Urban Contemporary, Store Displays, Fixtures, Supplies

HARE CLOTHIER (CLO)
171 Gadsden St. (m-b)
Chester, SC 29706
803-581-3262 / Fax: 803-581-3263
Sales: $1 Million-$10 Million
SHULER ROBERTSON (Co-Owner)
GERRY ROBERTSON (Co-Owner) & Buys Store Displays, Fixtures, Supplies
MARK HUEY-Men's Sportswear, Furnishings, Accessories, Dress Shoes, Casual Shoes, Athletic Footwear, Work Boots, Urban Contemporary

JUDGE KELLER'S STORE (CLO)
367 College Ave. (p)
Clemson, SC 29631
864-654-6446
Sales: $500,001-$1 Million
LEONARD KELLER (Owner) & Buys Men's Casualwear, T-shirts, Sweatshirts, Store Displays, Fixtures, Supplies

MR. KNICKERBOCKER (MW-2)
354 College Ave. (m)
Clemson, SC 29631
864-654-4203 / Fax: 864-654-4225
Sales: $1 Million-$10 Million
Website: www.mrknickerbocker.com
JAMES SPEARMAN (Owner)
DAVID SPEARMAN (G.M.M.) & Buys Men's, Young Men's & 8 to 20 Boys' Wear, Store Displays, Fixtures, Supplies

ADAIR'S MEN'S SHOP (MW)
100 Musgrove St. (m-b)
Clinton, SC 29325
864-833-0138
Sales: $500,001-$1 Million
JAMES R. ADAIR (Owner) & Buys Men's Wear, Casual Shoes, Dress Shoes, Work Shoes, Formalwear, Store Displays, Fixtures, Supplies

THE ARMY NAVY STORE (AN)
(CAROLINA SURPLUS SALES)
1621 Main St. (bud)
Columbia, SC 29201
803-252-1350 / Fax: 803-252-1354
Sales: $500,001-$1 Million
JOHN RATLIFF (Co-Owner) & Buys Men's Athletic Footwear, Activewear
ANDREW D. ZALKIN (Co-Owner) & Buys Men's & Boys' Wear, Footwear, Accessories, Furnishings, Store Displays, Fixtures, Supplies

BRITTONS, INC. (CLO)
2818 Devine St. (b)
Columbia, SC 29205
803-771-2700 / Fax: 803-765-2528
Website: www.brittonsofcolumbia.com
ANDREW LEVINSON (President & G.M.M.) & Buys Men's Overcoats, Suits, Tailored Jackets, Tailored Slacks, Raincoats, Sweaters, Sport Shirts, Outer Jackets, Casual Slacks, Leather Apparel, Furnishings, Belts, Jewelry, Store Displays, Fixtures, Supplies

BUMS SPORTSWEAR (MW)
(HARMON SPORTSWEAR, INC.)
2700 Broad River Rd. (p)
Columbia, SC 29210
803-798-4100 / Fax: 803-750-1750
Sales: $500,000-$1 Million
DON HARMON (Co-Owner) & Buys Men's Sportswear
BARBARA SUMMERS (Co-Owner) & Buys Men's Sportswear

EXTRA MILE (SP)
3223 Devine St., #1
Columbia, SC 29206
803-254-7027 / Fax: 803-254-4823
Website: www.theextramile.com
LAYTON GWINN (Owner) & Buys Activewear, Athletic Footwear

FUN WEAR (MW-3)
100 Columbiana Center (b)
Columbia, SC 29210
803-732-7221
MICHAEL MEANS (Owner) & Buys Men's Wear, Urban Contemporary, Store Displays, Fixtures, Supplies

GRANGER OWINGS, INC. (MW)
1333 Main St. (p-m-b)
Columbia, SC 29201
803-252-6714 / Fax: 803-748-8509
Sales: $500,001-$1 Million
Website: www.grangerowings.com
BILL OWINGS (Co-Owner) & Buys Men's Wear, Leather Apparel, Footwear, Store Displays, Fixtures, Supplies
JIM ROGERS (Co-Owner) & Buys Men's Wear, Leather Apparel, Footwear, Store Displays, Fixtures, Supplies
VAUGHN GRANGER (Co-Owner) & Buys Men's Wear, Leather Apparel, Footwear, Store Displays, Fixtures, Supplies

LOURIE'S, INC. (MW-2)
P.O. Box 1427 (b)
1601 Main St.
Columbia, SC 29202
(DLS Outfitters)
803-765-9200 / Fax: 803-256-1906
Sales: $1 Million-$10 Million
Website: www.louries.com
JOEL LOURIE (President)
JERRY STAFFORD-Men's Overcoats, Suits, Tailored Jackets, Tailored Slacks, Raincoats, Big & Tall Men's Wear, Men's Sport Shirts, Casual Slacks, Active Apparel, Outerwear, Leather Apparel, Furnishings, Headwear, Accessories, Footwear, Store Displays, Fixtures, Supplies

MARK'S MENSWEAR (MW)
1625 Main St.
Columbia, SC 29201
803-779-0729
ALLEN RIVKIN-Men's Sportswear, Furnishings, Accessories, Dress Shoes, Casual Shoes, Dress Boots, Store Displays, Fixtures, Supplies

MAYO'S SUIT CITY (MW)
(MAYO'S)
6539 Two Notch Rd. (m-b)
Columbia, SC 29223
803-786-1123 / Fax: 803-754-7168
Sales: $500,001-$1 Million
ALAN BERRY (V.P.) & Buys Men's Sportswear, Furnishings, Accessories, Footwear, Store Displays, Fixtures, Supplies

MOE LEVY'S (CLO)
1300 Assembly St. (p-m)
Columbia, SC 29201
803-252-2857 / Fax: 803-252-9504
Sales: $1 Million-$10 Million
HAROLD B. RITTENBERG (Partner) & Buys Men's Sweaters, Sport Shirts, Leather Jackets, Casual Slacks, Active Apparel, Furnishings, Headwear, Accessories, Outerwear, Work Clothes, Young Men's Wear, Urban Contemporary, Boys' Sweaters, Footwear, Store Displays, Fixtures, Supplies
FLORENCE LEVY (Partner) & Buys Men's Sweaters, Sport Shirts, Leather Jackets, Casual Slacks, Active Apparel, Furnishings, Headwear, Accessories, Outerwear, Work Clothes, Young Men's Wear, Urban Contemporary, Boys' Sweaters, Footwear, Store Displays, Fixtures, Supplies

NEW YORK STYLE (MW)
1300 Main St. (m)
Columbia, SC 29201
803-254-5235
IKE DEWNANI (Owner) & Buys Men's Sportswear, Furnishings, Accessories, Store Displays, Fixtures, Supplies

SPORTS ACTIONS (SP-2)
5550 Forest Dr. (m)
Columbia, SC 29206
803-787-1323
Sales: $100,001-$500,000
JIM YOUNG PAIK (Owner) (@ 803-929-1990) & Buys Boys' Footwear, Men's Footwear, Leather Goods, Licensed Apparel, Men's Casualwear, Accessories, Outerwear, Sportswear, Young Men's Apparel

STRICTLY RUNNING (SP)
736 Harden St.
Columbia, SC 29205
803-799-4786
Sales: $100,001-$500,000
NORMAN FERRIS (Owner) & Buys Activewear, Athletic Footwear

TODD & MOORE, INC. (SG-2)
620 Huger St.
Columbia, SC 29201
803-765-0150 / Fax: 803-252-7049
G. MOORE (Co-Owner) & Buys Men's & Boys' Athletic Apparel, Athletic Footwear, Store Displays, Fixtures, Supplies
CHUCK TODD (Co-Owner) & Buys Men's & Boys' Athletic Apparel, Athletic Footwear, Store Displays, Fixtures, Supplies

SOUTH CAROLINA - Columbia

UNIVERSITY BOOK STORE (SP)
(UNIVERSITY OF SOUTH CAROLINA)
1400 Greene St.
Columbia, SC 29201
803-799-7406 / Fax: 803-777-8673
Website: www.scbookstore.com
DANA SENTERFEIT (Mdse. Mgr.) & Buys Activewear, Licensed Apparel

WEATHERS OF COLUMBIA, INC. (MW)
2710 Devine St. (b-h)
Columbia, SC 29205
803-771-6485 / Fax: 803-254-9343
Sales: $1 Million-$10 Million
MARION SCOTT (Co-Owner & President) & Buys Store Displays, Fixtures, Supplies
ALAN THOMAS (Co-Owner) & Buys Men's Wear, Leather Apparel, Footwear, Accessories, Furnishings
LEONARD FABRIZIO (Co-Owner) & Buys Men's Wear, Leather Apparel, Footwear, Accessories, Furnishings

ABRAMS' DEPARTMENT STORES (DEPT)
P.O. Box 867 (p-m-b)
318 Laurel St.
Conway, SC 29526
843-248-9198
Sales: $500,001-$1 Million
SAMUEL L. ABRAMS (Owner & G.M.M.) & Buys Men's Sweaters, Sport Shirts, Outer Jackets, Leather Jackets, Casual Slacks, Active Apparel, Furnishings, Headwear, Accessories, Young Men's Wear, 8 to 20 Boys' Wear, Footwear, Store Displays, Fixtures, Supplies

HABERDASHERY GENTLEMEN'S CLOTHIER (MW)
1028 3rd Ave. (m-b)
Conway, SC 29526
843-248-9999 / Fax: 843-248-3510
Sales: $500,001-$1 Million
RUSSELL FOWLER (Owner) & Buys Men's Sportswear, Furnishings, Accessories, Dress Shoes, Casual Shoes, Store Displays, Fixtures, Supplies

MEN'S WORLD (MW)
1015 Pearl St. (m)
Darlington, SC 29532
843-393-5681 / Fax: 843-393-5686
Sales: $100,001-$500,000
ANN GARLAND (Owner) & Buys Men's Big & Tall Clothing, Sportswear, Furnishings, Accessories, Footwear, Store Displays, Fixtures, Supplies

ROBINSON CO., INC. (DEPT)
P.O. Box 387 (m-b)
215 W. Main St.
Easley, SC 29641
864-855-0017 / Fax: 864-859-1821
Sales: $1 Million-$10 Million
ALFRED ROBINSON (President) & Buys Men's Overcoats, Suits, Tailored Jackets, Tailored Slacks, Raincoats, Sweaters, Sport Shirts, Outer Jackets, Leather Apparel, Casual Slacks, Active Apparel, Furnishings, Headwear, Belts, Small Leather Goods, Fragrances, Young Men's Wear, Footwear, Store Displays, Fixtures, Supplies
MARGOT ROBINSON-Store Displays, Fixtures, Supplies

EDGEFIELD FACTORY OUTLET (CLO)
115 Courthouse Sq. (m)
Edgefield, SC 29824
803-637-9944
Sales: $100,001-$500,000
JUSTINE LONG (Owner) & Buys Men's Sportswear, Furnishings, Accessories, Footwear, Urban Contemporary, Store Displays, Fixtures, Supplies

CLOTHING WORLD, INC. (CLO)
P.O. Box 370
Hwy. I -20, Rt. 53
Elgin, SC 29045
803-736-6576 / Fax: 803-736-1062
Sales: $1 Million-$10 Million
MIKE JAMES (Owner) & Buys Men's & Boys' Wear, Footwear, Accessories, Furnishings, Store Displays, Fixtures, Supplies

CLOTHING UNLIMITED (MW)
1657 W. Palmetto St. (p)
Florence, SC 29501
843-667-9671 / Fax: 843-667-4449
MARK BUTLER (Owner) & Buys Men's Sportswear, Dress Shirts, Ties, Belts, Hosiery, Headwear, Urban Contemporary, Store Displays, Fixtures, Supplies

HEAT STREET (CLO)
2419 2nd Loop Rd.
Florence, SC 29501
843-661-0602 / Fax: 843-661-6222
LLOYD MITCHELL (Owner) & Buys Sunglasses, Men's Footwear, Surf & Swimwear, T-shirts, Imprinted Sportswear, Urban Streetwear
RENEE MILES-Sunglasses, Men's Footwear, Surf & Swimwear, T-shirts, Imprinted Sportswear, Urban Streetwear

HOFFMAN & HOFFMAN (MW)
2618 2nd Loop Rd. (b)
Florence, SC 29501
843-669-9009 / Fax: 843-669-9009
CHARLES HOFFMAN (Owner) & Buys Men's Sportswear, Furnishings, Accessories, Dress Shoes, Casual Shoes, Athletic Footwear, Boots, Store Displays, Fixtures, Supplies
BONNIE HOFFMAN-Men's Sportswear, Furnishings, Accessories, Dress Shoes, Casual Shoes, Athletic Footwear, Boots, Store Displays, Fixtures, Supplies

JEAN'S GLORY (MW)
108 N. Dargan St. (p)
Florence, SC 29501
843-667-1653
Sales: $100,001-$500,000
SANG CHONG PARK (Owner) & Buys Men's Sportswear, Furnishings, Accessories, Footwear, Urban Contemporary, Store Displays, Fixtures, Supplies

ROYAL KNIGHT FORMAL WEAR (MW-2)
Florence Mall (m-b)
Florence, SC 29501
843-662-8702
Sales: $500,001-$1 Million
HENRY REVELL (Owner) & Buys Men's, Young Men's & Boys' Formalwear, Footwear, Store Displays, Fixtures, Supplies

TOMLINSON'S STORE, INC. (DEPT-12)
P.O. Box 870 (bud-p-m)
1309 E. Palmetto St.
Florence, SC 29503
843-669-1854 / Fax: 843-662-4364
Sales: $10 Million-$50 Million
RICK TOMLINSON (Chmn.)
GENE BARBER (President & G.M.M.) & Buys Men's Wear, Leather Apparel, Young Men's & Boys' Wear, Urban Contemporary, Footwear, Store Displays, Fixtures, Supplies

HAMRICK'S (CLO-23)

742 Peachoid Rd. (p-m)
Gaffney, SC 29341
864-489-5769 / Fax: 864-487-0954
Sales: $10 Million-$50 Million
Website: www.hamricks.com
Retail Locations: TN, NC, GA, SC

BARRY HAMRICK (Owner)
DINAH HAMRICK (V.P. & G.M.M.)
PAUL CARNEY (Opers. Mgr.) & Buys Store Displays, Fixtures, Supplies
DANNETTA HILL (Real Estate Contact)
JOHN L. HUMPHREY-Men's Suits, Tailored Jackets, Tailored Slacks, Raincoats, Big & Tall Men's Wear, Sweaters, Sport Shirts, Outer Jackets, Leather Apparel, Casual Slacks, Active Apparel, Furnishings, Accessories, Young Men's Wear
MICHELLE FLANY-8 to 20 Boys' Wear
MICHELLE FIPPS-Children's Accessories

ALWYN'S (CLO)

P.O. Box 492 (bud-p)
914 Front St.
Georgetown, SC 29440
843-546-4070
Sales: $100,001-$500,000

ALWYN GOLDSTEIN (Owner) & Buys Men's & Boys' Wear, Accessories, Furnishings, Footwear, Store Displays, Fixtures, Supplies

BALLEW & SCOTT CUSTOM CLOTHIERS (MW)

213 N. Main St. (m-b)
Greenville, SC 29601
864-242-4240 / Fax: 864-242-4249
Sales: $1 Million-$10 Million

JOE BALLEW (Co-Owner) & Buys Men's Sportswear, Furnishings, Accessories, Footwear, Store Displays, Fixtures, Supplies
BUTCH SCOTT (Co-Owner) & Buys Men's Sportswear, Furnishings, Accessories, Footwear, Store Displays, Fixtures, Supplies

BELK, INC. - WESTERN DIV. (DEPT-56)

14 S. Main St. (bud-p-m-b-h)
Greenville, SC 29601
(Belk Stores Services)
864-235-3148 / Fax: 864-235-2596
Website: www.belk.com
Retail Locations: AL, AR, GA, KY, MS, SC, TX, TN

LINDA ZWERN (Chmn.)
LARS PETERSEN (President)
WILLIAM L. WILSON (Sr. V.P. & Real Estate Contact) (@ 704-357-1000, Ext.: 3082)
RONALD SHEALY (V.P.-Mdse. & G.M.M.-Men's & Boys')
SCOTT HOLTZCLAW-Men's Tailored Jackets, Neckwear, Suits, Raincoats, Big & Tall Men's Wear
JAMIE OLIVER-Men's Slacks, Big & Tall Men's Slacks
DAVID ADCOCK-Men's Signature Sportswear, Better Sportswear
ROBIN EAGAR-Men's Signature Sportswear, Better Sportswear
MARGARET POLESON-Men's Dress Shirts, Robes, Gloves, Underwear, Hosiery, Headwear, Accessories
GERARD HORSTMANN-Young Men's Wear

SUSAN CARLY (D.M.M.-Children's)
TRIP HEEKS-8 to 20 Boys' Wear
SONA INGRAM-Boys' & Toddlers' Clothing & Accessories

FRED BROWN (D.M.M.-Shoes)
KEVIN FERGUSON-Men's & Boys' Dress Shoes, Casual Shoes, Western Shoes, Athletic Footwear, Boots, Slippers, Sandals

BROCKMAN'S MENSWEAR, INC. (MW)

Lake Forest Shopping Center (b)
1362 N. Pleasantburg Dr.
Greenville, SC 29609
864-244-1760 / Fax: 864-292-3742

JERRY BROCKMAN (Owner) & Buys Men's Sportswear, Furnishings, Accessories, Store Displays, Fixtures, Supplies

GEORGE'S BOOTERY (FW-2)

1417 Laurens Rd., #C (p-m)
Greenville, SC 29607
864-370-9990

GEORGE MARIANOS (Owner) & Buys Men's Western & Casual Boots, Dress Shoes, Casual Shoes, Store Displays, Fixtures, Supplies

GREGORY'S FORMAL WEAR (MW-6)

2021 Augusta St.
Greenville, SC 29605
864-235-8524 / Fax: 864-239-0011
Website: www.gregorysformalwear.com

DAVID GREGORY (Co-Owner) & Buys Men's, Young Men's & Boys' Formalwear, Accessories
TODD GREGORY (Co-Owner) & Buys Men's, Young Men's & Boys' Formalwear, Accessories
BUDDY GREGORY (Co-Owner) & Buys Men's, Young Men's & Boys' Formalwear, Accessories

JACK RUNNION LTD. (MW)

530 Haywood Rd. (h)
Greenville, SC 29607
864-297-5610 / Fax: 864-297-4007
Sales: $500,000-$1 Million

JACK RUNNION (Owner) & Buys Men's Sportswear, Furnishings, Accessories, Footwear, Store Displays, Fixtures, Supplies

LORICK WORLD OF FASHION (CLO)

1041 W. Blue Ridge Dr. (m-b)
Greenville, SC 29609
864-242-4130 / Fax: 864-467-1328

JACK ATKINSON (President & Owner) & Buys Men's Jeans, Shirts, Shorts, Hosiery, Belts, Denim Jackets, Store Displays, Fixtures, Supplies

RUSH WILSON LTD. (MW)

23 W. North St. (b)
Greenville, SC 29601
864-232-2761 / Fax: 864-232-7203
Sales: $1 Million-$10 Million
Website: www.rushwilson.com

RUSH WILSON (President) & Buys Men's Suits, Tailored Jackets, Tailored Slacks, Raincoats, Sportswear, Leather Apparel, Furnishings, Accessories, Footwear, Store Displays, Fixtures, Supplies
RUSH WILSON, III-Men's Suits, Tailored Jackets, Tailored Slacks, Raincoats, Sportswear, Leather Apparel, Furnishings, Accessories, Footwear, Store Displays, Fixtures, Supplies

STYLES OF NEW YORK (MW)

2 S. Main St. (m)
Greenville, SC 29601
864-271-4195
Sales: $500,001-$1 Million

MR. MATAI (Owner) & Buys Men's Wear, Sportswear, Furnishings, Accessories, Footwear, Store Displays, Fixtures, Supplies

THE UPTOWN DOWNTOWN (CLO)

203 N. Main St. (p-m-b)
Greenville, SC 29601
864-271-4245 / Fax: 864-271-4482

ELIZABETH BATSON (Owner & G.M.M.) & Buys Men's Wear, Footwear, Accessories, Furnishings, Urban Contemporary, Store Displays, Fixtures, Supplies

SOUTH CAROLINA - Greenwood

DAVID LINDSEY CLOTHIER (MW)
404 Main St. (b)
Greenwood, SC 29646
864-229-8004 / Fax: 864-229-6770
Sales: $500,001-$1 Million
- DAVID LINDSEY (Owner) & Buys Men's Sportswear, Furnishings, Accessories, Footwear, Store Displays, Fixtures, Supplies
- ED MOORE-Men's Sportswear, Furnishings, Accessories, Footwear, Store Displays, Fixtures, Supplies

GENTLEMEN'S CHOICE (MW)
206 N. Main St. (b)
Greenwood, SC 29646
864-223-5050
Sales: $500,001-$1 Million
- ROBERT RAY (Co-Owner) & Buys Leather Goods, Men's Big & Tall Apparel, Men's & Boys' Apparel, Men's Casualwear, Men's Denim Apparel, Men's Formalwear, Men's Accessories, Men's Hosiery, Men's Outerwear, Men's Sportswear, Men's Suits, Men's Swimwear, Men's Underwear
- JAY PENDERGRASS (Co-Owner) & Buys Leather Goods, Men's Big & Tall Apparel, Men's & Boys' Apparel, Men's Casualwear, Men's Denim Apparel, Men's Formalwear, Men's Accessories, Men's Hosiery, Men's Outerwear, Men's Sportswear, Men's Suits, Men's Swimwear, Men's Underwear
- FRANKIE CONNELL (Co-Owner) & Buys Leather Goods, Men's Big & Tall Apparel, Men's & Boys' Apparel, Men's Casualwear, Men's Denim Apparel, Men's Formalwear, Men's Accessories, Men's Hosiery, Men's Outerwear, Men's Sportswear, Men's Suits, Men's Swimwear, Men's Underwear

SUPERSTYLE OF NEW YORK (MW)
403 Main St. (m)
Greenwood, SC 29646
864-223-6784 / Fax: 864-224-0727
Sales: $500,001-$1 Million
- VICTOR KARAM (Owner) & Buys Men's Sportswear, Furnishings, Accessories, Footwear, Store Displays, Fixtures, Supplies

BAILES-COLLINS (MW)
715 E. Wade Hampton Blvd. (m)
Greer, SC 29651
864-877-3671 / Fax: 864-879-0026
Sales: $1 Million-$10 Million
- GENE COLLINS (President) & Buys Men's Sportswear, Big & Tall Men's Wear, Furnishings, Headwear, Accessories, Footwear, Urban Contemporary, Store Displays, Fixtures, Supplies

GREGORY'S BOUTIQUE, INC. (MW-3)
114 W. Poinsett St. (p)
Greer, SC 29650
864-877-5121 / Fax: 864-877-5195
Sales: $1 Million-$10 Million
- J. W. GREGORY (Owner) & Buys Men's Wear, Leather Apparel, Young Men's Wear, Shirts, Ties, Footwear, Urban Contemporary, Store Displays, Fixtures, Supplies

SMITH & JAMES, INC. (MW-1)
222 Trade St. (m)
Greer, SC 29651
864-877-6525 / Fax: 864-877-0551
Sales: $100,001-$500,000
- BERNARD C. PRICE (President) & Buys Men's Overcoats, Suits, Tailored Jackets, Tailored Slacks, Raincoats, Sweaters, Sport Shirts, Outer Jackets, Leather Apparel, Casual Slacks, Active Apparel, Furnishings, Headwear, Accessories, Footwear, Store Displays, Fixtures, Supplies

FUNKY BEACH (SP)
Beach Market
2 N. Forest Beach Rd.
Hilton Head, SC 29928
843-341-3865 / Fax: 843-363-9440
- LEE WOON (Owner) & Buys Beach Apparel, Men's Swimwear, Headwear, Sandals

KNICKER'S / HARBOURTOWN CLOTHING (MW)
149 Lighthouse Rd.
Hilton Head, SC 29928
888-604-3481 / Fax: 888-604-3483
- ROBERT BOWES (Owner)
- JOCK MILLER-Men's Wear, Sportswear

A SHORE THING, INC. (SP-4)
(Embroidery Division)
32 Shelter Cove Ln.
Hilton Head Island, SC 29928
843-689-9513 / Fax: 843-689-9513
Website: www.shorething.com
- PAUL TEBRAKE (Co-Owner)
- RUTH TEBRAKE (Co-Owner) & Buys Activewear

HARBORTOWN TOYS (KS)
147 E. Lighthouse Rd. (m-b)
Hilton Head Island, SC 29928
843-671-3254 / Fax: 843-671-1495
- BILL CUNNINGHAM (Mgr.)

HILTON HEAD (CLO-7)
P.O. Box 6379 (bud-p-m-b)
90 Beach City Rd.
Hilton Head Island, SC 29938
843-341-3881 / Fax: 843-842-4226
Sales: $1 Million-$10 Million
Website: www.hhpve.com
- JORGE SALGADO-Men's Golf Apparel, Shirts, T-shirts, Fleecewear, Hats, Store Displays, Fixtures, Supplies
- VICKY JONES-Men's Golf Apparel, Shirts, T-shirts, Fleecewear, Hats, Store Displays, Fixtures, Supplies

LATITUDES LIMITED GIFT (CLO)
(CROWNE PLAZA RESORT)
130 Shipyard Dr.
Hilton Head Island, SC 29928
843-842-2400 / Fax: 843-785-8463
- MARY WYSOCKI (@ 843-341-1843)-Boys' Apparel, Boys' Swimwear, Accessories, Footwear, Hats, Men's Apparel, Men's Surf & Swimwear, Resortwear, T-shirts

S.M. BRADFORD CO. (MW)
Shelter Cove Harbor
149 Lighthouse Rd.
Hilton Head Island, SC 29928
843-785-3200 / Fax: 843-671-6979
- CLAYTON EMMERT (Owner) & Buys Upscale Menswear, Furnishings, Accessories, Footwear
- SUE DeLOACH (Mgr.)

BEACH TOWN (SP-2)
1009 Ocean Blvd.
Isle of Palm, SC 29451
843-886-9845
- MICHAEL FRAGUS (Co-Owner) & Buys Boys' Apparel, Boys' Swimwear, Sunglasses, Accessories, Footwear, Hats, Men's Apparel, Men's Surf & Swimwear, Resortwear, T-shirts
- EMILY FRAGUS (Co-Owner) & Buys Boys' Apparel, Boys' Swimwear, Sunglasses, Accessories, Footwear, Hats, Men's Apparel, Men's Surf & Swimwear, Resortwear, T-shirts
- DANIELLE BROWN-Boys' Apparel, Boys' Swimwear, Sunglasses, Accessories, Footwear, Hats, Men's Apparel, Men's Surf & Swimwear, Resortwear, T-shirts

EVERGREEN (MW)
510 Calhoun St.
Johnston, SC 29832
803-275-4288
- SOO KIM (Owner) & Buys Men's Suits, Sportswear, Dress Shirts, Ties, Hosiery, Belts, Store Displays, Fixtures, Supplies

WOFFORD'S MENSWEAR (MW)
412 Calhoun St. (b)
Johnston, SC 29832
803-275-2173
Sales: Under $100,000
HENRY D. WOFFORD, SR. (Owner) & Buys Men's Overcoats, Suits, Tailored Jackets, Tailored Slacks, Raincoats, Sportswear, Furnishings, Headwear, Accessories, Footwear, Store Displays, Fixtures, Supplies

C. TUCKER'S DEPARTMENT STORE (DEPT)
P.O. Box 383 (p-m)
125 Main St.
Kingstree, SC 29556
843-355-6821
Sales: $500,001-$1 Million
TAB A. BLAKELY (Owner) & Buys Men's Sportswear, Furnishings, Headwear, Belts, Young Men's Wear, Urban Contemporary, Store Displays, Fixtures and Supplies

ATHLETIC WAREHOUSE (SP-5)
210 Northpark Sq.
Lancaster, SC 29720
803-416-9595 / Fax: 803-416-9596
JIM GUY (Owner) & Buys Activewear, Athletic Footwear

KORNBLUT'S DEPARTMENT STORE, INC. (DEPT)
103 E. Main St. (p-m)
Latta, SC 29565
843-752-5384
Sales: $500,001-$1 Million
MOSES KORNBLUT (President) & Buys Men's Sportswear, Furnishings, Headwear, Accessories, Young Men's Wear, Dress Shoes, Casual Shoes, Store Displays, Fixtures, Supplies

BARGAIN FAIR (MW)
207 Fleming St. (p)
Laurens, SC 29360
864-984-6831
TOM SMITH (Owner) & Buys Men's Work Clothes, Jeans, Shirts, Underwear, Belts, Hosiery, Work Shoes, Store Displays, Fixtures, Supplies

WOLPERT'S DEPARTMENT STORE, INC. (DEPT)
4111 Main St. (m-b)
Loris, SC 29569
843-756-5272 / Fax: 843-756-0202
Sales: $500,001-$1 Million
EUGENE MILLS (Owner) & Buys Men's Suits, Sweaters, Sport Shirts, Outer Jackets, Leather Apparel, Casual Slacks, Active Apparel, Dress Shirts, Ties, Underwear, Headwear, Belts, Young Men's & Boys' Wear, Big & Tall Men's Wear, Urban Contemporary, Footwear, Store Displays, Fixtures, Su

SCHWARTZ'S DEPARTMENT STORE (MW)
7 W. Boyce St. (m)
Manning, SC 29102
803-435-2602
Sales: $100,001-$500,000
DAVID SCHWARTZ (Owner) & Buys Men's Headwear, Accessories, Furnishings, Footwear, Store Displays, Fixtures, Supplies

GRICE'S MENSWEAR, INC. (MW)
202 N. Main St. (m)
Marion, SC 29571
843-423-6141 / Fax: 843-423-6194
Sales: $500,001-$1 Million
H. M. GRICE (Owner) & Buys Men's Sportswear, Furnishings, Accessories, Footwear, Store Displays, Fixtures, Supplies
PERRY GRICE (V.P.) & Buys Men's Sportswear, Furnishings, Accessories, Footwear, Store Displays, Fixtures, Supplies

BARRONS (CLO)
(BARRONS MONCKS CORNER)
P.O. Box 1117 (p-m-b)
331 E. Main St.
Moncks Corner, SC 29461
843-761-8088 / Fax: 843-899-2829
Sales: $1 Million-$10 Million
MANUEL COHEN (President) & Buys Men's Overcoats, Suits, Tailored Jackets, Tailored Slacks, Raincoats, Sweaters, Sport Shirts, Outer Jackets, Leather Apparel, Casual Slacks, Active Apparel, Furnishings, Headwear, Accessories, Footwear, Urban Contemporary, Hunting Accessories
ELINOR COHEN-Store Displays, Fixtures, Supplies

DENIM COUNTRY (CLO)
Rt. 1 (bud-p)
P.O. Box 72
Mount Croghan, SC 29727
843-672-5257
Sales: $100,001-$500,000
MARY ANN NICHOLSON (Co-Owner) & Buys Men's Sweaters, Sport Shirts, Outer Jackets, Denim Jackets, Jeans, Casual Slacks, Active Apparel, Dress Shirts, Ties, Underwear, Hats, Young Men's & 8 to 20 Boys' Wear, Urban Contemporary, Store Displays, Fixtures, Supplies
MACK NICHOLSON (Co-Owner) & Buys Men's Sweaters, Sport Shirts, Outer Jackets, Denim Jackets, Jeans, Casual Slacks, Active Apparel, Dress Shirts, Ties, Underwear, Hats, Young Men's & 8 to 20 Boys' Wear, Store Displays, Fixtures, Supplies

GWYNN'S OF MT. PLEASANT (CLO)
Village Point Shopping Center (b)
916 Houston Northcutt Blvd.
Mount Pleasant, SC 29464
843-884-9518 / Fax: 843-849-7990
Website: www.gwynns.com
MARSHALL SIMON, JR. (President) & Buys Men's Sweaters, Sport Shirts, Outer Jackets, Casual Slacks, Active Apparel, Furnishings, Headwear, Accessories, Footwear, Urban Contemporary, Store Displays, Fixtures, Supplies
LYNN SIMON (V.P.) & Buys Men's Sweaters, Sport Shirts, Outer Jackets, Casual Slacks, Active Apparel, Furnishings, Headwear, Accessories, Footwear, Urban Contemporary, Store Displays, Fixtures, Supplies

STAGECOACH III LTD. (CLO)
Wando Crossing Shopping Ctr. (p-m)
1483 Hwy. 17 North
Mount Pleasant, SC 29464
843-884-7913 / Fax: 843-881-6403
BILL LUHN (Owner) & Buys Men's Wear, Leather Coats, Footwear, Young Men's Wear, 8 to 20 Boys' Wear, Store Displays, Fixtures, Supplies
KEITH LIPSKY (Mgr.) & Buys Men's Wear, Leather Coats, Footwear, Young Men's Wear, 8 to 20 Boys' Wear, Store Displays, Fixtures, Supplies

B. WALLACE & CO. (CLO)
(WILLIAM WALLACE JR. CORP.)
9672 N. Kings Hwy. (b)
Myrtle Beach, SC 29572
843-692-0888 / Fax: 843-467-2809
Sales: $1 Million-$10 Million
WILLIAM WALLACE (C.E.O.) & Buys Men's Wear, Leather Apparel, Big & Tall Men's Wear, Footwear
CHUCK SWANGER-Men's Wear, Leather Apparel, Big & Tall Men's Wear, Footwear

BARGAIN BEACHWEAR (SP-9)
1616 Executive Ave.
Myrtle Beach, SC 29577
843-626-9339 / Fax: 843-626-2108
Sales: $501,000-$1 Million
SAMUEL LANIADO (President) & Buys Activewear
MARTY LANLIDO-Men's & Boys' Swimwear, Shorts, T-Shirts, Footwear

SOUTH CAROLINA - Myrtle Beach

EAGLES BEACHWEAR (CLO-17)

1000 S. Kings Hwy.
Myrtle Beach, SC 29577
843-448-0416 / Fax: 843-626-0155

BOB HUGHES (Real Estate Contact) (@ 843-626-0155)

MICHAEL BOTON-Boys' Apparel & Swimwear, Sunglasses, Accessories, Hats, Footwear, Men's Apparel, Men's Surf & Swimwear

MARSHA ADI-Boys' Apparel & Swimwear, Sunglasses, Accessories, Hats, Footwear, Men's Apparel, Men's Surf & Swimwear

FORMAL WEAR OF MYRTLE BEACH (CLO)

1108 N. Kings Hwy. (m)
Myrtle Beach, SC 29577
843-448-8639 / Fax: 843-448-8639
Sales: $1 Million-$10 Million

NICKOLAS RAISIS (Owner) (@ 803-449-2829) & Buys Store Displays, Fixtures, Supplies, Men's Formalwear, Ties, Accessories, Footwear, Young Men's Formalwear, 8 to 20 Boys' Wear, Boys' Formalwear

JOHN RAISIS (V.P. & Mgr.) & Buys Men's Formalwear, Ties, Accessories, Footwear, Young Men's Formalwear, 8 to 20 Boys' Wear, Boys' Formalwear

ANDREW RAISIS (V.P. & Mgr.) & Buys Men's Formalwear, Ties, Accessories, Footwear, Young Men's Formalwear, 8 to 20 Boys' Wear, Boys' Formalwear

JAMIN' LEATHER (CLO & MO & OL)

4015 Hwy. 501 (p-m)
Myrtle Beach, SC 29579
843-903-3936 / Fax: 843-903-3938
Website: www.jaminleather.com

JAMIE JOSEPH (Sls. Mgr.) & Buys Leather Apparel, Small Leather Goods, Overcoats, Jackets, Boots, Accessories, Swimwear, T-shirts, Headwear

THE MEN'S STORE (MW)

(LMG, INC.)
5001 N. Kings Hwy. (b)
Myrtle Beach, SC 29577
843-449-8610 / Fax: 843-449-5832

LARRY GRIFFIN (Owner) & Buys Men's Tailored Jackets, Tailored Slacks, Sportswear, Furnishings (No Underwear or Gloves), Belts, Store Displays, Fixtures, Supplies

MIKE'S DEPARTMENT STORE, INC. (DEPT-2)

(WINDY HILL CENTER)
P.O. Box 1211 (m)
511 S. Kings Hwy.
Myrtle Beach, SC 29577
843-448-2769 / Fax: 843-448-5832
Sales: $500,000-$1 Million

MIKE SHAMAH (Owner) & Buys Men's T-shirts, Beachwear, Swimwear, Shorts, Store Displays, Fixtures, Supplies

MYRTLE BEACH TENNIS CLUB (SP)

P.O. Box 29572-7111
Hwy. 17 Bypass North
Myrtle Beach, SC 29577
843-449-4486 / Fax: 843-449-0932

JOHN MACK (Mgr.) & Buys Activewear, Athletic Footwear, Licensed Apparel

SWIMSUIT STATION (SP)

1616 Executive Ave.
Myrtle Beach, SC 29577
843-626-5866 / Fax: 843-626-2108

JEANETTE LANIADO (Owner) & Buys Swimwear

BERGENS (MW)

1208 Caldwell St. (p-m)
Newberry, SC 29108
803-276-3113
Sales: $1 Million-$10 Million

CHARLES BYRD (Co-Owner) & Buys Men's Overcoats, Suits, Tailored Jackets, Tailored Slacks, Raincoats, Big & Tall Men's Wear, Outer Jackets, Sweaters, Sport Shirts, Leather Apparel, Casual Slacks, Active Apparel, Headwear, Accessories, Furnishings, Dress Shoes, Casual Shoes, Store Displays, Fixtures, Supplies

EDDIE PORTER (Co-Owner) & Buys Men's Overcoats, Suits, Tailored Jackets, Tailored Slacks, Raincoats, Big & Tall Men's Wear, Outer Jackets, Sweaters, Sport Shirts, Leather Apparel, Casual Slacks, Active Apparel, Young Men's Wear, Headwear, Accessories, Furnishings, Dress Shoes, Casual Shoes, Store Displays, Fixtures, Supplies

BOULINEAU'S FOODS PLUS (DEPT)

(BOULINEAU'S, INC.)
212 Sea Mountain Hwy. (p)
North Myrtle Beach, SC 29582
843-249-3556 / Fax: 843-249-8839

FRANK BOULINEAU (Owner) & Buys Men's, Young Men's & Boys' Swimwear, Beach Shoes, Boots, Store Displays, Fixtures, Supplies

MYRTLE BEACH T-SHIRTS (SP-4)

4718 Bearfoot Landing
North Myrtle Beach, SC 29582
843-626-7223 / Fax: 843-448-6298

JIM HENSLEY (Owner) & Buys T-shirts, Headwear

DEAN'S LTD. (MW)

(GEORGE'S ENTERPRISES, INC.)
1185 Russell St. (bud-p-m-b-h)
Orangeburg, SC 29115
803-536-6902 / Fax: 803-535-0295

GEORGE DEAN (Owner) & Buys Big & Tall Men's Wear, Sportswear, Urban Contemporary Clothing, Furnishings, Accessories, Store Displays, Fixtures, Supplies

JEANS GLORY (MW)

1115 Russell St. (p-m)
Orangeburg, SC 29115
803-536-4174 / Fax: 803-516-0350

SUNNY KIMM (Owner) & Buys Men's Sportswear, Furnishings, Accessories, Footwear, Store Displays, Fixtures, Supplies

MARINE CORPS EXCHANGE 0160 (PX)

(MCCS)
P.O. Box 5100
Parris Island, SC 29905
843-525-3302 / Fax: 843-228-2551
Sales: $10 Million-$50 Million

ROBERT ALLEN (G.M.M.)

DAN DePACE-Tailored Jackets & Slacks, Overcoats, Suits, Raincoats, Big & Tall Men's Wear, Sweaters, Sportswear, Sport Shirts, Outer Jackets, Leather Apparel, Casual Slacks, Active Apparel, Furnishings, Dress Shirts, Ties, Robes, Underwear, Hosiery, Gloves, Headwear, Accessories, Belts, Small Leather Goods, Young Men's Wear

BROCK'S, INC. (MW)

219 E. Main St. (m-b)
Pickens, SC 29671
864-878-9541
Sales: $500,001-$1 Million

GLEN BROCK (Owner) & Buys Men's Sportswear, Furnishings, Belts, Footwear, Work Clothing, Work Shoes, Boots, Hunting Apparel, Boys' Wear, Store Displays, Fixtures, Supplies

PISTOL CREEK WEST (MW-2)

423 Oak Rd. (p-m-b)
Piedmont, SC 29673
864-220-3500
Sales: $500,001-$1 Million

ROBERT TEDFORD (Owner) & Buys Men's Wear, Boys' Wear, Sportswear, Furnishings, Accessories, Footwear, Store Displays, Fixtures, Supplies

LANDY TEDFORD-Men's Wear, Boys' Wear, Sportswear, Furnishings, Accessories, Footwear, Store Displays, Fixtures, Supplies

BOONE'S READY TO WEAR (WW)

(FRANK N. BOONE)
601 Saluda St. (m)
Rock Hill, SC 29730
803-327-1650

FRANK N. BOONE (Owner) & Buys Men's & Boys' Western Wear, Store Displays, Fixtures, Supplies

WASHBURN & CO. (CLO-6)
(THE OOPS CO.)
3709 S. Church St. Ext. (bud-m)
Roebuck, SC 29376
864-576-5071 / Fax: 864-576-4988
RUSTY WASHBURN (Owner) & Buys Men's Sportswear, Furnishings, Belts, 8 to 20 Boys' Wear, Store Displays, Fixtures, Supplies
SALLY CHAMBERS (V.P.) & Buys Men's Sportswear, Furnishings, Accessories, Boys' Clothing, Furnishings, Accessories, Sportswear

C.B. FORREST & SON (CLO)
101 N. Main St. (p-m)
Saluda, SC 29138
864-445-7080 / Fax: 864-445-3707
Sales: $1 Million-$10 Million
EARL FORREST (Co-Owner) & Buys Men's Overcoats, Suits, Raincoats, Sweaters, Sport Shirts, Outer Jackets, Leather Apparel, Casual Slacks, Active Apparel, Furnishings, Headwear, Belts, Small Leather Goods, Fragrances, Big & Tall Men's Wear, Boys' Wear, Students' Wear, Footwear, Store Displays, Fixtures, Supplies
BRAD FORREST (Co-Owner) & Buys Men's Overcoats, Suits, Raincoats, Sweaters, Sport Shirts, Outer Jackets, Leather Apparel, Casual Slacks, Active Apparel, Furnishings, Headwear, Belts, Small Leather Goods, Fragrances, Big & Tall Men's Wear, Boys' Wear, Students' Wear, Footwear, Store Displays, Fixtures, Supplies

BERGEN'S DEPARTMENT STORE (DEPT)
P.O. Box 813 (p-m)
105 N. Townsville St.
Seneca, SC 29679
864-882-2745 / Fax: 864-882-0282
Sales: $1 Million-$10 Million
JAKE BERGEN (President)
ROBERT BERGEN-Men's Sweaters, Sport Shirts, Outer Jackets, Leather Apparel, Casual Slacks, Active Apparel, Dress Shirts, Ties, Robes, Underwear, Headwear, Belts, Young Men's & Boys' Wear, Men's & Boys' Dress Shoes, Casual Shoes, Shoes, Store Displays, Fixtures, Supplies

HARRIS SPORTING GOODS, INC. (SG)
P.O. Box 1195 (b)
991 Bypass 123
Seneca, SC 29679
864-882-3391 / Fax: 864-882-3399
JOEL HARRIS (Owner) & Buys Men's & Boys' Sports Apparel, Athletic Footwear, Store Displays, Fixtures, Supplies

YOUNG'S FASHIONS (MW-2)
235 E. Main St. (m-b)
Seneca, SC 29678
864-882-9505 / Fax: 864-226-9588
SOON KANG (Owner) & Buys Men's Sportswear, Furnishings, Accessories, Footwear, Urban Contemporary, Boys' Wear 4 to 20

HI-STYLE FASHION (MW)
173 E. Main St. (m)
Spartanburg, SC 29306
864-573-6601
PETER SUYANNI (Owner) & Buys Men's Suits, Dress Shirts, Ties, Accessories, Men's Shoes, Boys' Wear, Store Displays, Fixtures, Supplies
RENI SUYANNI-Men's Suits, Dress Shirts, Ties, Accessories, Men's Shoes, Boys' Wear, Store Displays, Fixtures, Supplies

JOHN GRAHAM STORES (DEPT-8)
(CAROLINA CASH COMPANY)
P.O. Box 1532
143 E. Main St.
Spartanburg, SC 29304
864-582-8459 / Fax: 864-542-8411
JOHN GRAHAM, III (President)
GREGG GRAHAM (V.P.) & Buys Men's, Young Men's & Boys' Wear, Accessories, Furnishings, Footwear, Store Displays, Fixtures, Supplies

PRICE'S STORE FOR MEN (MW)
196 Main St. (m-b)
Spartanburg, SC 29306
864-582-5701
Sales: $500,000-$1 Million
HARRY PRICE (President) & Buys Men's Overcoats, Suits, Tailored Jackets, Tailored Slacks, Raincoats, Sweaters, Sport Shirts, Outer Jackets, Leather Apparel, Casual Slacks, Active Apparel, Furnishings, Headwear, Belts, Small Leather Goods, Big & Tall Men's Wear, Footwear, Store Displays

SAM EVATT'S, INC. (MW)
246 E. Blackstock Rd. (b)
Spartanburg, SC 29301
864-574-6777 / Fax: 864-574-6765
SAM EVATT (Owner) & Buys Men's Sportswear, Furnishings, Accessories, Footwear, Store Displays, Fixtures, Supplies

THOMAS & SONS FORMALWEAR (MW-5)
276 S. Church St. (b-des)
Spartanburg, SC 29306
800-845-7088 / Fax: 864-583-2195
Sales: $1 Million-$10 Million
Website: www.thomasandsons.com
SWOFFORD THOMAS (President & Real Estate Contact) & Buys Men's Apparel, Men's Formalwear, Men's Accessories, Men's Hosiery, Men's Suits, Men's Footwear
DAVID THOMAS (V.P.-Opers.) & Buys Men's Apparel, Men's Formalwear, Men's Accessories, Men's Hosiery, Men's Suits, Men's Footwear
DERRICK THOMAS (Gen. Mgr.) & Buys Men's Apparel, Men's Formalwear, Men's Accessories, Men's Hosiery, Men's Suits, Men's Footwear

BERGER'S MEN'S STORE (MW)
P.O. Box 1077
Main St.
Sumter, SC 29151
803-775-2481
STEVE BERGER (President & Owner) & Buys Men's Sportswear, Furnishings, Accessories, Boys' Suits
ROBIN BERGER-Men's Sportswear, Furnishings, Accessories, Boys' Suits

NEW YORK HI STYLE (MW-2)
17 N. Main St. (m)
Sumter, SC 29150
803-775-8726 / Fax: 803-905-4299
DANNY ADVANI (Owner) & Buys Men's Sportswear, Furnishings, Accessories, Boys' Wear 4 to 7 & 8 to 20, Store Displays, Fixtures, Supplies

REAGAN'S GREEN ACRES (WW)
2441 Jereco Rd. (m)
Sumter, SC 29153
803-469-0859 / Fax: 803-469-3510
JOYCE REAGAN (Co-Owner) & Buys Men's & Boys' Western Wear, Boots
BOB REAGAN (Co-Owner) & Buys Men's & Boys' Western Wear, Boots

STANLEY WELCH CLOTHIERS (CLO)
434 Gurgnard Dr., #A (b)
Sumter, SC 29150
803-775-1832 / Fax: 803-773-2821
Sales: $1 Million-$10 Million
STANLEY WELCH (Owner) & Buys Men's Sportswear, Furnishings, Headwear, Jewelry, Belts, Small Leather Goods, Men's Footwear, Urban Contemporary, Store Displays, Fixtures, Supplies
CHIP BRACALENTE (Mgr.) & Buys Men's Sportswear, Furnishings, Headwear, Jewelry, Belts, Small Leather Goods, Men's Footwear, Urban Contemporary, Store Displays, Fixtures, Supplies

THREE T'S UNLIMITED (CLO)
11 S. Main St. (m)
Sumter, SC 29150
803-773-1448
WILLIAM WHITTLETON (Owner) & Buys Men's & Boys' Suits, Jeans, T-shirts, Caps, Belts, Small Leather Goods, Dress Shoes, Store Displays, Fixtures, Supplies

UNIVERSITY SHOP, INC. (MW)

672 Bultman Dr. (m-b)
Sumter, SC 29150
803-773-7113
Sales: $1 Million-$10 Million

HALSELL ROBERTS (Owner) & Buys Men's Overcoats, Suits, Tailored Jackets, Sport Coats, Tailored Slacks, Sweaters, Sport Shirts, Leather Apparel, Casual Slacks, Accessories, Men's Footwear, Store Displays, Fixtures, Supplies

DAVID DICKSIN (G.M.M.) & Buys Men's Overcoats, Suits, Tailored Jackets, Sport Coats, Tailored Slacks, Sweaters, Sport Shirts, Leather Apparel, Casual Slacks, Accessories, Men's Footwear, Store Displays, Fixtures, Supplies

GIANTS BEACHWEAR (MW-4)

(M & S, INC.)
1001 Hwy. 17 North
Surfside Beach, SC 29575
843-238-4255

MOSHE SHARVIT (Owner) & Buys Men's Beach Wear, Boys' Beach Wear, Men's & Boys' Beach Shoes & Sandals, Store Displays, Fixtures, Supplies

HARRY FROM, INC. (CLO)

101 W. Main St. (p)
Union, SC 29379
864-427-6511
Sales: $1 Million-$10 Million

GLORIA GOLDBERG (Co-Owner)

MONTY SMITH (Mgr.) & Buys Toddler to Size 7 Boys' Wear, Footwear, Store Displays, Fixtures, Supplies

NEW YORK SUPER STYLES (MW)

215 S. Gadberry St. (m)
Union, SC 29379
864-427-7273

ABDUL CHOUDRY (Owner) & Buys Men's Dress Shirts, Sport Shirts, T-shirts, Hosiery, Jeans, Belts, Urban Contemporary, Store Displays, Fixtures, Supplies

TYLER BROTHERS TRUE VALUE (DEPT)

(V & S VARIETY)
P.O. Box 97 (p)
116 Railroad Ave.
Wagener, SC 29164
803-564-3174 / Fax: 803-564-3214
Sales: $1 Million-$10 Million

AL TYLER, JR. (President) & Buys Store Displays, Fixtures, Supplies

JOHN TYLER (G.M.M.) & Buys Men's Overcoats, Suits, Tailored Jackets, Tailored Slacks, Raincoats, Sweaters, Sport Shirts, Outer Jackets, Casual Slacks, Leather Apparel, Furnishings, Headwear, Accessories, Big & Tall Men's Wear, 8 to 20 Boys' Wear, Men's Work Shoes, Shoes, Boys' Shoes

MOORE'S MEN'S (MW-2)

116 E. Main St. (m-b)
Walhalla, SC 29691
864-638-2054 / Fax: 864-882-1118

MARSHAL CHILBRESS (Owner) & Buys Men's Sportswear, Furnishings, Accessories, Footwear, Big & Tall Men's Wear, Store Displays, Fixtures, Supplies

RUDY COBB-Men's Sportswear, Furnishings, Accessories, Footwear, Big & Tall Men's Wear, Store Displays, Fixtures, Supplies

YOUNG'S FASHION (MW)

112 Congress St. (m)
Winnsboro, SC 29180
803-635-3672

YOUNG PYON (Owner) & Buys Men's Sportswear, Furnishings, Belts, Footwear, Urban Contemporary, Store Displays, Fixtures, Supplies

MEN'S SHOP (MW)

49 N. Congress St. (m-b)
York, SC 29745
803-684-4121 / Fax: 803-684-2956

RONNIE BAILES (Owner) & Buys Men's Sportswear, Furnishings, Accessories, Footwear, Store Displays, Fixtures, Supplies

HITCH'N POST (WW)

2601 SE 6th Ave. (m-b)
Aberdeen, SD 57401
605-229-1655 / Fax: 605-229-1685
Sales: $500,000-$1 Million

TERRY LARSON (Owner) & Buys Men's Western Wear, Overcoats, Suits, Raincoats, Outer Jackets, Dress Shirts, Gloves, Headwear, Belts, Jewelry, Boots, Store Displays, Fixtures, Supplies

THE MAIN (MW)

P.O. Box 1441 (p-m-b)
321 S. Main St.
Aberdeen, SD 57401
605-225-7232 / Fax: 605-225-8785
Sales: $500,000-$1 Million

STEVE FRANK (President) & Buys Men's Footwear, Men's Suits, Sweaters, Outer Jackets, Leather Coats, Sport Shirts, Active Apparel, Dress Shirts, Ties, Hosiery, Hats, Accessories, Young Men's Wear, Urban Contemporary, Store Displays, Fixtures, Supplies

DON HEINRICH (G.M.M.) & Buys Men's Suits, Sweaters, Outer Jackets, Leather Coats, Sport Shirts, Active Apparel, Dress Shirts, Ties, Hosiery, Hats, Accessories, Young Men's Wear, Store Displays, Fixtures, Supplies

WEBB CO. (CLO)

315 S. Main St. (m)
Aberdeen, SD 57401
605-225-1141

ROBERT WEBB (Owner) & Buys Men's, Tailored Slacks, Tailored Jackets, Casual Slacks, Active Apparel, Headwear, Hosiery, Ties, Footwear, Dress Shoes, Casual Shoes, Athletic Footwear, Boots, Store Displays, Fixtures and Supplies

JOHN WEBB-Men's, Tailored Slacks, Tailored Jackets, Casual Slacks, Active Apparel, Headwear, Hosiery, Ties, Footwear, Dress Shoes, Casual Shoes, Athletic Footwear, Boots, Store Dislays, Fixtures and Supplies

MAURICE WEBB-Men's, Tailored Slacks, Tailored Jackets, Casual Slacks, Active Apparel, Headwear, Hosiery, Ties, Footear, Dress Shoes, Casual Shoes, Athletic Footwear, Boots, Store Displays, Fixtures and Supplies

PETE'S CLOTHING & WESTERN WEAR (WW)

500 State St. (m)
Belle Fourche, SD 57717
605-892-4773 / Fax: 605-892-4219

PETER KRUSH (Owner) & Buys Men's & Boys' Western Wear, Related Accessories, Men's & Boys' Western Boots, Men's Formal Wear, Accessories, Work Boots, Dress Shirts, Store Displays, Fixtures, Supplies

LEE & HANSON, INC. (MW)

720 Main St. (bud-p-m)
Britton, SD 57430
605-448-5242

ROGER FURMAN (Owner) & Buys Men's Wear, Sportswear, Furnishings, Accessories, Footwear, Work Boots, Rubber Footwear, Store Displays, Fixtures and Supplies

FERGEN'S MENSWEAR (MW)

(BIGGY CO., INC.)
414 Main Ave. (m)
Brookings, SD 57006
605-692-2622 / Fax: 605-692-7380

STEVE KIRKEY (Owner) & Buys Men's Sportswear, Furnishings, Accessories, Dress Shoes, Casual Shoes, Slippers, Boots, Urban Contemporary, Store Displays, Fixtures, Supplies

RAY'S WESTERN WEAR & SADDLERY (WW)

Hwy. 16 West (m)
Chakiblain, SD 57325
605-734-6046 / Fax: 605-734-5915

RAYMOND STECKELBERG (Owner) & Buys Men's & Boys' Western Wear, Related Accessories, Men's & Boys' Western Boots, Store Displays, Fixtures, Supplies

ANDERSON'S (SP-3)

123 S. Main St.
Chamberlain, SD 57325
605-734-6852 / Fax: 605-734-6852

WILLIAM GIESLER (Co-Owner)

MIKE GIESELER (Co-Owner) & Buys Activewear, Athletic Footwear, Licensed Apparel

PERRY ANDERSON (Mgr.) & Buys Activewear, Athletic Footwear, Licensed Apparel

JULI'S COUNTRY CASUAL (CLO)

P.O. Box 1337 (m)
205 Main St.
Eagle Butte, SD 57625
605-964-3733
Sales: $1 Million-$10 Million

JULI HASKELL (Owner) & Buys Men's Sportswear, Casual Western Wear, Accessories, Boots, Urban Contemporary, Store Displays, Fixtures, Supplies

THE PLAINS (DEPT)

P.O. Box 380 (p)
Hwy. 212
Eagle Butte, SD 57625
605-964-4610
Sales: $100,001-$500,000

SHARON K. BOEHRS (Co-Owner)

SHAWN BOEHRS (Co-Owner) & Buys Men's Tailored Jackets, Tailored Slacks, Raincoats, Sweaters, Sport Shirts, Outer Jackets, Casual Slacks, Active Apparel, Furnishings, Footwear, Athletic Footwear, Headwear, Accessories, Young Men's & Boys' Wear, Urban Contemporary, Big & Tall Men's Wear, Leather Vests, Western Wear, Related Accessories, Boots, Store Displays, Fixtures, Supplies

COUNTRY CLOSET (CLO)

122 W. 1st Ave. (m)
Faith, SD 57626
605-967-2330 / Fax: 605-967-2249

PAUL PETERSON (Co-Owner) & Buys Men's & Boys' Western Wear, Related Accessories, Men's & Boys' Western Boots, Slippers, Casual Shoes, Sandals, Store Displays, Fixtures, Supplies

SHAWN PETERSON (Co-Owner) & Buys Men's & Boys' Western Wear, Related Accessories, Men's & Boys' Western Boots, Slippers, Casual Shoes, Sandals, Store Displays, Fixtures, Supplies

DIAMOND D WESTERN WEAR (WW)

P.O. Box 195 (m)
114 N. Deadwood
Fort Pierce, SD 57532
605-223-2958

DAVE DAHL (Owner) & Buys Men's & Boys' Western Wear, Related Accessories, Men's & Boys' Western Boots, Store Displays, Fixtures, Supplies

OSBORN'S CLOTHING CO. (MW)

(OSBORN'S CHAMPS)
328 Dakota Ave. South (p-m-b)
Huron, SD 57350
605-352-8576 / Fax: 605-352-8577
Sales: $1 Million-$10 Million

JOHN OSBORN (President) & Buys Men's, Young Men's & Boys' Wear, Urban Contemporary, Leather Apparel, Western Wear, Footwear, Store Displays, Fixtures, Supplies

STAN'S MEN'S SHOP, INC. (MW)

105 N. Eagan Rd. (m)
Madison, SD 57042
605-256-2728
Website: www.stansmensshop.com

RICHARD FAWBUSH (Owner) & Buys Men's & Young Men's Wear, Store Displays, Fixtures, Supplies

SOUTH DAKOTA - Mitchell

MERCHANDISE OUTLET STORE (WW-2)
203 N. Main St. (m)
Mitchell, SD 57301
605-996-3431
MONICA CROSS (Owner) & Buys Men's Western Apparel, Boots, Related Furnishings & Accessories, Store Displays, Fixtures, Supplies

MICHAEL'S TOGGERY (MW)
211 N. Main St. (m)
Mitchell, SD 57301
605-996-3782 / Fax: 605-996-1934
LEE MICHAEL (Co-Owner) & Buys Men's & Young Men's Wear, Urban Contemporary, Leather Apparel, Store Displays, Fixtures, Supplies

ANDERSON'S FAMILY SHOE STORE (FW)
314 Main St. (m)
Mobridge, SD 57601
605-845-3578 / Fax: 605-845-2578
Sales: $500,001-$1 Million
GARY ANDERSON (Owner) & Buys Men's & Boys' Athletic Footwear, Men's Dress Shoes, Casual Shoes, Slippers, Work Boots, Accessories, Store Displays, Fixtures, Supplies
CHERYL ANDERSON-Men's & Boys' Athletic Footwear, Men's Dress Shoes, Casual Shoes, Slippers, Work Boots, Accessories, Store Displays, Fixtures, Supplies

WESTERN RANCHER BOOT & SADDLE SHOP (WW)
221 Main St. (m)
Mobridge, SD 57601
605-845-2330
Sales: $500,001-$1 Million
Website: www.westernrancher.net
RON LANDIS (Co-Owner) & Buys Clothing, Sportswear, Furnishings, Headwear, Accessories, Athletic Footwear, Men's, Young Men's & Boys' Western Wear, Related Furnishings & Accessories, Western Boots, Store Displays, Fixtures, Supplies
ALAN LANDIS (Co-Owner) & Buys Clothing, Sportswear, Furnishings, Headwear, Accessories, Athletic Footwear, Men's, Young Men's & Boys' Western Wear, Related Furnishings & Accessories, Western Boots, Store Displays, Fixtures, Supplies

ALS OASIS, INC. (DEPT)
1000 E. Hwy. 16 (m-b)
Oacoma, SD 57365
605-734-6051 / Fax: 605-734-6927
Sales: $10 Million-$50 Million
DEE GEDDES (President)
GERALDINE DOMINIACK-Men's Sportswear, Headwear, Furnishings, Accessories, Young Men's & Boys' Wear, Store Displays, Fixtures, Supplies
NANCY KNIPPLING-Men's Sportswear, Headwear, Furnishings, Accessories, Young Men's & Boys' Wear, Store Displays, Fixtures, Supplies

ANDERSON'S (SP-3)
907 E. Sioux Ave.
Pierre, SD 57501
605-224-7114 / Fax: 605-224-7114
WILLIAM GIESLER (Owner)
PERRY ANDERSON (Mgr.) & Buys Activewear, Athletic Footwear, Licensed Apparel

DAKOTAMART OF PIERRE, INC. (GM & SG)
(LYNN, INC.)
120 W. Sioux Ave. (m)
Pierre, SD 57501
605-224-8871 / Fax: 605-224-5670
Sales: $10 Million-$50 Million
Website: www.dakotamart.com
ERROL PETERSON (Mgr.) & Buys Store Displays, Fixtures, Supplies
CHRIS ANDERSON-Men's & Boys' Sportswear, Furnishings, Accessories

LORI'S CLOTHING (CLO)
P.O. Box 695
313 Main St.
Platte, SD 57369
605-337-3929 / Fax: 605-337-3929
LORI LUCAS (Owner) & Buys Men's Sportswear, Urban Contemporary, Furnishings, Accessories, Store Displays, Fixtures, Supplies

BLACK HILLS GOLD JEWELRY, INC. (JWLY-5)
P.O. Box 6400
5125 Hwy. 16 South
Rapid City, SD 57701
605-721-3700 / Fax: 605-394-3750
Sales: $1 Million-$10 Million
Website: www.blackhillsgoldbycoleman.com
DWIGHT SOBCZEK (President & Owner)
DUANE SOBCZEK-Jewelry, Watches

RCC WESTERN STORES, INC. (WW-21 & OL)
P.O. Box 1139 (m-b)
324 E. Boulevard
Rapid City, SD 57701
605-342-7737 / Fax: 605-342-0743
Sales: $10 Million-$50 Million
Website: www.rccwestern.com
Retail Locations: TN, KY, IN, IA, WI, MN, SD, ND
ROBERT HOOVER (President)
CRAIG WEIDE-Overcoats, Suits, Raincoats, Outerjackets, Leather Apparel, Men's Western Clothing, Sport Shirts, Dress Shirts,Active Apparel, Store Displays, Fixtures, Supplies
CHUCK PAULSON (Mdse. Mgr.) & Buys Men's Headwear, Footwear, Western Boots
TODD MUELLER-Denim, Men's Ties, Robes, Underwear, Hosiery, Gloves, Belts, Jewelry, Fragrances
BOB HOOPER (Real Estate Contact)

SEELEY, INC. (MW)
2001 W. Main St., #A3 (b)
Rapid City, SD 57702
605-342-0225 / Fax: 605-341-1200
Sales: $1 Million-$10 Million
LEONARD BACHMAN (President) & Buys Men's Wear, Accessories, Furnishings, Footwear, Store Displays, Fixtures, Supplies
MARK BACHMAN-Men's Wear, Accessories, Furnishings, Footwear, Store Displays, Fixtures, Supplies

WESTERN WAY WORK WAREHOUSE (MW-2)
(G & N ENTERPRISES, INC.)
(WORK WEARHOUSE)
(WESTERN WOMAN)
2255 N. Haines (p-m)
Rapid City, SD 57701
605-341-4322 / Fax: 605-341-4322
Sales: $1 Million-$10 Million
HARVEY GREENFIELD (Owner) & Buys Western Wear, Men's Sportswear, Furnishings, Accessories, Young Men's Wear, 7 to 20 Boys' Wear, Store Displays, Fixtures, Supplies
JIM GREENFIELD (Gen. Mgr.) & Buys Western Wear, Men's Sportswear, Furnishings, Accessories, Young Men's Wear, 7 to 20 Boys' Wear, Men's Footwear, Store Displays, Fixtures, Supplies

RETTEDAL'S DEPARTMENT STORE (DEPT)
P.O. Box 362
551 Main St.
Scotland, SD 57059
605-583-4115
Sales: $500,001-$1 Million

DEAN RETTEDAL (Owner) & Buys Sweaters, Sport Shirts, Outer Jackets, Casual Slacks, Active Apparel, Dress Shirts, Ties, Underwear, Hosiery, Gloves, Headwear, Belts, Small Leather Goods, Dress Shoes, Casual Shoes, Shoes, Athletic Footwear, Work Boots, Dress Boots, Western Boots, Store

ATHLETIC EDGE (SP-2)
(C & S ENTERPRISES)
1614 S. Sycamore St.
Sioux Falls, SD 57110
605-575-1084 / Fax: 605-371-8721

CINDY GEYER (Owner) & Buys Activewear, Athletic Footwear, Licensed Apparel

BALDWIN SUPPLY CO. (CLO-7)
P.O. Box 1464 (p-m)
1400 N. Industrial Ave.
Sioux Falls, SD 57104
605-332-5632 / Fax: 605-331-4161

DAVE CAMPBELL (Owner) & Buys Store Displays, Fixtures, Supplies

TAMMY ELLEFSON-Men's Work Shirts, Jeans, Headwear, Accessories, Boots

DAUBY'S SPORT SHOP, INC. (SG)
2720 W. 41st St.
Sioux Falls, SD 57105
605-332-8041 / Fax: 605-332-6627

DENNIS KRIER (Owner) & Buys Men's Teamwear, Accessories, Footwear, Store Supplies

BRIAN SANDRO (Asst. Mgr.) & Buys Men's Teamwear, Accessories, Footwear, Store Supplies

THE GREAT OUTDOOR STORE, INC. (CLO)
235 S. Phillips Ave. (m)
Sioux Falls, SD 57104
605-335-1132 / Fax: 605-335-5730

DEANN ECHOLS (Owner) & Buys Men's Sportswear, Belts, Hosiery, T-shirts, Outdoor Clothing, Sandals, Store Displays, Fixtures, Supplies

HALBERSTADT'S CLOTHIERS (MW-4)
Empire Mall (b)
Sioux Falls, SD 57103
605-361-2619 / Fax: 605-362-8683

JEFF HALBERSTADT (Owner) & Buys Men's Sportswear, Furnishings, Accessories, Footwear, Store Displays, Fixtures, Supplies

LEWIS DRUG STORE (DEPT-8)
2701 S. Minnesota Ave., #1 (m-b)
Sioux Falls, SD 57105
605-367-2800 / Fax: 605-367-2876
Website: www.truevalue.com

MARY ANSON-Men's Sportswear, Furnishings, Boys' Wear, Store Displays, Fixtures, Supplies

NORMAN'S MENSWEAR (MW)
2621 S. Minnesota Ave. (m)
Sioux Falls, SD 57105
605-336-7270 / Fax: 605-336-0845
Sales: $1 Million-$10 Million

TOM HENRY (Owner) & Buys Men's Wear, Leather Apparel, Accessories, Furnishings, Store Displays, Fixtures, Supplies

DON THE CLOTHIER (MW)
1603 Main St. (p-m)
Tyndall, SD 57066
605-589-3252 / Fax: 605-589-3452
Sales: $1 Million-$10 Million

MARK HOUSE (Co-Owner) & Buys Men's Sportswear, Furnishings, Leather Apparel, Dress Shirts, Boots, Slippers, Sandals, Store Displays, Fixtures, Supplies

TERESA HOUSE (Co-Owner) & Buys Men's Sportswear, Furnishings, Leather Apparel, Men's Footwear, Store Displays, Fixtures, Supplies

JANE'S COUNTRY (MW)
221 S. Main St. (m)
Wagner, SD 57380
605-384-5633

JANE WILLIAMS (Owner) & Buys Men's Sportswear, Furnishings, Accessories, Footwear, Store Displays, Fixtures, Supplies

MARTY'S (CLO)
210 S. Main St. (p-m)
Winner, SD 57580
605-842-3130
Sales: $100,001-$500,000

MARTIN FLAKUF (Owner) & Buys Clothing, Sportswear, Furnishings, Headwear, Accessories, Store Displays, Fixtures, Supplies

KNUTSON WESTERN STORE (WW)
208 Walnut St.
Yankton, SD 57078
605-665-6889 / Fax: 605-665-6829

LYLE KNUTSON (Co-Owner) & Buys Western Wear, Related Furnishings, Headwear, Boots, Accessories, Store Displays, Fixtures, Supplies

KAREN KNUTSON (Co-Owner) & Buys Western Wear, Related Furnishings, Headwear, Boots, Accessories, Store Displays, Fixtures, Supplies

THE GLOBE CLOTHIERS (CLO)
2101 Broadway Ave. (m-b)
Yanton, SD 57078
605-665-3297 / Fax: 605-665-0599
Sales: $100,001-$500,000

JIM GEVENS (Owner) & Buys Men's Sportswear, Furnishings, Accessories, Men's Dress Shoes, Casual Shoes, Store Displays, Fixtures, Supplies

TENNESSEE - Alcoa

PROFFITT'S DEPARTMENT STORES (DEPT-26)
(SAKS INC.)
P.O. Box 9388 (m-b)
760 Kingston Pike
Alcoa, TN 37701
865-983-7000 / Fax: 865-981-9514
Sales: $100 Million-$500 Million
Website: www.proffitts.com
Retail Locations: GA, KY, NC, SC, TN, VA, WV
R. BRAD MARTIN (Chmn. & C.E.O.)
TONI BROWNING (President & C.E.O.-Proffitts)
BOBBIE EDWARDS (Visual Mdsg. Dir.) & Buys Store Displays, Fixtures
FORREST ASHWORTH (Purch. Mgr.) (@ 601-968-4400) & Buys Supplies
ERIC FARRIS (Real Estate Contact) (@ 901-937-2113)

RICK THOMAS (D.M.M.) & Buys Men's Suits, Dress Shirts, Men's Sweaters, Sport Shirts, Casual Slacks
PEGGY HILLIARD-Tailored Suits
JIM HARRING-Sportswear
DAVID LUTNER-Furnsishings
MR. LAUREN HOWARD-Ties, Accessories
BILL GADBOLD-Young Men's Wear
JIM BAKER-Boys Wear, Casual Slacks
JEFF USEFORGE-8 to 20 Boys Wear, Accessories, Furnishings, Footwear
TIM FRANKLIN (@ 865-981-6322)-Size 8 to 20 Boys' Wear

WYNN'S (CLO-2)
Midland Shopping Center (m)
P.O. Box 70
Alcoa, TN 37701
865-983-2714 / Fax: 865-977-9230
Website: www.wynnsporting.com
JANICE SNYDER (Owner)
MIKE COUGHLIN (President) & Buys Men's Tailored Slacks, Sportswear, Furnishings, Headwear, Accessories, Footwear, Big & Tall Men's Wear, Store Displays, Fixtures, Supplies
ROB JONES (V.P.) & Buys Men's Tailored Slacks, Sportswear, Furnishings, Headwear, Accessories, Footwear, Big & Tall Men's Wear, Store Displays, Fixtures, Supplies

GRESHAM'S FINE MEN'S CLOTHING (MW)
214 Word Cir. (b)
Brentwood, TN 37027
615-370-9413 / Fax: 615-370-9638
Website: www.greshamsfinemens.qpg.com
EARL GRESHAM (Owner) & Buys Men's Shirts, Pants, Sport Coats, Belts, Ties, Headwear, Footwear

WILLIAM KING CLOTHIERS (MW-2)
534 State St. (h)
Bristol, TN 37620
423-968-9383 / Fax: 423-968-4313
WILLIAM KING JR. (Owner) & Buys Men's Sportswear, Dress Shirts, Underwear, Hosiery, Small Leather Goods, Store Displays, Fixtures, Supplies

B & B DEPARTMENT STORE (DEPT)
26 S. Washington St. (p)
Brownsville, TN 38012
731-772-9733
LOUIS BADDOUR (Owner) & Buys Men's Sportswear, Furnishings, Headwear, Belts, Small Leather Goods, Footwear, Young Men's Wear, 8 to 20 Boys' Wear, Store Displays, Fixtures, Supplies

MARKHAM DEPARTMENT STORE (DEPT)
222 Main St. North (p-m)
Carthage, TN 37030
615-735-0184 / Fax: 615-735-0184
Sales: $100,001-$500,000
B. L. MARKHAM, SR. (Owner) & Buys Men's Overcoats, Suits, Tailored Jackets, Tailored Slacks, Raincoats, Sportswear, Furnishings, Headwear, Accessories, Footwear, Young Men's Shop, 8 to 20 Boys' Wear, Big & Tall Men's Wear, Urban Contemporary, Leather Apparel, Store Displays, Fixtures, Supplies

ARGUS BIG & TALL (MW)
2200 Hamilton Place Blvd.
Chattanooga, TN 37421
423-899-4298 / Fax: 423-899-4298
ROBERT COHEN (Owner) & Buys Big & Tall Men's Wear, Men's Wear, Furnishings, Accessories

BRAINERD ARMY STORE (AN)
5102 Brainerd Rd. (p)
Chattanooga, TN 37411
423-892-0422 / Fax: 423-892-0422
BILL HONEYCUTT (Owner) & Buys Men's & Boys' Work Clothes, Thermal Underwear, Socks, Footwear, Store Displays, Fixtures, Supplies

BRUCE BAIRD & CO., INC. (MW)
735 Broad St. (m-b)
Chattanooga, TN 37402
423-265-8821 / Fax: 423-756-3610
BRUCE BAIRD (Owner) & Buys Men's Overcoats, Suits, Tailored Jackets, Tailored Slacks, Sweaters, Sport Shirts, Outer Jackets, Leather Apparel, Furnishings, Headwear, Accessories, Footwear, Store Displays, Fixtures, Supplies

CHATTANOOGA SPORTSWEAR (MW)
5210 Brainerd Rd. (p)
Chattanooga, TN 37411
423-499-4947 / Fax: 423-499-4929
JIN KIM (Owner) & Buys Men's Sportswear, Headwear, Footwear, Furnishings, Accessories, Young Men's Wear, 8 to 20 Boys' Wear, Store Displays, Fixtures, Supplies

COOLEY'S, INC. (CLO)
P.O. Box 15397 (m-b)
Chattanooga, TN 37415
423-877-4554 / Fax: 423-877-3057
Sales: $500,000-$1 Million
JAMES H. COOLEY, JR. (President) & Buys Men's Formal Wear, Overcoats, Suits, Tailored Jackets, Tailored Slacks, Raincoats, Sportswear, Furnishings, Robes, Accessories, Leather Apparel, Dress Footwear, Store Displays, Fixtures, Supplies

MARGARET'S CHILDREN'S FASHIONS (KS)
5010 Rossville Blvd. (b)
Chattanooga, TN 37407
423-867-2006 / Fax: 423-877-5363
NELL CHRISTNACHT (Co-Owner) & Buys 8 to 10 Boys' Wear, Footwear, Store Displays, Fixtures, Supplies
MARGARET CHRISTNACHT (Co-Owner) & Buys 8 to 10 Boys' Wear, Footwear, Store Displays, Fixtures, Supplies

YACOUBIAN TAILOR (CLO)
721 Broad St. (b)
Chattanooga, TN 37402
423-265-0187 / Fax: 423-265-1097
JOHN YACOUBIAN (Owner) & Buys Men's Suits, Tailored Clothing, Raincoats, Sportswear, Leather Apparel, Furnishings, Accessories, Store Displays, Fixtures, Supplies

BRIGGS' CLOTHIERS (MW)
323 N. Riverside Dr. (m-b)
Clarksville, TN 37040
931-647-6444 / Fax: 931-647-9515
Sales: $100,001-$500,000
ERNIE BRIGGS (President) & Buys Men's & Young Men's Wear, Boys' Wear, Dress Footwear, Store Displays, Fixtures, Supplies
TOM SCHMITTOU (G.M.M.) & Buys Men's & Young Men's Wear, Boys' Wear, Dress Footwear, Store Displays, Fixtures, Supplies

TENNESSEE - Clarksville

GRANDPA'S GENERAL MERCHANDISE (DG)

1894 Fort Campbell Blvd. (m)
Clarksville, TN 37042
931-647-0251 / Fax: 931-648-9696
Sales: $1 Million-$10 Million

JACKIE LANGFORD (President) & Buys Men's Sportswear, Furnishings, Accessories, Boys' Wear, Store Displays, Fixtures, Supplies

MELBA TEDDER (G.M.M.) & Buys Men's Overcoats, Raincoats, Sport Shirts, Outer Jackets, Leather Apparel, Casual Slacks, Active Apparel, Underwear, Hosiery, Gloves, Headwear, Belts, Casual Footwear

NEW YORK NEW YORK (MW)

1610 Fort Campbell Blvd. (bud-p)
Clarksville, TN 37042
931-647-6090

ANDY MAHBUBANI (Owner) & Buys Men's Sportswear, Furnishings, Accessories, Footwear, Young Men's Wear, Urban Contemporary, 8 to 20 Boys' Wear, Store Displays, Fixtures, Supplies

HARDWICK MEN'S STORE, INC. (MW)

95 1st St. NE (b)
Cleveland, TN 37311
423-479-1286 / Fax: 423-339-1877
Sales: Under $100,000

JOE WILLIAMS (Owner)

BRUCE HAYES (Mgr.) & Buys Men's Headwear, Store Displays, Fixtures, Supplies

HIXON'S FURNISHINGS FOR MEN, INC. (MW)

200 Paul Huss Pkwy. (m-b)
Cleveland, TN 37312
423-479-4545 / Fax: 423-472-1261

DAVID H. HIXON, III (Owner) & Buys Men's Sportswear, Formal Wear, Accessories, Swimwear, Store Displays, Fixtures, Supplies

PAMELA HIXON-Men's Sportswear, Formal Wear, Accessories, Swimwear, Store Displays, Fixtures, Supplies

TOWN SQUIRE (MW)

1717 Keith St. NW
Cleveland, TN 37311
423-472-6012 / Fax: 423-472-2568

LARRY McDANIEL (Owner & Mgr.) & Buys Men's Wear, Leather Apparel, Footwear, Big & Tall Men's Wear, Urban Contemporary, Store Displays, Fixtures, Supplies

PIGG & PARSONS, INC. (MW)

117 W. 7th St. (m-b)
Columbia, TN 38401
931-388-0601 / Fax: 931-840-6199
Sales: $500,000-$1 Million

DAVID B. JACKSON (Owner) & Buys Men's Sportswear, Furnishings, Headwear, Accessories, Footwear, Store Displays, Fixtures, Supplies

ROBERSON'S DEPARTMENT STORE (DEPT)

428 E. Broad St. (m-b)
Cookeville, TN 38501
931-526-4412
Sales: $500,000-$1 Million

WILLIAM F. ROBERSON (President) & Buys Men's Sportswear, Furnishings, Boys' Wear, Leather Apparel, Headwear, Accessories, Footwear, Store Displays, Fixtures, Supplies

ROBERT ROBERSON (V.P.) & Buys Men's Sportswear, Furnishings, Boys' Wear, Leather Apparel, Headwear, Accessories, Footwear, Store Displays, Fixtures, Supplies

HILL'S (CLO)

56 S. Main St. (p-m-b)
Crossville, TN 38555
931-484-6189 / Fax: 931-707-9043
Sales: $1 Million-$10 Million

MARTHA HILL (President & G.M.M.) & Buys Men's, Young Men's & Boys' Wear, Store Displays, Fixtures, Supplies

FUSSELL'S SHOP (CLO)

103 N. Main St. (bud-p-m)
Dickson, TN 37055
615-446-3724
Sales: $500,000-$1 Million

ANN F. BASS (President & Owner) & Buys 8 to 20 Boys' Wear, Store Displays, Fixtures, Supplies

LEROY WINSTEAD-Men's & Young Men's Jeans, Denim & Western Wear

MARVIN TUMMINS-8 to 20 Boys' Wear

PHIL JONES-Men's Sweaters, Sport Shirts, Active Apparel, Dress Shirts, Men's Outer Jackets, Robes, Underwear, Hosiery, Gloves, Accessories, Young Men's Wear, Leather Apparel

JAMES DONEGAN-Men's Overcoats, Suits, Tailored Jackets, Tailored Slacks, Raincoats, Casual Slacks, Ties, Headwear, Big & Tall Men's Wear, Store Displays, Fixtures and Supplies

M & M DEPARTMENT STORE (DEPT)

P.O. Box 757 (m)
Donelson Pkwy.
Dover, TN 37058
931-232-5432
Sales: $500,000-$1 Million

DIANE MARTIN (Owner) & Buys Men's Sweaters, Sport Shirts, Furnishings, Headwear, Accessories, Footwear, Store Displays, Fixtures, Supplies, 8 to 20 Boys' Wear

BARBARA MARSHAL-Men's Sweaters, Sport Shirts, Furnishings, Headwear, Accessories, Footwear, Store Displays, Fixtures, Supplies, 8 to 20 Boys' Wear, Urban Contemporary

E. T. REAVIS & SON (CLO & OL)

P.O. Box 198 (bud-p-m)
Dresden, TN 38225
731-364-2405
Sales: $100,001-$500,000
Website: www.etreavis.com

TOM REAVIS (Owner) & Buys Men's Sportswear, Work Wear, Furnishings, Accessories, Headwear, Young Men's Wear, Size 7 & Up Boys' Wear, Footwear, Store Displays, Fixtures, Supplies

MISTER B MEN'S SHOP (MW-2)

113 Popular St. (p-m-b)
Dresden, TN 38225
731-364-2012
Sales: $500,000-$1 Million

MIKE PARRISH (Owner) & Buys Men's Sportswear, Furnishings, Accessories, Footwear, Store Displays, Fixtures, Supplies

MANNERS MEN'S SHOP, INC. (MW)

575 Mall Blvd., #A (m-b)
Dyersburg, TN 38024
901-285-4452
Sales: $100,001-$500,000

ERNEST BLALOCK (Owner) & Buys Men's, Young Men's & Boys' Wear, Leather Apparel, Store Displays, Fixtures, Supplies

SIR RICHARD'S (MW)

2700 Lake Rd. (m-b)
Dyersburg, TN 38024
731-285-1721 / Fax: 731-285-1878
Sales: $100,001-$500,000

RICHARD CARRAWAY (Owner) & Buys Men's Overcoats, Suits, Tailored Jackets, Tailored Slacks, Raincoats, Sweaters, Sport Shirts, Outer Jackets, Leather Apparel, Casual Slacks, Active Apparel, Furnishings, Headwear, Accessories, Store Displays, Fixtures & Supplies

GERALD PRESLAR (G.M.M.) & Buys Men's Overcoats, Suits, Tailored Jackets, Tailored Slacks, Raincoats, Sweaters, Sport Shirts, Outer Jackets, Leather Apparel, Casual Slacks, Active Apparel, Furnishings, Headwear, Accessories

MICKEY LAWSON (CLO)

128 E. College St. (m-b)
Fayetteville, TN 37334
931-433-1131

MICKEY LAWSON (Owner) & Buys Men's Sportswear, Furnishings, Accessories, Athletic Footwear, Casual Shoes, Young Men's Wear, Footwear, Store Displays, Fixtures, Supplies

TENNESSEE - Franklin

PIGG & PEACH, INC. (MW)
400 Main St. (m-b)
Franklin, TN 37064
615-794-3855
BILL PEACH (Owner) & Buys Men's Suits, Sportswear, Furnishings, Headwear, Accessories, Footwear, Store Displays, Fixtures, Supplies

GATLINBURG FACTORY OUTLET (CLO-2)
610 Parkway (m)
Gatlinburg, TN 37738
865-430-3281 / Fax: 865-436-7439
MIKE MALKA (Owner) & Buys Men's Sportswear, Furnishings, Accessories, Young Men's Wear, 8 to 20 Boys' Wear, Store Displays, Fixtures, Supplies
UZI MAMAN (Mgr.) & Buys Men's Sportswear, Furnishings, Accessories, Young Men's Wear, Urban Contemporary, 8 to 20 Boys' Wear, Store Displays, Fixtures, Supplies

JONATHAN'S (CLO)
733 Parkway (m-b)
Gatlinburg, TN 37738
865-436-3179 / Fax: 865-436-6422
JONATHAN MILLER (President) & Buys Men's Wear, Footwear, Boys' T-shirts, Store Displays, Fixtures, Supplies
DEBBIE FLEMING (V.P.) & Buys Men's Wear, Footwear, Boys' T-shirts, Store Displays, Fixtures, Supplies

TAILOR SHOP, INC. (MW)
1323 Tusculum Blvd. (m)
Greeneville, TN 37745
423-638-3071
Sales: $100,001-$500,000
DAVID HAWK (Owner) & Buys Men's Sportswear, Accessories, Furnishings, Headwear, Store Displays, Fixtures, Supplies

JEANS & THINGS (CLO-2)
114 E. Main St. (p-m)
Henderson, TN 38340
731-989-5407
JIMMY CLIFFORD (Owner) & Buys Men's T-shirts, Jeans, Store Displays, Fixtures, Supplies

TRAIL WEST, INC. (CLO-7 & OL)
1183 W. Main St. (m-b)
Hendersonville, TN 37075
615-264-2955 / Fax: 615-264-7030
ED SMITH (Owner) & Buys Men's Western Wear, Western Accessories, Furnishings, Western Headwear, Boots, Store Displays, Fixtures, Supplies

PUCKETT & MAYNORD APPAREL STORE, INC. (CLO)
24 E. Main St. (m)
Hohenwald, TN 38462
931-796-3554
KEN MAYNORD (Owner) & Buys Men's Tailored Jackets, Tailored Slacks, Sportswear, Furnishings, Accessories, Urban Contemporary, Store Displays, Fixtures, Supplies

BRASHER'S, INC. (SP)
367 Vann Dr., #A (b-des)
Jackson, TN 38305
731-668-0505
Sales: $1 Million-$10 Million
EARL C. WALKER, JR. (President)
ROB BEASENBURG (Mgr.) & Buys Formal Wear, Special Occasion Wear, Related Accessories

NANDO JONES DEPARTMENT STORE, INC. (DEPT)
111 W. Lafayette St. (m)
Jackson, TN 38301
901-423-9625
Sales: $500,000-$1 Million
WES FORSYTHE (President & G.M.M.) & Buys Men's Overcoats, Suits, Tailored Jackets, Tailored Slacks, Raincoats, Sweaters, Sport Shirts, Outer Jackets, Casual Slacks, Furnishings, Belts, Jewelry, Footwear, Boys' Clothing, Sportswear, Accessories, Big & Tall Men's Wear, Store Displays, Fixtures, Supplies
GAY JONES FORSYTHE-Men's Overcoats, Suits, Tailored Jackets, Tailored Slacks, Raincoats, Sweaters, Sport Shirts, Outer Jackets, Casual Slacks, Furnishings, Belts, Jewelry, Footwear, Boys' Clothing, Sportswear, Accessories, Big & Tall Men's Wear, Store Displays, Fixtures, Supplies

MASENGILL'S SPECIALTY SHOP (CLO)
246 E. Main St. (m-b)
Johnson City, TN 37601
423-926-9633 / Fax: 423-928-4431
AMBERS WILSON, JR. (President) & Buys Men's Sweaters, Sport Shirts, Outer Jackets, Active Apparel, Furnishings, Accessories, Store Displays, Fixtures, Supplies

WISEMAN'S CLOTHING (CLO)
6001 Unico Dr.
Johnson City, TN 37601
423-926-0691 / Fax: 423-926-2980
Sales: $1 Million-$10 Million
JOHNNY FARNER (Co-Owner) & Buys Store Displays, Fixtures, Supplies
ELLEN FARNER (Co-Owner) & Buys Store Displays, Fixtures, Supplies
REBECCA HONIGMAN-Store Displays, Fixtures, Supplies
DENISE WEBB-Men's Sportswear, Western Wear, Furnishings, Headwear, Accessories, Leather Apparel, Footwear, 8 to 20 Boys' Wear

BLAKELY-MITCHELL CO. (MW-2)
240 Broad St. (m)
Kingsport, TN 37660
423-245-8351
Sales: $100,001-$500,000
TED TESTERMAN (President) & Buys Store Displays, Fixtures, Supplies, Men's Wear, Men's Dress Shoes
BILL TESTERMAN (V.P.) & Buys Men's Wear, Men's Dress Shoes

NOTE:-Balance Of Buying Performed at BLAKELY-MITCHELL CO., Bristol, Va - See Listing.

AMERICAN CLOTHING CO. (CLO & OL)
(JOHN H. DANIEL CO.)
P.O. Box 2006 (m-b)
120 W. Jackson Ave.
Knoxville, TN 37901
865-523-6212 / Fax: 865-523-6435
Sales: $1 Million-$10 Million
Website: www.americanclothing.cc
COLEMAN BRYAN (President) & Buys Men's Sportswear, Dress Shirts, Overcoats, Suits, Sport Coats, Tailored Slacks, Big & Tall Men's Wear, Sweaters, Sport Shirts, Outer Jackets, Casual Slacks, Active Apparel, Raincoats, Ties, Footwear
REID SLOCUM-Store Displays, Fixtures, Supplies

BOWLIN ENTERPRISES (CLO)
P.O. Box 22171
Knoxville, TN 37933
865-966-8785 / Fax: 865-966-8794
DARRELL BOWLIN (Owner) & Buys Dive Apparel & Accessories, Men's Surf & Swimwear, Outdoor Gear & Apparel, T-shirts
CHERRY WILLIAMSON-Dive Apparel & Accessories, Men's Surf & Swimwear, Outdoor Gear & Apparel, T-shirts

COACHMAN CLOTHIERS, INC. (MW)
9700 Kingston Pike, #13 (b)
Knoxville, TN 37922
865-690-5805
DAVID DILL (Co-Owner) & Buys Men's Sportswear, Furnishings, Accessories, Footwear, Store Displays, Fixtures, Supplies
GAIL DILL (Co-Owner) & Buys Men's Sportswear, Furnishings, Accessories, Footwear, Store Displays, Fixtures, Supplies

GOODY'S FAMILY CLOTHING, INC. (CLO-297)

P.O. Box 22000 (bud-m)
400 Goody's Ln.
Knoxville, TN 37922
865-966-2000 / Fax: 865-777-4165
Sales: Over $1 Billion
Website: www.goodysonline.com
Retail Locations: NY, VA, WV, NC, SC, GA, FL, AL, TN, MS, KY, OH, IN, IL, MO, AR, OK, TX, NC, SC, GA, TN

ROBERT GOODFRIEND (Chmn. & C.E.O)
LANA CAIN KRAUTER (President) & Buys Men's and Boys' Clothing, Shoes
DAVID R. MULLINS (Exec. V.P.-Stores)
JOHN WISE (V.P.-Visual Presentation) & Buys Store Displays, Fixtures, & Supplies
JOHN PAYNE (Sr. V.P.& G.M.M.)
STEVE CAUTHEN (Real Estate Contact)
ALLEN MARKWAY (V.P. & D.M.M.-Men's) & Buys Men's Casual Slacks, Dress Shirts, Outer Jackets, Blazers
DOUG STONE-Young Men's Wear, Men's Furnishings, Accessories
KRIS RICE-Men's Denim
BARRY COMBS-Men's Sportwear, Activewear, Boys' Wear

M.S. McCLELLAN & CO., INC. (CLO)

5614 Kingston Pike (b)
Knoxville, TN 37919
865-584-3492 / Fax: 865-584-7515
Sales: $1 Million-$10 Million

MATTHEW S. McCLELLAN (Owner) & Buys Men's Wear, Leather Apparel, Footwear, Store Displays, Fixtures, Supplies
DAN KOCKS (G.M.M.) & Buys Men's Wear, Leather Apparel, Footwear, Store Displays, Fixtures, Supplies

McMILLAN CLOTHING STORE (MW)

1643 Cumberland Ave.
Knoxville, TN 37916
865-637-1384
Website: www.allvol.com

DONNA KENDRICK-Casual & Boys' Urban Contemporary

MEN OF MEASURE CLOTHING (MW-4)

7922 Kingston Pike (m-b)
Knoxville, TN 37919
865-694-8189
Sales: $1 Million-$10 Million
Website: www.menof.com

HENRY M. BARKER (Co-Owner)
JACK S. PHILLIPS (Co-Owner) & Buys Big & Tall Men's Overcoats, Suits, Tailored Jackets, Tailored Slacks, Raincoats, Sweaters, Sport Shirts, Outer Jackets, Leather Apparel, Casual Slacks, Active Apparel, Furnishings, Belts, Small Leather Goods, Fragrances, Store Displays, Fixtures, Supplies
AUGIE BARKER (Co-Owner) & Buys Big & Tall Men's Overcoats, Suits, Tailored Jackets, Tailored Slacks, Raincoats, Sweaters, Sport Shirts, Outer Jackets, Leather Apparel, Casual Slacks, Active Apparel, Furnishings, Belts, Small Leather Goods, Fragrances, Store Displays, Fixtures, Supplies

UNIVERSITY BOOK & SUPPLY STORE (SP-7)

University Ctr.
Knoxville, TN 37996
865-974-3364 / Fax: 865-974-4233
Sales: $10 Million-$20 Million
Website: http://bookstore.asa.utk.edu

MIKE ROOS (Dir.)
GAIL HEDRICK (Head Dir.) & Buys Activewear, Athletic Footwear, Golf Apparel, Licensed Apparel, Pants, Jackets, Hosiery

MACON DEPARTMENT STORE (DEPT)

(HUDSON'S DEPARTMENT STORE)
201 Public Sq. (p-m-b)
Lafayette, TN 37083
615-666-3859 / Fax: 615-666-9388

TERRY HUDSON (Owner) & Buys Men's & Boys' Wear, Footwear, Store Displays, Fixtures, Supplies

MOORE'S (MW)

(JIM MOORE CO.)
39 NW Public Sq. (m)
Lawrenceburg, TN 38464
931-762-3116
Sales: $100,001-$500,000

JAMES Y. MOORE, JR. (Owner) & Buys Men's Wear, Footwear, Young Men's Wear, Store Displays, Fixtures, Supplies

WHITE'S & COMPANY DEPARTMENT STORE, INC. (DEPT)

306 Crews St. (p-m)
Lawrenceburg, TN 38464
931-762-3818 / Fax: 931-762-8686

JOHN WHITE (President) & Buys Men's Overcoats, Tailored Slacks, Sweaters, Sport Shirts, Leather Apparel, Active Apparel, Belts, Footwear, Men's Big & Tall Wear, Furnishings, Headwear, Jewelry, Boys' Wear, Store Displays, Fixtures, Supplies

DAVIS DRY GOODS CO. (DG)

(HANCOCKS)
(DAVIS DRY GOODS)
40 S. Main St. (m)
Lexington, TN 38351
731-968-3351 / Fax: 731-968-3366

ELWOOD SMALL (Co-Owner) & Buys Men's Wear, Young Men's Wear, Jeans, Shirts, Men's Work Shoes, Boys' Wear, Store Displays, Fixtures, Supplies
CAROL SMALL (Co-Owner) & Buys Men's Wear, Young Men's Wear, Jeans, Shirts, Men's Work Shoes, Boys' Wear, Store Displays, Fixtures, Supplies

DUGGAN'S MEN'S STORE (MW)

162 Foot Hills Mall (m-b)
Maryville, TN 37801
865-983-4350

KENNETH DUGGAN (Owner) & Buys Men's Overcoats, Suits, Tailored Jackets, Tailored Slacks, Raincoats, Sweaters, Sport Shirts, Outer Jackets, Casual Slacks, Dress Shirts, Ties, Hosiery, Underwear, Headwear, Belts, Jewelry, Footwear, Store Displays, Fixtures, Supplies

McELHINEY'S MEN'S SHOP (MW)

2336 Cedar Ave. (m)
McKenzie, TN 38201
731-352-7172

DANNY McELHINEY (Owner) & Buys Men's Sportswear, Furnishings, Accessories, Headwear, Young Men's Wear, Urban Contemporary, Footwear, Store Displays, Fixtures, Supplies

MEDLIN'S STORE, INC. (CLO)

15050 S. Highland Dr. (m)
McKenzie, TN 38201
731-352-7110

TOMMY MEDLIN (Owner) & Buys Men's Sportswear, Furnishings, Belts, 8 to 20 Boys' Wear, Big & Tall Men's Wear, Leather Apparel, Footwear, Store Displays, Fixtures, Supplies

A. SCHWAB, INC. (DEPT)

163 Beale St. (bud-p)
Memphis, TN 38103
901-523-9782

ABE SCHWAB (President)
ELEANOR SCHWAB BRESLOW-Men's Work Clothes, Dress Shirts, Underwear, Belts, Hats, Footwear, Urban Contemporary, Store Displays, Fixtures, Supplies

CIRCLE SALES (MW)

101 S. Main St. (p-m)
Memphis, TN 38103
901-523-2211

SAMUEL SALKY (Owner) & Buys Men's Sportswear, Furnishings, Leather Apparel, Footwear, Store Displays, Fixtures, Supplies

TENNESSEE - Memphis

FASHION UNLIMITED (CLO-2)
59 S. Main St. (m)
Memphis, TN 38103
901-527-5770
KYONG HONG (Owner) & Buys Men's Wear, Accessories, Furnishings

GREG'S STORE FOR MEN (MW-10)
1710 N. Shelby Oaks
Memphis, TN 38134
901-384-3287 / Fax: 901-384-3283
LESLIE BAER (Partner) & Buys Men's Sportswear, Furnishings, Accessories, Headwear, Young Men's Wear, Boys' Wear, Footwear, Store Displays, Fixtures, Supplies
LARRY WOLF (Partner) & Buys Men's Sportswear, Furnishings, Accessories, Headwear, Young Men's Wear, Boys' Wear, Footwear, Store Displays, Fixtures, Supplies

I. ROSEN'S (MW-2)
539 Perkins Ext. (m-b)
Memphis, TN 38117
901-683-4591 / Fax: 901-763-2008
Sales: $1 Million-$10 Million
STEVEN ROSEN (Co-Owner) & Buys Men's Overcoats, Suits, Tailored Jackets, Tailored Slacks, Raincoats, Sweaters, Sport Shirts, Outer Jackets, Casual Slacks, Leather Apparel, Furnishings, Headwear, Accessories, Men's Shoes, Young Men's Wear, Boys' Wear, Store Displays, Fixtures, Supplies
MILTON ROSEN (Co-Owner) & Buys Men's Overcoats, Suits, Tailored Jackets, Tailored Slacks, Raincoats, Sweaters, Sport Shirts, Outer Jackets, Casual Slacks, Leather Apparel, Furnishings, Headwear, Accessories, Men's Shoes, Young Men's Wear, Boys' Wear, Store Displays, Fixtures, Supplies

JAMES DAVIS (MW)
(DAVIS-WEINBERG CO.)
400 Grove Park Rd. (b)
Memphis, TN 38117
901-767-4640 / Fax: 901-682-3338
Sales: $1 Million-$10 Million
VAN WEINBERG (President & G.M.M.)
MONTE STEWART (Gen. Mgr.) & Buys Men's Sportswear, Leather Apparel, Furnishings, Headwear, Accessories, Store Displays, Fixtures, Supplies
JOE AUGUSTINE-Men's Sportswear, Leather Apparel, Furnishings, Headwear, Accessories, Store Displays, Fixtures, Supplies

KWON'S CORP. (CLO)
2240 Lamar Ave. (p)
Memphis, TN 38114
901-454-5010
SOK KWON (Owner) & Buys Men's Sportswear, Furnishings, Accessories, Footwear, Young Men's Wear, 8 to 20 Boys' Wear, Store Displays, Fixtures, Supplies

LANSKY AT THE PEABODY (GM)
(PEABODY HOTEL MEN'S SHOP))
92 S. Front St. (b)
Memphis, TN 38103
901-525-5401 / Fax: 901-525-1476
Sales: $1 Million-$10 Million
Website: www.lanskybros.com
BERNARD LANSKY (Chmn.) & Buys Men's Sportswear, Furnishings, Headwear, Accessories, Store Displays, Fixtures, Supplies
HAL LANSKY (President & G.M.M.) & Buys Men's Sportswear, Furnishings, Headwear, Accessories, Store Displays, Fixtures, Supplies

MARTY'S, LLC (MW-11)
(SHELMAR, INC.)
3106 Norbrook Dr.
Memphis, TN 38116
901-345-8525 / Fax: 901-345-7682
VIDIT PURBHOO (Owner) & Buys Men's, Young Men's & Boys' Clothing, Leather Apparel, Footwear
BARON GILLARD-Store Displays, Fixtures, Supplies
STEVE BAER-Men's T-shirts, Active Apparel, Accessories

MEMPHIS IMPRINT (CLO)
632 S. Highland St. (m)
Memphis, TN 38111
901-323-2382 / Fax: 901-323-0204
ROBERT BASS (Owner)
LINDA AVERY (Mgr.) & Buys Young Men's Outer Jackets, Fleecewear, Store Displays, Fixtures, Supplies

MITCHELL'S STORES, INC. (CLO)
20 S. Mid America Mall (p)
Memphis, TN 38103
901-525-1296 / Fax: 901-525-9322
Sales: $500,000-$1 Million
C. O. MITCHELL (Owner) & Buys Men's Coats, Suits, Overcoats, Footwear, 8 to 20 Boys' Wear, Store Displays, Fixtures, Supplies
STEVE MITCHELL-Men's Coats, Suits, Overcoats, Footwear, 8 to 20 Boys' Wear, Store Displays, Fixtures, Supplies

OAK HALL (MW)
6150 Poplar Ave., #146
Memphis, TN 38119
901-761-3580 / Fax: 901-761-5731
BILL LEVY (Owner) & Buys Men's Wear, Furnishings, Accessories, Footwear
ROGER HAGSTRON-Footwear

TAN LINE SWIMWEAR (SP-3)
6099 Mount Moria Rd. Ext.
Memphis, TN 38115
901-795-9300
RANDY FARRIS (Co-Owner) & Buys Sunglasses, Fashion Accessories, Apparel, Men's Surf & Swimwear, Resortwear, T-shirts
CASSANDRA FARRIS (Co-Owner) & Buys Sunglasses, Fashion Accessories, Apparel, Men's Surf & Swimwear, Resortwear, T-shirts

THE UNIVERSITY STORE (SP)
University of Memphis
506 University Dr.
Memphis, TN 38152
901-678-2011 / Fax: 901-678-5447
Website: www.bkstore.com/umemphis
BETH CAIN (Mgr.)
RODNEY MERRIWETHER (Asst. Mgr.) & Buys Fleece, Jackets, Hosiery, T-shirts

VILLAGE MART (CLO-4)
4055 American Way (m-b)
Memphis, TN 38118
901-365-3557 / Fax: 901-363-8111
MAHMUD ABRAHAM (Owner) & Buys Men's & Boys' Wear, Store Displays, Fixtures, Supplies

R.J. BURROW DEPARTMENT STORE (DEPT)
1082 S. Main St. (m)
Milan, TN 38358
731-686-1161 / Fax: 731-723-3999
RICHARD J. BURROW (Owner) & Buys Men's Wear, Footwear, Store Displays, Fixtures, Supplies

DAWSON'S, INC. (CLO)
1720 W. Andrew Johnson Hwy. (m-b)
Morristown, TN 37814
423-586-5732 / Fax: 423-586-5735
Sales: $100,001-$500,000
HERMAN WEST (Owner) & Buys Men's Sportswear, Furnishings, Accessories, Young Men's Wear, Store Displays, Fixtures, Supplies

HADDAD'S DEPARTMENT STORE (DEPT)
69 Crigger Cir. (m)
Munford, TN 38058
901-837-8025 / Fax: 901-837-6514
Sales: $100,001-$500,000
DAVID HADDAD (Partner) & Buys Men's Suits, Tailored Slacks, Sweaters, Sport Shirts, Casual Slacks, Active Apparel, Furnishings, Headwear, Accessories, Casual Shoes, Young Men's Wear, Store Displays, Fixtures, Supplies

PIGG & PARSONS OF MURFREESBORO, INC. (MW-1)
810 NW Broad St. (m-b)
Murfreesboro, TN 37129
615-893-7593 / Fax: 615-867-0655
Sales: $500,000-$1 Million
MARTY BELK (G.M.M.) & Buys Men's Wear, Footwear, Store Displays, Fixtures, Supplies

ATHLETE'S HOUSE INTERNATIONAL (SG)
1700 Portland Ave. (p)
Nashville, TN 37212
615-298-4495 / Fax: 615-292-7465
DAVID GRAESLIN (Owner) & Buys Active Apparel, Sportswear, Accessories, Furnishings

FRIEDMANS, INC. (AN)
2101 21st Ave. South (p-m)
Nashville, TN 37212
615-297-3343 / Fax: 615-242-1456
Sales: $1 Million-$10 Million
FRANK FRIEDMAN (President) & Buys Men's Sweaters, Leather Apparel, Furnishings (Except Gloves), Young Men's Wear, Belts, Store Displays, Fixtures, Supplies

GENESCO, INC. (FW-759 & MO)
(JARMAN)
(JOHNSTON & MURPHY)
(JOURNEY'S KIDZ)
(UNDERGROUND STATION)
(NAUTICA
(JOURNEY'S)
P.O. Box 731 (bud-p-m-b)
1415 Murfreesboro Pike
Nashville, TN 37217
615-367-8505 / Fax: 615-367-8579
Sales: $500 Million-$1 Billion
Website: www.genesco.com
Retail Locations: AL, AK, AR, AZ, CA, CO, CT, DE, DC, FL, GA, HI, ID, IA, IL, IN, KS, KY, LA, ME, MD, MA, MI, MN, MS, MO, MT, NE, NV, NH, NJ, NM, NY, NC, ND, OH, OK, OR, PA, RI, SC, SD, TN, TX, UT, VT, VA, WA, WI, WY
BEN T. HARRIS (Chmn. & C.E.O.)
HAL PENNINGTON (President & C.O.O.)
MARIO GALLIONE (V.P. & G.M.M. - Journeys)
BLAINE LUCAS (G.M.M. - Johnston & Murphy) & Buys Boys' Footwear, Men's Footwear, Men's Accessories, Men's Apparel, Hosiery

J. MICHAEL'S CLOTHIERS, INC. (MW)
2525 West End Ave., #200
Nashville, TN 37203
615-321-0686 / Fax: 615-320-1201
Website: www.jmichael.org
MIKE MAHAFFEY (Owner) & Buys Men's Sportswear, Furnishings, Accessories, Young Men's Wear
JIM BRANDON-Footwear, Men's Sportswear, Furnishings, Accessories, Young Men's Wear
TOM REPASS-Men's Sportswear, Furnishings, Accessories, Young Men's Wear

LEVY'S, INC. (MW)
3900 Hillsboro Rd., #36 (b-h)
Nashville, TN 37215
615-383-2800 / Fax: 615-383-7600
Sales: $1 Million-$10 Million
Website: www.levysclothes.com
DAVID W. LEVY (President & G.M.M.) & Buys Men's Overcoats, Suits, Tailored Jackets, Tailored Slacks, Raincoats
ELLEN LEVY-Jewelry, Small Leather Goods, Sweaters, Sport Shirts, Outerwear, Furnishings, Casual Slacks, Active Apparel, Dress Shirts, Ties, Robes, Underwear, Hosiery, Gloves, Headwear, Belts, Store Displays, Fixtures and Supplies

McPHERSON'S MEN'S SHOP, INC. (MW)
5920 Charlotte Pike (m)
Nashville, TN 37209
615-356-4886 / Fax: 615-356-4846
Sales: $1 Million-$10 Million
PAUL BARLAR (Owner) & Buys Men's Overcoats, Suits, Tailored Jackets, Tailored Slacks, Raincoats, Sweaters, Sport Shirts, Outer Jackets, Casual Slacks, Active Apparel, Furnishings, Headwear, Accessories, Big & Tall Men's Wear, Footwear, Store Displays, Fixtures, Supplies

NASHVILLE SPORTING GOODS CO (SG)
169 8th Ave. North (h)
Nashville, TN 37203
615-259-4241 / Fax: 615-259-4149
ROBERT BUTLER (Owner) & Buys Active Apparel, Sportswear, Footwear

OXFORD SHOP OF NASHVILLE, INC. (MW)
4001 Hillsboro Rd. (b)
Nashville, TN 37215
615-383-4442
ERIC VIARS (Co-Owner) & Buys Men's Sportswear, Furnishings, Accessories, Footwear, Store Displays, Fixtures, Supplies
DAVID GARRIS (Co-Owner) & Buys Men's Sportswear, Furnishings, Accessories, Footwear, Store Displays, Fixtures, Supplies

OXFORD WEARHOUSE (MW-3)
235 5th Ave. North (m-b)
Nashville, TN 37219
615-256-8430 / Fax: 615-256-0903
TOMMY BABIT (Owner) & Buys Men's Sportswear, Furnishings, Accessories, Footwear, Store Displays, Fixtures, Supplies

PETWAY REAVIS (MW)
506 Church St.
Nashville, TN 37219
615-255-6409
JOHN MINTON (Owner & President) & Buys Men's Sportswear, Furnishings, Accessories, Footwear, Store Displays, Fixtures, Supplies

R. JOSEPH MENSWEAR (MW)
2010 Glen Echo Rd.
Nashville, TN 37215
615-298-2100 / Fax: 615-269-4131
Website: www.josephmenswear.com
RICHARD ORGA (Owner) & Buys Men's Sportswear, Furnishings, Accessories, Footwear, Store Displays, Fixtures, Supplies
KENNETH IBES (Mgr.)

SAM'S CLOTHING & SHOES (MW)
(SAM'S GENERAL MERCHANDISE, INC.)
227 5th Ave. North (p-m-b)
Nashville, TN 37219
615-242-6301 / Fax: 615-383-4836
BERNIE LANDAU (Co-Owner) & Buys Young Men's Wear, Footwear, Store Displays, Fixtures, Supplies
STAN LANDAU (Co-Owner) & Buys Young Men's Wear, Urban Contemporary, Footwear, Store Displays, Fixtures, Supplies

NEWPORT DRY GOODS (DG-2)
(MORRISTOWN DRY GOODS)
255 E. Main St. (p)
Newport, TN 37821
423-623-2921 / Fax: 423-623-4397
Sales: $1 Million-$10 Million
JAMES CARROLL KYKER (Owner) & Buys Men's Tailored Slacks, Sweaters, Sport Shirts, Casual Slacks, Active Apparel, Dress Shirts, Ties, Belts, 8 to 20 Boys' Wear, Footwear, Store Displays, Fixtures, Supplies

PHILLIPS' APPAREL (CLO)
19816 Alberta St. (m)
Oneida, TN 37841
423-569-5130 / Fax: 423-569-9177
STEVE PHILLIPS (Co-Owner) & Buys Men's Sportswear, Tailored Jackets, Tailored Slacks, Dress Shirts, Ties, Belts, Footwear, Young Men's & Boys' Clothing, Store Displays, Fixtures, Supplies
GINA PHILLIPS (Co-Owner) & Buys Men's Sportswear, Tailored Jackets, Tailored Slacks, Dress Shirts, Ties, Belts, Footwear, Young Men's & Boys' Clothing, Urban Contemporary, Store Displays, Fixtures, Supplies

BILL'S MEN'S SHOP (MW)
612 Tennessee Ave. South (p)
Parsons, TN 38363
731-847-6439
DONNA BOX (Owner) & Buys Men's Sportswear, Furnishings, Accessories, Footwear, Young Men's Wear, Footwear, Urban Contemporary, Store Displays, Fixtures, Supplies

TENNESSEE - Pigeon Forge

CLOTHING WORLD (CLO-3 & WW & OL)
2828 Parkway
Pigeon Forge, TN 37863
865-428-4656 / Fax: 865-453-7727
Sales: $500,000-$1 Million
STONEY C. DUNCAN (Owner) & Buys Men's Sportswear, Headwear, Young Men's Wear, 8 to 20 Boys' Wear

STAGES WEST, INC. (CLO & OL)
2765 Parkway (p-m-b)
Pigeon Forge, TN 37863
865-453-8086 / Fax: 865-429-0669
Website: www.stageswest.com
MARLENE HOUSER (Owner) & Buys Men's & Boys' Footwear, Western Wear, Urban Contemporary, Store Displays, Fixtures, Supplies

PATE'S DEPARTMENT STORE (DEPT)
P.O. Box 309 (p)
208 Main St.
Rutherford, TN 38369
731-665-7459 / Fax: 901-665-6320
Sales: $500,000-$1 Million
JOE F. PATE (Co-Owner) & Buys Men's, Young Men's & Boys' Wear, Footwear, Store Displays, Fixtures, Supplies
BRADLEY PATE (Co-Owner) & Buys Men's, Young Men's & Boys' Wear, Urban Contemporary, Footwear, Store Displays, Fixtures, Supplies

GRISHAM'S (MW-2)
700 Main St. (m-b)
Savannah, TN 38372
731-925-2315
BRUCE GRISHAM (Owner) & Buys Men's Sportswear, Clothing, Furnishings, Footwear, Store Displays, Fixtures, Supplies

CANTRELL'S MEN'S & LADIES' SPORTSWEAR (CLO)
115 W. Main St. (m-b)
Smithville, TN 37166
615-597-4120
PHILLIP WAYNE CANTRELL (President) & Buys Men's Sportswear, Furnishings, Accessories, Leather Apparel, Footwear, Urban Contemporary, Store Displays, Fixtures, Supplies

J.D.'S MEN'S CLOTHING (MW)
210 Cedar Ave. (m)
South Pittsburg, TN 37380
423-837-7222 / Fax: 423-837-0959
J. D. LLOYD (Owner) & Buys Men's Wear, Accessories, Furnishings

LAD & DAD, INC. (MW)
2023 Memorial Blvd. (m-b)
Springfield, TN 37172
615-384-7668
Sales: $500,000-$1 Million
GARY DIORIO (Partner) & Buys Men's Sportswear, Furnishings, Accessories, Urban Contemporary, Store Displays, Fixtures, Supplies

DEBBIE'S YOUTH SHOP (KS)
102 S. Court Sq. (m-b)
Trenton, TN 38382
731-855-2600
DEBBIE FINCH (Owner) & Buys 8 to 20 Boys' Wear, Footwear, Urban Contemporary, Store Displays, Fixtures, Supplies

WESTWIN, INC. (CLO-3)
1032 S. High St. (m-b)
Trenton, TN 38382
731-855-1032 / Fax: 731-855-1037
WINTER HODGES (Owner) & Buys Men's Sportswear, Furnishings, Accessories, Young Men's Wear, Footwear, Store Displays, Fixtures, Supplies

CLYDE PHILLIPS' MEN'S SHOP (MW)
125 W. Lincoln St. (m)
Tullahoma, TN 37388
931-455-2061
Sales: $100,001-$500,000
JAMES S. PHILLIPS (Owner) & Buys Men's Overcoats, Suits, Tailored Jackets, Tailored Slacks, Raincoats, Sportswear, Leather Apparel, Furnishings, Belts, Jewelry, Fragrances, Footwear, Store Displays, Fixtures, Supplies

BENNETT'S, INC. (MW)
122 S. 1st St. (p)
Union City, TN 38261
731-885-2851 / Fax: 731-885-5317
Sales: $100,001-$500,000
RAIFORD TARVER (Owner) & Buys Men's Overcoats, Suits, Tailored Jackets, Tailored Slacks, Raincoats, Sweaters, Sport Shirts, Outer Jackets, Casual Slacks, Active Apparel, Leather Apparel, Dress Shirts, Ties, Robes, Underwear, Hosiery, Gloves, Headwear

FIVE SEASONS, INC. (CLO)
627 E. Reelfoot Ave. (b)
Union City, TN 38261
731-885-2772 / Fax: 731-885-2191
Sales: $500,000-$1 Million
Website: www.fiveseasonsonline.com
ROBERT J. KEATHLEY (President)
BARRY KEATHLEY (Mgr.) & Buys Men's Overcoats, Suits, Tailored Jackets, Tailored Slacks, Raincoats, Sweaters, Sport Shirts, Outer Jackets, Leather Apparel, Casual Slacks, Active Apparel, Dress Shirts, Robes, Underwear, Gloves, Footwear, Big & Tall Men's Wear, Young Men's Wear, Store D
J.R. SEALS-Men's Ties, Hosiery, Belts, Jewelry, Small Leather Goods, Fragrances

HAMMER'S CLOTHING STORE (CLO-9)
102 1st Ave. SE (p)
Winchester, TN 37398
931-967-3787 / Fax: 931-962-0717
Sales: $1 Million-$10 Million
JOSHUA HAMMER (Partner) & Buys Men's & Boys' Wear, Leather Apparel, Footwear, Urban Contemporary, Store Displays, Fixtures, Supplies
EARL HAMMER (Partner) & Buys Men's & Boys' Wear, Leather Apparel, Footwear, Store Displays, Fixtures, Supplies
NOTE-Buying of Men's & Boys' Wear Also Performed In Albertsville, AL - See Listing.

BIG & TALL MEN'S SHOP (MW)

3291 S. 14th St. (m-b)
Abilene, TX 79605
915-692-7310
Sales: $500,001-$1 Million

LARRY RUSHING (Owner) & Buys Men's Big & Tall Apparel, Sportswear, Furnishings, Golf Apparel, Swimwear, Skiwear, Accessories, Store Displays, Fixtures & Supplies

F & S CLOTHIERS (MW)

(SHOES OF ABILENE)
4102 Buffalo Gap Rd. (m)
Abilene, TX 79605
915-698-7061 / Fax: 915-698-7063
Sales: $500,001-$1 Million

BILL STANLEY (Owner) & Buys Men's Sportswear, Furnishings, Headwear, Accessories, Dress Shoes, Casual Shoes, Formalwear, Store Displays, Fixtures, Supplies

KARLA BROWN (Manager) & Buys Men's Sportswear, Furnishings, Headwear, Accessories, Dress Shoes, Casual Shoes, Formalwear, Store Displays, Fixtures, Supplies

KIDS CLOSET (KS)

317 E. Main St. (m-b)
Alice, TX 78332
361-664-4772 / Fax: 361-664-4772

ESMERALDA SAENZ (Owner) & Buys Infant to Size 7 Boys' Wear, Footwear, Related Accessories, Furnishings, Store Displays, Fixtures, Supplies

MORTON'S CACTUS JACK'S (CLO)

6921 Hwy. 67 East
Alvarado, TX 76009
817-790-2381 / Fax: 817-790-3300
Sales: $500,001-$1 Million

JOEL MORTON (Co-Owner) & Buys Men's Suits, Tailored Jackets, Tailored Slacks, Raincoats, Sportswear, Furnishings, Headwear, Accessories, Boys' Wear, Men's & Boys' Western Wear, Big & Tall Men's Wear, Western Boots, Work Boots

KELLY MORTON (Co-Owner) & Buys Store Displays, Fixtures, Supplies

BOWMAN'S DEPARTMENT STORE (DEPT)

118 W. Sealy (m-b)
Alvin, TX 77511
281-585-3212 / Fax: 281-585-8084

RUTH BOWMAN (Owner) & Buys Men's & Boys' Wear, Accessories, Furnishings, Store Displays, Fixtures & Supplies

CATTLEMAN WESTERN STORE (WW)

314 S. Gordon (m)
Alvin, TX 77511
281-585-5626 / Fax: 281-585-5627

ALBERT JENNINGS (Owner) & Buys Men's & Boys' Clothing, Young Men's Wear, Big & Tall Wear, Sportswear, Ties, Accessories, Western Boots, Store Displays, Fixtures, Supplies

JEFF MILLIGAN-Men's & Boys' Clothing, Young Men's Wear, Big & Tall Wear, Sportswear, Ties, Accessories, Western Boots, Store Displays, Fixtures, Supplies

WELLBORN'S DEPARTMENT STORE (DEPT)

210 E. House St. (m)
Alvin, TX 77511
281-331-3125 / Fax: 281-585-8532
Sales: $500,001-$1 Million

DAVID JIRCIK (Mgr.) & Buys Men's Wear, Sportswear, Accessories, Furnishings, Boys' & Students' Wear, Footwear, Store Displays, Fixtures, Supplies

COATS CLOTHIERS BIG & TALL (MW)

2500 Coulter, #106 (m)
Amarillo, TX 79106
806-359-6511 / Fax: 806-359-6616
Sales: $500,001-$1 Million

LYNDAL COATS (Owner) & Buys Big & Tall Men's Sportswear, Furnishings, Footwear, Store Displays, Fixtures, Supplies

RAFFKIND'S (MW-2)

7701 I-40 West, #344 (m-b)
Amarillo, TX 79160
806-353-1334 / Fax: 806-353-9780
Sales: $1 Million-$10 Million
Website: www.raffkinds.com

GEORGE RAFFKIND (President) & Buys Men's Overcoats, Suits, Tailored Jackets, Tailored Slacks, Raincoats, Sweaters, Outer Jackets, Sport Shirts, Casual Slacks, Furnishings, Swimwear, Dress Shirts, Ties, Underwear, Jewelry, Hosiery, Accessories, Belts, Fragrances, Robes, Gloves, Headwear, Small Leather Goods, Footwear, Store Displays, Fixtures, Supplies

ERIC CURBYN (Manager) & Buys Men's Overcoats, Suits, Tailored Jackets, Tailored Slacks, Raincoats, Sweaters, Outer Jackets, Sport Shirts, Casual Slacks, Furnishings, Swimwear, Dress Shirts, Ties, Underwear, Jewelry, Hosiery, Accessories, Belts, Fragrances, Robes, Gloves, Headwear, Small Leather Goods, Footwear, Store Displays, Fixtures, Supplies

TOP NOTCH OUTFITTERS (CLO)

2617 Wolflin Vlg. (m)
Amarillo, TX 79109
806-353-9468 / Fax: 806-353-3158
Sales: $500,001-$1 Million

TIM BROSIOR (Co-Owner) & Buys Men's Sportswear, Sweaters, Sportshirts, Outer Jackets, Casual Shirts, Active Apparel, Outdoor Clothing, Footwear, Store Displays, Fixtures, Supplies

WALKING SHOP (FW)

4151 W. 34th St. (m-b)
Amarillo, TX 79109
806-353-1051 / Fax: 806-353-1980
Sales: $100,001-$500,000

RAY HINDMAN (Owner)

TRUDY HINDMAN-Men's Orthopedic Shoes, Men's Comfort Footwear, Store Displays, Fixtures & Supplies

CLIFF'S MENSWEAR (MW)

229 N. Velasco St. (m)
Angleton, TX 77515
979-849-4041

CLIFF TUBB (Owner) & Buys Men's Sportswear, Furnishings, Accessories, Store Displays, Fixtures & Supplies

ATHLETIC ATTIC (SP-12)

3811 S. Cooper St., # 2302
Arlington, TX 76015
817-557-4232
Sales: $2 Million-$5 Million

HOWARD GOTTLIEB (Co-Owner) & Buys Licensed Apparel, Activewear

ALAN NOBLITT (V.P.-Opers.) & Buys Athletic Footwear

CASUAL LAKE (CLO)

2441 S. Collins
Arlington, TX 76014
817-794-5040

EUGENE BROWN (Mgr.) & Buys Men's Sportswear, Dress Shirts, Ties, Gloves, Accessories, Headwear, Young Men's Wear, 8 to 20 Boys' Wear, Store Displays, Fixtures, Supplies

ENSY TAILOR & CLOTHIER, INC. (MW)

4001 W. Green Oaks Blvd. (b)
Arlington, TX 76016
817-483-1464 / Fax: 817-516-0704

ENSY HADAVAND (President) & Buys Men's Sportswear, Furnishings, Footwear, Accessories, Store Displays, Fixtures, Supplies

TEXAS - Arlington

HERMAN'S MEN'S SHOP, INC. (MW)
212 W. Main St. (m)
Arlington, TX 76010
817-274-8411
Sales: $500,001-$1 Million
RON HERMAN (President)
DAVE HERMAN-Men's Sport Coats, Sweaters, Sport Shirts, Outer Jackets, Casual Slacks, Furnishings, Small Leather Goods, Footwear, Store Displays, Fixtures, Supplies

THE MAN'S SHOP (MW)
100 S. West St. (m-b)
Arlington, TX 76010
817-548-7224 / Fax: 817-548-7224
Sales: $500,001-$1 Million
WALLY HARDIN (Owner) & Buys Men's Suits, Tailored Jackets, Tailored Slacks, Raincoats, Sportswear, Furnishings, Leather Apparel, Suede Apparel, Footwear, Urban Contemporary, Store Displays, Fixtures, Supplies

LONE STAR WESTERN WEAR (WW-2)
1115 E. Tyler (m-b)
Athens, TX 75751
903-677-5775 / Fax: 903-677-3158
JOE MASSO (Owner) & Buys Men's, Young Men's & Boys' Western Wear, Men's Sportswear, Headwear, Accessories, Leather & Suede Apparel, Boots, Store Displays, Fixtures, Supplies

ALLDAYS DEPARTMENT STORE (DEPT)
116 E. Hiram (m-b)
Atlanta, TX 75551
903-796-2176 / Fax: 903-796-7025
Sales: $1 Million-$10 Million
ROB ALLDAY (President)
RICK STUBBS (V.P.) & Buys Men's Sportswear, Accessories, Furnishings, Footwear, Store Displays, Fixtures, Supplies

KENNEDY SHOES & WESTERN STORE (WW & FW)
118 E. Main St. (m)
Atlanta, TX 75551
903-796-6621
Sales: $100,001-$500,000
GEORGE KENNEDY (Co-Owner) & Buys Men's Western Wear, Boys' Western Wear, Men's & Boys' Boots, Related Accessories, Furnishings, Store Displays, Fixtures, Supplies
DEBBIE KENNEDY (Co-Owner) & Buys Men's Western Wear, Boys' Western Wear, Men's & Boys' Boots, Related Accessories, Furnishings, Store Displays, Fixtures, Supplies

ALLENS BOOT CENTER (WW-2)
1522 S. Congress Ave. (m-b)
Austin, TX 78704
512-440-8828 / Fax: 512-447-0582
Sales: $1 Million-$10 Million
STEVE GREENBERG (President) & Buys Men's & Boys' Western Shirts, Jeans, Headwear, Belts, Leather Western Jackets, Footwear, Store Displays, Fixtures, Supplies

THE CADEAU (CLO-2)
(CADEAU, INC.)
2316 Guadalupe St. (m-b)
Austin, TX 78705
512-477-7276 / Fax: 512-477-1403
JEANETTE NASSOUR (Owner) & Buys Men's Sportswear, Furnishings, Accessories, Footwear, Store Displays, Fixtures, Supplies

CAPRA & CAVELLI (MW)
3500 Jefferson St., #110
Austin, TX 78731
512-450-1919 / Fax: 512-450-1919
KEN MILLER-Men's Apparel, Accessories

FITTING STOOL, INC. (FW-5 & OL)
2525 W. Anderson Ln. (b)
Austin, TX 78750
512-323-6518 / Fax: 512-258-2758
Sales: $1 Million-$10 Million
Website: www.fittingstool.com
MIKE MURPHY (President)
CHARLES BANKS (C.E.O.)
PAUL DICKS-Men's Footwear, Leather Goods, Watches, Accessories, Men's Apparel, Hosiery, Furnishings

GATLIN & ESTRELLA CLOTHIERS (CLO)
The Village at Westlake (b-h)
701 Capital of Texas Hwy. South, #D480
Austin, TX 78746
512-328-4438 / Fax: 512-327-2567
Website: www.oxfordshop.com
LARRY GATLIN (Co-Owner) & Buys Suits, Sport Coats, Sportswear, Accessories, Furnishings, Footwear, Store Displays
BUDDY ESTRELLA (Co-Owner) & Buys Suits, Sportcoats, Sportswear, Accessories, Furnishings, Men's Footwear, Store Displays

HORACE'S FORMAL WEAR (MW)
3742 Far West Blvd., #112 (b)
Austin, TX 78731
512-794-8384 / Fax: 512-794-8385
Sales: $500,001-$1 Million
Website: www.horacesformalwear.com
MICHAEL DANKS (Owner) & Buys Men's & Boys' Formal Wear, Footwear, Related Accessories, Furnishings, Store Displays, Fixtures, Supplies

KARAVEL SHOES (FW)
5525 Burnet Rd. (m-b)
Austin, TX 78756
512-459-7603 / Fax: 512-459-5243
Website: www.karavelshoes
RICK KARAVEL (Owner) & Buys Men's Casual Shoes, Walking Shoes, Athletic Footwear, Work Shoes, Dress Shirts, Hosiery, Store Displays, Fixtures, Supplies

ROOSTER ANDREWS SPORTING GOODS (SG-2)
P.O. Box 300099 (m)
3901 Guadalupe St.
Austin, TX 78703
512-454-9642 / Fax: 512-454-9935
Website: www.roosterandrews.com
ROOSTER ANDREWS (President & Owner)
GRIFF ANDREWS-Men's Sport Shirts, Athletic Apparel, Active Apparel, Fleece, Hosiery, Athletic Footwear

SCOTT-WYNNE OUTFITTERS (CLO & OL)
(SCOTT-WYNNE CO., INC.)
3810 Medical Pkwy., #157 (p-m)
Austin, TX 78756
512-419-7667 / Fax: 512-419-9744
Website: www.outfits.com
MARIETTA SCOTT (Owner) & Buys Men's Overcoats, Raincoats, Sweaters, Outer Jackets, Casual Slacks, Dress Shirts, T-shirts, Outerwear, Underwear, Headwear, Furnishings, Urban Contemporary, Accessories, Belts, Jewelry, Store Displays, Fixtures, Supplies

THE TEXAS CLOTHIER, INC. (MW)
2905 San Gabriel (b)
Austin, TX 78705
512-478-4956 / Fax: 512-478-8631
Sales: $1 Million-$10 Million
Website: www.texasclothier.com
DAIN HIGDON (Owner) & Buys Men's Sportswear, Furnishings, Footwear, Accessories, Store Displays, Fixtures and Supplies

UNIVERSITY CO-OP SOCIETY (SP)
(UNIVERSITY OF TEXAS)
2244 Guadalupe
Austin, TX 78705
512-476-7211 / Fax: 512-478-7901
Sales: $10 Million-$20 Million
Website: www.universitycoop.com
GEORGE MITCHELL (President)
KRISTINE SALAZAR (V.P.-Mdsg.) & Buys Men's Activewear
TONY GUAJARDO-Men's & Boys' Wear

WALLY'S (MW)
2727 Exposition Blvd. (m-b)
Austin, TX 78703
512-476-2423 / Fax: 512-476-8522
Sales: $500,001-$1 Million
WALLY SHOWALTER (Owner) & Buys Men's Sportswear, Furnishings, Accessories, Men's Footwear, Store Displays, Fixtures & Supplies

WHOLE EARTH PROVISION CO. (SP-7)
1010 W. 11th St. (m-b)
Austin, TX 78703
512-476-4811 / Fax: 512-476-3301
Website: www.wholeearthprovision.com
JACK JONES (Owner)
STORMIE WOLFGRAHAM (Dir.-Shoe Dept.)
ROD PENROD (Warehouse Mgr.) (@ 512-476-4811) & Buys Store Displays, Fixtures and Supplies
KEVIN LEWIS-Footwear, Outer Wear, Accessories
LAURA KINMEN-Men's & Boys' Outdoor Active Apparel

AZLE WESTERN WEAR (WW)
161 Industrial (m-b)
Azle, TX 76020
817-444-2855
Sales: $1 Million-$10 Million
ROBERT CLAUSSEN (President) & Buys Men's & Boys' Western Wear, Related Furnishings, Headwear, Accessories, Boots, Store Displays, Fixtures
BOB BROWN (Mgr.) & Buys Store Supplies

WILD BILL'S WESTERN WEAR (WW-2)
1708 6th St. (bud-p-m-b)
Bay City, TX 77414
979-244-5205 / Fax: 979-244-5322
Sales: $1 Million-$10 Million
BILL NEWTON (Owner) & Buys Men's & Boys' Western Wear, Related Furnishings, Headwear, Accessories, Boots, Store Displays, Fixtures, Supplies

ANDERSON'S SHOE & SADDLE (WW)
102 E. Texas Ave. (m)
Baytown, TX 77520
281-422-8385 / Fax: 281-422-5480
Sales: $1 Million-$10 Million
LINDA PUTMAN (Owner) & Buys Men's & Boys' Western Wear, Men's Leather Apparel, Men's Suede Apparel, Related Accessories, Furnishings, Footwear, Store Displays, Fixtures, Supplies

THE BRANDERY IRON (WW)
6565 Eastex (m)
Beaumont, TX 77706
409-892-5761 / Fax: 409-899-9566
DIANE CUPPS (Owner) & Buys Men's Western Wear, Related Accessories, Furnishings, Leather Apparel, Suede Apparel, Boots, Store Displays, Fixtures, Supplies

BUTCH HOFFER (CLO)
136 Parkdale Mall (b-h)
Beaumont, TX 77706
409-892-9311 / Fax: 409-892-9313
Sales: $1 Million-$10 Million
BUTCH HOFFER (C.E.O.) & Buys Men's Wear, Furnishings, Accessories, Footwear, Store Displays, Fixtures, Supplies
LEWIS HOFFER-Men's Wear, Furnishings, Accessories, Footwear, Store Displays, Fixtures, Supplies

CHARLES HOFFER CO. (MW)
P.O. Box 7054 (b)
6250 Ivanhoe, #22
Beaumont, TX 77726
409-866-3349
Sales: $500,001-$1 Million
CHARLES HOFFER (President)
MURRAY HOFFER (G.M.M.) & Buys Men's Ties, Robes, Underwear, Headwear, Active Apparel, Accessories, Footwear, Store Displays, Fixtures, Supplies
STEPHEN HOFFER-Men's Sweaters, Sport Shirts, Outer Jackets, Casual Slacks, Big &Tall Wear, Boys' Wear
STEWART HOFFER-Boys' Wear

GEORGE WILSON (MW)
(NORMAN'S, INC.)
4132 Dowlen Rd. (b)
Beaumont, TX 77706
409-898-0919 / Fax: 409-898-2278
Sales: $1 Million-$10 Million
CHARLES T. NORMAN (President) & Buys Men's Wear, Sportswear, Big & Tall Men's Wear, Furnishings, Headwear, Accessories, Store Displays, Fixtures, Supplies
JASON NORMAN-Men's Footwear

NORMAN'S MEN'S FASHIONS (MW)
122 Gateway Dr. (m-b)
Beaumont, TX 77701
409-833-0363 / Fax: 409-833-0404
Sales: $1 Million-$10 Million
CHARLIE NORMAN (President)
CECIL WELLS (V.P.) & Buys Men's Clothing, Sportswear, Furnishings, Headwear, Accessories, Men's Footwear, Men's Big & Tall, Store Displays, Fixtures & Supplies
BETTY NORMAN (Secy. & Treas.)

SAM'S WESTERN STORE (WW)
5090 College St. (m)
Beaumont, TX 77707
409-842-2625 / Fax: 409-842-4699
DAVID BERTINO (Owner) & Buys Men's Western Wear, Related Accessories, Furnishings, Leather Apparel, Suede Apparel, Boots, Store Displays, Fixtures, Supplies

COCHRAN, BLAIR & POTTS, INC. (CLO)
221 E. Central Ave.
Belton, TX 76513
254-939-3333 / Fax: 254-939-3588
Sales: $500,001-$1 Million
ROB POTTS (President) & Buys Men's & Young Men's Wear, Footwear, Men's Western Wear, Store Displays, Fixtures, Supplies

SCHIGUT'S DEPARTMENT STORE (DEPT)
216 E. Central (m)
Belton, TX 76513
254-939-5991 / Fax: 254-939-5991
Sales: $500,001-$1 Million
RICHARD SCHIGUT (Owner) & Buys Men's Sweaters, Sport Shirts, Outer Jackets, Casual Slacks, Dress Shirts, Ties, Underwear, Gloves, Headwear, Belts, Footwear, Big & Tall Men's Wear, Store Displays, Fixtures, Supplies

MARTIN'S DEPARTMENT STORE (DEPT)
209 Main St. (m)
Big Lake, TX 76932
915-884-2113 / Fax: 915-884-2793
Sales: $500,000-$1 Million
JIMMY MARTIN (Co-Owner) & Buys Men's Sportswear, Sweaters, Sport Shirts, Outer Jackets, Casual Slacks, Active Apparel, Western Wear, Furnishings, Headwear, Footwear, Work Boots, Accessories, Big & Tall Men's Wear, Young Men's Wear, Store Displays, Fixtures, Supplies
BRYAN MARTIN (Co-Owner) & Buys Men's Overcoats, Suits, Tailored Jackets, Tailored Slacks, Raincoats, Sportswear, Sweaters, Sport Shirts, Outer Jackets, Casual Slacks, Boys' Jeans, Furnishings, Dress Shirts, Ties, Robes, Underwear, Hosiery, Gloves, Hats, Accessories, Belts, Jewelry, Sma

WARD'S WESTERN WEAR, INC. (WW)
212 Rummels (m-b)
Big Spring, TX 79720
915-267-8512 / Fax: 915-267-7959
Sales: $100,001-$500,000
SHANE WARD (Manager) & Buys Men's Western Wear, Boots, Boys' Western Wear, Furnishings, Accessories, Store Displays, Fixtures, Supplies

BOB'S WESTERN WEAR (WW)
521 N. Main St. (m)
Borger, TX 79007
806-273-2741
Sales: $100,001-$500,000
NEAL FARMER (Owner) & Buys Men's Western Wear, Furnishings, Related Accessories, Headwear, Footwear, Young Men's Wear, Store Displays, Fixtures, Supplies

TEXAS - Borger

R & K MENSWEAR (MW)
517 Main St. (p-m-b)
Borger, TX 79007
806-273-7761 / Fax: 806-274-9351
GINA SMITH (Owner) & Buys Men's Sportswear, Furnishings, Footwear, Headwear, Accessories, Urban Contemporary, Boys' Wear, Store Displays, Fixtures, Supplies

THE HOSS & BOSS WESTERN WEAR (WW)
1501 E. Walker (m-b)
Breckenridge, TX 76424
254-559-3524
SHEILA GUY (Owner) & Buys Men's & Boys' Western Wear, Related Accessories, Furnishings, Boots, Store Displays, Fixtures, Supplies

HUB CLOTHIERS, INC. (MW)
111 W. Walker St. (m)
Breckenridge, TX 76424
254-559-3611
Sales: $500,001-$1 Million
TED GOLDSMITH (Owner) & Buys Men's Overcoats, Suits, Tailored Jackets, Tailored Slacks, Raincoats, Big & Tall Wear, Sportswear, Sweaters, Sport Shirts, Outer Jackets, Leather Apparel, Casual Slacks, Active Apparel, Furnishings, Dress Shirts, Ties, Robes, Underwear, Hosiery, Gloves

BODE & TONN (MW)
101 E. Main St. (b)
Brenham, TX 77833
979-836-5400 / Fax: 979-836-5400
Sales: $1 Million-$10 Million
HARRY E. GRIMM (Co-Owner) & Buys Men's Overcoats, Suits, Raincoats, Big & Tall Men's Wear, Sportswear, Sweaters, Sport Shirts, Outer Jackets, Casual Slacks, Furnishings, Footwear, Hats, Belts, Fragrances, Urban Contemporary, Store Displays
GLORIA COOKIE GRIMM (Co-Owner) & Buys Men's Overcoats, Suits, Raincoats, Big & Tall Men's Wear, Sportswear, Sweaters, Sport Shirts, Outer Jackets, Casual Slacks, Furnishings, Footwear, Hats, Belts, Fragrances, Urban Contemporary, Store Displays

J & O MENSWEAR (MW)
2370 N. Expwy., #1242 (b)
Brownsville, TX 78526
956-546-5317 / Fax: 956-546-1035
Sales: $500,001-$1 Million
NAOMI CALAPA (President)
CAMILLE MARROQUIN (Sales Mgr.) & Buys Leather Goods, Men's Apparel, Men's Big & Tall Apparel, Men's Formalwear, Men's Designer Apparel, Men's Accessories, Men's Hosiery, Men's Outerwear, Men's Sleepwear, Men's Sportswear, Men's Suits, Young Men's Apparel

LA CASA DEL NYLON (DEPT)
1304 E. Adam (p-m)
Brownsville, TX 78520
956-546-4133 / Fax: 956-546-2960
ISRAEL LIZKA (Owner) & Buys Men's Wear, Sportswear, Accessories, Furnishings, Shoes, Store Displays, Fixtures, Supplies

LOS 4 REYES (DG)
1104 E. Elizabeth St. (m)
Brownsville, TX 78520
956-542-7158 / Fax: 956-982-4381
Sales: $1 Million-$10 Million
HARRY HOLZMAN (Owner & President)
MIKE FURGATCH (G.M.M.) & Buys Men's Sweaters, Sport Shirts, Outer Jackets, Casual Slacks, Active Apparel, Dress Shirts, Underwear, Hosiery, Gloves, Belts, Fragrances, Young Men's Wear, Footwear

MR. JOHN'S MAN'S SHOP (MW)
2200 Bola Chica Blvd., #31 (m-b)
Brownsville, TX 78521
956-546-4541 / Fax: 956-546-4542
Sales: $500,000-$1 Million
JAMES JOHN (Owner) & Buys Men's Sportswear, Furnishings, Accessories, Headwear, Footwear, Store Displays, Fixtures, Supplies

HERITAGE MENSWEAR - BIG & TALL (MW)
117 N. Main St. (m-b)
Bryan, TX 77803
979-822-6575 / Fax: 779-822-6575
ROBERT DODSON (Owner) & Buys Men's Wear, Sportswear, Accessories, Furnishings, Footwear, Big & Tall Men's Wear, Store Displays, Fixtures, Supplies
CURTIS CAMARILLO (Mgr.) & Buys Men's Wear, Sportswear, Accessories, Furnishings, Footwear, Big & Tall Men's Wear, Store Displays, Fixtures, Supplies

C.B. FINCHER'S WESTERN WEAR (WW)
12208 S. Fwy. (m)
Burleson, TX 76028
817-293-0620 / Fax: 817-293-4011
C.B. FINCHER (Owner)
JACK FINCHER-Men's Western Wear, Related Furnishings, Headwear, Boots, Accessories, Store Displays, Fixtures, Supplies
BEVERLY HAVIS-Men's Western Wear, Related Furnishings, Headwear, Boots, Accessories, Store Displays, Fixtures, Supplies

CAMP LONGHORN (CLO)
1 Longhorn Rd. (p)
Burnet, TX 78611
512-793-2811 / Fax: 512-793-6732
DONNA ROBERTSON-Men's & Boys' T-shirts, Casual Shirts, Shorts, Headwear, Active Apparel, Store Displays, Fixtures, Supplies

WEST TEXAS WESTERN STORE, INC. (WW-2)
1206 23rd St. (p-m)
Canyon, TX 79015
806-655-9612 / Fax: 806-655-9613
Website: www.westernhats.com
SANDY MARTIN (Owner) & Buys Men's Western Wear, Related Accessories, Furnishings, Headwear, Jeans, Store Displays, Fixtures, Supplies
TERRY MARTIN-Men's Footwear, Western Boots
TRACY MARTIN-Men's Footwear, Western Boots

CALLAHAN'S GENERAL STORES (GM-2)
200 S. Bell Blvd. (m-b)
Cedar Park, TX 78613
512-335-8585 / Fax: 512-335-1223
VERLIN CALLAHAN (President & Co-Owner)
RICHARD CALLAHAN (Store Mgr.) & Buys Store Displays, Fixtures, Supplies
DORIS PEARSON-Men's, Young Men's & Boys' Western Wear, Cowboy Hats, Cowboy Boots

SAYE'S (CLO)
219 S. Keary (m)
Clarendon, TX 79226
806-874-3844
TERRY ASKEW (Owner) & Buys Men's Wear, Sportswear, Furnishings, Accessories, Men's Western Shirts, Belts, Jeans, Underwear, Work Apparel, Young Men's & Boys' Western Shirts, Jeans, Store Displays, Fixtures, Supplies

WITMER'S MENSWEAR (MW)
1909 W. Broadway (m-b)
Clarksville, TX 75426
903-427-5740 / Fax: 903-427-5740
Sales: $500,001-$1 Million
ERNEST WITMER (Owner) & Buys Men's Wear, Men's Sportswear, Furnishings, Accessories, Western Boots

BJ'S WESTERN WEAR (WW)
410 W. 5th St. (b)
Clifton, TX 76634
254-675-8113 / Fax: 254-675-8166
Sales: $500,001-$1 Million
Website: www.bjwestern.com
JULIA CONLEY (Owner) & Buys Men's, Young Men's & Boys' Western Wear, Sportswear, Accessories, Bolo Ties, Footwear, Store Displays, Fixtures, Supplies

TEXAS A & M BOOKSTORE (SP)
(BARNES & NOBLE #572)
Memorial Student Ctr.
College Station, TX 77844
979-845-8681 / Fax: 979-845-6512
LEN SCOGGINS (Mgr.)
MARC ECKHART (Mgr.) & Buys Jackets, Hosiery, Athletic Footwear

POTTER WESTERN STORE (WW)

2106 Hwy. 71 South (m-b)
Columbus, TX 78934
979-732-2288
Sales: $100,001-$500,000

HENRY POTTER, JR. (Owner) & Buys Men's Raincoats, Dress Shirts, Ties, Gloves, Belts, Jewelry, Boys' Clothing, Cowboy Hats, Cowboy Boots, Store Displays, Fixtures, Supplies

BENJAMIN'S (CLO-2)

(BENJAMIN'S SURF, INC.)
10534 S. Padre Island Dr. (m)
Corpus Christi, TX 78418
361-937-2608 / Fax: 361-937-3816

BENJAMIN LISKA (President) & Buys Men's Sportswear, Furnishings, Accessories, Boys' Wear, Men's Footwear, Boys' Footwear
CAROLINE LISKA-Store Displays, Fixtures, Supplies

JACK ENGLISH MENSWEAR (CLO)

3636 S. Alameda (b)
Corpus Christi, TX 78411
361-853-0361 / Fax: 361-854-0662
Sales: $100,001-$500,000

JACK ENGLISH (President & G.M.M.) & Buys Men's Overcoats, Suits, Tailored Jackets, Tailored Slacks, Raincoats, Sportswear, Sweaters, Sport Shirts, Outer Jackets, Casual Slacks Furnishings, Accessories, Footwear

OCEAN TREASURES (CLO-9)

(SEA TREASURES)
(BU-JON'S)
14049 S. Padre Island Dr. (m)
Corpus Christi, TX 78418
361-949-7558 / Fax: 361-949-0210
Sales: $1 Million-$10 Million

BOB BEAUREGARD (Owner) & Buys Store Displays, Fixtures, Supplies
ROBIN FELTS (Mgr.) & Buys Men's Sportswear
CHRISTY CAMPBELL-Men's Footwear, Sportswear, Furnishings, Accessories

SWIMMIN' STUFF (SP & MO)

2033 Airline Rd., #2
Corpus Christi, TX 78412
361-993-5570 / Fax: 361-993-0419
Sales: $100,001-$500,000

MARLENE DALY (President & G.M.M.) & Buys Activewear, Athletic Apparel, Imprintable Apparel

WILLIAM'S FASHION SHOES (FW & OL & MO)

(MANLEY JUE, INC.)
3849 S. Alameda St. (bdes)
Corpus Christi, TX 78411
361-851-0094 / Fax: 361-851-6744
Sales: $500,001-$1 Million
Website: www.williams-shoes.com

WILLIAM H. JUE (Owner) & Buys Men's Footwear, Leather Goods, Watches, Men's Accessories, Men's Apparel, Hosiery
LYNN AMPARAN (Mgr.)

GREEN'S (CLO)

126 W. 5th Ave. (bud-p-m-b)
Corsicana, TX 75110
903-874-4891 / Fax: 903-874-6445

LUCILLE GREEN (Owner)
MARSHALL PURIFOY-Men's, Young Men's & Boys' Wear, Leather Apparel, Suede Apparel, Sportswear, Accessories, Furnishings, Footwear, Store Displays, Fixtures, Supplies

BEN'S WESTERN WEAR (WW)

109 N. Front (b)
Cotulla, TX 78014
830-879-2526 / Fax: 830-879-3388
Website: www.benswesternwear.com

STEWART MARTIN (Owner) & Buys Men's & Boys' Western Wear, Related Sportswear, Accessories, Furnishings, Boots, Store Displays, Fixtures, Supplies

ARMY & AIR FORCE EXCHANGE SERVICE (PX-1763 & OL)

P.O. Box 660202 (bud-p-m-b-h)
3911 S. Walton Walker Blvd.
Dallas, TX 75236
214-312-2011 / Fax: 214-312-6392
Sales: Over $1 Billion
Website: www.aafes.com
Retail Locations: AZ, AK, AZ, AR, CA, CO, CT, DE, DC, FL, GA, HI, ID, IL, IN, IA, KS, KY, LA, ME, MD, MA, MI, MN, MS, MO, MT, NE, NV, NH, NJ, NM, NY, NC, ND, OH, OK, OR, PA, RI, SC, SD, TN, TX, UT, VT, VA, WA, WV, WI, WY, International Locations on Military Bases

CHARLES MILLER (Sr. Planner)
STEVE DANNER (Visual Mktg. Spec. Planner) & Buys Store Displays, Fixtures, Supplies
JIM MOON (V.P. & G.M.M.-Softlines)
DAVE BOW (Category Team Mgr.)
HAZEL GREEN-Military Wear
PAM BAUR-Army Uniforms
ANTHONY WILLIAMS-Young Men's Trendsetter Sportswear, Shirts, Pants, Polo, Young Men's Coordinates, Flannel Shirts, FUBU
OPEN-Men's Dress Apparel, Suits, Sportcoats, Dress Shirts, Ties, Haggar, Belts, Suspenders, Big & Tall Men's Wear, Palmland, Polo
CHRIS TYLER-Men's Athletic Apparel, Licensed Apparel
STEPHANIE McCULLOUGH-Men's Raincoats, Outerwear, Leather Jackets, Jeans, Sweaters, Shorts, T-shirts, Swimwear, Headwear, Gloves
MIKE McMICHAEL-Men's Pajamas, Robes, Underwear, Hosiery, T-shirts
DAVE LUMBLEY (Div. Merch. Mgr.)
DIANA POULSON (Mdse. Mgr.-Children's Wear)
MARK BROWN-Boys' Clothing, Shorts, Coordinates, Swimwear, Sweaters, Outerwear, Dress Shirts, Casual Slacks, Sweaters, Robes, Pajamas, Knit Shirts, T-shirts, Shorts, Underwear, Accessories
ALICA SCOTT (Mgr.-Footwear)
JIM TRUSSEL-Footwear
NATASHA LEE-Children's Shoes
JASON MOORE-Men's Shoes
RAY DOWNS-Military Footwear

THE ARMY STORE (AN)

10606 Garland Rd. (m)
Dallas, TX 75218
214-328-1341 / Fax: 214-328-4134
Website: www.thearmystore.net

MIKE GREEN (President) & Buys Men's Sportswear, Furnishings, Men's Headwear, Accessories, Boys' Wear, Leather Apparel, Suede Apparel, Footwear, Store Displays, Fixtures, Supplies

TEXAS - Dallas

BILLYE LITTLE & ASSOCIATES (RB)
P.O. Box 585251
2300 Stemmons Fwy.
Dallas, TX 75258
214-634-0691 / Fax: 214-688-7414
BILLYE LITTLE (Executive) & Buys Men's Sportswear, Leather Apparel, Suede Apparel, Furnishings, Headwear, Accessories, 8 to 20 Boys' Wear, Urban Contemporary, Footwear

BOOT TOWN, INC. (WW-25)
13625 Neutron
Dallas, TX 75224
972-788-1301 / Fax: 972-788-4897
Sales: $1 Million-$10 Million
PENNY PRITCHER (Owner & President) & Buys Men's & Boys' Western Wear, Furnishings, Headwear, Accessories, Boots
HAROLD RODEN-Men's & Boys' Western Wear, Furnishings, Headwear, Accessories, Boots

CHILDREN'S APPAREL SERVICE (RB)
P.O. Box 585868 (b)
Apparel Mart, #3A51
Dallas, TX 75258
214-634-2821 / Fax: 214-634-1638
Sales: $1 Million-$10 Million
Website: www.childrensapparelserv.com
Retail Locations: TX
JOLENE DUCOMMUN (Mdse. Mgr.) & Buys 8 to 20 Boys' Clothing, Sportswear, Accessories, Furnishings

CORPORATE TRADITIONS, INC. (MW)
1140 Empire Central, #170 (m-b-h)
Dallas, TX 75247
214-638-5050 / Fax: 214-905-1313
Website: www.corptrad.com
ANITA GREEN (Owner) & Buys Men's Sportswear, Furnishings, Accessories, Footwear, Store Displays, Fixtures, Supplies

CULWELL & SON (MW & OL)
6319 Hillcrest (b)
Dallas, TX 75205
214-522-7000 / Fax: 214-521-7329
Sales: $10 Million-$50 Million
Website: www.culwell.com
CHARLES BURGIN (Vice Chmn.) & Buys Men's Formal Wear, Custom Apparel, Suits, Sport Coats
MIKE CULWELL (President) & Buys Store Displays, Fixtures, Supplies
PATRICIA BLANKINSHIP-Young Men's & Boys' Wear
JAY BURGIN-Men's Sportswear, Accessories, Furnishings, Dress Shirts, Ties, Belts, Footwear

DAN'S BIG & TALL SHOP (MW-3 & OL)
11312 LBJ Fwy., #100
Dallas, TX 75238
214-221-8255 / Fax: 214-221-0254
Website: www.bigtalldirect.com
ROBERT SCHLEIN (Owner) & Buys Big & Tall Men's Wear, Related Accessories, Furnishings, Store Displays, Fixtures, Supplies

DANIEL TAYLOR CLOTHIER, INC. (MW)
3699 McKinney Ave., #313 (b)
Dallas, TX 75204
214-521-0433 / Fax: 214-521-0435
DANIEL TAYLOR (Owner) & Buys Men's Sportswear, Furnishings, Accessories, Men's Footwear, Store Displays, Fixtures, Supplies

DAVID'S DEPARTMENT STORE (DEPT)
(LOS MORITOS CORP)
128 Dallas W. Shopping Ctr. (p)
Dallas, TX 75212
214-630-3530 / Fax: 214-630-2920
DAVID ESQUENAZI (President) & Buys Men's & Boys' Wear, Leather Apparel, Sportswear, Accessories, Furnishings, Footwear, Store Displays, Fixtures, Supplies

FORTY FIVE TEN, INC. (MW)
4510 McKinney Ave.
Dallas, TX 75205
214-559-4510 / Fax: 314-559-4507
Website: www.fortyfiveten.com
BRIAN BOLKE-Apparel

H.D.'S CLOTHING CO. (CLO)
3018 Greenville Ave. (m-b)
Dallas, TX 75206
214-821-5255 / Fax: 214-823-3644
Sales: $500,001-$1 Million
Website: www.hdsclothing.com
VICKI DeMARCO (Co-Owner) & Buys Men's Sportswear, Jeans, Young Men's Wear, Urban Contemporary, Footwear, Accessories, Furnishings, Store Displays, Fixtures, Supplies
HARRY DeMARCO (Co-Owner) & Buys Men's Sportswear, Accessories, Furnishings, Jeans, Outer Jackets, Young Men's Wear, Footwear, Store Displays, Fixtures, Supplies

HAROLD'S (CLO-47 & MO & OL)
(OLD SCHOOL CLOTHING CO.)
5919 Maple Ave. (b)
Dallas, TX 75235
214-366-0600 / Fax: 972-366-1061
Sales: $10 Million-$50 Million
Website: www.harolds.com
HUGH MILLER (President)
JODI LANEY (Visual Mdsg. Coord.) & Buys Store Displays, Fixtures, Supplies
LEON MORRISON (D.M.M.-Men's)
GARTH HALL-Men's Sweaters, Sport Shirts, Active Apparel, Headwear, Men's Outer Jackets, Dress Shirts
LEE McCOLLUGN-Men's Belts, Jewelry, Small Leathers, Fragrances, Furnishing, Sportswear
COURTNEY CUTHREW-Belts, Hosiery, Shoes

JUST ADD WATER (CLO-11)
2990 Congressman Ln.
Dallas, TX 75220
214-956-8686 / Fax: 214-351-1609
Website: www.justaddwater.com
RON McCULLARS (Owner) & Buys Beachwear, Surf & Swimwear, Wet Suits, Headwear, Sandals, Flip Flops

JUST JUSTIN BOOTS (CLO & MO & OL)
(BOOTS FOR LESS)
2461 N. Stemmans
Dallas, TX 75207
214-630-2858 / Fax: 214-630-2402
Website: www.bootsforless.com
JIMMY VELIS (President)
JIM CURRIER (Gen. Mgr.) & Buys Men's Western Clothing, Furnishings, Accessories, Boys' T-shirts, Store Displays, Fixtures, Supplies, Men's Footwear, Cowboy Boots, Dress Boots

KEN'S MAN'S SHOP (MW)
309 Preston Royal (b)
Dallas, TX 75230
214-369-5367 / Fax: 214-369-6657
Website: www.kensmansshop.com
KEN HELFMAN (President) & Buys Men's Overcoats, Suits, Tailored Jackets, Tailored Slacks, Raincoats, Sportswear, Sweaters, Sport Shirts, Outer Jackets, Leather Apparel, Casual Slacks, Furnishings, Headwear, Footwear, Accessories, Store Displays, Fixtures, Supplies
JERRI HELFMAN (V.P.) & Buys Men's Overcoats, Suits, Tailored Jackets, Tailored Slacks, Raincoats, Sportswear, Sweaters, Sport Shirts, Outer Jackets, Leather Apparel, Casual Slacks, Furnishings, Headwear, Footwear, Accessories, Store Displays, Fixtures, Supplies

TEXAS - Dallas

THE KENT SHOP OF TEXAS (MW)

5342 Belt Line Rd. (h)
Dallas, TX 75254
972-233-1752 / Fax: 972-233-1754
Sales: $1 Million-$10 Million

OSKAR MEDINA (Gen. Mgr.)

ROD TRAPP-Men's Overcoats, Suits, Tailored Jackets, Tailored Slacks, Formalwear, Raincoats, Sweaters, Sport Shirts, Sportswear, Furnishings, Accessories, Outer Jackets, Leather Apparel, Casual Slacks, Active Apparel, Dress Shirts, Ties, Robes, Underwear, Hosiery, Gloves, Footwear, Belts, Jewelry, Small Leather Goods, Fragrances, Urban Contemporary, Golf Apparel, Store Displays, Fixtures and Supplies

LEATHER BY BOOTS - DALLAS (CLO)

2525 Wycliff Ave., #124
Dallas, TX 75219
214-528-3865 / Fax: 214-528-7881
Website: www.leathernetwork.com/lbbpage

DEAN WALRADT (Owner) & Buys Men's Wear, Sport Shirts, Casual Slacks, Furnishings, Accessories, Gloves, Underwear, Footwear

LEATHER LOBBY (CLO-2)

(KARA COLLECTIONS, LLC)
Southwest Center Mall (p-m-b)
3662 W. Camp Wisdom Rd., #1034
Dallas, TX 75237
972-298-4442 / Fax: 972-298-4442

KAY SAWANT-Leather Apparel, Small Leather Goods

LEVINE'S (DEPT-12)

511 W. Jefferson St. (bud-p-m-b)
Dallas, TX 75208
214-948-7396
Sales: $10 Million-$50 Million

DONALD DISMORE (Partner) & Buys Men's & Boys' Wear, Footwear, Store Displays, Fixtures, Supplies

LOMBARDO CUSTOM APPAREL (MW-2)

8315 Preston Rd. (b-h)
Dallas, TX 75225
214-265-8488 / Fax: 214-265-9289
Sales: $1 Million-$10 Million
Website: www.lombardocustom.com

JAY LOMBARDO (President & Owner) & Buys Men's Overcoats, Suits, Tailored Jackets & Slacks, Raincoats, Big & Tall Men's Wear, Sweaters, Sport Shirts, Outer Jackets, Leather Apparel, Casual Slacks, Active Apparel, Furnishings, Dress Shirts, Ties, Robes, Underwear, Hosiery, Gloves, Headwear, Accessories, Belts, Jewelry, Boys' Sportswear, Furnishings, Accessories, Footwear

FORREST GIBBS (G.M.M.) & Buys Men's Overcoats, Suits, Tailored Jackets & Slacks, Raincoats, Big & Tall Men's Wear, Sweaters, Sport Shirts, Outer Jackets, Leather Apparel, Casual Slacks, Active Apparel, Furnishings, Dress Shirts, Ties, Robes, Underwear, Hosiery, Gloves, Headwear, Accessories, Belts, Jewelry, Boys' Sportswear, Furnishings, Accessories, Footwear

ANDY SMITH-Sportswear, Sweaters, Sport Shirts, Ties, Accessories, Belts, Jewelry, Small Leather Goods

LUKE'S LOCKER (SG-3 & FW)

3607 Oak Lawn Ave. (m-b)
Dallas, TX 75219
214-528-1290 / Fax: 214-522-5696
Website: www.lukeslocker.com

MATT LUCAS (President) & Buys Men's Casual Clothing, Athletic Apparel, Tank Tops, T-shirts, Shorts, Active Apparel, Running Apparel, Athletic Footwear

MARVIN BROWN CLOTHING, INC. (MW)

5500 Greenville Ave., #702 (b)
Dallas, TX 75206
214-369-1133 / Fax: 214-368-5811
Sales: $1 Million-$10 Million

MARVIN BROWN (Owner) & Buys Men's Wear, Leather Apparel, Accessories, Furnishings, Sportswear, Footwear, Store Displays, Fixtures, Supplies

MDC GIFTSHOP (MW)

(HOWARD CROW CO.)
2201 Stemmons Fwy. (m-b)
Dallas, TX 75207
214-651-8395 / Fax: 214-748-3427

NANCY BOWLING (Mdse. Mgr.) & Buys Men's Sportswear, Outerwear, Accessories, Furnishings, Footwear, Store Displays, Fixtures, Supplies

MG INTERNATIONAL MENSWEAR (MW-9)

(BIG & TALL FASHIONS)
(INTL. SUIT WAREHOUSE)
5850 LBJ Frwy. (m-des)
Dallas, TX 75240
214-360-0422 / Fax: 214-696-1655
Retail Locations: TX

MIKE GHANI (President & Real Estate Contact) & Buys Men's Sportswear, Big & Tall Men's Wear, Furnishings, Accessories, Young Men's Wear, Urban Contemporary, Footwear, Store Displays, Fixtures & Supplies

MISTER TUXEDO (MW)

6625 Snider Plz. (m-b)
Dallas, TX 75205
214-363-1871 / Fax: 214-363-8755

HAROLD BELL (Owner) & Buys Men's & Boys' Formal Wear, Related Accessories, Furnishings, Footwear, Formal Shoes, Store Displays, Fixtures, Supplies

N. ALLAGE FASHIONS (MW)

1517 Main St. (m-b)
Dallas, TX 75201
214-742-6246 / Fax: 214-742-8437
Sales: $1 Million-$10 Million

NAHIDEH ALLAGE (President) & Buys Men's Sportswear, Furnishings, Accessories, Men's Footwear, Store Displays, Fixtures, Supplies

TEXAS - Dallas

NEIMAN MARCUS (DEPT-35 & MO & OL)
(Div. of THE NEIMAN MARCUS GROUP)
1618 Main St. (b)
Dallas, TX 75201
214-741-6911 / Fax: 214-573-6136
Sales: Over $1 Billion
Website: www.neimanmarcus.com
Retail Locations: AZ, CA, CO, DC, FL, GA, HI, MA, MI, MN, MO, NJ, NV, NY, OH, PA, TX, VA, WI

BURTON M. TANSKY (Chmn. & C.E.O.)
KAREN KATZ (C.E.O.- Stores Div.)
JIM GOLD (Sr. V.P. & G.M.M.)
SARA BOOHAM (Visual Coord.) (@ 214-573-5380) & Buys Store Displays, Fixtures
WAYNE HUSSEY (Real Estate Contact) (@ 214-761-2417)

JENNIFER JORDAN (D.M.M. - Men's) & Buys Men's Neckwear
NATHAN JOHNSON-Men's Special Collections, Brioni Special Orders, Brioni Stock
PHILIP JORDAN-Valentino, Dolce & Gabbana, Donna Karan, Hugo Boss, Designer, Giorgio Armani/Mani By Giorgio Armani, Giorgio Armani Borgonuovo-Black Label, Giorgio Armani/Mani Staple Stock
ERIK WILKINSON-Men's Classifications
BRIAN CARL (@ 214-761-2714)-Men's Customized Fashions, Special Orders

SCOTT FRADIN (V.P. & D.M.M.)
WILL SWILLE-Shirts
AINSLEY CHARLES-Men's Designer & Basic Shirts
STEVE CROSS-Men's Underwear, Hosiery, Leather Accessories, Pajamas
RANA JAYNE-Men's Neckwear
SLOANE PHILLIPS-Men's Accessories, Jewelry
CONNIE CLARK-Polo, Ferragamo, Turnbull Asser Shirts & Neckwear, Dress Shirts

GREG MADDEL-Men's Sport Shirts, Sweaters, Casual Slacks
CHRIS SPIEKER-Men's Progressive, Collections, Designer Swimwear, Men's Culture Collections, Contemporary, Bridge & Designer Wear, Men's Contemporary, Sportswear
CAROLYN CANNON-Men's Polo Sportswear
STACY FERTITTA-Gentlemen's Collections

LESLIE FAUST (V.P. & D.M.M.)
STEVE CROSS-Men's Footwear

SCOTT FRADIN (V.P. & D.M.M.)
KIM DIANGELO-Men's Fragrances

POCKETS (MW)
(POCKETS, INC.)
9669 N. Central Expwy. (b)
Dallas, TX 75231
214-368-1167 / Fax: 214-368-1208
Sales: $1 Million-$10 Million
Website: www.pocketsmenswear.com

DAVID SMITH (Owner)
DOUG DUCKWORTH (G.M.M.) & Buys Men's Tailored Slacks, Raincoats, Sweaters, Sport Shirts, Outer Jackets, Casual Slacks, Active Apparel, Leather Apparel, Men's Robes, Underwear, Hosiery, Headwear, Belts, Jewelry, Small Leather Goods, Store Displays, Fixtures, Supplies
FRED BESSINGER-Men's Overcoats, Suits, Tailored Jackets, Dress Shirts, Ties, Store Displays, Fixtures, Supplies, Men's Tailored Slacks, Raincoats, Sportswear, Sweaters, Sport Shirts, Outer Jackets, Casual Slacks, Active Apparel, Leather Apparel, Men's Robes, Underwear, Hosiery, Headwear, Belts, Jewelry, Small Leather Goods
SHARON KUHL-Men's Accessories

ROBERT TALBOT (MW)
87 Highland Park Vlg. (m-b-h)
Dallas, TX 75205
214-526-6800
Sales: $100,001-$500,000

ROBERT TALBOT (Owner) & Buys Men's Shirts, Ties, Shearling Coats, Small Leather Goods, Underwear, Hosiery, Store Displays

RUN ON (SP-4)
5400 E. Mockingbird Ln., #114
Dallas, TX 75206
214-821-0909 / Fax: 214-821-1365
Sales: $1 Million-$10 Million
Website: www.runontexas.com

BOB WALLACE (Owner) & Buys Running Footwear, Apparel

SEBASTIAN'S CLOSET (MW-2)
5100 Belt Line Rd., #540 (b-des)
Dallas, TX 75254
972-387-0888 / Fax: 972-458-8762
Sales: $1 Million-$10 Million

TIM
BOB LEAMY (Owner) & Buys Men's Sportswear, Footwear, Furnishings, Accessories

STANLEY KORSHAK (DEPT)
(CRESCENT RETAIL, INC.)
500 Crescent Ct., #100 (b)
Dallas, TX 75201
214-871-3600 / Fax: 214-871-3617
Sales: $1 Million-$10 Million
Website: www.stanleykorshak.com

CRAWFORD BROCK (President)
ROSE CLARK (G.M.M.) & Buys Men's Sportswear, Furnishings, Accessories, European Fashions
RAJAN PATEL (Visual & Fashion Dir.) & Buys Store Displays, Fixtures, Supplies

SWEET MANUFACTURING, INC. (MW)
4949 Beeman Ave. (m)
Dallas, TX 75223
214-887-1260 / Fax: 214-887-1266
Sales: $1 Million-$10 Million

HAROLD SWEET (Co-Owner & President) & Buys Men's Big & Tall Apparel, Casualwear, Formalwear, Accessories, Hosiery, Outerwear, Sportswear, Suits, Swimwear, Sleepwear
CAROL KING (Co-Owner & Store Mgr.) & Buys Men's Big & Tall Apparel, Casualwear, Formalwear, Accessories, Hosiery, Outerwear, Sportswear, Suits, Swimwear, Sleepwear

TALL-E-HO MENSWEAR (MW-2)
650 Preston Forest Cir. (b)
Dallas, TX 75230
214-691-3700 / Fax: 214-691-3700
Sales: $1 Million-$10 Million

DAVID KEATON-Big & Tall Men's Overcoats, Suits, Tailored Jackets, Tailored Slacks, Raincoats, Sweaters, Sport Shirts, Outer Jackets, Casual Slacks, Leather Apparel, Active Apparel, Dress Shirts, Ties, Robes, Underwear, Hosiery, Gloves, Headwear, Belts, Small Leather Goods, Jewelry, Fragrances, Store Displays, Fixtures & Supplies

THE TIE-COON (MW)
4015 Villanova (m-b)
Dallas, TX 75225
214-369-8437 / Fax: 214-369-4949
Website: www.thetiecoon.com

MICHAEL GARZA (Mgr.) & Buys Men's Accessories, T-shirts, Ties, Small Leather Goods, Store Displays, Fixtures, Supplies

UNIK (MW)
1514 Elm St. (m-b)
Dallas, TX 75201
214-742-9829 / Fax: 214-742-9829

MARK KIM (Owner) & Buys Men's Sportswear, Furnishings, Accessories, Belts, Men's Footwear, Store Displays, Fixtures, Supplies

TEXAS - Dallas

UNION JACK CLOTHING (MW)
3920 Cedar Springs (m)
Dallas, TX 75219
214-528-9600 / Fax: 214-521-5705
Website: www.unionjackdallas.com
RICHARD LONGSTAFF (Owner) & Buys Men's Sportswear, Activewear, Swimwear, Clubwear, Belts, Underwear, Footwear, Young Men's Wear, Men's Footwear, Accessories, Furnishings, Store Displays, Fixtures, Supplies
KIM JOHNSON (Manager) & Buys Men's Sportswear, Activewear, Swimwear, Clubwear, Belts, Underwear, Footwear, Young Men's Wear, Men's Footwear, Accessories, Furnishings, Store Displays, Fixtures, Supplies

DAVID'S WESTERN STORE (WW-3)
1410 S. FM 51 (m-b)
Decatur, TX 76234
940-627-3949 / Fax: 940-627-3536
Sales: $1 Million-$10 Million
Website: www.nationalroperssupply.com
DAVID ISHAM (Owner)
KAY DAVID (Mdse. Mgr.) & Buys Men's Western Wear, Sportswear, Furnishings, Accessories, 8 to 18 Boys' Western Wear, Sportswear, Footwear, Store Displays, Fixtures, Supplies

GUARANTEE STORE (DEPT)
704 S. Main St. (p-m)
Del Rio, TX 78840
830-775-0588 / Fax: 830-775-5757
MICHAEL STOOL (President) & Buys Men's Sportswear, Furnishings, Headwear, Accessories, Boys' Wear, Students' Wear, Leather Apparel, Suede Apparel, Urban Contemporary, Store Displays, Fixtures, Supplies

KEMPER'S COWBOY SHOP (WW)
P.O. Box 221 (p)
Denison, TX 75021
903-465-1266
Sales: $500,001-$1 Million
BENNY R. KEMPER (President) & Buys Men's Western Suits, Tailored Jackets, Tailored Slacks, Gloves, Belts, Jewelry, Footwear
ROLF W. KEMPER (G.M.M.) & Buys Men's Ties, Store Displays, Fixtures, Supplies

FOSTER'S SADDLE SHOP, INC. (WW)
6409 Hwy. 35 East (m)
Denton, TX 76207
940-383-1549 / Fax: 940-591-0072
Sales: $1 Million-$10 Million
BILL FOSTER (Owner) & Buys Western Apparel
SHIRLEY PHILLIPS-Western Headwear
LISA FOSTER-Men's, Boys' & Young Men's Western Wear, Leather Apparel, Accessories, Furnishings, Footwear, Store Displays, Fixtures and Supplies
MARK FOSTER-Men's, Boys' & Young Men's Boots, Western Headwear

J.T. CLOTHIERS (MW)
2430 I 35 East
Denton, TX 76205
940-387-0761 / Fax: 940-387-5041
Sales: $500,001-$1 Million
JAMES TRITT (Owner) & Buys Men's Wear, Sportswear, Sport Shirts, Activewear, Furnishings, Accessories, Footwear

RUSSELL'S (DEPT)
(Div. of DUNLAPS)
908 W. University (m-b)
Denton, TX 76201
940-387-6121 / Fax: 940-387-6124
Sales: $1 Million-$10 Million
Website: www.dunlaps.com
CATHY FAULKNER (Mgr.) & Buys Tailored Jackets, Tailored Slacks, Sweaters, Sport Shirts, Outer Jackets, Casual Slacks, Active Apparel, Furnishings, Accessories, Leather Apparel, Footwear, Young Men's & Boys' Wear

NOTE:-Store Displays, Fixtures, Supplies Bought at DUNLAPS, Ft. Worth, TX.

WELDON SADDLE SHOP (WW)
345 E. Hickory (m)
Denton, TX 76201
940-382-1921 / Fax: 940-387-1643
Website: www.weldonswestern.com
KIPPIE WICKINSON-Men's & Boys' Western Wear, Related Accessories, Furnishings, Headwear, Footwear, Boots, Store Displays, Fixtures, Supplies
DANA BURR-Men's & Boys' Western Wear, Related Accessories, Furnishings, Headwear, Footwear, Boots, Store Displays, Fixtures, Supplies

DARDEN-SPARKS DEPARTMENT STORE (MW)
P.O. Box 120 (p-m)
205 Main St.
Deport, TX 75435
903-652-4515
DAWNE DARDEN (Co-Owner) & Buys Men's Sportswear, Furnishings, Accessories, Footwear, Store Displays, Fixtures, Supplies
JUANITA SPARKS (Co-Owner)

HARMAN'S DEPARTMENT STORE (DEPT)
100 S. Broadway (p-m)
Dimmit, TX 79027
806-647-4638 / Fax: 806-647-4638
BILL HARMAN (Owner) & Buys Men's Suits, Tailored Jackets, Tailored Slacks, Coats, Sportswear, Denim Apparel, Furnishings, Small Leather Goods, Formal Wear, Footwear, Headwear, Young Men's & Boys' Wear, Store Displays, Fixtures, Supplies

ALDRICH'S, INC. (MW)
608 Dumas Ave. (m)
Dumas, TX 79029
806-935-5616 / Fax: 806-934-1656
Sales: $500,001-$1 Million
SAM ALDRICH (Owner) & Buys Men's Sportswear, Furnishings, Accessories, Store Displays, Fixtures, Supplies

ABASCAL'S WESTERN WEAR (WW-2)
(LA CASA BLANCA, INC.)
P.O. Box 929 (m)
2125 Garrison
Eagle Pass, TX 78852
830-773-8697 / Fax: 830-773-3343
Sales: $500,001-$1 Million
AMADU ABASCAL, JR. (President) & Buys Men's Suits, Tailored Jackets, Overcoats, Men's Sport Shirts, Outer Jackets, Casual Slacks, Leather Apparel, Dress Shirts, Belts, Footwear, Store Displays, Fixtures, Supplies

DON LUIS MENSWEAR (MW)
330 Main St. (m)
Eagle Pass, TX 78852
830-773-9119
LUIS VIELMA (Owner) & Buys Men's Wear, Leather Apparel, Accessories, Furnishings, Footwear, Urban Contemporary, Store Displays, Fixtures, Supplies

RISKIND'S (DEPT)
364 Main St. (m-b)
Eagle Pass, TX 78852
(Henry Doneger)
830-773-2373 / Fax: 830-773-2560
Sales: $1 Million-$10 Million
DAN RISKIND (President & G.M.M.) & Buys Boys' Wear, Accessories, Furnishings, Store Displays, Fixtures, Supplies

GREER'S WESTERN (WW)
(J.B. GREER CORP.)
1414 E. Main St. (p)
Eastland, TX 76448
254-629-3989 / Fax: 915-532-4099
Sales: $1 Million-$10 Million
JERRY GREER (Owner) & Buys Men's, Young Men's & Boys' Western Wear, Boots, Leather Apparel, Related Accessories, Furnishings, Store Displays, Fixtures, Supplies

AMPY'S WESTERN STORE, INC. (WW)
214 E. San Antonio (p)
El Paso, TX 79901
915-542-0788 / Fax: 915-532-4099
Sales: $1 Million-$10 Million
SARAH MARQUEZ (Owner) & Buys Men's & Boys' Western Apparel, Furnishings, Accessories, Store Displays, Fixtures, Supplies

TEXAS - El Paso

BARGAIN SHOP (MW)

204 E. San Antonio Ave. (p-m)
El Paso, TX 79901
915-532-7411

MAY DAYOUB (Owner) & Buys Men's Sportswear, Furnishings, Accessories, Footwear, Store Displays, Fixtures & Supplies

BAZAAR UNIFORMS & MEN'S STORE (CLO)

304 E. Overland (p-m)
El Paso, TX 79901
915-544-7340 / Fax: 915-544-7341

CHRISTOPHER JOSEPH (Owner) & Buys Men's Wear, Sportswear, Accessories, Furnishings, Uniforms, Footwear, Store Displays, Fixtures, Supplies

BERKO, INC. (DEPT)

(EL ENCANTO)
310 S. El Paso St. (p-m-b)
El Paso, TX 79901
915-533-7186 / Fax: 915-544-0534
Sales: $1 Million-$10 Million

MICHIE ESQUENAZI (Co-Owner) & Buys Men's Overcoats, Suits, Raincoats, Big & Tall, Sportswear, Furnishings, Belts, Jewelry, Footwear, Young Men's Wear, Boys' Wear, Baptismal Clothing, School Uniforms, Outerwear, Store Displays, Fixtures, Supplies

HENRY ESQUENAZI (Co-Owner) & Buys Men's Overcoats, Suits, Raincoats, Big & Tall, Sportswear, Furnishings, Belts, Jewelry, Footwear, Young Men's Wear, Boys' Wear, Baptismal Clothing, School Uniforms, Outerwear, Store Displays, Fixtures, Supplies

COWTOWN BOOT COMPANY (WW-12 & OL)

11401 Gateway Blvd. West
El Paso, TX 79936
915-593-2929 / Fax: 915-593-2249
Sales: $1 Million-$10 Million
Website: www.cowtownboots.com
Retail Locations: TX, AZ, NV, NM

JOE CALCATERRA (Owner) & Buys Men's & Boys' Western Wear, Related Accessories, Furnishings, Footwear, Boots, Store Dispalys

EL RANCHO ALTO (WW)

(A & S SALES CO.)
114 S. Mesa (p-m)
El Paso, TX 79901
915-544-3545

WAFA SALAMEH (Owner) & Buys Store Displays, Fixtures, Supplies

ALI SALAMEH (Mgr.) & Buys Men's Wear, Western Wear, Jeans, Sportswear, Accessories, Furnishings

ERENE (FW)

417 S. Oregon (bud-p)
El Paso, TX 79901
915-532-3575 / Fax: 915-532-3672
Sales: $1 Million-$10 Million

JOE LEWIS RODRIGUEZ (Owner) & Buys Men's Footwear, Boys' Footwear, Store Displays, Fixtures, Supplies

FASHION CORNER (MW)

321 E. San Antonio (m-b)
El Paso, TX 79901
915-533-0878

TONY DAYOUB (Owner) & Buys Men's Sportswear, Furnishings, Accessories, Young Men's Wear, Store Displays, Fixtures, Supplies

HOLLAND DEPT. STORE (DEPT-2)

402 S. El Paso St. (bud-p-m)
El Paso, TX 79901
915-532-2274 / Fax: 915-544-4228
Sales: $1 Million-$10 Million

SAL HOLLAND (Owner) & Buys Men's Sportswear, Dress Shirts, Underwear, Gloves, Headwear, Young Men's & Boys' Wear, Store Displays, Fixtures, Supplies

JAMES HOLLAND (V.P.) & Buys Men's Sportswear, Dress Shirts, Underwear, Gloves, Headwear, Young Men's & Boys' Wear, Store Displays, Fixtures, Supplies

ROCKS T-SHIRTS (CLO)

4005 Leavell
El Paso, TX 79904
915-562-4798 / Fax: 915-566-0387

BOB SIMPSON (Owner) (@ 915-566-2889)

PAM HIETZ-Men's T-shirts, Active Apparel, Store Displays, Fixtures, Supplies

SEVILLE FASHIONS, INC. (MW & CLO)

(GRANDADDY BLUES)
210 E. San Antonio (m)
El Paso, TX 79901
915-542-0827 / Fax: 915-533-0949
Sales: $1 Million-$10 Million

JOHN DAVID ABOUD (President) & Buys Men's Sportswear, Furnishings, Headwear, Accessories, Leather Apparel, Footwear, Work Boots, Store Displays, Fixtures, Supplies

TEXAS STORE (CLO-7)

(Div. of RICHARD ROSEN, INC.)
210 S. Mesa (bud-p-m)
El Paso, TX 79901
915-533-7923 / Fax: 915-533-5160
Sales: $10 Million-$50 Million

RICHARD J. ROSEN (President) & Buys Men's Wear

MARK ROSEN (V.P.) & Buys Men's Suits, Sport Shirts, Casual Slacks, Furnishings, Headwear, Boys' Wear, Men's Overcoats, Sweaters, Belts, Tailored Slacks, Jeans, Small Leather Goods, Young Men's Wear, Leather Apparel, Footwear, Store Displays, Fixtures, Supplies

UNION-FASHION CLOTHING CO., INC. (CLO)

1 Union Fashion Ctr. (b)
El Paso, TX 79901
915-532-8282 / Fax: 915-533-6022
Sales: $10 Million-$50 Million

ENOCH KIMMELMAN (Owner) & Buys Men's Sportswear, Headwear, Clothing, Furnishings, Accessories, Store Displays

NOTE-Footwear is a Leased Department.

VIRTUAL RAGS.COM (CLO & OL)

11394 James Watt Dr., #511 (bud-p-m-b-des)
El Paso, TX 79936
915-592-3972 / Fax: 915-595-2017
Sales: $1 Million-$10 Million
Website: www.virtualrags.com

RICHARD KOON (Owner) & Buys Men's Sweaters, Sport Shirts, Outer Jackets, Casual Slacks, Active Apparel, Boys' Sportswear, Store Displays, Fixtures, Supplies

DILDY'S (WW)

Hwy. 290 (m)
Elgin, TX 78621
512-285-4337

LEE DILDY (Owner) & Buys Men's Western Wear, Big & Tall Men's Wear, Western Boots, Related Accessories, Furnishings, Store Displays, Fixtures, Supplies

JACK POFF MEN'S & BOYS' WEAR (MW)

116 W. Knox (m-b)
Ennis, TX 75119
972-875-7521

MAUREEN POFF (Owner) & Buys Store Displays

JACK POFF (Mgr.) & Buys Men's Sportswear, Furnishings, Accessories, Men's Footwear

INTERNATIONAL MANUFACTURING GROUP (FW)

(THE BOOTJACK)
1201 W. Park St.
Farr, TX 78502
956-783-1183 / Fax: 956-783-5734

GEORGE MASSO (President)

THOMAS REAM-Western Boots, Store Displays, Fixtures, Supplies

L & M RANCH WEAR (WW-2)

205 E. Main St. (m)
Florence, TX 76527
254-793-2388

BERNARD MILLER (Owner) & Buys Men's Underwear, Hosiery, Men's & Boys' Jeans, Western Shirts, Accessories, Big & Tall Men's Jeans, Western Shirts, Footwear, Store Displays, Fixtures, Supplies

TEXAS - Fort Worth

ARMY-NAVY STORE (AN-5)

514 N. Beach St. (m)
Fort Worth, TX 76111
817-838-3090 / Fax: 817-838-7409
Sales: $1 Million-$10 Million
Website: www.evensoutfitter.com

JIM EVANS (Owner) & Buys Men's Sportswear, Work Clothes, Accessories, Furnishings, Footwear, Store Displays, Fixtures, Supplies

DAVID'S KING-SIZE CLOTHES, INC. (MW)

6730 Camp Bowie (m)
Fort Worth, TX 76116
817-731-3691

KAY LYNN DUVINSKI (Owner) & Buys Boots, Related Accessories, Furnishings, Store Displays

MICHELE ALLARD (G.M.M.) & Buys Big & Tall Men's Wear, Store Displays, Fixtures, Supplies

DILLARD'S DEPARTMENT STORES, INC. - FORT WORTH DIV. (DEPT-59 & OL & MO)

4501 N. Beach St. (m-b)
Fort Worth, TX 76137
817-831-5111 / Fax: 817-831-5114
Website: www.dillards.com
Retail Locations: TX

DRUE CORBUSIER (President)

TONY MENZIE (G.M.M.)

WEST CHERRY (V.P.-Real Estate) (@ 501-376-5567)

JOHN TITTLE (D.M.M.-Men's Sportswear, Furnishings & Access.) & Buys Men's Knit Shirts, Sport Shirts, Murano

JOAN HOUX-Men's Underwear, Socks, Pajamas, Robes

LUCY HUGHES-Men's Underwear, Socks, Pajamas, Robes

JAMIE SCHERER-Men's Accessories, Belts, Small Leather Goods

LYNN GIBSON-Men's Tommy Hilfiger, Men's Coordinates, Big & Tall Men's Sportswear & Furnishings

ROBERT BAUHOFFER-Men's Shorts, Casual Slacks, Active Sportswear, Swimwear, Sweaters, Outerwear, Leather Apparel, Outdoor Apparel

KRISTIE SHAW-Men's Perry Ellis, Claiborne For Men, Advance Sportswear

LINDA WRIGHT-Men's Polo, Daniel Cremieux, Nautica

SUSAN RINDERKNECHT-Men's Denim Apparel, Denim Shorts, Levis, Tommy Jeans, Polo Denim, Guess, Nautica Denim

CATHY BUCHANAN (D.M.M.-Men's Fragrances)

VAL OFFILL-Men's Fragrances

NANETTE ARGABRITE (D.M.M.-Footwear)

CANDY WILHITE-Boys' Footwear

LAURA WYNN-Men's Footwear

KAREN MORENO (D.M.M.)

VAL OFFILL-Moderate 8 to 20 Boys' Outerwear, Sweaters, Accessories, 8 to 20 Boys' Dresswear

MIKE FOOTE-Better 8 to 20 Boys' Wear, 3 to 7 Boys' Sportswear, Boys' Swimwear

DON FUNICELLA (Visual Dir.) & Buys Store Displays, Fixtures, Supplies

NOTE:-For Buyers of Men's Tailored Clothing, Dress Shirts, Gloves & Ties, See Our Listing For Dillard's in Little Rock, AR.

DUNLAP CO. (DEPT-56)

200 Bailey Ave. (m)
Fort Worth, TX 76107
817-336-4985 / Fax: 817-347-0245
Sales: $100 Million-$500 Million
Website: www.dunlaps.com
Retail Locations: AL, AZ, AK, CO, KS, LA, MI, ME, NM, OK, TX, VA

REGINAL MARTIN (Chmn.)

EDWARD MARTIN (President)

CURTIS WHEAT (Dir.-Planning & Construction) & Buys Store Displays, Fixtures

RUSSELL MARTIN (Real Estate Contact) (@ 817-347-0217)

CHRIS RIFLER (Mdse. Mgr.) & Buys Promotional Men's, Young Men's & Boys' Wear

KIM LUCE-Men's Footwear

FAME MENSWEAR (MW-2)

4200 S. Fwy., #23 (m-b)
Fort Worth, TX 76115
817-921-5198 / Fax: 817-921-5198

ABDULLAH AZIZ (Co-Owner) & Buys Men's & Boys' Wear, Furnishings, Accessories, Footwear, Store Displays, Fixtures, Supplies

ABDEL AZIZ (Co-Owner) & Buys Men's & Boys' Wear, Furnishings, Accessories, Footwear, Store Displays, Fixtures, Supplies

FAST FORWARD (MW-20)

(ACTION CONCEPTS, INC.)
7503 Flagstone, #30 (p-m-b)
Fort Worth, TX 76118
817-589-1346 / Fax: 817-589-9449
Website: www.fastforward.com

JERRY ANDERSON (Co-Owner) & Buys Young Men's Active Apparel, T-shirts, Swimwear, Athletic Footwear, Store Displays, Fixtures, Supplies

BRANDON BATTON (Co-Owner)

MICHAEL BEEDLE-Young Men's Activewear, T-shirts, Swimwear, Urban Contemporary, Athletic Footwear

FINCHER'S WESTERN STORES, INC. (WW)

115 E. Exchange (p)
Fort Worth, TX 76106
817-624-7302 / Fax: 817-624-1992
Sales: $500,001-$1 Million
Website: www.fincherswhitefront.com

HOYT T. FINCHER, JR. (Owner) & Buys Men's Western Wear, Related Accessories

TEXAS - Fort Worth

JOHN L. ASHE, INC. (MW)

1540 S. University Dr., #105 (b-des)
Fort Worth, TX 76107
817-335-4551 / Fax: 817-335-4554
Sales: $1 Million-$10 Million

STEVE BRATTELI (Chmn. & G.M.M.) & Buys Men's Overcoats, Suits, Tailored Jackets, Tailored Slacks, Raincoats, Sweaters, Sport Shirts, Outer Jackets, Casual Slacks, Active Apparel, Furnishings, Headwear, Accessories, Leather Apparel, Suede Apparel, Footwear

M.L. LEDDY'S BOOT & SADDLERY (CLO-3)

2455 N. Main St. (m-b)
Fort Worth, TX 76106
817-624-3149 / Fax: 817-625-2725
Sales: $1 Million-$10 Million
Website: www.leddys.com

WILSON FRANKLIN (President) & Buys Men's Western Wear, Furnishings, Headwear, Accessories, Leather Apparel, Boots, Store Displays, Fixtures, Supplies

MARK DUNLAP (V.P.) & Buys Men's Western Wear, Resort Wear, Furnishings, Headwear, Accessories, Leather Apparel, Boots, Store Displays, Fixtures, Supplies

STRIPLING & COX (DEPT-4)

(Div. of DUNLAP CO.)
200 Bailey (m-b)
Fort Worth, TX 76107
817-336-4985 / Fax: 817-347-6245
Sales: $10 Million-$50 Million
Website: www.dunlaps.com

ED MARTIN (President)

REG MARTIN (V.P.)

CHRIS RIEFLER-Men's Sportswear, Furnishings & Accessories, Young Men's Wear, 8 to 20 Boys' Wear

ANGELA MURRELL (@ 817-336-4985)-Fragrances

KIM LUCE-Men's Footwear

NOTE-Store Displays, Fixtures & Supplies Bought at DUNLAP CO., Ft. Worth, TX.

WIMBERLY ARMY STORE, INC. (AN)

2466 E. Lancaster (p-m)
Fort Worth, TX 76103
817-531-1641
Sales: $500,001-$1 Million

DAVID WIMBERLY (Owner) & Buys Men's Government Issue Clothing, Footwear, Jeans, Boys' Camouflage Apparel, Store Displays, Fixtures, Supplies

ELLISON WESTERN WEAR (WW)

P.O. Box 434 (m)
Franklin, TX 77856
979-828-3380 / Fax: 979-828-3110

CHARLES ELLISON (Owner) & Buys Men's Western Sportswear, Work Clothes, Outerwear, Furnishings, Cowboy Boots, Boys' Wear, Store Displays, Fixtures, Supplies

KNOPP & METZGER DRY GOODS, INC. (DG)

261 W. Main St. (m)
Fredericksburg, TX 78624
830-997-2251 / Fax: 830-997-4027

JAMES METZGER (President)

JOHN METZGER (Mdse. Mgr.) & Buys Men's Sportswear, Furnishings, Headwear, Accessories, Footwear, Boys' & Students' Wear, Store Displays, Fixtures, Supplies

INGRAM'S (CLO)

705 Main St. (m)
Friona, TX 79035
806-250-3291 / Fax: 806-250-5191
Sales: $500,001-$1 Million

SYLVIA INGRAM (Owner) & Buys Men's & Boys' Wear, Sportswear, Accessories, Furnishings, Store Displays, Fixtures, Supplies

COL. BUBBIE'S (AN)

(STRAND SURPLUS SENTER)
(KKM, INC.)
2202 Strand (p-m)
Galveston, TX 77550
409-762-7397 / Fax: 409-762-7396
Website: www.colbubbie.com

MEYER REISWERG (Owner) & Buys Men's Army Surplus, Boys' Wear, Men's Footwear, Camouflage, Store Displays, Fixtures, Supplies

L.S. MORRISON & CO. (DEPT)

(MORRISON DEPARTMENT STORE)
118 Houston St. (m-b)
George West, TX 78022
361-449-1511

ROSS BROWN (Owner) & Buys Men's & Boys' Workclothes, T-shirts, Golf Apparel, Shirts, Hosiery, Sport Shirts, Small Leather Goods, Store Displays, Fixtures, Supplies

GOLD'S DEPARTMENT STORE (DEPT)

109 W. 7th St. (p-m-b)
Georgetown, TX 78626
512-930-5171 / Fax: 512-863-8319
Sales: $500,000-$1 Million

MORTON GOLD (Co-Owner) & Buys Men's Overcoats, Suits, Tailored Jackets, Tailored Slacks, Raincoats, Sportswear, Sweaters, Sport Shirts, Outer Jackets, Casual Slacks, Active Apparel, Furnishings, Headwear, Accessories, Footwear, Young Men's & Boys' Wear, Western Wear, Boots, Store Disp

IRWIN GOLD (Co-Owner) & Buys Men's Overcoats, Suits, Tailored Jackets, Tailored Slacks, Raincoats, Sportswear, Sweaters, Sport Shirts, Outer Jackets, Casual Slacks, Active Apparel, Furnishings, Headwear, Accessories, Footwear, Young Men's & Boys' Wear, Western Wear, Boots

PRATHOS STORE, INC. (CLO)

153 E. Austin (p)
Giddings, TX 78942
979-542-3259 / Fax: 979-542-5140

BETTY PRATHOS (Owner)

WILLIAM GLAISER-Men's & Boys' Clothing, Sportswear, Furnishings, Headwear, Accessories, Footwear, Store Displays, Fixtures, Supplies

THE BEACHCOMBER (SP)

1406 Park Rd., #36
Graford, TX 76449
940-779-2938 / Fax: 940-779-3087

PEGGIE PERRYMAN (Owner) & Buys Boys' Apparel & Swimwear, Sunglasses, Footwear, Hats, Men's Apparel, Men's Surf & Swimwear, Resortwear, T-shirts

BOAZ DEPARTMENT STORE (DEPT)

P.O. Box 269 (p-m)
507 Elm St.
Graham, TX 76450
940-549-1150
Sales: $500,001-$1 Million

PETE SHABAY (President & Owner)

NEIL OLIVER (Mgr.) & Buys Men's Suits, Tailored Jackets, Tailored Slacks, Big & Tall Men's Wear, Sweaters, Sport Shirts, Outer Jackets, Casual Slacks, Active Apparel, Furnishings, Accessories, Boys' Wear, Men's Footwear, Store Displays, Fixtures, Supplies

ACTON MEN'S SHOP (MW)

3220 Fall Creek Hwy. (m)
Granbury, TX 76049
817-326-2225

LEE BERGEMAN (Owner) & Buys Men's Sportswear, Furnishings, Accessories, Store Displays, Fixtures, Supplies

NEW YORK STORE (WW)

P.O. Box 325 (p-m)
308 E. Galbraith
Hebronville, TX 78361
361-527-3412 / Fax: 361-527-3037
Sales: $500,001-$1 Million

MARGARITA ELLISON-Men's & Boys' Western Wear, Urban Contemporary, Related Accessories, Furnishings, Western Boots, Store Displays, Fixtures & Supplies

SCHWARZ DEPARTMENT STORE, INC. (DEPT)

P.O. Box 535 (m)
641 10th St.
Hempstead, TX 77445
979-826-2466 / Fax: 979-826-6675
Sales: $500,001-$1 Million

HARRY D. SCHWARZ, III (President)
MARY YBARRA (Asst. Mgr.) & Buys Men's Wear, Accessories, Sportswear, Furnishings, Young Men's Wear, Boys' Clothing, Men's Footwear, Store Displays, Fixtures, Supplies

SALMON-ROSS DEPARTMENT STORE (WW)

114 Pecan St. (p)
Hico, TX 76457
254-796-4424

GLEN ROSS (Co-Owner) & Buys Men's Western Wear, Sportswear, Furnishings, Small Leather Goods, Young Men's & Boys' Wear, Footwear
MRS. PAT ROSS (Co-Owner) & Buys Store Displays, Fixtures, Supplies

GEORGE'S CASUAL & WESTERN WEAR (WW & CLO)

56 W. Elm St. (b)
Hillsboro, TX 76645
254-582-8618
Sales: $10 Million-$50 Million

JEAN FARQUHAR (Co-Owner) & Buys Men's Sportswear, Furnishings, Accessories, Boys' Wear
GEORGE FARQUHAR (Co-Owner) & Buys Men's Sportswear, Furnishings, Accessories, Boys' Wear, Western Clothing, Related Accessories, Boots

ACTIVE ATHLETE (SP-2)

9428 Cullen Blvd., #A
Houston, TX 77051
713-738-7860 / Fax: 713-738-1110
Sales: $2 Million-$5 Million

DANNY VISHNU (Co-Owner) & Buys Activewear, Athletic Footwear, Athletic Apparel, Licensed Apparel
PAUL VISHNU (Co-Owner) & Buys Activewear, Athletic Footwear, Athletic Apparel, Licensed Apparel

AL'S FORMAL WEAR (CLO-150)

7807 Main St.
Houston, TX 77030
713-791-1888 / Fax: 713-791-1692
Sales: $10 Million-$50 Million
Website: www.alsformalwear.com
Retail Locations: LA, NM, OK, TX

ALAN GAYLOR (Owner) & Buys Store Displays, Fixtures, Supplies
MELINDA GORDON-Men's & Boys' Formal Wear, Footwear, Related Accessories, Furnishings, Store Displays, Fixtures, Supplies
ELIS RUSHEFSKY (Real Estate Contact)

BILL WALKER CLOTHIER LTD. (CLO)

1141 Uptown Park Blvd., #1 (m)
Houston, TX 77056
713-871-9811 / Fax: 713-871-9449

BILL WALKER (Owner) & Buys Store Displays, Fixtures, Supplies, Men's Wear, Sportswear, Furnishings, Accessories
SHELLEY WALKER-Men's Wear, Sportswear, Furnishings, Accessories

BUCK'S THE BIG MAN'S STORES (MW)

5900 N. Freeway (p)
Houston, TX 77076
713-691-6713 / Fax: 713-691-0224
Sales: $500,001-$1 Million

MELVIN BUCK (Owner) & Buys Big & Tall Men's Suits, Sportswear, Dress Shirts, Ties, Robes, Underwear, Hosiery, Belts, Footwear, Store Displays, Fixtures, Supplies

THE CHILDREN'S COLLECTION (KS-2)

1717 Post Oak Blvd. (m-b)
Houston, TX 77056
713-622-4350 / Fax: 713-622-4523

VICKI BERNSTEIN (V.P. & Dir.-Stores) & Buys Store Displays, Fixtures, Supplies
REBECCA CHAPMAN-8 to 20 Boys' Clothing, Sportswear, Furnishings, Accessories
KRISTI VARNDELL-Boys' Footwear

FOLEY'S (DEPT-70)

(MAY DEPARTMENT STORES)
1110 Main St. (m-b)
Houston, TX 77002
(May Merchandising Corp.)
713-405-7033 / Fax: 713-405-7069
Sales: Over $1 Billion
Website: www.foleys.com
Retail Locations: CO, LA, NM, OK, TX

ANDREW PICKMAN (President & C.E.O.)
JON GUNNERSON (Sr. V.P. & G.M.M.-Men's)
BOB BETHA (Real Estate Contact)
LOU CAPORALE (D.M.M.-Men's Clothing, Furnishings, Accessories)
SARAH VIERVILLE-Better Clothing, Sport Coats, Tailored Slacks
APRIL DERICK-Dress Shirts
CHRISTI WIATREK-Men's Sleepwear, Robes, Underwear, Hosiery
JAMES CARCASI-Men's Neckwear
CLIFF COOPER-Men's Gloves, Headwear, Accessories
DOUG TIFFAN-Suits, Top Coats, Raincoats

TAFFY BEASLEY (D.M.M.-Men's Sportswear)
SCOTT FRANCIA-Men's Knitwear, Izod, Wovens, Guess, Calvin Klein, Outerwear, Leather
JASON DALRY-Men's Activewear, Swimwear
TIM KNOTT-Men's Polo, Claiborne for Men, Nautica
LACY GRANATO-Men's Sport Shirts
CLARK REYNOLDS-Tommy Hilfiger, Jones New York

BLAKE GARNER (D.M.M.-Young Men's) & Buys Young Men's Denim
JAMES STARKE-8 to 20 Boys' Tops, Collections
PATTY CHUBON-8 to 20 Boys' Bottoms, Accessories
ANTHONY WESTROP-Young Men's Knits

DREW REICH (G.M.M.-Cosmetics)
CHRISTINA O'FARRELL-Men's Fragrances

BARBARA HORNE (D.M.M.)
ROBERT CLARK-Men's Shoes
STACY LINDSEY-Boys' Shoes

STEVE VIESER (V.P.-Visual Mdse. Presentations)
BEN RUEHL-Store Fixtures, Supplies

TEXAS - Houston

GEORGIO'S (MW-3)
213 Sharpstown Ctr.
Houston, TX 77036
713-772-9076 / Fax: 713-772-0210
EDDIE SROUR (Owner) & Buys Men's Sportswear, Furnishings, Accessories, Footwear, Urban Contemporary, Store Displays, Fixtures, Supplies

GEOVANNI'S BIG & TALL (MW)
127 Sharpstown Ctr.
Houston, TX 77036
713-771-6988
FRED ELFAADI (Owner) & Buys Men's Big & Tall Wear, Accessories, Furnishings, Footwear

GORDON'S MAN'S STORE (MW)
518 Broadway (m-b)
Houston, TX 77012
713-926-5018 / Fax: 713-926-2181
DAVE DONAHOE (Owner) & Buys Men's Furnishings, Work Clothes, Western Wear, Boys' Western Apparel, Men's & Boys' Western Boots, Footwear, Store Displays, Fixtures, Supplies

HAMILTON SHIRT CO., INC. (CLO)
P.O. Box 37113 (m-b-h)
Houston, TX 77237
713-780-8222 / Fax: 713-780-8224
Sales: $1 Million-$10 Million
JIM HAMILTON (Owner) & Buys Men's Ties, Shirts, Hosiery, Belts, Store Displays, Fixtures, Supplies

HAROLD'S IN THE HEIGHTS (CLO)
350 W. 19th St. (m-b-h)
Houston, TX 77008
713-864-2647 / Fax: 713-864-9830
Sales: $1 Million-$10 Million
Website: www.haroldsintheheights.com
HAROLD WIESENTHAL (Co-Owner)
DARRYL WIESENTHAL (Co-Owner) & Buys Men's Suits, Sportswear, Leather Apparel, Furnishings, Accessories, Big & Tall Men's & Boys' Wear, Store Displays, Fixtures, Supplies
MICHAEL WIESENTHAL (Co-Owner) & Buys Men's Suits, Sportswear, Leather Apparel, Furnishings, Accessories, Big & Tall Men's & Boys' Wear, Store Displays, Fixtures, Supplies
JIM PIERCE-Men's Footwear

KAPLAN'S BEN HUR (DEPT)
P.O. Box 7989 (m-b)
2125 Yale St.
Houston, TX 77270
713-861-2121 / Fax: 713-861-2967
Sales: $500,000-$1 Million
Website: www.kaplansbenhur.com
MARTIN KAPLAN (President)
DALE GRASSMAN-Men's Sweaters, Sport Shirts, Casual Slacks, Dress Shirts, Ties, Robes, Underwear, Belts, Jewelry, Store Displays, Fixtures, Supplies
MIKE BRASWELL-Men's Sweaters, Sport Shirts, Casual Slacks, Dress Shirts, Ties, Robes, Underwear, Belts, Jewelry, Store Displays, Fixtures, Supplies

LUCHO, INC. (MW)
1121 Uptown Park Blvd. (des)
Houston, TX 77056
713-961-3577 / Fax: 713-961-0971
Sales: $1 Million-$10 Million
PATRICIA STURION (Gen. Mgr.)
L. LUCHO-Leather Goods, Men's Casualwear, Formalwear, Hosiery, Outerwear, Sportswear, Suits, Accessories

M. PENNER FOR MEN (MW)
2950 Kirby Dr.
Houston, TX 77098
713-527-8200 / Fax: 713-527-9648
Sales: $1 Million-$10 Million
Website: www.mpenner.com
MURRY PENNER (President) & Buys Leather Goods, Men's Big & Tall Apparel, Casualwear, Denim Apparel, Formalwear, Accessories, Hosiery, Outerwear, Sportswear, Suits, Swimwear
MORRIS PENNER (G.M.M.) & Buys Leather Goods, Men's Big & Tall Apparel, Casualwear, Denim Apparel, Formalwear, Accessories, Hosiery, Outerwear, Sportswear, Suits, Swimwear

MANNY SIMON'S MENSWEAR (MW)
6635 Harrisburg Blvd. (m)
Houston, TX 77011
713-926-7809
Sales: $100,001-$500,000
HARRY SIMON (Owner) & Buys Men's Tailored Slacks, Sport Shirts, Outer Jackets, Casual Slacks, Dress Shirts, Ties, Underwear, Belts, Small Leather Goods, Men's Footwear, Big & Tall Men's Wear, Store Displays, Fixtures, Supplies

THE MEN'S WEARHOUSE (MW-475)
(K&G MEN'S CENTER)
(MOORES)
(SUIT MAX)
5803 Glenmont (p-m-b)
Houston, TX 77081
713-295-7200 / Fax: 713-664-7140
Sales: $900 Million
Website: www.menswearhouse.com
Retail Locations: TX, WA, OR, GA, MI, NY, CA
GEORGE ZIMMER (Founder & C.E.O.)
ERIC LANE (President)
RICHARD GOLDMAN (Exec. V.P.)
ROBERT E. ZIMMER (Sr. V.P.)
TOM JENNINGS (V.P.)
SCOTT NORRIS (D.M.M.)
JIM ZIMMER (Sr. V.P.) & Buys Men's Suits, Tailored Jackets, Big & Tall Men's Wear
ED STEINER-Men's Dress Shirts
TONY FINOCHIARO-Men's Sweaters, Sport Shirts
STEVE DONALDSON-Men's Casual Slacks, Tailored Slacks
SCOTT NORRIS-Men's Ties, Overcoats, Raincoats, Leather Jackets, Hosiery, Jewelry, Gloves, Belts, Small Leather Goods
MIKE BATLIN-Men's Footwear, Gloves, Belts, Small Goods
STEVE ROTHCHILD (Dir.-Real Estate)

MR. Z. (MW)
9660 Hillcroft St. (m-b)
Houston, TX 77096
713-661-2383
Sales: $1 Million-$10 Million
JOEL ZIMMERMAN (President) & Buys Men's Overcoats, Suits, Tailored Jackets, Tailored Slacks, Sweaters, Sport Shirts, Leather Apparel, Casual Slacks, Sportswear, Furnishings, Dress Shirts, Robes, Underwear, Ties, Hosiery, Big & Tall Men's Wear, Young Men's & Boys' Wear, Accessories, Footwear

NORTON DITTO (MW)

(HIGHLAND VILLAGE)
4060 Westhiemer Blvd. (b-h)
Houston, TX 77027
713-688-9800 / Fax: 713-621-3875
Sales: $10 Million-$50 Million
Website: www.nortonditto.com

DICK HITE (President)
PHIL DITTO (V.P. & G.M.M.) & Buys Men's Formalwear, Overcoats, Suits, Tailored Jackets, Tailored Slacks, Raincoats, Sport Shirts, Outer Jackets, Casual Slacks, Active Apparel, Accessories
ROGER McMAHAN (Mgr.)
LARRY ADAMS (Visual Mdsr.) & Buys Store Displays, Fixtures, Supplies
GINA LEIKER-Men's Furnishings, Sportswear, Leather Apparel

NOTE-Footwear Is a Leased Department.

OSHMAN'S (SG-80 & OL)

(Div. of GART SPORTS)
2302 Maxwell Ln.
Houston, TX 77023
713-928-3171 / Fax: 713-967-8228
Sales: $100 Million-$500 Million
Website: www.oshmans.com
Retail Locations: AZ, CA, FL, KS, LA, MI, NM, OK, SC, TN, TX

ALVIN LUBETKIN (President & C.E.O.)
BRUCE AIRSMAN (V.P.-Apparel Mdsg.)
KERRY DIVINE (Dir.-Creative Svces. & Visual Mdsg.) & Buys Store Displays, Fixtures, Supplies
BETTY BROADFOOT-Men's Sport Shirts, Sweaters, Casual Slacks, Shorts, Swimwear, T-shirts, Jeans, Tank Tops, Outerwear, Golf Apparel, Apparel, Big & Tall Men's Wear
CLINT PIERCE-Men's Logo & Fleece, 8 to 20 Boys' Wear, Men's Fitness, Running & Cycling Wear
KATHY METCALFE-Men's Ski Wear, Boys' Apparel, Ski Boots, Urban Contemporary, 8 to 20 Boys Wear
MICHAEL McGUINN (Sr. V.P.-Footwear) & Buys Men's Footwear, Hiking Boots, Sneakers, Training Shoes
BOBBY RAMMER-Men's Outdoor & Casual Footwear, Men's & Boys' Hosiery

PALACE BOOT SHOP, INC. (WW)

1212 Prairie Ave. (m)
Houston, TX 77002
713-224-1411 / Fax: 713-224-7919

LAKIS XYDIS (Partner) & Buys Men's & Boys' Western Apparel, Related Furnishings, Headwear, Accessories, Dress Shoes, Casual Shoes, Boots, Moccasins, Store Displays, Fixtures, Supplies
STEVE XYDIS (Partner) & Buys Men's & Boys' Western Apparel, Related Furnishings, Headwear, Accessories, Dress Shoes, Casual Shoes, Boots, Moccasins, Store Displays, Fixtures, Supplies

RODOLFO FESTARI FOR MEN, INC. (MW)

1712 Post Oak Blvd. (m-b-h)
Houston, TX 77056
713-626-1234 / Fax: 713-993-0984
Sales: $1 Million-$10 Million

RODOLFO FESTARI (Owner) & Buys Men's Italian Furnishings, Sportswear, Accessories, Men's Leather Dress Shoes, Boots, Store Displays, Fixtures, Supplies

SAM'S CLOTHIERS, INC. (CLO)

3330 Hill Croft (p-m-b)
Houston, TX 77057
713-952-7474 / Fax: 713-975-7746
Sales: $500,001-$1 Million

SAM CALIMERA (Owner) & Buys Men's Footwear
BILL HICKL (Fin. Ofcr.) & Buys Men's Wear, Sportswear, Furnishings, Accessories, Store Displays, Fixtures, Supplies

SHINING STARZ (CLO)

6101 Hersch Rd. (m)
Houston, TX 77026
713-631-5510 / Fax: 713-692-9676

DUNSTAN MARSHALL (Owner) & Buys Men's Wear, Urban Contemporary, Headwear, Footwear, Accessories

SHUDDE BROTHERS, INC. (SP)

905 Trinity (m-b-h)
Houston, TX 77007
713-223-2191
Website: www.shudde.com

NEAL SHUDDE (Owner) & Buys Men's Headwear, Western, Dress & Casual Hats, Accessories, Store Displays, Fixtures, Supplies

NOTE-Only Headwear is Carried at This Store.

STAGE STORES, INC. (CLO-617)

(PALAIS ROYAL)
(BEALLS)
(STAGE)
P.O. Box 35167 (m)
10201 Main St.
Houston, TX 77025
(Directives West-L.A.)
(Henry Doneger)
713-667-5601 / Fax: 713-663-9573
Sales: Over $1 Billion
Website: www.stagestoresinc.com
Retail Locations: AL, AZ, AR, CO, FL, KS, LA, MS, MO, NM, OK, TX

JAMES SCARBOROUGH (C.E.O. & President)
ROBERT FLOUM (Exec. V.P.)
GOUGH GRUBBS (V.P.-Dist. & Admin.)
JULIE BLACKMORE (V.P.-Purch. & Store Opers.) & Buys Store Fixtures, Supplies
JEN WILKSON (Visual Mdsg. Mgr.) & Buys Store Displays
SETH BOOTH (Real Estate Contact)
DENNIS ABRAMCZYK (G.M.M.)
MELANIE ADAMS-Men's Knits, Sweaters, Wovens
DOUG CULVER-Men's Dress Shirts, Ties, Furnishings, Accessories
MELONEY APPLEBY-Men's Shorts, Jeans, Suits, Big & Tall
SHIRLEY TIJARINA-Men's Outerwear

HESS CSUY (D.M.M.-Young Men's Collections)
ANITA VON FELDT-Young Men's Knits, Wovens
DAVID AVER-8 to 20 Boys' Wear

JULIE USRY (D.M.M.-Footwear)
OPEN-Men's & Boys' Work Footwear
DAN STRODE-Men's Athletic Footwear

GILL GIFFORD (V.P. & D.M.M.-Accessories & Gifts)
KIM STEWART-Men's Fragrances
NANETTE SAHA-Men's Fine Jewelry

STELZIG OF TEXAS (CLO & WW)

(STELZIG SADDLERY CO., INC.)
3123 Post Oak Blvd. (p-m)
Houston, TX 77056
713-629-7779 / Fax: 713-629-8661
Website: www.stelzigoftexas.com

FRANCES STELZIG-BUTLER (President) & Buys Men's Sportswear, Western Wear, Accessories, Boys' Blue Jeans, Men's & Boys' Footwear, Boots, Store Displays, Fixtures, Supplies

TEXAS - Houston

TAGHI'S, INC. (CLO)
5116 Westheimer Rd. (b)
Houston, TX 77056
713-963-0884 / Fax: 713-963-0880

A. TAGHI (Owner) & Buys Men's Sportswear, Furnishings, Accessories, Footwear, Urban Contemporary, Store Displays, Fixtures, Supplies

TAILOR'S TOUCH (MW)
9898 Southwest Fwy. (m-b)
Houston, TX 77074
713-777-3187 / Fax: 713-777-3188

MANUEL RIAN (Owner) & Buys Men's Sportswear, Furnishings, Accessories, Store Displays, Fixtures & Supplies

VELLERIANO ITALY (MW)
(HOUSTON EUROPEAN STYLE, INC.)
5085 Westheimer, #2860
Houston, TX 77056
713-552-1188 / Fax: 713-552-1343

PATRICIA PORTO (Owner) & Buys Men's Overcoats, Suits, Tailored Jackets & Slacks, Raincoats, Big & Tall Wear, Sportswear, Sweaters, Outer Jackets, Leather Apparel, Casual Slacks, Active Apparel, Furnishings, Dress Shirts, Ties, Robes, Underwear, Hosiery, Gloves, Headwear, Accessories, Belts, Jewelry, Small Leather Goods, Young Men's Wear, Boys' Sportswear, Furnishings, Accessories, Footwear, Store Displays, Fixtures, Supplies

DANIELLO PENEDA (Mgr.) & Buys Men's Overcoats, Suits, Tailored Jackets & Slacks, Raincoats, Big & Tall Wear, Sportswear, Sweaters, Outer Jackets, Leather Apparel, Casual Slacks, Active Apparel, Furnishings, Dress Shirts, Ties, Robes, Underwear, Hosiery, Gloves, Headwear, Accessories, Belts, Jewelry, Small Leather Goods, Young Men's Wear, Boys' Sportswear, Furnishings, Accessories, Footwear, Store Displays, Fixtures, Supplies

VENTURA'S FORMAL WEAR (CLO)
(VENTURA'S BRIDAL SALON)
102 N. Loop At Yale (m-b)
Houston, TX 77008
713-880-2788 / Fax: 713-880-5544
Website: www.venturasbridal.com

FRANK VENTURA (President) & Buys Men's Formal Wear, Men's & Boys' Footwear, Furnishings, Accessories, Store Displays, Fixtures, Supplies

TASKA VENTURA (V.P.) & Buys Men's Formal Wear, Men's & Boys' Footwear, Furnishings, Accessories, Store Displays, Fixtures, Supplies

VILLAGE CLOTHIERS (CLO)
2411 Rice Blvd.
Houston, TX 77005
713-520-9096 / Fax: 713-520-6618
Website: www.villageclothier.com

CHARLES PRITCHETT (Owner) & Buys Men's Wear, Accessories, Furnishings

VINCE FORD CUSTOM APPAREL (MW)
5615 Richmond Ave.
Houston, TX 77057
713-974-6321 / Fax: 713-977-3339

VINCENT FORD (Owner) & Buys Men's Wear, Accessories, Furnishings, Footwear

WOLF PAWN & DEPARTMENT STORE (DEPT)
2701 Dowling St. (p)
Houston, TX 77004
713-659-7656 / Fax: 713-659-3239
Sales: $1 Million-$10 Million

BERNARD WOLF (Owner)

ARTIE NEWSOME-Men's Sportswear, Furnishings, Headwear, Accessories, Young Men's Wear, Leather Apparel, Men's Footwear

RAYMOND BURGOIS-Store Displays, Fixtures, Supplies

ZINDLER'S BIG & TALL (MW)
(ZINDLER'S, INC.)
7887 Katy Fwy., #340 (m-b)
Houston, TX 77024
713-629-0663 / Fax: 713-629-5159
Website: www.tallbig.com

KENNETH W. ZINDLER (President & G.M.M.) & Buys Big & Tall Men's Overcoats, Suits, Tailored Jackets, Tailored Slacks, Dress Shirts, Sportswear, Sport Coats, Furnishings, Headwear, Accessories, Footwear

ED KANE BOOT & WESTERN WEAR (WW)
6306 Aldine Bender (m)
Humble, TX 77396
281-441-3158

ED KANE (Owner) & Buys Men's Western Boots, Men's, Young Men's & Boys' Western Wear, Leather Apparel, Related Accessories, Furnishings, Store Displays, Fixtures, Supplies

DELORES KANE (Mgr.) & Buys Men's, Young Men's & Boys' Western Wear, Leather Apparel, Related Accessories, Furnishings, Store Displays, Fixtures, Supplies

FOOTACTION USA (SG-500)
(FOOTSTAR)
7880 Bent Branch Dr., #100
Irving, TX 75063
972-501-5000 / Fax: 972-501-5002
Website: www.footaction.com
Retail Locations: TX, CA, LA, NC, NV, NY, VA

SHAWN NEVILLE (President)

KEN MOODY (Dir. & Brand Mgr.)

DAN GOLDSTEIN (Dir.-Product Liquidation)

JERRY VESSEN (Visual Mdsr. & Real Estate Contact) & Buys Men's Fashion & Athletic Apparel

STEVE KENDALL (Real Estate Contact)

KEITH JOHNSON (D.M.M.-Men's Running, Casual & Outdoor)

BRIAN BURNETT (D.M.M.-Men's Basketball & X-Training)

KEITH JOHNSON-Men's Crosstraining & Fitness Footwear, Men's Running, Walking & Specialty Footwear

RODNEY DYER-Men's Hiking, Casual & Canvas Footwear

GREG MULKEY-Men's Dress Shoes, Casual Shoes, Boots

GEOFF TESSE-Men's Running, Walking & Specialty Footwear

JUSTIN ROBBINS (D.M.M.-Children's Footwear)

GABRIELLA GARZA-GRANDE-Boys' Footwear, Men's Hosiery, Shoecare, Accessories

DAVE NEEHAN (D.M.M.-Apparel & Accessories)

TOM AUSTIN-Men's Athletic Apparel

JIM McCONNELL-Licensed Apparel, Headwear

TONY HUTCHINSON-Men's Hosiery, Shoecare, Accessories

NEIMAN MARCUS DIRECT (MO & OL)
(NEIMAN MARCUS BY MAIL)
(HORCHOW)
(TRIFLES)
(CHEF'S CATALOG)
5950 Colwell Blvd.
Irving, TX 75039
972-969-3100 / Fax: 972-969-3212
Sales: $100 Million-$500 Million
Website: www.nmdirect.com

KAREN KATZ (President & C.E.O.-NM Direct)

GERALD BARNES (Sr. V.P. & G.M.M.-Apparel, Accessories, Men's)

DAVID ALTMAN (V.P. & D.M.M.- Sportswear) & Buys Designer Sportswear, Couture

JEANE ROZAS-Men's Leisure Sportswear, Knitwear, Neckwear, Young Men's Wear, Boys' Wear

KIM LINDER-Boys' Wear

ZALE CORP. (JWLY-2300)
901 W. Walnut Hill Ln.
Irving, TX 75038
972-580-4000 / Fax: 972-580-5551
Sales: Over $1 Billion
Website: www.zalecorp.com
Retail Locations: MA, RI, NH, ME, VT, CT NJ, NY, PA, DE, VA, MD, WV, NC, SC, GA, FL AL IN,ID AZ, NV, CA, HI, OR, WA, MS, KY, OH, IN, MI, IA,WI, MN, SD., ND, MT,IL, MO, KS, NE, LA, AR, OK, TX, CO, WY, UT, NM, AK, CA, PR

ROBERT J. DINICOLA (Chmn.)
MARY FORTE (President & C.E.O.)
TERRY GHIORZI-Men's Jewelry & Watches

P.N. ASHY STORE (CLO)
137 E. Houston St. (p)
Jasper, TX 75951
409-384-4332
Sales: $500,001-$1 Million

MARY ASHY (Owner) & Buys Men's Work Clothing, Outer Wear, Western Shirts, Big & Tall, Men's Robes, Underwear, Hosiery, Young Men's Wear, Men's Footwear, Boots, 8 to 20 Boys' Wear, Store Displays, Fixtures, Supplies

WEST BEAR CREEK (GM)
406 Main St. (p)
Junction, TX 76849
915-446-2514 / Fax: 914-446-2761

TOM JOHNSON (Co-Owner) & Buys Men's Jeans, Tops, Underwear, Hosiery, Outerwear, Western Clothing, Furnishings, Accessories, Boots, Store Displays, Fixtures & Supplies
LINDA JOHNSON (Co-Owner) & Buys Men's Jeans, Tops, Underwear, Hosiery, Outerwear, Western Clothing, Furnishings, Accessories, Boots, Store Displays, Fixtures & Supplies
KAREN BASSETT-Men's Jeans, Tops, Underwear, Hosiery, Outerwear, Western Clothing, Furnishings, Accessories, Boots, Store Displays, Fixtures & Supplies

ACADEMY CORP. (CLO-75 & SG)
(ACADEMY SPORTS & OUTDOORS)
1800 N. Mason Rd. (p-m)
Katy, TX 77449
281-646-5200 / Fax: 281-646-5204
Sales: $50 Million-$100 Million
Website: www.academy.com
Retail Locations: TX, OK, LA, MS, AL, TN, FL

ARTHUR GOCHMAN (Dir.-Opers.)
ROBERT FRENNEA (Exec. V.P.-Apparel)
IRENE GALINEX (Dir.-Mdsg.) & Buys Store Displays, Fixtures, Supplies
KATHY KING (Real Estate Contact)
BETH MENUET (V.P.-Footwear)
JENELLE WILLIAMS-Athletic Footwear
KEVIN CHAPMAN-Men's Work Boots, Rubber Footwear, Men's Casual Footwear
MARISSA KULLER-Kids' Footwear
TERRI BOLTON-Men's & Boys' Licensed Apparel
JAKE SLIGHT-Men's Workwear, Men's & Boys' Casual Clothing, Sportswear, Activewear, Boys' Wear, Golf Apparel
DEEDEE SEDULE-Men's & Boys' Swimwear, 8 to 20 Boys Wear
MARGARET BOWMEN-Active Apparel

HILL COUNTRY WESTERN WEAR (WW)
219 Junction Hwy. (b)
Kerrville, TX 78028
830-257-7333 / Fax: 830-792-4740
Sales: $100,001-$500,000

LINDA LASHLEY TRISCH (Owner) & Buys Men's Western Clothing, Sportswear, Accessories, Furnishings, Headwear, Young Men's & Boys' Western Wear, Men's & Boys' Western Boots

SCHREINER'S (DEPT)
(THE DUNLAP CO.)
736 Water St. (m-b)
Kerrville, TX 78028
830-896-1212 / Fax: 830-896-1210
Sales: $1 Million-$10 Million

JAMES SHULTS (Gen. Mgr.) & Buys Men's Sportswear, Accessories, Furnishings, Big & Tall Men's Wear, Store Displays, Fixtures, Supplies

SAXON'S MENSWEAR (SP)
1801 E. Center Expwy., #4 (m-b)
Killeen, TX 76541
254-699-3905 / Fax: 254-699-3489
Sales: $500,001-$1 Million

GUS GARCIA (Partner) & Buys Men's Formal Wear & Related Accessories, Footwear, Young Men's & Boys' Formal Wear, Big & Tall Men's Formal Wear, Store Displays, Fixtures, Supplies
TOM SAITO (Partner) & Buys Men's Formal Wear & Related Accessories, Footwear, Young Men's & Boys' Formal Wear, Big & Tall Men's Formal Wear, Store Displays, Fixtures, Supplies

SUE'S WESTERN LAND (WW)
Hwy. 96 South (m-b)
Kirbyville, TX 75956
409-423-5152 / Fax: 409-423-6264
Sales: $500,001-$1 Million

BRET KEMP (Owner) & Buys Men's, Young Men's & Boys' Western Wear, Urban Contemporary, Related Accessories, Furnishings, Footwear, Big & Tall Men's Western Wear, Store Displays, Fixtures, Supplies

CINDY & RICARDO (CLO)
River Dr. Mall, #D15 (p-m-b)
Laredo, TX 78040
956-727-5101 / Fax: 956-727-3742
Sales: $1 Million-$10 Million

RICARDO GARZA (Co-Owner) & Buys Young Men's Sportswear, Dress Shirts, Small Leather Goods, Footwear
ALMA GARZA (Co-Owner) & Buys Young Men's Sportswear, Dress Shirts, Small Leather Goods, Footwear

DON ANTONIO'S MENSWEAR (MW)
P.O. Box 664 (p-m)
1111 Iturbide St.
Laredo, TX 78040
956-723-3648 / Fax: 956-723-3640

FERNANDO A. SALINAS (Owner) & Buys Men's Suits, Tailored Jackets, Tailored Slacks, Raincoats, Sportswear, Furnishings, Hats, Headwear, Accessories, Store Displays, Fixtures, Supplies

JOE BRAND, INC. (CLO-2)
P.O. Box 1220 (m-b)
5300 San Dario Ave., #260
Laredo, TX 78042
956-722-0771 / Fax: 956-722-0125
Sales: $1 Million-$10 Million

SEYMOUR DEUTSCH (C.E.O.) & Buys Men's & Young Men's Wear, Furnishings, Accessories, Store Supplies, Fixtures
VICTOR CANALES-Men's & Young Men's Wear, Furnishings, Accessories, Store Supplies, Fixtures
RICARDO LAZARO-Store Displays

NOTE-Footwear Is a Leased Department.

JUVENCIO'S MENSWEAR, INC. (MW)
4500 San Bernardo Ave. (m-b)
Laredo, TX 78041
956-722-6303 / Fax: 956-722-2464
Sales: $500,001-$1 Million

JUVENCIO DeANDA (Owner) & Buys All Men's, Young Men's, Big & Tall Men's Wear, Urban Contemporary, Leather Apparel, Men's Footwear, Store Displays, Fixtures, Supplies

TEXAS - Laredo

LA FAMA (MW-2)
(SULAK'S)
(EL PORVENIR)
(NORTON & SONS, INC.)
P.O. Box 118 (bud-p-m)
Laredo, TX 78042
956-726-3636 / Fax: 956-723-0241

LES NORTON-Men's Shoes

ROBERT NORTON (@ 210-723-4837)-Men's Overcoats, Suits, Tailored Jackets, Tailored Slacks, Raincoats, Sportswear, Sweaters, Sport Shirts, Outer Jackets, Casual Slacks, Active Apparel, Leather Jackets, Furnishings, Dress Shirts, Ties, Underwear, Accessories, Hosiery, Gloves, Headwear, Belts, Jewelry, Fragrances, Young Men's & Boys' Suits, Store Displays, Fixtures, Supplies

NOTE:-Shoes Are Only Carried in One Store Location.

LOS DOS LAREDOS (DEPT-3)
(SAMSON'S)
(NORTONS)
(NORTON STORES, INC.)
P.O. Box 1044 (p)
402 Convent Ave.
Laredo, TX 78042
956-723-5244 / Fax: 956-722-1520
Sales: $1 Million-$10 Million

LARRY NORTON (Co-Owner) & Buys Men's Athletic Footwear, Men's & Boys' Wear, Sportswear, Accessories, Furnishings, Store Displays, Fixtures, Supplies

RICHARD NORTON (Co-Owner) (@ 956-725-3200) & Buys Men's & Boys' Wear, Urban Contemporary, Sportswear, Accessories, Furnishings, Men's Footwear, Store Displays, Fixtures, Supplies

MIKE'S WESTERN WEAR, INC. (WW)
4519 San Bernardo Ave. (m-b)
Laredo, TX 78041
956-722-0927 / Fax: 956-791-6453

MIKE JACAMAN (Co-Owner) & Buys Men's & Boys' Western Clothing, Boots, Sportswear, Furnishings, Headwear, Accessories, Store Displays, Fixtures, Supplies

SIROS, INC. (SP-3)
1112 Hidalgo
Laredo, TX 78040
956-723-8132 / Fax: 956-723-8189
Sales: $5 Million-$10 Million

MARK CONNELLY (President)

MARIO PEREZ (Mgr.) & Buys Activewear, Athletic Footwear

ZORBA, INC. (FW-7)
902 E. Hillside Rd. (b)
Laredo, TX 78041
956-726-9122 / Fax: 956-726-0658
Sales: $1 Million-$10 Million

JOSE LUIS MARTINEZ (President)

JOSE MARTINEZ, JR.-Boys' Footwear, Men's Footwear, Licensed Apparel, Watches, Hosiery

EDDIE'S COWBOY STORE (WW)
624 Ave. H (p)
Levelland, TX 79336
806-894-4158
Sales: $500,001-$1 Million

EDDIE COURTNEY (Owner) & Buys Men's & Boys' Western Wear, Related Accessories, Furnishings, Western Boots, Store Displays, Fixtures, Supplies

LEWIE'S, INC. (DEPT)
P.O. Box 9155 (p)
1500 Hwy. 90
Liberty, TX 77575
936-336-2121 / Fax: 409-336-9263
Sales: $1 Million-$10 Million

LEWIE MAJORS (Owner) & Buys Men's Sweaters, Work Clothes, Casual Slacks, Outer Jackets, Active Apparel, Leather Jackets, Sportswear, Underwear, Hosiery, Gloves, Headwear, Belts, Jewelry, Small Leather Goods, Fragrances, Western Shirts, Young Men's Wear, 8 to 20 Boys' Wear, Big & Tall Men's Wear, Men's & Boys' Footwear, Store Displays, Fixtures, Supplies

SHERRI BIRDWELL-Men's Sweaters, Work Clothes, Casual Slacks, Outer Jackets, Active Apparel, Leather Jackets, Sportswear, Underwear, Hosiery, Gloves, Headwear, Belts, Jewelry, Small Leather Goods, Fragrances, Western Shirts, Young Men's Wear, Urban Contemporary, 8 to 20 Boys' Wear, Big & Tall Men's Wear, Men's & Boys' Footwear, Store Displays, Fixtures, Supplies

HASSE'S, INC. (CLO)
105 E. Young St. (p-m-b)
Llano, TX 78643
915-247-4147 / Fax: 915-247-4148
Sales: $500,000-$1 Million

PAUL SCHUESSLER (Owner & Mgr.) & Buys Men's & Boys' Western Wear, Men's Sportswear, Furnishings, Headwear, Accessories, Boys' Wear, Men's & Boys' Footwear, Store Displays, Fixtures, Supplies

ARMY-NAVY STORE (AN-2)
1018 Loop 281
Longview, TX 75604
903-297-7006 / Fax: 903-297-0014
Sales: $100,001-$500,000

WALTER MIDDLETON (Mgr. & Owner) & Buys Hunting Clothing, T-shirts, Camouflage, Outdoor Apparel, Belts, Headwear, Boots

C & C WESTERN WEAR, INC. (WW)
1700 N. Eastman Rd. (m)
Longview, TX 75601
903-753-8991 / Fax: 903-753-8360
Website: www.mikescustomhalters.com

CAROLYN CHILDRESS-HELMS (Owner) & Buys Men's Western Boots

FREIDA CARTER (Mgr.) & Buys Men's Western Boots, Men's & Boys' Western Wear, Related Accessories, Furnishings, Store Displays, Fixtures, Supplies

GABRIEL'S MENSWEAR (MW)
405 W. Loop 281, #2A (p-m-b)
Longview, TX 75604
903-663-1471 / Fax: 903-663-6865

SAM GAWRIEH (Owner) & Buys Men's Sportswear, Dress Shirts, Ties, Belts, Headwear, Boys' Suits, Men's Footwear, Store Displays, Fixtures & Supplies

HURWITZ MEN'S SHOP (MW)
2002 Judson Rd. (m-b)
Longview, TX 75605
903-753-4474 / Fax: 903-753-0716
Sales: $500,001-$1 Million

STEVE BRATTELI (Owner) & Buys Men's Overcoats, Tailored Jackets, Tailored Slacks, Raincoats, Sportswear, Sweaters, Sport Shirts, Casual Slacks, Outer Jackets, Leather Apparel, Active Apparel, Furnishings, Dress Shirts, Ties, Robes, Underwear, Hosiery, Gloves, Headwear, Accessories, Bi

BRANDING IRON COWBOY OUTFITTERS (WW)
3320 34th St. (m)
Lubbock, TX 79410
806-785-0500
Sales: $1 Million-$10 Million
Website: www.cowboy-outfitter.com

EDWARD ISAAC (Owner) & Buys Men's & Boys' Western Wear, Related Accessories, Furnishings, Western Boots, Store Displays, Fixtures, Supplies

BUD'S MEN'S SHOP (MW)
2811 50th St. (m)
Lubbock, TX 79413
806-797-2554 / Fax: 806-797-4735

BERNARD BARASCH (Owner) & Buys Men's Sportswear, Furnishings, Accessories, Store Displays, Fixtures, Supplies

DOLLAR WESTERN WEAR (WW-6)
5011 Slide Rd. (p-m-b)
Lubbock, TX 79414
806-793-2818 / Fax: 806-793-0595
Sales: $1 Million-$10 Million

MICHAEL KAHN (C.E.O.) & Buys Men's, Young Men's & 8 to 20 Boys' Western Wear, Related Furnishings, Headwear, Accessories, Boots, Store Displays, Fixtures, Supplies

THE FAMOUS DEPARTMENT STORES (DEPT)

1213 Ave. G (bud-p)
Lubbock, TX 79401
806-763-5711
Sales: $100,001-$500,000

SADALLAH MOSES (Owner) & Buys Men's Sportswear, Furnishings, Formal Wear, Big & Tall Men's Wear, Young Men's Wear, Boys' Shirts, Jeans, Men's & Boys' Footwear, Store Displays, Fixtures, Supplies

H. G. THRASH CLOTHIER, INC. (MW)

2010 Broadway (m-b)
Lubbock, TX 79401
806-741-0303 / Fax: 806-744-4271
Sales: $1 Million-$10 Million
Website: www.hgthrash.com

HOWARD THRASH (Owner) & Buys Men's Sportswear, Furnishings, Accessories, Footwear, Store Displays, Fixtures, Supplies

LINGUIST BIG & TALL (MW)

(THOMAS A. LINGUIST LTD., INC)
4816 W. 50th St. (m-b)
Lubbock, TX 79414
806-795-2154

THOMAS LINGUIST (Owner) & Buys Men's Big & Tall Clothing, Sportswear, Furnishings, Accessories, Store Displays, Fixtures, Supplies

MALOUF'S (MW-2)

8201 Quaker Ave., #106 (m-b-des)
Lubbock, TX 79424
806-794-9500 / Fax: 806-798-3428
Sales: $1 Million-$10 Million
Website: www.maloufs.com

JOHN B. MALOUF (Chmn. & President) & Buys Men's Overcoats, Suits, Tailored Jackets, Tailored Slacks, Raincoats, Big & Tall Wear, Men's Sweaters, Sportswear, Sport Shirts, Outer Jackets, Leather Apparel, Casual Slacks, Active Apparel, Furnishings, Headwear, Accessories, Belts, Jewelry, Small Leather Goods, Big & Tall Men's Wear, Men's Footwear

SAM MALOUF (Partner Mgr.) & Buys Men's Overcoats, Suits, Tailored Jackets, Tailored Slacks, Raincoats, Big & Tall Wear, Men's Sweaters, Sportswear, Sport Shirts, Outer Jackets, Leather Apparel, Casual Slacks, Active Apparel, Furnishings, Headwear, Accessories, Belts, Jewelry, Small Leather Goods, Big & Tall Men's Wear, Men's Footwear

CARL COFFEE (Mgr.) & Buys Men's Overcoats, Suits, Tailored Jackets, Tailored Slacks, Raincoats, Big & Tall Wear, Men's Sweaters, Sportswear, Sport Shirts, Outer Jackets, Leather Apparel, Casual Slacks, Active Apparel, Furnishings, Headwear, Accessories, Belts, Jewelry, Small Leather Goods, Big & Tall Men's Wear, Men's Footwear

KARL NIMTZ (Visual Display Mgr.) & Buys Store Displays, Fixtures, Supplies

CLARK'S DEPARTMENT STORE (DEPT)

(Div. of DUNLAP CO.)
3043 S. John Redditt (m-b)
Lufkin, TX 75904
936-639-3146 / Fax: 936-634-8020
Sales: $1 Million-$10 Million

JIM CLARK (G.M.M.) & Buys Men's Sweaters, Sport Shirts, Outer Jackets, Leather Apparel, Active Apparel, Sportswear, Furnishings, Headwear, Accessories, Young Men's Wear, Boys' Wear, Men's Leather Apparel

ALANA THOMPSON (Mgr.) & Buys Men's Sweaters, Sport Shirts, Outer Jackets, Leather Apparel, Active Apparel, Sportswear, Furnishings, Headwear, Accessories, Young Men's Wear, Boys' Wear, Men's Leather Apparel

M.F. COLLINS-Men's Footwear

NOTE-Buying of Store Displays, Fixtures, Supplies is Performed at THE DUNLAP CO., Ft. Worth, TX.

JIM WILLIAMS' MENSWEAR (MW)

4405 S. Medford (m-b)
Lufkin, TX 75901
936-634-3555 / Fax: 936-634-3551
Sales: $100,001-$500,000

JIM WILLIAMS (Owner) & Buys Men's Sportswear, Furnishings, Accessories, Footwear, Big & Tall Men's Wear, Young Men's Wear, Store Displays, Fixtures, Supplies

LUFKIN ARMY & NAVY STORE (AN-2)

717 N. Timberland Dr.
Lufkin, TX 75901
936-634-7557 / Fax: 936-637-6860
Sales: $100,001-$500,000

KEITH GILBERT (Owner) & Buys Men's Activewear, Camouflage, Outdoor Apparel, Hunting Apparel, Boots

HARRIS WESTERN, INC. (WW)

19743 I-35 South (m)
Lytle, TX 78052
830-772-3616 / Fax: 830-709-4136
Sales: $1 Million-$10 Million
Website: www.harriswesterninc.com

GEORGE HARRIS (President) & Buys Store Displays, Fixtures, Supplies

SCOTT HARRIS (V.P.)

JOLINDA RICHARDS (G.M.M.) & Buys Men's Western Wear, Men's Overcoats, Tailored Jackets, Sport Shirts, Outer Jackets, Leather Apparel, Casual Slacks, Dress Shirts, Ties, Gloves, Headwear, Belts, Jewelry, Big & Tall Men's Western Wear, Boys' Western Clothing, Accessories, Men's Footwear, B

ROWAN'S WESTERN WEAR (WW)

P.O. Box 571 (p-m)
Hwy. 90 & 175
Mabank, TX 75147
903-887-3618 / Fax: 903-887-3618
Sales: $1 Million-$10 Million

DONNIE ROWAN (Co-Owner) & Buys Men's, Young Men's, Big & Tall Men's & Boys' 8 to 20 Western Wear, Sportswear, Western Hats, Accessories, Furnishings, Western & Work Boots, Store Displays, Fixtures, Supplies

SHEILA ROWAN (Co-Owner) & Buys Men's, Young Men's, Big & Tall Men's & Boys' 8 to 20 Western Wear, Sportswear, Western Hats, Accessories, Furnishings, Western & Work Boots, Store Displays, Fixtures, Supplies

SALEM'S FASHION (CLO)

514 Hwy. 281 (b)
Marble Falls, TX 78654
830-693-3250 / Fax: 830-693-7331
Sales: $1 Million-$10 Million

JOHN SALEM, SR. (President) & Buys Men's Suits, Tailored Jackets, Tailored Slacks, Sportswear, Dress Shirts, Ties, Underwear, Hosiery, Gloves, Accessories, Men's Footwear, Store Displays, Fixtures, Supplies

SUSAN JUDICE (Mgr.) & Buys Men's Suits, Tailored Jackets, Tailored Slacks, Sportswear, Dress Shirts, Ties, Underwear, Hosiery, Gloves, Accessories, Men's Footwear, Store Displays, Fixtures, Supplies

ERNIE'S (MW)

301 N. Washington Ave. (m-b)
Marshall, TX 75670
903-935-2705 / Fax: 903-935-5589
Sales: $500,001-$1 Million

ERNIE SEMETY (Owner) & Buys Men's Wear, Sportswear, Furnishings, Accessories, Young Men's Wear, Big & Tall Men's Wear, Men's Boots, Men's Footwear, Store Displays, Fixtures, Supplies

TEXAS - McAllen

JOE BRAND (MW-2)

2200 S. 10th St. (m-b)
McAllen, TX 78503
956-682-8311 / Fax: 956-682-0528
Sales: $1 Million-$10 Million

MEL MEDINA, SR. (Owner)

MEL MEDINA, JR. (G.M.M.) (@ 210-682-8311) & Buys Men's Overcoats, Suits, Tailored Jackets, Tailored Slacks, Formal Wear, Western Wear, Raincoats, Sportswear, Big & Tall Men's Wear, Sweaters, Sport Shirts, Outer Jackets, Casual Slacks, Active Apparel, Furnishings, Headwear, Accessories, Young Men's Wear, 8 to 20 Boys' Wear, Men's & Boys' Western Wear, Store Displays, Fixtures & Supplies

JORGE MEDINA (G.M.M.) & Buys Men's Overcoats, Suits, Tailored Jackets, Tailored Slacks, Formal Wear, Western Wear, Raincoats, Sportswear, Big & Tall Men's Wear, Sweaters, Sport Shirts, Outer Jackets, Casual Slacks, Active Apparel, Furnishings, Headwear, Accessories, Young Men's Wear, 8 to 20 Boys' Wear, Men's & Boys' Western Wear

KALIFA'S WESTERN WEAR (WW)

122 S. 17th St. (m)
McAllen, TX 78501
956-687-5392 / Fax: 956-630-4524
Sales: $1 Million-$10 Million

ABDALA KALIFA (Owner) & Buys Men's Western Wear, Related Accessories, Furnishings, Work Boots, Western Boots, Dress Boots, Store Displays, Fixtures, Supplies

MAN'S SHOP (MW-4)

14 S. Main St. (m-b)
McAllen, TX 78501
956-686-1777 / Fax: 956-686-2477

DAVID WESTERMAN (President)

NEIL WESTERMAN (Secy. & Treas.) & Buys Men's & Young Men's Wear, Urban Contemporary, Sportswear, Accessories, Furnishings, Men's Footwear, Store Displays, Fixtures, Supplies

McALLEN SPORTS (SG)

109 S. 17th (bud-p)
McAllen, TX 78501
956-687-3773 / Fax: 956-682-1394
Website: www.mcallensports.com

JORGE SALCINES (Owner) & Buys Men's & Boys' Wear, Sandals, T-shirts, Athletic Footwear, Hosiery, Store Displays, Fixtures & Supplies

NEW YORK STORE WESTERN WEAR (WW)

(CEDAR HEIGHTS, INC.)
1309 S. 10th St. (m-b)
McAllen, TX 78501
956-682-5702 / Fax: 956-682-5983
Sales: $500,001-$1 Million

HENRY MARINA (President) & Buys Men's Overcoats, Western Wear, Jeans, Tailored Slacks, Raincoats, Sweaters, Sport Shirts, Outer Jackets, Casual Slacks, Active Apparel, Neckwear, Furnishings, Headwear, Accessories, Big & Tall Men's Wear, Men's & Boys' Footwear, Young Men's & Boys' Wear

OLGA MARINA (Consultant) & Buys Men's Overcoats, Western Wear, Jeans, Tailored Slacks, Raincoats, Sweaters, Sport Shirts, Outer Jackets, Casual Slacks, Active Apparel, Neckwear, Furnishings, Headwear, Accessories, Big & Tall Men's Wear, Men's & Boys' Footwear, Young Men's & Boys' Wear

PADRE STYLE, INC. (CLO-2)

1120 W. Lindberg, #A (p)
McAllen, TX 78501
956-682-9754 / Fax: 956-687-1591
Sales: $1 Million-$10 Million

ZETTA FAIR (Co-President) & Buys Men's Sweaters, Active Apparel, Sport Shirts, Outer Jackets, Leather Apparel, Casual Slacks, Store Displays, Fixtures, Supplies

LARRY FAIR (Co-President) & Buys Active Apparel, Sportswear, Denim, Store Displays, Fixtures

LAURA VASQUEZ-Boys' Wear, Boys' Denim & Sportswear

TRAPPINGS (MW)

4300 N. 10th St. (m-b)
McAllen, TX 78504
956-630-2548 / Fax: 956-630-2120
Sales: $500,001-$1 Million

LORI GOLDMAN (Owner) & Buys Men's Sportswear, Men's Wear, Furnishings, Accessories, Men's Footwear, Store Displays, Fixtures & Supplies

HORSE & RIDER (WW-4)

(THE ACTION CO.)
P.O. Box 8008 (m-b)
1425 N. Tennessee St.
McKinney, TX 75069
972-542-8700 / Fax: 972-562-7300
Sales: $10 Million-$50 Million
Website: www.theactioncompany.com

DONALD MOTSENBOCKER (President)

MELINDA CORN-Western Wear, Related Accessories, Furnishings, Boots, Shoes, Store Displays, Fixtures & Supplies

KARNER'S DEPARTMENT STORE (DEPT)

109 E. Commerce St. (p-m)
Mexia, TX 76667
254-562-3827 / Fax: 254-562-5901
Sales: $1 Million-$10 Million

PEGGY WILSON (Owner) & Buys Men's Wear, Sportswear, Accessories, Furnishings, Boys' Wear, Students' Wear, Men's Footwear, Boys' Footwear, Store Displays, Fixtures & Supplies

GEORGE'S MEN'S SHOPS (MW-2)

Hwy. 180 East (p)
Brazos Shopping Ctr.
Mineral Wells, TX 76067
940-325-3737
Sales: $100,001-$500,000

GEORGE W. SMITH (Owner) & Buys Men's Sportswear, Furnishings, Accessories, Urban Contemporary, Store Displays, Fixtures, Supplies

MARYANN SMITH-Men's Sportswear, Furnishings, Accessories, Urban Contemporary, Store Displays, Fixtures, Supplies

MISSION WESTERN WEAR (WW)

617 Conway (m)
Mission, TX 78572
956-581-2116 / Fax: 956-585-6782

ARIEL HINOJOSA (Co-Owner) & Buys Men's Western Clothing, Sportswear, Furnishings, Accessories, Work Shoes, Boots, Store Displays, Fixtures, Supplies

PAULA HINOJOSA (Co-Owner) & Buys Men's Western Clothing, Sportswear, Furnishings, Accessories, Work Shoes, Boots, Store Displays, Fixtures, Supplies

BRAGG'S WESTERN (WW)

1014 W. 1st St.
Mount Pleasant, TX 75455
903-572-5560 / Fax: 903-572-9236

KIM ROGERS (Owner) & Buys Men's Western Wear, Related Accessories, Furnishings, Boots, Boys' Western Wear, Store Displays, Fixtures, Supplies

GLYN'S WESTERN WEAR (WW)

(GLYN'S WESTERN STORE, INC.)
206 N. Jefferson (p)
Mount Pleasant, TX 75455
903-572-3232

DON ALEXANDER (Owner & Mgr.) & Buys Men's Western Suits, Sportswear, Accessories, Headwear, Work Clothes, Boots, Big & Tall Men's Wear, Young Men's Wear, Boys' Wear, Store Displays, Fixtures, Supplies

McLAINE'S MENSWEAR, INC. (MW)
113 E. Main St. (p-m)
Nacogdoches, TX 75961
936-564-6911
Sales: $100,001-$500,000
DICK McLAINE (Owner) & Buys Men's Sportswear, Furnishings, Accessories, Store Displays, Fixtures, Supplies

MIZE DEPARTMENT STORE (DEPT)
108 E. Hospital (p)
Nacogdoches, TX 75961
936-564-8346 / Fax: 936-564-7344
Sales: $1 Million-$10 Million
MIKE BAY (President) & Buys Men's Wear, Sportswear, Accessories, Furnishings, Young Men's Wear, Store Displays, Fixtures, Supplies, Men's Footwear, Boys' Footwear
BROOKE DeWITT-Boys' Wear & Accessories

SHAW DEPARTMENT STORE (DEPT)
115 E. Main St. (p)
Nacogdoches, TX 75961
936-564-8219
Sales: $500,001-$1 Million
TERRY STRONG (Mgr.) & Buys Men's & Young Men's Sportswear, Furnishings, Accessories, Footwear, Boys' Jeans, Store Displays, Fixtures, Supplies

P. NEMIR DRY GOODS (DG & OL)
107 E. Washington Ave. (p-m)
Navasota, TX 77868
409-825-3369
Website: www.pnemir.com
ROBERT L. NEMIR, JR. (Owner) & Buys Men's, Young Men's & Boys' Wear, Work Clothes, Jeans, Accessories, Footwear, Store Displays, Fixtures & Supplies

WESTERN IMAGE (WW)
310 Pauls Rd. (m)
New Boston, TX 75570
903-628-2050
Sales: $100,001-$500,000
KIM WALDRUM (Owner) & Buys Men's Western Wear, Related Accessories, Furnishings, Boots, Store Displays, Fixtures, Supplies

BOXCAR ENTERPRISES, INC. (MW)
1259 Loop 337 (m)
New Braunfels, TX 78130
830-620-0411 / Fax: 830-606-6760
DARWIN HARRIS (Owner) & Buys Men's Sportswear, Footwear, Accessories, Urban Contemporary, Store Displays, Fixtures, Supplies

DUCKY'S (CLO)
272 S. Union (m)
New Braunfels, TX 78130
830-609-7422 / Fax: 830-620-5650
DOUGLAS HEILMANN (Owner) & Buys Men's Sport Shirts, Active Apparel, Headwear, Swimwear, Sandals, Store Displays, Fixtures, Supplies

HIGH BREHM HAT & WESTERN WEAR (WW)
1279 E. Common (m-b)
New Braunfels, TX 78130
830-629-2531
DONNIE SHAW (Owner) & Buys Men's Western Wear, Work Boots, Headwear, Accessories, Store Displays, Fixtures, Supplies

HEINSOHN'S STORE (DEPT)
Box 21. Rt. 2 (p)
New Ulm, TX 78950
979-732-5081
LESLIE F. HEINSOHN (Owner) & Buys Men's Western Sportswear, Work Boots, Western Boots, Furnishings, Store Displays, Fixtures, Supplies

JIM'S TALL & BIG MAN'S SHOP, INC. (MW)
423 N. Grant (p-m)
Odessa, TX 79761
915-333-1071
Sales: $100,001-$500,000
JIM E. SIMPSON (Owner)
GLADYS SIMPSON (President) & Buys Big & Tall Men's Overcoats, Suits, Tailored Jackets, Tailored Slacks, Raincoats, Sweaters, Sport Shirts, Outer Jackets, Casual Slacks, Active Apparel, Furnishings, Belts, Store Displays, Fixtures, Supplies
DAVID SIMPSON (V.P.) & Buys Big & Tall Men's Overcoats, Suits, Tailored Jackets, Tailored Slacks, Raincoats, Sweaters, Sport Shirts, Outer Jackets, Casual Slacks, Active Apparel, Furnishings, Belts, Store Displays, Fixtures, Supplies

TERRY'S MEN'S FASHIONS (MW)
2648 MacArthur Dr. (m-b)
Orange, TX 77630
409-883-2010 / Fax: 409-883-9168
Sales: $500,001-$1 Million
Website: www.terrysfashions.com
TERRY LANDRY (Owner) & Buys Men's Overcoats, Suits, Tailored Jackets, Tailored Slacks, Raincoats, Sweaters, Sport Shirts, Outer Jackets, Leather Apparel, Casual Slacks, Furnishings, Dress Shirts, Ties, Robes, Underwear, Hosiery, Gloves, Hats, Headwear, Belts, Jewelry, Small Leather

WESTERN STORE, INC. (WW)
1107 W. Green St. (m)
Orange, TX 77630
409-886-3771 / Fax: 409-886-3771
KATIE LUCIA (President) & Buys Men's Western Clothing, Accessories, Sportswear, Furnishings, Boots, Boys' Western Wear, Store Displays, Fixtures, Supplies

TOTAH BROTHERS (MW)
209 W. Oak St.
Palestine, TX 75801
903-729-4136 / Fax: 903-729-2151
ANGI TOTAH (Co-Owner)
ANDY TOTAH (Co-Owner) & Buys Men's Wear, Accessories, Furnishings, Shoes

WAYNES WESTERN WEAR (WW)
1504 N. Hobart St. (m-b)
Pampa, TX 79065
806-665-2925 / Fax: 806-665-0624
CAROL STRIBLING (Owner) & Buys Men's & Boys' Western Wear, Western Boots, Related Accessories, Furnishings

L.O. HAMMONS MEN'S STORE (MW)
27 Lamar (m-b)
Paris, TX 75460
903-785-2113
Sales: $500,001-$1 Million
NEIL BRATTELI (Co-Owner) & Buys Men's Wear, Furnishings, Accessories, Footwear, Store Displays, Fixtures, Supplies
NANCY BRATTELI (Co-Owner) & Buys Men's Wear, Furnishings, Accessories, Footwear, Store Displays, Fixtures, Supplies

NOLAN'S MENSWEAR (MW)
5018 Fairmont Pkwy.
Pasadena, TX 77505
281-487-8782 / Fax: 281-991-3546
Website: www.nolansmenswear.com
MAX IVENS-Men's Wear, Suits, Sportswear, Furnishings, Accessories, Footwear

SHELTON CLEANERS & MENSWEAR (MW)
208 S. Oak St. (m)
Pearsall, TX 78061
830-334-2343
Sales: $100,001-$500,000
HOWARD SHELTON (Owner) & Buys Men's Wear, Sportswear, Acessories, Furnishings, Store Displays, Fixtures, Supplies

CAVENDERS (WW)
324 Rusk St. (p)
Pittsburgh, TX 75686
903-856-5367 / Fax: 903-856-5569
Sales: $500,001-$1 Million
DAVID HOOVER (Owner) & Buys Men's Western Wear, Boots, Related Accessories, Furnishings, Leather Apparel, Store Displays, Fixtures, Supplies

GEBO DISTRIBUTING CO., INC. (GM-16)
P.O. Box 850 (bud)
Plainview, TX 79072
806-293-4212 / Fax: 806-293-3992
Sales: $1 Million-$10 Million
MIKE McCARTHY (President & C.E.O.)
KEN FINCHER-Men's & Boys' Sportswear, Casual Western Wear, Accessories, Furnishings, Work Boots, Western Boots

MASSO'S DEPARTMENT STORE (DEPT)
105 E. 6th (m)
Plainview, TX 79072
806-293-2092 / Fax: 806-293-0768
Sales: $500,001-$1 Million
JACOB MASSO (Owner) & Buys Men's & Boys' Wear, Western Wear, Sportswear, Accessories, Furnishings, Footwear, Boots, Store Displays, Fixtures, Supplies

RAGLANDS WESTERN WEAR (WW)
3209 Olton Rd. (p)
Plainview, TX 79072
806-296-7524
AUSTIN RAGLAND (Owner)
RONNY RAGLAND-Men's, Young Men's & Boys' Western Wear, Related Accessories, Furnishings, Boots, Casual Shoes, Store Supplies, Fixtures

CIRCA 2000 BY MIKE ZACK, INC. (MW)
5800 Legacy Dr., #C5
Plano, TX 75024
972-673-0920 / Fax: 972-673-0569
Sales: $500,001-$1 Million
MIKE ZACK (Co-Owner) & Buys Men's Wear, Sportswear, Accessories, Furnishings, Footwear, Boys' Sportswear

J.C. PENNEY CO. (DEPT-1300 & MO & OL)
6501 Legacy Dr. (p-m-b)
Plano, TX 75024
972-431-1000 / Fax: 972-431-9205
Sales: $30 Billion
Website: www.jcpenney.com
Retail Locations: AZ, AK, AZ, AR, CA, CO, CT, DE, DC, FL, GA, HI, ID, IL, IN, IA, KS, KY, LA, ME, MD, MA, MI, MN, MS, MO, MT, NE, NV, NH, NJ, NM, NY, NC, ND, OH, OK, OR, PA, RI, SC, SD, TN, TX, UT, VT, VA, WA, WV, WI, WY
ALLEN QUESTROM (Chmn. & C.E.O.)
KEN HICKS (President & C.O.O. - Stores)
VANESSA CASTAGNA (Exec. V.P. - J.C. Penney)
MIKE TAXTER (Exec. V.P. & Dir. - Stores)
MIKE BOYSLEM (President-Catalog & Distribution)
JOHN IRVIN (Exec. V.P. - J.C. Penney Direct)
KIRK BELL (Store. Mdse. Plng. Coord.)

LANA CAIN KRAUTER (Exec. V.P. & G.M.M. - Men's & Children's)
CLARKE McNAUGHS (D.M.M.-Men's)
HAL CAUSEY-Headwear, Gloves, Robes, Sleepwear
TOM COLVER-Leather Goods, Belts, Accessories
SUZETTE FUSCO-Men's Dress Shirts, Ties
MARY JEAN MAVRO-Men's Underwear, Hosiery

CINDY STARK (D.M.M.-Men's Clothing & Sportswear)
MIKE STRANGE-Men's Woven Apparel, Izod, Hunt Club
THORSTEN WEBER-Sport Shirts, Fleece, Big & Tall Menswear
MARCI SARTER-Swimwear, Outerwear
JAMES GROSS-Crazy Horse, J. Ferrar
SAM SOUAN-Suits, Custom-Fit Suits, Sport Coats, Tailored Collections, Dress Trousers

STEVE LAWRENCE (Exec. V.P.-Young Men's) & Buys Young Men's Sportswear, Workwear, Men's Athletic Apparel & Accessories
HAL CAUSEY-Men's Hosiery
DERRICK FLOWERS-Collections
BRIAN McNAMARA-Jeans, Western Wear, Slacks, Shorts
OPEN-Fleece, Men's Athletic Apparel & Accessories

JOE PETRONE (D.M.M.-Boys' Apparel)
WALT MEYERS-4 to 20 Boys' Outerwear, Swimwear, Athletic Apparel, Team Apparel, Boys' Underwear, Sleepwear, Hosiery & Accessories
LISA MILLER-Levi's, Dockers
JAN GRADY-4 to 7 Boys' Tops, Collections
AARON BONHAM-8 to 20 Boys' Tops, Sweaters, Husky Boys' Suits, Sportcoats, National Brand Collections, Boys' Suits, Dress Up Apparel, Coordinates
JEFFREY BERGUS (Cor. Brand Mgr.-Arizona Jeans)

DAN EDMONSON (Div. V.P.-Family Footwear)
LARRY PIETENPOL-Boys' Athletic Footwear, Boys' Shoes, Men's Athletic Footwear
JIM FALCONE-Men's Shoes, Slippers, Hiking Boots, Sandals, Casual Shoes
TIM CULVER-Men's Rugged Sporting Apparel

GARY LUNDBERG (Purch. Mgr.) & Buys Store Displays, Fixtures
CHUCK FOUGHTY (V.P. & Dir.-Store Environment)
MICHAEL LOWENKRUN (Real Estate Contact)

DOWDY'S MEN'S & BOYS' WEAR (MW)
(DOWDY, INC.)
P.O. Box C (p-m)
115 N. Main St.
Pleasanton, TX 78064
830-569-8791 / Fax: 830-569-8793
Sales: $500,001-$1 Million
CRAIG DOWDY (President) & Buys Men's, Young Men's & Boys' Wear, Urban Contemporary, Accessories, Furnishings, Sportswear, Western Wear, Western Boots, Store Displays, Fixtures, Supplies
SARAH EVANS-Men's Footwear

SHARK ATTACK (SP-2)
441 W. Cotter Ave.
Port Aransas, TX 78373
361-749-6379
Sales: $501,000-$1 Million
DAN MEERBEEK (Owner) & Buys Licensed Apparel, Activewear, Surfwear, Swimwear

ROY'S WESTERN WEAR, INC. (WW)
7600 Twin City Hwy. (m-b)
Port Arthur, TX 77642
409-727-2061 / Fax: 409-727-8142
Sales: $500,001-$1 Million
DAVID BADGETT (Owner) & Buys Men's, Young Men's & Boys' 8 to 20 Western Wear, Clothing, Ties, Headwear, Belts, Boots, Jewelry, Small Leather Goods, Store Displays, Fixtures, Supplies

MELSTAN, INC. (WW)
111 N. Ann St. (m)
Port Lovaca, TX 77979
361-552-5441 / Fax: 361-552-4416
TURNEY W. CRAWFORD (President) & Buys Store Displays, Fixtures, Supplies
STANLEY DIERLMAN (V.P.) & Buys Men's Western Wear, Boots, Furnishings, Accessories, Store Displays, Fixtures and Supplies
MINDY DIERLMAN-Men's Western Wear, Boots, Urban Contemporary, Furnishings, Accessories

TWINS FASHIONS (WW)
210 E. Main St. (p-m)
Post, TX 79356
806-495-3387
LOVETA JOSEY (Co-Owner) & Buys Men's & Boys' Western Wear, Underwear, Dress Shirts, Socks, Boots, Store Displays, Fixtures, Supplies
ROY JOSEY (Co-Owner) & Buys Men's & Boys' Western Wear, Underwear, Dress Shirts, Socks, Boots, Store Displays, Fixtures, Supplies

M. NIETO, INC. (WW)
P.O. Box 1929 (m)
Presidio, TX 79845
915-229-3220 / Fax: 915-229-4500
Sales: $500,001-$1 Million
MARIO NIETO (President) & Buys Men's Western Wear, Related Accessories, Furnishings, Boots, Store Displays, Fixtures, Supplies

SPENCER BROTHERS, INC. (DEPT)
P.O. Box 2079 (p-m-b)
Presidio, TX 79845
915-229-3324 / Fax: 915-229-4216
Sales: $500,001-$1 Million
MARY SPENCER (Co-Owner) & Buys Store Displays, Fixtures, Supplies
JOE SPENCER (Co-Owner)
CARLOS SPENCER (Co-Owner) & Buys Men's Sportswear, Furnishings, Accessories, Swimwear, Young Men's & Boys' Wear, Footwear, Store Displays, Fixtures & Supplies

TUMBLEWEED WESTERN WEAR (WW)
205 W. 3rd St. (m-b)
Quanah, TX 79252
940-663-5916
Sales: $100,001-$500,000
VICKIE LINDSEY (Owner) & Buys Men's Western Wear, Related Accessories, Furnishings, Western Boots, Cowboy Hats, Store Displays, Fixtures & Supplies

CLASSIC TAILOR SHOP (CLO)
2000 N. Plano (m-b)
Richardson, TX 75082
972-235-5770
AL ABUSAAD (Owner) & Buys Men's Suits, Store Displays, Fixtures, Supplies

DAD & LADS STORE (MW)
(JOHN HOLLINSWORTH, INC.)
2160 N. Coit Rd., # 130 (p-m-b)
Richardson, TX 75080
972-231-3497 / Fax: 972-231-3498
JIM C. SCOTT (President) & Buys Men's & Boys' Wear, Sportswear, Accessories, Furnishings, Footwear, Young Men's Store Displays, Fixtures, Supplies

J.C. RAMIREZ CO., INC. (WW)
P.O. Box 217 (m)
Roma, TX 78584
956-849-1541 / Fax: 956-849-4076
Sales: $1 Million-$10 Million
CECILIA BENAVIDES (Co-Owner) & Buys Men's & Boys' Western Wear, Related Accessories, Furnishings, Cowboy Hats, Footwear, Store Displays, Fixtures, Supplies
NOEL BENAVIDES (Co-Owner) & Buys Men's & Boys' Western Wear, Related Accessories, Furnishings, Cowboy Hats, Footwear, Urban Contemporary, Store Displays, Fixtures, Supplies

RAMIREZ VARIETY STORE, INC. (CLO)
707 Estrella St.
Roma, TX 78584
956-849-1231
MANUEL RAMIREZ (President)
ALFREDO RAMIREZ (G.M.M.) & Buys Men's Dress Shirts, Underwear, Hosiery, Gloves, Belts, Jewelry, Small Leather Goods, Headwear, Shirts, Work Shoes, Work Boots, Store Displays, Fixtures, Supplies

OWL WESTERN WEAR (CLO)
2989 Hwy. 304 (bud-p)
Rosanky, TX 78953
512-321-7330 / Fax: 512-237-2277
DONNA BARTSCH (Owner) & Buys Men's Tailored Jackets, Sportswear, Casual Wear, Western Wear, Ties, Headwear, Belts, Fragrances, Big & Tall Men's Wear, Young Men's Wear, Urban Contemporary, 8 to 20 Boys' Wear, Men's & Boys' Footwear, Store Displays, Fixtures, Supplies

THE CORRAL (WW)
(JACK & BARBARA HEITMAN, INC.)
2605 1st St. (m)
Rosenberg, TX 77471
281-341-0900 / Fax: 281-633-0900
JACK HEITMAN (Co-Owner) & Buys Men's, Young Men's & Boys' 8 to 20 Western Wear, Headwear, Furnishings, Western Accessories, Leather Apparel, Boots, Store Displays, Fixtures, Supplies
BARBARA HEITMAN (Co-Owner) & Buys Men's, Young Men's & Boys' 8 to 20 Western Wear, Headwear, Furnishings, Western Accessories, Leather Apparel, Boots, Store Displays, Fixtures, Supplies

BILL'S MAN'S SHOP (MW)
137 W. Beauregard Ave. (p)
San Angelo, TX 76903
915-655-7545 / Fax: 915-655-9546
EDDIE FOWLER (Owner) & Buys Men's, Young Men's & Boys' Wear, Big & Tall Men's Wear, Western Wear, Boots, Furnishings, Accessories, Store Displays, Fixtures, Supplies

GABRIEL'S (CLO)
2225 W. Beauregard Ave. (b)
San Angelo, TX 76901
915-949-1982 / Fax: 915-949-1984
Sales: $1 Million-$10 Million
TOM WOMACK (Co-Owner) & Buys Men's Overcoats, Suits, Tailored Jackets, Tailored Slacks, Raincoats, Sweaters, Sport Shirts, Outer Jackets, Casual Slacks, Furnishings, Headwear, Accessories, Footwear, Store Displays, Fixtures, Supplies
DEBBIE TRONCUSO (Co-Owner) & Buys Men's Overcoats, Suits, Tailored Jackets, Tailored Slacks, Raincoats, Sweaters, Sport Shirts, Outer Jackets, Casual Slacks, Furnishings, Headwear, Accessories, Footwear, Store Displays, Fixtures, Supplies

MAHON'S MEN'S SHOP (MW)
2214 W. Beauregard (m)
San Angelo, TX 76901
915-949-6031
Sales: $100,001-$500,000
BRYAN MAHON (Owner) & Buys Men's Overcoats, Suits, Tailored Jackets, Tailored Slacks, Raincoats, Sweaters, Sport Shirts, Outer Jackets, Casual Slacks, Furnishings, Footwear, Headwear, Accessories, Big & Tall Men's Wear, Store Displays, Fixtures & Supplies
MONTE MAHON-Men's Overcoats, Suits, Tailored Jackets, Tailored Slacks, Raincoats, Sweaters, Sport Shirts, Outer Jackets, Casual Slacks, Furnishings, Footwear, Headwear, Accessories, Big & Tall Men's Wear, Store Displays, Fixtures & Supplies

MR. BOOTS SAN ANGELO, INC. (WW)
2130 W. Beauregard (m)
San Angelo, TX 76901
915-949-3921 / Fax: 915-942-0046
Sales: $1 Million-$10 Million
JAMES TIMM (President) & Buys Men's Western Wear, Related Accessories, Furnishings, Boots, Boys' Western Wear, Store Displays, Fixtures, Supplies
DAVID TIMM (V.P.) & Buys Men's Western Wear, Related Accessories, Furnishings, Boots, Boys' Western Wear, Store Displays, Fixtures, Supplies

TEXAS - San Antonio

ALL ASHORE FASHION SWIMWEAR (CLO)

11745 IH-10 West
San Antonio, TX 78230
210-691-0100 / Fax: 210-494-6300

LES ROBBINS (Owner) & Buys Beachwear, Activewear, Surf & Swimwear, Wetsuits, Headwear, Sandals, Flip Flops

BEACON'S (CLO)

(ABELMAN ENTERPRISES, INC.)
321 N. New Braunfels (p-m)
San Antonio, TX 78202
210-223-3311 / Fax: 210-223-2223
Sales: $1 Million-$10 Million

ARTHUR ABELMAN (President) & Buys Men's Sportswear, Furnishings, Headwear, Accessories, Footwear, Men's Big & Tall Wear, Young Men's Wear, School Uniforms, Store Displays, Fixtures, Supplies

ALVIN ABELMAN (Secy. & Treas.) & Buys Men's Sportswear, Furnishings, Headwear, Accessories, Footwear, Men's Big & Tall Wear, Young Men's Wear, School Uniforms, Store Displays, Fixtures, Supplies

JOSEPH'S, INC. (MW-2)

7400 San Pedro (m-b)
San Antonio, TX 78216
210-344-9285 / Fax: 210-227-7451
Sales: $1 Million-$10 Million

STEVE RUBIN (President)

DAVID RUBIN (V.P.) & Buys Men's Overcoats, Suits, Tailored Jackets, Tailored Slacks, Raincoats, Big & Tall Wear, Sportswear, Sweaters, Sport Shirts, Outer Jackets, Leather Apparel, Casual Slacks, Active Apparel, Furnishings, Dress Shirts, Ties, Robes, Underwear, Hosiery, Gloves, Headwear, Accessories, Belts, Jewelry, Small Leather Goods, Fragrances, Boys' Clothing, Sportswear, Furnishings, Accessories, Footwear, Store Displays, Fixtures, Supplies

LANE HEDGEPETH CLOTHIER (MW)

13751 Castle Grove (m-b)
San Antonio, TX 78231
210-341-6766 / Fax: 210-341-6766
Sales: $100,001-$500,000

LANE HEDGEPETH (Owner) & Buys Men's Sportswear, Furnishings, Accessories, Footwear, Casual Wear

NATIONAL ARMY SURPLUS CO., INC. (AN-2)

5600 Bandera Rd. (m)
San Antonio, TX 78238
210-680-3322 / Fax: 210-680-3368

GRACE DIAMOND (President) & Buys Men's Sportswear, Furnishings, Accessories, Footwear, Boys' Wear, Urban Contemporary, Store Displays, Fixtures, Supplies

PENNER'S, INC. (MW)

311 W. Commerce St. (b)
San Antonio, TX 78205
210-226-2487 / Fax: 210-222-0101
Sales: $1 Million-$10 Million
Website: www.pennersinc.com

MARK B. PENNER (President) & Buys Men's Overcoats, Suits, Tailored Jackets, Tailored Slacks, Raincoats, Sweaters, Sport Shirts, Outer Jackets, Casual Slacks, Furnishings, Headwear, Accessories, Footwear, Store Displays, Fixtures, Supplies, Men's Overcoats, Suits, Tailored Jackets, Tailored Slacks, Raincoats, Sweaters, Sport Shirts, Outer Jackets, Casual Slacks, Furnishings, Headwear, Accessories, Footwear, Store Displays, Fixtures, Supplies

RUN-A-WAY RUNNERS' STORE (SP)

3428 N. Saint Mary's
San Antonio, TX 78212
210-826-1888 / Fax: 210-732-1332
Sales: $100,001-$500,000

JOHN PURNELL (Owner) & Buys Activewear, Athletic Footwear

SATEL'S, INC. (MW-2)

5100 Broadway (b)
San Antonio, TX 78209
210-822-3376 / Fax: 210-824-3386
Website: www.satels.com

JAMES SATEL (Co-Owner) & Buys Men's Wear, Sportswear, Accessories, Furnishings, Leather Apparel, Dress Shoes, Casual Shoes, Store Displays, Fixtures, Supplies

TOFFE SATEL-Men's Wear, Sportswear, Accessories, Furnishings, Leather Apparel, Dress Shoes, Casual Shoes, Store Displays, Fixtures, Supplies

T-SHIRTS UNLIMITED (CLO)

(J.R. ENTERPRISES)
2436 SW 36th St.
San Antonio, TX 78237
210-431-3420 / Fax: 210-431-0013

JIM SMITH (Co-Owner) & Buys Men's & Boys' T-shirts, Headwear, Outer Jackets, Store Displays, Fixtures, Supplies

CANDY SMITH (Co-Owner) & Buys Men's & Boys' T-shirts, Headwear, Outer Jackets, Store Displays, Fixtures, Supplies

TIES.COM (OL)

7959 Fredericksburg Rd., #119 (m-b)
San Antonio, TX 78229
210-614-8433 / Fax: 210-614-8434
Sales: $100,001-$500,000
Website: www.ties.com

KATHY MARROU (President & G.M.M.)

CHRIS MARROU (Co-Owner)

MOLLY MIRRAGE (Designer) & Buys Men's and Boys' Ties

JANINE CHAVEZ (Mgr.) & Buys Men's and Boys' Ties

TODDS, INC. (MW)

7400 San Pedro, #222 (b)
San Antonio, TX 78216
210-349-6464 / Fax: 210-349-0302
Sales: $1 Million-$10 Million

ANDRES SZITA (Owner & G.M.M.) & Buys Men's Overcoats, Suits, Tailored Jackets, Tailored Slacks, Raincoats, Sportswear, Sweaters, Sport Shirts, Outer Jackets, Leather Jackets, Casual Slacks, Furnishings, Dress Shirts, Ties, Robes, Underwear, Hosiery, Gloves, Accessories, Belts, Jewelry, Small Leather Goods, Fragrances, Dress Shoes, Store Displays, Fixtures, Supplies

VIA MILANO, INC. (MW)

802 Northstar Dr. (b-des)
San Antonio, TX 78216
210-377-0207 / Fax: 210-377-4229
Sales: $500,001-$1 Million

KAZEM AHMADI (Owner) & Buys Leather Goods, Men's Big & Tall Apparel, Casualwear, Denim Apparel, Formalwear, Accessories, Hosiery, Outerwear, Sportswear, Suits, Swimwear, Boys' Wear

HARRY'S DEPARTMENT STORE (DEPT-2)

403 E. Wallace (p)
San Saba, TX 76877
915-372-3636 / Fax: 915-372-5832
Sales: $1 Million-$10 Million

LORENA TERRY (Co-Owner) & Buys Men's Wear, Sportswear, Accessories, Furnishings, Boys' & Students' Wear, Boots, Shoes, Store Displays, Fixtures, Supplies

DAVID PARKER (Co-Owner) & Buys Men's Wear, Sportswear, Accessories, Furnishings, Boys' & Students' Wear, Boots, Shoes, Store Displays, Fixtures, Supplies

D & D SUPPLY (CLO)

12th St. & Ave. C (m)
Seagraves, TX 79359
806-387-2149 / Fax: 806-387-2849

JUDY SELLERS (Co-Owner) & Buys Men's Casual Slacks, Active Apparel, Belts, Fragrances, Footwear, Store Displays, Fixtures, Supplies

DON SELLERS (Co-Owner) & Buys Men's Casual Slacks, Active Apparel, Belts, Fragrances, Footwear, Store Displays, Fixtures, Supplies

B & T SPORTS (SP)

227 Main St.
Sealy, TX 77474
979-885-4716 / Fax: 979-885-3035
Sales: $100,001-$500,000

LARRY KUCIEMBA (President) & Buys Athletic Apparel, Activewear, Imprintable Apparel

SADDLE SHOP (WW)

2517 N. Austin St. (p-m-b)
Seguin, TX 78155
830-379-1760
Sales: $100,001-$500,000

RONNIE ASHLEY (Co-Owner) & Buys Western Clothing, Men's Raincoats, Big & Tall Men's Wear, Outer Jackets, Dress Shirts, Gloves, Headwear, Belts, Footwear, Boots, Young Men's Wear, Boys' Clothing, Store Displays, Fixtures, Supplies

CONNIE ASHLEY (Co-Owner) & Buys Western Clothing, Men's Raincoats, Big & Tall Men's Wear, Outer Jackets, Dress Shirts, Gloves, Headwear, Belts, Footwear, Boots, Young Men's Wear, Boys' Clothing, Store Displays, Fixtures, Supplies

SPORTS ETC. (SP)

P.O. Box 1007
205 E. Montana Dr.
Shiner, TX 77984
361-594-2812 / Fax: 361-594-2812
Sales: Under $100,000

DONALD POHLER (Owner) & Buys Athletic Apparel, Activewear, Licensed Apparel

HACKFELD'S (CLO)

3219 College Ave. (m-b)
Snyder, TX 79549
915-573-6763 / Fax: 915-573-7374
Sales: $100,001-$500,000

JACKIE HACKFIELD (Co-Owner) & Buys Men's Western Wear, Sport Shirts, Accessories, Young Men's T-shirts, Boots, Store Displays, Fixtures & Supplies

KEITH HACKFIELD (Co-Owner) & Buys Men's Western Wear, Sport Shirts, Accessories, Young Men's T-shirts, Boots, Store Displays, Fixtures & Supplies

ON THE BEACH (CLO)

2105 Padre Blvd. (m)
South Padre Island, TX 78597
956-761-1194 / Fax: 956-761-7036

GENE BAGLEY (Owner) & Buys Men's Swimsuits, Shorts, Sport Shirts, Slacks, Hosiery, Footwear, Urban Contemporary, Store Displays, Fixtures, Supplies

TATE'S (CLO)

P.O. Box 2490
700 Padre Blvd.
South Padre Island, TX 78597
956-761-9541 / Fax: 956-761-4549

TATE CELAYA (Owner) & Buys Men's Wear, Sportswear, Accessories, Furnishings, Men's Footwear, Store Displays, Fixtures, Supplies

CATES' MEN'S & BOYS' WEAR (MW)

221 Main St. (p-m-b)
Spearman, TX 79081
806-659-3426 / Fax: 808-659-2496

ALFRED AVILA (Co-Owner) & Buys Men's & Young Men's Wear, Footwear, Accessories, Furnishings, Boots, Boys' Wear, Store Displays, Fixtures, Supplies

CINDY AVILA (Co-Owner) & Buys Men's & Young Men's Wear, Footwear, Accessories, Furnishings, Boots, Boys' Wear, Store Displays, Fixtures, Supplies

SWIM SHOPS OF THE SOUTHWEST (SP-2)

5010 Louetta Rd., #M
Spring, TX 77379
281-376-4460 / Fax: 281-251-1459

JOHN VOGEL (Co-Owner) & Buys Apparel, Accessories, Swimwear, Sandals

RUSS GARNEY (Co-Owner) & Buys Apparel, Accessories, Swimwear, Sandals

RETAIL CONCEPTS, INC. (SG-15)

(SUN & SKI SPORTS)
(UNIVERSAL SKI & SPORTS)
4001 Greenbriare, #100 (p-m-b)
Stafford, TX 77477
281-340-5000 / Fax: 281-340-5020
Website: www.sunandski.com
Retail Locations: TX, NC, MO, OH, FL, TN, OK, GA, MD, CA, NY

BARRY GOLDWARE (President)

RICK STEINLE-Men's & Boys' Watersport Apparel, Snow Ski Apparel

TRICIA KUBECZKA-Men's & Boys' Snow Ski Apparel

JOHN JARRETT-Men's & Boys' Outdoor Camping Accessories

BRAD THOMPSON-Footwear, Ski Accessories, Men's & Boys' Cycling Apparel

MARTY CHAMBERS (Dist. Ctr. Mgr.) & Buys Store Displays, Fixtures and Supplies

CHICK ELMS' GRAND ENTRY WESTERN STORE (WW)

1695 S. Loop (m)
Stephenville, TX 76401
254-968-3920 / Fax: 254-968-3920

CHICK ELMS (Co-Owner) & Buys Cowboy Hats

CINDRA ELMS (Co-Owner) & Buys Men's & Boys' Western Wear, Accessories, Furnishings, Footwear, Store Displays, Fixtures, Supplies

R.P.'S WESTERN OUTLET (WW-2)

1355 S. Loop (bud-m)
Stephenville, TX 76401
254-968-6612

RON PACK (Owner) & Buys Men's Western Wear, Accessories, Footwear, Furnishings, Store Displays, Fixtures, Supplies

BUISON, INC. (CLO)

(BUI-YAH-KAH)
1254 Misty Lake Ct. (m-b)
Sugarland, TX 77478
281-242-2014 / Fax: 281-242-6001

HAI BUI (V.P.) & Buys Men's Sportswear, Accessories, Furnishings, Footwear, Boys' Sportswear, Store Displays, Fixtures, Supplies

CIRCLE E WESTERN, INC. (WW)

300 Shannon Rd. (p)
Sulphur Springs, TX 75482
903-885-4481 / Fax: 903-439-3274

MICKEY EDDINS (Owner) & Buys Men's & Young Men's Western Clothing, Sportswear, Leather Apparel, Dress Shirts, Ties, Underwear, Gloves, Headwear, Accessories, 8 to 20 Boys' Shirts, Jeans

CURT MORRIS-Men's & Young Men's Western Clothing, Sportswear, Leather Apparel, Dress Shirts, Ties, Underwear, Gloves, Headwear, Accessories, 8 to 20 Boys' Shirts, Jeans, Footwear, Boots, Store Displays, Fixtures, Supplies

ODOM'S BIG & TALL MENSWEAR (MW)

Box 23, Rt. 4 (b)
Sulphur Springs, TX 75482
903-885-8982
Sales: $100,001-$500,000

DONNA ODOM (Owner) & Buys Men's Big & Tall Clothing, Sportswear, Furnishings, Accessories, Footwear, Store Displays, Fixtures, Supplies

WESTERN STORE (WW)

118 S. Main St. (m)
Sweeny, TX 77480
979-548-3100
Sales: $500,001-$1 Million

DONALD BARBER-Men's Western Jeans, Shirts, Belts, Footwear, Cowboy Hats, Store Displays, Fixtures & Supplies

MARY BARBER (Owner) & Buys Men's Western Jeans, Shirts, Belts, Footwear, Cowboy Hats, Store Displays, Fixtures & Supplies

DANDY WESTERN WEAR (WW)

I 20 & Hopkins Rd. (p-m-b)
Sweetwater, TX 79556
915-235-4456
Sales: $1 Million-$10 Million

MARTY FOUST (Owner) & Buys Men's Western Wear, Accessories, Furnishings, Footwear, Cowboy Hats, Store Displays, Fixtures, Supplies

TEAGUE SUPPLY (CLO)
Box 147G (bud-p)
Rt. 3
Teague, TX 75860
254-739-2445
Sales: $500,001-$1 Million
JOYCE GONZALES-Men's & Boys' Blue Jeans, T-shirts, Shorts, Gloves, Headwear, Accessories, Store Displays, Fixtures and Supplies
STEVE EUBANKS (Co-Owner) & Buys Footwear, Boots
ROBERT EUBANKS (Co-Owner)
BETH BEENE (Mgr.) & Buys Men's & Boys' Blue Jeans, T-shirts, Shorts, Gloves, Headwear, Accessories, Store Displays, Fixtures and Supplies
BILLY BEENE (Co-Owner) & Buys Store Displays, Fixtures, Supplies

CY LONG MENSWEAR (MW)
1401 S. 31st St. (m-b)
Temple, TX 76504
254-778-4301
Sales: $500,001-$1 Million
CY LONG (Owner) & Buys Men's Sportswear, Furnishings, Accessories, Big & Tall Men's Wear, Men's Footwear, Store Displays, Fixtures, Supplies

COUNTRY STORE (MW)
210 W. Moore St. (m)
Terrell, TX 75160
972-563-3813 / Fax: 972-551-1000
Sales: $1 Million-$10 Million
MARIE RISINGER (Owner) & Buys Men's Tailored Slacks, Tailored Jackets, Sportswear, Accessories, Furnishings, Footwear, Store Displays, Fixtures, Supplies

CANON & WILLIAMS (MW)
4026 Summerhill Rd.
Texarkana, TX 75503
903-791-6354 / Fax: 903-794-7032
Website: www.canonandwilliams.com
JUDGE CANNON (Owner) & Buys Men's and Boys' Clothing, Suits, Sportcoats, Furnishings, Accessories, Footwear

LACY DRY GOODS (DG)
P.O. Box 127 (m)
Turkey, TX 79261
806-423-1155
Sales: $500,001-$1 Million
HUBERT PRICE (President) & Buys Men's Sportswear, Furnishings, Accessories, Footwear, Boys' Wear, Store Displays, Fixtures, Supplies
DELORES PRICE-Men's Sportswear, Furnishings, Accessories, Footwear, Boys' Wear, Urban Contemporary, Store Displays, Fixtures, Supplies

ARMY & NAVY STORE OF TYLER (AN-2)
1201 SE Loop 323 (p)
Tyler, TX 75701
903-592-0548 / Fax: 903-592-1645
Sales: $1 Million-$10 Million
WALTER MIDDLETON (Owner) & Buys Men's Work Clothing, Western Wear, Boys' Shorts, Footwear, T-shirts, Shorts, Headwear, Hosiery, Underwear, Store Displays, Fixtures, Supplies

CAVENDER'S BOOT CITY (WW-42 & OL)
2025 W. Southwest Loop 323 (m)
Tyler, TX 75701
903-561-4992 / Fax: 903-561-4849
Sales: $50 Million-$100 Million
Website: www.cavenders.com
Retail Locations: TX
MIKE CAVENDER (Co-Owner) (@ 903-509-9509)
SHARON BILES (Real Estate Contact) (@ 713-524-4646)
DAVID KING-Men's Western Wear, Boys' Western Wear, Related Accessories, Furnishings, Footwear, Store Displays, Fixtures & Supplies

GRAND CHILDREN (KS)
114 E. 8th St. (b)
Tyler, TX 75701
903-592-4827 / Fax: 903-592-4838
SUZANNE CALHOUN (Owner) & Buys 8 to 20 Boys' Wear, Related Accessories, Furnishings, Store Displays, Fixtures, Supplies

JOYNER & FRY (MW)
102 E. 8th St. (m-b)
Tyler, TX 75701
903-597-3721
Sales: $1 Million-$10 Million
STEVE FRY (Owner) & Buys Men's Wear, Leather Apparel, Accessories, Furnishings, Footwear, Urban Contemporary, Store Displays, Fixtures, Supplies

M.A. SIMMS CAPRANCH & CO., INC. (SP-2)
2018 S. Broadway
Tyler, TX 75701
903-592-3452 / Fax: 903-595-6607
MOLLY NELSON (Co-Owner) & Buys Store Displays, Fixtures, Supplies
BRETT NELSON (Co-Owner) & Buys Men's Sportswear, Furnishings, Accessories
SHARON HUNTER-Boys' Footwear, Sportswear, Furnishings, Accessories

PENICK & CHANCE, INC. (MW)
(PAUL'S BIG & TALL)
(P.C.'S MENSWEAR)
4574 S. Broadway (m-b)
Tyler, TX 75703
903-561-6505 / Fax: 903-561-2784
PAUL CHANCE (Owner) (@ 903-561-6373) & Buys Men's Sweaters, Sport Shirts, Outer Jackets, Casual Slacks, Active Apparel, Accessories, Big & Tall Men's Furnishings, Dress Shirts, Underwear, Hosiery, Jewelry, Small Leather Goods, Fragrances, Footwear, Store Displays, Fixtures, Supplies
CHARLES HAMILTON (Mgr.) & Buys Men's Suits, Tailored Jackets, Tailored Slacks, Overcoats, Raincoats, Big & Tall Men's Wear, Sportswear, Sweaters, Sport Shirts, Outer Jackets, Leather Apparel, Casual Slacks, Active Apparel, Furnishings, Dress Shirts, Ties, Robes, Underwear, Hosiery, Gloves, Headwear, Accessories, Belts, Small Leathers

SUIT SOURCE USA (MW & OL)
4955 Profit Dr., #2
Tyler, TX 75707
903-561-6036 / Fax: 903-561-8848
Website: www.suitsource.com
MAC SYMES (Owner) & Buys Men's Formal Wear, Suits, Blazers, Sport Coats, Tuxedos, Big & Tall Wear

FRANK'S WESTERN WEAR (WW)
1017 Pat Booker, #C
Universal City, TX 78148
210-658-0551 / Fax: 210-658-0541
ROBERT TRUJILLO (Co-Owner) & Buys Men's & Boys' Western Wear, Related Accessories, Furnishings, Footwear, Store Displays, Fixtures, Supplies

JULIEN'S (CLO)
200 N. Getty (b-h)
Uvalde, TX 78801
830-278-2925 / Fax: 830-278-9759
Sales: $500,001-$1 Million
DOROTHY WINSTON (Owner) & Buys Men's, Young Men's & Boys' Wear, Urban Contemporary, Sportswear, Accessories, Furnishings, Footwear, Store Displays, Fixtures, Supplies

HIGH-BREHM HAT & WESTERN WEAR (WW)
6603 N. Navarro St. (m)
Victoria, TX 77904
361-575-4972 / Fax: 361-573-6825
KELLY HIGH (Owner) & Buys Men's, Young Men's & Boys' Western Wear, Men's Leather Apparel, Related Accessories, Furnishings, Footwear, Boots, Store Displays, Fixtures, Supplies

MELVIN'S GLOBE CLOTHIERS, INC. (MW)
6320 Navarro St. (m-b)
Victoria, TX 77904
361-575-2698 / Fax: 361-575-4922
Sales: $1 Million-$10 Million
Website: www.melvinsvictoria.com
MELVIN DUSEK (Chmn.)
RANDY HUTSON (President) & Buys Men's Overcoats, Suits, Tailored Jackets, Tailored Slacks, Raincoats, Sportswear, Furnishings, Headwear, Accessories, Footwear, Big & Tall Men's Wear, Store Displays, Fixtures, Supplies

RATHER'S, INC. (MW)
2523 N. Laurent (m-b)
Victoria, TX 77901
361-573-6421
Sales: $100,001-$500,000
JAMES C. RATHER (Owner) & Buys Men's Wear, Sportswear, Accessories, Furnishings, Big & Tall Men's Wear, Store Displays, Fixtures, Supplies

BAR B WESTERN STORE (WW)
1080 N. Main St. (b)
Vidor, TX 77662
409-769-4558 / Fax: 409-769-9451
JAMES E. BOND (President) & Buys Men's Sportswear, Furnishings, Accessories, Footwear, Boots, Leather Apparel, Boys' Wear, Store Displays, Fixtures, Supplies

HUB CLOTHIER (MW)
(DALLAS APPAREL, INC.)
506 Austin Ave. (m)
Waco, TX 76702
254-754-8611
Sales: $1 Million-$10 Million
TONY MARTIN (Owner) & Buys Men's Sportswear, Furnishings, Accessories, Footwear, Young Men's Wear, Boys' Wear, Store Displays, Fixtures, Supplies

RITCHIE'S WESTERN WEAR (WW)
(TRIPLE R WESTERN WEAR, INC.)
4533 W. Waco Dr. (m-b)
Waco, TX 76710
254-776-8036 / Fax: 254-776-8698
Sales: $1 Million-$10 Million
Website: www.texsource.com
ALAN RITCHIE (Owner)
MIKE RITCHIE (G.M.M.) & Buys Men's & Boys' Western Wear, Related Accessories, Furnishings, Footwear, Store Displays, Fixtures, Supplies

SALESMAN'S SAMPLE OUTLET (MW)
(JIM DEAL, INC.)
4306 Memorial Dr. (m)
Waco, TX 76711
254-752-8305 / Fax: 254-752-0517
Sales: $1 Million-$10 Million
LINDA DEAL (Co-Owner) & Buys Men's Big & Tall, Leather Apparel
CAL DEAL (Co-Owner) & Buys Men's Sportswear, Furnishings, Accessories

HUB CLOTHES (CLO & OL)
112 W. Dallas (m)
Weatherford, TX 76086
817-594-2762 / Fax: 817-599-6121
Sales: $1 Million-$10 Million
BUTCH HOTT (Owner) & Buys Men's Tailored Jackets, Tailored Slacks, Raincoats, Sportswear, Sweaters, Sport Shirts, Outer Jackets, Casual Slacks, Active Apparel, Furnishings, Dress Shirts, Ties, Underwear, Hosiery, Headwear, Accessories, Belts, Small Leather Goods, Footwear, Boots

BOOTS 'N' JEANS, INC. (WW)
2005 W. Expwy., #83 (m)
Weslaco, TX 78596
956-968-8150 / Fax: 956-969-3486
MARTIN MASSO (Co-Owner) & Buys Men's Western Wear, Accessories, Furnishings, Men's Footwear, Boots, Young Men's Wear, Boys' Wear, Store Displays, Fixtures, Supplies

LIONEL WESTERN WEAR, INC. (WW)
332 S. Texas (m)
Weslaco, TX 78596
956-968-2552 / Fax: 956-477-5166
Sales: $1 Million-$10 Million
SANDRA O. PENA (Owner) & Buys Men's Western Wear, Related Accessories, Furnishings, Boots, Store Displays, Fixtures, Supplies

BROWSE SHOP WESTERN WEAR (WW & CLO)
1111 E. Scott (p)
Wichita Falls, TX 76303
940-766-0972 / Fax: 940-766-1140
Sales: $1 Million-$10 Million
M. W. OLIVER (Owner & G.M.M.) & Buys Men's Western Wear, Sportswear, Tailored Jackets, Tailored Slacks, Footwear, Big & Tall Men's Wear, Boots, Store Displays, Fixtures, Supplies
MARLENE ERMIS-Men's Western Wear, Sweaters, Sport Shirts, Outer Jackets, Casual Slacks, Tailored Jackets, Tailored Slacks, Raincoats, Dress Shirts, Suits, Ties, Underwear, Hosiery, Gloves, Headwear, Belts, Jewelry, Small Leather Goods, Leather Apparel, Footwear, Boots, Young Men's Wear, Boys' Wear

COOLEY'S WESTERN WEAR (WW)
4300 Kemp Blvd. (p)
Wichita Falls, TX 76308
940-691-6012 / Fax: 940-691-6034
Sales: $1 Million-$10 Million
JOHN COOLEY (Owner) & Buys Men's Western Wear, Related Accessories, Furnishings, Footwear, Boots, Store Displays, Fixtures & Supplies
CARRI COOLEY (Mgr.) & Buys Men's Western Wear, Related Accessories, Furnishings, Footwear, Boots, Store Displays, Fixtures & Supplies

SAMMY'S WESTERN WEAR (WW)
P.O. Box 713 (m)
Winnie, TX 77665
409-296-2351
WILFRED LE BLANC (Co-Owner) & Buys Men's Western Wear, Accessories, Furnishings, Footwear, Boots, Store Displays, Fixtures, Supplies
ELOISE LE BLANC (Co-Owner) & Buys Men's Western Wear, Accessories, Furnishings, Footwear, Boots, Store Displays, Fixtures, Supplies

ANDREA'S (WW)
P.O. Box 743 (p-m-b)
Woodsboro, TX 78393
361-543-4832
ANDIE ROOKE (Owner) & Buys Men's & Boys' Western Wear, Related Accessories, Furnishings, Footwear, Urban Contemporary, Store Displays, Fixtures & Supplies

J.B. BEST & CO. (CLO)
P.O. Box 6 (m)
120 S. Charlton
Woodville, TX 75979
409-283-2124
Sales: $500,001-$1 Million
JAMES BEST (Partner) & Buys Men's Overcoats, Suits, Tailored Jackets, Tailored Slacks, Raincoats, Sportswear, Furnishings, Headwear, Accessories, Footwear, Big & Tall Men's Wear, Young Men's & Boys' Wear, Urban Contemporary, Store Displays, Fixtures & Supplies
HUNTLEY KENESSON (Partner) & Buys Store Displays, Fixtures, Supplies

LONE STAR STORE (CLO)
(LONE STAR DRY GOODS)
P.O. Box 2831
Zapata, TX 78076
956-765-4325
JUAN GARZA (Owner) & Buys Men's & Boys' Wear, Urban Contemporary, Western Wear, Footwear, Furnishings, Accessories, Store Displays, Fixtures, Supplies

UTAH - Altamont

COUNTRY FLAIR (CLO)

P.O. Box 437 (p)
15250 W. 4000 N.
Altamont, UT 84001
435-454-3418

BRENT WALKER (Co-Owner)
JESSIE WALKER (Co-Owner) & Buys Footwear
COURTNEY THEENER-Men's Coats, Sportswear, Hosiery, Straw Hats, T-shirts, Fleece, Active Apparel, Accessories, Young Men's Wear & Boys' Wear, Store Displays, Fixtures, Supplies

JOHNSTOWN LTD. (MW)

144 S. Main St. (b)
Bountiful, UT 84010
801-294-0516

JOHN HEPWORTH (Owner & Mgr.) & Buys Men's Sportswear, Furnishings, Accessories, Footwear, Store Displays, Fixtures, Supplies

JOLLEY'S RANCHWEAR, INC. (CLO)

52 N. Main (p-m)
Cedar City, UT 84720
435-586-8108 / Fax: 435-586-4208
Sales: $1 Million-$10 Million

STEVE JOLLEY (Owner) & Buys Men's Western Sportswear, Accessories, Furnishings, Boys' Wear, Footwear, Store Displays, Fixtures, Supplies

MR. R MENSWEAR (MW)

74 N. Main St. (m-b)
Cedar City, UT 84720
435-586-2494 / Fax: 435-586-0859

ALAN CARDON (President) & Buys Men's Suits, Furnishings, Headwear, Accessories, Footwear, Store Displays, Fixtures, Supplies

SUMMIT MERCANTILE (WW)

P.O. Box 8 (p-m)
16 S. Main St.
Coalville, UT 84017
435-336-2421 / Fax: 435-336-1233
Sales: $1 Million-$10 Million

JAMES BLONQUIST (President) & Buys Men's Western Wear & Work Clothes, Footwear, Related Accessories, Store Displays, Fixtures, Supplies

DCR DEPARTMENT STORE (DEPT)

135 N. Main St. (bud)
Fillmore, UT 84631
435-743-5115 / Fax: 435-743-5124

CRAIG BARTHOLOMEW (Owner) & Buys Men's Sportswear, Furnishings, Boys' Wear, Boots, Store Displays, Fixtures, Supplies

OUTPOST MERCANTILE (DEPT-2)

P.O. Box 99 (p)
Fort Duchesne, UT 84026
435-722-3211 / Fax: 435-353-4566
Sales: $500,000-$1 Million

MYRON DUNCAN (Owner) & Buys Men's Clothing, Sportswear, Store Displays, Fixtures, Supplies

JJ'S FAMILY STORE (CLO)

133 Main St. (m)
Huntington, UT 84528
435-687-9029
Sales: $1 Million-$10 Million

JESSE BRINKERHOFF (Owner) & Buys Men's Sportswear, Jeans, Western Wear, Underwear, Hosiery, Gloves, Accessories, Young Men's Wear, 8 to 20 Boys' Wear, Sportswear, Furnishings, Accessories, Store Displays, Fixtures, Supplies
JANETTE FLORENSON-Urban Contemporary, Boots

DUKE'S CLOTHING (CLO)

39 W. Center St. (p-m)
Kanab, UT 84741
435-644-2700 / Fax: 435-644-5185

SAM AIKEN (Owner) & Buys Men's Sportswear, Furnishings, Western Hats, Belts, Wallets, Young Men's Wear, Boys' Shirts, Jeans, T-shirts, Fleece, Active Apparel, Footwear, Store Displays, Fixtures, Supplies
CINDY AIKEN-Men's Sportswear, Furnishings, Western Hats, Belts, Wallets, Young Men's Wear, Boys' Shirts, Jeans, T-shirts, Fleece, Active Apparel

DIAMOND T WESTERN WEAR (WW)

451 N. Main St. (m-b)
Layton, UT 84041
801-546-1301 / Fax: 801-546-1301
Sales: $100,001-$500,000

TOM BROUGH (Owner) & Buys Men's & Boys' Western Wear, Related Accessories, Boots, Footwear, Store Displays, Fixtures, Supplies

BROADBENT & SON (DEPT)

128 N. 100 E. (p-m-b)
Lehi, UT 84043
801-768-9201

JOHN S. BROADBENT (Owner) & Buys Men's & Boys' Wear, Footwear, Store Displays, Fixtures, Supplies
BETTY BROADBENT-Men's & Boys' Wear, Footwear, Store Displays, Fixtures, Supplies

KATER SHOP, INC. (MW)

81 N. Main St. (m)
Logan, UT 84321
435-752-1195 / Fax: 435-753-6032
Sales: $1 Million-$10 Million
Website: www.missionoutfitters.com

M. LYNN HICKEN (Co-Owner) & Buys Men's Overcoats, Suits, Tailored Jackets, Tailored Slacks, Raincoats, Sweaters, Sport Shirts, Casual Slacks, Furnishings, Store Displays, Fixtures, Supplies
STEVE HICKEN (Co-Owner) & Buys Men's Overcoats, Suits, Tailored Jackets, Tailored Slacks, Raincoats, Sweaters, Sport Shirts, Casual Slacks, Furnishings, Store Displays, Fixtures, Supplies

LEVEN'S (MW)

69 N. Main St.
Logan, UT 84323
435-752-7032 / Fax: 435-713-4443
Sales: $1 Million-$10 Million

DAVID WILLIAMS (Owner) & Buys Men's Suits, Sportswear, Outerwear, Accessories, Footwear, Formal Wear, Young Men's Wear, Boys' Wear, Store Displays, Fixtures, Supplies

THE SPORTSMAN (CLO & SP)

129 N. Main St. (p-m-b)
Logan, UT 84321
435-752-0211 / Fax: 435-755-8663
Sales: $1 Million-$10 Million

RUSS FJELSTEAD (Owner) & Buys Men's & Young Men's Sportswear, Active Apparel, Accessories, Furnishings, Headwear, Footwear, Store Displays, Fixtures, Supplies
MARK FJELSTEAD (Mgr.) & Buys Men's & Young Men's Sportswear, Active Apparel, Accessories, Furnishings, Headwear, Footwear, Store Displays, Fixtures, Supplies
KRISTAN FJELSTEAD-Men's & Young Men's Sportswear, Active Apparel, Accessories, Furnishings, Headwear, Footwear, Store Displays, Fixtures, Supplies

UTAH STATE UNIVERSITY BOOKSTORE (SP)

(UTAH STATE UNIVERSITY)
University Blvd.
UMC 0200
Logan, UT 84322
435-797-1666 / Fax: 435-797-3793
Sales: $2 Million-$5 Million

DAVE HANSEN (Assoc. Mgr.)
LORI CANO-Activewear, Outerwear, Licensed Apparel

JENSEN'S DEPARTMENT STORE (DEPT)
29 N. Main St. (p-m)
Manti, UT 84642
435-835-3131 / Fax: 435-835-3132
Sales: $1 Million-$10 Million
JOHN JENSEN (Owner) & Buys Men's Sportswear, Furnishings, Headwear, Accessories, Young Men's Wear, Boys' Wear, Leather Apparel, Footwear, Store Displays, Fixtures, Supplies

THE T-SHIRT SHOP (GM)
38 N. Main St.
Moab, UT 84532
435-259-5271
Website: www.moabtshirts.com
DOROTHY BYRD (Owner) & Buys Men's T-shirts, Headwear, Souvenirs

TUCKER'S EMPORIUM (WW)
30 W. Main St. (m)
Mount Pleasant, UT 84647
435-462-3488
LOIS TUCKER (Owner) & Buys Men's, Young Men's & Boys' Western Wear, Related Accessories, Jeans, Store Displays, Fixtures, Supplies

DAHLE'S BIG & TALL (CLO-14)
6107 South State St. (b)
Murray, UT 84107
801-261-1554 / Fax: 801-892-2556
Sales: $1 Million-$10 Million
Website: www.dahles.com
ALLAN DAHLE (Chmn. & Co-Owner)
ROBERT DAHLE (President-Men's Div.) & Buys Big & Tall Men's Wear, Store Displays, Fixtures, Supplies
BUD SHEHAN (V.P.-Adv.) & Buys Big & Tall Men's Wear, Sportswear, Leather Apparel, Furnishings, Accessories

THE FREEDOM CO. (MW)
6061 S. State St.
Murray, UT 84107
801-266-5858 / Fax: 801-266-1516
Website: www.freedomco.com
JONI SIEBERT (Owner) & Buys Men's Work Uniforms, Medical Uniforms, Medical Shoes, Apparel for Corporate, Restaurants & Hotels, Store Displays, Fixtures, Supplies

A-1 MEDICAL SUPPLY (CLO-3)
134 31st St. (m)
Ogden, UT 84401
801-394-4455 / Fax: 801-394-6060
JO ANN PERUCCA (Owner) (@ 801-479-3577) & Buys Men's Medical Uniforms, Medical Shoes, Store Displays, Fixtures, Supplies

C.W. CROSS CO., INC. (WW)
2246 Washington Blvd. (b)
Ogden, UT 84401
801-394-5773 / Fax: 801-627-0415
Website: www.crosswestern.com
CRAIG CROSS (Co-Owner) & Buys Men's Footwear, Men's, Young Men's & Boys' Western Wear, Leather Apparel, Related Accessories, Furnishings, Store Displays, Fixtures, Supplies
TONY CROSS (Co-Owner) & Buys Men's, Young Men's & Boys' Western Wear, Leather Apparel, Related Accessories, Furnishings, Store Displays, Fixtures, Supplies

MILLER'S SKI & CYCLE HAUS (SG)
834 Washington Blvd. (b)
Ogden, UT 84404
801-392-3911 / Fax: 801-392-8666
Sales: $100,001-$500,000
ALAN MILLER (President & Owner) & Buys Ski Wear, Sweaters, Outer Jackets, Underwear, Hosiery, Gloves, Headwear, Store Displays, Fixtures, Supplies

QUALITY FASHION APPAREL (SP)
50 E. 4600 S. (m)
Ogden, UT 84405
801-393-0929
STANLEY PAULSEN-Formal Wear & Related Accessories, Furnishings, Footwear, Store Displays, Fixtures, Supplies

SMITH & EDWARDS CO. (DEPT)
3936 N. Hwy. 126 (p-m)
Ogden, UT 84404
801-731-1120 / Fax: 801-731-2113
ALBERT SMITH (Owner)
JAMES B. SMITH (President) & Buys Men's Western Sportswear, Furnishings, Leather Apparel, Boys' Wear, Boys' Footwear, Store Displays, Fixtures, Supplies
STEVE SMITH-Men's Footwear

ALLEN'S TUXEDOS (MW-2)
1027 N. State St. (p)
Orem, UT 84057
801-224-8956
ALLEN PRESTON (President & Owner) & Buys Formal Wear & Related Accessories, Furnishings, Footwear, Store Displays, Fixtures, Supplies

BJORN STOVA (CLO-3)
(STEIN ERIKSEN, INC.)
7815 E. Royal St.
Park City, UT 84060
435-645-0760 / Fax: 435-645-7191
Website: www.steineriksen.com
FRANCOISE ERIKSEN (Owner) & Buys Men's Ski Apparel, Sportswear, Headwear, Belts, Footwear, Store Displays, Fixtures, Supplies

DUGINS WEST, INC. (CLO)
P.O. Box 2008 (p-m)
Park City, UT 84068
435-649-4200
ROBERT DUGINS (Owner) & Buys Men's & Boys' T-shirts, Store Displays, Fixtures, Supplies

NANRON, INC. (CLO-2)
(HILDA'S)
541 Main St. (b-h)
Park City, UT 84060
435-649-7321 / Fax: 435-649-0241
MARY BLACK (Owner) & Buys Men's Sportswear, Furnishings (No Underwear), Accessories, Footwear, Dress Shoes, Athletic Footwear, Slippers, Sandals

SOMETHING TO CROW ABOUT (CLO-2)
43 S. Main St. (p-m)
Payson, UT 84651
801-465-4770 / Fax: 801-465-2872
Sales: $500,001-$1 Million
DALE LeBARON (Owner) & Buys Men's & 8 to 20 Boys' Wear, Footwear, Furnishings, Accessories, Store Displays, Fixtures, Supplies

RICHARD'S TOGGERY (CLO)
42 E. Main St. (m-b)
Price, UT 84501
435-637-1164 / Fax: 435-637-8216
MARLENE GHIRARDELLI (Owner)
GREG GHIRARDELLI (Mgr.) & Buys Men's & Young Men's Sportswear, Leather Apparel, Furnishings, Boys' Jeans, Belts, Small Leather Goods, Fragrances, T-shirts, Fleece, Active Apparel, Store Displays, Fixtures, Supplies

CHRISTENSEN'S DEPARTMENT STORES (DEPT-3)
P.O. Box 97 (m)
39 N. Main St.
Richfield, UT 84701
435-896-6466 / Fax: 435-896-6621
ALAN CHRISTENSEN (Partner) & Buys Men's Sportswear, Furnishings, Young Men's Wear, Boys' Wear, Footwear
DAVID CHRISTENSEN (Partner) & Buys Men's Sportswear, Furnishings, Young Men's Wear, Boys' Wear, Footwear, Store Displays, Fixtures, Supplies

BEACH BREAK (SP-2)
1770 Red Cliffs Dr., #185
Saint George, UT 84790
435-674-2430 / Fax: 801-574-3544
MARTHA LUCIA (Co-Owner) & Buys Skiwear
LEN LUCIA (Co-Owner) & Buys Skiwear

UTAH - Salt Lake City

A.A. CALLISTER CO. (CLO-2)

3615 S. Redwood Rd. (p)
Salt Lake City, UT 84119
801-973-7058 / Fax: 801-973-6799
Sales: $1 Million-$10 Million
Website: www.callister.com

EDWARD F. CALLISTER (President)
A. A. CALLISTER (C.E.O.)
MARY ANN KNAPHUS (Exec. V.P.) & Buys Men's Hats, Footwear, Men's Western Suits, Dusters, Leather Apparel, Riding Wear, Ties, Headwear, Young Men's Wear, Boys' Western Shirts, Jeans, Hats, Store Displays, Fixtures, Supplies
DANNETTE HAMMOND-Men's Hats, Footwear, Men's Western Suits, Dusters, Leather Apparel, Riding Wear, Ties, Headwear, Young Men's Wear, Boys' Western Shirts, Jeans, Hats, Store Displays, Fixtures, Supplies
CHERILYN SIMAGND-Boots, Hats, Accessories

COPPER RIVET, INC. (CLO-11)

3424 S. State St., #F (b)
Salt Lake City, UT 84115
801-487-0650 / Fax: 801-487-0781
Sales: $10 Million-$50 Million

AMY WOLFE (President) & Buys Store Design
TED YOUNG (V.P.) & Buys Young Men's Sweaters, Sport Shirts, Casual Slacks, Active Apparel, Leather Apparel, Hosiery, Headwear, Belts, Boys' Sportswear
LAURA THOMAS-Accessories, Furnishings

GINGISS FORMAL WEAR (SP-5)

6970 S. Highland Dr. (m-b-des)
Salt Lake City, UT 84121
801-943-4100 / Fax: 801-957-1287
Sales: $1 Million-$10 Million

LONNIE BAIRD (President) & Buys Men's Tuxedos, Footwear, Formal Furnishings, Headwear, Accessories, Boys' Tuxedos, Store Displays, Fixtures, Supplies
SHON BAIRD (Mgr.) & Buys Men's Tuxedos, Footwear, Formal Furnishings, Headwear, Accessories, Boys' Tuxedos, Store Displays, Fixtures, Supplies

GREAT SALT LAKE COUNSEL (CLO-2)

525 Foothill Blvd.
Salt Lake City, UT 84113
801-582-3663 / Fax: 801-582-7401
Website: www.gslc-bsa.org

CHRIS SMALLWOOD (Mgr.) & Buys 12 to Adult Scout Uniforms

JMR CHALKGARDEN (CLO-6)

149 W. 200 S.
Salt Lake City, UT 84101
801-355-8199 / Fax: 801-355-3852
Sales: $1 Million-$10 Million

JEFF BARNARD (Mgr.) & Buys Men's Wear, Young Men's Wear, Boys' Jeans & Tops, Leather Apparel, Urban Contemporary, Store Displays, Fixtures
RICHARD BARNARD (Mgr.) & Buys Men's Footwear, Accesories

MODA ITALIA, INC. (MW)

105 E. South Temple (b)
Salt Lake City, UT 84111
801-355-8828 / Fax: 801-532-4884
Sales: $500,001-$1 Million

ANTONIO SCIAMMARELLA (Owner) & Buys Men's Imported Sportswear (Custom Tailored from Italy), Furnishings, Accessories, Store Displays, Fixtures, Supplies

MR. MAC (CLO-2)

(MAC'S OF MIDVILLE)
5690 S. Redwood Rd. (p-m)
Salt Lake City, UT 84123
801-966-6400 / Fax: 801-966-6482
Sales: $1 Million-$10 Million
Website: www.mrmac.com

SCOTT CHRISTENSEN (Co-Owner) & Buys Men's Wear, Young Men's Wear, Boys' Wear, Leather Apparel
STAN CHRISTENSEN (Co-Owner) & Buys Men's Footwear, Furnishings, Accessories
WAYNE WARE (Comptroller) & Buys Store Displays, Fixtures, Supplies

SHOPPER'S BOOT CORRAL & WESTERN WEAR (CLO)

(WORLD ENTERPRISES, INC.)
3400 S. Redwood Rd. (m-b)
Salt Lake City, UT 84119
801-974-5603 / Fax: 801-974-5603

MARY GUSTAFSON (President) & Buys Boys' Apparel, Boys' Footwear, Men's Footwear, Leather Goods, Men's Accessories, Men's Apparel, Hosiery
JULIE O'BRIEN-Boys' Apparel, Boys' Footwear, Men's Footwear, Leather Goods, Men's Accessories, Men's Apparel, Hosiery

SKAGGS' (MW-12)

3828 S. Main St.
Salt Lake City, UT 84115
801-261-4400 / Fax: 801-284-4752
Website: www.skaggscompanies.com

DON SKAGGS (Owner)
CLARK EVANS (Mgr.) & Buys Men's Work Uniforms

SUNDANCE CATALOG (MO-2)

3865 W. 2400 S.
Salt Lake City, UT 84120
801-973-2711 / Fax: 801-973-4989
Sales: $1 Million-$10 Million
Website: www.sundancecatalog.com

BRUCE WILLARD (President) & Buys Men's Sweaters, Jewelry, Accessories
HILLARY LAMBERT-Men's Sweaters, Jewelry, Accessories

UTAH WOOLEN MILLS (CLO)

59 W. South Temple (b)
Salt Lake City, UT 84101
801-364-1851 / Fax: 801-364-1854
Sales: $1 Million-$10 Million

BART STRINGHAM (President) & Buys Men's Wear, Accessories, Dress Shirts, Store Displays, Fixtures, Supplies

FAMILY STORE, INC. (CLO-3)

(MICHAEL'S FLORSHEIM SHOP)
(SHOPPER'S WESTERN WEAR & BOOT CORRAL)
P.O. Box 65809 (bud-p-m-b-des)
4860 S. Redwood Rd.
Taylorsville, UT 84123
801-964-1600 / Fax: 801-965-1600
Sales: $1 Million-$10 Million

PAUL KINGSTON (President) & Buys Boys' Apparel, Boys' Footwear, Leather Goods, Men's Footwear, Licensed Apparel, Watches, Men's Accessories, Men's Apparel, Hosiery
MARY GUSTAFSON (G.M.) & Buys Boys' Apparel, Boys' Footwear, Leather Goods, Men's Footwear, Licensed Apparel, Watches, Men's Accessories, Men's Apparel, Hosiery

THE BULL RING (WW)

1801 W. Hwy. 40 (b-h)
Vernal, UT 84078
435-789-9474 / Fax: 435-789-7969
Sales: $500,001-$1 Million

LANCE GARDNER (Owner) & Buys Men's & Boys' Western Wear, Furnishings, Accessories, Boots, Store Displays, Fixtures, Supplies

CHRISTENSEN'S DEPARTMENT STORE (DEPT)

(DKC, INC.)
1149 W. Hwy. 40 (m)
Vernal, UT 84078
435-781-1571 / Fax: 435-781-1573
Sales: $1 Million-$10 Million

DAVID CHRISTENSEN (Owner & President) & Buys Men's Wear, Leather Apparel, Furnishings, Accessories, Young Men's Wear, Boys' Wear, Footwear, Store Displays, Fixtures, Supplies

THE AMERICAN COWBOY (WW)
(UNIVERSAL EQUESTRIAN CENTER)
1450 W. 400 N. (m-b)
West Bountifull, UT 84087
801-295-7433 / Fax: 801-295-7182

DON CHRISTENSEN (Owner)
JED CHRISTENSEN (Mgr.) & Buys Men's Western Wear, Related Accessories, Footwear, Store Displays, Fixtures, Supplies

VERMONT - Barre

THE HOMER FITTS CO. (DEPT)
P.O. Box 465 (m)
159 N. Main St.
Barre, VT 05641
802-476-3144 / Fax: 802-476-3146
Sales: $1 Million-$10 Million
Website: www.homerfitts.com
EDWARD J. CORRIGAN (President) & Buys Men's Wear, Leather Apparel, Store Displays, Fixtures, Supplies
JULIANNE MONTY (G.M.M.) & Buys Men's Wear, Leather Apparel, Store Displays, Fixtures, Supplies

SHAFFE'S MEN'S SHOP (MW)
475 Main St. (m)
Bennington, VT 05201
802-442-2521
Sales: $100,001-$500,000
DAVID SHAFFE (Owner) & Buys Men's Sportswear, Furnishings & Accessories

SPORTS & GRAPHICS (CLO)
451 Main St. (m)
Bennington, VT 05201
802-447-0020 / Fax: 802-442-4732
Sales: $1 Million-$10 Million
TOM HUSSER (Owner) & Buys Men's, Young Men's & Boys' Imprintable Apparel

SHAPIRO'S (CLO)
18 Park St. (m)
Brandon, VT 05733
802-247-5505
Sales: $100,001-$500,000
DAVID HOWELLS (Owner) & Buys Intimate Apparel, Swimwear, Boys' Wear, Suits, Sportswear, Accessories, Store Displays, Fixtures, Supplies
CINDY McTAGGERT-Intimate Apparel, Swimwear, Boys' Wear, Suits, Sportswear, Accessories, Store Displays, Fixtures, Supplies

BURROW'S SPORT SHOP (CLO)
105 Main St. (m-b)
Brattleboro, VT 05301
802-254-9430 / Fax: 802-254-9683
Sales: $100,001-$500,000
SHERI WOODWORTH (Co-Owner) & Buys Men's & Boys' Skiwear, Sportswear, Ski Headwear, Accessories, Store Displays, Fixtures, Supplies
BOB WOODWORTH (Co-Owner) & Buys Men's & Boys' Skiwear, Sportswear, Ski Headwear, Accessories, Store Displays, Fixtures, Supplies

SAM'S DEPARTMENT STORES, INC. (DEPT-3)
74 Main St. (m)
Brattleboro, VT 05301
802-254-2933 / Fax: 802-254-5355
STANLEY BOROFSKY (President) & Buys Men's Overcoats, Raincoats, Sportswear, Furnishings, Headwear, Accessories, Young Men's Wear, Leather Apparel, Store Displays, Fixtures & Supplies
BRADLEY BOROFSKY-Men's Overcoats, Raincoats, Sportswear, Furnishings, Headwear, Accessories, Young Men's Wear, Leather Apparel, Men's & Boys' Footwear
MARILYN GILL-Boys' Wear

COMMON THREADS (CLO)
3 Main St.
Burlington, VT 05401
802-865-7910 / Fax: 802-860-1929
DAVID CORY (Owner) & Buys Beachwear, Swimwear, Headwear
JOANNA LAWRENCE-Beachwear, Swimwear, Headwear

DEPATIE'S STORE (MW)
139 Main St. (p-m)
Enosburg Falls, VT 05450
802-933-8900
STEPHEN DEPATIE (Co-Owner)
KEVIN DEPATIE (Co-Owner) & Buys Buys Men's Sportswear, Accessories, Dress Shoes, Casual Shoes, Casual Wear, Furnshings, Athletic Footwear, Boots, Work Shoes, Big & Tall Men's Wear, Store Displays, Fixtures, Supplies

PHIL'S, INC. (MW)
18 Main St. (m)
Essex Junction, VT 05452
802-878-3319 / Fax: 802-879-5119
Website: www.philstradingpost.com
MATT COHEN (Owner & Mgr.) & Buys Men's Wear, Young Men's Wear, Leather Apparel, Sportswear, Accessories, Furnishings, Headwear, Dress Shoes, Work Boots, Store Displays, Fixtures, Supplies

CARL DURFEE'S (CLO)
34 Main St. (p-m)
Fair Haven, VT 05743
802-265-3313 / Fax: 802-265-3313
MARY MARTIN (Owner) & Buys Men's Sportswear, Furnishings, Headwear, Belts, Young Men's Shirts, Trousers & Jeans, 8 to 18 Boys' Wear, Store Displays, Fixtures, Supplies

THE BARN (CLO)
(NEW ENGLAND SHOE BARN)
(W.R.G., INC.)
Rts. 11 & 100 (m)
Londonderry, VT 05148
802-824-5000
WALTER GENSER (Owner) & Buys Men's Overcoats, Tailored Jackets, Sportswear, Dress Shirts
BETTY GENSER-Men's Dress Shoes, Athletic Footwear, Work Shoes

THE ORVIS CO., INC. (CLO-25 & MO & OL)
Rt. 7A (b)
Manchester, VT 05254
802-362-3622 / Fax: 802-362-3525
Sales: $200 Million
Website: www.orvis.com
Retail Locations: GA, VT, NY, TX, NJ, MA, VA, IL WA, CT, MI, PA, CO, MO, GA, UT, WY, AZ, UK
LEIGH PERKINS, SR. (Chmn.)
LEIGH "PERK" PERKINS, JR. (President & C.E.O.)
DAVID PERKINS (Sr. V.P.)
GEORGE HASKINS (Real Estate Contact) (@ 802-362-8661)
SHARON McNAMARA (V.P. & Catalog Mdse. Mgr.)
TOM KERR (Product Dev.-Retail & Catalog) & Buys Men's Sportcoats, Woven Shirts, Leather Apparel, Outerwear
MARK TEMPLETON (Produc Dev.-Retail & Catalog) & Buys Men's Sportcoats, Raincoats, Sportswear, Leather Apparel
CYNTHIA PAQUETTE (Prod. Development Spec.) & Buys Furnishings & Footwear for Men

SOX MARKET, INC. (CLO)
Manchester Ctr. (p-m)
Rt. 7A
Manchester, VT 05255
802-362-5500
Sales: $1 Million-$10 Million
MICHAEL ADLER (Owner) (@ 802-862-6464, Ext.: VM) & Buys Men's, Boys' & Young Men's Hosiery, Store Displays, Fixtures, Supplies

THE VERMONT COUNTRY STORE (MO & CLO-2 & OL)
P.O. Box 1108 (m)
Manchester Center, VT 05255
802-362-4667 / Fax: 802-362-8288
Sales: $10 Million-$50 Million
Website: www.vermontcountrystore.com
ROBERT ALLEN (President)
TARA SABOL-Men's & Boys' Wear, Footwear, Robes, Underwear, Hosiery, Headwear, Furnishings, Accessories, Small Leather Goods

ARTHUR'S DEPARTMENT STORE (DEPT)
(BREAULT ENTERPRISES)
63 Main St. (m-b)
Morrisville, VT 05661
802-888-3125 / Fax: 802-888-3126
ARTHUR BREAULT (President) & Buys Store Displays, Fixtures, Supplies
THERESA BREAULT (V.P.) & Buys Boys' Clothing, Sportswear, Furnishings, Accessories, Leather Apparel
JEFF MOSER (Gen. Mgr.) & Buys Men's Overcoats, Suits, Tailored Jackets, Tailored Slacks, Raincoats, Sportswear, Furnishings, Headwear, Accessories, Young Men's Shop, Urban Contemporary

MILLER'S COUNTRY OUTFITTERS (CLO)
P.O. Box 781 (m)
Rt. 100
Morrisville, VT 05661
802-888-4589
BRENT MILLER (Owner) & Buys Men's Sportswear, Underwear, Hosiery, Gloves, Headwear, Belts, Dress Shoes, Athletic Footwear, Work Shoes, Young Men's Wear, Store Displays, Fixtures, Supplies

NEEDLEMAN'S BRIDE & FORMAL, INC. (CLO-2)
1 Main St. (p-m)
Newport, VT 05855
802-334-8000 / Fax: 802-334-0170
Sales: $500,000 - $1 Million
Website: www.needlemansbridal.com
MARVIN NEEDLEMAN (Co-Owner) & Buys Men's Wear, Formal Wear, Dress Shoes, Store Displays, Fixtures, Supplies
CAROL NEEDLEMAN (Co-Owner) & Buys Men's Wear, Formal Wear, Dress Shoes, Store Displays, Fixtures, Supplies
MARK NEEDLEMAN (Co-Owner) & Buys Men's Wear, Formal Wear, Dress Shoes, Store Displays, Fixtures, Supplies

DAN & WHIT'S GENERAL STORE (GM)
(FRASER'S GENERAL STORE)
P.O. Box 157 (b)
319 Main St.
Norwich, VT 05055
802-649-1950
Sales: $1 Million-$10 Million
JACK FRASER (Co-Owner)
GEORGE FRASER (Co-Owner)
RON SWIFT-Dress Shoes, Athletic Footwear, Boots, Store Displays, Fixtures, Supplies
LINDA CONRAD-Men's Work Clothes, Boys' T-shirts, Jeans, Sweats

BODYGEARS (SP & MO & OL)
112 Woodstock Ave.
Rutland, VT 05701
802-775-2747
Sales: $501,000-$1 Million
Website: www.bodygears.com
MARY SHEROWSKI (Mgr.) & Buys Active Apparel, Running & Dancing Shoes, Hosiery

LINDHOLM'S SPORT CENTER (MW)
2 S. Main St. (m)
Rutland, VT 05701
802-773-6000
Sales: $500,000-$1 Million
JUSTIN LINDHOLM (Owner) & Buys Men's Sports Clothing, Hunting & Fishing Apparel

CAPLAN'S ARMY STORE (AN & SP)
457 Railroad St. (m)
Saint Johnsbury, VT 05819
802-748-3236 / Fax: 802-748-5259
DAVID CAPLAN (Owner)
GARY ELY (Mgr.) & Buys Men's Wear, Young Men's Wear, Outerwear, Hunting & Fishing Apparel, Store Supplies, Fixtures
RODGER DETH (Asst. Mgr.) & Buys Men's Wear, Young Men's Wear, Outerwear, Hunting & Fishing Apparel, Store Supplies, Fixtures

THE ALPINE SHOP, INC. (CLO-2 & SP)
1184 Williston Rd. (b)
South Burlington, VT 05403
802-862-2714 / Fax: 802-862-0598
Sales: $1 Million-$10 Million
Website: www.alpineshopvt.com
SCOTT RIELEY (Co-Owner) & Buys Men's Sportswear, Shorts, Running Apparel, Skiwear, Footwear, Store Displays, Fixtures, Supplies
PEG RIELEY (Co-Owner) & Buys Men's Sportswear, Shorts, Running Apparel, Skiwear, Footwear, Store Displays, Fixtures, Supplies

WARREN STORE, INC. (DEPT)
284 Main St. (p-m-b)
Warren, VT 05674
802-496-3864 / Fax: 802-496-7233
WARREN HOLDINGS (Owner) & Buys Men's Outerwear, Sportswear, Store Displays, Fixtures, Supplies
JIM HILTON-Men's Outerwear, Suits, Sportswear, Accessories, Knitwear, Hosiery, Furnishings

VIRGIN ISLANDS - Kinghill Saint Croix

THE LE BARON (MW)

P.O. Box 1299 (m)
Sunny Isle Shopping Ctr.
Kinghill Saint Croix, VI 00851
340-778-5800 / Fax: 340-778-5585

ARNOLD HELENSE (Owner) & Buys Men's Suits, Tailored Jackets, Tailored Slacks, Sport Shirts, Casual Slacks, Furnishings, Dress Shirts, Ties, Hosiery, Accessories, Belts, Jewelry, Small Leather Goods, Fragrances, Shoes, Young Men's Wear, 8 to 20 Boys' Wear, Store Displays, Fixtures, Supplies

BUCANEER BEACH BOUTIQUES (SP-2)

P.O. Box 218
Christiansted
Saint Croix, VI 00820
340-773-2898 / Fax: 340-778-8215
Sales: $100,001-$500,000

PATRICIA L. ARMSTRONG (Owner) & Buys Swimwear, Sunglasses, Beach Footwear, Sportswear

CARIBBEAN CLOTHING CO. (MW)

Christiansted (b)
41 Queen Cross St.
Saint Croix, VI 00820
340-773-5012 / Fax: 340-773-7391

MARK FERDSCHNEIDER (Owner) & Buys Men's & Young Men's Contemporary Sweaters, Sport Shirts, Casual Slacks, Dress Shirts, Ties, Underwear, Hats, Belts, Urban Contemporary, Store Displays, Fixtures, Supplies

MID ISLAND MENSWEAR (MW)

P.O. Box 7043 (m-b)
Sunny Isle
Saint Croix, VI 00823
340-778-2795 / Fax: 340-778-2795

MAHMUD A. IDHEILEH (Owner) & Buys Men's Wear, Urban Contemporary, Store Displays, Fixtures, Supplies

SAMIRA'S FASHIONS (DEPT)

223 Sunshine Mall (p-m-b)
3 La Villa Reine Shopping Center
Saint Croix, VI 00840
340-778-4740 / Fax: 340-778-3842
Sales: $1 Million-$10 Million

SAMIH ASHWASH (Owner) & Buys Men's Wear, Urban Contemporary, Store Displays, Fixtures, Supplies

BIG PLANET, INC. (CLO-3)

P.O. Box 8325 (b)
Saint John, VI 00831
340-776-6638 / Fax: 340-779-4330

PRETLOW PRETLOWMAJETT (Owner) & Buys T-shirts, Sport Shirts, Walking Shorts, Sandals, Urban Contemporary, Store Displays, Fixtures, Footwear, Supplies

ASFOUR DEPARTMENT STORE (DEPT-2)

Charlotte Amalie (b)
Veterans Dr.
Saint Thomas, VI 00802
340-774-4565 / Fax: 340-776-3060
Sales: $1 Million-$10 Million

ABRAHAM ASFOUR (Owner) & Buys Men's & Boys' Wear, Urban Contemporary, Store Displays, Fixtures, Supplies

BAREFOOT TRADING CO. (MW)

P.O. Box 9258 (m)
Saint Thomas, VI 00801
340-775-3611 / Fax: 340-776-3851

TONY BUETTNER (Owner) & Buys Men's Shorts, Sport Shirts, Footwear, Swimwear, Store Displays, Fixtures, Supplies

YVONNE QUESTEL (Mgr.) & Buys Men's Shorts, Sport Shirts, Footwear, Swimwear, Store Displays, Fixtures, Supplies

COSMOPOLITAN, INC. (CLO-8 & OL)

P.O. Box 6578 (b)
Charlotte Amalie
Saint Thomas, VI 00804
340-776-2040 / Fax: 340-776-1885
Sales: $1 Million-$10 Million
Website: www.cosmopolitan.vi

CARY TENENBAUM (Owner) & Buys Men's Tailored Slacks, Sport Shirts, Casual Slacks, Dress Shirts, Ties, Robes, Underwear, Hosiery, Belts, Active Apparel, Headwear, Footwear, Swimwear, Store Supplies, Fixtures, Supplies

CUCKOO'S NEST (CLO)

International Plz.
Saint Thomas, VI 00802
340-776-4005 / Fax: 340-776-4005

HELEN KIRWAN (Owner) & Buys Men's Accessories

L & C MILLINER (DEPT)

P.O. Box 7691 (bud-p-b)
Charlotte Amalie
Saint Thomas, VI 00801
340-774-2608 / Fax: 340-774-3989
Sales: $1 Million-$10 Million

LESLIE MILLINER (President) & Buys Men's Suits, Tailored Jackets, Tailored Slacks, Sport Shirts, Casual Slacks, Furnishings, Headwear, Accessories, Boys' Wear, Store Displays, Fixtures, Supplies

MONSIEUR CREOLE, INC. (DEPT)

P.O. Box 4650 (m)
Charlotte Amalie
Saint Thomas, VI 00803
340-774-2630 / Fax: 340-776-3715
Sales: $100,001-$500,000

BEVERLY MAGRAS (Owner) & Buys Men's Raincoats, Sweaters, Casual Slacks, Sport Shirts, Accessories, Boys' Clothing, Store Displays, Fixtures, Supplies

PAMPERED PIRATE, INC. (CLO)

P.O. Box 590 (m-b)
Charlotte Amalie
Saint Thomas, VI 00804
340-775-5450 / Fax: 340-774-5371

GREG JOHNSON (Owner) & Buys Men's Ties, Store Displays, Fixtures, Supplies

PLAYERS (CLO)

(RUNNING STATION, INC.)
P.O. Box 11726 (m-b)
Charlotte Amalie
Saint Thomas, VI 00801
340-776-4540

JOSE BELCHER (Co-Owner) & Buys Men's Active Apparel, Surf Wear, Store Displays, Fixtures, Supplies

VAUGHN BELCHER (Co-Owner) & Buys Men's Active Apparel, Urban Contemporary, Surf Wear, Store Displays, Fixtures, Supplies

THE RITZ CARLTON (CLO)

6900 Great Bay
Saint Thomas, VI 00802
340-775-3333 / Fax: 340-775-4444

CHARLENE DICK-Beach Apparel, Surf Swimwear, Wet Suits, Headwear, Beach Shoes

SHELL SEEKERS, INC. (CLO)

(OUTRIGGER)
P.O. Box 8417
Saint Thomas, VI 00801
340-774-4370 / Fax: 340-776-0345

LINDA CONSOLVO (Owner) & Buys Men's Sportswear, Beachwear, Store Displays, Fixtures, Supplies

TWIN CITY DEPARTMENT STORE (DEPT)

Charlotte Amalie (bud)
78 Main St.
Saint Thomas, VI 00802
340-774-0095 / Fax: 340-776-8923

ELAIS EL-HAJ (Co-Owner)

FAHED EL-HAJ (Co-Owner) & Buys Men's, Young Men's & Boys' Wear, Urban Contemporary, Store Displays, Fixtures, Supplies

UNDERWATER SAFARIS (CLO)

P.O. Box 139
Tortola, VI 99999
287-494-3235 / Fax: 284-494-5322

MAUREEN GREEN (Owner)

CARINA BRUCE-Beachwear, Surf & Swimwear, Wet Suits, Headwear, Beach Shoes

KEGLEY & CO. (MW)

127 E. Main St.
Abingdon, VA 24210
276-628-1108

DUKE KEGLEY (President) & Buys Men's Sportswear, Furnishings, Accessories, Footwear, Store Displays, Fixtures, Supplies

WAILES (DEPT)

P.O. Box 509 (b)
139 Ambriar Plz.
Amherst, VA 24521
434-946-5344 / Fax: 434-946-5313

PAUL WAILES (Owner) & Buys Men's & Young Men's Wear, Accessories, Furnishings, Footwear, Store Displays, Fixtures, Supplies

SAM'S CUSTOM SHOP (MW)

7308 Little River Tnpk.
Annandale, VA 73008
703-354-6589 / Fax: 703-941-4743

ANNA KASSAR (Owner) & Buys Men's Overcoats, Suits, Tailored Jackets, Tailored Slacks, Store Supplies

CASUAL ADVENTURE (SP)

3451 N. Washington Blvd. (m-b)
Arlington, VA 22201
703-527-0600 / Fax: 703-524-9090
Sales: $1 Million-$10 Million
Website: www.casualadventure.com

DAVE HAGGERTY (Gen. Mgr.) & Buys Men's Sportswear, Outdoor Clothing, Footwear, Store Displays, Fixtures, Supplies

HECHT'S (DEPT-74)

(Div. of THE MAY DEPT. STORES CO.)
(STRAWBRIDGE'S)
685 N. Glebe Rd. (m)
Arlington, VA 22203
(May Merchandising Corp.)
703-558-1200 / Fax: 703-247-2346
Sales: Over $1 Billion
Website: www.hechts.com
www.strawbridges.com
Retail Locations: VA, DC, MD, NC

FRANK GUZZETTA (President)
DAVID GLICK (Sr. V.P. & G.M.M.)

CHUCK HOGAN (D.M.M.) (@ 703-558-1846) & Buys Men's Furnishings, Men's Wear & Men's Accessories
DARREN PROSTER-Men's Sweaters, Knits, Better Knitwear
MELANIE OLLIC-Men's Sport Shirts, Julian, Gant, Chaps
CHRIS CAVALLINE-Men's Activewear
DON DeFABIO-Men's Collections
DAVE HANNETT-Men's Accessories, Gloves, Small Leather Goods
CATHLEEN TOBIN-Men's Underwear, Hosiery, Pajamas, Robes
MARVIN SCHIFF-Men's Overcoats, Suits, Raincoats
MARK JOHNSON-Men's Pants, Jeans
DEBBIE BRASCHNWEITZ-Men's Pants, Sport Coats
MARY NOONE-Men's Neckwear
LISA THURSTON-Men's Dress Shirts
CHRISTIAN LIOWINDOWSKY-Men's Fragrances
ANGELA WEBBER-Men's Shoes

DERRICK LUPINO (Sr. V.P. & G.M.M.) & Buys Children's
DEBBIE KELLY-Boys' Shoes
JASON GLENN-8 to 20 Boys' Tops
KIM WARGOSKY-2 to 7 Boys' Wear, Accessories
NICOLE ROBERTS-Young Men's Tops
MIKE TRIVETT-Young Men's & Boys' Bottoms

JIM APRUZZEFE (V.P.-Visual Mdsg. & Creative Planning) & Buys Store Displays
JOHN CORNWELL (Dir.-Maintenance & Construction & Real Estate Contact) & Buys Store Fixtures
JOE GIAMMONA-Store Supplies

MEN'S SHOP LTD. (MW)

2156 Crystal Plaza Arc (m)
Arlington, VA 22202
703-415-0330
Sales: $100,001-$500,000

MR. KANAWATI (Owner) & Buys Men's Sportswear, Furnishings, Accessories

D. REYNOLDS STORE (MW)

111 S. Bridge St. (p)
Bedford, VA 24523
540-586-8315
Sales: $500,001-$1 Million

DALE WELLS (Owner)
RUTH F. CROUCH (G.M.M.) & Buys Men's Suits, Sweaters, Sport Shirts, Outer Jackets, Casual Slacks, Active Apparel, Footwear, Work Clothes, Store Displays, Fixtures, Supplies
W. J. KLUNK-Men's Suits, Sweaters, Sport Shirts, Outer Jackets, Casual Slacks, Active Apparel, Footwear, Work Clothes, Store Displays, Fixtures, Supplies

MAGIC MART (DEPT-20)

(AMMAR'S, INC.)
710 S. College Ave.
Bluefield, VA 24605
276-322-4686 / Fax: 276-326-1060
Sales: $50 Million-$100 Million
Website: www.magicstores.com
Retail Locations: VA, WV, GA, KY, IN, LA, TX, MS

R.F. AMMAR (President)
TREY AMMAR (V.P.)
RICHARD AMMAR (Real Estate Contact)
JOHN HAWKINS (Svce. Mgr.) & Buys Store Displays, Fixtures, Supplies
ROBERT LUTHER-Men's Sportswear, Furnishings, Boys' Wear, Urban Contemporary
LISA PURDUE-Men's Underwear, Hosiery, Gloves, Headwear
JAMES HILLYER-Men's Jewelry, Small Leather Goods
DOUG HORN-Footwear
MIKE KITTE-Men's Fragrances

BLAKELY - MITCHELL CO. (MW-2)
517 State St. (b)
Bristol, VA 24201
276-669-0116 / Fax: 276-669-0117
Sales: $1 Million-$10 Million

TED W. TESTERMAN (Owner) & Buys Men's Overcoats, Suits, Tailored Jackets, Tailored Slacks, Raincoats, Sweaters, Sport Shirts, Outer Jackets, Casual Slacks, Active Apparel, Furnishings, Headwear, Accessories, Young Men's Wear, Big & Tall Men's Wear, Men's Footwear, Store Displays, Fixtures, Supplies

HUGH E. TESTERMAN (President) & Buys Men's Overcoats, Suits, Tailored Jackets, Tailored Slacks, Raincoats, Sweaters, Sport Shirts, Outer Jackets, Casual Slacks, Active Apparel, Furnishings, Headwear, Accessories, Young Men's Wear, Big & Tall Men's Wear, Men's Footwear, Store Displays, Fixtures, Supplies

BILL E. TESTERMAN (V.P.) & Buys Men's Overcoats, Suits, Tailored Jackets, Tailored Slacks, Raincoats, Sweaters, Sport Shirts, Outer Jackets, Casual Slacks Active Apparel, Furnishings, Headwear, Accessories, Young Men's Wear, Big & Tall Men's Wear, Men's Footwear, Store Displays, Fixtures, Supplies

BURRIS (CLO-2)
(J. CASEY'S, INC.)
19819 Main St. (m)
Buchanan, VA 24066
540-254-2221 / Fax: 540-254-9849
Sales: $500,001-$1 Million

PETER D. BURRIS (President) & Buys Men's Sweaters, Sport Shirts, Casual Slacks, Leather Apparel, Active Apparel, Footwear, Accessories, Urban Contemporary, Store Displays, Fixtures, Supplies

CHANTILLY CASH & CARRY (DEPT)
13941 Lee Jackson Hwy. (p-m)
Chantilly, VA 22021
703-378-5310 / Fax: 703-378-5310

JAMES KIM (Owner) & Buys Men's T-shirts, Fleece, Levi's & Wrangler Shirts, Work Boots, Western Footwear, Store Displays, Fixtures, Supplies

ELJO'S (MW)
3 Elliewood Ave. (b)
Charlottesville, VA 22903
434-295-5230 / Fax: 434-979-3532
Website: www.eljos.com

MYLES THURSTON (Owner) & Buys Men's Sportswear, Furnishings, Accessories, Footwear, Store Displays, Fixtures, Supplies

HEIDI'S PERFECT FIT (MW)
1311 Wertland St. (m-b)
Charlottesville, VA 22903
434-295-8777 / Fax: 434-979-3727

MEHDI AKBAR (Owner) & Buys Men's Formal Wear, Shoes, Furnishings, Accessories, Store Displays, Fixtures, Supplies

MEN'S & BOYS' SHOP (MW)
410 E. Main St. (b)
Charlottesville, VA 22902
434-296-6924

L. MICHAEL KIDD (Owner) & Buys Store Displays, Fixtures, Supplies, Men's Overcoats, Suits, Tailored Jackets, Tailored Slacks, Sportswear, Ties, Headwear, Belts, Footwear, Jewelry, Small Leather Goods, Leather Apparel, Boys' Wear

THE YOUNG MEN'S SHOP (MW)
241 Zan Rd. (m)
Charlottesville, VA 22902
434-975-3131 / Fax: 434-975-5225
Sales: $1 Million-$10 Million
Website: www.theyoungmensshop.com

HARRY MARSHALL (President) & Buys Men's Overcoats, Suits, Tailored Jackets, Tailored Slacks, Raincoats, Big & Tall, Sweaters, Sport Shirts, Outer Jackets, Casual Slacks, Gloves, Headwear, Belts, Hosiery, Jewelry, Small Leather Goods, Footwear, Store Displays, Fixtures, Supplies

MARSHALL PRYOR (V.P.) & Buys Boys' Formalwear, Suits, Tailored Jackets

THE LEATHER LADY (CLO)
2331 Vicker Ave.
Chesapeake, VA 23324
757-494-1316
Website: www.theleatherlady.com

HOLLY ANN HAMILTON (Owner) & Buys Chaps, Men's Leather Apparel & Accessories

TOM'S BEACH SUPPLY (GS)
66380 Maddox Blvd.
Chincoteague, VA 23336
757-336-3480

ALBERTA LITTLE (Co-Owner)

STEVE COSSETTO (Co-Owner) & Buys T-shirts, Shorts, Swimwear, Beach Footwear

SHERMAN'S, INC. (CLO)
P.O. Box 6111 (m)
106 N. Franklin St.
Christiansburg, VA 24073
540-382-3182 / Fax: 540-382-3182

J. E. SHERMAN (President)

RANDY SHERMAN (V.P.)

MIKE SHERMAN-Men's Overcoats, Suits, Tailored Jackets, Tailored Slacks, Raincoats, Sweaters, Sport Shirts, Casual Slacks, Outer Jackets, Leather Apparel, Furnishings, Accessories, Men's Footwear, Store Supplies

HITE'S, INC. (CLO-2)
P.O. Box 130 (m-b)
Clarksville, VA 23927
434-374-5914 / Fax: 434-374-9418
Sales: $1 Million-$10 Million

DALE HITE (President) & Buys Men's Sportswear, Furnishings & Accessories, Footwear, Store Displays, Fixtures, Supplies

TOPS & BOTTOMS, INC. (CLO-4 & SP)
P.O. Box 950 (m)
Clintwood, VA 24228
276-679-5643 / Fax: 276-679-5644
Sales: $1 Million-$10 Million

BOB PHIPPS (Owner)

JOELLE KENT (G.M.M.) & Buys Men's Overcoats, Hosiery, Swimwear, Licensed Active Apparel, Sport Shirts, Outer Jackets, Active Apparel, Men's Headwear, Jewelry, Boys' Clothing, Sportswear, Accessories, Athletic Footwear, Store, Displays, Fixtures, Supplies

ADOLPH'S (MW)
648 Southpark Blvd., #B (m-b)
Colonial Heights, VA 23834
804-520-0141
Sales: $1 Million-$10 Million

JIM RUBLE (President) & Buys Store Displays, Fixtures, Supplies, Men's, Young Men's & Boys' Wear, Accessories, Footwear

GLEN G. HEARNS-Men's, Young Men's & Boys' Wear, Urban Contemporary, Accessories, Footwear

ROOKLIN'S, INC. (DEPT)
239 N. Maple Ave. (m)
Covington, VA 24426
540-965-4851 / Fax: 540-962-9642
Sales: $500,001-$1 Million

WOODROW ROOKLIN (President) & Buys Store Displays, Fixtures, Supplies

MICHAEL WARWICK (V.P.) & Buys Men's Wear, Furnishings, Accessories, Men's Footwear, Store Displays, Fixtures, Supplies

HELEN ROOKLIN (Secy.) & Buys Urban Contemporary, Store Displays, Fixtures, Supplies

ABE KOPLEN CLOTHING CO. (MW)
214 N. Union St. (p-m)
Danville, VA 24541
434-791-2237 / Fax: 434-791-2402
Sales: $1 Million-$10 Million

BARRY KOPLEN (G.M.M.) & Buys Men's Wear, Footwear, Young Men's & Boys' Wear, Urban Contemporary, Leather Apparel, Store Displays, Fixtures, Supplies

GLEN-MORE CLOTHES CO. (MW-2)
309 Main St. (m-b)
Danville, VA 24541
434-793-5037
Sales: $1 Million-$10 Million

DAVID SAYERS (Owner) & Buys Store Displays, Fixtures, Supplies

ANN BEYER (Secy. & Treas.) & Buys Men's Sports Coats, Outer Jackets, Casual Slacks, Dress Shirts, Accessories, Hosiery

HARRISON THROCKMORTON-Men's wear, Sportcoats, Outer Jackets, Casual Slacks, Dress Shirts, Accessories, Hosiery, Men's Footwear

J. BERMAN, INC. (MW)
P.O. Box 1595 (m-b)
406 Main St.
Danville, VA 24543
434-793-2051 / Fax: 434-799-1022
Sales: $1 Million-$10 Million
JAY D. BERMAN (President) & Buys Men's Overcoats, Suits, Tailored Jackets, Tailored Slacks, Raincoats, Big & Tall Men's Wear, Sweaters, Sport Shirts, Outer Jackets, Leather Apparel, Casual Slacks, Active Apparel, Furnishings, Headwear, Accessories, Footwear, Store Displays, Fixtures, Supplies

PATCHWORK PLUS (SP)
17 Killdeer Ln. (m)
Dayton, VA 22821
540-879-2505 / Fax: 540-879-2310
KEN REEVES (President & Co- Owner)
PHYLLIS REEVES (Co-Owner) & Buys Men's Straw Hats
JUDITH HEATWOLE-Men's Straw Hats, Dress Hats

LATINO'S MEXICAN STORE (CLO & MO)
3190 Main St. (bud)
Exmore, VA 23350
757-442-9293
ALBERTO BRIONES (Owner) & Buys Men's Wear, Clothing, Sportswear, Casual Slacks, Active Apparel, Footwear, Boys' Wear, Boys' Sportswear, Men's & Boys' Mexican Apparel

LYNFORD UNIFORMS, INC. (CLO-2)
9683 Lee Hwy.
Fairfax, VA 22031
703-591-5876 / Fax: 703-591-5890
EVELYN OVERCASH (Owner) & Buys Store Displays, Fixtures, Supplies, Men's Uniforms, Related Footwear
AUDREY HALL-Men's Uniforms, Related Footwear

UNIVERSITY RHO & SWIM (CLO)
10631 Braddock (m)
Fairfax, VA 22032
703-278-8202 / Fax: 703-278-8845
Sales: $100,001-$500,000
Website: www.rhoandswim.com
CANDY SCHADLE (Owner) & Buys Men's Swimsuits, Shorts, Sweaters, Polo, T-shirts, Licensed Jackets, Swim Sandals, Store Displays, Fixtures & Supplies

STEVEN WINDSOR, INC. (MW-3)
6535 Arlington Blvd. (m-b)
Falls Church, VA 22042
703-533-9784 / Fax: 703-533-9787
Sales: $1 Million-$10 Million
RON MANENDORF (Exec. V.P. & G.M.M.) & Buys Men's Big, Tall & Short Overcoats, Suits, Tailored Jackets, Tailored Slacks, Raincoats, Sweaters, Sport Shirts, Outer Jackets, Casual Slacks, Leather Apparel, Active Apparel, Dress Shirts, Ties, Gloves, Robes, Underwear, Hosiery, Headwear, Belts, Small Leather Goods, Jewelry, Store Displays, Fixtures, Supplies

RED FRONT TRADING CO. (MW)
P.O. Box 294 (m)
119 N. Main St.
Farmville, VA 23901
434-392-6410
Sales: $100,001-$500,000
MR. CARTER (Owner) & Buys Men's Work Clothes, Levi's, Tops, Winter Hosiery, Gloves, Underwear, Store Displays, Fixtures & Supplies

WESTERN WAYS, INC. (WW)
17952 Forest Rd. (m)
Forest, VA 24551
434-385-8011 / Fax: 434-385-6979
GREG HOBSON (Co-Owner) & Buys Western Shirts, Jeans, Outer Jackets, Accessories, Boots, English Clothing, Store Displays, Fixtures & Supplies
DIANA HOBSON (Co-Owner) & Buys Western Shirts, Jeans, Outer Jackets, Accessories, Boots, English Clothing, Store Displays, Fixtures & Supplies

CARLTON FOR MEN, INC. (MW)
Westwood Ctr. (b)
2011 Plank Rd.
Fredericksburg, VA 22401
540-373-0023
CARLTON SIMMS (Owner) & Buys Men's Suits, Sportswear, Furnishings, Casual Slacks, Accessories, Footwear

THE SCOTSMAN (MW-7)
(BURTON'S MENSWEAR, INC.)
P.O. Box 7043 (bud)
350 Landsdowne Rd.
Fredericksburg, VA 22404
540-371-1776 / Fax: 540-371-4605
ROBERT BURTON (Owner) (@ 540-972-5321)
NEIL BURTON (@ 804-231-0793)-Men's Sportswear, Robes, Underwear, Hosiery, Gloves, Belts, Boys' Clothing, Sportswear, Furnishings, Tailored Jackets, Big & Tall Men's Wear, Urban Contemporary, Footwear, Store Displays, Fixtures, Supplies

TIM'S MART (CLO)
1010 Caroline St.
Fredericksburg, VA 22401
540-371-5325
TIMOTHY PARKS (Owner & G.M.M.) & Buys Men's Suits, Tailored Jackets, Tailored Slacks, Raincoats, Sportswear, Furnishings, Headwear, Dress Shoes, Accessories, Size 8 to 20 Boys' Wear, Store Displays, Fixtures, Supplies

STOKES STORES (DEPT)
533 E. Main St. (p)
Front Royal, VA 22630
540-635-4437
Sales: $500,000-$1 Million
BERNARD STOKES (President)
ANDREW STOKES (Mgr.) & Buys Men's Work Clothes, Small Leather Goods, Jeans, Jackets, Coats, Belts, Footwear, Underwear, Western Wear, Big & Tall Men's Wear, Hosiery, Raincoats, Active Apparel, T-shirts, Gloves, Store Displays, Fixtures, Supplies

CHRIS' DEPARTMENT STORE (DEPT)
148 E. Jackson St. (bud-p-m-b)
Gate City, VA 24251
276-386-7611
Sales: $100,001-$500,000
CHRIS MAYA (Co-Owner) & Buys Men's Sportswear, Furnishings, Western Wear, Boys' Wear, Accessories, Footwear, Store Displays, Fixtures, Supplies
MARY NELL MAYA (Co-Owner) & Buys Men's Sportswear, Furnishings, Western Wear, Boys' Wear, Accessories, Footwear, Store Displays, Fixtures, Supplies

STYLE SHOP (CLO)
123 E. Jackson St. (m)
Gate City, VA 24251
276-386-3141
RUTH RHOTON (Owner) & Buys Men's Outer Jackets, Pants, Underwear, Hosiery, Shirts, Ties, Store Displays, Fixtures & Supplies

VIRGINIA - Glen Allen

S & K FAMOUS BRANDS, INC. (MW-240 & OL)
P.O. Box 31800 (m)
11100 W. Broad St.
Glen Allen, VA 23060
804-346-2500 / Fax: 804-346-2627
Sales: $100 Million-$500 Million
Website: www.skmenswear.com
Retail Locations: AZ, AR, CA, CO, CT, DE, DC, FL, GA, VA, NC, NY, NJ, MA
STUART C. SIEGEL (Chairman & C.E.O.)
STEWART CASEN (President & C.O.O.)
WALT BARE (Real Estate Contact)
ROBERT VIDETIC (V.P. & D.M.M.) & Buys Men's Overcoats, Suits, Tailored Jackets, Tailored Slacks, Raincoats
PAUL GARY (Sr. V.P.) & Buys Men's Sportswear
JON VINEGAR (V.P. & D.M.M.) & Buys Men's Dress Shoes, Casual Shoes, Dress Shirts, Ties, Accessories
HOWARD ROSE-Furnishings, Belts, Accessories, Small Leather Goods, Jewelry

PEACE FROGS RETAIL, INC. (CLO)
7546 John Clayton Memorial Hwy.
Gloucester, VA 23061
804-695-1314 / Fax: 804-695-1714
Sales: $500,001-$1 Million
Website: www.peacefrogs.com
CATESBY JONES (Owner)
NICOLE BAKER-Men's Sportswear, T-shirts, Sandals, Jewelry, Store Displays, Fixtures, Supplies

CARDINAL CAP & JACKET (MO)
(CARDINAL INDUSTRIES, INC.)
P.O. Box 1430 (m)
Hwy. 460
Grundy, VA 24614
276-935-4545 / Fax: 276-935-4970
Sales: $1 Million-$10 Million
LLEWELLYN SHORTRIDGE (President)
TERESA DAMRON-Men's Nylon Water Repellent Jackets, Headwear,T-shirts, Emblems & Decals

BENTON - KNIGHT LTD. (CLO)
28 S. King St. (b)
Hampton, VA 23669
757-723-0521
Sales: $1 Million-$10 Million
ALFRED BENTON-KNIGHT II (President & G.M.M.) & Buys Men's Sportswear, Leather Apparel, Furnishings, Accessories, Dress Shoes, Young Men's Wear, Store Displays, Fixtures, Supplies

GEAR, INC. (MW)
(MUGLERS OF PHOEBUS)
123 E. Mellen St. (m-b)
Hampton, VA 23663
757-723-6431 / Fax: 757-723-5934
Sales: $500,001-$1 Million
Website: www.muglers.com
DON GEAR (Owner) & Buys Men's Wear, Big & Tall Men's Wear, Uniforms, Related Footwear, Furnishings, Accessories, Store Displays, Fixtures, Supplies

GENTS OF HAMPTON (MW)
(BARO, INC.)
Coliseum Mall
Hampton, VA 23666
757-826-5240 / Fax: 757-480-4465
Sales: $500,001-$1 Million
ROY ORLEANS-Men's & Young Men's Wear, Footwear, Accessories, Furnishings, Boys' Wear, Store Displays, Fixtures, Supplies

SUNNYSIDE STORE, INC. (DEPT)
2788 Fancy Gap Hwy. (p-m-b)
Hillsville, VA 24343
276-728-2031
Sales: $500,001-$1 Million
NORMAN SEMONES (Owner) & Buys Men's Wear, Work Shoes, Boys' Wear, Urban Contemporary, Accessories, Furnishings, Store Displays, Fixtures, Supplies

MARK & JAY'S (MW)
5294 Oaklawn Blvd. (m)
Hopewell, VA 23860
804-458-1727
Sales: $500,000-$1 Million
HOWARD S. COHEN (Owner) & Buys Men's Wear, Leather Apparel, Accessories, Furnishings, Dress Shoes, Casual Shoes, Work Shoes, Store Displays, Fixtures, Supplies

PERRY'S SPECIALTY SHOP, INC. (CLO)
321 Main St. (m)
Lawrenceville, VA 23868
434-848-4423 / Fax: 434-848-2598
Sales: $500,001-$1 Million
PERRY LUCY (Owner) & Buys Men's Sportswear, Urban Contemporary, Furnishings, Accessories, Shoes, Store Displays, Fixtures, Supplies

ALVIN - DENNIS (MW)
102 W. Washington St. (b)
Lexington, VA 24450
540-463-5383
ALVIN CARTER (Owner) & Buys Men's Sportswear, Furnishings, Headwear, Accessories, Leather Apparel, Footwear, Store Displays, Fixtures, Supplies

COLLEGE TOWN SHOP (CLO)
111 W. Nelson St. (m-b)
Lexington, VA 24450
540-463-2731
MARTHA DERRICK (Co-Owner) & Buys Men's Sportswear, Furnishings, Accessories, Footwear, Store Displays, Fixtures & Supplies
BUDDY DERRICK (Co-Owner) & Buys Men's Sportswear, Furnishings, Accessories, Footwear

YOGI BEAR JELLY STONE PARK (DEPT)
P.O. Box 191 (p)
Hwy. 211
Luray, VA 22835
540-743-4002 / Fax: 540-743-2111
Website: www.campluray.com
JOHN RUST (Co-Owner)
NANCY RUST (Co-Owner) & Buys Men's & Boys' T-shirts, Sandals, Store Displays, Fixtures, Supplies

FAMOUS, INC. (MW)
1019 Main St. (p)
Lynchburg, VA 24504
434-846-7515
Sales: $500,001-$1 Million
LYLE CHEEK (Co-Owner) & Buys Men's Sportswear, Furnishings, Accessories, Men's Footwear, Store Displays, Fixtures & Supplies
KEITH CHEEK (Co-Owner) & Buys Men's Sportswear, Furnishings, Accessories, Men's Footwear, Store Displays, Fixtures & Supplies

GQ SPORTSWEAR (MW)
5 Wadsworth St. (m)
Lynchburg, VA 24501
434-846-6601
BHAGU KIRPALANI (Owner) & Buys Men's T-shirts, Active Apparel, Headwear, Shorts, Store Displays, Fixtures & Supplies

NICE AS NEW, INC. (CLO)
2828 Linkhorne (p-m)
Lynchburg, VA 24503
434-384-3997 / Fax: 434-384-9433
FLO WILDER (Co-Owner) & Buys Men's & Boys' Wear, Accessories, Furnishings, Store Displays, Fixtures, Supplies
SANDRA BURNS (Co-Owner) & Buys Men's & Boys' Wear, Accessories, Furnishings, Store Displays, Fixtures, Supplies

R. COFFEE LTD., INC. (MW)
4925 Boonsboro Rd. (m-b)
Lynchburg, VA 24503
434-384-0518 / Fax: 434-384-1397
Sales: $500,001-$1 Million
RICK COFFEE (Owner) & Buys Men's Sportswear, Furnishings, Accessories, Shoes, Store Displays, Fixtures, Supplies

ARMY & NAVY STORE (AN)

219 E. Main St. (b)
Marion, VA 24354
276-783-3832 / Fax: 540-782-1910
Sales: $1 Million-$10 Million

BRAD MULLEN (Owner) & Buys Men's & Boys' Jeans, Tops, Hosiery, Underwear, Men's Military Apparel, Hunting Apparel, Men's Footwear, Store Displays, Fixtures & Supplies

BALDWIN'S FASHIONS (CLO-2)

111 Main St. (m)
Marion, VA 24354
276-783-4641 / Fax: 276-783-2936

MELITA SUTHERS (Owner) (@ 276-228-5251) & Buys Toddler to Size 4 Boys' Wear

SUE BYRD (Mgr.) & Buys Boys' Wear 4 to 7, Store Displays, Fixtures, Supplies

BOTTOMS UP (CLO)

P.O. Box 820
Marion, VA 24354
276-783-5331 / Fax: 276-783-5331

EDWARD POE (Owner) & Buys Men's Jeans, Shirts, Denim Apparel, Jackets, Hosiery, Small Leather Goods, Young Men's Wear, Size 8 to 16 Boys' Wear, Men's & Boys' Shoes, Store Displays, Fixtures, Supplies

ERNIE SULLINS' OUTLET STORE (CLO-3)

1587 N. Main St. (m)
Marion, VA 24354
276-783-6300 / Fax: 276-782-3900
Sales: $1 Million-$10 Million

ERNIE SULLINS (Owner) (@ 888-785-5467) & Buys Men's Suits, Tailored Jackets, Tailored Slacks, Sportswear, Urban Contemporary, Furnishings, Belts, Boys' Wear 4 to 7, Store Displays, Fixtures, Supplies

FAUSTO'S CLOTHIERS, INC. (CLO)

212 E. Main St., #B (b)
Marion, VA 24354
276-783-4711 / Fax: 276-783-4711
Sales: $500,001-$1 Million

FAUSTO OBREGON (Owner) & Buys Men's Sportswear, Furnishings, Accessories, Footwear, Tailored Clothing, Store Displays, Fixtures, Supplies

STONE & CO. (MW)

P.O. Box 5144
213 Aaron St.
Martinsville, VA 24112
276-632-6142 / Fax: 276-666-1223

BOB STONE (Owner) & Buys Men's Sportswear, Golf Apparel Shirts, T-shirts, Accessories, Footwear, Boys' Sportswear

GOLFDOM (SG)

8203 Watson St.
McLean, VA 22102
703-790-8844 / Fax: 703-790-8871

BUDDY CHRISTENSEN-Men's & Boys' Sportswear, Golf Apparel, Footwear, Accessories

JAMES CLOTHIERS (MW-2)

(JAMES LTD.)
1767 International Dr., #M (m-b)
McLean, VA 22102
703-883-1444 / Fax: 703-883-9551

MIKE COLEN (Co-Owner) & Buys Men's Wear, Furnishings, Accessories, Dress Shoes, Store Displays, Fixtures, Supplies

JAMES COLEN (Co-Owner) & Buys Men's Wear, Furnishings, Accessories, Dress Shoes, Store Displays, Fixtures, Supplies

SID COLEN (Co-Owner) & Buys Men's Wear, Furnishings, Accessories, Dress Shoes, Store Displays, Fixtures, Supplies

McLEAN CLOTHIERS, INC. (MW)

1349 Chain Bridge Rd.
McLean, VA 22101
703-734-0241 / Fax: 703-821-1428

VIN NEWGEN (Owner) & Buys Men's Clothing, Sportswear, Furnishings, Accessories, Store Displays, Fixtures & Supplies

NORDSTROM - EAST COAST DIV. (DEPT-24)

8075 Tysons Corner Ctr. (m-b)
McLean, VA 22102
703-761-1121 / Fax: 703-761-1121
Website: www.nordstrom.com
Retail Locations: VA, NC, SC, FL, GA, NJ, PA, NY

PAUL DOHERTY (D.M.M.-Men's Div.) (@ 730-761-3556)

JUSTIN SIMPSON (@ 703-761-3549)-Men's Clothing

KARYN ARMSTRONG (@ 703-761-3561)-Men's Sportswear

TRACY WELLS (@ 703-761-3473)-Men's Furnishings, Accessories

ALEX NAVARRO-Young Men's Wear

PATTIE MILLER (@ 703-761-3560)-Men's Faconnable

SANDY QUOMG (D.M.M.-Kids' Wear) (@ 703-761-3508)

MICHAEL NEAL (@ 703-761-3513)-Boys' Wear

ALLISON WHITT (@ 703-761-3559)-Men's Rail

DEBIE BARELA (D.M.M.-Cosmetics & Fragrances)

LAURA SHEEHAN-Men's Fragrances

ANDREW MARCUS (D.M.M.-Footwear)

STEVE HARRISON-Men's Footwear

SCOTT BOYLE (Regional Display Mgr.) & Buys Store Displays, Fixtures, Supplies

SUN TAILORING (MW)

2001 International Dr. (b)
McLean, VA 22101
703-761-1122 / Fax: 703-761-1122

SUN KANG (Owner) & Buys Men's Sportswear, Furnishings, Accessories, Footwear, Store Displays, Fixtures, Supplies

BEECROFT & BULL LTD. (MW-5)

10325 Warwick Blvd. (b)
Newport News, VA 23601
757-596-0951 / Fax: 757-596-7825
Sales: $1 Million-$10 Million

MORRIS BEECROFT (Owner) (@ 757-428-0283) & Buys Men's Wear, Leather Apparel, Dress Shoes, Casual Shoes

CRAIG BEECROFT-Men's Wear, Leather Apparel, Dress Shoes, Casual Shoes

BRIAN BEECROFT-Men's Wear, Leather Apparel, Dress Shoes, Casual Shoes

DEYONG'S WESTERN WEAR (WW)

(DEYONG'S WORKBOOT)
6139 Jefferson Ave., #G (bud-p-m-b-des)
Newport News, VA 23605
757-838-2323 / Fax: 757-838-2043
Sales: $500,001-$1 Million
Website: www.deyongs.com

ADAM DEYONG (Partner) & Buys Men's Footwear, Leather Goods, Men's Apparel

JEFF DEYONG (Partner) & Buys Men's Footwear, Leather Goods, Men's Apparel

BARBARA DEYONG (Partner) & Buys Men's Footwear, Leather Goods, Men's Apparel

G.I. JOE ARMY SURPLUS (AN)

3610 Washington Ave.
Newport News, VA 23601
757-244-3610

DONALD JACKSON (Owner) & Buys Men's & Boys' Military Wear, Shoes, Related Accessories, Store Displays, Fixtures & Supplies

MANHATTAN (MW)

403 Granby St., #B
Norfolk, VA 23510
757-640-0001 / Fax: 757-640-0455

DANIEL LEE (Owner) & Buys Men's Urban Contemporary Clothing, Accessories, Sportswear, Footwear

R & B'S CLOTHING (CLO)

6159 Sewells Point Rd.
Norfolk, VA 23513
757-852-9111 / Fax: 757-852-9112

TRUDY RIDDICK (Owner) & Buys Men's Wear, Urban Contemporary, Sportswear, Furnishings, Accessories

VIRGINIA - Norfolk

STAMOR CORP. (MW-19)

(FINE'S MEN'S SHOPS)
(STREET STUFF)
1164 Azalea Garden Rd. (p)
Norfolk, VA 23502
757-857-6013 / Fax: 757-857-4603
Sales: $10 Million-$50 Million

MITCHELL A. FINE (President)
BOB LEE (Visual Display Mgr.) & Buys Store Displays, Fixtures, Supplies
MARK GARRETT-Men's Sportswear, Sweaters, Sport Shirts, Active Apparel, Dress Shirts, Urban Contemporary
CATHY COWELL-Men's Accessories

STARK & LEGUM, INC. (MW)

739 Granby St. (p)
Norfolk, VA 23510
757-627-1018 / Fax: 757-626-3912
Sales: $500,001-$1 Million
Website: www.menhats.com

CHARLES LEGUM (President & G.M.M.) & Buys Men's Overcoats, Suits, Tailored Jackets, Tailored Slacks, Raincoats, Sportswear, Furnishings, Headwear, Accessories, Leather Apparel, Footwear, Store Displays, Fixtures, Supplies
BRYN SCOLA-Headwear
ROGER HARRISON-Headwear

ULLMAN & EMANUEL, INC. (CLO)

(ACTSCHUL'S)
427 Granby St. (p-m)
Norfolk, VA 23510
757-622-2317 / Fax: 757-622-5514
Sales: $1 Million-$10 Million

RICHARD EMANUEL (V.P.) & Buys Men's Overcoats, Leather Outerwear, Suits, Tailored Jackets, Tailored Slacks, Raincoats, Sweaters, Sport Shirts, Outer Jackets, Casual Slacks, Active Apparel, Furnishings, Headwear, Accessories, Young Men's Wear, Dress Shoes, Store Displays, Fixtures, Supplies

JAXON'S, INC. (CLO)

P.O. Box 197 (p-m)
Parksley, VA 23421
757-665-5967 / Fax: 757-665-6390
Sales: $1 Million-$10 Million

JANICE HART (Co-Owner) & Buys Men's Overcoats, Suits, Sportswear, Furnishings, Swimwear, Small Leather Goods, Fragrances, Young Men's Wear, Boys' Wear, Belts, Footwear, Store Displays, Fixtures, Supplies

MR. KING'S CLOTHES (MW-2)

30 W. Washington St.
Petersburg, VA 23803
804-861-0581 / Fax: 804-861-5125

KIM KI DONG (Co-Owner) & Buys Men's & Boys' Clothing, Sportswear, Footwear, Accessories, Store Displays
KIM SUK SOO (Co-Owner) & Buys Men's & Boys' Clothing, Sportswear, Footwear, Accessories, Store Displays

ARMY-NAVY STORE (AN)

1817 High St.
Portsmouth, VA 23704
757-397-7452 / Fax: 757-397-4101

IRVING FRANK (Mgr.) & Buys Activewear, Hunting Apparel, Footwear, Boots

ROGERS CLOTHES, INC. (CLO)

3134 Western Branch Blvd. (m)
Portsmouth, VA 23701
757-484-1020

AUBREY CUTHRELL (President) & Buys Men's Sportswear, Furnishings, Accessories, Store Displays, Fixtures & Supplies

ALEX & DANA (MW)

2 Main St. NE (m)
Pulaski, VA 24301
540-980-1111 / Fax: 540-980-6161

ALEX RYGAS (Owner) & Buys Men's Sportswear, Furnishings, Accessories, Store Displays, Fixtures & Supplies

MARINE CORPS EXCHANGE (PX)

P.O. Box 229 (p-m-b)
M.W.R. 0120
Quantico, VA 22134
703-640-8800 / Fax: 703-640-6708
Sales: $10 Million-$50 Million

VICKI BARTLETT (Exchange Officer)
JACKIE PARKER-Men's Overcoats, Suits, Tailored Jackets, Tailored Slacks, Raincoats, Sweaters, Sport Shirts, Outer Jackets, Casual Slacks, Active Apparel, Big & Tall Men's Wear, Urban Contemporary
CATHY HARMAN-Men's & Boys' Footwear
HOPE THOMPSON-Young Men's Wear, Furnishings, Accessories
KRISTINE STOYKS-Boys' Wear

THE MARINE SHOP (CLO)

(HARRY D. ELMS, INC.)
300 Potomac Ave. (m)
Quantico, VA 22134
703-640-7195 / Fax: 703-640-6809
Sales: $1 Million-$10 Million
Website: www.themarineshop.com

MAJ. HARRY ELMS, SR. (President) & Buys Military Uniforms, Military Footwear, Related Accessories, Furnishings, Store Displays, Fixtures, Supplies

DJR ENTERPRISES (CLO)

1012 W. Main St. (p-m-b)
Radford, VA 24141
540-639-9386 / Fax: 540-633-0504
Sales: $1 Million-$10 Million
Website: www.djrnet.com

DAVID McDANIEL (President) & Buys Sportswear, Urban Contemporary, Accessories, Furnishings, Store Displays, Fixtures, Supplies

GARRETT'S, INC. (CLO)

1124 E. Main St. (m-b)
Radford, VA 24141
540-639-3841 / Fax: 540-639-5089
Sales: $500,001-$1 Million

MEG WEDDLE (Owner) & Buys Men's Wear, Dress Shoes, Casual Shoes, Accessories, Furnishings, Store Displays, Fixtures, Supplies

RESTON CUSTOM TAILOR (MW)

2260 Hunters Woods Plz., #B (m)
Reston, VA 20191
703-860-3560 / Fax: 703-860-4068

WAGNER CORDOVA (Owner) & Buys Men's Sportswear, Furnishings, Accessories, Store Displays, Fixtures & Supplies

CURY'S, INC. (CLO)

P.O. Box 1225 (m-b)
1517 Front St.
Richlands, VA 24641
276-963-6100 / Fax: 276-963-6418
Sales: $500,001-$1 Million
Website: www.curys.com

ROD CURY (Owner) & Buys Men's & Young Men's Wear, Accessories, Furnishings, Men's Dress Shoes, Casual Shoes, Store Displays, Fixtures, Supplies

707 MEN'S SHOP (MW)

(BAXANI CORP.)
310 E. Broad St. (m)
Richmond, VA 23219
804-643-0859 / Fax: 804-643-0859

CHARLES BAXANI (President) & Buys Men's Urban Contemporary, Furnishings (No Underwear), Accessories, Shoes, Store Displays, Fixtures, Supplies

ATLANTIC TANNING (CLO-6)

710 N. Hamilton St., #100
Richmond, VA 23221
804-353-5300 / Fax: 804-359-5008
Website: www.atlantictanning.net

DARA FRIEDLANDER-Men's Surf & Swimwear

VIRGINIA - Richmond

CHILDREN'S WEAR DIGEST (KS-3 & MO & OL)
3607 Mayland Ct.
Richmond, VA 23233
804-270-7401 / Fax: 804-270-7405
Website: www.cwdkids.com
PHILIP KLAUS, JR. (C.E.O.) & Buys Size 4 to 18 Boys' Wear
SUSAN GILES (V.P.) & Buys Size 4 to 18 Boys' Wear
MARY LOU BEAN-Size 4 to 18 Boys' Wear

DISCO SPORTS, INC. (SG)
8813 Three Chopt Rd. (m)
Richmond, VA 23229
804-285-4242 / Fax: 804-673-4055
Website: www.discosports.com
GAIL HELD (Owner) & Buys Men's & Boys' Athletic Apparel, Licensed Apparel, Footwear

DIXIE SPORTS (DEPT-5)
2400 Westwood Ave. (p-m)
Richmond, VA 23230
804-353-4953 / Fax: 804-355-4269
Sales: $1 Million-$10 Million
Website: www.bococksports.com
KEN CARAVATTI (Owner) & Buys Store Displays, Fixtures, Supplies
SHAWN ROMER-Men's & Boys' Sportswear, Active Apparel, Apparel, Athletic Apparel, Athletic Footwear, Headwear

FRANCO'S FINE CLOTHIER (CLO-3)
5321 Lakeside Ave. (p-m-b)
Richmond, VA 23228
804-264-2994 / Fax: 804-262-1225
Sales: $1 Million-$10 Million
Website: www.francos.com
FRANCO AMBROGI (Owner) & Buys Men's Suits, Formal Wear, Footwear, Sportswear, Leather Apparel, Furnishings, Belts, Jewelry, Small Leather Goods, Fragrances, Young Men's Wear, Boys' Wear, Store Displays, Fixtures, Supplies
MARK AMBROGI-Men's Suits, Formal Wear, Footwear, Sportswear, Leather Apparel, Furnishings, Belts, Jewelry, Small Leather Goods, Fragrances, Young Men's Wear, Boys' Wear, Store Displays, Fixtures, Supplies

HULL STREET OUTLET, INC. (AN)
3820 Jefferson Davis Hwy. (p-m-b)
Richmond, VA 23234
804-275-9239 / Fax: 804-275-8926
Sales: $500,000-$1 Million
FRED FINN (Mgr.) & Buys Men's & Boys' Wear, Urban Contemporary, Boots, Store Displays, Fixtures, Supplies
JERRY FINN-Men's & Boys' Wear, Urban Contemporary, Boots, Store Displays, Fixtures, Supplies

J. ALTIS LTD. (MW)
Stoney Point Shopping Ctr.
Richmond, VA 23235
804-272-7731 / Fax: 804-272-4435
JIM ALTIS (Owner) & Buys Men's & Young Men's Wear, Men's Dress Shoes, Casual Shoes, Furnishings, Accessories, Store Displays, Fixtures, Supplies

LITTLE PEEPS (KS)
550 E. Grace St. (p)
Richmond, VA 23219
804-649-4800 / Fax: 804-225-9707
Sales: $100,001-$500,000
LARRY PROCTOR (Owner) & Buys Boys' Wear, Furnishings, Accessories, Footwear, Headwear, Hosiery

PANTS PLUS (MW)
(JEANS PLUS)
214 E. Broad St. (bud-p-m)
Richmond, VA 23219
804-225-8857
Sales: $100,001-$500,000
B. S. JIANDANI (Owner) & Buys Men's Overcoats, Suits, Raincoats, Sportswear, Furnishings, Dress Shoes, Casual Shoes, Jewelry, Small Leather Goods, Young Men's Wear & Boys' Wear, Store Displays, Fixtures, Supplies

PETER BLAIR, INC. (MW)
5718 Grove Ave. (b-h)
Richmond, VA 23226
804-288-8123 / Fax: 804-288-4678
Sales: $100,001-$500,000
ED CLEAVENER (Co-Owner) & Buys Men's Sportswear, Furnishings, Accessories, Footwear, Store Displays, Fixtures, Supplies
RICHARD FOWLKES, II (Co-Owner) & Buys Men's Sportswear, Furnishings, Accessories, Footwear, Store Displays, Fixtures, Supplies

SEA DREAM LEATHER CO. (MW-11)
3304 W. Broad St. (b)
Richmond, VA 23230
804-359-3521 / Fax: 804-359-0442
JIM STORIE (President) & Buys Men's Leather Wear, Small Leather Goods, Footwear, Urban Contemporary
RAY TOLSON (Secy. & Treas.) & Buys Store Displays, Fixtures & Supplies

SHEVEL'S, INC. (MW-2)
Willow Lawn Shopping Ctr. (b)
Richmond, VA 23230
804-282-9594 / Fax: 804-282-4460
ROBERT SIFF (Owner) & Buys Men's Suits, Furnishings, Accessories, Leather Apparel, Footwear, Store Displays, Fixtures and Supplies

SOUL STATION (CLO)
(SUNNY LIM, INC.)
429 E. Broad St. (m-b)
Richmond, VA 23219
804-788-1758 / Fax: 804-788-0023
SUNNY LIM (President & G.M.M.) & Buys Men's Wear, Suits, Sportswear, Furnishings, Accessories, Footwear, Urban Contemporary, Store Displays, Fixtures, Supplies

VATEX AMERICA (CLO)
2935 Hermitage Rd. (m-b)
Richmond, VA 23220
804-353-9010 / Fax: 804-353-8939
Website: www.vatex.com
JERRY GORDE (C.E.O.)
CHRISTINE GIBSON-Men's Urban Contemporary, Boys' 4 to 7 & 8 to 20 Casual Wear

CMT SPORTING GOODS CO., INC. (SG-4)
3473 Brandon Ave. SW (m)
Roanoke, VA 24018
540-343-5533 / Fax: 540-343-2915
Website: www.cmtsports.com
BARBARA SWINDELL-Men's & Boys' Athletic Apparel, Licensed Apparel, Team Clothing, Athletic Footwear, Store Displays, Fixtures & Supplies

DAVIDSON'S (MW-2)
412 S. Jefferson (m-b-des)
Roanoke, VA 24011
540-343-2441 / Fax: 540-345-6021
Sales: $1 Million-$10 Million
Website: www.fineclothiers.com
LARRY DAVIDSON (President) & Buys Men's Overcoats, Outer Jackets, Suits, Tailored Jackets, Tailored Slacks, Sweaters
BRUCE YOUNG (V.P.-Operations) & Buys Activewear, Gloves, Headwear, Belts, Small Leather Goods, Store Displays, Fixtures, Supplies
DAVID WHITE-Men's Sport Shirts, Dress Shirts, Ties, Casual Slacks

FINK'S JEWELERS, INC. (JWLY-15)
(FINK'S)
(GARIBALDI & BRUNS)
P.O. Box 12906
3545 Electric Rd.
Roanoke, VA 24018
540-342-2991 / Fax: 540-343-1570
Sales: $10 Million-$50 Million
Website: www.finks.com
ALVIN FINK (Chairman)
MARC FINK (President & C.E.O.)
DEBBIE SMITH-Jewelry
SCEVA GWYN-Watches

VIRGINIA - Roanoke

JOHN NORMAN CO. (CLO-2)
(JOSEPH & JOSHUA, INC.)
4222 Electric Rd. (m-b)
Roanoke, VA 24014
540-989-3105
JEFF WENDELL (President) & Buys Men's Furnishings, Accessories & Swimwear, Store Displays, Fixtures & Supplies
GEORGE HENDRICK-Men's Furnishings, Accessories & Swimwear, Store Displays, Fixtures & Supplies

MIKE GLASSNER, INC. (JWLY-7)
(GLASSNER JEWELERS)
3807 Brandon Ave. SW, #2010
Roanoke, VA 24018
540-989-0024 / Fax: 540-989-7489
Sales: $1 Million-$10 Million
JERRY B. MCBRIDE (President)
SCOTT BEVERIDGE (V.P.) & Buys Watches
SHERI BEVERIDGE (V.P.) & Buys Jewelry

NEW YORK FASHIONS, INC. (MW)
30 W. Campbell Ave. (m)
Roanoke, VA 24011
540-345-3320 / Fax: 540-345-3320
HARRY MAGHERA (Owner) & Buys Men's Sportswear, Furnishings, Accessories, Footwear, Store Displays, Fixtures & Supplies

SAM'S ARMY NAVY (AN)
(SAM'S ON THE MARKET, INC.)
304 Market St. (p-m)
Roanoke, VA 24011
540-342-7300 / Fax: 540-345-0432
Sales: $500,001-$1 Million
Website: www.samsmarket.com
JEFF GOLDSTEIN (Mgr.) & Buys Men's Casual Wear, Work Clothes, Underwear, Hosiery, Belts, Uniforms, Jeans, Work Shoes, Boots, Store Displays, Fixtures & Supplies
THOMAS V. ANDERTON SR. (Owner)

BOOT'VIL (WW)
8625 Seminole Trl.
Ruckersville, VA 22968
434-985-4574 / Fax: 434-985-5019
Website: www.boot-vil.com
MARY ANNE SIMPSON (Owner) & Buys Men's & Boys' Western Wear, Footwear, Furnishings, Accessories, Headwear

THOMPSON'S SUITS (MW)
(QUALITY CLOTHES, INC.)
2049 E. Main St. (m-b)
Salem, VA 24153
540-986-0050 / Fax: 540-986-1324
Sales: $1 Million-$10 Million
Website: www.thompsonsclothing.com
FRANK THOMPSON (Owner) & Buys Men's Wear, Dress Shoes, Accessories, Furnishings, Store Displays, Fixtures, Supplies

GARRETT, LLC (KS)
110 E. Union St.
Sandston, VA 23150
804-762-4455 / Fax: 804-217-8999
MARIE GARRETT (Owner) & Buys Men's Apparel, Furnishings, Accessories & Footwear

STERNHEIMER BROTHERS, INC. (MW-55 & OL)
(A & N STORES)
5501 Ferncroft Rd. (p)
Sandston, VA 23150
804-226-1324 / Fax: 804-222-4894
Sales: $50 Million-$100 Million
Website: www.anstores.com
Retail Locations: VA
MARK A. STERNHEIMER (President)
ROSS STERNHEIMER (Exec. V.P. & Real Estate Contact)
RON BRITT (G.M.M.) & Buys Store Displays, Fixtures, Supplies
HARRIET MILLS-Men's Sportswear, Accessories, Furnishings
JAMES MASTIN-Men's Footwear

COLEMAN'S OUTDOORS (SG)
137 Main St. (m)
Scottsville, VA 24590
434-286-2547 / Fax: 434-286-2547
Sales: $100,001-$500,000
MARK STEVENS (Owner) & Buys Outdoor Clothing, Overcoats, Hunting Clothing, Outer Jackets, Raincoats, Work Apparel, Boots, Camoflauge Clothing, Store Displays, Fixtures, Supplies
PAM STEVENS-Outdoor Clothing, Overcoats, Hunting Clothing, Outer Jackets, Raincoats, Work Apparel, Boots, Camoflauge Clothing, Store Displays, Fixtures, Supplies

PEEBLES, INC. (DEPT-140)
1 Peebles St. (p-m-b)
South Hill, VA 23970
434-447-5200 / Fax: 434-447-5302
Sales: $50 Million-$100 Million
Website: www.peebles.com
Retail Locations: NY, PA, OH, IN, MO, KY, WV, VA, MD, NJ, DE, AL, SC, NC, TN
MIKE MOORMAN (C.E.O.)
RON PALMORE (G.M.M.)
BEN HAUBENREISER (D.M.M.)
KEN YOUNG (@ 804-447-5357)-Men's Shoes
RANDY WILSON-Active Wear, Collections
JOHN GALO-Men's Ties, Robes, Underwear, Hosiery, Gloves, Headwear, Footwear
JEFF CLARK-Young Men's Wear
STEVE MANNING-Suit Separates, Pants

JOHN BOWER (D.M.M.) & Buys Boys' Wear
CAROL DUNN (Visual Display Mgr.) & Buys Store Displays
JOANNE FARNSWORTH (Real Estate Contact)

PAPILLON STORE (MW-6)
(ALLIED INTERNATIONAL CORP.)
45191 Columbia Pl.
Sterling, VA 20166
703-444-5515 / Fax: 703-444-6493
Website: www.alliedint.com
CHAUN AKHAVAN-Men's Dress Shirts, Ties, Accessories, Store Displays, Fixtures, Supplies

BEASLEY'S (CLO)
4200 Holland Rd. (b)
Stuart, VA 24171
276-694-3518 / Fax: 276-694-8066
Sales: $500,001-$1 Million
RICHARD MARTIN (Owner) & Buys Sportswear, Dress Shirts, Ties, Underwear, Hosiery, Gloves, Belts, Headwear, Small Leather Goods, Footwear, Store Displays, Fixtures, Supplies

RICHARDSON & NASH CLOTHIERS (MW)
126 N. Main St. (m-b)
Suffolk, VA 23434
757-539-2422 / Fax: 757-539-2429
Sales: $500,001-$1 Million
SCOTT NASH (Co-Owner) & Buys Men's Sportswear, Furnishings, Accessories, Store Displays, Fixtures & Supplies
BOBBY RICHARDSON (Co-Owner) & Buys Men's Sportswear, Furnishings, Accessories, Store Displays, Fixtures & Supplies

THE FASHION GALLERY (CLO)
(C.D. WILSON)
P.O. Box 586
4719 Lee Hwy.
Verona, VA 24482
540-248-4292 / Fax: 540-248-5753
LINDA F. WILSON-HOLDEN (Owner) & Buys Men's Wear, Men's Furnishings, Accessories, Footwear

ACREDALE SADDLERY (WW)
5248 Indian River Rd.
Virginia Beach, VA 23464
757-467-3183 / Fax: 757-426-1263
BETTE DAVIS (President & Owner) & Buys Store Displays, Fixtures & Supplies
PEGGY STEIN-Men's & Boys' Western Wear, Related Accessories, Furnishings, Boots

DAN RYAN'S FOR MEN (MW)
(H. RYAN & SON LTD.)
764 Hilltop North Shopping Ctr. (m)
Virginia Beach, VA 23451
757-425-0660 / Fax: 757-428-5760
DAN RYAN (Owner) & Buys Men's Wear, Dress Shoes, Furnishings, Accessories, Jewelry, Fragrances, Store Displays, Fixtures & Supplies

VIRGINIA - Virginia Beach

THE FUNKY BEAT (GM)
Fairfield Shopping Ctr.
Virginia Beach, VA 23462
757-467-8834 / Fax: 757-474-4043
DEAN WORKMAN (Owner) & Buys Men's Wear, Sportswear, Boys' Wear, Footwear, Accessories, Active Apparel, Surf Wear

MARC LANCE MENSWEAR (MW)
4000 Virginia Beach Blvd. (m-b)
Virginia Beach, VA 23452
757-340-9831 / Fax: 757-340-0235
Sales: $1 Million-$10 Million
STANLEY FURMAN (President & Co-Owner) & Buys Men's Sportswear, Dress Shirts, Ties, Robes, Accessories, Dress Shoes, Store Displays, Fixtures, Supplies
JERRY EPSTEIN (Co-Owner) & Buys Men's Sportswear, Urban Contemporary, Dress Shirts, Ties, Robes, Accessories, Dress Shoes, Store Displays, Fixtures, Supplies
GIGI EPSTEIN-Men's Sportswear, Dress Shirts, Ties, Robes, Accessories, Dress Shoes, Store Displays, Fixtures, Supplies

NEXCOM (PX-115)
(NAVY EXCHANGE SERVICE COMMAND)
3280 Virginia Beach Blvd. (bud-p-m-b)
Virginia Beach, VA 23452
757-463-6200 / Fax: 757-631-3888
Sales: $50 Million-$100 Million
Website: www.navy-nex.com
ROBERT McGINTY (Chief Mdsg. Ofcr.)
LITA SOHN (G.M.M.) (@ 757-631-3816)
MAX ALLEN (D.M.M.) (@ 757-631-4575)
DONALD JERASA-Men's Sportswear, Collections
MARK PRICE-Men's Overcoats, Raincoats, Outer Jackets, Leather Apparel, Small Leather Goods, Dress Shirts, Ties, Robes, Underwear, Hosiery, Gloves, Sweaters
SCOTT POTERT-Tailored Separates, Denim
RON REID-Young Men's Wear, Men's Active Apparel

BARBARA DIVJAK (D.M.M.) & Buys Children's Wear
MELINDA KATZ-8 to 20 Boys' Wear, Sportswear, Furnishings, Accessories

MIKE PATCH (D.M.M.)
BETH KELSEY-Jewelry
AMY BELL-Fragrances
LORETTA A. LAMBERT (D.M.M.) & Buys Frangrances
RON JOHANSEN (D.M.M.-Footwear) (@ 757-631-3806) & Buys Men's & Boys' Footwear
BILL MARX-Athletic Footwear
RICHARD CRAMER-Men's and Boy's Footwear

NANETTE RIOPASAKIS (Visual Mdsg. Specialist) & Buys Store Displays, Fixtures, Supplies

SHIRT TALES (CLO-2)
2010 Atlantic Ave. (p)
Virginia Beach, VA 23451
757-422-5321 / Fax: 757-428-0323
ANGELO RICCIO (Owner) & Buys Shorts, T-shirts, Polo Shirts, Hats, Sandals, Store Displays, Fixtures, Supplies

THE SHORE STORE (CLO-2)
(LAR JAC CORP.)
1014 Atlantic Ave. (p-m-b)
Virginia Beach, VA 23451
757-428-6141 / Fax: 757-425-1069
Sales: $1 Million-$10 Million
LARRY BRANCH (Owner) & Buys Men's & Boys' Sportswear, Shorts, Accessories, Furnishings, Men's Footwear, Store Displays, Fixtures, Supplies

URBAN WEAR (CLO-2)
701 Lynnhaven Pkwy.
Virginia Beach, VA 23452
757-631-9027 / Fax: 757-631-0060
Sales: $100,001-$500,000
VIVIENT TOMAYUM (Owner) & Buys Urban Contemporary, Jeans, T-shirts, Woven Shirts, Sportswear, Store Displays, Fixtures & Supplies

RICHARDSON'S (MW)
706 Main St. (m)
West Point, VA 23181
804-843-2760 / Fax: 804-843-2716
Sales: $500,001-$1 Million
SAM RICHARDSON (Owner) & Buys Men's Sportswear, Furnishings, Accessories, Footwear, Store Displays, Fixtures, Supplies

D. M. WILLIAMS LTD. (CLO-2)
Merchant Sq. (b)
Williamsburg, VA 23185
757-220-0456 / Fax: 757-220-0456
DON WILLIAMS (Owner) & Buys Men's Leather Apparel, Men's Wear, Accessories, Furnishings, Dress Shoes, Casual Shoes, Store Displays, Fixtures, Supplies

R. BRYANT LTD. (MW-2)
429 Duke Of Gloucester St. (b)
Williamsburg, VA 23185
757-253-0055 / Fax: 757-259-0705
Sales: $1 Million-$10 Million
RUSTY BRYANT (Owner) & Buys Men's Wear, Accessories, Furnishings, Men's Footwear, Store Displays, Fixtures, Supplies

BELL CLOTHES (CLO)
122 N. Loudoun St. (m-b)
Winchester, VA 22601
540-667-1430 / Fax: 540-667-3662
Sales: $1 Million-$10 Million
IRVIN SHENDOW (President) & Buys Men's Suits, Tailored Jackets, Clothing, Tailored Slacks, Sweaters, Outer Jackets, Gloves, Headwear, Accessories, Fragrances, Sport Shirts, Casual Slacks, Furnishings, Dress Shoes, Young Men's & Boys' Wear, Big & Tall Men's Wear, Store Displays, Fixtures, Supplies

THE WORKINGMAN'S STORE & TOTAL IMAGE (CLO)
325 W. Boscawen St. (p)
Winchester, VA 22601
540-662-2263 / Fax: 540-662-9399
Sales: $1 Million-$10 Million
Website: www.thetotalimage.net
BOBBY AMBERGI-Sweaters, Accessories, Sport Shirts, Casual Slacks, Jeans, Boys' Clothing, Sportswear, Big & Tall Men's Wear, Western Clothing, Work Shoes, Boots, Casual Shoes
JO ELLEN BOYCE-Footwear, Work Apparel

HARMON'S (CLO)

P.O. Box 113 (m-b)
Hwy. 58 West
Woodlawn, VA 24381
276-236-4884 / Fax: 276-238-1115
Website: www.harmonsstore.com

G. H. HARMON (Owner) & Buys Men's, Young Men's & Boys' Wear, Big & Tall Men's Wear, Furnishings, Accessories, Men's Footwear, Boys' Footwear

SHERRI HARMON-Store Displays, Fixtures, Supplies

OLD FORT WESTERN STORE (WW)

2028 E. Lee Hwy.
Wytheville, VA 24382
276-223-1118 / Fax: 276-223-0936
Sales: $500,001-$1 Million

HOWARD HART (Partner) & Buys Men's Western Clothing, Sportswear, Furnishings, Headwear, Boots, Accessories, Young Men's Wear, 8 to 20 Boys' Wear

LARRY BALL (Partner) & Buys Men's Western Clothing, Sportswear, Furnishings, Headwear, Boots, Accessories, Young Men's Wear, 8 to 20 Boys' Wear

CAROL BALL-Men's Western Clothing, Sportswear, Furnishings, Headwear, Boots, Accessories, Young Men's Wear, 8 to 20 Boys' Wear

MASCAR, INC. (CLO)

(IGNATIUS)
1215 George Washington Hwy., #C (m-b)
Yorktown, VA 23693
757-596-6919 / Fax: 757-596-6919
Sales: $500,001-$1 Million

IGNATIUS MASCARENHES (Owner) & Buys Men's Sportswear, Furnishings, Accessories, Store Displays, Fixtures, Supplies

WAUGH'S MEN'S STORE, INC. (MW)
110 E. Heron St. (b)
Aberdeen, WA 98520
360-533-3880 / Fax: 360-533-3884
Sales: $500,000-$1 Million
Website: www.waughsmensstoreandmore.com
RAY ERICKS (President) & Buys Men's Sweaters, Sport Shirts, Outer Jackets, Active Apparel, Men's Overcoats, Suits, Tailored Jackets, Tailored Slacks, Casual Slacks, Leather Apparel, Furnishings, Headwear, Dress Shirts, Casual Slacks, Athletic Footwear, Boots, Accessories, Young Men's

COUNTRY SQUARE (FW-2)
4053 Auburn Way North (b-des)
Auburn, WA 98002
253-859-1400 / Fax: 253-859-0604
Sales: $500,001-$1 Million
DENNIS NIRSCHL (Partner) & Buys Boys' Apparel, Boys' Footwear, Men's Footwear, Leather Goods, Licensed Apparel, Watches, Men's Accessories, Men's Apparel
DANA NIRSCHL (Partner) & Buys Boys' Apparel, Boys' Footwear, Men's Footwear, Leather Goods, Licensed Apparel, Watches, Men's Accessories, Men's Apparel
SHAWN NIRSCHL (Mgr.) & Buys Boys' Apparel, Boys' Footwear, Men's Footwear, Leather Goods, Licensed Apparel, Watches, Men's Accessories, Men's Apparel

ROTTLE'S DEPARTMENT STORE, INC. (DEPT)
226 E. Main St. (m)
Auburn, WA 98002
253-833-2750 / Fax: 253-939-9514
Sales: $500,000-$1 Million
JOHN ROTTLE (President) & Buys Store Displays, Fixtures, Supplies
DONALD A. ROTTLE (C.E.O.)
JIM ROTTLE (G.M.M.) & Buys Men's Sportswear, Furnishings, Accessories
CHRIS JENSEN-Footwear

UNIFORM STATION (CLO)
226 1st St. NE (m)
Auburn, WA 98002
253-735-4372 / Fax: 253-735-4091
SHARON DOUGHERTY-SMITH (Owner) & Buys Medical Uniforms, Work Clothes, Work Shoes, Store Displays, Fixtures, Supplies

ORIGINAL JOHN'S, INC. (WW & FW)
P.O. Box 387 (p-m)
601 E. Main St.
Battle Ground, WA 98604
360-687-2551 / Fax: 360-687-9876
BRIAN HABERMAN (Owner) & Buys Men's Western Wear, Work Clothes, Footwear, Store Displays, Fixtures, Supplies

ALBERT LTD. (CLO)
224 Bellevue Sq., #M (m-b)
Bellevue, WA 98004
425-455-2970 / Fax: 425-454-9653
DICK BROWN (Owner) & Buys Suits, Tailored Jackets, Tailored Slacks, Dress Shirts, Tuxedos, Classical & Traditional Men's Wear, Sportswear, Casual Slacks, Sport Shirts, Sweaters, Accessories, Golf Apparel, Store Displays, Fixtures, Supplies

SYLVIA'S SWIMWEAR (SP)
14100 NE 20th St.
Bellevue, WA 98007
425-747-1131 / Fax: 425-747-8924
Sales: $1 Million-$10 Million
Website: www.goswim.com
SYLVIA BAILEY (Co-Owner) & Buys Swimwear, Accessories
SCOTT POWELL (Co-Owner) & Buys Swimwear, Accessories

THE FORMAL HOUSE (MW)
1400 N. State St.
Bellingham, WA 98225
360-733-2560 / Fax: 360-733-2631
Website: www.formalhouse.com
MARK NEEDAM (Owner) & Buys Tuxedos, Footwear, Accessories

GARY'S MENSWEAR, INC. (MW)
128 W. Holly St. (m-b)
Bellingham, WA 98225
360-733-2180 / Fax: 360-734-4104
Sales: $1 Million-$10 Million
BARBARA LUPO (Co-Owner) & Buys Clothing, Sportswear, Furnishings, Accessories, Shoes, Store Displays, Fixtures, Supplies
GARY LUPO (Co-Owner) & Buys Clothing, Sportswear, Furnishings, Accessories, Shoes, Urban Contemporary, Store Displays, Fixtures, Supplies

GOFF'S DEPARTMENT STORE (DEPT)
674 Peace Portal Dr.
Blaine, WA 98230
360-332-6663
Sales: $100,001-$500,000
MURRAY GOFF (Owner)
GREG GOFF-Men's, Young Men's & Boys' Wear, Furnishings, Accessories, Store Displays, Fixtures, Supplies

BETH WEST (WW)
(BETH, INC.)
18002 Bothell-Everett Hwy. SE, #7 (p)
Bothell, WA 98012
425-745-6867 / Fax: 425-481-2384
LANCE BREWER (President) & Buys Men's Western Wear, Related Accessories Furnishings, Western Boots
JACQUELINE BREWER-Store Displays, Fixtures, Supplies

PAUL RICHARDS CLOTHING (CLO)
10127 Main St. (b)
Bothell, WA 98011
425-486-4303
PAUL RICHARDS (Owner) & Buys Men's Wear, Furnishings, Accessories, Sportswear, Dress Shirts, Store Displays, Fixtures and Supplies

STOWE'S SHOES & CLOTHING (DEPT)
420 E. Fairhaven (m)
Burlington, WA 98233
360-755-0570 / Fax: 360-755-9441
Sales: $1 Million-$10 Million
PEGGY STOWE (President) & Buys Men's Dress, Casual & Athletic Footwear, Underwear, Store Displays, Fixtures & Supplies
JODY BURKE-Men's Sportswear, Dress Shirts, Ties, Robes, Accessories, Casual Slacks, Small Leather Goods
DON NESBLET-Men's Boots

CENTERVILLE WESTERN STORE (WW-7)
1500 Lum Rd. (m)
Centralia, WA 98531
360-736-4800 / Fax: 360-736-8148
Website: www.centervillenw.com
DICK BAKER (Owner) & Buys Men's Western Wear, Leather Apparel, Boys' Wear, Footwear, Store Displays, Fixtures, Supplies, Books, Safety Shoe Retail

BARTEL'S (CLO-2)
(MOUNT-CATE APPAREL, INC.)
486 N. Market Blvd. (p-m-b)
Chehalis, WA 98532
360-748-0277 / Fax: 360-748-0302
Sales: $500,001-$1 Million
JOE MOUNT (Owner) & Buys Men's Wear, Sportswear, Furnishings, Accessories, Young Men's Wear, Footwear, Store Displays, Fixtures, Supplies

SUNBIRD SHOPPING CENTER, INC. (MW-2)
1757 N. National Ave. (p-m)
Chehlais, WA 98532
360-748-3337 / Fax: 360-748-3331
Sales: $1 Million-$10 Million
GUS SALLOWM (Owner) & Buys Work Clothing, Underwear, Headwear, Belts, Work Shoes, Store Displays, Fixtures and Supplies

CARRY ALL (CLO)
(SHIRT SHOP PLUS)
140 E. Woodin Ave. (p)
Chelan, WA 98816
509-682-5789 / Fax: 509-682-9084
Sales: $500,001-$1 Million
SHIRLEY VAUGHN (Owner) & Buys T-shirts, Shorts, Headwear, Pants, Gloves, Store Displays, Fixtures, Supplies

WASHINGTON - Chelan

CHELAN DEPARTMENT STORE (DEPT)
206 W. Woodin Ave. (p-m)
Chelan, WA 98816
509-682-2216 / Fax: 509-682-5513
TINA ASHBY (Owner) & Buys Sport Shirts, Casual Slacks, Active Apparel, Dress Shirts, Ties, Underwear, Hose Gloves, Belts, Jeans, T-shirts, Fleece & Shorts, Boys' Jeans 7 & Up, Store Displays, Fixtures and Supplies

COMPANY 107 (MW)
P.O. Box 40 (m)
107 E. Woodin Ave.
Chelan, WA 98816
509-682-4311
Sales: $100,001-$500,000
JACQUE ODEN (Owner) & Buys Men's Sweaters, Sport Shirts, Outer Jackets, Leather Apparel, Casual Slacks, Active Apparel, Furnishings, Accessories, Urban Contemporary, Store Displays, Fixtures, Supplies

LEE MORRIS CO. (CLO)
844 Sixth St. (m-b)
Clarkston, WA 99403
509-758-2092 / Fax: 509-758-0276
Sales: $100,001-$500,000
JOHN DESIMONE (Co-Owner) & Buys Men's Sportswear, Furnishings, Young Men's Wear, Big & Tall Men's Wear, Casual Footwear, Slippers, Store Displays, Fixtures, Supplies
SALLY DESIMONE (Co-Owner) & Buys Men's Sportswear, Furnishings, Young Men's Wear, Big & Tall Men's Wear, Casual Footwear, Slippers, Store Displays, Fixtures, Supplies

THE CLOTHES HORSE (CLO)
103 S. Main St. (m)
Colfax, WA 99111
509-397-3067 / Fax: 509-397-2622
Sales: $100,001-$500,000
LYNN CRISP (Owner) & Buys Clothing, Sportswear, Furnishings, Headwear, Footwear, Accessories, Young Men's Wear, Store Displays, Fixtures, Supplies

CONCRETE DEPARTMENT STORE (DEPT)
45880 Main St. (p-m)
Concrete, WA 98237
360-853-8700 / Fax: 360-853-8700
BETTE LARSON (Owner) & Buys Jeans, T-shirts, Sport Shirts, Dress Shirts, Ties, Robes, Underwear, Hosiery, Gloves, Headwear, Belts, Small Leathers, Footwear, Store Displays, Fixtures and Supplies

CHRISTENSEN'S DEPARTMENT STORE (DEPT)
P.O. Box 189 (p-m)
101 Mashell Ave. North
Eatonville, WA 98328
360-832-3621 / Fax: 360-832-8442
RICK CHRISTENSEN (Owner) & Buys Men's Overcoats, Tailored Jackets, Tailored Slacks, Raincoats, Sweaters, Sport Shirts, Outer Jackets, Casual Slacks, Active Apparel, Furnishings, Headwear, Dress Footwear, Work Footwear, Athletic Footwear, Slippers, Accessories, Young Men's & Size 8 to 20 Boys' Wear, Urban Contemporary, Work Wear, Store Displays, Fixtures, Supplies

MOSER'S CLOTHING STORE (MW)
118 E. 4th Ave. (bud-p-m-b)
Ellensburg, WA 98926
509-925-1272
JOHN MOSER (Owner) & Buys Men's Wear, Sportswear, Furnishings, Accessories, Young Men's Wear, Store Displays, Fixtures and Supplies, Work Clothing, T-shirts, Fleece & Shorts

GEESEY'S (MW)
17 Basin NW (m)
Ephrata, WA 98823
509-754-3411 / Fax: 509-754-0763
Sales: $100,001-$500,000
HAROLD GEESEY (Owner) & Buys Men's Wear, Leather Apparel, Young Men's Wear, Footwear, Boots, Athletic Footwear, Slippers, Store Displays, Fixtures, Supplies

SOUND SAFETY PRODUCTS (MW-3)
3602 Broadway (m-b)
Everett, WA 98201
425-743-7463 / Fax: 425-259-3019
Website: www.worknmore.com
DON VAN TROJEN (Owner) & Buys Safety Clothes, Boots, Store Displays, Fixtures & Supplies, Equipment, Outerwear

ZUMIEZ, INC. (MW-80 & OL)
1420 80th St. SW, #A (m)
Everett, WA 98203
425-551-1500 / Fax: 425-551-1555
Sales: $50 Million-$100 Million
Website: www.zumiez.com
Retail Locations: AK, CA, CO, ID, IL, MN, MT, NY, OR, UT, WA, WI
TOM CAMPION (Owner)
RICK BROOKS (C.F.O.)
JIM Bob HUME (Merch. Mgr.) & Buys Men's Wear, Young Men's Wear, Sportswear
ANDY ESPENEL-Men's Wear, Accessories
JOSH BURAH-Snowboard Apparel
Adam GERKIN-Skateboard Apparel
SUSI HUXTABLE-Juniors, Footwear

MERAS MENSWEAR & TUX SHOP (MW)
7716 Pioneer Way
Gig Harbor, WA 98335
253-851-3366
A. MERAS (Owner) & Buys Clothing, Sportswear, Furnishings, Accessories, Store Displays, Fixtures, Supplies

BITAR'S LA VOGUE DEPARTMENT STORE (DEPT)
623 Simpson Ave. (p-m-b)
Hoquiam, WA 98550
360-532-2310
Sales: $500,000-$1 Million
DANIEL B. BITAR (Co-Owner)
WILLIAM L. BITAR (Co-Owner) & Buys Men's Work Footwear, Buys Store Displays, Fixtures, Supplies
EDWARD C. BITAR (Co-Owner & G.M.M.) & Buys Men's Leather Jackets, Boys' & Students Wear, Big & Tall Men's Wear, Young Men's Wear, Urban Contemporary, Dress Footwear

GRANGE SUPPLY, INC. (DG)
145 NE Gilman Blvd. (p)
Issaquah, WA 98027
425-392-6469 / Fax: 425-392-2348
LEE ELLIS (Mgr.) & Buys Men's Work Clothes, Western Wear, T-shirts, Active Apparel, Boys' Jeans, Footwear, Headwear, Store Displays, Fixtures & Supplies

BASIN DEPARTMENT STORE (DEPT)
111 W. 1st St. (p)
Kennewick, WA 99336
509-586-6309 / Fax: 509-783-4059
STUART LOGG (President) & Buys Men's, Young Men's & Boys' Wear, Big & Tall Men's Wear, Footwear, Work Wear, Western Wear, Store Displays, Fixtures, Supplies

MOSS BAY MERCANTILE (MW)
7 Lake Short Plz. (m)
Kirkland, WA 98033
425-827-1116
Sales: $100,001-$500,000
DICK HARLOW (Owner) & Buys Clothing, Sportswear, Dress Shirts, Ties, Hosiery, Belts, Store Displays, Fixtures, Supplies

THE STAR STORE (CLO)
P.O. Box 307
201 1st St.
Langley, WA 98260
360-221-5223 / Fax: 360-221-5224
Sales: $100,001-$500,000
TAMAR FELTON (Owner) & Buys Men's & Boys' Wear, Young Men's Wear, Footwear, Store Displays, Fixtures, Supplies

THE HAT SHOP (CLO)

(WOOD SHOP)
719 Front St.
Leavenworth, WA 98826
509-548-4442 / Fax: 509-548-7906

KAREN RIEKE (Owner) & Buys Men's Hats, Store Displays, Fixtures, Supplies

BOB'S MERCHANDISE, INC. (CLO)

1111 Hudson St. (bud-p)
Longview, WA 98632
360-425-3870 / Fax: 360-636-4334
Sales: $1 Million-$10 Million

BOB SCHLECHT (President)

DAVE HOLMA (Mgr.) & Buys Store Displays, Fixtures, Supplies

KURT HENDRICKSON-Men's Overcoats, Sweaters, Outer Jackets, Furnishings, Headwear, Accessories, Work Boots, Men's Active Apparel, Young Men's Wear, Urban Contemporary, Athletic Footwear, Casual Slacks, Sport Shirts, Boys' Wear Size 8 to 20

UNIFORM EXPRESS (MW)

1339 Commerce St., #208 (m)
Longview, WA 98632
360-425-5460 / Fax: 360-425-9141

CINDY NORDSTROM (Partner) & Buys Medical, Restaurant & Police Uniforms, Related Footwear, Store Displays, Fixtures, Supplies

MARJORIE MIDDLETON (Partner) & Buys Medical, Restaurant & Police Uniforms, Related Footwear, Store Displays, Fixtures, Supplies

WALL STREET CUSTOM CLOTHIERS (CLO & OL)

2448 76th Ave. SE, #101B (m-b)
Mercer Island, WA 98040
206-232-6122 / Fax: 206-236-6780
Sales: $1 Million-$10 Million
Website: www.wallstreetclothiers.com

DALE DUNNING (President) & Buys Men's Ties, Belts, Suspenders, Furnishings, Casual Slacks, Sport Shirts, Custom Clothing, Dress Shirts, Casual Slacks, Accessories, Footwear, Store Displays, Fixtures, Supplies

RAWSON'S (CLO)

P.O. Box 1310 (m)
212 2nd Ave. South
Okanogan, WA 98840
509-422-4247 / Fax: 509-422-0611

RICHARD RAWSON (Co-Owner) & Buys Men's Wear, Leather Apparel, Young Men's & Boys' Wear, Urban Contemporary, Footwear, Store Displays, Fixtures, Supplies

BONNIE RAWSON (Co-Owner) & Buys Men's Wear, Leather Apparel, Young Men's & Boys' Wear, Urban Contemporary, Footwear, Store Displays, Fixtures, Supplies

PRINCE'S, INC. (DEPT)

1000 23rd Ave. (bud-p-m-b)
Oroville, WA 98844
509-476-3651 / Fax: 509-476-3164

JIM PRINCE (Owner) & Buys Men's Leather Jackets, Young Men's Wear, Big & Tall Men's & Boys' Wear, Accessories, Furnishings, Footwear, Store Supplies, Fixtures

MARILYN PRINCE-Store Displays

GRIGG'S DEPARTMENT STORES (DEPT)

801 W. Columbia St. (p-m-b)
Pasco, WA 99301
509-547-0566 / Fax: 509-547-4387
Sales: $1 Million-$10 Million

CHARLIE GRIGG (Owner) & Buys Store Displays, Fixtures, Supplies

DEBORAH HARDEN-Men's & Boys' Wear, Accessories, Furnishings

BEN BUSH-Footwear

ATHLETE'S CHOICE (SP)

215 W. 1st St.
Port Angeles, WA 98362
360-452-8661

TODD CLAYTON (Owner) & Buys Activewear, Licensed Apparel, Athletic Footwear

BROWN'S, INC. (CLO)

112 W. Front St. (m-b)
Port Angeles, WA 98362
360-457-4150 / Fax: 360-452-6298
Sales: $500,001-$1 Million
Website: www.brownsoutdoor.com

LARRY BROWN (Owner) & Buys Outdoor Clothes, Long Underwear, Sweaters, Belts, Boots, Store Displays, Fixtures and Supplies

EVAN BROWN-Outdoor Clothes, Long Underwear, Sweaters, Belts, Boots, Store Displays, Fixtures and Supplies

SWAIN'S GENERAL STORE, INC. (DEPT-3)

602 E. 1st St. (m)
Port Angeles, WA 98362
360-452-2357 / Fax: 360-452-7561
Sales: $1 Million-$10 Million
Website: www.swainsinc.com

BECKY GEDLUND (Owner)

TODD ANGEVINE-Men's Sport Shirts, Active Apparel, Dress Shirts, Ties, Robes, Hosiery, Gloves, Raincoats, Big & Tall Men's Wear, Men's Underwear, Accessories, Boys' Wear, Store Displays, Fixtures & Supplies, Children & Infant Clothes, Paint, Hardware

MIKE MUDD-Footwear

ERIC HEDIN-Store Displays, Fixtures and Supplies

TOGGERY, INC. (MW)

105 E. 1st St. (b)
Port Angeles, WA 98362
360-457-4303 / Fax: 360-457-0138
Sales: $1 Million-$10 Million
Website: gotham@tenforward.com

ROY E. GOTHAM (Owner) & Buys Men's & Young Men's Suits, Sportswear, Furnishings, Accessories, Big & Tall Men's Wear, Store Displays, Fixtures, Supplies

DAVE MURPHY (Mgr.) & Buys Men's & Young Men's Suits, Sportswear, Furnishings, Accessories, Big & Tall Men's Wear, Store Displays, Fixtures, Supplies

NORTHWEST MAN (MW-2)

(The Clothes Horse)
912 Water St. (m-b)
Port Townsend, WA 98368
360-385-6734 / Fax: 360-385-6734

GAIL BOULTER (Owner) & Buys Men's Accessories, Furnishings, Casual Footwear, Store Displays, Fixtures & Supplies

KEN VOGEL CLOTHING (CLO)

400 E. Main (p-m)
Pullman, WA 99163
509-332-0505 / Fax: 509-334-9134

KEN VOGEL (Owner) & Buys Tailored Jackets, Tailored Slacks, Sportswear, Furnishings, Headwear, Accessories, Store Displays, Fixtures, Supplies

STUDENT'S BOOK CORP. (SP-3)

(WASHINGTON STATE UNIVERSITY)
NE 700 Thatuna St.
Pullman, WA 99163
509-332-2537 / Fax: 509-332-8239
Sales: $100,001-$500,000
Website: www.wsubookie.net

PAT WRIGHT (Mgr.) & Buys Books

KELLI DAHMEN (Dept. Mgr.) & Buys Activewear, Fleecewear, Jackets, Hosiery, Shorts, Hats, Golf Apparel, Athletics

DENNIS SALES CO., INC. (MW-2)

(DENNIS CO.)
146 5th St. (p-m)
Raymond, WA 98577
360-942-2427 / Fax: 360-942-2932

GARY DENNIS (Owner)

BRENT DENNIS (V.P.) & Buys Store Displays, Fixtures, Supplies

LISA KLEMP (Secy. & Treas.) & Buys Men's Sweaters, Sport Shirts, Outer Jackets, Casual Slacks, Active Apparel, Furnishings, Headwear, Footwear, Accessories, Boys' Wear

WASHINGTON - Redmond

EDDIE BAUER, INC. (CLO-600 & MO & OL)

(Div. of THE SPIEGEL GROUP)
P.O. Box 97000 (b)
15010 NE 36th St.
Redmond, WA 98052
425-882-6100 / Fax: 425-556-7689
Sales: Over $3 Billion
Website: www.eddiebauer.com
Retail Locations: AZ, AK, AZ, AR, CA, CO, CT, DE, DC, FL, GA, HI, ID, IL, IN, IA, KS, KY, LA, ME, MD, MA, MI, MN, MS, MO, MT, NE, NV, NH, NJ, NM, NY, NC, ND, OH, OK, OR, PA, RI, SC, SD, TN, TX, UT, VT, VA, WA, WV, WI, WY

- FABIAN MANSSON (President & C.E.O.)
- KATHY BOYET (Mdse. Mgr.)
- S. RONALD GASTON (Sr. V.P. & C.F.O.)
- OPEN (Visual Presentation & Creative Services) & Buys Store Displays, Fixtures, Supplies
- DIANE JEFFRIES-Men's Shirts, Men's Outerwear
- MARK BORISON (Real Estate Contact)
- BARBARA CAALIM-Men's Knit Shirts
- SUSANA DOLEZAL-Men's Woven Shirts, Accessories
- DIANE SUMNER-Men's Sweaters, Outerwear, Active Apparel

REDMOND WORK & WESTERN WEAR (WW)

7829 Leavy Way (p-m-b)
Redmond, WA 98052
425-883-3484 / Fax: 425-881-5637
Sales: $500,000-$1 Million

- JOE HONG (Owner) & Buys Men's & Boys' Western Wear, Overcoats, Suits, Tailored Slacks, Leather Apparel, Active Apparel, Gloves, Belts, Footwear, Store Displays, Fixtures, Supplies

SPORTEES, INC. (CLO & OL)

16725 Cleveland St. (b)
Redmond, WA 98052
425-882-1333 / Fax: 425-881-5926
Sales: $500,001-$1 Million
Website: www.sportees.com

- BRIAN HOWE (Owner) & Buys Men's Shirts, Jackets, Sweaters, Footwear, Store Displays, Fixtures, Supplies

RENTON WESTERN WEAR, INC. (WW-2 & OL)

724 S. 3rd St. (p)
Renton, WA 98055
425-255-3922 / Fax: 425-225-7711
Sales: $1 Million-$10 Million
Website: www.rentonww.com

- JERRY KAVESH (Co-Owner) & Buys Men's & Boys' Western Wear, Related Accessories, Furnishings, Footwear, Store Displays, Fixtures, Supplies

SHIRTZ TO GO, INC. (CLO-2)

P.O. Box 997 (p)
77 Wells Ave. South
Renton, WA 98057
425-235-7114 / Fax: 425-235-7143
Website: www.shirtztogo.com

- MICK SCHLOFF (President) & Buys Men's T-shirts, Fleece, Urban Contemporary, Store Displays, Fixtures, Supplies

THE OUTFITTERS (CLO)

56 N. Clark Ave. (m)
Republic, WA 99166
509-775-3350
Sales: $100,001-$500,000

- KATHLEEN HARCOURT (Owner) & Buys Men's Work Wear, Western Wear, Accessories, Furnishings, Boys' Wear, Footwear, Store Displays, Fixtures, Supplies

DAWSON - RICHARDS TUX SHOP (CLO)

1350 Jadwin St., #B (m)
Richland, WA 99352
509-943-0652 / Fax: 509-943-6199
Sales: $1 Million-$10 Million

- GARY MILLER (Owner) & Buys Men's Formalwear, Furnishings, Accessories, Footwear

BON MARCHE (DEPT-42)

(Div. of FEDERATED DEPT. STORES, INC.)
620 Northgate Mall (p-m-b)
Seattle, WA 98101
(Federated Merchandising Group)
206-406-2222 / Fax: 206-506-6007
Sales: $500 Million-$1 Billion
Website: www.federated-fds.com

- DAN EDELMAN (Chmn. & C.E.O.)
- ERIC SALUS (President)
- GARY GROSSBLATT (Sr. V.P.-Men's & Children's)
- KATHY KALDAL (D.M.M.-Moderate Men's) & Buys Men's Overcoats, Suits, Tailored Jackets, Tailored Slacks, Raincoats, Men's Dress Shirts, Ties
- MARIA PERRY (D.M.M.-Men's Furnishings,)
- CLARK BERNARD-Men's Robes, Underwear, Hosiery, Men's Gloves, Headwear, Belts, Jewelry, Small Leather Goods
- BOBBY BUI-Sweaters, Knit Shirts
- JEFF WEISS-Men's Collections, Men's Polo, Men's Nautica, Men's Casual Slacks, Men's Levi's, Haggar Slacks, Dockers, Men's Outerwear, Outer Jackets, Men's Active Apparel, Men's Swimwear, Sweaters, Knit Shirts
- STAN FRIEDLANDER (D.M.M.-Young Men's & Boys') & Buys Young Men's Sweaters, Woven Shirts, Accessories, Knits, Young Men's Levis, Denims, Casual Slacks, Outerwear
- THOMAS HOLT-Young Men's Collections, Status Apparel, Men's Collection Sportswear

BUTCH BLUM (MW-2)

1408 5th Ave. (m-b)
Seattle, WA 98101
206-622-5760 / Fax: 206-622-6664
Sales: $1 Million-$10 Million
Website: www.butchblumworld.com

- BUTCH BLUM (Owner)
- JOHN RICHARDS-Men's Sportswear, Accessories
- ROYAL ROLES-Men's Furnishings
- MARESA PATTERSON-Store Displays, Fixtures
- CAROLYN FENNER-Supplies

BYRNIE UTZ HATS (SP)

310 Union (p-m-b)
Seattle, WA 98101
206-623-0233
Sales: $500,001-$1 Million

- PAUL FERRY (Owner) & Buys Hats, Gloves, Umbrellas, Store Displays, Fixtures and Supplies

CC FILSON CO. (SG)

1555 4th Ave. South
Seattle, WA 98134
206-223-4906 / Fax: 206-624-4539
Website: www.filson.com

- STEVE MATSON (Owner)
- MELANIE SWOBODA-Men's Wear, Rugged Outdoor Clothing, Footwear, Luggage, Wallets, Accessories

EBBET'S FIELD FLANNELS (SP & MO & OL)

P.O. Box 4858 (m-b-des)
562 1st Ave. South
Seattle, WA 98104
206-382-7249 / Fax: 206-382-4411
Sales: $1 Million-$10 Million
Website: www.ebbets.com

- JERRY COHEN (President)
- LISA COOPER (V.P.-Opers.) & Buys Men's Apparel

FEDERAL ARMY & NAVY SURPLUS, INC. (AN & OL)

2112 1st Ave. (m)
Seattle, WA 98121
206-443-1818 / Fax: 206-727-4844
Sales: $1 Million-$10 Million
Website: www.gr8gear.com

- HENRY SCHALOUM (Co-Owner) & Buys Men's Sportswear, Shirts, Underwear, Gloves, Headwear, Belts, Boots, Young Men's & 8 to 20 Boys' Wear, Military Surplus, Store Displays, Fixtures, Supplies
- JACK SCHALOUM (Co-Owner) & Buys Men's Sportswear, Shirts, Underwear, Gloves, Headwear, Belts, Boots, Young Men's & 8 to 20 Boys' Wear, Military Surplus, Store Displays, Fixtures, Supplies

WASHINGTON - Seattle

FIORINI SPORTS (SG)

4720 University Village Pl. (b)
Seattle, WA 98105
206-523-9610 / Fax: 206-523-0058
Sales: $1 Million-$10 Million
Website: www.fiorinisports.com

JEFF FIORINI (President) & Buys Footwear, Store Displays, Fixtures, Supplies
PAT McDONALD (Mgr.) & Buys Footwear, Store Displays, Fixtures, Supplies
JULIE VILL-Men's, Young Men's & Boys' Sweaters, Sport Shirts, Outer Jackets, Headwear, Active Apparel, Skiwear

THE FORUM (MW)

601 Union St. (b)
Seattle, WA 98101
206-233-9695
Sales: $500,000-$1 Million

VOULA XENOS (President) & Buys Men's Overcoats, Suits, Tailored Jackets, Tailored Slacks, Raincoats, Sportswear, Sweaters, Outer Jackets, Leather Apparel, Casual Slacks, Active Apparel, Furnishings, Dress Shirts, Ties, Robes, Underwear, Hosiery, Gloves, Accessories, Belts, Urban Contem
SPIRO XENOS (V.P.) & Buys Men's Overcoats, Suits, Tailored Jackets, Tailored Slacks, Raincoats, Sportswear, Sweaters, Outer Jackets, Leather Apparel, Casual Slacks, Active Apparel, Furnishings, Dress Shirts, Ties, Robes, Underwear, Hosiery, Gloves, Accessories, Belts, Urban Contem

LEROUX'S FINE APPAREL (CLO)

(MICHAEL J. SMITH, INC.)
3220 W. McGraw (b)
Seattle, WA 98199
206-283-0377 / Fax: 206-283-0142
Sales: $500,000-$1 Million

ALEXANDRA SMITH (Co-Owner) & Buys Men's Sportswear, Sweaters, Sport Shirts, Outer Jackets, Casual Slacks, Active Apparel, Footwear, Furnishings, Accessories, Store Displays, Fixtures, Supplies
MICHAEL SMITH (Co-Owner) & Buys Men's Overcoats, Suits, Tailored Jackets, Tailored Slacks, Raincoats, Sportswear, Men's Sweaters, Sport Shirts, Outer Jackets, Casual Slacks, Active Apparel, Footwear, Furnishings, Accessories, Store Displays, Fixtures, Supplies
GREG CARNESE (Mgr.) & Buys Men's Sportswear, Sweaters, Sport Shirts, Outer Jackets, Casual Slacks, Active Apparel, Footwear, Furnishings, Accessories, Store Displays, Fixtures, Supplies

LEROY MENSWEAR (MW)

204 Pike St. (p)
Seattle, WA 98101
206-682-1033
Sales: $500,001-$1 Million

LEROY SHUMATE (Owner) & Buys Men's & Young Men's Overcoats, Suits, Tailored Jackets, Tailored Slacks, Raincoats, Sportswear, Sweaters, Sport Shirts, Outer Jackets, Leather Apparel, Furnishings, Accessories, Casual Slacks, Active Apparel, Dress Shirts, Ties, Hosiery, Gloves, Headwear

MARIO'S OF SEATTLE (CLO-2)

1513 6th Ave. (b-h)
Seattle, WA 98101
206-223-1461 / Fax: 206-625-9285
Website: www.marios.com

MARIO BISIO (Owner) & Buys Men's Wear, Sportswear, Furnishings, Accessories, Footwear
PATRICK ANGUS-Store Displays, Fixtures and Supplies

NORDSTROM, INC. (DEPT-132 & OL & MO)

500 Pine St. (b)
Seattle, WA 98101
206-628-2111 / Fax: 206-373-4354
Sales: Over $1 Billion
Website: www.nordstrom.com
Retail Locations: AK, AZ, CA, CO, CT, FL, GA HI, IL, IN, KS, MD, MI, MM, NY, NJ, NY, OH, OR, PA, RI, TX, UT, VA, WA, NC, MO

BLAKE W. NORDSTROM (President-Nordstrom.com)
LAURIE BLACK (President-Nordstrom Rack Group)
JIM BRAMLEY (President-Nordstrom.com)
PETER E. NORDSTROM (President-Full Line Mdsg. Strategy)
ERIK B. NORDSTROM (Exec. V.P. & Full Line Stores)
MARCI SCOTT (V.P.-Corp. Merchandising Mgr.) (@ 206-373-4555)
CATHY ANDERSON (D.M.M.-NW Men's Division) (@ 206-373-2982)
BILL BRENNER-Men's Clothing
RON McNEIL (@ 206-373-2176)-Men's Suits, Sportscoats
LAUREL IRVING (@ 206-373-2145)-Men's Faconnable
RICK DEARDEUFF (@ 206-373-2177)-Men's Sweaters, Sport Shirts, Outer Jackets, Leather Apparel, Casual Slacks, Corporate Casual, Sportswear
LISA STELL (@ 206-373-2142)-Men's Furnishings, Shirts, Ties, Belts, Misc.
KRIS WANLASS-Young Men's Wear
ERIN VAN MOORHEM (@ 206-373-2259)-Boys' Clothing
LISA CODY (@ 206-373-2175)-The Rail (NW)
ROLAND THIELE (Corp. Display Mgr.)
NANCY WEBBER (Interior Planner) & Buys Store Displays, Fixtures, Supplies
NOTE:-Each store has its own footwear buyer

SUPER JOCK & JILL (SG)

7210 E. Green Lake Dr. (p)
Seattle, WA 98115
206-522-7711 / Fax: 206-524-3952
Website: www.superjocknjill.com

CHET JAMES (Owner) & Buys Running Apparel, Athletic Footwear, Store Displays, Fixtures and Supplies

TOMMY BAHAMA (CLO)

1809 7th Ave., #806
Seattle, WA 98101
206-622-8688
Website: www.tommybahama.com
Retail Locations: AL, AZ, CA, FL, HI, IL, MO, NV, TX

TONY MARGOLIS (President & C.E.O.)
GEORGE SANTACROCE (President- Retail Div.) & Buys Men's Footwear, Shirts, Pants, Accessories

WASHINGTON - Seattle

UNIVERSITY BOOK STORE (SP-9)
4326 University Way NE
Seattle, WA 98105
206-634-3400 / Fax: 206-634-0810
Sales: $50 Million-$100 Million
Website: www.ubookstore.com
BRIAN PEARCE (Gen. Mgr.)
KATE HARPER-Activewear

WINTERS FORMAL WEAR, INC. (SP-6)
310 Broadway East (m-b)
Seattle, WA 98102
206-324-3171 / Fax: 206-726-8377
Website: www.winterstux.com
MR. COHEN (Owner) & Buys Men's & Boys' Formal Wear, Related Footwear, Store Displays, Fixtures, Supplies
SERENA COHEN-Men's & Boys' Formal Wear, Related Footwear, Store Displays, Fixtures, Supplies

YANKEE PEDDLER LTD. (CLO)
4218 E. Madison (b)
Seattle, WA 98112
206-324-4218 / Fax: 206-324-0399
Sales: $100,001-$500,000
LYNNE PARROTT (President) & Buys Men's Sportswear, Furnishings' Store Displays, Fixtures, Supplies

ZEBRACLUB, INC. (CLO)
1901 1st Ave. (m)
Seattle, WA 98101
206-448-7452 / Fax: 206-441-6664
Website: www.zebraclub.com
BAILEE MARTIN (Mgr.) & Buys Men's Sport Coats, Sport Shirts, Outer Jackets, Active Apparel, Furnishings, Accessories, Footwear, Young Men's Wear, Urban Contemporary, Store Displays, Fixtures, Supplies

OLIVER-HAMMER CLOTHES SHOP (MW)
817 Metcalf (m)
Sedro Wooley, WA 98284
360-855-0395 / Fax: 360-855-1466
Sales: $1 Million-$10 Million
DYRK MEYER (Co-Owner & Mgr.) & Buys Men's Raincoats, Sportswear, Sweaters, Sport Shirts, Outer Jackets, Casual Slacks, Active Apparel, Furnishings, Accessories, Belts, Small Leather Goods, Footwear, Work Wear, Sportswear

GENERAL STORE, INC. (DEPT)
N. 2424 Division (bud)
Spokane, WA 99207
509-444-8005 / Fax: 509-328-2120
Sales: $1 Million-$10 Million
BILL BARANY (President) & Buys Store Displays, Fixtures, Supplies
TERRI MITCHELL-Men's & Boys' Utility Clothing, Casual Wear, Footwear, Urban Contemporary

HAMER'S, INC. (MW-4)
N. 1112 Washington St. (b)
Spokane, WA 99201
509-326-1060 / Fax: 509-326-2798
Sales: $1 Million-$10 Million
DAVID T. HAMER (President) & Buys Men's & Young Men's Suits, Sportswear, Leather Goods, Boys' Wear, Footwear

MR. TUX (CLO-7)
(Div. of MOSBY'S, INC.)
13216 E. Sprigus (m-b)
Spokane, WA 99206
509-927-8786 / Fax: 509-893-8844
Website: www.mr-tux.com
JOHN MOSBY (Owner) & Buys Men's & Young Men's Formal Wear, Footwear, Related Furnishings, Accessories, Store Displays, Fixtures, Supplies

WHITE'S BOOTS, INC. (FW & OL & MO)
4002 E. Ferry Ave. (m-b)
Spokane, WA 99202
509-535-2422 / Fax: 509-535-2423
Sales: $10 Million-$50 Million
Website: www.whitesoutdoor.com
SKIP MARCH (President)
TERRY MARCH (Warehouse Buyer) & Buys Boys' Footwear, Men's Footwear, Leather Goods, Watches, Men's Accessories, Men's Apparel, Hosiery

DUFFLE BAG, INC. (DEPT-3 & MO)
P.O. Box 99308 (p)
8207 S. Tacoma Way
Tacoma, WA 98499
253-588-4433 / Fax: 253-581-3642
Sales: $1 Million-$10 Million
Website: www.theduffiebag.com
DIANE SIGEL (C.E.O.) & Buys Men's Active Apparel, Underwear, Hosiery, Gloves, Headwear, Belts, Footwear, Store Displays, Fixtures & Supplies

KRAFF'S DISTINCTIVE CLOTHING FOR MEN (CLO & MO)
P.O. Box 232 (m-b)
111 S. Toppenish Ave.
Toppenish, WA 98948
509-865-3000 / Fax: 509-865-1004
Website: www.kraffspendleton.com
DAN JOHNSON (Owner) & Buys Men's Overcoats, Suits, Tailored Jackets, Tailored Slacks, Raincoats, Sportswear, Sweaters, Sport Shirts, Outer Jackets, Casual Slacks, Leather Apparel, Active Apparel, Furnishings, Dress Shirts, Ties, Robes, Underwear, Hosiery, Gloves, Headwear, Accessories, Belts, Small Leather Goods, Jewelry, Big & Tall Men's Wear, Young Men's Wear, Footwear, Store Displays, Fixtures, Supplies

ATHLETE'S CORNER (SG-4)
1112 NE 78th St. (m)
Vancouver, WA 98665
360-574-1010 / Fax: 360-574-4868
Website: www.athletescorner.com
KIRK JABUSCH (Owner) & Buys Men's Active Apparel, Young Men's Active Apparel, Boys' Active Apparel, Footwear, Store Displays, Fixtures, Supplies
MARGARET JABUSCH-Men's Active Apparel, Young Men's Active Apparel, Boys' Active Apparel, Footwear, Store Displays, Fixtures, Supplies

THE COUNTRY STORE (DEPT & OL)
20211 Vashon Hwy. SW (m)
Vashon, WA 98070
206-463-3655 / Fax: 206-463-3679
Sales: $500,001-$1 Million
Website: www.tcsag.com
VY BIEL (Owner) & Buys Men's Sportswear, Underwear, Gloves, Hosiery, T-shirts, Headwear, Raincoats, Footwear, Boys' Wear, Boys' Footwear, Store Displays, Fixtures, Supplies

NEW YORK STORE WESTERN OUTFITTERS (WW)
2254 E. Isaacs Ave. (bud-p-m-b-h)
Walla Walla, WA 99362
509-529-3600
Sales: $500,001-$1 Million
Website: www.westernoutfitterdeal.com
JOHN SAUL (President) & Buys Men's, Young Men's & Boys' Western Wear, Related Furnishings, Accessories, Big & Tall Men's Wear, Footwear, Store Displays, Fixtures, Supplies

SPORLEDERS (CLO & OL)
(WALLA WALLA CLOTHING)
51 E. Main St. (m-b)
Walla Walla, WA 99362
509-525-4783 / Fax: 509-525-4794
Sales: $1 Million-$10 Million
Website: www.wallawallaclothing.com
KELLY RICHARDS (Co-Owner)
CRAIG RICHARDS (Co-Owner) & Buys Men's Overcoats, Suits, Tailored Jackets, Tailored Slacks, Raincoats, Sweaters, Sport Shirts, Outer Jackets, Leather Apparel, Casual Slacks, Active Apparel, Furnishings, Accessories, Store Displays, Fixtures, Supplies

KIDS COUNT TOO (KS)
2 S. Wenatchee Ave. (m-b)
Wenatchee, WA 98801
509-665-7600 / Fax: 509-665-0481
Sales: $500,001-$1 Million

GROVER COLLINS (Co-Owner) & Buys 8 to 20 Boys' Wear, Furnishings, Accessories, Footwear, Store Displays, Fixtures, Supplies

MARCY COLLINS (Co-Owner) & Buys 8 to 20 Boys' Wear, Furnishings, Accessories, Footwear, Store Displays, Fixtures, Supplies

MILLS BROTHERS, INC. (MW)
10 S. Wenatchee Ave. (m-b)
Wenatchee, WA 98801
509-662-2650 / Fax: 509-664-1839
Sales: $500,000-$1 Million

SAM M. MILLS (Owner) & Buys Men's Sportswear, Formalwear, Furnishings, Headwear, Accessories, Fragrances, Big & Tall Men's Wear, Store Displays, Fixtures, Supplies

RON FELTY (Footwear Mgr.) & Buys Footwear, Formalwear

STAN'S MERRY MART, INC. (CLO)
733 S. Wenatchee Ave. (bud-p)
Wenatchee, WA 98801
509-662-5858 / Fax: 509-663-4830
Sales: $1 Million-$10 Million

ETHEL WRIGHT-Men's Tailored Slacks, Sportswear, Sweaters, Sport Shirts, Outer Jackets, Casual Slacks, Active Apparel, Furnishings, Accessories, Footwear, Big & Tall Men's Wear, Young Men's Wear, Boys' Wear, Store Displays

HILDABOB'S (CLO)
P.O. Box 699 (m)
231 Riverside Ave.
Winthrop, WA 98862
509-996-3279

ROBERT MAUGHAN (Partner) & Buys Men's Sportswear, Sweaters, Sport Shirts, Active Apparel, Dress Shirts, Headwear, Jewelry, Store Displays, Fixtures, Supplies

HILDA ROSENBERG (Partner) & Buys Men's Sportswear, Sweaters, Sport Shirts, Active Apparel, Dress Shirts, Headwear, Jewelry, Store Displays, Fixtures, Supplies

GENIE, INC. (CLO)
667 Central Ave. (m)
Barboursville, WV 25504
304-733-2799 / Fax: 304-733-4250
JEAN SPURLOCK (Co-Owner)
DARRELL SPURLOCK (Co-Owner)
DEBBIE BLACK (Mgr.) & Buys Men's & Boys' Wear, T-shirts, Fleece, Sweat Pants, Jackets, Hosiery, Store Displays, Fixtures, Supplies

HERNDON WESTERN WEAR CO. (WW)
(J & S WESTERN WEAR, INC.)
6006 Rt. 60 East (b)
Barboursville, WV 25504
304-736-9191
Sales: $100,001-$500,000
SANDY VOWELL (Owner) & Buys Men's Western Wear, Sweaters, Western Shirts, Outer Jackets, Leather Apparel, Casual Slacks, Furnishings, Accessories, Footwear, Young Men's Wear, Boys' Wear, Store Displays, Fixtures, Supplies

HARRY'S MEN'S SHOP, INC. (MW)
311 Neville (m)
Beckley, WV 25802
304-253-3400
MAX LEWIN (Owner) & Buys Men's Overcoats, Suits, Tailored Jackets, Tailored Slacks, Outer Jackets, Dress Shirts, Ties, Robes, Underwear, Gloves, Belts, Small Leather Goods, Jewelry, Store Displays, Fixtures, Supplies

STRADERS, INC. (DEPT)
37 W. Main St. (m-b-h)
Buckhannon, WV 26201
304-472-2320
WILLIAM OURS (President) & Buys Men's Overcoats, Suits, Tailored Jackets, Tailored Slacks, Raincoats, Sportswear, Sweaters, Sport Shirts, Outer Jackets, Leather Apparel, Furnishings, Dress Shirts, Ties, Robes, Underwear, Hosiery, Gloves, Headwear, Accessories, Young Men's & Boys' 8 to 20 Wear, Big & Tall Men's Wear, Footwear, Store Supplies, Fixtures
WANDA ZINKBFOOS-Store Displays

BUFFALO SHOPPING CENTER (DEPT)
P.O. Box 10 (p)
Buffalo, WV 25033
304-937-2621 / Fax: 304-937-2688
FAYE WALTER-Men's & Boys' Work Clothes, T-shirts, Underwear, Fleece, Hosiery, Footwear, Store Displays, Fixtures, Supplies

CALVIN'S, INC. (MW)
(ESTEP'S-THE NU LOOK)
700 Lee St. East (h)
Charleston, WV 25301
304-346-8008
TOM ESTEP (President) & Buys Men's Suits, Tailored Jackets, Sportswear, Furnishings, Accessories, Boys' Suits, Dress Shoes, Urban Contemporary, Store Displays, Fixtures, Supplies

CHARLESTON DEPARTMENT STORE, INC. (DEPT-2 & OL)
1661 W. Washington St. (b)
Charleston, WV 25312
304-346-6793 / Fax: 304-346-6797
Sales: $1 Million-$10 Million
Website: www.charlestondeptstore.com
BARRY OGRIN (President)
TOM KING-Men's Wear, Sportswear, Shirts, Pants, Footwear, Accessories
TASHA ELLIS-Boys' Wear, Sportswear, Shirts, Pants, Footwear, Accessories

KELLEY'S MEN'S SHOP, INC. (MW & OL & MO)
108 W. Washington St. (m-b)
Charleston, WV 25302
304-343-9415 / Fax: 304-345-7107
Sales: $1 Million-$10 Million
Website: www.kelleys.com
KEN WALDECK (Owner) & Buys Active Apparel
TOM CUTLIP (D.M.M.) & Buys Outer Jackets, Leather Apparel, Casual Slacks, Belts, Jewelry, Small Leather Goods, Fragrances, Overcoats, Suits
ARGYLE McMILLION (D.M.M.) & Buys Men's Sweaters, Sport Shirts, Dress Shirts, Ties
ED DOAK-Men's Tailored Slacks
GARY GIBBONS-Men's Footwear
TRISH FENNEKEN-Robes, Gloves, Underwear, Hosiery
ED DOAK (Display Mgr.) & Buys Store Displays, Fixtures, Supplies

LA GRANGE LEATHERS, INC. (CLO)
1037 Charleston Town Ctr. (p-m-b)
Charleston, WV 25389
304-345-6906 / Fax: 304-345-6906
Website: www.alexrossboots.com
MR. LANNIE BRYANT (Owner) & Buys Men's Leather Outerwear, Boys' Leather Outerwear, Footwear, Store Displays, Fixtures, Supplies

SAYER BROTHERS, INC. (CLO-3)
P.O. Box 1829 (m)
Charleston, WV 25327
304-925-4900 / Fax: 304-925-2828
Sales: $500,000-$1 Million
FARRIS SAYER (President) & Buys Men's & Boys' Footwear, Men's Sportswear, Furnishings, Headwear, Accessories, 8 to 20 Boys' Wear, Store Displays, Fixtures, Supplies
DAVID SAYER (V.P.) & Buys Men's & Boys' Footwear, Men's Sportswear, Furnishings, Headwear, Accessories, 8 to 20 Boys' Wear, Store Displays, Fixtures, Supplies
CHRIS HUSSON (G.M.M.) & Buys Men's & Boys' Footwear, Men's Sportswear, Furnishings, Headwear, Accessories, 8 to 20 Boys' Wear, Store Displays, Fixtures, Supplies

YOUNG'S DEPARTMENT STORE, INC. (DEPT)
1613 W. Washington St. (p-m-b)
Charleston, WV 25312
304-343-1011 / Fax: 304-343-1011
HELEN OATRIDGE (Owner) & Buys Store Displays, Fixtures, Supplies, Footwear
JAMES L. OATRIDGE (V.P.) & Buys Footwear, Men's, Young Men's & Boys' Sportswear, Urban Contemporary, Underwear, Hosiery, Belts, Small Leather Goods, Big & Tall Men's Wear

MARIO'S MENSWEAR (MW)
P.O. Box 663 (b)
Fairmont, WV 26554
304-366-1740 / Fax: 304-367-1575
Sales: $100,001-$500,000
MARIO LIBONATI (Owner) & Buys Men's Overcoats, Suits, Tailored Jackets, Tailored Slacks, Sportswear, Sweaters, Sport Shirts, Outer Jackets, Casual Slacks, Accessories, Dress Shirts, Ties, Hosiery, Footwear, Store Displays, Fixtures, Supplies

WEISBERGER'S CLOTHING (CLO)
709 Main St. (p)
Follansbee, WV 26037
304-527-0414
Sales: $500,000-$1 Million
ARNOLD PLITTMAN (President) & Buys Men's Sportswear, Leather Apparel, Furnishings, Headwear, Accessories, Young Men's Wear, Footwear, Store Displays, Fixtures, Supplies

KEN-LU CLOTHING, INC. (CLO)
P.O. Box 386 (m)
Gilbert, WV 25621
304-664-3213 / Fax: 304-664-2031
GLEMA MEADE (Owner) & Buys Men's Overcoats, Suits, Tailored Jackets, Tailored Slacks, Sportswear, Sweaters, Sport Shirts, Outer Jackets, Casual Slacks, Leather Apparel, Active Apparel, Dress Shirts, Ties, Robes, Underwear, Hosiery, Gloves, Belts, Small Leather Goods, Fragrances, Footwear, Big & Tall Men's Wear, Young Men's Wear, Store Displays, Fixtures, Supplies

GLENN'S SPORTING GOODS (SG)

1051 4th Ave. (m)
Huntington, WV 25701
304-523-7766 / Fax: 304-523-7907

JIM BRUMFIELD (Owner) & Buys Men's Outer Jackets, Hats, Footwear, Sportswear, Sport Shirts, Headwear

WORKINGMAN'S FAMILY STORE (MW-2)

140 5th Ave. (p-m)
Huntington, WV 25701
304-522-3404 / Fax: 304-522-3415

JERRY FURBEE (Owner) & Buys Big & Tall Men's Wear, Men's Tailored Slacks, Sweaters, Sport Shirts, Outer Jackets, Casual Slacks, Active Apparel, Dress Shirts, Ties, Robes, Underwear, Hosiery, Headwear, Belts, Small Leather Goods, Work Clothing, Jeans, Footwear, Store Displays, Fixtures, Supplies

WRIGHT'S (MW)

P.O. Box 388 (b)
4th Ave. & 10th St.
Huntington, WV 25708
304-525-7834 / Fax: 304-525-7848
Sales: $1 Million-$10 Million

CHARLES A. JAMBE (Owner) & Buys Men's Overcoats, Suits, Tailored Jackets, Tailored Slacks, Raincoats, Sweaters, Sport Shirts, Outer Jackets, Casual Slacks, Leather Apparel, Active Apparel, Dress Shirts, Ties, Robes, Underwear, Hosiery, Gloves, Headwear, Belts, Footwear, Store Displays, Fixtures, Supplies

SHAPIRO'S STORE, INC. (CLO)

P.O. Box 400 (m-b)
6167 Armstrong St.
Keyser, WV 26726
304-788-6112 / Fax: 304-788-1656

STEVEN SHAPIRO (Owner) & Buys Men's Formal Wear, Related Footwear, Young Men's Formal Wear

McCORMICK'S, INC. (DEPT)

P.O. Box 627 (p-m-b)
112 Jefferson Ave.
Logan, WV 25601
304-752-4190 / Fax: 304-752-2190
Sales: $1 Million-$10 Million

DAVID McCORMICK (President) & Buys Store Displays, Fixtures, Supplies

JOHN HOWERTON (Asst. Mgr.) & Buys Men's Wear, Big & Tall Men's Wear, Footwear, Young Men's Wear, All Leather Apparel

ELLIS DEPARTMENT STORES, INC. (DEPT)

P.O. Box 98 (m-b)
336 Main St.
Madison, WV 25130
304-369-2211 / Fax: 304-369-7005

CHARLES ELLIS, JR. (President) & Buys Men's, Young Men's & Boys' Wear, Footwear, Accessories, Store Displays, Fixtures, Supplies

MAN CLOTHING & JEWELRY CO. (DEPT-2)

209 Main St. (p-m-b)
Man, WV 25635
304-583-7051 / Fax: 304-583-7667
Sales: $1 Million-$10 Million

JEAN S. COOK (President)

MARY GRAHAM (V.P.) & Buys Men's Sportswear, Furnishings, Headwear, Accessories, Footwear, Boys' Wear, Store Displays, Fixtures, Supplies

MEN'S SHOP (MW)

US 219 North (p-m)
Marlinton, WV 24954
304-799-6423

CHRIS BURNS (Co-Owner) & Buys Men's Work Clothes, Jeans, Tops, Underwear, Hosiery

JOANNA BURNS (Co-Owner) & Buys Men's Work Clothes, Jeans, Tops, Underwear, Hosiery

KIPLING SHOE CO., INC. (FW-4)

P.O. Box 187 (m)
1221 Main St.
Milton, WV 25541
304-743-5721 / Fax: 304-743-1226
Sales: $1 Million-$10 Million

CARROLL OSBURN (President & G.M.)

BECKY SMITH (Mgr.) & Buys Boys' Apparel, Boys' Footwear, Men's Footwear, Leather Goods

ARMY STORE (AN)

137 Pleasant St. (m)
Morgantown, WV 26505
304-296-4316 / Fax: 304-292-2295
Website: www.adventuresedge.org

JAN KIGER (Owner) & Buys Men's Work Clothes, Jeans, Tops, Hosiery

DANIEL'S MEN'S STORE, INC. (MW)

P.O. Box 1140 (b)
419 High St.
Morgantown, WV 26505
304-296-7202 / Fax: 304-296-1252
Sales: $1 Million-$10 Million

SAUL RADMAN (Owner) & Buys Men's Sportswear, Furnishings, Accessories, Big & Tall Men's Wear

RICHARD WHITELOCK (G.M.M.) & Buys Men's Overcoats, Suits, Tailored Jackets, Tailored Slacks, Raincoats, Footwear

GABRIEL BROTHERS, INC. (CLO-27)

55 Scott Ave. (p-m-b)
Morgantown, WV 26508
304-292-6965 / Fax: 304-292-3191
Website: www.gabrielbrothers.com
Retail Locations: MD, OH, PA, VA, WV

JOHN GABRIEL (V.P.)

JIM BARGER (Real Estate Contact)

DIANE HUTCHINSON-Boy's Wear, Accessories, Furnishings

BRET JOSEPHS-Men's & Boys' Footwear

RON GABRIEL-Men's Wear

ANDY VERDAR-Store Displays, Fixtures, Supplies

REINER & CORE (CLO)

374 High St. (m-b)
Morgantown, WV 26505
304-296-4383 / Fax: 304-292-0351

RANDY WILDMAN (President) & Buys Men's Overcoats, Suits, Tailored Jackets, Tailored Slacks, Raincoats, Sportswear, Sweaters, Sport Shirts, Outer Jackets, Casual Slacks, Active Apparel, Leather Jackets, Furnishings, Accessories, Dress Shirts, Ties, Robes, Underwear, Hosiery, Gloves, Headwear, Belts, Small Leather Goods, Jewelry, Fragrances, Footwear, Store Displays, Fixtures, Supplies

BLAKE'S KIDDIE KORRAL & ATTIC (KS)

305 Jefferson Ave. (m-b)
Moundsville, WV 26041
304-845-1411
Sales: $100,001-$500,000

HILDA BLAKE (Owner) & Buys Boys' Clothing, Sportswear, Accessories, Belts, Footwear, Store Displays, Fixtures, Supplies

RUTTENBERG'S CLOTHING (CLO-2)

238 Jefferson Ave. (p)
Moundsville, WV 26041
304-845-1940
Sales: $500,000-$1 Million

ILENE RUTTENBERG (Owner) & Buys Men's Sportswear, Sweaters, Sport Shirts, Outer Jackets, Casual Slacks, Active Apparel, Furnishings, Footwear, Young Men's & Boys' Wear, Belts, Small Leather Goods, Hats, T-shirts, Store Displays, Fixtures, Supplies

MASON'S (MW)

P.O. Box 129 (m-b)
244 North St.
New Martinsville, WV 26155
304-455-5357
Sales: $100,001-$500,000

DONALD E. MASON (Owner) & Buys Men's Work Wear & Tuxedos

WEST VIRGINIA - Parkersburg

HORNOR & HARRISON (MW & OL)

2709 Murdoch Ave. (m-b)
Parkersburg, WV 26101
304-422-8459 / Fax: 304-422-8271
Sales: $1 Million-$10 Million

DEAN R. BOONE (President) & Buys Men's Formalwear, Overcoats, Suits, Tailored Jackets, Tailored Slacks, Raincoats, Footwear

DAVID BOONE (V.P.) & Buys Men's Sportswear, Sweaters, Sport Shirts, Outer Jackets, Casual Slacks, Active Apparel, Furnishings, Headwear, Accessories, Big & Tall Men's Wear, Store Displays, Fixtures, Supplies

WHY NOT SHOP (CLO)

P.O. Box 400
Slatyfork, WV 26291
304-572-1200

BERYL MINGHING (Owner) & Buys Swimwear, Sunglasses, Footwear, Hats, Skate Apparel, T-shirts, Imprinted Sportswear

WORKINGMAN'S STORE (MW-2)

1201 Grand Central (p-m)
Vienn, WV 26105
304-295-2340 / Fax: 304-295-2345
Website: www.workingmans.com

DAVID SCHRAMM (Owner) & Buys Men's Work Clothes, Jeans, Tops, Underwear, Hosiery, Footwear, Safety Shoes

J.C. TEC & CO., INC. (WW)

(THE SILVER SPUR)
12 Commerce Dr. (m)
Westover, WV 26505
304-296-7575 / Fax: 304-296-9105

GARY DICKSON (President) & Buys Men's Western Wear, Boots, Boys' Western Sport Shirts, Dress Shirts, Boots, Store Displays, Fixtures, Supplies

SPORT YOUR COLORS (SP)

1615 Warwood Ave.
Wheeling, WV 26003
304-277-2777
Sales: $100,001-$500,000

DEBRA DUFFY (Co-Owner)

LARRY DUFFY (Co-Owner) & Buys Activewear, Athletics, Golf Apparel

GREENBRIER (MW)

(CHECKS)
(SAM & SEAN'S COLLECTION)
(GOLF SHOP)
(THE GREENBRIER SHOP)
(POLO RALPH LAUREN)
300 W. Main St.
White Sulphur Springs, WV 24986
304-536-7806 / Fax: 304-536-7893
Website: www.greenbrier.com

STEPHEN BALDWIN (Dir. - Retail Opers.) & Buys Men's Wear, Sportswear, Formalwear, Accessories

ALBERT'S ARMY STORE (AN)

133 3rd Ave. (p)
Williamson, WV 25661
304-235-3190

IVAN ALBERT (Mgr.) & Buys Men's & Boys' Work Clothes, Men's Work Shoes, Store Displays, Fixtures, Supplies

JP TOGS (CLO)
106 N. 1st St. (m)
Abbotsford, WI 54405
715-223-4112 / Fax: 715-223-4112
Sales: $100,001-$500,000
JOEL HOPPERDIETZEL (Owner) & Buys Men's Sportswear, Jeans, T-shirts, Furnishings, Headwear, Accessories, Young Men's Wear, Boys' Sportswear, Furnishings, Accessories, Footwear, Store Displays, Fixtures, Supplies

B BAR 10 WESTERN STORE (WW & OL)
9685 Hwy. B
Amherst, WI 54406
715-824-3750 / Fax: 715-824-2331
Website: www.bbar10.com
MELISSA B. SHIELDS (Co-Owner) & Buys Men's Western Sweaters, Active Apparel, Jewelry, Fragrances, Men's Overcoats, Suits, Tailored Jackets, Tailored Slacks, Raincoats, Sport Shirts, Outer Jackets, Leather Apparel, Boots, Hats, Dress Shirts, Belts, Big & Tall Men's Western Wear, Boys' Western Wear, Store Displays, Fixtures, Supplies
LAINE SHIELDS (Co-Owner) & Buys Men's Western Sweaters, Active Apparel, Jewelry, Fragrances, Men's Overcoats, Suits, Tailored Jackets, Tailored Slacks, Raincoats, Sport Shirts, Outer Jackets, Leather Apparel, Boots, Hats, Dress Shirts, Belts, Big & Tall Men's Western Wear, Boys' Western Wear, Store Displays, Fixtures, Supplies

GUYS SHOP (MW)
820 5th Ave. (m)
Antigo, WI 54409
715-623-2666
Sales: $100,001-$500,000
CHARLES EBERT (Owner) & Buys Men's Overcoats, Suits, Tailored Jackets, Tailored Slacks, Leather Jackets, Raincoats, Sweaters, Sport Shirts, Outer Jackets, Casual Slacks, Active Apparel, Furnishings, Headwear, Accessories, Young Men's Wear, Big & Tall Men's Wear, Store Displays, Fixtures, Supplies

MARK PASCH LTD. (MW)
333 W. Brown Deer Rd. (h)
Bayside, WI 53217
414-351-5634 / Fax: 414-351-5634
Sales: $1 Million-$10 Million
Website: www.markpaschltd.com
MARK PASCH (Owner) & Buys Men's Furnishings, Dress Shirts, Underwear, Hosiery, Accessories, Footwear, Store Displays, Fixtures, Supplies
MARIO CRIVELLO (Mgr.) & Buys Men's Sportswear, Furnishings, Accessories

ESKIMO COMFORT (CLO)
199 Broadway (m)
Berlin, WI 54923
920-361-2424
Sales: $100,001-$500,000
ED YANKOWSKI (Co-Owner) & Buys Store Displays, Fixtures, Supplies
SUE YANKOWSKI (Co-Owner) & Buys Store Displays, Fixtures, Supplies
TOM YANKOWSKI-Men's Coats, Jackets, Outer Jackets, Gloves, Headwear, Snowmobile Suits, Hunting Clothes, Moccasins, Big & Tall Men's Wear, Outer Jackets, Hunting Clothes, Snowmobile Suits

B & G GOLF, BOWLING & RACQUET SPORTS (SG-5)
12730 W. Burleigh Rd. (m-b)
Brookfield, WI 53005
262-781-6506 / Fax: 262-781-5385
Sales: $1 Million-$10 Million
Website: www.bggolf.com
MICHAEL STORTS (President & Owner)
SCOTTY GUNDERSON-Men's Golf Apparel Shoes

RIDERS IN STORM (MW)
13875 W. North Ave. (m)
Brooksfield, WI 53005
262-789-9893
CARY KLINGKAMMER (Owner) & Buys Men's T-shirts, Jeans, Shorts, Store Displays, Fixtures, Supplies
JASON KLINGKAMMER-Men's T-shirts, Jeans, Shorts, Store Displays, Fixtures, Supplies

SCHMIDT'S CLOTHING, INC. (CLO)
503 N. Madison Ave. (m)
Chilton, WI 53014
920-849-4716 / Fax: 920-849-4716
Sales: $100,001-$500,000
RITA HOLST (President) & Buys Men's Sweaters, Sport Shirts, Outer Jackets, Casual Slacks, Active Apparel, Big & Tall Wear, Furnishings, Headwear, Belts, Jewlery, Small Leather Goods, Store Displays, Fixtures, Supplies

RADA'S MENSWEAR (MW)
322 N. Bridge St. (m)
Chippewa Falls, WI 54729
715-723-6466 / Fax: 715-723-6466
RICHARD RADA (Owner) & Buys Men's Overcoats, Suits, Tailored Jackets, Tailored Slacks, Raincoats, Sweaters, Sport Shirts, Outer Jackets, Leather Apparel, Casual Slacks, Active Apparel, Furnishings, Headwear, Accessories, Young Men's Wear, Big & Tall Men's Wear, Store Displays, Fixtures, Supplies

R. STOLTENBERG & SON (DEPT)
1060 Hickory St. (bud-p-m)
Cleveland, WI 53015
920-693-8741
EARL STOLTENBERG (President) & Buys Men's Sportswear, Furnishings, Accessories, Store Displays, Fixtures, Supplies

DRETZKA'S DEPARTMENT STORE CO., INC. (DEPT)
4746 S. Packard Ave. (bud-p-m-b)
Cudahy, WI 53110
414-744-8832
Sales: $100,001-$500,000
Website: www.snuggies.com
JOHN DRETZKA (President & G.M.M.)
MARY A. TAMSEN-Men's Footwear, Boys' Apparel, Accessories

CAS (MW)
1355 2nd Ave. (b)
Cumberland, WI 54829
715-822-2421
CASIMIR (Owner) & Buys Men's Sportswear, Furnishings, Headwear, Accessories, Store Displays, Fixtures, Supplies

BRADLEY'S DEPARTMENT STORE (DEPT)
(WW BRADLEY & CO., INC.)
222 E. Walworth Ave. (p)
Delavan, WI 53115
262-728-3421 / Fax: 262-728-1459
Sales: $100,001-$500,000
WILLIAM M. McKOY (President & G.M.M.) & Buys Men's Sweaters, Sport Shirts, Outer Jackets, Casual Slacks, Active Apparel, Furnishings, Headwear, Accessories, Young Men's Wear, 7-12 Boys' Wear, Store Displays, Fixtures, Supplies

ZEGERS' CLOTHIERS, INC. (MW)
124 N. Broadway (m-b)
DePere, WI 54115
920-339-0053 / Fax: 920-339-0081
DON ZEGERS (Owner) & Buys Clothing, Sportswear, Furnishings, Headwear, Accessories, Store Displays, Fixtures, Supplies

KOZELKA'S MENSWEAR (CLO-2)
133 N. Iowa St. (p-m)
Dodgeville, WI 53533
608-935-3507 / Fax: 608-935-3335
BILL WALL (Owner) & Buys Men's Sportswear, Furnishings, Accessories, Men's & Boys' Activewear

WISCONSIN - Dodgeville

LANDS' END, INC. (MO & CLO-17 & OL)
(LAND'S END KIDS)
(COMING HOME)
(BEYOND BUTTONDOWNS)
(Div. Of SEARS)
5 Lands' End Ln. (p-m)
Dodgeville, WI 53595
608-935-9341 / Fax: 608-935-4291
Sales: Over $1.3 Billion
Website: www.landsend.com

MINDY MEADS (President & C.E.O.)
JEFF A. JONES (Exec. V.P. & C.O.O.)

ERIC KAYSER (V.P. & G.M.M.-Men's)
JOE HUDSON-Men's Dress Slacks, Sport Coats, Woven Bottoms, Swimwear, Tailored Clothing, Men's Dress Shirts, Men's Ties
CHRISTOPHER FUNK-Men's Woven Shirts, Dress Shirts, 8 to 16 Boys' Clothing, Sportswear, Furnishings, Accessories
DENISE KSIEZ-Footwear, Neckwear
REGINA BAKKA-Men's Hosiery, Underwear, Belts, Accessories, Dress Shirts
PATTIE A. SIMIGRAN (V.P. & G.M.M.-Co-Ed & Kids' Division)
GEOFF WERNER (V.P.) & Buys Co-Ed Outerwear
OPEN-Co-Ed Knit Shirts
CAROLE SPELIC-Boys' Outerwear

CALLAN'S SKOGMO STORE (DEPT)
113 W. Main St. (p)
Durand, WI 54736
715-672-8750 / Fax: 715-672-8756
Sales: $100,001-$500,000

HELEN H. CALLAN (President)
DAN CALLAN (G.M.M.) & Buys Men's & Boys' Wear, Footwear, Store Displays, Fixtures, Supplies

TOWN & COUNTRY SHOP (CLO)
301 E. Wall St. (b)
Eagle River, WI 54521
715-479-4060

ROSE LULICH (Owner) & Buys Sportswear, Store Displays, Fixtures, Supplies

GALLERY (WW)
2619 E. Clairemont Ave. (m-b-h)
Eau Claire, WI 54701
715-835-6451 / Fax: 715-835-7766

TOM STREETS (Owner) & Buys Men's Formal Wear, Store Displays, Fixtures, Supplies

MULDOON'S, INC. (MW)
1506 S. Hastings (m)
Eau Claire, WI 54701
715-832-3502 / Fax: 715-832-6798
Website: www.muldoons.com

JOHN MULDOON (Owner) & Buys Men's Sportswear, Furnishings, Headwear, Accessories, Store Displays, Fixtures, Supplies

J. ROBERT'S MENSWEAR (MW-2)
17 S. Wisconsin St. (m)
Elkhorn, WI 53121
262-723-2610 / Fax: 262-723-1820
Sales: $100,001-$500,000
Website: www.jrobertsmenswear.com

MARILYN SCHOBERG (Co-Owner)
JAMES SCHOBERG (Co-Owner) & Buys Men's Sportswear, Furnishings, Headwear, Footwear, Accessories, Store Displays, Fixtures, Supplies

ON DECK SPORTSWEAR (MW-5)
P.O. Box 280 (m-b)
Fish Creek, WI 54212
920-868-9091 / Fax: 920-868-2660
Sales: $1 Million-$10 Million
Website: www.ondeckclothing.com

MITCH LARSON (Owner) & Buys Men's Sportswear, Furnishings, Headwear, Accessories, Store Displays, Fixtures, Supplies

BRAUER'S (CLO)
116 S. Main St. (b)
Fond Du Lac, WI 54935
920-921-1234
Sales: $100,001-$500,000

MICHAEL EGLI (President) & Buys Men's Sportswear, Furnishings, Headwear, Accessories, Footwear, Store Displays, Fixtures, Supplies

WATER FRONT SHOP (CLO-1)
(ABBEY MANAGEMENT. CORP.)
The Abbey Resort (bud-p-m-b)
Fontana, WI 53125
262-275-6811 / Fax: 262-275-3264
Sales: $1 Million-$10 Million
Website: www.theabbeyresort.com

JENNIFER DOANE (G.M.M.) & Buys Men's Sportswear, Hosiery, Accessories, Big & Tall Men's Wear, Sweatshirts, T-shirts, Store Displays, Fixtures, Supplies

STUART'S CLOTHING STORES, INC. (MW-2)
100 N. Main St.
Fort Atkinsan, WI 53538
920-568-1181

JOHN STUART (Owner) & Buys Men's Sportswear, Furnishings, Headwear, Accessories, Store Displays, Fixtures, Supplies

C.A. GROSS CO., INC. (MW)
P.O. Box 991 (b)
130 N. Adams St.
Green Bay, WI 54305
920-435-8336 / Fax: 920-436-3822
Sales: $500,000-$1 Million

JAMES BOPRAY (President) & Buys Men's Furnishings, Accessories, Store Displays, Fixtures, Supplies
ROBERT STEIN (Secy.)
MICHAEL HAGERTY (Treasurer) & Buys Men's Sportswear, Footwear
TOM BROSTEAU (G.M.M.) & Buys Men's Clothing

CONARD LTD. (MW)
(J & S CONARD LTD.)
844 Willard Dr. (m)
Green Bay, WI 54304
920-494-5700 / Fax: 920-494-3124
Sales: $500,000-$1 Million

JOHN D. CONARD (President)
MIKE CONARD-Men's Overcoats, Suits, Tailored Jackets, Tailored Slacks, Raincoats, Sweaters, Sport Shirts, Outer Jackets, Casual Slacks, Active Apparel, Furnishings, Headwear, Accessories, Big & Tall Men's Wear, Young Men's Wear, Store Displays, Fixtures, Supplies

DENIS SPORT SHOP, INC. (SG-2)
940 Hansen Rd. (m-b)
Green Bay, WI 54301
920-429-9220 / Fax: 920-429-9279

JOHN DENIS (Owner) & Buys Men's & Boys' Activewear, Outerwear, Athletic Uniforms, Headwear, Gloves

DU BOIS FORMAL WEAR (MW-5)
127 S. Broadway
Green Bay, WI 54303
920-432-1754 / Fax: 920-432-1754
Website: www.duboisformalwear.com

AMY BIEBEL (Co-Owner)
JIM DuBOIS (Co-Owner) & Buys Men's Tuxedos, Dress Shirts, Ties, Belts, Jewelry, Footwear, Accessoriews, Furnishings, Store Displays, Fixtures, Supplies

JASON LOUIS MEN'S CLOTHING (MW)
933 Anderson Dr.
Green Bay, WI 54304
920-499-9555 / Fax: 920-499-9569
Website: www.jasonlouis.com

LOUIS FAUST (Co-Owner)
TODD MEYER (Co-Owner) & Buys Men's Accessories, Furnishings, Footwear

WISCONSIN - Green Bay

REGGIE WHITE'S ALL PRO (SG)
1931 Holmgren Way
Green Bay, WI 54304
920-497-6210 / Fax: 920-497-5962
Website: www.reggiesproshop.com
SHERRIE TANNER (Owner) & Buys Hats, T-shirts, Sportswear, Licensed Apparel

SCANLAN JEWELERS, INC. (JWLY-3)
2350 E. Mason St., #31
Green Bay, WI 54302
920-465-9829 / Fax: 920-465-3890
Sales: $1 Million-$10 Million
DAVID SCANLAN (President)
JUDY SCANLAN (Treas. & Secy.) & Buys Jewelry, Watches

MICHAEL'S FOOTWEAR (FW)
5427 S. 108th St.
Hales Corners, WI 53130
414-425-3260
MICHAEL A. SAJDAK (Owner) & Buys Men's Footwear, Work Boots
AL SAJDAK (G.M.) & Buys Men's Footwear, Work Boots

SHERPER'S, INC. (MW-2)
10730 W. Janesville Rd. (bud-p-m-b-h)
Hales Corners, WI 53130
414-425-6888 / Fax: 414-425-1210
GARY SHERPER (President) & Buys Men's Sportswear, Leather Apparel, Furnishings, Young Men's Wear, Big & Tall Men's Wear
KEN ZIRKELBACH (V.P.) & Buys Men's Sportswear, Leather Apparel, Furnishings, Young Men's Wear, Big & Tall Men's Wear, Men's Footwear, Store Displays, Fixtures and Supplies

PERSONALIZED PRODUCTS (SP)
30 E. Sumner St.
Hartford, WI 53027
262-673-6300 / Fax: 262-673-6707
CURTIS GUNST (Owner) & Buys Imprintable Activewear

BOTTOM HALF CLOTHING (CLO-2)
1810 Crooks Ave. (m)
Kaukauna, WI 54130
920-766-4832 / Fax: 920-759-2646
Sales: $1 Million-$10 Million
DON GRISSMAN (Owner) & Buys Men's Sportswear, Furnishings, Accessories

GINO'S MENSWEAR, INC. (MW)
7507 41st Ave. (m-b)
Kenosha, WI 53142
262-694-2588 / Fax: 262-694-1760
Sales: $500,000-$1 Million
GINO DeBARTOLO (Owner) & Buys Men's Sportswear, Leather Apparel, Furnishings, Accessories
TONY DeBARTOLO-Men's Sportswear, Leather Apparel, Furnishings, Accessories, Store Displays, Fixtures and Supplies

S.J. CRYSTAL'S MEN'S SHOP (MW)
6916 Green Bay Rd. (m-b)
Kenosha, WI 53142
262-694-7356 / Fax: 262-694-4041
Website: www.sjcrystals.com
LEWIS ACETO (Owner) & Buys Men's Sportswear, Furnishings, Accessories

SUPER SPORTS (SP)
3206 80th St.
Kenosha, WI 53142
262-694-9206 / Fax: 262-694-9227
Sales: $500,001-$1 Million
BRIAN PORTILIA (Owner) & Buys Activewear, Athletic Apparel, Licensed Apparel, Athletic Footwear

ART IMIG'S CLOTHIERS (MW)
795 Woodlake Rd., #D (b)
Kohler, WI 53044
920-459-4190 / Fax: 920-459-4192
Sales: $500,000-$1 Million
ARTHUR R. IMIG (President) & Buys Men's Sportswear, Leather Apparel, Accessories, Store Displays, Fixtures, Supplies
ROBERT J. IMIG (G.M.M.) & Buys Men's Sportswear, Leather Apparel, Accessories, Store Displays, Fixtures, Supplies

DESMOND'S FORMAL WEAR (MW)
P.O. Box 1447 (m)
400 Main St.
La Crosse, WI 54601
608-781-7770 / Fax: 608-784-6856
Website: www.desmonds.com
JOHN DESMOND (Owner)
TIM DESMOND (Mgr.) & Buys Suits, Ties, Dress Shirts, Suspenders, Jackets, Tuxedos, Shoes

P & R AWARDS (SP)
2300 State Rd.
La Crosse, WI 54601
608-782-8140 / Fax: 608-782-8148
PHIL SCHWEKE (Co-Owner) & Buys Activewear
RUTH SCHWEKE (Co-Owner) & Buys Activewear

SALEM MARKOS & SONS, INC. (CLO-1)
313 Pearl St. (p-m)
LaCrosse, WI 54601
608-782-6210
Sales: $100,001-$500,000
SALEM MARKOS, II (V.P.) & Buys Men's Tailored Slacks, Jeans, Hosiery, Gloves, Headwear, Work Wear, Big & Tall Wear, Sweaters, Sport Shirts, Outer Jackets, Sportswear, Leather Apparel, Ties, Underwear, Belts, Jewelry, Small Leather Goods, Store Displays, Fixtures, Supplies

SUNSEEKERS TANNING & SWIMWEAR (SP)
116 5th Ave. South
Lacrosse, WI 54605
608-782-4646 / Fax: 608-784-5809
THERESA WEIBEL (Co-Owner) & Buys Boys' Swimwear, Swimwear, Men's Swimwear, Men's Surf & Swimwear
JEFFREY WEIBEL (Co-Owner) & Buys Boys' Swimwear, Swimwear, Men's Swimwear, Men's Surf & Swimwear

FLEMING'S LTD. (CLO)
711 Main St. (b)
Lake Geneva, WI 53147
262-248-4637
Website: www.flemingsltd.com
MAUREEN LANNON (Co-Owner)
KEVIN FLEMING (Co-Owner) & Buys Men's Casual Wear, Urban Contemporary Casual Wear, Headwear

OVERLAND SHEEPSKIN CO. (CLO)
741 W. Main St. (m-b)
Lake Geneva, WI 53147
262-248-1916
Website: www.overlandsheepskinco.com
MARIE VAN DER STERREN (Mgr.) & Buys Men's Sheepskin Coats, Leather Coats, Hats

WALKER'S CLOTHING (MW)
125 W. Maple St. (p-m)
Lancaster, WI 53813
608-723-4700 / Fax: 608-723-7881
STEVEN J. WALKER (President) & Buys Men's Wear, Young Men's Wear, Footwear, Store Displays, Fixtures, Supplies

D.W. ZEMKE, INC. (MW)
708 S. Whitney Way (b)
Madison, WI 53711
608-274-6447
Sales: $500,000-$1 Million
DAVID ZEMKE (President) & Buys Men's Sportswear, Furnishings, Headwear, Accessories, Footwear, Store Displays, Fixtures, Supplies

WISCONSIN - Madison

FAMOUS FOOTWEAR (FW-860)
(BROWN SHOES, INC.)
7010 Mineral Point Rd. (p-m)
Madison, WI 53717
608-829-3668 / Fax: 608-829-3353
Website: www.famousfootwear.com
Retail Locations: PR, GA, MS, TX, MI, CA, ID, OH, WA, VA, WI, TN, MD

RON FROMM (C.E.O.)
RICK AUSICK (Sr. V.P. & G.M.M.)
SCOTT JENNERICH (Real Estate Contact)
TOM SICARI (V.P. & D.M.M.-Athletics) & Buys Boys' Athletic Footwear, Dress Shoes, Casual Shoes, Boots, Shoes Accessories, Slippers, Hosiery, Headwear
MIKE KISSLING-Men's Athletic Footwear, Dress Shoes, Casual Shoes, Boots

JAZZMAN (MW)
340 State St. (m-b)
Madison, WI 53703
608-256-2062 / Fax: 608-256-1846

PAUL STRONG (Owner) & Buys Men's Sportswear, Furnishings, Accessories

LITTLE LUXURIES, INC. (SP)
214 State St.
Madison, WI 53703
608-255-7372 / Fax: 608-251-4140

JANICE DURAND (Owner) & Buys Men's Ties, Small Leather Goods, Hats, Gloves, Store Displays, Fixtures, Supplies

MOMENTS TO CHERISH (SP)
2990 Kahill Main (m)
Madison, WI 53711
608-274-5683

CELESTE BURDS (Co-Owner) & Buys Men's Formal Wear, Tuxedos, Accessories, Footwear
KIM NOONAN (Co-Owner) & Buys Men's Formal Wear, Tuxedos, Accessories, Footwear

RUNDELL'S, INC. (MW)
7475 Mineral Point Rd. (m)
Madison, WI 53717
608-829-2532 / Fax: 608-829-2719
Sales: $500,000-$1 Million

JUDITH RUNDELL (President) & Buys Store Displays, Fixtures, Supplies
JAMES C. RUNDELL (Secy. & Treas.) & Buys Men's Overcoats, Suits, Tailored Jackets, Tailored Slacks, Raincoats, Sportswear, Furnishings, Headwear, Accessories, Big & Tall Men's Wear
JONATHAN RUNDELL-Men's Leather Apparel

WINTERSILKS (MO & OL)
14 S. Carroll St. (m)
Madison, WI 53703
608-280-9000
Website: www.wintersilks.com

CHRIS VIG (President)
JAY SAFTCHICK (V.P.-Mdsg.) & Buys Men's Silk Active Apparel, Furnishings, Headwear

WOLDENBERG'S (MW)
702 N. Midvale Blvd. (b)
Madison, WI 53705
608-238-4020 / Fax: 608-233-4222
Sales: $500,000-$1 Million

MICHAEL PRUE (Owner) & Buys Men's Overcoats, Suits, Tailored Jackets, Tailored Slacks, Raincoats, Sportswear, Furnishings, Headwear, Accessories, Footwear, Store Displays, Fixtures, Supplies

BALDWIN'S MENSWEAR (MW)
816 S. 8th St. (m)
Manitowoc, WI 54220
920-684-9272
Sales: $100,001-$500,000

DONALD J. KADERABEK (Owner) & Buys Men's Wear, Store Displays, Fixtures, Supplies

DAN'S TOG SHOP, INC. (MW)
N89, W16389 Main St. (m)
Menomonee Falls, WI 53051
262-251-3820 / Fax: 262-255-6460
Sales: $500,001-$1 Million
Website: www.shoppingthevillage.com

ROBERT BAER (President) & Buys Men's Overcoats, Suits, Tailored Jackets, Tailored Slacks, Raincoats, Sweaters, Sport Shirts, Outer Jackets, Casual Slacks Active Apparel, Furnishings, Headwear, Accessories, Store Displays, Fixtures, Supplies

EL PASO WESTERN GEAR (WW)
N87 W16459 Jacobson Dr. (m)
Menomonee Falls, WI 53051
262-251-2110

ZORY ABRAMOVICH (Owner) & Buys Men's Western Clothing, Related Furnishings, Headwear, Accessories, Boots

KOHL'S DEPARTMENT STORES (DEPT-428)
N56 W17000 Ridgewood Dr. (m)
Menomonee Falls, WI 53051
262-703-7000 / Fax: 262-703-6255
Sales: $3.68 Billion
Website: www.kohls.com
Retail Locations: AR, CO, CT, DE, GA, IL, ID, IA, KS, OK, PA, SC, SD, MD, MI, MN, MO, NB, NJ, NY, NC, ND, OH, TN, TX, VA, WI

LARRY MONTGOMERY (Chmn. & C.E.O.)
R. LAWRENCE MONTGOMERY (Vice Chmn. & C.E.O.)
KEVIN B. MANSELL (President)
ARLENE MEIER (C.O.O.)
OPEN (Exec. V.P. & G.M.M.-Softlines)
DON BRENNAN (Sr. V.P. & D.M.M.-Men's Wear)
JILL SOLTAU-Men's Active Apparel, Sweaters, Sport Shirts, Jeans & Denim
TAMMY LITZAU-Men's Dress Shirts, Ties
ALEX TOMMY-Sport Coats, Tailored Jackets, Tailored Slacks, Casual Slacks
OPEN-Men's Robes, Underwear, Hosiery, Gloves, Headwear, Belts, Jewelry, Small Leather Goods
MARILYN SCHEUER-Young Men's Wear
KELLY KRAETSCH-Men's Outerwear, Overcoats, Raincoats

MIKE JOHNSON (V.P. & D.M.M.-Children's Wear)
ROBYN DEARDORFF-Infants & Toddlers Basics & Sleepwear
JESSICA WOODWARD-8 to 20 Boys'

MEGAN HOPKINS (D.M.M.-Footwear)
JOHN WELLMAN-Men's Footwear
STEVE PHILLIPS-Boys' Footwear

JERRY NEAL (Dir.-Visual Presentation) & Buys Store Displays, Fixtures, Supplies

COFFIN'S DEPARTMENT STORE (DEPT)
230 Main St. East (m)
Menomonie, WI 54751
715-235-5088

JAMES COFFIN (Owner) & Buys Men's Sportswear, Furnishings, Accessories

MARK BERMAN & SON LTD. (CLO)
11920 N. Port Washington Rd. (b)
Mequon, WI 53092
262-241-8010 / Fax: 262-241-5592
Website: www.bermanbasics.com

MARK H. BERMAN (President) & Buys Men's Overcoats, Suits, Tailored Jackets, Tailored Slacks, Headwear
MICHAEL S. BERMAN-Men's Sportswear, Furnishings, Accessories, Young Men's Wear, 8 to 20 Boys' Wear
KAYE KIPEN BERMAN-Men's Sportswear, Accessories

WISCONSIN - Merrill

GUYS SHOP (MW)

913 E. Main St. (m)
Merrill, WI 54452
715-536-8211 / Fax: 715-539-0062

JACK KREINSCHMIDT (Owner) & Buys Men's Sportswear, Furnishings, Accessories

A. GOLDMANN & SONS (DEPT)

(SAM PIVAR'S & SONS)
930 W. Mitchell St. (bud)
Milwaukee, WI 53204
414-645-9100 / Fax: 414-645-4480
Sales: $1 Million-$10 Million

MILTON PIVAR (Co-Owner) & Buys Men's Sportswear, Furnishings, Accessories, Footwear, Young Men's Wear, 8 to 20 Boys' Wear
JERRY LEWIS (Co-Owner) & Buys Men's Sportswear, Furnishings, Accessories, Footwear, Young Men's Wear, 8 to 20 Boys' Wear

BAGLEY'S MENSWEAR (MW)

7608 W. Hampton Ave. (p)
Milwaukee, WI 53218
414-463-2880 / Fax: 414-463-3485
Sales: $500,000-$1 Million

ALLAN BAGLEY (Owner) & Buys Men's Overcoats, Suits, Tailored Jackets, Tailored Slacks, Raincoats, Big & Tall Men's Wear, Sweaters, Sport Shirts, Outer Jackets, Casual Slacks, Leather Apparel, Active Apparel, Furnishings, Headwear, Accessories
ROBERT BAGLEY-Store Displays, Fixtures, Supplies
MIKE SULLIVAN (G.M.M.) & Buys Men's Overcoats, Suits, Tailored Jackets, Tailored Slacks, Raincoats, Big & Tall Men's Wear, Sweaters, Sport Shirts, Outer Jackets, Casual Slacks, Leather Apparel, Active Apparel, Furnishings, Headwear, Accessories

CARSON PIRIE SCOTT (DEPT-57)

(Div. of SAKS INCORPORATED)
(BERGNER'S)
(THE BOSTON STORE)
331 W. Wisconsin Ave. (m-b)
Milwaukee, WI 53203
414-347-1152 / Fax: 414-347-5117
Sales: Over $1 Billion
Website: www.saksincorporated.com
Retail Locations: MA, CT, WA, ID, UT, NM, MO, NY, MD

KRIS WILLIAMS-Newborn 0-9 Months, J. Seymour Newborn/Infant, Infants 12-24 Months
JENNIFER PADUCH-Boys 8-20 Furnishings, Toddler Boyswear 2-4, J. Seymour 2-4, Boys Basics Private Brand, J. Seymour Boys 4-7
ANTHONY J. BUCCINA (President)
MICHAEL MACDONALD (C.E.O. & Chairman)
MIKE NEMOIR (G.M.M.-Herne)
BUSTER CROOK (G.M.M.-Men's & Children's Wear)
PETER GOUSSIOS (V.P. & D.M.M.-Men's Clothing)
JIM DUNCAN-Men's Suits, Tailored Jackets, Tailored Slacks, Outerwear, Rainwear, Leather Coats, Dress Coats
JAN BOIE-Men's Casual Slacks, Tommy Hilifger Jeans, Polo Jeans, Calvin Klein, Mens Guess?, Nautica Jeans, Updated Denim (DKNY), Girbaud Denim
ANDRE GRIGGS-Men's Dress Shirts, Neckwear
SANDY GIESENSCHLAG-Men's Hosiery, Underwear, Robes, Accessories, Loungewear, Belts, Seasonal Accessories, Small Leather Goods
KEITH YANKO-Men's Branded Sports Coats, Branded Slacks, Levi Dockers, Big & Tall, Separates, Casual Pants
ELLEN SAKE-Men's Sportshirts, Caribbean Joe, Cezani, Consensus, Columbia Sportswear, Izod, Chaps Denim
BRIAN GROVER (V.P. & D.M.M.-Young Men's & Men's Sportswear)
JOHN STEFENS-Men's Knits, Sweaters, Men's Wovens
NICOLE HOPKINSON-Young Men's Collections, Active Sportswear
KELLY CORDILL-Men's Updated & Contemporary Sportswear, Nautica, Designers, Claiborne, Tommy Hilfiger, Polo - Ralph Lauren, Perry Ellis
RON LABARRE (D.M.M.-Childrens, Boys, Basics & Accessories)
JEFF Nesbit-Boys' 8-20 Active, Denim, Tommy Hilfiger
RICK SCHLENTHER (V.P.-Visual Mdsg.)
STEVE PETERSEN (Dir.-Visual Mdsg.) & Buys Store Fixtures & Supplies
JOHN CORE (Visual Mdsg. Asst.) & Buys Store Displays
BRIAN J. MARTIN (Real Estate Contact)

DETOUR CLOTHING STORE (CLO)

1300 E. Brady St.
Milwaukee, WI 53202
414-273-5156 / Fax: 414-273-5167
Website: www.detouronline.com

JASON MEYER (Mgr.) & Buys Men's Denim, Tops, Pants, Outwear, Accessories

HERBERGER'S (DEPT-40)

(Div. of SAKS INCORPORATED)
331 W. Wisconsin Ave. (p-m)
Milwaukee, WI 53203
414-347-1152 / Fax: 414-347-5080
Sales: $100 Million-$500 Million
Website: www.saksincorporated.com
Retail Locations: MN, WI, MT, ND, NE SD, CO, IA, WI, WY

ANTHONY J. BUCCINA (President)
MIKE NEMOIR (G.M.M.-Men's)
DAVID DEVINE (D.M.M.-Men's Outerwear)
NICOLE HOPKINSON-Active Apparel
KELLY CORDILL-Men's Casual Bottoms, Suits, Dress Shirts, Ties
ANDREA GORDON-Men's Collections, Better Sportswear
CATRINA JACOBSON-Men's Furnishings, Accessories
KATHY O'BRYANT-Men's Mainstream/Main Floor Sportswear (Moderate Sportswear)
BRIAN GROVER (V.P./D.M.M.) & Buys Young Men's
RON LABARRE (D.M.M.-Children's)
JENNIFER TADUCH-8 to 20 Boys' Wear
RICK SCHLENTHER
STEVE PETERSEN (Dir.-Visual Mdsg.) & Buys Fixtures, Supplies
JOHN CORE (Visual Mdsg. Asst.) & Buys Store Displays

JACK L. MARCUS, INC. (DEPT & MO)

5300 W. Fon Du Lac Ave. (p)
Milwaukee, WI 53216
800-236-2611 / Fax: 414-438-4987
Sales: $1 Million-$10 Million

DEBRA MARCUS WALTON (President)
ANDREA R. BERRY (G.M.M.)
KAREN SCHMERIN-Men's Sportswear, Furnishings, Accessories, Boys' Wear, Footwear, Store Displays, Fixtures, Supplies

JOHNNIE WALKER'S STORES, INC. (MW-1)

234 W. Wisconsin Ave. (p-m)
Milwaukee, WI 53203
414-271-7746 / Fax: 414-271-7748
Sales: $1 Million-$10 Million

JAY KODNER (President) & Buys Men's & Young Men's Fashion Clothing, Sportswear, Headwear, Footwear, Outerwear, Jewelry, Accessories, Store Displays, Fixtures, Supplies

WISCONSIN - Milwaukee

LES MOISE, INC. (CLO-2)
151 E. Silver Spring Dr.
Milwaukee, WI 53217
414-964-5330 / Fax: 414-964-5734
CLEM ROSMANN (Owner) & Buys Apparel, Sportswear, Headwear, Footwear
RICK ROSMANN (Mgr.) & Buys Apparel, Sportswear, Headwear, Footwear
JODY DEIBEL-Sportswear, Headwear, Footwear, All Related Apparel

RICHARD BENNETT TAILORS (CLO)
2500 N. Mayfair Rd. (h)
Milwaukee, WI 53226
414-774-4850 / Fax: 414-774-4853
ELMER MILLER (Owner) & Buys Men's Sportswear, Furnishings, Accessories, Store Displays, Fixtures, Supplies
DAVID MILLER-Men's Sportswear, Furnishings, Accessories, Store Displays, Fixtures, Supplies

ROGER STEVENS CORP. (MW)
428 E. Wisconsin Ave. (b)
Milwaukee, WI 53202
414-277-9010 / Fax: 414-277-8533
STEPHEN SCHROEDER (Owner) & Buys Men's & Young Men's Sportswear, Leather Apparel, Furnishings, Accessories, Store Displays, Fixtures, Supplies

SONNY'S FOR MEN, INC. (MW-2)
(MR. SONNY'S, INC.)
825 N. Jefferson Ave. (b)
Milwaukee, WI 53202
414-276-5566 / Fax: 414-276-5566
Sales: $500,000-$1 Million
MELODY GENSLER (Co-Owner) & Buys Men's Sportswear, Swimwear, Dress Shirts, Underwear, Hosiery, Accessories, Footwear, Store Displays, Fixtures and Supplies
ROBERT GENSLER (Co-Owner) & Buys Men's Sportswear, Swimwear, Dress Shirts, Underwear, Hosiery, Accessories, Footwear

UNIVERSITY OF WISCONSIN MILWAUKEE BOOKSTORE (SP)
(UNIVERSITY OF WISCONSIN)
P.O. Box 725
Milwaukee, WI 53201
414-229-4201 / Fax: 414-229-6194
Sales: $500,001-$1 Million
LINDA HAUSLADEN (Exec. Dir.) & Buys Activewear

CLOTHES CONNECTION (CLO)
(JMI, INC.)
P.O. Box 181 (m)
Minocqua, WI 54548
715-356-2484 / Fax: 715-356-9121
JOHN MORRIS (Owner) & Buys Men's Sportswear, Belts, Young Men's Wear, Store Displays, Fixtures, Supplies

ROSS SPORTSWEAR (CLO)
P.O. Box 1050 (b)
503 Oneida Ave.
Minocqua, WI 54548
715-356-3861 / Fax: 715-358-2125
Sales: $100,001-$500,000
WILLIAM R. ROSS, JR. (Owner) & Buys Men's Sportswear, Furnishings, Headwear, Accessories, Footwear, Store Displays, Fixtures, Supplies

PAUL'S MENSWEAR (MW)
P.O. Box 430 (m)
1000 17th Ave.
Monroe, WI 53566
608-325-3125 / Fax: 608-325-3126
Sales: $100,001-$500,000
PAUL E. PAULSON (President & G.M.M.) & Buys Men's & Young Men's Wear, Urban Contemporary, Pants & Jeans, Footwear, Store Displays, Fixtures, Supplies

BILL PAUL LTD. (MW-3)
112 W. Wisconsin Ave. (b)
Neenah, WI 54956
920-722-1171 / Fax: 920-725-4550
Sales: $1 Million-$10 Million
WILLIAM F. PAUL (Owner)
DENNIS VERSECKI-Men's Sportswear, Furnishings, Headwear, Accessories, Leather Apparel, Men's Footwear, Store Displays, Fixtures, Supplies

CHAPPELL SPORTS, INC. (SP)
18600 W. National Ave.
New Berlin, WI 53146
262-679-9101 / Fax: 262-679-3353
Sales: $500,001-$1 Million
LENNY CHAPPELL (Owner)
JOANNE CHAPPEL (G.M.M.) & Buys Activewear

MARKMAN'S DEPARTMENT STORE (DEPT)
207 W. North Water (p-m)
New London, WI 54961
920-982-2466
GARY MARKMAN (Owner) & Buys Men's Suits, Raincoats, Sweaters, Sport Shirts, Outer Jackets, Leather Apparel, Casual Slacks, Furnishings, Fragrances, Store Displays, Fixtures, Supplies

J & F HABERDASHERY LTD. (MW)
1073 Summit Ave. (m-b)
Oconomowoc, WI 53066
262-567-7070 / Fax: 262-567-7104
PAUL FOBIAN (Owner) & Buys Men's Tuxedos, Sportswear, Furnishings, Accessories

CLOTHES FOR HIM (MW)
160 McGregor Plz. (p-m)
Platteville, WI 53818
608-348-5356 / Fax: 608-348-5205
Sales: $100,001-$500,000
SPENCER CHARLSON (Co-Owner) & Buys Men's & Young Men's Wear, Men's Footwear, Big & Tall Men's Wear, Store Displays, Fixtures, Supplies
SHEILA CHARLSON (Co-Owner) & Buys Men's & Young Men's Wear, Men's Footwear, Big & Tall Men's Wear, Store Displays, Fixtures, Supplies

ANCHOR MENSWEAR (MW)
121 N. Franklin St. (b)
Port Washington, WI 53074
262-284-0909 / Fax: 262-284-0902
SCOTT SCHWIEZER (Owner) & Buys Men's Sportswear, Furnishings, Headwear, Accessories, Urban Contemporary, Store Displays, Fixtures, Supplies

D.W. MENSWEAR (MW)
P.O. Box 218 (p-m)
125 W. Cook St.
Portage, WI 53901
608-742-7745
Sales: $100,001-$500,000
DOUG WILLIAMS (Owner) & Buys Men's Sportswear, Furnishings, Licensed Apparel, Headwear, Belts, Jewelry, Fragrances, Footwear, Store Displays, Fixtures, Supplies

EULBERG'S LTD. (MW)
P.O. Box 279 (m)
128 W. Cook St.
Portage, WI 53901
608-742-8524 / Fax: 608-742-1761
Sales: $500,000-$1 Million
DAVID W. EULBERG (President) & Buys Men's Sweaters, Sport Shirts, Outer Jackets, Casual Slacks, Leather Apparel, Furnishings, Headwear, Accessories, Store Displays, Fixtures, Supplies

KOZELKA'S MENSWEAR (MW)
120 N. Beaumont Rd. (p)
Prairie du Chien, WI 53821
608-326-6016 / Fax: 608-326-4990
THOMAS KOZELKA (Co-Owner)
RICHARD KOZELKA (Co-Owner)
GARY KOZELKA-Men's Wear, Furnishing, Footwear & Accessories

WALL STREET FOR CHILDREN (KS)
130 E. Black Hawk Ave. (m)
Prairie du Chien, WI 53821
608-326-2604 / Fax: 608-326-4448
KENNETH WALL (Co-Owner) & Buys Size 8 to 20 Boys' Wear, Store Displays, Fixtures, Supplies
JUDY WALL (Co-Owner) & Buys Size 8 to 20 Boys' Wear

ATTITUDE (MW)
5820 Durand Ave. (m)
Racine, WI 53403
262-554-2157 / Fax: 262-554-3190
JAMIE BASQUEZ (Owner) & Buys Urban Contemporary, Store Displays, Fixtures, Supplies

HARRY'S TAILOR SHOP (MW)
3015 Douglas Ave. (m)
Racine, WI 53402
262-639-4954
HARRY DERDERIAN (Owner) & Buys Men's Suits,Tailored Jackets, Tailored Slacks, Big & Tall Men's Wear

ROGAN'S SHOES, INC. (FW-28)
1750 Ohio St. (m-b)
Racine, WI 53405
262-637-3613 / Fax: 262-637-0613
Sales: $10 Million-$50 Million
Website: www.rogansshoes.com
Retail Locations: IL, MN, WI
DAVE ROGAN (President) & Buys Boys' Footwear, Men's Footwear, Leather Goods, Accessories, Hosiery
MARK ROGAN (Exec. V.P.)
TOM ROGAN (V.P.-Purch.) & Buys Boys' Footwear, Men's Footwear, Leather Goods, Accessories, Hosiery

TINY'S BIG & TALL (MW-2)
2026 Lathrop Ave. (p)
Racine, WI 53405
262-634-2814 / Fax: 262-632-8605
HOWARD COOK (Owner) & Buys Men's Sportswear, Big & Tall Men's Wear, Footwear, Swimwear, Furnishings, Accessories
JIM COOK-Men's Sportswear, Big & Tall Men's Wear, Footwear, Swimwear, Furnishings, Accessories

DeBYLE'S, INC. (CLO-2)
P.O. Box 128 (b)
9 S. Brown St.
Rhinelander, WI 54501
715-362-4406 / Fax: 715-362-1772
Sales: $1 Million-$10 Million
DWAYNE DeBYLE (President & G.M.M.) & Buys Men's Sportswear, Leather Apparel, Accessories, Boys' & Students Wear, Young Men's Wear, Urban Contemporary, Store Displays, Fixtures, Supplies

G.B. HERON'S (MW)
2900 College Dr. (m-b)
Rice Lake, WI 54868
715-234-3633 / Fax: 715-234-4873
Sales: $100,001-$500,000
Website: www.gbherons.com
JOLENE DOYLE (Owner) & Buys Men's Sportswear, Leather Apparel, Accessories, Footwear, Store Displays, Fixtures, Supplies

SURPLUS OUTLET (MW)
7 S. Main St. (b)
Rice Lake, WI 54868
715-234-3491 / Fax: 715-234-9207
Sales: $100,001-$500,000
TOM KAMRATH (Owner) & Buys Men's Sportswear, Work Clothing, Leather Apparel, Footwear, Big & Tall Men's Wear

GENTLEMAN'S QUARTER, INC. (MW)
109 S. Main St. (m-b)
Shawand, WI 54166
715-524-6100 / Fax: 715-524-6100
Sales: $100,001-$500,000
JEFF KIRCHNER (Owner) & Buys Men's Sportswear, Furnishings, Headwear, Footwear, Accessories, Store Displays, Fixtures, Supplies

HARLEY'S (MW)
(BRILL-RYAN ENTERPRISES., INC.)
4009 N. Oakland Ave. (b-h)
Shorewood, WI 53211
414-332-3404 / Fax: 414-332-2854
Sales: $1 Million-$10 Million
Website: www.harleys4men.com
TIM RYAN (President) & Buys Men's Sportswear, Big & Tall Men's Wear, Furnishings, Accessories, Store Displays, Fixtures and Supplies
PERRY NEWSOM-Men's Sportswear, Big & Tall Men's Wear, Furnishings, Accessories, Store Displays, Fixtures and Supplies

SPOONER MERCANTILE CO. (DEPT)
145 Walnut St. (m)
Spooner, WI 54801
715-635-3343 / Fax: 715-635-8062
Sales: $100,001-$500,000
BARRY BENSON (Owner) & Buys Men's Overcoats, Suits, Tailored Jackets, Tailored Slacks, Sweaters, Sport Shirts, Outer Jackets, Raincoats, Big & Tall Men's Wear, Casual Slacks, Active Apparel, Furnishings, Headwear, Accessories, Men's Footwear, Young Men's & Boys' Wear, Urban Contemporary (Denim Only), Boys' Shoes, Store Displays, Fixtures, Supplies

SPOONER OUTLET, INC. (MW)
209 Walnut St. (bud-m)
Spooner, WI 54801
715-635-3883 / Fax: 715-635-2450
Website: www.spooneroutlet.com
BRUCE SHARRON (Co-Owner)
ROGER SHARRON, JR. (Co-Owner) & Buys Men's Wear, Footwear, Accessories, Boys' T-shirts, Store Displays, Fixtures, Supplies

PARKINSON'S (MW)
1000 Main St. (m-b)
Stevens Point, WI 54481
715-345-0250 / Fax: 715-341-0242
JIM LUKOWICZ (Co-Owner) & Buys Men's Sportswear, Furnishings, Headwear, Accessories, Store Displays, Fixtures, Supplies
ROSE LUKOWICZ (Co-Owner) & Buys Men's Sportswear, Furnishings, Headwear, Accessories, Store Displays, Fixtures, Supplies

SELBO MENSWEAR (MW)
144 E. Main St. (b)
Stoughton, WI 53589
608-873-5355
PAUL SELBO (Owner) & Buys Men's Sportswear, Footwear, Furnishings, Accessories

NORTHWEST OUTLET, INC. (MW)
1814 Belknap St. (m)
Superior, WI 54880
715-392-9838 / Fax: 715-392-1452
Sales: $1 Million-$10 Million
Website: www.nwoutlet.com
DAVE MILLER (President)
LEN PASKE-Men's Overcoats, Rainwear, Sportswear, Underwear, Belts, Small Leather Goods, Boys' Clothing, Sportswear, Store Displays, Fixtures, Supplies
DON HOBSON-Men's Hosiery, Gloves, Headwear, Footwear

BURNSTAD BROTHERS, INC. (CLO)
701 E. Clifton St. (m-b)
Tomah, WI 54660
608-372-6335 / Fax: 608-372-4062
KENT BURNSTAD (Owner)
RITA BURNSTAD-Store Displays, Fixtures, Supplies
BARBARA MANGENE-Men's Sportswear, Dress Shirts, Hosiery, Small Leather Goods, Swimwear, Store Displays, Fixtures, Supplies

TOMAH CASH MERCANTILE CO. (DEPT)
914 Superior Ave. (m-b)
Tomah, WI 54660
608-372-2171 / Fax: 608-372-4242
Sales: $1 Million-$10 Million
JOHN H. ROSE (President) & Buys Store Displays, Fixtures, Supplies
MARK ROSE-Men's Footwear, Men's Wear
DON FLETCHER-Men's Wear
KERRY ROSE-8 to 20 Boys' Wear
SALLY ROSE-8 to 20 Boys' Wear

WISCONSIN - Two Rivers

EVANS DEPARTMENT STORES (DEPT-2)
(EVAN, INC.)
1816 Washington St. (p-m)
Two Rivers, WI 54241
920-793-3705 / Fax: 920-793-2421
Sales: $1 Million-$10 Million
Website: www.evanstoybox.com
ALLAN EVANOFF (Owner) & Buys Men's Sweaters, Sport Shirts, Active Apparel, Furnishings, Headwear, Belts, Boys' Clothing, Sportswear, Store Displays, Fixtures, Supplies
HEIDI EVANOFF (Secy. & Treas.) & Buys Men's Sweaters, Sport Shirts, Active Apparel, Furnishings, Headwear, Belts, Boys' Clothing, Sportswear, Store Displays, Fixtures, Supplies

SCHROEDER BROTHERS CO. (DEPT)
P.O. Box 296 (m-b)
1623 Washington St.
Two Rivers, WI 54241
920-793-2241 / Fax: 920-794-7702
Sales: $500,000-$1 Million
JOHN SCHROEDER (President) & Buys Men's & Boys' Outerwear, Store Displays, Fixtures, Supplies
TIM SCHROEDER-Boys' Wear
FRANK BIRR-Men's Sportswear, Furnishings, Headwear, Footwear

CENTER STAGE (CLO)
118 S. Main St. (m-b)
Viroqua, WI 54665
608-637-3114 / Fax: 608-637-6181
DOROTHY HOFFLAND (Owner)
PAMELA SKREDE (Mgr.) & Buys Men's Wear, Footwear, Young Men's Wear, Urban Contemporary Pants, 8 to 20 Boys' Wear, Footwear
STEVEN SKREDE (Mgr.) & Buys Men's Wear, Footwear, Young Men's Wear, Urban Contemporary Pants, 8 to 20 Boys' Wear, Footwear, Store Displays, Fixtures and Supplies

FELIX'S, INC. (CLO)
102 S. Main St. (m)
Viroqua, WI 54665
608-637-7152 / Fax: 608-637-8706
Sales: $500,000-$1 Million
STEPHEN FELIX (President & Owner) & Buys Men's Sportswear, Young Men's Wear, Accessories, Footwear, Store Displays, Fixtures, Supplies

MR. G'S, INC. (CLO-5)
120 N. Main St. (p)
Viroqua, WI 54665
608-637-8271 / Fax: 608-637-8377
GENE GABRYSIAK (Owner) & Buys Men's Sportswear, Dress Shirts, Underwear, Hosiery, Swimwear, Footwear, Accessories, Furnishings, Store Displays, Fixtures, Supplies

FISCHER'S DEPARTMENT STORE (DEPT)
P.O. Box 168 (p)
210 E. Main St.
Watertown, WI 53094
920-261-6965 / Fax: 920-261-6986
Sales: $1 Million-$10 Million
NELSON FISCHER (President) & Buys Store Displays, Fixtures, Supplies
TODD FISCHER (Mdse. Mgr.) & Buys Men's Overcoats, Suits, Tailored Jackets, Tailored Slacks, Raincoats, Big & Tall Men's Wear, Sweaters, Sport Shirts, Outer Jackets, Leather Apparel, Casual Slacks, Active Apparel, Furnishings, Headwear, Belts, Jewelry, Small Leather Goods
BARBARA FISCHER-Store Displays, Supplies
LYNN MALLACH-Store Displays, Supplies

LARES FASHIONS (CLO)
245 W. Main St.
Waukesha, WI 53186
262-524-0446 / Fax: 262-506-0060
ARENIO LARES (Owner) & Buys Men's Dress Shirts, Casual Slacks, Sportswear

SURPLUS OUTLET STORE (MW)
330 W. Main St. (p-m)
Waukesha, WI 53186
262-542-5811 / Fax: 978-336-2407
LARRY TARKINOW (Owner) & Buys Men's Work Clothes, Hunting Apparel

BAESEMAN'S, INC. (MW)
1002 S. 3rd Ave. (m)
Wausau, WI 54401
715-842-0928 / Fax: 715-842-0929
TOM ROSSI (Mgr.) & Buys Men's Outdoor Wear, Hunting Apparel, Boots, Footwear, Store Displays, Fixtures, Supplies

ST. CLAIR'S MENSWEAR (MW)
(DAVID P. JAHNKE, INC.)
P.O. Box 56 (m-b)
307 3rd St.
Wausau, WI 54402
715-842-3621 / Fax: 715-842-8575
Sales: $500,000-$1 Million
Website: www.stclairsmenswear.com
DAVID P. JAHNKE (Owner) & Buys Men's Overcoats, Suits, Tailored Jackets, Tailored Slacks, Raincoats, Sweaters, Sport Shirts, Outer Jackets, Leather Apparel, Casual Slacks, Activewear, Furnishings, Belts, Store Displays, Fixtures, Supplies

FOX'S MENSWEAR (MW-2)
P.O. Box 167 (b)
2500 N. Mayfair Rd.
Wauwatosa, WI 53226
414-771-9898
PETER FOX (Owner) & Buys Men's Wear, Suits, Tailored Jackets, Tailored Slacks, Sportswear, Slacks, Young Men's Wear, Urban Contemporary, Store Displays, Fixtures, Supplies

RODIEZ'S RUNNING STORE (SP)
10903 W. Lincoln Ave.
West Allis, WI 53227
414-321-1154 / Fax: 414-321-1152
ANTHONY RODIEZ (President) & Buys Running Apparel, Athletic Footwear

SAGER'S MEN'S APPAREL, INC. (MW)
101 S. Main St. (m)
West Bend, WI 53095
262-334-4318 / Fax: 262-334-5148
DONALD SAGER (Co-Owner) & Buys Men's & Young Men's Sportswear, Leather Apparel, Furnishings, Headwear, Accessories, Store Displays, Fixtures, Supplies
SCOTT SAGER (Co-Owner) & Buys Men's & Young Men's Sportswear, Leather Apparel, Furnishings, Headwear, Accessories, Store Displays, Fixtures, Supplies

WEST BEND WOOLEN MILLS STORE (CLO)
(BADGER MERCANTILE COMPANY)
1125 E. Washington St. (m)
West Bend, WI 53095
262-334-7052 / Fax: 262-334-1870
MIKE WINKLER (Co-Owner) & Buys Men's Sportswear, Furnishings, Winter Headwear, Belts, Big & Tall Men's Wear, Young Men's & Boys' Wear, Store Displays, Fixtures, Supplies
STEVE WINKLER (Co-Owner) & Buys Store Displays, Fixtures, Supplies

BRUCE PAUL GOODMAN - THE FASHIONABLE CLOTHIER (CLO)
314 E. Silver Springs Dr. (b)
Whitefish Bay, WI 53217
414-962-0405
BRUCE PAUL GOODMAN (Owner) & Buys Men's Sportswear, Furnishings, Accessories, Store Displays, Fixtures, Supplies

LEFFINGWELL'S MENSWEAR (MW)
141 W. Main St. (m)
Whitewater, WI 53190
262-473-2181
HARRY LEFFINGWELL (Owner) & Buys Men's Sportswear, Furnishings, Headwear, Footwear, Accessories, Young Men's Wear, Store Displays, Fixtures, Supplies

DE MARCO'S (MW-5)

601 SE Wyoming Blvd. (m)
Casper, WY 82609
307-266-5201 / Fax: 307-266-5201

ROBERT MARCOVITZ (Co-Owner)
LEN MARCOVITZ (Co-Owner)
DAVE MARCOVITZ (Co-Owner) & Buys Men's Sportswear, Furnishings, Accessories, Footwear, Urban Contemporary, Young Men's Wear, Store Displays, Fixtures, Supplies

LOU TAUBERT RANCH OUTFITTERS (CLO-2)

125 E. 2nd St. (b)
Casper, WY 82601
307-234-2500 / Fax: 307-237-1218
Sales: $1 Million-$10 Million

LOUIS TAUBERT, JR. (C.E.O.) & Buys Men's, Young Men's & Boys' Wear, Western Wear, Leather Apparel, Footwear, Western Boots, Store Displays, Fixtures, Supplies

CORRAL WEST RANCHWEAR (WW-97)

4519 Frontier Mall Dr. (bud-p-m-b)
Cheyenne, WY 82009
307-632-0951 / Fax: 307-632-4032
Sales: $10 Million-$50 Million
Website: www.corralwest.com
Retail Locations: AZ

LESLIE A. BALL (President)
LORI GATES-Men's, Young Men's & Boys' Western Hats, Footwear, Western Boots
RON THRING-Men's Western Wear, Leather Jackets, Young Men's & Boys' Western Wear

SIERRA TRADING POST, INC. (MO & DG-3 & OL)

5025 Campstool Rd. (p-m-b)
Cheyenne, WY 82007
307-775-8050 / Fax: 307-775-8301
Website: www.sierratradingpost.com

KEITH RICHARDSON (Owner)
KEN WALTER (Mgr.) & Buys Men's Outdoor Clothing, Footwear, Store Displays, Fixtures, Supplies

JR'S FASHIONS FOR MEN (MW)

1225 Sheridan Ave. (m)
Cody, WY 82414
307-587-2891

JERRY POSEY (Owner) & Buys Men's Sportswear, Furnishings, Slippers
JIM HERMAN (Asst. Mgr.) & Buys Store Displays, Fixtures, Supplies

DUBOIS MERCANTILE, INC. (DEPT)

118 E. Main St. (p-m)
Dubois, WY 82513
307-455-2455

WAYNE STEINERT (Owner) & Buys Men's & Boys' Jeans, Sport Shirts, Casual Slacks, T-shirts, Dress Shirts, Hosiery, Underwear, Store Displays, Fixtures, Supplies
ROBIN STEINERT-Footwear

BOOT & SADDLE SHOP, INC. (CLO)

300 S. Gillette Ave. (p-m-b)
Gillette, WY 82716
307-682-3749

JAMES NOECKER (President & Owner) & Buys Men's Wear, Sportswear, Furnishings, Accessories, Western Wear, Footwear, Western Boots, Store Displays, Fixtures and Supplies

PROBST WESTERN STORE (WW)

547 Greybull Ave. (m-b)
Greybull, WY 82426
307-765-2171 / Fax: 307-765-2161

JEFFREY PROBST (President) & Buys Men's & Boys' Western Wear, Hosiery, Footwear, Outdoor Clothing, Store Displays, Fixtures, Supplies
TYSON PROBST-Men's & Boys' Western Wear, Hosiery, Footwear, Outdoor Clothing, Store Displays, Fixtures, Supplies

WILLIAMS' DEPARTMENT STORE (DEPT)

522 Greybull Ave. (p-m)
Greybull, WY 82426
307-765-2321 / Fax: 307-765-2321

JOHN WILLIAMS (President & Owner) & Buys Tailored Jackets, Tailored Slacks, Sportswear, Furnishings, Footwear, Boots, Accessories, Young Men's Wear, Urban Contemporary, Boys' Wear, Store Displays, Fixtures and Supplies

JACK DENNIS OUTDOOR SHOP (SG-2 & OL)

P.O. Box 3369 (b)
Jackson, WY 83001
307-733-3270 / Fax: 307-733-4540

LARRY BASHFORD-Outer Jackets, Overcoats, Gloves, Hats, Hosiery, Ski Wear (All Outdoor Clothing), Boots, Store Displays, Fixtures, Supplies

SIRK ENTERPRISES (CLO-3)

P.O. Box 983 (p)
Jackson, WY 83001
307-733-2221 / Fax: 307-739-9642
Website: www.sirkshirts.com

RICK HOLLINGSWORTH (Owner) & Buys Men's Sportswear, Dress Shirts, Accessories, Furnishings, Store Displays, Fixtures & Supplies

SAWAYA'S KEMMERER SHOE STORE, INC. (MW)

921 Pine St. (m)
Kemmerer, WY 83101
307-877-3588 / Fax: 307-877-9822

JOHN SAWAYA (Owner) & Buys Tailored Jackets, Tailored Slacks, Raincoats, Sweaters, Sport Shirts, Outer Jackets, Sport Shirts, Active Apparel, Casual Apparel, Work Apparel, Dress Shirts, Ties, Underwear, Hosiery, Work Gloves, Belts, Small Leather Goods, Jewelry, Western Wear, Western Boots, Young Men's & Boys' Wear, Footwear, Store Displays, Fixtures, Supplies

LINTON SUPPLY CO. (DG-2)

(LINTON'S BIG R STORES)
455 S. Absaroka St. (m)
Powell, WY 82435
307-754-9521 / Fax: 307-754-3964

JIM LINTON (President & Gen. Mgr.)
JACKIE McKAY-Men's Western Shirts, Ties, Hats, Tailored Slacks, Headwear, Jeans, Work Clothes, Underwear, Raincoats, Hosiery, Small Leather Goods, Outer Jackets, Boys' Jeans, Western Shirts, Western Boots, Footwear, Store Displays, Fixtures, Supplies

KELLEY'S SHOES, INC. (FW)

(KELLEY'S SHOE ANNEX)
P.O. Box 6396 (bdes)
447 N. Front St.
Rock Springs, WY 82901
307-362-2311 / Fax: 307-382-5427
Sales: $500,001-$1 Million

C.L. RUSSELL (President) & Buys Boys' Footwear, Men's Footwear, Leather Goods, Men's Accessories, Hosiery
BRAD RUSSELL (V.P.) & Buys Boys' Footwear, Men's Footwear, Leather Goods, Men's Accessories, Hosiery
GAY LYNN RUSSELL-Boys' Footwear, Men's Footwear, Leather Goods, Men's Accessories, Hosiery

DAN'S WESTERN WEAR (WW)

P.O. Drawer D (p)
226 N. Main
Sheridan, WY 82801
307-672-9378

ELEANOR CHADWICK (Co-Owner) & Buys Men's & Big & Tall Men's Western Work Clothes
DEANNA GEORGE (Co-Owner) & Buys Men's & Big & Tall Men's Western Work Clothes, Men's Leather Apparel, Boots, Accessories, Store Displays, Fixtures, Supplies

THE MEN'S SHOP (MW)

P.O. Box 803 (m)
121 N. Main
Sheridan, WY 82801
307-674-9742
Sales: $100,001-$500,000

JOHN P. DAY, SR. (President & G.M.M.) & Buys Men's Suits, Tailored Slacks, Tailored Jackets, Raincoats, Sweaters, Sport Shirts, Outer Jackets, Casual Slacks, Furnishings, Headwear, Belts, Small Leather Goods, Store Displays, Fixtures and Supplies

LEE'S TEES (CLO-3)

P.O. Box 159
1 Village Centre
Teton Village, WY 83025
307-733-9197 / Fax: 307-733-1240
Website: www.leestees.com

LEE GARDNER (Owner) & Buys Activewear

GODDARD STORES, INC. (CLO)

2042 Main St. (p-m)
Torrington, WY 82240
307-532-2635 / Fax: 307-532-7455

KAREN BANDEMER-Men's Sportswear, Dress Shirts, Underwear, Hosiery, Small Leather Goods, Fragrances, Swimwear, Ties, Belts, Gloves, T-shirts, Fleece, Active Apparel, Young Men's Wear, Boys' Wear, Store Displays, Fixtures, Supplies

HUNGRY JACK'S GENERAL STORE, INC. (DEPT)

P.O. Box 255 (p)
Hwy. 22
Wilson, WY 83014
307-733-3561

KEVIN ROICE (Co-Owner) & Buys Men's Work Clothing, Footwear, Sportswear, Furnishings, Store Displays, Fixtures, Supplies

JANA ROICE (Co-Owner) & Buys Men's Work Clothing, Sportswear, Furnishings, Store Displays, Fixtures, Supplies

Men's & Boys' Wear Buyers in Canada

ALBERTA - Calgary

BOUTIQUE OF LEATHERS LTD. (CLO-15)

6012 3rd St. SW (m-b)
Calgary, AB T2H 0H9
403-259-2726 / Fax: 403-255-2641
Sales: $1 Million-$10 Million
Website: www.boutiqueofleathers.com

BARRY LAMMLE (President) & Buys Men's Leather Jackets, Pants, Gloves, Belts, Small Leather Goods
KARI CARR (Mkt. Mgr.) & Buys Men's Leather Jackets, Pants, Gloves, Belts, Small Leather Goods

GORD'S RUNNING STORE LTD. (SP)

919 Centre St. NW
Calgary, AB T2E 2P6
403-270-8606 / Fax: 403-283-8341
Website: www.gordsrunningstore.com

GORD HOBBINS (Owner) & Buys Activewear, Athletic Footwear, Boys' Wear, Accessories

MacLEOD BROTHERS LTD. (MW-2)

415 60th Ave. SE, #13 (m-b-des)
Calgary, AB T2H 2J5
403-253-1811 / Fax: 403-255-7469
Sales: $1 Million-$10 Million

KEN BENNETT (Owner) & Buys Leather Goods, Men's Apparel, Men's Big & Tall Apparel, Men's Casualwear, Men's Denim Apparel, Men's Accessories, Men's Hosiery, Men's Outerwear, Men's Sportswear, Men's Suits, Men's Swimwear, Men's Underwear

MARK'S WORK WEARHOUSE LTD. (MW-300)

(L'EQUIPEUR)
(WORK WORLD)
1035 64th Ave., #30 (m-b)
Calgary, AB T2H 2J7
403-255-9220 / Fax: 403-255-6005
Sales: $300 Million
Website: www.marks.com
Retail Locations: AB, BC, MB, NB, NF, NS, NT, ON, QC, PE, SK

GARTH MITCHELL (President & C.E.O.)
PAUL WILSON (C.O.O.-Mark's Div.)
MICHAEL STRACHAN (C.O.O.-Work World & Sr. V.P.- Mktg.)
RICK HARRISON (Sr. V.P.-Mdsg.)
RICHARD FAUST-Men's Tops, Outerwear
IAIN SUMMERS-Men's Bottoms
JENNY McCULLOCH-Men's Accessories
DARREN TEES-Workwear
RON IWAMOTO-Men's Footwear

SWIM CO. (SP-10)

6403 Burbank Rd.
Calgary, AB T2H 2L1
403-259-6113 / Fax: 403-253-6667
Website: www.swimco.com

STEVE FORSETH-Men's Swimwear
STACY FINK-Children's, Athletic
KRISTIN SKAGGS-Street Wear, Shoes, Accessories
KITTY LIU-Swimwear
DAVID BACON (Co-Owner)
LORI BACON (Co-Owner)
AMANDA WENSLEY-Junior Swimwear

BELOW THE BELT (CLO-26)

(LEVI'S)
5611 87th St. (m)
Edmonton, AB T6E 6H7
780-469-5301 / Fax: 780-465-7862
Retail Locations: CA

JANET PAYNE (President) & Buys Young Men's Sportswear, Casual Wear, Belts, Small Leather Goods, Men's Footwear
DEREK PAYNE (Real Estate Contact) & Buys Store Displays, Fixtures and Supplies

GOLD BRICK JEWELRY LTD. (JWLY-7)

(DALE'S JEWELERS)
(GOLD BRICK)
10551 114th St.
Edmonton, AB T5H 3J6
780-428-7169 / Fax: 780-425-8307
Sales: $1 Million-$10 Million

FRANK FARKAS (President) & Buys Jewelry, Watches

HENRY SINGER FASHION GROUP (MW-3)

#160 Manulife Pl. (b-des)
10180 101 St.
Edmonton, AB T5J 3S4
780-420-0909 / Fax: 780-425-5905
Sales: $10 Million-$50 Million
Website: www.henrysinger.com

FRED SINGER (President) & Buys Leather Goods, Men's & Boys' Apparel, Men's Casualwear, Men's Denim Apparel, Men's Formalwear, Men's Accessories, Men's Hosiery, Men's Outerwear, Men's Sportswear, Men's Suits, Footwear

RUNNING ROOM LTD. (FW-62 & OL)

9750 47th Ave. (m-b-des)
Edmonton, AB T6E 5P3
780-439-3099 / Fax: 780-433-6433
Sales: $10 Million-$50 Million
Website: www.runningroom.com
Retail Locations: MN

JOHN STANTON (President)
DANA LOZINIK (V.P.-Purch.) & Buys Boys' Apparel, Boys' Footwear, Men's Apparel, Men's Footwear, Leather Goods, Licensed Apparel, Watches, Men's Accessories, Hosiery
KEVIN HIGA (Real Estate Contact)

BLACK & LEE TUXEDOS (MW-12)

8920 Fraisenton Ct. (m-b-des)
Burnaby, BC V5J 5H8
604-688-2481 / Fax: 604-688-5951
Sales: $1 Million-$10 Million
Website: www.blackandlee.com

PAT RATTENBURY (President & Co-Owner)
JIM RENTMEESTER (Co-Owner) & Buys Men's Big & Tall Apparel, Men's Apparel, Men's Casualwear, Men's Formalwear, Men's Accessories, Men's Hosiery, Men's Suits, Footwear
PETER MERALI (Gen. Mgr. & Real Estate Contact) & Buys Men's Big & Tall Apparel, Men's Apparel, Men's Casualwear, Men's Formalwear, Men's Accessories, Men's Hosiery, Men's Suits, Footwear
CLARKE RATTENBURY (Sls. Mgr.)

WESTERN ATHLETIC LTD. (SP)

117 2544 Douglas
Burnaby, BC V5C 5W7
604-291-0788 / Fax: 604-291-7344

HENRY SOMERS (Co-Owner) & Buys Activewear, T-shirts, Shorts, Caps
KEN GARDINER (Co-Owner) & Buys Activewear, T-shirts, Shorts, Caps

FIELDS (CLO-120)

(Div. of HUDSON'S BAY CO.)
766 Clieeden Pl. (p-m)
Delta, BC V3M 6C7
604-523-6566 / Fax: 604-523-4700
Retail Locations: AB, BC, MB, SK

LEANNE NAISCHNIDTS (Mgr. & Real Estate Contact)
IAN Officer (G.M.M.)
CICILIA ROBINSON-Men's Wear
DEBBIE DOUGLAS-Boys' Wear
HARRAS GARCHO-Footwear
SANDE CHAN-Accessories, Furnishings

UNIVERSAL STORES (CLO-2)
700 W. 3rd Ave.
Prince Rupert, BC V8J 1M4
250-624-6743 / Fax: 250-624-5642
JACK PAYNE (President)
CINDY PAYNE-Men's Overcoats, Sportswear, Furnishings, Belts, Boys' Sportswear, Accessories, Jeans, Footwear

BOOTLEGGER (CLO-117)
(Div of COMARK, INC.)
4460 Jacombs Rd.
Richmond, BC V6V 2C5
604-276-8400 / Fax: 604-276-8516
Website: www.bootlegger.com
Retail Locations: CA
RICHARD SCHULTE (President)
KIM INNES (G.M.M.)
JILL JANKOWSKI (Gen. Mgr.)
PAUL BURREL-Men's Jeans
JOHN JENELIN-Men's Casual Shirts
TRACY BAKER-4 to 7 Boys' Outerwear, Men's Outer Jackets, Leather Apparel, Men's Bottoms
Eng OTTO-Boys' Bottoms
P. J. CZANK-Men's Belts, Small Leather Goods
ROGER CYR (Real Estate Contact)

STERLING SHOES, INC. (FW-66)
(B-CODE)
(FREEDMAN SHOES)
(JONEVE)
(SHOE WAREHOUSE)
2580 Viscount Way (m-b)
Richmond, BC V6V 1N1
604-270-6114 / Fax: 604-278-7751
Sales: $10 Million-$50 Million
Retail Locations: CA
JEREMY HOROWITZ (President) & Buys Boys' Footwear, Men's Footwear, Leather Goods, Watches, Men's Accessories, Hosiery
MAGDA CANDERAN (G.M.) & Buys Boys' Footwear, Men's Footwear, Leather Goods, Watches, Men's Accessories, Hosiery
KATHY CENTANI-Men's Footwear
NICKI PETERSON-Boys' Footwear
MANNIE DRUCKER (Real Estate Contact)

CHAPY'S (CLO-3)
833 W. Pender St. (m-b)
Vancouver, BC V6C 1K7
604-685-6207 / Fax: 604-685-8589
TED CHAPMAN (President)
JANET CHAPMAN-Men's Overcoats, Suits, Tailored Jackets, Tailored Slacks, Raincoats, Sportswear, Furnishings, Slippers

FORERUNNER'S (SP)
3504 4th Ave. West
Vancouver, BC V6R 1N8
604-732-4535 / Fax: 604-734-0786
PETER BUTLER (Owner) & Buys Activewear, Athletic Footwear

HILL'S OF KERRISDALE (CLO)
2125 W. 41st Ave. (b)
Vancouver, BC V6M 1Z3
604-266-9177 / Fax: 604-266-6834
ROSS HILL (President) & Buys Men's Tailored Jackets, Tailored Slacks, Sportswear, Furnishings, Small Leather Goods, Belts, Boys' Sportswear, Furnishings, Accessories, Denim, Footwear, Store Displays, Fixtures and Supplies
JAMES S. HILL (C.E.O.) & Buys Men's Tailored Jackets, Tailored Slacks, Sportswear, Furnishings, Small Leather Goods, Belts, Boys' Sportswear, Furnishings, Accessories, Jeans, Footwear, Store Displays, Fixtures and Supplies

LADY SPORT (SP)
3545 4th Ave. West
Vancouver, BC V6R 1N9
604-733-1173 / Fax: 604-733-1595
Website: www.ladysport.bc.ca
BRETT DAVIDSON (Owner) & Buys Activewear, Athletic Footwear

LEONE (CLO)
757 W. Hastings St., #112 (b)
Vancouver, BC V6C 1A1
604-683-1132 / Fax: 604-683-8535
Website: www.leone.ca
ALBERTO LEONE (President)
BERNARD MANTOI (Gen. Mgr.) & Buys Men's Overcoats, Suits, Tailored Jackets, Tailored Slacks, Raincoats, Sportswear, Furnishings, Headwear, Accessories, Footwear, Store Displays, Fixtures & Supplies

LUGARO (JWLY-7)
(LUGARO JEWELERS)
404-935 Marine Dr.
Vancouver, BC V7P 1S3
604-986-0320 / Fax: 604-986-8151
Sales: $1 Million-$10 Million
Website: www.lugaro.com
STEVE AGOPIAN (President) & Buys Jewelry, Watches
CLARA AGOPIAN (V.P.) & Buys Jewelry, Watches

MURRAY GOLDMAN LTD. (CLO-4)
910 Richards St.
Vancouver, BC V6B 3C1
604-687-2221 / Fax: 604-687-2215
Sales: $1 Million-$10 Million
MURRAY GOLDMAN (President)
DAVID GOLDMAN (V.P.) & Buys Young Men's Accessories, Furnishings, Sportswear, Casual Slacks, Footwear, Store Displays, Fixtures and Supplies

ALPINE MEADOWS (SP)
Ambleside Ln.
West Vancouver, BC V7T 2Y9
604-921-8120
DAVE WONG (Owner) & Buys Activewear, Athletic Footwear

BEN MOSS JEWELERS WESTERN CANADA LTD. (JWLY-50 & OL)
Canwest Global Center
300-201 Portage Ave.
Winnipeg, MB R3B 3K6
204-947-6682 / Fax: 204-988-0148
Sales: $10 Million-$50 Million
Website: www.benmoss.com
Retail Locations: Canada
BRENT TREPEL (President & C.E.O.)
SANDRA DANBERY (G.M.M.) & Buys Jewelry, Watches
MERV MOKNOWED (Real Estate Contact) (@ 204-988-0148)

BOCHAW LTD. (MW)
(RAGAZZI FINE CLOTHING & CASUAL WEAR)
897 Corydon Ave., #100 (m-b)
Winnipeg, MB R3M 0W7
204-488-8080 / Fax: 204-487-7843
Sales: $1 Million-$10 Million
GERRY SCERBO (President) & Buys Men's Leather Goods, Men's Casualwear, Men's Denim Apparel, Men's Formalwear, Men's Accessories, Men's Hosiery, Men's Outerwear, Men's Sportswear, Men's Suits, Men's Swimwear
BRUCE RAYBURN (Store Mgr.) & Buys Men's Leather Goods, Men's Casualwear, Men's Denim Apparel, Men's Formalwear, Men's Accessories, Men's Hosiery, Men's Outerwear, Men's Sportswear, Men's Suits, Men's Swimwear

HANFORD DREWIT (MW)
354 Broadway (b)
Winnipeg, MB R3C 0T2
204-957-1640 / Fax: 204-956-2660
Sales: $1 Million-$10 Million
Website: www.hanforddrewit.ca
PAUL STILLER (Owner) & Buys Men's Big & Tall Apparel, Men's Apparel, Men's Casualwear, Men's Denim Apparel, Men's Formalwear, Men's Accessories, Men's Hosiery, Men's Outerwear, Men's Sportswear, Men's Suits, Men's Swimwear, Men's Sleepwear
PETER HENRY (Store Mgr.) & Buys Men's Big & Tall Apparel, Men's Apparel, Men's Casualwear, Men's Denim Apparel, Men's Formalwear, Men's Accessories, Men's Hosiery, Men's Outerwear, Men's Sportswear, Men's Suits, Men's Swimwear, Men's Sleepwear

MANITOBA - Winnipeg

SAAN STORES (DEPT-227 & KS-6)
(SAAN FOR KIDS)
P.O. Box 9400
1370 Sony Pl.
Winnipeg, MB R3C 3C3
204-474-5300 / Fax: 204-474-5216
Sales: $100 Million-$500 Million
Website: www.saan.ca
Retail Locations: AB, BC, MB, NF, NW, NS, ON, PE, PO, SK, YU, NB

A. COHEN (President & V.P.-Mdsg.)
NORM NOLAN (G.M.M.)
FRED PENNELL-Men's Tailored Slacks, Raincoats, Sweaters, Outer Jackets, Casual Slacks, Active Apparel, Denim Wear, Leather Apparel, T-shirts, Dress Slacks
JOE DRAUDE-Men's Ties, Robes, Underwear, Belts, Workwear, Rubber Rainsuits
DEBBIE RURARZ-8 to 18 Boys' Clothing, Boys' Outerwear, Boys' Underwear
SILVANO CENDOU-Boys' Footwear
AL DODD (D.M.M.-Footwear)
JOHN PERREIRA-Men's Footwear
CARI-LYN REBIZANT (Real Estate Contact)

V & S DEPARTMENT STORES (DEPT-667)
1530 Gamble Pl.
Winnipeg, MB R3T 1N6
204-453-9511 / Fax: 204-452-6615
Website: www.truserv.ca

LEO CHARRIER (C.E.O.)
CARRIE DIACOS-Men's Sportshirts, Outer Jackets, Casual Slacks, Active Apparel, Leather Apparel, T-shirts, Furnishings, Headwear, Belts, 8 to 16 Boys' Jeans, Footwear

JACK CALP'S MENSWEAR LTD. (MW)
8 Charlotte St. (p-m-b)
Saint John, NB E2L 2H4
506-634-8535 / Fax: 506-648-9808

NORMAN CALP (President) & Buys Men's Overcoats, Suits, Tailored Jackets, Tailored Slacks, Raincoats, Furnishings, Accessories
BONNIE CALP-Men's Sportswear, Overcoats, Suits, Tailored Jackets, Tailored Slacks, Raincoats, Furnishings, Accessories

WESCAL DEPARTMENT STORE (DEPT)
P.O. Box 310 (p-m)
Bay Roberts, NF A0A 1G0
709-786-2155 / Fax: 709-786-9369

CALVIN SPENCER (Owner)
DEBBIE YOUNG-Men's Raincoats, Sweaters, Active Apparel, Ties, Robes, Underwear, Hosiery, Gloves, Accessories, Men's & Boys' Footwear
EILEEN MARTIN-Men's Raincoats, Sweaters, Active Apparel, Ties, Robes, Underwear, Hosiery, Gloves, Accessories, Men's & Boys' Footwear

RIFF'S LTD. (DEPT-30)
2 Hardy Ave. (p-m)
Grand Fall Windsor, NF A2A 2P9
709-489-5631 / Fax: 709-489-7689
Retail Locations: CA

SANDRA WHITE (@ 709-468-2403)-Men's Footwear
IVAR RIFF (President & Real Estate Contact)
PAUL McDONALD-Men's Overcoats, Tailored Slacks, Tailored Jackets, Suits, Raincoats, Sportshirts, Outer Jackets, Casual Slacks, Active Apparel, Furnishings, Accessories

CHARM DIAMOND CENTRES (JWLY-65)
(CRESCENT GOLD & DIAMONDS)
140 Portland St.
Dartmouth, NS B2Y 1J1
902-463-7177 / Fax: 902-466-5472
Sales: $10 Million-$50 Million
Website: www.charmdiamondcenters.com
Retail Locations: NF, NS, ON, PE, NB

LAWRENCE HARTNETT-Jewelry
JIM MAHON-Jewelry
RICHARD D. CALDER (President) & Buys Jewelry, Watches
MARY RYAN (Real Estate Contact)
TROY CALDER-Watches

COLWELL BROTHERS, INC. (CLO-3)
P.O. Box 275 (b-des)
Halifax, NS B3J 2N7
902-423-7139 / Fax: 902-422-5483

ANDREW COLWELL (Owner) & Buys Men's Casual Clothing & Sportswear, Related Accessories & Furnishings
MARK CHERRY-Men's Casual Clothing & Sportswear, Related Accessories & Furnishings

MARITIME CAMPUS STORE LTD. (SP)
(UPAC)
6238 Quinpool Rd.
Halifax, NS B3L 1A3
902-423-6523 / Fax: 902-455-9777
Website: www.maritimecampusstore.promocan.com

LOUISE RIEDEL (Co-Owner) & Buys Activewear, Ski Apparel, Apparel, Swimwear
JURGEN RIEDEL (Co-Owner) & Buys Activewear, Ski Apparel, Apparel, Swimwear

SUPER TOUCH LTD. (CLO-4)
(ISLANDS)
116 King St. (bud-p-m)
North Sidney, NS B2A 3R7
902-794-4997 / Fax: 902-794-4997

JOHN MORRELL (G.M.M.)
MARIE McCORMICK-Men's & Boys' T-shirts, Swimwear

THE OLD MILL (CLO & MO)
P.O. Box 99 (bud-p-m-b-h)
Hwy. #4S
Blyth, ON N0M 1H0
519-523-4595 / Fax: 519-523-4565
Sales: $100,001-$500,000
Website: www.theoldmill.ca

GLENYCE SNELL (Owner) & Buys Men's Leather Apparel & Accessories, Footwear

BOLTON'S MENSWEAR (MW)
15 Allan Dr. (m-b)
Bolton, ON L7E 2B5
905-857-5383
Sales: $100,001-$500,000

JOHN SPANO (Owner) & Buys Men's & Young Men's Suits, Tailored Jackets, Tailored Slacks, Casuals, Denims, Sportswear, Active Apparel, Footwear

ROBBIE'S (SP)
83 Clarence St.
Brampton, ON L6W 1S5
905-451-1167 / Fax: 905-451-1179

ROBBIE KNARR (Owner)
TED KNAAR-Activewear, Licensed Apparel

ZELLER'S, INC. (DEPT-500)
(HUDSON'S BAY CO.)
8925 Torbram Rd. (p-m)
Brampton, ON L6T 4G1
905-792-4400 / Fax: 905-792-4730
Sales: $4.6 Billion
Website: www.zellers.com
Retail Locations: AB, BC, MB, NB, NF, NS, ON, PE, QC, SK

THOMAS HAIG (President & C.E.O.)
PAM DANIS (G.M.M.) (@ 905-792-4738)
SEAN MacDONALD (Sr. Buyer) & Buys Active Apparel, Sportswear, Shorts, Activeware, Licensed, Swimwear
JOHAN DuPLOOY (@ 905-792-4555)-Men's Overcoats, Outerwear, Raincoats, Denim
MICHAEL STASZAK (@ 905-792-4470)-Men's Ties, Belts, Dress Shirts, Accessories, Sleepwear, Workwear
MARY ANN MILIC (@ 905-792-4456)-Knits, Men's Sportswear, Sweaters, Casual Pants, Dress Pants
MIKE GEARY-Pants
KATRINA TUFFORD-Boys' Sportswear, Sleepwear-0-3x
ZENTA PASTINS (Asst. Buyer) & Buys Infant's Boys'-0-3x Layette
DENNIS FORTIER (Sr. Buyer) & Buys Men's Basics, Furnishings, Men's Underwear, Hosiery
JASETT KING (Asst. Buyer) & Buys Boys' Basics, Infants Accessories
LINA MARANDO (Sr. Buyer-Boys' Wear, Sleepwear & Outerwear)
JOSIE MATTHEWS (Asst. Buyer) & Buys Boys' Outerwear, Sleepwear 4-16
ANNTIONETTE MARINO (Asst. Buyer) & Buys Boys' Separates 4-16
OLGA BUCCIARELLI (Replenishment Analyst) & Buys Boys' Outerwear, Sleepwear, Accessories
ERIN ROIRDOM (Replenishment Analyst) & Buys Boys' Activewear, Separates & Licensed Departments
CARLOS MAIATO-Men's & Boys' Footwear

NORTH BY NORTHWEST (CLO-5 & OL)
7 Chamberlin Dr. (m)
Cambridge, ON N1T 1L8
519-621-9942 / Fax: 519-622-5936
Sales: $1 Million-$10 Million
Website: www.northbynorthwest.net

RUSS SIGURDSON (Owner) & Buys Men's Outer Jackets, Accessories, Footwear, Boys' Outer Jackets

BARCLAY'S STORE FOR MEN (MW-5)
(LAS BRISES CASUALS)
939 Lawrence Ave. East (m-b)
Don Mills, ON M3C 1P8
416-445-9219 / Fax: 416-445-3111
Sales: $100,001-$500,000

STEVEN FLOMEN (Co-Owner) & Buys Men's & Young Men's Suits, Tailored Jackets, Tailored Slacks, Raincoats, Overcoats, Dress Shirts & Accessories, Sportswear
AVRUM FLOMEN (Co-Owner) & Buys Men's & Young Men's Suits, Tailored Jackets, Tailored Slacks, Raincoats, Overcoats, Dress Shirts & Accessories, Sportswear

BATA (SP-158 & SG-93)
(ATHLETE'S WORLD)
(BATA)
2 Concorde Pl.
Don Mills, ON M3C 1K3
416-446-2020 / Fax: 416-446-2175
Website: www.bata.com
Retail Locations: ON, NF, NB, BC, AB, SW, SK, NT, PE, NS, QC, MB, YT

DAVE RICHER (V.P.-Mdsg.-Athletes World)
DAVID BLACK (Real Estate Contact)
BARRY WILLIAMS-Athletic Footwear
LIONEL SIMS (G.M.M.)
CHRIS NG-Activewear

TILLEY ENDURABLES (CLO-4 & MO & OL)
900 Don Mills Rd. (b)
Don Mills, ON M3C 1V6
416-441-6141 / Fax: 416-444-3866
Sales: $100,001-$500,000
Website: www.tilley.com

JEANNE SCHEUFLER-Men's Travel Apparel
RICKI KLORFINE-Travel Accessories

BIKINI BAY (CLO)
2 Ashwarren Rd.
Downsview, ON M3J 1Z5
416-638-8838 / Fax: 416-638-4843

LIDIA KISLIUK (Owner) & Buys Swimwear, Sandals

CANLY SHOES (FW-3)
4517 Chesswood Dr. (m-b)
Downsview, ON M3J 2V6
416-630-5802 / Fax: 416-631-9886
Sales: $1 Million-$10 Million

ESTHER BURSTEIN (Partner) & Buys Boys' Apparel, Boys' Footwear, Men's Footwear, Leather Goods, Men's Accessories
JACOB BURSTEIN (Partner) & Buys Boys' Apparel, Boys' Footwear, Men's Footwear, Leather Goods, Men's Accessories

TOWN SHOES LTD. (FW-63 & OL)
(SHOE CO.)
44 Kodiak Cres. (m-b)
Downsview, ON M3J 3G5
416-638-5011 / Fax: 416-638-3847
Sales: $50 Million-$100 Million
Website: www.theshoecompany.com
Retail Locations: BC, ON, SK

HARVEY ROUTBARD (President) & Buys Boys' Apparel, Boys' Footwear, Men's Footwear, Leather Goods, Men's Accessories, Men's Apparel, Hosiery
ALAN SIMPSON (C.O.O.)
PETER GERHARDT (Real Estate Contact)

BILL MILES' MEN'S FASHION LTD. (MW)
2966 Bloor West (m-b)
Etobicoke, ON M8X 1B7
416-239-4410
Sales: $100,001-$500,000

WILLIAM MILES (Owner) & Buys Men's Overcoats, Suits, Tailored Jackets, Slacks, Sportswear, Furnishings & Accessories
RON ORR (G.M.M.) & Buys Men's Overcoats, Suits, Tailored Jackets, Slacks, Sportswear, Furnishings & Accessories

MOORE'S CLOTHING FOR MEN (MW-113)
(THE MEN'S WAREHOUSE)
129 Carlingview Dr.
Etobicoke, ON M9W 5E7
416-798-8082 / Fax: 416-798-4662
Sales: $100,001-$500,000
Website: www.mooresclothing.com
Retail Locations: AB, ON, MB, BC

DAVE STARRETT (President)
DANNY ADDARIO-Men's Suits, Sportcoats, Blazers, Neckwear
MARIO CANDIDO-Men's Sportswear, Outerwear
BILL KINGSTON-Men's Dress & Casual Pants, Shorts, Footwear
RAY RIDEOUT-Men's Dress Shirts & Accessories

McTAGGART'S (CLO-9)
578 Scott St. (m)
Fort Frances, ON P9A 1H4
807-274-7706 / Fax: 807-274-9209
Sales: $1 Million-$10 Million

JOHN McTAGGART (President & G.M.M.)
RICHARD BOILEAU (D.M.M.)
ELLIE DEROWARD-Footwear
ALAN CAIN-Men's Suits, Tailored Jackets, Tailored Slacks, Raincoats, Sweaters, Outer Jackets, Casual Slacks, Active Apparel, Accessories, 8 to 18 Boys' Wear

BIG & TALL MEN'S SHOP BY GILBERT (MW)
439 King West (bud-p-m-b-h)
Hamilton, ON L8P 1B8
905-528-8238 / Fax: 905-528-4158
Sales: $100 Million-$500 Million
Website: www.bigtallxtall.com
STELLA LAZICH (Co-Owner)
GILBERT LAZICH (Co-Owner) & Buys Big & Tall Men's Wear, Footwear
TED LAZICH (Dir.- e-Commerce)
TOM LAZICH (G.M.M.) & Buys Suits, Tailored Jackets & Slacks, Raincoats, Big & Tall Wear, Sweaters, Sport Shirts, Outer Jackets, Active Apparel, Furnishings, Dress Shirts, Ties, Robes, Underwear, Hosiery, Gloves, Headwear, Accessories, Belts, Store Displays, Fixtures and Supplies

HOUSE OF GOLD JEWELERS (SP-4)
117 Main St. East
Hawkesbury, ON K6A 1A1
613-632-8892 / Fax: 613-632-5225
Sales: $1 Million-$10 Million
Website: www.hardensjewelers.com
WILLIAM F. HARDEN (President) & Buys Jewelry, Watches

LIMESTONE & IVY (CLO-3)
(FANCY THAT)
48-50 Princess St. (m-b)
Kingston, ON K7L 1A4
613-549-4489 / Fax: 613-531-9358
Sales: $100,001-$500,000
INGER SPARRING (Owner)
DAN SPARRING (@ 613-342-5631)-Men's & Young Men's Footwear

STAR MEN'S SHOPS (MW-3)
213 King St. West (m)
Kitchener, ON N2G 1B1
519-744-5271 / Fax: 519-744-5273
Sales: $1 Million-$10 Million
GORDON STRAUSS (Owner) & Buys Men's Tailored Suits, Jackets, Slacks, Raincoats, Overcoats, Casual Slacks, Sportswear, Dress Shirts, Ties, Robes, Underwear, Hosiery, Belts, Young Men's Contemporary Wear

LOGO SPORTS, INC. (SP)
1105 Wellington Rd. South
London, ON N6E 1V4
519-649-1850 / Fax: 519-657-4145
PETER SMITH (Co-Owner) & Buys Licensed Apparel
PAT SMITH (Co-Owner) & Buys Licensed Apparel

RUNNER'S CHOICE (SP)
207 Dundas St.
London, ON N6A 1G4
519-672-5928 / Fax: 519-672-2761
Website: www.runnerschoice.on.ca
PAUL ROBERTS (Owner) & Buys Activewear, Athletic Footwear

KNOT SHOP (MW-13)
145 Renfrew Dr., #130 (m-b-des)
Markham, ON L3R 9R6
905-470-6290 / Fax: 905-479-2546
Sales: $1 Million-$10 Million
Website: www.tie-rack.com
ROY BISHKO (President)
JUDY PAUL (V.P.)
RANDY BROWN-Men's Apparel, Accessories

RUNNING FREE (SP-3)
708 Denison St.
Markham, ON L3R 1C1
905-477-7871 / Fax: 905-477-9447
Website: www.runningfree.ca
NICK CAPPA (Co-Owner) & Buys Activewear, Athletic Footwear, Apparel
JOHN POSCA (Co-Owner) & Buys Activewear, Athletic Footwear, Apparel

TRI MARK (SP)
8688 Woodbine Ave.
Markham, ON L3R 8B9
905-475-1712 / Fax: 800-668-8605
Website: www.trimarksportswear.com
NANCY LAM (@ Ext. 301)-Activewear, Sportswear

TUXEDO ROYALE (MW-16)
185 Konrad Crescent
Markham, ON L3R 8T9
905-474-0304 / Fax: 905-474-1697
Website: www.tuxedoroyale.com
IVAN J. ZICHY (President)
KEVIN SLANEY (V.P.) & Buys Men's Formal Wear, Furnishings, Accessories, Footwear

UNIVERSITY CLASS (CLO)
234 Hood Rd. (m)
Markham, ON L3R 3K8
905-479-9929 / Fax: 905-940-9180
Sales: $100,001-$500,000
MR. MAKOS (Opers. Mgr.) & Buys Men's & Boys' Casual Wear, Active Apparel

ELEGANT FASHIONS, INC. (CLO)
900 Rathburn Rd. West, # D2 (m)
Mississuaga, ON L5C 4L4
905-897-0233 / Fax: 905-554-2814
Sales: $100,001-$500,000
MRS. SATI SEEPERSAUD (Owner) & Buys 4 to 17 Boys' Casual Wear, Active Apparel

KIDDIE KOBBLER LTD. (FW-25)
68 Roberson Rd., # 106 (m-b)
Nepean, ON K2H 8P5
613-820-0505 / Fax: 613-820-8250
Sales: $1 Million-$10 Million
Retail Locations: CA, ON, QC
FRED NORMAN (President) & Buys Boys' Apparel, Boys' Footwear, Licensed Apparel, Sporting Goods
CARMEN MACALUSO (V.P.) & Buys Boys' Apparel, Boys' Footwear, Licensed Apparel, Sporting Goods

ANDRE FOR MEN (MW)
5150 Yonge St. (b)
North York, ON M2N 6N2
416-250-7411
Sales: $100,001-$500,000
J. LEE (Owner) & Buys Men's Dress & Casual Wear, Accessories

BROWN'S (CLO-2)
(BROWN'S SHORT MAN)
1975 Avenue Rd. (b)
North York, ON M5M 4A3
416-489-1975 / Fax: 416-485-3155
Website: www.shortmanbrown.com
LOU BROWN (Owner) & Buys Men's Clothing, Accessories, Shoes
GERRY GINSBERG-Men's Clothing, Accessories, Shoes

JORDAN'S APPAREL (MW)
2501 Steeles Ave. West (p)
North York, ON M3J 2P1
416-667-1175
Sales: $100,001-$500,000
LEWIS JORDAN (Owner) & Buys Men's Sportswear, Accessories, Boys' Wear, Young Men's Wear

SI VOUS PLAY SPORTS (SP-6)
1 Yorkgate Blvd.
North York, ON M3N 3A1
416-650-5665 / Fax: 416-650-5658
FRANK COLAROSSI (Owner) & Buys Activewear, Athletic Footwear, Licensed Apparel

SYD SILVER FORMALS (MW-16)
79 Wingold Ave. (b-h)
North York, ON M6B 1P8
416-256-4784 / Fax: 416-256-3005
Sales: $100,001-$500,000
Website: www.sydsilver.com
MICHAEL SILVER (President)
SAL CAIRA (G.M.M.) & Buys Men's Formal Wear & Related Accessories, Footwear, Furnishings

BURROWS' (MW)
200 Lakeshore Rd. East
Oakville, ON L6J 1H6
905-842-0232 / Fax: 905-842-0548
Sales: $100,001-$500,000
Website: www.burrowsclothiers.com
RONALD BURROWS (President) & Buys Men's Overcoats, Suits, Tailored Jackets, Tailored Slacks, Raincoats, Sportswear, Furnishings, Headwear, Accessories, Footwear

E.R. FISHER LTD. (MW-2)
113 Sparks St. Mall
Ottawa, ON K1P 5B5
613-232-9636 / Fax: 613-232-4560
Sales: $100,001-$500,000
TONY FISHER (Owner)
PETER FISHER-Men's Overcoats, Suits, Tailored Jackets, Tailored Slacks, Raincoats, Sweaters, Sportshirts, Outer Jackets, Leather Apparel, Casual Slacks, Dress Shirts, Ties Robes, Underwear, Hosiery, Gloves

PUERTA DEL SOL (CLO)
335 Cumberland (b)
Ottawa, ON K1N 7J3
613-789-4372 / Fax: 613-789-2895
Sales: $100,001-$500,000
TANYA CAPPELLETTO (Owner) & Buys Men's & Boys' T-shirts, Swimwear, Active Apparel, Footwear

LIPSON'S STORES (CLO-2)
289 Main St. (p-m)
Picton, ON K0K 2T0
613-476-6080 / Fax: 613-476-5975
Sales: $100,001-$500,000
JOHN DAVID LIPSON (Owner) & Buys Men's & Young Men's Suits, Tailored Slacks, Coats, Sportswear, Furnishings, Boys' Casual Wear, Footwear

FRASER'S CLOTHES SHOPS (CLO-5 & OL)
P.O. Box 550 (b)
Renfrew, ON K7V 4B1
613-432-2211 / Fax: 613-432-8193
Sales: $1 Million-$10 Million
Website: www.frasersclothesshops.com
MIKE WALSH (G.M.M.) & Buys Men's Sportswear, Furnishings, Accessories, 6 to 18 Boys' Sportswear, Clothing, Furnishings, Accessories, Footwear
DOUG COLLINS-Men's Suits, Tailored Jackets, Tailored Slacks

ARLIE'S SPORT SHOP (SP)
(BOATHOUSE ROW)
188 Bunting Rd.
Saint Catharines, ON L2M 3Y1
905-684-8134 / Fax: 905-684-4142
ARLIE KATZMAN (Owner) & Buys Downhill Skiing Apparel
ROSS GARLICK (Gen. Mgr.)
JAMIE KATZMAN-Athletic Footwear
WARREN BURGER-Skiwear, Activewear, Licensed Apparel

QUICK STEP (SP)
285 Saint Paul St.
Saint Catharines, ON L2R 3M8
905-685-3988
ED JANG (Mgr.) & Buys Activewear, Athletic Footwear, Licensed Apparel

MUGFORD LTD. (FW-4)
(COPPERFIELDS)
(MUGFORD SHOES)
429 Talbot St. (m-b)
Saint Thomas, ON N5P 1C1
519-631-0755 / Fax: 519-633-9029
Sales: $1 Million-$10 Million
DONALD MUGFORD (President)
MERLE MUGFORD-Men's Footwear, Leather Goods, Accessories, Apparel

EURO VERVE CO. LTD. (RB)
2360 Midland Ave., #5 (m-b)
Scarborough, ON M1S 1P8
416-321-6235 / Fax: 416-321-6879
Sales: $100,001-$500,000
ALAN HO (Managing Director) & Buys Men's Active Apparel, Casual Apparel, Athletic Apparel, Sweaters

JEAN MACHINE (CLO-33)
(SUNRISE RECORDS)
4069 Gordon Baker Rd. (p)
Scarborough, ON M1W 2P3
416-498-6601
Sales: $100,001-$500,000
Website: www.jeanmachine.com
Retail Locations: QC, ON
ROY S. PERLMAN (Owver) & Buys Young-Men's Denim Pants, Jackets, Belts, Hosiery, Headwear
MALCOLM H. PERLMAN (President)
PERRY WOODMAN (Real Estate Contact)

LIGHTMAN'S (MW)
3270 Danforth Ave. (p)
Scarborough, ON M1L 1C3
416-694-6967 / Fax: 416-694-6967
KEN LIGHTMAN (Owner) & Buys Men's Work Clothes, Work Shoes

SPORTS FANTASY (SP-2)
300 Borough Dr.
Scarborough, ON M1P 4P5
416-296-0194 / Fax: 416-296-0857
Sales: $1 Million-$10 Million
Website: www.sportsfantasyinc.com
ANGELO IOANNIDES (Owner) & Buys Activewear, Licensed Apparel

ANTHONY MENSWEAR & IMPORTED SHOES (MW & FW)
ANDREW'S FORMAL WEAR
1558 Eglinton West (b-h)
Toronto, ON M6E 2G8
416-789-4913 / Fax: 416-783-8181
Sales: $100,001-$500,000
Website: www.andrewsformals.com
ANTHONY ALAMPI (Owner) & Buys Men's & Boys' Formal Wear, Footwear
NICK ALAMPI-Men's & Boys' Formal Wear, Footwear

ONTARIO - Toronto

THE BAY DEPARTMENT STORES (DEPT-99)
(Div. of HUDSON'S BAY CO.)
401 Bay St., 7th Fl. (p-m-b)
Toronto, ON M5H 2Y4
416-861-6437 / Fax: 416-861-6538
Sales: $2.6 Billion
Website: www.hbc.com
Retail Locations: AB, BC, MB, NB, NS, ON, QC, SK

GEORGE J. HELLER (President & C.E.O.-Hudson's Bay Co.)
MARC CHOUINARD (President & C.E.O.-The Bay) (@ 416-861-4809)
ROB CANNON (G.M.M.-Men's & Children's)
TONY WALDRON-Men's Collections, Formal Wear, Accessories
WAYNE KRZYZEWSKI-Men's Suits, Tailored Jackets
MARK PITTMAN-Mens Ties, Dress Shirts
TERRI McMENANIN-Men's Robes, Hosiery, Pajamas, Underwear

KAREN ADAMS (D.M.M.- Young Men's Collections)
TONY WALDRON-Young Men's Accessories, Separates, Budget
GARY McCRIGHT-Young Men's Wear, Activewear, Denim

IAN BAILLIE (D.M.M.-Men's Sportswear)
BOB CASEY-Men's Casual Outerwear, Casual Slacks, Dockers, Budget Pants & Outerwear, Denims, Dress Slacks
JIM MONTERIO-Men's Sportswear, Separates, Budget Sportswear, Fleecewear, Men's Sweaters, Swimwear, Budget Sweaters & Swimwear
VIC SCHGAL-Men's Collections
JOEL BRANCH-Men's Moderate & Better, Sportswear Collection

DES BRADY (G.M.M.-Men's Footwear & Boys)
ANDREW VASARINSH-Men's & Boys' Seasonal Footwear
DUANE McFARLAND-Men's Footwear

DAVID AMEN (D.M.M.-Boys' Wear)
ANJU MENON-7 to 16 Boys' Wear

EDGAR CHAU (Visual Presentation) & Buys Store Displays, Fixtures and Supplies
ANN SHAW (Real Estate Contact) (@ 416-861-4822)

BEATTIE'S (MW-2 & KS & OL)
430 Eglinton Ave. West (m-b)
Toronto, ON M5M 1A2
416-481-4459 / Fax: 416-481-6837
Sales: $100,001-$500,000
Website: www.beattiesonline.com

DAVID HADDEN (Owner) & Buys Men's Sportswear, Furnishings & Accessories, Boys' Wear & Accessories, Footwear, School Uniforms

BELLISSIMO (MW)
882 Eglinton Ave. West (b)
Toronto, ON M6C 2B6
416-782-4780 / Fax: 416-781-5739
Sales: $500,001-$1 Million
Website: www.bellissimomensclothier.com

TONY BELLISSIMO (Owner) & Buys Men's Sportswear, Furnishings & Accessories, Young Men's Wear, Footwear

BOOMER (MW)
309 Queen St. West (m)
Toronto, ON M5V 2A4
416-598-0013

DAN MOLENAAR (Co-Owner) & Buys Men's Sportswear, Furnishings & Accessories, Young Men's Wear
DIANE MOLENAAR (Co-Owner) & Buys Men's Sportswear, Furnishings & Accessories, Young Men's Wear

BRAND'S OF TORONTO (MW)
2095 Yonge St. (bud-p)
Toronto, ON M4S 2A4
416-489-7644
Sales: $100,001-$500,000

SIMON BRAND (Owner) & Buys Men's Sportswear, Furnishings & Accessories, Young Men's Wear

THE BRICK SHIRT HOUSE LTD. (SP)
112 Cumberland St. (m-b)
Toronto, ON M5R 1A6
416-964-7021 / Fax: 416-964-7021
Sales: $500,001-$1 Million

ALAN GOOUCH (President) & Buys Leather Goods, Men's Apparel, Men's Big & Tall Apparel, Men's Casualwear, Men's Designer Apparel, Men's Formalwear, Men's Accessories, Men's Hosiery, Men's Sportswear
DEBORAH GOOUCH (V.P.) & Buys Leather Goods, Men's Apparel, Men's Big & Tall Apparel, Men's Casualwear, Men's Designer Apparel, Men's Formalwear, Men's Accessories, Men's Hosiery, Men's Sportswear

CASA LANALGO (CLO)
715 College (m-b)
Toronto, ON M6G 1C2
416-536-4393 / Fax: 416-536-9396

CARLOS LANALGO (Owner) & Buys Men's Sportswear, Accessories, Young Men's Wear, Boys' Wear & Accessories

CLUB MONACO (CLO-80 & OL)
(Div. of RALPH LAUREN)
430 King St. West (p-m-b)
Toronto, ON M5V 1L5
416-585-4101 / Fax: 416-585-4176
Website: www.clubmonaco.com
Retail Locations: BC, MB, NS, ON, QC

JOHN MEHAS (President)
TERESA McGUIRE (Dir.-Men's Product Dev.)
MIKE McGOWAN (Mdse. Mgr.) & Buys Men's Fleecewear, Knits,Tops,Sweaters
PAUL YUN-SANJ-Men's Outerwear, Coats, Sports Shirts, Denim, Casual Slack, Young Men's, Blazers,Tailored Slacks
GENE MESSINA (Real Estate Contact) (@ 201-531-6684)

THE COOP (MW)
3287 Yonge St. (b)
Toronto, ON M4N 2L8
416-544-9944 / Fax: 416-544-1425
Sales: $100,001-$500,000
Website: www.cooping.com

JOHN CORALLO (President) & Buys Men's Sportswear, Furnishings, Accessories, Young Men's Wear
VEV KLINE (Secy.) & Buys Men's Sportswear, Furnishings, Accessories, Young Men's Wear

CRAWFORD'S CLOTHES LTD. (KS)
508 Lawrence Ave. West, #A (m-b)
Toronto, ON M6A 1A1
416-782-8137 / Fax: 416-916-5127

PAUL SPIER (Owner) & Buys Boys' Clothing, Sportswear, Furnishings, Young Men's Wear

GRAFTON - FRASER, INC. (MW-241)
(JACK FRASER)
(TIMBERLAND)
(TIP TOP TAILOR)
(GEORGE RICHARDS)
(GRAFTON & CO.)
(MR. BIG & TALL)
(THE SUIT EXCHANGE)
44 Apex Rd. (m-b-des)
Toronto, ON M6A 2V2
416-780-9922 / Fax: 416-780-2158
Sales: $100 Million-$500 Million

GLENN STONEHOUSE (Owner & C.E.O.)
BOB CHRISTIE (Real Estate Contact)
MEL McLEAN (Gen. Mgr. & G.M.M.-George Richards, Mr. Big & Tall)
MIKE KOSMYNKA (Gen. Mgr.-Suit Exchange)
MICHAEL WAITZER (Gen. Mgr.-Tip Top Tailor)
NORM COOPER (G.M.M.-Mr. Big & Tall, George Richards)
CHRIS CAMERON (G.M.M.-Grafton & Co.)
BARRIE REID (G.M.M.-Jack Fraser)

ONTARIO - Toronto

HARRY DAVID LTD. (MW)

220 Augusta Ave. (bud-p)
Toronto, ON M5T 2L6
416-593-9719 / Fax: 416-593-8747

JACK CARRUSCA (Owner) & Buys Men's Work Clothes, Denims, T-shirts, Accessories, Footwear

HARRY ROSEN (MW-17)

77 Bloor St. West, #1600 (b-h)
Toronto, ON M5S 1M2
416-935-9200 / Fax: 416-515-7067
Website: www.harryrosen.com

HARRY ROSEN (Exec. Chairman) (@ 416-935-9202)
LAURENCE ROSEN (Chmn. & C.E.O.)
PETER STANSFIELD (President & C.O.O.)
JEFF FARBSTEIN (G.M.M. & V.P.)

HARRIET GOODMAN (Mdse. Mgr.) & Buys Men's Sportswear, Outerwear
DAVID VOSKO (Mdse. Mgr.) & Buys Footwear, Ties, Dress Shirts, Hosiery, Belts, Jewelry, Small Leather Goods, Fragrances
VIKASH BHATTI-Overcoats
SHANNON STEWART-Sweaters

GREG HELPS (National Display Mgr.) & Buys Store, Displays, Fixtures, Supplies
MARK TEIXEIRA (Store Planning & Design) & Buys Store, Displays, Fixtures, Supplies

HIGHER GROUND CLOTHING LTD. (CLO)

2488 Yonge St.
Toronto, ON M4P 2H5
416-486-2488

KEVIN ROHER (Owner) & Buys Skiwear, Hiking Apparel
GREG SNODDY (Mgr.) & Buys Skiwear, Hiking Apparel

HOLT RENFREW & CO. LTD. (CLO-10)

60 Bloor St. West, #300 (m-b-h)
Toronto, ON M4W 3B8
416-922-2333 / Fax: 416-922-3240
Sales: $100 Million-$500 Million
Website: www.holtrenfrew.com

CHRIS JAMUF-Men's Designer Clothing, Sportswear, Men's Branded Clothing & Sportswear, Men's Demin
SARAH ATTETTURE-Men's Accessories, Furnishings, Private Label Clothing, Intimates, Gifts,
Robes, Underwear, Hosiery, Belts, Gloves
DON MAH-Men's Outerwear, Private Label Sportswear
SHELLEY ROZENWALD (V.P. & G.M.M.-Fragrances)
ANNA MARIA ALONZO-Men's Fragrances

HUDSON'S BAY CO. (DEPT-50 & OL)

(ZELLERS)
(THE BAY)
(FIELDS)
(HBC OUTFITTERS)
401 Bay St., #700
Toronto, ON M5H 2Y4
416-861-6112 / Fax: 416-861-4334
Sales: Over $7 Billion
Website: www.hbc.com
Retail Locations: AB, BC, MB, NB, NF, NS, ON, QC, SK

GEORGE J. HELLER (President & C.E.O.)
MARC CHOUINARD (President & C.O.O.-The Bay)
THOMAS HAIG (President & C.O.O.-Zellers)
DON RODGER (V.P.-Real Estate) (@ 416-861-6976)

INTERNATIONAL CLOTHIERS, INC. (MW-120)

111 Orfus Rd. (m)
Toronto, ON M6A 1M4
416-785-1771 / Fax: 416-785-9156
Sales: $10 Million-$50 Million
Website: www.internationalclothiers.com

ISSAC BENNETT (Chmn. & President & Real Estate Contact) & Buys Boys' Apparel, Leather Goods, Men's Apparel, Men's Casualwear, Men's Denim Apparel, Men's Formalwear, Men's Outerwear, Men's Sportswear, Men's Suits
DONNA EDWARD-Boys' Apparel, Leather Goods, Men's Apparel, Men's Casualwear, Men's Denim Apparel, Men's Formalwear, Men's Outerwear, Men's Sportswear, Men's Suits

JEROME'S GENTLEMEN'S APPAREL (MW)

2480 Yonge St. (b-des)
Toronto, ON M4P 2H5
416-489-2494 / Fax: 416-489-2531

JEROME STARR (President) & Buys Men's Overcoats, Suits, Tailored Jackets, Tailored Slacks, Raincoats, Sportswear, Furnishings, Accessories, Footwear, Store, Displays, Fixtures, Supplies

KINGSPORT CLOTHIER TO EXTRA TALL OR LARGER MEN (MW)

243 Eglinton Ave. West (m-b)
Toronto, ON M4R 1B1
416-482-2803 / Fax: 416-482-2289
Sales: $1 Million-$10 Million
Website: www.kingsport-bigandtall.com

L. FREEDMAN (President) & Buys Big & Tall Men's Overcoats, Suits, Tailored Jackets, Tailored Slacks, Raincoats, Sweaters, Sportshirts, Outer Jackets, Casual Slacks, T-shirts, Dress Slacks, Ties, Robes, Underwear, Hosiery, Gloves, Headwear, Belts, Small Leather Goods, Store, Displays, Fixtures, Supplies
HERSCH FREEDMAN (V.P.) & Buys Big & Tall Men's Overcoats, Suits, Tailored Jackets, Tailored Slacks, Raincoats, Sweaters, Sportshirts, Outer Jackets, Casual Slacks, T-shirts, Dress Slacks, Ties, Robes, Underwear, Hosiery, Gloves, Headwear, Belts, Small Leather Goods, Store, Displays, Fixtures, Supplies

KORRY'S CLOTHIERS (MW)

569 Danforth Ave. (b-des)
Toronto, ON M4K 1P9
416-463-1115 / Fax: 416-463-1880
Sales: $1 Million-$10 Million
Website: www.korrys.com

SAUL KORMAN (Owner & President) & Buys Men's Sportswear, Furnishings, Accessories, Young Men's Wear, Store Displays, Fixtures & Supplies

MARC LAURENT (CLO)

151 Bloor St. West (b-h)
Toronto, ON M5S 1S4
416-928-9124 / Fax: 416-928-0039
Sales: $1 Million-$10 Million
Website: www.marclaurent.com

MILA BENDAYAN (President) & Buys Men's Overcoats, Suits, Tailored Jackets, Tailored Slacks, Raincoats, Men's Sportswear, Sweaters, Sportshirts, Outer Jackets, Casual Slacks, Jeans, T-shirts, Leather Apparel, Dress Slacks, Ties, Gloves, Hosiery, Belts, Footwear, Store, Displays, Fixtures, Supplies
GREG MADESKER-Men's Overcoats, Suits, Tailored Jackets, Tailored Slacks, Raincoats, Men's Sportswear, Sweaters, Sportshirts, Outer Jackets, Casual Slacks, Jeans, T-shirts, Leather Apparel, Dress Slacks, Ties, Gloves, Hosiery, Belts, Footwear, Store, Displays, Fixtures, Supplies

NEW YORK, NEW YORK (MW)

123 Queen St. West (m)
Toronto, ON M5H 2M9
416-364-1791 / Fax: 416-364-5073

NAT MANSOUR (Owner) & Buys Men's Overcoats, Tailored Jackets, Tailored Slacks, Raincoats, Sportswear, Furnishings, Accessories, Footwear

ONTARIO - Toronto

OVER THE RAINBOW (MW)

101 Yorkville Ave. (m-b-h)
Toronto, ON M5R 1C1
416-967-7448 / Fax: 416-968-2457

JOEL CARMEN (Owner) & Buys Men's Wear, Young Men's Wear, Urban Contemporary, Sportswear

PACE ACHESON CLOTHIERS (MW)

BCE Pl. (m-b-h)
181 Bay St.
Toronto, ON M5J 2T3
416-361-0211 / Fax: 416-361-0156
Sales: $1 Million-$10 Million

DAVID PACE (President) & Buys Men's Overcoats, Suits, Tailored Jackets, Tailored Slacks, Raincoats, Sportswear, Furnishings, Headwear, Accessories, Store Displays, Fixtures, Supplies

SALVATI MENSWEAR, INC. (MW)

138 Cumberland (b-h)
Toronto, ON M5R 1A6
416-961-3309 / Fax: 416-961-4052
Sales: $1 Million-$10 Million
Website: www.salvati.ca

JOHN SALVATI (President) & Buys Men's Overcoats, Suits, Tailored Jackets, Tailored Slacks, Raincoats, Sportswear, Dress Slacks, Ties, Belts, Fragrances, Footwear, Store, Displays, Fixtures, Supplies

SEARS CANADA, INC. (DEPT-117)

222 Jarvis St. (p-m)
Toronto, ON M5B 2B8
416-362-1711 / Fax: 416-941-2501
Sales: Over $1 Billion
Website: www.sears.ca
Retail Locations: AB, BC, MB, NB, NS, NF, ON, QC, SK

MARK COHEN (Chmn. & C.E.O.)
KEN NIXON (V.P. & Real Estate Contact) (@ 416-941-3774)
GLEN COOK-Men's Formal Wear
MARK MILANDU-Men's Accessories
SUZANNE SPERLING-Men's Activewear, Swimwear
PANSY WATSON-Men's Sportswear, Outerwear
DINO FINELLI-Men's Footwear
MIKE NIELSON-Boys' Activewear, Swimwear
FRANK CHOUINARU-Size 8-18 Boys' Wear
TERRY SKINNER-Boys' Footwear

WALTER BEAUCHAMP TAILORS LTD. (MW)

145 Wellington West (b-h)
Toronto, ON M5J 1H8
416-595-5454 / Fax: 416-595-7087
Website: www.walterbeauchamp.com

TERRY BEAUCHAMP (Owner) & Buys Men's Tailored Suits, Tailored Jackets, Tailored Slacks, Custom Dress Shirts & Accessories
MARY McGUIGAN-Men's Tailored Suits, Tailored Jackets, Tailored Slacks, Custom Dress Shirts & Accessories

EDDIE BAUER, INC. (CLO-39 & MO & OL)

(Div. of SPIEGEL OF CANADA)
201 Aviva Park Dr.
Vaughan, ON L4L 9C1
905-851-6700 / Fax: 905-851-6437
Website: www.eddiebauer.com
Retail Locations: AB, BC, MB, NB, NF, NS, SK, Japan, Germany

RICK FERSCH (President)
MARK COMSTOCK (Real Estate Contact) (@ 905-851-4859)
MARK BLACKWELL (Real Estate Contact) (@ 425-755-6100)
NOTE-All Buying Is Performed at Eddie Bauer In Seattle, WA-See Listing

G.H. DECHENE & FILS, INC. (CLO-5)

4080 Blvd. St. Anne (bud-p)
Beauport, QC G1C 2J3
418-667-0801 / Fax: 418-667-0143
Sales: $1 Million-$10 Million

ERIC DECHENE (President) & Buys Casual Slacks, Sportswear, Footwear

LES BOUTIQUES SAN FRANCISCO, INC. (CLO-150 & KS-19 & DEPT-4)

(Div. of SAN FRANCISCO GROUP)
(FRISCO)
(LES AILES DE LA MODE)
(SAN FRANCISCO MAILLOTS)
(WEST COAST)
50 Rue De Lauzon (bud-p-m-b-h)
Boucherville, QC J4B 1E6
450-449-1313 / Fax: 450-449-1317
Sales: $200 Million
Website: www.bsf.ca
Retail Locations: QC, NF, BC

PAUL DeLAGE ROBERGE (President & C.E.O.)
CAMILLE ROBERGE (V.P.)
JULIEN HOULE (V.P.)
MICHELLE GENEREUX (Dir.-West Coast)
MONIQUE PARENT (Dir.-Frisco)

PANTORAMA INDUSTRIES, INC. (CLO-207)

(VINTAGE BLUE)
(ROBERTO)
(AUTHENTIC LEVIS)
(LEVIS)
(Di GALA)
(1850 LEVIS)
2 Lake Rd.
Dollard Des Ormeaux, QC H9B 3H9
514-421-1850 / Fax: 514-684-3159
Website: www.pantorama.com
Retail Locations: AB, NB, NF, NS, ON, QC

ROBERT WEXLER (Chmn.)
SIDNEY APTACKER (President) & Buys Men's Sweaters, Sportcoats, Outer Jackets, Denim, Casual Slacks, Hosiery
JACQUES BOUZAGLOU-Men's Footwear
MYETTE VINCENT-Men's Sweaters, Sportcoats, Outer Jackets, Denim, Casual Slacks, Hosiery
SOL STRINGFIELD (Real Estate Contact)

CAVEAU DES JEANS LTEE. (CLO-20)

84 Lois St.
Hull, QC J8Y 3R4
819-777-7670 / Fax: 819-777-8889
Website: www.caveaudesjeans.ca
Retail Locations: QC

MARIO LANTHIER (Owner) & Buys Men's Apparel, Sportswear, Accessories, Furnishings

LE JEAN BLEU, INC. (CLO-57)

1895 46th Ave.
Lachine, QC H8T 2N9
514-631-3300 / Fax: 514-631-3553
Website: www.jeanbleu.com

ALLAN BERLACH (President)
JANE COLTON-Men's & Young Men's Denim Shirts, Pants, Sweaters, Outer Jackets, Active Apparel, T-shirts, Hosiery, Headwear, Belts, Footwear

A. GOLD & SONS LTD. (CLO-10)

2050 Rue DeBleury St., #100
Montreal, QC H3A 2N9
514-288-4653 / Fax: 514-288-6804

MICHAEL GOLD (Managing Dir.)
PIERRE PELTIER-Men's Tailored Jackets, Tailored Slacks
SYLVIAN HINSE-Men's Sportswear
GAIL GOLD-Ties, Neckwear
JULIE TREMBLAY-Men's Belts, Hosiery
PIERRE LEGAULT-Men's Footwear

BOUTIQUE ENDURANCE (SP)

6579 Saint Denis St.
Montreal, QC H2S 2S1
514-272-9267 / Fax: 514-272-2252
Website: www.endurance.montreal.ca

PIERRE LEVEILLE (Owner) & Buys Activewear, Athletic Footwear

BOUTIQUE NRJ (CLO)
1382 St. Catherine West
Montreal, QC H3G 1P8
514-875-6464 / Fax: 514-875-6868
MOSHE SIMHON (Owner) & Buys Men's & Boys' Denim, Levis
MAYER BEZKIN (President) & Buys Men's & Boys' Denim, Levis

CLASSY FORMAL WEAR (MW-57)
8211 17th Ave.
Montreal, QC H1Z 4J9
514-728-6200 / Fax: 514-728-9850
Website: www.classy.ca
Retail Locations: AB, NS, MB, ON, QC, NB, BC
WILLIAM JAHNKE (President & Real Estate Contact)
BARBARA PRANKE (Mdse. Mgr.) & Buys Men's Formal Wear & Related Accessories, Footwear, 8 to 16 Boys' Formal Wear & Accessories, Footwear

ERNEST & JONATHAN (MW-36)
9200 Meilleur, #101 (m)
Montreal, QC H2N 2A9
514-858-5258 / Fax: 514-858-5255
Website: www.ernest.ca
Retail Locations: AB, BC, MB, NB, NF, NS, NT, ON, QC, PE, SK
GILLES CALESTAGNE-Men's & Young Men's Suits, Sportswear, Furnishings, Headwear, Accessories
ERNEST MARTIN (Real Estate Contact)

JEANS EXPERTS (CLO-27)
5000 Buchan St., # 501 (p)
Montreal, QC H4P 1T2
514-731-7146 / Fax: 514-731-6994
Sales: $10 Million-$50 Million
Website: www.jeansexperts.com
JACOB CRUDO (President)
ANNETTE CRUDO (V.P.)
SHARONA CRUDO (Secy.) & Buys Men's & Young Men's Denim Shirts, Jackets, Pants, Sweaters, Sportswear, 8 to 18 Boys' Wear

JOSEPH SHAMIE & FILS, LTEE. (CLO)
3921 Ontario St. East
Montreal, QC H1W 1S8
514-527-2477 / Fax: 514-527-2478
RAYMOND SHAMIE (Co- Owner) & Buys Men's Overcoats, Suits, Tailored Jackets, Tailored Slacks, Raincoats, Sportswear, Furnishings, Headwear, 8 to 16 Boys' Wear
MICHAEL SHAMIE (Co-Owner) & Buys Men's Overcoats, Suits, Tailored Jackets, Tailored Slacks, Raincoats, Sportswear, Furnishings, Headwear, 8 to 16 Boys' Wear

LE CHATEAU (MW-150)
5695 Ferrier St. (bud-p-m)
Montreal, QC H4P 1N1
514-738-7000 / Fax: 514-342-0851
Sales: $161 Million
Website: www.lechateau.ca
Retail Locations: NB, NF, NS, NT, ON, QC, SK, YT
JANE SILVERSTONE SEGAL (President)
FRANCO ROCCHI (V.P.-Sales)
BARBARA POSIEWCO-Men's Wear
ENRICO DESY-Men's Shoes
LEE ALBERT (Real Estate Contact) (@ 514-843-8417, Ext.: 257)

LES VETEMENTS TATOO CLOTHING, INC. (MW-15)
(USA)
(OMBRE)
488 Montpellier (m)
Montreal, QC H4N 2G7
514-747-4720 / Fax: 514-747-9345
Sales: $1 Million-$10 Million
ALLAN BRAND (President & Real Estate Contact) & Buys Men's Overcoats, Suits, Tailored Jackets, Tailored Slacks, Raincoats, Sportswear, Furnishings, Headwear, Belts

NEON CLOTHING COMPANY OF CANADA, INC. (MW)
6565 St. Hubert St.
Montreal, QC H2S 2M5
514-274-1221 / Fax: 514-274-8590
IRVING TAJFEL (Owner) & Buys Men's Sportswear, Accessories, Furnishings
MARSHA BERMAN-Men's Sportswear, Accessories, Furnishings

OLD RIVER (MW-10)
9850 Tolhurst, #201 (m-b)
Montreal, QC H3L 2Z8
514-843-5520 / Fax: 514-843-4501
Sales: $10 Million-$50 Million
Website: www.oldriver.ca
PATRICK EDERY-Leather Goods, Men's Apparel, Men's Big & Tall Apparel, Men's Casualwear, Men's Denim Apparel, Men's Formalwear, Men's Accessories, Men's Hosiery, Men's Outerwear, Men's Sportswear, Men's Suits, Men's Swimwear, Men's Underwear, Young Men's Apparel

AVALANCHE MODE (SP)
2930 Hamel Blvd., #117
Quebec, QC G1P 2J2
418-877-5584 / Fax: 418-877-6400
FRANCINE POULINE (Owner) & Buys Men's Skiing Apparel

ALDO GROUP, INC. (FW-518)
(ALDO)
905 Rue Hodge (des)
Saint Laurent, QC H4N 2B3
514-747-2536 / Fax: 514-747-7993
Sales: $100 Million-$500 Million
Website: www.aldoshoes.com
Retail Locations: QC, AB, ON, NS, PE, MB, BC, NF, SK, NB
ALDO BENSADOUN (President & C.E.O.)
DIANNE BIBEAU (Dir.-Mdse.) & Buys Men's Footwear, Leather Goods, Watches, Men's Accessories, Hosiery
VITO RIPA (D.M.M.-Footwear) & Buys Boys' Footwear
MARY-ANDREE BOUTIN (Real Estate Contact)

BROWN'S SHOE SHOPS, INC. (FW-35)
790 Begin St. (b-des)
Saint Laurent, QC H4M 2N5
514-334-5000 / Fax: 514-745-3250
Sales: $50 Million-$100 Million
Website: www.brownsshoes.com
Retail Locations: AB, BC, ON, QC
MICHAEL BROWNSTEIN (President & G.M.M.)
MORTON BROWNSTEIN (C.E.O.)
JEAN MARC BAILLARGEN-Men's Footwear
ANNIE COHEN-Boys' Apparel, Men's Apparel
JOCELYNE HAMEL-Men's Accessories
TONY ICHKHAN-Boys' Footwear

BIZOU INTERNATIONAL, INC. (JWLY-63)
(BIZOU)
615 Rte. Cameron
Saint Marie Debauce, QC G6E 1B1
418-387-8481 / Fax: 418-387-8404
Sales: $10 Million-$50 Million
Website: www.bizou.com
MARCEL LABRECQUE (President) & Buys Jewelry, Watches
LUCIE LABRECQUE-Jewelry, Watches

BENTLEY UNIC LEATHERS (CLO-250)
(Div. of BENTLEY LEATHERS)
3200 Griffath
St. Laurent, QC H4T 2B3
514-341-9333 / Fax: 514-685-3746
Website: www.shopbentley.com
ANDY CHELMINSKI (President)
CAROL SATEL-Slippers
REINA MALTONI-Gloves

QUEBEC - Villie Saint Laurent

ROSSY (DEPT)

(MICHAEL ROSSY LTD.)
450 Blvd. Lebeau
Villie Saint Laurent, QC H4N 1R7
514-335-6255 / Fax: 514-335-9690
Website: www.rossy.qc.ca

MICHAEL ROSSY, JR. (V.P.) & Buys Men's Overcoats, Tailored Slacks, Raincoats, Sweaters, Outer Jackets, Active Apparel, 6 to 18 Boys' Sportswear, Footwear

IMPRESSIONS IN THREAD (SP)

950 Arcola Ave.
Regina, SK S4N 0F5
306-347-8072 / Fax: 306-565-0613

SHAWN LACHAMBRE (Mgr.) & Buys Activewear

Mail Order Index

MAIL-ORDER INDEX

A

ABC DISTRIBUTING CO., INC.	North Miami	FL
ABERCROMBIE & FITCH CO.	Reynoldsburg	OH
ALAN FURMAN & CO., INC.	Rockville	MD
ALPHA SHIRT CO.	Philadelphia	PA
AMERICAN HEALTH CARE APPAREL LTD.	Easton	PA
AMWAY CORP.	Ada	MI
ARTHUR BEREN SHOES, INC.	San Francisco	CA
AUSSIE DOGS	San Clemente	CA

B

BACHRACH CLOTHING	Decatur	IL
BAILEY'S	Laytonville	CA
BANANA REPUBLIC	San Francisco	CA
BEACH HOUSE SWIMWEAR	Ft. Myers	FL
BEN SILVER CORP., THE	Charleston	SC
BERGDORF GOODMAN	New York	NY
BILL'S KHAKIS	Reading	PA
BILLS WHEELS, INC.	Santa Cruz	CA
BLAIR CORP.	Warren	PA
BLUE & GOLD SPORTS SHOP	Mishawaka	IN
BODYGEARS	Rutland	VT
BRIGADE QUARTERMASTERS LTD.	Kennesaw	GA
BROOKS BROTHERS	New York	NY
BROWN & HAWKINS DEPT. STORE	Seward	AK

C

CABLE CAR CLOTHIERS	San Francisco	CA
CAPRIOLA'S	Elko	NV
CARDINAL CAP & JACKET	Grundy	VA
CASTLE UNIFORMS	Fayetteville	NC
CASUAL MALE CORP.	Canton	MA
CHADWICK'S OF BOSTON	West Bridgewater	MA
CHILDREN'S WEAR DIGEST	Richmond	VA
CLOSET, THE	Joplin	MO
CLOTHES POST, INC.	Petoskey	MI
COWBOY CENTER	Miami	FL
CRUISIN' USA	Saint Louis	MO
CUSTOM CAPS & SHIRTS	Sparks	NV

D

DAVENPORT & CO.	Springfield	MA
DAVIDSON SHOES	Canandaiqua	NY
DESANTIS COLLECTION, THE	Boca Raton	FL
DILLARD'S DEPT. STORES, INC. - FORT WORTH DIV.	Fort Worth	TX
DILLARD'S DEPT. STORES, INC. - LITTLE ROCK DIV.	Little Rock	AR
DILLARD'S DEPT. STORES, INC. - PHOENIX DIV.	Tempe	AZ
DILLARD'S DEPT. STORES, INC. - ST. LOUIS DIV.	Saint Louis	MO
DUFFLE BAG, INC.	Tacoma	WA
DUNN'S RETAIL GRAND JUNCTION	Burnville	MN

E

EBBET'S FIELD FLANNELS	Seattle	WA
EDDIE BAUER, INC.	Vaughan	ON
EDDIE BAUER, INC.	Redmond	WA

F

F1 MARKETING GROUP, INC.	Mamaroneck	NY
FITNESS STUFF, INC.	Gresham	OR
FLAP HAPPY, INC.	Santa Monica	CA
FORMAL FASHIONS, INC.	Tempe	AZ
FOX RACING, INC.	Morgan Hill	CA
FRENCH CREEK SHEEP & WOOL CO.	Elverson	PA
FRIEDMAN'S SHOES	Atlanta	GA
FUN WEAR BRANDS, INC.	Estes Park	CO

G

GALCO SALES CO., INC.	Cleveland	OH
GALLIGASKINS	Juneau	AK
GARNET HILL	Franconia	NH
GENESCO, INC.	Nashville	TN
GOHN BROTHERS	Middlebury	IN
GORSUCH LTD.	Vail	CO
GREAT OUTDOOR CLOTHING	Incline Village	NV
GUMP'S, INC.	San Francisco	CA

H

HABAND COMPANY	Oakland	NJ
HARDY & HARDY, INC.	Destin	FL
HAROLD'S	Dallas	TX
HATSHACK.COM	Atlanta	GA
HEBRON SPORTS & FASHION, INC.	Doraville	GA
HOT 'N' SPICY LINGERIE CO.	Baton Rouge	LA
HOUSE OF TYROL, INC.	Cleveland	GA

I

IMAGES ALIVE LTD.	Deerfield	IL
INDUSTRIAL SHOE CO.	Santa Ana	CA
INTERMOUNTAIN SAFETY SHOES	Golden	CO
INTERNATIONAL MALE	San Diego	CA

J

J. CREW GROUP, INC.	New York	NY
J.C. PENNEY CO.	Plano	TX
J.J. HAT CENTER, INC.	New York	NY
JACK L. MARCUS, INC.	Milwaukee	WI
JAMIN' LEATHER	Myrtle Beach	SC
JAS TOWNSEND & SON, INC.	Pierceton	IN
JAZZERTOGS	Carlsbad	CA
JEFFERIES SOCKS	Burlington	NC
JOS. A. BANK CLOTHIERS, INC.	Hampstead	MD
JUST JUSTIN BOOTS	Dallas	TX

K

K.U. BOOKSTORES	Lawrence	KS
KALAMAZOO REGALIA	Kalamazoo	MI
KALE UNIFORM, INC.	Chicago	IL
KAST-A-WAY SWIMWEAR	Cincinnati	OH
KELLEY'S MEN'S SHOP, INC.	Charleston	WV
KENNETH COLE PRODUCTIONS, INC.	New York	NY
KINGSIZE	New York	NY
KOALA MEN'S SWIMWEAR	Sherman Oaks	CA
KRAFF'S DISTINCTIVE CLOTHING FOR MEN	Toppenish	WA

L

L.L. BEAN, INC.	Freeport	ME
LANDAU'S	Princeton	NJ
LANDS' END, INC.	Dodgeville	WI
LATINO'S MEXICAN STORE	Exmore	VA
LEBO'S SHOE STORE, INC.	Charlotte	NC
LIBERTYVILLE SADDLE SHOP	Libertyville	IL

MAIL-ORDER INDEX

Online Retailers Index

ONLINE RETAILER INDEX

Retailer	City	State
2BIGFEET.COM	Albany	GA

A

Retailer	City	State
ABC DISTRIBUTING CO., INC.	North Miami	FL
ABERCROMBIE & FITCH CO.	Reynoldsburg	OH
ALA MOANA CENTER-HILO HATTIE	Honolulu	HI
ALAMO STYLES, INC.	Franklin	MA
ALAN FURMAN & CO., INC.	Rockville	MD
ALAN'S SHOES, INC.	Tucson	AZ
ALCALA WESTERN WEAR	Chicago	IL
ALLIE BROTHERS TAILORS	Livonia	MI
ALLOY	New York	NY
ALLURE	Philadelphia	PA
ALPINE SHOP LTD.	Kirkwood	MO
ALTERNATIVE SHOES, INC.	Chicago	IL
AMERICA'S SHIRT	Indianapolis	IN
AMERICAN CLOTHING CO.	Knoxville	TN
AMERICAN EAGLE OUTFITTERS	Warrendale	PA
APEX, INC.	Pawtucket	RI
ARISTOKIDS, INC.	Palm Beach	FL
ARMY & AIR FORCE EXCHANGE SERVICE	Dallas	TX
ARMY NAVY	Whitehall	PA
ARNOLD'S MENS STORE, INC.	Indianapolis	IN
ATHLETE'S FOOT, THE	Kennesaw	GA
AUDACE	Fort Lauderdale	FL

B

Retailer	City	State
B BAR 10 WESTERN STORE	Amherst	WI
BACHRACH CLOTHING	Decatur	IL
BAILEY'S	Laytonville	CA
BALLY, INC.	New Rochelle	NY
BANANA REPUBLIC	San Francisco	CA
BAR-TED ARMY & NAVY STORE	Astoria	NY
BARBARA'S BOATIQUE, INC.	Fort Lauderdale	FL
BARRINGTON OUTFITTERS	Barrington	MA
BARRY MANUFACTURING CO.	Chamblee	GA
BEACHWOOD PRO SHOP	La Porte	IN
BEATTIE'S	Toronto	ON
BELK STORES SERVICES, INC.	Charlotte	NC
BEN MOSS JEWELERS WESTERN CANADA LTD.	Winnipeg	MB
BEN SILVER CORP., THE	Charleston	SC
BIG R, INC.	Lamar	CO
BIKERLEATHER.COM	Clifton	NJ
BILL'S KHAKIS	Reading	PA
BLACK BIRD SHOPPING CENTER, INC.	Medford	OR
BLAIR CORP.	Warren	PA
BLOOMINGDALE'S	New York	NY
BLUEFLY.COM	New York	NY
BODYGEARS	Rutland	VT
BONNEY & GORDON STORE FOR MEN	Sacramento	CA
BOOT BARN	Orange	CA
BOOT HILL	Hillsboro	OR
BOSCOV'S DEPT. STORE, INC.	Reading	PA
BRIGADE QUARTERMASTERS LTD.	Kennesaw	GA
BRINE'S SPORTING GOODS.	Cambridge	MA
BRODY'S BOYS' & YOUNG MEN'S WEAR	West Bloomfield	MI
BROOKS BROTHERS	New York	NY
BROWN SHOE COMPANY, INC.	Saint Louis	MO
BUCHHEIT, INC.	Perryville	MO
BURDINES	Miami	FL
BURLINGTON COAT FACTORY	Burlington	NJ
BURTON UNIFORM CORP.	Weymouth	MA
BUSY BEE DEPT. STORE	Springfield	MO

C

Retailer	City	State
C. ORRICO, INC.	Palm Beach	FL
CABLE CAR CLOTHIERS	San Francisco	CA
CALIFORNIA DRAWSTRINGS	New Orleans	LA
CAMP ROBINSON CANTEEN	North Little Rock	AR
CANNON BEACH OUTDOOR WEAR	Cannon Beach	OR
CASHMERES ETC., INC.	Bay Harbour Islands	FL
CASTLE SUPERSTORE CORP.	Phoenix	AZ
CASUAL MALE CORP.	Canton	MA
CATHAY KAI, INC.	Aiea	HI
CAVENDER'S BOOT CITY	Tyler	TX
CHADWICK'S OF BOSTON	West Bridgewater	MA
CHARLESTON DEPT. STORE, INC.	Charleston	WV
CHILDREN'S WEAR DIGEST	Richmond	VA
CHIMERE INTERNATIONAL	Naples	FL
CIRCLE M WESTERN STORE	Mountain Grove	MO
CLOSET, THE	Joplin	MO
CLOTHING WORLD	Pigeon Forge	TN
CLUB MONACO	Toronto	ON
COSMOPOLITAN, INC.	Saint Thomas	VI
COUNTRY GENERAL STORE	Van Nuys	CA
COUNTRY STORE, THE	Vashon	WA
COWBOY CENTER	Miami	FL
COWTOWN BOOT COMPANY	El Paso	TX
CRAZY SHIRTS, INC.	Aiea	HI
CRUISIN' USA	Saint Louis	MO
CULWELL & SON	Dallas	TX

D

Retailer	City	State
D & L HOUSE OF LEATHER, INC.	West Yarmouth	MA
DALE'S SHIRT WHEEL	San Jose	CA
DAN'S BIG & TALL SHOP, INC.	Dallas	TX
DAN'S BOOTS & SADDLES	Los Ranchos de Albuque	NM
DARTMOUTH CO-OP SOCIETY	Hanover	NH
DAVID STEPHEN CO.	San Francisco	CA
DAWAHARE'S	Lexington	KY
DELBERT'S CLOTHING, INC.	Arthur	IL
DESANTIS COLLECTION, THE	Boca Raton	FL
DEXTER SHOE CO.	Hagerstown	MD
DICK AVARD'S HABERDASHERY	Nashua	NH
DICK'S CLOTHING & SPORTING GOODS	Pittsburgh	PA
DILLARD'S DEPT. STORES, INC. - FORT WORTH DIV.	Fort Worth	TX
DILLARD'S DEPT. STORES, INC. - LITTLE ROCK DIV.	Little Rock	AR
DILLARD'S DEPT. STORES, INC. - PHOENIX DIV.	Tempe	AZ
DILLARD'S DEPT. STORES, INC. - ST. LOUIS DIV.	Saint Louis	MO
DISCOVERY CHANNEL STORES	Berkeley	CA
DOM'S OUTDOOR OUTFITTERS	Livermore	CA
DONECKER'S, INC.	Ephrata	PA
DORR MILL STORE	Guild	NH
DUKE UNIVERSITY STORES	Durham	NC
DUNCAN MEN'S STORE	Denver	CO

E

Retailer	City	State
E-BOOT.COM	Carnesville	GA

ONLINE RETAILER INDEX

E. T. REAVIS & SON	Dresden	TN
EASTERN CLOTHING	Watertown	MA
EASTERN MOUNTAIN SPORTS, INC.	Peterborough	NH
EBBET'S FIELD FLANNELS	Seattle	WA
EDDIE BAUER, INC.	Redmond	WA
EDDIE BAUER, INC.	Vaughan	ON
EL MUNDO FOR MEN	Cannon Beach	OR
EMBROIDERY SHOP	Rockland	ME
ENTERPRISE 99	Los Angeles	CA
ERMENEGILDO ZEGNA CORP.	New York	NY

F

FAMILY BRITCHES, INC.	Chappaqua	NY
FANBUZZ.COM	Minnetonka	MN
FANWEAR.COM	Bedford Hills	NY
FEATHERHILL WESTERN SHOP	Lenhartsville	PA
FEDERAL ARMY & NAVY SURPLUS, INC.	Seattle	WA
FELL CO., THE	Highland Park	IL
FINE KICKS	Pasadena	CA
FITNESS STUFF, INC.	Gresham	OR
FITTING STOOL, INC.	Austin	TX
FLEMINGTON DEPT. STORE	Flemington	NJ
FRASER'S CLOTHES SHOPS	Renfrew	ON
FREEMAN INTERNATIONAL	Montvale	NJ
FRENCH CREEK SHEEP & WOOL CO.	Elverson	PA
FRIEDMAN'S SHOES	Atlanta	GA

G

G & L CLOTHING CO.	Des Moines	IA
G.Q. FASHION	Thomasville	GA
GAP, INC., THE	San Francisco	CA
GARNET HILL	Franconia	NH
GATOR SHOP	Gainesville	FL
GEORGE'S APPAREL, INC.	Manchester	NH
GERALD SAMPTER CLOTHIER, INC.	Fremont	NE
GRANT BOYS, INC., THE	Costa Mesa	CA
GRAY'S, INC.	Kitty Hawk	NC
GREG LARSON SPORTS	Brainerd	MN
GUMP'S, INC.	San Francisco	CA

H

HABAND COMPANY	Oakland	NJ
HADDAD'S, INC.	Monroe	LA
HAROLD'S	Dallas	TX
HATSHACK.COM	Atlanta	GA
HATVANTAGE	Atlanta	GA
HEBRON SPORTS & FASHION, INC.	Doraville	GA
HIRSHLEIFER'S ETC.	Manhasset	NY
HJ FOSS	Golden	CO
HORNOR & HARRISON	Parkersburg	WV
HOT 'N' SPICY LINGERIE CO.	Baton Rouge	LA
HOT TOPIC, INC.	City of Industry	CA
HOWARD - KNIGHT'S TALL & BIG	Lexington	KY
HUB CLOTHES	Weatherford	TX
HUDSON'S BAY CO.	Toronto	ON
HUFFMAN'S BIG & TALL	Modesto	CA

I

INTERNATIONAL MALE	San Diego	CA

J

J-RAY SHOES	Mobile	AL
J. CREW GROUP, INC.	New York	NY
J. KLEINBAUER, INC.	Selinsgrove	PA
J.C. PENNEY CO.	Plano	TX
JACK DENNIS OUTDOOR SHOP	Jackson	WY
JAMIN' LEATHER	Myrtle Beach	SC
JAX	Fort Collins	CO
JAY STEVENS APPAREL FOR BIG OR TALL MEN	Oklahoma City	OK
JEANS WESTERNER, INC.	Montrose	CO
JEDLICKA'S SADDLERY	Santa Barbara	CA
JESSE BROWN'S OUTDOORS	Charlotte	NC
JIM HERRON LTD.	Springfield	IL
JIM'S FORMAL WEAR	Trenton	IL
JOHN HELMER HABERDASHER	Portland	OR
JOHNSTON'S CLOTHIERS	Wichita	KS
JUST JUSTIN BOOTS	Dallas	TX
JWT STORES, INC.	Ship Bottom	NJ

K

K.U. BOOKSTORES	Lawrence	KS
KATHY KAREN CHILDRENS SHOPPE	Dunmore	PA
KAUFMAN'S TALL & BIG MEN'S SHOP	Englewood	CO
KELLEY'S MEN'S SHOP, INC.	Charleston	WV
KENNETH COLE PRODUCTIONS, INC.	New York	NY
KEPP'S MENS SHOPS OF FLORIDA, INC.	Naples	FL
KIDDIE WEAR	Boca Raton	FL
KIK-WEAR, INC.	Los Angeles	CA
KING'S WESTERN WEAR, INC.	Studio City	CA
KINGSIZE	New York	NY
KOALA MEN'S SWIMWEAR	Sherman Oaks	CA
KRAMER'S MENSWEAR	Honolulu	HI
KRANSON CLOTHES, INC.	Wilkes-Barre	PA

L

L. STRAUSS BIG & TALL MEN'S CLOTHING, INC.	Louisville	KY
L.L. BEAN, INC.	Freeport	ME
LAMEY-WELLEHAN	Lewiston	ME
LANDS' END, INC.	Dodgeville	WI
LEVINE'S FAMILY SHOES	Clearwater	FL
LIBERTY STORE	Auburn	NY
LIBERTYVILLE SADDLE SHOP	Libertyville	IL
LOCAL MOTION	Honolulu	HI

M

MACY'S EAST	New York	NY
MACY'S WEST	San Francisco	CA
MADISON INTERNATIONAL, INC.	Beverly Hills	CA
MAIN STREET MENS WEAR	Hutchinson	KS
MANNY'S ON S.U. CAMPUS, INC.	Syracuse	NY
MARK SHALE	Woodridge	IL
MARK, FORE & STRIKE	Boca Raton	FL
MARSHALL FIELD'S	Minneapolis	MN
MARTY SHOES, INC.	Secaucus	NJ
MAUS & HOFFMAN, INC.	Fort Lauderdale	FL
MC SPORTING GOODS, INC.	Grand Rapids	MI
MCPHERSON'S DRY GOODS CO.	Salmon	ID
MICHELSON JEWELERS, INC.	Paducah	KY

ONLINE RETAILER INDEX

MILBERN CLOTHING CO.	Saint Paul	MN
MILLS, INC.	San Francisco	CA
MOE SPORTS SHOPS, INC.	Ann Arbor	MI
MOHAN CUSTOM CLOTHIERS	Beaverton	OR

N

NAPLES BEACH HOTEL & GOLF CLUB	Naples	FL
NATHAN'S MEN'S STORE	Lakeland	FL
NATIONAL FOOTWEAR	Allentown	PA
NAUTICAL BOATIQUE, INC.	Miami	FL
NEIMAN MARCUS	Dallas	TX
NEIMAN MARCUS DIRECT	Irving	TX
NFL SHOP	San Francisco	CA
NIKE, INC.	Beaverton	OR
NORDSTROM - LOS ANGELES DIV.	Redondo Beach	CA
NORDSTROM NORTHERN DIV. - CITY REGION	San Francisco	CA
NORDSTROM, INC.	Seattle	WA
NORM THOMPSON	Hillsboro	OR
NORTH BY NORTHWEST	Cambridge	ON

O

OLD NAVY CLOTHING CO.	San Francisco	CA
ORVIS CO., INC., THE	Manchester	VT
OSHMAN'S	Houston	TX
OVERLAND SHEEPSKIN	Fairfield	IA
OVERTON'S, INC.	Greenville	NC
OXMAN SURPLUS, INC.	Santa Fe Springs	CA

P

P. NEMIR DRY GOODS	Navasota	TX
PACIFIC EYES & T'S	Vista	CA
PACIFIC SUNWEAR, INC.	Anaheim	CA
PALM BEACH GOLF CENTER, INC.	Palm Beach Gardens	FL
PARADISE JEWELERS	Athol	MA
PATRICK JAMES, INC.	Fresno	CA
PAUL FREDRICK	Fleetwood	PA
PAYLESS SHOE SOURCE, INC.	Topeka	KS
PEBBLE BEACH GOLF SHOP	Pebble Beach	CA
PENN STATE BOOK STORE ON CAMPUS	University Park	PA
PERLIS	New Orleans	LA
PFI WESTERN STORE	Springfield	MO
PIONEER WESTERN WEAR & MORE	Fredericktown	MO
PLEASURE CHEST LTD.	West Hollywood	CA
POLO GEAR	Wellington	FL
POMEROY'S MENS STORES, INC.	Mesa	AZ
POMPANO BEACH GOLF SHOP	Pompano Beach	FL
PORTA BELLA	New York	NY
PRINCETON SPORTS	Columbia	MD
PRINCETON UNIVERSITY STORE	Princeton	NJ
PRO SPORTSWORLD, INC.	Modesto	CA

R

R & R MEN'S WEAR	Palm Springs	CA
RAINS DEPT. STORE	Ojai	CA
RCC WESTERN STORES, INC.	Rapid City	SD
RENTON WESTERN WEAR, INC.	Renton	WA
REYER'S SHOE STORE	Sharon	PA
REYN'S MENSWEAR, INC.	Kamuela	HI
RICHARD DAVID FOR MEN	Sedona	AZ
RICHARD'S GEMS & JEWELRY	Miami	FL
RIFLESSI	New York	NY
RITCHIE SWIMWEAR	Davie	FL
ROAD RUNNER SPORTS, INC.	San Diego	CA
ROD'S WESTERN PALACE, INC.	Columbus	OH
RODES CO.	Louisville	KY
ROLO SAN FRANCISCO, INC.	San Francisco	CA
RUNNING ROOM LTD.	Edmonton	AB
RURAL KING SUPPLY CO., INC.	Mattoon	IL

S

S & K FAMOUS BRANDS, INC.	Glen Allen	VA
SAGESPORT, INC.	Kings Mountain	NC
SAM'S WESTERN WEAR	Riverside	CA
SCHNEE'S BOOTS, INC.	Bozeman	MT
SCOTT-WYNNE OUTFITTERS	Austin	TX
SCOTTISH LION IMPORT SHOP, THE	North Conway	NH
SEARS, ROEBUCK & CO.	Hoffman Estates	IL
SELBY SHOES	West Palm Beach	FL
SHEPLER'S	Wichita	KS
SHOE PAVILION, INC.	Pinole	CA
SHORT SIZES, INC.	Cleveland	OH
SHUTTLE PRODUCTS INTERNATIONAL INC.	Indialantic	FL
SIERRA TRADING POST, INC.	Cheyenne	WY
SKECHERS U.S.A., INC.	Manhattan Beach	CA
SMALLWOOD'S, INC.	Fort Lauderdale	FL
SMITH & HAWKEN	Novato	CA
SNOOZY'S COLLEGE BOOKSTORE	Birmingham	AL
SOLDIER CITY	Turnersville	NJ
SOUTH MOON UNDER	Berlin	MD
SPENCER GIFTS, INC.	Egg Harbor Township	NJ
SPENCER'S WESTERN WORLD, INC.	Pinella	FL
SPIEGEL OUTLET STORES	Downers Grove	IL
SPIEGEL, INC.	Downers Grove	IL
SPORLEDERS	Walla Walla	WA
SPORTEES, INC.	Redmond	WA
SPORTIF USA	Sparks	NV
SPORTS FAN	Denver	CO
SPORTS HUT	Wayzata	MN
SPORTS MANIA	Jacksonville	FL
STAFFORD'S	Thomasville	GA
STAG SHOP, INC.	Grenada	MS
STAGES WEST, INC.	Pigeon Forge	TN
STERNHEIMER BROTHERS, INC.	Sandston	VA
STRAUS CO.	Fargo	ND
STRIDE RITE CORP., THE	Lexington	MA
SUAYAS'	Miami	FL
SUIT SOURCE USA	Tyler	TX
SUNUP SUNDOWN, INC.	Fort Lauderdale	FL
SWEETWATER SURF SHOP	Wrightsville Beach	NC
SWIM AND RUN SHOP, INC.	Boise	ID

T

TANINO CRISCI AMERICA	New York	NY
TARGET DIRECT	Woodbury	MN
TEAM ONE NEWPORT	Newport	RI
TIES.COM	San Antonio	TX
TILLEY ENDURABLES	Don Mills	ON
TILLY'S SPORTSWEAR	Irvine	CA
TITUSVILLE BARGAIN STORE	Titusville	PA

ONLINE RETAILER INDEX

Buying Office Index

BUYING OFFICES INDEX

Alphabetical Company Index

ALPHABETICAL INDEX

A

ALPHABETICAL INDEX

Name	City	State
AIRBRUSH MAGIC	Saint Petersburg	FL
AL BASKIN CO.	Woodridge	IL
(See MARK SHALE)		
AL GAUDIO'S	Belle Vernon	PA
AL JAKE, INC.	West New York	NJ
AL JOHNSON	Minneapolis	MN
AL MAGOON'S	Lawrence	MA
AL WEISS MEN'S CLOTHING	Los Angeles	CA
AL'S 5 AND 10	Mobile	AL
AL'S ARMY STORE	Orlando	FL
AL'S FORMAL WEAR	Houston	TX
AL'S MEN'S SHOP	Brooklyn	NY
AL'S SHOP	Santa Ana	CA
AL-BAR RANCH	Mishawaka	IN
THE ALAMO II	Normal	IL
ALAMO SHOES	Berwyn	IL
ALAMO STYLES	Franklin	MA
ALAN BILZERIAN	Boston	MA
ALAN DAVID	New York	NY
ALAN FURMAN & CO., INC.	Rockville	MD
ALAN'S	Carthage	MS
(See COGHLAN FASHIONS FOR MEN)		
ALAN'S SHOES, INC.	Tucson	AZ
ALANDALES, INC.	Culver City	CA
ALASKA COMMERCIAL CO.	Anchorage	AK
ALBERT LTD.	Bellevue	WA
ALBERT'S	Rayville	LA
ALBERT'S ARMY STORE	Williamson	WV
ALBERT'S MEN'S SHOP	Newport	KY
ALBERT'S PROSPECT	Cleveland	OH
ALCALA WESTERN WEAR	Chicago	IL
ALDER'S WIDE SHOES, INC.	Pleasant Hill	CA
ALDO	Saint Laurent	QC
(See ALDO GROUP, INC.)		
ALDO GROUP, INC.	Saint Laurent	QC
ALDO'S MENSWEAR	Amherst	NY
(See ALDO'S UOMO)		
ALDO'S UOMO	Amherst	NY
ALDRICH'S, INC.	Dumas	TX
ALEX & DANA	Pulaski	VA
ALEX SEBASTIAN	Costa Mesa	CA
ALEX'S FASHION CENTER	Balboa Island	CA
ALEX'S MR. ESQUIRE, INC.	Brooklyn	NY
ALEXANDER DAVIS MENS CLOTHING	Boise	ID
(See M. ALEXANDER, INC.)		
ALEXANDER'S SHOE STORE	Costa Mesa	CA
ALEXANDER'S STORE	Blairsville	GA
ALEXANDER'S, INC.	Nogales	AZ
ALEXANDREA'S	Raleight	NC
ALFRED OLSON CO.	Milaca	MN
ALI'S MARKETING MANAGEMENT	Kissimmee	FL
ALICE'S WONDERLAND	Greeley	PA
ALL ABOUT TENNIS	Tempe	AZ
ALL AMERICAN BOY	San Francisco	CA
ALL AMERICAN JEANS, INC.	New Orleans	LA
(See RUBENSTEIN BROTHERS)		
ALL AMERICAN SPORTS FAN	Fresno	CA
ALL AMERICAN SWIM SUPPLY	Florence	AL
ALL AMERICAN TEAM SHOP	San Francisco	CA
ALL ASHORE FASHION SWIMWEAR	San Antonio	TX
ALL PRO SPORTS	Encino	CA
ALL SPORT	Harrisonville	MO
ALL SPORTS, INC.	Lexington	KY
ALL SWEATS	Barbourville	KY
ALL-PRO ATHLETIC SHOE, INC.	North Hollywood	CA
ALLAN REYNOLDS' SHOES	Cleveland	MS
ALLDAYS DEPARTMENT STORE	Atlanta	TX
ALLEN & BELL'S DEPARTMENT STORE	Clare	MI
ALLEN COLLINS	West Waterford	CT
ALLEN COLLINS, INC.	West Hartford	CT
ALLEN'S	Leominster	MA
(See THE WILLIAM A. ALLEN CO., INC.)		
ALLEN'S MENSWEAR	Freeport	IL
ALLEN'S OF HASTINGS	Hastings	NE
ALLEN'S OF SAN JUAN	Mayaguez	PR
ALLEN'S TUXEDOS	Orem	UT
ALLENS BOOT CENTER	Austin	TX
ALLIE BROTHERS TAILORS	Livonia	MI
ALLIED INTERNATIONAL CORP.	Sterling	VA
(See PAPILLON STORE)		
ALLOY	New York	NY
ALLURE	Philadelphia	PA
ALMACENES RIVIERA	Rio Piedras	PR
ALOHA PARADISE	Jacksonville	FL
ALPHA & OMEGA	Clinton	NC
ALPHABET SHOP	Sarasota	FL
ALPINE MEADOWS	West Vancouver	BC
ALPINE SHOP LTD.	Kirkwood	MO
THE ALPINE SHOP, INC.	South Burlington	VT
ALPINE SPORTS CENTER	Big Bear Lake	CA
ALS OASIS, INC.	Oacoma	SD
ALTERNATIVE SHOES, INC.	Chicago	IL
ALTO'S, INC.	Virginia	MN
ALUMNI SHOP FOR HIM & HER	Morgan City	LA
ALVAREZ BROS. CO., INC.	Orange	CA
(See ARMY-NAVY STORE)		
ALVIN - DENNIS	Lexington	VA
ALVIN'S STORES	Panama City Beach	FL
ALWYN'S	Georgetown	SC
AMAZONIA'S SWEATERS	Keystone	CO
AMBASSADOR SHOP	Oklahoma City	OK
AMELIA INN GIFT SHOP	Amelia Island	FL
AMELIA ISLAND CLOTHING CO.	Amelia Island	FL
AMERICA'S 1 BIG & TALL	Jensen Beach	FL
AMERICA'S FASHIONS	Newark	NJ
AMERICA'S HALLOWEEN HEADQUARTERS	Egg Harbor Township	NJ
(See SPENCER GIFTS, INC.)		
AMERICA'S SHIRT	Indianapolis	IN
AMERICAN APPAREL SHOPS, INC.	Ashland	KY
(See STARS AND STRIPES CLOTHIERS)		
AMERICAN APPAREL SHOPS, INC.	Ashland	KY
THE AMERICAN BAG	Spring Hill	FL
AMERICAN CLOTHING CO.	Knoxville	TN
THE AMERICAN COWBOY	West Bountifull	UT
AMERICAN EAGLE OUTFITTERS	Warrendale	PA
AMERICAN FASHIONS	New Orleans	LA
AMERICAN FORMAL & BRIDAL	Kansas City	MO
AMERICAN HEALTH CARE APPAREL	Easton	PA
AMERICAN IMAGE SPORTS	Cambridge	MA
AMERICAN MALE & CO.	Oswego	IL
AMERICAN MAN BIG & TALL	Albuquerque	NM
AMERICAN OUTFITTERS	Waukegan	IL
AMERICAN OUTFITTERS	Bedford	PA
AMERICAN PANTS CO.	Bensalem	PA
AMERICAN RAG CIE	Los Angeles	CA
AMERICAN RETAIL GROUP	Duluth	MN
(See MAURICE'S, INC.)		
AMERICAN RETAIL GROUP	Ontario	CA
(See ANCHOR BLUE)		
AMERICAN RUGBY SUPPLY, INC.	Elk Grove Village	IL
(See RUGBY CUSTOM SPORTSWEAR CO.)		
AMIN'S, INC.	Truth or Consequences	NM
AMITYVILLE MEN'S SHOP, INC.	Amityville	NY
AMMAR'S, INC.	Bluefield	VA
(See MAGIC MART)		
AMPY'S WESTERN STORE, INC.	El Paso	TX
AMUNDSON CLOTHING STORE	Decorah	IA
AMWAY CORP.	Ada	MI
ANANIAS, INC.	Sunrise	FL
ANCHOR BLUE	Ontario	CA
ANCHOR MENSWEAR	Port Washington	WI

ALPHABETICAL INDEX

ALPHABETICAL INDEX

B

ALPHABETICAL INDEX

ALPHABETICAL INDEX

ALPHABETICAL INDEX

ALPHABETICAL INDEX

ALPHABETICAL INDEX

ALPHABETICAL INDEX

Name	City	State
BUSY BEE DEPARTMENT STORE	Springfield	MO
BUSY BEE MERCANTILE CO.	Quincy	IL
BUTCH BLUM	Seattle	WA
BUTCH HOFFER	Beaumont	TX
BUTCHER & CO.	Elk City	OK
(See JONES' MENSWEAR)		
BUTCHER'S MENSWEAR	Weatherford	OK
BUTLER'S PROMOTIONS, INC.	Aitkin	MN
BUTTON DOWN	San Francisco	CA
BUTTONS & BOWS, INC.	Paradise	CA
BUTTROSS DEPARTMENT STORE	Canton	MS
BUTTS' DRY GOODS	Thorndale	TX
BUY FOR LESS	Douglas	GA
BUY OR DYE, INC.	Boston	MA
BUY RITE	Huntington Park	CA
BUY-A-TUX	Chicago	IL
BUZZELL'S CLOTHING STORE	Caribou	ME
BY GEORGE SHEILA'S	Helena	MT
BYER'S MEN'S SHOP	Trenton	NJ
BYRNIE UTZ HATS	Seattle	WA
C		
C & C FEED	Jennings	LA
C & C SPORTS	Evansville	IN
C & C WESTERN WEAR, INC.	Longview	TX
C & G SPORTING GOODS	Panama City	FL
C & H WESTERN WEAR	High Ridge	MO
C & K CLOTHING	Mountain Home	AR
C & K CLOTHING	West Plains	MO
C & K DISTRIBUTORS, INC.	McCook	NE
(See DENIM & DUDS)		
C & K FASHIONS	Chicago	IL
C & S ENTERPRISES	Sioux Falls	SD
(See ATHLETIC EDGE)		
C & S SUPPLY CO., INC.	Mankato	MN
C & W JOHNSTON, INC.	Lake Placid	NY
(See RUTHIE'S RUN)		
C'EST LA VIE SPORTSWEAR	Southfield	MI
C-MART	East Chicago	IN
C-MART DISCOUNT WAREHOUSE	Forest Hill	MD
C. GOLDSTEIN'S & SON INC.	Milledgeville	GA
C. L. NEWMAN CO., INC.	Salem	OR
(See LES NEWMAN'S WORK & OUTDOOR CLOTHING)		
C. ORRICO, INC.	Palm Beach	FL
C. TUCKER'S DEPARTMENT STORE	Kingstree	SC
C.A. GROSS CO., INC.	Green Bay	WI
C.B. FINCHER'S WESTERN WEAR	Burleson	TX
C.B. FORREST & SON	Saluda	SC
C.B.'S SALTWATER OUTFITTERS	Sarasota	FL
C.D. WILSON	Verona	VA
(See THE FASHION GALLERY)		
C.D.N. SPORTS, INC.	Passaic	NJ
(See OLYMPIC TOWN)		
C.E. ROTH FORMAL WEAR	Allentown	PA
C.E. SMITH & ASSOCIATES	Denver	CO
(See SKAGGS TUXALL UNIFORM & EQUIPMENT, INC.)		
C.H. MARTIN, INC.	Staten Island	NY
C.J. MINERAL AND BEAD	Ormond Beach	FL
C.L. CARNAHAN CORP.	Lakewood	NY
C.R. JEWELERS DIAMOND OUTLET	Coral Springs	FL
C.S.W.W.	Great Falls	MT
C.V.'S DEPARTMENT STORE	Stephens	AR
C.W. CROSS CO., INC.	Ogden	UT
CABANA SHOP	Lauderdale Sea	FL
CABARET	Los Angeles	CA
CABERSON'S COMPANIES, INC.	Tulsa	OK
(See ABERSON'S MEN'S)		
CABLE CAR CLOTHIERS	San Francisco	CA
CACTUS TRADING, INC.	New York	NY
(See SILVER TRADING)		
THE CADEAU	Austin	TX
CADEAU, INC.	Austin	TX
(See THE CADEAU)		
CADET NECKWEAR TIE CORNER	Philadelphia	PA
CAHILL & SWAIN, INC.	Winston-Salem	NC
CAHILL'S SPORTING GOODS	Troy	NY
CAJUN CLOTHING CO.	New Orleans	LA
(See PERLIS)		
CAL'S STORES	San Diego	CA
(See CALIFORNIA SPORTS)		
CAL'S WESTERN STORE	Lafayette	LA
CALHOUN COUNTY COOPERATIVE	Calhoun City	MS
CALICO CAT	Laurel	MS
(See TOM CAT, INC.)		
CALICO COW	Alturas	CA
(See ARDIE'S CLASSIE LASSIE)		
CALIFORNIA BIG & TALL	San Francisco	CA
(See ROCHESTER BIG & TALL CLOTHING, INC.)		
CALIFORNIA DAZE	Phoenix	AZ
CALIFORNIA DRAWSTRINGS	New Orleans	LA
CALIFORNIA FASHION MALL	Birmingham	AL
CALIFORNIA KIDS & TEENS	Alta Loma	CA
CALIFORNIA SPORTS	San Diego	CA
CALIFORNIA SURPLUS MART	Los Angeles	CA
CALIFORNIA UNIFORM	Los Angeles	CA
(See UNIFORMS, INC.)		
CALL JEWELERS, INC.	Phoenix	AZ
CALLAHAN'S GENERAL STORES	Cedar Park	TX
CALLAN'S SKOGMO STORE	Durand	WI
CALVIN'S, INC.	Charleston	WV
CAM'S	Wallace	ID
(See RULLMAN'S)		
CAMARA'S CLOTHIER	Turlock	CA
CAMBRIDGE LTD.	Tulsa	OK
THE CAMBRIDGE SHOP	Birmingham	AL
CAMERON CLOTHING	Vinton	IA
CAMILLO TUXEDOS	Norwalk	CT
(See CAMILLO, INC.)		
CAMILLO, INC.	Norwalk	CT
CAMIRE'S ATHLETIC SOLES & LEVIS	Wakefield	RI
CAMOUFLAGE CLOTHING	New York	NY
CAMP HILTON HEAD	Hilton Head Island	SC
CAMP LONGHORN	Burnet	TX
CAMP ROBINSON CANTEEN	North Little Rock	AR
CAMPAU CLOTHING CO., INC.	Hamtramck	MI
CAMPBELL SUPPLY CO.	Sioux Falls	SD
CAMPBELL'S IN THE VILLAGE	Stockton	CA
CAMPUS ATHLETIC	Tucson	AZ
CAMPUS CLASSICS	Mount Laurel	NJ
CAMPUS COLORS, INC.	Highland Park	IL
CAMPUS SPORTS	Charlotte	NC
CANADY'S SPORTS CENTER, INC.	Wilmington	NC
CANAL JEAN CO., INC.	New York	NY
CANAL MENSWEAR	Passaic	NJ
CANDY CANE'S CHILDREN'S SHOP	Los Angeles	CA
CANFIELD'S, INC.	Omaha	NE
CANLY SHOES	Downsview	ON
CANNON BAY BEACH CLUB	Cannon Beach	OR
CANNON BEACH OUTDOOR WEAR	Cannon Beach	OR
CANNON'S MEN'S SHOP	Goldsboro	NC
CANON & WILLIAMS	Texarkana	TX
CANON WESTERN WEAR	Canon City	CO
CANTERBURY	Cranston	RI
CANTERBURY CLOTHIERS LTD., INC.	Akron	OH
CANTERBURY LEATHER SHOP	Orleans	MA
CANTRELL'S MEN'S & LADIES SPORTSWEAR	Smithville	TN
CANYON BEACHWEAR	Santa Monica	CA
CANYON VILLAGE MARKETPLACE	Grand Canyon	AZ
CAPE HORN CORNER	Red Lion	PA
CAPE TIP SPORTSWEAR	Provincetown	MA
CAPIN & CO.	Nogales	AZ
CAPITA'S CLOTHING OUTLET	Berwick	PA

ALPHABETICAL INDEX

ALPHABETICAL INDEX

ALPHABETICAL INDEX

ALPHABETICAL INDEX

D

ALPHABETICAL INDEX

ALPHABETICAL INDEX

ALPHABETICAL INDEX

E

ALPHABETICAL INDEX

ALPHABETICAL INDEX

ALPHABETICAL INDEX

ALPHABETICAL INDEX

G

ALPHABETICAL INDEX

ALPHABETICAL INDEX

ALPHABETICAL INDEX

H

ALPHABETICAL INDEX

ALPHABETICAL INDEX

ALPHABETICAL INDEX

I

ALPHABETICAL INDEX

J

ALPHABETICAL INDEX

ALPHABETICAL INDEX

ALPHABETICAL INDEX

K

ALPHABETICAL INDEX

ALPHABETICAL INDEX

L

ALPHABETICAL INDEX

ALPHABETICAL INDEX

ALPHABETICAL INDEX

M

ALPHABETICAL INDEX

ALPHABETICAL INDEX

ALPHABETICAL INDEX

ALPHABETICAL INDEX

ALPHABETICAL INDEX

Name	City	State
MORLEE'S MEN SHOP, INC.	Jersey City	NJ
MORRIS & SONS	Chicago	IL
MORRIS BROTHERS	New York	NY
MORRIS CLOTHING CO.	Gordon	NE
MORRIS MEN'S SHOP	Albany	NY
MORRIS' MENSWEAR	Ithaca	NY
MORRIS, INC.	Greenfield	IN
MORRISON DEPARTMENT STORE	George West	TX
(See L.S. MORRISON & CO.)		
MORRISTOWN DRY GOODS	Newport	TN
(See NEWPORT DRY GOODS)		
MORRY'S LTD.	Salem	OR
MORRY'S MEN'S STORE, INC.	Salem	OR
(See MORRY'S LTD.)		
MORT WALLIN OF LAKE TAHOE	Las Vegas	NV
MORTON'S ARMY & NAVY	Cedarhurst	NY
MORTON'S CACTUS JACK'S	Alvarado	TX
MOSER'S CLOTHING STORE	Ellensburg	WA
MOSES FOR MEN, INC.	Butte	MT
MOSES' DEPARTMENT STORE	Gulfport	MS
MOSHER'S	Newton Centre	MA
MOSKOW'S, INC.	Whiteville	NC
MOSS BAY MERCANTILE	Kirkland	WA
MOTTAGHI & SON, INC.	Washington	DC
(See SOLBIATO)		
MT. OLIVER MEN'S SHOP	Pittsburgh	PA
MOUNT-CATE APPAREL, INC.	Chehalis	WA
(See BARTEL'S)		
MOUNTAIN MERCANTILE TRUE VALUE	Caliente	NV
MOUNTAIN MUNCHKIN	Alamosa	CO
MOUNTAIN SPORTS	Flagstaff	AZ
MOUNTAIN TEES	Breckenridge	CO
MOUNTAIN TOPS, INC.	Kennebunk	ME
MOUNTAIN VIEW	Campbell	CA
MOUNTAIN WEST CLOTHING, INC.	Plains	MT
MOUNTAIN WEST T & TRADING CO.	Manitou Springs	CO
(See MANITOU SPRINGS T-SHIRT CO.)		
THE MOVIN MAN	Columbus	GA
MOYER'S	Ord	NE
MP SURPLUS, INC.	Pinckard	AL
MR COOL	Little Rock	AR
(See CRK ENTERPRISE, INC.)		
MR. ALAN, INC.	Boston	MA
MR. ALBERT'S MEN'S WORLD	Cleveland	OH
(See ALBERT'S PROSPECT)		
MR. B'S WEARHOUSE	Schoolcraft	MI
MR. B.	Des Moines	IA
MR. BIG & TALL	Carmichael	CA
MR. BIG & TALL	Toronto	ON
(See GRAFTON - FRASER, INC.)		
MR. BLACKWELL'S	Springfield	MO
MR. BOOTS SAN ANGELO, INC.	San Angelo	TX
MR. BURCH FORMAL WEAR	Birmingham	AL
MR. CARROLL	Hasbrouck Heights	NJ
(See CARROLL'S FASHIONS)		
MR. CASUAL & SUITS UNLIMITED, INC.	Albuquerque	NM
MR. CURLEY, INC.	Salisbury	MD
MR. EDDIE, INC.	Wilmette	IL
MR. FASHION, INC.	Asbury Park	NJ
MR. FORMAL, INC.	Portland	OR
(See THE TUX SHOP)		
MR. G'S CLOTHING	Cherokee	IA
MR. G'S, INC.	Viroqua	WI
MR. HYDE'S LEATHER	Canton	OH
MR. JIM'S HIS SHOP, INC.	Goodland	KS
MR. JOHN'S	Oklahoma City	OK
MR. JOHN'S BEACH STORE	Charleston	SC
MR. JOHN'S MAN'S SHOP	Brownsville	TX
MR. K STORES, INC.	Gastonia	NC
MR. KAY'S, INC.	Chicago	IL
MR. KICKS	Jacksonville	FL
(See SHEL-MAR, INC.)		
MR. KING'S CLOTHES	Petersburg	VA
MR. KNICKERBOCKER	Clemson	SC
MR. MAC	Salt Lake City	UT
MR. MAN	Newark	NJ
MR. NEAT'S FORMAL WEAR, INC.	Loveland	CO
MR. NED, INC.	New York	NY
MR. OOLEY'S	Oklahoma City	OK
MR. PANOSIAN'S	Elmira	NY
(See PANOSIAN'S, INC.)		
MR. R MENSWEAR	Cedar City	UT
MR. RAGS	Long Beach	CA
MR. RIC	Vallejo	CA
MR. SID	Newton Centre	MA
MR. SONNY'S, INC.	Milwaukee	WI
(See SONNY'S FOR MEN, INC.)		
MR. TONY MEN'S SHOP	Miami	FL
MR. TUX	Spokane	WA
MR. WICKS, INC.	Little Rock	AR
MR. Z.	Houston	TX
MRCKANO	Lachine	QC
(See LE JEAN BLEU, INC.)		
MT. VERNON CLOTHING CO., INC.	Mount Vernon	IA
(See BAUMAN'S)		
MUGFORD LTD.	Saint Thomas	ON
MUGFORD SHOES	Saint Thomas	ON
(See MUGFORD LTD.)		
MUGLERS OF PHOEBUS	Hampton	VA
(See GEAR, INC.)		
MULDOON'S, INC.	Eau Claire	WI
MULTI-LINE INDUSTRIES, INC.	Bowdon	GA
MUR-LEE, INC.	Lynbrook	NY
MURDOCK'S OF CARSON CITY, INC.	Carson City	NV
MURRAY GOLDMAN LTD.	Vancouver	BC
MURRAY'S CORNER, INC.	Brooklyn	NY
MURRAY'S SHOES, INC.	Bloomington	IL
MURRAY'S STORE	Marceline	MO
MURRAY'S TOGGERY SHOP, INC.	Nantucket	MA
MURRELL'S MENSWEAR	Edmonton	KY
MY GENERATION GRAPHICS	Sarasota	FL
MYATT'S SHOES & SPORTS	Nampa	ID
MYER & STONE CO.	Steubenville	OH
MYKLEBUST'S	Lewiston	ID
MYRTLE BEACH T-SHIRTS	North Myrtle Beach	SC
MYRTLE BEACH TENNIS CLUB	Myrtle Beach	SC

N

Name	City	State
N & R DEPARTMENT STORE, INC.	South Haven	MI
N. ALLAGE FASHIONS	Dallas	TX
N. LANDAU HYMAN JEWELERS	Allentown	PA
N. PEAL	New York	NY
N. SCHLOSSBERG & SON	Baltimore	MD
N.J. CARAWAY & CO., INC.	Logansport	LA
N.Y.C. CLOTHING	East Elmhurst	NY
(See ACTIVE WEARHOUSE, INC.)		
NADLER BROTHERS	Ames	IA
(See T. GALAXY CORP.)		
NADLER'S	Cincinnati	OH
NAFZIGER'S	Nampa	ID
NAISH HAWAII LTD.	Kailua	HI
NAMAN'S DEPARTMENT STORE	Mobile	AL
NAME BRANDS, INC.	Tulsa	OK
THE NAME DROPPER	Montgomery	AL
NANA CO.	Santa Monica	CA
NANA'S KIDDIE SHOPPE	Orlando	FL
NANDO JONES DEPARTMENT STORE, INC.	Jackson	TN
NANNY'S	Sanibel Island	FL
NANRON, INC.	Park City	UT
NANTUCKET SPORTS LOCKER	Nantucket	MA
NAPIER BROTHERS' CLOTHING	Lancaster	KY
NAPLES BEACH HOTEL & GOLF CLUB	Naples	FL
NAPOLEON, INC.	New York	NY

ALPHABETICAL INDEX

ALPHABETICAL INDEX

O

ALPHABETICAL INDEX

ALPHABETICAL INDEX

Name	City	State
PARR OF ARIZONA	Phoenix	AZ
PARSOW'S, INC.	Omaha	NE
PARTNERS LTD.	Lafayette	LA
PARTNERS MEN'S STORE	Little Rock	AR
PARTS UNKNOWN	Oxnard	CA
PARVIZI	Flint	MI
PASEO FASHIONS	Azusa	CA
PASTEL	Palm Beach	FL
PATAGONIA	Ventura	CA
PATCHWORK PLUS	Dayton	VA
PATE'S DEPARTMENT STORE	Rutherford	TN
PATERSON MEN'S SHOP, INC.	Paterson	NJ
PATI'S FORMAL WEAR	New Kensington	PA
PATRICK JAMES, INC.	Fresno	CA
PATRICK'S	Centreville	AL
PATRICK'S OF RED RIVER	Red River	NM
PATTERSON'S BACKBAY DANCEWEAR, INC.	Burlington	MA
PATTERSON'S MENSWEAR	Bemidji	MN
PAUL ARROW'S PANTS SHOP, INC.	East Liverpool	OH
PAUL BUNYAN'S	Little Rock	AR
PAUL FREDRICK	Fleetwood	PA
PAUL FREDRICK MEN'S STYLE	Fleetwood	PA
(See PAUL FREDRICK)		
PAUL JARDIN OF USA	Woodland Hills	CA
PAUL MANN SALES	Melbourne	FL
PAUL RICHARDS CLOTHING	Bothell	WA
PAUL SIMON CO.	Charlotte	NC
PAUL SMITH, INC.	New York	NY
PAUL STUART	New York	NY
PAUL'S BIG & TALL	Tyler	TX
(See PENICK & CHANCE, INC.)		
PAUL'S FASHIONS, INC.	Berlin	NJ
PAUL'S FINE CLOTHING, INC.	Cheshire	CT
PAUL'S MENSWEAR	Monroe	WI
PAUL'S MENSWEAR, INC.	Evansville	IN
PAUL'S WESTERN STORE, INC.	Henryetta	OK
PAULS MEN'S SHOP	Taos	NM
PAULUCCI'S TAILOR & MENSWEAR	Lewiston	ID
PAYLESS SHOE SOURCE, INC.	Topeka	KS
PEABODY HOTEL MEN'S SHOP)	Memphis	TN
(See LANSKY AT THE PEABODY)		
PEACE FROGS RETAIL, INC.	Gloucester	VA
PEACOCK'S MENSWEAR, INC.	Dublin	GA
PEARL FACTORY	Honolulu	HI
(See THE SULTAN CO.)		
PEARSON'S DEPARTMENT STORES	Kinston	NC
PEBBLE BEACH GOLF SHOP	Pebble Beach	CA
PEBBLE BEACH TENNIS SHOP	Pebble Beach	CA
PEDLEY, INC.	Martinez	CA
PEEBLES, INC.	South Hill	VA
PEGASUS DIAMOND OUTLET	Phoenix	AZ
(See PEGASUS DIAMONDS)		
PEGASUS DIAMONDS	Phoenix	AZ
PEGASUS LEATHER CO.	Sausalito	CA
PEGGY'S PAYSON PLACE	Payson	AZ
PEIGHT SUPPLY	Belleville	PA
(See PEIGHT'S COUNTRY STORE)		
PEIGHT'S COUNTRY STORE	Belleville	PA
PELICAN ROOST	Captiva	FL
PELICAN SWIM & SKI	Whitehouse	NJ
PENICK & CHANCE, INC.	Tyler	TX
PENLAND & SONS DEPARTMENT STORE	Marshall	NC
PENN STATE BOOK STORE ON CAMPUS	University Park	PA
PENN STATE UNIVERSITY	University Park	PA
(See PENN STATE BOOK STORE ON CAMPUS)		
PENN-DEL MANAGEMENT CO.	Philadelphia	PA
PENNELL'S, INC.	Brunswick	ME
PENNER'S, INC.	San Antonio	TX
PENNYWORTH'S, INC.	Lynn	MA
PENROD INTERNATIONAL	Miami	FL
PEOPLES CLOTHING STORE	Boone	IA
PEOPLES CLOTHING STORE	Durham	NC
PEOPLES DEPARTMENT STORES, INC.	Franklin	NC
PEOPLES STORE	Manistique	MI
THE PEOPLES STORE OF CHARLESTON, INC.	Charleston	SC
PEPE'S MENSWEAR & TAILOR SHOP	Toledo	OH
PEPIN'S MEN'S APPAREL	New Bedford	MA
PEPS OF ASPEN, INC.	Aspen	CO
(See BOOGIE'S DINER)		
PERFECT SHOES	Santa Ana	CA
PERLIS	New Orleans	LA
PERRY ELLIS	New York	NY
(See SALANT CORPORATION)		
PERRY'S DEPARTMENT STORE	Louisville	MS
PERRY'S SPECIALTY SHOP, INC.	Lawrenceville	VA
PERRYMAN WESTERN WEAR	Phoenix	AZ
PERSIMMON TREE	Newport Beach	CA
PERSONALIZED PRODUCTS	Hartford	WI
THE PERUVIAN CONNECTION LTD.	Tonganoxie	KS
PETE SMITH, INC.	Destin	FL
PETE'S CLOTHING & WESTERN WEAR	Belle Fourche	SD
PETE'S SPORTSWEAR, INC.	El Segundo	CA
PETER BLAIR, INC.	Richmond	VA
PETER CLOTHIERS	Overland Park	KS
PETER DANIEL, INC.	Barrington	IL
PETER ELLIOT	New York	NY
PETER HARRIS	Latham	NY
PETER HARRIS CLOTHES	Latham	NY
(See HUCK FINN CLOTHES, INC.)		
PETER ISLAND RESORT	Duluth	GA
PETER NAGY ENTERPRISES, INC.	Orange	NJ
PETER'S MALE APPAREL, INC.	Brunswick	GA
PETER'S STORE FOR MEN, INC.	Chagrin Falls	OH
PETERSEN'S CLOTHING & ACCESSORIES	Boise	ID
(See PETERSEN'S ENTERPRISES)		
PETERSEN'S ENTERPRISES	Boise	ID
PETWAY REAVIS	Nashville	TN
PFI WESTERN STORE	Springfield	MO
PHANTOM	Santa Cruz	CA
(See BILLS WHEELS, INC.)		
PHELPS - DODGE MERCANTILE CO.	Morenci	AZ
PHIDIPPIDES	Metairie	LA
PHIDIPPIDES	Atlanta	GA
PHIDIPPIDES SPORTS CENTER	Concord	NC
PHIL'S MEN'S SHOP, INC.	Fairfield	CA
PHIL'S SQUIRE SHOPPE	Greenwood	MS
PHIL'S WEAR-HOUSE	Van Nuys	CA
PHIL'S, INC.	Essex Junction	VT
PHILIP KOENIG	Bronx	NY
PHILIP WOLFE HABERDASHER, INC.	Providence	RI
PHILIPS	Fort Lauderdale	FL
(See CARRIAGE CLOTHIERS)		
PHILLIP GALL'S OUTDOOR SHOP	Lexington	KY
PHILLIP STEWART CUSTOM	Portland	OR
PHILLIP'S MEN'S SHOP	Salisbury	MD
PHILLIPS COWBOY SHOP	Carlsbad	NM
PHILLIPS VARIETY STORE	Royston	GA
PHILLIPS' APPAREL	Oneida	TN
PHILLIPS' MEN'S SHOP, INC.	Laurel	DE
PHILLY'S KIDS	Philadelphia	PA
PHILS BOYS' & GIRLS' WEAR	Abbeville	LA
PHOENIX FASHIONS FOR BUSINESS	Cartersville	GA
PHYLLIS' JEANS & APPAREL	Rostrauer	PA
PHYSICAL ACTIVEWEAR	New York	NY
(See RICHIE'S CLOTHING)		
PIA'S SCANDANAVIAN WOOLENS	Anchorage	AK
PIBES	Arecibo	PR
PICK-N-SAVE SHOES	Mobile	AL
(See SMART SHOE STORES, INC.)		
PIER 17 MARINA, INC.	Jacksonville	FL
PIER GROUP	Montauk	NY
PIERRE PART STORE, INC.	Pierre Part	LA

ALPHABETICAL INDEX

ALPHABETICAL INDEX

ALPHABETICAL INDEX

ALPHABETICAL INDEX

ALPHABETICAL INDEX

S

ALPHABETICAL INDEX

ALPHABETICAL INDEX

ALPHABETICAL INDEX

ALPHABETICAL INDEX

ALPHABETICAL INDEX

ALPHABETICAL INDEX

ALPHABETICAL INDEX

T

ALPHABETICAL INDEX

ALPHABETICAL INDEX

ALPHABETICAL INDEX

Name	City	State
TUCKER ENTERPRISES	Tucson	AZ
TUCKER'S EMPORIUM	Mount Pleasant	UT
TUCKER'S GATEWAY SHOP-O-RAMA	Benton	KY
TUMBLEWEED WESTERN WEAR	Quanah	TX
TUNA ENTERPRISES	Kissimmee	FL
TUPELO HONEY	Miami	FL
TURLEY'S	West Burlington	IA
TURNBALL & ASSER CUSTOM CLOTHIERS	New York	NY
TURTURICI NEW GENERATIONS	San Carlos	CA
TUX INTERNATIONAL	Short Hills	NJ
THE TUX SHOP	Portland	OR
TUXEDO CENTER, INC.	Hollywood	CA
TUXEDO DEN, INC.	Redding	CA
TUXEDO HOUSE	Lutherville Timonium	MD
TUXEDO JUNCTION	Williamsville	NY
TUXEDO JUNCTION	Honolulu	HI
TUXEDO JUNCTION EAST (See TUXEDO JUNCTION WEST)	Las Vegas	NV
TUXEDO JUNCTION WEST	Las Vegas	NV
TUXEDO JUNCTION, INC. (See TUXEDO JUNCTION WEST)	Las Vegas	NV
TUXEDO PALACE	Las Vegas	NV
TUXEDO ROYALE	Markham	ON
TUXEDO ZONE, INC.	Baltimore	MD
TUXEDO/THE BRIDAL CONNECTION (See BIG GUYS TUXEDO)	Victorville	CA
TUXEDOS BY ROSE	North Bergen	NJ
TUXES & TAILS	Indianapolis	IN
TWEEDS CLOTHING	New Hyde Park	NY
TWIN CITY DEPARTMENT STORE	Saint Thomas	VI
TWIN CITY SURPLUS, INC.	Reno	NV
TWINS FASHIONS	Post	TX
TWISTED PINE FUR & LEATHER	Breckenridge	CO
TWO BLONDES	Mary Esther	FL
TWO BROTHERS MENSWEAR	Chicago	IL
TWO FASHION CORP.	Mount Vernon	NY
TWO GUYS CLOTHING	Youngstown	OH
TYLER BROTHERS TRUE VALUE	Wagener	SC
TYNDALL'S FORMALWEAR	Durham	NC
TYROL SKI & SPORTS, INC.	Rochester	MN
TYRONE	Roslyn	NY
TYRONE'S TAILORING & FORMAL WEAR	Orlando	FL
TYSON'S MENSWEAR, INC.	Port Charlotte	FL
TYSONS MENS WEAR, INC. (See CAPTAIN'S LANDING)	Punta Gorda	FL

U

Name	City	State
U-SHOP POPULAR FASHIONS	Kosciusko	MS
U.B. CARPENTER DEPARTMENT STORES	Jonesville	LA
U.S. CAVALRY	Radcliff	KY
U.S. MEN'S FASHIONS	Chicago	IL
U.S. SPACE-ROCKET	Huntsville	AL
U2 JOSEF'S FUNWEAR	Panama City Beach	FL
UCLA STUDENTS' STORE	Los Angeles	CA
UDELCO, INC.	Orangeburg	NY
UGO'S, INC.	East Longmeadow	MA
UJENA SWIMWEAR (See THE SWIMWEAR COMPANY)	Tampa	FL
ULBRICH & KRAFT (See MOBERLY & KLENNER)	Bloomington	IL
ULLMAN & EMANUEL, INC.	Norfolk	VA
ULTA MODA FASHIONS	Hopewell Junction	NY
ULTIMA MODA BY HAL	Encino	CA
ULTIMATE SPORTSFAN, INC.	Orlando	FL
ULTRA DIAMOND FLAGSHIP STORE (See ULTRA STORES, INC.)	Chicago	IL
ULTRA DIAMOND OUTLETS (See ULTRA STORES, INC.)	Chicago	IL
ULTRA STORES, INC.	Chicago	IL
UMBERTO INTERNATIONAL CLOTHIER	Long Beach	CA
UNC STUDENT STORE	Chapel Hill	NC
UNCLE BILLY'S GENERAL STORE	Hilo	HI
UNCLE BILLY'S HILO BAY HOTEL (See UNCLE BILLY'S GENERAL STORE)	Hilo	HI
UNCLE MILTY'S	Clearwater	FL
UNCLE SAM'S SAFARI OUTFITTERS, INC.	Manchester	MO
UNDER WARES FOR HIM	New York	NY
UNDERCOVER BY ROLO (See ROLO SAN FRANCISCO, INC.)	San Francisco	CA
UNDERGROUND MENSWEAR, INC.	Detroit	MI
UNDERGROUND STATION (See GENESCO, INC.)	Nashville	TN
UNDERNEATH.COM	Atlanta	GA
UNDERWATER SAFARIS	Tortola	VI
UNDERWEAR HOUSE	Miami	FL
UNIFIRST CORP.	Wilmington	MA
UNIFORM EXPRESS	Longview	WA
THE UNIFORM SHOP	Bakersfield	CA
UNIFORM STATION	Auburn	WA
UNIFORMITY	Boise	ID
UNIFORMS BY MALIA	Aiea	HI
UNIFORMS, INC.	Los Angeles	CA
UNIK	Dallas	TX
UNION	New York	NY
UNION JACK CLOTHING	Dallas	TX
UNION WAR SURPLUS STORE, INC.	San Pedro	CA
UNION-FASHION CLOTHING CO., INC.	El Paso	TX
UNIQUE DESIGN	Newark	NJ
UNIQUE FASHIONS	Brooklyn	NY
UNIQUE HANDBAGS AND FASHIONS	Coatesville	PA
UNITED COLORS OF BENETTON	Los Angeles	CA
UNITED MEN'S STORE (See DAVID BARRY'S TALL & BIG)	Birmingham	AL
UNITED MENSWEAR	Detroit	MI
UNITED MEN'S FASHIONS	Buffalo	NY
UNITED MENS, INC.	Birmingham	AL
UNITED SPORTS APPAREL	Stevensville	MI
UNIV. OF ALABAMA (See SNOOZY'S COLLEGE BOOKSTORE)	Birmingham	AL
UNIVERSAL BOOT SHOPS	San Diego	CA
UNIVERSAL EQUESTRIAN CENTER (See THE AMERICAN COWBOY)	West Bountifull	UT
UNIVERSAL GEAR, INC.	Washington	DC
UNIVERSAL SKI & SPORTS (See RETAIL CONCEPTS, INC.)	Stafford	TX
UNIVERSAL STORES	Prince Rupert	BC
UNIVERSALGEAR.COM (See UNIVERSAL GEAR, INC.)	Washington	DC
UNIVERSITY BOOK & SUPPLY, INC.	Cedar Falls	IA
UNIVERSITY BOOK & SUPPLY STORE	Knoxville	TN
UNIVERSITY BOOK CENTER	College Park	MD
UNIVERSITY BOOK STORE	Seattle	WA
UNIVERSITY BOOK STORE	Columbia	SC
UNIVERSITY BOOK STORE	Amherst	MA
UNIVERSITY BOOK STORE	Norman	OK
UNIVERSITY BOOKSTORE	Kent	OH
THE UNIVERSITY BOOKSTORE	West Lafayette	IN
UNIVERSITY CLASS	Markham	ON
UNIVERSITY CO-OP SOCIETY	Austin	TX
UNIVERSITY OF ALABAMA (See UNIVERSITY SUPPLY STORE)	Tuscaloosa	AL
UNIVERSITY OF ARIZONA BOOKSTORE	Tucson	AZ
UNIVERSITY OF ARKANSAS BOOKSTORE	Fayetteville	AR
UNIVERSITY OF ARKANSAS LITTLE ROCK BOOKSTORE	Little Rock	AR
UNIVERSITY OF CALIFORNIA-LA (See UCLA STUDENTS' STORE)	Los Angeles	CA
UNIVERSITY OF CENTRAL FLORDIA KNIGHTWEAR	Orlando	FL
UNIVERSITY OF COLORADO (See CU BOOKSTORE)	Boulder	CO
UNIVERSITY OF FLORIDA (See UNIVERSITY OF FLORIDA BOOK STORES)	Gainesville	FL
UNIVERSITY OF FLORIDA BOOK STORES	Gainesville	FL
UNIVERSITY OF GEORGIA BOOK STORE	Athens	GA

ALPHABETICAL INDEX

V

ALPHABETICAL INDEX

ALPHABETICAL INDEX

ALPHABETICAL INDEX

X

Y

ALPHABETICAL INDEX